T0236500

Lecture Notes in Computer Science 9696

Commenced Publication in 1973
Founding and Former Series Editors:
Gerhard Goos, Juris Hartmanis, and Jan van Leeuwen

Editorial Board

David Hutchison
Lancaster University, Lancaster, UK
Takeo Kanade
Carnegie Mellon University, Pittsburgh, PA, USA
Josef Kittler
University of Surrey, Guildford, UK
Jon M. Kleinberg
Cornell University, Ithaca, NY, USA
Friedemann Mattern
ETH Zurich, Zürich, Switzerland
John C. Mitchell
Stanford University, Stanford, CA, USA
Moni Naor
Weizmann Institute of Science, Rehovot, Israel
C. Pandu Rangan
Indian Institute of Technology, Madras, India
Bernhard Steffen
TU Dortmund University, Dortmund, Germany
Demetri Terzopoulos
University of California, Los Angeles, CA, USA
Doug Tygar
University of California, Berkeley, CA, USA
Gerhard Weikum
Max Planck Institute for Informatics, Saarbrücken, Germany

More information about this series at http://www.springer.com/series/7410

Mark Manulis · Ahmad-Reza Sadeghi
Steve Schneider (Eds.)

Applied Cryptography and Network Security

14th International Conference, ACNS 2016
Guildford, UK, June 19–22, 2016
Proceedings

Springer

Editors
Mark Manulis
Department of Computer Science
University of Surrey
Guildford
UK

Steve Schneider
Department of Computer Science
University of Surrey
Guildford
UK

Ahmad-Reza Sadeghi
CASED
Technische Universität Darmstadt
Darmstadt, Hessen
Germany

ISSN 0302-9743   ISSN 1611-3349   (electronic)
Lecture Notes in Computer Science
ISBN 978-3-319-39554-8   ISBN 978-3-319-39555-5   (eBook)
DOI 10.1007/978-3-319-39555-5

Library of Congress Control Number: 2015958852

LNCS Sublibrary: SL4 – Security and Cryptology

© Springer International Publishing Switzerland 2016
This work is subject to copyright. All rights are reserved by the Publisher, whether the whole or part of the material is concerned, specifically the rights of translation, reprinting, reuse of illustrations, recitation, broadcasting, reproduction on microfilms or in any other physical way, and transmission or information storage and retrieval, electronic adaptation, computer software, or by similar or dissimilar methodology now known or hereafter developed.
The use of general descriptive names, registered names, trademarks, service marks, etc. in this publication does not imply, even in the absence of a specific statement, that such names are exempt from the relevant protective laws and regulations and therefore free for general use.
The publisher, the authors and the editors are safe to assume that the advice and information in this book are believed to be true and accurate at the date of publication. Neither the publisher nor the authors or the editors give a warranty, express or implied, with respect to the material contained herein or for any errors or omissions that may have been made.

Printed on acid-free paper

This Springer imprint is published by Springer Nature
The registered company is Springer International Publishing AG Switzerland

Preface

The 14th International Conference on Applied Cryptography and Network Security, ACNS 2016, took place June 19–22, 2016, in Guildford, UK, and was organized by the Surrey Centre for Cyber Security (SCCS) at the University of Surrey.

ACNS is an annual conference focusing on original research in applied cryptography, cyber security, and privacy. Both academic research with high relevance to real-world problems and developments in industrial and technical frontiers fall within the scope of the conference.

ACNS 2016 received 183 submissions, all of which were reviewed by the Program Committee. Each of the 49 Program Committee members was assigned an average of 11 submissions for review. Each paper was assigned to at least three reviewers, while submissions co-authored by Program Committee members were assigned to at least four reviewers. The Program Committee was helped by the reports and opinions of 138 external reviewers. The submission process was not anonymous and author names were visible to all reviewers. The review process was organized and managed through EasyChair. The reviewers were asked to declare any conflicts of interest for all submissions in the beginning of the process. The selection process was very competitive and after highly interactive discussions and a careful deliberation, 35 papers were selected by the Program Committee for presentation at the conference. This puts the acceptance rate of ACNS 2016 at 19 %.

The ACNS 2016 program included two invited talks: "Securing Positioning: From GPS to IoT" by Srdjan Capkun from ETH Zurich and "Foundations of Hardware-Based Attested Computation and Applications of SGX" by Bogdan Warinschi from Bristol University. The prize for the Best Student Paper was awarded to Elena Kirshanova and Friedrich Wiemer for their paper "Parallel Implementation of BDD Enumeration for LWE" co-authored with Alexander May.

ACNS 2016 was organized by Mark Manulis and Ahmad-Reza Sadeghi, who served as program chairs, selected the Program Committee, and led their efforts in choosing papers that you will find in this volume, and by Steve Schneider, who served as general chair and was helped in the local organization by Anna-Lisa Ferrara and Shujun Li.

The ACNS 2016 chairs would like to thank everyone who contributed to the success of the conference. We are grateful to the Program Committee and external reviewers for their commitment, hard work, and enthusiasm to ensure that each paper received a thorough and fair review. Last but not least, we wish to thank all conference participants for making ACNS 2016 an enjoyable experience.

June 2016

Mark Manulis
Ahmad-Reza Sadeghi
Steve Schneider

ACNS 2016

14th International Conference on Applied Cryptography and Network Security
Guildford, UK, June 19–22, 2016

General Chair

Steve Schneider   University of Surrey, UK

Program Chairs

Mark Manulis   University of Surrey, UK
Ahmad-Reza Sadeghi   TU Darmstadt, Germany

Program Committee

Frederik Armknecht   University of Mannheim, Germany
Giuseppe Ateniese   Stevens Institute of Technology, USA
Elias Athanasopoulos   Vrije Universiteit Amsterdam, The Netherlands
Man Ho Au   Hong Kong Polytechnic University, China
Liqun Chen   Hewlett-Packard Laboratories, UK
Sherman S.M. Chow   Chinese University of Hong Kong, China
Mauro Conti   University of Padua, Italy
Lucas Davi   TU Darmstadt, Germany
Alexandra Dmitrienko   ETH Zurich, Switzerland
Michael Franz   University of California, Irvine, USA
Sebastian Gajek   NEC Laboratories Europe, Germany
Jens Groth   University College London, UK
Goichiro Hanaoka   AIST, Japan
Feng Hao   Newcastle University, UK
Michael Huth   Imperial College London, UK
Tibor Jager   Ruhr University Bochum, Germany
Yier Jin   University of Central Florida, USA
Aniket Kate   Purdue University, USA
Stefan Katzenbeisser   TU Darmstadt, Germany
Negar Kiyavash   University of Illinois, USA
Vladimir Kolesnikov   Bell Laboratories, USA
Mark Manulis   University of Surrey, UK
Ivan Martinovic   University of Oxford, UK

Azalia Mirhoseini	Rice University, USA
Atsuko Miyaji	JAIST, Japan
Payman Mohassel	University of Calgary, Canada
Jörn Müller-Quade	Karlsruhe Institute of Technology, Germany
David Naccache	Ecole Normale Superieure, France
Michael Naehrig	Microsoft Research Redmond, USA
Hamed Okhravi	MIT Lincoln Laboratory, USA
Claudio Orlandi	Aarhus University, Denmark
Panos Papadimitratos	KTH Royal Institute of Technology, Sweden
Thomas Peyrin	Nanyang Technological University, Singapore
Bertram Poettering	Ruhr University Bochum, Germany
Bart Preneel	KU Leuven, Belgium
Jeyavijayan Rajendran	University of Texas at Dallas, USA
Christian Rechberger	Technical University of Denmark, Denmark
Peter Y. Ryan	University of Luxembourg, Luxembourg
Rei Safavi-Naini	University of Calgary, Canada
Thomas Schneider	TU Darmstadt, Germany
Ozgur Sinanoglu	NYU Abu Dhabi, UAE
Douglas Stebila	McMaster University, Canada
Thorsten Strufe	TU Dresden, Germany
Gang Tan	Penn State University, USA
Vanessa Teague	University of Melbourne, Australia
Mehdi Tibouchi	NTT Secure Platform Laboratories, Japan
Ivan Visconti	University of Salerno, Italy
Wenyuan Xu	University of South Carolina, USA
Moti Yung	Snapchat, USA
Jianying Zhou	Institute for Infocomm Research, Singapore

External Reviewers

Dirk Achenbach

Sk Subidh Ali

Moreno Ambrosin

Kanishka Ariyapala

Afonso Arriaga

Tomer Ashur

Nuttapong Attrapadung

Saikrishna Badrinarayanan

David Barrera

Marc Beunardeau

David Bigelow

Begül Bilgin

Kaidel Bjoern

Jonathan Bootle

Joppe Bos

Colin Boyd

Ferdinand Brasser

Brandon Broadnax

Luigi Catuogno

Andrea Cerulli

Pyrros Chaidos

Sze Yiu Chau

Zhuo Chen

Michele Ciampi

Alberto Compagno

Heng Cui

Daniel Demmler

Alexander Detrano

Fraser Dickin

Christoph Dobraunig

Benjamin Dowling
Maria Eichelseder
Keita Emura
Hossein Fereidooni
Manuel Fersch
Houda Ferradi
Yuichi Futa
Rémi Géraud
Essam Ghadafi
Lorenzo Grassi
Stefano Guarino
Gus Gutoski
Britta Hale
Stephan Häuser
Matt Henricksen
Felix Heuer
Jialin Huang
Matthias Huber
Siam Hussain
Jean-Louis Huynen
Chandrakumar Holenarasipursuresh
Panagiotis Ilia
Vincenzo Iovino
Morshed Islam
Hakon Jacobsen
Angela Jäschke
Dirmanto Jap
Mahavir Jhawar
Sachhidh Kannan
Bhavana Kanukurthi
Arun Kanuparthi
Ghassan Karame
Pierre Karpman
Nikolaos Karvelas
Taechan Kim
Ágnes Kiss
Alexander Koch
Stefan Koelbl
Matthias Krause
Russell W.F. Lai
Kim Laine
Chhagan Lal
Charles Lamech
Sebastian Lauer
Hoon Wei Lim
Shen Liu

Xiruo Liu
Patrick Longa
Jiqiang Lu
Stefan Lucks
Daniel Masny
Takahiro Matsuda
Bodhisatwa Mazumdar
Florian Mendel
Alfred Menezes
Vasily Mikhalev
Vladislav Mladlenov
Paweł Morawiecki
Pedro Moreno-Sanchez
Matthias Nagel
Ivica Nikolic
Go Ohtake
Kazumasa Omote
Cristina Onete
Jiaxin Pan
Panagiotis Papadopoulos
Arpita Patra
Umberto Ferraro Petrillo
Antigoni Polychroniadou
Ivan Pryvalov
Kim Ramchen
Sadegh Riazi
Peter B. Roenne
Stefanie Roos
Arnab Roy
Sujoy Sinha Roy
Bita Rouhani
Vladimir Rozic
Tim Ruffing
Yusuke Sakai
Hani Salah
Jacob Schuldt
Alexander Senier
Hwajeong Seo
Setareh Sharifian
Siang Meng Sim
Luisa Siniscalchi
Juraj Somorovsky
Ebrahim Songhori
Riccardo Spolaor
Richard Skowyra
Marjan Skrobot

Chunhua Su
Somayeh Taheri
Katsuyuki Takashima
Qiang Tang
Tyge Tiessen
Elmar Tischhauser
Thao Tran
Pengwei Wang
Qingju Wang
Xiuhua Wang
Xueyang Wang
Marcel Winandy
Miao Xu

Jia Xu
Shota Yamada
Rupeng Yang
Muhammad Yasin
Shaza Zeitouni
Dongrui Zeng
Liang Feng Zhang
Tao Zhang
Zongyang Zhang
Yongjun Zhao
Luying Zhou
Michael Zohner

Contents

Authentication and Key Establishment

On the Security of the Algebraic Eraser Tag Authentication Protocol

Simon R. Blackburn[1] and M.J.B. Robshaw[2(✉)]

[1] Information Security Group, Royal Holloway University of London,
Egham TW20 0EX, UK
[2] Impinj, 400 Fairview Ave. N., Suite 1200, Seattle, WA 98109, USA
matt.robshaw@impinj.com

Abstract. The Algebraic Eraser has been gaining prominence as Secur-eRF, the company commercializing the algorithm, increases its marketing reach. The scheme is claimed to be well-suited to IoT applications but a lack of detail in available documentation has hampered peer-review. Recently more details of the system have emerged after a tag authentication protocol built using the Algebraic Eraser was proposed for standardization in ISO/IEC SC31 and SecureRF provided an open public description of the protocol. In this paper we describe a range of attacks on this protocol that include very efficient and practical tag impersonation as well as partial, and total, tag secret key recovery. Most of these results have been practically verified, they contrast with the 80-bit security that is claimed for the protocol, and they emphasize the importance of independent public review for any cryptographic proposal.

Keywords: Algebraic Eraser · Cryptanalysis · Tag authentication · IoT

1 Introduction

Extending security features to RAIN RFID tags[1] and other severely constrained devices in the *Internet of Things* is not easy. However the different pieces of the deployment puzzle are falling into place. Over-the-air (OTA) commands supporting security features have now been standardized [11] and both tag and reader manufacturers can build to these specifications knowing that interoperability will follow. The OTA commands themselves are crypto-agnostic so parallel work on a range of cryptographic interfaces, so-called *cryptographic suites*, is ongoing within ISO/IEC SC31. These cryptographic suites provide the detailed specifications that allow algorithms such as the AES [14,23], PRESENT-80 [8,15], and Grain-128a [1,16] to be used on even the most basic of RFID devices.

---

[1] Following the creation of the RAIN Industry Alliance, UHF RFID tags are increasingly branded as RAIN RFID tags. These RFID tags operate at 860–960 MHz and are far more constrained than the HF RFID tags that are familiar from public transport and NFC applications.

© Springer International Publishing Switzerland 2016
M. Manulis et al. (Eds.): ACNS 2016, LNCS 9696, pp. 3–17, 2016.
DOI: 10.1007/978-3-319-39555-5_1

For symmetric cryptography a range of lighter alternatives to the Advanced Encryption Standard (AES) [23] have received a high level of cryptanalytic attention over several years. While the AES will always be an important implementation option, some of these alternative algorithms may be appropriate for certain use-cases. To those not in the field the cost and performance advantages provided by these new algorithms might appear slight. But the requirements of the RAIN RFID market are such that even a minor degradation in the read range or a small percentage increase in silicon price can eliminate the business case for adding security to many use-cases.

Turning to asymmetric cryptography there are several work items in ISO/IEC 29167 that describe public-key solutions. Parts 29167-12 [17] and 29167-16 [18] describe tag authentication based on elliptic curve cryptography, though they carry significant implementation challenges for RAIN RFID. 29167-17 [19] provides another elliptic-curve tag authentication solution with the additional property that compact pre-computed coupons can be used to provide implementation advantages. In 29167-20 [20], however, we encounter an alternative to elliptic curves: 29167-20 proposes a method for asymmetric tag authentication that is based on *braid groups*. This proposal is based on the *Algebraic Eraser* (AE) key agreement protocol [3,25]. SecureRF, the company commercializing (and owning the trademark to) the Algebraic Eraser, claims significant implementation advantages for the Algebraic Eraser over solutions that use elliptic curves. In particular the Algebraic Eraser is claimed to be well-suited to deployments as part of the Internet of Things.

Note. The Algebraic Eraser has been proposed for use in many environments. However the commentary and descriptions in this paper will use the typical RFID setting of an Interrogator (or reader) interacting with a Tag. This provides the closest match with the terms used in the protocol [25].

Related Work

Until recently, crucial details about the Algebraic Eraser and any associated cryptographic protocol were not available. This made independent security analysis and performance evaluation difficult. (See [12,13,21,22,24] for what little exists in the published literature.) However, in October 2015 SecureRF provided a detailed public description of the Algebraic Eraser tag authentication protocol [9,25]. This means that the protocol can now be publicly reviewed and discussed. The published description includes a specific set of system parameters, a set of test vectors, and a description of the tag authentication protocol. However SecureRF do not disclose how the system parameters were generated, an aspect of the technology that is known to be of crucial importance. Indeed, some of the attacks in this paper are able to exploit structure in the system parameters that have been proposed for standardization.

While general documentation [3] describes the Algebraic Eraser in terms of braid groups, company presentations [4,6] distance the technology from previous cryptographic proposals that use braid groups. Instead the security of the Algebraic Eraser is said to depend on a problem called the *simultaneous conjugacy separation search problem* [4] and sample parameter sizes have been published for different security levels. In [25] the parameters are claimed to correspond to an 80-bit security level, though a precise security model is not provided. Most likely the intention is that the work effort to recover a private key from the corresponding public key should be roughly equivalent to 2^{80} operations.

The tag authentication protocol in [25] is based upon a Diffie–Hellman-like key agreement scheme. Very recently Ben-Zvi, Blackburn, and Tsaban [7] presented an innovative cryptanalysis of the underlying key agreement protocol.[2] Using only information that is exchanged over the air, and avoiding the hard problem upon which the security of the Algebraic Eraser key agreement protocol is claimed to be based, Ben-Zvi *et al.* provide a method for deriving the shared secret key. Using non-optimized implementations they successfully recovered—in under eight hours—the shared secrets generated using the Algebraic Eraser key agreement protocol with parameters provided by SecureRF that were intended to provide 128-bit security [6].

Since then Anshel, Atkins, Goldfeld and Gunnells (researchers associated with SecureRF) have posted a technical response [2] to the Ben-Zvi–Blackburn–Tsaban (BBT) attack. This is not the place to comment on that document, except to highlight one feature that is relevant for our work here.

In [2] Anshel *et al.* consider the implications of the BBT attack and state that the attack would not apply to one of two profiles proposed for standardization [20]. Section 4.2 of Anshel *et al.* [2] reveals that the profile claimed to be secure is one where "... an attacker never has access to one of the public keys ..." [2]. However the idea that it is reasonable for the security of a public key scheme to depend on the public key being hidden is very strange. While it is true Tag public keys could be delivered to interrogators out-of-band, the security of the scheme should not depend on the Interrogator keeping those keys secret. Indeed, if we trust an Interrogator not to reveal the Tag public key then we can trust the Interrogator with a symmetric key and there would be no need to use the Algebraic Eraser at all! So while two of the five attacks described in this paper use the Tag public key for the required calculations, we see no limitation in assuming that the tag public key is, as the name implies, public.

Finally, we should point out a recent posting of Atkins and Goldfeld [5] that suggests modifications to the tag authentication protocol in the light of the results of this paper.

Our Contribution

In this work we derive a range of new and very efficient attacks on the tag authentication protocol [25]. We side-step the bulk of the mathematical machinery behind the Algebraic Eraser, but observe some curious features of the Algebraic Eraser that cause significant failures in this protocol. In particular we provide the following attacks against the variant that is currently proposed for standardization:

---

[2] The results in this paper are entirely independent of the work in Ben-Zvi *et al* [7].

1. Tag impersonation of a target tag with success probability $\approx 2^{-7}$ after 273 queries against the target tag and storage $\approx 2^{16}$ bits.
2. Tag impersonation of a target tag with 100 % success rate after $\approx 2^{15}$ queries against the target tag and using $\approx 2^{23}$ bits of storage.
3. Full recovery of a tag private key matrix (see Sect. 3.3) with negligible work after running the tag authentication protocol 33 times against the target tag.
4. Tag impersonation of a target tag with 100 % success rate, using Attack 3 and a small pre-computed look-up table of around 128 64-bit words. The on-line work in the attack is negligible while the off-line pre-computation for current parameter sizes is also negligible. This attack uses (a non-heuristic part of) an attack due to Kalka, Teicher and Tsaban [21] together with a novel application of a certain permutation group algorithm.
5. Complete tag private key (or equivalent key) recovery—recovering both the tag private matrix and the secret tag conjugate set (see Sect. 3.3)—building on Attack 3 and requiring a work effort of 2^{49} operations and storage $\approx 2^{48}$ 64-bit words for one of the parameter choices proposed for standardization that is claimed to provide 80-bit security.

Our attacks avoid using any heuristic methods, and apply for all parameter sets of the size proposed in the standard (not just the specific given parameters). These failures in the tag authentication protocol severely undermine claims for an 80-bit security level. We conclude that the protocol is unsuitable for both deployment and standardization in its current form.

Our paper is structured as follows. In Sect. 2 we provide an overview of the Algebraic Eraser tag authentication protocol with the mathematical formalities following in Sect. 3. The attacks are described in Sects. 4, 5, 6, and 7 respectively and we close the paper with our conclusions.

2   Algebraic Eraser and Tag Authentication

The Algebraic Eraser does not use familiar mathematics and a description can be, at first sight, somewhat complicated. However, for our attacks we will only need the basic tools that we provide in Sect. 3. For a more complete view the reader is referred to both the general description of the Algebraic Eraser [3] and the specific protocol details in [25].

As mentioned in the Introduction, at the core of the Algebraic Eraser is a key agreement protocol. Using the familiar protocol flow that dates back to Diffie–Hellman [10], an Interrogator and Tag exchange public keys. Then, by each applying their own secret component to the other public key, both Interrogator and Tag can arrive at a shared common secret key value. To turn this key agreement protocol into a tag authentication protocol, the Interrogator specifies a portion of the shared secret that should be returned by the Tag. The correctness of this response can be verified by the Interrogator. This is illustrated in Table 1 and described more technically in Sect. 3.4.

Table 1. An outline of the Algebraic Eraser tag authentication scheme [25]. The underlying key agreement protocol is used to derive a shared secret. The Interrogator instructs the Tag, using byte index s and bit-length l, to extract an authentication token t of length l from this shared secret.

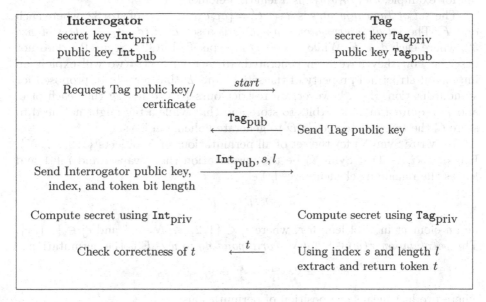

We will refer to the portion of the secret key returned by the Tag as an authentication token t. In [25] the Interrogator indicates to the Tag how to construct t by sending a starting index s and length l during the message exchange between Interrogator and Tag. The protocol description neither specifies nor gives guidelines on s and l. Clearly a fake tag will always be able to fool an Interrogator with probability 2^{-l} but the field specifying the length l in [25] is eight bits long so we have $0 \leq l \leq 255$. This certainly covers all the natural choices. Note that generating an authentication token t by revealing parts of a shared secret means that the Interrogator will need to generate and use different public keys at each tag authentication. While this is alluded to in Section B.1.2 of [25] it is unclear whether the ensuing performance penalty in storage and transaction time is always reflected in published performance figures.

3   Some Technical Details

This section reviews some of the technical details of the protocol. We describe only as much of the detail as we need to describe our attacks.

3.1   System Parameters

The protocol specifies some system parameters, the *key space*, as follows.

Let N be a small positive integer; [25] mandates that $N = 10$. Let $B = \{b_1, b_2, \ldots, b_{N-1}\}$ be an alphabet of size $N - 1$ (the b_i are known as *Artin generators*). Let F be the set of all formal strings in the disjoint union $B \cup B^{-1}$. So, for example, $b_2 b_1^{-1} b_1 b_4 b_2^{-1}$ is a length 5 element of F.

The *set of Tag conjugates* is a set $C = \{c_1, c_2, \ldots, c_{32}\}$ of size 32, where each $c_i \in F$. The *set of Interrogator conjugates* is a set $D = \{d_1, d_2, \ldots, d_{32}\}$ of size 32, where each $d_i \in F$. While C and D are specified in [25] SecureRF does not describe how they have been generated. In fact, in Sect. 4 we will exploit an important structural property of the sets C and D that have been proposed for standardization. Here, however, we restrict ourselves to noting that each of C and D require around 90 Kbits to store and that while a tag might not need to store C the Interrogator needs D to generate ephemeral keys.

We write $\mathrm{Sym}(N)$ for the set of all permutations of N objects $\{1, 2, \ldots, N\}$. Let $s_i = (i, i+1) \in \mathrm{Sym}(N)$ be the permutation that swaps i and $i+1$ and leaves the remaining elements fixed. Let

$$w = b_{i_1}^{\epsilon_1} b_{i_2}^{\epsilon_2} \cdots b_{i_r}^{\epsilon_r}$$

be an element in F of length r, where $i_j \in \{1, 2, \ldots, N-1\}$ and $\epsilon_j \in \{-1, 1\}$. The *permutation* $\pi(w) \in \mathrm{Sym}(N)$ *corresponding to* $w \in F$ is the permutation

$$\pi(w) = s_{i_1}^{\epsilon_1} s_{i_2}^{\epsilon_2} \cdots s_{i_r}^{\epsilon_r} = s_{i_1} s_{i_2} \cdots s_{i_r}$$

where product means composition of permutations.

Finally, the protocol [25] specifies using arithmetic in the finite field $\mathbb{F}_{256}$ and defines a specific sequence of $N = 10$ non-zero elements in $\mathbb{F}_{256}$, called *T-values*, and a specific $N \times N$ matrix M_* with entries in $\mathbb{F}_{256}$ called a *seed matrix*. This choice of parameter sizes is denoted B10F256 and, according to Section B.3, is intended to provide 80-bit security.

Another set of parameters, denoted B16F256, has been independently provided by SecureRF to the first author. The same underlying field is used for both parameter sets but the matrices, the set of T-values, and the permutations are defined for $N = 16$ rather than $N = 10$. The parameters B16F256 are intended to provide 128-bit security.

3.2   E-Multiplication

E-multiplication is the public key operation, analogous to finite field exponentiation in Diffie–Hellmann, that lies at the heart of the Algebraic Eraser. It takes two parameters as input. The first parameter is a pair (M, σ) where M is an $N \times N$ matrix over $\mathbb{F}_{256}$ and $\sigma \in \mathrm{Sym}(N)$ is a permutation. The second parameter is a string $w \in F$. The output is a pair (M', σ') where M' is an $N \times N$ matrix over $\mathbb{F}_{256}$ and $\sigma' \in \mathrm{Sym}(N)$. We write

$$(M, \sigma) * w = (M', \sigma').$$

The permutation σ' is easy to define: $\sigma' = \sigma \, \pi(w)$. The matrix M' is computed by first finding a certain $N \times N$ matrix $\phi(\sigma, w)$ with entries in $\mathbb{F}_{256}$, and then setting $M' = M\phi(\sigma, w)$. We do not specify the details of how $\phi(\sigma, w)$ is defined, but just give the following details. To compute $\phi(\sigma, w)$, we replace the symbols b_i and b_i^{-1} in w by certain fixed matrices and their inverses. These matrices have entries in a polynomial ring in N variables, and the last row of all these matrices is all zero apart from the final entry which is 1. We multiply our matrices together (obtaining a matrix whose last row is all zero apart from the final entry which is 1). We evaluate each entry of this product (which is a ratio of two polynomials in N variables) by replacing each variable by one of the T-values to form the matrix $\phi(\sigma, w)$ with entries in $\mathbb{F}_{256}$. We use σ to decide which T-value replaces each variable in this process.

We note four properties that follow from the way E-multiplication is defined:

1. If w is the concatenation of strings w' and w'' then

$$(M, \sigma) * w = ((M, \sigma) * w') * w''. \tag{1}$$

  In fact E-multiplication has other nice properties related to the fact that E-multiplication is derived from the action of a braid group. However we do not need these properties here.

2. The matrix $\phi(\sigma, w)$ only depends on σ and w (and on the T-values, which are fixed).

3. The entries of the last row of $\phi(\sigma, w)$ are all zero, except the final entry which is 1.

4. The following linearity property follows from our partial description of E-multiplication:

$$\text{If } (M_1, \sigma) * w = (M_1', \sigma') \text{ and } (M_2, \sigma) * w = (M_2', \sigma')$$
$$\text{then } (a_1 M_1 \oplus a_2 M_2, \sigma) * w = (a_1 M_1' \oplus a_2 M_2', \sigma') \tag{2}$$

  for any $a_1, a_2 \in \mathbb{F}_{256}$.

3.3   Private and Public Keys

The Tag private key has two components.

1. The first component is an $N \times N$ matrix K_T over $\mathbb{F}_{256}$ that is generated from the seed matrix M_*. During the key generation process a random degree 9 polynomial $p(x)$ over $\mathbb{F}_{256}$ is selected and we set $K_T = p(M_*)$. See Section B.1.2 of [25]. The parameters are chosen so that the probability of recovering K_T by guessing the polynomial $p(x)$ is $(2^{-8})^{10} = 2^{-80}$.

2. The second component of the private key is a string $c \in F$ that is obtained by concatenating at least 16 of the Tag conjugates and their inverses. (The inverse of a word $b_{i_1}^{\epsilon_1} b_{i_2}^{\epsilon_2} \cdots b_{i_r}^{\epsilon_r}$ is the word $b_{i_r}^{-\epsilon_r} b_{i_{r-1}}^{-\epsilon_{r-1}} \cdots b_{i_1}^{-\epsilon_1}$.)

The matrix K_T and the string c form the *private key* of the Tag. The Tag's *public key* is defined to be

$$(M_T, \sigma_T) = (K_T, 1) * c$$

where 1 is the identity permutation.

When interacting with the Tag, the Interrogator generates an ephemeral private and public key, using the set of Interrogator conjugates rather than Tag conjugates. This means that the Interrogator's private key is an $N \times N$ matrix K_I over $\mathbb{F}_{256}$ and a concatenation d of at least 16 of the Interrogator conjugates and their inverses. The Interrogator's public key is

$$(M_I, \sigma_I) = (K_I, 1) * d.$$

3.4   Authenticating a Tag

The Tag authentication protocol runs as follows. The Interrogator requests the Tag's public key (M_T, σ_T). The Interrogator also generates an ephemeral private key and sends the corresponding public key (M_I, σ_I) to the Tag. The Tag computes the shared key

$$(K_T M_I, \sigma_I) * c$$

and the Interrogator computes the shared key

$$(K_I M_T, \sigma_T) * d.$$

The function ϕ and the parameters of the scheme are designed so that these values are equal. The Interrogator requests that part of the shared key be returned to the Interrogator and authenticates the Tag if the Tag replies correctly. Though the shared key is a matrix-permutation pair, the permutation is easy to compute from public material (it is just a product of two public permutations: $\sigma_I \sigma_T = \sigma_T \sigma_I$). So the matrix is the only non-public part of the shared key.

We note that all the attacks in this paper use knowledge of the shared secret key generated during the tag authentication protocol. It is a minor detail, but since [25] restricts the length of the authentication token ($l \leq 255$) an attacker might need to repeat tag authentication using three different choices for s and $l = 255$ before recovering the entire shared secret (as the shared matrix is represented by a sequence of $8 \times N(N-1) = 720$ bits). This three-fold increase in the work effort is included in our estimates.

4   Basic Tag Impersonation

In a tag authentication protocol, an attacker can always run the tag authentication protocol against a target tag at will. The goal would be to derive enough information so that the attacker can impersonate the target tag to a genuine Interrogator in a future run of the tag authentication protocol. We now describe a simple impersonation attack of this type.

Suppose an attacker chooses a permutation σ and a set of matrices M_i, for $0 \leq i \leq N(N-1) = 90$. The matrices are chosen so that they form a basis for the space of all $N \times N$ $\mathbb{F}_{256}$ matrices for which the last row begins with $N-1$ zero values. Taken together, the matrices and the single permutation σ provide $N(N-1) + 1 = 91$ spoof Interrogator public keys that are used in 91 runs of the tag authentication protocol against the target Tag. This yields 91 shared secrets S_i, for $0 \leq i \leq N(N-1)$, remembering from Sect. 3.4 that we will need to include a further factor of three in any work effort computation.

Now suppose the attacker attempts to impersonate the target Tag to a genuine Interrogator and receives a random public key (M_I, σ_I), where $\sigma_I = \sigma$. Emulating the target Tag, the attacker computes a_i for $0 \leq i \leq N(N-1)$, so that

$$M_I = \bigoplus_{i=0}^{N(N-1)} a_i M_i.$$

The linearity observed in Eq. 2 of Sect. 3.2 guarantees that the secret S that would be computed by a genuine tag can also be computed as

$$S = \bigoplus_{i=0}^{N(N-1)} a_i S_i.$$

The attacker will be able to extract the correct authentication token from S and fool the Interrogator with 100 % certainty.

As described, the attack requires that the Interrogator choose a public key with $\sigma_I = \sigma$. At first sight, for the parameters in [25], it appears that since $N! \approx 2^{21.8}$ the probability a genuine Interrogator chooses the hoped-for σ_I is around $2^{-21.8}$. However closer analysis reveals additional structure in the conjugate sets C and D. In particular, all the permutations generated by C have five fixed points, as do all the permutations generated by D. This means that the space of possible permutations that might be encountered from a genuine Interrogator is reduced from $N!$ to $(N/2)! \approx 2^7$. The probability a genuine Interrogator chooses the hoped-for σ_I is therefore greater than 2^{-7}.

For those that prefer certainty, it is obvious an attacker can increase his success probability by performing more off-line interrogation of the target Tag using different σ. This gives a variety of trade-offs, with the extreme being an attacker who will be able to emulate the target tag with 100 % certainty after interrogating that tag around $91 \times 3 \times 5! < 2^{15}$ times.

5 Tag Private Matrix Recovery

The security of the Algebraic Eraser tag authentication protocol depends on the secrecy of two components: the $N \times N$ private $\mathbb{F}_{256}$-matrix K_T and the tag string $c \in F$. In fact, both of these need to be kept secret: in the section below we provide details of a very efficient tag impersonation attack if K_T is known; moreover, K_T can be recovered from the public key if c is known. In Section B.3 of [25] parameters are chosen so that the work effort to recover K_T by guessing the polynomial $p(x)$ used to construct it is equal to the claimed security level of 2^{80} operations.

Exploiting the linearity observed in Eq. 2 of Sect. 3.2 we show how a differential cryptanalytic attack can recover the entirety of the secret matrix K_T after

11 tag authentications. Taking into account protocol constraints and parameters specified in [25] we will need 33 tag authentications in practice, but in the following description we will set aside the factor of three for clarity.

To begin, the attacker authenticates a target Tag using any Interrogator public key (A, σ) and stores the shared secret S that results. The attacker then authenticates the same tag with N related public keys that use the same permutation σ and matrices $P_1, \ldots, P_N$ constructed as follows.

Let $E_{i,j}$ be the $N \times N$ matrix that is all zero, except its (i, j) entry which is 1. Set $P_t = A \oplus E_{t,N}$ for $1 \leq t \leq N$. The attacker challenges the target tag with the ten public keys (P_t, σ), for $1 \leq t \leq N$, and stores the secret matrices S_t that result.

One can observe that $S = K_T A V$ and $S_t = K_T P_t V$, for $1 \leq t \leq N$, where the matrix $V = \phi(\sigma, c)$ will depend on σ and the Tag's secret product c in a complicated way; the last row of V is all zero, except its last entry which is 1, by a property of E-multiplication stated above. However neither P_t nor V depend on K_T and we observe that

$$S \oplus S_t = (K_T A V) \oplus (K_T P_t V) = K_T (A \oplus P_t) V = K_T E_{t,N} V.$$

Since the last row of V has a special form, $S \oplus S_t$ will be zero everywhere except in the last column, for $1 \leq t \leq N$. Further, the values in this last column will correspond to the tth column of the tag secret matrix K_T. Taken together, the entirety of the tag secret matrix K_T can be recovered column-by-column and something that is intended to require 2^{80} operations can be accomplished with negligible work after $N + 1 = 11$ interactions with the target Tag, or 33 tag authentications if we take into account the protocol constraints in [25].

This attack has been confirmed using the parameters and examples given in [25]. It has also been confirmed on parameter sets of the form B16F256 that have been supplied by SecureRF. In this latter case, with N=16, we are required to perform 17 interactions with the target Tag, or 136 tag authentications if we respect protocol considerations and only recover at most 255 bits in each interaction. Recall that parameter sets of the form B16F256 are intended to provide 128-bit security.

The linearity property that facilitates this attack appears intrinsic to the definition of the Algebraic Eraser and thus hard to avoid; increasing the size of parameters will not provide any significant additional security.

6   Efficient Tag Impersonation

Even though the tag impersonation attack of Sect. 4 is already very effective, a more efficient attack can be designed using the result of Sect. 5. This new attack is more efficient in terms of all three measures of tag queries, computation, and storage.

Recall that $d_1, d_2, \ldots, d_{32} \in F$ are the interrogator conjugates. Define their corresponding permutations $g_i \in \text{Sym}(N)$ by $g_i = \pi(d_i)$. We already observed in Sect. 4 that these permutations are highly structured and have five fixed points.

Algorithm 1. Constructing a lookup table

1: Construct a table indexed by the $N!$ permutations in $\mathrm{Sym}(N)$, with all entries empty.
2: Add 'terminate' to the entry corresponding to the identity permutation.
3: Let L be a list that contains just the identity permutation.
4: **while** L non-empty **do**
5:     Let g be the first element in L.
6:     **for** $i \in \{1, 2, \ldots, 32\}$ and $e \in \{-1, 1\}$ **do**
7:         Compute gg_i^e.
8:         **if** the table entry indexed by gg_i^e is still empty **then**
9:             Change this entry to (i, e).
10:            Add gg_i^e to L.
11:    Remove g from L.

Stage 0: A pre-computation stage. Build an oracle which, when given a permutation $\sigma \in \mathrm{Sym}(N)$ that lies in the subgroup of $\mathrm{Sym}(N)$ generated by the g_i, returns r (a small integer), $i_1, i_2, \ldots, i_r \in \{1, 2, \ldots, 32\}$ and $\epsilon_1, \ldots, \epsilon_r \in \{-1, 1\}$ such that

$$\sigma = g_{i_1}^{\epsilon_1} g_{i_2}^{\epsilon_2} \cdots g_{i_r}^{\epsilon_r}.$$

Since $N! = 10! \leq 2^{22}$, we can build a very efficient oracle by constructing a lookup table of size $N!$ which contains the pair i_r and ϵ_r for each permutation σ that can be written as a product of the g_i (and a termination string for the identity permutation). The table may be constructed by using Algorithm 1.

Since each permutation g is added to the list L at most once, constructing the table takes at most about $N! \times 32 \times 2 \approx 2^{28}$ operations. Once the table is constructed, the oracle works on input σ by using the table to find the last element in a product of the permutations g_i and their inverses that is equal to σ. It then multiplies σ by the inverse of this last element, and iterates until it reaches the identity permutation. The oracle returns the shortest expression of the form we want (though we do not need this). The oracle is very efficient: just a few table lookups and permutation compositions are needed.

The subgroup generated by the permutations g_i in [25] is extremely small (as these permutations all fix the same five points). So building the table for the oracle above is extremely fast. We have implemented Algorithm 1 in C. It takes just 0.014 s to generate the table, and resulting oracle takes an average of under 0.00005 seconds to answer typical query, running on a 2.7 GHz i7 MacBook Pro. So the pre-computation stage takes a negligible time to complete, and the resulting oracle is extremely fast in practice.

Note that Algorithm 1 and the resulting oracle are very efficient even if the permutations d_i generate the whole of the symmetric group (the worst case for the pre-computation). Experiments with our implementation show that the table is constructed in 66 s, and the resulting oracle answers a typical query in an average of under 0.0015 s. So the pre-computation is always efficient.

For situations where it becomes impossible to store (in RAM) a table of length equal to the order of the subgroup generated by the permutations g_i, for example if N is much larger, we would suggest first using standard Schreier–Sims techniques (see Seress [26, Chap. 4], for example) and then the powerful heuristic approach of Kalka, Teicher and Tsaban [21], to construct the oracle. Note that the pre-computed oracle can be used whenever the same set of reader conjugates are used. Since the reader conjugate set D is a public system parameter [25] an oracle can be collaboratively computed and shared over the Internet.

Stage 1: Interact with the Tag as in Sect. 5 to obtain the Tag's public key (M_T, σ_T) and then its secret key K_T.

Stage 2: Impersonate the Tag using the techniques of Phase 2 of the attack of Kalka, Teicher and Tsaban [21, Section 3.2.2]. The details are as follows.

When a legitimate interrogator queries (M_I, σ_I), query the oracle to obtain $i_1, i_2, \ldots, i_r \in \{1, 2, \ldots, 32\}$ and $\epsilon_1, \ldots, \epsilon_r \in \{-1, 1\}$ such that

$$\sigma_I = g_{i_1}^{\epsilon_1} g_{i_2}^{\epsilon_2} \cdots g_{i_r}^{\epsilon_r}.$$

Define

$$w = d_{i_1}^{\epsilon_1} d_{i_2}^{\epsilon_2} \cdots d_{i_r}^{\epsilon_r}.$$

Compute the matrix L_1 that is the result of the following E-multiplication:

$$(K_T M_I, \sigma_I) * w^{-1}.$$

Compute the matrix L_2 that is the result of the following E-multiplication:

$$(K_T^{-1} M_T, \sigma_T) * w.$$

The shared key is $(L_1 L_2, \sigma_T \sigma_I)$. This derivation has been implemented and confirmed.

7   Full Private Key Recovery

Given the extreme effectiveness of the tag impersonation attack of Sect. 6 the need for a full key recovery attack on the Algebraic Eraser tag authentication protocol is questionable. Under normal circumstances one might prefer a key-recovery attack so that recovered keys could be inserted into a cloned device, thereby exploiting the storage and performance advantages of the original algorithm. However, in our attacks, the pre-computed look-up table is small and impersonation is exceptionally fast; in fact it would be interesting to compare the performance of the impersonation attack to the computation required by the legitimate tag.

Nevertheless, to illustrate that a complete key recovery attack does exist we outline a basic attack using a *meet-in-the-middle* technique. While the attack in this section is already very effective (2^{48} storage and 2^{49} time for one of the parameter choices proposed for standardization) we believe that more analysis could reveal more practical variants.

To start, we will say that Tag conjugate products $c, c' \in F$ are *equivalent*, which we write as $c \equiv c'$, if

$$(I, 1) * c = (I, 1) * c'$$

where I is the $N \times N$ identity matrix and where 1 is the identity permutation. The definition of E-multiplication shows that when V is any fixed invertible matrix $c \equiv c'$ if and only if

$$(V, 1) * c = (V, 1) * c'.$$

In particular, when $V = K_T$ and c are the two components of the Tag private key, a private key consisting of K_T and c' will produce the same Tag public key if, and only if, $c \equiv c'$ (because K_T is invertible). Since all shared keys can be derived from the public key and the interrogator's secret information, replacing c by c' in the Tag makes no difference to any of the shared keys computed by the Tag in the protocol. So to recover the full secret key of the Tag we need only find $c' \in F$ that is equivalent to c.

Assume that the Tag's secret product c of conjugates has length 16, as allowed by [25]. There are $2 \times 32 = 2^6$ possibilities for each term in the product, and so there are $2^{6 \times 16} = 2^{96}$ possibilities for c. We now describe a simple meet-in-the-middle technique that will recover an equivalent product c' using a look-up table with $\sqrt{2^{96}} = 2^{48}$ entries. The attack extends in a natural way to longer products of conjugates.

Suppose now that an attacker has recovered the Tag private matrix K_T by the attack of Sect. 5. Clearly the attacker has the Tag's public key (M_T, σ_T). The attacker then searches for products $c' \in F$ of Tag conjugates that are equivalent to c by finding c' such that $(K_T, 1) * c' = (M_T, \sigma_T)$. We write $c' = w_1'(w_2')^{-1}$ where the w_i are length eight products of Tag conjugates and their inverses. Note that

$$(K_T, 1) * w_1' = (M_T, \sigma_T) * w_2'.$$

For each of the 2^{48} possibilities for w_1', we compute $(K_T, 1) * w_1'$. We store the results in such a way that it is easy to find w_1' if we are given $(K_T, 1) * w_1'$. For example, we could use an array of pairs $((K_T, 1) * w_1', w_1')$, sorted by its first component.

For each of the 2^{48} possibilities for w_2', we compute $(M_T, \sigma_T) * w_2$ and check whether this value occurs as the first of a pair in our array. Once we find such a value w_2, we set $c' = w_1'(w_2')^{-1}$ where w_1' is the second element of the pair we have found in the array. Note that

$$(K_T, 1) * c' = ((K_T, 1) * w_1') * (w_2')^{-1} = ((M_T, \sigma_T) * w_2') * (w_2')^{-1} = (M_T, \sigma_T),$$

and so c' and K_T form a private key that produces the Tag's public key. Hence $c \equiv c'$, and we have found an equivalent private key for the Tag.

Small-scale variants of this attack—using a reduced Tag conjugate set C and shorter products—have been successfully implemented for the parameter sets B10F256 given in [25].

8 Conclusion

The Algebraic Eraser has been on the periphery of the cryptographic literature for nearly ten years. However the designers have not made it easy for independent researchers to analyze the scheme. The reason for this approach is unclear, but the consequence has been a lack of independent peer-review.

It is too soon to determine whether or not secure schemes can be built around the mechanisms seen in the Algebraic Eraser. Certainly it is always interesting to see new techniques based on different hard problems. But any performance claims for the Algebraic Eraser are premature without a more complete understanding of the security that is delivered. The work of Ben-Zvi *et al.* [7] and that presented in this paper suggest that a lack of independent analysis has hindered the algorithm proponents from seeking out alternative viewpoints and, critically, from recognizing some very effective attacks. These have only become apparent as the profile of the algorithm has been raised and details about the algorithm have been made public.

It is hard to avoid the conclusion that the Algebraic Eraser should not be used or standardized in its current form. If future versions are proposed, and [5] provides hints that this may be the case, then it is important that a full and detailed specification be made publicly available. Just as for the parent algorithm, we believe any variants should not be used until there has been sufficient independent public cryptanalysis.

References

1. Ågren, M., Hell, M., Johansson, T., Meier, W.: Grain-128a: a new version of grain-128 with optional authentication. Int. J. Wirel. Mob. Comput. **5**(1), 48–59 (2011). Inderscience
2. Anshel, I., Atkins, D., Goldfeld, D., Gunnels, P.: Defeating the Ben-Zvi, Blackburn, and Tsaban Attack on the Algebraic Eraser. http://arxiv.org/pdf/1601.04780v1.pdf, http://eprint.iacr.org/2016/044.pdf
3. Anshel, I., Anshel, M., Goldfeld, D., Lemieux, S.: Key agreement, the Algebraic Eraser and Lightweight Cryptography. Contemporary Mathematics 418, pp. 1–34 (2006). www.securerf.com/wp-content/uploads/2014/03/SecureRF-Technical-White-Paper-06-with-Appendix-A-B.pdf
4. Atkins, D.: Algebraic Eraser: A lightweight, efficient asymmetric key agreement protocol for use in no-power, low-power, and IoT devices. www.csrc.nist.gov/groups/ST/lwc-workshop2015/papers/session8-atkins-paper.pdf
5. Atkins, D., Goldfeld, D.: Addressing the Algebraic Eraser Diffie–Hellman over-the-Air Protocol. http://eprint.iacr.org/2016/205.pdf (Pre-print)
6. Atkins, D., Gunnells, P.E.: Algebraic Eraser: A lightweight, efficient asymmetric key agreement protocol for use in no-power, low-power, and IoT devices. www.csrc.nist.gov/groups/ST/lwc-workshop2015/presentations/session8-atkins-gunnell.pdf
7. Ben-Zvi, A., Blackburn, S.R., Tsaban, B.: A Practical Cryptanalysis of the Algebraic Eraser. 7 October 2015. http://eprint.iacr.org/2015/1102 (Pre-print)
8. Bogdanov, A., Knudsen, L.R., Leander, G., Paar, C., Poschmann, A., Robshaw, M.J.B., Seurin, Y., Vikkelsoe, C.: PRESENT: an ultra-lightweight block cipher. In: Paillier, P., Verbauwhede, I. (eds.) CHES 2007. LNCS, vol. 4727, pp. 450–466. Springer, Heidelberg (2007)
9. Cryptography Stack Exchange. Posting, November 18 2015. http://crypto.stackexchange.com/questions/30644/status-of-algebraic-eraser-key-exchange

10. Diffie, W., Hellman, M.: New Directions in Cryptography. IEEE Trans. Inf. Theor. **IT–22**(6), 644–654 (1976)
11. EPCglobal. EPC Radio Frequency Identity Protocols, Generation 2 UHF RFID. Specification for RFID Air Interface Protocol for Communications at 860 MHz-960 MHz Version 2.0.1. www.gs1.org/gsmp/kc/epcglobal/uhfc1g2
12. Goldfeld, D., Gunnells, P.: Defeating the Kalka-Teicher-Tsaban linear algebra attack on the Algebraic Eraser, arXiv:1202.0598, February 2012
13. Gunnells, P.: On the cryptanalysis of the generalized simultaneous conjugacy search problem and the security of the Algebraic Eraser, arXiv:1105.1141, May 2011
14. ISO/IEC 29167-10:2015 - Information technology - Automatic identification and data capture techniques - Part 10: Crypto suite AES-128 security services for air interface communications
15. ISO/IEC 29167-11:2014 - Information technology - Automatic identification and data capture techniques - Part 11: Crypto suite PRESENT-80 security services for air interface communications
16. ISO/IEC 29167-13:2015 - Information technology - Automatic identification and data capture techniques - Part 13: Crypto suite Grain-128a security services for air interface communications
17. ISO/IEC 29167-12:2015 - Information technology - Automatic identification and data capture techniques - Part 12: Crypto suite ECC-DH security services for air interface communications
18. ISO/IEC 29167-16 - Information technology - Automatic identification, data capture techniques - Part 16: Crypto suite ECDSA-ECDH security services for air interface communications
19. ISO/IEC 29167-17:2015 - Information technology - Automatic identification and data capture techniques - Part 17: Crypto suite cryptoGPS security services for air interface communications
20. ISO/IEC 29167-20 - Information technology - Automatic identification, data capture techniques - Part 20: Crypto suite Algebraic Eraser security services for air interface communications. Working Draft
21. Kalka, A., Teicher, M., Tsaban, B.: Short expressions of permutations as products and cryptanalysis of the Algebraic Eraser. Adv. Appl. Math. **49**, 57–76 (2012)
22. Myasnikov, A., Ushakov, A.: Cryptanalysis of the Anshel-Anshel-Goldfeld-Lemieux key agreement protocol. Groups Complex. Crypt. **1**, 63–75 (2009)
23. National Institute of Standards and Technology. FIPS 197: Advanced Encryption Standard, November 2001
24. SecureRF Corporation. Corporate materials. www.securerf.com
25. SecureRF Corporation. Algebraic Eraser OTA Authentication. 5 October 2015. www.securerf.com/wp-content/uploads/2015/10/Algebraic_Eraser_Over-the-Air_Authentication.pdf. Also posted at [9]
26. Seress, Á.: Permutation Group Algorithms. Cambridge University Press, Cambridge (2003)

A Cryptographic Analysis of UMTS/LTE AKA

Stephanie Alt[1], Pierre-Alain Fouque[2], Gilles Macario-rat[4],
Cristina Onete[3], and Benjamin Richard[4(✉)]

[1] DGA Bruz, Bruz, France
s.alt@free.com
[2] IRISA, University of Rennes 1, Rennes, France
pierre-alain.fouque@ens.fr
[3] INSA/IRISA Rennes, Rennes, France
cristina.onete@gmail.com
[4] Orange Labs, Chatillon, France
{gilles.macariorat,benjamin.richard}@orange.com

Abstract. Secure communications between mobile subscribers and
their associated operator networks require mutual authentication and
key deri-vation protocols. The 3GPP standard provides the AKA protocol
for just this purpose. Its structure is generic, to be instantiated with a set
of seven cryptographic algorithms. The currently-used proposal instantiates these by means of a set of AES-based algorithms called MILENAGE;
as an alternative, the ETSI SAGE committee submitted the TUAK algorithms, which rely on a truncation of the internal permutation of Keccak.

In this paper, we provide a formal security analysis of the AKA protocol in its complete three-party setting. We formulate requirements
with respect to both Man-in-the-Middle (MiM) adversaries, i.e. key-
indistinguishability and impersonation security, and to local untrusted
serving networks, denoted "servers", namely state-confidentiality and
soundness. We prove that the unmodified AKA protocol attains these
properties as long as servers cannot be corrupted. Furthermore, adding
a unique server identifier suffices to guarantee all the security statements
even in in the presence of corrupted servers. We use a modular proof approach: the first step is to prove the security of (modified and unmodified)
AKA with generic cryptographic algorithms that can be represented as
a unitary pseudorandom function –PRF– keyed either with the client's
secret key or with the operator key. A second step proceeds to show that
TUAK and MILENAGE guarantee this type of pseudorandomness, though
the guarantee for MILENAGE requires a stronger assumption. Our paper
provides (to our knowledge) the first complete, rigorous analysis of the
original AKA protocol and these two instantiations. We stress that such
an analysis is important for any protocol deployed in real-life scenarios.

Keywords: Security proof · AKA protocol · TUAK · MILENAGE

1 Introduction

Transmitting confidential and authenticated data between two parties across
an insecure channel is a fundamental goal in cryptography. Secure channels are
usually obtained by means of an authenticated key-exchange (AKE) protocol.

© Springer International Publishing Switzerland 2016
M. Manulis et al. (Eds.): ACNS 2016, LNCS 9696, pp. 18–35, 2016.
DOI: 10.1007/978-3-319-39555-5_2

AKE protocols generally consist of two phases. During the first phase, the parties authenticate each other and exchange data that enables them to compute a master key. The latter is then used to derive one or several secret keys, as well as other useful values. In a second phase, the derived keys are used to construct the secure channel between the parties, guaranteeing the confidentiality, integrity, and authentication of the data they exchange.

In this paper, we focus on the Authentication and Key Agreement protocol (AKA) used in 3G and 4G networks, more specifically the 3G UMTS AKA (Universal Mobile Telecommunications System) and 4G EPS AKA (Evolved Packet System) protocol[1]. The AKA protocol is used in a greater context in the 3rd Generation Partnership Project (3GPP), which aims to develop the specifications for the next generation mobile systems. The security of the system is covered by Technical Specifications 33 (TS 33) and 35 (TS 35)[2], from both an architectural and a security-algorithm standpoint.

The AKA Protocol. Initially developed in the 1990s, AKA uses symmetric keys exclusively, in a mobile-network context which imposes a peculiar architecture. In this setup, mobile *clients* subscribe to a single *operator*, which provides them with mobile services (messaging, calls, Internet use, etc.). Services are provided across a secure channel, not by the operator, but by an intermediate *local* network operator (which we call *server* to avoid confusion). The server and operator are affiliated together for domestic use. However, if the client is abroad, service is provided by a server affiliated with a different operator. Thus, servers are only trusted to provide services, but they must not learn the client's long-term secrets (known only to the client and the operator); by contrast, servers do learn short-term secret values, such as session keys, which are necessary for the transmission of the required service. Consequently, unlike the classical two-party AKE setting, the AKA protocol requires three participants.

One specificity of the subscriber-operator architecture is that clients are associated both with a unique client-key and with their operator's key, which is shared with all the other clients (a potentially very large number) of that operator. Clients minimize the risk of compromising the shared key by only storing a (one-way) function of that, and the client key, never the operator key in clear.

The design of the AKA protocol is influenced by three important constraints. One is that (current and older) SIM cards, cannot generate (pseudo)random numbers. Thus, freshness has to be guaranteed without client randomness. The second constraint is that the (necessary) communication[3] between servers and operators in the roaming scenario is usually expensive. In the AKA protocol, operators generate *batches* of *authentication vectors* for the server, thus

---

[1] We stress that while AKA is an instance of authenticated key-exchange, AKE denotes a larger class of protocols, including e.g. TLS/SSL, PACE/EAC, etc.

[2] See http://www.3gpp.org/DynaReport/33-series.htm and http://www.3gpp.org/DynaReport/35-series.htm.

[3] Notably, since the server is not trusted, it needs information from the client's operator to provide service to the client.

minimizing costs. Finally, mobile channels are notoriously noisy, requiring the protocol to be robust with respect to noise. As a result of these constraints, the AKA protocol is *stateful*, with the authentication depending on an updatable *sequence number*, which is accepted within a tolerance interval.

TUAK and MILENAGE. In this paper we focus on the *provable security* of AKA. The latter is constructed using symmetric-key primitives, namely a set of seven cryptographic functions, denoted $\mathcal{F}_1, \ldots, \mathcal{F}_5, \mathcal{F}_1^*, \mathcal{F}_5^*$. We closely follow the design of these algorithms, as well as that of the protocol, in our analysis.

Originally, 3GPP put forward a proposal for an AES-encryption-based algorithm set, called MILENAGE [1]. As an alternative to MILENAGE, the ETSI SAGE committee proposed another set of algorithms called TUAK [2], which relies on a truncation of Keccak's internal permutation. The winner of the SHA-3 hash function competition, Keccak offers both higher performance, in hardware and software, than AES, and resistance to many generic attacks. While the TUAK algorithms inherit Keccak's superior performance, they do not use the Keccak permutation in a usual, black-box way, but rather rely on something akin to a Merkle-Damgård construction. Instead, the internal permutation is truncated, then used in a cascade, which makes previous results harder to use. We cannot simply use the same assumptions for the truncated version as we would for the original permutation, either. Our analysis of the key indistinguishability, as well as client- and respectively server-impersonation resistance of the protocol concerns both the classical MILENAGE-based version, and the one using TUAK.

Related Work. At its core, the AKA protocol provides authenticated key exchange (AKE), a primitive first modelled by Bellare and Rogaway [8]. We use the Bellare-Pointcheval-Rogaway (BPR) extension of this model [7]; however, the three-party setting and lack of randomness on the prover side do not allow us to simply "import" their model, as we explain in more detail below.

Few papers give a security proof for AKA, especially when instantiated with MILENAGE. Gilbert provides an out-of-context proof for MILENAGE [11], showing it operates as a kind of counter mode for key derivation. It is unclear whether this suffices to guarantee security for AKA at large; indeed, we show in this paper that MILENAGE is not quite as versatile as TUAK. The closest results to a security proof of AKA (see below) use automated (formal) verification.

In 2003, Zhang [15] described an important server-corruption attack against AKA and advised against the use of sequence numbers as state. He also presented a stateless modification of the protocol called AP-AKA and proved its security in Shoup's model. In the full version of this paper, we show that AP-AKA is still vulnerable to a particular type of replay attack. Server corruptions are a highly relevant threat in a post-Snowden cryptographic era, in which intelligence agencies have been known to substitute and backdoor algorithms, and store massive amounts of data. We take such attacks into account into our definitions. We also extend a countermeasure from Zhang [15], which features the addition, in the authentication string, of a unique server-specific identifier, and we show how to incorporate it within the existent MILENAGE and TUAK specifications.

The security proof of Lee et al. [13] is complementary to ours as they focus on the LTE (Long-term Evolution) protocol in 4G networks (similar to AKA, but using different identifiers and key-management), rather than the handshake itself. Lee et al. analyse the *privacy* of LTE, rather than the *security* of AKA (as we do). Their main result is that in the absence of server corruptions, LTE attains a weak untraceability against an active MiM adversary. We discuss their work in more detail in the full version. Though this is not made explicit, Lee et al.'s result implies the impersonation resistance of LTE and some security of the derived session keys; however, their proofs hold for an important modification of AKA, as we discuss in more detail in the full version. A surprising problem is that [13] cannot capture IMSI-catcher attacks (which directly impact privacy *without* server corruptions); this is because, contrary to real-world scenarios, they assume that once a TMSI is allocated, the IMSI will never again appear in clear. Finally, their proofs reduce the privacy of AKA to some assumptions on the functions which are akin to the unitary function G that we use; however, they do not analyse TUAK and MILENAGE to verify whether these suites actually guarantee those required properties.

Arapinis et al. [5] focus on the client privacy of the AKA protocol by automated verification in ProVerif [10]; however, they only assess a *modified* version, which randomizes the sequence number. This fundamental modification makes their results inapplicable to the original protocol. Our attempts to extend this analysis to that of the true protocol by using a state-permissive tool called StatVerif [6] were not fruitful, as discussed in the full paper.

Our Contributions. We present four main contributions: (a) fully-formalized definitions for the security of AKA in the three party setting; (b) security proofs indicating that the current AKA protocol does not attain full security in the presence of server corruptions (due to the attack of Zhang [15]); (c) we show how to attain full security by simply adding a unique server identifier in the authentication; (d) we prove that our security statements hold for both protocol instantiations (TUAK and MILENAGE). In particular, we analyse two somewhat-similar versions of the protocol: the original AKA scheme and a slight variation of it of our own design, which we also analyse. We detail our contributions below.

Security Model. We first define a threat model and five game-based security notions for the 3-party AKA protocol, three with respect to a Man-in-the-Middle –MiM– adversary (akin to BPR security, but with three parties, allowing server corruptions for the *strong*, as opposed to the *weak* property), and two with respect to malicious servers. These properties are:

1. **Key-indistinguishability:** the derived session keys are indistinguishable from random by a MiM attacker placed between the client and a server with black-box access to all operators.
2. **Client- and server-impersonation:** a MiM attacker cannot impersonate honest servers (to the client), or clients (to an honest server). Due to the identification phase, AKA resists client impersonations better than server impersonations.

3. **State-confidentiality:** (malicious) servers cannot learn: the client's secret key, the operator's secret key, nor their state. The malicious server may interact with both operators and clients, but we only address the AKA handshake (not the secure-channel primitives).
4. **Soundness:** (malicious) servers cannot authenticate to the client unless they are explicitly given authenticating information by a legitimate operator.

Security Proofs. We analyse the security of two versions of AKA: the current one, and our modification of it. In the full version, we also show that the AP-AKA version of the protocol, due to Zhang, is vulnerable to a replay attack. We prove that, under the assumption that the seven cryptographic functions behave as a unitary function G that is pseudorandom when keyed with the client key, the *current* AKA version guarantees: weak key-indistinguishability; weak server-impersonation resistance; strong client-impersonation resistance; and soundness. If furthermore the algorithms behave as a PRF called G^*, when keyed with the operator key, AKA also guarantees state confidentiality. For our modification of the AKA protocol, we prove, under the same assumptions: state-indistinguishabi-lity, soundness, as well as strong key-indistinguishability, server- and client-impersonation security. This first proof step, reducing protocol security to that of a unitary function, allows us to define a sufficient security requirement for the underlying sub-algorithms.

TUAK and MILENAGE. The second step of the proof is to show that both TUAK and MILENAGE behave as the required functions G and G^*. This can be proved for TUAK under the standard assumption that the (un-)truncated Keccak permutation is a good PRF [9,12]. By contrast, proving that MILENAGE can be modelled as a unitary PRF when keyed with the operator key requires the pseudorandomness of a keyed AES-version of a classic Davies-Meyer construction for MILENAGE, which seems a stronger assumption than just assuming the pseudorandomness of the underlying AES permutation.

AKA Privacy. Several papers indicate privacy problems for AKA, e.g. [3–5,14]. The last of these is a recent result, indicating that privacy can be attacked at a lower level than the protocol layer (by leakage at a physical layer). Since AKA is known not to provide strong privacy, and it is moreover unclear whether it *can* even hope to provide it considering such leaks at lower layers, we choose to restrict ourselves to the subject of AKA security, rather than its privacy.

2 The AKA Protocol

Mobile 3G networks use the variant of AKA fully depicted in Fig. 1, allowing the client and the server to output session keys (CK, IK), which are then used to secure future message-exchanges. The same protocol is the backbone of the 4G LTE protocol; however, for LTE the client is associated with an identifier called GUTI (see 3GPP TS 23.003, release 13), as opposed to the tuple of permanent and temporary identifiers we describe below. The use of GUTIs make no difference for our analysis. More significantly, the session keys CK, IK from the 3G protocol are only used as key material for a key derivation function KDF, which outputs the true session key.[4] Our proofs work similarly for this new key derivation, but we would need an additional reduction to KDF security.

This protocol features two main *active* actors: the client (in 3GPP terminology ME/USIM) and the server (denoted VLR). The third, only selectively-active party is the operator (denoted HLR). The tripartite setup of AKA was meant for roaming, for which the server providing mobile coverage is not the client's operator, and may be subject to different legislation and vulnerabilities than the latter. Thus, although the server is trusted to provide services across a secure channel, it must not learn long-term sensitive information about either clients or their home operators. Using the server as a mere proxy would ideal; however, the server/operator communication is (financially) expensive.

Section 3 describes in detail the setup of the three parties. Clients C and operators Op use both the client's secret key sk_C and the operator's secret key sk_{Op}[5]. The client and operator also keep track of sequence numbers Sqn_C (resp. $Sqn_{Op,C}$), updated after each successful authentication (by a simple, predictable procedure, e.g. incrementing them by a fixed value). If the states are too far apart, the client prompts a re-synchronization. The three parties: clients, servers, and operators, also know the client's permanent identifier IMSI. Clients and servers must keep track of tuples (IMSI, TMSI, LAI), the last two values forming a unique temporary identifier, which is updated at every session.

The AKA protocol, depicted in Fig. 1, proceeds in several subparts. The first two protocol exchanges are between the client C and the server S over an *insecure channel* and they make up the *user identification* step. At the end of this phase, the server will associate C with an identifier, either the permanent International Mobile Subscriber Identity IMSI or the tuple of a Temporary Mobile Subscriber Identity TMSI and the Local Area Identifier LAI of the server issuing the latest TMSI. The identification procedure is vital to the client's privacy; however, as we focus here only on the *security* of AKA, we just associate each client with a unique user ID UID (as we explain at the end of this section). Once the server associates the client with an identifier UID, it proceeds either to the *authentication vector generation* step (detailed in the set ① of instructions in Fig. 1), or to the *authenticated key-exchange* part (detailed in instruction sets ②-④). The former of these is run by the server and the operator of the client C over a *secure channel*, and it provides the server S with authentication and key-exchange material for a batch of AKA sessions with C; whenever S runs out of AKE material, it re-runs the vector generation step. For each session, Op prepares an authentication vector AV consisting of: a fresh random value R; a server-authentication string Mac_S (authenticating R and the value $Sqn_{Op,C}$); a client-authentication string Mac_C (authenticating R only); the session keys CK

---

[4] This key, denoted K_{asme}, is computed as: $K_{asme} = KDF(CK\|IK, ID_{SN}, Sqn \oplus AK, const)$, with ID_{SN} the serving operator network identity.

[5] Technically speaking, the client never stores this value in clear; instead it uses a pseudorandom value Top_C computed from the client and operator keys.

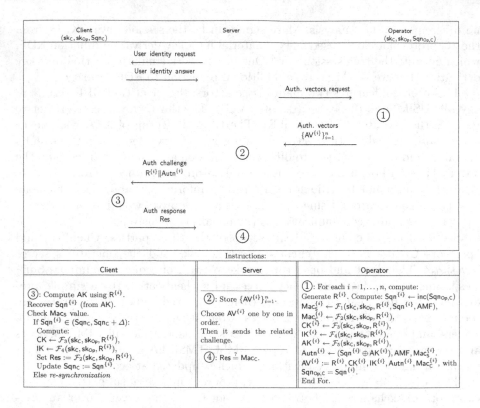

Fig. 1. The AKA procedure.

and IK; and a one-time-pad encryption of $Sqn_{Op,C}$ with a pseudorandom string AK. The values Mac_S, Mac_C, CK, IK, AK are output by cryptographic algorithms denoted $\mathcal{F}_1, \ldots, \mathcal{F}_5$ respectively. The AKA protocol also features the algorithms $\mathcal{F}_1^*, \mathcal{F}_5^*$ for re-synchronization. All algorithms take as input the client key sk_C, the operator key sk_{Op}, and the random value R; in addition, $\mathcal{F}_1$ and $\mathcal{F}_1^*$ also use the operator's and resp. the client's sequence number. The server is given a batch of vectors of the form: $AV = (R, CK, IK, Mac_S, Mac_C, AMF, AK \oplus Sqn_{Op,C})$, in which AMF is a public authentication management field managed by the operator.

The *authenticated-key-exchange* step allows clients and servers to mutually authenticate and compute session keys over an *insecure channel*. The server chooses the next AV from the latest batch, using the random R and the string $Autn = (Sqn_{Op,C} \oplus AK) \| AMF \| Mac_S$ as a challenge. The client uses R to compute AK and recover $Sqn_{Op,C}$. If the received Mac_S verifies and $Sqn_{Op,C}$ is within a predefined distance Δ of Sqn_C, then C computes (CK, IK) and the value Mac_C, sending this last value to S. If the two sequence numbers are too far apart, then C forces a re-synchronization, described below. Else, the client updates Sqn_C to $Sqn_{Op,C}$, and S verifies the received authentication value with respect to the Mac_C sent by Op. If Mac_C verifies, then S sends an acknowledgement to Op and runs a TMSI *re-allocation*. During the optional *re-synchronization*, the client uses Sqn_C

to compute values $\mathsf{Mac}_\mathsf{S}^*$ and $\mathsf{AK}^* \oplus \mathsf{Sqn}_\mathsf{C}$ as Op did, using the session R, but algorithms $\mathcal{F}_1^*$ and $\mathcal{F}_5^*$ (not $\mathcal{F}_1$ and $\mathcal{F}_5$). If $\mathsf{Mac}_\mathsf{S}^*$ verifies, Op resets $\mathsf{Sqn}_{\mathsf{Op,C}}$ to Sqn_C and sends to S another batch of AV as before. The protocol restarts.

Following successful key exchange, the client and server run the TMSI *reallocation*. The server sends an (unauthenticated) encryption of a new, randomly chosen TMSI (which is unique per server) to the client C, using the agreed-upon key CK. Encryption is done by means of the A5/3 algorithm (see 3GPP TS 43.020, release 12), run in cipher mode. The new TMSI value, called $\mathsf{TMSI_{new}}$, is only permanently saved by S if acknowledged by the client; else, both $\mathsf{TMSI_{new}}$ and $\mathsf{TMSI_{old}}$ are retained and can be used in the next protocol run.

Identities and Reallocation. Though in this paper we stick close to the AKA protocol, one simplification we make throughout is associating each client with a single, unique UID, which we consider public. In practice, UID is the user's IMSI, which is used in case a TMSI value is not traceable to an IMSI. From the point of view of security, any attack initiated by mismatching TMSI values (i.e. replacing one value by another) is equivalent to doing the same with IMSI values.

Another important feature of AKA that we abstract in this analysis is the TMSI reallocation. If the TMSI system were flawless (a newly-allocated TMSI is reliable and non-modifiable by an active MiM), then we could prove a stronger degree of server impersonation than we currently do. As discussed in Sect. 3, an active MiM can inject false TMSI values, which make servers request an IMSI value; if the MiM reuses this value, it can impersonate servers by offline relays. The use of the TMSI in AKA is undone by using IMSIs as a backup for TMSIs; also, insecurities in using TMSIs translate to the identification by IMSI.

3   Security Model

In this section, we propose a security model with respect to two types of adversaries: an active MiM with access to the insecure channel between the client and the server; and a malicious server, which also has access to operators. Our security notions are: key-indistinguishability for the session keys CK, IK, and client- and server-impersonation resistance. With respect to servers, we also require the key-confidentiality of the client's long term data $\mathsf{sk_C}, \mathsf{sk_{Op}}, \mathsf{Sqn_C}$, and soundness. We use similar oracles for all the definitions. While we cannot use a basic BPR syntax [7] in this three-party setting, we guarantee a same kind of security with respect to MiM attackers. While our server-impersonation model is slightly weaker than that for client-impersonation, this has no impact on the key-indistinguishability for the session keys. For clarity, we include here only intuitive description of the oracles, and leave the formalization for the full version.

Set Up and Participants. We consider a set $\mathcal{P}$ of participants, which are either a server S_i or a mobile client C_i. Operators Op are not modelled as active parties; in all security games with respect to MiM adversaries, operators are black-box algorithms within each server S_i. For security with respect servers, the operators are oracles which malicious servers may query. We assume there are n_C clients, n_S servers, and n_{Op} operators. For MiM models, servers contain "copies" of all operators; the copies are assumed to be synchronized with respect to client state, though their output might depend on which server queries them. We associate each client with: a unique identifier UID, long-term static keys $(\text{sk}_{UID}, \text{sk}_{Op})$, and an ephemeral state st_{UID} which is a sequence number Sqn_{UID}. Each of the n_S servers has black-box access to operator algorithms (or oracles for state-confidentiality and soundness) $\text{Op}_1, \ldots, \text{Op}_{n_{Op}}$, initialised with long-term keys (sk_{Op_i}) and tuples $(\text{UID}, \text{sk}_C, \text{Sqn}_{Op,C})$, the last value dynamically updated. For simplicity, we assume that the key space of all operators is identical.

Security Against MiM Adversaries. In our model, the clients and servers may run concurrent executions of the protocol Π. We denote the j-th execution of the protocol by party P as P_j, associated with a session ID sid, a partner ID pid (consisting either of one or of multiple elements), and an accept/reject bit accept (explained in detail in Sect. 4). In this case P_j is a handle, used by a MiM adversary $\mathcal{A}$ to access the oracles below so as to schedule message deliveries, send tampered messages, or interact arbitrarily with any party. We also use a function G, which we model as a PRF. For a more detailed description, see our full version.

- CreateCl(Op): creates a new user C associated with a unique identifier UID, a key sk_{UID} drawn independently and uniformly at random from a key space $\mathcal{S}$, the key sk_{Op} of operator Op, and a sequence number Sqn stored in st_{UID}. The adversary is given UID and Sqn_{UID}. The operator Op is given $(\text{UID}, \text{sk}_{UID}, \text{Op}, \text{Sqn}_{UID})$, and initializes $\text{st}_{Op,UID} := \text{Sqn}_{UID}$, saving the entry $(\text{UID}, \text{sk}_{UID}, \text{sk}_{Op}, \text{st}_{Op,UID})$ in its database.
- NewInstance(P): instantiates a new instance of Π for party P, thus creating the handle P_j, which is made available to the adversary.
- Execute(P, i, P', j): simulates an execution of Π between the initiating instance P_i and the instance P'_j outputting the transcript τ.
- Send(P, i, m): sends message m to instance P_i, which outputs a response m'.
- Reveal(P, i): outputs the session key(s) K of instance P_i.
- Corrupt(P): If P is a client, return the key sk_C, but not sk_{Op}[6]. If P is a server, return sk_{Op}, giving the adversary access to oracle OpAccess. Corrupted parties become *adversarially controlled*.
- OpAccess(S, C): gives the adversary access to the local copy of all the operators stored "inside" a corrupted server S; the adversary receives as output the message Op returns if S queries Op concerning a client C.

---

[6] In this we keep faithful to the implementation of AKA, which protects sk_{Op} from the user by storing a 1-way function of sk_{Op} and sk_C in the SIM card. Another approach would be to reveal an intermediate, AKA-specific value denoted Top_C upon corruption. In the interest of generality, we keep the model at a higher level of abstraction than the peculiarities of AKA. We also note that in our proofs, a common first step is to give the adversary access to a broader corruption oracle, which also reveals sk_{Op}, with no security loss.

– StReveal(C, i, bit_S): returns the state of a client C_i if $\text{bit}_S = 0$ or the state of an operator with respect to a client if $\text{bit}_S = 1$.

We consider two classes of adversaries $\mathcal{A}$, *weak* and *strong*, depending on whether $\mathcal{A}$ may corrupt servers or not. We model three requirements with respect to MiM adversaries.

The notion of *key indistinguishability* demands that the session keys for each execution be indistinguishable from random bitstrings of equal length. The corresponding game is played as follows. The challenger generates the keys of all the n_{Op} operators and the n_C clients; then it gives the n_S servers S_i black-box access to the operators. The adversary may query any of the oracles above, and finally issue a single *Test* query on a fresh instance P_i, which returns either the real keys this instance computed, or random ones of the same length. Strong adversaries can gain oracle access to the copies of the operators in that server. We say that an instance is *fresh* if, and only if: neither the party, nor the partner is corrupted, and no key-reveal was done either on this party, nor on the partner. We define *partner* instances as having the same *session ID* sid, which will consist of a random number R, the client key sk_C, the operator key sk_{Op}, and the sequence number used in the successful server authentication $Sqn_{Op,C}$[7].

Finally, $\mathcal{A}$ determines whether the returned keys were real or random, and wins if, and only if its response is correct. The adversary's advantage is defined as:

$$\mathsf{Adv}_\Pi^{\mathsf{K.Ind}}(\mathcal{A}) := |\Pr[\mathcal{A} \text{ wins}] - 1/2|.$$

Definition 1 [Weak/Strong Key-Indistinguishability]. *A key-agreement protocol Π is $(t, q_{exec}, q_{res}, q_G, \epsilon)$-weakly key-indistinguishable (resp. $(t, q_{exec}, q_{res}, q_s, q_{Op}, q_G, \epsilon)$-strongly-key-indistinguishable) if no adversary running in time t, creating at most q_{exec} party instances with at most q_{res} resynchronizations per instance, (corrupting at most q_s servers and making at most q_{Op} OpAccess queries per operator per corrupted server for strong security), and making at most q_G queries to function G, has an advantage $\mathsf{Adv}_\Pi^{\mathsf{K.Ind}}(\mathcal{A}) > \epsilon$.*

We also consider *impersonation* attacks, in which $\mathcal{A}$ aims to impersonate a partner of a fresh instance. Again, the game begins by generating keys; then $\mathcal{A}$ gains access to all the oracles (except server corruption/operator access for weak adversaries). When $\mathcal{A}$ stops, she *wins* if, and only if, there exists an instance (server-instance S_i for client-impersonation, client-instance C_i for the server-impersonation) that ends in an accepting state and is *fresh*, subject to an offline/online relay attack described below. The adversary's advantage is:

$$\mathsf{Adv}_\Pi^{\mathsf{C.Imp}}(\mathcal{A}) := \Pr[\mathcal{A} \text{ wins}], \text{ and respectively } \mathsf{Adv}_\Pi^{\mathsf{S.Imp}}(\mathcal{A}) := \Pr[\mathcal{A} \text{ wins}].$$

Definition 2 [Weak/Strong Impersonation security]. *A key-agreement protocol Π is $(t, q_{exec}, q_{res}, q_G, \epsilon)$-weak-impersonation-secure (resp. $(t, q_{exec}, q_{res}, q_s,$*

---

[7] This choice of pid and sid makes our security guarantee non-composable; however, the design of AKA makes it hard to define pids based only on publicly-known values.

$q_{Op}, q_G, \epsilon)$-*strong-impersonation secure) if no adversary running in time t, creating at most q_{exec} party instances with at most q_{res} resynchronizations per instance, (corrupting at most q_s servers and making at most q_{Op}* OpAccess *queries per operator per corrupted server for strong security), and making at most q_G queries to the function G, has an advantage* $\mathsf{Adv}_\Pi^{C.Imp}(\mathcal{A}) \geq \epsilon$ *or* $\mathsf{Adv}_\Pi^{S.Imp}(\mathcal{A}) \geq \epsilon$.

Though AKA is claimed to provide mutual authentication, its design introduces a vulnerability, leading to a subtle difference between the *client*-impersonation and *server*-impersonation guarantees. In fact, the protocol allows $\mathcal{A}$ to run a MiM attack resembling a relay attack. Servers can be impersonated even if we rule out online relays (an adversary just forwards messages from a server to a client instance, and vice versa): $\mathcal{A}$ merely performs an out-of-order (offline) relay as described in the third scenario of Fig. 2, as explained below. This is the gap between the client- and the server-impersonation guarantees for the AKA protocol. Our server-impersonation model rules out both offline and online relays, whereas client-impersonation only rules out online relays.

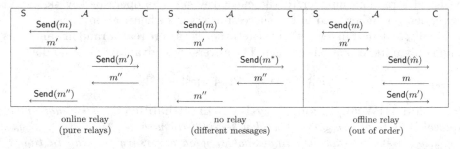

online relay
(pure relays)

no relay
(different messages)

offline relay
(out of order)

Fig. 2. Examples of Online and Offline relays. For the AKA protocol, the message m is the client's UID, which the adversary can learn. The message m' is a valid authentication challenge, and the message m'' is the authentication response. The message $\hat{m}$ is the UID request message, whereas m^* is a random message.

Security Against Servers. We also formalize the notions of *state-confidentiality* and *soundness* with respect to a malicious server S. The former requirement demands that (malicious) servers cannot learn the values: sk_C, sk_{Op}, and the tuple $(\mathsf{Sqn}_C, \mathsf{Sqn}_{Op,C})$. We use a similar model as for the MiM-adversary model, except that now the adversary has oracle access to the operators. We preserve the oracles UReg, NewInstance, Execute, Send, Reveal, StReveal described above, and add the following two oracles (with a modification of Corrupt):

- Corrupt(P) $\rightarrow$ S: if P is a client, behave as in the MiM model. If P is an operator, return sk_{Op} and the tuples $S = (\mathsf{UID}, \mathsf{sk}_{UID}, \mathsf{st}_C, \mathsf{st}_{Op,C})$ of all clients C subscribing to Op.
- OpAccess(S, C) $\rightarrow$ m: simulates querying C's operator on behalf of C for a single session, returning the message m that Op outputs to a corrupted S.

As opposed to key-indistinguishability, which guarantees the security of the session keys, state confidentiality protects the client- and operator long-term states against malicious servers. The state-confidentiality game begins by generating client- and operator material. The adversary can use her oracles arbitrarily, finally outputting a tuple: $(P_i, sk^*_{UID}, sk^*_{Op}, st^*_{UID}, st^*_{Op,UID})$ for an uncorrupted client with identifier UID such that no partner of any instance of P has ever been corrupted. We say $\mathcal{A}$ and wins if at least one of the values: $sk^*_{UID}, sk^*_{Op}, st^*_{UID}, st^*_{Op,UID}$ is equal to the client's real $sk_{UID}, sk_{Op}, st_{UID}, st_{Op,UID}$. The advantage of $\mathcal{A}$ is: $Adv_{\Pi}^{St.Conf}(\mathcal{A}) := Pr[\mathcal{A} \text{ wins}]$.

Definition 3 [State-confidentiality]. *A key-agreement protocol Π is $(t, q_{exec}, q_{res}, q_{Op}, q_G, \epsilon)$-state-confidential if no adversary running in time t, creating at most q_{exec} party instances with at most q_{res} resynchronizations per instance, making at most q_{Op} OpAccess queries and q_G queries to G, has an advantage $Adv_{\Pi}^{St.Conf}(\mathcal{A}) \geq \epsilon$.*

We also require the property of *soundness*, which demands that malicious servers cannot make an uncorrupted client instance terminate in an accepting state without help from the operator. This game resembles impersonation-security, but the adversary is now a legitimate server with operator access, interacting with the state-confidentiality oracles arbitrarily, making q_{Op} OpAccess queries per client. The adversary wins if, and only if, there exist $(q_{Op} + 1)$ uncorrupted client instances that terminate in an accepted state. We also restrict this notion with respect to offline replay attacks, as for server-impersonation. The advantage of $\mathcal{A}$ is defined as: $Adv_{\Pi}^{Sound}(\mathcal{A}) := Pr[\mathcal{A} \text{ wins}]$.

Definition 4 [Soundness]. *A key-agreement protocol Π is $(t, q_{exec}, q_{res}, q_{Op}, q_G, \epsilon)$-server-sound if no adversary running in time t, creating at most q_{exec} party instances with at most q_{res} resynchronizations per instance, making at most q_{Op} queries to any operator Op and at most q_G queries to the function G, has an advantage $Adv_{\Pi}^{Sound}(\mathcal{A}) \geq \epsilon$.*

4   Security of the AKA Protocol

In this section, we focus on the *current, unmodified* version of the AKA protocol with respect to the five properties formalized in Sect. 3.

In particular, parties P (clients C and servers S) run sessions of the protocol, thus creating party *instances* denoted P_i. An instance is said to finish in an *accepting* state if and only if it auhenticates its partner. Each instance keeps track of a partner- and a session-ID.

The partner ID pid of an accepting client instance C_i is S (this reflects the lack of server identifiers); server instances S_i, have a pid corresponding to a unique UID. The session ID sid of each instance consists of: UID, R, and the value Sqn that is agreed upon during the session. In the absence of resynchronization, the session ID is $(UID, R, Sqn_{Op,C})$. During re-synchronization, the operator updates $Sqn_{Op,C}$ to the client's Sqn_C; this update is taken into account in the sid. Any two partners (same sid) with accepting states compute session keys $(CK\|IK)$.

A Unitary Function G**.** We analyse the security of AKA in two steps. First, we reduce it to the pseudorandomness of an intermediate, unitary function G. This function models the suite of seven algorithms used in AKA; each algorithm is a specific call to G. For the state-confidentiality property we must also assume the pseudorandomness of the related unitary function G^*, which is the same as G, but we key it with the operator key $\mathsf{sk_{Op}}$ rather than the client key sk. This first step gives a sufficient condition to provide AKA security for any suite of algorithms intended to be used within it. As a second step (showed in the full version), we prove that both TUAK and MILENAGE, guarantee this property.

We note that the pseudorandomness of G implies the pseudorandomness of each sub-algorithm, but is a strictly stronger property, which is necessary since the session keys CK and IK, computed by two different algorithms on the same input, *must* be independent.

4.1   Provable Security Guarantees

The existing AKA protocol only attains the weaker versions of key-indistinguishability, client-, and server-impersonation resistance. The protocol also guarantees state-confidentiality and soundness with respect to malicious servers.

Denote by Π the AKA protocol described in Sect. 2, but in which the calls to the internal cryptographic functions $\mathcal{F}_1, \ldots, \mathcal{F}_5, \mathcal{F}_1^*, \mathcal{F}_5^*$ are replaced by calls to the function $G : \{0,1\}^\kappa \times \{0,1\}^d \times \{0,1\}^t \times \{0,1\}^t \to \{0,1\}^n$, in which κ is a security parameter, d is a positive integer strictly larger than the size of the operator key, and t indicates the block size of an underlying pseudo-random permutation. As we detail in the full paper, the exact values of d, t, and n differ for TUAK and MILENAGE; however, the construction of G is somewhat similar.

We denote by $\mathcal{S}_\mathsf{C} := \{0,1\}^\kappa$ the key-space for the client keys and by $\mathcal{S}_\mathsf{Op} := \{0,1\}^e$, the key space for operator keys, for some specified $e < d$ (in practice $e = 256$). Our system features n_C clients, n_S servers and n_Op operators.

Security Statements. We group the five security statements that we prove for the AKA protocol into two theorems. The first groups the properties of: weak key-indistinguishability, strong client- and weak server-impersonation resistance, and soundness with respect to servers. The second theorem is that for state-confidentiality, which requires an additional assumption. We defer the proofs for the full version.

Our security statements are phrased with respect to an adversary $\mathcal{A}$ trying to break (in some way) the security of Π, which runs in time t, creates at most q_exec party instances with at most q_res resynchronizations per instance, and makes at most q_G queries to the function G. Furthermore, in the case of strong MiM adversary, it can also corrupt at most q_s servers and make at most q_Op OpAccess queries per operator per corrupted server. For the *legitimate-and-malicious* adversary, we quantify $\mathcal{A}$ in terms of the maximal number q_Op of queries to the oracle OpAccess, and the similar $q_\mathsf{exec}, q_\mathsf{res}$ and q_G queries.

The function G is defined as above.

Theorem 1 [W.K.Ind, S.C.Imp, W.S.Imp, Sound].   *For the protocol Π using the unitary function G described above, the following properties hold:*

W.K.Ind. *For any $(t, q_{exec}, q_{res}, q_G)$-adversary $\mathcal{A}$ against the W.K.Ind-security of Π winning with advantage $\mathsf{Adv}_{\Pi}^{\mathsf{W.K.Ind}}(\mathcal{A})$ there exists a $(t' \approx O(t), q' = q_G + q_{exec}(2 + q_{res}))$-adversary $\mathcal{A}'$ against the pseudorandomness of G with:*

$$\mathsf{Adv}_{\Pi}^{\mathsf{W.K.Ind}}(\mathcal{A}) \leq n_C \cdot \left(\frac{q_{exec}^2}{2^{|R|}} + \mathsf{Adv}_G^{\mathsf{prf}}(\mathcal{A}') \right).$$

S.C.Imp. *For any $(t, q_{exec}, q_{res}, q_s, q_{Op}, q_G)$-adversary $\mathcal{A}$ against the S.C.Imp-security of Π, winning with advantage $\mathsf{Adv}_{\Pi}^{\mathsf{S.C.Imp}}(\mathcal{A})$, there exists a $(t' \approx O(t), q' = 5 \cdot q_s \cdot q_{Op} + q_G + q_{exec}(q_{res} + 2))$-adversary $\mathcal{A}'$ against the pseudorandomness of G such that:*

$$\mathsf{Adv}_{\Pi}^{\mathsf{S.C.Imp}}(\mathcal{A}) \leq n_C \cdot \left(2 \cdot \mathsf{Adv}_G^{\mathsf{prf}}(\mathcal{A}') + \frac{(q_{exec} + q_s \cdot q_{Op})^2}{2^{|R|}} + \frac{q_{exec} \cdot q_{res}}{2^{|Res|}} + \frac{1}{2^{\kappa}} \right).$$

W.S.Imp. *For any $(t, q_{exec}, q_{res}, q_G)$-adversary $\mathcal{A}$ against the W.S.Imp-security of Π, winning with advantage $\mathsf{Adv}_{\Pi}^{\mathsf{W.S.Imp}}(\mathcal{A})$, there exists a $(t' \approx t, q = q_{exec} \cdot (q_{res} + 2) + q_G)$-adversary $\mathcal{A}'$ against the pseudorandomness of G such that:*

$$\mathsf{Adv}_{\Pi}^{\mathsf{W.S.Imp}}(\mathcal{A}) \leq n_C \cdot \left(\mathsf{Adv}_G^{\mathsf{prf}}(\mathcal{A}') + \frac{q_{exec} \cdot q_{res}}{2^{|Macs|}} + \frac{1}{2^{\kappa}} \right).$$

Sound. *For any $(t, q_{exec}, q_{res}, q_{Op}, q_G, \epsilon)$-adversary $\mathcal{A}$ against the soundness of Π, winning with advantage $\mathsf{Adv}_{\Pi}^{\mathsf{Sound}}(\mathcal{A})$, there exists a $(t' \approx t, q' = 5 \cdot q_{Op} + q_G + n_C \cdot q_{exec}(2 + q_{res}))$-adversary $\mathcal{A}'$ against the pseudorandomness of G such that:*

$$\mathsf{Adv}_{\Pi}^{\mathsf{Sound}}(\mathcal{A}) \leq n_C \cdot \left(2 \cdot \mathsf{Adv}_G^{\mathsf{prf}}(\mathcal{A}') + \frac{q_{exec} \cdot q_{res}}{2^{|Macs|}} + \frac{1}{2^{\kappa}} \right).$$

Theorem 2 [St.Conf-resistance].   *For the protocol Π using the unitary functions G, G^*, for any $(t, q_{exec}, q_{res}, q_{Op}, q_G, q_{G^*})$-adversary $\mathcal{A}$ against the St.Conf-security of Π, winning with advantage $\mathsf{Adv}_{\Pi}^{\mathsf{St.Conf}}(\mathcal{A})$, there exist: a $(t' \approx O(t), q' = q_G + q_{exec}(5 + q_{res}))$-prf-adversary $\mathcal{A}_1$ on G and $(t' \approx O(t), q' = q_{G^*})$-prf-adversary $\mathcal{A}_2$ on G^* such that:*

$$\mathsf{Adv}_{\Pi}^{\mathsf{St.Conf}}(\mathcal{A}) \leq n_C \cdot \left(\frac{1}{2^{|sk_C|}} + \frac{1}{2^{|sk_{Op}|}} + \frac{2}{2^{|Sqn|}} + \mathsf{Adv}_G^{\mathsf{prf}}(\mathcal{A}_1) + \mathsf{Adv}_{G^*}^{\mathsf{prf}}(\mathcal{A}_2) \right).$$

MILENAGE and TUAK. Our second step is to prove that TUAK and MILENAGE both behave as the generic function G. Due to space constraints, we only propose two theorems of the pseudorandomness of these functions and leave all the details to the full paper. Notably, as opposed to TUAK (whose symmetric design allows a lot more leeway), the MILENAGE algorithms require a stronger assumption to prove the PRF property for G^* (which is keyed with sk_{Op}).

Theorem 3 [prf-security for TUAK algorithms]. *For the generalization of the TUAK algorithms G_{tuak} (resp. G^*_{tuak}) keyed with the subscriber key (resp. the operator key) and the functions f and f^* two different truncated keyed internal permutation of* Keccak, *for any (t,q)-adversary $\mathcal{A}$ against the pseudorandomness of the function f (resp. f^*), then there exists a $(t' \approx t, q' = q)$-adversary $\mathcal{A}'$ such that:*

$$\mathsf{Adv}^{\mathsf{prf}}_{G_{\mathsf{tuak}}}(\mathcal{A}) = \mathsf{Adv}^{\mathsf{prf}}_{f}(\mathcal{A}') \qquad \mathsf{Adv}^{\mathsf{prf}}_{G^*_{\mathsf{tuak}}}(\mathcal{A}) = \mathsf{Adv}^{\mathsf{prf}}_{f^*}(\mathcal{A}').$$

Theorem 4 [prf-security for MILENAGE algorithms]. *For the generalization of the MILENAGE algorithms G_{mil1} and G_{mil2} (resp. G^*_{mil1} and G^*_{mil2}) keyed with the subscriber key (resp. the operator key) and the function f (resp. f^*) the AES algorithm (resp. a keyed version of a classic Davies-Meyer), for any (t,q)-adversary $\mathcal{A}$ against the pseudorandomness of the function f (resp. f^*), then there exists a $(t' \approx 3 \cdot t, q' = 3 \cdot q)$-adversary $\mathcal{A}'$ such that:*

$$\mathsf{Adv}^{\mathsf{prf}}_{G_{\mathsf{mil1}}}(\mathcal{A}) = \mathsf{Adv}^{\mathsf{prf}}_{f}(\mathcal{A}')(= \mathsf{Adv}^{\mathsf{prf}}_{G_{\mathsf{mil2}}}(\mathcal{A})), \mathsf{Adv}^{\mathsf{prf}}_{G^*_{\mathsf{mil1}}}(\mathcal{A}) = \mathsf{Adv}^{\mathsf{prf}}_{f^*}(\mathcal{A}')(= \mathsf{Adv}^{\mathsf{prf}}_{G^*_{\mathsf{mil2}}}(\mathcal{A})).$$

4.2 Vulnerabilities of the AKA Protocol

In the three-party mobile setting, the server is authenticated by the client if it presents credentials (authentication vectors) generated by the client's operator. The properties of state-confidentiality and soundness, which the AKA protocol guarantees, indicate that servers cannot learn the client's long-term data, and that they cannot authenticate without the operator-generated data.

However, Zhang [15] and Zhang and Fang [16] pointed out that once a server is corrupted, it can obtain legitimate authentication data from the client's operator, and then use this data to set up a False Base Station (FBS), which can lead to a malicious, unauthorised server authenticating to the client. As a result, the AKA protocol does not guarantee strong key-indistinguishability, nor strong server-impersonation resistance.

The main attack strategy is also depicted in Fig. 3. In a first step, the client C is assumed to be in the LAI corresponding to a server S^*, which will later be corrupted. The server receives a batch of authentication vectors $(\mathsf{AV}_1, \ldots, \mathsf{AV}_n)$, using some of them (vectors $\mathsf{AV}_1, \ldots, \mathsf{AV}_k$) to provide service to that client (and learn what services this client has provided, etc.). Subsequently, the client moves to a different LAI, outside the corrupted network's area. The adversary $\mathcal{A}$ has corrupted the server S^* and learned the remaining vectors $\mathsf{AV}_{k+1}, \ldots, \mathsf{AV}_n$; this adversary then uses this authentication data to authenticate to the client, *in its new location*. This immediately breaks the server-impersonation guarantee. Moreover, since authentication vectors also contain the short-term session keys, key-indistinguishability is breached, too. This attack is particularly dangerous since a single server corruption can affect a very large number of clients. Moreover, server corruption is easily practiced in totalitarian regimes, in which mobile providers are subject to the state, and partial data is furthermore likely to be leaked upon using backdoored algorithms.

Such attack do not, however, affect client-impersonation resistance, since the server cannot use an authentication vector from the server to respond to a

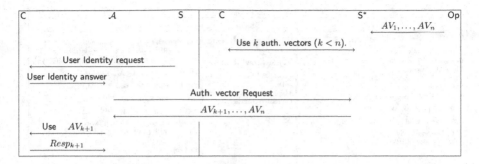

Fig. 3. The attack of Zhang and Fang. On the right hand side, the client is in the vulnerable network, interacting with the server S^*. The server uses up authentication vectors $\mathsf{AV}_1, \ldots \mathsf{AK}_k$. Then, the server S^* is corrupted, and the adversary $\mathcal{A}$ learns $\mathsf{AV}_{k+1}, \ldots, \mathsf{AV}_n$, which it uses in a second attack phase (on the left).

freshly-generated authentication challenge (the random value for the two authentication vectors is different).

5   Additional Security with Few Modifications

The main reason server-corruption attacks are effective is that servers associated with a specific geographic area (like a country, a region, etc.) can re-use authentication vectors given by the operator in a different geographic area, impersonating the legitimate server associated with that area. This vulnerability, however, is easily fixed as long as the client's device is aware of its geographical location. Our solution is to add a unique server identifier, denoted Id_S, to the input of each of the cryptographic functions, thus making any leftover authentication tokens un-replayable in the wrong area. We stress that this is a minor modification to the protocol, as servers are already associated with a unique LAI identifier.

We also show in the full version how to include Id_S in the computation of each of the cryptographic algorithms. We present our modified protocol in Fig. 4.

Security of the Modified AKA Protocol. This modification still (trivially) preserves the properties of strong client-impersonation resistance, soundness, and state confidentiality. However, the modification yields in addition strong key-indistinguishability and server-impersonation resistance, as we detail below. The proofs are given in the full version.

Theorem 5 [S.K.Ind, S.S.Imp]. *For the modified protocol Π using the unitary function G described in Sect. 4, the following properties also hold:*

S.K.Ind. *For any* $(t, q_{\mathsf{exec}}, q_{\mathsf{res}}, q_s, q_{\mathsf{Op}}, q_G)$-*adversary* $\mathcal{A}$ *against the* S.K.Ind-*security of* Π *winning with advantage* $\mathsf{Adv}_{\Pi}^{\mathsf{S.K.Ind}}(\mathcal{A})$ *there exists a* $(t' \approx$

Instructions:		
Client	Server	Operator
(3): Compute AK using $R^{\{i\}}$. Recover $\mathsf{Sqn}^{\{i\}}$ (from AK). Check Mac_S value. If $\mathsf{Sqn}^{\{i\}} \in (\mathsf{Sqn}_C, \mathsf{Sqn}_C + \Delta)$: Compute: $\mathsf{CK} \leftarrow \mathbf{Upd\_F_3}(\mathsf{sk}_C, \mathsf{sk}_{Op}, R^{\{i\}}, \mathsf{Ids})$, $\mathsf{IK} \leftarrow \mathbf{Upd\_F_4}(\mathsf{sk}_C, \mathsf{sk}_{Op}, R^{\{i\}}, \mathsf{Ids})$, Set $\mathsf{Res} := \mathbf{Upd\_F_2}(\mathsf{sk}_C, \mathsf{sk}_{Op}, R^{\{i\}}, \mathsf{Ids})$. Update $\mathsf{Sqn}_C := \mathsf{Sqn}^{\{i\}}$. Else *re-synchronization*	(2): Store $\{AV^{\{i\}}\}_{i=1}^n$. Choose $AV^{\{i\}}$ one by one in order. Then, it forges and sends the related challenge. ———— (4): $\mathsf{Res} \overset{?}{=} \mathsf{Mac}_C$.	(1): For each $i = 1, \ldots, n$, compute: Generate $R^{\{i\}}$. Compute: $\mathsf{Sqn}^{\{i\}} \leftarrow \mathsf{inc}(\mathsf{Sqn}_{Op,C})$ $\mathsf{Mac}_S^{\{i\}} \leftarrow \mathbf{Upd\_F_1}(\mathsf{sk}_C, \mathsf{sk}_{Op}, R^{\{i\}}, \mathsf{Sqn}^{\{i\}}, \mathsf{AMF}, \mathsf{Ids})$, $\mathsf{Mac}_C^{\{i\}} \leftarrow \mathbf{Upd\_F_2}(\mathsf{sk}_C, \mathsf{sk}_{Op}, R^{\{i\}}, \mathsf{Ids})$, $\mathsf{CK}^{\{i\}} \leftarrow \mathbf{Upd\_F_3}(\mathsf{sk}_C, \mathsf{sk}_{Op}, R^{\{i\}}, \mathsf{Ids})$, $\mathsf{IK}^{\{i\}} \leftarrow \mathbf{Upd\_F_4}(\mathsf{sk}_C, \mathsf{sk}_{Op}, R^{\{i\}}, \mathsf{Ids})$, $\mathsf{AK}^{\{i\}} \leftarrow \mathbf{Upd\_F_5}(\mathsf{sk}_C, \mathsf{sk}_{Op}, R^{\{i\}}, \mathsf{Ids})$, $\mathsf{Autn}^{\{i\}} \leftarrow (\mathsf{Sqn}^{\{i\}} \oplus \mathsf{AK}), \mathsf{AMF}, \mathsf{Mac}_S$. $AV^{\{i\}} := (R^{\{i\}}, \mathsf{CK}^{\{i\}}, \mathsf{IK}^{\{i\}}, \mathsf{Autn}^{\{i\}}, \mathsf{Mac}_C^{\{i\}})$, with $\mathsf{Sqn}_{Op,C} = \mathsf{Sqn}^{\{i\}}$. End For.

Fig. 4. The modified instructions of our variant.

$O(t), q' = 5 \cdot q_s \cdot q_{Op} + q_G + q_{exec}(q_{res} + 2))$-*adversary $\mathcal{A}'$ against the pseudo-randomness of G with:*

$$\mathsf{Adv}_\Pi^{\mathsf{S.K.Ind}}(\mathcal{A}) \leq n_C \cdot \left(\frac{(q_{exec} + q_s \cdot q_{Op})^2}{2^{|R|}} + 2 \cdot \mathsf{Adv}_G^{\mathsf{prf}}(\mathcal{A}') \right).$$

S.S.Imp. *For any $(t, q_{exec}, q_{res}, q_s, q_{Op}, q_G)$-adversary $\mathcal{A}$ against the S.S.Imp-security of Π, winning with advantage $\mathsf{Adv}_\Pi^{\mathsf{S.S.Imp}}(\mathcal{A})$, there exists a $(t' \approx O(t), q' = 5 \cdot q_s \cdot q_{Op} + q_G + q_{exec}(2 + q_{res}))$-adversary $\mathcal{A}'$ against the pseudo-randomness of G such that:*

$$\mathsf{Adv}_\Pi^{\mathsf{S.S.Imp}}(\mathcal{A}_{\mathbb{G}_0}) \leq n_C \cdot \left(\frac{q_{exec} \cdot q_{res}}{2^{|\mathsf{Mac}_S|}} + \frac{1}{2^\kappa} + 2 \cdot \mathsf{Adv}_G^{\mathsf{prf}}(\mathcal{A}') \right).$$

Each of the two bounds above depend linearly on the number of clients n_C; while this number can be as large as, potentially, six billion, the size of the secret keys (128 or 256 bits) and of the random value (128 bits) can still make the bound negligible. The linear factor n_C, however, highlights the importance of using authentication strings longer than 128 bits for authentication.

References

1. 3GPP: 3G Security, Specification of the MILENAGE algorithm set: an example algorithm set for the 3Gpp. Authentication and key generation functions f1, f1*, f2, f3, f4, f5 and f5*; Document 2: algorithm specification. TS 35.206, 3rd Generation Partnership Project (3GPP), June 2007
2. 3GPP: 3G Security, Specification of the TUAK algorithm set: a 2nd example for the 3Gpp. Authentication and key generation functions f1, f1*, f2, f3, f4, f5 and f5* – Document 1: algorithm specification. TS 35.231, 3rd Generation Partnership Project (3GPP), June 2013
3. Shaik, A., Borgaonkar, R., Asokan, N., Niemi, V., Seifert, J.-P.: Practical attacks against privacy and availability in 4G/LTE mobile communication systems. In: Accepted to NDSS 2016 (2016)

 4. Arapinis, M., Chothia, T., Ritter, E., Ryan, M.: Analysing unlinkability and anonymity using the applied Pi calculus. In: Proceedings of the CSF 2010, pp. 107–121 (2010)
 5. Arapinis, M., Mancini, L.I., Ritter, E., Ryan, M., Golde, N., Redon, K., Borgaonkar, R.: New privacy issues in mobile telephony: fix and verification. In: Proceedings of ACM CCS
 6. Arapinis, M., Ritter, E., Ryan, M.D.: StatVerif: verification of stateful processes. In: Proceedings of CSF 2011, pp. 33–47 (2011)
 7. Bellare, M., Pointcheval, D., Rogaway, P.: Authenticated key exchange secure against dictionary attacks. In: Preneel, B. (ed.) EUROCRYPT 2000. LNCS, vol. 1807, pp. 139–155. Springer, Heidelberg (2000)
 8. Bellare, M., Rogaway, P.: Entity authentication and key distribution. In: Stinson, D.R. (ed.) CRYPTO 1993. LNCS, vol. 773, pp. 232–249. Springer, Heidelberg (1994)
 9. Bertoni, G., Daemen, J., Peeters, M., Van Assche, G.: On the indifferentiability of the sponge construction. In: Smart, N.P. (ed.) EUROCRYPT 2008. LNCS, vol. 4965, pp. 181–197. Springer, Heidelberg (2008)
10. Blanchet, B.: Automatic verification of security protocols in the symbolic model: the verifier ProVerif. In: Aldini, A., Lopez, J., Martinelli, F. (eds.) FOSAD VII. LNCS, vol. 8604, pp. 54–87. Springer, Heidelberg (2014)
11. Gilbert, H.: The security of "One-Block-to-Many" modes of operation. In: Johansson, T. (ed.) FSE 2003. LNCS, vol. 2887, pp. 376–395. Springer, Heidelberg (2003)
12. Hall, C., Wagner, D., Kelsey, J., Schneier, B.: Building PRFs from PRPs
13. Lee, M., Smart, N., Warinschi, B., Watson, G.: Anonymity guarantees of the UMTS/LTE authentication and connection protocol. Int. J. Inf. Sec. 13(6), 513–527 (2014)
14. Strobel, D.: IMSI catcher. In: Seminar Work, Ruhr-Universitat Bochum (2007)
15. Zhang, M.: Provably-Secure Enhancement on 3Gpp. Authentication and Key Agreement Protocol. In: IACR Cryptology ePrint Archive 2003, p. 92 (2003). http://eprint.iacr.org/2003/092
16. Zhang, M., Fang, Y.: Security analysis and enhancements of 3GPP authentication and key agreement protocol. IEEE Trans. Wirel. Commun. 4(2), 734–742 (2005)

Low-Cost Mitigation Against Cold Boot Attacks for an Authentication Token

Ian Goldberg[1], Graeme Jenkinson[2(✉)], and Frank Stajano[2]

[1] University of Waterloo, Waterloo, Canada
[2] University of Cambridge, Cambridge, UK
gcj21@cl.cam.ac.uk

Abstract. Hardware tokens for user authentication need a secure and usable mechanism to lock them when not in use. The Pico academic project proposes an authentication token unlocked by the proximity of simpler wearable devices that provide shares of the token's master key. This method, however, is vulnerable to a cold boot attack: an adversary who captures a running Pico could extract the master key from its RAM and steal all of the user's credentials. We present a cryptographic countermeasure—bivariate secret sharing—that protects all the credentials except the one in use at that time, even if the token is captured while it is on. Remarkably, our key storage costs for the wearables that supply the cryptographic shares are very modest (256 bits) and remain *constant* even if the token holds thousands of credentials. Although bivariate secret sharing has been used before in slightly different ways, our scheme is leaner and more efficient and achieves a new property—cold boot protection. We validated the efficacy of our design by implementing it on a commercial Bluetooth Low Energy development board and measuring its latency and energy consumption. For reasonable choices of latency and security parameters, a standard CR2032 button-cell battery can power our prototype for 5–7 months, and we demonstrate a simple enhancement that could make the same battery last for over 9 months.

Keywords: Hardware authentication token · Cold boot attack · Memory remanence · Bivariate secret sharing · Bluetooth low energy

1 Introduction

In 2014 the influential FIDO industry consortium published version 1.0 of its Universal Authentication Framework specification [1], which defines a token-based authentication system intended to replace passwords. The token itself might be unlocked with a variety of methods, such as biometrics. In 2011, Stajano proposed Pico [2], a system with similar goals and architecture (replacing passwords by a token that locally stores a different credential per verifier) but with

---

I. Goldberg—On sabbatical at the University of Cambridge while this work was being carried out.

© Springer International Publishing Switzerland 2016
M. Manulis et al. (Eds.): ACNS 2016, LNCS 9696, pp. 36–57, 2016.
DOI: 10.1007/978-3-319-39555-5_3

a proximity-based secret-sharing method for unlocking the token (as originally proposed in 2001 by Desmedt et al. [3]) that would also allow continuous authentication (similar to what Corner and Noble [4] first demonstrated in 2002). In this work we revisit the security of the Pico token-unlocking proposal, improving its resilience against memory readout attacks such as "cold boot" [5]. We use the Pico terminology throughout, since this is the reference design that we are improving upon; however, our techniques might also be applied to FIDO UAF or to any other security token that requires locking when not in possession of its user, provided it adopted the proximity-based secret-sharing technique called "Threshold things that think" by Desmedt et al. [3] and "Picosiblings" by Stajano [2]. In this introduction we first set the scene by summarizing the relevant features of Pico. We then explain what additional security benefits we provide with our work.

The Pico is a security token containing hundreds of login credentials, stored in encrypted form in the token's permanent memory. Because the Pico's aim is to allow people to authenticate without having to remember secrets, by design its storage is not unlocked by a PIN or password but rather by the presence of other small wearable devices, the Picosiblings, using a k-out-of-n secret sharing scheme to reconstruct the strong master key that decrypts the Pico's storage.[1] Without the master key, which is not stored in the Pico, the encrypted credentials are unreadable. The intention is that, if adversaries capture the Pico, they will not be able to read its secrets, not even if they also capture a few Picosiblings. No protection is offered by the scheme, though, if the adversary manages to capture the Pico and at least k Picosiblings.

To avoid storing the master key in the Pico, the master key is securely erased immediately after having been reconstructed and used. The decrypted credentials themselves are securely erased after a short interval. Whenever the Pico needs to use any of its credentials (again), the master key must be reconstructed to allow their decryption, but reconstruction can only happen if at least k Picosiblings are within range. Therefore a group of k Picosiblings creates an aura of safety around its wearer, within which the Pico can unlock its credentials.

The privacy of the wearer would be under threat if a passive observer could recognize the Picosiblings by their transmissions, thereby identifying the wearer and tracking their location. The security of the credentials would be under threat if an active attacker could impersonate the target Pico to the Picosiblings and persuade them to release their shares of the master key. For this reason, the communications between a Pico and its Picosiblings must be authenticated and encrypted, and the Picosiblings must only respond to their own Pico.

The primary focus of this paper is to protect the Pico against cold boot attacks. A cold boot attack consists of capturing the running device while plaintext secrets

---

[1] In Pico, for additional security, some special shares are supplied by user biometrics and by a network server [2], and different shares may have different weights [6]. The work described in this paper is independent of these features and therefore for simplicity in what follows we shall ignore these aspects here and treat all shares equally unless otherwise noted.

are in RAM, power-cycling it without allowing a clean shutdown and then exploiting data remanence to read its secrets from RAM, as described by Halderman et al. [5]. We generalize the threat model, beyond the literal cold boot, to any other potential means of reading the secrets present in RAM at the time the running Pico is captured, regardless of whether they involve power-cycling the device. The plaintext secrets under threat would include the credentials themselves, the reconstructed master key used to decrypt them and the shares of the master key received from the Picosiblings.

1.1 Highlights

Although the individual techniques we use (secret sharing, bivariate polynomials, etc.) have been proposed before, our variant is original, the way we combine them is original, and the protection features we achieve have not previously appeared in the literature. We also build a working prototype and measure its performance. In particular:

We design a new internal architecture for the Pico security token and a communication protocol between Pico and Picosiblings that, besides meeting all the security and privacy requirements in the original Pico paper,[2] additionally protect the Pico from cold boot attacks. The hundreds of credentials on the Pico are never all exposed in plaintext, even within the device: the Pico only unlocks the credentials in use at the time. This minimizes exposure to any memory readout attacks, however performed.

We partition the Pico credential database into independently encrypted bins. Crucially, our protection scheme is such that the additional key storage cost per Picosibling is *constant* with respect to the number of bins.

Whether the credentials in the Pico are public keys or symmetric keys [7], we achieve the above without resorting to public-key primitives, so as to facilitate energy-efficient implementation and to avoid introducing a failure point under the threat that quantum computing might one day break today's public-key cryptosystems.

We validate our design with a prototype implementation using commercial off-the-shelf Bluetooth Low Energy parts that demonstrates most of the above features. Working Picosiblings had never been implemented in hardware before and thus our prototype, besides offering enhanced security, is the first concrete instantiation of Picosiblings on which performance measurements can be conducted.

2   The Problem

In the original design for Pico, as summarized above, the credential storage is encrypted by a master key that in turn is assembled from cryptographic shares received from the Picosiblings. If adversaries steal a Pico that has been switched off, they will not be able to recover the master key (which only exists in temporary storage), nor any of the user's credentials (stored in permanent storage, but

---

[2] We repeat these requirements in Sect. 2 for the convenience of the reader.

encrypted under the master key), nor any of the received shares (which need to be cached in some readable form until at least k of them have been assembled). The problem, however, is that they might steal a running Pico, with received shares or decrypted secrets in RAM, and somehow find a way of reading these shares or secrets while they lie in RAM in plaintext.

A more subtle problem is that, in order to communicate securely with the Picosiblings, the Pico needs to store, permanently, some Pico-to-Picosiblings communication keys. Since the master key that unlocks the storage of the Pico is reconstructed from shares supplied by the Picosiblings, it is clear that the communication keys to talk to the Picosiblings cannot be encrypted under the master key, or they would be inaccessible when the Pico boots up. But if they are stored in plaintext and accessible to attackers who capture the Pico, then such attackers would be in a position to impersonate the Pico to the Picosiblings and therefore obtain the shares from them. Stannard and Stajano [8] acknowledge this threat and invoke some amount of tamper resistance in order to address it. Clearly, if the Pico's processor and memory are all enclosed in a tamper-resistant perimeter, any memory-readout attacks will fall outside the adversary model. However it is hard for us as independent researchers to constructively validate the strength of this defense because tamper-resistant system-on-chip devices are usually only sold to corporations, under NDA and in large volumes.

To protect the security and privacy (including location privacy) of the owner of the Pico, the original design [2] called for a protocol providing the following features:

- The Pico can ascertain the presence of any of its Picosiblings in the vicinity.
- The Picosibling responds to its master Pico but not to any other Pico.
- At each ping, the Picosibling sends its k-out-of-n share to the Pico, in a way that does not reveal it to eavesdroppers.
- An eavesdropper can detect the bidirectional communications between Pico and Picosiblings but not infer identities or long-term pseudonyms.
- The Pico can detect and ignore old replayed messages.
- The Pico can detect and ignore relay attacks (e.g. with Hancke-Kuhn [9]).

Most of these properties were offered in Stannard and Stajano's protocol [8]; however, as our current work redefines the communication between Pico and Picosiblings, these properties must be preserved.

2.1   Attacker Model

- We assume the attacker can listen to some of the communications between Pico and Picosiblings, but not to those of their initial setup and pairing ("secure at first use").
- We assume the attacker can send messages to the Pico and/or Picosiblings, but not during initial setup and pairing.

– We assume the attacker can capture and read out the content of a Pico (whether on or off) and fewer than k Picosiblings, but only after initial setup and pairing has taken place.[3]
– As a concession to the considerations above, we assume it is possible for the defender to use low-cost tamper-proofing facilities of the kind in use in smart-cards and phone SIMs in order to provide a small amount of permanent storage that the adversary cannot read, even after acquiring physical control of the device.[4] We assume however that the adversary is otherwise able to read out the bulk storage (flash) and workspace (RAM) of the captured device.

The attacker wins if she can extract all the credentials in plaintext out of a captured Pico or if she can use a captured Pico to authenticate as its owner (the former implies the latter).

3   Our Solution in a Nutshell

Our core idea is to partition the encrypted storage of the Pico into many small bins, each holding just a few credentials (ideally just one, subject to technical limitations), and to redesign the secret sharing scheme and the communication protocol with the Picosiblings so that only one bin gets decrypted at a time.

Instead of one master key for the whole Pico we now have as many master keys as there are bins. These are, again, reconstructed from shares supplied by the Picosiblings, but now the Pico must first ask for the shares that are relevant to a particular bin.

We keep the communication keys with the Picosiblings in tamper-resistant storage from which the adversary cannot economically extract them. (We could conceivably also store a "master key to encrypt the whole RAM" in there as well; however, in the absence of a dedicated cryptoprocessor, the decrypted RAM, or at least the current block of decrypted RAM, would then have to be written out in some workspace in order to be used, and we have assumed that the adversary could access that.)

This means that even an adversary who can read the memory of our Pico (except for the Picosibling communication keys held in tamper-resistant storage) can at most acquire the credentials of one of the bins. We therefore protect the security token from cold boot attacks even when it is not possible (for reasons of cost, performance or simply because the manufacturers will not sell us any potentially suitable hardware) to resort to enclosing the whole processor and RAM into a tamper-resistant enclosure.

---

[3] The number of devices compromised by the attacker can never go down (the attacker cannot "unlearn" the secrets of a device he previously compromised) and any Picosibling that he ever compromised counts towards the quota that cannot reach k in our adversary model.

[4] Note that such protected storage would be needed by Pico to protect the communication keys with the Picosiblings regardless of cold boot protection, as acknowledged by Stannard and Stajano [8].

The trade-off of our approach is that, whereas previously when the master key had been reconstructed all the credentials were available instantly, here the Pico must first decide which bin of credentials to decrypt, then request the shares of the relevant bin key from the nearby Picosiblings and only then, after a round trip, will it be able to decrypt the relevant credentials. This introduces latency. User acceptability of an alternative security mechanism is largely unaffected by the level of security it offers (which is unobservable by most users anyway) but is dramatically affected by waiting time. For this reason, besides developing the crypto, we implemented our system on commercial off-the-shelf Bluetooth LE development boards in order to measure whether the latency and power consumption of our approach would be acceptable in a realistic setting.

4   A New Secret Sharing Scheme for Authentication Tokens

4.1   The Pico Credential Database

A Pico stores a potentially large number N of user credentials, grouped into 256 bins.[5] The value 256 is a parameter of the system; it is straightforward to make it larger, at the cost of somewhat increased implementation complexity. For each account the user has, there is one *(userid, credential)* pair. The user may, but does not have to, use a different userid for every account. The user may also have several accounts with the same service, obviously with distinct userids.

The original Pico design [2] was vulnerable to a cold boot attack: the entire credential database was encrypted with a single master key, shared across the Picosiblings using Shamir secret sharing [10]. While the Pico was being unlocked, that key, and so the entire set of credentials, could be exposed. To mitigate this attack, in our design we encrypt the credentials in each bin with their own *bin key*.

Doing this in a naive way, however, would require the Picosiblings to each store shares of hundreds of keys, which is far too much—we want the Picosibling storage requirements to be very small. To this end, we use a *keying polynomial* $K(y)$ of degree r, and set the encryption key for bin β to $K(\beta)$. The keying polynomial $K(y)$ is shared to the Picosiblings in the manner described in Sect. 4.2.

The choice of the polynomial degree r is important: the Picosiblings will each have to store $r + 1$ key-sized entries, so we would like to keep r small. However, if the Pico is ever actively unlocking *more than r bins at the same time*, then at least $r + 1$ values of $K(\beta_i)$ will be in memory simultaneously. A cold boot attack at that point will be able to recover the entire polynomial K, and thus decrypt *all* of the bins. Note that this is not to say that credentials from at most r bins can be unlocked at any time in the Pico; once the Pico unlocks a bin (reconstructs the bin key $K(\beta_i)$ and decrypts the desired credential(s) in the bin), the Pico will wipe the key (and the shares that constructed it) from

---

[5] If $N \le 256$ then each credential has its own bin and can be decrypted independently of the others. If $N > 256$ then some bins may contain more than one credential, which will be encrypted and decrypted together.

memory. It is only if the Pico is *actively receiving shares* of more than r bin keys at the same time that the fatal problem arises.

We can therefore choose r to be quite small, and simply program the Pico to never request more than r key reconstructions in parallel. Indeed, $r = 1$ is a perfectly reasonable choice, and results in each Picosibling having to store only two key-sized values—256 bits in total. (Note that $r = 0$ corresponds to the original Pico strategy [2] of encrypting every credential with the same key.)

Appendix A presents the schema for the Pico credential database.

4.2 Bivariate Secret Sharing

The secret to be shared across the Picosiblings (say there are n Picosiblings) is the above keying polynomial, which is an arbitrary degree-r polynomial $K(y) = \sum_{j=0}^{r} k_j y^j$.

The possible inputs y for this polynomial are bin identifiers (β_i), which are values in a small finite field $\mathbb{F}$. In our implementation, we choose $\mathbb{F} = GF(2^8)$, so the number of bins is $|\mathbb{F}| = 256$, and each bin identifier is a single byte. However, the outputs of the polynomial should be encryption keys, which should of course be much larger than 8 bits. Therefore, we select the coefficients k_j of the keying polynomial from a *vector space* $\mathbb{V}$ over $\mathbb{F}$; in particular, we choose $\mathbb{V} = \mathbb{F}^{16}$, so that the elements of $\mathbb{V}$ are vectors (arrays) of 16 bytes (128 bits). Thus we write $K(y) \in \mathbb{V}[y]$.

In order to share an entire polynomial $K(y)$, rather than a single encryption key as in the original design, we now have the Pico create a *bivariate polynomial* $F(x,y)$ of degree $(k - 1, r)$—that is, of degree $k - 1$ in x and of degree r in y: $F(x, y) = \sum_{i=0}^{k-1} \sum_{j=0}^{r} a_{ij} x^i y^j$. For a univariate polynomial, k points $y_i = f(\alpha_i)$ define a unique polynomial f of degree $k - 1$. The equivalent statement for a bivariate polynomial is that k univariate polynomials $f_i(y) = F(\alpha_i, y)$ of degree r define a unique bivariate polynomial F of degree $(k - 1, r)$.

A bivariate secret sharing scheme for n participants (the Picosiblings, in our case) is defined as follows. Let $\mathbb{F}$ be a finite field; $\mathbb{V}$ be a vector space over $\mathbb{F}$; k, r, and n be non-negative integers with $1 \leq k \leq n$; and $\alpha_1, \ldots, \alpha_n$ be arbitrary distinct non-zero elements of $\mathbb{F}$. (The α_i are the Picosibling identifiers selected by the Pico. Although our protocol never requires these identifiers to leave the Pico—even the Picosiblings never learn their own identifiers—they are not security sensitive, in the sense that their knowledge would not help an adversary guess any of the shares.) As above, the secret to be shared is the univariate polynomial $K(y) = \sum_{j=0}^{r} k_j y^j \in \mathbb{V}[y]$.

For $0 \leq j \leq r$, set $a_{0j} = k_j$, and for $1 \leq i \leq k - 1$ and $0 \leq j \leq r$, select a_{ij} uniformly at random from $\mathbb{V}$. Then construct the bivariate polynomial $F(x, y) \in \mathbb{V}[x, y]$ as above.

For each $1 \leq i \leq n$, compute the degree-r polynomial $f_i(y) = F(\alpha_i, y) \in \mathbb{V}[y]$, and send $f_i(y)$ (the *share*) to participant i. Note that the amount of storage this requires at each participant is $r + 1$ elements of $\mathbb{V}$.

In a typical secret-sharing protocol, k participants would combine their shares to recover the shared secret *polynomial* $K(y)$. Our scenario is slightly different, however; for a specified bin identifier β, we wish to reconstruct just the single *value* $K(\beta) \in \mathbb{V}$, and not the whole polynomial $K(y)$. To accomplish this reconstruction, we will send the value β to k Picosiblings. Each Picosibling i will reply with $v_{\beta i} = f_i(\beta) = F(\alpha_i, \beta)$—a single value in $\mathbb{V}$. We then perform Lagrange interpolation on the $(\alpha_i, v_{\beta i})$ pairs in the usual way to recover $F(0, \beta) = K(\beta)$.

We can achieve proactivity [11] by periodically creating n shares of the zero polynomial, and sending them to the Picosiblings to add to their existing shares (queueing them on the Pico until the next time each Picosibling is encountered—this is safe, since the queued value reveals no information about either the old or new value of the share of the keying polynomial). To remove a Picosibling from the scheme, the same mechanism is used, except the removed Picosibling is not sent a share of the zero polynomial. To add a Picosibling to the scheme, k existing Picosiblings get together to reconstruct F, a new and unused $\alpha_{n+1} \neq 0$ is picked, and $F(\alpha_{n+1}, y)$ is sent to the new Picosibling.

4.3   Picosibling Protocol

We now develop a protocol based on the above bivariate secret sharing scheme that allows individual bins in the Pico credential database to be unlocked as needed.

Enrollment. When a new Picosibling is enrolled to a Pico, the Pico executes a pairing protocol with the Picosibling in order to establish a random shared symmetric communication key CK_i that will be used to protect all communication between the Pico and that Picosibling. The pairing mechanism is outside the scope of the current discussion; see Krause [12] for a description of the proposed pairing mechanisms for Picos and Picosiblings. At pairing time, the Pico also selects an arbitrary unused non-zero $\alpha_i \in \mathbb{F}$ to serve as that Picosibling's *Picosibling identifier*. The Pico will store each of the communication keys CK_i in its small tamper-proof memory, while the α_i are not sensitive, and need not be protected in this manner. If the tamper-proof memory is extremely tight, the CK_i can each be derived from a single master 128-bit secret CK^* as $CK_i = \text{CBC-MAC}_{CK^*}(\alpha_i)$; in that case, only the 128-bit CK^* needs to be stored in tamper-proof memory.

The first batch of at least k Picosiblings will be enrolled at the time the Pico is initialized. At this time, the Pico will create the keying polynomial $K(y)$, use it to encrypt the credential database, and send shares of $K(y)$ to the Picosiblings as described above. Later, new Picosiblings can be enrolled by having the Pico communicate with k existing Picosiblings to reconstruct the entirety of the bivariate polynomial $F(x, y)$ that produces the shares of the keying polynomial $K(y) = F(0, y)$. The Pico will then send the new Picosibling the coefficients $f_{i0}, f_{i1} \in \mathbb{V}$ of its share of the keying polynomial.

Query Share. When the user attempts to authenticate to a service, the Pico will look up the bin identifier β associated with the credential for that service in its credential database. The Pico will then attempt to construct the bin key $K(\beta)$ by communicating with each of k nearby Picosiblings. This communication will be protected using the above symmetric communication keys CK_i.

The Pico sends the value β to each Picosibling; the Picosibling evaluates its share $v_{\beta i} = f_{i0} + \beta * f_{i1}$ of the keying polynomial for the specified bin and returns the value $v_{\beta i}$ to the Pico.

The Pico (which knows the value of α_i associated with each Picosibling) then uses Lagrange interpolation to find the bin key $K(\beta) = \sum_{i=1}^{k} v_{\beta i} \prod_{\substack{1 \le j \le k \\ j \ne i}} \frac{\alpha_j}{\alpha_j - \alpha_i}$.

The bin key is then used to decrypt the desired credential in bin β of the Pico credential database. Once the credential is accessed, the shares and the reconstructed $K(\beta)$ can be deleted from memory.

The bin key reconstruction process is when the Pico is at its most vulnerable: if it has received some, but not all, of the k shares it has requested, then an adversary cold booting the Pico at that point could recover some shares of the bin key, and capturing up to $k-1$ Picosiblings (which is within the threat model) would reveal the bin key to the adversary. However, unlike the original Pico design, *only* the credentials in that bin are revealed, and not all credentials in the Pico. One might be tempted to use a technique such as that of TRESOR [13] to do the entirety of the bin key reconstruction and bin decryption in CPU registers; being able to do so would add even more security to our proposal. We could not experiment with this idea because in our prototype the role of the Pico was played by a BLE-capable Android phone whose non-Intel CPU did not support the AES-NI instruction set required by TRESOR.

Query Presence. Once the credential has been used, the Pico enters into a continuous authentication mode with the service. [2] The continuous authentication uses an ephemeral key and, therefore, no longer needs access to the credential database. However, if the Pico is out of range of its siblings it automatically locks and pauses any active sessions.

While the Pico is in continuous authentication mode, it periodically sends heartbeat requests to its nearby Picosiblings. As long as k Picosiblings respond to the heartbeat, the Pico will maintain continuous authentication to the service. These siblings do not necessarily have to be the devices that initially provided shares to unlock the credential, although it is reasonable for the Pico to try to contact those devices first.

5   Prototype Implementation

To validate and measure the performance of our cryptographic design, we implemented our scheme on a realistic hardware development platform for wearable devices.

To our knowledge, this is the first time that working Picosiblings as dedicated devices have been prototyped. Our self-imposed implementation constraints attempt to limit the burden imposed on the user in various dimensions (size, weight, maintenance, obtrusiveness, cost, etc.). More specifically, Picosiblings should:

- Be small enough to be attached (unobtrusively) to a range of items that users already frequently carry (such as wallets, phones, and keys).
- Be able to be integrated into items that users carry or wear.
- Operate for many months without charging or replacing batteries.
- Be cheap to purchase and replace.

Whilst somewhat vague, these non-functional requirements introduce a set of constraints against which the success of our prototype implementation can be measured.

The Pico and its Picosiblings are heavily asymmetric, with Picosiblings being both heavily constrained (in terms of size and therefore battery capacity) and poorly resourced (in terms of memory, computation power, and user interface features). Recognizing this, our implementation is optimized around the most resource-constrained devices—the Picosiblings.

A defining architectural choice for Picosiblings is the wireless communication protocol. Low-cost, low-power wireless communication is a key enabling technology for the Internet of Things (IoT). Of the numerous wireless standards employed in IoT applications, Bluetooth Low Energy (BLE) is the closest match to Pico's requirements. BLE is specifically targeted at scenarios exhibiting significant asymmetry, and has been designed around the performance of off-the-shelf button-cell batteries. BLE also supports a privacy feature, in which hardware addresses are encrypted over the air, in order to avoid tracking of devices [14]; this feature also meshes well with our requirements.

5.1 BLE Picosibling Service

In contrast to Bluetooth classic (essentially a cable replacement), BLE is targeted at applications that transmit only a few octets of data at frequencies ranging from once a second to every few days, weeks, or months. Such applications typically send only a limited range of primitive data types; for example, representing the value of a temperature sensor. In BLE, server state is made available through sets of *characteristics*. Characteristics group together state (both readable and writable) and metadata such as name and access permissions. Readable characteristics expose the historic or current state recorded by the service. For example, a simple light switch service may expose the state of the light (either on or off). Writable characteristics are commonly used to command behaviour; for example, turning a light on or off. Characteristics and associated behaviours are grouped together into reusable components called services. Clients can interrogate a service's characteristics and associated metadata to determine how to interact with the service; this can be viewed as a implementation of the well-known Service Oriented Architecture (SOA) pattern:

A paradigm for organizing and utilizing distributed capabilities that may be under the control of different ownership domains. It provides a uniform means to offer, discover, interact with and use capabilities to produce desired effects consistent with measurable preconditions and expectations [15].

The following sections provide an overview of the BLE Picosibling service.[6]

Enrollment. To enroll a new Picosibling, it must be first awoken and made discoverable by the Pico. In our prototype implementation, unenrolled Picosiblings are woken up by the user pressing a button. However, as the design matures, such UI elements will be removed. As with commercial BLE beacon devices, awakening the device from sleep will be performed by the user tapping the device (which is detected by a MEMS accelerometer). Once awake, the Picosibling enters the BLE general advertising mode. Whilst in this mode, the Picosibling can accept a connection event from the Pico. Once connected, the Picosibling's exposed state can be read and written.

With weaknesses in BLE pairing mechanisms well documented [16], enrollment of Picosiblings is based upon the principle of "secure at first use". To enroll a new Picosibling, the Pico writes into it its unique communication key CK_i and share $f_i(y)$. The Picosibling's communication key is exposed by the BLE service as a single 16-byte (128-bit) write-only characteristic. When this characteristic is written, the Picosibling performs key diversification[7] to generate a further two keys. These keys provide authenticated encryption (encrypt-then-MAC) for messages sent over the air. Transmitted messages contain counters to prevent reflection and replay attacks.

As noted in Sect. 4.2, storage for the share requires $r + 1$ elements of $\mathbb{V}$. In this case, values in $\mathbb{V}$ are vectors (arrays) of 16 elements of $\mathbb{F}$; that is, arbitrary 16-byte (128-bit) values. Thus, the share $f_i(y)$ is represented in the BLE profile as a single 32-byte write-only characteristic.

Query Share/Presence. To query the Picosibling's share, the Pico writes the value β (encrypted and MAC'd using the keys established at enrollment) into a write-only characteristic. This characteristic is 48 bytes in length, with 16 bytes for each of the initialization vector (IV), encrypted payload, and a message authentication code (MAC). On writing the characteristic, the value is decrypted and verified using the keys established at enrollment. The decrypted payload is a binary packed data structure containing a counter (whose value is even for communication from the Pico to the Picosibling, and odd in the opposite

---

[6] This description is intended to capture the essential features of our implementation rather than act as a formal specification.

[7] The communication key is diversified by performing a CBC-MAC (using the AES coprocessor) on two fixed values (1 and 2). The Picosibling does not possess a source of cryptographically strong randomness, and therefore is not trusted to generate random keys.

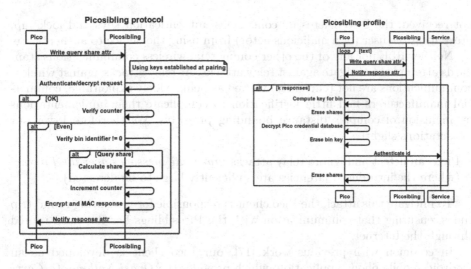

Fig. 1. Overview of the Picosibling protocol implementation (left) and the Picosibling profile implementation (right) in BLE, as UML sequence diagrams.

direction), a share flag (set to 1 when the Pico is querying the value of a share, and 0 when it is merely querying presence), and an 8-bit bin identifier β.

Using the bin identifier β, the Picosibling evaluates its share $f_i(\beta)$.[8] The Picosibling share (encrypted and MAC'd) is returned to the Pico by updating a 64-byte read-only characteristic (16 bytes for the IV, 32 bytes for the encrypted payload, including the share and the incremented counter, and 16 bytes for the MAC). Changes to this value are automatically reported as a BLE notification to the Pico.

Querying the Picosibling's presence is achieved as described above, querying the Picosibling while setting the share flag to 0.

Figure 1 (left) shows an overview of the BLE Picosibling profile query share and presence behaviour.

Our prototype Picosiblings have been developed using an off-the-shelf BLE development kit from Texas Instruments (TI), described in Appendix B.

5.2 BLE Picosibling Profile

A BLE profile specifies the behaviour of the client (in our case, the Pico). Figure 1 (right) gives an overview of the client behaviour when querying the Picosiblings' shares. Querying presence is largely the same, except that if k responses are

---

[8] As an optimization, computation in $GF(2^8)$ is performed with two precomputed 256-byte tables. The first provides provides a lookup $i \mapsto g^i$ and the second $g^i \mapsto i$ for a generator g. Note that although the CC2541 device contains 256 KB of flash, there is not a free 64 KB segment capable of holding a 256 * 256 B lookup table required for precomputing the entire multiplication table in $GF(2^8)$.

not received, the Pico deletes its continuous authentication keys and locks up, preventing the user (or a malicious actor) from using the device to authenticate.

Neither BLE nor any of the other commercial wireless communications standards attempts to mitigate against relay attacks. As relay attacks against wireless communications are not (currently) viewed as being widely exploitable, commercial manufacturers find little justification to complicate their implementations by inclusion of complex distance bounding protocols. We therefore lower our expectations slightly:

– Pico can detect and ignore relay attacks *that route messages over the Internet* (where the introduced latencies are sufficiently large to be detected).

To mitigate this attack the Pico client is responsible for measuring round trip times, ensuring that communication with the Picosiblings has not been routed through the Internet.

In common with previous work [17], our Pico client is developed as an Android mobile phone application, which provides the *Quasi-Nothing-To-Carry* property of the evaluation framework defined by Bonneau et al. [18]. Our minimal implementation of Pico supports:

– Requesting Picosibling shares to unlock entries in the credential database (see Appendix A) and
– querying Picosiblings for user presence.

No other features of Pico are implemented in our prototype client.

6 Performance Evaluation

In contrast to typical BLE applications such as remote sensing, where communication is infrequent and therefore battery life is measured in months or even years, Pico continually communicates with its Picosiblings to verify that the user, once authenticated, remains present. Thus a key objective of prototyping is to estimate the impact that the protocol of Sect. 4.3 has on the Picosibling's battery life. Following the detailed guidance given in TI Application Note AN092 [19], we have produced estimates of battery lifetime under representative conditions with the focus on assessing the broad feasibility of our architectural choices.

As a first step, we derive an upper bound estimate on battery lifetime. This corresponds to an active but unused Picosibling; that is, a Picosibling that the user is carrying with them but is not one of the k-out-of-n used by Pico when querying a share or user presence. In contrast to Bluetooth classic, BLE is a connectionless protocol. As a connection-oriented channel is never established, there is little cost in dropping and re-establishing connections only when there is useful data to send [20]. When not communicating, Picosiblings enter a low-power sleep mode.[9] Although Picosiblings spend the majority of their time asleep, they periodically wake up, advertising their presence to respond to requests from the Pico

---

[9] As detailed in Kamath and Lindh [19], when sleeping the device enters Power Mode 2 where the current consumed is $1\,\mu A$.

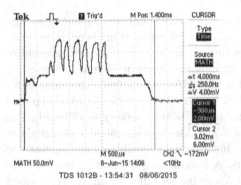 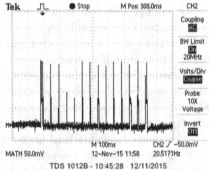

Fig. 2. Left: Oscilloscope trace of current consumed by BLE Picosibling during periodic wakeup, advertising its presence. Right: Oscilloscope trace of the current consumed by a BLE Picosibling when the Pico is querying its presence. (Note the differences in the horizontal scale.)

device. The time between wakeups, t_w, is a parameter of our system. As mentioned in Sect. 3, this time controls how long (after the user initiates a login to a service) the Pico may have to wait before being able to contact its Picosiblings, and thus complete the login. We want this latency to be low, but frequent wakeups will decrease battery life. We analyze this tradeoff next.

Figure 2 shows an oscilloscope trace of current consumption[10] during the period in which the Picosibling is advertising its presence to the Pico device. As is evident from Fig. 2, current consumption varies markedly as the Picosibling transitions between different operating states (notably transmitting and receiving, but also waking up and preparing for sleep).

We measured the average current during the advertising period to be 10.42 mA. The time between advertising events is t_w; the advertising period is 4.02 ms, with the Picosibling being asleep (and drawing 1 μA) the remainder of the time. Thus, we estimate the total average current of an active but unused Picosibling as

$$\frac{((t_w - 4.02\,\text{ms}) * 1\,\mu\text{A} + (4.02\,\text{ms} * 10.42\,\text{mA}))}{t_w} = 1\,\mu\text{A} + \frac{41.9}{t_w}\,\mu\text{As}.$$

In the original design [2], Picosibling shares are used to construct a single full-disk encryption (FDE) key. This FDE key protects the Pico credential database when the user is not present. In contrast, our scheme requires that decryption keys are reconstructed on demand; that is, when the user authenticates with a given service. As keys are reconstructed in the flow of the overall authentication process, response latency is critical. Sasse et al. [21] report that average completion time for username and password authentication is on the order of ten seconds.[11] In our prototype implementation, we chose $t_w = 1\,\text{s}$, so that the Pico

---

[10] Measured as the voltage across a 1 KΩ resistor.
[11] This value was produced by applying the KLM-GOMS methodology (a modelling approach for predicting how long it takes an expert user to accomplish a task on a computing system) [22].

reconstructs the encryption keys within one second under ideal conditions and within two to three seconds with some radio interference. This process involves little cognitive effort from the user and is therefore unlikely to be seen as a major burden. This value of t_w yields an average current of about $43\,\mu\text{A}$.

Assuming $55\,\text{mAh}$ is the capacity of a CR1616 battery (see Appendix B for hardware details), that gives an expected battery lifetime of $55\,\text{mAh}/43\,\mu\text{A} = 1300\,\text{h}$, or 53 days. Assuming the capacity of a CR2032 battery is $230\,\text{mAh}$, this results in an expected battery lifetime of $230\,\text{mAh}/43\,\mu\text{A} = 5300\,\text{h}$, or 220 days.

Our estimates indicate that an active but unused Picosiblings can operate on a CR2032 battery for over seven months. A Picosibling interacting with a Pico will, however, of course have a somewhat lower battery life; we analyze this effect next. Figure 2 shows the current consumed by the Picosibling when the Pico is querying its presence. Querying presence requires the client (Pico) to write a single BLE characteristic, with the response returned via a BLE notification. However, the captured trace exhibits multiple interactions between the Pico and the Picosibling. Whilst additional messages (for example for setting up the BLE connection) are expected, the sheer number of interactions was somewhat confusing. On detailed investigation we determined that the TI BLE stack limits the MTU of user data to 20 bytes (the minimum allowable in the BLE specification). Thus, when writing or reading characteristics greater than 20 bytes, the communication is broken into multple packets. As the TI BLE stack is provided as a binary library, this parameter could not be changed and the presence of these additional messages is a limitation of our current implementation. We could improve on this, and thus save time and energy, but only if we had the ability to modify the library.

Figure 2 shows that the Picosibling responds to a query in about 680 ms. This could be significantly reduced, saving energy, if more data could be sent in each packet. Note that querying a Picosibling's share requires exactly the same set of interactions with the Pico, and therefore takes approximately the same time. The additional processing time required to evaluate the share is tiny in comparison.

Once a Pico is unlocked, it enters continuous authentication mode. In this mode, the Pico polls its Picosiblings to ensure that at least k of them remain in the Pico's vicinity. How often this polling is done is governed by t_c, another parameter of our system. Again, a higher t_c will increase the battery life. This time, the tradeoff is not to interactive latency, however, but to how long a Pico will stay unlocked after leaving the aura of its Picosiblings. (Note that t_c must be a multiple of t_w, as communication can only occur when the Picosibling wakes up.)

Similar to the above, we compute the average current for a Picosibling undergoing continuous authentication to be $\frac{823}{t_c}\,\mu\text{A}\,\text{s}$. This is in addition to the above cost of waking up every t_w, so the total average current is $1\,\mu\text{A} + \frac{41.9}{t_w}\,\mu\text{A}\,\text{s} + \frac{823}{t_c}\,\mu\text{A}\,\text{s}$. (Although, again, the numerator 823 could be significantly smaller with an improved BLE stack with a higher MTU.)

If we retain $t_w = 1\,\text{s}$, and set $t_c = 30\,\text{s}$, then the average current is $70\,\mu\text{A}$. If we are satisfied with $t_c = 60\,\text{s}$, the average current is $57\,\mu\text{A}$. With a CR1616 battery, the latter figure would give an expected battery lifetime of 960 h, or 40 days; with a CR2032 battery, the battery life would increase to 4000 h, or over 165 days. This value is within the performance requirements for Picosiblings outlined in Sect. 5 (and would be even higher with a better BLE stack).

It should also be noted that, under normal circumstances, Pico automatically logs users out of services when they are away from the terminal used to access those services. Thus, the Pico does not need to confirm the presence of its Picosiblings continuously. If a user, for example, is actively logged into a service only half of the time, the lifetime of a CR2032 battery would be over 190 days with our current implementation.

Additionally, the Picosiblings could use a MEMS accelerometer to notice that they are not being worn (when, for example, the user is asleep), and go to sleep themselves for that entire time, without waking up every t_w.

Extending the above example, if the user sleeps 8 h per day, and is actively logged into a service for half of her waking hours, the lifetime of a CR2032 battery would be over 280 days.

7 Related Work

The most obviously related work is Pico: the relevant papers from Stajano and his group [2,6–8,17] have been extensively referred to throughout the text.

Laurie and Singer [23] argue that it is impossible to have a system which is both general purpose and trustworthy. Their requirements for a trusted authentication device (which they refer to as the Neb) closely match those of Pico. However, in contrast to Pico, the Neb does not attempt to mitigate loss or theft of the device.

FIDO (Fast IDentity Online), an open industry alliance of vendors, including a who's who of major players such as Alibaba, American Express, ARM, Google, Intel, Mastercard, Microsoft, PayPal, Samsung and Visa, released two sets of specifications for online authentication: UAF (Universal Authentication Framework) [1] and U2F (Universal Second Factor) [24]. Both involve authenticating to online services with a device. UAF replaces passwords entirely by allowing users to authenticate from a FIDO-enabled device, such as a smartphone. It involves registering the user's device to online services and selecting a biometric authentication action, such as swiping a finger, performed on the device. Pico and FIDO share commonalities in both the problem they are addressing and their approaches, though it should be noted that Pico predates the FIDO specifications by over 3 years.

Müller et al.'s TRESOR [13] is closely related to our present work in purpose: it too is a low-cost protection against cold boot attacks. Their approach is totally different, however: it works by running the encryption fully within the CPU registers, with creative use of the debug registers as crypto storage. We considered how to overcome the restrictions on the limited register space available, and we would have liked to offer defense in depth by combining their approach with ours, but were not able to do so because TRESOR is specific to Intel processors supporting the AES-NI instruction set.

There is prior art on sensing the proximity of a user-worn tag to infer user presence and lock and unlock devices, from Want et al.'s Active Badge [25], through Landwehr's patent [26, 27], and to Corner and Noble's "Zero-interaction authentication" [4], the first system in which the user-worn token provided the cryptographic key to unlock the target device. Sharing the key among multiple devices was first suggested by Desmedt et al. [3]. Peeters defended a PhD [28] on this topic and, among other contributions, showed how to securely store a share in a wearable device that does not offer a secure storage hardware primitive [29]. We did not use it because capturing enough wearables was outside our threat model, but this is another result that might be profitably combined with our design to provide defense in depth.

Bivariate secret sharing has been used in prior works; for example, by Cachin et al. [30] and by Tassa and Dyn [31]. In those works, the secret to be shared was a scalar, and the bivariate polynomial was used to effectively make *shares of shares* of the secret. In contrast, in our work, the secret to be shared is itself the univariate keying polynomial $K(y)$. This polynomial is not acting in a secret-sharing capacity; $K(0)$ is not special—it is merely the bin key for bin number 0.

Proactive secret sharing was introduced by Herzberg et al. [11], and mobile proactive secret sharing (MPSS) by Schultz et al. [32]. Those schemes require relatively heavyweight commitment and public-key primitives. Our system does not require such primitives, because our threat model is less general. In particular, in our setting, the *dealer* (the entity creating the shares from the secret) is the Pico itself, which is assumed to be trusted—there is no need for the Picosiblings to verify that the shares they receive are consistent. Similarly, although we allow for a mobile adversary that can compromise Picosiblings over time, we assume that once an adversary compromises a Picosibling, it cannot be "uncompromised"; that is, the set of compromised Picosiblings is non-decreasing. This allows us to use relatively simple protocols for Picosibling addition and removal, as we do not need to deal with cases where the adversary compromises $k - 1$ Picosiblings before a removal, and a *different* $k - 1$ Picosiblings afterwards. (MPSS, on the other hand, does go to great effort to deal with such cases.)

8   Conclusions

The remarkable industry momentum gathering behind the FIDO alliance suggests a strong convergence towards replacing passwords with a personal authentication token. If that premise is accepted, the next problem is how to lock and unlock the token to protect it against unauthorized use. While FIDO UAF [1] offers static unlocking, Pico [2] adopts the proximity-based threshold scheme pioneered by Desmedt et al. [3], using it as a platform for continuous authentication.

We found Pico vulnerable to a cold boot attack: an adversary who captured a running Pico and was able to read its RAM would be able to steal all the credentials of the user. We designed and prototyped a low-cost mitigation for this vulnerability, without resorting to the silver bullet of making the whole security token tamper-proof. Bootstrapping all security from a small amount of tamper-resistant flash memory (which Pico requires anyway, regardless of our contribution), we protect the user's credentials against an adversary who may read out all the flash and RAM of a running token. Our new secret sharing scheme, based on a bivariate polynomial, allows only a small fraction of the credentials to be exposed at a time. Our solution scales to a high number of credentials while imposing only a constant (and small) storage cost on the Picosiblings.

We have prototyped our cryptographic design on COTS hardware and measured its performance in terms of power consumption and latency. Our Picosibling prototype lasts for 165–220 days (depending on how frequently the user is authenticated to a service) on a CR2032 button-cell battery, with an observed authentication latency of 2–3 s. We also show how a simple accelerometer detecting when the Picosibling is not being worn could increase the battery life by about 50 %. Fixing gratuitous inefficiencies in the BLE stack would increase it further.

We trust readers will agree that our prototype, though not yet ready for prime time, soundly demonstrates the viability of our design: if it were made into a commercial product, battery life and latency could be improved even further.

Acknowledgements. We thank Rob Harle for his advice on selecting a Bluetooth Low Energy development platform. We thank David Llewellyn-Jones for insightful comments on the comparative security of our scheme with respect to related work. Jenkinson and Stajano thank the European Research Council for funding this research through grant StG 307224 (Pico). Goldberg thanks NSERC for grant RGPIN-341529.

Appendix A Schema of the Pico Credential Database

Table 1 shows the schema of the Pico credential database. Each row in this database is indexed by a hash of the service's identifier $H(ID_S)$. Each of the N

Table 1. Schema of the Pico credential database. Depending on the scenario, credentials may be public/private key pairs or symmetric keys shared with the service. Note that Google and Expedia end up in the same bin, that the user shares the same userid for Expedia and Amazon, and that the user has two distinct Twitter accounts, which she distinguishes by the userid.

Hash of service's identifier	Bin identifier	Encrypted credential	Userid
$H(ID_{Google})$	0x1e	$\{cred_{Google,jane.doe}\}_{K(0x1e)}$	jane.doe
$H(ID_{Amazon})$	0x75	$\{cred_{Amazon,jane257}\}_{K(0x75)}$	jane257
$H(ID_{Twitter})$	0x57	$\{cred_{Twitter,@jane}\}_{K(0x57)}$	@jane
...	...	...	...
$H(ID_{Expedia})$	0x1e	$\{cred_{Expedia,jane257}\}_{K(0x1e)}$	jane257
$H(ID_{Twitter})$	0x32	$\{cred_{Twitter,@tattoophile}\}_{K(0x32)}$	@tattoophile

rows in the Pico credential database contains a 1-byte bin identifier $\beta_1, \ldots, \beta_N$, an encrypted credential, and other information required to identify the account to the user. Note that if $N > 256$, then there will be multiple credentials in the same bin; those credentials will be encrypted with the same key. A cold boot attack during a bin key reconstruction will reveal all of the credentials in the bin, and not just the credential being actively requested—but only a fraction of one percent of all the credentials, and not all of them, as in the previous design.

Appendix B Hardware Prototype Platform

Our prototype Picosiblings have been developed using an off-the-shelf BLE development kit from Texas Instruments (TI), shown in Fig. 3. The TI development board is built around a power-optimised system-on-chip (SoC) solution targeting BLE and proprietary 2.4 GHz RF applications [33]. The development kit includes a hardware debugger and full source code for Operating System (OSAL) and Hardware Abstraction Layers (HAL). The BLE protocol stack is provided as a set of binary libraries. Software for the platform is built using the third-party IAR Embedded Workbench toolchain.

The CC2541's main features include:

- High-performance low-power 8-bit 8051 processor
- 256 KB flash and 8 KB RAM (retained in all power states)
- Peripherals including watchdog and general-purpose timers, 2x USART, I2C, and AES coprocessor
- 6 mm x 6 mm QFN40 package

Fig. 3. Texas Instruments CC2541DK-MINI Bluetooth Low Energy development kit.

In volume, the CC2541 SoC is priced at approximately \$4. However, assuming price falls in line with trends witnessed with classic Bluetooth, it can be expected to approach the \$2–3 range as the technology becomes ubiquitous.

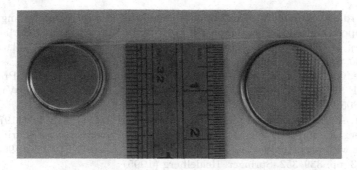

Fig. 4. The two standard coin batteries we used. Left: CR1616 (16 mm diameter, 1.6 mm thickness, ≈55 mAh). Right: CR2032 (20 mm diameter, 3.2 mm thickness, ≈230 mAh).

As the CC2541 SoC requires relatively few additional discrete components the bill of materials for a Picosibling built using this device could comfortably sit in the $3–4 range. This is, arguably, sufficiently cheap for users not to worry about purchasing and replacing devices.

Standard button-cell CR1616 and CR2032 batteries (shown in Fig. 4) are reasonable batteries to use in our scenario, as their size makes them well suited to wearable electronics and embedding in jewellery.

References

1. FIDO Alliance: FIDO UAF complete specifications FINAL 1.0, December 2014
2. Stajano, F.: Pico: no more passwords!. In: Christianson, B., Crispo, B., Malcolm, J., Stajano, F. (eds.) Security Protocols XIX. LNCS, vol. 7114, pp. 49–81. Springer, Heidelberg (2011)
3. Desmedt, Y., Burmester, M., Safavi-Naini, R., Wang, H.: Threshold Things That Think (T4): Security requirements to cope with theft of handheld/handless internet devices. In: Proceedings of Symposium on Requirements Engineering for Information Security (2001)
4. Corner, M.D., Noble, B.D.: Zero-interaction authentication. In: Proceedings of ACM MobiCom 2002, pp. 1–11, 23–28 September 2002
5. Halderman, J.A., Schoen, S.D., Heninger, N., Clarkson, W., Paul, W., Calandrino, J.A., Feldman, A.J., Appelbaum, J., Felten, E.W.: Lest we remember: Cold-boot attacks on encryption keys. Commun. ACM **52**(5), 91–98 (2009)
6. Stafford-Fraser, Q., Stajano, F., Warrington, C., Jenkinson, G., Spencer, M., Payne, J.: To have and have not: Variations on secret sharing to model user presence. In: Proceedings of UPSIDE workshop of UBICOMP 2014, September 2014
7. Stajano, F., Christianson, B., Lomas, M., Jenkinson, G., Payne, J., Spencer, M., Stafford-Fraser, Q.: Pico without public keys. In: Christianson, B., Švenda, P., Matyáš, V., Malcolm, J., Stajano, F., Anderson, J. (eds.) Security Protocols 2015. LNCS, vol. 9379, pp. 195–211. Springer, Heidelberg (2015). doi:10.1007/978-3-319-26096-9_21

8. Stannard, O., Stajano, F.: Am I in good company? A privacy-protecting protocol for cooperating ubiquitous computing devices. In: Christianson, B., Malcolm, J., Stajano, F., Anderson, J. (eds.) Security Protocols 2012. LNCS, vol. 7622, pp. 223–230. Springer, Heidelberg (2012)

9. Hancke, G.P., Kuhn, M.G.: An RFID distance bounding protocol. In: Proceedings of IEEE SECURECOMM 2005, pp. 67–73. IEEE Computer Society, Washington, DC (2005)

10. Shamir, A.: How to share a secret. Commun. ACM **22**(11), 612–613 (1979)

11. Herzberg, A., Jarecki, S., Krawczyk, H., Yung, M.: Proactive secret sharing or: how to cope with perpetual leakage. In: Coppersmith, D. (ed.) CRYPTO 1995. LNCS, vol. 963, pp. 339–352. Springer, Heidelberg (1995)

12. Krause, F.M.A.: Designing Secure & Usable Picosiblings: An exploration of potential pairing mechanisms. Master's thesis, Wolfson College, University of Cambridge (2014)

13. Müller, T., Freiling, F.C., Dewald, A.: TRESOR runs encryption securely outside RAM. In: 20th USENIX Security Symposium, USENIX (2011)

14. Gomez, C., Oller, J., Paradells, J.: Overview and evaluation of bluetooth low energy: an emerging low-power wireless technology. Sensors **12**(9), 11734–11753 (2012)

15. MacKenzie, C.M., Laskey, K., McCabe, F., Brown, P.F., Metz, R., Hamilton, B.A.: Reference model for service oriented architecture 1.0. OASIS Standard (2006)

16. Ryan, M.: Bluetooth: with low energy comes low security. In: 7th USENIX Workshop on Offensive Technologies, Berkeley, CA, USENIX (2013)

17. Stajano, F., Jenkinson, G., Payne, J., Spencer, M., Stafford-Fraser, Q., Warrington, C.: Bootstrapping adoption of the pico password replacement system. In: Christianson, B., Malcolm, J., Matyáš, V., Švenda, P., Stajano, F., Anderson, J. (eds.) Security Protocols 2014. LNCS, vol. 8809, pp. 172–186. Springer, Heidelberg (2014)

18. Bonneau, J., Herley, C., van Oorschot, P.C., Stajano, F.: The quest to replace passwords: a framework for comparative evaluation of web authentication schemes. In: Proceedings of the 2012 IEEE Symposium on Security and Privacy, SP 2012, pp. 553–567. IEEE Computer Society, Washington, DC (2012)

19. Kamath, S., Lindh, J.: Measuring Bluetooth Low Energy Power Consumption. Texas Instruments application note AN092, Dallas (2010)

20. Heydon, R.: Bluetooth Low Energy The Developer's Handbook. Prentice Hall, Upper Saddle River (2013)

21. Sasse, M.A., Steves, M., Krol, K., Chisnell, D.: The great authentication fatigue – and how to overcome it. In: Rau, P.L.P. (ed.) CCD 2014. LNCS, vol. 8528, pp. 228–239. Springer, Heidelberg (2014)

22. Card, S.K., Moran, T.P., Newell, A.: The keystroke-level model for user performance time with interactive systems. Commun. ACM **23**(7), 396–410 (1980)

23. Laurie, B., Singer, A.: Choose the red pill and the blue pill: A position paper. In: Proceedings of the 2008 Workshop on New Security Paradigms, NSPW 2008, pp. 127–133. ACM, New York (2008)

24. Alliance, F.: FIDO U2F Spec Package, May 2015

25. Want, R., Hopper, A., Falcao, V., Gibbons, J.: The active badge location system. ACM Trans. Inf. Syst. **10**(1), 91–102 (1992)

26. Landwehr, C.E.: Protecting unattended computers without software. In: Proceedings of the 13th Annual Computer Security Applications Conference, pp. 274–283. IEEE Computer Society, Washington, DC (1997)

27. Landwehr, C.E., Latham, D.L.: Secure identification system US Patent 5,892,901, filed 1997-06-10, granted 1999-04-06 (1999)
28. Peeters, R.: Security architecture for things that think. Ph.D. thesis, KU Leuven (2012)
29. Simoens, K., Peeters, R., Preneel, B.: Increased resilience in threshold cryptography: sharing a secret with devices that cannot store shares. In: Joye, M., Miyaji, A., Otsuka, A. (eds.) Pairing 2010. LNCS, vol. 6487, pp. 116–135. Springer, Heidelberg (2010)
30. Cachin, C., Kursawe, K., Lysyanskaya, A., Strobl, R.: Asynchronous verifiable secret sharing and proactive cryptosystems. In: 9th ACM Conference on Computer and Communications Security, pp. 88–97 (2002)
31. Tassa, T., Dyn, N.: Multipartite Secret Sharing by Bivariate Interpolation. In: 33rd International Colloquium on Automata, Languages and Programming, pp. 288–299 (2006)
32. Schultz, D., Liskov, B., Liskov, M.: MPSS: Mobile proactive secret sharing. ACM Trans. Inf. Syst. Secur. 13(4), 34:1–34:32 (2010)
33. Instruments, T.: CC2541 SimpleLink Bluetooth Smart and Proprietary Wireless MCU. Web page

Two More Efficient Variants of the J-PAKE Protocol

Jean Lancrenon, Marjan Škrobot[✉], and Qiang Tang

SnT, University of Luxembourg, Luxembourg, Luxembourg
{jean.lancrenon,marjan.skrobot,qiang.tang}@uni.lu

Abstract. Recently, the password-authenticated key exchange protocol J-PAKE of Hao and Ryan (Workshop on Security Protocols 2008) was formally proven secure in the algebraic adversary model by Abdalla et al. (IEEE S&P 2015). In this paper, we propose and examine two variants of J-PAKE - which we call RO-J-PAKE and CRS-J-PAKE - that each makes the use of two less zero-knowledge proofs than the original protocol. We show that they are provably secure following a similar strategy to that of Abdalla et al. We also study their efficiency as compared to J-PAKE's, also taking into account how the groups are chosen. Namely, we treat the cases of subgroups of finite fields and elliptic curves. Our work reveals that, for subgroups of finite fields, CRS-J-PAKE is indeed more efficient than J-PAKE, while RO-J-PAKE is much less efficient. On the other hand, when instantiated with elliptic curves, both RO-J-PAKE and CRS-J-PAKE are more efficient than J-PAKE, with CRS-J-PAKE being the best of the three. Regardless of implementation, we note that RO-J-PAKE enjoys a looser security reduction than both J-PAKE and CRS-J-PAKE. CRS-J-PAKE has the tightest security proof, but relies on an additional trust assumption at setup time.

Keywords: Password-authenticated key exchange · J-PAKE · Efficiency · Random oracle · Common reference string · Zero-knowledge proof

1 Introduction

The objective of *Password-Authenticated Key Exchange* (PAKE) is to allow secure authenticated communication over insecure networks between two or more parties who only share a low-entropy password. Many different protocols have been proposed in the literature to accomplish this. Among them, the J-PAKE protocol [18] has been implemented due to its patent-free nature.

J-PAKE is quite unique because it integrates Non-Interactive Zero-Knowledge proofs of knowledge (NIZKs in the rest of the paper) - specifically, Schnorr proofs of knowledge [28] - effectively into its design. However, the presence of these proofs is actually one of the main arguments of J-PAKE's detractors: Indeed, they add more exponentiations to a protocol that already contains many. A question that can be asked therefore is whether variants of J-PAKE using less proofs of knowledge can be found, and how they compare in terms of efficiency to the original protocol.

© Springer International Publishing Switzerland 2016
M. Manulis et al. (Eds.): ACNS 2016, LNCS 9696, pp. 58–76, 2016.
DOI: 10.1007/978-3-319-39555-5_4

1.1 Our Contribution

We answer these questions by exhibiting two new protocols - which we call RO-J-PAKE and CRS-J-PAKE - that are very similar to J-PAKE, but each use two less zero-knowledge proofs. We explicitly prove the security of RO-J-PAKE, following a similar strategy to that of Abdalla et al. in their recent analysis of J-PAKE [5], and show how the proof can be adapted to the case of CRS-J-PAKE. We also provide a more refined analysis of these protocols' efficiency relative to J-PAKE's. We do this by explicitly examining costs depending on which groups are used to deploy the protocol. This is especially important for RO-J-PAKE, since it requires hashing into the group in question. Indeed, while on paper, this appears to have no importance, in practice it requires some attention. We treat the cases of Elliptic Curve (EC) groups and Subgroups of Finite Fields (SFFs), since all three protocols require the Decisional Diffie-Hellman (DDH) assumption to hold. In more detail, our findings are as follows:

- *In terms of provable security:* RO-J-PAKE and CRS-J-PAKE are asymptotically as secure as J-PAKE, and against the same kind of adversaries, namely, algebraic adversaries. However, RO-J-PAKE enjoys a looser security proof than J-PAKE and CRS-J-PAKE, essentially because of the addition of a random oracle. CRS-J-PAKE has the tightest proof of the three protocols. See the theorem bounds in Sect. 4.
- *In terms of computational and communication efficiency:* The apparent computational gain in efficiency that RO-J-PAKE and CRS-J-PAKE enjoy due to their having two less zero-knowledge proofs than J-PAKE can be summarized as follows:

- When all three protocols are instantiated with ECs, CRS-J-PAKE and RO-J-PAKE cost a total of about 8 group-sized exponentiations less than J-PAKE. CRS-J-PAKE has a slight edge over RO-J-PAKE, because the latter requires hashing into an EC group. However, experimental results (see Sect. 2.4) using recent research by Brier et al. [13] shows that this edge can be practically ignored.
- When all three protocols are instantiated with SFFs, CRS-J-PAKE takes 8 group-sized exponentiations less than J-PAKE, but RO-J-PAKE suffers from two additional exponentiations of size comparable to that of the base field's prime - which is typically way larger than the actual group - thus making it much less efficient than J-PAKE in practice, see Table 2. This is also due to the need to hash into a SFF. Thus, unless an efficient hashing method is devised, this instantiation of RO-J-PAKE may only have theoretical interest.
- Regardless of the group instantiation, both RO-J-PAKE and CRS-J-PAKE are more efficient than J-PAKE in terms of communication, as they both send four less group elements and two less scalars than J-PAKE does.

RO-J-PAKE and CRS-J-PAKE have a few other (dis)advantages related to their deployability, and that are worth mentioning. See Sect. 2.4 for more details.

1.2 Related Work

PAKE in general has been very heavily studied in the past twenty years. We briefly indicate some landmark papers here, and refer to Pointcheval's survey [27] for more complete references. PAKE was introduced by Bellovin and Meritt in [10]. Their EKE protocol was the first of its kind. It was later followed by Jablon's SPEKE protocol [19]. The first viable formal security models for PAKE appeared in [8,12]. A year later, Katz et al. [21] demonstrated that PAKE could be practically realized without random oracles, but at the expense of assuming a Common Reference String (CRS) to be in place. Meanwhile, Goldreich et al. [15] showed that PAKE could be realized in a reasonable security model, solely based on general complexity assumptions, and without any form of trusted setup. Finally, Canetti et al. introduced universally composable PAKE in [14].

Some other work has been devoted to making PAKE more practical for deployment. For instance, in [25] MacKenzie has revisited the PAK protocol [24], showing how to optimize the underlying protocols with EC and SFF implementations. The use of short exponents has also been considered, see [26]. Yet another line of research involved determining the lowest communication costs for standard-model-secure, CRS-based PAKE, see [20,22]. More recently, work by Abdalla et al. [6] has shown that the computation costs (in terms of number of exponentiations) of many of these protocols can be diminished as well.

The work most relevant to ours is that by Hao and Ryan [18] introducing J-PAKE. The protocol has been deployed a few times (e.g. in Firefox sync [2], OpenSSL [3], and the Thread network protocol [4]), mainly because of its simplicity and patent-free nature, but a formal analysis of its security had remained elusive until the work of Abdalla et al. in [5]. Our work is heavily inspired by theirs.

1.3 Organization

The rest of the paper is organized as follows. Section 2 describes our new protocols, and contains a detailed analysis of their efficiency when deployed with EC and SFF. Then, in Sect. 3, we review the PAKE security model from [7], which is used to prove our protocols' security in Sect. 4. Finally, we conclude the paper in Sect. 5.

2 The RO-J-PAKE and CRS-J-PAKE Protocols

In this section we describe the RO-J-PAKE and CRS-J-PAKE protocols, which are presented in Figs. 1 and 2, respectively. In addition, we present the practical considerations when these protocols are deployed.

2.1 Notation

For a given security parameter k, let $\mathbb{G}$ be a finite multiplicative group[1] of prime order q, such that $|q| := k$. Being the strongest assumption necessary, we

---

[1] As previously mentioned, the group of interest is either a SFF or EC group. Throughout this paper, protocols will be presented multiplicatively.

will assume the Decisional Square Diffie Hellman (DSDH, see paragraph 3.2) holds over $\mathbb{G}$. Let H_0 be a full-domain hash mapping $\{0,1\}^*$ to $\mathbb{G}$. H_1 is a hash function from $\{0,1\}^*$ to $\{0,1\}^k$. A function f is used to ensure that both parties sort values identically. This can be done in various ways (e.g. using max or min functions). Let $a \leftarrow A$ denote selecting a uniformly at random from A.

2.2   The RO-J-PAKE Protocol

As described in [18] and analyzed in [5], the original J-PAKE protocol consists of two message rounds. In the first round, each party generates two random group elements and sends them together with corresponding NIZK proofs of the chosen exponents. A client receives X_3 and X_4 values and computes $\alpha :=$ $(X_1X_3X_4)^{x_2pw}$, while a server receives X_1 and X_2 values and computes $\beta :=$ $(X_1X_2X_3)^{x_4pw}$. In the second round, the client and the server exchange these α and β values, again with corresponding NIZK proofs. In order to compute the shared secret, both parties first cancel the $g^{x_2x_4pw}$ factor from the received value, and then exponentiate what is left to either x_2 (client) or x_4 (server). If everything goes according to the protocol's specification, both parties end up with $K := (X_1X_3)^{x_2x_4pw}$.

We observed that the exponents x_1 and x_3 are never explicitly used to compute α, β, or K. Parties only need to use the X_1 and X_3 values to generate what can be considered as a random base $T_K = g^{(x_1+x_3)}$ for a Diffie-Hellman (DH) transform. Our idea is to exploit this fact and change the protocol such that the number of NIZK proofs in protocol can be reduced. However, as in the proof of the original J-PAKE (see [5]), we still need to know the discrete logs of X_1 and X_3 for the reduction to work (i.e. in order to simulate the protocol in a sound way). A solution for this is to employ a random oracle taking as input fresh messages from each party to provide a random base with exponents known only to the simulator. This idea gives rise to the RO-J-PAKE protocol below.

Protocol Description. A mathematical description of RO-J-PAKE is shown in Fig. 1. Next, we rephrase the protocol informally. In the description below, we will assume that the client and server always check if the received message is well-formed and if the validity of NIZK proof holds under appropriate label.

After initialization in which public parameters are fixed and a password different from zero is shared between the client and server, the protocol runs in two phases. In the first phase, each party generates one group element and corresponding NIZK proof and sends them – along with its ID – to the other party. In the second phase, upon receiving the first message, both parties compute a common base D as $H_0(f(A, B, X_1, X_2))$. Then, each party computes and sends to other party its commit message that consists of $\alpha := (DX_2)^{x_1pw}$ and corresponding NIZK proof π_α under label l_A in case of client, and $\beta := (DX_1)^{x_2pw}$ and π_β under label l_B in case of server. Upon receipt of the second message, each party derives a shared secret K, which should be an element of group $\mathbb{G}$, and then a bit-string sk, which will act as a session key.

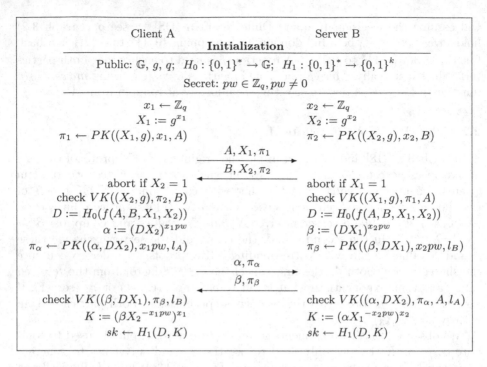

Fig. 1. The RO-J-PAKE protocol. The value of labels are $l_A := (A, B, X_1, X_2)$ and $l_B := (B, A, X_2, X_1)$. PK generates NIZK proofs and VK verifies them.

The purpose of function f is to preserve the symmetry and keep the protocol within two message rounds by making sure that both parties sort values identically and compute the same D. In Sect. 2.4, we discuss the instantiation of the hash function H_0, while H_1 can be seen as a computational randomness extractor (see Sect. 3.2).

It is worth mentioning that RO-J-PAKE's design prevents the weird-but-benign case of *swapping instances* which happens in the original J-PAKE protocol if the values X_1 and X_2 (or X_3 and X_4 in case of server) are flipped. In that case, the NIZK proof π_β (or π_α resp.) from second message round would still be valid (since the base for the β and α values stay as intended), however, the derived keys would not be the same. A simple solution, proposed in [5], is to expand the NIZK proof labels and add to them all the received values. In RO-J-PAKE, the swapping case does not occur even with the labels left out. However, we strongly advise using the labels in NIZK proofs to ensure that the messages from different rounds are bound together. This additionally makes the proof significantly tighter.

2.3   The CRS-J-PAKE Protocol

The observation that J-PAKE's $X_1 X_3$ value can be in a sense replaced by a random group element that neither party has control over can be exploited in another direction as well: We can simply add to the protocol's setup a randomly generated value $U \in \mathbb{G}$ that is fixed once and for all, and plays the role of $X_1 X_3$ in J-PAKE and D in RO-J-PAKE for all protocol executions. Hence, we can also consider the CRS-J-PAKE protocol, described fully below. Just like RO-J-PAKE, we eliminate two of the NIZK proofs by design. The name comes from the value U, which is a Common Reference String (CRS). In particular, it carries with it an underlying secret - i.e. the discrete log u of U to the base g - which must be unknown to all parties. In the security proof however, the simulator does get access to u, similarly to the way it knows the discrete logs of the outputs of hash values in the case of RO-J-PAKE (by programming the RO in this way).

Since we no longer need to hash into the underlying group, in contrast to RO-J-PAKE, CRS-J-PAKE has no efficiency issues with respect to a hash implementation. However, the need to generate and trust the hard-coded value U poses its own deployment issues, as also shown in Sect. 2.4.

Protocol Description. CRS-J-PAKE is shown in Fig. 2. In comparison to RO-J-PAKE, the major difference is the adoption of the common reference string U, which will be securely chosen in the initialization phase and be hard-coded into the protocol implementation. The purpose of function f is the same as in RO-J-PAKE, it keeps the protocol within two message rounds. As in RO-J-PAKE, swapping instance case does not occur by design.

2.4   Practical Considerations

In theory, for J-PAKE and the two new variants, the modular exponentiations are the predominant factors in the computation. Hence, the computational cost is estimated based on counting the number of such modular exponentiations. Note that it takes one exponentiation to generate a Schnorr NIZK proof and two to verify it [28]. Referring to the protocol specifications in Figs. 1, 2, and Fig. 1 from [5], we summarize their complexities in Table 1.

In practice however, counting the modular exponentiations is insufficient, in particular for RO-J-PAKE. This is because the true speed depends highly on how H_0 - which lands into the protocol's underlying group - is computed. Thus, we further discuss the computational complexity with respect to two different instantiations. It is important to recall that for the security proofs to be valid, $\mathbb{G}$ must be such that the DDH assumption is believed to hold, see [11] for examples.

– **SFF instantiation.** Here, we assume that $\mathbb{G}$ is deployed as the q-order subgroup of $GF(p)^*$, where $p = rq + 1$ and p and q are both prime. Thus, we have $|r| = |p| - |q|$. Standard techniques implement H_0 by first hashing into $GF(p)^*$, which is truly cheap, and then *exponentiating the result by* r, which depends on $|r|$. In particular Table 1, indicates that J-PAKE is more efficient

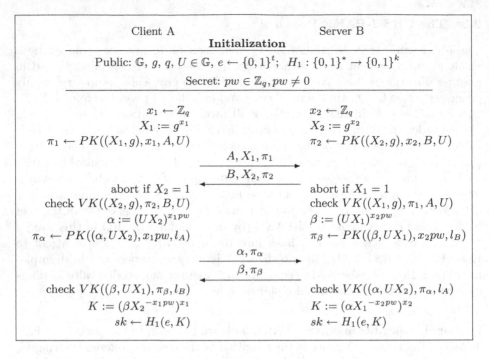

Fig. 2. The CRS-J-PAKE protocol. The labels $l_A := (A, B, X_1, X_2, U)$, $l_B := (B, A, X_2, X_1, U)$ and $l = f(A, B, X_1, X_2)$.

than RO-J-PAKE if and only if $28|q| \leq 20|q| + 2|r|$, i.e. if and only if $4|q| \leq |r|$. In other words, J-PAKE is better than RO-J-PAKE provided that a single $|r|$-bit exponentiation costs more than 4 $|q|$-bit ones. Since Table 2 shows that in general, $|r|$-bit exponentiations cost *way more* than that, J-PAKE is definitely the better option when using SFFs[2]. Note that CRS-J-PAKE would be better than J-PAKE in this setting.

– **EC instantiation.** We carried out an experiment based on a Win7 64-bit operating system, with Intel(R) Core(TM) i7-5600U CPU@2.60 GHz and 8.0 GB RAM. In our test, we assumed the EC is over prime field $GF(p)$ with $|p| = 256$, and took $\mathbb{G}$ to be an EC group of prime order q with $|q| > 160$. H_0 was implemented using the recently discovered hashing algorithms of Brier et al. [13]. We found that an exponentiation takes on average 0.001383 s, while hashing a message into the EC group only takes 0.000086 s. (For reference, the source codes are listed in the full paper.) This shows that hashing is about 16 times cheaper than exponentiating. Hence, using ECs, both RO-J-PAKE and CRS-J-PAKE are definitely more efficient than J-PAKE.

---

[2] Table 2 contains some NIST-recommended parameters, but even in theory the situation seems hopeless. Indeed, from [11] we see that for the DDH to reasonably hold in a SFF, we actually need $10|q| > |p| = |r|$, rendering the $4|q| \leq |r|$ requirement unachievable.

Table 1. The efficiency comparison between J-PAKE, RO-J-PAKE and CRS-J-PAKE.

Protocol	Complexity	
	Communication	Computation
J-PAKE	$12 \times \mathbb{G} + 6 \times \mathbb{Z}_q$	$28|q|$-bit exp
RO-J-PAKE	$8 \times \mathbb{G} + 4 \times \mathbb{Z}_q$	$20|q|$-bit exp $+ 2\, H_0$
CRS-J-PAKE	$8 \times \mathbb{G} + 4 \times \mathbb{Z}_q$	$20|q|$-bit exp

Table 2. Cost of an $|r|$-bit exponentiation compared to a $|q|$-bit one. E.g, for a 2048-bit modulus and 224-bit exponents, one $|r|$-bit exponentiation costs a bit over 8 $|q|$-bit ones. One sees the ratio getting much worse as the NIST-recommended [1] parameters grow.

$|p|$	$|q|$	$|r|$	$|r|/|q|$
1024	160	856	5.35
2048	224	1824	8.14
3072	256	2816	11

Further Deployment Notes for Practitioners. On one hand, in favor of the new protocols, both are most-likely patent-free, like their big brother. Indeed, the structure of all three is essentially the same, having nothing really to do with that of EKE [10] or SPEKE [19]. For instance, none of the "J-PAKE"s perform any password-keyed encryption (like EKE) nor do they hash the password to get a commonly agreed-upon base (like SPEKE). The password is not even encrypted, as is done in many PAKEs that are standard-model-secure, e.g. [20,21].

On the other hand, RO-J-PAKE and CRS-J-PAKE also have specific implementation issues to deal with for their security proofs to be of any use.

- **The random oracle model.** All three protocols' theoretical security relies on the random oracle model which is implicitly present in the security of the Schnorr NIZK proofs. However, RO-J-PAKE uses it arguably more than the other two, because of H_0. This does not point to any particular weakness, but care must always be taken when selecting the hash function in practice. It also introduces a additional degradation factor in the security proof.
- **The CRS.** It is important to understand that CRS-J-PAKE's security relies crucially on the CRS U being generated *randomly* and *such that* $\log_g(U)$ *remains unknown to attackers*. This should be done in a trustworthy way [17]. For instance, a trusted authority can be asked to generate U by selecting u at random, setting $U = g^u$, and throwing u away, or even selecting a purely random string μ, and checking that μ encodes good U, without needing to "handle" u at all. This is an option for large institutions trying to deploy this protocol internally for employees. Another option would be for a predetermined set of users to jointly compute U, with the drawback that any additional user would have to trust the generated value.

3 Model

To prepare for the proofs, we outline the security model from [7] and present the complexity assumptions and cryptographic building blocks.

3.1 Model

Participants, Passwords and Initialization. Each principal U comes from either the *Clients* or *Servers* set, which are finite, disjoint, nonempty sets. We assume that each client $A \in Clients$ is in possession of a password pw_A, while each server $B \in Servers$ holds a vector of the passwords of all clients $pw_B = \langle pw_A \rangle_{A \in Clients}$. Before the execution of a protocol, an initialization phase occurs, in which public parameters are fixed and for each client a secret pw_A is drawn uniformly (and independently) at random from a finite set **Passwords** of size N and given to all servers.

Protocol Execution. The protocol P specifies how principals react to network messages. Since in reality each principal may run multiple executions of P with different partners, each principal is allowed an unlimited number of *instances* executing P. We denote client instances by A^i and server instances by B^j. In this model, a bit b is flipped at the beginning of the game. To assess P's security, we assume that an adversary $\mathcal{A}$ has total network control, i.e. $\mathcal{A}$ provides inputs to instances, via the following *queries*:

- **Send**(U^i, M): $\mathcal{A}$ sends message M to instance U^i. As a response, U^i processes M according to P and outputs a reply. This query models active attacks.
- **Execute**(A^i, B^j): This triggers an honest run of P between A^i and B^j, and its transcript is given to $\mathcal{A}$. It covers passive eavesdropping on protocol flows.
- **Reveal**(U^i): $\mathcal{A}$ receives the current value of the session key sk_U^i. This captures session key leakage.
- **Test**(U^i): If $b = 1$, $\mathcal{A}$ gets sk_U^i. Otherwise, it receives a random string from the session key space. This query measures sk_U^i's semantic security.
- **Corrupt**(U): pw_U is given to $\mathcal{A}$. This models compromise of the long-term key.

Partnering. An instance U^i accepts if it holds a session key sk_U^i, a session ID sid_U^i and a partner ID pid_U^i. An instance U^i terminates if it will not send nor receive any more messages. Instances A^i and B^j are partnered if: (1) both accept; (2) $sid_A^i = sid_B^j \neq \bot$; (3) $pid_A^i = B$ and $pid_B^j = A$; (4) $sk_A^i = sk_B^j$; and (5) no other instance accepts with the same *sid*.

Freshness. Freshness captures the idea that the adversary should not trivially know the session key being tested. An instance U^i is said to be fresh with forward secrecy if: (1) it accepts; (2) no **Reveal** query was made to U^i nor to its partner U^{ij}; and (3) no **Corrupt**(U') query was made before U^i defined its session key sk_U^i, and a **Send**(U^i, M) query was made at some point, for any U'.

Advantage of the Adversary. We say that $\mathcal{A}$ wins and breaks the ake security of P, if upon making **Test** queries to fresh instances U^i that have terminated, $\mathcal{A}$ outputs a bit b', such that $b' = b$, where b is the bit selected at the beginning of the protocol. We denote the probability of this event by $\mathbf{Succ}_\mathrm{P}^{ake}(\mathcal{A})$. The ake-advantage of $\mathcal{A}$ in breaking P is $\mathbf{Adv}_\mathrm{P}^{ake}(\mathcal{A}) = 2\,\mathbf{Succ}_\mathrm{P}^{ake}(\mathcal{A}) - 1$.

3.2   Cryptographic Building Blocks

We state the hardness assumptions upon which the security of our protocols rests, and introduce other useful building blocks.

Let $\mathcal{D}$ be a probabilistic algorithm trying to break a hardness assumption while running in time t and let $\varepsilon \in [0,1]$. We say that the assumption holds over $\mathbb{G}$ if there does not exist a (t, ε)-solver for polynomial t and non-negligible ε. For any x, y and z from $\mathbb{Z}_q$, set $DH_g(g^x, g^y) := g^{xy}$, $SDH_g(g^x) := g^{x^2}$ and $TGDH_g(g^x, g^y, g^z) := g^{xyz}$. Let $\mathcal{C}$ be a challenger.

Decision Diffie-Hellman (DDH). We say that $\mathcal{D}$ is a (t, ε)-DDH solver if $\mathbf{Adv}_{g,\mathbb{G}}^{ddh}(\mathcal{D}) := \mathbf{Succ}_{g,\mathbb{G}}^{ddh}(\mathcal{D}) - \frac{1}{2} \geq \varepsilon$, where $\mathbf{Succ}_{g,\mathbb{G}}^{ddh}(\mathcal{D}) := \Pr[b' = b]$ in the following game.

$\mathcal{C}$ flips a bit b, and chooses uniformly at random values x, y, and z in $\mathbb{Z}_q$. Then, $X := g^x$ and $Y := g^y$ are computed and, Z is set as follows: $Z := g^z$ if b is equal to 0 and $Z := DH_g(X, Y)$ otherwise. Now, $\mathcal{D}$ gets as input (g, X, Y, Z) and tries to distinguish whether Z is the real Diffie-Hellman value $DH_g(X, Y)$ or a random group element of $\mathbb{G}$. At the end of the game, $\mathcal{D}$ outputs a bit b'.

Decision Square Diffie-Hellman (DSDH). We say $\mathcal{D}$ is a (t, ε)-DSDH solver if $\mathbf{Adv}_{g,\mathbb{G}}^{dsdh}(\mathcal{D}) := \mathbf{Succ}_{g,\mathbb{G}}^{dsdh}(\mathcal{D}) - \frac{1}{2} \geq \varepsilon$, where $\mathbf{Succ}_{g,\mathbb{G}}^{dsdh}(\mathcal{D}) := \Pr[b' = b]$ in the following game.

First x and y are chosen uniformly at random from $\mathbb{Z}_q$ and a bit b is flipped by $\mathcal{C}$. Let $X := g^x$. If the bit b that $\mathcal{C}$ holds is equal to 0, then $Y := g^y$. Otherwise, set $Y := SDH_g(X)$. Now, $\mathcal{D}$ gets as input (g, X, Y) and tries to distinguish whether Y is a square Diffie-Hellman value or a random group element of $\mathbb{G}$. At the end of the game, $\mathcal{D}$ outputs a bit b'.

Decision Triple Group Diffie-Hellman (DTGDH). We say $\mathcal{D}$ is a (t, ε)-DTGDH solver if $\mathbf{Adv}_{g,\mathbb{G}}^{dtgdh}(\mathcal{D}) := \mathbf{Succ}_{g,\mathbb{G}}^{dtgdh}(\mathcal{D}) - \frac{1}{2} \geq \varepsilon$, where $\mathbf{Succ}_{g,\mathbb{G}}^{dtgdh}(\mathcal{D}) := \Pr[b' = b]$ in the following game.

$\mathcal{C}$ chooses x, y, z, and w uniformly at random in $\mathbb{Z}_q$ and flips a bit b. $\mathcal{C}$ computes $X := g^x$, $Y := g^y$, and $Z := g^z$. The value W is set to g^w if $b = 0$, or $W := TGDH_g(X, Y, Z)$ otherwise. $\mathcal{D}$ gets $(g, X, Y, Z, DH_g(X, Y), DH_g(X, Z), DH_g(Y, Z), W)$, and tries to tell whether W is a Triple Diffie-Hellman value or a random group element. At the end of the game, $\mathcal{D}$ outputs bit a b'.

Random Oracle. In the random oracle model [9], hash functions are modeled as public, random functions - with co-domain $\{0,1\}^k$ or some particular group - that the adversary has query access to. Answers to new input are selected randomly, while answers to previous inputs are repeated, see Fig. 3.

Common Reference String (CRS). In the CRS model, a public, trusted value – called the CRS – is selected at setup time, and given to all participants and the adversary. To CRS may be associated an underlying trapdoor, which the simulator gets access to during the security proof.

Simulation-Sound Extractable NIZK Proofs (SE-NIZK). We keep the discussion here informal; for more details on SE-NIZK, we refer to [5,16].

Let $\mathcal{R}$ be an efficiently computable relation with a binary output and two inputs (x,w), where x and w are called the statement and the witness, respectively. Let $\mathcal{L}$ be the NP-language that consist of statements with respect to $\mathcal{R}$: $\mathcal{L} = \{x \mid \exists w, \mathcal{R}(x,w) = 1\}$. A NIZK proof system $(Setup, PK, VK)$ for $\mathcal{R}$ is a two-party protocol, where on input w a prover is able to prove to a verifier that some statement x is the member of $\mathcal{L}$ without revealing w. In practice, the prover produces a proof $\pi \leftarrow PK(x, w, l)$ for some label l. Anyone holding x, π, and l can check the proof by running algorithm $VK(x, \pi, l)$, which outputs 1 if the proof is valid, and 0 otherwise.

We say that $(Setup, PK, VK)$ is SE-NIZK if *(unbounded) zero-knowledge* (UZK) and *simulation-sound-extractability* (SE) both hold. Informally, UZK ensures that simulated proofs are indistinguishable from real one, while SE guarantees that there exists an *Ext* algorithm that can extract a witness from any adversary-generated proof, even if the adversary can see simulated proofs. These properties are typically enabled in NIZK proof systems by generating a trapdoor for some additional CRS at setup time. However, this is not the case for Schnorr proofs [28], which are used to instantiate SE-NIZK in J-PAKE. Fortunately, it was shown in [5] that under certain conditions Schnorr proofs satisfy both properties: ZK stems from the programmability of the RO, while for SE the adversary has to be assumed *algebraic*, and all the bases used in protocol must be hard-linear.

Computational Randomness Extractor. In the original J-PAKE paper [18], the hash function used for key derivation is implicitly modeled as a random oracle. However, it was shown in [5] that a computational randomness extractor for random group elements [23] is sufficient. Such a randomness extractor is a function $ext_R : \{0,1\}^t \times \mathbb{G} \to \{0,1\}^k$, for some $t \geq 0$. The extractor is said to be secure if a polynomial-time adversary $\mathcal{A}$'s advantage in distinguishing $ext_R(r,e)$ from a random bitstring in $\{0,1\}^k$ given r, and where (r,e) is randomly sampled from $\{0,1\}^t \times \mathbb{G}$, is negligible. For more details, see [5].

4   Security Analysis

In this section we present the security proofs for RO-J-PAKE and CRS-J-PAKE. Due to their similarity with the J-PAKE protocol, we are able to structure the proofs in the vein of [5] with the goal to simplify proofreading. The proofs that are demonstrated here are slightly simpler than the original J-PAKE proof. This is true even in case the labels l_A and l_B only contain the identity of the originator of the NIZK proofs π_α and π_β, as in the original J-PAKE.

Throughout our analysis, we will assume that the NIZK proofs used in are SE-NIZK. This is crucial, since it will allow the simulator to tell apart correct and incorrect password guesses and simulate all queries made by the adversary. As in J-PAKE, we keep Schnorr proofs of knowledge as the instantiation of SE-NIZK in our protocols. In [5], they are shown to be SE-NIZK in the algebraic adversary model with random oracles under one additional condition: the hard-linearity property of bases used in proof must be exhibited. Since the security of our protocols rests on the the same hardness assumptions as those in [5], the hard-linearity property of bases is preserved. Additionally, for the proofs to go through, it is as well crucial that the discrete logs of D in RO-J-PAKE (from the RO) and of U in CRS-J-PAKE (the CRS) are known to the simulator.

4.1   Proof of Security for RO-J-PAKE

To exhibit the security of RO-J-PAKE, we will bound the adversarial advantage in attacking the ake security of the studied protocols by using sequence-of-games approach. Starting from the original attack game $\mathbf{G}_0$ – which is played between a challenger $\mathcal{C}$ and an adversary $\mathcal{A}$ – we will make a small change to a corresponding protocol $\mathbf{P}_0$ and thus define the next game. Our goal is to prove that $\mathcal{A}$'s advantage is proportional to that of the "dummy" online guesser by showing that $\mathcal{A}$ has negligible advantage to distinguish between two successive games with the exception of game $\mathbf{G}_4$, where guessing-the-right-password event occurs with non-negligible probability.

Going further, the challenger $\mathcal{C}$ takes the role of a simulator that executes the protocol for $\mathcal{A}$. The protocol execution begins by an initialization phase. Then, the simulator gives to $\mathcal{A}$ all public values generated in the initialization phase. Upon receiving an oracle query from $\mathcal{A}$, $\mathcal{C}$ will respond by executing the appropriate algorithm as in Fig. 3. All state information generated during the execution of protocol will be recorded by the simulator.

Theorem 1. *Consider **RO-J-PAKE** as specified in Fig. 1, with a password set of size N. Let $\mathcal{A}$ be an adversary that runs in time at most t, and makes at most n_{se}, n_{ex}, n_{re}, n_{te}, n_{h0} queries of type **Send**, **Execute**, **Reveal**, **Test** and RO queries to H_0. It holds that*

$$Adv_{\text{ro}-\text{j}-\text{pake}}^{ake}(\mathcal{A}) \leq \frac{n_{se}}{N} + O\Bigg(\frac{(n_{se} + n_{ex} + n_{ho})^2}{q} + \frac{n_{h0}^2}{q} + Adv_{g,\mathbb{G}}^{dsdh}(t')$$
$$+ (n_{ex} + n_{se}^2)Adv_{g,\mathbb{G}}^{dtgdh}(t') + 2n_{h0}n_{se}Adv_{g,\mathbb{G}}^{ddh}(t')$$
$$+ (n_{re} + n_{te})Adv_{ext_R}^{comp}(t') + Adv_{NIZK}^{uzk}(t') + Adv_{NIZK}^{ext}(t')\Bigg),$$

and where $t' = O(t + (n_{se} + n_{ex} + n_{ho})t_{exp})$ with t_{exp} being the time required for an exponentiation in $\mathbb{G}$.

Proof. From now on, the values that are received by an honest party and possibly coming from $\mathcal{A}$ will be denoted as X_1', α', etc. We say that instance is *matching* if $X_1 = X_1'$ and $X_2 = X_2'$. In that case, the client's hash output D_A will be equal to the server's D_B. Also, we say that instances are *fully matching*, if both message rounds are honestly forwarded by $\mathcal{A}$.

Game G_0 (Original protocol): This game is faithful to Fig. 1.

Game G_1 (Simulation and extraction): As defined in Sect. 3, we simulate **Send, Execute, Reveal, Corrupt,** and **Test** queries that $\mathcal{A}$ may make, with the difference now that for **Send** queries, the simulator runs an extractor Ext, which takes as input a NIZK proof that is produced by $\mathcal{A}$, and outputs a corresponding witness. If the extraction fails, so does $\mathcal{A}$. Also, all hash queries to H_0 are answered by maintaining a list $\mathcal{L}_{h0}$ (see Fig. 3).

From now on, we assume that an instance receiving a non-valid NIZK proof aborts. More importantly, the simulator – by running the extractor Ext – can obtain discrete logs x_1', x_2', $x_1'pw'$, and $x_2'pw'$ (and thus pw') from corresponding NIZK proofs that are generated by $\mathcal{A}$. Note that we assume that the simulator knows the discrete logarithms of the outputs of H_0 queries.

$$\mathbf{Adv}_{\text{ro}-\text{j}-\text{pake}}^{ake}(\mathcal{A}) = \mathbf{Adv}_{P_1}^{ake}(\mathcal{A}) + O\left(\mathbf{Adv}_{NIZK}^{uzk}(t') + \mathbf{Adv}_{NIZK}^{ext}(t')\right) . \quad (1)$$

H_0: For each hash query $H_0(w)$, if the same query was previously asked, the simulator retrieves the record (w, D, d) from the list $\mathcal{L}_{h0}$ and answers with D. Otherwise, the answer D is chosen according to the following rule:

⋆ **Rule $H_0^{(1)}$**
    Choose $d \leftarrow \mathbb{Z}_q$. Compute $D := g^d$ and write the record (w, D, d) to $\mathcal{L}_{h0}$.

Fig. 3. Simulation of the hash function H_0

Game G_2 (Force uniqueness and avoid collisions): In this game, collisions on the partial transcript $((A, X_1, \pi_1), (B, X_2, \pi_2))$ and the H_0 random oracle are avoided.

More precisely, if a value X_1 or X_2 is repeated in the protocol execution or has already appeared in the random oracle query made by $\mathcal{A}$, the protocol halts and $\mathcal{A}$ fails. The same happens if the outputs of distinct H_0 random oracle queries coincide. Both events are bounded with the birthday paradox:

$$\mathbf{Adv}_{P_1}^{ake}(\mathcal{A}) = \mathbf{Adv}_{P_2}^{ake}(\mathcal{A}) + O\left(\frac{(n_{se} + n_{ex} + n_{h0})^2}{q}\right) + O\left(\frac{n_{h0}^2}{q}\right) . \quad (2)$$

Game $\mathbf{G}_3$ (Allow instance linking): Same as $\mathbf{G}_2$.

As we can see in Fig. 1, the values A, B, X_1 and X_2 are all included in the labels l_A and l_B. This renders the game $\mathbf{G}_3$ from the J-PAKE proof unnecessary.

$$\mathbf{Adv}_{P_2}^{ake}(\mathcal{A}) = \mathbf{Adv}_{P_3}^{ake}(\mathcal{A}) . \quad (3)$$

Game $\mathbf{G}_4$ (Check password guesses): If before a **Corrupt** query, $\mathcal{A}$ makes a **Send** query to a non-matching instance containing α' or β' that corresponds to a correct password guess, the protocol halts and $\mathcal{A}$ succeeds.

The crucial observation here is that the simulator can check whether the password guess is correct or not. This is so, since the simulator can obtain discrete logs of X_1', X_2', α' and β' by running Ext on the corresponding NIZK proofs. The extraction does not work for the value coming from a reduction, which we will call a *simulated value*, otherwise the simulator could break the hardness assumption trivially. To determine if the password guess is correct, the simulator can proceed as follows: (1) if both X_1' and α' (or X_2' and β' in the case of server impersonation) come from $\mathcal{A}$, the simulator extracts two discrete logs from the corresponding NIZK proofs (e.g. x_1' from π_1 and $x_1' pw'$ from π_α), divides them and checks whether the result is equal to pw_A; or (2) if one of the values that instance receives is a simulated value (X_1' or α' and X_2' or β'), the simulator extracts one discrete log of the value coming from $\mathcal{A}$ and combines it with the correct password pw_A to perform a check against the simulated value.

$$\mathbf{Adv}_{P_3}^{ake}(\mathcal{A}) \leq \mathbf{Adv}_{P_4}^{ake}(\mathcal{A}) . \quad (4)$$

Game $\mathbf{G}_5$ (Randomize session keys for wrong password guesses): In case of an false password guess to a non-matching instance, K is set randomly.

The proof is split into two parts. In the first, we set K randomly only in the non-matching client instances in case of a wrong guess – we will call those *target* client instances. We construct an algorithm $\mathcal{D}$ that given a tuple $\langle X, Y \rangle$, where $X \leftarrow g^x$ and $Y \in \mathbb{G}$, attempts to break the DSDH assumption by running $\mathcal{A}$ as a subroutine. The algorithm $\mathcal{D}$ simulates the protocol for $\mathcal{A}$ by setting K randomly for all target client instances, and computing K normally for all other client instances as follows.[3]

---

[3] Due to the labels l_A and l_B, the random self-reducibility of the DSDH assumption can be used. This affects the tightness of the proof: we do not need to use a hybrid argument, so the factor n_{se} in front of $\mathbf{Adv}_{g,\mathbb{G}}^{dsdh}(\mathcal{D})$ in the Theorem 1 does not appear.

For a given DSDH instance $\langle X, Y \rangle$, any client instance A^i chooses $a, b \leftarrow \mathbb{Z}_q^*$ and sets $X_1 = X^a g^b$. When A^i receives a $\mathbf{Send}(A^i, (B, X_2', \pi_2'))$ query, the simulator extracts x_2' from π_2', computes D_A and sets $\alpha = X^{a(d'+x_2')pw_A} g^{b(d'+x_2')pw_A}$. After receiving $\mathbf{Send}(A^i, (\beta', \pi_\beta'))$ and extracting a witness from π_β', the client instance A^i computes $K = X^{ad'x_2'pw'} g^{bd'x_2'pw'} Y^{a^2 x_2'(pw'-pw_A)} X^{2abx_2'(pw'-pw_A)} g^{b^2 x_2'(pw'-pw_A)}$. Note that the value pw' is obtained by dividing extracted witnesses from the NIZK proofs $pw' = Ext(\pi_\beta')/Ext(\pi_2')$, while d' comes from the list $\mathcal{L}_{h0}$ (see Fig. 3). In case of matching instances or a correct password guess $K = X^{d_A pw_A x_2'} g^{bd'x_2'pw'}$, since pw' is equal to pw_A. If Y is a real DSDH challenge, then the value K will be computed as in $\mathbf{G}_4$. On the other hand, if Y is random and an incorrect password guess is made, then K will be random, since $x_2' \neq 0$ (checked in the protocol, see Fig. 1) and $a(pw'-pw_A) \neq 0$.

Now we show that the simulation is sound for any instance of B that generates X_2 and receives possibly simulated X_1' or α'. If any of the two received values is not from A^i, the simulator can extract a witness from the NIZK proof and check whether the password is correct or not. Moreover, if both received values are from A^i, the instances are matching, otherwise π_α would not be valid. Thus, there is no need to check the password in this case. Since the reduction for the second part of proof in case of relevant server instances is analogous, we get the following bound:

$$\mathbf{Adv}_{P_4}^{ake}(\mathcal{A}) = \mathbf{Adv}_{P_5}^{ake}(\mathcal{A}) + \mathbf{Adv}_{g,\mathbb{G}}^{dsdh}(t') \ . \tag{5}$$

Game $\mathbf{G}_6$ (Randomize session keys for paired instances): In case of a matching instance, set K randomly (and matching instances get the same K).

We use DTGDH (see Sect. 3.2) in a hybrid argument. We build an algorithm $\mathcal{D}$ that randomly chooses indexes $i, j \leftarrow \{1, 2, \ldots, n_{se}\}$ and simulates the protocol by computing K randomly for all (lexicographically) previous instances $(A^{i'}, B^{j'})$ that are fully matching, and setting K normally for all later $(A^{i'}, B^{j'})$.

For (A^i, B^j), A^i sets $X_1 = X$, B^j sets $X_2 = Y$, and the value Z is the output of $H_0(A^i, B^j, X, Y)$. If A^i and B^j match, A^i sets $\alpha = (DH_g(X, Z)DH_g(X, Y))^{pw_A}$ and B^j sets $\beta = (DH_g(Y, Z)DH_g(X, Y))^{pw_A}$. If they fully match, the shared secret is computed as $K = W^{pw_A}$. If $W = g^{xyz}$ then this simulates computing K normally. If W is random, then K is random since $pw_A \neq 0$.

We now need to check if the simulation is sound for other possible queries to A^i and B^j. If A^i (resp. B^j) receives non-simulated values X_2' and β' (resp. X_1' and α'), it can extract witnesses from the NIZK proofs, check the password guess, and respond accordingly. If A^i (resp. B^j) receives an X_2' (resp. X_1') value from $\mathcal{A}$ and a simulated β (resp. α), π_β (resp. π_α) would not be valid due to the labels l_B (resp. l_A). Conversely, if after the first message flow the instances are matching ($X_1 = X_1'$ and $X_2 = X_2'$), but α' or β' are from $\mathcal{A}$, the password guess will be wrong. In case a password guess is correct and the simulation continues, a $\mathbf{Corrupt}$ query has been made due to $\mathbf{G}_4$. Since the simulator can extract x_1' or x_2' in case of impersonation, K can be computed as $\mathcal{A}$ expects it to be.

Therefore,

$$\mathbf{Adv}^{ake}_{\Gamma_5}(\mathcal{A}) - \mathbf{Adv}^{ake}_{P_6}(\mathcal{A}) + (n_{ex} + n_{se}^2)\mathbf{Adv}^{dlydlh}_{g,\mathbb{G}}(t') \ . \tag{6}$$

Game G_7 (Randomize α and β): If there was no **Corrupt** query, set α and β randomly in all instances. In the case of a correct password guess to a non-matching instance (after **Corrupt** query), compute K as the other party would.

Again the proof is split into two parts. Firstly, using a reduction from DDH, the α values are set randomly. We construct an algorithm $\mathcal{D}$ that randomly chooses $i \leftarrow \{1, 2, \ldots, n_{se}\}$ and $j \leftarrow \{1, 2, \ldots, n_{ho}\}$, and simulates the protocol for $\mathcal{A}$ by setting an exponent $x_1 pw_A$ in α to be random for all client instances prior to A^i and computing α normally for all client instances after A^i as follows.[4]

A^i sets $X_1 = X$, and the challenge Y is embedded as the output of the jth $H_0(A, B, X_1, X_2')$ query. After receiving **Send**$(A^i, (B, X_2', \pi_2'))$, the simulator extracts x_2' to compute $\alpha = Z^{pw_A} X^{x_2' pw_A}$. Clearly, if Z is random, so is α, and if $Z = DH_g(X, Y)$, α is computed as in G_6. If $\mathcal{A}$ succeeds (by guessing b or the correct password), $\mathcal{D}$'s guess to the DDH challenger is $b_1' = 1$, and 0 otherwise.

Note that upon receiving β which corresponds to a correct password guess (either from $\mathcal{A}$ or from B), the simulator can make other instances of A compute the key as $\mathcal{A}$ or B would, even if α is random. This is possible since it can extract x_2', $x_2' pw'$ from the proofs, check the password guess, and run A accordingly.

We now show the simulation is sound for any instance of B that generates X_2 and receives a possibly simulated X_1' or α' from A^i: (1) if both values are from A^i, set K randomly (due to G_6); (2) if either value is not from A^i, the simulator can extract witnesses from the proof, checks if the password is correct (and satisfies G_4) or not (and sets K randomly due to G_5); (3) if some α' corresponding to a correct password guess submitted to an instance of B is not from A^i and the execution continues (a **Corrupt** query has been made), the discrete log of X_1 is known and the simulator can compute the shared secret K_B as $\mathcal{A}$ would.

Since the reduction for the second part of proof in case of relevant server instances is analogous, we get the following bound:

$$\mathbf{Adv}^{ake}_{P_6}(\mathcal{A}) = \mathbf{Adv}^{ake}_{P_7}(\mathcal{A}) + 2n_{ho}n_{se}\mathbf{Adv}^{ddh}_{g,\mathbb{G}}(t') \ . \tag{7}$$

Game G_8 (Randomize sk): Set sk randomly in all instances in which K is set randomly (the matching instances get the same sk).

Remember that sk is computed as $H_1(D, K)$ and that D is the output of a random oracle. The games are computationally indistinguishable, since K is random and H_1 is a computational randomness extractor.

$$\mathbf{Adv}^{ake}_{P_7}(\mathcal{A}) = \mathbf{Adv}^{ake}_{P_8}(\mathcal{A}) + (n_{re} + n_{te})\mathbf{Adv}^{comp}_{extR}(t') \ . \tag{8}$$

This concludes the proof. □

---

[4] In addition to factor n_{se}, which appears in the proof of original J-PAKE [5], there is a security degradation of factor n_{ho}, since in this reduction the simulator also needs to guess the "right" random oracle query.

4.2   Proof of Security for CRS-J-PAKE

Due to its very high similarity with the proof from Sect. 4.1, we will only state the theorem bound. The main idea behind the proof is that instead of knowing the discrete logs of H_0's output, the simulator knows the discrete log of parameter U. For more proof details, we refer the reader to the full paper.

Theorem 2. *Consider **CRS-J-PAKE** (see Fig. 2) with a password set of size N and fixed public value U. Let $\mathcal{A}$ be an adversary that runs in time at most t, and makes at most n_{se}, n_{ex}, n_{re}, n_{te}, n_{h0} queries of type **Send**, **Execute**, **Reveal**, and **Test**. It holds that*

$$Adv^{ake}_{crs-j-pake}(\mathcal{A}) \leq \frac{n_{se}}{N} + O\left(\frac{(n_{se}+n_{ex})^2}{q} + (n_{ex}+n_{se}^2)Adv^{dtgdh}_{g,\mathbb{G}}(t')\right.$$
$$+ Adv^{dsdh}_{g,\mathbb{G}}(t') + 2n_{se}Adv^{ddh}_{g,\mathbb{G}}(t') + (n_{re}+n_{te})Adv^{comp}_{ext_R}(t')$$
$$\left. + Adv^{uzk}_{NIZK}(t') + Adv^{ext}_{NIZK}(t')\right),$$

and where $t' = O(t + (n_{se} + n_{ex} + n_{ho})t_{exp})$ with t_{exp} being the time required for an exponentiation in $\mathbb{G}$.

5   Conclusion

In this paper, we proposed two new variants of J-PAKE, showed that the security proof from [5] can be adapted to cover our proposals, and compared the overall efficiency of all three protocols when instantiated with ECs or SFFs. Since RO-J-PAKE using SFFs is the least efficient because of the implementation of the hash function H_0, it would be interesting to see if it can be proven secure using a large SFF (and therefore, a "small r"), all while using a short-exponent-type complexity assumption (e.g. as in [26]).

Acknowledgments. We thank the anonymous reviewers for their helpful comments. The first and third authors are supported by the National Research Fund, Luxembourg (projects CORE-AToMS and INTER-Sequoia for the first, and project CORE-BRAIDS (junior track) for the second). The third author is also supported by the University of Luxembourg in an internal project REQUISITE. We want to thank Husen Wang for his help with respect to the EC instantiation in Sect. 2.4.

References

1. BlueKrypt (2015). http://www.keylength.com/en/4/
2. Firefox Sync (2015). https://www.mozilla.org/en-US/firefox/sync/
3. OpenSSL (2015). https://www.openssl.org/
4. Thread Protocol (2015). http://threadgroup.org/
5. Abdalla, M., Benhamouda, F., MacKenzie, P.: Security of the J-PAKE password-authenticated key exchange protocol. In: 2015 IEEE Symposium on Security and Privacy, SP 2015, pp. 571–587. IEEE Computer Society (2015)

6. Abdalla, M., Benhamouda, F., Pointcheval, D.: Public-Key encryption indistinguishable under plaintext-checkable attacks. In: Katz, J. (ed.) PKC 2015. LNCS, vol. 9020, pp. 332–352. Springer, Heidelberg (2015)
7. Abdalla, M., Fouque, P.-A., Pointcheval, D.: Password-Based authenticated key exchange in the three-party setting. In: Vaudenay, S. (ed.) PKC 2005. LNCS, vol. 3386, pp. 65–84. Springer, Heidelberg (2005)
8. Bellare, M., Pointcheval, D., Rogaway, P.: Authenticated key exchange secure against dictionary attacks. In: Preneel, B. (ed.) EUROCRYPT 2000. LNCS, vol. 1807, pp. 139–155. Springer, Heidelberg (2000)
9. Bellare, M., Rogaway, P.: Random oracles are practical: a paradigm for designing efficient protocols. In: ACM Conference on Computer and Communications Security, pp. 62–73. ACM Press (1993)
10. Bellovin, S.M., Merritt, M.: Encrypted key exchange: password-based protocols secure against dictionary attacks. In: 1992 IEEE Symposium on Research in Security and Privacy, SP 1992, pp. 72–84 (1992)
11. Boneh, D.: The decision diffie-hellman problem. In: Buhler, J.P. (ed.) ANTS 1998. LNCS, vol. 1423, pp. 48–63. Springer, Heidelberg (1998)
12. Boyko, V., MacKenzie, P.D., Patel, S.: Provably secure password-authenticated key exchange using diffie-hellman. In: Preneel, B. (ed.) EUROCRYPT 2000. LNCS, vol. 1807, pp. 156–171. Springer, Heidelberg (2000)
13. Brier, E., Coron, J.-S., Icart, T., Madore, D., Randriam, H., Tibouchi, M.: Efficient indifferentiable hashing into ordinary elliptic curves. In: Rabin, T. (ed.) CRYPTO 2010. LNCS, vol. 6223, pp. 237–254. Springer, Heidelberg (2010)
14. Canetti, R., Halevi, S., Katz, J., Lindell, Y., MacKenzie, P.: Universally composable password-based key exchange. In: Cramer, R. (ed.) EUROCRYPT 2005. LNCS, vol. 3494, pp. 404–421. Springer, Heidelberg (2005)
15. Goldreich, O., Lindell, Y.: Session-Key generation using human passwords only. In: Kilian, J. (ed.) CRYPTO 2001. LNCS, vol. 2139, pp. 408–432. Springer, Heidelberg (2001)
16. Groth, J.: Simulation-Sound NIZK proofs for a practical language and constant size group signatures. In: Lai, X., Chen, K. (eds.) ASIACRYPT 2006. LNCS, vol. 4284, pp. 444–459. Springer, Heidelberg (2006)
17. Groth, J., Ostrovsky, R.: Cryptography in the multi-string model. In: Menezes, A. (ed.) CRYPTO 2007. LNCS, vol. 4622, pp. 323–341. Springer, Heidelberg (2007)
18. Hao, F., Ryan, P.: J-PAKE: authenticated key exchange without PKI. Trans. Comput. Sci. 11, 192–206 (2010)
19. Jablon, D.P.: Strong password-only authenticated key exchange. ACM SIGCOMM Comput. Commun. Rev. 26(5), 5–26 (1996)
20. Jiang, S., Gong, G.: Password based key exchange with mutual authentication. In: Handschuh, H., Hasan, M.A. (eds.) SAC 2004. LNCS, vol. 3357, pp. 267–279. Springer, Heidelberg (2004)
21. Katz, J., Ostrovsky, R., Yung, M.: Efficient password-authenticated key exchange using human-memorable passwords. In: Pfitzmann, B. (ed.) EUROCRYPT 2001. LNCS, vol. 2045, pp. 475–494. Springer, Heidelberg (2001)
22. Katz, J., Vaikuntanathan, V.: Round-Optimal password-based authenticated key exchange. In: Ishai, Y. (ed.) TCC 2011. LNCS, vol. 6597, pp. 293–310. Springer, Heidelberg (2011)
23. Krawczyk, H.: Cryptographic extraction and key derivation: the HKDF scheme. In: Rabin, T. (ed.) CRYPTO 2010. LNCS, vol. 6223, pp. 631–648. Springer, Heidelberg (2010)

24. MacKenzie, P.: The PAK Suite: Protocols for Password-Authenticated Key Exchange. DIMACS Technical report 2002-46 (2002)
25. MacKenzie, P.D.: More efficient password-authenticated key exchange. In: Naccache, D. (ed.) CT-RSA 2001. LNCS, vol. 2020, pp. 361–377. Springer, Heidelberg (2001)
26. MacKenzie, P.D., Patel, S.: Hard bits of the discrete log with applications to password authentication. In: Menezes, A. (ed.) CT-RSA 2005. LNCS, vol. 3376, pp. 209–226. Springer, Heidelberg (2005)
27. Pointcheval, D.: Password-Based authenticated key exchange. In: Fischlin, M., Buchmann, J., Manulis, M. (eds.) PKC 2012. LNCS, vol. 7293, pp. 390–397. Springer, Heidelberg (2012)
28. Schnorr, C.-P.: Efficient identification and signatures for smart cards. In: Brassard, G. (ed.) CRYPTO 1989. LNCS, vol. 435, pp. 239–252. Springer, Heidelberg (1990)

Hash-Based TPM Signatures
for the Quantum World

Megumi Ando[1]([✉]), Joshua D. Guttman[1], Alberto R. Papaleo[1], and John Scire[2]

[1] The MITRE Corporation, Bedford, MA, USA
{mando,guttman,apapaleo}@mitre.org
[2] Stevens Institute of Technology, Hoboken, NJ, USA
jscire@stevens.edu

Abstract. Trusted Platform Modules (TPMs) provide trust and attestation services to the platforms they reside on, using public key encryption and digital signatures among other cryptography operations. However, the current standards mandate primitives that will be insecure in the presence of quantum computers. In this paper, we study how to eliminate these insecure primitives. We replace RSA-based digital signatures with a hash-based scheme. We show that this scheme can be implemented using reasonable amounts of space on the TPM. We also show how to protect the TPM from rollback attacks against these state-sensitive signature operations.

Keywords: Post-quantum · Trusted Platform Module (TPM) · Attestation Identity Key (AIK) · Merkle trees

1 Introduction

A Trusted Platform Module (TPM) is a low-cost cryptographic microprocessor for enabling trusted computing functionalities. TPMs follow a set of global industry standards laid out by the Trusted Computing Group (TCG) also called the TCG standards (versions 1.2 and 2.0). As of this writing, there are a number of vendors which supply hardware TPMs: AMD, Atmel, Broadcom, IBM, Infineon, Intel, Lenovo, National Semi, Nationz, Qualcomm, STMicroelectronics, Samsung, Sinosun, Texas Instruments, Nuvoton Technology, and Fuzhou Rockchip [24]; and most personal computers and a few mobile devices (with the notable exception of Apple computers) are shipped with a TPM [21]. It is assumed that a TPM is implicitly trustworthy and tamper-resistant. This trust is bootstrapped to enable two trusted computing capabilities, secure encrypted storage and remote attestation, explained below.

1.1 Secure Encrypted Storage

Costing a couple of dollars each, a TPM is an inexpensive solution for securing sensitive data even under the threat that the hosting platform may become

© Springer International Publishing Switzerland 2016
M. Manulis et al. (Eds.): ACNS 2016, LNCS 9696, pp. 77–94, 2016.
DOI: 10.1007/978-3-319-39555-5_5

corrupted [21]. This is achieved by storing sensitive information outside the TPM only in encrypted form, with the corresponding encrypting TPM key either in the TPM's hardware-protected area or also encrypted by another TPM key. In this way, a TPM serves as a tamper-resistant hardware Root-of-Trust for Storage (RTS) [2,14,21].[1]

Because the TPM has a limited amount of non-volatile RAM (NVRAM), only a few special TPM keys are kept in protected space within the TPM. Other keys are stored in encrypted form in unprotected areas on the platform. They exist in unencrypted form only transiently as needed and only within the TPM. The storage keys thus form a key hierarchy (a tree), where each non-root key is encrypted under its parent key.

In TPM version 2.0, the encryption of child nodes can be done either symmetrically or asymmetrically [2,21]. Thus, we can trivially avoid a quantum-insecure storage mechanism by using only symmetric storage keys. A single caveat to the solution is duplication, or a mechanism for transferring or backing up TPM keys. Currently, duplication is handled by decrypting a specific key (or even an entire subtree) and then re-encrypting it with the public portion of another TPM's RSA key [2,14,21]. Symmetric encryption cannot replace RSA encryption without preplacing shared TPM keys across platforms.

1.2 Attestation

A platform state measurement indicates whether a platform is in an expected state and therefore still trustworthy. Through a separate mechanism, the hash of this measurement can be written into special TPM registers called Platform Configuration Registers (PCRs). This is done using a trusted hardware component: a Root-of-Trust for Measurement (RTM; e.g., Intel TXT for boot measurements) [20].

A TPM can be used for securely reporting the measurement stored in the PCRs [2,10,14,17,20,21]; and so it serves also as a hardware Root-of-Trust for Reporting (RTR). This is done using two types of TPM keys: an Attestation Identity Key (AIK) and an Endorsement Key (EK). An AIK is an asymmetric signature key corresponding to a user and or application on the platform and is used for enabling anonymity. There may be many AIKs per platform. To be useful, an AIK must satisfy the property that it is infeasible for an adversary to forge a valid signature (under the key) using any information stored on the platform outside of the TPM. An EK is an asymmetric encryption key with the unforgeability property that it is infeasible for an adversary to create a valid encryption under the key. It is unique to the platform, created randomly, and properly certified by the manufacturer. The EK is kept inside the TPM, never leaves the TPM, and is used for certifying AIKs as genuine.

The AIK is used to sign a quote, which includes the measurements stored in the PCRs as well as a verifier-provided nonce for freshness. For the signed

---

[1] Note that while a TPM can guarantee confidentiality and detect modification of securely stored data, it cannot retrieve secured data in the event that data is damaged; some other mechanism should be implemented to mitigate data loss.

quote to be meaningful, the AIK itself is certified in order to prove that the AIK belongs to a genuine TPM. The signed quote, along with the AIK's certificate, is sent to a verifying party.

Each TPM is shipped with a vendor-certified EK (version 1.2) or Primary Seed (version 2.0) [2,14,21]. All AIKs are securely derived from this key or seed as needed and certified by a trusted Privacy-CA (PCA). The Direct Anonymous Attestation (DAA) protocol also ensures anonymity [6]. This alternative does not require a trusted third party but incurs a large cost in cryptographic complexity instead.

1.3 Our Contributions

Current TPM solutions were designed to be secure against classical adversaries, as opposed to quantum adversaries. This is problematic since some of the trust arguments rely on the intractability of computational problems with known efficient quantum algorithms. For example, TPM keys were originally (in version 1.2) all RSA keys, which are insecure given Shor's quantum integer factorization scheme [22], and both PCA and DAA protocols use RSA encryption.

This paper presents our initial investigation into architecting a quantum-secure TPM. We have identified the following set of current TPM mechanisms to be those which rely on RSA and, thus, known to be vulnerable to quantum-attacks:

1. Secure (encrypted) storage
2. Duplication
3. TPM signing keys
4. PCA protocol
5. DAA protocol
6. Encrypted transport session

(By encrypted transport session, we mean transporting information, e.g., a TPM command, securely to a TPM.)

Although RSA is insecure in a post-quantum era, there are some notable alternatives without any known attacks. One such alternative is hash-based digital signature schemes, such as Merkle's tree authentication using a one-time signature (OTS) scheme. We claim that Merkle tree signatures are a practical alternative to RSA authentication, solving issues 3 and 4 above. (**Disclaimer:** The signing-based PCA protocol described in this paper is weaker than the original; we lose repudiability of a claim that two AIKs are linked.)

In this paper:

- We present our hash-based TPM signing key construction: QUAntum Secure Hash (QUASH). Given the space limitation of the TPM, our solution offloads most of the storage to the untrusted platform in a way that preserves security.
- We also show that our solution prevents replay attacks; it prevents a particular OTS key from being used to sign multiple messages.
- Lastly, we provide recommendations for system parameters.

1.4 Related Work

Efficient quantum algorithms [11,22] break RSA, Digital Signature Algorithm (DSA), and Elliptic Curve Digital Signature Algorithm (ECDSA) in a quantum-world setting [4]. Fortunately, a number of cryptographic techniques are believed to be quantum-secure despite these known algorithms, including: hash-based, code-based, lattice-based, and multivariate-quadratic-equations cryptography [1,4]. In this paper, we propose a hash-based TPM signing solution, whose security relies solely on the existence of collision-resistant hash functions and pseudorandom number generators and assess its practicality as a system. Our approach for storing data outside the TPM is similar to the technique presented in [19] for creating virtual monotonic counters for TPMs.

Lattice-based cryptography provides a strong alternative candidate for enabling quantum-secure TPM signatures. A recent paper [1] presents an efficient signature scheme Tightly-secure Efficient Signatures from standard LAttices (TESLA) that relies on the intractability of standard lattices as opposed to ideal lattices. The paper presents *fixed* parameters for quantum-security. Our approach uses an efficient, stateful hash-based signature scheme (e.g., [7,8,23]) as a primitive. It has the benefit that its security is based solely on the existence of collision-resistant hash functions and pseudorandom number generators, whereas the lattice-based approach relies on the intractability of lattice problems. However, our hash-based approach has a key management problem that the lattice-based approach avoids. A more in-depth comparison between our approach and one that uses this lattice-based signature scheme is outside the scope of this paper.

Road Map: Sect. 2 contains our problem statement (the definitions and system model we adopt for our construction) and the technical background necessary for understanding our post-quantum attestation solution. In Sects. 3 and 4, we provide our main results: our hash-based TPM signing key construction, QUASH, and a practicality assessment of this solution. In Sect. 5, we conclude with a summary of our work.

2 Problem Statement and Preliminaries

Our goal is to architect hash-based TPM signing keys, defined below.

Unlike the RSA signature scheme, the most efficient hash-based signature schemes maintain some key state information to work.[2] At a minimum, the leaf number is needed in order to avoid reusing an OTS key pair; and some auxiliary information is required for efficient signing. We also introduce the notion of an Endorsement *Signing* Key (ESK), which is a vendor-certified TPM *signing* key for certifying AIKs.

Definition 1. *A tamper-evident hash-based AIK is a TPM signing key with the additional property that it is infeasible for an adversary to change an AIK state value without the change being detected.*

---

[2] A recent paper [5] presents a practical stateless hash-based signature scheme.

Definition 2. *The hash-based ESK is an unforgeable TPM signing key derived from a Primary Seed, with the property that it is infeasible for an adversary to change the ESK state value. (A Primary Seed is a large random number which is created by the vendor and protected by the TPM.)*

If the number of AIKs is limited and relatively small, we can simply store all required key state information within the protected NVRAM space of the TPM. Our goal is to extend this solution to the case where an *unbounded* number of AIKs can be created, despite the hard space limit within the NVRAM. We do this by storing the key state information outside of the TPM in balanced binary (e.g., red-black trees or treaps) hash trees and by keeping only digests of the state information within the NVRAM for integrity protection.

Our construction, QUASH, has the following set of desirable properties.

– **Tamper-evidence: prevention of OTS key reuse.** The key state information is integrity-protected by storing hash digests in the TPM NVRAM. Thus, our tamper-evident signing solution prevents an OTS key from being used more than once, a concern if we use hash-based signatures.
– **Availability: localization of data loss.** While a TPM can guarantee confidentiality and data modification detection of securely stored data, it cannot retrieve secured data in the event that encrypted data is lost. Thus, a modification to any of the AIKs' state information renders *multiple* AIKs unusable. Given "registers" for holding multiple integrity check values within the TPM's NVRAM, we minimize the number of AIKs that are lost when the state information of a single AIK is corrupted.
– **Efficiency: TPM space requirements.** We show that our construction can work with a space-limited TPM, despite using a hash-based signature scheme requiring key state storage and producing large signatures.
– **Efficiency: integrity checks.** Looking up and updating key state information on the platform is efficient. Our solution uses a balanced binary tree structure that requires only $\mathcal{O}(\log N)$ steps, where N denotes the number of AIKs. More critically, the integrity checks executed by the TPM are efficient, also requiring only $\mathcal{O}(\log N)$ steps.
– **Efficiency: AIK re-generation.** Hash-based signatures require generating fresh OTS keys post-provisioning since only a finite number of OTS keys can be created at set-up time. We amortize the key re-generation time by creating fresh OTS keys for a subsequent Merkle tree during signing.

2.1 System Model

We assume that the TPM is trusted and tamper-resistant, but the hosting platform is untrusted. The TPM's functionalities are augmented to include hash-based capabilities. Specifically, it can create a Merkle signature scheme key, integrity check a current AIK state, and sign a message using such an integrity-checked current key state. Additionally, its NVRAM is equipped with a small number of special registers, which we call Integrity Registers.

In today's implementation, the TPM's NVRAM is used for storing root keys for certificate chains, the EK (an RSA encryption key), the expected measurement of the machine launch state, and decryption keys used before the disk is made available [9]. The minimum NVRAM size required by the TPM (version 1.2) spec is 1280 bytes [18]. We assume that the TPM RAM size is also fairly limited.

2.2 Merkle Tree Authentication

Merkle tree authentication is specified by two algorithms: a one-time signature (OTS) scheme and a Merkle signature scheme. Merkle signature schemes differ from each other in their traversal algorithms for constructing the "next authentication path" efficiently. We describe the Merkle signature scheme generically, intentionally hiding the details for the traversal algorithm for readability, and also because it is well-understood how the traversal time and storage size vary depending on the algorithm used, see [4].[3]

Moreover, real experimental results reveal that the overall performance of a tree authentication scheme (using a state-of-the-art traversal algorithm) is dominated by the performance of the underlying OTS scheme [16]. While the original Lamport-Diffie scheme (LD-C in this paper) was shown to be optimal in number of hash computations [3], LDWM is the usual go-to OTS scheme, because it decreases both the signature and storage sizes.

Within the context of this paper, $h(\cdot)$ is a cryptographic one-way hash function, and $r(\cdot)$ is a cryptographically secure pseudorandom number generator (PRNG) as defined below.

Definition 3. *A cryptographic hash function $h : \{0,1\}^* \rightarrow \{0,1\}^n$ maps arbitrary length strings to strings of length n, such that the following properties are satisfied:*

- *(Easy to compute) Given any $x \in \{0,1\}^*$, it is easy to compute its hash $y = h(x)$.*
- *(Pre-image resistance) Given any y in the image, it is computationally infeasible to find any x such that $h(x) = y$.*
- *(Second pre-image resistance) Given a $x_1 \in \{0,1\}^*$, it is computationally infeasible to find any $x_2 \neq x_1$ such that $h(x_2) = h(x_1)$.*
- *(Collision resistance) It is computationally infeasible to find any pair $x_1, x_2 \in \{0,1\}^*$ such that $h(x_2) = h(x_1)$.*

Definition 4. *A cryptographically secure pseudorandom number generator*

$$r : \{0,1\}^m \rightarrow \{0,1\}^n$$

is a function that generates an n-bit output from a truly random m-bit seed and satisfies the next-bit test: Given the first polynomial number of output bits, it is computationally infeasible to to predict the next bit of the output with probability non-negligibly larger than $\frac{1}{2}$.

---

[3] Merkle's original construction requires $\mathcal{O}(H^2)$ space and $\mathcal{O}(H)$ time [15], but recent constructions provide more efficient results [7,8,13,23].

Setup. A Merkle signature scheme (MSS) public key is equivalent to the result of the following computation. First we initialize a tree of constant branching factor D and height H and generate D^H OTS key pairs. The OTS key pairs are derived from the hash of the AIK name id, the re-generation number i, the leaf index ℓ, and the private-value index j: The AIK seed for AIK id is

$$s_{\mathrm{AIK}}(id) = h(id);$$

the seed for the i-th Merkle tree for id is

$$s_{\mathrm{MSS}}(id, i) = s_{\mathrm{AIK}}(id)|i = h(id)|i;$$

and the seed for the ℓ-th leaf of the i-th Merkle tree for id is

$$s_{\mathrm{LEAF}}(id, i, \ell) = s_{\mathrm{MSS}}(id, i)|\ell = h(id)|i|\ell.$$

The concatenation of a leaf seed and a private-value index is inputted into the pseudorandom number generator $r(\cdot)$ to create an OTS private key value.[4] We store the hash of the ℓ-th OTS public key in the ℓ-th leaf of the tree, and the value of each non-leaf node is computed as the hash of the concatenation of its children's stored values. The MSS public key corresponds to the root value of this tree.

The approach above–computing values for all D^H leaves and subsequently hashing up the Merkle tree–is unnecessarily space consuming in practice. The convention is to keep a much smaller number of hashes in a stack, see [4].

Signing. Given a leaf in the Merkle tree, its authentication path is the sequence of sibling nodes along the path from it to the root. For example, the authenticating path for leaf 12 in Fig. 1(a) is $(\nu(11), \nu(6), \nu(1))$, where $\nu(i)$ denotes the hash value at node i.

An MSS signature is valid iff two conditions hold: the OTS signature σ verifies, and the OTS public key value y is consistent with the MSS public key Y and an authentication branch B. Thus, an MSS signature Σ is the quadruple:

$$\Sigma = (\ell, \sigma, y, B), \tag{1}$$

where ℓ denotes the leaf index number. The OTS public key y and signature σ can be computed from the OTS setup and signing algorithms, respectively. A traversal algorithm is implemented to compute the next authentication path B, and some key state information is saved to do this efficiently.

Because MSS setup is time-consuming, we recommend amortizing the cost of generating the next Merkle tree during signing. A single call to the signing algorithm should produce a signature, while doing a little bit of computation for incorporating *one* additional leaf in setting up the next tree, see Fig. 1(b). We

---

[4] In general, the OTS keys do not have to be derived from the same parent seed. We do so here to save storage space.

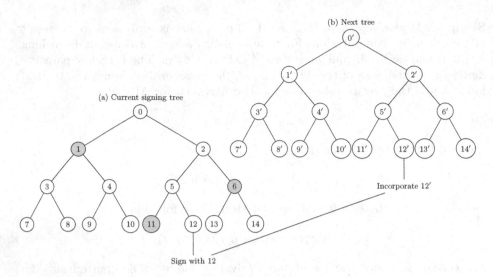

Fig. 1. (a) The nodes for node 12's authentication path are in green. (b) Computation for the next tree during is amortized during signing. During signing using leaf i, leaf i' for the next tree is created and incorporated into the next tree's stack.

could increase or decrease the key re-generation rate according to how fast the OTS keys are being used. This would require some other mechanism for determining the key usage rate and slight modifications to the key_state structure below.

> The key_state object has the following fields:
>
> - ID $\triangleq$ TPM signing key id
> - parent $\triangleq$ parent TPM signing key id
> - iter $\triangleq$ tree iteration or re-generation number
> - height $\triangleq$ height of Merkle tree
> - bfactor $\triangleq$ branching factor of Merkle tree
> - ots $\triangleq$ OTS scheme used
> - lparam $\triangleq$ loop parameter for the OTS scheme, see appendix
> - leaf $\triangleq$ leaf number (for signing)
> - stack $\triangleq$ stack for next tree
> - state $\triangleq$ initial state for next tree
> - cur_state $\triangleq$ saved state for updating the current tree's auth. path

ID stores the MSS key's unique id. parent stores the id of the key's parent. iter stores the re-generation number. height and bfactor store the tree's height and constant branching factor, respectively. ots and lparam store the OTS scheme and its corresponding loop parameter. leaf stores the leaf index. stack stores the stack for setting up the next tree. state stores the initial saved state for the next tree, which includes the first authentication path. cur_state

stores auxiliary state structures for tree traversal algorithms that are more optimal and may include the authentication path for the next signature. An instance
of a key_state object is initialized with iter and leaf set to 1; lparam set to
⊥; and with state and cur_state empty.

3   QUAntum Secure Hash (QUASH)

The MSS setup algorithm must be executed within the TPM. Otherwise malicious software may swap out the real public key with any value, including a MSS
public key created from its choice for the seed. The MSS signing algorithm must
also be executed within the TPM, since the purpose of having a TPM signing key
is to prove (to some verifier) that some function (e.g., construction of a quote)
was carried out by a trusted component.

However, (stateful) hash-based digital signature schemes are space-intensive,
requiring key state and producing large signatures. Thus, the design challenge is
to offload the key state storage to the untrusted platform in a way that preserves
security. We outline the main design challenges here:

- **Key state must be stored outside TPM:** A single key_state object for
  an AIK of branching factor 2 and height 20 takes 4 KB of space, see Table 1
  in Sect. 4. To support even twenty such AIKs, either the TPM's NVRAM size
  must increase by an order of magnitude, or we must store the required key
  state information outside of the TPM in such a way that the overall solution
  remains secure.
- **Preventing rollbacks:** Rollbacks must be carefully managed, since the AIK
  key states are stored on the untrusted platform, and an OTS key is secure only
  if it is used once.[5]
- **Efficient integrity checks:** To prevent rollback attacks and issues from
  unintended data corruptions, we keep hash chains of the AIKs' key states in
  the protected space. These hashes are kept in special registers in the TPM's
  NVRAM and are used for integrity checks prior to key creation and signing.
  Since the integrity checks must be computed by the resource-limited TPM,
  the naive approach of computing the hash chain directly from the AIKs' key
  states is impractical; a more efficient method is needed.
- **Resiliency from data corruption:** Each TPM Integrity Register holds
  a compressed representation of a group of AIKs' key state information.
  Thus, damage to a single key state in the group could render all AIKs in
  the group useless. Our solution allows for recovery of AIKs and TPM registers
  where possible and minimizes the number of AIKs that are unrecoverable.

---

[5] Encrypting the AIKs' state information does not prevent rollbacks; an adversary
could restore an AIK to a previous state by writing over its current encrypted state
with a saved previous encrypted state.

3.1   Data Structures

State Storage Trees. The AIKs' state information is organized in balanced binary trees outside of the TPM. Each node in a State Storage Tree corresponds to an AIK and contains the information necessary for signing under this key. Specifically, each node stores a pair: a key_state object k (introduced in Sect. 2.2) and a subtree hash. The subtree hash is the hash of the concatenation of k and the subtree hashes of the node's children.[6]

Integrity Registers. Digests of last good key states are stored in the TPM's NVRAM in registers, which we call Integrity Registers.

Group Membership. The key states of a group of AIKs are hash-chained together to create a single hash digest. Thus, damage to any key state in the group can render all of the keys in this group useless. To mitigate this kind of data loss, an AIK belongs to multiple groups, where the hash chain of each group is stored in a separate Integrity Register. Given $(d \cdot I)$ Integrity Registers, each key state object belongs to I groups. Group membership is decided by the hash value of the key id. A key id is a member of group G_i^b if the i-th d-ary symbol of its hash is b:

$$G_i^b = \{id : i\text{-th } d\text{-ary symbol of } h(id) \text{ is } b\}. \tag{2}$$

For every group G_i^b, there is a corresponding State Storage Tree T_i^b for maintaining the state information of the AIKs in G_i^b and a corresponding Integrity Register R_i^b for storing the tree hash of T_i^b. We denote by trees(id) a list of State Storage Trees to which id belongs, ordered lexicographically:

$$\texttt{trees}(id) = \{T_i^b : id \in G_i^b\}. \tag{3}$$

For example, if $d = 2$, $i = 2$, and the hash of id ends in 01, id belongs to groups G_0^1 and G_1^0. The State Storage Trees trees(id) = (T_0^1, T_1^0) and corresponding Integrity Registers R_0^1 and R_1^0 are shaded in Fig. 2 below.

3.2   AIK Methods

We describe our methods for creating and certifying AIKs and signing under AIKs using the data structures described in the previous subsection. In Sect. 3.3, we show that our solution is tamper-evident and thwarts forgeries. Our practicality assessment of our solution is given in Sect. 4.

---

[6] The AIK seeds are never stored anywhere. The Primary Seed s_0, i.e., the "unsalted ESK seed," is the only seed stored in the TPM's NVRAM. A TPM signing key seed is generated from s_0 as needed and only in the protected space in the TPM.) .

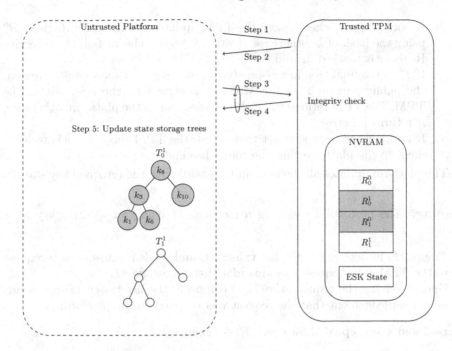

Fig. 2. State Storage Trees track AIK key state information. Integrity Registers in the TPM's NVRAM store integrity check values.

AIK Creation. To create a new identity key id,

1. The platform determines the list $\text{trees}(id)$ and sends a request to create an AIK to the TPM via a TPM interface, such as the TCG Software Stack (TSS). The request contains id, the parent id, the OTS scheme, and the Merkle tree height and branching factor.
2. Upon receiving the request, the TPM computes the list $\text{trees}(id)$ and sends an acknowledgement that the request was received to the platform.

Steps 3 and 4 are repeated for every $T_i^b \in \text{trees}(id)$:

3. The platform computes what the authentication path for node $h(id) \in T_i^b$ will be after the node is inserted into the tree. It sends this authentication path to the TPM.
4. To check the integrity of the authentication path, the TPM ensures that (i) the hashes along the authentication path are consistent with each other, and (ii) the hash at the root is equal to the value stored in the Integrity Register R_i^b corresponding to T_i^b.
   a. For the first authentication path that passes both integrity checks, the TPM instantiates a new **key_state** object k using the MSS setup method. The AIK seed s is determined from the parent signing key seed s_P and id, e.g., $s = s_P || id$.[7] The TPM computes the hash of the key state k and returns k and the public key Y to the the platform.

---

[7] If the parent key is not the ESK, this is determined recursively.

b. If both integrity checks pass, the TPM updates the Integrity Register R_i^b using the hash of k; otherwise, if either integrity checks fail, the Integrity Register is marked invalid.

c. If T_i^b is the final tree in trees(id): if a new key was successfully created, the public portion Y of the MSS key is signed by the ESK within the TPM. The TPM returns the ESK endorsement to the platform; otherwise, it returns an error.

d. If nothing has been sent yet this round, the TPM sends an acknowledgment to the platform that the round has ended.

5. The platform updates all the trees in trees(id) with the returned key state k.

Signing. The protocol for signing a message M using an identity key id is similar:

1. The platform determines the list trees(id) and sends a sign-message request to the TPM. The request contains id and the message M.

2. Upon receiving the request, the TPM computes the list trees(id) and sends an acknowledgement that the request was received to the platform.

Steps 3 and 4 are repeated for every $T_i^b \in$ trees(id):

3. The platform computes the authentication path for node $h(id) \in T_i^b$. It sends this authentication path and the key state k stored at node $h(id) \in T_i^b$ to the TPM.

4. To check the integrity of the authentication path, the TPM ensures that (i) the hash of k and the hashes along the authentication path are consistent with each other, and (ii) the hash at the root is equal to the value stored in the Integrity Register R_i^b corresponding to T_i^b.

a. For the first authentication path that passes both integrity checks, the TPM signs the message M using the MSS signing method and k.

b. If both integrity checks pass, the TPM updates the Integrity Register R_i^b using the updated MSS object k; otherwise, if either integrity checks fail, the Integrity Register is marked invalid.

c. If T_i^b is the final tree in trees(id): if M was successfully signed, the TPM returns the signature and the updated key state k' to the platform; otherwise, it returns an error.

d. If the signature used the "last leaf" in the current Merkle tree, the public portion Y of the next MSS key is signed by the ESK and this newly created ESK endorsement is also sent to the platform.

e. If nothing has been sent yet this round, the TPM sends an acknowledgment to the platform that the round has ended.

5. The platform updates all the trees in trees(id) with the returned key state k.

Signing a Key Handle. Each AIK must be certified as having been created by a legitimate TPM. This is done by signing each AIK public value using the ESK. The ESK itself is certified by the vendor, perhaps using a message authentication code (MAC) derived from the Primary Seed s_0.[8]

The ESK is a TPM hash-based signing key whose seed is derived from s_0 and some user-inputted salt. Both s_0 and the ESK state information is kept in the TPM's NVRAM and never leaves the protected space.

Key and Register Recovery. The TPM itself does not provide a mechanism for recovering data lost during storage, transmission, or processing. Even a low bit error rate can render all AIKs useless without some means of recovering AIKs (when possible) and reverting Integrity Registers to useable states. Here, we describe how this can be accomplished.

First, for each State Storage Tree, the platform computes the hash chain value from scratch (i.e., from the key states, as opposed to from the subtree hashes) and sends an AIK recovery request to the TPM along with the tree hashes. The TPM responds with the set B of State Storage Trees which did not pass the integrity checks and resets the corresponding Integrity Registers. (By resetting, we mean that the registers reflect the valid integrity value corresponding to an empty State Storage Tree.) For every tree $t \in B$, for every node $v \in t$, the platform checks if there exists a State Storage Tree $t' \notin B$, and $t' \in \mathtt{trees}(id)$, where id is the id of v. Note that this can be computed efficiently from the hash of id. If t' exists, the platform marks the AIK as recoverable.

For every tree $t \in B$ and recoverable node $v \in t$, the platform sends to the TPM a request to add node v to t, along with an authenticating path for v in t and a proof of correctness for v (i.e., a tree $t' \notin B$, and $t' \in \mathtt{trees}(id)$ and an authenticating path for v on t'). If the proof verifies, the TPM updates the corresponding Integrity Register accordingly; otherwise, the register is marked as invalid.

From above, we see that AIKs in damaged State Storage Trees can be recovered from undamaged State Storage Trees. An AIK id is recoverable iff there exists a State Storage Tree in $\mathtt{trees}(id)$ that passes all integrity checks. In other words, an AIK is *unrecoverable* iff

$$t \in \mathtt{trees}(id) \implies t \in B.$$

For a fixed number N of AIKs, increasing d and I decreases the chance of an AIK being unrecoverable. However, this obviously increases the number of Integrity Registers in the TPM's NVRAM.

3.3   Correctness and Security Proofs

We provide sketches of correctness and security proofs for our construction here.

---

[8] Note that ESK may periodically require a fresh certificate.

Lemma 1. *If an authenticating path passes both integrity checks (step 4 for both AIK setup and signing), then the path does not contain any unauthorized modifications.*

Proof. If the hash value in the Integrity Register holds the intended value, then in order for an adversary to modify the path, it must do so in such a way that the final tree hash at the root retains this intended value. This is infeasible by the (second pre-image resistance) property of the hash function, see Def. 3.

Moreover, if an Integrity Register holds a valid value, it must be the intended value; since the Integrity Register is protected by the TPM, and the TPM updates the register with a valid value iff all integrity checks on the corresponding authenticating branch pass. (**Remark:** Thus when an integrity checks fails for a State Storage Tree T_i^b, the corresponding Integrity Register R_i^b must be marked invalid in order for Lemma 1 and Corollaries 1 and 2 to hold, see step 4b in AIK creation and signing.) □

Corollary 1 (Tamper-resistance). *Any unauthorized modification of an AIK's key state information (stored outside the TPM) is detectable.*

Corollary 2 (Unforgeability). *It is infeasible for an adversary to forge a signature under a properly certified AIK.*

Theorem 1 (Correctness). *Let id be any hash-based AIK with at least one authentication path which passes both integrity checks. Given any message M of any arbitrarily length, a signature on M under AIK id verifies.*

Proof. Let p be the first authenticating path that passes both integrity checks. From Lemma 1, p does not not contain any unauthorized modifications. Thus, the AIK's key state is the intended key state, and so any signature under it verifies. □

4   Practicality Assessment

4.1   Space Analysis

We first determine how much space is needed for storing a key state object. The hash output size is assumed to be (256 bits or) 32 bytes. Eight of the key_state object fields—ID, parent, iter, height, bfactor, ots, lparam, and leaf—take up very little space. For concreteness, we have allotted 4 bytes for each of these fields; so $8 \times 4 = 32$ bytes are needed for storing all of these fields.

The maximum total storage size is dominated by the storage requirements for the remaining fields—stack, state, and cur_state—which depend on the traversal algorithm being used and the dimensions of the Merkle tree. We use the state-of-the-art traversal scheme from [8]; and our Merkle tree is binary with height $H =$ height.

During Merkle tree setup, an initial state consisting of H "authentication" nodes, $H - 2$ "treehash" nodes, and a single "retain" node are stored [8], hence, $2H - 1$ nodes. The `stack` for this computation requires a maximum of H nodes.

Additionally, the traversal algorithm requires storing at most $3.5H - 4$ nodes in `cur_state` at any given step [8]. Thus, the total maximum space (in bytes) required for storing a key state object is bounded by $\Gamma(H) =$

$$32 + (32 \times (6.5H - 5)) = 208H - 128. \tag{4}$$

Table 1 shows the key state storage size for binary Merkle trees of various sizes.

Table 1. Key state storage size in KB.

		Targeted Range		
		$H = 15$	$H = 20$	$H = 25$
# OTS keys	2^H	$3 \cdot 10^4$	$1.05 \cdot 10^6$	$33.55 \cdot 10^6$
Storage size $\Gamma(H)$	$208H - 128$	3.0 KB	4.0 KB	5.1 KB

TPM Space for AIK Creation. Here, we provide an estimate for the TPM space needed to create an AIK. This estimation is meant to approximate the maximum space used by a space-efficient implementation.

In the analysis below, a unit is 32 bytes. For simplicity, we assume that the Merkle trees are binary of height H; we use the traversal algorithm described in [8] and the space-efficient [12] SHA-256 for the hash function; the space required for running the PRNG likewise is minimal; and the length of each OTS private x-value is 1 unit.

In creating a TPM signing key, the maximum resident TPM space is needed when the public key is being signed. We estimate the space required as follows:

- 1 unit for storing the public key (input);
- $\Gamma(H) = 6.5H - 4$ units for storing the ESK key state (input), see (4);
- 1 unit for storing the leaf index ℓ (output);
- $N(ots)$ units for the maximum OTS signature σ size (output);
- $N(ots)$ units for the maximum OTS public-key portion y size (output); and
- H units for the maximum authentication path size (output);

where the loop parameter $N(ots)$ depends on the OTS scheme. At this point, we need not retain the input authentication path, the newly created key state, its hash, nor the updated register value. (**Remark:** In order to save TPM space, the newly created AIK state is returned to the platform before signing the retained public key value using the ESK state, see **AIK Creation** in Sect. 3.2.)

We need only negligible scratch space for running the MSS signing method: Only negligible additional space (beyond the space allotted for storing the output) is required for computing the OTS signature and public-key. Likewise, only negligible additional space (beyond space for storing the inputted ESK state) is required for updating `cur_state`, `state`, and `stack`.

Table 2 shows the maximum TPM space needed for creating an AIK of various sizes. Note that the total space required is not impacted by the number N of AIKs; (unless N is impractically large).

Table 2. TPM space required for AIK creation in KB: In LD-C, the complement of the message is also encoded to prevent man-in-the-middle attacks. LD-Z [15] encodes the zero count of the message digest to prevent forgeries.

	LD-C	LD-Z	LDWM $w = 2$	LDWM $w = 4$	LDWM $w = 8$
$H = 15$	36.4	20.5	12.1	7.9	5.8
$H = 20$	37.6	21.7	13.3	9.1	7.0
$H = 25$	38.8	22.9	14.5	10.3	8.2

TPM Space for AIK Signing. The maximum space in the TPM needed for signing a message is identical to that of setup.

4.2   Time Analysis

Since the State Storage Trees are balanced binary hash trees,

- Determining (the key state and) the authentication path takes $I \cdot \log(N)$ time, where N is the number of AIKs, and an id belongs to I groups.
- Determining the root value from (the key state and) the authentication path also takes $I \cdot \log(N)$ time.
- To update a State Storage Tree, only the nodes along a path to the root need to be reevaluated. Moreover, reevaluating a subtree hash requires only one hash operation. So, updating the State Storage Trees takes $I \cdot \log(N)$ time.

There are traversal algorithms that require $\mathcal{O}(H)$ space and $\mathcal{O}(H)$ time with low constant factors [8,23]. Therefore, by using an optimal traversal algorithm, the cost of MSS signing is dominated by the cost of executing the underlying OTS scheme once. Amortizing the re-generation cost only increases the signing time by roughly a factor of two.

The only time-inefficient step is MSS setup, which necessarily requires time proportional to the number of OTS keys created at setup time. For the ESK, this can occur at provisioning time. For AIKs, we would like to set up on-the-fly, as needed. To mitigate this setup cost, we can setup a new AIK with a small Merkle tree and ramp up its size for subsequent tree(s).

5   Conclusion

We conclude that our construction for hash-based TPM signing keys is practical, if a state-of-the-art traversal algorithm, such as [8], is implemented.

QUASH can be implemented with a fairly small NVRAM: If an ESK Merkle tree includes roughly 6.5 million OTS key pairs, it can certify 100 AIKs, each requiring at most $(2^{16} =)$ 65 thousand re-generations without needing to be re-certified by the vendor. This can be accomplished by setting a binary Merkle tree height to 23. Given these Merkle tree parameters, the maximum storage space required for storing the `key_state` object is 4.7 KB. Supporting 6 Integrity Registers would require an additional 192 bytes.

Acknowledgment. The authors would like to thank Anna Lysyanskaya for her suggestion on how to derive the ESK from a Primary Seed and Chris Eliopoulos Alicea, Joseph J. Ferraro, John D. Ramsdell, and the anonymous reviewers for helpful comments.

References

1. Alkim, E., Bindel, N., Buchmann, J., Dagdelen, Ö.: TESLA: Tightly-Secure Efficient Signatures from Standard Lattices. Cryptology ePrint Archive, Report 2015/755 (2015)
2. Arthur, W., Challener, D., Goldman, K.: A Practical Guide to TPM 2.0: Using the Trusted Platform Module in the New Age of Security. Apress, Berkeley (2015)
3. Barak, B., Mahmoody-Ghidary, M.: Lower bounds on signatures from symmetric primitives. In: Proceedings of the 48th Annual IEEE Symposium on Foundations of Computer Science, pp. 680–688, October 2007
4. Bernstein, D.J., Buchmann, J., Dahmen, E. (eds.): Post-Quantum Cryptography. Springer Science & Business Media, Heidelberg (2009)
5. Bernstein, D.J., et al.: SPHINCS: practical stateless hash-based signatures. In: Oswald, E., Fischlin, M. (eds.) EUROCRYPT 2015, Part I. LNCS, vol. 9056, pp. 368–397. Springer, Heidelberg (2015)
6. Brickell, E., Camenisch, J., Chen, L.: Direct anonymous attestation. In: Proceedings of the 11th ACM Conference on Computer and Communications Security, CCS 2004, pp. 132–145. ACM, New York, NY, USA (2004)
7. Buchmann, J., Dahmen, E., Hülsing, A.: XMSS–a practical forward secure signature scheme based on minimal security assumptions. In: Yang, B.-Y. (ed.) PQCrypto 2011. LNCS, vol. 7071, pp. 117–129. Springer, Heidelberg (2011)
8. Buchmann, J., Dahmen, E., Schneider, M.: Merkle tree traversal revisited. In: Buchmann, J., Ding, J. (eds.) PQCrypto 2008. LNCS, vol. 5299, pp. 63–78. Springer, Heidelberg (2008)
9. Challener, D., Yoder, K., Catherman, R., Safford, D., Van Doorn, L.: A Practical Guide to Trusted Computing. Pearson Education, Upper Saddle River (2007)
10. Coker, G., Guttman, J., Loscocco, P., Herzog, A., Millen, J., O'Hanlon, B., Ramsdell, J., Segall, A., Sheehy, J., Sniffen, B.: Principles of remote attestation. Int. J. Inf. Secur. **10**(2), 63–81 (2011)
11. Grover, L.K.: A fast quantum mechanical algorithm for database search. In: Proceedings of the Twenty-eighth Annual ACM Symposium on Theory of Computing, STOC 1996, pp. 212–219. ACM, New York, NY, USA (1996)
12. Ideguchi, K., Owada, T., Yoshida, H.: A study on RAM requirements of various SHA-3 Candidates on Low-cost 8-bit CPUs. IACR Cryptology ePrint Archive (2009)
13. Jakobsson, M., Leighton, T., Micali, S., Szydlo, M.: Fractal merkle tree representation and traversal. In: Joye, M. (ed.) CT-RSA 2003. LNCS, vol. 2612, pp. 314–326. Springer, Heidelberg (2003)
14. Kinney, S.: Trusted Platform Module Basics: Using TPM in Embedded Systems. Elsevier Inc., Burlington (2006)
15. Merkle, R.C.: Advances in Cryptology–CRYPTO 1989 Proceedings, chapter A Certified Digital Signature, pp. 218–238 (1990)
16. Naor, D., Shenhav, A., Wool, A.: One-Time Signatures Revisited: Have They Become Practical? IACR Cryptology ePrint Archive (2005)

17. Parno, B., McCune, J.M., Perrig, A.: Bootstrapping trust in commodity computers. In: 2010 IEEE Symposium on Security and Privacy (SP), pp. 414–429. IEEE, May 2010

18. Parno, B., McCune, J.M., Perrig, A.: Bootstrapping Trust in Modern Computers. Springer Science & Business Media, New York (2011)

19. Sarmenta, L.F., van Dijk, M., O'Donnell, C.W., Rhodes, J., Devadas, S.: Virtual monotonic counters and count-limited objects using a TPM without a trusted OS. In: Proceedings of the First ACM Workshop on Scalable Trusted Computing, STC 2006, pp. 27–42. ACM, New York, NY, USA (2006)

20. Scarlata, V., Rozas, C., Wiseman, M., Grawrock, D., Vishik, C.: Trusted Computing: Ein Weg zu neuen IT-Sicherheitsarchitekturen, chapter TPM Virtualization: Building a General Framework, pp. 43–56. Vieweg+Teubner (2008)

21. Segall, A.: Trusted platform modules: When, Why, and How to Use Them. Version: 21 June 2015

22. Peter, W.: Shor.: polynomial-time algorithms for prime factorization and discrete logarithms on a quantum computer. SIAM Rev. **41**(2), 303–332 (1999)

23. Szydlo, M.: Merkle tree traversal in log space and time. In: Cachin, C., Camenisch, J.L. (eds.) EUROCRYPT 2004. LNCS, vol. 3027, pp. 541–554. Springer, Heidelberg (2004)

24. TCG: TCG Vendor ID Registry, September 2015. http://www.trustedcomputing group.org

Signatures with Advanced Properties

Fuzzy Signatures: Relaxing Requirements and a New Construction

Takahiro Matsuda[1]([✉]), Kenta Takahashi[2], Takao Murakami[1], and Goichiro Hanaoka[1]

[1] National Institute of Advanced Industrial Science and Technology (AIST), Tokyo, Japan
{t-matsuda,takao-murakami,hanaoka-goichiro}@aist.go.jp
[2] Hitachi, Ltd., Yokohama, Japan
kenta.takahashi.bw@hitachi.com

Abstract. Takahashi et al. (ACNS 2015) introduced the notion of *fuzzy signature*, which is a signature scheme that allows a signature to be generated using "fuzzy data" (i.e. a noisy string such as a biometric feature) as a signing key, without using any additional user-specific data (such as a helper string in the context of fuzzy extractors). They gave a generic construction of a fuzzy signature scheme from the combination of an ordinary signature scheme with some homomorphic properties regarding keys and signatures, and a new primitive that they call linear sketch, and showed a concrete instantiation based on the Waters signature scheme (EUROCRYPT 2005). A major weakness of their scheme is that fuzzy data is assumed to be distributed uniformly, and another is that it has somewhat large public parameter (proportional to the security parameter), and requires bilinear groups, and either (or both) of these properties could be barriers for implementation and/or practical use.

In this paper, we revisit the results of Takahashi et al.: We show that in their generic construction, the requirements on each of the building blocks can be relaxed in several aspects. More specifically, our relaxation for the underlying linear sketch scheme allows us to use a new linear sketch scheme (that we propose) for a fuzzy key setting different from that of Takahashi et al., for which we only require that the average min-entropy of fuzzy data is high (under the situation some part of its information is leaked). Furthermore, our relaxation on the underlying signature scheme enables us to now use the Schnorr signature scheme as a building block. Our concrete instantiation of a fuzzy signature scheme is, although relying on a random oracle, arguably much more practical than the scheme by Takahashi et al. The latter relaxation routes through a variant of related key security for signature schemes.

Keywords: Fuzzy signature · Schnorr signature · Biometrics

1 Introduction

1.1 Background and Motivation

As the information society grows rapidly, the public key infrastructure (PKI) plays a more significant role as an infrastructure for managing digital certificates.

© Springer International Publishing Switzerland 2016
M. Manulis et al. (Eds.): ACNS 2016, LNCS 9696, pp. 97–116, 2016.
DOI: 10.1007/978-3-319-39555-5_6

It is also expected to be widely used for personal use such as national IDs and e-government services. One of the biggest risks in the PKI, which needs to be considered in the personal use, lies in a user's private key [8]; since the user's identity is verified based only on his/her private key, the user needs to protect the private key in a highly secure manner. For example, the user is required to store his/her private key into a smart card (or USB token), and remember a password to activate the key. Such an approach, however, can reduce the usability, especially for elderly people in an aging society.

One of the promising approaches to fundamentally solve this problem is to use *biometric data* (e.g. fingerprint, face, and iris) as a private key. Since a user's biometrics is a part of human body, it can offer a more secure and usable way to link the individual with his/her private key (i.e. it is not forgotten unlike passwords and is much harder to steal than cards). Also, a sensor that captures multiple biometrics simultaneously (e.g. face and iris [4]; fingerprint and finger-vein [13]) has been widely developed to obtain a large amount of entropy at one time, and a recent study [11] has shown that very high accuracy (e.g. the false acceptance rate (FAR) is 2^{-133} (resp. 2^{-87}) when the false rejection rate (FRR) is 0.055 (resp. 0.0053)) can be achieved by combining four finger-vein features.

However, since biometric data is noisy data that fluctuates each time it is captured, it cannot be directly used as a private key. In this paper, we call such a noisy string *fuzzy data*.

Fuzzy Signature. Takahashi et al. [15] introduced a concept of digital signature called *fuzzy signature* to address this issue. Fuzzy signature consists of three algorithms $(\mathsf{KG_{FS}}, \mathsf{Sign_{FS}}, \mathsf{Ver_{FS}})$.[1] First, the key generation algorithm $\mathsf{KG_{FS}}$ takes a noisy string x as input, and outputs a verification key vk. Then, the signing algorithm $\mathsf{Sign_{FS}}$ takes another noisy string x' and a message m as input, and outputs a signature σ. Finally, the verification algorithm $\mathsf{Ver_{FS}}$ verifies whether σ is a valid signature (on a message m) or not, using the verification key vk. If x is close to x', σ is verified as valid. As discussed in [15], the key difference between fuzzy signatures and digital signatures using a *fuzzy extractor* [7], is that the former does not need user-specific auxiliary data (called a "helper string" in the context of fuzzy extractors) to generate a signature σ. Thus, a fuzzy signature scheme can be used to realize a biometric version of the PKI that does not require a user to carry a dedicated device containing the helper string, which is preferable in terms of the usability.

We note that a fuzzy signature scheme has a public parameter (generated by the setup algorithm) that is needed for signing messages. However, it is not user-specific, and thus the user need not carry it by himself/herself. In contrast, in fuzzy-extractor-based signature schemes, the auxiliary data (which can be made public, but) is user-specific, and has to be present at the time of signing together with the user (signer) himself/herself. Hence, it has to be carried out by the user, or stored somewhere in a remote server and a signing device has

---

[1] To be precise, a fuzzy signature scheme also has the "setup" algorithm for generating a public parameter that is shared by all users, as explained shortly.

to be on-line when generating a signature. More in-depth discussions between fuzzy signatures and fuzzy-extractor-based signatures can be found in [15].

Overview of the Results of Takahashi et al. [15] *and Our Motivation.* In this paper, we build on the results of Takahashi et al., and give new results on fuzzy signatures. To better explain and understand our motivation and results, let us briefly recall the technical results in [15]: In addition to formally define fuzzy signatures, Takahashi et al. formalized what they call a *fuzzy key setting*, which formalizes some necessary information about the setting over which fuzzy data is considered, e.g. the metric space to which fuzzy data belongs, the threshold with which two sampled data are considered close/far, the distribution from which each fuzzy data is assumed to be drawn, how the fluctuation of fuzzy data is modeled, etc. A fuzzy signature scheme is associated with such a fuzzy key setting.

Takahashi et al. also introduced a tool that they call *linear sketch*, which is a kind of a pair of linear encoding and error correction methods, that is associated with a fuzzy key setting. They then gave a generic construction of a fuzzy signature scheme for a fuzzy key setting from a combination of a linear sketch scheme (associated with the same fuzzy key setting) and an ordinary signature scheme that has some homomorphic properties regarding keys and signatures. They then specified a concrete fuzzy key setting in which a fuzzy data is distributed uniformly over some metric space, and showed a linear sketch scheme for it, and also showed an ordinary signature scheme based on the Waters signature scheme [16] that can be used with the linear sketch in their generic construction. By using these concrete linear sketch scheme and the signature scheme, Takahashi et al. [15] showed a concrete instantiation of a fuzzy signature scheme for the above fuzzy key setting.

Since Takahashi et al.'s fuzzy signature scheme is based on the Waters signature scheme [16], it has somewhat large public parameter (where the number of group elements in the parameter is proportional to the security parameter), and requires bilinear groups. Therefore, either (or both) of these properties, namely large parameter size and the use of bilinear groups, could be barriers for implementation (especially in computationally limited devices) and/or practical use. More importantly, they assume that fuzzy data is distributed uniformly (over some metric space). This is quite a strong assumption, and thus potentially limits the usefulness of their result. For example, biometric information, which is one of the main targets of fuzzy signatures, is typically not at all uniformly distributed. The same is true for other fuzzy data such as data produced from physically unclonable functions (PUFs).

This motivates us to study whether we can overcome these weaknesses of the fuzzy signature scheme in [15], and come up with a more efficient and easier-to-implement fuzzy signature scheme, while only requiring a more plausible requirement for fuzzy data, e.g. requiring only high min-entropy for the distribution of fuzzy data, which is a necessary requirement (because otherwise a signature can be forged by guessing the fuzzy data used as a signing key).

1.2 Our Contributions

In this paper, we show that in the generic construction of a fuzzy signature scheme shown by Takahashi et al. [15], the requirements on each of the building blocks used in their generic construction, can be relaxed in several aspects: Our relaxation for the underlying linear sketch scheme allows us to use a new linear sketch scheme (that we propose) for a different fuzzy key setting from that of Takahashi et al. As a result, *we only need to require that the (average) min-entropy of the distribution of fuzzy data is high (under the situation where some part of its information is leaked)*. This is our main contribution in this paper. Furthermore, our relaxation on the underlying signature scheme enables us to widen the class of signature schemes that can be used as a building block in the construction by Takahashi et al. In particular, from our relaxations, we can now use the Schnorr signature scheme [14] together with our proposed linear sketch scheme, to obtain a new concrete fuzzy signature scheme. Although our new concrete fuzzy signature scheme is secure only in the random oracle model, unlike the concrete fuzzy signature scheme by Takahashi et al. based on the Waters signature scheme [16], our concrete fuzzy signature scheme based on the Schnorr scheme does not need bilinear groups, is much more efficient, simpler, easier-to-implement, and hence more suitable for practical use, than the scheme in [15]. Below, we explain more technical details of our results.

Relaxing the Requirements on the Linear Sketch Scheme. As mentioned earlier, this primitive can be understood as a pair of linear encoding and error correction method. It is associated with a fuzzy key setting and an abelian group $(\mathcal{K}, +)$, and consists of two algorithms: "Sketch" and "DiffRec" (where the latter stands for "difference reconstruction"). The first algorithm can be used to generate a "sketch" c of an element $s \in \mathcal{K}$ using a fuzzy data x. The second algorithm takes as input two sketches c and c', where c (resp. c') is supposedly a sketch of an element $s \in \mathcal{K}$ (resp. $s' \in \mathcal{K}$) generated by using a fuzzy data x (resp. x'), and outputs the difference $\Delta s = s - s'$ if the two fuzzy data x and x' are "close" (according to the threshold t specified in the fuzzy key setting). It was also required in [15] that a linear sketch scheme satisfies additional "linearity" and "simulatability" properties that are used in the security proof for the generic construction of a fuzzy signature scheme in [15].

In Sect. 5, we introduce four relaxations to the original definition in [15]. (1) We allow a setup algorithm that outputs a public parameter shared by all algorithms in the scheme. (2) We allow the algorithms to be probabilistic. (3) We relax the property called linearity, which is a kind of functional requirement and was originally defined like correctness (without errors), into some distributional notion. (4) We relax the property called simulatability, which is a kind of confidentiality notion, into some average-case indistinguishability-type notion.

Although each relaxation is simple and may not sound so important, the combination of them guides us to constructing a new linear sketch scheme based on a well-known universal hash function family satisfying linearity. The confidentiality (average-case indistinguishability) of our proposed linear sketch scheme follows from the leftover hash lemma [7,9]. The biggest merit of this linear sketch scheme, compared to the one in [15], is that we can remove the assumption that fuzzy data is distributed uniformly. Interestingly, if any of our four relaxations is not introduced and the previous definition by [15] is used, our construction does not satisfy some of the requirements, and thus our relaxations are actually essential. For more details, see Sect. 5.

Relaxing the Requirements on the Underlying Signature Scheme. In Sect. 6, we show that in the generic construction of a fuzzy signature scheme shown by Takahashi et al. [15], if we can assume that the underlying signature scheme satisfies a notion of security against some kind of related key attack with respect to addition, denoted by Φ^{add}-RKA* security, and formally defined in Sect. 3.2, then one of the homomorphic properties regarding keys (and signatures) required in the construction of [15], can be removed. Interestingly, we show that if a signature scheme satisfies the standard EUF-CMA security and the homomorphic properties required in the construction of [15], then the scheme is automatically Φ^{add}-RKA* secure, while the converse is not necessarily true. Therefore, although our security proof for the generic construction requires a seemingly stronger "RKA" security for the underlying signature scheme, it is in fact a strict relaxation of the security proof by [15], and thus potentially widen the class of signature schemes that can be used as a building block for the generic construction of [15]. As a merit of our "relaxation", we show that the original Schnorr signature scheme [14] can be shown to satisfy the Φ^{add}-RKA* security in the random oracle model. For more details, see Sect. 3.2.

New Security Proof for Takahashi et al.'s Generic Construction from Relaxed Assumptions. In Sect. 6, we show a new security proof for the generic construction of a fuzzy signature scheme by Takahashi et al. [15], from exactly the same primitives, but with our relaxed (and hence weaker) assumptions. More specifically, we prove that if the underlying signature scheme satisfies our RKA security notion and has a relaxed homomorphic property, and the linear sketch scheme satisfies all the relaxed requirements we introduce, then the constructed fuzzy signature scheme is secure. The approach for the proof (e.g. the ordering of games in the sequence of games argument) is very similar to, and proceeds very closely to, the original security proof by [15]. Therefore, our contribution in this security proof is to clarify that a security proof from weaker assumptions is in fact possible, and clarify those assumptions for the underlying signature scheme and the linear sketch scheme. For more details, see Sect. 6.

1.3 Paper Organization

The rest of the paper is organized as follows: In Sect. 2, we review the basic notation, definitions, and facts. In Sect. 3.2, we review definitions for ordinary signatures, and introduce a new RKA security definition. We also show that the Schnorr signature scheme satisfies our RKA security notion. In Sect. 4, we review the definitions for fuzzy signatures, together with the definition of a fuzzy key setting. In Sect. 5, we introduce our relaxed definitions for a linear sketch. We then specify a concrete fuzzy key setting which requires that the distribution of fuzzy data is only of high (average) min-entropy (in the presence of some kind of leakage), and propose a new construction of a linear sketch scheme. In Sect. 6, we give a new security proof for the generic construction of a fuzzy signature scheme by Takahashi et al. [15], based on our relaxed requirements for the building blocks. In Sect. 7, we give the full description of our Schnorr-based fuzzy signature scheme. In Sect. 8, we discuss the plausibility of our fuzzy key setting, and some open problems.

Due to the space limitation, the proofs of the theorems and lemmas in this paper are omitted and will be given in the full version, and we only give some high-level explanations for them in this proceedings version.

2   Preliminaries

In this section, we recall the basic notation, definitions and facts.

Basic Notation. $\mathbb{N}$, $\mathbb{Z}$, and $\mathbb{R}$ denote the sets of all natural numbers, all integers, and all real numbers, respectively. If $n \in \mathbb{N}$, then we define $[n] := \{1, \ldots, n\}$. Throughout the paper, we use the bold font to denote a vector (such as $\boldsymbol{x}$ and $\boldsymbol{\alpha}$). If $a \in \mathbb{R}$, then "$\lfloor a \rceil$" denotes the integer that is the nearest to a (the rounding operation). We extend the definition of "$\lfloor \cdot \rceil$" to allow it to take a real vector $\boldsymbol{a} = (a_1, a_2, \ldots)$ as input, by $\lfloor \boldsymbol{a} \rceil := (\lfloor a_1 \rceil, \lfloor a_2 \rceil, \ldots)$.

"$x \leftarrow y$" denotes that y is (deterministically) assigned to x. If S is a finite set, then "$|S|$" denotes its size, and "$x \leftarrow_{\mathsf{R}} S$" denotes that x is chosen uniformly at random from S. If $\varPhi$ is a distribution (over some set), then "$x \leftarrow_{\mathsf{R}} \varPhi$" denotes that x is chosen according to the distribution $\varPhi$. For a function $f : D \to R$ and an element $y \in R$, we denote by "$f^{-1}(y)$" the set of preimages of y under f, namely, $f^{-1}(y) := \{x \in D | f(x) = y\}$. If x and y are bit-strings, then "$|x|$" denotes the bit-length of x, and "$(x||y)$" denotes the concatenation of x and y. "(P)PTA" stands for a *(probabilistic) polynomial time algorithm*.

If $\mathcal{A}$ is a probabilistic algorithm, then "$y \leftarrow_{\mathsf{R}} \mathcal{A}(x)$" denote that $\mathcal{A}$ computes y by taking x as input and using an internal randomness that is chosen uniformly at random. If furthermore $\mathcal{O}$ is a (possibly probabilistic) algorithm or a function, then "$\mathcal{A}^{\mathcal{O}}$" denotes that $\mathcal{A}$ has oracle access to $\mathcal{O}$. Throughout the paper, "k" denotes a security parameter. A function $f(\cdot) : \mathbb{N} \to [0, 1]$ is said to be *negligible* if for all positive polynomials $p(\cdot)$ and all sufficiently large k, we have $f(k) < 1/p(k)$.

2.1   Basic Definitions Related to Probability and Entropy

Definition 1. *([7]) Let $(\mathcal{X}, \mathcal{Y})$ be a joint distribution defined over the set $X \times Y$. The* average *min-entropy of $\mathcal{X}$ given $\mathcal{Y}$, denoted by $\widetilde{\mathbf{H}}_\infty(\mathcal{X}|\mathcal{Y})$, is defined by $\widetilde{\mathbf{H}}_\infty(\mathcal{X}|\mathcal{Y}) := -\log_2(\mathbf{E}_{y \leftarrow_{\mathsf{R}} \mathcal{Y}}[\max_{x' \in X} \Pr[\mathcal{X} = x' | \mathcal{Y} = y]])$.*

Definition 2. *Let $\mathcal{X}$ and $\mathcal{X}'$ be distributions defined over the same set X. The statistical distance between $\mathcal{X}$ and $\mathcal{X}'$, denoted by $\mathbf{SD}(\mathcal{X}, \mathcal{X}')$, is defined by $\mathbf{SD}(\mathcal{X}, \mathcal{X}') := \frac{1}{2} \sum_{z \in X} |\Pr[\mathcal{X} = z] - \Pr[\mathcal{X}' = z]|$. We say that $\mathcal{X}$ and $\mathcal{X}'$ are statistically indistinguishable, if $\mathbf{SD}(\mathcal{X}, \mathcal{X}')$ is negligible.*

2.2   Universal Hash Function Family and the Leftover Hash Lemma

Here, we first recall the definition of a universal hash function family, then its concrete construction, and finally the leftover hash lemma [9].

Definition 3. *Let $\mathcal{H} = \{h_z : D \to R\}_{z \in Z}$ be a family of hash functions, where Z denotes the seed space of $\mathcal{H}$. We say that $\mathcal{H}$ is a universal hash function family if for all $x, x' \in D$ such that $x \neq x'$, we have $\Pr_{z \leftarrow_R Z}[h_z(x) = h_z(x')] \leq 1/|R|$.*

A Concrete Construction with Linearity. In this paper, we will use the following concrete construction of a universal hash function family $\mathcal{H}_{lin}$ whose domain is $\mathbb{F}_{p^n}$ and whose range is $\mathbb{F}_p$, where $\mathbb{F}_p$ is a finite field with prime order p and $n \in \mathbb{N}$. Note that $\mathbb{F}_{p^n}$, when viewed as a vector space, is isomorphic to the vector space $(\mathbb{F}_p)^n$. Let $\psi : (\mathbb{F}_p)^n \to \mathbb{F}_{p^n}$ be an isomorphism of the vector spaces, and ψ^{-1} be its inverse, which are both computable in time polynomial of $n \cdot \log_2(p)$.

Let the seed space be $Z = \mathbb{F}_{p^n}$, the domain be $D = (\mathbb{F}_p)^n$, and the range be $R = \mathbb{F}_p$. For each $z \in Z$, define the function $h_z : D \to R$ as follows: On input $\boldsymbol{x} \in (\mathbb{F}_p)^n$, $h_z(\boldsymbol{x})$ computes $y \leftarrow \psi(\boldsymbol{x}) \cdot z$, where the operation "$\cdot$" is the multiplication in the extension field $\mathbb{F}_{p^n}$. Let $(y_1, \ldots, y_n) = \psi^{-1}(y)$. The output of $h_z(\boldsymbol{x})$ is $y_1 \in \mathbb{F}_p$. The family $\mathcal{H}_{lin}$ consists of the hash functions $\{h_z\}_{z \in Z}$.

It is well-known (see, e.g. [3]) that $\mathcal{H}_{lin}$ is a universal hash function family. Furthermore, for every $z \in Z$, h_z satisfies linearity, in the following sense:

$$\forall \boldsymbol{x}, \boldsymbol{x}' \in (\mathbb{F}_p)^n \text{ and } \alpha, \beta \in \mathbb{F}_p : \quad \alpha \cdot h_z(\boldsymbol{x}) + \beta \cdot h_z(\boldsymbol{x}') = h_z(\alpha \cdot \boldsymbol{x} + \beta \cdot \boldsymbol{x}').$$

Leftover Hash Lemma. Roughly speaking, the leftover hash lemma [9] states that a universal hash function family is a good (strong) randomness extractor. Here, we recall a version of the leftover hash lemma shown by Dodis et al. [7] that allows leakage from the inputs to a universal hash function.

Lemma 1. *([7]) Let $\mathcal{H} = \{h_z : D \to R\}_{z \in Z}$ be a universal hash function family. Let U_Z and U_R be the uniform distributions over Z and R, respectively. Furthermore, let $(\mathcal{X}, \mathcal{Y})$ be a joint distribution, where the support of $\mathcal{X}$ is contained in D. Then, when z is chosen uniformly as $z \leftarrow_R Z$, it holds that*

$$\mathbf{SD}\Big((z, h_z(\mathcal{X}), \mathcal{Y}), (U_Z, U_R, \mathcal{Y})\Big) \leq \frac{1}{2}\sqrt{2^{-\tilde{\mathbf{H}}_\infty(\mathcal{X}|\mathcal{Y})} \cdot |R|}.$$

3   Definitions for (Ordinary) Signatures

In this section, we first review the definitions for (ordinary) signature schemes (Sect. 3.1). We then give the definition of our variant of related key attacks security (which we call RKA* security) and some facts on it (Sect. 3.2).

3.1   Structural Properties

Syntax and Correctness. We model a signature scheme Σ as a quadruple of the PPTAs (Setup, KG, Sign, Ver) that are defined as follows: Setup is the setup algorithm that takes 1^k as input, and outputs a public parameter pp; KG is the key generation algorithm that takes pp as input, and outputs a verification/signing key pair (vk, sk); Sign is the signing algorithm that takes pp, sk, and a message m as input, and outputs a signature σ; Ver is the verification algorithm that takes pp, vk, m, and σ as input, and outputs either $\top$ ("accept") or $\bot$ ("reject").

We require for all $k \in \mathbb{N}$, all pp output by Setup(1^k), all (vk, sk) output by KG(pp), and all messages m, we have Ver$(pp, vk, m, \mathsf{Sign}(pp, sk, m)) = \top$.

Simple Key Generation Process. Here we formalize what we call the *simple key generation process* property, which says that the key generation algorithm KG first picks a secret key sk uniformly at random from the secret key space, and then computes the corresponding verification key vk deterministically from sk.[2]

Definition 4. *Let $\Sigma = $ (Setup, KG, Sign, Ver) be a signature scheme. We say that Σ has a* simple key generation process *if each pp output by Setup specifies a secret key space $\mathcal{K}_{pp}$, and there exists a deterministic PTA KG$'$ such that the key generation algorithm KG(pp) can be written as follows:*

$$\mathsf{KG}(pp) : [sk \leftarrow_{\mathsf{R}} \mathcal{K}_{pp}; \ vk \leftarrow \mathsf{KG}'(pp, sk); \ \text{Return } (vk, sk).]. \tag{1}$$

Homomorphic Properties. Here, we review the homomorphic properties regarding keys (and signatures) of a signature scheme used by Takahashi et al. [15]. We also define a weaker version (which we simply call the *weak homomorphic* property) that only requires the first two requirements out of the three, which is sufficient for our security proof in Sect. 6 to go through.

Definition 5. *Let $\Sigma = $ (Setup, KG, Sign, Ver) be a signature scheme with a simple key generation process (i.e. there is a deterministic PTA KG$'$ in Definition 4). We say that Σ is* homomorphic *if it satisfies the following three properties:*

1. *For all parameters pp output by Setup, the signing key space $\mathcal{K}_{pp}$ constitutes an abelian group $(\mathcal{K}_{pp}, +)$.*
2. *There exists a deterministic PTA M_{vk} that takes a public parameter pp (output by Setup), a verification key vk (output by KG(pp)), and a "shift" $\Delta sk \in \mathcal{K}_{pp}$ as input, and outputs the "shifted" verification key vk'.*
   We require for all pp output by Setup and all $sk, \Delta sk \in \mathcal{K}_{pp}$, it holds that

$$\mathsf{KG}'(pp, sk + \Delta sk) = \mathsf{M}_{vk}(pp, \mathsf{KG}'(pp, sk), \Delta sk). \tag{2}$$

---

[2] Takahashi et al. [15] defined this property as part of the homomorphic property (Definition 5). We separate it for our convenience.

3. *There exists a deterministic PTA* $\mathsf{M_{sig}}$ *that takes a public parameter pp (output by* Setup*), a verification key vk (output by* $\mathsf{KG}(pp)$*), a message m, a signature* σ*, and a "shift"* $\Delta sk \in \mathcal{K}_{pp}$ *as input, and outputs a "shifted" signature* σ'*. We require for all pp output by* Setup*, all messages m, and all* $sk, \Delta sk \in \mathcal{K}_{pp}$*, the following two distributions are identical:*

$$\{\sigma' \leftarrow_R \mathsf{Sign}(pp, sk + \Delta sk, m) : \sigma'\}, \quad and$$

$$\{\sigma \leftarrow_R \mathsf{Sign}(pp, sk, m); \ \sigma' \leftarrow \mathsf{M_{sig}}(pp, \mathsf{KG}'(pp, sk), m, \sigma, \Delta sk) : \sigma'\}. \quad (3)$$

Furthermore, we require that for all pp output by Setup*, all* $sk, \Delta sk \in \mathcal{K}_{pp}$*, and all* (m, σ) *satisfying* $\mathsf{Ver}(pp, \mathsf{KG}'(pp, sk), m, \sigma) = \top$*, it holds that*

$$\mathsf{Ver}(pp, \mathsf{KG}'(pp, sk + \Delta sk), m, \mathsf{M_{sig}}(pp, \mathsf{KG}'(pp, sk), m, \sigma, \Delta sk)) = \top. \quad (4)$$

If Σ *satisfies only the first two properties, then we say that* Σ *is* weakly homomorphic.

Schnorr Signature Scheme. Our concrete instantiation of a fuzzy signature scheme is based on the Schnorr signature scheme [14] and thus we review it here. Let GGen be a "group generator" that takes 1^k as input and outputs the description $\mathcal{G} = (\mathbb{G}, p, g)$ of a cyclic group $\mathbb{G} = \langle g \rangle$ with prime order $p = \Theta(2^k)$. Using the group generator GGen as a building block, the Schnorr signature scheme $\Sigma_{\mathsf{Sch}} = (\mathsf{Setup_{Sch}}, \mathsf{KG_{Sch}}, \mathsf{Sign_{Sch}}, \mathsf{Ver_{Sch}})$ is constructed as in Fig. 1.

It was shown by Pointcheval and Stern [12] that the Schnorr scheme is EUF-CMA secure in the random oracle model where H is modeled as a random oracle, under the DL assumption (which requires that given $\mathcal{G} = (\mathbb{G}, p, g)$ and g^x for a randomly chosen $x \in \mathbb{Z}_p$, it is hard to compute x). Furthermore, it should be clear from the relation between a signing key sk and the corresponding verification key $vk = g^{sk}$ that the Schnorr scheme admits a simple key generation process $\mathsf{KG}'(sk) = vk$ with the signing key space $\mathbb{Z}_p$, and furthermore given y and a "shift" Δsk, we can obtain a "shifted" verification key $vk' = \mathsf{KG}'(sk + \Delta sk) := (vk) \cdot g^{\Delta x}$, which results in $g^{sk} \cdot g^{\Delta sk} = g^{sk + \Delta sk} = \mathsf{KG}'(sk + \Delta sk)$. Hence, the following lemma holds:

Lemma 2. *The Schnorr signature scheme* Σ_{Sch} *(in Fig. 1) satisfies the weak homomorphic property in the sense of Definition 5.*

$\mathsf{Setup_{Sch}}(1^k)$:	$\mathsf{Sign_{Sch}}(pp, sk, m)$:	$\mathsf{Ver_{Sch}}(pp, vk, m, \sigma)$:
$\quad \mathcal{G} := (\mathbb{G}, p, g) \leftarrow \mathsf{GGen}(1^k)$	$\quad x \leftarrow sk$	$\quad y \leftarrow vk$
$\quad$ Let $H : \{0,1\}^* \rightarrow \mathbb{Z}_p$	$\quad r \leftarrow_R \mathbb{Z}_p$	$\quad (h, s) \leftarrow \sigma$
$\quad\quad$ be a hash function.	$\quad R \leftarrow g^r$	$\quad R \leftarrow g^s \cdot y^{-h}$
$\quad$ Return $pp \leftarrow (\mathcal{G}, H)$.	$\quad h \leftarrow H(R\|m)$	$\quad$ If $H(R\|m) = h$ then
$\mathsf{KG_{Sch}}(pp)$:	$\quad s \leftarrow r + x \cdot h \bmod p$	$\quad\quad$ return $\top$ else return $\bot$.
$\quad x \leftarrow_R \mathbb{Z}_p; \quad y \leftarrow g^x$	$\quad$ Return $\sigma \leftarrow (h, s)$.	
$\quad$ Return $(vk, sk) \leftarrow (y, x)$.		

Fig. 1. The Schnorr signature scheme Σ_{Sch}.

3.2   A Variant of Related Key Attacks Security

RKA* *Security.* Here, we introduce an extension of EUF-CMA security for signature schemes, which we call RKA* security[3], that considers security against an adversary who may mount a kind of related-key attacks (RKA). Like the popular definition of RKA security for signature schemes by Bellare et al. [1], RKA* is defined with respect to a class of functions that captures an adversary's ability to modify signing keys. Our definition, however, has subtle differences from the definition of [1]. The main difference is that in our definition, an adversary is allowed to modify the verification key under which its forgery is verified, while we do not allow an adversary to use a message as its forgery if it is already signed by the signing oracle.

Formally, let $\Sigma = (\mathsf{Setup}, \mathsf{KG}, \mathsf{Sign}, \mathsf{Ver})$ be a signature scheme with a simple key generation process, namely, there exists a deterministic PTA KG' such that KG can be written as Eq. (1). Let Φ be a class of functions both of whose domain and the range are the signing key space of Σ. For Σ, Φ, and an adversary $\mathcal{A}$, consider the following Φ-RKA* experiment $\mathsf{Expt}_{\Sigma,\mathcal{A}}^{\Phi\text{-}\mathrm{RKA}^*}(k)$:

$$\mathsf{Expt}_{\Sigma,\mathcal{A}}^{\Phi\text{-}\mathrm{RKA}^*}(k) : [\ pp \leftarrow_{\mathrm{R}} \mathsf{Setup}(1^k); \ (vk, sk) \leftarrow_{\mathrm{R}} \mathsf{KG}(pp);$$

$$\mathcal{Q} \leftarrow \emptyset; \ (\phi', m', \sigma') \leftarrow_{\mathrm{R}} \mathcal{A}^{\mathcal{O}_{\mathsf{Sign}}(\cdot,\cdot)}(pp, vk); \ vk' \leftarrow \mathsf{KG}'(pp, \phi'(sk));$$

$$\text{If } \phi' \in \Phi \wedge m' \notin \mathcal{Q} \wedge \mathsf{Ver}(pp, vk', m', \sigma') = \top \text{ then return 1 else return 0}],$$

where $\mathcal{O}_{\mathsf{Sign}}$ is the signing oracle which takes (the description of) a function $\phi \in \Phi$ and a message m as input, updates the "used message list" $\mathcal{Q}$ by $\mathcal{Q} \leftarrow \mathcal{Q} \cup \{m\}$, and returns a signature $\sigma \leftarrow_{\mathrm{R}} \mathsf{Sign}(pp, \phi(sk), m)$.

Definition 6. *We say that a signature scheme Σ is Φ-RKA* secure if for all PPTA adversaries $\mathcal{A}$, $\mathsf{Adv}_{\Sigma,\mathcal{A}}^{\Phi\text{-}\mathrm{RKA}^*}(k) := \Pr[\mathsf{Expt}_{\Sigma,\mathcal{A}}^{\Phi\text{-}\mathrm{RKA}^*}(k) = 1]$ is negligible.*

Note that if we consider Φ to be consisting only of the identity function, then we recover the standard EUF-CMA security for a signature scheme.

The Class of Functions. In this paper, we will treat RKA* security with respect to addition, which is captured by the following functions (where $\mathcal{K}$ denotes the signing key space of a signature scheme that we assume constitutes an abelian group):

Addition: $\Phi^{\mathrm{add}} := \{\phi_a^{\mathrm{add}} | a \in \mathcal{K}\}$, where $\phi_a^{\mathrm{add}}(x) = x + a$.

Sufficient Conditions for Φ^{add}-RKA Security.* It turns out that any EUF-CMA secure signature scheme (with a simple key generation process) that satisfies the three requirements of the homomorphic property (Definition 5) is automatically Φ^{add}-RKA* secure, and hence these are sufficient conditions for Φ^{add}-RKA* security. (Due to the space limitation, we provide its proof in the full version.)

---

[3] The asterisk (*) indicates that the notion is different from that of Bellare et al. [1].

Theorem 1. *Any* EUF-CMA *secure signature scheme (with a simple key generation process) satisfying the homomorphic property (Definition 5) is Φ^{add}-RKA* secure.*

Φ^{add}-RKA* *Security of the Schnorr Signature Scheme.* As we mentioned in the previous subsection, the Schnorr signature scheme Σ_{Sch} admits a simple key generation process, and is weakly homomorphic, where its signing key space is the abelian group $(\mathbb{Z}_p, +)$. The following theorem formally states that the Schnorr signature scheme satisfies Φ^{add}-RKA* security. The proof can be shown very similarly to the proof of the EUF-CMA security of the Schnorr scheme using the general forking lemma of Bellare and Neven [2], and its Φ^{add}-weak-RKA security shown in [10]. We provide its proof in the full version.

Theorem 2. *If the DL assumption holds with respect to* GGen, *then the Schnorr signature scheme Σ_{Sch} (in Fig. 1) is Φ^{add}-RKA* secure in the random oracle model where H is modeled as a random oracle.*

4   Definitions for Fuzzy Signatures

In this section, we recall the definitions of a fuzzy key setting (Sect. 4.1) and a fuzzy signature scheme (Sect. 4.2), both of which are from [15].

4.1   Formalization of Fuzzy Key Setting

A fuzzy key setting specifies a metric space to which fuzzy data (such as biometric data) belongs, the threshold with which two sampled fuzzy data are considered close/far, the distribution from which each fuzzy data is assumed to be sampled, and the error distribution that models "fluctuation" of fuzzy data. The false acceptance rate (FAR) and the false rejection rate (FRR), are also defined. The formalization of [15] adopts the so-called *universal error model*, which assumes that for all objects U that produce fuzzy data that we are interested in, if U produces a data x at the first measurement (e.g. at the registration), and the same object is measured next time, then the measured data x' follows the distribution $\{e \leftarrow_{\mathsf{R}} \Phi;\ x' \leftarrow x + e : x'\}$. (That is, Φ is the same, regardless of individual U.)

Formally, a fuzzy key setting $\mathcal{F}$ consists of $((\mathsf{d}, X), t, \mathcal{X}, \Phi, \epsilon)$, each of which is defined as follows:

(d, X): This is a metric space, where X is a space to which a possible fuzzy data x belongs, and $\mathsf{d} : X^2 \to \mathbb{R}$ is the corresponding distance function. We furthermore assume that X constitutes an abelian group.

t: $(\in \mathbb{R})$ This is the threshold value, determined by a security parameter k. Based on t, the false acceptance rate (FAR) and the false rejection rate (FRR) are determined. We require that $\mathtt{FAR} := \Pr[x, x' \leftarrow_{\mathsf{R}} \mathcal{X} : \mathsf{d}(x, x') < t]$ is negligible in k.

$\mathcal{X}$: This is a distribution of fuzzy data over X.

Φ: This is an error distribution (see the above explanation).

ϵ: $(\in [0, 1])$ This is an error parameter that represents FRR. We require that for all $x \in X$, $\mathtt{FRR} := \Pr[e \leftarrow_{\mathsf{R}} \Phi : \mathsf{d}(x, x + e) \geq t] \leq \epsilon$.

4.2 Fuzzy Signature

A fuzzy signature scheme Σ_{FS} for a fuzzy key setting $\mathcal{F} = ((\mathsf{d}, X), t, \mathcal{X}, \Phi, \epsilon)$ consists of the four algorithms $(\mathsf{Setup}_{\mathsf{FS}}, \mathsf{KG}_{\mathsf{FS}}, \mathsf{Sign}_{\mathsf{FS}}, \mathsf{Ver}_{\mathsf{FS}})$:

$\mathsf{Setup}_{\mathsf{FS}}$: This is the setup algorithm that takes the description of the fuzzy key setting $\mathcal{F}$ and 1^k as input (where k determines the threshold value t of $\mathcal{F}$), and outputs a public parameter pp.

$\mathsf{KG}_{\mathsf{FS}}$: This is the key generation algorithm that takes pp and a fuzzy data $x \in X$ as input, and outputs a verification key vk.

$\mathsf{Sign}_{\mathsf{FS}}$: This is the signing algorithm that takes pp, a fuzzy data $x' \in X$, and a message m as input, and outputs a signature σ.

$\mathsf{Ver}_{\mathsf{FS}}$: This is the (deterministic) verification algorithm that takes pp, vk, m, and σ as input, and outputs either $\top$ ("accept") or $\bot$ ("reject").

Correctness. We require that for all $k \in \mathbb{N}$, all pp output by $\mathsf{Setup}_{\mathsf{FS}}(\mathcal{F}, 1^k)$, all $x, x' \in X$ such that $\mathsf{d}(x, x') < t$, and all messages m, it holds that $\mathsf{Ver}_{\mathsf{FS}}(pp, \mathsf{KG}_{\mathsf{FS}}(pp, x), m, \mathsf{Sign}_{\mathsf{FS}}(pp, x', m)) = \top$.

EUF–CMA *Security.* EUF–CMA security of a fuzzy signature scheme is defined in a similar manner to that of an ordinary signature scheme, reflecting the universal error model of a fuzzy key setting.

For a fuzzy signature scheme Σ_{FS} for a fuzzy key setting $\mathcal{F} = ((\mathsf{d}, X), t, \mathcal{X}, \Phi, \epsilon)$ and an adversary $\mathcal{A}$, consider the following experiment $\mathsf{Expt}_{\Sigma_{\mathsf{FS}}, \mathcal{F}, \mathcal{A}}^{\mathrm{EUF\text{-}CMA}}(k)$:

$$\mathsf{Expt}_{\Sigma_{\mathsf{FS}}, \mathcal{F}, \mathcal{A}}^{\mathrm{EUF\text{-}CMA}}(k) : [\ pp \leftarrow_{\mathsf{R}} \mathsf{Setup}_{\mathsf{FS}}(\mathcal{F}, 1^k);\ x \leftarrow_{\mathsf{R}} \mathcal{X};\ vk \leftarrow_{\mathsf{R}} \mathsf{KG}_{\mathsf{FS}}(pp, x);$$

$$\mathcal{Q} \leftarrow \emptyset;\ (m', \sigma') \leftarrow_{\mathsf{R}} \mathcal{A}^{\mathcal{O}_{\mathsf{Sign}_{\mathsf{FS}}}(\cdot)}(pp, vk) :$$

$$\text{If } m' \notin \mathcal{Q} \wedge \mathsf{Ver}_{\mathsf{FS}}(pp, vk, m', \sigma') = \top \text{ then return 1 else return 0}],$$

where $\mathcal{O}_{\mathsf{Sign}_{\mathsf{FS}}}$ is the signing oracle that takes a message m as input, and operates as follows: It updates $\mathcal{Q}$ by $\mathcal{Q} \leftarrow \mathcal{Q} \cup \{m\}$, samples $e \leftarrow_{\mathsf{R}} \Phi$, computes a signature $\sigma \leftarrow_{\mathsf{R}} \mathsf{Sign}_{\mathsf{FS}}(pp, x + e, m)$, and returns σ.

Definition 7. *We say that a fuzzy signature scheme Σ_{FS} is* EUF–CMA *secure if for all PPTA adversaries $\mathcal{A}$,* $\mathsf{Adv}_{\Sigma_{\mathsf{FS}}, \mathcal{F}, \mathcal{A}}^{\mathrm{EUF\text{-}CMA}}(k) := \Pr[\mathsf{Expt}_{\Sigma_{\mathsf{FS}}, \mathcal{F}, \mathcal{A}}^{\mathrm{EUF\text{-}CMA}}(k) = 1]$ *is negligible.*

5 Linear Sketch

In this section, we introduce our new definitions for the primitive called *linear sketch* that was first formalized by Takahashi et al. [15], which plays an important role in the generic construction in [15]. We then propose a new construction of a linear sketch for a concrete fuzzy key setting in which the distribution of fuzzy data has high average min-entropy (in the presence of leakage).

On the Treatment of Real Numbers. Below, we use real numbers to represent and process fuzzy data. We assume that a suitable representation with sufficient accuracy is chosen to encode the real numbers whenever they need to be treated by the algorithms considered below. (If an algorithm takes a real number as input, its running time is with respect to the encoded version of the input.)

5.1   Our Relaxed Definition

Informally speaking, a linear sketch is associated with a fuzzy key setting and an abelian group $(\mathcal{K}, +)$, and consists of two algorithms: "Sketch" and "DiffRec" whose functionalities are explained shortly. It was also required in [15] that a linear sketch scheme satisfies additional "linearity" and "simulatability" properties that are used in the security proof for the generic construction of a fuzzy signature scheme in [15].

We introduce four relaxations to the original definition in [15]: **(1)** We introduce a setup algorithm that produces a public parameter, which is used by the two main algorithms Sketch and DiffRec, and also by the auxiliary algorithm M_c that is used for defining "linearity"; **(2)** We allow the sketching algorithm Sketch, and the auxiliary algorithm M_c, to be probabilistic (as opposed to defining them as deterministic algorithms in [15]); **(3)** We relax the linearity property to some weaker "distributional" variant, while in [15] it was defined like correctness that needs to be satisfied without any failure; **(4)** We relax the simulatability property, which captures confidentiality of sketches produced by Sketch, to a weaker variant that we call "average-case indistinguishability".

Formally, our definition of a linear sketch scheme is as follows:

Definition 8. *Let $\mathcal{F} = ((\mathsf{d}, X), t, \mathcal{X}, \varPhi, \epsilon)$ be a fuzzy key setting. We say that a tuple of PPTAs $\mathcal{S} = (\mathsf{Setup}, \mathsf{Sketch}, \mathsf{DiffRec})$ is a* linear sketch *scheme for $\mathcal{F}$, if it satisfies the following three properties:*

Syntax and Correctness: *Each algorithm of $\mathcal{S}$ has the following interface:*
  - Setup *is the "setup" algorithm that takes the description $\varLambda$ of an abelian group $(\mathcal{K}, +)$ as input, and outputs a public parameter pp (which we assume contains the information of $\varLambda$).*
  - Sketch *is the "sketching" algorithm that takes pp, an element $s \in \mathcal{K}$, and a fuzzy data $x \in X$ as input, and outputs a "sketch" c.*
  - DiffRec *is the (deterministic) "difference reconstruction" algorithm that takes pp and two values c, c' (supposedly output by Sketch) as input, and outputs the "difference" $\Delta s \in \mathcal{K}$.*

  We require that for all $x, x' \in X$ such that $\mathsf{d}(x, x') < t$, all (descriptions of) abelian groups $\varLambda = (\mathcal{K}, +)$, all pp output by $\mathsf{Setup}(\varLambda)$, and all $s, \Delta s \in \mathcal{K}$, it holds that $\mathsf{DiffRec}(pp, \mathsf{Sketch}(pp, s, x), \mathsf{Sketch}(pp, s + \Delta s, x')) = \Delta s$.

Linearity: *There exists a PPTA M_c satisfying the following: For all abelian groups $\varLambda = (\mathcal{K}, +)$, all pp output by $\mathsf{Setup}(\varLambda)$, all $x, e \in X$ such that $\mathsf{d}(x, x + e) < t$, and for all $s, \Delta s \in \mathcal{K}$, the following two distributions are statistically indistinguishable (in the security parameter k that is associated with t in $\mathcal{F}$):*

$$\{c \leftarrow_\mathsf{R} \mathsf{Sketch}(pp, s, x); \ c' \leftarrow_\mathsf{R} \mathsf{Sketch}(pp, s + \Delta s, x + e) : (c, c')\}, \quad and$$
$$\{c \leftarrow_\mathsf{R} \mathsf{Sketch}(pp, s, x); \ c' \leftarrow_\mathsf{R} M_c(pp, c, \Delta s, e) : (c, c')\} \tag{5}$$

Average-Case Indistinguishability: *For all abelian groups $\varLambda = (\mathcal{K}, +)$, the following two distributions are statistically indistinguishable (in the security parameter k that is associated with t in $\mathcal{F}$):*

$$\{pp \leftarrow_R \mathsf{Setup}(\Lambda); \ x \leftarrow_R \mathcal{X}; \ s \leftarrow_R \mathcal{K}; \ c \leftarrow_R \mathsf{Sketch}(pp,s,x) : (pp,s,c)\}, \ \ and$$
$$\{pp \leftarrow_R \mathsf{Setup}(\Lambda); \ x \leftarrow_R \mathcal{X}; \ s,s' \leftarrow_R \mathcal{K}; \ c \leftarrow_R \mathsf{Sketch}(pp,s,x) : (pp,s',c)\}$$
$$\tag{6}$$

Here are a couple of remarks:

- The word "average-case" of average-case indistinguishability is due to the property that its definition guarantees that the element s in a sketch c is hidden only when it is chosen randomly from $\mathcal{K}$.
- As mentioned just above Definition 8, our definition is obtained by relaxing the definition in [15] in several regards. (In the full version, we provide the original definitions for a linear sketch given in [15] for a comparison.) In particular, we can cast any linear sketch that satisfies the definition in [15] by defining the public parameter pp to be the description of an abelian group Λ itself: Then, the linearity property (resp. simulatability) in the sense of [15] implies the linearity property (resp. average-case indistinguishability) in our definition.

5.2 Our New Construction

Here, we propose a new construction of a linear sketch scheme for a concrete fuzzy key setting. We first specify the fuzzy key setting with which our scheme is associated, and then give our construction.

Specific Fuzzy Key Setting. Here, we specify a concrete fuzzy key setting $\mathcal{F} = ((\mathsf{d}, X), t, \mathcal{X}, \Phi, \epsilon)$ for which our linear sketch scheme and our Schnorr-based fuzzy signature scheme are constructed.

Metric space (d, X): The space X is defined by $X := [0,1)^n \subset \mathbb{R}^n$, where $n \in \mathbb{N}$ is a parameter specified by the context (e.g. an object from which we measure fuzzy data) and a security parameter k. The distance function $\mathsf{d} : X \times X \to \mathbb{R}$ is the L_∞-norm. Namely, for $\boldsymbol{x} = (x_1, \ldots, x_n) \in X$ and $\boldsymbol{x}' = (x'_1, \ldots, x'_n) \in X$, we define $\mathsf{d}(\boldsymbol{x}, \boldsymbol{x}') := \|\boldsymbol{x} - \boldsymbol{x}'\|_\infty := \max_{i \in [n]} |x_i - x'_i|$. Note that X forms an abelian group with respect to coordinate-wise addition (modulo 1).

Threshold t: For a security parameter k, we require the threshold $t \in \mathbb{R}$, where $(1/(2t)) \in \mathbb{N}$, to satisfy

$$k \le \lfloor -n \log_2(2t) \rfloor. \tag{7}$$

Distribution $\mathcal{X}$: An efficiently samplable distribution over X that satisfies the assumption on the average min-entropy that we state later.

Error distribution Φ **and Error parameter** ϵ: Φ is any efficiently samplable (according to k) distribution over X such that $\mathsf{FRR} \le \epsilon$ for all $x \in X$.

Other than the requirement on $\mathcal{X}$, the above specification of the fuzzy key setting is essentially the same as the one used in [15].[4] Takahashi et al. required $\mathcal{X}$

---

[4] Actually, [15] set the security parameter k to be exactly $\lfloor -n \log_2(2t) \rfloor$. However, we need more strict threshold for t, so that we can use the leftover hash lemma in the proof of Theorem 3 (given in the full version).

to be the uniform distribution. However, this is a somewhat strong requirement, and may not be suitable for potential applications of fuzzy signature schemes. In this work, we succeed in relaxing the requirement on $\mathcal{X}$, from the uniform distribution to a distribution with sufficiently high average min-entropy.

More specifically, let $\mathcal{X}'$ be the "scaled-up" version of $\mathcal{X}$, namely, $\mathcal{X}'$ is the distribution obtained by multiplying the integer $1/(2t) \in \mathbb{N}$ to the outcome of the distribution $\mathcal{X}$. Since $\mathcal{X}$ is a distribution over $[0,1)^n$, $\mathcal{X}'$ is a distribution over $[0,1/(2t))^n$. Now, let us divide $\mathcal{X}'$ into the "integer" part $\mathcal{X}'_{in}$ and the "decimal" part $\mathcal{X}'_{de}$. Namely, let $\boldsymbol{x}' = (x'_1, \ldots, x'_n)$ be a vector produced from $\mathcal{X}'$. Then, $\mathcal{X}'_{in}$ is the distribution of the n-dimensional vector whose i-th element is the integer part of x'_i. Similarly, $\mathcal{X}'_{de}$ is the distribution of the n-dimensional vector whose i-th element is the decimal part of x'_i. Note that the joint distribution $(\mathcal{X}'_{in}, \mathcal{X}'_{de})$ contains the same information as $\mathcal{X}'$ (and hence as $\mathcal{X}$).

The requirement we impose on the distribution $\mathcal{X}$ of fuzzy data, is that we have $\widetilde{\mathbf{H}}_\infty(\mathcal{X}'_{in}|\mathcal{X}'_{de}) \geq \log p + \omega(\log k)$, where p is the order of the field over which we consider the universal hash $\mathcal{H}_{lin}$. (We note that $\widetilde{\mathbf{H}}_\infty(\mathcal{X}'_{in}|\mathcal{X}'_{de}) = \widetilde{\mathbf{H}}_\infty(\mathcal{X}'|\mathcal{X}'_{de}) = \widetilde{\mathbf{H}}_\infty(\mathcal{X}|\mathcal{X}'_{de})$. Furthermore, since p will also be the order of the group over which the Schnorr scheme is constructed, we typically set $p = \Theta(2^k)$, equivalently $\log p = \Theta(k)$.) We would like to emphasize that this requirement is arguably much more relaxed than requiring that $\mathcal{X}$ is the uniform distribution over X (which was done in [15]). We discuss the plausibility of this requirement later in Sect. 8.

Our Construction. Let $\mathcal{F} = ((\mathsf{d}, X), t, \mathcal{X}, \Phi, \epsilon)$ be the fuzzy key setting as defined above. Let $\mathbb{F}_p$ be a finite field with prime order p satisfying $p \geq 1/(2t)$. Here, we identify $\mathbb{F}_p$ with $\mathbb{Z}_p$, and thus we freely interpret an element in the former set as an element in the latter set, and vice versa. Let $\mathcal{H}_{lin} = \{ h_z : (\mathbb{F}_p)^n \to \mathbb{F}_p \}_{z \in \mathbb{F}_{p^n}}$ be the universal hash function family with linearity that we reviewed in Sect. 2. For each $z \in \mathbb{F}_{p^n}$ and $s \in \mathbb{F}_p$, we define "$h_z^{-1}(s)$" as the set of preimages of s under h_z. That is, $h_z^{-1}(s) := \{\boldsymbol{\alpha} \in (\mathbb{F}_p)^n | h_z(\boldsymbol{\alpha}) = s\}$. Hence, the notation "$\boldsymbol{\alpha} \leftarrow_{\mathsf{R}} h_z^{-1}(s)$" means that we choose a vector $\boldsymbol{\alpha}$ uniformly from the set $h_z^{-1}(s)$ (which can be performed in time polynomial of $n \cdot \log_2(p)$). Furthermore, for notational convenience, let $T := 1/(2t) \in \mathbb{N}$.

Then, using these, our linear sketch scheme $\mathcal{S} = (\mathsf{Setup}, \mathsf{Sketch}, \mathsf{DiffRec})$ for $\mathcal{F}$ and the additive group $(\mathbb{Z}_p, +)$ $(=: \Lambda)$ is constructed as described in Fig. 2 (left), where we also give a description of the auxiliary algorithm $\mathsf{M_c}$ for convenience. The output space of Sketch is $(\mathbb{R}_p)^n$, where $\mathbb{R}_p := \mathbb{R}/p\mathbb{R}$.

The following guarantees that our construction satisfies all the requirements.

Theorem 3. *The linear sketch scheme $\mathcal{S}$ in Fig. 2 (left) for the fuzzy key setting $\mathcal{F}$ that we specified above, satisfies all the properties of Definition 8.*

Due to the space limitation, we provide the formal proof in the full version. Roughly speaking, the correctness follows from the linearity of the universal hash family $\mathcal{H}_{lin}$ and a simple algebra; The linearity property of $\mathcal{S}$ follows from

Setup($\Lambda = (\mathbb{Z}_p, +)$) :
    $z \leftarrow_R \mathbb{F}_{p^n}$; $pp \leftarrow (\Lambda, z)$
    Return pp.
Sketch($pp, s, \boldsymbol{x}$) : (where $s \in \mathbb{Z}_p$ and $\boldsymbol{x} \in [0, 1)^n$)
    $\boldsymbol{\alpha} \leftarrow_R h_z^{-1}(s)$; $\boldsymbol{c} \leftarrow \boldsymbol{\alpha} + T \cdot \boldsymbol{x}$ [†]
    Return $\boldsymbol{c} \in (\mathbb{R}_p)^n$.
DiffRec($pp, \boldsymbol{c}, \boldsymbol{c}'$) :
    $\Delta \boldsymbol{c} \leftarrow \boldsymbol{c}' - \boldsymbol{c}$ [†]; $\Delta s \leftarrow h_z(\lfloor \Delta \boldsymbol{c} \rceil)$
    Return $\Delta s \in \mathbb{F}_p$.

$\mathsf{M}_c(pp, \boldsymbol{c}, \Delta s, \boldsymbol{e})$:
    $\Delta \boldsymbol{\alpha} \leftarrow_R h_z^{-1}(\Delta s)$
    $\boldsymbol{c}' \leftarrow (\boldsymbol{c} + \Delta \boldsymbol{\alpha} + T \cdot \boldsymbol{e})$ [†]
    Return $\boldsymbol{c}' \in (\mathbb{R}_p)^n$.

Fig. 2. Our proposed linear sketch scheme $\mathcal{S} = (\mathsf{Setup}, \mathsf{Sketch}, \mathsf{DiffRec})$ for the fuzzy key setting $\mathcal{F}$ (left), and the auxiliary algorithm M_c for showing the linearity property (right). [†] The operation "+" (resp. "−") in $(\mathbb{R}_p)^n$ are the coordinate-wise addition (resp. subtraction) in $\mathbb{R}_p$.

the linearity of $\mathcal{H}_{lin}$ and the simple observation that $\{\boldsymbol{\alpha} \leftarrow_R h_z^{-1}(s); \Delta \boldsymbol{\alpha} \leftarrow_R h_z^{-1}(\Delta s) : \boldsymbol{\alpha} + \Delta \boldsymbol{\alpha}\}$ yields the uniform distribution over the set $h_z^{-1}(s + \Delta s)$ for any $z \in \mathbb{F}_{p^n}$ and $s, \Delta s \in \mathbb{F}_p$; The high-level ideas for the proof for the average-case indistinguishability are as follows: Note that the distribution $D = \{z \leftarrow_R \mathbb{F}_{p^n}; \boldsymbol{x} \leftarrow_R \mathcal{X}; s \leftarrow_R \mathbb{F}_p; \boldsymbol{\alpha} \leftarrow_R h_z^{-1}(s); \boldsymbol{c} \leftarrow \boldsymbol{\alpha} + T \cdot \boldsymbol{x} : (z, s, \boldsymbol{c})\}$, which corresponds to the first distribution in Eq. (6), is equivalent to $D' = \{z \leftarrow_R \mathbb{F}_{p^n}; \boldsymbol{x} \leftarrow_R \mathcal{X}; \boldsymbol{\alpha} \leftarrow_R (\mathbb{F}_p)^n; \boldsymbol{c} \leftarrow \boldsymbol{\alpha} + T \cdot \boldsymbol{x} : (z, s = h_z(\boldsymbol{\alpha}), \boldsymbol{c})\}$. Now, define the joint distribution $(A, C) := \{\boldsymbol{x} \leftarrow_R \mathcal{X}; \boldsymbol{\alpha} \leftarrow_R (\mathbb{F}_p)^n; \boldsymbol{c} \leftarrow \boldsymbol{\alpha} + T \cdot \boldsymbol{x} : (\boldsymbol{\alpha}, \boldsymbol{c})\}$. In the full proof, we show that $\widetilde{\mathbf{H}}_\infty(A|C) = \widetilde{\mathbf{H}}_\infty(\mathcal{X}'_{in} | \mathcal{X}'_{de})$. This, together with our requirement on $\mathcal{X}$, allows us to invoke the leftover hash lemma to conclude that D' is statistically close to some distribution D''. We will then show that this D'' is equivalent to the distribution corresponding to the second one in Eq. (6).

6   Generic Construction and Our New Security Proof

In this section, we revisit the generic construction for a fuzzy signature scheme by Takahashi et al. [15], which uses a linear sketch and a signature scheme as building blocks, and show its new security proof.

The Generic Construction by Takahashi et al. [15]. Let $\mathcal{F} = ((d, X), t, \mathcal{X}, \Phi, \epsilon)$ be a fuzzy key setting, and let $\mathcal{S} = (\mathsf{Setup}_l, \mathsf{Sketch}, \mathsf{DiffRec})$ be a linear sketch for $\mathcal{F}$. Let $\Sigma = (\mathsf{Setup}_s, \mathsf{KG}, \mathsf{Sign}, \mathsf{Ver})$ be a signature scheme with a simple key generation process (i.e. there exists a deterministic PTA KG'). We assume that Σ is weakly homomorphic (as per Definition 5), namely, its signing key space (given pp) is an abelian group $(\mathcal{K}_{pp}, +)$, and has the additional algorithm M_{vk}. Using $\mathcal{S}$ and Σ, the generic construction of a fuzzy signature scheme $\Sigma_{FS} = (\mathsf{Setup}_{FS}, \mathsf{KG}_{FS}, \mathsf{Sign}_{FS}, \mathsf{Ver}_{FS})$ for the fuzzy key setting $\mathcal{F}$, originally proposed by Takahashi et al. [15], is constructed as in Fig. 3.

$\mathsf{Setup}_{\mathsf{FS}}(\mathcal{F}, 1^k):$	$\mathsf{Sign}_{\mathsf{FS}}(pp, x', m):$	$\mathsf{Ver}_{\mathsf{FS}}(pp, VK, m, \sigma):$
$pp_s \leftarrow_{\mathsf{R}} \mathsf{Setup}_s(1^k)$	$(pp_s, pp_l) \leftarrow pp$	$(pp_s, pp_l) \leftarrow pp$
Let $\Lambda := (\mathcal{K}_{pp_s}, +).$	$\widetilde{sk} \leftarrow_{\mathsf{R}} \mathcal{K}_{pp_s}$	$(vk, c) \leftarrow VK$
$pp_l \leftarrow_{\mathsf{R}} \mathsf{Setup}_l(\Lambda)$	$\widetilde{vk} \leftarrow \mathsf{KG}'(pp_s, \widetilde{sk})$	$(\widetilde{vk}, \widetilde{\sigma}, \widetilde{c}) \leftarrow \sigma$
Return $pp \leftarrow (pp_s, pp_l).$	$\widetilde{\sigma} \leftarrow_{\mathsf{R}} \mathsf{Sign}(pp_s, \widetilde{sk}, m)$	If $\mathsf{Ver}(pp_s, \widetilde{vk}, m, \widetilde{\sigma}) = \bot$
$\mathsf{KG}_{\mathsf{FS}}(pp, x):$	$\widetilde{c} \leftarrow_{\mathsf{R}} \mathsf{Sketch}(pp_l, \widetilde{sk}, x')$	$\qquad$ then return $\bot$.
$(pp_s, pp_l) \leftarrow pp$	Return $\sigma \leftarrow (\widetilde{vk}, \widetilde{\sigma}, \widetilde{c}).$	$\Delta sk \leftarrow \mathsf{DiffRec}(pp_l, c, \widetilde{c})$
$sk \leftarrow_{\mathsf{R}} \mathcal{K}_{pp_s}$		If $\mathsf{M}_{\mathsf{vk}}(pp_s, vk, \Delta sk) = \widetilde{vk}$
$vk \leftarrow \mathsf{KG}'(pp_s, sk)$		$\qquad$ then return $\top$ else return $\bot$.
$c \leftarrow_{\mathsf{R}} \mathsf{Sketch}(pp_l, sk, x)$		
Return $VK \leftarrow (vk, c).$		

Fig. 3. The generic construction of a fuzzy signature scheme Σ_{FS} for a fuzzy key setting $\mathcal{F}$ by Takahashi et al. [15], which combines a linear sketch scheme $\mathcal{S}$ for $\mathcal{F}$ and a weakly homomorphic signature scheme Σ.

Our New Security Proof. Takahashi et al. [15] required that the underlying signature scheme Σ to be homomorphic (not just weak one) and EUF-CMA secure. Here, we show that if we can assume the Φ^{add}-RKA* security for Σ, then we only need to require it to satisfy the "weak homomorphic property" (which does not require the algorithm $\mathsf{M}_{\mathsf{sig}}$) in Definition 5. Our result is in fact a relaxation of the requirements in Takahashi et al.'s construction, because as we showed in Theorem 1, an EUF-CMA secure signature scheme that satisfies the homomorphic property is automatically Φ^{add}-RKA* secure, while a Φ^{add}-RKA* secure signature scheme is not necessarily homomorphic.

Theorem 4. *If Σ is weakly homomorphic and is Φ^{add}-RKA* secure, and $\mathcal{S}$ is a linear sketch scheme for $\mathcal{F}$ (in the sense of Definition 8), then the fuzzy signature scheme Σ_{FS} for $\mathcal{F}$ constructed as in Fig. 3 is EUF-CMA secure.*

Due to the space limitation, we give the formal proof in the full version. As mentioned earlier, our security proof follows very similarly to that of [15]. Our proof is via the sequence of games argument. We gradually change the original EUF-CMA security experiment for an adversary $\mathcal{A}$ against our construction of a fuzzy signature scheme by using the weakly homomorphic property of Σ, and the linearity property and average-case indistinguishability of $\mathcal{S}$, so that if $\mathcal{A}$ is still successful in the final game, we can use $\mathcal{A}$ to break the Φ^{add}-RKA* security of the underlying signature scheme Σ. The main difference from the security proof in [15] is that the Φ^{add}-RKA* security of Σ allows us to combine two of the games in the sequence of the games considered in the security proof in [15] in one step. For the details, see the proof in the full version.

7 Instantiation

Here, we show a concrete instantiation of a fuzzy signature scheme by using the Schnorr signature scheme (Fig. 1) and the linear sketch scheme proposed in Sect. 5.2 as the building blocks in the generic construction in Sect. 6.

$\mathsf{Setup}_{\mathsf{FS}}(\mathcal{F}, 1^k):$	$\underline{\mathsf{Sign}_{\mathsf{FS}}(pp, \boldsymbol{x}', m):}$	$\underline{\mathsf{Ver}_{\mathsf{FS}}(pp, VK, m, \sigma):}$
$\quad \mathcal{G} := (\mathbb{G}, p, g) \leftarrow \mathsf{GGen}(1^k)$	$\widetilde{sk} \leftarrow_{\mathrm{R}} \mathbb{Z}_p$	$(vk, \boldsymbol{c}) \leftarrow VK$
$\quad$ Let $H : \{0,1\}^* \to \mathbb{Z}_p$	$\widetilde{vk} \leftarrow g^{\widetilde{sk}}$	$(\widetilde{vk}, \widetilde{h}, \widetilde{s}, \widetilde{\boldsymbol{c}}) \leftarrow \sigma$
$\qquad$ be a hash function.	$r \leftarrow_{\mathrm{R}} \mathbb{Z}_p$	$R \leftarrow g^{\widetilde{s}} \cdot (vk)^{-\widetilde{h}}$
$\quad z \leftarrow_{\mathrm{R}} \mathbb{F}_{p^n}$	$R \leftarrow g^r$	If $H(R\|m) \neq \widetilde{h}$ then return $\perp$.
$\quad$ Return $pp \leftarrow (\mathcal{G}, z, H)$.	$\widetilde{h} \leftarrow H(R\|m)$	$\Delta \boldsymbol{c} \leftarrow \widetilde{\boldsymbol{c}} - \boldsymbol{c}$ [†]
$\underline{\mathsf{KG}_{\mathsf{FS}}(pp, \boldsymbol{x}):}$	$\widetilde{s} \leftarrow r + x \cdot \widetilde{h} \bmod p$	$\Delta sk \leftarrow h_s(\lfloor \Delta \boldsymbol{c} \rceil)$
$\quad sk \leftarrow_{\mathrm{R}} \mathbb{Z}_p$	$\boldsymbol{\alpha}' \leftarrow_{\mathrm{R}} h_z^{-1}(\widetilde{sk})$	If $vk \cdot g^{\Delta sk} = \widetilde{vk}$ then
$\quad vk \leftarrow g^{sk}$	$\widetilde{\boldsymbol{c}} \leftarrow \boldsymbol{\alpha}' + T \cdot \boldsymbol{x}'$ [†]	$\qquad$ return $\top$ else return $\perp$.
$\quad \boldsymbol{\alpha} \leftarrow_{\mathrm{R}} h_z^{-1}(sk)$	$\sigma \leftarrow (\widetilde{vk}, \widetilde{h}, \widetilde{s}, \widetilde{\boldsymbol{c}})$.	
$\quad \boldsymbol{c} \leftarrow \boldsymbol{\alpha} + T \cdot \boldsymbol{x}$ [†]	Return σ.	
$\quad$ Return $VK \leftarrow (vk, \boldsymbol{c})$.		

Fig. 4. The proposed Schnorr-based fuzzy signature scheme. [†] The operation "$+$" (resp. "$-$") in $(\mathbb{R}_p)^n$ are the coordinate-wise addition (resp. subtraction) in $\mathbb{R}_p$.

Let $\mathcal{F} = ((d, X), t, \mathcal{X}, \Phi, \epsilon)$ be the fuzzy key setting we specified in Sect. 5, and suppose the dimension of the fuzzy data space is n. Let GGen be a group generator (which we assume to produce a description of a group whose order is p). Let $\mathcal{H}_{lin} = \{h_z : (\mathbb{F}_p)^n \to \mathbb{F}_p\}_{z \in \mathbb{F}_{p^n}}$ be the universal hash family with linearity that we introduce in Sect. 2. (As in previous sections, we identify $\mathbb{F}_p$ with $\mathbb{Z}_p$.) Let $H : \{0,1\}^* \to \mathbb{Z}_p$ be a cryptographic hash function. Using these building blocks, we construct a fuzzy signature scheme $\Sigma_{\mathsf{FS}} = (\mathsf{Setup}_{\mathsf{FS}}, \mathsf{KG}_{\mathsf{FS}}, \mathsf{Sign}_{\mathsf{FS}}, \mathsf{Ver}_{\mathsf{FS}})$ for the fuzzy key setting $\mathcal{F}$ as in Fig. 4.

The following statement on security is obtained as a corollary of Theorems 2, 3 and 4, and Lemma 2.

Theorem 5. *If the DL assumption holds with respect to* GGen*, then the fuzzy signature scheme* Σ_{FS} *in Fig. 4 is* EUF−CMA *secure in the random oracle model where H is modeled as a random oracle.*

Although our scheme is secure only in the random oracle model due to the reliance on the Schnorr scheme, it has several practical advantages compared to the concrete instantiation based on the Waters signature scheme shown in [15]: Our scheme does not require bilinear maps, and the verification key size can be much shorter than that in [15]. More importantly, our scheme works for the fuzzy key setting in which fuzzy data cannot be assumed to be distributed uniformly over the data space (which was required in [15]), but that only its average min-entropy (given some parts of the fuzzy data) is sufficiently high.

8   Discussion

On the Plausibility of Our Requirement on the Distribution of Fuzzy Data. As we have seen in the previous sections, in this work we have succeeded in relaxing the requirement on the distribution of fuzzy data than the one required by Takahashi et al. [15], and have given a more efficient concrete instantiation of a fuzzy signature scheme based on the Schnorr scheme, which is secure in the random oracle model under the DL assumption.

A natural question would be whether practical fuzzy key settings can satisfy our requirement, especially the requirement on the average min-entropy in the presence of leakage (the "decimal" part of the "scaled-up version" of fuzzy data, $\widetilde{\mathbf{H}}_\infty(\mathcal{X}'_{in}|\mathcal{X}'_{de})$ in our notation). In the biometric setting, which is one of the main motivations for considering fuzzy signature schemes (and thus is one of the most important settings that should be captured by the formalization of fuzzy data settings), a well-known approach to measure the biometric entropy is *discrimination entropy* proposed by Daugman [5]. He considered a distribution of a Hamming distance m between two iriscodes (well-known iris features [6]) that are extracted from two different irises, and showed that it can be quite well approximated using the binomial distribution $B(n,p)$, where $n = 249$ and $p = 0.5$. He referred to the parameter n ($= 249$) as a discrimination entropy. The probability that two different iriscodes exactly match can be approximated to be 2^{-249}. This is a positive news for us, and for the future of related research.

However, of course, that the probability of two different iriscodes matching is approximated as 2^{-249}, does not necessarily mean that using iriscode x as fuzzy data gives us 249-bit security. Especially, in our case, we need to take into account the leakage (information leaked from the "decimal" part $\mathcal{X}'_{de}$), when the data is cast into our setting. We have to choose the threshold t by taking into account various other things, such as FAR and FRR. (Note that an adversary does not have to estimate the original iriscode x, but only has to estimate an iriscode $\tilde{x}$ that is sufficiently close to x.) Therefore, it seems not so easy to use the results from [5,6] just as it is.

If a single biometric feature does not have enough entropy, then one of the promising solutions to the problem would be to combine multiple biometric features. For example, Murakami et al. [11] recently showed that by combining four finger-vein features, FAR $= 2^{-133}$ (resp. FAR $= 2^{-87}$) can be achieved in the case when FRR $= 0.055$ (resp. FRR $= 0.0053$). Also, a multibiometric sensor that simultaneously acquires multiple biometrics (e.g. iris and face [4]; finger-print and finger-vein [13]) has also been widely developed. Thus, we believe that using multiple biometrics is a promising direction for increasing entropy without affecting usability (which is also an important factor in practice).

It is also important to note that (an approximation of) $\widetilde{\mathbf{H}}_\infty(\mathcal{X}'_{in}|\mathcal{X}'_{de})$ could be experimentally estimated by using real fuzzy data (in a similar manner done in [11]). This is an important feature in order for fuzzy signature schemes (and security systems based on them) to be used in practice.

Open Problems. It would be important to tackle the problem of whether we can realize the fuzzy key setting required in our work by some practical biometric settings/systems. It is also worth tackling whether further relaxing the requirement than our specific fuzzy key setting is possible, or considering settings that are different from ours. For example, can we construct a fuzzy signature scheme with other types of metric spaces (e.g. Euclid distance, hamming distance, edit distance, etc.)? It would also be worth clarifying whether we can construct more fuzzy signature schemes based on other existing signature schemes.

Acknowledgement. The authors would like to thank the anonymous reviewers for their invaluable comments and suggestions.

References

1. Bellare, M., Cash, D., Miller, R.: Cryptography secure against related-key attacks and tampering. In: Lee, D.H., Wang, X. (eds.) ASIACRYPT 2011. LNCS, vol. 7073, pp. 486–503. Springer, Heidelberg (2011)
2. Bellare, M., Neven, G.: Multi-signatures in the plain public-key model and a general forking lemma. In: CCS 2006, pp. 390–399 (2006)
3. Cheraghchi, M.: Capacity achieving codes from randomness condensers (2011). http://arxiv.org/pdf/0901.1866v2.pdf. Preliminary version appeared in ISIT 2009
4. Connaughton, R., Bowyer, K.W., Flynn, P.J.: Fusion of face and iris biometrics, Chapter 12. In: Burge, M.J., Bowyer, K.W. (eds.) Handbook of Iris Recognition, pp. 219–237. Springer, London (2013)
5. Daugman, J.: The importance of being random: Statistical principles of iris recognition. Pattern Recogn. **36**(2), 279–291 (2003)
6. Daugman, J.: How iris recognition works. IEEE Trans. Circ. Syst. Video Technol. **14**, 21–30 (2004)
7. Dodis, Y., Ostrovsky, R., Reyzin, L., Smith, A.: Fuzzy extractors: How to generate strong keys from biometrics and other noisy data. SIAM J. Comput. **38**(1), 97–139 (2008)
8. Ellison, C., Schneier, B.: Ten risks of PKI: What you're not being told about public key infrastructure. Comput. Secur. J. **16**(1), 1–7 (2000)
9. Håstad, J., Impagliazzo, R., Levin, L., Luby, M.: Construction of a pseudorandom generator from any one-way function. SIAM J. Comput. **28**(4), 1364–1396 (1999)
10. Morita, H., Schuldt, J.C.N., Matsuda, T., Hanaoka, G., Iwata, T.: On the security of the schnorr signature scheme and DSA against related-key attacks. In: Kwon, S., Yun, A. (eds.) ICISC 2015. LNCS, vol. 9558, pp. 20–35. Springer, Heidelberg (2016). doi:10.1007/978-3-319-30840-1_2
11. Murakami, T., Ohki, T., Takahashi, K.: Optimal sequential fusion for multibiometric cryptosystems. Elsevier Information Fusion (To appear)
12. Pointcheval, D., Stern, J.: Security proofs for signature schemes. In: Maurer, U.M. (ed.) EUROCRYPT 1996. LNCS, vol. 1070, pp. 387–398. Springer, Heidelberg (1996)
13. Raghavendra, R., Raja, K.B., Surbiryala, J., Busch, C.: A low-cost multimodal biometric sensor to capture finger vein and fingerprint. In: IJCB 2014, pp. 1–7 (2014)
14. Schnorr, C.-P.: Efficient identification and signatures for smart cards. In: Brassard, G. (ed.) CRYPTO 1989. LNCS, vol. 435, pp. 239–252. Springer, Heidelberg (1990)
15. Takahashi, K., Matsuda, T., Murakami, T., Hanaoka, G., Nishigaki, M.: A signature scheme with a fuzzy private key. In: Malkin, T., Kolesnikov, V., Lewko, A., Polychronakis, M. (eds.) ACNS 2015. LNCS, vol. 9092, pp. 105–126. Springer, Heidelberg (2015). doi:10.1007/978-3-319-28166-7_6
16. Waters, B.: Efficient identity-based encryption without random oracles. In: Cramer, R. (ed.) EUROCRYPT 2005. LNCS, vol. 3494, pp. 114–127. Springer, Heidelberg (2005)

Foundations of Fully Dynamic Group Signatures

Jonathan Bootle, Andrea Cerulli[✉], Pyrros Chaidos, Essam Ghadafi,
and Jens Groth

University College London, London, UK
{jonathan.bootle.14,andrea.cerulli.13,pyrros.chaidos.10,
e.ghadafi,j.groth}@ucl.ac.uk

Abstract. Group signatures are a central cryptographic primitive that
has received a considerable amount of attention from the cryptographic
community. They allow members of a group to anonymously sign on
behalf of the group. Membership is overseen by a designated group
manager. There is also a tracing authority that can revoke anonymity
by revealing the identity of the signer if and when needed, to enforce
accountability and deter abuse. For the primitive to be applicable in
practice, it needs to support fully dynamic groups, i.e. users can join and
leave at any time. In this work we take a close look at existing security
definitions for fully dynamic group signatures. We identify a number of
shortcomings in existing security definitions and fill the gap by providing
a formal rigorous security model for the primitive. Our model is general
and is not tailored towards a specific design paradigm and can therefore,
as we show, be used to argue about the security of different existing
constructions following different design paradigms. Our definitions are
stringent and when possible incorporate protection against maliciously
chosen keys. In the process, we identify a subtle issue inherent to one
design paradigm, where new members might try to implicate older ones
by means of back-dated signatures. This is not captured by existing models. We propose some inexpensive fixes for some existing constructions
to avoid the issue.

Keywords: Group signatures · Security definitions

1 Introduction

Group signatures, put forward by Chaum and van Heyst [CvH91], are a fundamental cryptographic primitive allowing a member of a group (administered by a
designated manager) to anonymously sign messages on behalf of the group. In the

The research leading to these results has received funding from the European Research Council under the European Union's Seventh Framework Programme (FP/2007-2013) / ERC Grant Agreement n. 307937 and EPSRC grant
EP/J009520/1.

P. Chaidos—Was supported by an EPSRC scholarship (EP/G037264/1 – Security
Science DTC).

© Springer International Publishing Switzerland 2016
M. Manulis et al. (Eds.): ACNS 2016, LNCS 9696, pp. 117–136, 2016.
DOI: 10.1007/978-3-319-39555-5_7

case of a dispute, a designated tracing manager can revoke anonymity by revealing the signer. In many settings it is desirable to offer flexibility in joining and leaving the group. In static group signatures [BMW03], the group population is fixed once and for all at the setup phase. Partially dynamic group signatures [BSZ05,KY06] allow the enrolment of members in the group at any time but members cannot leave once they have joined. A challenging problem in group signatures is that of revocation, i.e. allowing removal of members from the group.

Related Work. After their introduction, a long line of research on group signatures has emerged. In the early years, security of group signatures was not well understood and early constructions were proven secure via informal arguments using various interpretations of their requirements.

Bellare et al. [BMW03] formalized the security definitions for static groups. In their model, the group manager (which also acts as the tracing authority) needs to be fully trusted. Later on, Bellare et al. [BSZ05] and Kiayias and Yung [KY06] provided formal security definitions for the more practical partially dynamic case. Also, [BSZ05] separated the tracing role from the group management. In both [BSZ05,KY06] models, members cannot leave the group once they have joined. More recently, Sakai et al. [SSE+12] strengthened the security definitions for partially dynamic groups by defining *opening soundness*, ensuring that a valid signature only traces to one user.

Group Signatures Without Revocation. Constructions of group signatures in the random oracle model [BR93] include [CS97, CM98, ACJT00, BBS04, CL04, CG04, NS04, FI05, FY04, KY05, DP06, BCN+10]. Constructions not relying on random oracles include [ACHdM05, Gro06, BW06, Gro07, BW07, AHO10].

Group Signatures With Revocation. Since revocation is an essential feature of group signatures, many researchers investigated the different approaches via which such a feature can be realized. One approach is for the group manager to change the group public key when members are removed and issue new group signing keys to all remaining legitimate members or allow them to update their old signing keys accordingly. This is the approach adopted by e.g. [TX03, CL02].

Bresson and Stern [BS01] realize revocation by requiring that the signer proves at the time of signing that her group membership certificate is not among those contained in a public revocation list. Another approach, which was adopted by e.g. [CL02, TX03, DKNS04, Ngu05], uses accumulators, i.e. functions that map a set of values into a fixed-length string and permit efficient proofs of membership.

Boneh et al. [BBS04] showed that their static group signature scheme supports revocation since it allows members to update their signing keys according to the changes in the group without the involvement of the manager. Camenisch and Groth [CG04] also gave a construction that supports revocation. Song [Son01] gave a fully dynamic group signature with forward security.

A different approach for revocation known as *Verifier Local Revocation* (VLR), which needs relaxation of some of the security requirements, considered by Brickell [Bri04], was subsequently formalized by Boyen and Shacham [BS04] and further used in e.g. [NF05, LV09, LLNW14]. In VLR, the revocation information (i.e. revocation lists) is only sent to the verifiers (as opposed to both verifiers and signers) who can check whether a particular signature was generated by a revoked member. A similar approach is also used in Direct Anonymous Attestation (DAA) protocols [BCC04]. *Traceable Signatures* [KTY04] extend this idea, as the group manager can release a trapdoor for each member, enabling their signatures to be traced back to the individual user.

More recently, Libert et al. [LPY12b,LPY12a] gave a number of efficient constructions of group signatures supporting revocation without requiring random oracles by utilizing the subset cover framework [NNL01] that was originally used in the context of broadcast encryption.

Shortcomings in Existing Models & Motivation. While the security of the static and partially dynamic group settings has been rigorously formulated [BMW03,BSZ05,KY06,SSE+12] and is now well understood, unfortunately, the security of their fully dynamic groups counterpart, which is more relevant to practice, has received less attention and is still lacking. In particular, the different design paradigms assume different (sometimes informal) models which do not necessarily generalize to other design approaches. This resulted in various models, the majority of which lack rigour. As a consequence, it can be difficult to compare the merits of the different constructions in terms of their security guarantees. Moreover, existing models place a large amount of trust in the different authorities and assume that their keys are generated honestly. This does not necessarily reflect scenarios arising in real applications. Furthermore, some existing models, as we show, fail to take into account some attacks which might be problematic for some applications of the primitive.

"He Who Controls the Present Controls the Past", (George Orwell). Consider a scenario where the new leadership of an organisation or country wants to justify an unpopular policy (e.g. layoffs or removal of personal freedoms). A way to do that would be to back-date documents justifying the policy: thus, any animosity for the policy would be towards the old leadership. The new leadership is only maintaining the status quo.

Re-framing this in technical terms, we show that the notion of traceability in existing models following the revocation list approach, where the group manager periodically publishes information (i.e. revocation lists) about members excluded from the group, is too weak. In those models, the life of the scheme spans over different intervals (epochs) at the start of which the manager updates the revocation lists. Signatures in those models are bound to a specific epoch. It is vital for functionality that old valid signatures (i.e. those produced at earlier epochs by then-legitimate members) are accepted by the verification algorithm.

The issue we identify in those models is that they allow members who joined at recent epochs to sign messages w.r.t earlier epochs during which they were not members of the group. In a sense this may be considered as an attack against traceability, as those members were not in the group at that interval. Technically however, the scenario we describe is allowed by the model: the underlying issue is a gap between one's interpretation of group signatures and what the definition implies. Our expectation is that a signature bound to epoch τ was produced by a member of the group *at that time*. Current definitions however, allows for all past, current, and future members, as long as they were not revoked at time τ.

One may dismiss this attack as theoretical, since the old leadership might appeal to the opener. However, this might not always be possible: the opener may be controlled by the new leadership, or in a business setting an outgoing CEO or board member might be disinterested or disincentivized from pursuing the issue. Another possible criticism might be that the weakness is trivial, and would be silently fixed in any construction using the model.

We show that some state of the art constructions, as [NFHF09,LPY12b, LPY12a], are susceptible to this attack. Specifically, their membership certificates are not bound to the epochs of their issuance. As a result, a member can sign w.r.t. earlier epochs. We stress that neither the authors of those schemes claimed their schemes were immune against such an issue nor that their models were supposed to capture such an attack. Thus, such an issue might not be a problem for the applications they originally had in mind, but only in a more general case.

In order to have strong security guarantees from the different constructions, a rigorous and unified security model is necessary. This is the aim of this work as we believe this is a challenging problem that needs to be addressed, especially given the relevance of the primitive.

Our Contribution. We take a close look at the security definitions of fully dynamic group signatures. We provide a rigorous security model that generalizes to the different design paradigms. In particular, our model covers both accumulator based and revocation list based approaches. Our model offers stringent security definitions and takes into account some attacks which were not considered by existing models. We give different flavors of our security definitions which capture both cases when the authorities' keys are adversarially generated and when such keys are honestly generated. We also show that our security definitions imply existing definitions for static and partially dynamic group signatures.

In the process, we identify a subtle difference between accumulator based and revocation list based approaches. Specifically, we identify a simple attack against traceability inherent to constructions following the latter approach and which is not captured by existing models. The attack allows a group member of to sign w.r.t. intervals prior to her joining the group. The security notion modelled by current definitions prevents users from signing only if they are explicitly revoked.

To address this, our traceability definition models a stricter security notion: users are not authorised to sign unless they are non-revoked and are active (i.e. part of the group) at the time interval associated with the signature. We note this is already implied in the accumulator based approach: the signer proves membership in the current version of the group at the time of signing. We also propose a number of possible fixes to this issue in some existing schemes.

Finally, we show that a fully dynamic group signature scheme obtained from the generic construction of accountable ring signatures given in [BCC+15] is secure w.r.t. the stronger variant of our security definitions.

Paper Organization. We present our model for fully dynamic group signatures in Sect. 2 and show that it implies existing definitions for static and partially dynamic group signatures. In Sect. 3 we analyse the security of three existing fully dynamic group signature schemes in our model.

Notation. A function $\nu(\cdot) : \mathbb{N} \rightarrow \mathbb{R}^+$ is negligible in the security parameter λ if for every polynomial $p(\cdot)$ and all sufficiently large values of λ, it holds that $\nu(\lambda) < \frac{1}{p(\lambda)}$. Given a probability distribution Y, we denote by $x \leftarrow Y$ the operation of selecting an element according to Y. If M is a probabilistic machine, we denote by $M(x_1, \ldots, x_n)$ the output distribution of M on inputs $(x_1, \ldots, x_n)$. By $[n]$ we denote the set $\{1, \ldots, n\}$. By PPT we mean running in probabilistic polynomial time in the relevant security parameter. For algorithms X and Y, $(x, y) \leftarrow \langle \mathsf{X}(a), \mathsf{Y}(b) \rangle$ denotes the the joint execution of X (with input a) and Y (with input b) where at the end X outputs x, whereas Y outputs y. By $\mathsf{X}^{\langle \cdot, \mathsf{Y}(b) \rangle}(a)$, we denote the invocation of Y (with input b) by X (with input a). Note that X does not get the private output of Y.

2   Syntax and Security of Fully Dynamic Group Signatures

The parties involved in a Fully Dynamic Group Signature (FDGS) are: a group manager $\mathcal{GM}$ who authorizes who can join the group; a tracing manager $\mathcal{TM}$ who can revoke anonymity by opening signatures; a set of users, each with a unique identity uid $\in \mathbb{N}$, who are potential group members. Users can join/leave the group at any time at the discretion of the group manager. We assume the group manager will regularly publish some information info_τ, associated with a distinct index τ (hereafter referred to as epoch). We assume that τ can be recovered given info_τ and vice versa (i.e. there is bijection between the epochs and associated information). The information depicts changes to the group, for instance, it could include the current members of the group (as in accumulator-based constructions) or those who have been excluded from the group (as, e.g. required by constructions based on revocation lists). As in existing models, we assume that anyone can verify the well-formedness and authenticity of the published group information. By combining the group information for the current epoch with that of the preceding one, any party can identify the list of members who have been revoked at the current epoch. We assume that the epochs preserve the order in which their corresponding information was published. More precisely, for all $\tau_1, \tau_2 \in \mathcal{T}$ ($\mathcal{T}$ being the space of epochs) we require that $\tau_1 < \tau_2$ if info_{τ_1} preceded info_{τ_2}.

Unlike existing models, which assume honestly generated authorities' keys, we separate the generation of the authorities' keys from that of the public parameters, which might need to be generated by a trusted party. This allows us (where appropriate) to define stringent security that protects against adversarial authorities who might generate their keys maliciously. Our definitions can be adapted straight away to work for the weaker setting where authorities' keys are generated honestly as in existing models. For the sake of generality, we define the group key generation as a joint protocol between the group and tracing managers. Clearly, it is desirable in some cases to avoid such interaction and allow authorities to generate their own keys independently. This is a special case of our general definition where the protocol is regarded as two one-sided protocols.

An $\mathcal{FDGS}$ scheme consists of the following polynomial-time algorithms:

- GSetup(1^λ) → param: is run by a trusted third party. On input a security parameter λ, it outputs public parameters param. The algorithm also initializes the registration table **reg**.
- ⟨GKGen$_{\mathcal{GM}}$(param), GKGen$_{\mathcal{TM}}$(param)⟩: is an interactive protocol between algorithms GKGen$_{\mathcal{GM}}$ and GKGen$_{\mathcal{TM}}$ run by $\mathcal{GM}$ and $\mathcal{TM}$, respectively, to generate their respective private keys as well as the rest of the group public key gpk. The input to both algorithms is the public parameters param. If completed successfully, the private output of GKGen$_{\mathcal{GM}}$ is a secret manager key msk, whereas its public output is a public key mpk, and the initial group information info. The private output of GKGen$_{\mathcal{TM}}$ is the secret tracing key tsk, whereas its public output is a public key tpk. The group public key is then set to gpk := (param, mpk, tpk).
- UKGen(1^λ) → (**usk**[uid], **upk**[uid]): outputs a secret/public key pair (**usk**[uid], **upk**[uid]) for user uid. We assume the public key table **upk** to be publicly available (possibly via PKI) so that anyone can get authentic copies of it.
- ⟨Join(info$_{\tau_{\text{current}}}$, gpk, uid, **usk**[uid]), Issue(info$_{\tau_{\text{current}}}$, msk, uid, **upk**[uid])⟩: is an interactive protocol between a user uid (who has already obtained a personal key pair, i.e. ran the UKGen algorithm) and the group manager $\mathcal{GM}$. Upon successful completion, uid becomes a member of the group. The final state of the Issue algorithm is stored in the registration table at index uid (i.e. **reg**[uid]), whereas that of the Join algorithm is stored in **gsk**[uid]. The epoch τ_{current} is part of the output of both parties.

  We assume that the protocol takes place over a secure (i.e. private and authentic) channel. The protocol is initiated by calling Join. The manager may update the group information after running this protocol. The registration table **reg** stores additional information used by the group manager and the tracing manager for updating and tracing, depending on the scheme specifics.
- UpdateGroup(gpk, msk, info$_{\tau_{\text{current}}}$, $\mathcal{S}$, **reg**) → info$_{\tau_{\text{new}}}$: is run by the group manager to update the group information while also advancing the epoch. It takes as input the group manager's secret key msk, a (possibly empty) set $\mathcal{S}$ of active members to be removed from the group and the registration table **reg**, it outputs a new group information info$_{\tau_{\text{new}}}$ and might also update the registration table **reg**. If there has been no changes to the group information, the algorithm returns ⊥ to indicate that no new information has been issued. The algorithm aborts if any uid ∈ $\mathcal{S}$ has not run the join protocol.
- Sign(gpk, **gsk**[uid], info$_\tau$, m) → Σ: on input the group public key gpk, a user's group signing key **gsk**[uid], the group information info$_\tau$ at epoch τ, and a message m, outputs a group signature Σ on m by the group member uid. If the user owning **gsk**[uid] is not an active member of the group at epoch τ, the algorithm returns ⊥.

- Verify(gpk, info$_\tau$, m, Σ) → 1/0: is a deterministic algorithm checking whether Σ is a valid group signature on m at epoch τ and outputs a bit accordingly.
- Trace(gpk, tsk, info$_\tau$, **reg**, m, Σ) → (uid, π_{Trace}): is a deterministic algorithm which is run by the tracing manager. It returns an identity uid > 0 of the group member who produced Σ plus a proof π_{Trace} attesting to this fact. If the algorithm is unable to trace the signature to a particular group member, it returns (0, π_{Trace}) to indicate that it could not attribute the signature.
- Judge(gpk, uid, info$_\tau$, π_{Trace}, **upk**[uid], m, Σ) → 1/0 : is a deterministic algorithm which on input the group public key gpk, a user identity uid, the group information at epoch τ, a tracing proof π_{Trace}, the user's public key **upk**[uid] (which is ⊥ if it does not exist), a message m, and a signature Σ, outputs 1 if π_{Trace} is a valid proof that uid produced Σ, and outputs 0 otherwise.

ADDITIONAL ALGORITHM. We will also use the following polynomial-time algorithm which is only used in the security games to ease composition.

IsActive(info$_\tau$, **reg**, uid) → 1/0 : returns 1 if the user uid is an active member of the group at epoch τ and 0 otherwise.

2.1 Security of Fully Dynamic Group Signatures

The security requirements of a fully dynamic group signature are: *correctness*, *anonymity*, *non-frameability*, *traceability* and *tracing soundness*. To define those requirements, we use a set of games in which the adversary has access to a set of oracles. The following global lists are maintained: HUL is a list of honest users; CUL is a list of corrupt users whose personal secret keys have been chosen by the adversary; BUL is a list of bad users whose personal and group signing keys have been revealed to the adversary; SL is a list of signatures obtained from the Sign oracle; CL is a list of challenge signatures obtained from the challenge oracle.

The details of the following oracles are given in Fig. 1.

AddU(uid) adds an honest user uid to the group at the current epoch.

CrptU(uid, pk) creates a new corrupt user whose public key **upk**[uid] is chosen by the adversary. This is called in preparation for calling the SndToM oracle.

SndToM(uid, M_{in}) used to engage in the Join-Issue protocol with the honest, Issue-executing group manager.

SndToU(uid, M_{in}) used to engage in the Join-Issue protocol with an honest, Join-executing user uid on behalf of the corrupt group manager.

ReadReg(uid) returns the registration information **reg**[uid] of user uid.

ModifyReg(uid, val) modifies the entry **reg**[uid], setting **reg**[uid] := val. For brevity we will assume ModifyReg also provides the functionality of ReadReg.

RevealU(uid) returns the personal secret key **usk**[uid] and group signing key **gsk**[uid] of group member uid.

Sign(uid, m, τ) returns a signature on the message m by the group member uid for epoch τ assuming the corresponding group information info$_\tau$ is defined.

AddU(uid)
. If uid ∈ HUL ∪ CUL Then Return ⊥.
. (usk[uid], upk[uid]) ← UKGen(1^λ).
. HUL := HUL ∪ {uid}, gsk[uid] :=⊥, $\text{dec}_{\text{Issue}}^{\text{uid}}$:= cont.
. $\text{st}_{\text{Join}}^{\text{uid}}$:= (τ_{current}, gpk, uid, usk[uid]).
. $\text{st}_{\text{Issue}}^{\text{uid}}$:= (τ_{current}, msk, uid, upk[uid]).
. ($\text{st}_{\text{Join}}^{\text{uid}}$, M_{Issue}, $\text{dec}_{\text{Join}}^{\text{uid}}$) ← Join($\text{st}_{\text{Join}}^{\text{uid}}$, ⊥).
. While ($\text{dec}_{\text{Issue}}^{\text{uid}}$ = cont and $\text{dec}_{\text{Join}}^{\text{uid}}$ = cont) Do
  ○ ($\text{st}_{\text{Issue}}^{\text{uid}}$, M_{Join}, $\text{dec}_{\text{Issue}}^{\text{uid}}$) ← Issue($\text{st}_{\text{Issue}}^{\text{uid}}$, M_{Issue}).
  ○ ($\text{st}_{\text{Join}}^{\text{uid}}$, M_{Issue}, $\text{dec}_{\text{Join}}^{\text{uid}}$) ← Join($\text{st}_{\text{Join}}^{\text{uid}}$, M_{Join}).
. If $\text{dec}_{\text{Issue}}^{\text{uid}}$ = accept Then reg[uid] := $\text{st}_{\text{Issue}}^{\text{uid}}$.
. If $\text{dec}_{\text{Join}}^{\text{uid}}$ = accept Then gsk[uid] := $\text{st}_{\text{Join}}^{\text{uid}}$.
. Return upk[uid].

SndToU(uid, M_{in})
. If uid ∈ CUL ∪ BUL Then Return ⊥.
. If uid ∉ HUL Then
  ○ HUL := HUL ∪ {uid}.
  ○ (usk[uid], upk[uid]) ← UKGen(1^λ).
  ○ gsk[uid] :=⊥, M_{in} :=⊥.
. If $\text{dec}_{\text{Join}}^{\text{uid}}$ ≠ cont Then Return ⊥.
. If $\text{st}_{\text{Join}}^{\text{uid}}$ is undefined
  ○ $\text{st}_{\text{Join}}^{\text{uid}}$:= (τ_{current}, gpk, uid, usk[uid]).
. ($\text{st}_{\text{Join}}^{\text{uid}}$, M_{out}, $\text{dec}_{\text{Join}}^{\text{uid}}$) ← Join($\text{st}_{\text{Join}}^{\text{uid}}$, M_{in})
. If $\text{dec}_{\text{Join}}^{\text{uid}}$ = accept Then gsk[uid] := $\text{st}_{\text{Join}}^{\text{uid}}$.
. Return (M_{out}, $\text{dec}_{\text{Join}}^{\text{uid}}$).

Trace(m, Σ, info_τ)
. Return (⊥, ⊥) if Verify(gpk, info_τ, m, Σ) = 0.
. Return (⊥, ⊥) if (m, Σ, τ) ∈ CL.
. Return Trace(gpk, tsk, info_τ, reg, m, Σ).

ReadReg(uid)
. Return reg[uid].

RevealU(uid)
. Return ⊥ if uid ∉ HUL \ (CUL ∪ BUL).
. BUL := BUL ∪ {uid}.
. Return (usk[uid], gsk[uid]).

CrptU(uid, pk)
. Return ⊥ if uid ∈ HUL ∪ CUL.
. CUL := CUL ∪ {uid}.
. upk[uid] := pk, $\text{dec}_{\text{Issue}}^{\text{uid}}$:= cont.
. Return accept.

SndToM(uid, M_{in})
. Return ⊥ if uid ∉ CUL.
. Return ⊥ if $\text{dec}_{\text{Issue}}^{\text{uid}}$ ≠ cont.
. $\text{st}_{\text{Issue}}^{\text{uid}}$:= (τ_{current}, msk, uid, upk[uid]).
. ($\text{st}_{\text{Issue}}^{\text{uid}}$, M_{out}, $\text{dec}_{\text{Issue}}^{\text{uid}}$) ← Issue($\text{st}_{\text{Issue}}^{\text{uid}}$, M_{in}).
. If $\text{dec}_{\text{Issue}}^{\text{uid}}$ = accept Then reg[uid] := $\text{st}_{\text{Issue}}^{\text{uid}}$.
. Return (M_{out}, $\text{dec}_{\text{Issue}}^{\text{uid}}$).

Sign(uid, m, τ)
. Return ⊥ if uid ∉ HUL or gsk[uid] =⊥ or info_τ =⊥.
. Return ⊥ if IsActive(info_τ, reg, uid) = 0.
. Σ ← Sign(gpk, gsk[uid], info_τ, m).
. SL := SL ∪ {(uid, m, Σ, τ)}.
. Return Σ.

Chal_b(info_τ, uid_0, uid_1, m)
. Return ⊥ if uid_0 ∉ HUL or uid_1 ∉ HUL.
. Return ⊥ if ∃b ∈ {0, 1} s.t. gsk[uid_b] =⊥.
. Return ⊥ if ∃b ∈ {0, 1} s.t. IsActive(info_τ, reg, uid_b) = 0.
. Σ ← Sign(gpk, gsk[uid_b], info_τ, m).
. CL := CL ∪ {(m, Σ, τ)}.
. Return Σ.

ModifyReg(uid, *val*)
. reg[uid] := *val*.

UpdateGroup(𝒮)
. Return UpdateGroup(gpk, msk, $\text{info}_{\tau_{\text{current}}}$, 𝒮, reg).

Fig. 1. Details of the oracles used in the security games

Chal_b(info_τ, uid_0, uid_1, m) is a left-right oracle for defining anonymity. The adversary chooses an epoch τ, the group information info_τ, two identities (uid_0, uid_1), and a message m and receives a group signature by member uid_b for b ← {0, 1} for the chosen epoch. It is required that both challenge users are active members at epoch τ. The adversary can only call this oracle once.

Trace(m, Σ, info_τ) returns the identity of the signer of the signature Σ on m w.r.t. info_τ if the signature was not obtained from the Chal_b oracle.

UpdateGroup(𝒮) allows the adversary to update the group. 𝒮 here is the set of the active members to be removed from the group.

The following security requirements are defined by the games in Fig. 2.

Correctness. This requirement guarantees that signatures produced by honest, non-revoked users are accepted by the Verify algorithm and that the honest tracing manager can identify the signer of such signatures. In addition, the Judge algorithm accepts the tracing manager's decision.

Experiment: $\mathbf{Exp}_{\mathcal{FDGS},\mathcal{A}}^{\mathsf{Corr}}(\lambda)$
- param $\leftarrow$ GSetup(1^λ); HUL := $\emptyset$.
- $\big((\mathsf{msk}, \mathsf{mpk}, \mathsf{info}), (\mathsf{tsk}, \mathsf{tpk})\big) \leftarrow \langle \mathsf{GKGen}_{\mathcal{GM}}(\mathsf{param}), \mathsf{GKGen}_{\mathcal{TM}}(\mathsf{param}) \rangle$.
- $\mathsf{gpk} := (\mathsf{param}, \mathsf{mpk}, \mathsf{tpk})$.
- $\big(\mathsf{uid}, m, \tau\big) \leftarrow \mathcal{A}^{\mathsf{AddU}, \mathsf{ReadReg}, \mathsf{UpdateGroup}}\big(\mathsf{gpk}, \mathsf{info}\big)$.
- If $\mathsf{uid} \notin \mathsf{HUL}$ or $\mathbf{gsk}[\mathsf{uid}] = \perp$ or $\mathsf{info}_\tau = \perp$ or $\mathsf{IsActive}(\mathsf{info}_\tau, \mathbf{reg}, \mathsf{uid}) = 0$ Then Return 0.
- $\Sigma \leftarrow \mathsf{Sign}(\mathsf{gpk}, \mathbf{gsk}[\mathsf{uid}], \mathsf{info}_\tau, m)$.
- If $\mathsf{Verify}(\mathsf{gpk}, \mathsf{info}_\tau, m, \Sigma) = 0$ Then Return 1.
- $(\mathsf{uid}^*, \pi_{\mathsf{Trace}}) \leftarrow \mathsf{Trace}(\mathsf{gpk}, \mathsf{tsk}, \mathsf{info}_\tau, \mathbf{reg}, m, \Sigma)$.
- If $\mathsf{uid} \neq \mathsf{uid}^*$ Then Return 1.
- If $\mathsf{Judge}(\mathsf{gpk}, \mathsf{uid}, \mathsf{info}_\tau, \pi_{\mathsf{Trace}}, \mathbf{upk}[\mathsf{uid}], m, \Sigma) = 0$ Then Return 1, Else Return 0.

Experiment: $\mathbf{Exp}_{\mathcal{FDGS},\mathcal{A}}^{\mathsf{Anon}\text{-}b}(\lambda)$
- param $\leftarrow$ GSetup(1^λ); HUL, CUL, BUL, SL, CL := $\emptyset$.
- $\big(\mathsf{st}_{\mathsf{init}}, \mathsf{msk}, \mathsf{mpk}, \mathsf{info}\big) \leftarrow \mathcal{A}^{\langle \cdot, \mathsf{GKGen}_{\mathcal{TM}}(\mathsf{param}) \rangle}(\mathsf{init} : \mathsf{param})$.
- Return 0 if $\mathsf{GKGen}_{\mathcal{TM}}$ did not accept or $\mathcal{A}$'s output is not well-formed.
- Parse the output of $\mathsf{GKGen}_{\mathcal{TM}}$ as $(\mathsf{tsk}, \mathsf{tpk})$ and set $\mathsf{gpk} := (\mathsf{param}, \mathsf{mpk}, \mathsf{tpk})$.
- $b^* \leftarrow \mathcal{A}^{\mathsf{AddU}, \mathsf{CrptU}, \mathsf{SndToU}, \mathsf{RevealU}, \mathsf{Trace}, \mathsf{ModifyReg}, \mathsf{Chal}_b}\big(\mathsf{play} : \mathsf{st}_{\mathsf{init}}, \mathsf{gpk}\big)$.
- Return b^*.

Experiment: $\mathbf{Exp}_{\mathcal{FDGS},\mathcal{A}}^{\mathsf{Non}\text{-}\mathsf{Frame}}(\lambda)$
- param $\leftarrow$ GSetup(1^λ); HUL, CUL, BUL, SL := $\emptyset$.
- $(\mathsf{st}_{\mathsf{init}}, \mathsf{info}, \mathsf{msk}, \mathsf{mpk}, \mathsf{tsk}, \mathsf{tpk}) \leftarrow \mathcal{A}(\mathsf{init} : \mathsf{param})$.
- Return 0 if $\mathcal{A}$'s output is not well-formed otherwise set $\mathsf{gpk} := (\mathsf{param}, \mathsf{mpk}, \mathsf{tpk})$.
- $\big(m, \Sigma, \mathsf{uid}, \pi_{\mathsf{Trace}}, \mathsf{info}_\tau\big) \leftarrow \mathcal{A}^{\mathsf{CrptU}, \mathsf{SndToU}, \mathsf{RevealU}, \mathsf{Sign}, \mathsf{ModifyReg}}\big(\mathsf{play} : \mathsf{st}_{\mathsf{init}}, \mathsf{gpk}\big)$.
- If $\mathsf{Verify}(\mathsf{gpk}, \mathsf{info}_\tau, m, \Sigma) = 0$ Then Return 0.
- If $\mathsf{Judge}(\mathsf{gpk}, \mathsf{uid}, \mathsf{info}_\tau, \pi_{\mathsf{Trace}}, \mathbf{upk}[\mathsf{uid}], m, \Sigma) = 0$ Then Return 0.
- If $\mathsf{uid} \notin \mathsf{HUL} \setminus \mathsf{BUL}$ or $(\mathsf{uid}, m, \Sigma, \tau) \in \mathsf{SL}$ Then Return 0 Else Return 1.

Experiment: $\mathbf{Exp}_{\mathcal{FDGS},\mathcal{A}}^{\mathsf{Trace}}(\lambda)$
- param $\leftarrow$ GSetup(1^λ); HUL, CUL, BUL, SL := $\emptyset$.
- $\big(\mathsf{st}_{\mathsf{init}}, \mathsf{tsk}, \mathsf{tpk}\big) \leftarrow \mathcal{A}^{\langle \mathsf{GKGen}_{\mathcal{GM}}(\mathsf{param}), \cdot \rangle}(\mathsf{init} : \mathsf{param})$.
- Return 0 if $\mathsf{GKGen}_{\mathcal{GM}}$ did not accept or $\mathcal{A}$'s output is not well-formed.
- Parse the output of $\mathsf{GKGen}_{\mathcal{GM}}$ as $(\mathsf{msk}, \mathsf{mpk}, \mathsf{info})$. Set $\mathsf{gpk} := (\mathsf{param}, \mathsf{mpk}, \mathsf{tpk})$.
- $\big(m, \Sigma, \tau\big) \leftarrow \mathcal{A}^{\mathsf{AddU}, \mathsf{CrptU}, \mathsf{SndToM}, \mathsf{RevealU}, \mathsf{Sign}, \mathsf{ReadReg}, \mathsf{UpdateGroup}}\big(\mathsf{play} : \mathsf{st}_{\mathsf{init}}, \mathsf{gpk}, \mathsf{info}\big)$.
- If $\mathsf{Verify}(\mathsf{gpk}, \mathsf{info}_\tau, m, \Sigma) = 0$ Then Return 0.
- $(\mathsf{uid}, \pi_{\mathsf{Trace}}) \leftarrow \mathsf{Trace}(\mathsf{gpk}, \mathsf{tsk}, \mathsf{info}_\tau, \mathbf{reg}, m, \Sigma)$.
- If $\mathsf{IsActive}(\mathsf{info}_\tau, \mathbf{reg}, \mathsf{uid}) = 0$ Then Return 1.
- If $\mathsf{uid} = 0$ or $\mathsf{Judge}(\mathsf{gpk}, \mathsf{uid}, \mathsf{info}_\tau, \pi_{\mathsf{Trace}}, \mathbf{upk}[\mathsf{uid}], m, \Sigma) = 0$ Then Return 1 Else Return 0.

Experiment: $\mathbf{Exp}_{\mathcal{FDGS},\mathcal{A}}^{\mathsf{Trace}\text{-}\mathsf{Sound}}(\lambda)$
- param $\leftarrow$ GSetup(1^λ); CUL := $\emptyset$.
- $(\mathsf{st}_{\mathsf{init}}, \mathsf{info}, \mathsf{msk}, \mathsf{mpk}, \mathsf{tsk}, \mathsf{tpk}) \leftarrow \mathcal{A}(\mathsf{init} : \mathsf{param})$.
- Return 0 if $\mathcal{A}$'s output is not well-formed otherwise set $\mathsf{gpk} := (\mathsf{param}, \mathsf{mpk}, \mathsf{tpk})$.
- $\big(m, \Sigma, \{\mathsf{uid}_i, \pi_{\mathsf{Trace}_i}\}_{i=1}^2, \mathsf{info}_\tau\big) \leftarrow \mathcal{A}^{\mathsf{CrptU}, \mathsf{ModifyReg}}\big(\mathsf{play} : \mathsf{st}_{\mathsf{init}}, \mathsf{gpk}\big)$.
- If $\exists i \in \{1, 2\}$ s.t. $\mathsf{Verify}(\mathsf{gpk}, \mathsf{info}_\tau, m, \Sigma) = 0$ Then Return 0.
- If $\mathsf{uid}_1 = \mathsf{uid}_2$ or $\mathsf{uid}_1 = \perp$ or $\mathsf{uid}_2 = \perp$ Then Return 0.
- If $\exists i \in \{1, 2\}$ s.t. $\mathsf{Judge}(\mathsf{gpk}, \mathsf{uid}_i, \mathsf{info}_\tau, \pi_{\mathsf{Trace}_i}, \mathbf{upk}[\mathsf{uid}_i], m, \Sigma) = 0$ Then Return 0.
- Return 1.

Fig. 2. Security games for fully dynamic group signatures

Formally, an $\mathcal{FDGS}$ scheme is *(perfectly) correct* if for all $\lambda \in \mathbb{N}$, the advantage

$$\mathsf{Adv}^{\mathrm{Corr}}_{\mathcal{FDGS},\mathcal{A}}(\lambda) := \Pr[\mathbf{Exp}^{\mathrm{Corr}}_{\mathcal{FDGS},\mathcal{A}}(\lambda) = 1]$$

is negligible (in λ) for all adversaries $\mathcal{A}$.

Note that the above definition of (perfect) correctness protects against even unbounded adversaries. If computational correctness suffices, i.e. when we consider correctness only against computationally-bounded adversaries, we can drop the last three lines from the correctness game in Fig. 2. Computational correctness of the Trace and Judge algorithms is implied by the other requirements.

(Full) Anonymity. This requires that signatures do not reveal the identity of the group member who produced them. In the game, the adversary, $\mathcal{A}$, can corrupt any user and fully corrupt the group manager by choosing her key. We require that both challenge users are active members of the group at the chosen epoch. Also, note that a Trace query on the challenge signature will fail.

As $\mathcal{A}$ can learn the personal secret and group signing keys of any user, including the challenge users, our definition captures full key exposure attacks.

The adversary chooses an epoch, the group information for that epoch, a message and two group members and gets a signature by either member and wins if she correctly guesses the member. Without loss in generality, we allow the adversary a single call to the challenge oracle. A hybrid argument (similar to that used in [BSZ05]) can be used to prove that this is sufficient.

Formally, an $\mathcal{FDGS}$ scheme is *(fully) anonymous* if for all $\lambda \in \mathbb{N}$, the advantage $\mathsf{Adv}^{\mathrm{Anon}}_{\mathcal{FDGS},\mathcal{A}}(\lambda)$ is negligible (in λ) for all PPT adversaries $\mathcal{A}$, where

$$\mathsf{Adv}^{\mathrm{Anon}}_{\mathcal{FDGS},\mathcal{A}}(\lambda) := \left| \Pr[\mathbf{Exp}^{\mathrm{Anon}\text{-}0}_{\mathcal{FDGS},\mathcal{A}}(\lambda) = 1] - \Pr[\mathbf{Exp}^{\mathrm{Anon}\text{-}1}_{\mathcal{FDGS},\mathcal{A}}(\lambda) = 1] \right|.$$

Non-Frameability. This ensures that even if the rest of the group as well as the tracing and group managers are fully corrupt, they cannot produce a signature that can be attributed to an honest member who did not produce it.

In the game, the adversary can fully corrupt both the group and tracing managers. She even chooses the keys of both managers. Thus, our definition is stronger than existing models. We just require that the framed member is honest.

Formally, an $\mathcal{FDGS}$ scheme is *non-frameable* if for all $\lambda \in \mathbb{N}$, the advantage

$$\mathsf{Adv}^{\mathrm{Non\text{-}Frame}}_{\mathcal{FDGS},\mathcal{A}}(\lambda) := \Pr[\mathbf{Exp}^{\mathrm{Non\text{-}Frame}}_{\mathcal{FDGS},\mathcal{A}}(\lambda) = 1]$$

is negligible (in λ) for all PPT adversaries $\mathcal{A}$.

Remark 1. In the game variant we give in Fig. 2, we allow the adversary to generate the tracing manager's key herself. While, as we show later, there are schemes which satisfy this strong variant of the definition, such definition might be too strong to be satisfied by some existing schemes. A weaker variant of the definition is where the tracing key is generated by the challenger rather than the adversary. This requires replacing lines 2–4 in the game in Fig. 2 by the following:

- $(\mathsf{st}_{\mathsf{init}}, \mathsf{info}, \mathsf{msk}, \mathsf{mpk}) \leftarrow \mathcal{A}^{\langle \cdot, \mathsf{GKGen}_{\mathcal{TM}}(\mathsf{param})\rangle}(\mathsf{init} : \mathsf{param})$
- Return 0 if $\mathcal{A}$'s output is not well-formed or $\mathsf{GKGen}_{\mathcal{TM}}$ did not accept
- Let $(\mathsf{tsk}, \mathsf{tpk})$ be the output of $\mathsf{GKGen}_{\mathcal{TM}}$. Set $\mathsf{gpk} := (\mathsf{param}, \mathsf{mpk}, \mathsf{tpk})$
- $\left(m, \Sigma, \mathsf{uid}, \pi_{\mathsf{Trace}}, \mathsf{info}_\tau\right) \leftarrow \mathcal{A}^{\mathsf{CrptU},\mathsf{SndToU},\mathsf{RevealU},\mathsf{Sign},\mathsf{ModifyReg}}\left(\mathsf{play} : \mathsf{st}_{\mathsf{init}}, \mathsf{gpk}, \mathsf{tsk}\right).$

Traceability. This ensures that the adversary cannot produce a signature that cannot be traced to an active member of the group at the chosen epoch. In the game, the adversary can corrupt any user and even chooses the tracing key of the tracing manager. The adversary is not given the group manager's secret key as this would allow her to create dummy users which are thus untraceable. Note that unlike [LPY12b, LPY12a, NFHF09], our definition captures that a member of the group should not be able to sign w.r.t. epochs prior to her joining the group since we do not restrict the adversary's forgery to be w.r.t. to the current epoch (i.e. the current version of the group information). The adversary wins if she produces a signature whose signer cannot be identified or is an inactive member at the chosen epoch. The adversary also wins if the Judge algorithm does not accept the tracing decision on the forgery.

Formally, an $\mathcal{FDGS}$ scheme is *traceable* if for all $\lambda \in \mathbb{N}$, the advantage

$$\mathsf{Adv}^{\mathsf{Trace}}_{\mathcal{FDGS},\mathcal{A}}(\lambda) := \Pr[\mathbf{Exp}^{\mathsf{Trace}}_{\mathcal{FDGS},\mathcal{A}}(\lambda) = 1]$$

is negligible (in λ) for all PPT adversaries $\mathcal{A}$.

Remark 2. To get an honestly-generated tracing key variant of the game in Fig. 2, we replace lines 2–5 in the game in Fig. 2 by the following lines:

- $\left((\mathsf{msk}, \mathsf{mpk}, \mathsf{info}), (\mathsf{tsk}, \mathsf{tpk})\right) \leftarrow \langle \mathsf{GKGen}_{\mathcal{GM}}(\mathsf{param}), \mathsf{GKGen}_{\mathcal{TM}}(\mathsf{param})\rangle$
- Set $\mathsf{gpk} := (\mathsf{param}, \mathsf{mpk}, \mathsf{tpk})$
- $\left(m, \Sigma, \tau\right) \leftarrow \mathcal{A}^{\mathsf{AddU},\mathsf{CrptU},\mathsf{SndToM},\mathsf{RevealU},\mathsf{Sign},\mathsf{ReadReg},\mathsf{UpdateGroup}}\left(\mathsf{play} : \mathsf{st}_{\mathsf{init}}, \mathsf{gpk}, \mathsf{info}, \mathsf{tsk}\right).$

Tracing Soundness. As recently defined by [SSE+12] in the context of partially dynamic group signatures, this requirement ensures that even if both the group and the tracing managers as well as all members of the group collude, they cannot produce a valid signature that traces to two different members. Such a requirement is vital for many applications. For example, applications where signers get rewarded or where we need to stop abusers shifting blame to others.

In the definition, the adversary can fully corrupt all parties involved and wins if she produces a valid signature and valid tracing proofs that the signature traces to different (possibly corrupt) users. We may also consider a stronger variant where the adversary wins by producing a signature that traces to different epochs.

Formally, an $\mathcal{FDGS}$ scheme has *tracing soundness* if for all $\lambda \in \mathbb{N}$,

$$\mathsf{Adv}_{\mathcal{FDGS},\mathcal{A}}^{\text{Trace-Sound}}(\lambda) := \Pr[\mathbf{Exp}_{\mathcal{FDGS},\mathcal{A}}^{\text{Trace-Sound}}(\lambda) = 1]$$

is negligible (in λ) for all PPT adversaries $\mathcal{A}$.

Remark 3. To get an honestly-generated tracing key variant of the game in Fig. 2, we replace lines 2–4 in the game in Fig. 2 by the following lines:

- $\left(\mathsf{st}_{\mathsf{init}}, \mathsf{msk}, \mathsf{mpk}, \mathsf{info}\right) \leftarrow \mathcal{A}^{\langle\cdot,\mathsf{GKGen}_{\mathcal{TM}}(\mathsf{param})\rangle}(\mathsf{init}:\mathsf{param})$
- Return 0 if $\mathsf{GKGen}_{\mathcal{TM}}$ did not accept or $\mathcal{A}$'s output is not well-formed
- Parse the output of $\mathsf{GKGen}_{\mathcal{TM}}$ as $(\mathsf{tsk},\mathsf{tpk})$ and set $\mathsf{gpk} := (\mathsf{param},\mathsf{mpk},\mathsf{tpk})$
- $\left(m, \Sigma, \{\mathsf{uid}_i, \pi_{\mathsf{Trace}_i}\}_{i=1}^{2}, \mathsf{info}_\tau\right) \leftarrow \mathcal{A}^{\mathsf{CrptU},\mathsf{ModifyReg}}\left(\mathsf{play}:\mathsf{st}_{\mathsf{init}},\mathsf{gpk},\mathsf{tsk}\right)$.

2.2 Comparison with Existing Models

Models used by accumulator-based constructions, e.g. [BS01, CL02, TX03, AST01, Ngu05, NFHF09], the vast majority of which are stated informally, are specific to that particular design paradigm and do not generalize to other construction approaches. Moreover, most of the them do not take into account some of the attacks that arise in a more formal setting. For instance, some models only protect against partially but not fully corrupt tracing managers and do not capture the tracing soundness requirement. On the other hand, models used by other design approaches, e.g. [NFHF09, LPY12b, LPY12a] are also specific to those approaches and have their own shortcomings. For instance, as discussed earlier, the models used by the state-of-the-art constructions by Libert et al. [LPY12b, LPY12a] and Nakanishi et al. [NFHF09] do not prevent a group member from being able to sign w.r.t. time intervals before she joined the group. This is an attack that can be problematic in some applications of the primitive. In the traceability game used in [NFHF09] as well as the misidentification game used in [LPY12b, LPY12a], the adversary is required to output a signature that is valid w.r.t. the current interval (epoch) and therefore the definitions do not capture the attack we highlight. We stress that the authors of the concerned models never claimed that their models cover such an attack as it might not be a problem for their intended applications.

The traceability issue we shed light on does not apply to accumulator based models. In these settings, when the group changes, an update is published containing a list of the currently active group members and most constructions work by having the signer prove membership in such a list. Therefore, even if a malicious member tries to sign w.r.t. an earlier version of the group information, she still has to prove she is a member of the group at the concerned interval.

In addition [NFHF09,LPY12b,LPY12a] only consider a partially but not fully corrupt tracing manager in the non-frameability game. Moreover, they do not capture the requirement that a signature should only trace to one member (i.e. tracing soundness). The latter is vital for many applications of the primitive.

Another distinction from existing models is that our model allows maliciously generated authorities' keys when applicable. Therefore, it offers more stringent security than existing models which rely on such keys being generated honestly.

2.3 Recovering Other Models

We give security reductions which relate our model to other well-known models for group signatures. All these models assume honest key generation, for both group and tracing managers, which is a special case of our model. We consider three models. First, the model for static group signatures given in [BMW03]. We then consider two models for partially dynamic groups from [BSZ05] and [KY06]. Due to lack of space, we present the technical details in the full paper [BCC+16].

Static Group Signatures [BMW03]. We note that we can recover static group signatures [BMW03] from our group signatures. We fix the group manager as the designated opener and include tsk in the group master secret key. In the setup, group members generate their key pairs and interact with the group manager to join the group. Their Open algorithm does not output proofs, as their model does not use a Judge algorithm, so we define a variant of our non-frameability game from Fig. 2 where we replace the last 4 lines in the game in Fig. 2 by the ones in Fig. 3.

- $\left(m, \Sigma, \mathsf{info}_\tau\right) \leftarrow \mathcal{A}^{\mathsf{CrptU,SndToU,RevealU,Sign,ModifyReg}}\left(\mathsf{play} : \mathsf{st}_{\mathsf{init}}, \mathsf{gpk}\right).$
- If $\mathsf{Verify}(\mathsf{gpk}, \mathsf{info}_\tau, m, \Sigma) = 0$ Then Return 0.
- $(\mathsf{uid}, \pi_{\mathrm{Trace}}) \leftarrow \mathsf{Trace}(\mathsf{gpk}, \mathsf{tsk}, \mathsf{info}_\tau, \mathbf{reg}, m, \sigma)$
- If $\mathsf{uid} \notin \mathsf{HUL} \setminus \mathsf{BUL}$ or $(\mathsf{uid}, m, \Sigma, \tau) \in \mathsf{SL}$ Then Return 0 Else Return 1.

Fig. 3. Modified non-frameability game.

This gives a sensible and compatible definition which allows us to recover the model from the fully dynamic scheme.

Static group signatures are just fully dynamic group signatures with no joining, issuing, or group updates. Correctness follows trivially from the correctness of the fully dynamic group signature scheme. [BMW03]-full-anonymity follows from (full) anonymity of the fully dynamic group signature scheme, while [BMW03]-full-traceability follows from our traceability and non-frameability requirements.

Partially Dynamic Group Signatures [BSZ05]. Fully dynamic group signatures also imply the partially dynamic group signatures of [BSZ05] in the case where nobody is removed from the group. Anonymity, non-frameability and traceability all follow from our corresponding definitions. Correctness follows trivially from the correctness of the fully dynamic group signature scheme.

Partially Dynamic Group Signatures [KY06]. Finally, we consider the partially-dynamic model of [KY06]. We fix the group manager as the designated opener and set (msk, tsk) to be the group master secret key. Our group info and registration table generalize their public state string. Their Join algorithm runs our user key-generation and Join/Issue algorithms. The membership certificate is then the user's public key along with the group information, and the membership secret is the user's private key. Again, their Open algorithm does not output proofs, and the model does not have a judge algorithm. Therefore, as in the case of [BMW03] we modify our non-frameability game from Fig. 2 where we replace the last 4 lines in the game in Fig. 2 with those in Fig. 3.

Correctness follows trivially from the correctness of the fully dynamic group signature scheme. Security against misidentification-attacks follows from traceability, security against framing-attacks follows from non-frameability, and anonymity follows from the (full) anonymity of the fully dynamic group signature.

3   On the Security of Some Existing Schemes

Here we take a closer look at some of the existing fully dynamic schemes and investigate whether or not they are secure using our proposed model.

We show that the state-of-the-art certificate-based schemes in [LPY12b, LPY12a, NFHF09] are all susceptible to an attack against traceability which allows any user to sign w.r.t. an epoch predating her joining. In our model this directly breaks traceability, as the signature is w.r.t. an epoch in which the signer was not active. We note that our attack does not contradict the original security proofs of the schemes, but instead highlights that our definition is stronger. We also show that it is easy to repair the schemes at a reasonable cost.

At first glance, our attack is the dual of a well known issue with many revocation systems. If a user is revoked and anonymity is maintained, the revoked user is able to produce back-dated signatures that still verify. The difference here is that while the revoked user *was* authorized to be part of the group for the epoch in question, in our attack the signing user was in fact *not* authorized to sign for the group. If the adversary is able to block the opening of this signature (e.g. via legal action), its existence would implicitly frame the group's past membership.

3.1   Libert et al. Schemes [LPY12b, LPY12a]

In [LPY12a], users are assigned leaves of a complete binary tree and given a membership certificate containing a unique tag identifying the user, and a commitment to the path from the root to the user's leaf in the tree. Note that the certificate is not bound to the epoch at which the user joined the group. In fact, users joining does not change info_τ or the epoch τ itself.

Revocation is based on the subset difference method [NNL01], using disjoint sets S_{k_i,u_i} for $i = 1, \ldots, m$ which cover non-revoked users. Sets are represented by two nodes, a node k_i and one of its descendants node u_i, and cover all leaves of the sub-tree rooted at node k_i which are not leaves of the sub-tree rooted at u_i. Revocations trigger epoch changes with info_τ updated with a new cover.

To sign, the group member anonymously proves that she holds a membership certificate, and that the node indicated by the certificate belongs to one of those sets. More precisely, the user proves that her leaf is a descendant of node k_i but not a descendant of node u_i for some $i \in [m]$.

Since user certificates are not bound to epochs and leaves are covered until their corresponding users are revoked, it is simple to break traceability: a user can join and then produce a signature for an epoch that predates her joining. A similar argument also applies to the variant of the scheme given in [LPY12b].

Theorem 1. *The fully dynamic scheme of Libert et al. [LPY12a] does not satisfy our traceability definition even w.r.t. honestly generated tracing manager's keys.*

Proof. Consider the following strategy in the traceability experiment: the adversary asks to join as a user uid_1 at epoch τ_1. User uid_1 gets assigned the leaf l_1. Then at a later epoch, τ_2, the adversary asks to join as a second user uid_2. Finally, the adversary signs using the credentials of uid_2 but for epoch τ_1.

We can check by inspection that all subproofs in the back-dated signature go through. The crucial observation is that at epoch τ_1, the leaf l_2 is not revoked and thus must be covered by one of the S_{k_i,u_i} sets. As the proof verifies and uid_2 used a legitimate certificate, opening the signature will be successful and indicate uid_2 as the signer. The adversary wins, as uid_2 was not active at epoch τ_1. $\square$

A possible countermeasure against the above attack is to regard unassigned leaves as revoked until they are assigned. This is simple to do as the scheme does not bound the number of revoked users. We do however need to re-examine the number of subsets required to express this, as the $2|\mathcal{R}| - 1$ bound for $|\mathcal{R}|$ revoked users may now seem impractical. If we assume leaves are allocated sequentially to users, we can bound the number of subsets by $2|\mathcal{R}_1| + log(|\mathcal{N} \setminus \mathcal{R}_2|)$ where $\mathcal{R}_2$ is the set of leaves pending allocation and $\mathcal{R}_1$ is the set of leaves allocated to users who were later revoked. Thus, our fix is only marginally more expensive than the base system and much more efficient than a naive analysis would indicate.

If proving set membership/intervals can be done efficiently (and depending on how the epoch counter is implemented), another possible fix is to bind membership certificates to the join epoch and then get the signer to prove that their join epoch is not later than the signing epoch.

3.2   Nakanishi et al. Scheme [NFHF09]

The scheme of Nakanishi et al. [NFHF09] is another certificate-based scheme in the random oracle model. It achieves constant time for both signing and signature verification, relative to the size of the group and the number of revoked users.

A user's group membership certificate consists of a signature on (x, ID) produced by the group manager, where x is a secret owned by the user and ID is a unique integer the manager assigned to her. The group manager can revoke users by issuing revocation lists info_τ. Each list consists of a sequence of *open* integer intervals (R_i, R_{i+1}) signed by the manager, whose endpoints are all the revoked ID's. At each epoch τ, a signer fetches the current info_τ and proves, as part of the signature, that her ID is contained in one interval of the revocation list. If the ID lies between two revoked users' identities, it means it is not an endpoint and so she has not been revoked.

As in other certificate-based constructions, verifiers only know of revoked members, not active ones and, similarly to [LPY12a], the time of joining is not taken into account. This allows users to sign with respect to any epoch prior to joining the group, which represents an attack against our traceability definition.

Theorem 2. *The Nakanishi et al. [NFHF09] fully dynamic group signature scheme does not satisfy our traceability definition.*

Proof. Let $\mathcal{A}$ be an adversary against the traceability game. The adversary adds user uid to the group at epoch τ. Since the user is not revoked, her ID is not an endpoint in any interval of the revocation list info_τ, as for all previous epochs. Therefore, $\mathcal{A}$ could easily produce valid signatures for uid to any epoch $\bar{\tau} < \tau$. Since these signatures trace back to a user which was inactive at the interval with which the signature is associated, $\mathcal{A}$ succeeds in the traceability game. $\square$

The scheme could be easily immunized against the above attack. A first solution, as for [LPY12a], is to initialize the revocation list with all ID's of users that have not joined the group yet. When the manager assigns an ID to a new user, he updates **reg** and the revocation list info_τ. This way, the signature size is not affected. On the other hand, revocation lists are now proportional to the size of the maximum number of users, instead of the number of revoked users.

An alternative countermeasure requires the group manager to include the joining epochs in the certificates by signing $(x, \text{ID}, \tau_{\text{join}})$, where x is a secret owned by user ID and τ_{join} is the joining epoch. A signer then needs to include in the signature a proof that τ_{join} is not greater than the signing epoch. To realize the latter, one can use membership proof techniques from [TS06, CCS08] which are already used in the original scheme. This would increase the cost of signing and verifying by only a constant factor. The new membership proof would require the group manager to provide signatures for every elapsed epoch, which could be appended, for instance, to the revocation list. This makes revocation lists grow linearly with the number of revoked users as well as the number of epochs.

3.3   Bootle et al. Scheme [BCC+15]

Recently, Bootle et al. [BCC+15] gave a generic construction of accountable ring signatures, where every signature can be traced back to a user in the ring. They also showed how one can obtain fully dynamic group signatures from accountable ring signatures. In addition, they gave an efficient instantiation in the random oracle model that is based on the DDH assumption. Their instantiation yields signatures of logarithmic size (w.r.t. the size of the ring), while signing is quasi-linear, and signature verification requires a linear number of operations. Bootle et al. claimed that their instantiation is more efficient than existing group signature schemes based on standard assumptions.

Each user has a secret key and an associated verification key. To sign, users first encrypt their verification key. Then, via a membership proof, they provide a signature of knowledge showing that the verification key belongs to the ring, and that they know the corresponding secret key. In the full version [BCC+16], we prove their construction is secure w.r.t. the stronger variant of our model.

References

[ACHdM05] Ateniese, G., Camenisch, J., Hohenberger, S., de Medeiros, B.: Practical group signatures without random oracles, IACR Cryptology ePrint Archive (2005)

[ACJT00] Ateniese, G., Camenisch, J.L., Joye, M., Tsudik, G.: A practical and provably secure coalition-resistant group signature scheme. In: Bellare, M. (ed.) CRYPTO 2000. LNCS, vol. 1880, pp. 255–270. Springer, Heidelberg (2000)

[AHO10] Abe, M., Haralambiev, K., Ohkubo, M.: Signing on elements in bilinear groups for modular protocol design. IACR Cryptology ePrint Archive (2010)

[AST01] Ateniese, G., Song, D., Tsudik, G.: Quasi-efficient revocation of group signatures. IACR Cryptology ePrint Archive 2001:101 (2001)

[BBS04] Boneh, D., Boyen, X., Shacham, H.: Short group signatures. In: Franklin, M. (ed.) CRYPTO 2004. LNCS, vol. 3152, pp. 41–55. Springer, Heidelberg (2004)

[BCC04] Brickell, E.F., Camenisch, J., Chen, L.: Direct anonymous attestation. In: Conference on Computer and Communications Security, CCS (2004)

[BCC+15] Bootle, J., Cerulli, A., Chaidos, P., Ghadafi, E., Groth, J., Petit, C.: Short accountable ring signatures based on DDH. In: Pernul, G., Y A Ryan, P., Weippl, E. (eds.) ESORICS 2015. LNCS, vol. 9326, pp. 243–265. Springer, Heidelberg (2015). doi:10.1007/978-3-319-24174-6_13

[BCC+16] Bootle, J., Cerulli, A., Chaidos, P., Ghadafi, E., Groth, J.: Foundations of fully dynamic group signatures. IACR Cryptology ePrint Archive (2016)

[BCN+10] Bichsel, P., Camenisch, J., Neven, G., Smart, N.P., Warinschi, B.: Get shorty via group signatures without encryption. In: Garay, J.A., De Prisco, R. (eds.) SCN 2010. LNCS, vol. 6280, pp. 381–398. Springer, Heidelberg (2010)

[BMW03] Bellare, M., Micciancio, D., Warinschi, B.: Foundations of group signatures: formal definitions, simplified requirements, and a construction based on general assumptions. In: Biham, E. (ed.) EUROCRYPT 2003. LNCS, vol. 2656. Springer, Heidelberg (2003)

[BR93] Bellare, M., Rogaway, P.: Random oracles are practical: a paradigm for designing efficient protocols. In: Conference on Computer and Communications Security - CCS (1993)

[Bri04] Brickell, E.: An efficient protocol for anonymously providing assurance of the container of a private key. Submitted to the Trusted Computing Group (2004)

[BS01] Bresson, E., Stern, J.: Efficient revocation in group signatures. In: Kim, K. (ed.) PKC 2001. LNCS, vol. 1992, pp. 190–206. Springer, Heidelberg (2001)

[BS04] Boneh, D., Shacham, H.: Group signatures with verifier-local revocation. In: Conference on Computer and Communications Security, CCS (2004)

[BSZ05] Bellare, M., Shi, H., Zhang, C.: Foundations of group signatures: the case of dynamic groups. In: Menezes, A. (ed.) CT-RSA 2005. LNCS, vol. 3376, pp. 136–153. Springer, Heidelberg (2005)

[BW06] Boyen, X., Waters, B.: Compact group signatures without random oracles. In: Vaudenay, S. (ed.) EUROCRYPT 2006. LNCS, vol. 4004, pp. 427–444. Springer, Heidelberg (2006)

[BW07] Boyen, X., Waters, B.: Full-domain subgroup hiding and constant-size group signatures. In: Okamoto, T., Wang, X. (eds.) PKC 2007. LNCS, vol. 4450, pp. 1–15. Springer, Heidelberg (2007)

[CCS08] Camenisch, J.L., Chaabouni, R., Shelat, A.: Efficient protocols for set membership and range proofs. In: Pieprzyk, J. (ed.) ASIACRYPT 2008. LNCS, vol. 5350, pp. 234–252. Springer, Heidelberg (2008)

[CG04] Camenisch, J.L., Groth, J.: Group signatures: better efficiency and new theoretical aspects. In: Blundo, C., Cimato, S. (eds.) SCN 2004. LNCS, vol. 3352, pp. 120–133. Springer, Heidelberg (2005)

[CL02] Camenisch, J.L., Lysyanskaya, A.: Dynamic accumulators and application to efficient revocation of anonymous credentials. In: Yung, M. (ed.) CRYPTO 2002. LNCS, vol. 2442, pp. 61–76. Springer, Heidelberg (2002)

[CL04] Camenisch, J.L., Lysyanskaya, A.: Signature schemes and anonymous credentials from bilinear maps. In: Franklin, M. (ed.) CRYPTO 2004. LNCS, vol. 3152, pp. 56–72. Springer, Heidelberg (2004)

[CM98] Camenisch, J.L., Michels, M.: A group signature scheme with improved efficiency. In: Ohta, K., Pei, D. (eds.) ASIACRYPT 1998. LNCS, vol. 1514, pp. 160–174. Springer, Heidelberg (1998)

[CS97] Camenisch, J.L., Stadler, M.A.: Efficient group signature schemes for large groups. In: Kaliski Jr., B.S. (ed.) CRYPTO 1997. LNCS, vol. 1294, pp. 410–424. Springer, Heidelberg (1997)

[CvH91] Chaum, D., van Heyst, E.: Group signatures. In: Davies, D.W. (ed.) EUROCRYPT 1991. LNCS, vol. 547, pp. 257–265. Springer, Heidelberg (1991)

[DKNS04] Dodis, Y., Kiayias, A., Nicolosi, A., Shoup, V.: Anonymous identification in Ad Hoc groups. In: Cachin, C., Camenisch, J.L. (eds.) EUROCRYPT 2004. LNCS, vol. 3027, pp. 609–626. Springer, Heidelberg (2004)

[DP06] Delerablée, C., Pointcheval, D.: Dynamic fully anonymous short group signatures. In: Nguyên, P.Q. (ed.) VIETCRYPT 2006. LNCS, vol. 4341, pp. 193–210. Springer, Heidelberg (2006)

[FI05] Furukawa, J., Imai, H.: An efficient group signature scheme from bilinear maps. In: Boyd, C., González Nieto, J.M. (eds.) ACISP 2005. LNCS, vol. 3574, pp. 455–467. Springer, Heidelberg (2005)

[FY04] Furukawa, J., Yonezawa, S.: Group signatures with separate and distributed authorities. In: Blundo, C., Cimato, S. (eds.) SCN 2004. LNCS, vol. 3352, pp. 77–90. Springer, Heidelberg (2005)

[Gro06] Groth, J.: Simulation-sound NIZK proofs for a practical language and constant size group signatures. In: Lai, X., Chen, K. (eds.) ASIACRYPT 2006. LNCS, vol. 4284, pp. 444–459. Springer, Heidelberg (2006)

[Gro07] Groth, J.: Fully anonymous group signatures without random oracles. In: Kurosawa, K. (ed.) ASIACRYPT 2007. LNCS, vol. 4833, pp. 164–180. Springer, Heidelberg (2007)

[KTY04] Kiayias, A., Tsiounis, Y., Yung, M.: Traceable signatures. In: Cachin, C., Camenisch, J.L. (eds.) EUROCRYPT 2004. LNCS, vol. 3027, pp. 571–589. Springer, Heidelberg (2004)

[KY05] Kiayias, A., Yung, M.: Group signatures with efficient concurrent join. In: Cramer, R. (ed.) EUROCRYPT 2005. LNCS, vol. 3494, pp. 198–214. Springer, Heidelberg (2005)

[KY06] Kiayias, A., Yung, M.: Secure scalable group signature with dynamic joins and separable authorities. IJSN 1(1/2), 24 (2006)

[LLNW14] Langlois, A., Ling, S., Nguyen, K., Wang, H.: Lattice-based group signature scheme with verifier-local revocation. In: Krawczyk, H. (ed.) PKC 2014. LNCS, vol. 8383, pp. 345–361. Springer, Heidelberg (2014)

[LPY12a] Libert, B., Peters, T., Yung, M.: Group signatures with almost-for-free revocation. In: Safavi-Naini, R., Canetti, R. (eds.) CRYPTO 2012. LNCS, vol. 7417, pp. 571–589. Springer, Heidelberg (2012)

[LPY12b] Libert, B., Peters, T., Yung, M.: Scalable group signatures with revocation. In: Pointcheval, D., Johansson, T. (eds.) EUROCRYPT 2012. LNCS, vol. 7237, pp. 609–627. Springer, Heidelberg (2012)

[LV09] Libert, B., Vergnaud, D.: Group signatures with verifier-local revocation and backward unlinkability in the standard model. In: Garay, J.A., Miyaji, A., Otsuka, A. (eds.) CANS 2009. LNCS, vol. 5888, pp. 498–517. Springer, Heidelberg (2009)

[NF05] Nakanishi, T., Funabiki, N.: Verifier-local revocation group signature schemes with backward unlinkability from bilinear maps. In: Roy, B. (ed.) ASIACRYPT 2005. LNCS, vol. 3788, pp. 533–548. Springer, Heidelberg (2005)

[NFHF09] Attrapadung, N., Emura, K., Hanaoka, G., Sakai, Y.: A revocable group signature scheme from identity-based revocation techniques: achieving constant-size revocation list. In: Boureanu, I., Owesarski, P., Vaudenay, S. (eds.) ACNS 2014. LNCS, vol. 8479, pp. 419–437. Springer, Heidelberg (2014)

[Ngu05] Nguyen, L.: Accumulators from bilinear pairings and applications. In: Menezes, A. (ed.) CT-RSA 2005. LNCS, vol. 3376, pp. 275–292. Springer, Heidelberg (2005)

[NNL01] Naor, D., Naor, M., Lotspiech, J.: Revocation and tracing schemes for stateless receivers. In: Kilian, J. (ed.) CRYPTO 2001. LNCS, vol. 2139, pp. 41–62. Springer, Heidelberg (2001)

[NS04] Nguyen, L., Safavi-Naini, R.: Efficient and provably secure trapdoor-free group signature schemes from bilinear pairings. In: Lee, P.J. (ed.) ASIACRYPT 2004. LNCS, vol. 3329, pp. 372–386. Springer, Heidelberg (2004)

[Son01] Song, D.X.: Practical forward secure group signature schemes. In: Conference on Computer and Communications Security, CCS (2001)

[SSE+12] Sakai, Y., Schuldt, J.C.N., Emura, K., Hanaoka, G., Ohta, K.: On the security of dynamic group signatures: preventing signature hijacking. In: Fischlin, M., Buchmann, J., Manulis, M. (eds.) PKC 2012. LNCS, vol. 7293, pp. 715–732. Springer, Heidelberg (2012)

[TS06]   Teranishi, I., Sako, K.: k-times anonymous authentication with a constant proving cost. In: Yung, M., Dodis, Y., Kiayias, A., Malkin, T. (eds.) PKC 2006. LNCS, vol. 3958, pp. 525–542. Springer, Heidelberg (2006)

[TX03]   Tsudik, G., Xu, S.: Accumulating composites and improved group signing. In: Laih, C.-S. (ed.) ASIACRYPT 2003. LNCS, vol. 2894, pp. 269–286. Springer, Heidelberg (2003)

A Lattice-Based Group Signature Scheme with Message-Dependent Opening

Benoît Libert[1], Fabrice Mouhartem[1(✉)], and Khoa Nguyen[2]

[1] École Normale Supérieure de Lyon, Lyon, France
fabrice.mouhartem@ens-lyon.fr
[2] Nanyang Technological University, Singapore, Singapore

Abstract. Group signatures are an important anonymity primitive allowing users to sign messages while hiding in a crowd. At the same time, signers remain accountable since an authority is capable of de-anonymizing signatures via a process called *opening*. In many situations, this authority is granted too much power as it can identify the author of any signature. Sakai *et al.* proposed a flavor of the primitive, called *Group Signature with Message-Dependent Opening* (GS-MDO), where opening operations are only possible when a separate authority (called "admitter") has revealed a trapdoor for the corresponding message. So far, all existing GS-MDO constructions rely on bilinear maps, partially because the message-dependent opening functionality inherently implies identity-based encryption. This paper proposes the first GS-MDO candidate based on lattice assumptions. Our construction combines the group signature of Ling, Nguyen and Wang (PKC'15) with two layers of identity-based encryption. These components are tied together using suitable zero-knowledge argument systems.

Keywords: Group signatures · Anonymity · Lattice assumptions

1   Introduction

GROUP SIGNATURES. Group signatures were introduced by Chaum and van Heyst in 1991 [15] as a technique allowing users to sign messages while retaining anonymity within a crowd of users they belong to. At the same, misbehaving group members cannot remain unpunished as an *authority*, called *opening authority*, is capable of tracing a signature to the user who generated it [5]. While such a tracing mechanism is necessary to ensure user accountability, it arguably grants excessive power to the opening authority which can retrieve the identity of any well-behaved user from his signature. To address this issue, Sakai *et al.* [40] suggested an extension, named *group signature with message dependent opening* (GS-MDO), which provides a refined balance between accountability and privacy. In GS-MDO systems, as formalized in [40], the identity of a signer can only be determined from two pieces of information: the opening authority's secret key and a message-specific token delivered by a separate authority called the *admitter*. Importantly, neither authority is able to trace any signature alone.

© Springer International Publishing Switzerland 2016
M. Manulis et al. (Eds.): ACNS 2016, LNCS 9696, pp. 137–155, 2016.
DOI: 10.1007/978-3-319-39555-5_8

Each opening operation has to be approved by the admitter who cannot identify signers by itself as it is denied access to the opening authority's secret key.

A different way to avoid centralizing the opening capability would be to split the opening authority's private key into several shares scattered among multiple servers using techniques from threshold cryptography [16]. This approach, however, requires all shareholders to run a distributed decryption protocol (indeed, any group signature implies a public-key encryption scheme [1]) at every single opening operation, even for identical messages. The GS-MDO primitive comes in handy when many signatures have to be opened on the same message. As a motivating example, we can think of access control gates in public transportation. In order to enter a metro station, the user can generate a signature (i.e., on a message specifying the date and time or his ride) proving his possession of a valid subscription without betraying his identity nor leaking any information on his habits (e.g., the frequency of his rides). If an accident occurs or a crime is committed, the police – which embodies the opening authority in this case – can request the opening tokens for to the time period of the incident and determine who was nearby at that time. In such a situation, the threshold opening approach would incur a substantial overhead to open all the signatures generated by commuters in a given time interval. In contrast, the GS-MDO primitive allows de-anonymizing all signatures corresponding to a given message – no matter how many users signed this message – without having the police interact any further with the public transportation company once the latter has revealed a message-specific token.

As another motivating application, we can think of anonymous comments posted on a blog engine, where a moderator can use a token to open all signatures related to forbidden messages. Yet another example consists of anonymous auctions where bidders sign the amount of their bid: in case of equalities, a single token allows identifying the multiple winners of the auction.

As such, message-dependent openings are relevant when the number of signatures to be opened is potentially high. Moreover, it can be seen as providing the dual functionality of *traceable* signatures [27]. As introduced by Kiayias, Tsiounis and Yung [27], traceable signatures allow the group manager to release a user-specific trapdoor using which all the signatures that user created can be identified. This extended capability allows delegating the tracing operation to parallel tracing agents who can detect all the transactions where a misbehaving user is involved without affecting the anonymity of honest users. Group signatures with message-dependent opening can be motivated in a similar way in that the distributed tracing process can be made with respect to the message rather than the users. If a signed message contains information about a specific suspicious transaction, releasing a message-specific trapdoor makes it possible to trace all parties involved in a given transaction determined by the signed message.

Lattice-based cryptography. Since the seminal results of Regev [39] and Gentry-Peikert-Vaikuntanathan [19], lattice-based cryptography has emerged (see [37] and references therein) as a promising alternative to discrete-logarithm or factoring-based technologies. This trend can be explained by the fact that lattices provide appealing advantages like simple arithmetic operations, their better asymptotic efficiency or their potential as candidates for post-quantum cryptography: indeed, quantum algorithms are not known to perform any better than classical ones for well-studied problems like *Learning With Errors* (LWE) or *Short Integer Solution* (SIS). Moreover, many advanced cryptographic functionalities (like full homomorphism [18]), which are elusive in the discrete logarithm setting, are enabled by these assumptions.

In this paper, we describe the first lattice-based realization of group signatures with message-dependent opening.

RELATED WORK. The pioneering work of Chaum an Van Heyst [15] inspired many group signature candidates in the nineties but practical and scalable constructions only came out in 2000. The first group signature that was both scalable and collusion-resistant was proposed by Ateniese, Camenisch, Joye and Tsudik [3] under the Strong RSA assumption. At that time, however, there was no precise definition of what it meant for a group signature to be secure. Security analyses were indeed conducted with respect to lists of sometimes redundant requirements. This state-of-affairs changed with the work of Bellare, Micciancio and Warinschi [5] who proposed a model synthesizing the security requirements into two properties named *anonymity* and *traceability*. In this model, Boneh, Boyen and Shacham [7] put forth a practical construction with very short signatures based on pairing-related assumptions. While the solution of [7] was in the random oracle model, constructions in the standard model came out in several works [10,11,23] inspired by the Groth-Sahai methodology [24].

Sakai *et al.* introduced the message-dependent opening functionality [40] in 2012. In their work, they provided evidence that GS-MDO schemes imply identity-based encryption (IBE) [8,41]. In the random oracle model, Ohara *et al.* [35] subsequently designed efficient GS-MDO schemes [35] based on non-standard assumptions in groups with a bilinear map. Libert and Joye [29] appealed to the same tools and the machinery of Groth-Sahai proofs [24] to build a GS-MDO system in the standard model.

While group signatures have attracted much attention in cryptography for many years, the first lattice-based proposal only appeared in 2010 in the work of Gordon, Katz and Vaikuntanathan [21]. While a simple counting argument suggests that no group signature can contain less than $\log N$ bits (where N is the number of group members), the Gordon *et al.* [21] construction had signatures of linear size in N. The desired logarithmic size was reached by Laguillaumie *et al.* [28] whose solution still remained quite costly. Although several substantial improvements were recently achieved [31,33,34], lattice-based group signatures are not yet competitive with pairing-based solutions. One of the cited reasons explaining this efficiency gap is the fact that *zero-knowledge proofs* [20] for lattice-related languages [6,32] remain less effective than those in groups with a bilinear map, where the rich underlying algebraic structure has proven very useful [24]. An illustration of the limited amount of algebraic structure of lattices is the absence of non-interactive zero knowledge (NIZK) proofs outside the random oracle model in the lattice setting (except for very specific languages [38]).

Even in the random oracle model, the design of lattice-based group signatures with extra properties remains a non-trivial problem. In particular, no GS-MDO system has been proposed so far. In fact, except the theoretical construction of Sakai *et al.* [40], all existing solutions [29,35,40] rely on bilinear maps. For the sake of not putting all one's eggs in the same basket, it is thus important to seek constructions based on different assumptions.

OUR CONTRIBUTION. We propose the first GS-MDO realization based on standard lattice assumptions. The security of our scheme is proved in the random oracle model under SIS and LWE assumptions. We design this scheme by extending the group signature scheme of Ling, Nguyen and Wang [33]. Not only does this scheme provide one of the most efficient candidates so far, its built-in zero-knowledge arguments turn out to be sufficiently flexible to accommodate our statements in the setting of message-dependent openings. Like [33], our construction proceeds by having each group member's signing key consist of a Boyen [9] signature for his identity $d \in \{0,1\}^{\ell}$. To sign a message M, the user encrypt his identity d using an IND-CCA encryption scheme derived from the Gentry-Peikert-Vaikuntanathan (GPV) IBE [19] via the Canetti-Halevi-Katz (CHK) paradigm [13]. Then, the user provides a ZK argument of possession of a Boyen signature for the message encrypted by the ciphertext, the message being embedded in the Fiat-Shamir challenge to make the proof non-interactive. Our scheme takes advantage of the fact that Ling *et al.* [33] used an IBE to encrypt the group member's identifier. We add a second encryption layer in order to encrypt the ciphertext under the identity M, which is the message to be signed. Therefore, the GS-MDO functionality can be achieved by combining two instances of the GPV IBE (one for the admitter and the second one for the opening authority). To reveal a message-specific token t_M, the admitter can simply output a private key for the identity M, then allowing the opener to retrieve the ciphertext hiding the identity. Then, using the encryption layer as in the Ling *et al.* scheme [33] allows us to adapt the underlying argument system to our purpose.

Now, the challenge is to prove that the entire double-encryption process was conducted properly. To this end, we can leverage the properties of Stern-like protocols [42] and translate the statements to be proved so as to apply the recently proposed framework of [30]. Our argument system, while addressing a more elaborate relation than in [33], is constructed in a simpler and more modular manner. In short, we reduce the entire statement into an assertion of the form $\mathbf{P} \cdot \mathbf{x} = \mathbf{v} \bmod q$, where $\mathbf{P}$ is a public matrix that depends on the group public key and the outer ciphertext layer, while $\mathbf{x}$ is a short vector which is constructed from the witness and has a special structure.

We can also notice that our technique can be used to enable message-dependent opening in the case of *dynamically growing groups* as well. For instance, the two-layer encryption method can be straightforwardly adapted to the dynamic group signature scheme from Libert *et al.* [30] which is also built upon the Ling *et al.* scheme [33] and also relies on Stern-like ZK arguments.

ROADMAP. To present our results, the rest of the paper is organized as follows. In Sect. 2, we first recall the necessary definitions and security notions. The supporting zero-knowledge argument system is constructed in Sect. 3. In Sect. 4, we present our lattice-based GS-MDO scheme.

2   Background

NOTATIONS. Matrices are denoted with bold upper-case letters $\mathbf{A}$ and vectors in bold lower-case letters $\mathbf{x}$. We assume that all vectors are column vectors. The concatenation of vectors $\mathbf{x} \in \mathbb{R}^k$ and $\mathbf{y} \in \mathbb{R}^m$ is denoted by $(\mathbf{x}\|\mathbf{y}) \in \mathbb{R}^{k+m}$. We denote the column concatenation of matrices $\mathbf{A} \in \mathbb{R}^{n \times k}$ and $\mathbf{B} \in \mathbb{R}^{n \times m}$ by $[\mathbf{A}|\mathbf{B}]$. If dimensions are compatible, $\langle \mathbf{u}, \mathbf{v} \rangle$ denote the inner product of vectors $\mathbf{u}$ and $\mathbf{v}$. The identity matrix of order k is denoted by $\mathbf{I}_k$, and $\mathbf{0}_\ell$ stands for the zero vector of dimension ℓ. If $\mathbf{A}$ is a full column rank matrix, we let $\widetilde{\mathbf{A}}$ denote its Gram-Schmidt orthogonalization. If $\mathbf{u} \in \mathbb{R}^n$, its Euclidean norm is denoted by $\|\mathbf{b}\|$ and this notation is extended to matrices $\mathbf{A} \in \mathbb{R}^{n \times m}$ with columns $(\mathbf{a}_i)_{i \leq m}$ by $\|\mathbf{A}\| = \max_{i \leq m} \|\mathbf{a}_i\|$. Finally, PPT stands for *Probabilistic Polynomial-Time*.

2.1   Lattices

A lattice Λ is a discrete subgroup of some space $\mathbb{R}^n$, which can be seen as the set of integer linear combinations of linearly independent vectors $(\mathbf{b}_i)_{i \leq n}$. Over a lattice Λ, and given a parameter $\sigma \in \mathbb{R}_+^*$, we define the Gaussian distribution of support Λ and parameter σ by $D_{\Lambda,\sigma}[\mathbf{b}] \sim \exp(-\pi \|\mathbf{b}\|^2/\sigma^2)$, for all $\mathbf{b} \in \Lambda$. We will use the fact that samples from $D_{\Lambda,\sigma}$ are short with overwhelming probability.

Lemma 1 ([4, Le. 1.5]). *For any lattice $\Lambda \subseteq \mathbb{R}^n$ and positive real number σ, we have $\mathrm{Pr}_{\mathbf{b} \hookleftarrow D_{\Lambda,\sigma}}[\|\mathbf{b}\| \leq \sqrt{n}\sigma] \geq 1 - 2^{-\Omega(n)}$.*

Gentry, Peikert and Vaikuntanathan [19] show that it is possible to efficiently sample from a Gaussian distribution on a lattice support given a sufficiently short basis of this lattice.

Lemma 2 ([12, Le. 2.3]). *There exists a PPT algorithm GPVSample that takes as inputs a basis $\mathbf{B}$ of a lattice $\Lambda \subseteq \mathbb{Z}^n$ and rational $\sigma \geq \|\widetilde{\mathbf{B}}\| \cdot \Omega(\sqrt{\log n})$, and outputs vectors $\mathbf{b} \in \Lambda$ with distribution $D_{\Lambda,\sigma}$.*

Definition 1. *Let $m \geq n \geq 1$ and $q \geq 2$. For a matrix $\mathbf{A} \in \mathbb{Z}_q^{n \times m}$, and a vector $\mathbf{u} \in \mathbb{Z}_q^n$, define $\Lambda_q(\mathbf{A}) := \{\mathbf{x} \in \mathbb{Z}^m : \exists \mathbf{s} \in \mathbb{Z}_q^n \ s.t. \ \mathbf{A}^T \cdot \mathbf{s} = \mathbf{x} \bmod q\}$ and*

$$\Lambda_q^\perp(\mathbf{A}) := \{\mathbf{x} \in \mathbb{Z}^m : \mathbf{A} \cdot \mathbf{x} = \mathbf{0} \bmod q\}, \quad \Lambda_q^{\mathbf{u}}(\mathbf{A}) := \{\mathbf{x} \in \mathbb{Z}^m : \mathbf{A} \cdot \mathbf{x} = \mathbf{u} \bmod q\}.$$

We also use an algorithm that jointly samples an uniform matrix $\mathbf{A}$ and a short basis of the lattice $\Lambda_q^\perp(\mathbf{A})$.

Lemma 3 ([2, Th. 3.2]). *There exists a PPT algorithm GenTrap that takes as inputs 1^n, 1^m and an integer $q \geq 2$ with $m \geq \Omega(n \log q)$, and outputs a matrix $\mathbf{A} \in \mathbb{Z}_q^{n \times m}$ and a basis $\mathbf{T}_\mathbf{A}$ of $\Lambda_q^\perp(\mathbf{A})$ such that $\mathbf{A}$ is within statistical distance $2^{-\Omega(n)}$ to $U(\mathbb{Z}_q^{n \times m})$, and $\|\widetilde{\mathbf{T}_\mathbf{A}}\| \leq \mathcal{O}(\sqrt{n \log q})$.*

The description of our scheme also uses an algorithm that extends a trapdoor for $\mathbf{A} \in \mathbb{Z}_q^{n \times m}$ to a trapdoor of any $\mathbf{B} \in \mathbb{Z}_q^{n \times m'}$ whose left $n \times m$ submatrix is $\mathbf{A}$.

Lemma 4 ([14, Le. 3.2]). *There exists a* PPT *algorithm* ExtBasis *that takes as inputs a matrix* $\mathbf{B} \in \mathbb{Z}_q^{n \times m'}$ *whose first m columns span* $\mathbb{Z}_q^n$, *and a basis* $\mathbf{T_A}$ *of* $\Lambda_q^{\perp}(\mathbf{A})$ *where* $\mathbf{A}$ *is the left* $n \times m$ *submatrix of* $\mathbf{B}$, *and outputs a basis* $\mathbf{T_B}$ *of* $\Lambda_q^{\perp}(\mathbf{B})$ *with* $\|\widetilde{\mathbf{T_B}}\| \leq \|\widetilde{\mathbf{T_A}}\|$.

2.2 Hardness Assumptions

We prove the security of our scheme in the ROM among the assumption that both algorithmic problems below are hard, in the sense that they cannot be solved by any PPT algorithm with non-negligible probability nor advantage respectively.

Definition 2. *Let* m, q, β *be functions of a parameter* n. *The Short Integer Solution problem* $\mathsf{SIS}_{m,q,\beta}$ *is as follows: Given* $\mathbf{A} \hookleftarrow U(\mathbb{Z}_q^{n \times m})$, *find* $\mathbf{x} \in \Lambda_q^{\perp}(\mathbf{A})$ *with* $0 < \|\mathbf{x}\| \leq \beta$.

Definition 3. *Let* q, α *be functions of a parameter* n. *For* $\mathbf{s} \in \mathbb{Z}_q^n$ *(a secret), the distribution* $A_{q,\alpha,\mathbf{s}}$ *over* $\mathbb{Z}_q^n \times \mathbb{Z}_q$ *is obtained by sampling* $\mathbf{a} \hookleftarrow U(\mathbb{Z}_q^n)$ *and (a noise)* $e \hookleftarrow D_{\mathbb{Z},\alpha q}$, *and returning* $(\mathbf{a}, \langle \mathbf{a}, \mathbf{s} \rangle + e)$. *The Learning With Errors problem* $\mathsf{LWE}_{q,\alpha}$ *is as follows: For* $\mathbf{s} \hookleftarrow U(\mathbb{Z}_q^n)$, *distinguish between arbitrarily many independent samples from* $U(\mathbb{Z}_q^n \times \mathbb{Z}_q)$ *and the same number of independent samples from* $A_{q,\alpha,\mathbf{s}}$.

If $q \geq \sqrt{n}\beta$ and $m, \beta \leq \mathsf{poly}(n)$, then standard worst-case lattice problems with approximation factors $\gamma = \widetilde{\mathcal{O}}(\beta\sqrt{n})$ reduce to $\mathsf{SIS}_{m,q,\beta}$ (see for instance [19, Se. 9]). Similarly, if $\alpha q = \Omega(\sqrt{n})$, then standard worst-case lattice problems with approximation factors $\gamma = \mathcal{O}(\alpha/n)$ quantumly reduce to $\mathsf{LWE}_{q,\alpha}$ (see [39] as well as [12,36] for classical analogues).

2.3 Group Signature with Message Dependent Opening

We use the syntax of Sakai *et al.* [40] to describe a GS-MDO, which extends the group signature's model of Bellare, Micciancio and Warinschi [5].

Definition 4 (GS-MDO). *A group signature with message-dependent opening is a tuple of algorithms* (Keygen, Sign, Verify, TrapGen, Open) *such that:*

Keygen$(1^\lambda, 1^N)$**:** *Given a security parameter* λ *and the number of group members* N, *outputs the group public key* gpk, *the opening key* ok, *the the admitter's private key* $\mathsf{msk}_{\mathsf{ADM}}$, *and a vector of user secret keys* $\mathbf{gsk} = (\mathbf{gsk}[d])_{d=0}^{N-1}$.

Sign$(\mathsf{gpk}, \mathbf{gsk}[d], M)$**:** *Given an user* d *secret key* $\mathbf{gsk}[d]$ *and a message* M, *issue a signature* Σ *for the message* M.

Verify$(\mathsf{gpk}, M, \Sigma)$**:** *Given a message* M *and a signature* Σ, *output 0 or 1.*

TrapGen$(\mathsf{gpk}, \mathsf{msk}_{\mathsf{ADM}}, M)$**:** *Given the admitter key* $\mathsf{msk}_{\mathsf{ADM}}$, *and a message* M, *output a token* t_M.

Open$(\mathsf{gpk}, \mathsf{ok}, \mathsf{t}_M, M, \Sigma)$**:** *Given the opening key* ok, *a message* M, *a token* t_M *for this message, and a signature* Σ, *return either* $d \in \mathbb{N}$, *or* $\perp$.

These algorithms must also verify the correctness property, meaning that for all $(\mathsf{gpk}, \mathbf{gsk}, \mathsf{ok}, \mathsf{msk_{ADM}}) \leftarrow \mathsf{Keygen}(1^\lambda, 1^N)$, for all $d \in \{0, \ldots, N-1\}$, and for all $M \in \{0,1\}^*$, we have w.h.p. $\mathsf{Verify}(\mathsf{gpk}, M, \mathsf{Sign}(\mathsf{gpk}, \mathbf{gsk}[d], M)) = 1$ and $\mathsf{Open}(\mathsf{gpk}, \mathsf{ok}, \mathsf{TrapGen}(\mathsf{gpk}, \mathsf{msk_{ADM}}, M), M, \mathsf{Sign}(\mathsf{gpk}, \mathbf{gsk}[d], M)) = d$.

Like in a classical group signature, the scheme must verify *Traceability* and *Anonymity*, but since the opening capability is split in two entities, namely the admitter and the opening authority (also known as the group manager), there therefore are two anonymity definitions: the *Opener Anonymity* and the *Admitter Anonymity*, which are formalized as follows.

Definition 5 (Traceability). *A GS-MDO scheme provides full traceability if, for any $\lambda \in \mathbb{N}$, any $N \in \mathsf{poly}(\lambda)$ and any PPT adversary $\mathcal{A}$ involved in the experiment below, it holds that $\mathbf{Adv}_{\mathcal{A}}^{\mathrm{trace}}(\lambda) = \Pr[\mathbf{Exp}_{\mathcal{A}}^{\mathrm{trace}}(\lambda, N) = 1] \in \mathsf{negl}(\lambda)$.*

$\underline{\mathit{Exp}_{\mathcal{A}}^{\mathit{trace}}(\lambda, N)}$

$(\mathsf{gpk}, \mathsf{ok}, \mathsf{msk_{ADM}}, \mathbf{gsk}) \leftarrow \mathsf{Keygen}(\lambda, N)$

$\mathsf{st} \leftarrow (\mathsf{ok}, \mathsf{msk_{ADM}}, \mathsf{gpk})$; $\mathcal{C} \leftarrow \emptyset$; $K \leftarrow \varepsilon$; $\mathit{Cont} \leftarrow \mathbf{true}$

while $(\mathit{Cont} = \mathbf{true})$ do

$\qquad (\mathit{Cont}, \mathsf{st}, j) \leftarrow \mathcal{A}^{\mathsf{Sign}(\mathbf{gsk}[\cdot], \cdot)}(\mathit{choose}, \mathsf{st}, K)$

$\qquad$ if $\mathit{Cont} = \mathbf{true}$ then $\mathcal{C} \leftarrow \mathcal{C} \cup \{j\}$; $K \leftarrow K \cup \{\mathbf{gsk}[j]\}$ end if

$(M^*, \sigma^*) \leftarrow \mathcal{A}^{\mathsf{Sign}(\mathbf{gsk}[\cdot], \cdot)}(\mathit{guess}, \mathsf{st})$

if $\mathsf{Verify}(\mathsf{gpk}, M^*, \sigma^*) = 0$ then *Return* 0

if $\mathsf{Open}(\mathsf{gpk}, \mathsf{ok}, \mathsf{TrapGen}(\mathsf{gpk}, \mathsf{msk_{ADM}}, M^*), M^*, \sigma^*) = \perp$ then *Return* 1

if $\exists j^* \in \{0, \ldots, N-1\}$ such that

$\qquad (\mathsf{Open}(\mathsf{gpk}, \mathsf{ok}, t_{M^*}, M^*, \sigma^*) = j^*) \wedge (j^* \notin \mathcal{C}) \wedge ((j^*, M^*)$ *not queried by* $\mathcal{A})$

$\qquad$ with $t_{M^*} \leftarrow \mathsf{TrapGen}(\mathsf{gpk}, \mathsf{msk_{ADM}}, M^*)$

then *Return* 1 else *Return* 0

Definition 6 (Admitter Anonymity). *A GS-MDO scheme provides full anonymity against the admitter if, for any $\lambda \in \mathbb{N}$, any $N \in \mathsf{poly}(\lambda)$ and any PPT adversary $\mathcal{A}$ involved in the experiment hereunder, we have*

$$\mathbf{Adv}_{\mathcal{A}}^{\mathrm{anon\text{-}adm}}(\lambda) = |\Pr[\mathbf{Exp}_{\mathcal{A}}^{\mathrm{anon\text{-}adm}}(\lambda, N) = 1] - 1/2| \in \mathsf{negl}(\lambda).$$

$\underline{\mathit{Exp}_{\mathcal{A}}^{\mathit{anon-adm}}(\lambda, N)}$

$(\mathsf{gpk}, \mathsf{ok}, \mathsf{msk_{ADM}}, \mathbf{gsk}) \leftarrow \mathsf{Keygen}(\lambda, N)$

$(\mathsf{st}, j_0, j_1, M^*) \leftarrow \mathcal{A}^{\mathcal{O}_{\mathsf{ok}}}(\mathit{choose}, \mathsf{gpk}, \mathbf{gsk}, \mathsf{msk_{ADM}})$

$b \leftarrow \{0,1\}$; $\quad \sigma^* \leftarrow \mathsf{Sign}(\mathsf{gpk}, \mathbf{gsk}[j_b], M^*)$

$b' \leftarrow \mathcal{A}^{\mathcal{O}_{\mathsf{ok}}}(\mathit{guess}, \mathsf{st}, \sigma^*)$

Return 1 if $b' = b$ and 0 otherwise

Here, $\mathcal{O}_{\mathsf{ok}}$ is an oracle that takes as input an arbitrary signature $\sigma \neq \sigma^*$ and uses ok and $\mathsf{msk_{ADM}}$ to return the identity of the signer.

Definition 7 (Opener Anonymity). *A GS-MDO scheme provides full anonymity against the opener if, for any $\lambda \in \mathbb{N}$, any $N \in \mathsf{poly}(\lambda)$ and any PPT adversary $\mathcal{A}$ involved in the experiment below, it holds that*

$$\mathbf{Adv}_{\mathcal{A}}^{\mathrm{anon\text{-}oa}}(\lambda) = |\Pr[\mathbf{Exp}_{\mathcal{A}}^{\mathrm{anon\text{-}oa}}(\lambda, N) = 1] - 1/2| \in \mathsf{negl}(\lambda).$$

$$\underline{Exp_{\mathcal{A}}^{anon-oa}(\lambda, N)}$$
$(\mathsf{gpk}, \mathsf{ok}, \mathsf{msk}_{\mathsf{ADM}}, \mathbf{gsk}) \leftarrow \mathsf{Keygen}(\lambda, N)$
$(\mathbf{st}, j_0, j_1, M^\star) \leftarrow \mathcal{A}^{\mathcal{O}_{\mathsf{msk}_{\mathsf{ADM}}}} (choose, \mathsf{gpk}, \mathbf{gsk}, \mathsf{ok})$
$b \hookleftarrow \{0, 1\}; \quad \sigma^\star \leftarrow \mathsf{Sign}(\mathsf{gpk}, \mathbf{gsk}[j_b], M^\star)$
$b' \leftarrow \mathcal{A}^{\mathcal{O}_{\mathsf{msk}_{\mathsf{ADM}}}} (guess, \mathbf{st}, \sigma^\star)$
$Return\ 1\ if\ b' = b\ and\ 0\ otherwise$

In the above notation, $\mathcal{O}_{\mathsf{msk}_{\mathsf{ADM}}}(.)$ is an oracle that returns trapdoors for arbitrary messages $M \neq M^\star$ chosen by the adversary.

2.4   Zero-Knowledge Arguments of Knowledge

We will work with statistical zero-knowledge argument systems, which are interactive protocols where the zero-knowledge property holds against *any* cheating verifier, while the soundness property only holds against *computationally bounded* cheating provers. More formally, let the set of statements-witnesses $R = \{(y, w)\} \in \{0, 1\}^* \times \{0, 1\}^*$ be an NP relation. A two-party game $\langle \mathcal{P}, \mathcal{V} \rangle$ is called an interactive argument system for the relation R with soundness error e if the following two conditions hold:

- **Completeness.** If $(y, w) \in R$ then $\Pr[\langle \mathcal{P}(y, w), \mathcal{V}(y) \rangle = 1] = 1$.
- **Soundness.** For any PPT $\widehat{\mathcal{P}}$, if $(y, w) \notin R$, then $\Pr[\langle \widehat{\mathcal{P}}(y, w), \mathcal{V}(y) \rangle = 1] \leq e$.

An argument system is called statistical zero-knowledge if for any $\widehat{\mathcal{V}}(y)$, there exists a PPT simulator $\mathcal{S}(y)$ producing a simulated transcript that is statistically close to the one of the real interaction between $\mathcal{P}(y, w)$ and $\widehat{\mathcal{V}}(y)$. A related notion is argument of knowledge, which requires the witness-extended emulation property. For protocols consisting of 3 moves (*i.e.*, commitment-challenge-response), witness-extended emulation is implied by *special soundness* [22], where the latter assumes that there exists a PPT extractor which takes as input a set of valid transcripts with respect to all possible values of the 'challenge' to the same 'commitment', and outputs w' such that $(y, w') \in R$.

Our statistical zero-knowledge arguments of knowledge (sZKAoK) are Stern-type [42]. In particular, they are Σ-protocols in the generalized sense considered in [6, 25] (where 3 valid transcripts are needed for extraction, instead of just 2).

3   The Underlying Zero-Knowledge Argument System

First of all, we recall that the protocol from [33] allows prover $\mathcal{P}$ to convince verifier $\mathcal{V}$ in ZK that $\mathcal{P}$ knows a valid message-signature pair $(d, \mathbf{z})$ for Boyen's signature scheme [9], and that the binary representation of d is honestly encrypted to a given ciphertext pair $(\mathbf{c}_1, \mathbf{c}_2)$. The strategy in [33] was to extend Stern's protocol [42] (via the Decomposition-Extension technique [32]) to prove the statement in a *ad-hoc* manner. However, their argument system was rather complicated, which makes it somewhat inflexible to be used as a sub-protocol in designing more advanced constructions.

The goal of this section is to construct the statistical zero-knowledge argument of knowledge (sZKAoK) underlying the GS-MDO scheme of Sect. 4. In our setting, the ciphertext component $\mathbf{c}_2$ is hidden, and $\mathcal{P}$ can additionally prove that the secret bits representing $\mathbf{c}_2$ are correctly encrypted to another given ciphertext pair $(\hat{\mathbf{c}}_1, \hat{\mathbf{c}}_2)$. By using the new strategy for Stern-like protocols, recently proposed in [30], we can handle the extended relation, yet the resulting argument system is obtained in a simpler and more modular manner than in [33].

More formally, let n, m, ℓ, q, β, b be positive integers and $k = \lceil \log q \rceil$. Let $\mathbf{H} = \mathbf{I}_\ell \otimes \left(1 \mid 2 \mid 4 \mid \cdots \mid 2^{k-1} \right) \in \mathbb{Z}_q^{\ell \times \ell k}$, and let bin : $\mathbb{Z}_q^\ell \to \{0,1\}^{\ell k}$ be the function mapping $\mathbf{w}$ to its component-wise binary decomposition $\mathrm{bin}(\mathbf{w})$. (Note that for all $\mathbf{w} \in \mathbb{Z}_q^\ell$, we have $\mathbf{H} \cdot \mathrm{bin}(\mathbf{w}) = \mathbf{w}$.) We define as well the binary decomposition function for integer bin : $\mathbb{N} \to \{0,1\}^*$.

The relation R_{gsmdo} associated with our protocol is then defined as follows.

Definition 8. *Define*

$$R_{\mathrm{gsmdo}} = \left\{ (\mathbf{A}, \{\mathbf{A}_i\}_{i=0}^\ell, \mathbf{B}, \mathbf{C}, \mathbf{G}, \hat{\mathbf{G}}, \mathbf{u}, \mathbf{c}_1, \hat{\mathbf{c}}_1, \hat{\mathbf{c}}_2), \mathbf{d}, \mathbf{z}, \mathbf{s}, \hat{\mathbf{s}}, \mathbf{e}_1, \hat{\mathbf{e}}_1, \mathbf{e}_2, \hat{\mathbf{e}}_2, \mathbf{c}_2 \right\}$$

as a relation where

$$\begin{cases} \mathbf{A}, \{\mathbf{A}_i\}_{i=0}^\ell, \mathbf{B}, \mathbf{C} \in \mathbb{Z}_q^{n \times m}; \ \mathbf{G} \in \mathbb{Z}_q^{n \times \ell}; \ \hat{\mathbf{G}} \in \mathbb{Z}_q^{n \times \ell k}; \ \mathbf{u} \in \mathbb{Z}_q^n; \ \mathbf{c}_1, \hat{\mathbf{c}}_1 \in \mathbb{Z}_q^m; \ \hat{\mathbf{c}}_2 \in \mathbb{Z}_q^{\ell k}; \\ \mathbf{d} = (d_1, \ldots, d_\ell) \in \{0,1\}^\ell; \ \mathbf{z} \in [-\beta, \beta]^{2m}; \ \mathbf{s}, \hat{\mathbf{s}} \in [-b, b]^n; \ \mathbf{e}_1, \hat{\mathbf{e}}_1 \in [-b, b]^m; \\ \mathbf{e}_2 \in [-b, b]^\ell; \ \hat{\mathbf{e}}_2 \in [-b, b]^{\ell k}; \ \mathbf{c}_2 \in \mathbb{Z}_q^\ell \end{cases}$$

satisfy

$$\begin{cases} \left[\mathbf{A} \mid \mathbf{A}_0 + \sum_{i=1}^\ell d_i \cdot \mathbf{A}_i \right] \cdot \mathbf{z} = \mathbf{u} \bmod q & (1) \\[2mm] \mathbf{c}_1 = \mathbf{B}^\top \cdot \mathbf{s} + \mathbf{e}_1 \bmod q; \quad \mathbf{c}_2 = \mathbf{G}^\top \cdot \mathbf{s} + \mathbf{e}_2 + \left\lfloor \frac{q}{2} \right\rfloor \cdot \mathbf{d} \bmod q & (2) \\[2mm] \hat{\mathbf{c}}_1 = \mathbf{C}^\top \cdot \hat{\mathbf{s}} + \hat{\mathbf{e}}_1 \bmod q; \quad \hat{\mathbf{c}}_2 = \hat{\mathbf{G}}^\top \cdot \hat{\mathbf{s}} + \hat{\mathbf{e}}_2 + \left\lfloor \frac{q}{2} \right\rfloor \cdot \mathrm{bin}(\mathbf{c}_2) \bmod q. & (3) \end{cases}$$

In Sect. 3.1, we present Stern's protocol from a high-level point of view, according to the abstraction of [30]. From the transformations performed in Sect. 3.2, we then show how to obtain a ZKAoK for R_{gsmdo} based on this abstract protocol.

3.1   Stern's Protocol, from a High-Level Viewpoint

Let $D, L, q \geq 2$ be positive integers and let VALID be a subset of $\{-1, 0, 1\}^L$. Suppose that $\mathcal{S}$ is a finite set such that one can associate every $\pi \in \mathcal{S}$ with a permutation T_π of L elements, satisfying the following condition:

$$\mathbf{x} \in \mathsf{VALID} \iff T_\pi(\mathbf{x}) \in \mathsf{VALID}. \tag{4}$$

We aim to construct a sZKAoK for the following abstract relation:

$$R_{\mathrm{abstract}} = \left\{ (\mathbf{P}, \mathbf{v}), \mathbf{x} \in \mathbb{Z}_q^{D \times L} \times \mathbb{Z}_q^D \times \mathsf{VALID} : \mathbf{P} \cdot \mathbf{x} = \mathbf{v} \bmod q. \right\}$$

Note that, Stern's original protocol corresponds to the special case when VALID $= \{\mathbf{x} \in \{0,1\}^L : \mathsf{wt}(\mathbf{x}) = k\}$ (where $\mathsf{wt}(\cdot)$ denotes the Hamming weight and $k < L$ is a given integer), $\mathcal{S} = \mathcal{S}_L$ - hereunder the set of all permutations of L elements, and $T_\pi(\mathbf{x}) = \pi(\mathbf{x})$.

The equivalence in (4) plays a crucial role in proving in ZK that $\mathbf{x} \in$ VALID: To do so $\mathcal{P}$ samples $\pi \hookleftarrow U(\mathcal{S})$ and lets $\mathcal{V}$ check that $T_\pi(\mathbf{x}) \in$ VALID, while the latter cannot learn any additional information about $\mathbf{x}$ thanks to the randomness of π. Furthermore, to prove in ZK that the linear equation holds, $\mathcal{P}$ samples a masking vector $\mathbf{r} \hookleftarrow U(\mathbb{Z}_q^L)$, sends $\mathbf{y} = \mathbf{x} + \mathbf{r} \bmod q$, and convinces $\mathcal{V}$ instead that $\mathbf{P} \cdot \mathbf{y} = \mathbf{P} \cdot \mathbf{r} + \mathbf{v} \bmod q$.

The interactive protocol between $\mathcal{P}(\mathbf{P}, \mathbf{v}, \mathbf{x})$ and $\mathcal{V}(\mathbf{P}, \mathbf{v})$, which employs a statistically hiding and computationally binding string commitment scheme COM (e.g., the SIS-based one from [26]), is described in Fig. 1.

---

1. **Commitment:** $\mathcal{P}$ samples $\mathbf{r} \hookleftarrow U(\mathbb{Z}_q^L)$, $\pi \hookleftarrow U(\mathcal{S})$ and randomness ρ_1, ρ_2, ρ_3 for COM. Then $\mathcal{P}$ sends the commitment CMT $= (C_1, C_2, C_3)$ to $\mathcal{V}$, where

$$C_1 = \mathsf{COM}(\pi, \mathbf{P} \cdot \mathbf{r}; \rho_1), \quad C_2 = \mathsf{COM}(T_\pi(\mathbf{r}); \rho_2), \quad C_3 = \mathsf{COM}(T_\pi(\mathbf{x} + \mathbf{r}); \rho_3).$$

2. **Challenge:** $\mathcal{V}$ sends a challenge $Ch \hookleftarrow U(\{1, 2, 3\})$ to $\mathcal{P}$.
3. **Response:** Depending on Ch, $\mathcal{P}$ sends the response RSP computed as follows:
   - $Ch = 1$: Let $\mathbf{t}_x = T_\pi(\mathbf{x})$, $\mathbf{t}_r = T_\pi(\mathbf{r})$, and RSP $= (\mathbf{t}_x, \mathbf{t}_r, \rho_2, \rho_3)$.
   - $Ch = 2$: Let $\pi_2 = \pi$, $\mathbf{y} = \mathbf{x} + \mathbf{r}$, and RSP $= (\pi_2, \mathbf{y}, \rho_1, \rho_3)$.
   - $Ch = 3$: Let $\pi_3 = \pi$, $\mathbf{r}_3 = \mathbf{r}$, and RSP $= (\pi_3, \mathbf{r}_3, \rho_1, \rho_2)$.

Verification: Receiving RSP, the verifier proceeds as follows:

   - $Ch = 1$: Check that $\mathbf{t}_x \in$ VALID and $C_2 = \mathsf{COM}(\mathbf{t}_r; \rho_2)$, $C_3 = \mathsf{COM}(\mathbf{t}_x + \mathbf{t}_r; \rho_3)$.
   - $Ch = 2$: Check that $C_1 = \mathsf{COM}(\pi_2, \mathbf{P} \cdot \mathbf{y} - \mathbf{v}; \rho_1)$, $C_3 = \mathsf{COM}(T_{\pi_2}(\mathbf{y}); \rho_3)$.
   - $Ch = 3$: Check that $C_1 = \mathsf{COM}(\pi_3, \mathbf{P} \cdot \mathbf{r}_3; \rho_1)$, $C_2 = \mathsf{COM}(T_{\pi_3}(\mathbf{r}_3); \rho_2)$.

In each case, $\mathcal{V}$ outputs 1 if and only if all the conditions hold. Otherwise, it outputs 0.

Fig. 1. A ZKAoK for the relation $\mathrm{R_{abstract}}$.

The properties of the given protocol is summarized in the following lemma.

Lemma 5. *The protocol in Fig. 1 is a* sZKAoK *for the relation* $\mathrm{R_{abstract}}$ *with perfect completeness, soundness error* $2/3$, *and communication cost* $\mathcal{O}(L \log q)$. *In particular:*

- *There exists an efficient simulator that, on input* $(\mathbf{P}, \mathbf{v})$, *outputs an accepted transcript which is statistically close to that produced by the real prover.*
- *There exists an efficient knowledge extractor that, on input a commitment* CMT *and 3 valid responses* $(\mathrm{RSP}_1, \mathrm{RSP}_2, \mathrm{RSP}_3)$ *to all 3 possible values of the challenge* Ch, *outputs* $\mathbf{x}' \in$ VALID *such that* $\mathbf{P} \cdot \mathbf{x}' = \mathbf{v} \bmod q$.

The proof of Lemma 5 employs standard simulation and extraction techniques for Stern-like protocols [17,26,31–33], and is available in the full version.

3.2 From R_{gsmdo} to $R_{abstract}$

We show that a sZKAoK for relation R_{gsmdo} in Definition 8 can be derived from the one for relation $R_{abstract}$ from Sect. 3.1. In the process, we employ the Decomposition-Extension technique from [32], which we will formalize as follows.

- For any positive integer i, denote by B_{2i} the set of all vectors in $\{0,1\}^{2i}$ having exactly i coordinates equal to 1, and denote by B_{3i} the set of all vectors in $\{-1,0,1\}^{3i}$ having exactly i coordinates equal to j, for every $j \in \{-1,0,1\}$.
- Define, for any integer $B > 0$, the number $\delta_B := \lfloor \log B \rfloor + 1$ and the sequence $B_1, \ldots, B_{\delta_B}$, where $B_j = \lfloor \frac{B+2^{j-1}}{2^j} \rfloor$ for all $j \in [\delta_B]$. As noted in [32,33], this sequence satisfies $\sum_{j=1}^{\delta_B} B_j = B$, and any integer in $[-B, B]$ can be expressed as a linear combination of the B_j's with coefficients in $\{-1,0,1\}$.
- Define the following matrices for any positive integers m, B:

$$\mathbf{H}_{m,B} = \begin{bmatrix} B_1 \ldots B_{\delta_B} & & & \\ & B_1 \ldots B_{\delta_B} & & \\ & & \ddots & \\ & & & B_1 \ldots B_{\delta_B} \end{bmatrix} \in \mathbb{Z}^{m \times m\delta_B},$$

and $\mathbf{H}_{m,B}^* = \left[\mathbf{H}_{m,B} | \mathbf{0}^{m \times 2m\delta_B} \right] \in \mathbb{Z}^{m \times 3m\delta_B}$.

Lemma 6 (Decomposition-Extension). *Let* m, B *be positive integers. Then, there exists an efficient algorithm that on input vector* $\mathbf{v} \in [-B, B]^m$*, outputs vector* $\mathbf{v}^* \in B_{3m\delta_B}$ *such that* $\mathbf{H}_{m,B}^* \cdot \mathbf{v}^* = \mathbf{v}$.

Proof. Let $\mathbf{v} = (v_1, \ldots, v_m)$, where $v_i \in [-B, B]$ for all $i \in [m]$. For each i, one can efficiently find $v_{i,1}, \ldots, v_{i,\delta_B} \in \{-1,0,1\}$ such that $\sum_{j=1}^{\delta_B} B_j \cdot v_{i,j} = v_i$.

Let $\mathbf{v}' = (v_{1,1}, \ldots, v_{1,\delta_B}, v_{2,1}, \ldots, v_{2,\delta_B}, \ldots, v_{m,1}, \ldots, v_{m,\delta_B}) \in \{-1,0,1\}^{m\delta_B}$, then $\mathbf{H}_{m,B} \cdot \mathbf{v}' = \mathbf{v}$. By appending $2m\delta_B$ suitable coordinates to $\mathbf{v}'$, one can obtain a vector $\mathbf{v}^* \in B_{3m\delta_B}$ such that $\mathbf{H}_{m,B}^* \cdot \mathbf{v}^* = \mathbf{v}$. $\square$

We now transform equations in Definition 8 into a unified equation of the form $\mathbf{P} \cdot \mathbf{x} = \mathbf{v} \bmod q$. Regarding Eq. (1), if we write $\mathbf{z}$ as $\mathbf{z} = (\mathbf{z}_1 \| \mathbf{z}_2)$, where $\mathbf{z}_1, \mathbf{z}_2 \in [-\beta, \beta]^m$, and let $\mathbf{z}_1^*, \mathbf{z}_2^* \in B_{3m\delta_\beta}$ be the vectors obtained by applying Lemma 6 to $\mathbf{z}_1, \mathbf{z}_2$, respectively, then we have:

$$\mathbf{u} = \left[\mathbf{A} \mid \mathbf{A}_0 + \sum_{i=1}^{\ell} d_i \cdot \mathbf{A}_i \right] \cdot \mathbf{z} = \mathbf{A} \cdot \mathbf{z}_1 + \mathbf{A}_0 \cdot \mathbf{z}_2 + \sum_{i=1}^{\ell} d_i \cdot \mathbf{A}_i \cdot \mathbf{z}_2 \bmod q$$

$$= (\mathbf{A} \cdot \mathbf{H}_{m,\beta}^*) \cdot \mathbf{z}_1^* + (\mathbf{A}_0 \cdot \mathbf{H}_{m,\beta}^*) \cdot \mathbf{z}_2^* + \sum_{i=1}^{\ell} (\mathbf{A}_i \cdot \mathbf{H}_{m,\beta}^*) \cdot (d_i \cdot \mathbf{z}_2^*) \bmod q$$

$$= \overline{\mathbf{A}} \cdot \bar{\mathbf{z}} \bmod q,$$

where

$$\begin{cases} \overline{\mathbf{A}} = \left[\mathbf{A} \cdot \mathbf{H}^*_{m,\beta} \mid \mathbf{A}_0 \cdot \mathbf{H}^*_{m,\beta} \mid \mathbf{A}_1 \cdot \mathbf{H}^*_{m,\beta} \mid \ldots \mid \mathbf{A}_\ell \cdot \mathbf{H}^*_{m,\beta}\right] \in \mathbb{Z}_q^{n \times (\ell+2)3m\delta_\beta} \\ \overline{\mathbf{z}} = \left(\mathbf{z}_1^* \| \mathbf{z}_2^* \| d_1 \cdot \mathbf{z}_2^* \| \ldots \| d_\ell \cdot \mathbf{z}_2^*\right) \in \{-1, 0, 1\}^{(\ell+2)3m\delta_\beta}. \end{cases}$$

Next, we extend $\mathbf{d} = (d_1, \ldots, d_\ell)$ to $\mathbf{d}^* = (d_1, \ldots, d_\ell, d_{\ell+1}, \ldots, d_{2\ell}) \in \mathsf{B}_{2\ell}$, and let $\mathbf{z}^* = \left(\overline{\mathbf{z}} \| d_{\ell+1} \cdot \mathbf{z}_2^* \| \ldots \| d_{2\ell} \cdot \mathbf{z}_2^*\right)$ and $\mathbf{A}^* = \left[\overline{\mathbf{A}} \mid \mathbf{0}^{n \times \ell 3m\delta_\beta}\right] \in \mathbb{Z}_q^{n \times (2\ell+2)3m\delta_\beta}$, then we have the following equation:

$$\mathbf{A}^* \cdot \mathbf{z}^* = \mathbf{u} \bmod q. \tag{5}$$

Meanwhile, we observe that (2) and (3) can be unified in the following form:

$$\begin{pmatrix} \mathbf{0} \\ \hline \lfloor \frac{q}{2} \rfloor \mathbf{I}_\ell \\ \hline \mathbf{0} \\ \hline \mathbf{0} \end{pmatrix} \mathbf{d} + \begin{pmatrix} \mathbf{0} \\ \hline -\mathbf{H} \\ \hline \mathbf{0} \\ \hline \lfloor \frac{q}{2} \rfloor \mathbf{I}_{\ell k} \end{pmatrix} \mathrm{bin}(\mathbf{c}_2) + \left(\begin{array}{c|cc} \mathbf{B}^\top & \multirow{2}{*}{$\mathbf{I}_{m+\ell}$} & \mathbf{0} \\ \mathbf{G}^\top & & \\ \hline \multirow{2}{*}{$\mathbf{0}$} & \mathbf{C}^\top & \multirow{2}{*}{$\mathbf{I}_{m+\ell k}$} \\ & \hat{\mathbf{G}}^\top & \end{array}\right) \begin{pmatrix} \mathbf{s} \\ \mathbf{e}_1 \\ \mathbf{e}_2 \\ \hat{\mathbf{s}} \\ \hat{\mathbf{e}}_1 \\ \hat{\mathbf{e}}_2 \end{pmatrix} = \begin{pmatrix} \mathbf{c}_1 \\ \mathbf{0}^\ell \\ \hat{\mathbf{c}}_1 \\ \hat{\mathbf{c}}_2 \end{pmatrix}.$$

For simplicity, we define $n_1 = 2m + \ell + \ell k$ and $m_1 = 2m + 2n + \ell + \ell k$. In the above unified equation, let $\mathbf{F}_1 \in \mathbb{Z}_q^{n_1 \times \ell}$, $\mathbf{F}_2 \in \mathbb{Z}_q^{n_1 \times \ell k}$, and $\mathbf{F}_3 \in \mathbb{Z}_q^{n_1 \times m_1}$ be the matrices associated with $\mathbf{d}$, $\mathrm{bin}(\mathbf{c}_2)$, and $\mathbf{e} = (\mathbf{s}\|\mathbf{e}_1\|\mathbf{e}_2\|\hat{\mathbf{s}}\|\hat{\mathbf{e}}_1\|\hat{\mathbf{e}}_1) \in [-b, b]^{m_1}$, respectively. Let $\mathbf{c} = \left(\mathbf{c}_1 \| \mathbf{0}^\ell \| \hat{\mathbf{c}}_1 \| \hat{\mathbf{c}}_2\right) \in \mathbb{Z}_q^{n_1}$, then the equation becomes:

$$\mathbf{F}_1 \cdot \mathbf{d} + \mathbf{F}_2 \cdot \mathrm{bin}(\mathbf{c}_2) + \mathbf{F}_3 \cdot \mathbf{e} = \mathbf{c} \bmod q.$$

We then extend $\mathrm{bin}(\mathbf{c}_2) \in \{0, 1\}^{\ell k}$ to vector $\mathrm{bin}^*(\mathbf{c}_2) \in \mathsf{B}_{2\ell k}$, and apply Lemma 6 to vector $\mathbf{e}$ to obtain $\mathbf{e}^* \in \mathsf{B}_{3m_1\delta_b}$. Furthermore, let $\mathbf{y}^* = \left(\mathbf{d}^* \| \mathrm{bin}^*(\mathbf{c}_2) \| \mathbf{e}^*\right)$, and $\mathbf{F}^* = \left[\mathbf{F}_1 | \mathbf{0}^{n_1 \times \ell} | \mathbf{F}_2 | \mathbf{0}^{n_1 \times nk} | \mathbf{F}_3 \cdot \mathbf{H}^*_{m_1, b}\right] \in \mathbb{Z}_q^{n_1 \times (2\ell+2\ell k+3m_1\delta_b)}$, then we have:

$$\mathbf{F}^* \cdot \mathbf{y}^* = \mathbf{c} \bmod q. \tag{6}$$

In the last step of our transformations, we let $L = (2\ell+2)3m\delta_\beta + 2\ell + 2\ell k + 3m_1\delta_b$ and $D = n + n_1$, and define matrix $\mathbf{P} = \left(\begin{array}{c|c} \mathbf{A}^* & \mathbf{0} \\ \hline \mathbf{0} & \mathbf{F}^* \end{array}\right) \in \mathbb{Z}_q^{D \times L}$, vector $\mathbf{x} = \begin{pmatrix} \mathbf{z}^* \\ \mathbf{y}^* \end{pmatrix} \in \{-1, 0, 1\}^L$, vector $\mathbf{v} = \begin{pmatrix} \mathbf{u} \\ \mathbf{c} \end{pmatrix} \in \mathbb{Z}_q^D$.

Equations (5) and (6) are now unified as:

$$\mathbf{P} \cdot \mathbf{x} = \mathbf{v} \bmod q. \tag{7}$$

Having obtained the desired Eq. (7), we now specify the set VALID to which $\mathbf{x}$ belongs, the set $\mathcal{S}$ and permutations of L elements $\{T_\pi : \pi \in \mathcal{S}\}$ for which the equivalence (4) holds.

- VALID: the set of all vectors $\mathbf{t} \in \{-1, 0, 1\}^L$ having the form:

$$\mathbf{t} = (\mathbf{t}_1 \| \mathbf{t}_2 \| g_1 \cdot \mathbf{t}_2 \| \ldots \| g_{2\ell} \cdot \mathbf{t}_2 \| \mathbf{g} \| \mathbf{t}_3 \| \mathbf{t}_4)$$

for some $\mathbf{t}_1, \mathbf{t}_2 \in \mathsf{B}_{3m\delta_\beta}$, $\mathbf{g} = (g_1, \ldots, g_{2\ell}) \in \mathsf{B}_{2\ell}$, $\mathbf{t}_3 \in \mathsf{B}_{2\ell k}$, $\mathbf{t}_4 \in \mathsf{B}_{3m_1\delta_b}$.

- $\mathcal{S} = \mathcal{S}_{3m\delta_\beta} \times \mathcal{S}_{3m\delta_\beta} \times \mathcal{S}_{2\ell} \times \mathcal{S}_{2\ell k} \times \mathcal{S}_{3m_1\delta_b}$.
- For $\pi = (\phi, \psi, \tau, \sigma, \eta) \in \mathcal{S}$ and $\mathbf{w} = (\hat{\mathbf{w}} \| \tilde{\mathbf{w}} \| \mathbf{w}_1 \| \ldots \| \mathbf{w}_{2\ell} \| \bar{\mathbf{w}} \| \ddot{\mathbf{w}} \| \breve{\mathbf{w}}) \in \mathbb{Z}_q^L$, where $\hat{\mathbf{w}}, \tilde{\mathbf{w}}, \mathbf{w}_1, \ldots, \mathbf{w}_{2\ell} \in \mathbb{Z}_q^{3m\delta_\beta}$, $\bar{\mathbf{w}} \in \mathbb{Z}_q^{2\ell}$, $\ddot{\mathbf{w}} \in \mathbb{Z}_q^{2\ell k}$, $\breve{\mathbf{w}} \in \mathbb{Z}_q^{3m_1\delta_b}$, we define:

$$T_\pi(\mathbf{w}) = (\phi(\hat{\mathbf{w}}) \| \psi(\tilde{\mathbf{w}}) \| \psi(\mathbf{w}_{\tau(1)}) \| \ldots \| \psi(\mathbf{w}_{\tau(2\ell)}) \| \tau(\bar{\mathbf{w}}) \| \sigma(\ddot{\mathbf{w}}) \| \eta(\breve{\mathbf{w}}))$$

as the permutation that transforms $\mathbf{w}$ as follows:
1. It rearranges the order of the 2ℓ blocks $\mathbf{w}_1, \ldots, \mathbf{w}_{2\ell}$ according to τ.
2. It then permutes block $\hat{\mathbf{w}}$ according to ϕ, blocks $\tilde{\mathbf{w}}$, $\{\mathbf{w}_i\}_{i=1}^{2\ell}$ according to ψ, block $\bar{\mathbf{w}}$ according to τ, block $\ddot{\mathbf{w}}$ according to σ, and block $\breve{\mathbf{w}}$ via η.

By inspection, it can be seen that

$$\mathbf{x} = (\mathbf{z}_1^* \| \mathbf{z}_2^* \| \mathbf{d}_1 \cdot \mathbf{z}_2^* \| \ldots \| \mathbf{d}_{2\ell} \cdot \mathbf{z}_2^* \| \mathbf{d}^* \| \mathsf{bin}^*(c_2) \| \mathbf{e}^*) \in \mathsf{VALID},$$

and that the property (4) is satisfied, as desired. As a result, we can obtain a sZKAoK for $\mathrm{R}_{\mathrm{gsmdo}}$ by running the protocol in Fig. 1 with common input $(\mathbf{P}, \mathbf{v})$ and prover's input $\mathbf{x}$.

Putting everything together, we have the following theorem.

Theorem 1. *There exists a Stern-type ZKAoK for the relation* $\mathrm{R}_{\mathrm{gsmdo}}$ *with perfect completeness, soundness error* $2/3$, *and communication cost* $\mathcal{O}(L \log q)$. *In particular:*

- *There exists an efficient simulator that, on input* $(\mathbf{A}, \{\mathbf{A}_i\}_{i=0}^\ell, \mathbf{B}, \mathbf{C}, \mathbf{G}, \hat{\mathbf{G}}, \mathbf{u}, \mathbf{c}_1, \hat{\mathbf{c}}_1, \hat{\mathbf{c}}_2)$, *outputs an accepted transcript which is statistically close to that produced by the real prover.*
- *There exists an efficient knowledge extractor that, on input a commitment* CMT *and 3 valid responses* $(\mathrm{RSP}_1, \mathrm{RSP}_2, \mathrm{RSP}_3)$ *to all 3 possible values of the challenge* Ch, *outputs a tuple* $(\mathbf{d}', \mathbf{z}', \mathbf{s}', \hat{\mathbf{s}}', \mathbf{e}_1', \hat{\mathbf{e}}_1', \mathbf{e}_2', \hat{\mathbf{e}}_2', \mathbf{c}_2')$ *such that:*

$$((\mathbf{A}, \{\mathbf{A}_i\}_{i=0}^\ell, \mathbf{B}, \mathbf{C}, \mathbf{G}, \hat{\mathbf{G}}, \mathbf{u}, \mathbf{c}_1, \hat{\mathbf{c}}_1, \hat{\mathbf{c}}_2), \mathbf{d}', \mathbf{z}', \mathbf{s}', \hat{\mathbf{s}}', \mathbf{e}_1', \hat{\mathbf{e}}_1', \mathbf{e}_2', \hat{\mathbf{e}}_2', \mathbf{c}_2') \in \mathrm{R}_{\mathrm{gsmdo}}.$$

The proof of Theorem 1 is straightforward. For simulation, we run the simulator of Lemma 5. For extraction, we run the knowledge extractor of Lemma 5, and then "backtrack" the described above transformations to obtain a satisfying witness for $\mathrm{R}_{\mathrm{gsmdo}}$. We thus omit the details.

4   A GS-MDO Scheme Based on Lattice Assumptions

Our scheme is described and analyzed in the model of Sakai *et al.* [40], which is described in Sect. 2.3.

Our GS-MDO scheme builds on the Ling *et al.* [33] group signature. In order to enable message-dependent openings, we add an encryption layer to the previous scheme using an IBE where the signed message serves as the receiver's identity. The *admitter*, which holds the master secret key for this IBE, is able to derive a message-specific token consisting of an IBE private key for this "identity". By itself, this information is insufficient to open the signature as it uncovers a second ciphertext embedded in the message space of the initial encryption layer. At the same time, the opening authority only has access to the external encryption layer which prevents it from identifying the signer without the message-specific token.

Now, the challenge is to prove that the entire double-encryption process was conducted properly while proving the knowledge of a Boyen signature at the same time. As demonstrated in Sect. 3, we solve this challenge by leveraging the properties of Stern-like protocols [42] and translating the statements to be proved so as to apply the technique of Sect. 3.

To encrypt the user's identity $d \in \{0,1\}^{\ell}$, we apply a multi-bit variant of the dual Regev system [19] and obtain a first-layer encryption

$$(\mathbf{c}_1, \mathbf{c}_2) = \left(\mathbf{B}^T \mathbf{s} + \mathbf{e}_1, \mathbf{G}^T \mathbf{s} + \mathbf{e}_2 + \lfloor q/2 \rfloor \cdot \mathsf{bin}(d)\right),$$

where $\mathbf{B} \in \mathbb{Z}_q^{n \times m}$ is the master public key of the underlying IBE, $\mathbf{e}_1, \mathbf{e}_2$ are small noise vectors and $\mathbf{G} \in \mathcal{H}_1(\mathsf{ovk}) \in \mathbb{Z}_q^{n \times \ell}$ is derived by hashing a one-time signature verification key (recall that, as in [33], we achieve anonymity in the CCA2 sense by applying the CHK paradigm [13] using ovk as the receiver's identity). Then, we use a second IBE layer to encrypt the binary decomposition of $\mathbf{c}_2 \in \mathbb{Z}_q^{\ell}$. In this second IBE instance, we use a matrix $\mathbf{C} \in \mathbb{Z}_q^{n \times m}$ and compute

$$(\hat{\mathbf{c}}_1, \hat{\mathbf{c}}_2) = \left(\mathbf{C}^T \hat{\mathbf{s}} + \hat{\mathbf{e}}_1, \hat{\mathbf{G}}^T \hat{\mathbf{s}} + \hat{\mathbf{e}}_2 + \lfloor q/2 \rfloor \cdot \mathsf{bin}(\mathbf{c}_2)\right),$$

for suitable noise vectors $\hat{\mathbf{e}}_1, \hat{\mathbf{e}}_2$ and where $\hat{\mathbf{G}} = \mathcal{H}_2(M) \in \mathbb{Z}_q^{n \times \ell \lceil \log q \rceil}$ is an IBE public key obtained by hashing the "identity" M. (Note that the two IBE layers use distinct random oracles $\mathcal{H}_1$ and $\mathcal{H}_2$.)

Now, the problem is to demonstrate the proper computation of $(\mathbf{c}_1, \mathbf{c}_2)$ and $(\hat{\mathbf{c}}_1, \hat{\mathbf{c}}_2)$. This can be achieved by proving knowledge of $\mathsf{bin}(\mathbf{c}_2) \in \{0,1\}^{\ell \lceil \log q \rceil}$, $\mathbf{s}, \hat{\mathbf{s}} \in \mathbb{Z}^n$, $\mathbf{e}_1, \hat{\mathbf{e}}_1 \in \mathbb{Z}^m$, $\mathbf{e}_2 \in \mathbb{Z}^{\ell}$, $\mathbf{e}_2 \in \mathbb{Z}^{\ell \lceil \log q \rceil}$ satisfying:

$$
\begin{pmatrix}
\mathbf{B}^T & \mathbf{I}_m & \mathbf{0} & & & & \mathbf{0} & \mathbf{0} \\
-\mathbf{G}^T & \mathbf{0} & -\mathbf{I}_\ell & & & & \mathbf{H} & -\lfloor q/2 \rfloor \cdot \mathbf{I}_\ell \\
& & & \mathbf{C}^T & \mathbf{I}_m & & \mathbf{0} & \mathbf{0} \\
& & & \hat{\mathbf{G}}^T & \mathbf{I}_{\ell \lceil \log q \rceil} & \lfloor q/2 \rfloor \cdot \mathbf{I}_{\ell \lceil \log q \rceil} & \mathbf{0} &
\end{pmatrix}
\cdot
\begin{pmatrix}
\mathbf{s} \\ \mathbf{e}_1 \\ \mathbf{e}_2 \\ \hat{\mathbf{s}} \\ \hat{\mathbf{e}}_1 \\ \hat{\mathbf{e}}_2 \\ \mathsf{bin}(\mathbf{c}_2) \\ \mathsf{bin}(d)
\end{pmatrix}
=
\begin{pmatrix}
\mathbf{c}_1 \\ \mathbf{0}_\ell \\ \hat{\mathbf{c}}_1 \\ \hat{\mathbf{c}}_2
\end{pmatrix},
$$

where $\mathbf{H}$ is defined as in Sect. 3. The second and fourth block relations ensure that that $\mathbf{c}_2$ is the message encrypted by $\hat{\mathbf{c}}_2$ while this hidden $\mathbf{c}_2$ encrypts $\mathsf{bin}(d)$. We are left with arguing knowledge of a Boyen signature on $\mathsf{bin}(d) \in \{0,1\}^{\ell}$, which can be achieved as in [33].

4.1 Description of the Scheme

The parameters are set in such a way that the Boyen signature and the GPV IBE scheme function properly and are secure. Let $n = \mathcal{O}(\lambda)$ be the lattice parameter, $N = 2^\ell = \mathsf{poly}(\lambda)$ be the number of group members, $q = \mathcal{O}(\ell \cdot n^2)$ be a prime modulus, $\beta = \widetilde{\mathcal{O}}(\sqrt{\ell n})$ be the infinity norm bound for signatures generated by Boyen's scheme [9], and b such that $q/b = \ell \cdot \widetilde{\mathcal{O}}(n)$ be the infinity norm bound for LWE noises sampled from error distribution χ.

Keygen$(1^\lambda, 1^N)$: This algorithm performs the following steps:
1. Generate a verification key $(\mathbf{A}, \mathbf{A}_0, \ldots, \mathbf{A}_\ell, \mathbf{u}) \in (\mathbb{Z}_q^{n \times m})^{\ell+2} \times \mathbb{Z}_q^n$ and a private key $\mathbf{T_A} \in \mathbb{Z}^{m \times m}$ for Boyen's signature scheme.
   Then for each $d \in \{0, \ldots, 2^\ell - 1\}$, define the corresponding private key $\mathbf{gsk}[d] = (\mathbf{v}_{d,1}^T \mid \mathbf{v}_{d,2}^T)^T \in \mathbb{Z}^{2m}$ to be the Boyen's signature for the message $\mathsf{bin}(d) = (d_1, \ldots, d_\ell) \in \{0, 1\}^\ell$ using the trapdoor $\mathbf{T_A}$.
2. Generate two encryption and decryption key pairs for the GPV-IBE scheme: the matrix $\mathbf{B} \in \mathbb{Z}_q^{n \times m}$ along with its trapdoor basis $\mathbf{T_B} \in \mathbb{Z}^{m \times m}$ and the matrix $\mathbf{C} \in \mathbb{Z}_q^{n \times m}$ with its trapdoor $\mathbf{T_C} \in \mathbb{Z}^{m \times m}$ using the GenTrap algorithm from Gentry *et al.* [19] described in Lemma 3.
3. Select a strong one-time signature $\Pi^{\mathsf{OTS}} = (\mathsf{OKeygen}, \mathsf{OSign}, \mathsf{OVer})$ and hash functions $\mathcal{H}_1 : \{0,1\}^* \to \mathbb{Z}_q^{n \times \ell}$, $\mathcal{H}_2 : \{0,1\}^* \to \mathbb{Z}_q^{n \times \ell \lceil \log q \rceil}$.
4. Output $\mathsf{ok} = \mathbf{T_B}$, $\mathsf{msk_{ADM}} = \mathbf{T_C}$, $\mathbf{gsk} = (\mathbf{gsk}[d])_{d=0}^{N-1}$ and

$$\mathsf{gpk} = \{\mathbf{A}, \{\mathbf{A}_i\}_{i=0}^\ell, \mathbf{u}, \mathbf{B}, \mathbf{C}, \Pi^{\mathsf{OTS}}, \mathcal{H}_1, \mathcal{H}_2\},$$

Sign$(\mathsf{gpk}, \mathbf{gsk}[d], M)$: To sign M using a group private key $\mathbf{gsk}[d]$,
1. Generate a key pair $(\mathsf{ovk}, \mathsf{osk}) \leftarrow \mathsf{OKeygen}(1^\lambda)$ for the signature Π^{OTS}.
2. Encrypt the message d with respect to the "identity" ovk using the GPV IBE [19]. Namely, let $\mathbf{G} = \mathcal{H}_1(\mathsf{ovk}) \in \mathbb{Z}_q^{n \times \ell}$. Sample $\mathbf{s} \hookleftarrow \chi^n; \mathbf{e}_1 \hookleftarrow \chi^m; \mathbf{e}_2 \hookleftarrow \chi^\ell$, and compute the ciphertext

$$\left(\mathbf{c}_1 = \mathbf{B}^T\mathbf{s} + \mathbf{e}_1, \mathbf{c}_2 = \mathbf{G}^T\mathbf{s} + \mathbf{e}_2 + \lfloor q/2 \rfloor \cdot \mathsf{bin}(d)\right) \in \mathbb{Z}_q^m \times \mathbb{Z}_q^\ell.$$

3. Using the GPV IBE again, encrypt the ciphertext $\mathbf{c}_2$ w.r.t the "identity" M. In other words, let $\hat{\mathbf{G}} = \mathcal{H}_2(M) \in \mathbb{Z}_q^{n \times \ell \lceil \log q \rceil}$, then sample $\hat{\mathbf{s}} \hookleftarrow \chi^n; \hat{\mathbf{e}}_1 \hookleftarrow \chi^m, \hat{\mathbf{e}}_2 \hookleftarrow \chi^{\ell \lceil \log q \rceil}$ and compute the ciphertext

$$\left(\hat{\mathbf{c}}_1 = \mathbf{C}^T\hat{\mathbf{s}} + \hat{\mathbf{e}}_1, \hat{\mathbf{c}}_2 = \hat{\mathbf{G}}^T\hat{\mathbf{s}} + \hat{\mathbf{e}}_2 + \lfloor q/2 \rfloor \cdot \mathsf{bin}(\mathbf{c}_2)\right) \in \mathbb{Z}_q^m \times \mathbb{Z}_q^{\ell \lceil \log q \rceil}.$$

4. Generate a NIZKAoK Π to prove the possession of a valid message-signature pair $(d, \mathbf{z})$ for Boyen's signature, and that $(\hat{\mathbf{c}}_1, \hat{\mathbf{c}}_2)$ is a correct encryption of $\mathbf{c}_2$ under the identity M, where $(\mathbf{c}_1, \mathbf{c}_2)$ is a correct encryption of $\mathbf{d} = \mathsf{bin}(d)$ under the identity ovk. To do this, run the interactive argument system for the relation $\mathsf{R_{gsmdo}}$ in Sect. 3 with public input $(\mathbf{A}, \{\mathbf{A}_i\}_{i=0}^\ell, \mathbf{B}, \mathbf{C}, \mathbf{G}, \hat{\mathbf{G}}, \mathbf{u}, \mathbf{c}_1, \hat{\mathbf{c}}_1, \hat{\mathbf{c}}_2)$ and prover's input $(\mathbf{d}, \mathbf{z}, \mathbf{s}, \hat{\mathbf{s}}, \mathbf{e}_1, \hat{\mathbf{e}}_1, \mathbf{e}_2, \hat{\mathbf{e}}_2, \mathbf{c}_2)$.

The protocol is repeated $t = \omega(\log n)$ times to get a negligible soundness error, and then made non-interactive using the Fiat-Shamir heuristic, which gives $\Pi = (\{\mathsf{Comm}_j\}_{j=1}^t, \mathsf{Chall}, \{\mathsf{Resp}_j\}_{j=1}^t)$, where

$$\mathsf{Chall} = \mathcal{H}(M, \mathsf{ovk}, \{\mathsf{Comm}_j\}_{j=1}^t, \mathbf{c}_1, \hat{\mathbf{c}}_1, \hat{\mathbf{c}}_2) \in \{1, 2, 3\}^t.$$

5. Compute a one-time signature $sig = \mathsf{OSign}(\mathsf{osk}; \mathbf{c}_1, \hat{\mathbf{c}}_1, \hat{\mathbf{c}}_2, \Pi)$.
6. Output $\Sigma = (\mathsf{ovk}, \mathbf{c}_1, \hat{\mathbf{c}}_1, \hat{\mathbf{c}}_2, \Pi, sig)$.

Verify$(\mathsf{gpk}, M, \Sigma)$: $\Sigma = (\mathsf{ovk}, \mathbf{c}_1, \hat{\mathbf{c}}_1, \hat{\mathbf{c}}_2, \Pi, sig)$ is verified w.r.t. M as follows:
1. If $\mathsf{OVer}(\mathsf{ovk}; sig; \mathbf{c}_1, \hat{\mathbf{c}}_1, \hat{\mathbf{c}}_2, \Pi) = 0$, return 0.
2. Verify the validity of the proof Π, if it fails, return 0.
3. If everything went correctly, then return 1.

TrapGen$(\mathsf{gpk}, \mathsf{msk}_{\mathsf{ADM}}, M)$: To generate a token t_M.
1. If a token for a message M was already queried, answer consistently.
2. Otherwise, derive a key for the identity M using the master secret key $\mathbf{T_C} \in \mathbb{Z}^{m \times m}$. Namely compute $\hat{\mathbf{G}} = \mathcal{H}_2(M)$, then using $\mathsf{SamplePre}$, compute a small-norm matrix $\mathbf{E}_M \in \mathbb{Z}^{m \times \ell \lceil \log q \rceil}$ such that $\mathbf{C} \cdot \mathbf{E}_M = \hat{\mathbf{G}}$.
3. Output $\mathsf{t}_M = \mathbf{E}_M$.

Open$(\mathsf{gpk}, \mathsf{ok}, \mathsf{t}_M, \Sigma, M)$: To open $\Sigma(\mathsf{ovk}, \mathbf{c}_1, \hat{\mathbf{c}}_1, \hat{\mathbf{c}}_2, \Pi, sig)$ using the opening key ok and the token for the message t_M, do the following:
1. Decrypt $(\hat{\mathbf{c}}_1, \hat{\mathbf{c}}_2)$ using t_M: $\mathbf{c}_2 = \mathbf{H} \cdot \lfloor (\hat{\mathbf{c}}_2 - \mathsf{t}_M^T \cdot \hat{\mathbf{c}}_1) \cdot (q/2) \rceil$.
2. Decrypt $(\mathbf{c}_1, \mathbf{c}_2)$ using $\mathsf{ok} = \mathbf{T_B} \in \mathbb{Z}^{m \times m}$, namely compute $\mathbf{G} = \mathcal{H}_1(\mathsf{ovk})$, and using $\mathsf{SamplePre}$ to get a short-norm matrix $\mathbf{F} \in \mathbb{Z}^{m \times \ell}$ such that $\mathbf{B} \cdot \mathbf{F} = \mathbf{G}$, and finally compute

$$d = (1 \mid 2 \mid 4 \mid \cdots \mid 2^{\ell-1}) \cdot \lfloor (\mathbf{c}_2 - \mathbf{F}^T \cdot \mathbf{c}_1) \cdot (q/2) \rceil.$$

3. Verify that d belongs to a valid user, if not return $\bot$, otherwise return d.

4.2   Security

The security of the above construction has been proven in the ROM under LWE and SIS assumptions as evidenced in the following theorems. The proofs of Theorems 2, 3 and 4 are available in the full version of the paper.

Theorem 2. *In the random oracle model, the above group signature scheme is fully traceable under the assumption that the SIS problem is hard.*

Theorem 3. *The above group signature scheme is fully anonymous against the admitter under the LWE assumption, and assuming that the one-time signature scheme Π^{OTS} is strongly unforgeable.*

Theorem 4. *The above group signature scheme is fully anonymous against the opener under the LWE assumption.*

Acknowledgements. The first author was funded by the "Programme Avenir Lyon Saint-Etienne de l'Université de Lyon" in the framework of the programme "Investissements d'Avenir" (ANR-11-IDEX-0007). Khoa Nguyen was supported by the "Singapore Ministry of Education under Research Grant MOE2013-T2-1-041".

References

1. Abdalla, M., Warinschi, B.: On the minimal assumptions of group signature schemes. In: López, J., Qing, S., Okamoto, E. (eds.) ICICS 2004. LNCS, vol. 3269, pp. 1–13. Springer, Heidelberg (2004)
2. Alwen, J., Peikert, C.: Generating shorter bases for hard random lattices. In: STACS 2009 (2009)
3. Ateniese, G., Camenisch, J., Joye, M., Tsudik, G.: A practical and provably secure coalition-resistant group signature scheme. In: Bellare, M. (ed.) CRYPTO 2000. LNCS, vol. 1880, pp. 255–270. Springer, Heidelberg (2000)
4. Banaszczyk, W.: New bounds in some transference theorems in the geometry of number. Mathematische Annalen (1993)
5. Bellare, M., Micciancio, D., Warinschi, B.: Foundations of group signatures: formal definitions, simplified requirements, and a construction based on general assumptions. In: Biham, E. (ed.) EUROCRYPT 2003. LNCS, vol. 2656, pp. 614–629. Springer, Heidelberg (2003)
6. Benhamouda, F., Camenisch, J., Krenn, S., Lyubashevsky, V., Neven, G.: Better zero-knowledge proofs for lattice encryption and their application to group signatures. In: Sarkar, P., Iwata, T. (eds.) ASIACRYPT 2014. LNCS, vol. 8873, pp. 551–572. Springer, Heidelberg (2014)
7. Boneh, D., Boyen, X., Shacham, H.: Short group signatures. In: Franklin, M. (ed.) CRYPTO 2004. LNCS, vol. 3152, pp. 41–55. Springer, Heidelberg (2004)
8. Boneh, D., Franklin, M.: Identity-based encryption from the weil pairing. In: Kilian, J. (ed.) CRYPTO 2001. LNCS, vol. 2139, pp. 213–229. Springer, Heidelberg (2001)
9. Boyen, X.: Lattice mixing and vanishing trapdoors: a framework for fully secure short signatures and more. In: Nguyen, P.Q., Pointcheval, D. (eds.) PKC 2010. LNCS, vol. 6056, pp. 499–517. Springer, Heidelberg (2010)
10. Boyen, X., Waters, B.: Compact group signatures without random oracles. In: Vaudenay, S. (ed.) EUROCRYPT 2006. LNCS, vol. 4004, pp. 427–444. Springer, Heidelberg (2006)
11. Boyen, X., Waters, B.: Full-domain subgroup hiding and constant-size group signatures. In: Okamoto, T., Wang, X. (eds.) PKC 2007. LNCS, vol. 4450, pp. 1–15. Springer, Heidelberg (2007)
12. Brakerski, Z., Langlois, A., Peikert, C., Regev, O., Stehlé, D.: On the classical hardness of learning with errors. In: STOC 2013. ACM (2013)
13. Canetti, R., Halevi, S., Katz, J.: Chosen-ciphertext security from identity-based encryption. In: Cachin, C., Camenisch, J.L. (eds.) EUROCRYPT 2004. LNCS, vol. 3027, pp. 207–222. Springer, Heidelberg (2004)
14. Cash, D., Hofheinz, D., Kiltz, E., Peikert, C.: Bonsai trees, or how to delegate a lattice basis. In: Gilbert, H. (ed.) EUROCRYPT 2010. LNCS, vol. 6110, pp. 523–552. Springer, Heidelberg (2010)
15. Chaum, D., van Heyst, E.: Group signatures. In: Davies, D.W. (ed.) EUROCRYPT 1991. LNCS, vol. 547, pp. 257–265. Springer, Heidelberg (1991)
16. Desmedt, Y., Frankel, Y.: Threshold cryptosystems. In: Brassard, G. (ed.) CRYPTO 1989. LNCS, vol. 435, pp. 307–315. Springer, Heidelberg (1989)
17. Ezerman, M.F., Lee, H.T., Ling, S., Nguyen, K., Wang, H.: A provably secure group signature scheme from code-based assumptions. In: Iwata, T., et al. (eds.) ASIACRYPT 2015. LNCS, vol. 9452, pp. 260–285. Springer, Heidelberg (2015)
18. Gentry, C.: Fully homomorphic encryption using ideal lattices. In: STOC (2009)

19. Gentry, C., Peikert, C., Vaikuntanathan, V.: Trapdoors for hard lattices and new cryptographic constructions. In: STOC 2008. ACM (2008)
20. Goldwasser, S., Micali, S., Rackoff, C.: The knowledge complexity of interactive proof-systems. In: STOC 1985. ACM (1985)
21. Gordon, S.D., Katz, J., Vaikuntanathan, V.: A group signature scheme from lattice assumptions. In: Abe, M. (ed.) ASIACRYPT 2010. LNCS, vol. 6477, pp. 395–412. Springer, Heidelberg (2010)
22. Groth, J.: Evaluating security of voting schemes in the universal composability framework. In: Jakobsson, M., Yung, M., Zhou, J. (eds.) ACNS 2004. LNCS, vol. 3089, pp. 46–60. Springer, Heidelberg (2004)
23. Groth, J.: Fully anonymous group signatures without random oracles. In: Kurosawa, K. (ed.) ASIACRYPT 2007. LNCS, vol. 4833, pp. 164–180. Springer, Heidelberg (2007)
24. Groth, J., Sahai, A.: Efficient non-interactive proof systems for bilinear groups. In: Smart, N.P. (ed.) EUROCRYPT 2008. LNCS, vol. 4965, pp. 415–432. Springer, Heidelberg (2008)
25. Jain, A., Krenn, S., Pietrzak, K., Tentes, A.: Commitments and efficient zero-knowledge proofs from learning parity with noise. In: Wang, X., Sako, K. (eds.) ASIACRYPT 2012. LNCS, vol. 7658, pp. 663–680. Springer, Heidelberg (2012)
26. Kawachi, A., Tanaka, K., Xagawa, K.: Concurrently secure identification schemes based on the worst-case hardness of lattice problems. In: Pieprzyk, J. (ed.) ASIACRYPT 2008. LNCS, vol. 5350, pp. 372–389. Springer, Heidelberg (2008)
27. Kiayias, A., Tsiounis, Y., Yung, M.: Traceable signatures. In: Cachin, C., Camenisch, J.L. (eds.) EUROCRYPT 2004. LNCS, vol. 3027, pp. 571–589. Springer, Heidelberg (2004)
28. Laguillaumie, F., Langlois, A., Libert, B., Stehlé, D.: Lattice-based group signatures with logarithmic signature size. In: Sako, K., Sarkar, P. (eds.) ASIACRYPT 2013, Part II. LNCS, vol. 8270, pp. 41–61. Springer, Heidelberg (2013)
29. Libert, B., Joye, M.: Group signatures with message-dependent opening in the standard model. In: Benaloh, J. (ed.) CT-RSA 2014. LNCS, vol. 8366, pp. 286–306. Springer, Heidelberg (2014)
30. Libert, B., Ling, S., Mouhartem, F., Nguyen, K., Wang, H.: Signature schemes with efficient protocols and dynamic group signatures from lattice assumptions. Cryptology ePrint Archive: Report 2016/101, January 2016
31. Libert, B., Ling, S., Nguyen, K., Wang, H.: Zero-knowledge arguments for lattice-basedaccumulators: Logarithmic-size ring signatures and group signatures without trapdoors. In: Eurocrypt 2016. LNCS. Springer (2016, To appear)
32. Ling, S., Nguyen, K., Stehlé, D., Wang, H.: Improved zero-knowledge proofs of knowledge for the ISIS Problem, and applications. In: Hanaoka, G., Kurosawa, K. (eds.) PKC 2013. LNCS, vol. 7778, pp. 107–124. Springer, Heidelberg (2013)
33. Ling, S., Nguyen, K., Wang, H.: Group signatures from lattices: simpler, tighter, shorter, ring-based. In: Katz, J. (ed.) PKC 2015. LNCS, vol. 9020, pp. 427–449. Springer, Heidelberg (2015)
34. Nguyen, P.Q., Zhang, J., Zhang, Z.: Simpler efficient group signatures from lattices. In: Katz, J. (ed.) PKC 2015. LNCS, vol. 9020, pp. 401–426. Springer, Heidelberg (2015)
35. Ohara, K., Sakai, Y., Emura, K., Hanaoka, G.: A group signature scheme with unbounded message-dependent opening. In: AsiaCCS 2013 (2013)
36. Peikert, C.: Public-key cryptosystems from the worst-case shortest vector problem. In: STOC 2009. ACM (2009)

37. Peikert, C.: A decade of lattice cryptography. Cryptology ePrint Archive: Report 2015/939, September 2015
38. Peikert, C., Vaikuntanathan, V.: Noninteractive statistical zero-knowledge proofs for lattice problems. In: Wagner, D. (ed.) CRYPTO 2008. LNCS, vol. 5157, pp. 536–553. Springer, Heidelberg (2008)
39. Regev, O.: On lattices, learning with errors, random linear codes, and cryptography. In: STOC 2005. ACM (2005)
40. Sakai, Y., Emura, K., Hanaoka, G., Kawai, Y., Matsuda, T., Omote, K.: Group signatures with message-dependent opening. In: Abdalla, M., Lange, T. (eds.) Pairing 2012. LNCS, vol. 7708, pp. 270–294. Springer, Heidelberg (2013)
41. Shamir, A.: Identity-based cryptosystems and signature schemes. In: Blakely, G.R., Chaum, D. (eds.) CRYPTO 1984. LNCS, vol. 196, pp. 47–53. Springer, Heidelberg (1985)
42. Stern, J.: A new paradigm for public key identification. IEEE Trans. Inf. Theory 42(6), 2757–2768 (1996)

Threshold-Optimal DSA/ECDSA Signatures and an Application to Bitcoin Wallet Security

Rosario Gennaro[1], Steven Goldfeder[2(✉)], and Arvind Narayanan[2]

[1] City College, City University of New York, New York, USA
rosario@cs.ccny.cuny.edu
[2] Princeton University, Princeton, USA
{stevenag,arvindn}@cs.princeton.edu

Abstract. While threshold signature schemes have been presented before, there has never been an optimal threshold signature algorithm for DSA. The properties of DSA make it quite challenging to build a threshold version. In this paper, we present a threshold DSA scheme that is efficient and optimal. We also present a compelling application to use our scheme: securing Bitcoin wallets. Bitcoin thefts are on the rise, and threshold DSA is necessary to secure Bitcoin wallets. Our scheme is the first general threshold DSA scheme that does not require an honest majority and is useful for securing Bitcoin wallets.

1 Introduction

Threshold signature schemes enable sharing signing power amongst n parties such that any subset of $t + 1$ can jointly sign, but any smaller subset cannot. This problem has received much attention in the cryptographic literature, and many such schemes have been designed. Some of these schemes produce signatures that are compatible with standard digital signature schemes. They replace only the signing algorithm and key generation algorithm, but the verification is compatible with the centralized signature schemes.

The Digital Signature Algorithm (DSA) is a very popular signature scheme, and a considerable amount of work has been done to build a threshold signing algorithm to produce a standard DSA signature. However, for reasons that we will elaborate in Sect. 4.2, building a threshold variant of DSA proved to be significantly difficult. While such schemes have been presented (e.g. [22,23,31]), they have serious drawbacks that make them unusable in practice: in particular no general scheme with an optimal number of servers is known. For the past 15 years, the problem has been mostly abandoned. The reason is twofold:

– As we discuss in Sect. 4.2 the technical difficulties in building a threshold-optimal variant of distributed DSA made this a challenging problem and it was not clear how to proceed from the solutions in [22,23,31].

© Springer International Publishing Switzerland 2016
M. Manulis et al. (Eds.): ACNS 2016, LNCS 9696, pp. 156–174, 2016.
DOI: 10.1007/978-3-319-39555-5_9

– There was never a pressing motivation to devise a solution for threshold DSA. Since there are optimal threshold schemes for other signature algorithms, one could choose a different scheme that was well suited for the problem at hand.

In recent years, a major application for threshold DSA signatures has arisen in the world of Bitcoin. Without a DSA/ECDSA threshold scheme, bitcoins are subject to a single point of failure and the risks of holding bitcoins are catastrophic. Motivated by this application, we tackle the technical challenges of threshold DSA, and present an efficient and optimal scheme.

The Motivation: Bitcoin's Security Conundrum. Bitcoin is a cryptographic e-cash system, by far the most widely used today. Unlike traditional banking transactions, Bitcoin transactions of any size can be fully automated – authorized only with a ECDSA signature. One's bitcoins are only as secure as the ECDSA key that can authorize their transfer; if this key is compromised, the bitcoins will be stolen. Unlike traditional banking transactions, once a Bitcoin transaction is enacted it is irreversible. Even if the coins are known to have been stolen, there is simply no way to reverse the offending transaction.

Indeed, the Bitcoin ecosystem is plagued by constant thefts. The statistics on Bitcoin hacks, thefts, and losses are extraordinary — there have been ten thefts of over 10,000 BTC each since mid-2011, and at least another thirty-four of over 1,000 BTC.[1] [4]. Kaspersky labs report detecting about a million infections per month of malware designed to search for and steal bitcoins [30].

The pervasiveness and regularity of these vulnerabilities highlight how Bitcoin is inherently theft-prone. For Bitcoin and cryptocurrencies to gain mainstream adoption, the current situation where a single rogue employee or a piece of malware can empty an organization's funds in hot storage instantly, irreversibly, and anonymously is simply untenable. Securing Bitcoin is equivalent to securing the keys that can authorize transactions. Instead of storing keys in a single location, keys should be split and signing should be authorized by a threshold set of computers. A breach of any number of machines up to the threshold will not allow the attacker to steal any money or glean any information about the key.

Since Bitcoin transactions use ECDSA keys, the only way to achieve this joint control is with an ECDSA threshold signature algorithm. While Bitcoin does have a built in "multi-signature" function for splitting control, using this severely compromises the confidentiality and anonymity of the participants as we explain in the full version of this paper.

Our Contributions. With a strong motivation for threshold DSA, we still lacked a scheme that was usable to secure Bitcoin keys. The best threshold signature scheme presented was that by Gennaro *et al.* [22]. That scheme, however, has a considerable setback. The key is distributed among n players such that a

---

[1] The majority, but not all, of these losses have been due to theft of keys.

group of size $t+1$ can jointly reconstruct the key. Yet, in order to produce a signature using their algorithm (without reconstructing the key), the participation of $2t+1$ players is required.[2]

This property of the scheme in [22] has various implications. First, requiring $n \geq 2t+1$ is very limiting in practice: for example it rules out an n-of-n sharing. Furthermore, the implications for a Bitcoin company that wants to distribute its signing power are severe. If the company chooses a threshold of t, then an attacker who compromises $t+1$ servers can steal all of the company's money. Yet, in order for the company to sign a transaction, they must set up $2t+1$ servers. In effect, they must double the number of servers, which makes the job of the attacker easier (as there are more servers for them to target).

Mackenzie and Reiter built a specialized scheme for the 2-of-2 signature case [31]. Yet no general DSA threshold scheme existed that did not suffer from these setbacks. In the full version of this paper, we sketch how to extend Mackenzie and Reiter to the multiparty case. While the extension does allow $t+1$ players to sign, it is quite inefficient as it requires $3t-1$ rounds of interaction, and the computation time and the storage grow with the number of players.

In this paper, we present a scheme that is both threshold-optimal and efficient. In particular:

1. It requires only $n \geq t+1$ servers.
2. The protocol requires only a constant number of rounds.
3. The computation time for each player is constant.[3]
4. Players require only a constant amount of storage.

Our scheme is practical and efficient. We implemented it and evaluated it, and it is the only scheme that is fully compatible with Bitcoin and efficient enough to now be a true candidate for any use case where a threshold signature scheme is desired. We have also spoken with various Bitcoin companies who confirmed that they are eager to incorporate our protocol to secure their systems.

2 Model, Definitions and Tools

In this section we introduce our communication model and provide definitions of secure threshold signature schemes.

COMMUNICATION MODEL. We assume that our computation model is composed of a set of n players $P_1, \ldots, P_n$ connected by a complete network of point-to-point channels and a broadcast channel.

---

[2] We note that throughout this paper we use the (t,n) notation consistently with how it's used in previous threshold signature works. In particular, a (t,n) signing scheme is secure against t colluding players and requires at least $t+1$ participants. In the Bitcoin multisignature notation, however, t-of-n refers to a scheme which is secure against $t-1$ malicious players and requires t participants to sign.

[3] That is to compute the players share, the computation time does not grow with the number of players. Players do however need to verify proofs from all players.

THE ADVERSARY. We assume that an adversary, $\mathcal{A}$, can corrupt up to t of the n players in the network. $\mathcal{A}$ learns all the information stored at the corrupted nodes, and hears all broadcasted messages. We consider two type of adversaries:

- *honest-but-curious:* the corrupted players follow the protocol but try to learn information about secret values;
- *malicious:* corrupted players to divert from the specified protocol in *any* (possibly malicious) way.

We assume that the network is "partially synchronous", meaning that the adversary speaks last in every communication round (a *rushing* adversary.) The adversary is modeled by a probabilistic polynomial time Turing machine.

Adversaries can also be categorized as *static* or *adaptive*. A static adversary chooses the corrupted players at the beginning of the protocol, while an adaptive one chooses them during the computation. In the following, for simplicity, we assume the adversary to be static, though the techniques from [13,28] can be used to extend our result to the adaptive adversary case.

Given a protocol $\mathcal{P}$ the *view* of the adversary, denoted by $\mathcal{VIEW}_{\mathcal{A}}(\mathcal{P})$, is defined as the probability distribution (induced by the random coins of the players) on adversary's knowledge, namely, the computational and memory history of all corrupted players, and the public communications and output of the protocol.

Signature Scheme. A signature scheme $\mathcal{S}$ is a triple of efficient randomized algorithms (Key-Gen, Sig, Ver). Key-Gen is the *key generator* algorithm: on input the security parameter 1^{λ}, it outputs a pair (y, x), such that y is the *public key* and x is the *secret key* of the signature scheme. Sig is the *signing* algorithm: on input a message m and the secret key x, it outputs *sig*, a signature of the message m. Since Sig can be a randomized algorithm there might be several valid signatures *sig* of a message m under the key x; with $\mathsf{Sig}(m, x)$ we will denote the set of such signatures. Ver is the *verification* algorithm. On input a message m, the public key y, and a string *sig*, it checks whether *sig* is a proper signature of m, i.e. if $sig \in \mathsf{Sig}(m, x)$.

The notion of security for signature schemes was formally defined in [25] in various flavors. The following definition captures the strongest of these notions: existential unforgeability against adaptively chosen message attack.

Definition 1. *We say that a signature scheme $\mathcal{S}$ =(Key-Gen,Sig,Ver) is unforgeable if no adversary who is given the public key y generated by Key-Gen, and the signatures of k messages $m_1, \ldots, m_k$ adaptively chosen, can produce the signature on a new message m (i.e., $m \notin \{m_1, \ldots, m_k\}$) with non-negligible (in λ) probability.*

Threshold Secret Sharing. Given a secret value x we say that the values $(x_1, \ldots, x_n)$ constitute a (t, n)-threshold secret sharing of x if t (or less) of these values reveal no information about x, and if there is an efficient algorithm that outputs x having $t + 1$ of the values x_i as inputs.

Threshold Signature Schemes. Let $S = ($Key-Gen, Sig, Ver$)$ be a signature scheme. A (t, n)-threshold signature scheme $\mathcal{TS}$ for S is a pair of protocols (Thresh-Key-Gen, Thresh-Sig) for the set of players $P_1, \ldots, P_n$.

Thresh-Key-Gen is a distributed key generation protocol used to jointly generate a pair (y, x) of public/private keys on input a security parameter 1^λ. At the end of the protocol, the private output of player P_i is a value x_i such that the values $(x_1, \ldots, x_n)$ form a (t, n)-threshold secret sharing of x. The public output of the protocol contains the public key y. Public/private key pairs (y, x) are produced by Thresh-Key-Gen with the same probability distribution as if they were generated by the Key-Gen protocol of the regular signature scheme S. It is sometimes acceptable to have a *centralized* key generation protocol, in which a trusted dealer runs Key-Gen to obtain (x, y) and shares x among the n players.

Thresh-Sig is the distributed signature protocol. The private input of P_i is the value x_i. The public inputs consist of a message m and the public key y. The output of the protocol is a value $sig \in$ Sig(m, x).

The verification algorithm for a threshold signature scheme is, therefore, the same as in the regular centralized signature scheme S.

Secure Threshold Signature Schemes

Definition 2. *We say that a (t, n)-threshold signature scheme $\mathcal{TS} = ($Thresh-Key-Gen, Thresh-Sig$)$ is* unforgeable, *if no malicious adversary who corrupts at most t players can produce, with non-negligible (in λ) probability, the signature on any new (i.e., previously unsigned) message m, given the view of the protocol* Thresh-Key-Gen *and of the protocol* Thresh-Sig *on input messages $m_1, \ldots, m_k$ which the adversary adaptively chose.*

This is analogous to the notion of existential unforgeability under chosen message attack as defined by Goldwasser, Micali, and Rivest [25]. Notice that now the adversary does not just see the signatures of k messages adaptively chosen, but also the internal state of the corrupted players and the public communication of the protocols. Following [25] one can also define weaker notions of unforgeability.

In order to prove unforgeability, we use the concept of *simulatable adversary view* [12, 26]. Intuitively, this means that the adversary who sees all the information of the corrupted players and the signature of m, could generate by itself all the other public information produced by the protocol Thresh-Sig. This ensures that the run of the protocol provides no useful information to the adversary other than the final signature on m.

Definition 3. *A threshold signature scheme $\mathcal{TS} = ($Thresh-Key-Gen, Thresh-Sig$)$ is* simulatable *if the following properties hold:*

1. *The protocol* Thresh-Key-Gen *is simulatable. That is, there exists a simulator SIM_1 that, on input a public key y, can simulate the view of the adversary on an execution of* Thresh-Key-Gen *that results in y as the public output.*
2. *The protocol* Thresh-Sig *is simulatable. That is, there exists a simulator SIM_2 that, on input the public input of* Thresh-Sig *(in particular the public key y and*

the message m), t shares $x_{i_1}, \ldots, x_{i_t}$, and a signature sig of m, can simulate the view of the adversary on an execution of Thresh-Sig *that generates sig as an output.*

Threshold Optimality. Given a (t, n)-threshold signature scheme, obviously $t + 1$ honest players are necessary to generate signatures. We say that a scheme is *threshold-optimal* if $t + 1$ honest players also suffice.

The main contribution of our work is to present a threshold-optimal DSA scheme for general t. The only known optimal scheme was in [31] for the case of $(1, 2)$-threshold (i.e. 2-out-of-2) threshold DSA. The protocol in [22,23] is not threshold-optimal as it requires $2t + 1$ honest players to compute a signature.

We point out that if we consider an honest-but-curious adversary, then it will suffice to have $n = t + 1$ players in the network to generate signatures (since all players will behave honestly, even the corrupted ones). But in the presence of a malicious adversary one needs at least $n = 2t + 1$ players in total to guarantee *robustness*, i.e. the ability to generate signatures even in the presence of malicious faults. In that sense our protocol improves over [22,23] where $n = 3t + 1$ players are required to guarantee robustness.

But we want to minimize the number of servers, and keep it at $n = t + 1$ even in the presence of malicious faults. In this case we give up on robustness, meaning that we cannot guarantee anymore that signatures will be provided. But we can still prove that our scheme is unforgeable. In other words, an adversary who corrupts almost all the players in the network can only create a denial of service attack, but not learn any information that would allow him to forge. This is another contribution of our paper, since it is not clear how to provide such "dishonest majority" analysis in the case of [22,23].

2.1   Additively Homomorphic Encryption

We assume the existence of an encryption scheme E which is additively homomorphic modulo a large integer N: i.e. given $\alpha = E(a)$ and $\beta = E(b)$, where $a, b \in Z_N$, there is an efficiently computable operation $+_E$ over the ciphertext space such that

$$\alpha +_E \beta = E(a + b \bmod N)$$

Note that if x is an integer, given $\alpha = E(a)$ we can also compute $E(xa \bmod N)$ efficiently. We refer to this operation as $x \times_E \alpha$. We denote the message space of E by $\mathcal{M}_E$ and the ciphertext space by $\mathcal{C}_E$.

With $\bigoplus_{i=1}^{t+1} \alpha_i$ we denote the summation over the addition operation $+_E$ of the encryption scheme: i.e. $\bigoplus_{i=1}^{t+1} \alpha_i = \alpha_1 +_E \ldots +_E \alpha_{t+1}$.

One instantiation of a scheme with these properties is Paillier's encryption scheme [35]. We recall the details of the scheme here.

- Key Generation: generate two large primes P, Q of equal length. and set $N = PQ$. Let $\lambda(N) = lcm(P - 1, Q - 1)$ be the Carmichael function of N. Finally choose $\Gamma \in Z_{N^2}^*$ such that its order is a multiple of N. The public key is (N, Γ) and the secret key is $\lambda(N)$.

- Encryption: to encrypt a message $m \in Z_N$, select $x \in_R Z_N^*$ and return $c = \Gamma^m x^N \bmod N^2$.
- Decryption: to decrypt a ciphertext $c \in Z_{N^2}$, let L be a function defined over the set $\{u \in Z_{N^2} : u = 1 \bmod N\}$ computed as $L(u) = (u-1)/N$. Then the decryption of c is computed as $L(c^{\lambda(N)})/L(\Gamma^{\lambda(N)}) \bmod N$.
- Homomorphic Properties: Given two ciphertexts $c_1, c_2 \in Z_{N^2}$ define $c_1 +_E c_2 = c_1 c_2 \bmod N^2$. If $c_i = E(m_i)$ then $c_1 +_E c_2 = E(m_1 + m_2 \bmod N)$. Similarly, given a ciphertext $c = E(m) \in Z_{N^2}$ and a number $a \in Z_n$ we have that $a \times_E c = c^a \bmod N^2 = E(am \bmod N)$.

2.2 Threshold Cryptosystems

In a (t, n)-threshold cryptosystem, there is a public key pk with a matching secret key sk which is shared among n players with a (t, n)-secret sharing. When a message m is encrypted under pk, $t+1$ players can decrypt it via a communication protocol that does not expose the secret key.

More formally, a public key cryptosystem $\mathcal{E}$ is defined by three efficient algorithms:

- key generation Enc-Key-Gen that takes as input a security parameter λ, and outputs a public key pk and a secret key sk.
- An encryption algorithm Enc that takes as input the public key pk and a message m, and outputs a ciphertext c. Since Enc is a randomized algorithm, there will be several valid encryptions of a message m under the key pk; with Enc(m, pk) we will denote the set of such ciphertexts.
- and a decryption algorithm Dec which is run on input c, sk and outputs m, such that $c \in$ Enc(m, pk).

We say that $\mathcal{E}$ is semantically secure if for any two messages m_0, m_1 we have that the probability distributions Enc(m_0) and Enc(m_1) are computationally indistinguishable.

A (t, n) threshold cryptosystem $\mathcal{TE}$, consists of the following protocols for n players $P_1, \dots, P_n$.

- A key generation protocol TEnc-Key-Gen that takes as input a security parameter λ, and the parameter t, n, and it outputs a public key pk and a vector of secret keys $(sk_1, \dots, sk_n)$ where sk_i is private to player P_i. This protocol could be obtained by having a trusted party run Enc-Key-Gen and sharing sk among the players.
- A threshold decryption protocol TDec, which is run on public input a ciphertext c and private input the share sk_i. The output is m, such that $c \in$ Enc(m, pk).

We point out that threshold variations of Paillier's scheme have been presented in the literature [2,15,16,27]. In order to instantiate our dealerless protocol, we must use the scheme from [27] as it is the only one that includes a dealerless key generation protocol that does not require $n \geq 2t + 1$.

3   Independent Trapdoor Commitments

A trapdoor commitment scheme allows a sender to commit to a message with information-theoretic privacy. i.e., given the transcript of the commitment phase the receiver, even with infinite computing power, cannot guess the committed message better than at random. On the other hand when it comes to opening the message, the sender is only computationally bound to the committed message. Indeed the scheme admits a *trapdoor* whose knowledge allows to open a commitment in any possible way (we will refer to this as the ability to *equivocate* the commitment). This trapdoor should be hard to compute efficiently.

Formally a (non-interactive) trapdoor commitment scheme consists of four algorithms KG, Com, Ver, Equiv with the following properties:

- KG is the key generation algorithm, on input the security parameter it outputs a pair pk, tk where pk is the public key associated with the commitment scheme, and tk is called the *trapdoor*.
- Com is the commitment algorithm. On input pk and a message M it outputs $[C(M), D(M)] = \mathsf{Com}(\mathsf{pk}, M, R)$ where R are the coin tosses. $C(M)$ is the commitment string, while $D(M)$ is the decommitment string which is kept secret until opening time.
- Ver is the verification algorithm. On input C, D and pk it either outputs a message M or $\perp$.
- Equiv is the algorithm that opens a commitment in any possible way given the trapdoor information. It takes as input pk, strings M, R with $[C(M), D(M)] = \mathsf{Com}(\mathsf{pk}, M, R)$, a message $M' \neq M$ and a string T. If $T = \mathsf{tk}$ then Equiv outputs D' such that $\mathsf{Ver}(\mathsf{pk}, C(M), D') = M'$.

We note that if the sender refuses to open a commitment we can set $D = \perp$ and $\mathsf{Ver}(\mathsf{pk}, C, \perp) = \perp$. Trapdoor commitments must satisfy the following properties

Correctness: If $[C(M), D(M)] = \mathsf{Com}(\mathsf{pk}, M, R)$ then $\mathsf{Ver}(\mathsf{pk}, C(M), D(M)) = M$.

Information Theoretic Security: For every message pair M, M' the distributions $C(M)$ and $C(M')$ are statistically close.

Secure Binding: We say that an adversary $\mathcal{A}$ wins if it outputs C, D, D' such that $\mathsf{Ver}(\mathsf{pk}, C, D) = M$, $\mathsf{Ver}(\mathsf{pk}, C, D') = M'$ and $M \neq M'$. We require that for all efficient algorithms $\mathcal{A}$, the probability that $\mathcal{A}$ wins is negligible in the security parameter.

Such a commitment is *non-malleable* [19] if no adversary $\mathcal{A}$, given a commitment C to a message m, is able to produce another commitment C' such that after seeing the opening of C to m, $\mathcal{A}$ can successfully decommit to a related message m' (this is actually the notion of non-malleability with respect to opening introduced in [17]). We are going to use a related property called *independence* and introduced in [24].

Consider the following scenario: an honest party produces a commitment C and the adversary, after seeing C, will produce another commitment C'

(which we require to be different from C in order to prevent the adversary from simply copying the behavior of the honest party and outputting an identical committed value). At this point the value committed by the adversary should be *fixed*, i.e. no matter how the honest party open his commitment the adversary will always open in a unique way.

The following definition takes into account that the adversary may see and output many commitments [14].

Independence: For any adversary $\mathcal{A} = (\mathcal{A}_1, \mathcal{A}_2)$ the following probability is negligible in k:

$$Prob \begin{bmatrix} \mathsf{pk}, \mathsf{tk} \leftarrow \mathsf{KG}(1^k) \; ; \; m_1, \ldots, m_t \leftarrow \mathcal{M} \\ r_1, \ldots, r_t \leftarrow \{0,1\}^k \; ; \; [c_i, d_i] \leftarrow \mathsf{Com}(\mathsf{pk}, m_i, r_i) \\ (\omega, \hat{c}_1, \ldots, \hat{c}_u) \leftarrow \mathcal{A}_1(\mathsf{pk}, c_1, \ldots, c_t) \text{ with } \hat{c}_j \neq c_i \forall i, j \\ m'_1, \ldots, m'_t \leftarrow \mathcal{M} \; ; \; d'_i \leftarrow \mathsf{Equiv}(\mathsf{pk}, \mathsf{tk}, m_i, r_i, m'_i) \\ (\hat{d}_1, \ldots, \hat{d}_u) \leftarrow \mathcal{A}_2(\mathsf{pk}, \omega, d_1, \ldots, d_t) \\ (\hat{d}'_1, \ldots, \hat{d}'_u) \leftarrow \mathcal{A}_2(\mathsf{pk}, \omega, d'_1, \ldots, d'_t) \\ \exists i : \bot \neq \hat{m}_i = \mathsf{Ver}(\mathsf{pk}, \hat{m}_i, \hat{c}_i, \hat{d}_i) \neq \mathsf{Ver}(\mathsf{pk}, \hat{m}'_i, \hat{c}_i, \hat{d}'_i) = \hat{m}'_i \neq \bot \end{bmatrix}$$

In other words even if the honest parties open their commitments in different ways using the trapdoor, the adversary cannot change the way he opens his commitments $\hat{C}_j$ based on the honest parties' openings.

Candidate Independent Trapdoor Commitments. As shown in [24] independence implies non-malleability. We point out that *all* non-malleable commitments in the literature are also independent ones.

The non-malleable commitment schemes in [17,18] are not suitable for our purpose because they are not "concurrently" secure, in the sense that the security definition holds only for $t = 1$ (i.e. the adversary sees only 1 commitment).

The stronger concurrent security notion of non-malleability for $t > 1$ is achieved by the schemes presented in [14,21,32]), and all these schemes can also be proven independent according to the definition presented above.

4   The Digital Signature Standard

We define a generic G-DSA signature algorithm as follows. The public parameters include a cyclic group $\mathcal{G}$ of prime order q generated by an element g, a hash function H defined from arbitrary strings into Z_q, and another hash function H' defined from $\mathcal{G}$ to Z_q.

- Secret Key x chosen uniformly at random in Z_q.
- Public Key $y = g^x$ computed in $\mathcal{G}$.
- Signing Algorithm on input an arbitrary message M, we compute $m = H(M) \in Z_q$. Then the signer chooses k uniformly at random in Z_q and computes $R = g^k$ in $\mathcal{G}$ and $r = H'(R) \in Z_q$. Then she computes $s = k^{-1}(m + xr) \bmod q$. The signature on M is the pair (r, s).

– Verification Algorithm On input $M, (r, s)$ and y, the receiver checks that $r, s \in Z_q$ and computes

$$R' = g^{ms^{-1} \bmod q} y^{rs^{-1} \bmod q} \text{ in } \mathcal{G}$$

and accepts if $H'(R') = r$.

The traditional DSA algorithm is obtained by choosing large primes p, q such that $q|(p-1)$ and setting $\mathcal{G}$ to be the subgroup of Z_p^* of order q. In this case the multiplication operation in $\mathcal{G}$ is multiplication modulo p. The function H' is defined as $H'(R) = R \bmod q$.

The ECDSA scheme is obtained by choosing $\mathcal{G}$ as a group of points on an elliptic curve of cardinality q. In this case the multiplication operation in $\mathcal{G}$ is the group operation over the curve. The function H' is defined as $H'(R) = R_x \bmod q$ where R_x is the x-coordinate of the point R.

4.1 Threshold DSA

As discussed in Sect. 2, in a (t, n)-threshold signature scheme the secret key is shared among n servers, in such a way that any t of them has no information about the secret key, while n players can sign a message using a communication protocol that does not require the secret key to be reconstructed. A scheme is threshold-optimal if exactly $n = t + 1$ honest players can sign.

For the case of DSA, in [22,23] Gennaro *et al.* present such a non-optimal scheme that requires $n = 2t + 1$ honest players to participate in a signature. In particular this prevents the classical "2-out-of-2" case where the key is split among 2 servers so that both must cooperate to sign, while 1 has no information about the secret key (in [22,23] if 1 server has no information about the key, then one would need 3 servers to sign). The 2-out-of-2 case is handled by [31].

The schemes of [22,31] are described for the specific case of the DSA scheme, but it is not hard to see that they both work for the generic G-DSA scheme, and therefore also for ECDSA. We present our scheme with the G-DSA notation.

4.2 The Technical Issues

The main technical issue in constructing threshold DSA signatures is dealing with the fact that *both* the secret key x and the nonce k have to remain secret. This means that in a threshold scheme, they must be shared among the servers. The protocol in [22] is based on Shamir's secret sharing [39], which means that both x and k are shared using polynomials of degree t. Due to the fact that k and x are multiplied to compute s, the end result is that s will be shared using a polynomial of degree $2t$, which requires $2t + 1$ honest players to reconstruct.

The protocol in [31] gets around the above problem by using a multiplicative sharing of the secret values in the protocol. This allows an efficient way to multiply k and x without incurring an increase of the number of players required to reconstruct. However it only works for 2 players.

Our first approach was to first extend the techniques in [31] to the case of t-out-of-t players, but that required $O(t)$ rounds and the use of Paillier's encryption scheme with a modulus $N = O(q^{3t-1})$. Moreover if one wanted to extend that to a t-out-of-n scheme using a combinatorial structure, it would require $O(n^t)$ storage, making it feasible only for small values of n and t. For comparison, we have included this scheme in the full version of this paper.

The scheme we present in the next section requires only 6 rounds, constant amount of storage from the players, and uses a Paillier modulus $N > q^8$.

5   Our Scheme

In this section, we describe our scheme in three parts. First we describe the initialization phase, in which some common parameters are chosen. Then we describe the key generation protocol, in which the parties jointly generate a DSA key pair $(x, y = g^x)$ with y public and x shared among the players. Finally, we describe the signature generation protocol.

In the following, we assume that if any player does not perform according to the protocol (e.g. by failing a ZK proof, or refusing to open a committed value), then the protocol aborts and stops.

5.1   Initialization Phase

In this phase, a common reference string containing the public information pk for an independent trapdoor commitment KG, Com, Ver, Equiv is selected and published. This could be accomplished by a trusted third party, who can be assumed to erase any secret information (i.e. the trapdoor of the commitment).[4] The common parameters $\mathcal{G}, g, q$ for the DSA scheme are assumed to be known.

5.2   Key Generation Protocol

Here we describe how the players can jointly generate a DSA key pair $(x, y = g^x)$ with y public and x shared among the players. The idea is to generate a public key E for an additively (mod N) homomorphic encryption scheme E, together with the secret key D in shared form among the players. The value N is chosen to be larger than q^8. Then a value x is generated, and encrypted with E, with the value $\alpha = E(x)$ made public. Note that this is an implicit (t, n) secret sharing of x, since the decryption key of E is shared among the players. We use independent trapdoor commitments KG, Com, Ver, Equiv to enforce the independence of the values contributed by each player to the selection of x (in the following, for simplicity we may drop the public key pk and the randomness input when describing the computation of a commitment and write $[C, D] = \mathsf{Com}(m)$)

---

[4] Another option is to use a publicly verifiable method that generates the public information, without the trapdoor being known. For example the public parameters in [18] could be generated by using a "random oracle" over some public information without anybody knowing the trapdoor.

More specifically, the scheme is described below. We assume that if any commitment opens to $\perp$ or if any of the ZK proofs fail, the protocol terminates without an output.

- The parties run the key generation protocol TEnc-Key-Gen for an additively homomorphic encryption scheme E. If using Paillier's encryption scheme, we can use the threshold version from [27] with $N > q^8$.
- Each player P_i selects a random value $x_i \in Z_q$, computes $y_i = g^{x_i} \in \mathcal{G}$ and $[C_i, D_i] = \mathsf{Com}(y_i)$;
- Each player P_i broadcasts C_i
- Each player P_i broadcasts
  - D_i which allows everybody to compute $y_i = \mathsf{Ver}(C_i, D_i)$.
  - $\alpha_i = E(x_i)$;
  - a ZK argument Π_i that states
    * $\exists\, \eta \in [-q^3, q^3]$ such that
    * $g^\eta = y_i$
    * $D(\alpha_i) = \eta$
  If any of the ZK arguments fails, the protocol terminates.
- The players compute $\alpha = \bigoplus_{i=1}^{t+1} \alpha_i$ and $y = \prod_{i=1}^{t+1} y_i$.

The public key for the DSA is set to y. We note that $y = g^x$ and that $\alpha = E(x')$ with $x' = x \bmod q$ since $x' = \sum_{i=1}^{t+1} x_i$ is computed modulo N, but since $N > q^8$, we have that x' is computed actually over the integers.

5.3   Signature Generation

We now describe the signature generation protocol, which is run on input m (the hash of the message M being signed) and the output of the key generation protocol described above. Here too, we assume that if any commitment opens to $\perp$ or if any of the ZK proofs fail, the protocol terminates without an output.

- Round 1
  Each player P_i
  - chooses $\rho_i \in_R Z_q$
  - computes $u_i = E(\rho_i)$ and $v_i = \rho_i \times_E \alpha = E(\rho_i x)$
  - computes $[C_{1,i}, D_{1,i}] = \mathsf{Com}([u_i, v_i])$ and broadcasts $C_{1,i}$
- Round 2
  Each player P_i broadcasts
  - $D_{1,i}$. This allows everybody to compute $[u_i, v_i] = \mathsf{Ver}(C_{1,i}, D_{1,i})$
  - a zero-knowledge argument $\Pi_{(1,i)}$ which states
    * $\exists\, \eta \in [-q^3, q^3]$ such that
    * $D(u_i) = \eta$
    * $D(v_i) = \eta D(E(x))$
  Players compute $u = \bigoplus_{i=1}^{t+1} u_i = E(\rho)$ and $v = \bigoplus_{i=1}^{t+1} v_i = E(\rho x)$, where $\rho = \sum_{i=1}^{t+1} \rho_i$ (over the integers)
- Round 3
  Each player P_i

- chooses $k_i \in_R Z_q$ and $c_i \in_R [-q^6, q^6]$
- computes $r_i = g^{k_i}$ and $w_i = (k_i \times_E u) +_E E(c_i q) = E(k_i \rho + c_i q)$
- computes $[C_{2,i}, D_{2,i}] = \mathsf{Com}(r_i, w_i)$ and broadcasts $C_{2,i}$

- Round 4
  Each player P_i broadcasts
  - $D_{2,i}$ which allows everybody to compute $[r_i, w_i] = \mathsf{Ver}(C_{2,i}, D_{2,i})$
  - a zero-knowledge argument $\Pi_{(2,i)}$ which states
    * $\exists\, \eta \in [-q^3, q^3]$ such that
    * $g^\eta = r_i$
    * $D(w_i) = \eta D(u) \bmod q$

  Players compute $w = \bigoplus_1^{t+1} w_i = E(k\rho + cq)$ where $k = \sum_{i=1}^{t+1} k_i$ and $c = \sum_{i=1}^{t+1} c_i$ (over the integers). Players also compute $R = \Pi_1^{t+1} r_i = g^k$ and $r = H'(R) \in Z_q$

- Round 5
  - players jointly decrypt w using TDec to learn the value $\eta \in [-q^7, q^7]$ such that $\eta = k\rho \bmod q$ and $\psi = \eta^{-1} \bmod q$
  - Each player computes

$$\sigma = \psi \times_E [(m \times_E u) +_E (r \times_E v)]$$
$$= \psi \times_E [E(m\rho) +_E E(r\rho x)]$$
$$= (k^{-1}\rho^{-1}) \times_E [E(\rho(m + xr))]$$
$$= E(k^{-1}(m + xr))$$
$$= E(s)$$

- Round 6
  The players invoke distributed decryption protocol TDec over the ciphertext σ. Let $s = D(\sigma) \bmod q$. The players output (r, s) as the signature for m.

Remark: The Size of the Modulus N. We note that in order for the protocol to be correct, all the homomorphic operations over the ciphertexts (which are modulo N), must not "conflict" with the operations modulo q of the DSA algorithms. We note that the values encrypted under E are $\sim q^7$. Indeed the ZK proofs guarantee that the values $k, \rho < q^3$. Moreover the "masking" value cq in the decryption of η is at most q^7, so the encrypted values in w_i are never larger than q^8. By choosing $N > q^8$ we guarantee that when we manipulate ciphertexts, all the operations on the plaintexts happen basically over the integers, without taking any modular reduction mod N.

Remark: The Distribution of Signatures. The adversary has the ability to affect the distribution of signatures by refusing to open his commitment if the signature is not to his liking. This leads to a possible loss of anonymity as an adversary can alter the distribution of the signatures in such a way that helps one distinguish the signatures made by this group.

In practice this is not a problem for Bitcoin. The only way one can affect distribution is by refusing to open, and if one of the players refused to open, we would detect that they are corrupted and reboot them. In the full version of this paper we analyze the anonymity lost under these assumptions. The anonymity in Bitcoin is linear in the number of users, and we find that the most the adversary can do is reduce the anonymity equivalently to halving the number of users.

5.4 Security Proof and Zero-Knowledge Arguments

A simulation based security proof and the details of how to implement the zero-knowledge proofs are presented in the full version of this paper.

6 Threshold Security for Bitcoin Wallets

In this section, we give an overview of Bitcoin, discuss the threat model, and show how threshold signatures provide a solution for the most pressing threats.

6.1 Bitcoin

Bitcoin is a decentralized digital currency [34]. Bitcoins are owned by *addresses*; an address is simply the hash of a public key. To transfer bitcoins from one address to another, a *transaction* is constructed that specifies one or more input addresses from which the funds are to be debited, and one or more output addresses to which the funds are to be credited. For each input address, the transaction contains a reference to a previous transaction which contained this address as an output address. In order for the transaction to be valid, it must be signed by the private key associated with each input address, and the funds in the referenced transactions must not have already been spent [6,34].

Each output of a transaction may only be referenced as the input to a single subsequent transaction. It is thus necessary to spend the entire output at once. It is often the case that one only wishes to spend part of an output that was received in a previous transaction. This is accomplished by means of a *change address* where one lists their own address as an output of the transaction.

While the sender could include their input address as the change address in the output, the best and recommended practice is to send the change to a newly generated addresses. The motivation for doing so is increased anonymity as it makes it harder to track which addresses are owned by which individuals.

A Bitcoin *wallet* is a software abstraction which seamlessly manages multiple addresses on behalf of a user. Users do not deal with the low level details of their addresses. They just see their total balance, and when they want to send bitcoins to another address, they specify the amount to be transferred. The wallet software chooses the input and change addresses and constructs the transaction.

Signed transactions are broadcast to the Bitcoin peer-to-peer network. They are validated by *miners* who group transactions together into *blocks*. Miners participate in a distributed consensus protocol that collects these blocks into an append-only global log called the *block chain*.

While the original Bitcoin paper does not specify which signature algorithm to use, the current implementation uses ECDSA over the secp256k1 curve [6–8].

6.2   Threat Model

To classify the problems, we distinguish between internal and external threats as well as between hot and cold wallets. While the term wallet is generally used loosely to refer to a software abstraction (as described in the previous section), we will use the term in the rest of the paper in a more precise sense.

Definition 4 (wallet). *A collection of addresses with the same security policy together with a software program or protocol that allows spending from those addresses in accordance with that policy.*

"Security policy" encompasses the ownership or access-control list and the conditions under which bitcoins in the wallet may be spent.

The terms *hot wallet* and *cold wallet* derive from the more general terms *hot storage*, meaning online storage, and *cold storage*, meaning offline storage.

Definition 5 (Hot wallet/Cold wallet). *A* hot wallet *is a wallet from which bitcoins can be spent without accessing cold storage. Conversely, a* cold wallet *is a wallet from which bitcoins cannot be spent without accessing cold storage.*

Note that these new definitions refer to the desired effect, not the method of achieving it. The desired effect of a business that maintains a hot wallet is the ability to spend bitcoins online without having to access cold storage.

Table 1. Taxonomy of threats

Adversary	Hot wallet	Cold wallet
Insider	Vulnerable by default; our methods are necessary	Reduces to physical security by default; our methods can help
External (network)	Reduces to network security by default; our methods can help	Safe

Table 1 shows four types of possible threats to Bitcoin wallets. Securing a cold wallet is a physical security problem. While a network adversary is unable to get to a cold wallet, traditional physical security measures can be used to protect it from insiders — for example, private keys printed on paper and stored in a locked safe with video surveillance.

In addition, our methods may be used to supplement physical security measures. Instead of storing the key in a single location, the business can store shares of the key in different locations. The adversary will thus have to compromise security in multiple locations in order to recover the key. Indeed, this is one use case where Bitcoin companies have expressed great interest in implementing our threshold signature scheme.

Protecting hot wallets from internal attackers is the most pressing problem. Our central claim is that due to the irreversibility of Bitcoin transactions, the level of insecurity of this threat category has no parallels in traditional finance or network security, necessitating Bitcoin-specific solutions. Whereas traditional banking systems can incorporate detection and recovery in their security measures, Bitcoin security must come from prevention; the irreversibility precludes any recovery options.

7 Implementation and Evaluation

In this section, we describe and evaluate our implementation of our protocol. We describe two different parts of our implementation. We also created a desktop Bitcoin wallet and android app that used threshold signatures for two factor authentication. The implementation details of the two factor applications are in the full version of this paper.

7.1 Our Protocol

We fully implemented our protocol in Java. We chose Java since it works well cross-platform, and in particular since it can run on mobile devices. We wrote our code as library functions that are easily called and incorporated into company's existing codebase.

We have released code for our threshold signing protocol[5] as well as for the two factor wallet[6]. We plan to update the repository shortly with code for the dealerless key generation protocol.

For the independent trapdoor commitment scheme, we implemented the second protocol in [21]. This protocol uses pairing based cryptography, and we used the Jpair library to facilitate this. For the underlying Paillier scheme, we use a modified version of the Java implementation of threshold Paillier in [36],

7.2 Runtime

We benchmarked our implementation on a machine with a 2.4 GHz Intel Core i7 Processor. Our implementation was extremely efficient. The time to generate a signature is a function of t, the number of players actively involved. We note that in the protocol, the time for each player to generate their shares is not affected by the number of other participants. However, players need to verify zero knowledge proofs and check commitments from all other players, and thus the runtime is affected by the number of players.

Our evaluation found that without checking proofs or commitments, each players runtime is 1.1 s. Checking proofs and commitments takes 0.5 s per player, and the runtime R in seconds is thus given by the following:

---

[5] https://github.com/citp/ThresholdECDSA.
[6] https://github.com/citp/TwoFactorBtcWallet.

$$R(t) = 1.1 + 0.5t$$

Not counting for network latency, this means if 3 participants are required to generate a signature (so $t = 2$), it takes $2.1\,s$ to generate a signature.

8   Conclusion

In this paper, we presented the first threshold-optimal signature scheme for DSA. We proved its security, implemented it, and evaluated it. Our scheme is quite efficient, and our implementation confirms that this scheme is ready to be used. Indeed, many Bitcoin companies have expressed great interest in our scheme as it provides a much needed solution to Bitcoin's security problem. We have open sourced our two-factor app and our general (t, n) signature code as well so that companies can benefit from our results and begin to use them immediately.

Acknowledgements. We would like to thank Dan Boneh, Joseph Bonneau, Edward W. Felten, Harry Kalodner, and Joshua Kroll for helpful input and feedback. We would also like to thank Harry Kalodner for his work in implementing the two factor wallet. We would like to thank Daniel Wichs for raising the question of how the adversary's ability to alter the signature distribution affects anonymity.

Rosario Gennaro is supported by NSF Grant 1545759. Steven Goldfeder is supported by the National Science Foundation Graduate Research Fellowship under grant number DGE 1148900. Arvind Narayanan is supported by NSF Grant CNS-1421689.

Refcrences

1. Andresen, G.: Github: Shared Wallets Design. https://gist.github.com/gavinandresen/4039433
2. Baudron, O., Fouque, P.-A., Pointcheval, D., Poupard, G., Stern, J.: Practical multi-candidate election system. In: PODC 2001
3. Barić, N., Pfitzmann, B.: Collision-free accumulators and fail-stop signature schemes without trees. In: Fumy, W. (ed.) EUROCRYPT 1997. LNCS, vol. 1233, pp. 480–494. Springer, Heidelberg (1997)
4. Bitcoin Forum member dree12, List of Bitcoin Heists (2013). https://bitcointalk.org/index.php?topic=83794.0
5. Bitcoin Forum member gmaxwell, Coinjoin: Bitcoin privacy in the real world (2013). https://bitcointalk.org/index.php?topic=279249.0
6. Bitcoin wiki: Transactions. https://en.bitcoin.it/wiki/Transactions
7. Bitcoin wiki: Elliptic Curve Digital Signature Algorithm. https://en.bitcoin.it/wiki/Elliptic_Curve_Digital_Signature_Algorithm
8. Bitcoin wiki: Secp256k1. https://en.bitcoin.it/w/index.php?title=Secp256k1
9. Bonneau, J., Narayanan, A., Miller, A., Clark, J., Kroll, J.A., Felten, E.W.: Mixcoin: anonymity for bitcoin with accountable mixes. In: Christin, N., Safavi-Naini, R. (eds.) FC 2014. LNCS, vol. 8437, pp. 486–504. Springer, Heidelberg (2014)
10. Camenisch, J., Kiayias, A., Yung, M.: On the portability of generalized schnorr proofs. In: Joux, A. (ed.) EUROCRYPT 2009. LNCS, vol. 5479, pp. 425–442. Springer, Heidelberg (2009)

11. Camenisch, J., Krenn, S., Shoup, V.: A framework for practical universally composable zero-knowledge protocols. In: Lee, D.H., Wang, X. (eds.) ASIACRYPT 2011. LNCS, vol. 7073, pp. 449–467. Springer, Heidelberg (2011)
12. Canetti, R., Security, U.C.: A new paradigm for cryptographic protocols. In: Proceedings of 42nd IEEE Symposium on Foundations of Computer Science (FOCS 2001) (2001)
13. Canetti, R., Gennaro, R., Jarecki, S., Krawczyk, H., Rabin, T.: Adaptive security for threshold cryptosystems. In: Wiener, M. (ed.) CRYPTO 1999. LNCS, vol. 1666, pp. 98–116. Springer, Heidelberg (1999)
14. Damgård, I., Groth, J.: Non-interactive and reusable non-malleable commitment schemes. In: Proceedings of 35th ACM Symposium on Theory of Computing (STOC 2003) (2003)
15. Damgård, I., Jurik, M.: A generalisation, a simplification and some applications of Paillier's probabilistic public-key system. In: Kim, K. (ed.) PKC 2001. LNCS, vol. 1992, pp. 119–136. Springer, Heidelberg (2001)
16. Damgård, I.B., Koprowski, M.: Practical threshold RSA signatures without a trusted dealer. In: Pfitzmann, B. (ed.) EUROCRYPT 2001. LNCS, vol. 2045, pp. 152–165. Springer, Heidelberg (2001)
17. Di Crescenzo, G., Ishai, Y., Ostrovsky, R.: Non-interactive and non-malleable commitment. In: Proceedings of 30th ACM Symposium on Theory of Computing (STOC 1998) (1998)
18. Di Crescenzo, G., Katz, J., Ostrovsky, R., Smith, A.: Efficient and non-interactive non-malleable commitment. In: Pfitzmann, B. (ed.) EUROCRYPT 2001. LNCS, vol. 2045, pp. 40–59. Springer, Heidelberg (2001)
19. Dolev, D., Dwork, C., Naor, M.: Non-malleable cryptography. SIAM J. Comp. 30(2), 391–437 (2000)
20. Fujisaki, E., Okamoto, T.: Statistical zero knowledge protocols to prove modular polynomial relations. In: Kaliski Jr., B.S. (ed.) CRYPTO 1997. LNCS, vol. 1294, pp. 16–30. Springer, Heidelberg (1997)
21. Gennaro, R.: Multi-trapdoor commitments and their applications to proofs of knowledge secure under concurrent man-in-the-middle attacks. In: Franklin, M. (ed.) CRYPTO 2004. LNCS, vol. 3152, pp. 220–236. Springer, Heidelberg (2004)
22. Gennaro, R., Jarecki, S., Krawczyk, H., Rabin, T.: Robust threshold DSS signatures. In: Maurer, U.M. (ed.) EUROCRYPT 1996. LNCS, vol. 1070, pp. 354–371. Springer, Heidelberg (1996)
23. Gennaro, R., Jarecki, S., Krawczyk, H., Rabin, T.: Secure distributed key generation for discrete-log based cryptosystems. In: Stern, J. (ed.) EUROCRYPT 1999. LNCS, vol. 1592, pp. 295–310. Springer, Heidelberg (1999)
24. Gennaro, R., Micali, S.: Independent zero-knowledge sets. In: Bugliesi, M., Preneel, B., Sassone, V., Wegener, I. (eds.) ICALP 2006. LNCS, vol. 4052, pp. 34–45. Springer, Heidelberg (2006)
25. Goldwasser, S., Micali, S., Rivest, R.L.: A digital signature scheme secure against adaptive chosen-message attacks. SIAM J. Comput. 17(2), 281–308 (1988)
26. Goldwasser, S., Micali, S., Rackoff, C.: The knowledge complexity of interactive proof-systems. SIAM. J. Comput. 18(1), 186–208 (1989)
27. Hazay, C., Mikkelsen, G.L., Rabin, T., Toft, T.: Efficient RSA key generation and threshold paillier in the two-party setting. In: Dunkelman, O. (ed.) CT-RSA 2012. LNCS, vol. 7178, pp. 313–331. Springer, Heidelberg (2012)
28. Jarecki, S., Lysyanskaya, A.: Adaptively secure threshold cryptography: introducing concurrency, removing erasures (Extended Abstract). In: Preneel, B. (ed.) EUROCRYPT 2000. LNCS, vol. 1807, pp. 221–242. Springer, Heidelberg (2000)

29. Johnson, D., Menezes, A., Vanstone, S.: The elliptic curve digital signature algorithm (ECDSA). Int. J. Inf. Secur. 1(1), 36–63 (2001)
30. Kaspersky Labs, Financial cyber threats in: 2013. Part 2: malware (2013). http://securelist.com/analysis/kaspersky-security-bulletin/59414/financial-cyber-threats-in-2013-part-2-malware/
31. MacKenzie, P., Reiter, M.: Two-party generation of DSA signatures. Int. J. Inf. Secur. 2, 218–239 (2004)
32. MacKenzie, P.D., Yang, K.: On simulation-sound trapdoor commitments. In: Cachin, C., Camenisch, J.L. (eds.) EUROCRYPT 2004. LNCS, vol. 3027, pp. 382–400. Springer, Heidelberg (2004)
33. Meiklejohn, S., Pomarole, M., Jordan, G., Levchenko, K., McCoy, D., Voelker, G.M., Savage, S.: A fistful of bitcoins: characterizing payments among men with no names. In: Proceedings of the 2013 Internet Measurement Conference. ACM (2013)
34. Nakamoto, S.: Bitcoin: a peer-to-peer electronic cash system. Consulted 1, 28 (2008)
35. Paillier, P.: Public-key cryptosystems based on composite degree residuosity classes. In: Stern, J. (ed.) EUROCRYPT 1999. LNCS, vol. 1592, pp. 223–238. Springer, Heidelberg (1999)
36. Paillier Threshold Encryption Toolbox. http://cs.utdallas.edu/dspl/cgi-bin/paalliertoolbox/manual.pdf
37. Pedersen, T.P.: Distributed provers with applications to undeniable signatures. In: Davies, D.W. (ed.) EUROCRYPT 1991. LNCS, vol. 547, pp. 221–242. Springer, Heidelberg (1991)
38. Rivest, R., Shamir, A., Adelman, L.: A method for obtaining digital signature and public key cryptosystems. Comm. ACM 21, 120–126 (1978)
39. Shamir, A.: How to share a secret. Comm. ACM 22, 612–613 (1979)

Legally Fair Contract Signing Without Keystones

Houda Ferradi, Rémi Géraud, Diana Maimuţ, David Naccache[⊠],
and David Pointcheval

École Normale Supérieure, 45 Rue D'Ulm, 75230 Paris Cedex 05, France
{houda.ferradi,remi.geraud,diana.maimut,david.naccache,
david.pointcheval}@ens.fr

Abstract. In two-party computation, achieving both fairness and guaranteed output delivery is well known to be impossible. Despite this limitation, many approaches provide solutions of practical interest by weakening somewhat the fairness requirement. Such approaches fall roughly in three categories: "gradual release" schemes assume that the aggrieved party can eventually reconstruct the missing information; "optimistic schemes" assume a trusted third party arbitrator that can restore fairness in case of litigation; and "concurrent" or "legally fair" schemes in which a breach of fairness is compensated by the aggrieved party having a digitally signed cheque from the other party (called the keystone).

In this paper we describe and analyse a new contract signing paradigm that doesn't require keystones to achieve legal fairness, and give a concrete construction based on Schnorr signatures which is compatible with standard Schnorr signatures and provably secure.

1 Introduction

When mutually distrustful parties wish to compute some joint function of their private inputs, they require a certain number of security properties to hold for that computation:

- *Privacy*: Nothing is learnt from the protocol besides the output;
- *Correctness*: The output is distributed according to the prescribed functionality;
- *Independence*: One party cannot make their inputs depend on the other parties' inputs;
- *Delivery*: An adversary cannot prevent the honest parties from successfully computing the functionality;
- *Fairness*: If one party receives output then so do all.

Any multi-party computation can be securely computed [4,6,14,15,24] as long as there is a honest majority [20]. In the case where there is no such majority,

© Springer International Publishing Switzerland 2016
M. Manulis et al. (Eds.): ACNS 2016, LNCS 9696, pp. 175–190, 2016.
DOI: 10.1007/978-3-319-39555-5_10

and in particular in the two-party case, it is (in general[1]) impossible to achieve both fairness and guaranteed output delivery [8,20].

Weakening Fairness. To circumvent this limitation, several authors have put forth alternatives to fairness that try and capture the practical context (*e.g.* contract-signing, bank transactions, etc.). Three main directions have been explored:

1. *Gradual release models*: The output is not revealed all at once, but rather released gradually (*e.g.* bit per bit) so that, if an abort occurs, then the adversary has not learnt much more about the output than the honest party. This solution is unsatisfactory because it is expensive and may not work if the adversary is more computationally powerful [11,16,17,22].
2. *Optimistic models*: A trusted server is setup but will not be contacted unless fairness is breached. The server is able to restore fairness afterwards, and this approach can be efficient, but the infrastructure requirements and the condition that the server be trusted limit the applicability of this solution [2,5,21]. In particular, the dispute-resolving third party must be endowed with functions beyond those usually required of a normal certification authority.
3. *Legally fair, or concurrent model*: The first party to receive output obtains an information dubbed the "keystone". The keystone by itself gives nothing and so if the first party aborts after receiving it, no damage has been done – if the second party aborts after receiving the result (say, a signature) then the first party is left with a useless keystone. But, as observed in [7] for the signature to be enforced, it needs to be presented to a court of law, and legally fair signing protocols are designed so that this signature *and* the keystone give enough information to reconstruct the missing data. Therefore, if the cheating party wishes to enforce its signed contract in a court of law, it by doing so reveal the signature that the first party should receive, thereby restoring fairness [7]. Legal fairness requires neither a trusted arbitrator nor a high degree of interaction between parties.

Lindell [20] also introduces a notion of "legally enforceable fairness" that sits between legal fairness and optimistic models: a trusted authority may force a cheating party to act in some fashion, should their cheating be attested. In this case the keystone consists in a digitally signed cheque for an frighteningly high amount of money that the cheating party would have to pay if the protocol were to be aborted prematurely and the signature abused.

Concurrent Signatures. Chen *et al.* [7] proposed a legally fair signature scheme based on ring signatures [1,23] and designated verifier signatures [19], that is proven secure in the Random Oracle Model assuming the hardness of computing discrete logarithms.

---

[1] See [17] for a very specific case where completely fair two-party computation can be achieved.

Concurrent signatures rely on a property shared by ring and designated verifier signatures called "ambiguity". In the case of two-party ring signatures, one cannot say which of the two parties produced the signature – since either of two parties could have produced such an ambiguous signature, both parties can deny having produced it. However, within the ring, if A receives a signature then she knows that it is B who sent it. The idea is to put the ambiguity-lifting information in a "keystone". When that keystone is made public, both signatures become simultaneously binding.

Concurrent signatures schemes can achieve legal fairness depending on the context. However their construction is not *abuse-free* [3,10]: the party A holding the keystone can always determine whether to complete or abort the exchange of signatures, and can demonstrate this by showing an outside party the signature from B with the keystone, before revealing the keystone to B.

Our Results. In this work we describe a new contract signing protocol that achieves legal fairness and abuse-freeness. This protocol is based on the well-known Schnorr signature protocol, and produces signatures *compatible* with standard Schnorr signatures. For this reason, and as we demonstrate, the new contract signing protocol is provably secure in the random oracle model under the hardness assumption of solving the discrete logarithm problem. Our construction can be adapted to other DLP schemes, such as most[2] of those enumerated in [18], including Girault-Poupard-Stern [12] and ElGamal [9].

2   Preliminaries

We assume the reader to be familiar with Schnorr signatures, that we recall in the appendix in the IACR ePrint version of this paper.

2.1   Concurrent Signatures

Let us give a more formal account of legal fairness as described in [7,20] in terms of concurrent signatures. Unlike classical contract-signing protocol, whereby contractors would exchange full-fledged signatures (*e.g.* [13]), in a concurrent signature protocol there are "ambiguous" signatures that do not, as such, bind their author. This ambiguity can later be lifted by revealing some additional information: the "keystone". When the keystone is made public, both signatures become simultaneously binding.

Let $\mathcal{M}$ be a message space. Let $\mathcal{K}$ be the keystone space and $\mathcal{F}$ be the keystone fix space.

Definition 1 (Concurrent signature). *A concurrent signature is composed of the following algorithms:*

---

[2] In a number of cases, *e.g.* DSA, the formulae of s do not lend themselves to security proofs.

- Setup(ℓ): *Takes a security parameter ℓ as input and outputs the public keys (y_A, y_B) of all participants, a function* KeyGen $: \mathcal{K} \to \mathcal{F}$, *and public parameters* pp *describing the choices of* $\mathcal{M}, \mathcal{K}, \mathcal{F}$ *and* KeyGen.
- aSign(y_i, y_j, x_i, h_2, M): *Takes as input the public keys y_1 and y_2, the private key x_i corresponding to y_i, an element $h_2 \in \mathcal{F}$ and some message $M \in \mathcal{M}$; and outputs an "ambiguous signature"*

$$\sigma = \langle s, h_1, h_2 \rangle$$

where $s \in \mathcal{S}, h_1, h_2 \in \mathcal{F}$.
- aVerify(σ, y_i, y_j, M): *Takes as input an ambiguous signature $\sigma = \langle s, h_1, h_2 \rangle$, public keys y_i and y_j, a message M; and outputs a boolean value, with the constraint that*

$$\mathsf{aVerify}\left(\sigma', y_j, y_i, M\right) = \mathsf{aVerify}\left(\sigma, y_i, y_j, M\right)$$

where $\sigma' = \langle s, h_2, h_1 \rangle$.
- Verify(k, σ, y_i, y_j, M): *Takes as input $k \in \mathcal{K}$ and σ, y_i, y_j, M as above; and checks whether* KeyGen(k) $= h_2$: *If not it terminates with output* False, *otherwise it outputs the result of* aVerify(σ, y_i, y_j, M).

A valid concurrent signature is a tuple $\langle k, \sigma, y_i, y_j, M \rangle$ that is accepted by the Verify algorithm. Concurrent signatures are used by two parties A and B in the following way:

1. A and B run Setup to determine the public parameters of the scheme. We assume that A's public and private keys are y_A and x_A, and B's public and private keys are y_B and x_B.
2. Without loss of generality, we assume that A initiates the conversation. A picks a random keystone $k \in \mathcal{K}$, and computes $f = $ KeyGen(k). A takes her own public key y_A and B's public key y_B and picks a message $M_A \in \mathcal{M}$ to sign. A then computes her ambiguous signature to be

$$\sigma_A = \langle s_A, h_A, f \rangle = \mathsf{aSign}(y_A, y_B, x_A, f, M_A).$$

3. Upon receiving A's ambiguous signature σ_A, B verifies the signature by checking that

$$\mathsf{aVerify}(s_A, h_A, f, y_A, y_B, M_A) = \mathsf{True}$$

If this equality does not hold, then B aborts. Otherwise B picks a message $M_B \in \mathcal{M}$ to sign and computes his ambiguous signature

$$\sigma_B = \langle s_B, h_B, f \rangle = \mathsf{aSign}(y_B, y_A, x_B, f, M_B)$$

then sends this back to A. Note that B uses the same value f in his signature as A did to produce σ_A.
4. Upon receiving B's signature σ_B, A verifies that

$$\mathsf{aVerify}(s_B, h_B, f, y_B, y_A, M_B) = \mathsf{True}$$

where f is the same keystone fix as A used in the previous steps. If the equality does not hold, then A aborts. Otherwise A sends keystone k to B.

At the end of this protocol, both $\langle k, \sigma_A \rangle$ and $\langle k, \sigma_B \rangle$ are binding, and accepted by the Verify algorithm.

Remark 1. Note that A has an the upper hand in this protocol: Only when A releases the keystone do both signatures become simultaneously binding, and there is no guarantee that A will ever do so. Actually, since A controls the timing of the keystone release (if it is released at all), A may only reveal k to a third party C but withhold it from B, and gain some advantage by doing so. In other terms, concurrent signatures can be *abused* by A [3,10].

Chen *et al.* [7] argue that there are situations where it is not in A's interest to try and cheat B, in which abuse-freeness is not necessary. One interesting scenario is credit card payment in the "four corner" model. Assume that B's signature is a payment to A. To obtain payment, A must channel *via* her acquiring bank C, which would communicate with B's issuing bank D. D would ensure that B receives both the signature and the keystone — as soon as this happens A is bound to her signature. Since in this scenario there is no possibility for A to keep B's signature private, fairness is eventually restored.

Example 1. A concurrent signature scheme based on the ring signature algorithm of Abe *et al.* [1] was proposed by Chen *et al.* [7]:

- Setup: On input a security parameter ℓ, two large primes p and q are selected such that $q|p - 1$. An element $g \in \mathbb{Z}_p^\times$ of order q is selected. The spaces $\mathcal{S} = \mathcal{F} = \mathbb{Z}_q$ and $\mathcal{M} = \mathcal{K} = \{0,1\}^*$ are chosen. Two cryptographic hash functions $H_1, H_2 : \{0,1\}^* \to \mathbb{Z}_q$ are selected and we set KeyGen $= H_1$. Private keys x_A, x_B are selected uniformly at random from $\mathbb{Z}_q$ and the corresponding public keys are computed as $g^{x_i} \bmod p$.
- aSign: The algorithms takes as input y_i, y_j, x_i, h_2, M, verifies that $y_i \neq y_j$ (otherwise aborts), picks a random value $t \in \mathbb{Z}_q$ and computes

$$h = H_2 \left(g^t y_j^{h_2} \bmod p \| M \right)$$
$$h_1 = h - h_2 \bmod q$$
$$s = t - h_1 x_i \bmod q$$

where $\|$ denotes concatenation. The algorithm outputs $\langle s, h_1, h_2 \rangle$.
- aVerify: This algorithm takes as input s, h_1, h_2, y_i, y_j, M and checks whether the following equation holds:

$$h_1 + h_2 = H_2 \left(g^s y_i^{h_1} y_j^{h_2} \bmod p \| M \right) \bmod q$$

The security of this scheme can be proven in the Random Oracle model assuming the hardness of computing discrete logarithms in $\mathbb{Z}_p^\times$.

2.2   Legal Fairness for Concurrent Signatures

A concurrent signature scheme is secure when it achieves existential unforgeability, ambiguity and fairness against an active adversary that has access to a signature oracle. We define these notions in terms of games played between the adversary $\mathcal{A}$ and a challenger $\mathcal{C}$. In all security games, $\mathcal{A}$ can perform any number of the following queries:

- KeyGen queries: $\mathcal{A}$ can receive a keystone fix $f = \mathsf{KeyGen}(k)$ where k is chosen by the challenger[3].
- KeyReveal queries: $\mathcal{A}$ can request that $\mathcal{C}$ reveals which k was chosen to produce a keystone fix f in a previous KeyGen query. If f was not a previous KeyGen query output then $\mathcal{C}$ returns $\perp$.
- aSign queries: $\mathcal{A}$ can request an ambiguous signature for any message of his choosing and any pair of users[4].
- SKExtract queries: $\mathcal{A}$ can request the private key corresponding to a public key.

Definition 2 (Unforgeability). *The notion of existential unforgeability for concurrent signatures is defined in terms of the following security game:*

1. *The* Setup *algorithm is run and all public parameters are given to $\mathcal{A}$.*
2. *$\mathcal{A}$ can perform any number of queries to $\mathcal{C}$, as described above.*
3. *Finally, $\mathcal{A}$ outputs a tuple $\sigma = \langle s, h_1, f \rangle$ where $s \in \mathcal{S}, h_1, f \in \mathcal{F}$, along with public keys y_C, y_D and a message $M \in \mathcal{M}$.*

$\mathcal{A}$ wins the game if aVerify *accepts σ and either of the following holds:*

- *$\mathcal{A}$ did not query SKExtract on y_C nor on y_D, and did not query aSign on (y_C, y_D, f, M) nor on (y_D, y_C, h_1, M).*
- *$\mathcal{A}$ did not query aSign on (y_C, y_i, f, M) for any $y_i \neq y_C$, and did not query SKExtract on y_C, and f is the output of* KeyGen: *either an answer to a KeyGen query, or $\mathcal{A}$ can produce a k such that $k = \mathsf{KeyGen}(k)$.*

The last constraint in the unforgeability security game corresponds to the situation where $\mathcal{A}$ knows one of the private keys (as is the case if $\mathcal{A} = A$ or B).

Definition 3 (Ambiguity). *The notion of ambiguity for concurrent signatures is defined in terms of the following security game:*

1. *The* Setup *algorithm is run and all public parameters are given to $\mathcal{A}$.*
2. *Phase 1: $\mathcal{A}$ can perform any number of queries to $\mathcal{C}$, as described above.*
3. *Challenge: $\mathcal{A}$ selects a challenge tuple (y_i, y_j, M) where y_i, y_j are public keys and $M \in \mathcal{M}$. In response, $\mathcal{C}$ selects a random $k \in \mathcal{K}$, a random $b \in \{0, 1\}$ and computes $f = \mathsf{KeyGen}(k)$. If $b = 0$, then $\mathcal{C}$ outputs*

$$\sigma_1 = \langle s_1, h_1, f \rangle = \mathsf{aSign}(y_i, y_j, x_i, f, M)$$

Otherwise, if $b = 1$ then $\mathcal{C}$ computes

$$\sigma_2 = \langle s_2, h_2, f \rangle = \mathsf{aSign}(y_j, y_i, x_i, f, M)$$

but outputs $\sigma_2' = \langle s_2, f, h_2 \rangle$ instead.

---

[3] The algorithm KeyGen being public, $\mathcal{A}$ can compute $\mathsf{KeyGen}(k)$ for any k of her choosing.

[4] Note that with this information and using KeyGen queries, $\mathcal{A}$ can obtain concurrent signatures for any message and any user pair.

4. *Phase 2: $\mathcal{A}$ can perform any number of queries to $\mathcal{C}$, as described above.*
5. *Finally, $\mathcal{A}$ outputs a guess bit $b' \in \{0,1\}$.*

$\mathcal{A}$ *wins the game if $b = b'$ and if $\mathcal{A}$ made no KeyReveal query on f, h_1 or h_2.*

Definition 4 (Fairness). *The notion of fairness for concurrent signatures is defined in terms of the following security game:*

1. *The Setup algorithm is run and all public parameters are given to $\mathcal{A}$.*
2. *$\mathcal{A}$ can perform any number of queries to $\mathcal{C}$, as described above.*
3. *Finally, $\mathcal{A}$ chooses two public keys y_C, y_D and outputs $k \in \mathcal{K}$ and $S = (s, h_1, f, y_C, y_D, M)$ where $s \in \mathcal{S}$, $h_1, f \in \mathcal{F}$, $M \in \mathcal{M}$.*

$\mathcal{A}$ *wins the game if aVerify(S) accepts and either of the following holds:*

– *f was output from a KeyGen query, no KeyReveal query was made on f, and Verify accepts $\langle k, S \rangle$.*
– *$\mathcal{A}$ can output $S' = (s', h_1', f, y_D, y_C, M')$ where aVerify(S') accepts and Verify(k, S) accepts, but Verify(k, S') rejects.*

This definition of fairness formalizes the idea that B cannot be left in a position where a keystone binds his signature to him while A's initial signature is not also bound to A. It does not, however, guarantee that B will ever receive the necessary keystone.

3 Legally Fair Co-signatures

3.1 Legal Fairness Without Keystones

The main idea builds on the following observation: Every signature exchange protocol is plagued by the possibility that the last step of the protocol is not performed. Indeed, it is in the interest of a malicious party to get the other party's signature without revealing its own. As a result, the best one can hope for is that a trusted third party can eventually restore fairness.

To avoid this destiny, the proposed paradigm does *not* proceed by sending A's signature to B and vice versa. Instead, we construct a *joint signature*, or *co-signature*, of both A and B. By design, there are no signatures to steal — and stopping the protocol early does not give the stopper a decisive advantage. More precisely, the contract they have agreed upon is the best thing an attacker can gather, and if she ever wishes to enforce this contract by presenting it to a court of law, she would confirm her own commitment to it as well as the other party's. Therefore, if one can construct co-signatures without intermediary individual signatures being sent, legal fairness can be achieved without keystones.

Since keystones can be used by the party having them to abuse the other [7], the co-signature paradigm provides an interesting alternative to concurrent signatures.

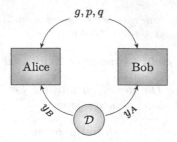

Fig. 1. Public directory $\mathcal{D}$ distributing the public keys.

3.2 Schnorr Co-signatures

To illustrate the new paradigm, we now discuss a legally fair contract-signing protocol built from the well-known Schnorr signature protocol, that produces signatures *compatible* with standard Schnorr signatures. This contract signing protocol is provably secure in the random oracle model under the hardness assumption of solving the discrete logarithm problem.

The construction can be adapted to other DLP schemes, such as most[5] of those enumerated in [18], including Girault-Poupard-Stern [12] and ElGamal [9].

- Setup: An independent (not necessarily trusted) authority generates a classical Schnorr parameter-set p, q, g which is given to A and B. Each user U generates a usual Schnorr public key $y_U = g^{x_U}$ and publishes y_U on a public directory $\mathcal{D}$ (see Fig. 1). To determine the co-signature public-key $y_{A,B}$ of the pair $\langle A, B \rangle$, a verifier consults $\mathcal{D}$ and simply computes $y_{A,B} = y_A y_B$. Naturally, $y_{A,B} = y_{B,A}$.
- Cosign: To co-sign a message m, A and B compute a common r and a common s, one after the other. Without loss of generality we assume that B initiates the co-signature.
  - During the first phase (Fig. 2), B chooses a private random number k_B and computes $r_B \leftarrow g^{k_B}$. He commits to that value by sending to A a message digest $\rho \leftarrow H(0\|r_B)$. A chooses a private random number k_A, computes $r_A \leftarrow g^{k_A}$ and sends r_A to B. B replies with r_B, which A checks against the earlier commitment ρ. Both parties compute $r \leftarrow r_A r_B$, and $e \leftarrow H(1\|m\|r)$, where m is the message to be co-signed.
  - During the second phase of the protocol, B sends $s_B \leftarrow k_B - ex_B \bmod q$ to A. A replies with $s_A \leftarrow k_A - ex_A \bmod q$. Both users compute $s \leftarrow s_A + s_B \bmod q$.
- Verify: As in the classical Schnorr signature, the co-signature $\{r, s\}$ is checked for a message m by computing $e \leftarrow H(m\|r)$, and checking whether $g^s y^e = r$ (Fig. 3). If the equality holds, then the co-signature binds both A and B to m; otherwise neither party is tied to m.

---

[5] In a number of cases, *e.g.* DSA, the formulae of s do not lend themselves to security proofs.

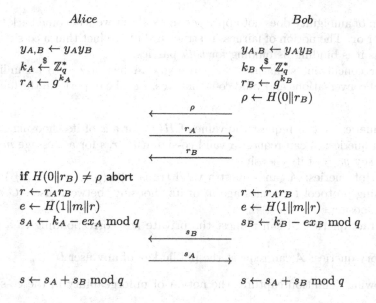

Fig. 2. Generating the Schnorr co-signature of message m.

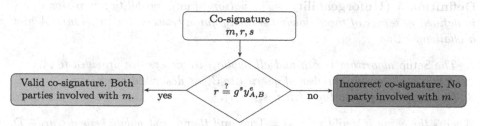

Fig. 3. Verification of a Schnorr co-signature m, r, s.

Remark 2. Note that during the co-signature protocol, A might decide not to respond to B: In that case, A would be the only one to have the complete co-signature. This is a breach of fairness insofar as A can benefit from the co-signature and not B, but the protocol is abuse-free: A cannot use the co-signature as a proof that B, and B alone, committed to m. Furthermore, it is not a breach of legal fairness: If A presents the co-signature in a court of law, she *ipso facto* reveals her commitment as well.

Remark 3. In a general fair-contract signing protocol, A and B can sign different messages m_A and m_B. Using the co-signature construction requires that A and B agree first on the content of a single message m.

3.3 Security Analysis

The security of the co-signature scheme essentially builds on the unforgeability of classical Schnorr signatures. Since there is only one co-signature output, the notion of ambiguity does not apply *per se* — albeit we will come back to that point later on. The notion of fairness is structural in the fact that a co-signature, as soon as it is binding, is binding for *both* parties.

As for concurrent signatures, an adversary $\mathcal{A}$ has access to an unlimited amount of conversations and valid co-signatures, *i.e.* $\mathcal{A}$ can perform the following queries:

- Hash queries: $\mathcal{A}$ can request the value of $H(x)$ for a x of its choosing.
- CoSign queries: $\mathcal{A}$ can request a valid co-signature r, s for a message m and a public key $y_{C,D}$ of its choosing.
- Transcript queries: $\mathcal{A}$ can request a valid transcript $(\rho, r_C, r_D, s_C, s_D)$ of the co-signing protocol for a message m of its choosing, between users C and D of its choosing.
- SKExtract queries: $\mathcal{A}$ can request the private key corresponding to a public key.
- Directory queries: $\mathcal{A}$ can request the public key of any user U.

The following definition captures the notion of unforgeability in the co-signing context:

Definition 5 (Unforgeability). *The notion of unforgeability for co-signatures is defined in terms of the following security game between the adversary $\mathcal{A}$ and a challenger $\mathcal{C}$:*

1. *The* Setup *algorithm is run and all public parameters are provided to $\mathcal{A}$.*
2. *$\mathcal{A}$ can perform any number of queries to $\mathcal{C}$, as described above.*
3. *Finally, $\mathcal{A}$ outputs a tuple $(m, r, s, y_{C,D})$.*

$\mathcal{A}$ wins the game if Verify$(m, r, s) =$ True *and there exist public keys $y_C, y_D \in \mathcal{D}$ such that $y_{C,D} = y_C y_D$ and either of the following holds:*

- *$\mathcal{A}$ did not query SKExtract on y_C nor on y_D, and did not query CoSign on $m, y_{C,D}$, and did not query Transcript on m, y_C, y_D nor m, y_D, y_C.*
- *$\mathcal{A}$ did not query Transcript on m, y_C, y_i for any $y_i \neq y_C$ and did not query SKExtract on y_C, and did not query CoSign on m, y_C, y_i for any $y_i \neq y_C$.*

We shall say that a co-signature scheme is unforgeable when the success probability of $\mathcal{A}$ in this game is negligible.

To prove that the Schnorr-based scheme described above is secure we use the following strategy: Assuming an efficient forger $\mathcal{A}$ for the co-signature scheme, we turn it into an efficient forger $\mathcal{B}$ for Schnorr signatures, then invoke the Forking Lemma to prove the existence of an efficient solver $\mathcal{C}$ for the discrete logarithm problem. All proofs hold in the Random Oracle model.

Since the co-signing protocol gives the upper hand to the last-but-one speaker there is an asymmetry: Alice has more information than Bob. Therefore we address two scenarios: When the attacker plays Alice's role, and when the attacker plays Bob's.

Theorem 1. *Let $\{y, g, p, q\}$ be a DLP instance. If $\mathcal{A}$ plays the role of Bob (resp. Alice) and is able to forge in polynomial time a co-signature with probability ϵ_F, then in the Random Oracle model $\mathcal{A}$ can break the DLP instance with high probability in polynomial time.*

Proof. The proof of this theorem is given in the appendix of the IACR ePrint of this paper. In the proof, this theorem is split in twain depending on whether $\mathcal{A}$ impersonates Bob or Alice.   □

4   Concurrent Co-signatures

4.1   Proofs of Involvment

We now address a subtle weakness in the protocol described in the previous section, which is not captured by the fairness property *per se* and that we refer to as the existence of "proofs of involvment". Such proofs are not valid co-signatures, and would not normally be accepted by verifiers, but they nevertheless are valid evidence establishing that one party committed to a message. In a legally fair context, it may happen that such evidence is enough for one party to win a trial against the other — who lacks both the co-signature, and a proof of involvment.

Example 2. In the co-signature protocol of Fig. 2, s_B is not a valid Schnorr signature for Bob. Indeed, we have $g^{s_B} y_B^e = r_B \neq r$. However, Alice can construct $s' = s_B + k_A$, so that m, r, s' forms a valid classical signature of Bob *alone* on m.

Example 2 illustrates the possibility that an adversary, while unable to forge a co-signature, may instead use the information to build a valid (mono-) signature. Note that Alice may opt for a weaker proof of involvment, for instance by demonstrating her possession of a valid signature using any zero-knowledge protocol.

A straightforward patch is to refrain from using the public keys y_A, y_B for both signature and co-signature — so that attempts at constructing proofs of involvment become vain. For instance, every user could have a key $y_U^{(1)}$ used for classical signature and for certifying a key $y_U^{(2)}$ used for co-signature[6]. If an adversary generates a classical signature from a co-signature transcript as in Example 2, she actually reveals her harmful intentions.

However, while this exposes the forgery — so that honest verifiers would reject such a signature — the perpetrator remains anonymous. There are scenarios in which this is not desirable, *e.g.* because it still proves that B agreed (with some unknown and dishonest partner) on m.

Note that the existence of proof of involvment is not necessary and depends on the precise choice of underlying signature scheme.

---

[6] The key $y_U^{(2)}$ may be derived from $y_U^{(1)}$ in some way, so that the storage needs of $\mathcal{D}$ are the same as for classical Schnorr.

4.2 Security Model

It is important to make extremely clear the security model that we are targeting. In this situation an adversary $\mathcal{A}$ (possibly Alice or Bob) tries to forged signatures from partial and/or complete traces of co-signature interactions, which can be of two kinds :

1. Co-signatures between two parties, at least one of which did not take part in the co-signature protocol;
2. (Traditional) signatures of either party.

$\mathcal{A}$ succeeds if and only if one of these forgeries is accepted, which can be captured as the probability of acceptance of $\mathcal{A}$'s outputs, and the victim (purported mono-signatory, or co-signatory) doesn't have a co-signature with $\mathcal{A}$[7].

Observe that due to the unforgeability of Schnorr signatures, the attacker must necessarily impersonate one of the co-signatories to achieve either of the two forgeries mentioned above (in fact, the strongest position is that of Alice, who has an edge over Bob in the protocol). This is the reason why the victim may have a co-signature of $\mathcal{A}$, so that this security model captures fairness.

In short, we propose to address such attacks in the following way:

1. By using a different key for co-signature and mono-signature;
2. By having Bob store specific co-signature-related information in non-volatile memory.

The reason for (1) is that it distinguishes between mono-signatures, and mono-signatures generated from partial co-signature traces. Thanks to this, it is easy for the verifier to detect a forgery, and perform additional steps.

The reason for (2) is twofold: On the one hand, it enables the verifier to obtain from Bob definitive proof that there was forgery; on the other hand, once the forgery has been identified, it makes it possible for the verifier to re-establish fairness binding the two real co-signatories together. Note that Bob is in charge of keeping this information secure, i.e. available and correct.

4.3 Concurrent Co-signatures

In the interest of fairness, the best we can ask is that if A tries to incriminate B on a message they both agreed upon, she cannot do so anonymously.

To enforce fairness on the co-signature protocol, we ask that the equivalent of a keystone is transmitted first; so that in case of dispute, the aggrieved party has a legal recourse. First we define the notion of an authorized signatory credential:

Definition 6 (Authorized signatory credential). *The data field*

$$\Gamma_{Alice,Bob} = \{Alice, Bob, k_A, \sigma_{x_A}(g^{k_A} \| Alice \| Bob)\}$$

---

[7] In particular, the question of whether Bob "intended" to sign is outside the scope of this security model.

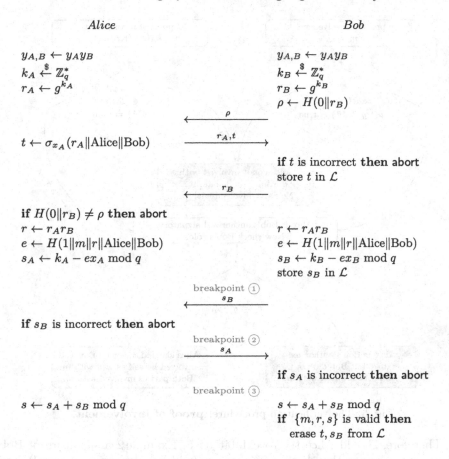

Fig. 4. The legally fair co-signature of message m.

is called an authorized signatory credential *given by Alice to Bob*, where σ_{x_A} is *some publicly known auxiliary signature algorithm using Alice's private key x_A as a signing key.*

Any party who gets $\Gamma_{\text{Alice,Bob}}$ can check its validity, and releasing $\Gamma_{\text{Alice,Bob}}$ is *by convention* functionally equivalent to Alice giving her private key x_A to Bob. A valid signature by Bob on a message m exhibited with a valid $\Gamma_{\text{Alice,Bob}}$ is *legally* defined as encompassing the meaning ($\Rightarrow$) of Alice's signature on m:

$$\{\Gamma_{\text{Alice,Bob}}, \text{signature by Bob on } m\} \Rightarrow \text{signature by Alice on } m$$

Second, the co-signature protocol of Fig. 2 is modified by requesting that Alice provide $t = \sigma_{x_A}(g^{k_A}\|\text{Alice}\|\text{Bob})$ to Bob. Bob stores this in a local non-volatile memory $\mathcal{L}$ along with s_B. For all practical purposes, $\mathcal{L}$ can be simply regarded as Bob's hard disk. Together, t and s_B act as a keystone enabling Bob (or a verifier, *e.g.* a court of law) to reconstruct $\Gamma_{\text{Alice,Bob}}$ if Alice exhibits a (fraudulent) signature binding Bob alone with his co-signing public key.

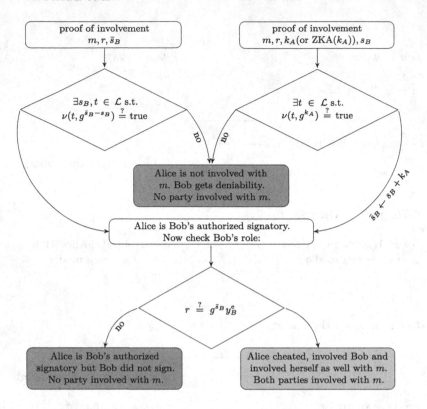

Fig. 5. The verification procedure: **proof of involvement**.

Therefore, should Alice try to exhibit as in Example 2 a signature of Bob alone on a message they both agreed upon (which is known as a fraud), the court would be able to identify Alice as the fraudster.

The modified signature protocol is described in Fig. 4. Alice has only one window of opportunity to try and construct a fraudulent signature of Bob: by stopping the protocol at breakpoint ② and using the information s_B[8].

Indeed, if the protocol is interrupted before breakpoint ①, then no information involving m was released by any of the parties: The protocol's trace can be simulated without Bob's help as follows

$$s_B, r \xleftarrow{\$} \mathbb{Z}_q$$
$$e \leftarrow H(1\|m\|r\|\text{Alice}\|\text{Bob})$$
$$r_B \leftarrow g^{s_B} y_B^e$$
$$r_A \leftarrow r r_B^{-1}$$
$$t \leftarrow \sigma_{x_A}(r_A\|\text{Alice}\|\text{Bob})$$
$$\rho \leftarrow H(0\|r_B)$$

---

[8] If Bob transmits a wrong or incorrect s_B, this will be immediately detected by Alice as $r_B \neq g^{s_B} y_B^e$. Naturally, in such a case, Bob never sent any information binding him to the contract anyway.

and Bob has only received from Alice the signature of a random integer.

If Alice and Bob successfully passed the normal completion breakpoint ③, *both* parties have the co-signature, and are provably committed to m.

5 Conclusion and Further Work

In this paper we described an alternative construction paradigm for legally fair contract signing that doesn't require keystones, but can be combined with them to provide additional power. The new paradigm produces co-signatures that bind a pair of users, and can be adapted to a number of DLP signature protocols. In the co-signature version of Schnorr's protocol, the resulting co-signatures have the same format as classical (single-user) signature. This paradigm guarantees fairness and abuse-freeness, and can be equipped with keystones to add functionalities such as whistleblower traceability.

Acknowledgments. This work was supported in part by the French ANR Project ANR-12-INSE-0014 SIMPATIC.

Appendix

The appendix is available in the IACR ePrint version of this paper.

References

1. Abe, M., Ohkubo, M., Suzuki, K.: 1-out-of-n signatures from a variety of keys. In: Zheng, Y. (ed.) ASIACRYPT 2002. LNCS, vol. 2501, pp. 415–432. Springer, Heidelberg (2002)
2. Asokan, N., Schunter, M., Waidner, M.: Optimistic protocols for fair exchange. In: ACM CCS 1997: 4th Conference on Computer and Communications Security, pp. 7–17. ACM Press, Zurich 1–4 April 1997
3. Baum-Waidner, B., Waidner, M.: Round-optimal and abuse-free optimistic multi-party contract signing. In: Welzl, E., Montanari, U., Rolim, J.D.P. (eds.) ICALP 2000. LNCS, vol. 1853, pp. 524–535. Springer, Heidelberg (2000)
4. Ben-Or, M., Goldwasser, S., Wigderson, A.: Completeness theorems for non-cryptographic fault-tolerant distributed computation (extended abstract). In: 20th Annual ACM Symposium on Theory of Computing, pp. 1–10. ACM Press, Chicago 2–4 May 1988
5. Cachin, C., Camenisch, J.L.: Optimistic fair secure computation. In: Bellare, M. (ed.) CRYPTO 2000. LNCS, vol. 1880, pp. 93–111. Springer, Heidelberg (2000)
6. Chaum, D., Crépeau, C., Damgård, I.: Multiparty unconditionally secure protocols (extended abstract). In: 20th Annual ACM Symposium on Theory of Computing, pp. 11–19. ACM Press, Chicago 2–4 May 1988
7. Chen, L., Kudla, C., Paterson, K.G.: Concurrent signatures. In: Cachin, C., Camenisch, J.L. (eds.) EUROCRYPT 2004. LNCS, vol. 3027, pp. 287–305. Springer, Heidelberg (2004)

8. Cleve, R.: Limits on the security of coin flips when half the processors are faulty (extended abstract). In: Hartmanis, J. (ed.) Proceedings of the 18th Annual ACM Symposium on Theory of Computing, May 28–30, Berkeley, California, USA, pp. 364–369. ACM (1986)

9. El Gamal, T.: A public key cryptosystem and a signature scheme based on discrete logarithms. In: Blakely, G.R., Chaum, D. (eds.) CRYPTO 1984. LNCS, vol. 196, pp. 10–18. Springer, Heidelberg (1985)

10. Garay, J.A., Jakobsson, M., MacKenzie, P.D.: Abuse-free optimistic contract signing. In: Wiener, M. (ed.) CRYPTO 1999. LNCS, vol. 1666, pp. 449–466. Springer, Heidelberg (1999)

11. Garay, J.A., MacKenzie, P.D., Prabhakaran, M., Yang, K.: Resource fairness and composability of cryptographic protocols. In: Halevi, S., Rabin, T. (eds.) TCC 2006. LNCS, vol. 3876, pp. 404–428. Springer, Heidelberg (2006)

12. Girault, M., Poupard, G., Stern, J.: On the fly authentication and signature schemes based on groups of unknown order. J. Cryptology 19(4), 463–487 (2006)

13. Goldreich, O.: A simple protocol for signing contracts. In: Chaum, D. (ed.) CRYPTO 1983, pp. 133–136. Plenum Press, New York (1983)

14. Goldreich, O.: Foundations of Cryptography: Basic Applications, vol. 2. Cambridge University Press, Cambridge (2004)

15. Goldreich, O., Micali, S., Wigderson, A.: How to play any mental game or a completeness theorem for protocols with honest majority. In: Aho, A. (ed.) 19th Annual ACM Symposium on Theory of Computing, pp. 218–229. ACM Press, New York 25–27 May 1987

16. Goldwasser, S., Levin, L.A.: Fair computation of general functions in presence of immoral majority. In: Menezes, A., Vanstone, S.A. (eds.) CRYPTO 1990. LNCS, vol. 537, pp. 77–93. Springer, Heidelberg (1991)

17. Gordon, S.D., Hazay, C., Katz, J., Lindell, Y.: Complete fairness in secure two-party computation. In: Ladner, R.E., Dwork, C. (eds.) 40th Annual ACM Symposium on Theory of Computing, pp. 413–422. ACM Press, Victoria 17–20 May 2008

18. Horster, P., Petersen, H., Michels, M.: Meta-El-Gamal signature schemes. In: ACM CCS 94: 2nd Conference on Computer and Communications Security, pp. 96–107. ACM Press, Fairfax (1994)

19. Jakobsson, M., Sako, K., Impagliazzo, R.: Designated verifier proofs and their applications. In: Maurer, U.M. (ed.) EUROCRYPT 1996. LNCS, vol. 1070, pp. 143–154. Springer, Heidelberg (1996)

20. Lindell, A.Y.: Legally-enforceable fairness in secure two-party computation. In: Malkin, T. (ed.) CT-RSA 2008. LNCS, vol. 4964, pp. 121–137. Springer, Heidelberg (2008)

21. Micali, S.: Simple and fast optimistic protocols for fair electronic exchange. In: Borowsky, E., Rajsbaum, S. (eds.) 22nd ACM Symposium Annual on Principles of Distributed Computing, pp. 12–19. Association for Computing Machinery, Boston 13–16 July 2003

22. Pinkas, B.: Fair secure two-party computation. In: Biham, E. (ed.) EUROCRYPT 2003. LNCS, vol. 2656, pp. 87–105. Springer, Heidelberg (2003)

23. Rivest, R.L., Shamir, A., Tauman, Y.: How to leak a secret. In: Boyd, C. (ed.) ASIACRYPT 2001. LNCS, vol. 2248, pp. 552–565. Springer, Heidelberg (2001)

24. Yao, A.C.C.: How to generate and exchange secrets (extended abstract). In: 27th Annual Symposium on Foundations of Computer Science, pp. 162–167. IEEE Computer Society Press, Toronto 27–29 October 1986

DoS Attacks and Network Anomaly Detection

Why Software DoS Is Hard to Fix: Denying Access in Embedded Android Platforms

Ryan Johnson[1,2]([⊠]), Mohamed Elsabagh[1], and Angelos Stavrou[1,2]

[1] George Mason University, Fairfax, VA 22030, USA
melsabag@gmu.edu
[2] Kryptowire, Fairfax, VA 22030, USA
{rjohnson,astavrou}@kryptowire.com

Abstract. A new class of software Denial of Service (DoS) attacks against Android platforms was recently discovered, where the attacks can force the victim device unresponsive, target and terminate other applications on the device, and continuously soft reboot the device [26]. After Google was informed of these DoS attacks, their attempt to resolve the problem did not adequately address the fundamental underlying attack principles. In this paper, we show that engineering software DoS defenses is challenging, especially for embedded and resource-constrained devices. To support our findings, we detail a revised DoS attack strategy for the latest version of Android. For our experimental evaluation, we demonstrate that the new class of DoS attacks are even more damaging to embedded Android devices. As part of our proof-of-concept attacks, we were able to render the Sony Bravia XBR-43X830C Android TV and the Amazon Fire TV Stick 1st generation devices permanently unusable. In addition, other devices, including the Moto 360 1st generation smartwatch, required flashing firmware images, whereas the Nvidia Shield Android TV and the Amazon Fire 7" Tablet required a factory reset to recover. Our attack is applicable to most Android devices and requires manual intervention to attempt to recover the device. The proposed attack strategy is more debilitating to devices that do not provide means for the end-user to easily access safe mode, recovery mode, or the ability flash firmware images. To mitigate the attack, we created an open-source defense application that has a 100 % prevention rate after a single soft reboot of the device while incurring less than 1.6 % performance overhead.

Keywords: Android · Dos attack · Dos defense · Mobile security

1 Introduction

The Android Operating System (OS) is becoming popular and pervasive to embedded platforms such as mini PCs, streaming media players, smart TVs, smartwatches, and infotainment systems. Despite the fact that most of the underlying Android framework remains the same among these devices, a common vulnerability may affect each platform differently. This is due to the devices having

© Springer International Publishing Switzerland 2016
M. Manulis et al. (Eds.): ACNS 2016, LNCS 9696, pp. 193–211, 2016.
DOI: 10.1007/978-3-319-39555-5_11

different form factors, hardware buttons, safe mode availability, and access to the recovery and fastboot modes. For instance, smartphones, the most mature of the Android platforms, are the best-equipped to deal with malicious applications since they generally provide both easy access to safe mode and recovery mode from a powered-off state by holding a combination of hardware buttons during boot. Some of the less mature or resource-constrained devices may lack or not provide easy access to these capabilities, which increases their exposure to Denial of Service (DoS) attacks.

Designing adequate defenses to software DoS attacks is difficult: in most cases, the resource under attack is shared and thus a trade-off between preventing the attack and allowing legitimate use of the resource is required in practice. If the attack countermeasure is not restrictive enough, it will enable a malicious actor to reduce the availability of the resource. On the other hand, if the attack countermeasure is too restrictive, it will limit legitimate usage of the resource. In the context of the DoS attack presented in this paper, the resource being attacked is availability of the device itself and, by extension, all of its constituent resources. Contrary to the software DoS, preventing DoS and Distributed DoS (DDoS) for network-based attacks is a well-researched area [27,28,31–33] and is known to be a difficult problem. There has been less research in application-level DoS attacks, which exploit inherent software design weaknesses, especially against Android [16,21,25,26].

In Android, intents are used for inter-process and intra-process communication. An intent is like a message that is sent by an app to itself or another app. An intent can contain data to be utilized by the receiving app to perform an action. Broadcast intents are sent to all apps that listen for a specific event or handle an action. Intents are a fundamental communication mechanism that are used by Android apps and can be abused since the Android OS does not put any limit on the amount or rate that intents can be directly sent from an app. Rapidly sending intents from a third-party app can result in various DoS attacks including making the target device unresponsive to the user, targeting and terminating other running apps, and forcing a soft reboot of the device. A soft reboot occurs whens the Android framework, residing in user space, crashes, but the Linux kernel continues execution. A soft reboot may appear to the user as a reboot since the Android boot animation is displayed during a soft reboot.

We informed Google of a novel class of intent-based DoS attacks on Android in September 2015, and they subsequently introduced fixes in Android to address them. We created variations of the intent-based DoS attacks that work around Google's fixes, making the attacks effective on the latest Android version. In this paper, we focus on the DoS attack to quickly and repeatedly soft reboot an Android device, which we refer to as the soft reboot cycle DoS attack, since it is the most severe of the DoS attacks. We provide results for the updated soft reboot cycle DoS attack on popular embedded Android devices. The underlying cause of the soft reboot is explained in conjunction with referencing Android Open Source Project (AOSP) Android 6 source code files. We also proposed changes to the Android framework to thwart the attacks, and we created an open-source

Android application that precludes the soft reboot cycle DoS attack from being
successful. This countermeasure application can be utilized by device manufacturers without making any modification to the Android framework. Device
manufacturers can utilize it as a system application in their next build or sign
the application with the device platform key to make it readily deliverable to
current devices.

2   Threat Model

We assume that the user side-loads the malicious application or downloads and
installs it from an official or third-party application marketplace. The code to
perform the soft reboot cycle DoS attack can be introduced by repackaging a popular application with malicious code. Repackaging Android applications is a popular method for distributing malware [29, 30, 34–36]. Social engineering is another
possible attack vector to deliver the malicious application [10, 13, 18, 23]. The
available approaches to remove an application depend on the specific Android
device. Safe mode prevents the execution of installed third-party applications.
If safe mode is available on the device, the user can boot into safe mode and
uninstall third-party applications. Android Debug Bridge (ADB) is a command-
line tool that allows the user to issue commands from a separate computing
device to an Android device or emulator. ADB comes disabled by default on
most devices. The user must specifically enable ADB in the Settings app, *and*
authorize the debug device that the Android device will be connected to [7]. If
ADB over a USB cable is enabled, then the user can obtain a list of all installed
third-party applications on the device using the `adb shell pm list packages`
`-3` command and uninstall them using ADB.

Certain devices will allow the user to boot into recovery mode and fastboot
mode from a powered-off or booting state using hardware buttons or screen
touches on smartwatches. The standard Android recovery mode allows a user to
perform a factory reset which wipes the data and cache partitions on the device
resulting in the removal of the user's installed applications. Fastboot mode allows
the user to flash firmware images to the device if the bootloader can be unlocked.
The soft reboot cycle DoS attack is persistent: once the attack is triggered, the
device becomes unresponsive and enters into soft reboot cycles. To summarize,
if all of the following four conditions are met, the user cannot remove an app
executing the soft reboot cycle DoS attack from the device:

1. No access to safe mode on the device.
2. ADB over USB is disabled prior to the attack.
3. The Android OS sends the `BOOT_COMPLETED` broadcast intent to third-party
   apps after the booting process completes[1].
4. There is no hardware-based method to enter a mode from a powered-off or
   booting state that will allow the user to perform a factory reset or flash
   firmware images.

---

[1] The only Android device that we have encountered that does not do this is the
Xiaomi Mi TV Box Mini [11].

If only the first 3 conditions are fulfilled, the user is forced to perform a factory reset or flash firmware images to recover the device from the attack.

3   Attack Method

Conceptual Attack Summary. A third-party Android app can soft reboot the Android OS by sending a large amount of intents rapidly. An Android app is composed of application components. An activity application component provides a Graphical User Interface (GUI) that allows the user to interact with the application. A service application component performs tasks in the background and does not present a GUI to the user. A broadcast receiver application component listens for specific events and state changes that occur within an app or the OS itself. The attack app contains the following application components: activity, service, and broadcast receiver.

The attack begins shortly after the Android OS boot process completes. The OS sends a broadcast intent, to indicate the fact that the boot process has completed, to broadcast receivers who have permission to receive it. The broadcast receiver in the attack app receives this broadcast intent and starts the service application component so it can execute in the background. The service application component then starts rapidly sending intents to start the activity application component. The intents being sent by the service contain specific flags which create an activity in its own task stack, so new activities are created even though the same activity already exists in a different task stack. Each started activity will send an intent to the service which will create more activities and the cycle repeats leading to a multiplicity the same activity being created.

The `system_server` process, an integral part of the Android framework, contains service threads that apps interact with using a client-server architecture. `system_server` creates the activity application components requested the by the service, and it also creates a socket pair to deliver the user's touch events to the app. Each activity that is created requires a single file descriptor from the `system_server` process for its end of the socket pair, although it can require two file descriptors if intents are sent rapidly since it will not be able to transfer the other socket to the app. Each process has a soft limit of file descriptors to prevent a single process from exhausting the resource. Once a process hits its soft limit for file descriptors, it cannot open or create files, pipes, or sockets.

A third-party app can create activities rapidly to force `system_server` to reach its soft limit of 1,024 file descriptors. When this occurs, `system_server` is constrained and can crash in a number of ways. The most common crash is due to `system_server` trying to create a system message dialog box indicating that the attacking app has crashed. A socket for this dialog box is required to obtain the user's input, but `system_server` will not be able to create it. This leads to an uncaught exception and results in a crash of `system_server`. This event causes the Android OS to soft reboot. The attacking app will again receive the broadcast intent that is sent out to apps indicating that the Android OS has completed the boot process. The attacking app again performs the attack to make the device soft reboot and this cycle will persistently occur until the user manually takes some action to prevent it.

Prior to Android 6, a third-party app was able to make the `system_server` process attack itself and eventually crash by creating a repeating alarm to have `system_server` send an intent every millisecond. Google, in response to our vulnerability disclosure, raised the minimum recurrence interval in between alarms to 60 s. This partially addressed the vulnerability, although they did not add a restriction on the amount or rate for all available means that an app can send intents. An app can still send an unrestricted amount of intents directly from an application component using the inherited methods of the `android.content.ContextWrapper` class. Without rate-limiting the sending of intents for all approaches available to an app or creating a reasonable limit on the amount of activity instances an app can concurrently have, the attack will be successful.

Soft Rebooting the Device. The interaction between the Reboot application, our malicious app, and `system_server` is shown in Fig. 1. Certain events have been omitted from Fig. 1 for clarity, such as the fact that the `com.android.server.am.ActivityManagerService` class creates all application components used by the attack app. In addition, only certain services within `system_server` are displayed. The Reboot application has a broadcast receiver application component (i.e., RebootReceiver in Fig. 1) to receive the `BOOT_COMPLETED` broadcast intent sent from `system_server`, so that the application can begin execution shortly after the Android OS completes the boot process (displayed as arrow 1 in Fig. 1). The app also listens for the

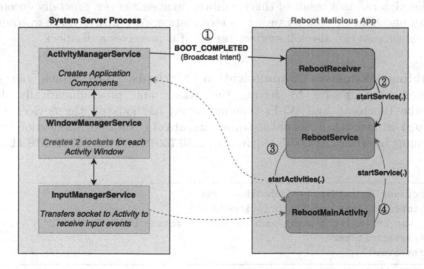

Fig. 1. Interaction between the Reboot malicious app and the `system_server` process. Dashed lines indicate indirect inter-process interactions.

android.hardware.usb.action.USB_STATE broadcast intent which is part of AOSP and does *not* require a permission. On all the devices we tested, this broadcast intent can be received prior to the BOOT_COMPLETED broadcast intent. Listing 1.1 shows how RebootReceiver should be declared in the app's AndroidManifest.xml file. It is important to ensure that the android:priority attribute be set to the maximum value (i.e., 999) in the intent-filter for the BOOT_COMPLETED action. Upon receiving this intent, RebootReceiver sends an intent to start the RebootService (displayed as arrow 2 in Fig. 1). RebootService will, first, create a thread to perform the attack, then return the START_STICKY constant in its onStartCommand method.

The thread that launches the attack will send a large number of intents to rapidly create numerous instances of activity application components (i.e., RebootMainActivity in Fig. 1) that are internal to the attacking app. The attack requires that the intents use the following two flags: FLAG_ACTIVITY_MULTIPLE_TASK and FLAG_ACTIVITY_NEW_TASK. These intent flags, when used together, create a new task stack containing a single activity even when a matching activity already exists within the attack application. The default behavior, without using these intent flags, is to push a new activity on top of the current task stack. Newly created instances of RebootMainActivity will attempt to start the RebootService in its onCreate method. The RebootService has already been created and is running, so it will just result in the execution of its onStartCommand method which will result in the creation of more instances of RebootMainActivity. This essentially creates an cycle of the two application components calling each other (displayed as arrows 3 and 4 in Fig. 1). The attack creates numerous instances of task stacks containing only a single activity. Each task stack will require system_server to allocate 1 to 2 file descriptors depending on the rate of the attack. The attack causes system_server to exhaust its file descriptors. As a result of this condition, system_server generally encounters an uncaught exception causing its termination. Alternatively, the watchdog daemon process can also kill system_server if it perceives a deadlock.

Disabling Wireless Communication Methods. The attack can be made more aggressive by having the attack app programmatically disable the Bluetooth and Wi-Fi communication methods on the device. The android.bluetooth.BluetoothAdapter.disable() Android Application Programming Interface (API) call requires the BLUETOOTH and the BLUETOOTH_ADMIN

```
1 <receiver android:name="RebootReceiver">
2   <intent-filter android:priority="999">
3     <action android:name="android.intent.action.BOOT_COMPLETED" />
4   </intent-filter>
5 </receiver>
```

Listing 1.1. Declaration of the RebootReceiver in the app's manifest.

permissions. This API call disables Bluetooth on the device so that any paired devices can no longer interact with the device. This will also preclude ADB over Bluetooth to the device for Android Wear devices. The android.net.wifi.WifiManager.setWifiEnabled(boolean) API call requires the ACCESS_WIFI_STATE and CHANGE_WIFI_STATE permissions. This API call can disable Wi-Fi so that other devices on the wireless network can be prevented from interacting with the target device over Wi-Fi, and it also prevents ADB over Wi-Fi which is present on certain Android devices.

4   Underlying Cause for the Soft Reboot

The intents sent by the attacking app have the FLAG_ACTIVITY_MULTIPLE_TASK and FLAG_ACTIVITY_NEW_TASK flags set, so a new starting window with a new task stack will be required for each activity. In this section, the classes that end with "Service" are contained within the system_server process. The com.android.server.wm.WindowManagerService class [4] creates a window for the activity and each window requires a pair of android.view.InputChannel objects to be created so that the input events from the input device files can be delivered to the activity window. Third-party applications cannot read directly from the input device files which are contained in the /dev/input directory, but system_server has permission to read from them since it belongs to the input group. Therefore, WindowManagerService creates a pair of sockets using the socketpair() system call, registers the input channel with the window via the com.android.server.input.InputManagerService class, and transfers the output channel to the application. This allows the application to consume and process input events from the user via system_server.

A socket pair requires a file descriptor for each end of the socket pair. Each created activity will initially make system_server use two file descriptors. It will then transfer one socket to the attacking app, although during the attack system_server is processing a deluge of intents and does not get a chance to transfer the socket. This results in system_server using two file descriptors per activity created which makes system_server get closer to approaching the soft limit of 1,024 per-process file descriptors set by the kernel. Once the soft limit is reached, system_server cannot open or create any new files, pipes, or sockets, and WindowManagerService will fail to create the starting window for each activity.

The attacking app will encounter an uncaught exception once its activities cannot be created. The attacking app uses an android.view.InputChannel object received from the WindowManagerService as a parameter to the android.view.InputEventReceiver constructor. The InputEventReceiver object is used to queue the received user events so that they can be stored while waiting to be consumed by the application. The InputChannel object that the application received will be null. So an exception will be thrown by the InputEventReceiver.nativeInit() native method in the attacking application which goes uncaught and causes it to terminate.

```
 1 Intent i = new Intent(this, RebootMainActivity.class);
 2 i.setFlags(Intent.FLAG_ACTIVITY_MULTIPLE_TASK | Intent.
       ↪ FLAG_ACTIVITY_NEW_TASK);
 3
 4 TaskStackBuilder tsb = TaskStackBuilder.create(this);
 5 for (int a = 0; a < 1024; a++)
 6   tsb.addNextIntent(i);
 7
 8 if (Build.VERSION.SDK_INT >= 23) {
 9   while (true)
10     tsb.startActivities();
11 } else {
12   PendingIntent pi = PendingIntent.getActivity(getApplicationContext()
       ↪ , 0, i, PendingIntent.FLAG_CANCEL_CURRENT);
13   AlarmManager am = (AlarmManager) this.getSystemService(Context.
       ↪ ALARM_SERVICE);
14   am.setRepeating(AlarmManager.ELAPSED_REALTIME_WAKEUP, 1, 1, pi);
15   tsb.startActivities();
16 }
```

Listing 1.2. Rapidly sending Intents using pending intents via AlarmManager and TaskStackBuilder, causing a soft reboot.

When the attacking app crashes, `ActivityManagerService` tries to display an `android.app.Dialog` object indicating that the attacking app has crashed. A socket will be required to deliver the user input to the window of the `Dialog` system message. `system_server` will not be able to create the socket, and an uncaught exception occurs. The `zygote` daemon process contains pre-loaded classes and resources and forks itself to create other applications quickly. `zygote` [6] starts `system_server` with the `--runtime-args` flag which provides the threads of `system_server` with an `UncaughtExceptionHandler` interface object of the type `com.android.internal.os.RuntimeInit.UncaughtHandler` [3]. It receives uncaught exceptions occurring within the threads of `system_server`. It only has one method and all of its code is within `try-catch-finally` blocks. The `finally` block calls the `android.os.Process.killProcess(int)` API call with an integer parameter that is the result of the `Process.myPid()` API call. Since the thread that has the uncaught exception occurs within `system_server`, this results in `system_server` both sending and receiving the `SIGKILL` signal, which results in its termination.

`zygote` is the parent process of `system_server`, so it will receive a `SIGCHLD` signal when `system_server` terminates. For each `SIGCHLD` signal that `zygote` receives, it will specifically check if the terminated child process is `system_server`. If `system_server` terminates, then `zygote` will send the `SIGKILL` signal to itself [5] which results in a soft reboot. The `init` process will then restart `zygote` since it is declared as a service in the `init.rc` file [2]. `zygote` will then restart `system_server`.

Listing 1.2 provides the source code to cause a soft reboot by rapidly sending intents. The attack uses `AlarmManager` to send an intent every millisecond in builds prior to Android 6. The `android.app.TaskStackBuilder` class is used to send 1,024 intents repeatedly for Android 6. The use of `TaskStackBuilder` requires Android 4.1 or above. The `Service.startActivities(Intent[])` API call can be used in place of `TaskStackBuilder` which requires Android 3.0 or above.

5 Attack Evaluation

We tested the soft reboot cycle DoS attack on various Android devices. Some of the newer Android platforms tend not have safe mode and some do not have easy access to recovery mode, so we focused on these devices. All of these devices were running a non-rooted stock version of the Android OS that came pre-installed on the device. All of these devices had ADB over USB disabled by default. Table 1 aggregates the results of the experimental data.

5.1 Sony Bravia XBR-43X830C Android TV

The Sony Bravia XBR-43X830C Android TV is vulnerable to the soft reboot cycle DoS attack, and there is no known way to recover. During our testing, the device was running Android 5.1.1 with a build fingerprint of `Sony/SVP4KDTV15_UC/SVP-DTV15:5.1.1/LMY48E.S63/2.473:user/release-keys`. The only way to perform a factory reset of the device is through the Settings app [14]. During the attack, the GUI becomes unresponsive to the infrared remote which prevents the user from reaching the Settings app to perform a factory reset. The device does have ADB over Wi-Fi, but this can be subverted since the attacking application disables Wi-Fi. This device does not have the ADB over USB

Table 1. Test devices and results summary.

Device	Build No	Android Version	Vulnerable	Recoverable
Sony Bravia XBR-43X830C TV	LMY48E.S63	5.1.1	Yes	No
Moto 360 1st Gen. Smartwatch	LDZ22O	5.1.1	Yes	Yes[a]
Amazon Fire TV Stick 1st Gen	JDQ39	4.2.2	Yes	No[b]
Xiaomi Mi Mini TV Box	KOT49H	4.4.2	No	Yes
Nvidia Shield Android TV	LMY47D	5.1	Yes	Yes[c]
Amazon Fire 7″ Tablet	LMY47O	5.1.1	Yes	Yes[c]
Devices prior to Android 4.1	-	< 4.1	Yes	Yes[c]

[a] Recovering requires crafting a special USB cable and flashing firmware images.
[b] Recovering requires ADB over USB, which is disabled by default, to be enabled prior to the attack.
[c] Recovering requires a *full* factory reset in recovery mode or flashing firmware images.

capability. The device also does not have safe mode, recovery mode, or fastboot mode. Therefore, the user is unable to uninstall the application, perform a factory reset, or flash firmware images. Booting to fastboot mode via ADB over Wi-Fi will show a black screen, but it will also soft brick the device as it will not boot properly after that. The device comes pre-installed with Google Play so the user can download apps, and they can also be installed via ADB over Wi-Fi.

5.2   Moto 360 1st Generation Smartwatch

The Moto 360 1st generation smartwatch is vulnerable to the soft reboot cycle DoS attack, although there is a way to recover via a modified USB cable that can be used to unlock the bootloader and flash firmware images to the device [12]. During our testing, the device was running Android 5.1.1 with a build fingerprint of `motorola/metallica/minnow:5.1.1/LDZ220/2006643:user/release-keys`. The device allows the user to directly install or uninstall apps using ADB over Bluetooth. When a user installs or uninstalls an app on an Android smartphone or tablet, which is paired with an Android Wear device, the accompanying Android Wear app, if present, will also be installed or uninstalled from the Android Wear device. The Moto 360 does not have a direct way to uninstall a particular application through its GUI. The user has about 8 s to perform some action on the device before the GUI becomes unresponsive. The user can initiate a factory reset through the GUI, but it will not have enough time to complete and be successful before the device soft reboots. The Moto 360 lacks a standard USB interface, so only ADB over Bluetooth is available. The attack app will disable Bluetooth to prevent communication with paired devices.

5.3   Amazon Fire TV Stick 1st Generation

The Amazon Fire TV Stick 1st generation is vulnerable to the soft reboot cycle DoS attack and can leave the device in an unusable state if ADB over USB is not enabled prior to the attack. The device runs Amazon Fire OS 3.0, which is a modified version of Android 4.2.2. The device we tested had a build fingerprint: `BRCM/montoya:4.2.2/JDQ39/54.1.2.2_user_122066120:user/release-keys`. If ADB over USB is enabled prior the attack, the user can list the installed third-party applications and uninstall them as the device is booting. The malicious application programmatically disables Bluetooth and Wi-Fi. This renders any paired devices ineffective and precludes ADB over Wi-Fi. There are no hardware buttons to force the device to boot into recovery mode or bootloader mode from a powered-off or booting state. This will effectively preclude the user from removing the application if ADB over USB is not enabled prior to the attack.

5.4   Xiaomi Mi TV Box Mini

The Xiaomi Mi TV Box Mini is not vulnerable to the soft reboot cycle DoS attack. The device we tested was running Android 4.4.2 and had a build

fingerprint of `Xiaomi/forrestgump/forrestgump:4.4.2/KOT49H/566:user/`
`release-keys`. Applications can be installed through the browser or a network-
connected device. Communication with the device is performed via a Bluetooth remote, and it contains no USB interfaces. The device does not send the
`BOOT_COMPLETED` broadcast intent to third-party applications, so the application
is unable to soft reboot the device after the devices completes the boot process.

5.5   Amazon Fire 7″ Tablet

The Amazon Fire 7″ Tablet is vulnerable to the soft reboot cycle DoS attack
if ADB over USB is not enabled prior to the attack. If ADB over USB is not
enabled prior to the attack, then the user must perform a factory reset of the
device or flash firmware images to the device. The device we tested was running Amazon Fire OS 5.0, which is a modified version of Android 5.1.1 and had
a build fingerprint of `Amazon/full_ford/ford:5.1.1/LMY47O/37.5.4.1_user_`
`541112720:user/release-keys`. The attacking app receives the `android.`
`hardware.usb.action.USB_STATE` broadcast intent because it is sent prior to
the `BOOT_COMPLETED` broadcast intent and does not require any permissions to
be able to receive it. This broadcast intent is received by the attacking app prior
to the Amazon launcher being displayed, so the user is precluded from unin-
stalling the app via the GUI. The device provides easy access to recovery mode
from a powered-off state by holding the volume down and power buttons during
boot.

5.6   Nvidia Shield Android TV

The Nvidia Shield Android TV device is vulnerable to the soft reboot cycle
DoS attack if ADB over USB is not enabled prior to the attack. The
device we tested was running Android 5.1.1 and had a build fingerprint of
`NVIDIA/foster_e/foster:5.1/LMY47D/35739_609.6420:user/release-keys`.
The device does not have safe mode and ADB over Wi-Fi can be programmatically disabled. The only way to recover is by performing a factory reset or
flashing firmware images to the device. There is a method to perform a factory
reset that is not published on Nvidia's website [1]. Alternatively, the user can
access the fastboot menu and flash firmware images.

5.7   General Android Mini PC Devices

Android mini PC devices are somewhat vulnerable to the soft reboot cycle DoS
attack since they generally lack safe mode. Some devices allow the user to push
a button during boot to enter recovery mode. In addition, some devices can
utilize the SD card to flash firmware images to the device. Whether the attack is
effective or not depends on the specific device and the mechanisms for recovery
it provides.

5.8 Android Devices Prior to Android 4.1

Safe mode was introduced in Android 4.1. Prior to Android 4.1, the user was forced to perform a factory reset via recovery mode or flash firmware images to remove an application that persistently soft rebooted the device. According to the Android Dashboard, devices running a version of Android prior to Android 4.1 made up 5.0 % of all Android devices as of March 7, 2016 [8].

6 Standalone Defense App

We developed an anti-reboot app (source available at [9]) that passively monitors intents sent by third-party apps on the system, and disables or uninstalls apps that attempt to flood the system with intents. The anti-reboot app observes intents by reading the system log buffer using `logcat` on the device, and parsing the log messages searching for intents. The app filters log messages using relevant log tags to reduce the amount of log messages it processes. For every observed intent, the sender's package name is logged and its total outbound intents count n is incremented. The anti-reboot app only considers intents that create new tasks, i.e., the `FLAG_ACTIVITY_NEW_TASK` and `FLAG_ACTIVITY_MULTIPLE_TASK` intent flags are set. It also ignores intents sent by system apps by filtering on the process User ID (UID) since system apps are assigned UIDs that are less than 10,000. Anti-reboot uses a one-level decay, where the intent count n is decreased by a constant c every second. This is intended to simulate the time a user would interact with a new activity before dismissing it. In other words, the value of c controls the tolerable persistence level of an offending app. For a period of t seconds, this results in an effective intent count $n' = n - ct$, and an effective sending rate $\rho = \frac{n'}{t} = \frac{n}{t} - c$. Finally, a monitored app is disabled or uninstalled if its corresponding n' exceeds a preset threshold (θ), which indicates that the monitored app has more than θ *active* task stacks.

6.1 Parameters Selection

There are two parameters that control the detection performance of the anti-reboot app: the intent decay c, and the cutoff threshold θ at which an app is disabled or uninstalled. The value of c controls the tolerance level of the defense to apps that persistently send multiple intents over time. While benign apps may create new tasks, such behavior typically lasts for only a very short period of time (i.e., short bursts) compared to attacking apps which need to be highly persistent in order to adversely affect the system. Therefore, the higher the value of c, the higher the tolerance and the more likely an attack may go undetected. A reasonable value of c would mimic the time it takes a user to click the recent tasks button and dismiss an activity off the screen, which takes about 2 s. Therefore, we set c to one intent every 2 s, i.e., $c = 0.5$.

Avoiding False Positives. The cutoff threshold θ controls when an attack is detected, based on the number of active task stacks s the attack app has created. Note that $s \leq n'$, since each task stack would hold at least one activity. Since an attack is detected if $n' \geq \theta$, setting θ to a very small value may result in faster detection at the expense of false positives (i.e., false alarms). Conversely, a very large value of θ results in lower detection rate. We can pick a reasonable value of θ by estimating an upper bound on n' for *benign* apps. Recent studies (e.g., [17,20]) have shown that the total number of activities declared in an app's manifest is less than 110 for the top 30 apps in the market, with a total of 60 foreground activities created on the device *per day* from the top 800 apps on the market. Therefore, we set $\theta = 200$, which allows 200 task stacks to be created at any point in time. This is more than three times the number (60) of task stacks that would be created, in the worst case, by benign apps if we assume each of the benign 60 activities was created in a new task stack and was never terminated.

In versions of Android earlier than 6.0, where `AlarmManager` does not have a minimum recurrence interval of 60 s, attacking apps can flood the system with activities using pending intents with short repeat intervals. To mitigate this, and in addition to observing intents, the anti-reboot app monitors the count and repeat interval of active pending intents being processed by the `AlarmManager`. It periodically retrieves a snapshot of the `AlarmManager` state by executing the `dumpsys alarm` command. Note that excessively running `dumpsys` can harm the overall system performance, while very long query periods can cause the attacks to go undetected. We empirically found that executing `dumpsys` every 500ms is suitable on the test devices used in this study. For each pending intent record, the anti-reboot app extracts the package name of the source app and the repeat interval. If the interval is less than a predefined threshold (set to 60 s as in Android 6.0), or the number of active pending intents of a source app is more than θ, the source app is flagged and is either disabled or uninstalled.

6.2   Detection Results

The anti-reboot app detected the soft reboot attack and identified the source of the attack 100 % of the time during out testing, even when the attack was in its most aggressive form. In many cases, we observed that the device reboots before the anti-reboot app gets a chance to disable or uninstall the attacking app. This is mainly due to the fact that the attacking app can request to start up to 5,500 new tasks in a single transaction using `Service.startActivities(Intent[])` API call. This quickly depletes the file descriptors of `system_server` which inhibits its capabilities and renders `system_server` unresponsive to any requests to disable or uninstall the offending app. To mitigate this, the anti-reboot app records the package name of offending apps along with a time stamp of when the attack was detected in persistent memory. It then checks when the system was soft rebooted, and if an offending app was detected within a 60 second period before the soft reboot, it disables the offending app after the soft reboot and informs the user. In addition, we confirm a soft reboot by checking to see if the Process

ID of system_server has changed, which occurs during a soft reboot. The user can re-enable disabled apps through the GUI of the anti-reboot app.

We emphasize that it is not possible to rate-limit the intents sent by processes, without changes to the OS itself. Even then, a balance has to be struck between usability and security. If the system sets overly strict limits on the sending rate of intents, apps may become unresponsive or sluggish, resulting in an overall degradation of the system performance and user experience. In addition, it is not straightforward to implement rate-limiting in a system that is heavily event-driven such as Android. If the system decides to silently drop intents, apps are likely to malfunction as a result of lost intents. Notifying apps that they are exceeding the rate-limit would require a back channel from system_server to the app, besides requiring the app to anticipate and handle the notification, which further complicates the design of both the OS and the apps. We are unaware if this attack have been used in "the wild." After informing Amazon of the DoS attack, they created a detection mechanism for it in the Amazon AppStore. Google did not respond to our question whether or not the attack app would make it through their vetting process to be available on Google Play.

6.3   Performance Evaluation

We tested the overhead introduced by the anti-reboot defense app by using the following two benchmarks: AnTuTu Benchmark v6.0.1 and BenchmarkPI v1.1. AnTuTu Benchmark provides an aggregate score that combines both multitasking, user experience, CPU and memory speeds, and 3D rendering performance. BenchmarkPI is a CPU time benchmark that computes π to the nth digit. We tested the defense app on the following devices: Nexus 5 running AOSP Android 6.0.1, Nvidia Shield Android TV running Android 5.1.1, Amazon Fire TV 1st generation running Android 4.2.2, and Amazon Fire 7″ tablet running Android 5.1.1. Under each scenario, we performed 20 runs and took the average of the resulting benchmark scores. We report the overhead as the percentage degradation in the aggregated average of the benchmark scores.

Figure 2 shows the overhead in the benchmark scores of AnTuTu Benchmark and BenchmarkPI. The overhead ranged from 0.8 % to 1.51 % for AnTuTu Benchmark and 0.14 % to 1.15 for BenchmarkPI. The overhead from the defense app is mainly due to the threads it spawns to continuously monitor the Android log and process the output of the dumpsys alarm command to record intent usage and attribute them to the app that sent them. Overall, the defense app introduced a small amount of overhead (less than 1.6 %) which we believe is acceptable for the service it provides.

6.4   Framework Defenses

We suggest changes be made to the ActivityManagerService class in the Android framework to prevent a single app from starting an arbitrarily large amount of activities. Currently, the amount of intents that can be sent to be processed by ActivityManagerService is only limited by the Android Binder

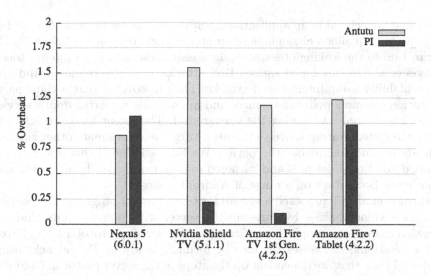

Fig. 2. Performance overhead based on AnTuTu Benchmark and BenchmarkPI scores.

transaction buffer size. On Android 6, this enables an app to send a around 5,500 intents to be processed by `ActivityManagerService` in a single transaction using the `Service.startActivities(Intent[])` API call. A limit of less than 400 concurrent activities should be imposed on each app to preclude it from soft rebooting the device. Alternatively, a proper rate for rate-limiting of intents can be established from empirical analysis of intent usage among third-party applications. We recommend that once the user selects to perform a factory reset of an Android Wear device that all third-party applications should be terminated so they cannot attempt to interfere with the factory reset process. In addition, introducing some delay before sending the `BOOT_COMPLETED` broadcast intent and similar intents to third-party apps can provide the user additional time to perform a factory reset through the Settings application.

7 Related Work

Researchers have previously discovered methods to perform a soft reboot of Android devices. Armando et al. [16] discovered a vulnerability that made the device reboot by repeatedly forking processes from the `zygote` process from a third-party app. Huang et al. [25] discovered flaws in the concurrency control within `system_server`. When a monitor lock is held for more than a certain time threshold (i.e., 60 s), the watchdog process will terminate `system_server` since it appears that the process has encountered a deadlock. Terminating `system_server` results in a soft reboot of the Android OS. They developed a static tool to identify risky use of monitor locks within `system_server` so they can be triggered.

Chin et al. [21] presented various DoS attacks by intercepting intents destined for another application. This is due to apps using implicit intents by using an action that is declared in an application component's intent filter, as opposed to using the fully qualified class name of an application component. Intent hijacking can lead to the leaking of sensitive data sent embedded in an intent object. Johnson et al. [26] developed various DoS attacks on device resources and system availability using intent-based attacks. They discovered that a third-party application can monopolize the camera and microphone resources from a service application component running the background. The intent-based attacks can render the system unresponsive to the user, target and terminate other running applications, and soft reboot the device. We have continued this research and proposed additional defenses and gathered experimental data by using the soft reboot cycle DoS attack on a range of Android devices.

Antunes et al. [15] proposed a system for testing server programs for resource exhaustion vulnerabilities by spraying the server with fuzzed inputs that are generated from a user-supplied specification of the server protocol. In [24], Groza et al. extends and formalizes the idea by formally modeling DoS attacks using cost-based rules that are dependent on the steps of the server protocol. Chang et al. [19] proposed a system that scans the source code of programs for potential code sites that may result in uncontrolled CPU time and stack consumption, and are influenced by untrusted input. Elsabagh et al. [22] proposed a system that models both the temporal and spatial information in resource consumption behavior of programs, and enforces the model at runtime. Extending such ideas to Android remains an open challenge, especially because of Android's uncoupled execution nature which heavily depends on inter-application communication.

8   Conclusion

By introducing a novel strategy for the soft reboot cycle DoS attack, we show that installing a third-party application, even with a limited set of permissions, can render certain Android devices unusable. In other cases, the user needed to perform a factory reset or flash firmware images to recover the victim device. Furthermore, we provide a detailed explanation as to the the underlying cause of the soft reboot that occurs in the Android framework. To support our claims, we reference the actual Android 6 source code and describe the mechanics of the attack strategy. To mitigate the attack, we leverage the existing Android framework to suggest changes that would either significantly reduce or eliminate the effects of the attacks. As a proof-of-concept, we implemented an open-source Android application that provides concrete countermeasures to prevent the attack and can be utilized by device manufacturers without modifying the device or the Android framework. As a final note, to ensure that our research is not misused, we informed Google and all of the affected device manufacturers listed in this paper so that Android devices can be made more secure.

References

1. Accessing SATV stock Recovery — nVidia Shield Android TV. http://forum. xda-developers.com/shield-tv/general/accessing-satv-stock-recovery-t3300211
2. Android Core Initialization Script. https://android.googlesource.com/platform/ system/core/+/android-6.0.0_r1/rootdir/init.rc
3. Android Core Runtime Init. https://android.googlesource.com/platform/frameworks/base/+/android-6.0.0_r1/core/java/com/android/internal/os/RuntimeInit. java
4. Android Core Window Manager Service. https://android.googlesource.com/ platform/frameworks/base/+/android-6.0.0_r1/services/core/java/com/android/ server/wm/WindowManagerService.java
5. Android Core Zygote. https://android.googlesource.com/platform/frameworks/ base/+/android-6.0.0_r1/core/jni/com_android_internal_os_Zygote.cpp
6. Android Core Zygote Init. https://android.googlesource.com/platform/frame works/base/+/android-6.0.0_r1/core/java/com/android/internal/os/ZygoteInit. java
7. Android Debug Bridge — Android Developers. http://developer.android.com/ tools/help/adb.html
8. Dashboards — Android Developers. http://developer.android.com/about/ dashboards/index.html
9. endlessrecursion/antireboot: A standalone App to defend againstreboot cycle DoS Attacks on Android. https://github.com/endlessrecursion/antireboot
10. Malware Uses SE Tricks to Enable Automatic App Installation. http://www. tripwire.com/state-of-security/latest-security-news/android-malware-uses-social-engineering-to-enable-automatic-app-installation/
11. Mi TV box Mini. http://xiaomi-mi.com/tv-box/xiaomi-mi-box-mini-tv-console/
12. Moto 360 adapter usb cable — How to Root Android. http://www.rootjunky.com/ moto-360-adapter-usb-cable/
13. OmniRAT Takes Over Android Devices Through Social EngineeringTricks. https://securityintelligence.com/news/omnirat-takes-over-android-devices-through-social-engineering-tricks/
14. SONY — eSupport - How to reset the Android TV to factorysettings. https://us. en.kb.sony.com/app/answers/detail/a_id/60594
15. Antunes, J., Neves, N.F., Veríssimo, P.J.: Detection and prediction of resource-exhaustion vulnerabilities. In: 19th International Symposium on Software Reliability Engineering, ISSRE 2008, pp. 87–96. IEEE (2008)
16. Armando, A., Merlo, A., Migliardi, M., Verderame, L.: Would you mind forking this process? a denial of service attack on android (and some countermeasures). In: Gritzalis, D., Furnell, S., Theoharidou, M. (eds.) SEC 2012. IFIP AICT, vol. 376, pp. 13–24. Springer, Heidelberg (2012)
17. Azim, T., Neamtiu, I.: Targeted and depth-first exploration for systematic testing of android apps. In: Proceedings of the 2013 ACM SIGPLAN International Conference on Object Oriented Programming Systems Languages & Applications, OOPSLA 2013, pp. 641–660. ACM (2013)
18. Bhattacharya, P., Yang, L., Guo, M., Qian, K., Yang, M.: Learning mobile security with labware. Secur. Priv. IEEE **12**(1), 69–72 (2014)
19. Chang, R., Jiang, G., Ivančić, F., Sankaranarayanan, S., Shmatikov, V.: Inputs of coma: static detection of denial-of-service vulnerabilities. In: Computer Security Foundations Symposium, CSF2009, 22nd IEEE, pp. 186–199. IEEE (2009)

20. Chen, X., Ding, N., Jindal, A., Hu, Y.C., Gupta, M., Vannithamby, R.: Smartphone energy drain in the wild: analysis and implications. In: Proceedings of the 2015 ACM SIGMETRICS International Conference on Measurement and Modeling of Computer Systems, pp. 151–164. ACM (2015)
21. Chin, E., Felt, A.P., Greenwood, K., Wagner, D.: Analyzing inter-application communication in android. In: Proceedings of the 9th International Conference on Mobile Systems, Applications, and Services, MobiSys 2011, pp. 239–252, ACM (2011)
22. Elsabagh, M., Barbará, D., Fleck, D., Stavrou, A.: Radmin: early detection of application-level resource exhaustion and starvation attacks. In: Bos, H., Monrose, F., Blanc, G. (eds.) Raid 2015. LNCS, vol. 9404, pp. 515–537. Springer, Heidelberg (2015). doi:10.1007/978-3-319-26362-5_24
23. Fedler, R., Schütte, J., Kulicke, M.: On the effectiveness of malware protection on android. Technical Report, Fraunhofer AISEC, Berlin (2013)
24. Groza, B., Minea, M.: Formal modelling and automatic detection of resource exhaustion attacks. In: Proceedings of the 6th ACM Symposium on Information, Computer and Communications Security, pp. 326–333. ACM (2011)
25. Huang, H., Zhu, S., Chen, K., Liu, P.: From system services freezing to system server shutdown in android: all you need is a loop in an app. In: Proceedings of the 22nd ACM SIGSAC Conference on Computer and Communications Security, pp. 1236–1247. ACM (2015)
26. Johnson, R., Elsabagh, M., Stavrou, A., Sritapan, V.: Targeted DoS on android: how to disable android in 10 seconds or less. In: Proceedings of the 10th International Conference on Malicious and Unwanted Software, pp. 239–252 (2015)
27. Liu, X., Yang, X., Lu, Y.: To filter or to authorize: network-layer dos defense against multimillion-node botnets. ACM SIGCOMM Comput. Commun. Rev. 38(4), 195–206 (2008)
28. Peng, T., Leckie, C., Ramamohanarao, K.: Survey of network-based defense mechanisms countering the dos and ddos problems. ACM Comput. Surv. 39(1), 3 (2007)
29. Potharaju, R., Newell, A., Nita-Rotaru, C., Zhang, X.: Plagiarizing smartphone applications: attack strategies and defense techniques. In: Barthe, G., Livshits, B., Scandariato, R. (eds.) ESSoS 2012. LNCS, vol. 7159, pp. 106–120. Springer, Heidelberg (2012)
30. Vidas, T., Christin, N.: Sweetening android lemon markets: measuring and combating malware in application marketplaces. In: Proceedings of the Third ACM Conference on Data and Application Security and Privacy, CODASPY 2013, pp. 197–208. ACM (2013)
31. Xiao, B., Chen, W., He, Y.: An autonomous defense against syn flooding attacks: detect and throttle attacks at the victim side independently. J. Parallel Distrib. Comput. 68(4), 456–470 (2008)
32. Yang, G., Gerla, M., Sanadidi, M.: Defense against low-rate tcp-targeted denial-of-service attacks. In: Proceedings of the Ninth International Symposium on Computers and Communications, ISCC 2004, vol. 1, pp. 345–350. IEEE (2004)
33. Yang, X., Wetherall, D., Anderson, T.: A dos-limiting network architecture. In: Proceedings of the 2005 Conference on Applications, Technologies, Architectures, and Protocols for Computer Communications, SIGCOMM 2005, pp. 241–252. ACM (2005)
34. Zheng, M., Sun, M., Lui, J.: Droid Analytics: a signature based analytic system to collect, extract, analyze and associate android malware. In: 2013 12th IEEE International Conference on Trust, Security and Privacy in Computing and Communications (TrustCom), pp. 163–171, July 2013

35. Zhou, W., Zhou, Y., Jiang, X., Ning, P.: Detecting repackaged smartphone applications in third-party android marketplaces. In: Proceedings of the Second ACM Conference on Data and Application Security and Privacy, CODASPY 2012, pp. 317–326 (2012)
36. Zhou, Y., Jiang, X.: Dissecting android malware: characterization and evolution. In: 2012 IEEE Symposium on Security and Privacy (SP), pp. 95–109, May 2012

Network Anomaly Detection
Using Unsupervised Feature Selection
and Density Peak Clustering

Xiejun Ni[1], Daojing He[1(✉)], Sammy Chan[2], and Farooq Ahmad[3]

[1] School of Computer Science and Software Engineering,
East China Normal University, Shanghai, China
djhe@sei.ecnu.edu.cn
[2] Department of Electronic Engineering,
City University of Hong Kong, Hong Kong, China
[3] Department of Computer Science,
COMSATS Institute of Information Technology, Lahore, Pakistan

Abstract. Intrusion detection systems (IDSs) play a significant role to effectively defend our crucial computer systems or networks against attackers on the Internet. Anomaly detection is an effective way to detect intrusion, which can discover patterns that do not conform to expected behavior. The mainstream approaches of ADS (anomaly detection system) are using data mining technology to automatically extract normal pattern and abnormal ones from a large set of network data and distinguish them from each other. However, supervised or semi-supervised approaches in data mining rely on data label information. This is not practical when the network data is large-scale. In this paper, we propose a two-stage approach, unsupervised feature selection and density peak clustering to tackle label lacking situations. First, the density-peak based clustering approach is introduced for network anomaly detection, which considers both distance and density nature of data. Second, to achieve better performance of clustering process, we use maximal information coefficient and feature clustering to remove redundant and irrelevant features. Experimental results show that our method can get rid of useless features of high-dimensional data and achieves high detection accuracy and efficiency in the meanwhile.

Keywords: Anomaly detection · Data mining · Feature selection · Maximal information coefficient · Density peak clustering

1 Introduction

Intrusion is a set of actions aiming to compromise the security of computer and network components in terms of confidentiality, integrity and availability [1]. Intrusion detection techniques can be classified into two categories:misuse detection (or signature-based detection) and anomaly detection. Misuse detection

© Springer International Publishing Switzerland 2016
M. Manulis et al. (Eds.): ACNS 2016, LNCS 9696, pp. 212–227, 2016.
DOI: 10.1007/978-3-319-39555-5_12

identifies intrusions based on patterns acquired from known attacks [2]. Anomaly detection discovers intrusions based on significant deviations from normal activities [3].

In early days, signature-based methods such as Snort [4], based on extensive knowledge of the particular characteristics of each attack, referred to as its signature are commonly applied. Such systems are highly effective in dealing with attacks for which they are programmed to defend unknown intrusion. Besides, they are not applicable for anomaly detection with large-scale network data because of the famous 4V [5]:

Volume. The scale and complexity of network data is beyond the Moores law which means the amount of traffic to be detected in every terminal increases rapidly. String matching based signature method is a computationally intensive task.

Variety. Network data usually is derived from various sources, where it is described in unstructured or semi-structured way. Proper integration is necessary to make uniform format.

Value. The value density of data is low. Anomaly detection problem usually faces with high dimensional network data. Some features of these data are useless in identifying anomaly.

Velocity. The detection needs response in real-time in order to detect attack or anomaly in time.

In addition, building new signatures require human experts' manual inspection which is not only expensive, but also induces a significant period of vulnerability between the discovery of a new attack and the construction of its signatures.

Patcha *et al.* [6] further categorizes anomaly detection methods into three categories: statistics-based, data mining-based and machine learning-based. Statistics-based method is difficult to adapt to the non-stationary variation of the network traffic, which leads to a high false positive rate [7]. To alleviates these shortcomings, a number of ADSs employ data mining techniques [8–12]. Data mining techniques aim to discover understandable patterns or models from given data sets [13]. It can efficiently identify profiles of normal network activities for anomaly detection, and build classifiers to detect attacks. Some earlier work show that these techniques can help to identify abnormal network activities efficiently.

Supervised anomaly intrusion detection approaches [8–10] highly rely on training data from normal activities, which are commonly used as data mining techniques. Since training data only contain historical activities, the profile of normal activities can only include the historical patterns of normal behavior. Therefore, new activities due to the change in the network environment or services are considered as deviations from the previously built profile, namely attacks. In addition, attack-free training data are not easy to obtain in real-world networks. The ADS trained by the data with hidden intrusions usually lacks the ability to detect intrusions.

To overcome the limitations of supervised anomaly-based systems, ADS employing unsupervised approaches has become a focus recently [14–17]. Unsupervised anomaly detection does not need attack-free training data. In distance-based methods, clusters are groups of data characterized by a small distance to the cluster center. However, a data point is always assigned to the nearest center, these approaches are not able to detect nonspherical clusters. In density-based spatial clustering methods, one chooses a density threshold, discards as noise the points in regions with densities lower than this threshold, and assigns to different clusters disconnected regions of high density. However, it can be nontrivial to choose an appropriate threshold.

Another challenge in ADS is feature selection. Many existing algorithms suffer from low effectiveness and low efficiency due to high dimensionality and large size of the data set. Hence, feature selection is essential for improving detection rate, since it can not only help reduce the computational cost but also improve the precision by removing irrelevant, mistaking and redundant features. However, in amount of data mining methods, features are selected based on the mutual information between feature and labels. Moreover, in many cases network data contain continuous variables which is challenging to measure the relation between features because the result greatly relies on the discretization methods.

Such limitations impose a serious bottleneck to unsupervised network anomaly detection problem. In this paper, we investigate anomaly detection problem in large scale and high-dimensional network data without labels and propose a new approach, called UFSDP (Unsupervised Feature Selection based Density Peak clustering) to tackle it. The major contributions of this paper are summarized as follows.

(1) We propose a new systematic framework that employs the density peak based clustering algorithm for network anomaly detection. This clustering algorithm has the advantage of extracting cluster centers and outlier points automatically. Besides, sampling adaptation is applied to improve the time and memory efficiency of the original clustering method in center selection stage.
(2) An unsupervised cluster-based feature selection mechanism is proposed before clustering procedure. We use two different ways to compute the relations for discrete and continuous attributes respectively. Different from other feature selection mechanism, we cluster the relevant features into groups according to their maximum redundancy from each other. Eventually redundant features are removed to make the feature number as least as possible.
(3) Extensive experiments are made to evaluate the performance of proposed method. Firstly, comparison are made over different classifiers by using original dataset and dataset with feature reduced by proposed selection algorithm. The proposed sampled-density peak clustering methodology is also compared with other clustering algorithms to evaluate its clustering performance in different credible metrics.

The rest of the paper proceeds as follows. Section 2 reviews related work. Section 3 describes our methodologies including unsupervised feature selection and density peak clustering respectively and highlights our motivation in using them. Section 4 presents our evaluation results and analysis. Section 5 finally summarizes our work.

2 Related Work

2.1 Unsupervised Anomaly Detection

Most of current network anomaly detection systems are supervised learning method. However, training data is typically expensive to obtain. Using unsupervised anomaly detection techniques, the system can be trained with unlabeled data and is capable of detecting previously unseen attacks.

Clustering, a ubiquitous unsupervised learning method, aims to group objects into meaningful subclasses. Therefore, network data generated from different attack mechanism or normal activities have distinct characteristics so each of them can be distinguished from others.

KMeans, a clustering method, is employed to detect unknown attacks and divide network data space effectively in [17]. However the performance and computation complexity of KMean method are sensitive to the predefined number of clusters and initialized cluster centers. Wei et al. [18] employs improved FCM algorithms to obtain an optimal k.

In [19], the authors proposed an anomaly detection method. This method utilizes a density-based clustering algorithm DBSCAN for modeling the normal activities of a user in a host.

Egilmez et al. [16] proposed a novel spectral anomaly detection method by developing a graph-based framework over wireless sensor networks. In their method, graphs are chosen to capture useful proximity information of measured data and employed to project the graph signals into normal and anomaly subspaces.

In [20], a SOM-based anomaly intrusion detection system was proposed, which could contract high-dimension data to lower dimension, meanwhile keeping the primary relationship between clustering and topology. But results is sensitive to parameters such as neuron number.

2.2 Feature Selection

The machine learning community has developed many solutions to address the curse of dimensionality problem in the form of feature selection and feature extraction. Different from feature extraction methods such as principal component analysis (PCA) [21] and linear discriminant analysis (LDA) [22], feature selection methods aim to choose a representative subset of all the features instead of creating a subset of new features by combinations of the existing features, which reserves the interpretability of attributes.

Feature selection can be briefly divided into three broad categories: the filter, embedded and wrapper approaches. In terms of feature selection, filter methods are commonly used.

Filter algorithms have low computational complexity, but the accuracy of the learning algorithms is not guaranteed. In [23], Peng *et al.* propose a minimal-redundancy-maximal-relevance (mRMR) criterion, which adds a feature to the final subset if it maximizes the difference between its mutual information with the class and the sum of its mutual information with each of the individual features already selected. Qu *et al.* [24] suggested a new redundancy measure and a feature subset merit measure based on mutual information concepts to quantify the relevance and redundancy among features. Song *et al.* [25] proposed a feature filter FAST based on the mutual information between features and minimum spanning tree is used to split features into clusters. Only one representative feature will be selected from every cluster to form the best discriminative feature subset. But when all weight value of edges is not high enough to arise split, it is not applicable.

In addition, it lacks an effective way to compute the mutual information between continuous features. Since continuous variables have unlimited values and the probability of any of them is not defined. Equal-width [26] divides continuous value into a number of bins with equal width, however it can be inaccurate since the width is an uncertainty. Others uses parzen window [27] to estimate the probability density distribution of two variables and employ integration computation. The actual distribution is unknown and the result highly relies on the selection of kernel function. FSFC [28] applies a new similarity measure, called maximal information compression index as the measurement of feature similarity and also predefines the number of selected features in the final feature subset.

3   Methodology

3.1   Feature Selection

Feature selection is a commonly used technique to select relevant features by reducing the data dimensionality and building effective prediction models. Feature selection can improve the performance of prediction models by alleviating the effect of the curse of dimensionality, enhancing the generalization performance, speeding up the learning process.

Relevance Definition. Suppose F denotes the set of whole features, F_i denotes an element of F, C denotes the target concept and S_i denotes the F-F_i. There are mainly three kinds of features:

Definition 1 (Strong correlation). F_i is strong relevant to target concept C if and only if

$$p(C|S_i, F_i) \neq p(C|S_i) \tag{1}$$

Strong relevant features can have impact on distribution of classification. Lacking strong relevant features, the result would be inaccurate.

Definition 2 (Weak correlation). F_i is weak relevant to target concept C if and only if

$$p(C|S_i, F_i) = p(C|S_i), \exists S_i' \subset S_i, p(C|S_i', F_i) \neq p(C|S_i') \qquad (2)$$

A weak relevant feature impacts the distribution of classification in some condition, but not necessary.

Definition 3 (Independent correlation). F_i is an independent feature if and only if

$$\forall S_i' \subset S_i, p(C|S_i', F_i) \neq p(C|S_i') \qquad (3)$$

Independent features do not influence the distribution of classification, so they are firstly removed in feature selection.

Mutual Information Calculation. In previous work [23,25], the symmetric uncertainty is used as the measure of correlation between two features. The symmetric uncertainty is defined as follows:

$$SU(F_i, F_j) = \frac{2 * Gain(F_i, F_j)}{H(F_i) + H(F_j)} \qquad (4)$$

$H(F_i)$ is the entropy of a discrete random variable $H(F_i)$, if $p(f)$ is the prior probabilities for all values of F_i, $H(F_i)$ is defined by:

$$H(F_i) = -\sum_{f \in F_i} p(f)\log_2 p(f) \qquad (5)$$

$H(F_i, F_j)$ is the conditional entropy of F_i with priori knowledge of all values of F_j. The smaller $H(F_i, F_j)$ is, the greater $Gain(F_i, F_j)$ is:

$$Gain(F_i, F_j) = H(F_i) - H(F_i|F_j) = H(F_j) - H(F_j|F_i) \qquad (6)$$

$Gain(F_i, F_j)$ means the contribution made by a known variable to reduce the uncertainty of an unknown variable, which can referred to another feature or the target concept.

Definition 4 (Relevancy). In supervised learning methods, features with low value of $SU(F_i, C)$ are firstly removed as independent ones. However, in unsupervised learning cases, the distribution of C are inaccessible. To deal with this problem, another measurement called ref is introduced to replace $SU(F_i, C)$ and their definition are as follows:

$$ref(F_i, C) = \frac{1}{n}\sum_{j=1}^{n} SU(F_i, F_j) \qquad (7)$$

$$ref(F_i, F_j) = SU(F_i, F_j) \qquad (8)$$

Discrete attributes such as *protocol_type* can directly be applied with afore-mentioned formulas. But continuous attributes such as *src_bytes* are uneasy to directly do so since their possible values are approximately infinite, and resulting in value $H(F_i)$ greater and value $SU(F_i, F_j)$ less than discrete attributes. As a result, it's challenging to compute relations between continuous features. Usually discretization operation is applied to map infinite values into finite values. However, most unsupervised discretization methods such as clustering and equal-width compute the relation in a rough way.

In this paper, the relation information between two continuous features are calculated using Maximal Information Coefficient (MIC) [29]. Methods such as mutual information estimators show a strong preference for some types of relations, but fails to describe well in other cases, which makes it unsuitable for identifying all potentially interesting relationships in a dataset. However, MIC has the ability to examine all potentially interesting relationships in a dataset independent of their form, which allows tremendous versatility in the search for meaningful insights.

MIC is based on the idea that if a relationship exists between two variables, then a grid can be drawn on the scatterplot of the two variables that divides the data to encapsulate that relationship. Given a finite dataset D of two dimensions, one of the dimensions named x-values and the other as y-values. Suppose x-values is divided into x bins and y-values into y bins, and we got a $x * y$ grid G, given by

$$I * (D, x, y) = argmaxI (D|G) \tag{9}$$

For each pair (x,y), the MIC algorithm finds the x by y grid with the highest induced mutual information. Then MIC algorithm normalizes the mutual information scores and compiles a matrix that stores $D|_G$. Then, the MIC(x,y) is the maximum value in the matrix.

Feature Cluster. After computing MI and MIC we get $ref(F_i, C)$ and $ref(F_i, F_j)$ from previous steps, then an intuitive clustering algorithm is proposed to filter those features. Firstly, features with low $ref(F_i, C)$ are removed since those features do not make obvious contribution for identifying. We set a *threshold1* for $ref(F_i, C)$. In this paper, we run algorithm multiple times and choose the best one. After that, redundant features are removed according to the value of $ref(F_i, F_j)$. We set *threshold2* for $ref(F_i, F_j)$, if $ref(F_i, F_j)$ exceeds *threshold2*, F_i and F_j can be regarded as redundant. Then we cluster those redundant features together. The details of the unsupervised feature selection algorithm for continuous features are given in Algorithm 1.

3.2   Density Peak Based Clustering

In distance-based methods, clusters are groups of data characterized by a small distance to the cluster center. However, a data point is always assigned to the nearest center, these approaches are not able to detect nonspherical clusters. In density-based spatial clustering methods, one chooses a density threshold,

---

Algorithm 1. Unsupervised continuous feature selection by MIC

Require: D=$\{F_0, F_1...F_{40}\}$ - the given dataset without label

$\quad\quad\quad\quad$ $\theta1$ - threshold for irrelevance

$\quad\quad\quad\quad$ $\theta2$ - threshold for redundancy

Ensure: S - selected feature subset

$\quad n = F_{continuous}.size()$

$\quad M[n][n] = \{0\}$ //initialize the relevance matrix M

$\quad$ **for** *each pair feature* $\{F_i, F_j\}$ **do**

$\quad\quad M[i][j] = M[j][i] = MIC[F_i][F_i]$

$\quad$ **end for**

$\quad F_{relevant} = \emptyset$

$\quad$ **for** $i = 0$ *to* n **do**

$\quad\quad M[i][i] = M[i][i] = Avg(M[i])$ // M[i][i] is the relevance score of feature Fi, equal

$\quad\quad$ to the average value of M[i][0].. M[i][1]...M[i][n-1]

$\quad\quad$ **if** $M[i][i] > \theta1$ **then**

$\quad\quad\quad F_{relevant} = F_{relevant} \cup F_i$

$\quad\quad$ **end if**

$\quad$ **end for**

$\quad$//=====Part1:Irrelevant Feature Removal=====

$\quad Feature\_cluster = \{\}$ $\quad\quad$ //a map

$\quad$ **for** *for each* F_i *in* $F_{relevant}$ **do**

$\quad\quad$ **if** $Feature\_cluster = \{\}$ **then**

$\quad\quad\quad Feature\_cluster = Feature\_cluster \cup \{i\}$

$\quad\quad$ **else**

$\quad\quad\quad float\ maxredundancy = 0.0, int\ maxindex = 0$

$\quad\quad\quad$ **for** *each* Fj *in* $Feature\_cluster$ **do**

$\quad\quad\quad\quad$ **if** $MIC[F_i][F_j] > maxreduncy$ **then**

$\quad\quad\quad\quad\quad maxredundancy = MIC[F_i][F_j]$

$\quad\quad\quad\quad\quad maxindex = F_j.index$

$\quad\quad\quad\quad$ **end if**

$\quad\quad\quad$ **end for**

$\quad\quad\quad$ **if** $maxredundancy < \theta2$ **then**

$\quad\quad\quad\quad Feature\_cluster = Feature\_cluster[i] \cup \{i\}$

$\quad\quad\quad$ **else**

$\quad\quad\quad\quad Feature\_cluster[maxindex].insert(i)$

$\quad\quad\quad$ **end if**

$\quad\quad$ **end if**

$\quad$ **end for**

$\quad$//=====Part2: Feature Clusters Construction=====

$\quad S = \emptyset$

$\quad$ **for** *each subset* S' *in* $Feature\_cluster$ **do**

$\quad\quad F_j = max_{F_k \in S'} M[k][k]$

$\quad\quad S = S \cup F_j$

$\quad$ **end for**

$\quad$//=====Part3: Feature Selection=====

$\quad$ **return** S

---

discards as noise the points in regions with densities lower than this threshold, and assigns to different clusters disconnected regions of high density. However, it can be nontrivial to choose an appropriate threshold.

Most clustering algorithms [14–17] need parameters predefined, such as cluster number, and the detection accuracy is sensitive to those parameters. In [30], Alex et al. develop a modern clustering method named Fast Search and Find of Density Peaks (DP). Given data samples, there are two variables that does this algorithm calculates for each data sample.

(1) local density ρ_i:

ρ_i measures the local density of a target point i by computing the number of points within the fixed radius to point i. There are two ways to compute local density.

In cut-off kernel,

$$\rho_i = \sum_{j \in I_s \setminus \{i\}} \chi(d_{ij} - d_c) \tag{10}$$

$$\chi(x) = \begin{cases} 1, x < 0; \\ 0, x \geq 0, \end{cases} \tag{11}$$

In Gaussian kernel,

$$\rho_i = \sum_{j \in I_s \setminus \{i\}} e^{-\left(\frac{d_{ij}}{d_c}\right)^2} \tag{12}$$

(2) minimum distance to high density point δ_i:

δ_i is measured by computing the minimum distance between point i and any other point with higher density. The points with higher value of local density and distance are selected as cluster center.

Cluster Center Selection. In original density peak clustering, the density and distance of all the data samples are computed primarily. During this procedure, the method maintains a matrix with float number for distance in size of N*N where N is the number of samples. When N is higher than 32000, the memory can not store the whole matrix at one pass. Memory constraints density peak clustering to applied in a larger scale dataset. We notice that if we downsample the network data randomly, the whole distribution of data become sparse but the position of cluster centers remains changed slightly. Because the original data points with high density are still higher than other points after unbiased downsampling. Given this, we use a portion of network data instead of whole dataset and obtain approximate centers.

Clustering Process. After the cluster centers have been found, every remaining point is assigned to the nearest center. The label assignment is performed in a single step.

4   Experiments and Analysis

4.1   Dataset and Preprocess

KDDCup99 dataset [31] is used as a benchmark which contains five million connection records processed from four gigabytes of compressed binary TCP dump data from seven weeks of network traffic. Due to the huge volume of original dataset, we use 10 % containing about 494021 records of this KDDCup99 dataset which is publicly available for experimental purpose. Attacks are broadly categorized in four groups such as Probes (information gathering attacks), DoS (denial of service), U2R (user to root) and R2L (remote to local). Each labeled record consists of 41 attributes (features) as depicted in Table 1 and one target value. Target value indicates the attack category name.

Algorithm 2. Data clustering by sampled Density-Peak algorithm

---

Require: D=$\{F_0, F_1...F_n\}$ - the dimension reduced dataset without label

   m - sample reduce factor   *Percent* - position of d_c

   $\theta1$ - threshold for density $\theta2$ - threshold for distance

Ensure: label - labels of data

   for $i = 0$ *to* N **do**

      if *random*.$(0, m) == 0$ **then**

         Sample.insert$(D[i])$

      end if

   end for

   =====Part1:Choose samples for centers =====

   List LL

   for *each pair* $(Sample[i], Sample[j])$ *in Samples* **do**

      $dist[i][j] = eculidean\_distance(Sample[i], Sample[j])$

      $LL.append(dist[i][j])$

   end for

   $d_c = percent * sorted(LL)$

   for *each i in Sample* **do**

      $Rho[i] = count_{j \in Sample \cap dist[i][j] < dc}(j)$

      $Delta[i] = min_{j \in Sample \cap Rho[j] > Rho[i]}(dist[i][j])$

   end for

   for *each i in Sample* **do**

      if $Rho[i] > \theta1 \cap Delta[i] > \theta2$ **then**

         Center.insert(i)

      end if

   end for

   =====Part2:Cluster center selection=====

   $Label = [N]$

   for *each i in D* **do**

      $Label[i] = min_{j \in Centers}(eculidean\_distance(D[i], Center[j]))$

   end for

   =====Part3:Labeling=====

   return *Label*

Table 1. Summay of the 41 attributes in KDDCup99 data sets

No	Feature name	Type	No	Feature name	Type
1	duration	C	22	is_guest_login	D
2	protocol_type	D	23	count	C
3	service	D	24	src_count	C
4	flag	D	25	serror_rate	C
5	src_bytes	C	26	srv_serror_rate	C
6	dst_bytes	C	27	rerror_rate	C
7	land	D	28	srv_rerror_rate	C
8	wrong_fragment	C	29	same_srv_rate	C
9	urgent	C	30	diff_srv_rate	C
10	hot	C	31	srv_diff_host_rate	C
11	num_failed_logins	C	32	dst_host_count	C
12	logged_in	D	33	dst_host_srv_count	C
13	num_compromised	C	34	dst_host_same_srv_rate	C
14	root_shell	D	35	dst_host_diff_srv_rate	C
15	su_attempted	D	36	dst_host_same_src_port_rate	C
16	num_root	C	37	dst_host_srv_diff_host_rate	C
17	num_file_creations	C	38	dst_host_serror_rate	C
18	num_shells	C	39	dst_host_srv_serror_rate	C
19	num_access_files	C	40	dst_host_rerror_rate	C
20	num_outbound_cmds	C	41	dst_host_srv_rerror_rate	C
21	is_hot_login	D			

Table 2. Specific of KDDCup99_10_percent

Attack category	Specific classes	No. of records
Normal	normal	97278
DoS	back,land,neptune,pod,smurf,teardrop	391458
Probe	ipsweep,nmapportsweep,satan	4107
R2L	ftpwriteguesspasswd,imap,multihop,phf,spy,warezclient...	1126
U2R	bufferoverflow,loadmodule,perl,rootkit	52
Total		494021

Since attributes in the KDD datasets include forms of continuous, discrete and symbolic with significantly varying resolution and ranges. In feature selection step, entropy and mutual information between discrete and symbolic attributes are computed without preprocessing. While in clustering stage, symbolic and discrete data are normalized and scaled. Firstly symbolic features like *protocol_type*, *services*, *flags* and *attack_names* were mapped to integer values ranging from

0 to $N - 1$ where N is the number of symbols. Secondly, min-max normalization process is implemented. Each of feature is linearly scaled to the range of $[0.0, 1.0]$ for the fairness between different attributes. As we see in Table 2, the 10 % of KDDCup99 is an imbalanced dataset, with 'neptune', 'normal' and 'smurf' greatly higher than other kinds. Therefore we downsample three kinds to ensure the relative balance with other attributes.

4.2 Performance Evaluation

To evaluate the effectiveness and performance of our proposed method, simulation experiments have been carried out. All experiments are executed on a computer with Intel I5 CPU, CPU clock rate of 3.20 GHz, 4 GB main memory. The algorithm proposed is implemented with Winpython-64bit using programming language Python 2.7.9. Several valuable utilities, MINE package [32] and Python open source machine learning library Scikit-learn, Numpy, SciPy, Matplotlib [33] are adopted during experiments.

In feature selection stage, we present the experimental results in terms of the classification accuracy and the the time gain from reduced data to original. Parameters of Alrogithm 1 are setup as following: $D=KDDCup99\_10\_percent$, $\theta 1=0.2$, $\theta 2=0.5$. After running Algorithm 1, we obtained selected discrete feature subset $\{2, 3, 4, 12\}$ and continuous feature subset $\{1, 8, 10, 23, 24, 25, 26, 27, 28, 29, 32, 33\}$, totally 16 features with 60.97 % reduction compared to original features numbers. Our experiment is set up as follows:

1. Comparison is carried out over our unsupervised method with other feature selection approaches, including supervised such as RFE, ExtraTreeClassifier.
2. Five classification algorithms are employed to classify data before and after feature selection. They are the tree-based DecisionTreeClassifier, ensemble learning method ExtraTreesClassifier, Random Forest Classifier algorithm and AdaboostClassifier and optimal margin-based Support Vector Machine, respectively.
3. We sampled those three categoreis to obtain a balanced dataset and the total number of samples is about 20000. Given that the result can be different every time, we run the comparision experiments 100 times on the same machine and then obtain average measured values.

Figure 1 records the classification accuracy of five classifier achieved on datasets reduced by four feature selection methods. From it we observed that

1. The original data without feature selection achieve the highest accuracy in most classifier situation since it reserves all information of the whole data.
2. Most feature selection methods can achieve a high accuracy and is close to original data. In most case, ensemble learning model, Random Forest and AdaBoost methods can achieve better detection accuracy compared with other model, such as Decision Tree, Support Vector Machine.

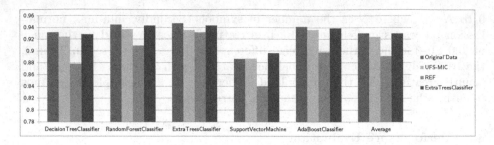

Fig. 1. Classification accuracy over different feature selection mehods

3. Compared with other supervised feature selection, MIC based-unsupervised feature selection acquire relatively high detection accuracy which is very close to the ExtraTreesClassifier with 0.4 % gap and to the original data with 0.6 % gap. Moreover, UFS-MIC achieves 3.3 % better than another supervised method RFE. The result shows that with absence of labels, the detection accuracy of proposed method is comparable with supervised approaches and thus suitable for network anomaly detection.

In the meanwhile, we record the time of running every classifier both features are selected and not. The detailed statistics in Table 3 illustrate that the proposed method efficiently reduces the time of running classification method on the reduced data. The average runtime benefit is considerable 14.44 % among different classifiers. In Decision Tree Classifier model, the benefit of 30.63 % is impressive.

Table 3. Runtime comparison between two datasets

	Orignal data	Reduced data	Time reduced
DecisionTreeClassifier	0.2520	0.1748	30.63 %
RandomForestClassifier	0.3969	0.3537	10.88 %
ExtraTreesClassifier	0.3782	0.3370	10.89 %
SupportVectorMachine	6.6171	5.8828	11.09 %
AdaBoostClassifier	22.4513	20.4912	8.73 %
Average	6.0191	5.4479	14.44 %

5   Conclusion

In this paper, we propose a two-stage framework for network anomaly detection. High-dimensional data commonly happens in network anomaly detection problems. Methods in solving these problem may suffer from curse of dimensionality.

In our first stage, we propose a sophisticated feature section method to get ride of irrelevant features and redundant features. By employing MIC approach, we solve the difficulty in calculating mutual information for continuous attributes. The experimental results show that this method achieves comparable accuracy with supervised methods and can effectively reduce the runtime of those methods with little sacrificing.

In the second stage, we introduce density peak based cluster. we have made a tradeoff that using fraction instead of the whole data samples to determine cluster centers approximatively. Experimental result shows that this method is efficient and achieve higher accuracy than other existing unsupervised methods generally.

Acknowledgement. This research is supported by the Pearl River Nova Program of Guangzhou (No. 2014J2200051), the National Science Foundation of China (Grants: 51477056 and 61321064), the Shanghai Rising-Star Program (No. 15QA1401700), the CCF-Tencent Open Research Fund, the Shanghai Knowledge Service Platform for Trustworthy Internet of Things (No. ZF1213), and the Specialized Research Fund for the Doctoral Program of Higher Education. Daojing He is the corresponding author of this article.

References

1. Heady, R., Luger, G.F., Maccabe, A., et al.: The architecture of a network level intrusion detection system. Department of Computer Science, College of Engineering, University of New Mexico (1990)
2. Barbara, D., Jajodia, S.: Applications of Data Mining in Computer Security. Springer Science & Business Media, New York (2002)
3. Eskin, E., Arnold, A., Prerau, M., et al.: A geometric framework for unsupervised anomaly detection. In: Barbará, D., Jajodia, S. (eds.) Applications of Data Mining in Computer Security, pp. 77–101. Springer, New York (2002)
4. Roesch, M.: Snort: lightweight intrusion detection for networks. LISA **99**(1), 229–238 (1999)
5. Camacho, J, Macia-Fernandez, G, Diaz-Verdejo, J., et al.: Tackling the big data 4 vs for anomaly detection. In: 2014 IEEE Conference on Computer Communications Workshops (INFOCOM WKSHPS), pp. 500–505. IEEE (2014)
6. Patcha, A., Park, J.M.: An overview of anomaly detection techniques: existing solutions and latest technological trends. Comput. Netw. **51**(12), 3448–3470 (2007)
7. Luo, Y.B., Wang, B.S., Sun, Y.P., et al.: FL-LPVG: an approach for anomaly detection based on flow-level limited penetrable visibility graph (2013)
8. Tran, Q.A., Duan, H., Li, X.: One-class support vector machine for anomaly network traffic detection. China Education and Research Network (CERNET), Tsinghua University, Main Building, vol. 310 (2004)
9. Hu, W., Hu, W.: Network-based intrusion detection using Adaboost algorithm. In: The 2005 IEEE/WIC/ACM International Conference on Web Intelligence, Proceedings, pp. 712–717. IEEE (2005)
10. Zhou, Q, Gu, L, Wang, C., et al.: Using an improved C4.5 for imbalanced dataset of intrusion. In: Proceedings of the 2006 International Conference on Privacy, Security, Trust: Bridge the Gap Between PST Technologies and Business Services, p. 67. ACM (2006)

11. Zhang, J., Zulkernine, M., Haque, A.: Random-forests-based network intrusion detection systems. IEEE Trans. Syst. Man Cybern Part C Appl. Rev. **38**(5), 649–659 (2008)
12. Tong, X., Wang, Z., Yu, H.: A research using hybrid RBF/Elman neural networks for intrusion detection system secure model. Comput. Phys. Commun. **180**(10), 1795–1801 (2009)
13. Hand, D.J., Mannila, H., Smyth, P.: Principles of Data Mining. MIT Press, Cambridge (2001)
14. Leung, K., Leckie, C.: Unsupervised anomaly detection in network intrusion detection using clusters. In: Proceedings of the Twenty-Eighth Australasian Conference on Computer Science, vol. 38, pp. 333–342. Australian Computer Society Inc (2005)
15. Zhang, J., Zulkernine, M.: Anomaly based network intrusion detection with unsupervised outlier detection. In: 2006 IEEE International Conference on Communications, ICC 2006, vol. 5, pp. 2388–2393. IEEE (2006)
16. Egilmez, H.E., Ortega, A.: Spectral anomaly detection using graph-based filtering for wireless sensor networks. In: 2014 IEEE International Conference on Acoustics, Speech and Signal Processing (ICASSP), pp. 1085–1089. IEEE (2014)
17. Jianliang, M., Haikun, S., Ling B.: The application on intrusion detection based on k-means cluster algorithm. In: 2009 International Forum on Information Technology and Applications, IFITA 2009, vol. 1, pp. 150–152. IEEE (2009)
18. Jiang, W., Yao, M., Yan, J.: Intrusion detection based on improved fuzzy c-means algorithm. In: 2008 International Symposium on Information Science and Engineering, ISISE 2008, vol. 2, pp. 326–329. IEEE (2008)
19. Oh, S.H., Lee, W.S.: An anomaly intrusion detection method by clustering normal user behavior. Comput. Secur. **22**(7), 596–612 (2003)
20. Huang, S.Y., Huang, Y.N.: Network traffic anomaly detection based on growing hierarchical SOM. In: 2013 43rd Annual IEEE/IFIP International Conference on Dependable Systems and Networks (DSN), pp. 1–2. IEEE (2013)
21. Wold, S., Esbensen, K., Geladi, P.: Principal component analysis. Chemometr. Intell. Lab. Syst. **2**(1), 37–52 (1987)
22. Yu, H., Yang, J.: A direct LDA algorithm for high-dimensional data with application to face recognition. Pattern Recogn. **34**, 2067–2070 (2001)
23. Peng, H., Long, F., Ding, C.: Feature selection based on mutual information criteria of max-dependency, max-relevance, and min-redundancy. IEEE Trans. Pattern Anal. Mach. Intell. **27**(8), 1226–1238 (2005)
24. Qu, G., Hariri, S., Yousif, M.: A new dependency and correlation analysis for features. IEEE Trans. Knowl. Data Eng. **17**(9), 1199–1207 (2005)
25. Song, Q., Ni, J., Wang, G.: A fast clustering-based feature subset selection algorithm for high-dimensional data. IEEE Trans. Knowl. Data Eng. **25**(1), 1–14 (2013)
26. Dougherty, J., Kohavi, R., Sahami, M.: Supervised and unsupervised discretization of continuous features. In: Machine Learning: Proceedings of the Twelfth International Conference, vol. 12, pp. 194–202 (1995)
27. Kwak, N., Choi, C.H.: Input feature selection by mutual information based on Parzen window. IEEE Trans. Pattern Anal. Mach. Intell. **24**(12), 1667–1671 (2002)
28. Mitra, P., Murthy, C.A., Pal, S.K.: Unsupervised feature selection using feature similarity. IEEE Trans. Pattern Anal. Mach. Intell. **24**(3), 301–312 (2002)
29. Reshef, D.N., Reshef, Y.A., Finucane, H.K., et al.: Detecting novel associations in large data sets. Science **334**(6062), 1518–1524 (2011)

30. Rodriguez, A., Laio, A.: Clustering by fast search and find of density peaks. Science **344**(6191), 1492–1496 (2014)
31. Cup, K.: Data. knowledge discovery in databases darpa archive (1999)
32. Albanese, D., Filosi, M.: Mine tool. https://github.com/minepy/minepy
33. Pedregosa, F., Varoquaux, G., Gramfort, A., et al.: Scikit-learn: machine learning in Python. J. Mach. Learn. Res. **12**, 2825–2830 (2011)

Deterministic and Functional Encryption

More Efficient Constructions
for Inner-Product Encryption

Somindu C. Ramanna[✉]

Laboratoire LIP, ENS de Lyon, Lyon, France
somindu.ramanna@ens-lyon.fr

Abstract. We propose new constructions for inner product encryption – IPE_1 and IPE_2, both secure under the eXternal Diffie-Hellman assumption (SXDH) in asymmetric pairing groups. The first scheme has constant-size ciphertexts whereas the second one is weakly attribute hiding. IPE_2 is derived from the identity-based encryption scheme of Jutla Roy (Asiacrypt 2013), that was extended from tag-based quasi-adaptive non-interactive zero-knowledge (QA-NIZK) proofs for linear subspaces of vector spaces over bilinear groups. The verifier common reference string (CRS) in these tag-based systems are split into two parts, that are combined during verification. We consider an alternate form of the tag-based QA-NIZK proof with a single verifier CRS that already includes a tag, different from the one defining the language. The verification succeeds as long as the two tags are unequal. Essentially, we embed a two-equation revocation mechanism in the verification. The new QA-NIZK proof system leads to IPE_1, a constant-sized ciphertext IPE scheme with very short ciphertexts. Both the IPE schemes are obtained by applying the n-equation revocation technique of Attrapadung and Libert (PKC 2010) to the corresponding identity based encryption schemes and proved secure under SXDH assumption. As an application, we show how our schemes can be specialised to obtain the first fully secure identity-based broadcast encryption based on SXDH with a trade-off among the public parameters, ciphertext and key sizes, all of them being sub-linear in the maximum number of recipients of a broadcast.

Keywords: Inner-product encryption · Attribute-hiding · Constant-size ciphertexts · Quasi-adaptive non-interactive zero knowledge proofs

1 Introduction

Inner product encryption (IPE) is a special form of the more general attribute-based encryption (ABE), which provides fine-grained access control to encrypted data. In ABE, a ciphertext is encrypted to some attribute $\mathbf{x}$ and a secret key is associated to some attribute $\mathbf{y}$ such that decryption succeeds iff some relation R on $\mathbf{x}, \mathbf{y}$ holds true i.e., $R(\mathbf{x}, \mathbf{y}) = 1$. The standard notion of security for ABE requires resistance to collusion attacks. More precisely, the privacy of a message encrypted to attribute $\mathbf{x}$ must not be compromised in the event of an attack by a group of users possessing secret keys for $\mathbf{y}_1, \mathbf{y}_2, \ldots, \mathbf{y}_q$ where

© Springer International Publishing Switzerland 2016
M. Manulis et al. (Eds.): ACNS 2016, LNCS 9696, pp. 231–248, 2016.
DOI: 10.1007/978-3-319-39555-5_13

$R(\mathbf{x}, \mathbf{y}_i) = 0$ for all $i = 1, \ldots, q$. Another useful security property, called *weak attribute hiding*, requires that given a ciphertext, the group of corrupt users unauthorised to decrypt the ciphertext, learn nothing about the attribute $\mathbf{x}$. In both cases, *adaptive security* allows users to be corrupted adaptively.

A simple form of ABE is identity-based encryption, where $\mathbf{x}$ and $\mathbf{y}$ represent identities and the relation R tests equality of identities. IPE is a more complex form with R testing orthogonality of $\mathbf{x}$ and $\mathbf{y}$ that are vectors in some inner product space. In other words, $R(\mathbf{x}, \mathbf{y}) = 1$ if $\langle \mathbf{x}, \mathbf{y} \rangle = 0$ and 0 otherwise. Though they appear restricted, inner products cover a wide range of functionalities useful in practice including polynomial functions, boolean formulae evaluating conjunctive and disjunctive normal forms, and identity-based broadcast encryption and revocation.

Most efficient constructions of IPE are based on pairings. A pairing $e : \mathbb{G}_1 \times \mathbb{G}_2 \to \mathbb{G}_T$ is a bilinear, non-degenerate and efficiently computable map defined over three groups $\mathbb{G}_1, \mathbb{G}_2, \mathbb{G}_T$ all having the same order. The common order of the groups may be composite or prime. Prime order pairings where $\mathbb{G}_1 \neq \mathbb{G}_2$ are called asymmetric. The best choices for implementation are *asymmetric pairings*, particularly those with no efficiently computable isomorphisms between $\mathbb{G}_1$ and $\mathbb{G}_2$ (called *Type-3 pairings*), from a point of view of security as well as efficiency. A consequence of the absence of efficient isomorphisms makes the decisional Diffie-Hellman (DDH) problem hard in both groups $\mathbb{G}_1$ and $\mathbb{G}_2$, collectively called the symmetric eXternal decisional Diffie-Hellman (SXDH) problem. We mainly focus on security under this assumption.

A powerful technique to obtain adaptive security for attribute-based encryption schemes is the dual system methodology introduced by Waters [Wat09]. Important features of the underlying algebraic structure that facilitate a dual system proof are *cancelling* and *parameter-hiding*. These features are explicitly available in composite order pairing groups that are not really suitable for practical deployment. A number of works have investigated the possibilities of translating the properties of composite order pairings to the prime-order setting, mostly in the context of dual system hierarchical IBE and ABE. However, the constructions resulting from these translations are not necessarily optimised in terms of various system parameters (such as ciphertext/key size, time required for decryption and so on). In contrast, direct constructions in the prime-order setting circumventing the route via composite order pairings, holds more promise in this regard. We believe that IPE as a cryptographic primitive is significant enough to justify attempts for direct constructions.

The goal of this work is to obtain new direct Type-3 pairing-based constructions of IPE that are efficient, adaptively secure with a focus on achieving either of the following properties – attribute-hiding or compact ciphertexts – from the SXDH assumption.

Our Contributions. We propose two new IPE schemes based on prime-order pairings named IPE_1 and IPE_2 – the former with constant-sized ciphertexts and the latter achieving weak attribute hiding, both secure under the SXDH assumption. The constructions are derived from quasi-adaptive non-interactive

Table 1. Constant-size ciphertext IPE.

Scheme	#pp	#cpr	#key	#dec
[CGW15]	$(2n+4)\|\mathbb{G}_1\| + \|\mathbb{G}_T\|$	$4\|\mathbb{G}_1\| + \|\mathbb{G}_T\|$	$(2n+2)\|\mathbb{G}_2\|$	$4[P] + 2n[M_2]$
$\mathcal{IPE}_1$	$(n+3)\|\mathbb{G}_1\| + \|\mathbb{G}_T\|$	$3\|\mathbb{G}_1\| + \|\mathbb{Z}_p\| + \|\mathbb{G}_T\|$	$(2n+1)\|\mathbb{G}_2\| + (n-1)\|\mathbb{Z}_p\|$	$3[P]+(2n-2)[M_2]+[E]$

Table 2. Attribute-hiding IPE.

Scheme	#pp	#cpr	#key	#dec
[CGW15]	$(2n+4)\|\mathbb{G}_1\| + \|\mathbb{G}_T\|$	$(2n+2)\|\mathbb{G}_1\| + \|\mathbb{G}_T\|$	$4\|\mathbb{G}_2\|$	$4[P] + 2n[M_1]$
$\mathcal{IPE}_2$	$(n+3)\|\mathbb{G}_1\| + \|\mathbb{G}_T\|$	$(n+1)\|\mathbb{G}_1\| + (n-1)\|\mathbb{Z}_p\| + \|\mathbb{G}_T\|$	$5\|\mathbb{G}_2\|$	$3[P] + (n+1)[M_1]$

zero knowledge (QA-NIZK) proofs of Jutla and Roy [JR13] and an IBE proposed in the same work (denoted $\mathcal{JR}\text{-}\mathcal{IBE}$ in the rest of the paper). $\mathcal{IPE}_2$ is obtained from $\mathcal{JR}\text{-}\mathcal{IBE}$ by a novel application of the n-equation revocation technique of Attrapadung and Libert [AL10]. But a constant-size ciphertext IPE cannot be constructed in a similar way from $\mathcal{JR}\text{-}\mathcal{IBE}$. To get around this problem, we propose a small tweak to the Jutla-Roy QA-NIZK proofs that leads to an alternate form of $\mathcal{JR}\text{-}\mathcal{IBE}$ (named $\mathcal{JR}\text{-}\mathcal{IBE}\text{-}\mathcal{D}$). The n-equation revocation method is then combined with $\mathcal{JR}\text{-}\mathcal{IBE}\text{-}\mathcal{D}$ to construct $\mathcal{IPE}_1$. QA-NIZK proofs were only known to yield IBE [JR13], hierarchical IBE (HIBE) [RS14b] and identity-based broadcast encryption [RS14a] but the question of whether they are useful in constructing other forms of ABE remained open. Thus, we (partially) settle an open question posed in [CGW15].

Tables 1 and 2 compare our constructions to those recently proposed by Chen et al. [CGW15]. The reason we do not include other previous constructions in the comparison is that the constructions in [CGW15] are the most efficient instantiations known so far and their constructions achieve security from the SXDH assumption. First, we define some abbreviations/notation we use in the comparison. #pp, #cpr and #key denote the sizes of public parameters, ciphertexts and keys respectively. #dec denotes the time required for decryption. $|X|$ denotes the size of representation of an element from X. [P], [M_i] (for $i = 1, 2$) and [E] respectively denote the time required for pairing operation, scalar multiplication in $\mathbb{G}_i$ (for $i = 1, 2$) and exponentiation in $\mathbb{G}_T$ respectively.

Note that both our schemes are at least as efficient as the corresponding instantiations in [CGW15]. The public parameters and decryption time are better in our schemes. The ciphertext size in both $\mathcal{IPE}_1$ and $\mathcal{IPE}_2$ are at least as short as those in [CGW15].

Quasi-Adaptive NIZK Proofs to IPE. Jutla and Roy [JR13] proposed constructions of quasi-adaptive non-interactive zero knowledge (QA-NIZK) proofs for linear equations over pairing groups that have a weaker soundness criterion called quasi-adaptive soundness. The difference with regular NIZKs is that the common reference string (CRS) is allowed to depend on the language.

These are useful in constructing a number of primitives, such as signatures, CCA2-secure public key encryption, commitment schemes and so on. From the signature scheme, they obtained an IBE using Naor's transform, which is the most efficient IBE known till date in terms of size of public parameters and ciphertexts achieving adaptive security under standard assumptions. Building upon this IBE, we obtain a weakly attribute hiding IPE scheme using the n-equation revocation method proposed in [AL10].

The NIZK construction that leads to the IBE is actually a split-CRS NIZK for tag-based languages, where the CRS for the verifier is split into two components. These two components are then combined using a public random tag ctag, which is also a parameter defining the language. We make a slight modification by combining the two components of the split-CRS with another tag ktag and only providing the combination as the CRS. This ensures that verification is successful unless the two tags are equal, thus making unconditional failure of verification a possibility. Nevertheless, the probability of failure is negligible and this small modification leads to an IBE scheme that has tags in both ciphertexts and keys. Decryption requires the two-equation revocation technique of Sahai and Waters [LSW08] as used in Waters' IBE [Wat09] and fails unconditionally with (negligible) probability equal to that of NIZK verification failure. The resulting IBE which we denote as $\mathcal{JR}\text{-}IBE\text{-}\mathcal{D}$, allows extension to primitives that were not possible from $\mathcal{JR}\text{-}IBE$, such as identity-based revocation schemes with small secret keys, constant-size ciphertext IBBE and so on. We present a construction of constant-size ciphertext IPE that can then be specialised to the afore-mentioned primitives. Unlike earlier constructions based on dual pairing vector spaces, specialising the IPE to specific cases actually leads to optimal constructions, i.e., these schemes are as efficient as direct constructions obtained from $\mathcal{JR}\text{-}IBE\text{-}\mathcal{D}$.

The reason for first constructing an IBE is two-fold. Firstly, it provides better intuition and acts as a basis for moving to inner product functionality. Second and most importantly, we do not know a direct generic transformation from QA-NIZK proofs to IBE, let alone IPE. To this end, there has been some recent work [JR15] that defines the so-called dual system simulation sound QA-NIZK proofs that explain the $\mathcal{JR}\text{-}IBE$ construction better in generic terms. It may be possible to explain our constructions too within this framework.

Application. As an application of IPE, we consider identity-based broadcast encryption (IBBE) wherein the goal is to securely broadcast an encrypted message to users associated with identities so that only a subset of *privileged* users can decrypt the message. Unlike the public key broadcast setting where the number of public keys varies polynomially with the security parameter, the number of valid identities in an IBBE are allowed to be exponential. Some direct constructions of adaptively secure constructions of IBBE schemes already exist in the literature [GW09, AL10, RS14a]. Most of these schemes require the number of privileged recipients for any broadcast to be bounded during setup (call this bound n). Previous schemes had either constant-sized ciphertexts or constant-sized keys with at least one out of public parameters, ciphertext, key having size depending linearly on n.

We show how to construct an IBBE from IPE_1 that achieves parameters, ciphertexts and keys all having size sublinear in n while maintaining security under static complexity assumptions. (Here, static means that the number of elements in instance is a constant). Due to lack of space, we present this discussion in the full version of this paper [Ram16].

Related Work. There have been several constructions of attribute encryption schemes based on pairings [SW05, GPSW06, OSW07, BSW07, Wat11, LW12], some focussing only on inner product encryption [KSW08, OT09, OT10, AL10]. Lattice-based constructions include ABE of [Boy13] for formulas and [GVW13, GGH+13] for circuits. We are mostly interested in constructions based on bilinear maps with prime order. Several approaches have been taken to constructing ABE schemes in the prime order pairing setting, most of them attempting to simulate properties of composite order pairings in suitably defined prime-order counterparts. A widely used technique is based on dual pairing vector spaces [OT08, OT09] which obtains all the nice theoretical properties but fails to preserve efficiency. The sparse DPVS technique introduced in [OT11] uses subgroups of sparse matrices (those mostly covered with zero entries) with the hope of improving efficiency. But the conversions are no longer generic and involve very complex security analysis. Another generic technique is that of dual system groups [CW13] that provides more efficient translations in the context of IBE. However, it does not extend to primitives that require anonymity or attribute-hiding. Two recent works [Wee14, Att14] present unifying frameworks for predicate encryption schemes fully secure within the dual system framework. These frameworks were defined in the composite order setting and later translated to prime-order groups [CGW15, Att15]. The new technique used in [CGW15] actually obtained very efficient and near-optimal constructions in the prime-order setting. Apart from translations from composite-order groups, there have been attempts at direct constructions of certain simple primitives such as IBE and HIBE. The approach of [JR13] is via QA-NIZK proofs. This was later extended to HIBE in [RS14b] and IBBE [RS14a]. Another interesting approach was to construct (H)IBE from message authentication codes (which is a symmetric primitive), examined in [BKP14]. But we do not know whether the last method extends to attribute-based encryption.

2   Preliminaries

This section introduces some notation followed by a review of pairings and related hardness assumptions. Also provided are definitions related to inner-product encryption.

2.1   Notation

The notation $x_1, \ldots, x_k \xleftarrow{\text{R}} \mathcal{X}$ indicates that elements $x_1, \ldots, x_k$ are sampled independently from the set $\mathcal{X}$ according to some distribution R. We use U to denote the uniform distribution. For a (probabilistic) algorithm $\mathcal{A}$, $y \xleftarrow{\text{R}} \mathcal{A}(x)$ means that y is chosen according to the output distribution of $\mathcal{A}$ on input x. $\mathcal{A}(x; r)$ denotes that $\mathcal{A}$ is run on input x with its internal random coins set to r. For two integers $a < b$, the notation $[a, b]$ represents the set $\{x \in \mathbb{Z} : a \le x \le b\}$. If $\mathbb{G}$ is a finite cyclic group, then $\mathbb{G}^\times$ denotes the set of generators of $\mathbb{G}$.

We denote vectors in $\mathbb{Z}_p^n$ by bold upright characters (e.g. $\mathbf{x}$). Inner product of two $\mathbb{Z}_p^n$-vectors $\mathbf{x} = (x_1, \ldots, x_n)$ and $\mathbf{y} = (y_1, \ldots, y_n)$ is given by $\langle \mathbf{x}, \mathbf{y} \rangle = \sum_{i=1}^{n} x_i y_i$.

2.2 Asymmetric Pairings and Hardness Assumptions

A bilinear pairing ensemble is a 7-tuple $\mathcal{G} = (p, \mathbb{G}_1, \mathbb{G}_2, \mathbb{G}_T, e, P_1, P_2)$ where $\mathbb{G}_1 = \langle P_1 \rangle$, $\mathbb{G}_2 = \langle P_2 \rangle$ are written additively and $\mathbb{G}_T$ is a multiplicatively written group, all having the same order p and $e : \mathbb{G}_1 \times \mathbb{G}_2 \to \mathbb{G}_T$ (the pairing) is a bilinear, non-degenerate and efficiently computable map. In a Type-3 pairing, $\mathbb{G}_1 \ne \mathbb{G}_2$ and no efficiently computable isomorphisms between $\mathbb{G}_1$ and $\mathbb{G}_2$ are known. The constructions we provide are based on such pairings.

The assumptions based on which the security of our constructions is proven are the decision Diffie-Hellman (DDH) assumptions in groups $\mathbb{G}_1$ and $\mathbb{G}_2$, called DDH1 and DDH2 respectively. Below, we describe these two assumptions. Technically speaking, the two assumptions are not in the standard form but can be shown to be equivalent. The reason we use the alternate forms is that they suit the requirements of our reductions and also to be in sync with the notation in [JR13].

Let $\mathcal{G} = (p, \mathbb{G}_1, \mathbb{G}_2, \mathbb{G}_T, e, P_1, P_2)$ be an asymmetric pairing ensemble and $\mathcal{A}$, a probabilistic polynomial time (PPT) algorithm $\mathcal{A}$ that outputs 0 or 1.

Assumption DDH1. Define a distribution $\mathcal{D}$ as follows: $P_1 \xleftarrow{\text{U}} \mathbb{G}_1^\times$; $b, s \xleftarrow{\text{U}} \mathbb{Z}_p$, $\mu \xleftarrow{\text{U}} \mathbb{Z}_p$; $\mathcal{D} = (\mathcal{G}, P_1, bP_1, bsP_1)$. The advantage of $\mathcal{A}$ in solving the DDH1 problem is given by

$$\mathsf{Adv}_{\mathcal{G}}^{\mathrm{DDH1}}(\mathcal{A}) = |\Pr[\mathcal{A}(\mathcal{D}, sP_1) = 1] - \Pr[\mathcal{A}(\mathcal{D}, (s + \mu)P_1) = 1]|.$$

Essentially, $\mathcal{A}$ has to decide whether $\mu = 0$ or $\mu \in_{\mathsf{U}} \mathbb{Z}_p$ given $(\mathcal{D}, (s + \mu)P_1)$. The (ε, t)-DDH1 assumption holds in $\mathcal{G}$ if for any adversary $\mathcal{A}$ running in time at most t, $\mathsf{Adv}_{\mathcal{G}}^{\mathrm{DDH1}}(\mathcal{A}) \le \varepsilon$.

Assumption DDH2. Let a distribution $\mathcal{D}$ be defined as follows: $P_2 \xleftarrow{\text{U}} \mathbb{G}_2^\times$, $r, c \xleftarrow{\text{U}} \mathbb{Z}_p$, $\gamma \xleftarrow{\text{U}} \mathbb{Z}_p$;

$$\mathcal{D} = (\mathcal{G}, P_2, rP_2, cP_2).$$

$\mathcal{A}$'s advantage in solving the DDH2 problem is given by

$$\mathsf{Adv}_{\mathcal{G}}^{\mathrm{DDH2}}(\mathcal{A}) = |\Pr[\mathcal{A}(\mathcal{D}, rcP_2) = 1] - \Pr[\mathcal{A}(\mathcal{D}, (rc + \gamma)P_2) = 1]|.$$

The (ε, t)-DDH2 assumption is that, for any t-time algorithm $\mathcal{A}$, $\mathsf{Adv}_{\mathcal{G}}^{\mathrm{DDH2}}(\mathcal{A}) \le \varepsilon$.

2.3 Inner Product Encryption (IPE)

Definition 1 (IPE). *Let V denote a vector space of dimension n over a field $\mathbb{F}$ and $\mathcal{M}$ denote the message space. An IPE scheme for inner products over V, is defined by four probabilistic algorithms –* Setup, Encrypt, KeyGen *and* Decrypt.

Setup*(κ, n) Takes as input a security parameter κ and the dimension of V. It outputs the public parameters $\mathcal{PP}$ and the master secret $\mathcal{MSK}$.*

KeyGen*$(\mathcal{MSK}, \mathbf{y})$ On input a vector $\mathbf{y} \in V$ and the master secret $\mathcal{MSK}$; this algorithm outputs a secret key $\mathcal{SK}_\mathbf{y}$ for $\mathbf{y}$.*

Encrypt*$(\mathcal{PP}, m, \mathbf{x})$ Takes as input a message m and an attribute vector $\mathbf{x} \in V$ and outputs a ciphertext C.*

Decrypt*$(\mathcal{PP}, C, \mathcal{SK}_\mathbf{y})$ If $\langle \mathbf{x}, \mathbf{y} \rangle = 0$, this algorithm returns the message m and $\perp$ otherwise.*

Correctness. The IPE scheme is said to satisfy the correctness condition if for all vectors $\mathbf{x}, \mathbf{y} \in V$ with $\langle \mathbf{x}, \mathbf{y} \rangle = 0$ and for all $m \in \mathcal{M}$, if $(\mathcal{PP}, \mathcal{MSK}) \xleftarrow{\text{R}}$ Setup(κ, n), $\mathcal{SK}_\mathbf{y} \xleftarrow{\text{R}}$ KeyGen$(\mathcal{MSK}, \mathbf{y})$, $C \xleftarrow{\text{R}}$ Encrypt$(\mathcal{PP}, m, \mathbf{x})$, then $\Pr[m = $ Decrypt$(\mathcal{PP}, C, \mathcal{SK}_\mathbf{y})] = 1$.

Definition 2 (Security). *The security definition for inner product encryption scheme that we consider is weak attribute hiding and adaptive security against chosen plaintext attacks. It is formalised in terms of the following game* ind-wah-cpa *between an adversary $\mathscr{A}$ and a challenger.*

Setup: *The challenger runs the* Setup *algorithm of the IPE and gives the public parameters to $\mathscr{A}$.*

Key Extraction Phase 1: *$\mathscr{A}$ makes a number of key extraction queries adaptively. For a query on a vector $\mathbf{y}$, the challenger responds with a key $\mathcal{SK}_\mathbf{y}$.*

Challenge: *$\mathscr{A}$ provides two pairs of messages and attribute vectors $m_0, \widehat{\mathbf{x}}_0$ and $m_1, \widehat{\mathbf{x}}_1$ with the restriction that if $\mathbf{y}$ is queried in the key extraction phase 1, then $\langle \widehat{\mathbf{x}}_0, \mathbf{y} \rangle \neq 0$ and $\langle \widehat{\mathbf{x}}_1, \mathbf{y} \rangle \neq 0$. The challenger chooses a bit β uniformly at random from $\{0, 1\}$, encrypts m_β to $\widehat{\mathbf{x}}_\beta$ and returns the resulting ciphertext $\widehat{C}$ to $\mathscr{A}$.*

Key Extraction Phase 2: *$\mathscr{A}$ makes more key extraction queries with the restriction that it cannot query a key for any vector $\mathbf{y}$ with $\langle \widehat{\mathbf{x}}_0, \mathbf{y} \rangle = 0$ or $\langle \widehat{\mathbf{x}}_1, \mathbf{y} \rangle = 0$.*

Guess: *$\mathscr{A}$ outputs a bit β'.*
If $\beta = \beta'$, then $\mathscr{A}$ wins the game. The advantage of $\mathscr{A}$ in winning the ind-wah-cpa *is given by*

$$\text{Adv}_{\text{IPE}}^{\text{ind-wah-cpa}}(\mathscr{A}) = \left| \Pr[\beta = \beta'] - \frac{1}{2} \right|.$$

The IPE scheme is said to be (ε, t, q)-IND-WAH-CPA secure if every t-time adversary making at most q key extraction queries has $\text{Adv}_{\text{IPE}}^{\text{ind-wah-cpa}}(\mathscr{A}) \leq \varepsilon$.

We also consider a slightly weaker form of adaptive security denoted IND-CPA-*security where attribute hiding property is not achieved. In the corresponding security game, denoted* ind-cpa, $\widehat{\mathbf{x}}_1 = \widehat{\mathbf{x}}_2$ *that is, there is only one challenge attribute vector* $\widehat{\mathbf{x}}$.

3   Variant of Jutla-Roy Split-CRS NIZK Proof and IBE

In this section, we suggest a small modification to QA-NIZK proofs of Jutla and Roy [JR13] and describe an IBE derived from it. We denote the IBE as $\mathcal{JR}$-$\mathcal{IBE}$-$\mathcal{D}$, the 'd' signifying a sort of 'dual' of the original scheme. $\mathcal{JR}$-$\mathcal{IBE}$-$\mathcal{D}$ forms the basis of our IPE construction with short ciphertexts. Since the QA-NIZK construction only points a way to the IBE construction, we provide an informal description of the modification required without delving into details of the construction or proof. For definitions and more details related to QA-NIZK proofs we refer to [JR13].

We are mainly interested in NIZK proofs for languages that are linear subspaces of vectors of $\mathbb{G}_2$-elements. [JR13] actually considers vectors over $\mathbb{G}_1$. Since $\mathbb{G}_1$ has shorter representation compared to $\mathbb{G}_2$, we prefer the ciphertext components to live in $\mathbb{G}_1$ and hence reverse the roles of $\mathbb{G}_1$ and $\mathbb{G}_2$ in our presentation. A linear subspace language is parameterised by an $t \times m$ matrix $\mathbf{A}$ of $\mathbb{G}_2$-elements and defined as

$$L_{\mathbf{A}} = \{\mathbf{x}^T \mathbf{A} \mid \mathbf{x} \in \mathbb{Z}_p^t\}.$$

A NIZK proof system for this language is a collection of four algorithms $(\mathsf{K}_0, \mathsf{K}_1, \mathsf{P}, \mathsf{V})$ where K_0 generates the common parameters (group descriptions for a pairing), K_1 generates CRS_p and CRS_v, the prover and verifier CRS's respectively, P generates a proof given a witness $\mathbf{x}$ for a candidate $\vec{Q} \in L_{\mathbf{A}}$ and V verifies that the proof is valid. Quasi-adaptiveness refers to the CRS being allowed to depend on the parameter, ($\mathbf{A}$ in the above case). Three notions – completeness, soundness and zero-knowledge – formalise the security requirements of a NIZK proof system. [JR13] starts with an efficient construction for this language and then extends it to what they call the split-CRS QA-NIZK system. The languages supported by such systems are characterised as

$$L_{\mathbf{A}, \vec{A}_1, \vec{A}_2} = \{\mathbf{x}^T \cdot [\mathbf{A} \mid \vec{A}_1 + \mathsf{ctag} \cdot \vec{A}_2] \mid \mathbf{x} \in \mathbb{Z}_p^t, \mathsf{ctag} \in \mathbb{Z}_p\},$$

with $\mathbf{A} \in \mathbb{G}_2^{t \times m}$, $\vec{A}_1, \vec{A}_2 \in \mathbb{G}_2^t$ are parameters defining the language. Writing $\mathbf{A}$ as $[\mathbf{A}_l \mid \mathbf{A}_r]$ with $\mathbf{A}_l \in \mathbb{G}_2^{t \times t}$ and $\mathbf{A}_r \in \mathbb{G}_2^{(m-t) \times t}$ and assuming that the number $(m - t)$ of equations in excess of the number of unknowns can be verified by just making additional randomised copies of the CRS [JR13], we only consider $\mathbf{A}_l$ in our descriptions. The algorithms of the split-CRS NIZK system are described below.

K_0: Generates the bilinear pairing parameters $\mathcal{G} = (p, \mathbb{G}_1, \mathbb{G}_2, \mathbb{G}_T, e, P_1, P_2)$.

K_1: Generates CRS as

$$\mathsf{CRS}_{p,0} = \begin{bmatrix} \mathbf{A}_l | \vec{A}_1 \end{bmatrix} \begin{bmatrix} \mathbf{u}_1 \\ b^{-1} \end{bmatrix} \qquad \mathsf{CRS}_{p,1} = \begin{bmatrix} \mathbf{A}_l | \vec{A}_2 \end{bmatrix} \begin{bmatrix} \mathbf{u}_2 \\ b^{-1} \end{bmatrix}$$

$$\mathsf{CRS}_{v,0} = \begin{bmatrix} b\mathbf{u}_1 \\ 1 \\ -b \end{bmatrix} P_1 \qquad \mathsf{CRS}_{v,1} = \begin{bmatrix} b\mathbf{u}_2 \\ 0 \\ 0 \end{bmatrix} P_1,$$

where $\mathbf{u}_1, \mathbf{u}_2 \xleftarrow{\mathsf{U}} \mathbb{Z}_p^t$ and $b \xleftarrow{\mathsf{U}} \mathbb{Z}_p^\times$. Note that $\mathsf{CRS}_{v,0}, \mathsf{CRS}_{v,1} \in \mathbb{G}_1^{t+2}$.

P: Suppose the candidate is $\vec{Q} = \mathbf{x}^T \cdot [\mathbf{A} | \vec{A}_1 + \mathsf{ctag} \cdot \vec{A}_2]$. The proof is given by

$$\vec{R} = \mathbf{x}^T (\mathsf{CRS}_{p,0} + \mathsf{ctag} \cdot \mathsf{CRS}_{p,1}).$$

V: Given a proof $\vec{R}$ for a candidate $\vec{Q}$, the verifier checks whether

$$e\left([\vec{R} \,|\, \vec{Q}], \mathsf{CRS}_{v,0} + \mathsf{ctag} \cdot \mathsf{CRS}_{v,1}\right)$$

equals 1_T, the identity of $\mathbb{G}_T$ or not indicating validity of the proof or otherwise, respectively. Here the pairing function e evaluated on vectors is nothing but the product of the component-wise evaluations.

Our Modification. We are now ready to propose our tweak to this split-CRS NIZK system. Instead of combining the verifier CRS's during verification, consider providing only one verifier CRS defined as

$$\mathsf{CRS}_v = \mathsf{CRS}_{v,0} + \mathsf{ktag}\,\mathsf{CRS}_{v,1}$$

where $\mathsf{ktag} \xleftarrow{\mathsf{U}} \mathbb{Z}_p$ is chosen in K_1. Verification is now done by testing whether

$$e\left([\vec{R} \,|\, \vec{Q}], \mathsf{CRS}_v\right)^{\frac{1}{(\mathsf{ctag} - \mathsf{ktag})}}$$

is 1_T only if $\mathsf{ctag} \neq \mathsf{ktag}$. Verification fails unconditionally if the two tags are equal. The modification weakens the quasi-adaptive soundness criterion since there is a probability that the verification algorithm fails. However, we make this modification only to make a transition to attribute-based encryption. Whether this NIZK system is actually useful for other purposes is beyond the scope of this work.

IBE. We now present the identity-based encryption scheme obtained from the above mentioned NIZK system.

$\mathsf{Setup}(\kappa)$: Let $\mathcal{G} = (p, \mathbb{G}_1, \mathbb{G}_2, \mathbb{G}_T, e, F_1, F_2)$ be a Type-3 pairing ensemble generated based on the security parameter κ. Choose $P_1 \xleftarrow{\mathsf{U}} \mathbb{G}_1^\times$, $P_2 \xleftarrow{\mathsf{U}} \mathbb{G}_2^\times$, $b \xleftarrow{\mathsf{U}} \mathbb{Z}_p^\times$, $\alpha_1, \alpha_2, u_1, u_2, v_1, v_2, w_1, w_2 \xleftarrow{\mathsf{U}} \mathbb{Z}_p$ and set $U_1 = (u_1 + bu_2)P_1$, $V_1 = (v_1 + bv_2)P_1$, $W_1 = (w_1 + bw_2)P_1$, $g_T = e(P_1, P_2)^{\alpha_1 + b\alpha_2}$. The parameters are given by

$$\mathcal{PP} : (P_1, bP_1, U_1, V_1, W_1, g_T)$$
$$\mathcal{MSK} : (P_2, \alpha_1, \alpha_2, u_1, u_2, v_1, v_2, w_1, w_2)$$

Encrypt($\mathcal{PP}, m, \mathsf{id}$): The ciphertext is given by $\mathcal{C} = (C_0, C_1, C_2, C_3, \mathsf{ctag})$ where

$$\mathsf{ctag}, s \xleftarrow{\mathsf{U}} \mathbb{Z}_p,$$
$$C_0 = m \cdot (g_T)^s,$$
$$C_1 = sP_1, \ C_2 = sbP_1, \ C_3 = s(U_1 + \mathsf{id}V_1 + \mathsf{ctag}W_1).$$

KeyGen($\mathcal{MSK}, \mathsf{id}$) Compute the secret key $\mathcal{SK}_{\mathsf{id}} = (K_1, K_2, K_3, K_4, K_5, \mathsf{ktag})$ as follows.

$$r, \mathsf{ktag} \xleftarrow{\mathsf{U}} \mathbb{Z}_p,$$
$$K_1 = rP_2, \ K_2 = (\alpha_1 + rw_1)\, P_2, \ K_3 = (\alpha_2 + rw_2)\, P_2$$
$$K_4 = r(u_1 + \mathsf{id}v_1 + \mathsf{ktag}w_1)P_2, \ K_5 = r(u_2 + \mathsf{id}v_2 + \mathsf{ktag}w_2)P_2.$$

Decrypt($\mathcal{C}, \mathcal{SK}_{\mathsf{id}}$): If $\mathsf{ctag} = \mathsf{ktag}$, return $\bot$. Otherwise compute

$$A = \left(\frac{e(C_3, K_1)}{e(C_1, K_4)e(C_2, K_5)} \right)^{\frac{1}{\mathsf{ctag}-\mathsf{ktag}}}$$

and recover the message as

$$m = \frac{C_0 \cdot A}{e(C_1, K_2)e(C_2, K_3)}.$$

The message m can be recovered in a single step involving 3 pairing operations.

Decryption involves the two-equation revocation technique of Sahai and Waters [LSW08] that was also used in Waters IBE [Wat09]. The scheme is adaptively secure under the SXDH assumption. Since $\mathcal{JR}\text{-}IB\mathcal{E}\text{-}\mathcal{D}$ is a special case of $IP\mathcal{E}_1$, its security is implied by that of $IP\mathcal{E}_1$. Hence we omit the proof.

4   IPE with Short Ciphertexts

In this section, we define our first IPE construction $IP\mathcal{E}_1$ with constant-size ciphertexts and show that it is adaptively secure. As mentioned earlier, we use the n-equation revocation technique of Attrapadung and Libert [AL10] to extend $\mathcal{JR}\text{-}IB\mathcal{E}\text{-}\mathcal{D}$ to support inner product encryption. Below is the description of the algorithms of $IP\mathcal{E}_1 = (IP\mathcal{E}_1.\mathsf{Setup}, IP\mathcal{E}_1.\mathsf{Encrypt}, IP\mathcal{E}_1.\mathsf{KeyGen}, IP\mathcal{E}_1.\mathsf{Decrypt})$.

$IP\mathcal{E}_1.\mathsf{Setup}(\kappa, n)$: Generate a Type-3 pairing $\mathcal{G} = (p, \mathbb{G}_1, \mathbb{G}_2, \mathbb{G}_T, e, F_1, F_2)$ based on the security parameter κ. Choose $P_1 \xleftarrow{\mathsf{U}} \mathbb{G}_1^{\times}$, $P_2 \xleftarrow{\mathsf{U}} \mathbb{G}_2^{\times}$, $b \xleftarrow{\mathsf{U}} \mathbb{Z}_p^{\times}$, $\alpha_1, \alpha_2, w_1, w_2 \xleftarrow{\mathsf{U}} \mathbb{Z}_p$, $\mathbf{u}_1 = (u_{1,1}, \ldots, u_{1,n})$, $\mathbf{u}_2 = (u_{2,1}, \ldots, u_{2,n}) \xleftarrow{\mathsf{U}} \mathbb{Z}_p^n$ and set $\mathbf{u} = (\mathbf{u}_1 + b\mathbf{u}_2)P_1$, $w = (w_1 + bw_2)$, $g_T = e(P_1, P_2)^{\alpha_1 + b\alpha_2}$. The parameters are given by

$$\mathcal{PP} : (P_1, bP_1, \mathbf{u}P_1, wP_1, g_T)$$
$$\mathcal{MSK} : (P_2, \alpha_1, \alpha_2, \mathbf{u}_1, \mathbf{u}_2, w_1, w_2)$$

$\mathcal{IPE}_1.\mathsf{Encrypt}(\mathcal{PP}, m, \mathbf{x} = (x_1, \ldots, x_n))$: Components of the ciphertext are computed as follows.

$$\mathsf{ctag}, s \xleftarrow{\mathsf{U}} \mathbb{Z}_p,$$
$$C_0 = m \cdot (g_T)^s,$$
$$C_1 = sP_1, \ C_2 = sbP_1, \ C_3 = s(\langle \mathbf{x}, \mathbf{u} \rangle + \mathsf{ctag} \cdot w)P_1.$$

Note that C_3 can be computed from $\mathbf{u}P_1$, wP_1 and ctag using $n + 1$ scalar multiplications. The ciphertext is given by $\mathcal{C} = (\mathbf{x}, C_0, C_1, C_2, C_3, \mathsf{ctag})$.

$\mathcal{IPE}_1.\mathsf{KeyGen}(\mathcal{MSK}, \mathbf{y} = (y_1, \ldots, y_n))$: The secret key for $\mathbf{y}$ is given by $\mathcal{SK}_\mathbf{y} = (K_1, K_2, K_3, (K_{4,i}, K_{5,i}, \mathsf{ktag}_i)_{i=2}^n)$ where

$$r, (\mathsf{ktag}_i)_{i=2}^n \xleftarrow{\mathsf{U}} \mathbb{Z}_p,$$
$$K_1 = rP_2, \ K_2 = (\alpha_1 + rw_1)P_2, \ K_3 = (\alpha_2 + rw_2)P_2,$$
For $i = 2, \ldots, n$,
$$K_{4,i} = r(-u_{1,1}\frac{y_i}{y_1} + u_{1,i} + \mathsf{ktag}_i w_1)P_2,$$
$$K_{5,i} = r(-u_{2,1}\frac{y_i}{y_1} + u_{2,i} + \mathsf{ktag}_i w_2)P_2.$$

$\mathcal{IPE}_1.\mathsf{Decrypt}(\mathcal{C}, \mathcal{SK}_\mathbf{y})$: Compute $\mathsf{ktag} = \sum_{i=2}^n x_i \mathsf{ktag}_i$. If $\mathsf{ctag} = \mathsf{ktag}$, return $\perp$. Otherwise let

$$A = \left(e(C_3, K_1)e(C_1, \sum_{i=2}^n x_i K_{4,i})^{-1}e(C_2, \sum_{i=2}^n x_i K_5)^{-1} \right)^{\frac{1}{\mathsf{ctag} - \mathsf{ktag}}}.$$

Recover the message as $m = \frac{C_0 \cdot A}{e(C_1, K_2)e(C_2, K_3)}$. As in the IBE, decryption can be done in a single step involving 3 pairings.

Correctness: Let $\mathcal{C} \xleftarrow{\quad} \mathcal{IPE}_1.\mathsf{Encrypt}(\mathcal{PP}, m, \mathbf{x} = (x_1, \ldots, x_n); s)$ where $\mathcal{C} = (\mathbf{x}, C_0, C_1, C_2, C_3, \mathsf{ctag})$ and let $\mathcal{SK}_\mathbf{y} \xleftarrow{\quad} \mathcal{IPE}_1.\mathsf{KeyGen}(\mathcal{MSK}, \mathbf{y} = (y_1, \ldots, y_n); r)$ with $\mathcal{SK}_\mathbf{y} = (K_1, K_2, K_3, (K_{4,i}, K_{5,i}, \mathsf{ktag}_i)_{i=2}^n)$. Suppose $\langle \mathbf{x}, \mathbf{y} \rangle = 0$ and $\mathsf{ktag} = \sum_{i=2}^n x_i \mathsf{ktag}_i \neq \mathsf{ctag}$. First, we look at the computation of A. We have

$$\sum_{i=2}^n x_i K_{4,i} = \sum_{i=2}^n x_i r(-u_{1,1}\frac{y_i}{y_1} + u_{1,i} + \mathsf{ktag}_i w_1)P_2$$

$$= r\left(-\frac{u_{1,1}}{y_1}\sum_{i=2}^n x_i y_i + \sum_{i=2}^n x_i u_{1,i} + w_1 \sum_{i=2}^n x_i \mathsf{ktag}_i \right) P_2$$

$$= r\left(-\frac{u_{1,1}}{y_1}(\langle \mathbf{x}, \mathbf{y} \rangle - x_1 y_1) + \langle \mathbf{x}, \mathbf{u}_1 \rangle - x_1 u_{1,1} + \mathsf{ktag} \cdot w_1 \right) P_2$$

$$= r(\langle \mathbf{x}, \mathbf{u}_1 \rangle + \mathsf{ktag} \cdot w_1) P_2.$$

Similarly, $\sum_{i=2}^n x_i K_{5,i} = r(\langle \mathbf{x}, \mathbf{u}_2 \rangle + \mathsf{ktag} \cdot w_1) P_2$. Combining the two, we get

$$e(C_1, \sum_{i=2}^n x_i K_{4,i})e(C_2, \sum_{i=2}^n x_i K_5) = e(P_1, P_2)^{rs(\langle \mathbf{x}, \mathbf{u} \rangle + \mathsf{ktag} \cdot w)}$$

implying that

$$A = \left(e(C_3, K_1) e(C_1, \sum_{i=2}^{n} x_i K_{4,i})^{-1} e(C_2, \sum_{i=2}^{n} x_i K_5)^{-1} \right)^{\frac{1}{\mathsf{ctag} - \mathsf{ktag}}} = e(P_1, P_2)^{rsw}.$$

The second stage of decryption recovers the message as shown below.

$$\frac{C_0 \cdot A}{e(C_1, K_2) e(C_2, K_3)} = \frac{m \cdot g_T^s \cdot A}{e(sP_1, (\alpha_1 + rw_1)P_2) e(sbP_1, (\alpha_2 + rw_2)P_2)}$$

$$= \frac{m \cdot e(P_1, P_2)^{(\alpha_1 + b\alpha_2)s} \cdot e(P_1, P_2)^{rsw}}{e(P_1, P_2)^{(\alpha_1 + b\alpha_2)s} e(P_1, P_2)^{rsw}}$$

$$= m$$

Before proving security, we describe algorithms that generate the necessary semi-functional objects for a dual system proof. These are required only in the proof.

$I\!P\!E_1.\mathsf{SFEncrypt}(\mathcal{PP}, \mathcal{MSK}, m, \mathbf{x})$: Generate $(\mathcal{C}' = (\mathbf{x}, C_0, C_1, C_2, C_3, \mathsf{ctag})) \xleftarrow{\text{R}} I\!P\!E_1.\mathsf{Encrypt}(\mathcal{PP}, m, \mathbf{x})$. Choose $\mu \xleftarrow{\text{U}} \mathbb{Z}_p$ and generate the semi-functional ciphertext components as follows.

$$C_0 \longleftarrow C_0 \cdot e(P_1, P_2)^{\mu \alpha_1},$$
$$C_1 \longleftarrow C_1 + \mu P_1, \quad C_3 \longleftarrow C_3 + \mu(\langle \mathbf{x}, \mathbf{u}_1 \rangle + \mathsf{ctag} \cdot w_1).$$

Return $\mathcal{C} = (\mathbf{x}, C_0, C_1, C_2, C_3, \mathsf{ctag})$ as the resulting semi-functional ciphertext.

$I\!P\!E_1.\mathsf{SFKeyGen}(\mathcal{PP}, \mathcal{MSK}, \mathbf{y})$: Let $SK'_{\mathbf{y}} = (K_1, K_2, K_3, (K_{4,i}, K_{5,i}, \mathsf{ktag}_i)_{i=2}^{n})$ be obtained by running $I\!P\!E_1.\mathsf{KeyGen}(\mathcal{MSK}, \mathbf{y})$. Pick $\gamma \xleftarrow{\text{U}} \mathbb{Z}_p$ and modify the components of $SK'_{\mathbf{y}}$ as follows:

$$K_2 \longleftarrow K_2 + \gamma P_2, \quad K_3 \longleftarrow K_3 - \tfrac{\gamma}{b} P_2.$$

The semi-functional key given by $SK'_{\mathbf{y}} = (K_1, K_2, K_3, (K_{4,i}, K_{5,i}, \mathsf{ktag}_i)_{i=2}^{n})$ is returned as output.

For a given pair of ciphertext and key satisfying ($\mathsf{ktag} = \sum_{i=2}^{n} x_i \mathsf{ktag}_i) \neq \mathsf{ctag}$ and $\langle \mathbf{x}, \mathbf{y} \rangle = 0$, decryption fails only when both are semi-functional since the message will be blinded by $e(P_1, P_2)^{\mu \gamma}$. It is easy to see that the rest of the semi-functional components get canceled.

We now prove that scheme $I\!P\!E_1$ is adaptively secure, formalised in the theorem below.

Theorem 1. *Scheme $I\!P\!E_1$ is (q, ε, t)-IND-CPA-secure if the $(\varepsilon_{\mathrm{DDH1}}, t_1)$-DDH1 and $(\varepsilon_{\mathrm{DDH2}}, t_2)$-DDH2 assumptions hold in the underlying pairing description $\mathcal{G}$ where $\varepsilon \leq \varepsilon_{\mathrm{DDH1}} + q \cdot \varepsilon_{\mathrm{DDH2}} + (1/p)$ and $t = \max(t_1, t_2) - O(q\rho)$, ρ being the maximum cost of scalar multiplication in either $\mathbb{G}_1$ or $\mathbb{G}_2$.*

Proof Sketch. Let G_0 denote the real security game ind-cpa (defined in Sect. 2.3). The proof proceeds though a sequence of games where we gradually change the distribution of the keys and challenge ciphertext provided to the adversary. At the end is the game where the attacker receives semi-functional encryption of a random message. We first change the ciphertext to semi-functional form and then the q keys provided as answers to the q queries to semi-functional form. There are essentially three main parts in the reduction.

Distinguishing normal and semi-functional ciphertexts: We show that an attacker's ability to distinguish between normal and semi-functional ciphertexts can be leveraged to solve the DDH1 problem. This is clear from the definition of semi-functional ciphertexts. P_1, bP_1 and sbP_1 come from the instance and are sufficient to simulate the correct environment. The DDH1 challenge is embedded in C_1 which is either normal or semi-functional according as the instance is real or random. Since no encoding of b is known in $\mathbb{G}_2$, the simulator itself cannot create a semi-functional key and detect the type of the challenge ciphertext.

Detecting whether k-th key is normal or semi-functional: This is the most crucial stage of the security reduction. Denote by $y_1, \ldots, y_q$ the queries made by the attacker. The first $k - 1$ keys returned are semi-functional and the last $q - k - 1$ keys are normal. The simulator is designed in a way that it can create both normal and semi-functional keys. The DDH2 challenge is embedded in the k-th key and particularly in component K_2. However, for the k-th key the simulator can only create a semi-functional ciphertext with $\mathsf{ctag} = \sum_{i=2}^{n} x_i \mathsf{ktag}_i$. This ensures that the simulator itself cannot detect the type of k-th key and trivially solve DDH2. Furthermore, the tags in the ciphertext and keys need to be uniformly and independently distributed in the attacker's view. This is achieved by setting them as

$$
\begin{pmatrix} \widehat{\mathsf{ctag}} \\ \mathsf{ktag}_2 \\ \vdots \\ \mathsf{ktag}_n \end{pmatrix} = \begin{pmatrix} -\widehat{x}_1 & -\widehat{x}_2 & -\widehat{x}_3 & \cdots & -\widehat{x}_n \\ y_2/y_1 & -1 & 0 & \cdots & 0 \\ y_3/y_1 & 0 & -1 & \cdots & 0 \\ \vdots & \vdots & \vdots & \ddots & \vdots \\ y_n/y_1 & 0 & 0 & \cdots & -1 \end{pmatrix} \begin{pmatrix} v_{2,1} \\ v_{2,2} \\ \vdots \\ v_{2,n} \end{pmatrix}
$$

where $\widehat{\mathsf{ctag}}$ is the tag associated with the challenge ciphertext for the challenge vector $\widehat{\mathbf{x}} = (\widehat{x}_1, \ldots, \widehat{x}_n)$ and $\mathsf{ktag}_2, \ldots, \mathsf{ktag}_n$ are the tags associated with the secret key for $\mathbf{y}_k$. The matrix has determinant $(-1)^n \langle \widehat{\mathbf{x}}, \mathbf{y}_k \rangle / y_1$ which is non-zero because all of $\mathscr{A}$'s queries are such that $\langle \widehat{\mathbf{x}}, \mathbf{y}_k \rangle \neq 0$. (Here y_1 is the first coordinate of $\mathbf{y}_k$). Hence all we need to do is choose $\mathbf{v}_2 = (v_{2,1}, \ldots, v_{2,n})$ uniformly from $\mathbb{Z}_p^n$ and also hide $\mathbf{v}_2$ information theoretically from the attacker. $\mathbf{v}_2$ is in fact embedded in the master secret key (and as a result in the public parameters) but masked by other additive terms. The argument repeated q times for each query gives a degradation of q in DDH2.

Distinguishing the real message from a random one: The last important step is an information theoretic argument to show that the message encrypted is random that is, the bit β is statistically hidden form the attacker. This is done by changing the setup and semi-functional key generation algorithms in such a way that all information provided to the attacker are independent of α_1. The only component that depends on α_1 is C_0 of the challenge ciphertext where the message has a blinding factor of $e(P_1, P_2)^{\mu\alpha_1}$. Since all other information is independent of α_1, $m_\beta \cdot e(P_1, P_2)^{\mu\alpha_1}$ is uniformly distributed in $\mathbb{G}_T$ and thus provides no hint to about β unless $\mu = 0$ which happens with probability $1/p$.

Refer to the full version [Ram16] for details of the proof.

5 Weakly Attribute-Hiding IPE

In this section, we present our second IPE construction $\mathcal{IPE}_2$ for inner products over $\mathbb{Z}_p^n$. Unlike $\mathcal{IPE}_1$, this construction is based on $\mathcal{JR}\text{-}\mathcal{IBE}$. While the n-equation revocation technique was used in [AL10] to obtain constant-size ciphertexts forgoing attribute-hiding, we use it here to anonymise ciphertexts by incorporating the technique into the encryption algorithm. We split the ciphertext component of $\mathcal{JR}\text{-}\mathcal{IBE}$ containing the identity hash into $n-1$ components corresponding to the entries of the attribute vector $\mathbf{x}$. For decryption, the relation $R(\mathbf{x}, \mathbf{y})$ can be verified by combining the ciphertext components using the secret vector $\mathbf{y}$ without knowing $\mathbf{x}$. Described below are the algorithms of $\mathcal{IPE}_2 = (\mathcal{IPE}_2.\mathsf{Setup}, \mathcal{IPE}_2.\mathsf{Encrypt}, \mathcal{IPE}_2.\mathsf{KeyGen}, \mathcal{IPE}_2.\mathsf{Decrypt})$.

$\mathcal{IPE}_2.\mathsf{Setup}(\kappa, n)$: Generate a Type-3 pairing $\mathcal{G} = (p, \mathbb{G}_1, \mathbb{G}_2, \mathbb{G}_T, e, F_1, F_2)$ based on the security parameter κ. Choose $P_1 \xleftarrow{\mathrm{U}} \mathbb{G}_1^\times$, $P_2 \xleftarrow{\mathrm{U}} \mathbb{G}_2^\times$, $b \xleftarrow{\mathrm{U}} \mathbb{Z}_p^\times$, $\alpha_1, \alpha_2, w_1, w_2 \xleftarrow{\mathrm{U}} \mathbb{Z}_p$, $\mathbf{u}_1, \mathbf{u}_2 \xleftarrow{\mathrm{U}} \mathbb{Z}_p^n$ and set $\mathbf{u} = \mathbf{u}_1 + b\mathbf{u}_2$, $w = w_1 + bw_2$ and $g_T = e(P_1, P_2)^{\alpha_1 + b\alpha_2}$. The parameters are given by

$$\mathcal{PP} : (P_1, bP_1, \mathbf{u}P_1, wP_1, g_T)$$
$$\mathcal{MSK} : (P_2, \alpha_1, \alpha_2, \mathbf{u}_1, \mathbf{u}_2, w_1, w_2)$$

$\mathcal{IPE}_2.\mathsf{Encrypt}(\mathcal{PP}, m, \mathbf{x} = (x_1, \ldots, x_n))$: The ciphertext is given by the tuple $\mathcal{C} = (C_0, C_1, C_2, (C_{3,i}, \mathsf{ctag}_i)_{i=2}^n)$ where

$$(\mathsf{ctag}_i)_{i=2}^n, s \xleftarrow{\mathrm{U}} \mathbb{Z}_p,$$
$$C_0 = m \cdot (g_T)^s,$$
$$C_1 = sP_1, \; C_2 = sbP_1,$$
$$C_{3,i} = s\left(-\frac{x_i}{x_1}u_1 + u_i + \mathsf{ctag}_i w\right)P_1 \text{ for } i = 2, \ldots, n.$$

Since $(u_i P_1)_{i \in [1,n]}$ and wP_1 are provided in $\mathcal{PP}$, each $C_{3,i}$ can be computed using 3 scalar multiplications.

$\mathcal{IPE}_2.\mathsf{KeyGen}(\mathcal{MSK}, \mathbf{y} = (y_1, \ldots, y_n))$: Secret key $\mathcal{SK}_{\mathbf{y}} = (K_1, K_2, K_3, K_4, K_5)$ is computed as follows.

$$r \xleftarrow{\mathrm{U}} \mathbb{Z}_p,$$
$$K_1 = rP_2, \; K_2 = (\alpha_1 + r\langle \mathbf{y}, \mathbf{u}_1 \rangle)P_2, \; K_3 = (\alpha_2 + r\langle \mathbf{y}, \mathbf{u}_2 \rangle)P_2$$
$$K_4 = rw_1 P_2, \; K_5 = rw_2 P_2.$$

$IPE_2.\mathsf{Decrypt}(\mathcal{C}, \mathcal{SK}_\mathbf{y}, \mathbf{y})$: Compute $\mathsf{ctag} = \sum_{i=2}^{n} y_i \mathsf{ctag}_i$. Recover the message as follows.

$$m = \frac{C_0 \cdot e(\sum_{i=2}^{n} y_i C_{3,i}, K_1)}{e(C_1, K_2 + \mathsf{ctag}K_4)e(C_2, K_3 + \mathsf{ctag}K_5)}.$$

Correctness. Let $\mathcal{C} \xleftarrow{\text{R}} IPE_2.\mathsf{Encrypt}(\mathcal{PP}, m, \mathbf{x} = (x_1, \ldots, x_n); s)$ and let $\mathcal{SK}_\mathbf{y} \xleftarrow{\text{R}} IPE_2.\mathsf{KeyGen}(\mathcal{MSK}, \mathbf{y} = (y_1, \ldots, y_n); r)$ where $\mathcal{C}$, $\mathcal{SK}_\mathbf{y}$ are given by $(C_0, C_1, C_2, (C_{3,i}, \mathsf{ctag}_i)_{i=2}^n)$, $\mathcal{SK}_\mathbf{y} = (K_1, K_2, K_3, K_4, K_5)$ respectively. Suppose $\langle \mathbf{x}, \mathbf{y} \rangle = 0$ and $\mathsf{ctag} = \sum_{i=2}^{n} y_i \mathsf{ctag}_i$. Let $A_1 = e(\sum_{i=2}^{n} y_i C_{3,i}, K_1)$ and $A_2 = e(C_1, K_2 + \mathsf{ctag}K_4)e(C_2, K_3 + \mathsf{ctag}K_5)$. Decryption is correct if $A_2/A_1 = (g_T)^s$. We have

$$
\begin{aligned}
A_1 &= e\left(\sum_{i=2}^{n} y_i C_{3,i}, K_1 \right) \\
&= e\left(\sum_{i=2}^{n} y_i s \left(-\frac{x_i u_1}{x_1} + u_i + \mathsf{ctag}_i w \right) P_1, r P_2 \right) \\
&= e\left(\left(-(\langle \mathbf{y}, \mathbf{x} \rangle - x_1 y_1)\frac{u_1}{x_1} + \langle \mathbf{y}, \mathbf{u} \rangle - y_1 u_1 + \mathsf{ctag} \cdot w \right) P_1, P_2 \right)^{rs} \\
&= e(P_1, P_2)^{rs(\langle \mathbf{y}, \mathbf{u} \rangle + \mathsf{ctag} \cdot w)},
\end{aligned}
$$

and

$$
\begin{aligned}
A_2 &= e(C_1, K_2 + \mathsf{ctag}K_4)e(C_2, K_3 + \mathsf{ctag}K_5) \\
&= e(sP_1, (\alpha_1 + r\langle \mathbf{y}, \mathbf{u}_1 \rangle) P_2 + \mathsf{ctag} \cdot r w_1 P_2) \\
&\quad \cdot e(sbP_1(\alpha_2 + r\langle \mathbf{y}, \mathbf{u}_2 \rangle) P_2 + \mathsf{ctag} \cdot r w_2 P_2) \\
&= e(P_1, (\alpha_1 + b\alpha_2)P_2)^s e(P_1, r(\langle \mathbf{y}, \mathbf{u}_1 \rangle + b\langle \mathbf{y}, \mathbf{u}_2 \rangle + \mathsf{ctag}(w_1 + bw_2))P_2)^s \\
&= (g_T)^s \cdot e(P_1, (\langle \mathbf{y}, \mathbf{u}_1 + b\mathbf{u}_2 \rangle + \mathsf{ctag} \cdot w)P_2)^{rs} \\
&= (g_T)^s \cdot e(P_1, P_2)^{rs(\langle \mathbf{y}, \mathbf{u} \rangle + \mathsf{ctag} \cdot w)}
\end{aligned}
$$

thus implying that $A_2/A_1 = (g_T)^s$, as desired.

Security. The theorem below summarises the security guarantee we obtain for IPE_2.

Theorem 2. *Scheme IPE_2 is (q, ε, t)-IND-WAH-CPA-secure if the $(\varepsilon_{\mathrm{DDH1}}, t_1)$-DDH1 and $(\varepsilon_{\mathrm{DDH2}}, t_2)$-DDH2 assumptions hold in the underlying pairing description $\mathcal{G}$ where $\varepsilon \leq \varepsilon_{\mathrm{DDH1}} + q \cdot \varepsilon_{\mathrm{DDH2}} + (1/p)$ and $t = \max(t_1, t_2) - O(q\rho)$, ρ being the maximum cost of scalar multiplication in either $\mathbb{G}_1$ or $\mathbb{G}_2$.*

The proof is more or less similar to the proof of Theorem 1 except for the information theoretic argument in the last step. In addition to showing that the blinding factor on the message is uniformly random in the attacker's view, we also need to prove that the attribute vector is hidden from the adversary. The solution is to simulate the key extraction queries in such a way that all information the attacker sees is independent of $\mathbf{u}_1$. Observe that $\mathbf{u}_1$ is part of the master secret and would also be used to define the semi-functional components for $C_{3,i}$. With all keys and parameters being independent of $\mathbf{u}_1$, one can argue that $C_{3,i}$ components are uniform and independent elements of $\mathbb{G}_1$ thus providing no hint about which attribute vector the challenge ciphertext is encrypted to. (This makes sense as the only ciphertext components determined by the attribute vector are $C_{3,i}$ for $i = 2, \ldots, n$). A detailed proof is provided in the full version [Ram16].

Acknowledgements. I would like to thank Benoit Libert and Palash Sarkar for helpful discussions as well as the reviewers of ACNS'16 for their valuable comments. This research was funded by the "Programme Avenir Lyon Saint-Etienne de l'Universite de Lyon" in the framework of the programme "Investissements d'Avenir" (ANR-11-IDEX-0007).

References

[AL10] Attrapadung, N., Libert, B.: Functional encryption for inner product: achieving constant-size ciphertexts with adaptive security or support for negation. In: Nguyen, P.Q., Pointcheval, D. (eds.) PKC 2010. LNCS, vol. 6056, pp. 384–402. Springer, Heidelberg (2010)

[Att14] Attrapadung, N.: Dual system encryption via doubly selective security: framework, fully secure functional encryption for regular languages, and more. In: Nguyen, P.Q., Oswald, E. (eds.) EUROCRYPT 2014. LNCS, vol. 8441, pp. 557–577. Springer, Heidelberg (2014)

[Att15] Attrapadung, N.: Dual system encryption framework in prime-order groups. IACR Cryptology ePrint Archive 2015:390 (2015)

[BKP14] Blazy, O., Kiltz, E., Pan, J.: (Hierarchical) identity-based encryption from affine message authentication. In: Garay, J.A., Gennaro, R. (eds.) CRYPTO 2014, Part I. LNCS, vol. 8616, pp. 408–425. Springer, Heidelberg (2014)

[Boy13] Boyen, X.: Attribute-based functional encryption on lattices. In: Sahai, A. (ed.) TCC 2013. LNCS, vol. 7785, pp. 122–142. Springer, Heidelberg (2013)

[BSW07] Bethencourt, J., Sahai, A., Waters, B.: Ciphertext-policy attribute-based encryption. In: IEEE Symposium on Security and Privacy, pp. 321–334. IEEE Computer Society (2007)

[CG13] Canetti, R., Garay, J.A. (eds.): CRYPTO 2013, Part II. LNCS, vol. 8043. Springer, Heidelberg (2013)

[CGW15] Chen, J., Gay, R., Wee, H.: Improved dual system ABE in prime-order groups via predicate encodings. In: Oswald, E., Fischlin, M. (eds.) EUROCRYPT 2015. LNCS, vol. 9057, pp. 595–624. Springer, Heidelberg (2015)

[CW13] Chen, J., Wee, H.: Fully, (almost) tightly secure IBE and dual system groups. In: Canetti, Garay (eds.) [CG13], pp. 435–460. Full version available as IACR Technical Report, 2013/803. http://eprint.iacr.org/2013/803

[GGH+13] Garg, S., Gentry, C., Halevi, S., Sahai, A., Waters, B.: Attribute-based encryption for circuits from multilinear maps. In: Canetti, Garay (eds.) [CG13], pp. 479–499

[GPSW06] Goyal, V., Pandey, O., Sahai, A., Waters, B.: Attribute-based encryption for fine-grained access control of encrypted data. In: Juels, A., Wright, R.N., De Capitani di Vimercati, S. (eds.) ACM Conference on Computer and Communications Security, pp. 89–98. ACM (2006)

[GVW13] Gorbunov, S., Vaikuntanathan, V., Wee, H.: Attribute-based encryption for circuits. In: Boneh, D., Roughgarden, T., Feigenbaum, J. (eds.) Symposium on Theory of Computing Conference, STOC 2013, Palo Alto, CA, USA, 1–4 June 2013, pp. 545–554. ACM (2013)

[GW09] Gentry, C., Waters, B.: Adaptive security in broadcast encryption systems (with short ciphertexts). In: Joux, A. (ed.) EUROCRYPT 2009. LNCS, vol. 5479, pp. 171–188. Springer, Heidelberg (2009)

[JR13] Jutla, C.S., Roy, A.: Shorter quasi-adaptive NIZK proofs for linear subspaces. In: Sako, K., Sarkar, P. (eds.) ASIACRYPT 2013, Part I. LNCS, vol. 8269, pp. 1–20. Springer, Heidelberg (2013)

[JR15] Jutla, C.S., Roy, A.: Dual-system simulation-soundness with applications to UC-PAKE and more. In: Iwata, T., Cheon, J.H. (eds.) ASIACRYPT 2015. LNCS, vol. 9452, pp. 628–653. Springer, Heidelberg (2015). doi: 10.1007/978-3-662-48797-6_26

[KSW08] Katz, J., Sahai, A., Waters, B.: Predicate encryption supporting disjunctions, polynomial equations, and inner products. In: Smart, N.P. (ed.) EUROCRYPT 2008. LNCS, vol. 4965, pp. 146–162. Springer, Heidelberg (2008)

[LSW08] Lewko, A.B., Sahai, A., Waters, B.: Revocation systems with very small private keys. IACR Cryptology ePrint Archive 2008:309 (2008)

[LW12] Lewko, A., Waters, B.: New proof methods for attribute-based encryption: achieving full security through selective techniques. In: Safavi-Naini, R., Canetti, R. (eds.) CRYPTO 2012. LNCS, vol. 7417, pp. 180–198. Springer, Heidelberg (2012)

[OSW07] Ostrovsky, R., Sahai, A., Waters, B.: Attribute-based encryption with non-monotonic access structures. In: Ning, P., De Capitani di Vimercati, S., Syverson, P.F. (eds.) ACM Conference on Computer and Communications Security, pp. 195–203. ACM (2007)

[OT08] Okamoto, T., Takashima, K.: Homomorphic encryption and signatures from vector decomposition. In: Galbraith, S.D., Paterson, K.G. (eds.) Pairing 2008. LNCS, vol. 5209, pp. 57–74. Springer, Heidelberg (2008)

[OT09] Okamoto, T., Takashima, K.: Hierarchical predicate encryption for inner-products. In: Matsui, M. (ed.) ASIACRYPT 2009. LNCS, vol. 5912, pp. 214–231. Springer, Heidelberg (2009)

[OT10] Okamoto, T., Takashima, K.: Fully secure functional encryption with general relations from the decisional linear assumption. In: Rabin, T. (ed.) CRYPTO 2010. LNCS, vol. 6223, pp. 191–208. Springer, Heidelberg (2010)

[OT11] Okamoto, T., Takashima, K.: Achieving short ciphertexts or short secret-keys for adaptively secure general inner-product encryption. In: Lin, D., Tsudik, G., Wang, X. (eds.) CANS 2011. LNCS, vol. 7092, pp. 138–159. Springer, Heidelberg (2011)

[Ram16] Ramanna, S.C.: More efficient constructions for inner-product encryption. Cryptology ePrint Archive, Report 2016/356 (2016). http://eprint.iacr.org/

[RS14a] Ramanna, S.C., Sarkar, P.: Efficient adaptively secure IBBE from standard assumptions. IACR Cryptology ePrint Archive 2014:380 (2014)

[RS14b] Ramanna, S.C., Sarkar, P.: Efficient (anonymous) compact HIBE from standard assumptions. In: Chow, S.S.M., Liu, J.K., Hui, L.C.K., Yiu, S.M. (eds.) ProvSec 2014. LNCS, vol. 8782, pp. 243–258. Springer, Heidelberg (2014)

[SW05]   Sahai, A., Waters, B.: Fuzzy identity-based encryption. In: Cramer, R. (ed.) EUROCRYPT 2005. LNCS, vol. 3494, pp. 457–473. Springer, Heidelberg (2005)

[Wat09] Waters, B.: Dual system encryption: realizing fully secure IBE and HIBE under simple assumptions. In: Halevi, S. (ed.) CRYPTO 2009. LNCS, vol. 5677, pp. 619–636. Springer, Heidelberg (2009)

[Wat11] Waters, B.: Ciphertext-policy attribute-based encryption: an expressive, efficient, and provably secure realization. In: Catalano, D., Fazio, N., Gennaro, R., Nicolosi, A. (eds.) PKC 2011. LNCS, vol. 6571, pp. 53–70. Springer, Heidelberg (2011)

[Wee14] Wee, H.: Dual system encryption via predicate encodings. In: Lindell, Y. (ed.) TCC 2014. LNCS, vol. 8349, pp. 616–637. Springer, Heidelberg (2014)

Attribute Based Encryption with Direct Efficiency Tradeoff

Nuttapong Attrapadung[1]([✉]), Goichiro Hanaoka[1], Tsutomu Matsumoto[2],
Tadanori Teruya[1], and Shota Yamada[1]

[1] National Institute of Advanced Industrial Science and Technology (AIST),
Tokyo, Japan
{n.attrapadung,hanaoka-goichiro,tadanori.teruya,
yamada-shota}@aist.go.jp
[2] Yokohama National University, Yokohama, Japan
tsutomu@ynu.ac.jp

Abstract. We propose the first fully secure unbounded Attribute-Based
Encryption (ABE) scheme such that the key size and ciphertext size can
be directly traded off. Our proposed scheme is parameterized by a positive integer d, which can be arbitrarily chosen at setup. In our scheme,
the ciphertext size is $O(t/d)$, the private key size is $O(md)$, and the public key size is $O(d)$, where t, m are the sizes of attribute sets and policies
corresponding to ciphertext and private key, respectively.

Our scheme can be considered as a generalization that includes two
of the state-of-the-art ABE instantiations, namely, the unbounded ABE
scheme and the ABE scheme with constant-size ciphertexts proposed by
Attrapadung (Eurocrypt 2014). Indeed, these two schemes correspond
to the two extreme cases of our scheme, that is, when setting $d = 1$ and
when setting d as the maximum size of allowed attribute sets, respectively. Furthermore, our scheme also yields a tradeoff between encryption and decryption time. Interestingly, when estimating efficiency using
numerical parameters, the decryption time is minimized at d being somewhere in the middle of the spectrum.

We believe that this tradeoff can provide advantages in applications
where size and/or time resources are concretely fixed in advance, as we
can flexibly adjust d to match available resources and thus make the most
of them. Such situations include, but are not limited to, implementations
of ABE in tiny hardware tokens.

Keywords: Attribute-based encryption · Efficiency tradeoff ·
Unbounded · Short ciphertext · Full security

1 Introduction

Attribute-based encryption (ABE), introduced by Sahai and Waters [23], is a
useful paradigm that generalizes traditional public key encryption. Instead of
encrypting to a target recipient, a sender can specify in a more general way

© Springer International Publishing Switzerland 2016
M. Manulis et al. (Eds.): ACNS 2016, LNCS 9696, pp. 249–266, 2016.
DOI: 10.1007/978-3-319-39555-5_14

about who should be able to view the message. In ABE for predicate R, which is a boolean function $R : \mathbb{X} \times \mathbb{Y} \to \{0, 1\}$, a private key, which is issued by an authority, is associated with an attribute $X \in \mathbb{X}$, while a ciphertext encrypting a message M is associated with an attribute $Y \in \mathbb{Y}$. A key for X can decrypt a ciphertext for Y if and only if $R(X, Y) = 1$. In this paper, we focus on ABE for boolean formulae predicate, which is one of the most useful ABE primitive, first considered by Goyal et al. [13]. For simplicity, we mainly consider the *key-policy* type of ABE [13][1]. In such a scheme, a key is associated with a boolean formula (a policy), while a ciphertext is associated with an assignment of boolean variables (an attribute set), and the decryption succeeds if and only if the assignment satisfies the formula. In what follows, we let t be the size of an attribute set corresponding to a ciphertext and m be the size of a policy corresponding to a private key.

Two of the state-of-the-art *fully-secure*[2] ABE schemes for boolean formulae were proposed by Attrapadung [2]:

1. The first scheme is the fully-secure *unbounded* ABE of [2]. Such a scheme has a (completely) unbounded property where every parameter does not require any maximum bound at the setup of the scheme. All the other ABE schemes for boolean formulae in the literature either have bounds in some parameters [10, 16,18–21,26] and/or only selectively secure[3] [15,17,22]. This scheme has an obvious advantage in that the scheme has scalability in their *functionality*, in particular, it works for any sizes of attribute sets and policies, and any number of attribute multi-use in one policy. In this scheme, the ciphertext size is $O(t)$ (or more precisely, ct group elements for a constant $c > 1$) and the key size is $O(m)$.

2. The second scheme is the fully-secure ABE with *constant-size ciphertexts* of [2]. All the other constant-size-ciphertext ABE schemes for boolean formulae in the literature are only selectively secure [6] or semi-adaptively secure[4] [11,24]. This scheme has an advantage of scalability in *efficiency*: it requires very short ciphertexts of size $O(1)$, regardless of any t, which is the size of an attribute set assigned to a ciphertext. On the downside, it requires the maximum bound for t, say T, to be fixed at the setup (but no bound is required for all the other parameters). Moreover, the key size is quite large as it becomes $O(mT)$.

Note that the above two schemes were originally proposed in composite-order groups in [2]. Their prime-order variants, which are considered more efficient (*cf.* [14]), were then subsequently obtained in [3].

---

[1] The other types are ciphertext-policy [8,25] and dual-policy [5] ABE.

[2] Full security (or also called adaptive security) is the standard security notion for ABE. In this notion, the adversary can adaptively query keys for any attribute X as long as $R(X, Y^*) = 0$ where Y^* is an adversarially and adaptively chosen attribute for the challenge ciphertext.

[3] Selective security refers to a weak notion where the adversary is required to announce the challenge ciphertext attribute Y^* upfront before seeing the public key.

[4] Semi-adaptive security is an intermediate notion between selective and full security.

Due to the drawback of the first scheme in that the ciphertext size is not constant (hence we may say that it lacks scalability in efficiency) and the drawbacks of the second scheme in that the key size is large and the attribute set size is bounded (and hence it lacks scalability in functionality), it is natural to seek for a new scheme with better scalability in both efficiency and functionality.

To this end, we consider the following important open problem:

Is it possible to achieve fully-secure *unbounded* ABE with *short ciphertext size* (less than t group elements)?

We note that constructing even only *selectively* secure ABE with the above property is also an open problem.

Our Contribution. In this paper, we answer the above question affirmatively by proposing a new fully-secure unbounded ABE scheme with a *direct tradeoff* between ciphertext and key size: the ciphertext size is $O(t/d)$ and the key size is $O(md)$, where the "adjusting parameter" d is any positive integer which can be arbitrarily chosen at setup. The efficiency comparison is shown in Table 1 below.

Table 1. Comparison among fully-secure KP-ABE

Scheme	|secret key|	|ciphertext|
Unbounded ABE of [2,3]	$O(m)$	$O(t)$
Constant-size-ciphertext ABE of [2,3]	$O(mT)$	$O(1)$
Our new schemes	$O(md)$	$O(t/d)$

† m is the size of policy associated to a private key.
t is the attribute set size associated to a ciphertext.
T is the maximum bound of t (if bounded).

Our tradeoff scheme can be thought of a generalization that includes both the unbounded ABE and the constant-size-ciphertext ABE of [2,3] as the two extreme cases on the spectrum over the tradeoff parameter d. That is, when setting $d = 1$, we recover the unbounded ABE, while setting $d = T$ (and thus posing the maximum bound of t) gives us back the constant-size-ciphertext ABE.

Adjusting d also consequently results in a tradeoff between encryption time and decryption time. We give the performance estimation in Sect. 4, where we show the efficiency comparison in details and more concretely in Tables 2, 3 and 4. Interestingly, as shown in Fig. 1, when estimating efficiency using numerical parameters, *e.g.,* from the 254-bit Barreto-Naehrig (BN) curve, the decryption time is minimized at d being somewhere in the middle of the spectrum.

Our Approach. Our new scheme is constructed based on Key-Policy over Doubly Spatial Encryption (KP-DSE) scheme, which is a primitive introduced also in [2] (with a prime-order version subsequently proposed in [3]). KP-DSE was shown to imply both the unbounded ABE and the constant-size-ciphertext ABE in [2]. We extend these implications by showing a new conversion from KP-DSE to KP-ABE with tradeoff, which is our goal. Applying this new conversion to the KP-DSE schemes of [2] and [3], we obtain a new KP-ABE with tradeoff in composite-order groups and prime-order groups, respectively.

Our idea for achieving the ciphertext of size $O(t/d)$ is to first partition the attribute set (of size t) associated to a ciphertext to t/d disjoint subsets each of size d. We then associate each subset by encoding it to an affine subspace in KP-DSE. Due to the efficiency of the concrete KP-DSE scheme of [2] where each affine space requires a corresponding ciphertext portion of constant size, the total ciphertext size is thus $O(t/d)$, the number of partitioned subsets. The fact that we require an affine subspace to encode a set of size d results in an increasing factor d for the key size, hence the tradeoff.

We describe our approach in details in Sect. 3. Before that, we give the definition of KP-DSE in Sect. 2.

Perspective. We believe that the tradeoff property of our scheme can provide advantages in real-world applications where size and/or time resources are concretely fixed in advance, as we can flexibly adjust d to match available resources and thus make the most of them. Such situations include, but are not limited to, implementations of ABE in tiny hardware tokens, such as secure applications for the Internet of Things.

2 Preliminaries

2.1 Definitions for ABE

Predicate Family. Let $R = \{R_\kappa : \mathbb{X}_\kappa \times \mathbb{Y}_\kappa \rightarrow \{0,1\} | \kappa \in \mathbb{N}^c\}$ be a predicate family where $\mathbb{X}_\kappa$ and $\mathbb{Y}_\kappa$ denote "key attribute" and "ciphertext attribute" spaces and c is some fixed constant. The index $\kappa = (n_1, n_2, \ldots, n_c)$ denotes some bounds for parameters specific to each predicate family.

ABE Syntax. An attribute-based encryption (ABE) scheme for predicate family R is defined by the following algorithms:

- Setup($1^\lambda, \kappa$) $\rightarrow$ (PK, MSK): takes as input a security parameter 1^λ and a family index κ of predicate family R, and outputs a master public key PK and a master secret key MSK.
- Encrypt($Y, M, $PK) $\rightarrow$ CT: takes as input a ciphertext attribute $Y \in \mathbb{Y}_\kappa$, a message $M \in \mathcal{M}$, and public key PK. It outputs a ciphertext CT.
- KeyGen($X, $MSK, PK) $\rightarrow$ SK: takes as input a key attribute $X \in \mathbb{X}_\kappa$ and the master key MSK. It outputs a secret key SK.
- Decrypt(CT, SK) $\rightarrow$ M: given a ciphertext CT with its attribute Y and the decryption key SK with its attribute X, it outputs a message M or $\perp$.

Correctness. Consider all indexes κ, all $M \in \mathcal{M}$, $X \in \mathbb{X}_\kappa$, $Y \in \mathbb{Y}_\kappa$ such that $R_\kappa(X, Y) = 1$. If Encrypt($Y, M, $PK) $\rightarrow$ CT and KeyGen($X, $MSK, PK) $\rightarrow$ SK where (PK, MSK) is generated from Setup($1^\lambda, \kappa$), then Decrypt(CT, SK) $\rightarrow$ M.

Security. The standard notion for ABE is called full security. We refer its definition to [2], as we do not work directly on it but rather use the embedding lemma for implications below (Lemma 1).

KP-ABE for Monotone Span Program Predicates. Let $\mathcal{U}$ be the universe of attributes. If $|\mathcal{U}|$ is of super-polynomial size, it is called large universe [13,22], otherwise, it is small universe. This predicate is indexed by $N \in \mathbb{N}$. In this predicate, the key attribute domain $\mathbb{X}_N$ is the set of all policies. A policy is specified by a monotone span program (or access structure) (A, π) where A is a matrix in $\mathbb{Z}_N^{m \times k}$ for some $m, k \in \mathbb{N}$, and π is a map $\pi : [1, m] \to \mathcal{U}$. The ciphertext attribute domain is the collection of all sets, S, of attributes in $\mathcal{U}$. For a set $S \subseteq \mathcal{U}$, let $A|_S$ be the sub-matrix of A that takes all the rows j such that $\pi(j) \in S$. We say that (A, π) accepts S if $(1, 0, \dots, 0) \in \mathsf{rspan}(A|_S)$, where $\mathsf{rspan}()$ denotes the row span. That is,

$$R_N^{\mathsf{KP\text{-}ABE}}((A, \pi), S) = 1 \iff (1, 0, \dots, 0) \in \mathsf{span}\{A_i | \pi(i) \in S\}.$$

In this paper, we consider unbounded KP-ABE, which is KP-ABE with large universe such that all parameters $|S|, m, k$ and the number of attribute re-use (the repetition in the range $\pi([1, m])$) are unbounded. It is well known that ABE for monotone span program implies ABE for monotone Boolean formulae [13].

2.2   KP-DSE

Our new KP-ABE scheme will use an implication from KP-DSE [2]. We briefly review it here.

Notions for Affine Spaces. Let $N, n, d \in \mathbb{N}$ where $0 \le d \le n$. Let $\boldsymbol{t}^\top$ be a vertical vector in $\mathbb{Z}_N^n$. Let $\boldsymbol{M} \in \mathbb{Z}_N^{n \times d}$ be a matrix whose columns are all linearly independent. An affine space in $\mathbb{Z}_N^n$ specified by a pair $(\boldsymbol{t}, \boldsymbol{M})$ is defined as $\boldsymbol{t}^\top + \mathsf{cspan}(\boldsymbol{M})$, where $\mathsf{cspan}()$ denotes the column span; more precisely, it is

$$\boldsymbol{t}^\top + \mathsf{cspan}(\boldsymbol{M}) = \{\boldsymbol{t}^\top + \boldsymbol{M}\boldsymbol{v}^\top | \boldsymbol{v} \in \mathbb{Z}_N^d\}.$$

Key-Policy over Doubly Spatial Encryption (KP-DSE). The predicate for KP-DSE is defined as follows. The predicate family is indexed by $(N, n) \in \mathbb{N}^2$. Define the key attribute domain $\mathbb{X}_{(N,n)}$ as the set of all pairs of an access matrix $A \in \mathbb{Z}_N^{m \times k}$ for any polynomial-size $m, k \in \mathbb{N}$ and a labelling map π that maps each row in $[1, m]$ to an affine space in $\mathbb{Z}_N^n$. Define the ciphertext attribute domain $\mathbb{Y}_{(N,n)}$ as the collection of all sets, T, of affine spaces in $\mathbb{Z}_N^n$. The predicate evaluation is defined by

$$R_{(N,n)}^{\mathsf{KP\text{-}DSE}}((A, \pi), T) = 1 \iff$$
$$(1, 0, \dots, 0) \in \mathsf{span}\{A_i | \exists Y \in T \text{ s.t. } \pi(i) \cap Y \neq \emptyset\}.$$

2.3   Embedding Lemma

The following useful lemma from [4,9] describes a sufficient criterion for implication from ABE for a given predicate to ABE for another predicate. We will use this lemma in Sect. 3.1 for showing that KP-DSE implies KP-ABE with tradeoff, which is our main proposal.

The lemma considers two arbitrary predicate families:

$$R_\kappa^{\mathsf{F}} : \mathbb{X}_\kappa \times \mathbb{Y}_\kappa \to \{0,1\}, \qquad R_{\kappa'}^{\mathsf{F}'} : \mathbb{X}_{\kappa'}' \times \mathbb{Y}_{\kappa'}' \to \{0,1\},$$

which is parametrized by $\kappa \in \mathbb{N}^c$ and $\kappa' \in \mathbb{N}^{c'}$ respectively. Suppose that there exists three efficient mappings

$$f_{\mathsf{p}} : \mathbb{Z}^{c'} \to \mathbb{Z}^c \qquad f_{\mathsf{e}} : \mathbb{X}_{\kappa'}' \to \mathbb{X}_{f_{\mathsf{p}}(\kappa')} \qquad f_{\mathsf{k}} : \mathbb{Y}_{\kappa'}' \to \mathbb{Y}_{f_{\mathsf{p}}(\kappa')}$$

which maps parameters, ciphertext attributes, and key attributes, respectively, such that for all $X' \in \mathbb{X}_{\kappa'}', Y' \in \mathbb{Y}_{\kappa'}'$,

$$R_{\kappa'}^{\mathsf{F}'}(X', Y') = 1 \quad \Leftrightarrow \quad R_{f_{\mathsf{p}}(\kappa')}^{\mathsf{F}}(f_{\mathsf{e}}(X'), f_{\mathsf{k}}(Y')) = 1. \qquad (1)$$

We can then construct an ABE scheme

$$\Pi' = \{\mathsf{Setup}', \mathsf{Encrypt}', \mathsf{KeyGen}', \mathsf{Decrypt}'\} \text{ for predicate } R_{\kappa'}^{\mathsf{F}'}$$

from an ABE scheme

$$\Pi = \{\mathsf{Setup}, \mathsf{Encrypt}, \mathsf{KeyGen}, \mathsf{Decrypt}\} \text{ for predicate } R_\kappa^{\mathsf{F}}$$

by letting

$$\mathsf{Setup}'(\lambda, \kappa') = \mathsf{Setup}(\lambda, f_{\mathsf{p}}(\kappa'))$$
$$\mathsf{Encrypt}'(\mathsf{PK}, M, X') = \mathsf{Encrypt}(\mathsf{PK}, M, f_{\mathsf{e}}(X')),$$
$$\mathsf{KeyGen}'(\mathsf{MSK}, \mathsf{PK}, Y') = \mathsf{KeyGen}(\mathsf{MSK}, \mathsf{PK}, f_{\mathsf{k}}(Y')),$$
$$\mathsf{Decrypt}'(\mathsf{CT}_{X'}, \mathsf{SK}_{Y'}) = \mathsf{Decrypt}(\mathsf{CT}_{f_{\mathsf{e}}(X')}, \mathsf{SK}_{f_{\mathsf{k}}(Y')}).$$

Lemma 1 (Embedding lemma [4,9]). *If Π is correct and secure, then so is Π'. This holds for both the cases of selective security and full security.*

2.4   Notations

Notation for Matrix in the Exponents. Vectors will be treated as either row or column matrices. When unspecified, we shall let it be a row vector. Let $\mathbb{G}$ be a group. Let $\boldsymbol{a} = (a_1, \ldots, a_n)$ and $\boldsymbol{b} = (b_1, \ldots, b_n) \in \mathbb{G}^n$. We denote $\boldsymbol{a} \cdot \boldsymbol{b} = (a_1 \cdot b_1, \ldots, a_n \cdot b_n)$, where '$\cdot$' is the group operation of $\mathbb{G}$. For $g \in \mathbb{G}$ and $\boldsymbol{c} = (c_1, \ldots, c_n) \in \mathbb{Z}^n$, we denote $g^{\boldsymbol{c}} = (g^{c_1}, \ldots, g^{c_n})$. We denote by $\mathbb{GL}_{p,n}$ the group of invertible matrices (the general linear group) in $\mathbb{Z}_p^{n \times n}$. Consider $\boldsymbol{M} \in \mathbb{Z}_p^{d \times n}$

(the set of all $d \times n$ matrices in $\mathbb{Z}_p$). Denote the transpose of M as $M^\top$. Denote $M^{-\top} = (M^\top)^{-1}$. We denote by g^M the matrix in $\mathbb{G}^{d \times n}$ of which its (i, j) entry is $g^{M_{i,j}}$, where $M_{i,j}$ is the (i, j) entry of M. For $Q \in \mathbb{Z}_p^{\ell \times d}$, we denote $(g^Q)^M = g^{QM}$. Note that from M and $g^Q \in \mathbb{G}^{\ell \times d}$, we can compute g^{QM} without knowing Q, since its (i, j) entry is $\prod_{k=1}^d (g^{Q_{i,k}})^{M_{k,j}}$. The same goes for g^M and Q. For $X \in \mathbb{Z}_p^{r \times c_1}$ and $Y \in \mathbb{Z}_p^{r \times c_2}$, we denote its pairing as:

$$e(g_1^X, g_2^Y) = e(g_1, g_2)^{Y^\top X} \in \mathbb{G}_T^{c_2 \times c_1}.$$

Projection Maps. As used in [3], $\left(\begin{smallmatrix} I_b \\ 0 \end{smallmatrix} \right)$ denotes the $(b+1) \times b$ matrix where the first b rows comprise the identity matrix while the last row is zero. It functions as a left-projection map. That is, $X \left(\begin{smallmatrix} I_b \\ 0 \end{smallmatrix} \right) \in \mathbb{Z}_p^{(d+1) \times d}$ is the matrix consisting of all left d columns of X for any $X \in \mathbb{Z}_p^{(d+1) \times (d+1)}$. Similarly, $\left(\begin{smallmatrix} 0 \\ 1 \end{smallmatrix} \right)$ is the $(b+1) \times 1$ matrix where the last row is 1; it functions as a right-projection map.

3   Our Key-Policy ABE Schemes

Main Idea for Our Scheme. The main idea for our new KP-ABE scheme is that we set an parameter d and partition the attribute set S to a disjoint union[5] as $S = S_1 \sqcup \cdots \sqcup S_\ell$ where $|S_j| \leq d$ for all $j \in [1, \ell]$ and $\ell = \lceil |S|/d \rceil$. We then represent each subset S_j by an affine space using an embedding method similar to the KP-ABE with constant-size ciphertext of [2] (which extends [6]). This method results in KP-DSE with the set of ℓ affine spaces in $\mathbb{Z}_N^{d+1}$. An implementation using the KP-DSE of [2] requires $O(\ell)$-size ciphertext for the set of ℓ affine spaces. Hence, we will achieve the ciphertext size of $O(\ell) = O(|S|/d)$ as desired.

Partitioned KP-ABE. As an intermediate predicate family, we define "partitioned KP-ABE" (for monotone span program). The purpose is only syntactic: to have a predicate family that is indexed also by the adjustable integer d. (The original definition has only index N specifying $\mathbb{Z}_N$). More precisely, it is indexed by $(N, d) \in \mathbb{N}^2$. The key attribute domain is the same as normal KP-ABE. The ciphertext attribute domain is the set of all collections of disjointed subsets of $\mathcal{U}$ each with size $\leq d$. The predicate evaluation is defined by

$$R_{(N,d)}^{\text{Partition-KP-ABE}}((A, \pi), U) = 1 \iff$$
$$(1, 0, \ldots, 0) \in \text{span}\{A_i | \exists W \in U \text{ s.t. } \pi(i) \in W\}.$$

(Here, U is a collection of disjointed subsets of $\mathcal{U}$ each with size $\leq d$.)

Partitioned KP-ABE implies Normal KP-ABE. Partitioned KP-ABE immediately implies KP-ABE by mapping ciphertext attribute as

$$S \mapsto \{S_1, \cdots S_\ell\}$$

---

[5] We denote by '$\sqcup$' the union of disjointed sets.

where $S = S_1 \sqcup \cdots \sqcup S_\ell$ where $|S_j| \le d$ for all $j \in [1, \ell]$ and $\ell = \lceil |S|/d \rceil$. To obtain a unique partition, we can arrange attributes in S in a lexicographical order as $S = \{b_1, \ldots, b_{|S|}\}$ and let $S_j = \{b_{(j-1)d+1}, \ldots, b_{jd}\}$ for all $j \in [1, \ell - 1]$ (and hence, $S_\ell = \{b_{(\ell-1)d+1}, \ldots, b_{|S|}\}$). Straightforwardly, we have the following lemma:

Lemma 2. *For any monotone access structure* $\mathbb{A} = (A, \pi)$*, any attribute set* S*, and* $\{S_j\}_j$ *defined as above, we have*

$$R_N^{\mathsf{KP\text{-}ABE}}((A, \pi), S) = 1 \quad \Longleftrightarrow \quad R_{(N,d)}^{\mathsf{Partition\text{-}KP\text{-}ABE}}((A, \pi), \{S_1, \cdots S_\ell\}) = 1.$$

Proof. This trivially holds since $\pi(i) \in S$ iff there exists $j \in [1, \ell]$ such that $\pi(i) \in S_j$.

3.1 Implication of Partitioned KP-ABE from KP-DSE

We now show that partitioned KP-ABE is implied from KP-DSE. The conversion is as follows.

- **Mapping Parameters.** We map $f_{\mathsf{p}} : (N, d) \mapsto (N, d+1)$. That is, we let the full dimension of affine spaces be $n = d + 1$.
- **Mapping Key Attributes.** Consider an access structure $\mathbb{A} = (A, \pi)$. Let m be the number of rows of the access matrix A. We map

$$f_{\mathsf{k}} : \mathbb{A} = (A, \pi) \mapsto \mathbb{A}' = (A, \pi')$$

where for $i = 1, \ldots, m$, we let $\pi'(i) = \mathsf{cspan}(\boldsymbol{X}^{(i)})$ where

$$\boldsymbol{X}^{(i)} := \begin{pmatrix} -\pi(i) & -\pi(i)^2 & \cdots & -\pi(i)^d \\ 1 & & & \\ & 1 & & \\ & & \ddots & \\ & & & 1 \end{pmatrix}.$$

In particular, each $\pi'(i)$ is an affine space passing through the point $\boldsymbol{0}^\top$ (*i.e.*, it is a vector space).

- **Mapping Ciphertext Attributes.** Consider a disjoint collection $\{S_1, \ldots, S_\ell\}$ where $|S_j| \le d$ for all $j \in [1, \ell]$. We map

$$f_{\mathsf{c}} : \{S_1, \ldots, S_\ell\} \mapsto \{\boldsymbol{y}^{(1)}, \ldots, \boldsymbol{y}^{(\ell)}\}$$

where for $j = 1, \ldots, \ell$, we let $\boldsymbol{y}^{(i)}$ be 0-dimensional affine space (a point) as

$$\boldsymbol{y}^{(j)} := (a_{j,0}, a_{j,1}, \ldots, a_{j,d})^\top.$$

where we define $a_{j,\iota}$ to be the coefficient of z^ι in $p_j(z) := \prod_{y \in S_j}(z - y) = a_{j,0} + a_{j,1}z + \cdots + a_{j,d}z^d$.

We show the following lemma for the above conversion. The implication from KP-DSE to KP-ABE will then follow from the embedding lemma.

Lemma 3. *For any monotone access structure* $\mathbb{A} = (A, \pi)$ *and a collection* $\{S_1, \ldots, S_\ell\}$ *where each* $|S_j| \leq d$, *we have*

$$R_d^{\text{Partition-KP-ABE}}(\mathbb{A}, \{S_1, \ldots, S_\ell\}) = 1 \iff$$
$$R_{f_p(d)}^{\text{KP-DSE}}(f_k(\mathbb{A}), f_c(\{S_1, \ldots, S_\ell\})) = 1.$$

Proof. From the definition of the KP-DSE predicate, to prove the statement of the theorem, it suffices to prove that for all $i \in [1, m], j \in [1, \ell]$,

$$\pi(i) \in S_j \iff \boldsymbol{y}^{(j)} \in \text{cspan}(\boldsymbol{X}^{(i)}) \tag{2}$$

Forward Direction $(\Rightarrow)$. Suppose $\pi(i) \in S_j$. Thus, $p_j(\pi(i)) = 0$ (by the definition of p_j). Therefore,

$$\begin{aligned}
\boldsymbol{X}^{(i)}(\boldsymbol{a}^{(j)})^\top &= \big(-(a_{j,1}\pi(i) + \cdots + a_{j,d}\pi(i)^d), a_{j,1}, \ldots, a_{j,d}\big)^\top \\
&= (a_{j,0}, a_{j,1}, \ldots, a_{j,d})^\top \\
&= \boldsymbol{y}^{(j)},
\end{aligned}$$

where we use the fact that $p_j(\pi(i)) = a_{j,0} + a_{j,1}\pi(i) + \cdots + a_{j,d}\pi(i)^d = 0$ in the second line. From this, we obtain that $\boldsymbol{y}^{(j)} \in \text{cspan}(\boldsymbol{X}^{(i)})$, which is the the right-hand side of (2), as desired. This concludes the forward part.

Backward Direction $(\Leftarrow)$. We prove by contrapositive. Suppose $\pi(i) \notin S_j$. Hence, $p_j(\pi(i)) \neq 0$. Suppose for contradiction that $\boldsymbol{y}^{(j)} \in \text{cspan}(\boldsymbol{X}^{(i)})$. Hence there is a linear combination $\boldsymbol{v}^\top = (v_1, \ldots, v_d)^\top$ such that

$$\boldsymbol{X}^{(i)}\boldsymbol{v}^\top = \boldsymbol{y}^{(j)}. \tag{3}$$

Thus, by our definitions of $\boldsymbol{X}^{(i)}, \boldsymbol{y}^{(j)}$, we must have that

$$\big(-(v_1\pi(i) + \cdots + v_d\pi(i)^d), v_1, \ldots, v_d\big)^\top = (a_{j,0}, a_{j,1}, \ldots, a_{j,d})^\top$$

But this implies that $p_j(\pi(i)) = 0$, a contradiction. Therefore, $\boldsymbol{y}^{(j)} \notin \text{cspan}(\boldsymbol{X}^{(i)})$. This concludes the proof for the backward part.

3.2 Our KP-ABE in Composite-Order Groups

In this subsection, we apply our KP-DSE-to-KP-ABE conversion above to the KP-DSE scheme in composite-order groups proposed in [2]. We use asymmetric groups instead of symmetric groups as defined for the original scheme in [2].

The scheme will use a composite-order asymmetric bilinear group generator $\mathcal{G}_{\text{composite}}$ which outputs $(\mathbb{G}_1, \mathbb{G}_2, \mathbb{G}_T, e, N, p_1, p_2, p_3) \xleftarrow{\$} \mathcal{G}_{\text{composite}}(\lambda)$, where $\mathbb{G}_1, \mathbb{G}_2, \mathbb{G}_T$ are of order $N = p_1 p_2 p_3$. The bilinear map takes the form $e : \mathbb{G}_1 \times \mathbb{G}_2 \to \mathbb{G}_T$. Let $\mathbb{G}_{1,p_i}, \mathbb{G}_{2,p_i}$ be the subgroup of order p_i of $\mathbb{G}_1, \mathbb{G}_2$ respectively. The scheme is as follows.

- Setup($1^\lambda, d$): Generate a composite-order group parameter as $(\mathbb{G}_1, \mathbb{G}_2, \mathbb{G}_T, e, N, p_1, p_2, p_3) \xleftarrow{\$} \mathcal{G}_{\text{composite}}(\lambda)$. Pick generators $g_1 \xleftarrow{\$} \mathbb{G}_{1,p_1}$, $g_2 \in \mathbb{G}_{2,p_1}$, and $Z_3 \xleftarrow{\$} \mathbb{G}_{2,p_3}$. Pick $\boldsymbol{h} = (h_0, h_1, \ldots, h_{d+1}, \phi_1, \phi_2, \phi_3, \eta) \xleftarrow{\$} \mathbb{Z}_N^{d+6}$ and $\alpha \xleftarrow{\$} \mathbb{Z}_N$. The public key is PK $= (g_1, g_2, e(g_1, g_2)^\alpha, g_1^{\boldsymbol{h}}, Z_3)$. The master secret key is MSK $= \alpha$.

- Encrypt(S, M, PK): Upon input a set $S \subseteq \mathbb{Z}_N$, do as follows.
  1. Let $\ell = \lceil |S|/d \rceil$. Partition S to a disjoint union as $S = S_1 \sqcup \cdots \sqcup S_\ell$ where $|S_j| \le d$ for all $j \in [1, \ell]$. For all $j \in [1, \ell]$, let $a_{j,\iota}$ be the coefficient of z^ι in $p_j(z) := \prod_{y \in S_j}(z - y)$.
  2. Pick $s, w, s_1, \ldots, s_\ell \xleftarrow{\$} \mathbb{Z}_N$. Output a ciphertext CT $= (C_0, C_1, C_2, C_3, C_4, \{C_{5,j}, C_{6,j}\}_{j \in [1,\ell]})$ where we let $C_0 = (e(g_1, g_2)^\alpha)^s M \in \mathbb{G}_T$ and

$$C_1 = g_1^s, \qquad\qquad\qquad C_2 = g_1^{s\eta},$$
$$C_3 = g_1^{s\phi_1 + w\phi_2}, \qquad\qquad C_4 = g_1^w,$$
$$C_{5,j} = g_1^{w\phi_3 + s_j(h_0 + h_1 a_{j,0} + \cdots + h_{d+1} a_{j,d})}, \qquad C_{6,j} = g_1^{s_j}$$

- KeyGen($(A, \pi), \text{MSK}, \text{PK}$): Upon input an access structure (A, π), where $A \in \mathbb{Z}_N^{m \times k}$ and $\pi : [1, m] \to \mathbb{Z}_N$ for some $m, k \in \mathbb{N}$, do as follows. Parse MSK $= \alpha$. Pick randomly $r, u, r_1, \ldots, r_m, v_2, \ldots, v_k \xleftarrow{\$} \mathbb{Z}_N$. Define $v_1 = r\phi_2$ and let $\boldsymbol{v} = (v_1, \ldots, v_k)$. Compute a secret key $\boldsymbol{K} = (K_1, K_2, K_3, \{K_{4,i}, K_{5,i}, \boldsymbol{K}_{6,i}\}_{i \in [1,m]})$ as

$$K_1 = g_2^{\alpha + r\phi_1 + u\eta},$$
$$K_2 = g_2^u,$$
$$K_3 = g_2^r,$$
$$K_{4,i} = g_2^{A_i \boldsymbol{v}^\top + r_i \phi_3},$$
$$K_{5,i} = g_2^{r_i},$$
$$\boldsymbol{K}_{6,i} = \left(g_2^{r_i h_0}, g_2^{r_i\left(h_2 - h_1 \pi(i)\right)}, \ldots, g_2^{r_i\left(h_{d+1} - h_1 \pi(i)^d\right)} \right).$$

Pick a randomness mask $\boldsymbol{R} \xleftarrow{\$} \mathbb{G}_{2,p_3}^{3+(d+3)m}$ (hence, $\boldsymbol{R}$ is of the same length as $\boldsymbol{K}$). Output a secret key SK $= \boldsymbol{K} \cdot \boldsymbol{R}$ (here, '$\cdot$' denotes the component-wise multiplication).

- Decrypt(CT, SK): Parse $(S, (A, \pi))$ from CT, SK. Assume (A, π) accepts S, so that the decryption can be performed. Let $I := \{i \in [1, m] | \pi(i) \in S\}$. From the property of LSSS, we have reconstruction coefficients $\{\mu_i\}_{i \in I}$ such that $\sum_{i \in I} \mu_i A_i \boldsymbol{v}^\top = v_1(= r\phi_2)$. Do as follows
  1. For all $i \in I$, do as follows. Let j_i be the index such that $\pi(i) \in S_{j_i}$. (There is such an index since $\pi(i) \in S$ for all $i \in I$). Parse $\boldsymbol{K}_{6,i} = (K_{6,i,0}, \ldots, K_{6,i,d})$. Compute

$$D_{6,i} := K_{6,i,0} \cdot K_{6,i,1}^{a_{j_1}} \cdots K_{6,i,d}^{a_{j_d}}.$$

(Also recall that $a_{j,\iota}$ be the coefficient of z^ι in $p_j(z) := \prod_{y \in S_j}(z - y)$.)

2. Compute $e(g_1, g_2)^{\alpha s} = L_1 L_2$ where

$$L_1 := e(C_1, K_1)e(C_2, K_2)^{-1}e(C_3, K_3)^{-1},$$
$$L_2 := \prod_{i \in I} \left(e(C_4, K_{4,i})e(C_{5,j_i}, K_{5,i})^{-1}e(C_{6,j_i}, D_{6,i}) \right)^{\mu_i}. \tag{4}$$

3. Finally compute $M \leftarrow C_0/e(g_1, g_2)^{\alpha s}$.

Security. The full security of the above scheme follows from the full security of the KP-DSE scheme in [2] and the embedding lemma for our KP-DSE-to-KP-ABE conversion. This is captured in the theorem below. We refer the Subgroup Decision Assumptions and the Expanded Diffie-Hellman Exponent (EDHE3, EDHE4) Assumptions to [2]. The notation $\mathsf{Adv}_{\mathcal{A}}^{P}(\lambda)$ denotes the advantage of an adversary $\mathcal{A}$ against the security of primitive or assumption P, in function of the security parameter λ. We also refer its precise definition for each assumption in [2].

Theorem 1. *The above KP-ABE is fully-secure under the Subgroup Decision Assumption 1,2,3, the $(d+1, \ell)$-EDHE3, and the $(d+1, m, k)$-EDHE4 Assumption (in asymmetric composite-order groups), where d is the adjustable integer, $\ell = \lceil |S|/d \rceil$, where S is the ciphertext query, and m, k are the maximum numbers of rows and columns of access matrices among all key queries, respectively. More precisely, for any ppt adversary $\mathcal{A}$, let q_1 denote the number of queries in phase 1, there exist ppt algorithms $\mathcal{B}_1, \mathcal{B}_2, \mathcal{B}_3, \mathcal{B}_4, \mathcal{B}_5$, whose running times are the same as $\mathcal{A}$ plus some polynomial times, such that for any λ,*

$$\mathsf{Adv}_{\mathcal{A}}^{\mathsf{KP\text{-}ABE}}(\lambda) \leq 2\mathsf{Adv}_{\mathcal{B}_1}^{\mathsf{SD1}}(\lambda) + (2q_1 + 3)\mathsf{Adv}_{\mathcal{B}_2}^{\mathsf{SD2}}(\lambda) + \mathsf{Adv}_{\mathcal{B}_3}^{\mathsf{SD3}}(\lambda)$$
$$+ q_1\mathsf{Adv}_{\mathcal{B}_4}^{(d+1,m,k)\text{-}\mathsf{EDHE4}}(\lambda) + \mathsf{Adv}_{\mathcal{B}_5}^{(d+1,\ell)\text{-}\mathsf{EDHE3}}(\lambda).$$

Proof. This follows immediately from the KP-DSE-to-KP-ABE implication (*i.e.*, Lemma 1 via Lemmas 2 and 3) and the security of KP-DSE of [2] (*i.e.*, Theorems 1, 11 and 12 in [2]).

3.3   Our KP-ABE in Prime-Order Groups

In this subsection, we apply our KP-DSE-to-KP-ABE conversion to the KP-DSE scheme in prime-order groups proposed in [3] (which is then converted from [2]). The security is based on the Matrix Diffie-Hellman Assumption with parameter $b \in \mathbb{N}$. When $b = 1$, we can use the SXDH Assumption, and when $b = 2$, we can use the Decision Linear Assumption.

The scheme will use a prime-order asymmetric bilinear group generator $\mathcal{G}_{\mathsf{prime}}$ which outputs $(\mathbb{G}_1, \mathbb{G}_2, \mathbb{G}_T, e, p) \xleftarrow{\$} \mathcal{G}_{\mathsf{prime}}(\lambda)$, where $\mathbb{G}_1, \mathbb{G}_2, \mathbb{G}_T$ are of order p. The bilinear map takes the form $e : \mathbb{G}_1 \times \mathbb{G}_2 \to \mathbb{G}_T$. The scheme is as follows.

- Setup($1^\lambda, d$): Run $(\mathbb{G}_1, \mathbb{G}_2, \mathbb{G}_T, e, p) \xleftarrow{\$} \mathcal{G}_{\mathsf{prime}}(\lambda)$. Pick generators $g_1 \xleftarrow{\$} \mathbb{G}_1$, $g_2 \xleftarrow{\$} \mathbb{G}_2$. Pick $\boldsymbol{H}_0, \boldsymbol{H}_1, \ldots, \boldsymbol{H}_{d+5}, \xleftarrow{\$} \mathbb{Z}_p^{(b+1)\times(b+1)}$. Pick $\boldsymbol{B} \xleftarrow{\$} \mathbb{GL}_{p,b+1} \subset$

$\mathbb{Z}_p^{(b+1)\times(b+1)}$. Choose $\tilde{D} \xleftarrow{\$} \mathbb{GL}_{p,b}$, define $D := \left(\begin{smallmatrix} \tilde{D} & 0 \\ 0 & 1 \end{smallmatrix}\right) \in \mathbb{GL}_{p,b+1}$ and $Z :=$
$B^{-\top}D$. Choose $\alpha \xleftarrow{\$} \mathbb{Z}_p^{(b+1)\times 1}$. Output

$$\mathsf{PK} = \left(e(g_1,g_2)^{\alpha^\top B\left(\begin{smallmatrix} I_b \\ 0 \end{smallmatrix}\right)}, g_1^{B\left(\begin{smallmatrix} I_b \\ 0 \end{smallmatrix}\right)}, \left\{ g_1^{H_i B\left(\begin{smallmatrix} I_b \\ 0 \end{smallmatrix}\right)} \right\}_{i\in[0,d+5]} \right),$$

$$\mathsf{MSK} = \left(g_2^{\alpha}, g_2^{Z\left(\begin{smallmatrix} I_b \\ 0 \end{smallmatrix}\right)}, \left\{ g_2^{H_i^\top Z\left(\begin{smallmatrix} I_b \\ 0 \end{smallmatrix}\right)} \right\}_{i\in[0,d+5]} \right).$$

- Encrypt$(S \subset \mathbb{Z}_p, M, \mathsf{PK})$: Upon input a set $S \subseteq \mathbb{Z}_p$, do as follows.
  1. Let $\ell = \lceil |S|/d \rceil$. Partition S to a disjoint union as $S = S_1 \sqcup \cdots \sqcup S_\ell$ where $|S_j| \le d$ for all $j \in [1,\ell]$. For all $j \in [1,\ell]$, let $a_{j,\iota}$ be the coefficient of z^ι in $p_j(z) := \prod_{y \in S_j}(z - y)$.
  2. Pick $s_0, w, s_1, \ldots, s_\ell \xleftarrow{\$} \mathbb{Z}_p^{b\times 1}$. Output a ciphertext as $\mathsf{CT} = (C_1, C_2, C_3, C_4, \{C_{5,j}, C_{6,j}\}_{j\in[1,\ell]}, C_0)$ where

$$C_1 = g_1^{B\left(\begin{smallmatrix} s_0 \\ 0 \end{smallmatrix}\right)},$$

$$C_2 = g_1^{H_{d+5} B\left(\begin{smallmatrix} s_0 \\ 0 \end{smallmatrix}\right)},$$

$$C_3 = g_1^{H_{d+2} B\left(\begin{smallmatrix} s_0 \\ 0 \end{smallmatrix}\right) + H_{d+3} B\left(\begin{smallmatrix} w \\ 0 \end{smallmatrix}\right)},$$

$$C_4 = g_1^{B\left(\begin{smallmatrix} w \\ 0 \end{smallmatrix}\right)},$$

$$C_{5,j} = g_1^{H_{d+4} B\left(\begin{smallmatrix} w \\ 0 \end{smallmatrix}\right) + (H_0 B + a_{j,0} H_1 B + \cdots + a_{j,d} H_{d+1} B)\left(\begin{smallmatrix} s_j \\ 0 \end{smallmatrix}\right)},$$

$$C_{6,j} = g_1^{B\left(\begin{smallmatrix} s_j \\ 0 \end{smallmatrix}\right)},$$

and $C_0 = e(g_1,g_2)^{\alpha^\top B\left(\begin{smallmatrix} s_0 \\ 0 \end{smallmatrix}\right)} \cdot M \in \mathbb{G}_T$.

- KeyGen$((A,\pi), \mathsf{MSK})$: Upon input an access structure (A,π), where $A \in \mathbb{Z}_N^{m\times k}$ and $\pi : [1,m] \to \mathbb{Z}_N$ for some $m, k \in \mathbb{N}$, do as follows. Parse $\mathsf{MSK} = \alpha$. Pick randomly $r, u, r_1, \ldots, r_m, v_2, \ldots, v_k \xleftarrow{\$} \mathbb{Z}_p^{b\times 1}$. Output a secret key $\mathsf{SK} = (K_1, K_2, K_3, \{K_{4,i}, K_{5,i}, K_{6,i,j}\}_{i\in[1,m], j\in[0,d]})$ where

$$K_1 = g_2^{\alpha + H_{d+2}^\top Z\left(\begin{smallmatrix} r \\ 0 \end{smallmatrix}\right) + H_{d+5}^\top Z\left(\begin{smallmatrix} u \\ 0 \end{smallmatrix}\right)},$$

$$K_2 = g_2^{Z\left(\begin{smallmatrix} u \\ 0 \end{smallmatrix}\right)},$$

$$K_3 = g_2^{Z\left(\begin{smallmatrix} r \\ 0 \end{smallmatrix}\right)},$$

$$K_{4,i} = g_2^{A_{i,1} H_{d+3}^\top Z\left(\begin{smallmatrix} r \\ 0 \end{smallmatrix}\right) + \sum_{j=2}^k A_{i,j} Z\left(\begin{smallmatrix} v_j \\ 0 \end{smallmatrix}\right) + H_{d+4}^\top Z\left(\begin{smallmatrix} r_i \\ 0 \end{smallmatrix}\right)},$$

$$K_{5,i} = g_2^{Z\left(\begin{smallmatrix} r_i \\ 0 \end{smallmatrix}\right)},$$

$$K_{6,i,0} = g_2^{H_0^\top Z\left(\begin{smallmatrix} r_i \\ 0 \end{smallmatrix}\right)},$$

$$\forall j\in[1,d] \quad K_{6,i,j} = g_2^{(H_{j+1}^\top - \pi(i)^j H_1^\top) Z\left(\begin{smallmatrix} r_i \\ 0 \end{smallmatrix}\right)}.$$

- Decrypt(CT, SK): Suppose (A, π) accepts the set S. Let $I = \{i \in [1, m] | \pi(i) \in S\}$. Compute coefficients $\{\mu_i\}_{i \in I}$ such that $\sum_{i \in I} \mu_i A_i = (1, 0, \ldots, 0)$. Do as follows

  1. For all $i \in I$, do as follows. Let j_i be the index such that $\pi(i) \in S_{j_i}$. (There is such an index since $\pi(i) \in S$ for all $i \in I$). Compute

$$D_{6,i} := K_{6,i,0} \cdot K_{6,i,1}^{a_{j_1}} \cdots K_{6,i,d}^{a_{j_d}}.$$

  (Also recall that $a_{j,\iota}$ be the coefficient of z^ι in $p_j(z) := \prod_{y \in S_j}(z - y)$.)

  2. Compute $e(g_1, g_2)^{\boldsymbol{\alpha}^\top B \binom{s_0}{0}} = L_1 \cdot L_2$ where

$$L_1 := e(C_1, K_1) e(C_2, K_2)^{-1} e(C_3, K_3)^{-1},$$

$$L_2 := \prod_{i \in I} \left(e(C_4, K_{4,i}) e(C_{5,\pi(i)}, K_{5,i})^{-1} e(C_{6,\pi(i)}, D_{6,i}) \right)^{\mu_i}.$$

  3. Finally compute $M \leftarrow C_0 / e(g_1, g_2)^{\boldsymbol{\alpha}^\top B \binom{s_0}{0}}$.

Security. The full security of the above scheme follows from the full security of the KP-DSE scheme in [3] and the embedding lemma for our KP-DSE-to-KP-ABE conversion. This is captured in the theorem below. We refer the Matrix Diffie-Hellman Assumption and the Expanded Diffie-Hellman Exponent Assumptions in prime-order subgroups (EDHE3p, EDHE4p) to [3, 12], respectively.

Theorem 2. *The above KP-ABE is fully-secure under the $\mathcal{D}_b$-Matrix-DH, $(d+1, \ell)$-EDHE3p, and $(d+1, m, k)$-EDHE4p Assumptions (in asymmetric prime-order groups), where d is the adjustable integer, $\ell = \lceil |S|/d \rceil$, where S is the ciphertext query, and m, k are the maximum numbers of rows and columns of access matrices among all key queries, respectively. More precisely, for any ppt adversary $\mathcal{A}$, let q_1 denote the number of queries in phase 1, there exist ppt algorithms $\mathcal{B}_1, \mathcal{B}_2, \mathcal{B}_3$, whose running times are the same as $\mathcal{A}$ plus some polynomial times, such that for any λ,*

$$\mathsf{Adv}_{\mathcal{A}}^{\mathsf{KP\text{-}ABE}}(\lambda) \leq (2q_1 + 3)\mathsf{Adv}_{\mathcal{B}_1}^{\mathcal{D}_b\text{-}\mathsf{MatDH}}(\lambda) +$$

$$q_1 \mathsf{Adv}_{\mathcal{B}_2}^{(d+1,m,k)\text{-}\mathsf{EDHE4p}}(\lambda) + \mathsf{Adv}_{\mathcal{B}_3}^{(d+1,\ell)\text{-}\mathsf{EDHE3p}}(\lambda).$$

Proof. This follows immediately from the KP-DSE-to-KP-ABE implication (*i.e.*, Lemma 1 via Lemma 2,3) and the security of the prime-order KP-DSE of [3] (*i.e.*, Theorem 3 in [3] via Theorem 11,12 in [2]). □

4   Efficiency Performance

Optimizing Decryption Time. The decryption time of our scheme can be optimized by reducing the number of pairings, which are the dominant operations. This is done by using the identity $\prod_i e(a_i, b) = e(\prod_i a_i, b)$, where we

Table 2. Comparison for asymptotic efficiency among KP-ABE

Scheme	$\|PK\|$	$\|SK\|$	$\|CT\|$	Enc time	Dec time		Unbounded?
					expo.	pair.	
Unbounded ABE of [2,3]	$O(1)$	$O(m)$	$O(t)$	$O(t)$	$O(m)$	$O(m)$	yes
Const.-$\|CT\|$ ABE of [2,3]	$O(T)$	$O(mT)$	$O(1)$	$O(T)$	$O(mT)$	$O(1)$	no, $T = \max t$
Our new schemes	$O(d)$	$O(md)$	$O(t/d)$	$O(t)$	$O(md)$	$O(\min\{m, t/d\})$	yes

bundle the group-$\mathbb{G}_1$ elements a_i that are paired to the same element of group $\mathbb{G}_2$ (here, it is b).

For simplicity here, we consider the composite-order scheme. The prime-order scheme can be done in a similar manner. In decryption, we can compute the element L_2 also as:

$$L_2 = e(C_4, \prod_{i \in I} K_{4,i}) \cdot \prod_{x=1}^{\ell} \left(e(C_{5,x}, \prod_{\substack{i \in I \\ \text{s.t.} j_i = x}} K_{5,i}^{-\mu_i}) e(C_{6,x}, \prod_{\substack{i \in I \cdot \\ \text{s.t.} j_i = x}} D_{6,i}^{\mu_i}) \right). \quad (5)$$

The original decryption as in Eq. (4) requires at most $2m + 4$ pairings, while the above alternative via Eq. (5) requires $2\ell + 4 = 2t/d + 4$ pairings. To minimize the decryption time, we choose the method of which the cost is the minimum of both.

Beside pairings, the total decryption time also include the cost for exponentiations, which is at most $md + m$ times. Hence, the total decryption time for the composite-order scheme is $c_1(md + m) + c_2(\min\{2m + 4, 2t/d + 4\})$, where c_1, c_2 are the costs for one exponentiation and one pairing, respectively. When fixing all parameters except d, this amount becomes $k_1 d + k_2/d + k_3$ for some constants k_1, k_2, k_3. This is minimized at d being somewhere in the middle (which will depend on k_1, k_2, k_3). This minimization will be depicted in Fig. 1(d) below. We also note that the min function is reflected at the sharp rigs at the leftmost parts of the graphs in Fig. 1(d).

Comparison for Asymptotic Efficiency. We provide a comparison of asymptotic efficiency among ABE schemes in Table 2. We consider fully-secure schemes that are either completely unbounded or admitting constant-size ciphertexts. The schemes that satisfy this criteria are the unbounded ABE of [2,3] and the

Table 3. Efficiency of our prime-order KP-ABE with $b = 1$. Here we use an example with $m = 40, t = 60$.

Adjust d	$\|PK\|$	$\|SK\|$	$\|CT\|$	Enc time		Dec time	
	(# of $\|\mathbb{G}_1\|$)	(# of $\|\mathbb{G}_2\|$)	(# of $\|\mathbb{G}_1\|$)	expo.($\mathbb{G}_1$)	expo.($\mathbb{G}_T$)	expo.($\mathbb{G}_2$)	pair.
General	$2d + 12$	$2md + 6m + 6$	$4t/d + 8$	$2t + 6t/d$	1	$2md + 2m$	$\min\left\{\begin{matrix}4m+8,\\4t/d+8\end{matrix}\right\}$
$d = 1$	14	326	248	480	1	160	168
$d = 4$	20	566	68	210	1	400	68
$d = 20$	52	1846	20	138	1	1680	20

Table 4. Concrete efficiency of our KP-ABE from Table 3 when instantiated using BN curves.

Adjust d	|PK| (bits)	|SK| (bits)	|CT| (bits)	Enc time expo($\mathbb{G}_1$)	expo($\mathbb{G}_T$)	Dec time expo($\mathbb{G}_2$)	pair.	total
General	$(2d+12)$ $\times 509$	$(2md+6m+6)$ $\times 255$	$(4t/d+8)$ $\times 509$	$(2t+6t/d)$ $\times 104$	1 $\times 164$	$(2md+2m)$ $\times 57$	$\min\left\{ \begin{smallmatrix} 4m+8, \\ 4t/d+8 \end{smallmatrix} \right\}$ $\times 342$	
$d=1$	7,126	83,130	126,232	49.8 ms	164 μs	9.1 ms	57.4 ms	66.5 ms
$d=4$	10,180	144,330	34,612	20 ms	164 μs	22.8 ms	23.2 ms	46 ms
$d=20$	26,468	470,730	10,180	14.2 ms	164 μs	95.7 ms	6.8 ms	102.5 ms

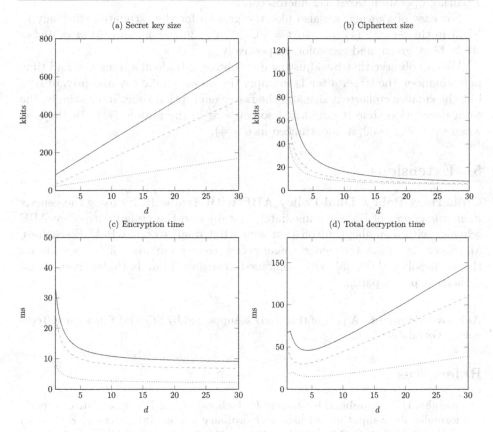

Fig. 1. Efficiency of our scheme when (1) $m=40, t=60$ (blue line), (2) $m=30, t=30$ (green dashed line), (3) $m=10, t=20$ (red dotted line). (Color figure online)

constant-size ciphertext scheme also of [2,3]. All the other schemes in the literature are either only selectively-secure or bounded in some parameters.

Concrete Efficiency. We provide the concrete efficiency of our KP-ABE scheme in prime-order groups. We use the instantiation where $b=1$, to maximize the efficiency, hence the scheme can be based on the SXDH Assumption [3]. To show concrete performance, we use an example with $m=40, t=60$ and vary $d = 1, 4, 20$ in Table 3. We note that we simply directly count the number of respective operations. This can be further improved by considering multi-exponentiation and multi-pairing algorithms (*e.g.*, [27]); we omit it here.

To obtain an even more concrete picture, we instantiate with the 254-bit Barreto-Naehrig (BN) curves in Table 4. Such curves admits the sizes of group elements as follows: $|\mathbb{G}_1| = 509$, $|\mathbb{G}_2| = 255$, and $|\mathbb{G}_T| = 2032$ bits [1]. As for the time performances in these curves, we refer to the implementation of [27], where exponentiations in $\mathbb{G}_1, \mathbb{G}_2, \mathbb{G}_T$ take $104, 57, 164$ microseconds, respectively, while a pairing operation takes 342 microseconds.

For ease of viewing, we also plot the graphs for the estimated efficiency in Fig. 1 in three cases: (1) $m = 40, t = 60$, (2) $m = 30, t = 30$, and (3) $m = 10, t = 20$, in blue, green, and red color, respectively.

We can observe that by adjusting d we obtain a tradeoff among size and time performances: the larger d tends to imply the larger public key and private keys but the smaller ciphertext size and the faster encryption time. Interestingly, the total decryption time is minimized somewhere in the middle (*e.g.*, in the case when $m = 40, t = 60$, it is optimized at $d = 4$).

5   Extensions

Ciphertext-Policy, Dual-Policy ABE with Tradeoff. By using the generic *dual conversion* of [7], we immediately obtain also the ciphertext-policy ABE schemes with a similar tradeoff (but somewhat dual) to our KP-ABE schemes. Moreover, by using the generic *dual-policy conversion* also of [7], we obtain the dual-policy ABE [5] with combined tradeoffs from both key-policy and ciphertext-policy parts.

Acknowledgement. A part of this study is supported by SECOM Science and Technology Foundation.

References

1. Aranha, D.F., Karabina, K., Longa, P., Gebotys, C.H., López, J.: Faster explicit formulas for computing pairings over ordinary curves. In: Paterson, K.G. (ed.) EUROCRYPT 2011. LNCS, vol. 6632, pp. 48–68. Springer, Heidelberg (2011)
2. Attrapadung, N.: Dual system encryption via doubly selective security: framework, fully secure functional encryption for regular languages, and more. In: Nguyen, P.Q., Oswald, E. (eds.) EUROCRYPT 2014. LNCS, vol. 8441, pp. 557–577. Springer, Heidelberg (2014)
3. Attrapadung, N.: Dual System Encryption Framework in Prime-Order Groups. IACR Cryptology ePrint Archive, 2015: 390 (2015). https://eprint.iacr.org/2015/390.pdf
4. Attrapadung, N., Hanaoka, G., Yamada, S.: Conversions among several classes of predicate encryption and applications to ABE with various compactness trade-offs. In: Iwata, T., et al. (eds.) ASIACRYPT 2015. LNCS, vol. 9452, pp. 574–600. Springer, Heidelberg (2015). doi:10.1007/978-3-662-48797-6_24

5. Attrapadung, N., Imai, H.: Dual-policy attribute based encryption. In: Abdalla, M., Pointcheval, D., Fouque, P.-A., Vergnaud, D. (eds.) ACNS 2009. LNCS, vol. 5536, pp. 168–185. Springer, Heidelberg (2009)
6. Attrapadung, N., Libert, B., de Panafieu, E.: Expressive key-policy attribute-based encryption with constant-size ciphertexts. In: Catalano, D., Fazio, N., Gennaro, R., Nicolosi, A. (eds.) PKC 2011. LNCS, vol. 6571, pp. 90–108. Springer, Heidelberg (2011)
7. Attrapadung, N., Yamada, S.: Duality in ABE: converting attribute based encryption for dual predicate and dual policy via computational encodings. In: Nyberg, K. (ed.) CT-RSA 2015. LNCS, vol. 9048, pp. 87–105. Springer, Heidelberg (2015)
8. Bethencourt, J., Sahai, A., Waters, B.: Ciphertext-policy attribute-based encryption. In: IEEE Symposium on Security and Privacy (S&P), pp. 321–334 (2007)
9. Boneh, D., Hamburg, M.: Generalized identity based and broadcast encryption schemes. In: Pieprzyk, J. (ed.) ASIACRYPT 2008. LNCS, vol. 5350, pp. 455–470. Springer, Heidelberg (2008)
10. Chen, J., Gay, R., Wee, H.: Improved dual system abe in prime-order groups via predicate encodings. In: Oswald, E., Fischlin, M. (eds.) EUROCRYPT 2015. LNCS, vol. 9057, pp. 595–624. Springer, Heidelberg (2015)
11. Chen, J., Wee, H.: Semi-adaptive attribute-based encryption and improved delegation for boolean formula. In: Abdalla, M., De Prisco, R. (eds.) SCN 2014. LNCS, vol. 8642, pp. 277–297. Springer, Heidelberg (2014)
12. Escala, A., Herold, G., Kiltz, E., Ràfols, C., Villar, J.: An algebraic framework for diffie-hellman assumptions. In: Canetti, R., Garay, J.A. (eds.) CRYPTO 2013, Part II. LNCS, vol. 8043, pp. 129–147. Springer, Heidelberg (2013)
13. Goyal, V., Pandey, O., Sahai, A., Waters, B.: Attribute-based encryption for fine-grained access control of encrypted data. In: ACM CCS 2006, pp. 89–98 (2006)
14. Guillevic, A.: Comparing the pairing efficiency over composite-order and prime-order elliptic curves. In: Jacobson, M., Locasto, M., Mohassel, P., Safavi-Naini, R. (eds.) ACNS 2013. LNCS, vol. 7954, pp. 357–372. Springer, Heidelberg (2013)
15. Hohenberger, S., Waters, B.: Attribute-based encryption with fast decryption. In: Kurosawa, K., Hanaoka, G. (eds.) PKC 2013. LNCS, vol. 7778, pp. 162–179. Springer, Heidelberg (2013)
16. Kowalczyk, L., Lewko, A.B.: Bilinear entropy expansion from the decisional linear assumption. In: Gennaro, R., Robshaw, M. (eds.) CRYPTO 2015. LNCS, vol. 9216, pp. 524–541. Springer, Heidelberg (2015)
17. Lewko, A., Waters, B.: Unbounded HIBE and attribute-based encryption. In: Paterson, K.G. (ed.) EUROCRYPT 2011. LNCS, vol. 6632, pp. 547–567. Springer, Heidelberg (2011)
18. Lewko, A., Waters, B.: New proof methods for attribute-based encryption: achieving full security through selective techniques. In: Safavi-Naini, R., Canetti, R. (eds.) CRYPTO 2012. LNCS, vol. 7417, pp. 180–198. Springer, Heidelberg (2012)
19. Lewko, A., Okamoto, T., Sahai, A., Takashima, K., Waters, B.: Fully secure functional encryption: attribute-based encryption and (hierarchical) inner product encryption. In: Gilbert, H. (ed.) EUROCRYPT 2010. LNCS, vol. 6110, pp. 62–91. Springer, Heidelberg (2010)
20. Okamoto, T., Takashima, K.: Fully secure functional encryption with general relations from the decisional linear assumption. In: Rabin, T. (ed.) CRYPTO 2010. LNCS, vol. 6223, pp. 191–208. Springer, Heidelberg (2010)
21. Okamoto, T., Takashima, K.: Fully secure unbounded inner-product and attribute-based encryption. In: Wang, X., Sako, K. (eds.) ASIACRYPT 2012. LNCS, vol. 7658, pp. 349–366. Springer, Heidelberg (2012)

22. Rouselakis, Y., Waters, B.: Practical constructions and new proof methods for large universe attribute-based encryption. In: ACM CCS 2013, pp. 463–474 (2013)
23. Sahai, A., Waters, B.: Fuzzy identity-based encryption. In: Cramer, R. (ed.) EURO-CRYPT 2005. LNCS, vol. 3494, pp. 457–473. Springer, Heidelberg (2005)
24. Takashima, K.: Expressive attribute-based encryption with constant-size cipher-texts from the decisional linear assumption. In: Abdalla, M., De Prisco, R. (eds.) SCN 2014. LNCS, vol. 8642, pp. 298–317. Springer, Heidelberg (2014)
25. Waters, B.: Ciphertext-policy attribute-based encryption: an expressive, efficient, and provably secure realization. In: Catalano, D., Fazio, N., Gennaro, R., Nicolosi, A. (eds.) PKC 2011. LNCS, vol. 6571, pp. 53–70. Springer, Heidelberg (2011)
26. Wee, H.: Dual system encryption via predicate encodings. In: Lindell, Y. (ed.) TCC 2014. LNCS, vol. 8349, pp. 616–637. Springer, Heidelberg (2014)
27. Zavattoni, E., Perez, L.D., Mitsunari, S., Sanchez-Ramirez, A., Teruya, T., Rodriguez-Henriquez, F.: Software implementation of an attribute-based encryption scheme. IEEE Trans. Comput. **64**(5), 1429–1441 (2015)

Turing Machines with Shortcuts: Efficient Attribute-Based Encryption for Bounded Functions

Xavier Boyen and Qinyi Li$^{(\boxtimes)}$

Queensland University of Technology, Brisbane, Australia
qinyi.li@student.qut.edu.au

Abstract. We propose a direct construction of attribute-based encryption (ABE) scheme for bounded multi-stack deterministic pushdown automata (DPDAs) and Turing machines that have polynomial runtime in the security parameter. Particularly, we show how to extend our construction to handle bounded DPDAs with two or more stacks, which leads to an ABE scheme for deterministic Turing machines (DTMs) with polynomial runtime.

Our ABE schemes have "input-specific" decryption runtime meaning that the decryption time depends on the semantics of attributes. If a machine halts prematurely on a certain input, its execution can be cut short. To the best of our knowledge, our ABE scheme is the first one that achieves this property and has security proofs based on standard cryptographic assumption.

The key technical ingredient we apply is a special graph encoding on the executions of bounded DPDAs with multi-stacks, allowing us to remember just enough of the execution history to enforce correct evaluation. The security of our scheme is shown to be based on the learning with errors (LWE) problem in the selective security model.

1 Introduction

Attribute-based encryption (ABE) enables the enforcement of complex access control conditions based on expressive decryption keys and ciphertext attributes. In a (key-policy) ABE scheme [15], a decryption key is associated with a Boolean predicate P from a family of predicates $\mathcal{P}$, and a message is encrypted with a public attribute string $\mathbf{w}$. Decryption succeeds iff $P(\mathbf{w}) = 1$. Designing ABE schemes with expressive and efficient access policies is of both theoretical and practical interest. On one hand, the research of ABE results in substantial advances in theoretical cryptography, such as functional encryption, garbling schemes and various of security proof techniques. With its plenty of applications in Cloud storage, access control, and outsourced computations etc., ABE has been shown a promising cryptographic primitive for the "Big Data" era in which huge amount of sensitive data needs to be securely stored and efficiently accessible in an expressive way.

© Springer International Publishing Switzerland 2016
M. Manulis et al. (Eds.): ACNS 2016, LNCS 9696, pp. 267–284, 2016.
DOI: 10.1007/978-3-319-39555-5_15

ABE with Input-Specific Decryption Complexity. Usually, the policy evaluation in decryption algorithms of ABE incurs a heavy computational overhead. As it is mentioned in [12], in most of the previously proposed ABE schemes whose polices are polynomial-size boolean formulas or boolean circuits, the policy evaluation always takes worst-case runtime. With the input-specific runtime, policy evaluation runs in the bare necessary time and could be very fast even for very large inputs. This property is crucial in most real world applications.

A simple example is the filter rule set in firewall systems. In a firewall system, the coming packets are inspected by filters according to a set of filtering rules. These filtering rules are usually sequentially arranged and will be applied to packets sequentially as well. Inspecting one packet under all rules is obviously inefficient. However, it is common practice to arrange the rules so that early accept/reject decisions can be made for most normal packets. As a consequence, decisions will hopefully be made very quickly for most of packets and, thus, efficiency increases. Our Turing machine-ABE scheme with input-specific runtime could see applications in complex filtering-based security systems for encrypted data.

From a practical perspective, it is desirable to design ABE schemes from standard cryptographic assumptions with efficient data access or decryption time. This serves for another motivation of us to design automata-based ABE scheme with input-specific decryption time. In the computation models of various automata, computations of an automaton would finish once it gets to an accept state after reading a prefix of inputs. However, this does not mean all the automata-based ABE schemes have input-specific decryption. In fact, the decryption time in the pairing-based ABE schemes in [2,26], depends on the length but not the content of input attributes, and thus, is not input-specific.

Most interestingly, it is a well-known (if poorly understood) phenomenon that most NP-complete problems exhibit a "phase transition" [9] from easy to hard to easy again, as a certain statistic of the input is varied (such as the ratio of number of clauses to number of variables in random 3-SAT instances). This is why SAT solvers work very well in practice, despite tackling problems that are formally NP-hard. Accordingly, our input-specific runtime constructions open the door to functional policy specifications that are technically NP-complete or NP-hard, but easily computable for inputs of practical interest.

Expressiveness of ABE. One of the central problems in ABE research is how to make predicates and policies ever more expressive. Most ABE schemes handle boolean formulas of polynomial size, with certain restrictions such as a monotonicity requirement. An advance over this model was provided with the pairing-based ABE schemes from [2,26] and lattice-based scheme from [6], where predicates attached to decryption keys are deterministic finite automata (DFAs), and attribute strings attached to ciphertexts are viewed as DFA input strings. Another recent breakthrough in that area came with the construction of ABE schemes for general boolean circuits with polynomial size [4,10,13], using different technical ideas such as multi-linear maps and/or lattices. Assuming the existence of Extractable Witness Encryption and Succinct Non-interactive

Arguments of Knowledge (SNARKS), two very strong and non-standard assumptions, Goldwasser et al. [12] proposed an ABE scheme for any polynomial-time Turing machines. An outstanding feature of the ABE schemes for DFAs from [2,26] and for Turing machines from [12] is that attribute strings could be arbitrarily long, which lead to various interesting applications, such as the innovative audit log system from [26]. However, it should be mentioned that the non-standard computational assumptions in [2,26] require fixing an a priori bound on the input length for the security reduction to obtain, and the construction of [12] came with a price of requirement of strong assumptions which have no satisfactory instantiations. In a different direction, ABE schemes for general circuits [4,10,13] provide obvious versatility benefits, as they enable predicates or policies to be any polynomial-size combinational (memoryless) function. For certain applications where policies have polynomial size, one could convert the policies into circuits on the fly and then apply the ABE schemes for circuits.

In this work, from the perspective of expressiveness of ABE, we focus on extending the notion of ABE for DFAs from [6,26] by providing *memory* taking the form of one or more push-down stacks—yielding a notion of ABE for (bounded) deterministic pushdown automata and Turing machines respectively.

Although the framework of [26] initiated the study of ABE schemes for automata (as opposed to the more traditional boolean formulas and circuits), it did not seem to support any mechanism for "read/write" tapes. Conceptually, two difficulties with implementing secure stack or tape machines are that configurations are exponentially many and time varying. One possible but not very satisfactory answer is to encode the entire memory (e.g., the stack or the tape) atomically into the atomic state or configuration of the machine. A related approach is to unroll an entire (bounded) Turing machine into a boolean circuit, e.g., so that a circuit-oriented ABE scheme [4,10,13] can be used; in this case it is the entire memory across the entire execution that is encoded "atomically" into the circuit as a function of its inputs.

A conceptually more desirable approach is to embrace the nature of the stack or tape as an attached memory, from which only the current element under the read/write head is accessible to the actual state machine, itself possibly very small. This approach requires guarantees that the portion of memory that is temporarily out of sight will not be tampered with—a non-trivial proposition. Our main contribution is to provide a secure way to attach stacks and tapes onto a "seed" ABE for DFA in a flexible and generic way. Based on this, we show how to realise ABE for deterministic state machines with multiple stacks (two stacks are enough to get a Turing machine, though additional stacks will increase efficiency). Our construction is based on the standard LWE assumption, rather than the pairing-based approach of [26].

1.1 Our Results

With above two motivations, we present a direct (key-policy) ABE scheme with input-specific decryption time for multi-stack deterministic pushdown automata

(DPDAs) that have polynomial (in security parameter) runtime. In particular, this yields a (key-policy) ABE scheme for deterministic Turing machines (DTMs) with polynomial (in security parameter) runtime through the equivalence between DTMs and DPDAs with two stacks. We refer to this special type of DPDAs and DTMs as bounded DPDAs and bounded DTMs, respectively, for short. To the best of our knowledge, our construction is the first ABE scheme which directly supports stack automata and has input-specific decryption time from standard cryptographic assumptions.

In our scheme, predicates or policies of users' decryption keys are directly expressed as bounded DPDAs. Messages are encrypted with polynomial-size attribute strings (the length of individual strings can vary). Decryption keys recover messages if and only if the automata recognize the strings attached to the ciphertexts. We prove the security of our scheme in the selective security model, based on the learning with errors problem (LWE).

In general, deterministic pushdown automata refer to single-stack machines. Deterministic pushdown automata with two stacks are much more powerful, being equivalent to deterministic Turing machines (DTMs). Our approach works with an arbitrary number of stacks; we will focus on constructing an ABE scheme for single-stack DPDAs and then show how to extend it easily to two (or more) stacks, to capture the full power of (bounded) deterministic Turing machines.

1.2   Our Approaches

Our approaches stem from the LWE-based ABE scheme for DFAs from [6]. We firstly give a quick review of stack and pushdown automata. A stack is a basic data structure which stores data in such a way that the most recently stored item is the first to be retrieved (also known as "last in, first out" access). Basically, stacks provide two principal operations: "push" a new element to the top of stack and "pop" the top-most element from stack. Stacks provide PDAs with additional memory space making PDAs more powerful than DFAs. A 3-Stack PDA is depicted in the Fig. 1.

We outline our approaches for 1-stack DPDAs. A deterministic pushdown automaton M with one stack is a 7-tuple: $M = (Q, \Sigma, \Gamma, \delta, s_0, z_0, F)$. The input

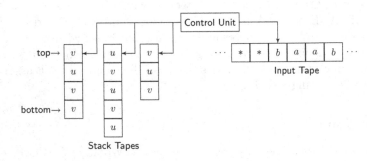

Fig. 1. A 3-Stack Pushdown Automaton

tape of M consists of symbols of an alphabet Σ. We write $\Sigma_\varepsilon = \Sigma \cup \varepsilon$ for the empty symbol ε. The finite internal states of M make up a set Q. $F \subseteq Q$ is a set of accept states. Γ is an alphabet of stack elements. For every execution, M starts from a unique initial state $s_0 \in Q$ and the stack is empty which is indicated by a bottom stack element $z_0 \in \Gamma$. For one computation process of M, a string $\mathbf{w}$ of symbols of Σ, which forms an input tape, is taken as an input. In one step of computation, M takes a current letter of input tape and the top stack element as input, does a stack operation and shifts its state according to a *deterministic* transition function $\delta : \Gamma \times Q \times \Sigma_\varepsilon \to \Gamma \times Q$. For instance, in the transition $\delta(u, s, b) \to (v, s')$, an automaton reads the symbol $b \in \Sigma$, changes the top stack element from u to v, and shifts its state from s to s'. Once M reaches some accept state $s_\omega \in F$, it stops and accepts $\mathbf{w}$. A PDA does not "remember" its execution history. A triple $(\gamma, s, \mathbf{w})$, which is called Instantaneous Description (ID), can be used to track the execution history of a PDA by capturing a "snapshot" of a PDA's execution status. In the ID, $\gamma \in \Gamma^*$ is the current stack contents with sequential order, $s \in Q$ is the current state, and $\mathbf{w} \in \Sigma^*$ is the remaining unread input. An accept ID is $(\gamma', s_\omega, \mathbf{w}')$ where $\gamma \in \Gamma^*$ is the stack contents, $s_\omega \in F$ is a accept state, and $\mathbf{w}' \in \Sigma^*$ is a suffix of $\mathbf{w}$.

The starting point of our construction is to naturally encode the input tapes and the transition function of PDAs into ciphertexts and decryption keys, respectively. We show the idea by describing a toy construction. Let ℓ be the upper bound of the length of all input strings. Let $\mathbf{S}_{z_0}$ and $\mathbf{A}_{s_0}$ be two publicly known matrices represent the unique initial stack element z_0 and state s_0 for all DPDAs. A lattice trapdoor of $[\mathbf{S}_{z_0}||\mathbf{A}_{s_0}]$ serves as the master secret key. A ciphertext of the input tape which contains an input string $\mathbf{w} = w_1 w_2 \ldots w_\ell \in \Sigma^\ell$ has the LWE form

$$\mathbf{s}^\top [\mathbf{S}_{z_0} || \mathbf{A}_{s_0} || \mathbf{G}_{w_1} || \mathbf{G}_{w_2} || \ldots || \mathbf{G}_{w_\ell}] + \boldsymbol{\nu}^\top$$

for a random secret vector $\mathbf{s} \xleftarrow{\$} \mathbb{Z}_q^n$, public matrices $\mathbf{G}_{w_i} \xleftarrow{\$} \mathbb{Z}_q^{n \times m}$, and noise vector $\boldsymbol{\nu}$ from some noise distribution χ. Note $[\mathbf{S}_{z_0}||\mathbf{A}_{s_0}||\mathbf{G}_{w_1}||\mathbf{G}_{w_2}||\ldots||\mathbf{G}_{w_\ell}]$ is just the matrix representation of ID $(s_0, z_0, w_1 w_2 \ldots w_\ell)$ for all the DPDAs in the beginning of execution.

The decryption key of a PDA $M = (Q, \Sigma, \Gamma, \delta, s_0, z_0, F)$ contains a set of low-norm transition matrices $\{\mathbf{R}_\delta\}$ such that a transition $\delta(u, s, b) \to (v, s')$ (where $s \notin F$) is mathematically abstracted as a matrix multiplication $[\mathbf{S}_u||\mathbf{A}_s||\mathbf{G}_b]\mathbf{R}_\delta = [\mathbf{S}_v||\mathbf{A}_{s'}] \pmod{q}$ (here we don't consider the ε transitions). These equations are inductively constructed. Firstly check if matrix $[\mathbf{S}_u||\mathbf{A}_s]$ exists with trapdoor (the first of this type of matrix is $[\mathbf{S}_{z_0}||\mathbf{A}_{s_0}]$ which does have trapdoor). If one of the sub-matrices of $[\mathbf{S}_u||\mathbf{A}_s]$ does not exist, sample it by "matrix-trapdoor" sampling algorithm TrapGen. Run TrapGen again to sample $\mathbf{S}_v$ and $\mathbf{A}_{s'}$ if they haven't been created. Then apply the lattice preimage sampling function SampleD to sample the low-norm transition matrix $\mathbf{R}_\delta$. Finally, each matrix $\mathbf{A}_{s_\omega}$ for $s_\omega \in F$ will be equipped with a decryption vector that allows decrypters to recover messages.

The decryption procedure works by following an accept execution path, sequentially applying the transition matrices $\mathbf{R}_\delta$ to linearly transform

$$\mathbf{s}^\top[\mathbf{S}_{z_0}||\mathbf{A}_{s_0}||\mathbf{G}_{w_1}||\mathbf{G}_{w_2}||\ldots||\mathbf{G}_{w_\ell}] + \boldsymbol{\nu}^\top$$

into

$$\mathbf{s}^\top[\mathbf{S}_u||\mathbf{A}_{s_\omega}||\mathbf{G}_{w_j}||\mathbf{G}_{w_{j+1}}||\ldots||\mathbf{G}_{w_\ell}] + \bar{\boldsymbol{\nu}}^\top,$$

(for some $u \in \Gamma$) which is the incomplete (in terms of stack configuration) matrix representation of an accept ID $(s_\omega, \boldsymbol{\gamma}, w_j w_{j+1}...w_\ell)$ where $1 \leq j$. The decryption vector of $\mathbf{A}_{s_\omega}$ then applies. We note the decryption does not need to read the whole input string.

Two problems make this toy construction insecure. Firstly, the concatenation matrix $[\mathbf{G}_{w_1}||\mathbf{G}_{w_2}||\ldots||\mathbf{G}_{w_\ell}]$ does not mathematically enforce any sequence between letters in the string. Secondly, no mechanism ensures the consistency of stack configurations. Different configurations may lead to the same execution result. For instance, consider two IDs $(uvz_0, s, w_1 w_2 w_3)$ and $(uvvz_0, s, w_1 w_2 w_3)$. A transition $\delta(u, s, w_1) \rightarrow (v, s')$ takes them to different next IDs, but they have the same transition equation. In particular, a transition equation only mirrors one piece of the whole execution of a DPDA and shows no connections with other transitions. On the other hand, this problem brought by "memoryless" description of DPDAs can be amended by including the whole execution history to each transition step, just as ID does. However, exponentially many IDs (within the input length bound ℓ) is impossible to be encoded in decryption keys.

Summing up, in order to securely embed bounded DPDAs with one or multiple stacks into decryption keys, we must take care to retain enough state to prevent malleability attacks while avoiding an exponential blow-up of the size of the decryption keys.

The Challenges of (Not) Keeping Memory. To figure out the minimal amount of state we need to keep in a pushdown automaton with respect to some input length bound, we notionally unroll all the possible execution paths of the automaton into a specially crafted low-dimensional space. The dimensions and coordinates of the space are determined so that the directed execution graph is *acyclic* (no directed cycles). Intuitively, the coordinates of this "execution graph space" represent the variables that the core state machine must remember about the stack/tape configuration. For example, one dimension could be a counter indicating how many symbols the machine has read from its second stack so far. The fewer the dimensions, the more risk that the graph of all possible unrolled executions, will contain directed cycles. If that happens, a malicious user can "jump" from one execution to another, yielding an illegal execution that could accept a word not in the language—an attack.

At one extreme, a machine whose core remembers nothing about the tapes corresponds to a very low-dimensional execution space (as the case of the toy construction). In this case, an adversary will be able to alter the stack tape or the input tape "out of sight" of the state machine, undetected, in order to take shortcuts/longcuts/sidecuts in the execution, throwing the machine into a configuration it should not have been able to reach from the given input. Conversely, a Turing machine whose state remembers everything, including the whole tape itself, can obviously be simulated as a mere DFA, albeit one with a huge state space, without danger of allowing an adversary to deviate from the execution. In this case the execution graph space will have (at least) one dimension for each possible cell. This will make the graph acyclic, but at the cost of requiring a state machine with exponentially many states.

Between those unworkable extremes, we devise an execution graph space of low constant dimension (function only of the *number* of stacks) that will always guarantee acyclicity. This gives us the variables that the core state machine will need to keep track of, to cryptographically ensure correct execution regardless of the size of the stack(s). Those variables enforce a set of constraints sufficient to ensure that users (performing the decryption) consistently proceed with the forward execution of the DPDA step by step, without having to remember unneeded data about the DPDA's previous steps. In our full construction, the actual execution of an automaton is based on the repeated application of transition equations similar to the toy construction. But each transition equation will carry (just) enough aforementioned variables so that the acyclic execution graphs can be correctly instantiated. We note that the transition equation (as in the toy construction) is a direct generalisaztion of the two-to-one recoding [13], itself ultimately based on lattice basis delegation [1,8].

Perhaps the most novel aspect of our ABE construction is the secure construction of (long, bidirectional) read/write tapes that do not require the entire configuration to be kept "in focus" at all times, unlike most other lattice-based public-key encryption scheme. We cryptographically enforce "big picture" consistency across space and time, using only local transformations or transitions with a short window of visibility. More specifically, there are a few transition steps involved in our constructions, implemented as *local* matrix multiplications. Once we ensure the current decryption step has been securely and honestly taken, it is automatically guaranteed that the previous decryption steps are securely taken, which by induction implies that the entire execution is *globally* correct. We prove all this using a game-based reductionist simulation from the LWE hardness assumption. The aforementioned execution graph and the selection of its dimensions to ensure acyclicity, are critical to the success of this simulation.

Relationship with ABE for Circuits. We emphasize that the pushdown automata in our scheme are subject to polynomial size input and polynomial execution time restrictions, and thus also admit (non unique) functionally equivalent polynomial size circuits. ABE schemes for general circuits like [4,10,13] can thus in theory achieve the same functionality by converting the bounded DPDA to DTM into an equivalent circuit beforehand. Our schemes provide a quite different and direct way to solve the problem, with an additional advantage of input-specific decryption time.

More specifically, the process of converting deterministic pushdown automata (especially with multiple stacks) into circuits is subtle. First, we need an actual algorithm, not just an existential equivalence. Second, the actually translated circuits can be optimised to have gates with small fan-in at the expense of depth, or be optimised for shallowness and require many gates, but not both. As both the height of the circuit and the number of gates and their fan-in affect the efficiency of circuit-based ABE schemes, a compromise would have to be struck.

A proper comparison with circuit-based ABE would require taking into account the exact cost of translating a DPDA or Turing machine into a circuit, not only in the sense of existential upper bounds, but also in the form of efficient algorithms that achieve them. A naive translation approach could result in a very noticeable penalty in the resulting Circuit ABE. Alas, an extensive literature search has failed to reveal any hypothetical TM-to-Circuit translators that would be markedly superior than the naive translation. For an ABE policy specified as a DPDA or a DTM, our construction sidesteps all issues related to translation and its tuning, and has the advantage of simplicity. Conversely of course, given an ABE policy as a circuit, it would be preferable to use a DTM for circuits rather translate it into a machine representation for our construction. Last but not least, the circuits conversion will certainly lose the advantage of input-specific decryption times from which many potential applications may get benefits in terms of efficiency.

The main contribution of our result is to show how the "simple" idea of *directly* embedding a bounded DPDA or DTM into an ABE system can actually be made to work, and proven secure in the reductionist simulation framework.

1.3   Other Related Works

The research on ABE can be traced back to the development of identity-based encryption (IBE). fuzzy IBE, a variant of IBE introduced in [23], triggered the birth of ABE. Various ABE schemes have been proposed based on multi-linear maps, bilinear maps and lattices [5,15,18,25]. While ABE enables complex access mechanism on encrypted data, it only provides privacy for the payload messages rather than attributes of the message. ABE is inadequate in some applications where the attributes themselves are considered to be sensitive. Predicate encryption (PE) has a similar structure to ABE but enjoys stronger privacy. PE hides the attributes of encrypted data as well for decryptors whose predicates of decryption are not satisfied by the attributes. Very recently, Gorbunov et al. [14] proposed a PE scheme for general circuits from standard LWE assumption by combining the key-homomorphic ABE scheme for circuits [4] and LWE-based fully homomorphic encryption. Functional encryption is a more powerful primitive which generalises ABE and PE. However, practical functional encryption schemes are only known for limited functionalities such as inner-product [17,20].

We note that the effort of improving (worst-case) decryption time of ABE schemes has been taken, for instance, in [16]. However, we are not aware of any existing ABE schemes from standard cryptographic assumptions that have the input-specific decryption time (the construction from [12] relies on SNARKS and extractable witness encryption, two very strong assumptions).

2 Preliminary

2.1 Lattices

We use the standard definitions of random integer lattices, discrete Gaussian distribution, the well-known lattice trapdoor techniques, and discrete Gaussian sampling algorithems. Particularly, we use the trapdoor generation algorithm TrapGen from [1,11,19] in the black-box way. The sampling algorithms SampleD and SampleExtend used in this paper are respectively the same as the SamplePre and SampLeft algorithms defined in [1]. We refer to the full version of this paper or above citations for details. The security of our constructions is based on the learning with errors (LWE) problem firstly introduced by Regev [22]. We refer to [7,21,22] for the definition and hardness results of the LWE problem.

2.2 Pushdown Automata

A *deterministic* **pushdown automaton** with one stack is a 7-tuple $(Q, \Sigma, \Gamma, \delta, s_0, z_0, F)$. Q is a finite set of states. $F \subseteq Q$ is the set of the accept states. Σ is the finite input alphabet. $\Sigma_\varepsilon = \Sigma \cup \{\varepsilon\}$ for the empty symbol ε. Γ is the finite stack alphabet. $\delta : \Gamma \times Q \setminus F \times \Sigma_\varepsilon \to \Gamma \times Q$ is the deterministic transition function. $z_0 \in \Gamma$ is the initial stack element and it is always at the bottom of the stack and never been removed. $s_0 \in Q$ is the unique start state. The reader is referred to the full version of this paper or the textbook [24] for the computational models of deterministic pushdown automata and Turing machines.

2.3 Definitions of Attribute-Based Encryption for PDAs

A key-policy attribute-based encryption scheme for PDAs consists of four algorithms (Setup, KeyGen, Encrypt, Decrypt). Setup takes as input a security parameter λ and a universal alphabet Σ_ε. It generates public parameters Pub and master secret key Msk. KeyGen uses Msk to generate decryption Sk_M for a given PDA machine M. Encrypt applies Pub to encrypt a message Msg under a string $\mathbf{w} \in \Sigma^*$, and produces the ciphertext $\mathsf{Ctx_w}$. Decrypt recovers the message from $\mathsf{Ctx_w}$ using Sk_M if M accepts $\mathbf{w}$, i.e. $\mathbf{w} \in L(M)$.

Security Model. We review the game-based selective security definition of (key-policy) ABE scheme for PDAs. Let $\mathcal{A}$ be the adversary, $\mathcal{B}$ be the challenger.

Initial. $\mathcal{A}$ submits a string $\mathbf{w}^* \in \Sigma^*$ as its challenge.

Setup. $\mathcal{B}$ runs algorithm Setup to generate the public parameters Pub and master secret key Msk and passes Pub to $\mathcal{A}$.

Phase 1. $\mathcal{A}$ adaptively issues the key generation queries for keys correspond to any PDA machine M of its choice. The only restriction is $\mathbf{w}^* \notin L(M)$. $\mathcal{B}$ runs the algorithm KeyGen(Pub, Msk, M) and returns Sk_M.

Challenge. $\mathcal{A}$ chooses a challenge message to be encrypted with $\mathbf{w}^*$. $\mathcal{B}$ flips a random coin $\gamma \in \{0,1\}$. If $\gamma = 1$, the challenge ciphertext is returned. Otherwise, a random element in the ciphertext space is returned.

Phase 2. This phase is exactly the same as **Phase 1**.
Guess. Finally, $\mathcal{A}$ outputs a guess bit γ' of γ. It wins if $\gamma' = \gamma$.

The advantage of $\mathcal{A}$ in the above game is defined as $|\Pr[\gamma' = \gamma] - \frac{1}{2}|$. We say a (Key-Policy) ABE scheme for PDAs is selectively secure if all PPT adversaries have at most a negligible advantage in the above game. In the stronger model named the adaptive security model, adversary submits the challenge string $\mathbf{w}^*$ in the **Challenge** phase.

3   Execution Graph of DPDAs

We now turn to explain the structure of the specially crafted execution graphs of DPDAs which are low-dimensional and acyclic. The execution graphs allow us to securely encode bounded DPDAs into decryption keys and to successfully overcome the difficulties of keeping execution history in memory. Without loss of generality, 1-Stack DPDAs are described in full detail. It is straightforward to extend the ideas to 2-Stack DPDAs and n-Stack DPDAs, by linearly increasing the dimension of the execution graphs so that they remain acyclic.

3.1   Descriptions of Execution Graph

The execution graph $G = (V, E)$ of a 1-Stack DPDA $M = (Q, \Sigma, \Gamma, \delta, s_0, z_0, F)$, with respect to the input length bound τ and running time bound η, consists of a set of vertices, denoted by V, and a set of edges denoted by E.

A vertex in V, which comprises of 5 variables, has form (u, s, j, t', t). The first coordinate $u \in \Gamma$ is the current top-most stack element. The second coordinate $s \in Q$ is the current state of DPDA. The third coordinate j, where $1 \leq j \leq \tau$, is the "input position" indicating currently the first $j - 1$ input symbols have been read by M, and the next symbol to be read is the jth one. The fourth and fifth coordinate t' and t, where $-1 \leq t' \leq 2\eta - 1$, $0 \leq t \leq 2\eta$ and $t' < t$, are "stack position tags" of u. t represents the stack position of current stack element u and t' represents the stack position of u's previous stack element. These stack position tags sequentially chain all current stack elements together in a logical way. During the transition (execution), the stack position tags change dynamically (in a way we specify later) so that the new top-stack element which is pushed in has a (logically) higher position than the previous top stack element, and the sequential relation between the stack element that is popped out, and rest of stack elements is removed. For the special stack element z_0 which will never be popped out, we assign the special tag value -1 to indicate that z_0 is always in the bottom of the stack.

The edges in E are defined by the input of transitions, either a symbol $b \in \Sigma$ or an empty symbol ε. The input symbol $b \in \Sigma$, which defines the outgoing edge of a vertex (s, u, j, t', t), is tied by input position j. We don't explicitly defines the input position for the ε input as it never appears in the input string.

The initial vertex of an execution graph of M is $(z_0, s_0, 1, -1, 0)$. Inductively, two vertices are connected to each other with respect to the type of transition, increasing of input position tags and increasing of stack positions. Let (u, s, j, t', t) be the current vertex for the top stack element $u \in \Gamma$, the state $s \in Q$, input position j and stack position tags t' and t for u and u's previous stack element respectively.

1. For a "push" transition $\delta(u, s, b) \rightarrow (v, s')$, $b \in \Sigma$ will define the outgoing edge. The next vertex will be defined as $(v, s', j+1, t+1, t+2)$ in which we increase the input position by 1, meaning that a non-empty symbol is read, and assign stack position tag $t+2$ to v and update u's position tag from t to $t+1$. There must be the case that $-1 \leq t' < t$. We write this relation as:

$$(u, s, j, t', t) \xrightarrow{b} (v, s', j+1, t+1, t+2)$$

   In the special case $t' = -1$, we have $u = z_0$.
2. For a "pop" transition $\delta(s, u, b) \rightarrow (s', v)$, $b \in \Sigma$ will define the outgoing edge. The next vertex will be defined as $(v, s', j+1, t'', t+1)$ in which we increase the input position by 1 and update v's stack position tag from t' to $t+1$ and v's previous tack element's stack position tag, say t'', is not change. There must be the case that $-1 \leq t'' < t' < t$. We write this relation as:

$$(u, s, j, t', t) \xrightarrow{b} (v, s', j+1, t'', t+1)$$

   In the special case $t'' = -1$, we have $v = z_0$.
3. For a ε "push" transition $\delta(u, s, \varepsilon) \rightarrow (v, s')$, ε symbol will define the outgoing edge. The next vertex will be defined as $(v, s', j, t+1, t+2)$ in which the input position stays unchanged, meaning that no input has been read in this transition. v is assigned the new stack position tag $t+2$ and u's position tag is updated from t to $t+1$. There must be the case that $-1 \leq t' < t < 2\eta$. We write this relation as:

$$(u, s, j, t', t) \xrightarrow{\varepsilon} (v, s', j, t+1, t+2)$$

   In the special case $t' = -1$, we have $u = z_0$.
4. For a ε "pop" transition $\delta(u, s, \varepsilon) \rightarrow (v, s')$, ε symbol will define the outgoing edge. The next vertex will be defined as $(s', v, j, t'', t+1)$ in which the input position stays unchanged, meaning that no input has been read in this transition. We update v's stack position tag from t' to $t+1$. v's previous tack element's stack position tag, say t'', is not change. There must be the case that $-1 \leq t'' < t' < t < 2\eta$. We write this relation as:

$$(u, s, j, t', t) \xrightarrow{\varepsilon} (s', v, j, t'', t+1)$$

   In the special case $t'' = -1$, we have $v = z_0$.

In a execution process with respect to a specific input, M will start from $(z_0, s_0, 1, -1, 0)$. It then follows the path defined by the input and ε transitions to travel between vertices. Once M reaches a vertex with some accept state s_ω, it stops and accepts the input. Otherwise, M stops and rejects the input if there is no transition with respect the current input or j, t', t reach the bounds.

To see why the execution graphs for 1-Stack DPDAs are acyclic, the coordinates of tuple (u, s, j, t', t), (input position j and stack position tags t', t) increase monotonically with at least one of them increasing at each step. t' decreases only when the top-most stack elements are popped out from the stack and its stack position tag is never going to be used again.

3.2   Matrix Representation

In our constructions, the execution graphs are instantiated by Matrices (recall the toy construction). However, matrix concatenation neither forces any sequential order to the individual matrices nor logically binds the individual matrices together. On the other hand, in execution graph, coordinates in a vertex are logically integrated, vertices and edges (specified by input symbols) are bound with respect to the input positions. In order to mitigate this problem, we use subscripts of matrices to denote the state, stack element and input symbols, and encode the input positions and stack position tags in the superscripts of matrices to tie concatenated matrices together logically.

Specifically, for a vertex (u, s, j, t', t), we encode it by matrix concatenation $[\mathbf{S}_u^{(t',t)} \| \mathbf{A}_s^{(t,j)}]$. $\mathbf{S}_u^{(t',t)} \in \mathbb{Z}_q^{n \times m}$ is the stack matrix of u with t as u's stack position tag and t' as the stack position tag of u's previous element. $\mathbf{A}_s^{(t,j)} \in \mathbb{Z}_q^{n \times m}$ is the state matrix of s. The superscript t ties $\mathbf{A}_s^{(t,j)}$ to $\mathbf{S}_u^{(t',t)}$, and j ties $\mathbf{A}_s^{(t,j)}$ to the jth input symbol, say b, which has matrix representation $\mathbf{G}_b^{(j)}$.

For expressing the transition equations that connect two vertices through an edge, we consider the following cases:

- $(u, s, j, t', t) \xrightarrow{b} (v, s', j+1, t+1, t+2)$ where the push transition $\delta(u, s, b) \to (v, s')$ for j^{th} input b happens: sample a low-norm transition matrix $\mathbf{R}_\delta^{(t',t,j)} \in \mathbb{Z}^{3m \times 3m}$ such that:

$$[\mathbf{S}_u^{(t',t)} \| \mathbf{A}_s^{(t,j)} \| \mathbf{G}_b^{(j)}] \mathbf{R}_\delta^{(t',t,j)} = [\mathbf{S}_u^{(t',t+1)} \| \mathbf{S}_v^{(t+1,t+2)} \| \mathbf{A}_{s'}^{(t+2,j+1)}] \pmod q$$

- $(u, s, j, t', t) \xrightarrow{b} (v, s', j+1, t'', t+1)$ where the pop transition $\delta(u, s, b) \to (v, s')$ for j^{th} input b happens: sample a low-norm transition matrix $\mathbf{R}_\delta^{(t',t,j)} \in \mathbb{Z}^{4m \times 2m}$ such that:

$$[\mathbf{S}_v^{(t'',t')} \| \mathbf{S}_u^{(t',t)} \| \mathbf{A}_s^{(t,j)} \| \mathbf{G}_b^{(j)}] \mathbf{R}_\delta^{(t',t,j)} = [\mathbf{S}_v^{(t'',t+1)} \| \mathbf{A}_{s'}^{(t+1,j+1)}] \pmod q$$

- $(u, s, j, t', t) \xrightarrow{\varepsilon} (v, s', j, t+1, t+2)$ where the push transition $\delta(u, s, \varepsilon) \to (v, s')$ for ε input happens: sample a low-norm transition matrix $\mathbf{R}_\delta^{(t',t,j)} \in \mathbb{Z}^{2m \times 3m}$ such that:

$$[\mathbf{S}_u^{(t',t)} \| \mathbf{A}_s^{(t,j)}] \mathbf{R}_\delta^{(t',t,j)} = [\mathbf{S}_u^{(t',t+1)} \| \mathbf{S}_v^{(t+1,t+2)} \| \mathbf{A}_{s'}^{(t+2,j)}] \pmod q$$

– $(u, s, j, t', t) \xrightarrow{\varepsilon} (s', v, j, t'', t + 1)$ where the push transition $\delta(u, s, \varepsilon) \rightarrow (v, s')$
for ε input happens: sample a low-norm transition matrix $\mathbf{R}_\delta^{(t',t,j)} \in \mathbb{Z}^{3m \times 2m}$
such that:

$$[\mathbf{S}_v^{(t'',t')} || \mathbf{S}_u^{(t',t)} || \mathbf{A}_s^{(t,j)}] \mathbf{R}_\delta^{(t',t,j)} = [\mathbf{S}_v^{(t'',t+1)} || \mathbf{A}_{s'}^{(t+1,j)}] \pmod{q}$$

In all above cases, if the state s' in the target vertex equals to some accept
state s_ω, we will simply use matrix $\mathbf{A}_\omega$ to denote it without any superscripts.
This is because the vertex (u, s_ω, j, t', t) must be the terminal of the execution
path and no next vertex exists.

The reason we use slightly different forms in the equations for push and pop
transition is that we update the stack position tags of the stack elements to keep
the actual transition equations compatible with the execution graphs such that
no direct cycles happen.

4   The ABE Scheme for Bounded 1-Stack DPDAs

4.1   Construction

Setup$(1^\lambda, 1^\tau, 1^\eta, \Sigma_\varepsilon = \{0, 1, \varepsilon\})$ On input of security parameter 1^λ, upper bound
$\tau = \tau(\lambda)$ of length of input string, upper bound $\eta = \eta(\lambda)$ of running time of
the pushdown automata, and the universal alphabet Σ_ε:
1. Pick 2τ matrices $\mathbf{G}_b^{(j)} \xleftarrow{\$} \mathbb{Z}_q^{n \times m}$ for $j \in [\tau]$ and $b \in \{0, 1\}$.
2. Sample $\mathbf{A} \in \mathbb{Z}_q^{n \times m}$ and its trapdoor $\mathbf{T_A} \in \mathbb{Z}^{m \times m}$ by TrapGen.
3. Pick $\mathbf{u} \xleftarrow{\$} \mathbb{Z}_q^n$.
4. Output Pub $= \left(\{\mathbf{G}_b^{(j)}\}_{b \in \{0,1\}, j \in [\tau]}, \mathbf{A}, \mathbf{u} \right)$ and Msk $= \mathbf{T_A}$.

KeyGen(Pub, Msk, $M = (Q, \Gamma, \delta, s_0, z_0, F))$)] On input of Pub, Msk and a 1-Stack
DPDA M, unroll M (up to the fixed bounds) into an execution graph:
1. Prepare for the initial vertex $(z_0, s_0, 1, -1, 0)$:
   (a) Run TrapGen to sample matrix $\mathbf{A}_{s_0}^{(0,1)}$ and its trapdoor.
   (b) Pick $\mathbf{S}_{z_0}^{(-1,0)} \xleftarrow{\$} \mathbb{Z}_q^{n \times m}$.
   (c) Sample $\mathbf{R} \in \mathbb{Z}^{m \times 2m}$ by SampleD such that $\mathbf{AR} = [\mathbf{S}_{z_0}^{(-1,0)} || \mathbf{A}_{s_0}^{(0,1)}]$
       $\pmod{q}$.
2. For a normal "push" transition $\delta(u, s, b) \rightarrow (v, s')$ that connects two vertices (u, s, j, t', t) and $(v, s', j + 1, t + 1, t + 2)$ through the edge b at input
   position j, the algorithm does:
   (a) The state matrix $\mathbf{A}_s^{(t,j)}$ with trapdoor and stack matrix $\mathbf{S}_u^{(t',t)}$ are
       already defined.
   (b) In case $s' \in Q \setminus F$, run TrapGen to sample matrix $\mathbf{A}_{s'}^{(t+2,j+1)}$ and its
       trapdoor if such state matrix has not been defined. If s' equals to
       some accept state $s_\omega \in F$, and the matrix $\mathbf{A}_{s_\omega}$ has not been defined,
       run TrapGen to sample it with trapdoor.
   (c) Pick $\mathbf{S}_u^{(t',t+1)}, \mathbf{S}_v^{(t+1,t+2)} \xleftarrow{\$} \mathbb{Z}_q^{n \times m}$ for $v \in \Gamma$ if this stack matrix has
       not been defined.

(d) Run SampleExtend to sample $\mathbf{R}_\delta^{(t',t,j)}$ with distribution $(D_{\mathbb{Z}^{3m}, \sigma})^{3m}$ such that if $s' \in Q \setminus F$:

$$[\mathbf{S}_u^{(t',t)} \| \mathbf{A}_s^{(t,j)} \| \mathbf{G}_b^{(j)}] \mathbf{R}_\delta^{(t',t,j)} = [\mathbf{S}_u^{(t',t+1)} \| \mathbf{S}_v^{(t+1,t+2)} \| \mathbf{A}_{s'}^{(t+2,j+1)}] \pmod q$$

or $s' = s_\omega$ for some $s_\omega \in F$:

$$[\mathbf{S}_u^{(t',t)} \| \mathbf{A}_s^{(t,j)} \| \mathbf{G}_b^{(j)}] \mathbf{R}_\delta^{(t',t,j)} = [\mathbf{S}_u^{(t',t+1)} \| \mathbf{S}_v^{(t+1,t+2)} \| \mathbf{A}_{s_\omega}] \pmod q.$$

3. For a normal "pop" transition $\delta(u, s, b) \rightarrow (v, s')$ that connects two vertices (u, s, j, t', t) and $(v, s', j+1, t'', t+1)$ through the input b at input position j, the algorithm does:
   (a) The state matrix $\mathbf{A}_s^{(t,j)}$ with trapdoor, stack matrices $\mathbf{S}_u^{(t',t)}$, $\mathbf{S}_v^{(t'',t')}$ are already defined.
   (b) In case that $s' \notin F$, run TrapGen to sample matrix $\mathbf{A}_{s'}^{(t+1,j+1)}$ and its trapdoor if such state matrix has not been defined. If s' is some accept state $s_\omega \in F$, and the matrix $\mathbf{A}_{s_\omega}$ has not been defined, run TrapGen to sample it with trapdoor.
   (c) Pick $\mathbf{S}_v^{(t'',t+1)} \xleftarrow{\$} \mathbb{Z}_q^{n \times m}$ if this stack matrix has not been defined.
   (d) Run SampleExtend to sample $\mathbf{R}_\delta^{(t',t,j)}$ with distribution $(D_{\mathbb{Z}^{4m}, \sigma})^{2m}$ such that if $s' \notin F$:

$$[\mathbf{S}_v^{(t'',t')} \| \mathbf{S}_u^{(t',t)} \| \mathbf{A}_s^{(t,j)} \| \mathbf{G}_b^{(j)}] \mathbf{R}_\delta^{(t',t,j)} = [\mathbf{S}_v^{(t'',t+1)} \| \mathbf{A}_{s'}^{(t+1,j+1)}] \pmod q$$

or $s' = s_\omega$ for some $s_\omega \in F$:

$$[\mathbf{S}_v^{(t'',t')} \| \mathbf{S}_u^{(t',t)} \| \mathbf{A}_s^{(t,j)} \| \mathbf{G}_b^{(j)}] \mathbf{R}_\delta^{(t',t,j)} = [\mathbf{S}_v^{(t'',t+1)} \| \mathbf{A}_{s_\omega}] \pmod q.$$

4. For a ε "push" transition $\delta(u, s, \varepsilon) \rightarrow (v, s')$ that connects two vertices (u, s, j, t', t) and $(v, s', j, t+1, t+2)$ through edge ε, the algorithm does:
   (a) The state matrix $\mathbf{A}_s^{(t,j)}$ with trapdoor and stack matrix $\mathbf{S}_u^{(t',t)}$ are already defined.
   (b) Run TrapGen to sample matrix $\mathbf{A}_{s'}^{(t+2,j)}$ and its trapdoor if $s' \notin F$ and such state matrix has not been defined. If s' is some accept state $s_\omega \in F$, and the matrix $\mathbf{A}_{s_\omega}$ has not been defined, run TrapGen to sample it with trapdoor.
   (c) Pick $\mathbf{S}_u^{(t',t+1)}, \mathbf{S}_v^{(t+1,t+2)} \xleftarrow{\$} \mathbb{Z}_q^{n \times m}$ if they haven't been defined.
   (d) Run SampleExtend to sample $\mathbf{R}_\delta^{(t',t,j)}$ with distribution $(D_{\mathbb{Z}^{2m}, \sigma})^{3m}$ such that if $s' \notin F$:

$$[\mathbf{S}_u^{(t',t)} \| \mathbf{A}_s^{(t,j)}] \mathbf{R}_\delta^{(t',t,j)} = [\mathbf{S}_u^{(t',t+1)} \| \mathbf{S}_v^{(t+1,t+2)} \| \mathbf{A}_{s'}^{(t+2,j)}] \pmod q$$

or $s' = s_\omega$ for some $s_\omega \in F$:

$$[\mathbf{S}_u^{(t',t)} \| \mathbf{A}_s^{(t,j)}] \mathbf{R}_\delta^{(t',t,j)} = [\mathbf{S}_u^{(t',t+1)} \| \mathbf{S}_v^{(t+1,t+2)} \| \mathbf{A}_{s_\omega}] \pmod q.$$

5. For a ε "pop" transition $\delta(u,s,b) \rightarrow (v,s')$ that connects two vertices (u,s,j,t',t) and $(v,s',j,t'',t+1)$ through the edge ε, the algorithm does:

   (a) The state matrix $\mathbf{A}_s^{(t,j)}$ with trapdoor, stack matrices $\mathbf{S}_u^{(t',t)}$, $\mathbf{S}_v^{(t'',t')}$ are already defined.

   (b) Run TrapGen to sample matrix $\mathbf{A}_{s'}^{(t+1,j)}$ and its trapdoor if $s' \notin F$ and such state matrix has not been defined. If s' is some accept state $s_\omega \in F$, and the matrix $\mathbf{A}_{s_\omega}$ has not been defined, run TrapGen to sample it with trapdoor.

   (c) Pick $\mathbf{S}_v^{(t'',t+1)} \xleftarrow{\$} \mathbb{Z}_q^{n \times m}$ if this stack matrix has not been defined.

   (d) Run SampleExtend to sample $\mathbf{R}_\delta^{(t',t,j)}$ with distribution $(D_{\mathbb{Z}^{3m},\sigma})^{2m}$ such that if $s' \notin F$:

   $$[\mathbf{S}_v^{(t'',t')}||\mathbf{S}_u^{(t',t)}||\mathbf{A}_s^{(t,j)}]\mathbf{R}_\delta^{(t',t,j)} = [\mathbf{S}_v^{(t'',t+1)}||\mathbf{A}_{s'}^{(t+1,j)}] \pmod{q}$$

   or $s' = s_\omega$ for some $s_\omega \in F$:

   $$[\mathbf{S}_v^{(t'',t')}||\mathbf{S}_u^{(t',t)}||\mathbf{A}_s^{(t,j)}]\mathbf{R}_\delta^{(t',t,j)} = [\mathbf{S}_v^{(t'',t+1)}||\mathbf{A}_{s_\omega}] \pmod{q}.$$

6. For all state matrices $\mathbf{A}_\omega$ of accept states $s_\omega \in F$, run SampleD to sample Gaussian vector $\mathbf{d}_{s_\omega}$ such that: $\mathbf{A}_{s_\omega}\mathbf{d}_{s_\omega} = \mathbf{u} \pmod{q}$.

7. Output the decryption key as:

$$\mathsf{Sk}_M = \left(\mathbf{R}, \{\mathbf{R}_\delta^{(t',t,j)}\}, \{\mathbf{d}_{s_\omega}\}_{s_\omega \in F}\right)$$

Encrypt(Pub, $\mathbf{w}$, Msg) The encryption algorithm takes as input the public parameters Pub, a binary string $\mathbf{w}$ with length $\ell \leq \tau$, and a message bit Msg $\in \{0,1\}$. Denote the ith bit of $\mathbf{w}$ by $\mathbf{w}[i]$. The algorithm then does:

1. Randomly select a vector $\mathbf{s} \xleftarrow{\$} \mathbb{Z}_q^n$.
2. Select a noise scalar $\nu_0 \leftarrow \chi$ and compute the scalar

$$c_0 = \mathbf{s}^\top \mathbf{u} + \nu_0 + \mathsf{Msg}\lfloor q/2 \rfloor.$$

3. Select a noise vector $\boldsymbol{\nu}_1 \leftarrow \chi^{(\ell+1)m}$, and compute the vector

$$\mathbf{c}_1^\top = \mathbf{s}^\top [\, \mathbf{A}||\mathbf{G}_{\mathbf{w}[1]}^{(1)} \,||\, \mathbf{G}_{\mathbf{w}[2]}^{(2)} \,||\, \cdots \,||\, \mathbf{G}_{\mathbf{w}[\ell-1]}^{(\ell-1)} \,||\, \mathbf{G}_{\mathbf{w}[\ell]}^{(\ell)} \,] + \boldsymbol{\nu}_1^\top.$$

4. Output the ciphertext for the attribute input string $\mathbf{w}$ as

$$\mathsf{Ctx}_{\mathbf{w}} = (c_0, \mathbf{c}_1).$$

Decrypt(Pub, Sk_M, $\mathsf{Ctx}_{\mathbf{w}}$, $\mathbf{w}$) On input Pub, decryption key Sk_M of automaton M, ℓ-length attribute string $\mathbf{w} = w_1 w_2 \ldots w_\ell$ and the ciphertext $\mathsf{Ctx}_{\mathbf{w}}$ encrypted by $\mathbf{w}$.

1. If $\mathbf{w} \notin L(M)$, return an error symbol $\bot$. Otherwise, unroll the execution graph of M, find the execution path from the start state s_0 to an accept state s_ω. Assume M digests the first $\ell' \leq \ell$ input symbols to get to s_ω. Collect all the transition matrices $\{\mathbf{R}_\delta^{t',t,j}\}$ (including $\mathbf{R}$) of the path and the vector $\mathbf{d}_{s_\omega}$.

2. Get the useful part of $\mathbf{c}_1$: $\bar{\mathbf{c}}_1^\top = \mathbf{s}^\top[\ \mathbf{A}\ \|\ \mathbf{G}_{\mathbf{w}[1]}^{(1)}\ \|\cdots\|\ \mathbf{G}_{\mathbf{w}[\ell']}^{(\ell')}\ ] + \bar{\boldsymbol{\nu}}_1^\top.$

3. Set $\mathbf{c}_{1,0}^\top = \bar{\mathbf{c}}_1^\top \underbrace{\begin{bmatrix} \mathbf{R} & & & \\ & \mathbf{I}_m & & \\ & & \ddots & \\ & & & \mathbf{I}_m \end{bmatrix}}_{\in \mathbb{Z}^{(\ell'+1)m \times (\ell'+2)m}} = \mathbf{s}^\top[\mathbf{S}_{z_0}^{(-1,0)}\|\mathbf{A}_{s_0}^{(0,1)}\|\mathbf{G}_{\mathbf{w}[1]}^{(1)}\|\cdots\|\mathbf{G}_{\mathbf{w}[\ell']}^{(\ell')}] +$

$\bar{\boldsymbol{\nu}}_{1,0}^\top.$

4. Sequentially apply the transition matrices to transfer $\mathbf{c}_{1,0}$ to get $\mathbf{c}_{1,end}^\top = \mathbf{s}^\top\mathbf{A}_{s_\omega} + \boldsymbol{\nu}_{1,end}^\top$. This can be done in an obvious way and the ciphertext part of stack matrices that come out with $\mathbf{A}_{s_\omega}$ at the last step is simply discarded.

5. Set $\Delta = c_0 - \mathbf{c}_{1,end}^\top\mathbf{d}_{s_\omega}$ and output output $\mathsf{Msg} = 0$ if $\|\Delta\| < q/4$, or $\mathsf{Msg} = 1$ otherwise.

4.2   Correctness and Parameters

We refer to the full version of this paper for the correctness and parameters selection of above scheme.

4.3   Security

Theorem 1. *The scheme is selectively secure if the* $LWE_{n,q,\chi}$ *problem is hard.*

We refer to the full version of this paper for the full proof. We also remark that as we consider attribute strings with bounded length, by relying on the sub-exponential hardness of the LWE problem and the standard "complexity leveraging" argument [3], above scheme is also adaptively secure.

5   Extensions to 2-Stack DPDAs (and Thus DTMs)

To extend the ABE scheme for 1-Stack DPDAs to handle two or more stacks (thus Turing machines), the execution graphs are correspondingly extended to represent additional memory and preserve acyclic property. This can be achieved by adding enough (linearly many) states. The resulting execution graphs have dimensions which are linearly more than the execution graphs of 1-Stack DPDAs in the number of stacks. The ABE schemes for multi-stacks DPDAs (Turing machines) are obtained by incorporating new execution graphs into matrix transition equations. Their security can be proved in a similar way of security proof of the ABE scheme for single stack DPDAs. We show in the full version of this paper the design of execution graphs for 2-Stack DPDAs and the matrix transition equations with respect to these graphs. The case of DPDAs with multiple stacks (more than two) follows readily.

6   Conclusion

In this paper, we present a (key-policy) attribute-based encryption scheme for deterministic multi-stack pushdown automata and, therefore, Turing machines, with polynomially bounded execution. Crucially, our scheme enjoys input-specific decryption time from standard cryptographic assumptions, in contrast to previous ABE schemes in which the decryption algorithms have always had worst-case runtime. We prove the security of our scheme based on the hardness of LWE problem in the selective security model.

An interesting open problem is to devise a technique whereby the benefits of input-specific complexity can be achieved for different classes of ABE, such as ABE for circuits. Another even more challenging problem is to design ABE schemes to handle a-priori unbounded automata or machines. The problem of handling non-deterministic Turing machines is also wide open.

Acknowledgement. The authors would like to thank Shweta Agrawal for insightful discussions, and the reviewers of ACNS 2016 for the helpful comments.

References

1. Agrawal, S., Boneh, D., Boyen, X.: Efficient lattice (H)IBE in the standard model. In: Gilbert, H. (ed.) EUROCRYPT 2010. LNCS, vol. 6110, pp. 553–572. Springer, Heidelberg (2010)
2. Attrapadung, N.: Dual system encryption via doubly selective security: framework, fully secure functional encryption for regular languages, and more. In: Nguyen, P.Q., Oswald, E. (eds.) EUROCRYPT 2014. LNCS, vol. 8441, pp. 557–577. Springer, Heidelberg (2014)
3. Boneh, D., Boyen, X.: Efficient selective identity-based encryption without random oracles. J. Cryptol. **24**(4), 659–693 (2011)
4. Boneh, D., Gentry, C., Gorbunov, S., Halevi, S., Nikolaenko, V., Segev, G., Vaikuntanathan, V., Vinayagamurthy, D.: Fully key-homomorphic encryption, arithmetic circuit ABE and compact garbled circuits. In: Nguyen, P.Q., Oswald, E. (eds.) EUROCRYPT 2014. LNCS, vol. 8441, pp. 533–556. Springer, Heidelberg (2014)
5. Boyen, X.: Attribute-based functional encryption on lattices. In: Sahai, A. (ed.) TCC 2013. LNCS, vol. 7785, pp. 122–142. Springer, Heidelberg (2013)
6. Boyen, X., Li, Q.: Attribute-based encryption for finite automata from LWE. In: Au, M.H., Miyaji, A. (eds.) ProvSec 2015. LNCS, vol. 9451, pp. 247–267. Springer, Heidelberg (2015)
7. Brakerski, Z., Langlois, A., Peikert, C., Regev, O., Stehlé, D.: Classical hardness of learning with errors. In: STOC 2013, pp. 575–584. ACM (2013)
8. Cash, D., Hofheinz, D., Kiltz, E., Peikert, C.: Bonsai trees, or how to delegate a lattice basis. In: Gilbert, H. (ed.) EUROCRYPT 2010. LNCS, vol. 6110, pp. 523–552. Springer, Heidelberg (2010)
9. Cheeseman, P., Kanefsky, B., Taylor, W.M.: Where the really hard problems are. In: IJCAI 1991, vol. 1, pp. 331–337. Morgan Kaufmann Publishers Inc. (1991)

10. Garg, S., Gentry, C., Halevi, S., Raykova, M., Sahai, A., Waters, B.: Candidate indistinguishability obfuscation and functional encryption for all circuits. In: FOCS 2013, pp. 40–49. IEEE (2013)
11. Gentry, C., Peikert, C., Vaikuntanathan, V.: Trapdoors for hard lattices and new cryptographic constructions. In: STOC 2008, pp. 197–206. ACM (2008)
12. Goldwasser, S., Kalai, Y.T., Popa, R.A., Vaikuntanathan, V., Zeldovich, N.: How to run turing machines on encrypted data. In: Canetti, R., Garay, J.A. (eds.) CRYPTO 2013, Part II. LNCS, vol. 8043, pp. 536–553. Springer, Heidelberg (2013)
13. Gorbunov, S., Vaikuntanathan, V., Wee, H.: Attribute-based encryption for circuits. In: STOC 2013, pp. 545–554. ACM (2013)
14. Gorbunov, S., Vaikuntanathan, V., Wee, H.: Predicate encryption for circuits from LWE. In: Gennaro, R., Robshaw, M. (eds.) CRYPTO 2015. LNCS, vol. 9216, pp. 503–523. Springer, Heidelberg (2015)
15. Goyal, V., Pandey, O., Sahai, A., Waters, B.: Attribute-based encryption for fine-grained access control of encrypted data. In: CCS 2006, pp. 89–98. ACM (2006)
16. Hohenberger, S., Waters, B.: Attribute-based encryption with fast decryption. In: Kurosawa, K., Hanaoka, G. (eds.) PKC 2013. LNCS, vol. 7778, pp. 162–179. Springer, Heidelberg (2013)
17. Katz, J., Sahai, A., Waters, B.: Predicate encryption supporting disjunctions, polynomial equations, and inner products. In: Smart, N. (ed.) EUROCRYPT 2008. LNCS, vol. 4965, pp. 146–162. Springer, Heidelberg (2008)
18. Lewko, A., Waters, B.: Unbounded HIBE and attribute-based encryption. In: Paterson, K.G. (ed.) EUROCRYPT 2011. LNCS, vol. 6632, pp. 547–567. Springer, Heidelberg (2011)
19. Micciancio, D., Peikert, C.: Trapdoors for lattices: simpler, tighter, faster, smaller. In: Pointcheval, D., Johansson, T. (eds.) EUROCRYPT 2012. LNCS, vol. 7237, pp. 700–718. Springer, Heidelberg (2012)
20. Okamoto, T., Takashima, K.: Adaptively attribute-hiding (hierarchical) inner product encryption. In: Pointcheval, D., Johansson, T. (eds.) EUROCRYPT 2012. LNCS, vol. 7237, pp. 591–608. Springer, Heidelberg (2012)
21. Peikert, C.: Public-key cryptosystems from the worst-case shortest vector problem: extended abstract. In: STOC 2009, pp. 333–342. ACM (2009)
22. Regev, O.: On lattices, learning with errors, random linear codes, and cryptography. In: STOC 2005, pp. 84–93. ACM (2005)
23. Sahai, A., Waters, B.: Fuzzy identity-based encryption. In: Cramer, R. (ed.) EUROCRYPT 2005. LNCS, vol. 3494, pp. 457–473. Springer, Heidelberg (2005)
24. Sipser, M.: Introduction to the Theory of Computation, vol. 2. Thomson Course Technology, Boston (2006)
25. Waters, B.: Ciphertext-policy attribute-based encryption: an expressive, efficient, and provably secure realization. In: Catalano, D., Fazio, N., Gennaro, R., Nicolosi, A. (eds.) PKC 2011. LNCS, vol. 6571, pp. 53–70. Springer, Heidelberg (2011)
26. Waters, B.: Functional encryption for regular languages. In: Safavi-Naini, R., Canetti, R. (eds.) CRYPTO 2012. LNCS, vol. 7417, pp. 218–235. Springer, Heidelberg (2012)

Offline Witness Encryption

Hamza Abusalah[1]([✉]), Georg Fuchsbauer[2], and Krzysztof Pietrzak[1]

[1] Institute of Science and Technology Austria, Klosterneuburg, Austria
{habusalah,pietrzak}@ist.ac.at
[2] Inria, ENS, CNRS and PSL Research University, Paris, France
georg.fuchsbauer@ens.fr

Abstract. Witness encryption (WE) was introduced by Garg et al. [GGSW13]. A WE scheme is defined for some NP language L and lets a sender encrypt messages relative to instances x. A ciphertext for x can be decrypted using w witnessing $x \in L$, but hides the message if $x \notin L$. Garg et al. construct WE from multilinear maps and give another construction [GGH+13b] using indistinguishability obfuscation (iO) for circuits. Due to the reliance on such heavy tools, WE can currently hardly be implemented on powerful hardware and will unlikely be realizable on constrained devices like smart cards any time soon.

We construct a WE scheme where *encryption* is done by simply computing a Naor-Yung ciphertext (two CPA encryptions and a NIZK proof). To achieve this, our scheme has a setup phase, which outputs public parameters containing an obfuscated circuit (only required for decryption), two encryption keys and a common reference string (used for encryption). This setup need only be run once, and the parameters can be used for arbitrary many encryptions. Our scheme can also be turned into a *functional* WE scheme, where a message is encrypted w.r.t. a statement and a function f, and decryption with a witness w yields $f(m, w)$.

Our construction is inspired by the functional encryption scheme by Garg et al. and we prove (selective) security assuming iO and statistically simulation-sound NIZK. We give a construction of the latter in bilinear groups and combining it with ElGamal encryption, our ciphertexts are of size 1.3 kB at a 128-bit security level and can be computed on a smart card.

Keywords: Witness encryption · Indistinguishability obfuscation · NIZK · Groth-Sahai proofs

1 Introduction

Witness Encryption. In an encryption scheme, the receiver needs to know some secret piece of information (the secret key) to decrypt. Garg, Gentry, Sahai

Research supported by the European Research Council, ERC starting grant (259668-PSPC) and ERC consolidator grant (682815 - TOCNeT).

© Springer International Publishing Switzerland 2016
M. Manulis et al. (Eds.): ACNS 2016, LNCS 9696, pp. 285–303, 2016.
DOI: 10.1007/978-3-319-39555-5_16

and Waters [GGSW13] propose the intriguing new notion of *witness encryption* (WE), where a scheme is defined for some NP language L with witness relation R: $L = \{x \,|\, \exists\, w : R(x, w) = 1\}$. The encryption algorithm takes an instance x (instead of a public key) and a message m and produces a ciphertext c. Using a witness w such that $R(x, w) = 1$, anyone can decrypt ciphertext c. Decryption is only possible if x is actually in the language and it is required that a ciphertext computed for some $x \notin L$ computationally hides the message m.

Applications. As shown in [GGSW13], from WE one can construct powerful cryptographic primitives such as identity-based encryption and attribute-based encryption [SW05] for circuits. But WE also allows for applications that were not possible before; for example, one can encrypt a message with respect to a puzzle, such that only someone who found a solution can decrypt. This puzzle can be any problem where solutions can be efficiently verified, like a crossword or Sudoku puzzle, or even the proof for some mathematical conjecture. Another application is asymmetric password-based encryption [BH15], which allows hashed passwords (for any password-hashing function already in place) to be used as public encryption keys and passwords to decrypt.

Constructing WE. Garg et al. [GGSW13] construct a WE scheme for the NP-complete language "exact set cover", which implies WE for any language $L \in$ NP via polynomial-time many-one reductions (a.k.a. Levin reductions). The security of this construction is based on a strong assumption on "approximate" multilinear maps as constructed in [GGH13a]. Subsequently, a construction of WE from indistinguishability obfuscation (iO) was given in [GGH+13b] and another one based on multilinear maps in [GLW14]. The only candidate construction of iO is also based on the approximate multilinear maps from [GGH13a].

Implementing multilinear maps as required for iO or WE is computationally very expensive, but a first—though far from practical—implementation exists [AHKM14], and it is conceivable that algorithmic and hardware progress yield practical implementations in the not too distant future.

Offline Witness Encryption. Given that WE is not even practical on high-end machines, it seems foolish to hope for an implementation on low-end devices like smart cards. In this paper we show however that it is possible to construct a WE scheme where *encryption* is very efficient, as the entire computationally hard work can be moved to a setup phase and—to a lesser extent—to the decryption process. This setup is either run by the sender *before* she knows the instance and the message for an encryption; or it is run by a trusted party once and for all and everyone can use the same parameters. The first case is reminiscent of online/offline encryption or signatures [EGM96], except that in our case, once generated, the parameters can be used for arbitrary many "online phases".

We call this concept *offline witness encryption* and define it as a tuple of three algorithms. The setup phase (which is not present in standard WE) takes as input only a security parameter 1^λ and outputs public parameters $(pp_e, pp_d) \leftarrow$ Setup(1^λ). To encrypt a message m for an instance x, one runs an encryption algorithm $c \leftarrow$ Enc(x, m, pp_e). Such ciphertext c can then be decrypted given a witness w, i.e., for which $R(x, w) = 1$ holds, as $m = \mathsf{Dec}(c, w, pp_\mathsf{d})$. The goal of offline WE is to keep the parameters pp_e for encryption and ciphertexts small and the Enc algorithm efficient.

Applications of Offline WE. In any application of witness encryption its offline variant can be used to make encryption practically efficient, if one accepts an additional setup phase. However, for applications like IBE and attribute-based encryption, as discussed in [GGSW13], system-wide parameters must be set up by a trusted party anyway. This party could therefore simply also generate the offline-WE parameters, meaning encryption can be made efficient without requiring any additional trust.

Bellare and Tung Hoang [BH15] define and construct *asymmetric* password-based encryption (A-PBE), where a hash of a password can be used as a public key to encrypt messages, which can then be decrypted using the password. Unlike its symmetric counterpart, A-PBE remains secure even when the server storing hashed passwords is compromised. In particular, they show that if hashed passwords are already deployed using an existing password-hashing function, witness encryption can be used to turn the hashed passwords into public keys.[1] The drawback of using WE is that both encryption and decryption are inefficient. Using offline WE where a trusted third party produces the system parameters in an offline phase, encryption can be made significantly more efficient, whereas decryption (and the one-time setup) remains inefficient.

The use of offline WE is therefore particularly appealing in scenarios where decryption is usually not done anyway, but ciphertexts are made public as a means of deterrent. Consider a scenario where a content provider lets subscribed users set up passwords and use them to access some content. The provider typically stores a hash of the password. In order to discourage subscribers from distributing their passwords and allowing others to access content, the provider could simply encrypt some sensitive user information (such as credit card details, etc.) under a user's hashed password and publish this ciphertext. As anyone who knows the password could decrypt, it is then in the user's interest to keep his password secret.

Our Construction. Our construction, as well as its proof, is inspired by the *functional encryption* scheme by Garg et al. [GGH+13b].

The parameters required for encryption $pp_\mathsf{e} = (crs, pk_1, pk_2)$ consist of two public keys of a standard public-key encryption (PKE) scheme and a common reference string for a non-interactive zero-knowledge (NIZK) proof system. The encryption $c = (x, c_1, c_2, \pi)$ of a message m for an instance x is simply a Naor-Yung [NY90, Sah99] CCA-secure encryption of the pair (x, m); that is, encryptions c_1 and c_2 of (x, m) under pk_1 and pk_2, respectively, together with a NIZK proof π showing that the two ciphertext c_1, c_2 encrypt the same message.

---

[1] Such a key consists of a pair (sa, hpw) of a salt and a hashed password $hpw = \mathsf{PH}(sa, pw)$ for a password-hashing function PH. Given a WE for the NP-language $\{(sa, \mathsf{PH}(sa, pw)) \mid pw\}$, messages are encrypted w.r.t. statements (sa, hpw) and can be decrypted using witness pw such that $hpw = \mathsf{PH}(sa, pw)$.

The setup algorithm samples two key pairs (sk_1, pk_1), (sk_2, pk_2) for the PKE scheme and a CRS for the NIZK proof system. The parameters pp_d required for decryption consist of the obfuscation $\tilde{D}$ of a circuit D defined as follows. On input a ciphertext $c = (x, c_1, c_2, \pi)$ and a string w, the circuit D

- checks if $R(x, w) = 1$ (i.e., w is a witness for $x \in L$);
- checks if π is a proof that c_1 and c_2 encrypt the same message; and
- if both checks pass, decrypts $(x', m) = \mathsf{PK.Dec}(sk_1, c_1)$ and outputs m if $x' = x$.

Given an (obfuscated) circuit as above, the decryption algorithm of our WE scheme simply evaluates $\tilde{D}((x, c_1, c_2, \pi), w)$, which will output the message m for any witness w with $R(x, w) = 1$.

We prove in Theorem 1 that the above is a secure offline-WE scheme (meaning that ciphertexts for $x \notin L$ computationally hide the message), assuming that the obfuscation satisfies the notion of *indistinguishability obfuscation* [BGI+01], the NIKZ is *statistically simulation-sound* [GGH+13b] and the PKE is semantically secure under chosen-plaintext attack (CPA).

Functional Witness Encryption. Functional witness encryption was proposed by Boyle et al. [BCP14] and its encryption algorithm takes as input a circuit f in addition to instance x and message m. A party knowing a witness w for x now does not learn m itself, but only the function $f(m, w)$. For example, x could be a labeled graph and a party knowing a t-clique in x can learn the labels of this clique (but no other labels). Indistinguishability-based security (there is also an extractability-based notion) requires that, even when $x \in L$, encryptions of (x, m_0, f_0) and (x, m_1, f_1) are indistinguishable if for all w with $R(x, w) = 1$ we have $f_0(m_0, w) = f_1(m_1, w)$.

In Sect. 4 we define an offline variant of functional witness encryption and give an instantiation by adapting the (obfuscated) decryption circuit of our OWE scheme: instead of outputting m when given a witness w, it parses m as a pair (f, m') and outputs $f(m', w)$. Encryption still consists of computing a Naor-Yung ciphertext, whereas for the scheme in [BCP14] the encryptor needs to perform iO-obfuscation.

Efficiency of Encryption. In Sect. 5 we propose a concrete instantiation of the encryption algorithm used by our OWE schemes. In order to avoid random oracles, we use Groth-Sahai proofs [GS08], which are perfectly sound NIZK proofs in the standard model for languages defined over bilinear groups. They let us prove that two ElGamal ciphertexts encrypt the same message. Using ideas from [GGH+13b] and making them efficient by translating them into the bilinear-group framework, we construct a statistically simulation-sound (SSS) proof system. Under the so-called SXDH assumption (which states that the decisional Diffie-Hellman problem holds in the base groups), the encryption scheme is CPA-secure and the proof system we construct is zero-knowledge.

In our instantiation a proof consists of 28 elements from a bilinear group and is computed by using bilinear-group exponentiations (but no pairings).

For a 128-bit security level, the size of the output of our encryption algorithm, comprising 2 ciphertexts and one SSS proof, is about 1.3 kB.

Handling Long Messages and Instances. ElGamal encryption is defined over a group $\mathbb{G}$ and encrypts elements from $\mathbb{G}$; we therefore need to encode the message (x, m) into $\mathbb{G}$. Using elliptic-curve-based groups, for 128-bit security the length of an element from $\mathbb{G}$ is 256 bits, and standard encoding techniques [FJT13] allow for encoding of 128 bits into one group element, which is prohibitively small for any meaningful application.

We could of course choose a larger group such that one group element fits the entire tuple (x, m), but this would become very inefficient for large values. The encryption procedure we construct in Sect. 5 will therefore allow to encrypt arbitrarily long messages by encrypting them block-wise. We then need to provide a proof for each 128-bit block separately; however, using some optimization, we manage to limit the growth of the ciphertext to 0.25 kB for every 128 bits of plaintext, meaning the ciphertext grows by a factor of 16 compared to the plaintext.

For offline WE (but not for its functional variant) a further optimization when handling large messages m is to use key encapsulation: when encrypting, the sender first picks a key k for a symmetric encryption scheme and generates a ciphertext $c = (c_K, c_M)$, where c_K is the WE encryption of (x, k), and c_M is the (secret-key) encryption of m under k. To decrypt (given a witness w), the receiver first decrypts c_K to learn k and then decrypts c_M to recover m.

Dealing with large instances x turns out more tricky. Instead of x we could encrypt a hash $y = H(x)$ using a collision-resistant hash function H, noting that x is input to the decryption algorithm, which can therefore check whether $y = H(x)$. However, to prove this construction secure, we require the notion of *differing-inputs obfuscation* (a.k.a. extractability obfuscation) [BGI+01, BCP14, ABG+13], which seems a much stronger assumption than indistinguishability obfuscation, as implausibility results in [GGHW14] show.

Related Work. Zhandry [Zha14] proposes the notion of *reusable witness encryption*, which is similar to offline WE. Apart from being a key-encapsulation scheme (which does not generalize to FWE), the main difference is that setup outputs parameters which are used for both encryption and decryption and additionally a master decryption key (which allows for CCA-type security).

Zhandry constructs reusable WE using multilinear maps (and no obfuscation), which makes decryption more efficient than ours. Although ciphertexts in [Zha14] are short, the parameters are not, and, more importantly, encryption is less efficient than ours as it requires the evaluation of a multilinear map whose level of multilinearity is linear in the number of gates of the circuit describing the NP relation R. Efficient encryption was our main motivation for introducing offline WE and for this reason our model has separate parameters for encryption and decryption.

2   Preliminaries

2.1   Notations and Conventions

Families of Circuits. A family of circuits $\{\mathcal{C}_\lambda\}_{\lambda \in \mathbb{N}}$ is of polynomial size if for some polynomial $p(\cdot)$ the size of every $C \in \mathcal{C}_\lambda$ is at most $|C| \leq p(\lambda)$.

Probabilistic Algorithms. If $\mathcal{X}$ is a finite set then $x \leftarrow \mathcal{X}$ denotes the process of sampling x uniformly at random from $\mathcal{X}$. Let $\mathcal{A}$ be a probabilistic polynomial-time (PPT) algorithm; then $\Pr[y \leftarrow \mathcal{A}(x)]$ denotes the probability that $\mathcal{A}(x)$ outputs y when run on uniformly sampled coins. We let $\Pr\left[x_1 \leftarrow \mathcal{X}_1; x_2 \leftarrow \mathcal{X}_2; \ldots : \varphi(x_1, x_2, \ldots) = 1\right]$ denote the probability that the predicate φ evaluated on $(x_1, x_2, \ldots)$ is true after the ordered execution of $x_1 \leftarrow \mathcal{X}_1$, $x_2 \leftarrow \mathcal{X}_2, \ldots$

Negligible Functions. A function $\nu \colon \mathbb{N} \to \mathbb{R}$ is called negligible if for every positive polynomial $p(\cdot)$, and all sufficiently large $n \in \mathbb{N}$, it holds that $\nu(n) \leq \frac{1}{p(n)}$. We write $f(\lambda) = \mathsf{negl}(\lambda)$ to mean that $f(\cdot)$ is negligible.

$\mathbf{Exp}_{\mathcal{A}}^{\mathsf{CPA}\text{-}b}(\lambda):$

$(sk, pk) \leftarrow \mathsf{Gen}(1^\lambda)$

$(m_0, m_1, st) \leftarrow \mathcal{A}_1(1^\lambda, pk)$ // we require $|m_0| = |m_1|$

$c_b \leftarrow \mathsf{Enc}(pk, m_b)$

Return $b' \leftarrow \mathcal{A}_2(st, c_b)$

Fig. 1. CPA-security game of public-key encryption

2.2   Public-Key Encryption

Our first ingredient is a standard public-key encryption scheme.

Definition 1 (PKE). *A public-key encryption scheme for a message space $\mathcal{M}$ is a tuple of PPT algorithms* (Gen, Enc, Dec). *Gen, on input a security parameter 1^λ, outputs a secret/public key pair* (sk, pk). *Enc, on input a public key pk and a message $m \in \mathcal{M}$, outputs a ciphertext c using randomness $r \in \{0,1\}^{\ell_{\mathsf{PK}}(\lambda)}$. Finally, Dec, on input a secret key sk and a ciphertext c, outputs $m \in \mathcal{M} \cup \{\bot\}$. Furthermore we require correctness and security:*

- *Correctness: For every $\lambda \in \mathbb{N}$, $m \in \mathcal{M}$ we have*

$$\Pr\left[(sk, pk) \leftarrow \mathsf{Gen}(1^\lambda); c \leftarrow \mathsf{Enc}(pk, m) \ : \ \mathsf{Dec}(sk, c) = m\right] = 1.$$

- *Indistinguishability under chosen-plaintext attacks (CPA): For every non-uniform PPT adversary $\mathcal{A} = (\mathcal{A}_1, \mathcal{A}_2)$ in $\mathbf{Exp}_{\mathcal{A}}^{\mathsf{CPA}\text{-}b}(\lambda)$ (Fig. 1) we have*

$$\left| \Pr\left[\mathbf{Exp}_{\mathcal{A}}^{\mathsf{CPA}\text{-}0}(\lambda) = 1\right] - \Pr\left[\mathbf{Exp}_{\mathcal{A}}^{\mathsf{CPA}\text{-}1}(\lambda) = 1\right] \right| = \mathsf{negl}(\lambda).$$

2.3 Indistinguishability Obfuscation

As a consequence of the impossibility of virtual black-box obfuscation, Barak et al. [BGI+12] proposed the weaker notion of indistinguishability obfuscation (iO), which guarantees that obfuscations of equivalent functionalities are computationally indistinguishable.

Definition 2 (Indistinguishability obfuscation [BGI+12,GGH+13b]). *A uniform PPT algorithm $i\mathcal{O}$ is an indistinguishability obfuscator for a family of polynomial-size circuits $\{\mathcal{C}_\lambda\}_{\lambda \in \mathbb{N}}$, if the following hold:*

- *For all $\lambda \in \mathbb{N}$, $C \in \mathcal{C}_\lambda$, $x \in \{0,1\}^\lambda$:* $\Pr\left[\widetilde{C} \leftarrow i\mathcal{O}(1^\lambda, C) : C(x) = \widetilde{C}(x)\right] = 1.$
- *For every non-uniform PPT adversary $\mathcal{A}$, there exists a negligible function $\nu(\cdot)$ such that for all $C_0, C_1 \in \mathcal{C}_\lambda$ such that $C_0(x) = C_1(x)$ for all x:*

$$\left| \Pr\left[\mathcal{A}(i\mathcal{O}(1^\lambda, C_0)) = 1\right] - \Pr\left[\mathcal{A}(i\mathcal{O}(1^\lambda, C_1)) = 1\right]\right| = \nu(\lambda). \tag{1}$$

Garg et al. [GGH+13b] provide a candidate iO construction for families of polynomial-size circuits.

2.4 Statistically Simulation-Sound NIZK

A non-interactive (NI) proof system for a language $L \in \mathsf{NP}$ consists of four PPT algorithms: a *common-reference string* (CRS) generator G, which on input 1^λ outputs a CRS; a prover P, which on input a CRS, a statement y and a witness w outputs a proof; and a verifier V, which on input a CRS, a statement and a proof outputs 0 or 1.

We require a proof system that satisfies completeness, statistical soundness, and zero-knowledge (ZK). Completeness means that, on input a statement and a witness, P outputs a proof that V accepts. Statistical soundness requires that no unbounded adversary can produce a proof of a false statement. Zero-knowledge means that a proof does not reveal any information (in a computational sense) about the witness used to compute it; this is formalized by requiring the existence of a simulator $S = (S_1, S_2)$ that can output a CRS and a proof for any statement, which are computationally indistinguishable from real ones.

A NIZK proof system is statistically simulation-sound (SSS) [GGH+13b] if no *unbounded* adversary can produce a valid proof for a statement $y' \notin L$ even when given a simulated proof for any other statement $y \neq y'$.

Definition 3 (SSS-NIZK). *A tuple of PPT algorithms $(G, P, V, S = (S_1, S_2))$ is a statistically simulation-sound non-interactive zero-knowledge (SSS-NIZK) proof system for $L \in \mathsf{NP}$ with witness relation R if the following hold:*

- *Perfect completeness: For every (y, w) such that $R(y, w) = 1$, it holds that*

$$\Pr\left[crs \leftarrow G(1^\lambda); \pi \leftarrow P(crs, y, w) : V(crs, y, \pi) = 1\right] = 1.$$

– *Statistical soundness:*

$$\Pr\left[crs \leftarrow \mathsf{G}(1^\lambda) \;:\; \exists\, (y,\pi) \text{ s.t. } y \notin L \wedge \mathsf{V}(crs,y,\pi) = 1\right] = \mathsf{negl}(\lambda).$$

– *Computational zero-knowledge:* For every (y,w) such that $R(y,w) = 1$, and non-uniform PPT adversary $\mathcal{A}$, it holds that

$$\big| \Pr\left[crs \leftarrow \mathsf{G}(1^\lambda); \pi \leftarrow \mathsf{P}(crs,y,w) \;:\; \mathcal{A}(crs,y,\pi) = 1\right] -$$
$$\Pr\left[(crs,\tau)\leftarrow\mathsf{S}_1(1^\lambda,y); \pi\leftarrow\mathsf{S}_2(crs,\tau,y) \;:\; \mathcal{A}(crs,y,\pi) = 1\right] \big| = \mathsf{negl}(\lambda). \quad (2)$$

– *Statistical simulation soundness:* For every y, it holds that

$$\Pr\left[\begin{array}{l} (crs,\tau) \leftarrow \mathsf{S}_1(1^\lambda,y); \\ \pi \leftarrow \mathsf{S}_2(crs,\tau,y) \end{array} : \begin{array}{l} \exists\, (y',\pi') \text{ s.t. } y' \neq y \wedge y' \notin L \\ \wedge\, \mathsf{V}(crs,y',\pi') = 1 \end{array} \right] = \mathsf{negl}(\lambda). \quad (3)$$

Garg et al. [GGH+13b] construct an SSS-NIZK scheme from any statistically sound NIZK scheme and any computationally hiding and perfectly binding non-interactive commitment scheme. In Sect. 5, we give an efficient instantiation of this, following their blueprint and using perfectly sound Groth-Sahai proofs [GS08] and ElGamal encryption as perfectly binding and computationally hiding commitment scheme. In particular, our SSS-NIZK proof system is for the following NP language.

Definition 4. *Let* $(\mathsf{PK.Gen}, \mathsf{PK.Enc}, \mathsf{PK.Dec})$ *be a public-key encryption scheme. We define the* NP *language* L_{enc} *and let* R_{enc} *denote its witness relation:*

$$L_{\mathsf{enc}} := \left\{ (pk_1, pk_2, c_1, c_2) \;\middle|\; \begin{array}{l} \exists\, (x, m, r_1, r_2) \text{ s.t. } c_1 = \mathsf{PK.Enc}(pk_1, (x,m); r_1) \\ \wedge\, c_2 = \mathsf{PK.Enc}(pk_2, (x,m); r_2) \end{array} \right\}$$
$$(4)$$

3   Offline Witness Encryption

A (standard) witness encryption scheme [GGSW13, BH15] is defined by an encryption algorithm Enc that takes a security parameter 1^λ, a statement x and a message m and outputs a ciphertext c; and a decryption algorithm Dec that on input a ciphertext c and a witness w outputs a message. Offline witness encryption allows for efficient encryption by outsourcing the resource-heavy computations to a setup phase, which is independent of the statement and message to be encrypted. There is a third algorithm Setup which on input a security parameter 1^λ outputs a pair of parameters: pp_{e}, which is used by Enc, and pp_{d}, which is used by Dec. In our formalization we follow the strengthened definition of witness encryption put forth by Bellare and Tung Hoang [BH15].

Definition 5 (Offline witness encryption). *An offline witness encryption (OWE) scheme for a language* $L \in \mathsf{NP}$ *with witness relation* $R : \mathcal{X} \times \mathcal{W} \to \{0,1\}$ *is a tuple of PPT algorithms* $\mathsf{OWE} = (\mathsf{Setup}, \mathsf{Enc}, \mathsf{Dec})$ *where:*

- $(pp_e, pp_d) \leftarrow \mathsf{Setup}(1^\lambda)$: *On input a security parameter* 1^λ, Setup *outputs parameters for encryption* pp_e *and parameters for decryption* pp_d.
- $c \leftarrow \mathsf{Enc}(1^\lambda, x, m, pp_e)$: *On input a security parameter* 1^λ, *a string* $x \in \mathcal{X}$, *a message* $m \in \mathcal{M}$, *and encryption parameters* pp_e, Enc *outputs a ciphertext* c.
- $\mathsf{Dec}(c, w, pp_d) \in \mathcal{M} \cup \{\bot\}$: *On input a ciphertext* c, *a string* $w \in \mathcal{W}$ *and decryption parameters* pp_d, Dec *outputs* $m \in \mathcal{M} \cup \{\bot\}$.

We require correctness and security:

- *Correctness: For all* $\lambda \in \mathbb{N}$, $(x, w) \in \mathcal{X} \times \mathcal{W}$ *such that* $R(x, w) = 1$, $m \in \mathcal{M}$:

$$\Pr\left[(pp_e, pp_d) \leftarrow \mathsf{Setup}(1^\lambda); c \leftarrow \mathsf{Enc}(1^\lambda, x, m, pp_e) \; : \; \mathsf{Dec}(c, w, pp_d) = m\right].$$

- *Security:* OWE *is selectively secure if for every non-uniform PPT adversary* $\mathcal{A} = (\mathcal{A}_1, \mathcal{A}_2)$ *in* $\mathbf{Exp}_{L,\mathcal{A}}^{\text{sel-WE-}b}(\lambda)$ *(Fig. 2) it holds that*

$$\left| \Pr\left[\mathbf{Exp}_{L,\mathcal{A}}^{\text{sel-WE-}0}(\lambda) = 1\right] - \Pr\left[\mathbf{Exp}_{L,\mathcal{A}}^{\text{sel-WE-}1}(\lambda) = 1\right]\right| = \mathsf{negl}(\lambda).$$

OWE *is adaptively secure if the same holds for* $\mathbf{Exp}_{L,\mathcal{A}}^{\text{adp-WE-}b}(\lambda)$ *(Fig. 3).*

$\underline{\mathbf{Exp}_{L,\mathcal{A}}^{\text{sel-WE-}b}(\lambda):}$

$(x, m_0, m_1, st) \leftarrow \mathcal{A}_1(1^\lambda)$
// We require $|m_0| = |m_1|$
$(pp_e, pp_d) \leftarrow \mathsf{Setup}(1^\lambda)$
$c_b \leftarrow \mathsf{Enc}(1^\lambda, x, m_b, pp_e)$
$b' \leftarrow \mathcal{A}_2(st, c_b, pp_e, pp_d)$
If $x \in L$, return 0
Return b'

$\underline{\mathbf{Exp}_{L,\mathcal{A}}^{\text{adp-WE-}b}(\lambda):}$

$(pp_e, pp_d) \leftarrow \mathsf{Setup}(1^\lambda)$
$(x, m_0, m_1, st) \leftarrow \mathcal{A}_1(1^\lambda, pp_e, pp_d)$
// We require $|m_0| = |m_1|$
$c_b \leftarrow \mathsf{Enc}(1^\lambda, x, m_b, pp_e)$
$b' \leftarrow \mathcal{A}_2(st, c_b)$
If $x \in L$, return 0
Return b'

Fig. 2. Selective-security game of WE   **Fig. 3.** Adaptive-security game of WE

We now present our construction of offline WE that we have outlined in the introduction and prove that it satisfies selective security.

Construction 1 (Offline WE). Let $\mathsf{PKE} = (\mathsf{PK.Gen}, \mathsf{PK.Enc}, \mathsf{PK.Dec})$ be a public-key encryption scheme, $\mathsf{NIZK} = (\mathsf{G}, \mathsf{P}, \mathsf{V})$ an SSS-NIZK scheme for L_{enc} (Definition 4), and $i\mathcal{O}$ an indistinguishability obfuscator for the family of polynomial-size circuits $\mathcal{D}_\lambda$ defined in (5) below. We construct an offline witness encryption scheme $\mathsf{OWE} = (\mathsf{Setup}, \mathsf{Enc}, \mathsf{Dec})$ for $L \in \mathsf{NP}$ that can be decided by a (circuit) witness relation $R : \{0,1\}^{\ell_x} \times \{0,1\}^{\ell_w} \to \{0,1\}$ as follows:

$(pp_e, pp_d) \leftarrow \mathsf{Setup}(1^\lambda)$: On input a security parameter 1^λ, do the following:

- $(sk_1, pk_1) \leftarrow \mathsf{PK.Gen}(1^\lambda)$ and $(sk_2, pk_2) \leftarrow \mathsf{PK.Gen}(1^\lambda)$.
- $crs \leftarrow \mathsf{NIZK.G}(1^\lambda)$.
- Construct the circuit $D_{sk_j, crs} \in \mathcal{D}_\lambda$ with $j = 1$

$$D_{sk_j, crs}(c, w):$$
1:   Parse c as $c = (x, c_1, c_2, \pi)$
2:   If $\mathsf{NIZK.V}(crs, (pk_1, pk_2, c_1, c_2), \pi) = 1$
       // Verify that π is a proof for (pk_1, pk_2, c_1, c_2).
       // w.r.t. L_{enc}, where (pk_1, pk_2) is hardcoded.   (5)
3:      $(\hat{x}, \hat{m}) := \mathsf{PK.Dec}(sk_j, c_j)$
4:      If $(\hat{x} = x) \wedge R(x, w) = 1$
5:         Return $\hat{m}$
6:   Return $\perp$

- $\tilde{D}_{sk_1, crs} \leftarrow i\mathcal{O}(1^\lambda, D_{sk_1, crs})$ after padding $D_{sk_1, crs}$ appropriately.[2]
- Set $pp_e = (crs, pk_1, pk_2)$ and $pp_d = \tilde{D}_{sk_1, crs}$.
- Output (pp_e, pp_d).

$c \leftarrow \mathsf{Enc}(1^\lambda, x, m, pp_e)$: On input a security parameter 1^λ, a string $x \in \{0,1\}^{\ell_x}$, a message $m \in \mathcal{M}$, and $pp_e = (crs, pk_1, pk_2)$, Enc does the following:
- $r_1, r_2 \leftarrow \{0,1\}^{\ell_{\mathsf{PK}}(\lambda)}$.
- $c_1 := \mathsf{PK.Enc}(pk_1, (x, m); r_1)$ and $c_2 := \mathsf{PK.Enc}(pk_2, (x, m); r_2)$.
- $\pi \leftarrow \mathsf{NIZK.P}(crs, (pk_1, pk_2, c_1, c_2), (x, m, r_1, r_2))$.
- Output $c := (x, c_1, c_2, \pi)$.

$\mathsf{Dec}(c, w, pp_d)$: On input a ciphertext $c = (x, c_1, c_2, \pi)$, a string $w \in \{0,1\}^{\ell_w}$ and parameters $pp_d = \tilde{D}_{sk_1, crs}$, Dec interprets $\tilde{D}_{sk_1, crs}$ as a circuit and outputs $m := \tilde{D}_{sk_1, crs}(c, w)$.

Theorem 1. $\mathsf{OWE} = (\mathsf{Setup}, \mathsf{Enc}, \mathsf{Dec})$ *in Construction 1 is a selectively-secure offline witness encryption scheme if* PKE *is a CPA-secure PKE scheme,* NIZK *an SSS-NIZK scheme, and* $i\mathcal{O}$ *an indistinguishability obfuscator for* $\mathcal{D}_\lambda$.

Proof. Assume towards contradiction that there exists a non-uniform PPT adversary $\mathcal{A}$ that distinguishes $\mathbf{Exp}_{L,\mathcal{A}}^{\text{sel-WE-0}}$ from $\mathbf{Exp}_{L,\mathcal{A}}^{\text{sel-WE-1}}$ with non-negligible probability. We reach a contradiction by first constructing a series of games $\mathbf{Exp}^{(i)}$ defined in Fig. 4, where by construction, $\mathbf{Exp}_{L,\mathcal{A}}^{\text{sel-WE-0}} = \mathbf{Exp}^{(0)}$ and $\mathbf{Exp}_{L,\mathcal{A}}^{\text{sel-WE-1}} = \mathbf{Exp}^{(6)}$, and then proving for $i = 0, 1, \ldots, 5$ that $\mathbf{Exp}^{(i)}$ and $\mathbf{Exp}^{(i+1)}$ are computationally indistinguishable.

$\mathbf{Exp}^{(1)}$ differs from $\mathbf{Exp}^{(0)}$ in that the CRS crs for the NIZK and the proof π are simulated rather than honestly generated. The zero-knowledge property of NIZK guarantees that honestly generated CRSs and proofs are indistinguishable from simulated ones by PPT adversaries.

---

[2] W.l.o.g. we assume that $|D_{sk_1, crs}| = |D_{sk_2, crs}|$; otherwise we always pad to the maximum possible length.

$\mathbf{Exp}^{(i)}(\lambda)$ $// \ i \in \{0, 1, 2, 3, 4, 5, 6\}$

$(x, m_0, m_1, st) \leftarrow \mathcal{A}_1(1^\lambda)$

$(sk_1, pk_1) \leftarrow$ PK.Gen$(1^\lambda);$ $(sk_2, pk_2) \leftarrow$ PK.Gen(1^λ)

$r_1, r_2 \leftarrow \{0, 1\}^{\ell_{\mathsf{PK}}(\lambda)}$

If $i \in \{0, 1, 2, 3\}$ $c_1 :=$ PK.Enc$(pk_1, (x, m_0); r_1)$
Elseif $i \in \{4, 5, 6\}$ $c_1 :=$ PK.Enc$(pk_1, (x, m_1); r_1)$

If $i \in \{0, 1\}$ $c_2 :=$ PK.Enc$(pk_2, (x, m_0); r_2)$
Elseif $i \in \{2, 3, 4, 5, 6\}$ $c_2 :=$ PK.Enc$(pk_2, (x, m_1); r_2)$

$y := (pk_1, pk_2, c_1, c_2)$
If $i \in \{0, 6\}$ $crs \leftarrow$ NIZK.G(1^λ)
Elseif $i \in \{1, 2, 3, 4, 5\}$ $(crs, \tau) \leftarrow$ NIZK.S$_1(1^\lambda, y)$

If $i \in \{0, 1, 2, 5, 6\}$ $D := D_{sk_j, crs}$ with $j = 1$ as defined in (5)
Elseif $i \in \{3, 4\}$ $D := D_{sk_j, crs}$ with $j = 2$ as defined in (5)

$\tilde{D} \leftarrow i\mathcal{O}(1^\lambda, D)$
Set $pp_e = (crs, pk_1, pk_2)$ and $pp_d = \tilde{D}$
If $i = 0$ $\pi \leftarrow$ NIZK.P$(crs, y, (x, m_0, r_1, r_2))$
Elseif $i = 6$ $\pi \leftarrow$ NIZK.P$(crs, y, (x, m_1, r_1, r_2))$
Elseif $i \in \{1, 2, 3, 4, 5\}$ $\pi \leftarrow$ NIZK.S$_2(crs, \tau, y)$

$c := (x, c_1, c_2, \pi)$
$b' \leftarrow \mathcal{A}_2(st, c, pp_e, pp_d)$
If $x \in L$, return 0
Return b'

Fig. 4. Hybrid games used in the proof of Theorem 1

Proposition 1. $\mathbf{Exp}^{(0)}(\lambda)$ and $\mathbf{Exp}^{(1)}(\lambda)$ are computationally indistinguishable if NIZK is zero-knowledge.

$\mathbf{Exp}^{(2)}$ differs from $\mathbf{Exp}^{(1)}$ in that the second ciphertext c_2 is generated as PK.Enc$(pk_2, (x, \underline{m_1}))$ rather than PK.Enc$(pk_2, (x, m_0))$. ($D_{sk_1, crs}$ and (π, crs) are the same as in $\mathbf{Exp}^{(1)}$.) The CPA-security of PKE for key pk_2 guarantees that this change is indistinguishable by PPT adversaries.

Proposition 2. $\mathbf{Exp}^{(1)}(\lambda)$ and $\mathbf{Exp}^{(2)}(\lambda)$ are computationally indistinguishable if PKE is CPA-secure.

$\mathbf{Exp}^{(3)}$ differs from $\mathbf{Exp}^{(2)}$ in that the circuit $D_{\underline{sk_2}, crs}$ is obfuscated instead of $D_{sk_1, crs}$. Statistical simulation-soundness of NIZK now guarantees that $D_{sk_1, crs}$ and $D_{sk_2, crs}$ are functionally equivalent when crs is simulated for the statement $y := (pk_1, pk_2, c_1, c_2)$. It then follows from the security of $i\mathcal{O}$ that their obfuscations are computationally indistinguishable.

Proposition 3. $\mathbf{Exp}^{(2)}(\lambda)$ and $\mathbf{Exp}^{(3)}(\lambda)$ are computationally indistinguishable if NIZK is statistically simulation-sound, and $i\mathcal{O}$ is secure.

$\mathbf{Exp}^{(4)}$ differs from $\mathbf{Exp}^{(3)}$ in that the first ciphertext c_1 is generated as PK.Enc$(pk_1, (x, \underline{m_1}))$ rather than PK.Enc$(pk_1, (x, m_0))$. ($D_{sk_2, crs}$ and (π, crs) are the same as in $\mathbf{Exp}^{(3)}$.) Now CPA security of PKE w.r.t. pk_1 implies that this change is computationally indistinguishable.

Proposition 4. $\mathbf{Exp}^{(3)}(\lambda)$ *and* $\mathbf{Exp}^{(4)}(\lambda)$ *are computationally indistinguishable if* PKE *is CPA-secure.*

$\mathbf{Exp}^{(5)}$ differs from $\mathbf{Exp}^{(4)}$ in that $D_{sk_1,crs}$ is obfuscated rather than $D_{sk_2,crs}$. Statistical simulation soundness of NIZK together with security of $i\mathcal{O}$ implies that this change is computationally indistinguishable.

Proposition 5. $\mathbf{Exp}^{(4)}(\lambda)$ *and* $\mathbf{Exp}^{(5)}(\lambda)$ *are computationally indistinguishable if* NIZK *is statistically simulation-sound, and* $i\mathcal{O}$ *is secure.*

$\mathbf{Exp}^{(6)}$ is the original game $\mathbf{Exp}_{L,\mathcal{A}}^{\text{sel-WE-1}}$, and differs from $\mathbf{Exp}^{(5)}$ in that the CRS and NIZK proof (crs, π) are honestly generated rather than simulated. By zero-knowledge of NIZK this change is computationally indistinguishable.

Proposition 6. $\mathbf{Exp}^{(5)}(\lambda)$ *and* $\mathbf{Exp}^{(6)}(\lambda)$ *are computationally indistinguishable if* NIZK *is zero-knowledge.*

Theorem 1 follows from Propositions 1–6. We formally prove Theorem 1 in the full version [AFP15]. $\qquad\square$

4 Offline Functional Witness Encryption

Boyle et al. [BCP14] consider both extractable and indistinguishability-based notions of FWE. We consider an offline version of their indistinguishability-based notion. Here the encryption algorithm takes input an instance x and a pair (m, f) of a message and a description of a circuit f and outputs a ciphertext c. A party knowing a witness w for x now does not learn m itself, but only the function $f(m, w)$. Security requires computational indistinguishability of encryptions of $(x, (m_0, f_0))$ and $(x, (m_1, f_1))$ as long as $f_0(m_0, w) = f_1(m_1, w)$ for all w with $R(x, w) = 1$.

Definition 6 (Offline FWE). OWE = (Setup, Enc, Dec) *from Definition 5 is an offline FWE scheme if the following hold:*

– *Correctness: For all* $\lambda \in \mathbb{N}$, $(x, w) \in \mathcal{X} \times \mathcal{W}$ *such that* $R(x, w) = 1$, $m \in \mathcal{M}$:

$$\Pr\left[\begin{array}{l}(pp_e, pp_d) \leftarrow \mathsf{Setup}(1^\lambda); \\ c \leftarrow \mathsf{Enc}(1^\lambda, x, m, pp_e); (m', f) := m\end{array} : \mathsf{Dec}(c, w, pp_d) = f(m', w)\right].$$

– *Security: OWE is selectively secure if for every non-uniform PPT adversary* $\mathcal{A} = (\mathcal{A}_1, \mathcal{A}_2)$ *in* $\mathbf{Exp}_{L,\mathcal{A}}^{\text{sel-FWE-}b}(\lambda)$ *(Fig. 5) we have*

$$\left|\Pr\left[\mathbf{Exp}_{L,\mathcal{A}}^{\text{sel-FWE-0}}(\lambda) = 1\right] - \Pr\left[\mathbf{Exp}_{L,\mathcal{A}}^{\text{sel-FWE-1}}(\lambda) = 1\right]\right| = \mathsf{negl}(\lambda).$$

$\mathbf{Exp}_{L,\mathcal{A}}^{\text{sel-FWE-}b}(\lambda):$

$(x, (m'_0, f_0), (m'_1, f_1), st) \leftarrow \mathcal{A}_1(1^\lambda)$ // we require that $|(m'_0, f_0)| = |(m'_1, f_1)|$
$(pp_e, pp_d) \leftarrow \mathsf{Setup}(1^\lambda); c_b \leftarrow \mathsf{Enc}(1^\lambda, x, (m'_b, f_b), pp_e)$
$b' \leftarrow \mathcal{A}_2(st, c_b, pp_e, pp_d)$
If $\exists w: (R(x, w) = 1 \wedge f_0(m'_0, w) \neq f_1(m'_1, w))$, return 0
Return b'

Fig. 5. Security game of selectively-secure witness encryption

Construction 2 (Offline functional WE). This construction is defined exactly as Construction 1, except that in the definition of the decryption circuit in Eq. (5) on page we replace

$$\text{Return } \hat{m}$$

with

$$\text{Parse } \hat{m} \text{ as } (\hat{m}', f) \text{ and return } f(\hat{m}', w).$$

Theorem 2. *Construction 2 is a selectively-secure offline functional witness encryption scheme under the same assumptions as in Theorem 1.*

The proof is analogous to the proof of Theorem 1.[3]

5   Instantiating Enc

We now show how to efficiently instantiate the encryption algorithm of both our offline-WE schemes over a bilinear group and prove its security under a standard assumption (SXDH) and without recurring to random oracles. We use ElGamal encryption [ElG84] for the public-key encryption scheme and build an SSS-NIZK proof system from Groth-Sahai proofs [GS08] following the abstract blueprint for it given in [GGH+13b].

5.1   Tools

Bilinear Groups. $\mathcal{G}$ is a bilinear-group generator if given a security parameter 1^λ it returns the description of a bilinear group $\Lambda = (p, \mathbb{G}, \mathbb{H}, \mathbb{T}, e, g, h)$ where:

---

[3] The only change to be made is in the proof of Proposition 3, which is the only time we use the fact that $\bar{x} \notin L$. In the description of $\mathcal{B}$, $\bar{m}_j$ is replaced by $(\bar{m}'_j, \bar{f}_j)$ for $j = 0, 1$. For Case 1 we now argue that $D_1((\bar{x}, \bar{c}_1, \bar{c}_2, \pi), w) = D_2((\bar{x}, \bar{c}_1, \bar{c}_2, \pi), w)$ for all π, w as follows: If $R(\bar{x}, w) = 0$ then both circuits output $\bot$. If $R(\bar{x}, w) = 1$ then by the winning condition for the security game we have $\bar{f}_0(\bar{m}'_0, w) = \bar{f}_1(\bar{m}'_1, w)$ for all w. Since $\bar{c}_1$ decrypts to $(\bar{x}, (\bar{m}'_0, \bar{f}_0))$ and $\bar{c}_2$ decrypts to $(\bar{x}, (\bar{m}'_1, \bar{f}_1))$, both circuits return $\bar{f}_0(\bar{m}'_0, w)$.

– $\mathbb{G}$, $\mathbb{H}$ and $\mathbb{T}$ are groups of prime order p, where p is of bit-length λ;
– $e\colon \mathbb{G} \times \mathbb{H} \to \mathbb{T}$ is a bilinear map, that is, $e(R^a, S^b) = e(R, S)^{ab}$ for all $R \in \mathbb{G}$, $S \in \mathbb{H}$, $a, b \in \mathbb{Z}_p$;
– g and h generate $\mathbb{G}$ and $\mathbb{H}$, resp., and $e(g, h)$ generates $\mathbb{T}$.

We use Type-3 bilinear groups [GPS08], in which no efficiently computable homomorphisms are assumed to exist between $\mathbb{G}$ and $\mathbb{H}$. We can therefore assume that the decisional Diffie-Hellman assumption (DDH) holds in $\mathbb{G}$, that is

$$\left| \Pr\left[\begin{array}{c} \Lambda \leftarrow \mathcal{G}(1^\lambda); a, b \leftarrow \mathbb{Z}_p : \\ 1 \leftarrow \mathcal{A}(\Lambda, g^a, g^b, g^{ab}) \end{array} \right] - \Pr\left[\begin{array}{c} \Lambda \leftarrow \mathcal{G}(1^\lambda); a, b, c \leftarrow \mathbb{Z}_p : \\ 1 \leftarrow \mathcal{A}(\Lambda, g^a, g^b, g^c) \end{array} \right] \right| = \mathsf{negl}(\lambda),$$

for any non-uniform PPT $\mathcal{A}$. We moreover assume DDH holds in $\mathbb{H}$, that is, the same holds with g replaced by h above. The SXDH assumption for a bilinear-group generator $\mathcal{G}$ is that DDH holds in both $\mathbb{G}$ and $\mathbb{H}$.

ElGamal Encryption. We use ElGamal encryption to encrypt message vectors in $\mathbb{G}^\ell$, for some fixed ℓ. A secret key $\boldsymbol{x} \leftarrow \mathbb{Z}_p^\ell$ defines a public key $\boldsymbol{X} \in \mathbb{G}^\ell$ via $X_i := g^{x_i}$ for $i = 1, \ldots, \ell$. A message $\boldsymbol{M} = (M_i)_{i=1}^\ell \in \mathbb{G}^\ell$ is encrypted under $\boldsymbol{X}$ by choosing $r \leftarrow \mathbb{Z}_p^*$ and setting

$$\boldsymbol{c} = (c_1, \ldots, c_\ell, c_{\ell+1}) := ((M_i \cdot X_i^r)_{i=1}^\ell, g^r). \tag{6}$$

Note that by using the same randomness for every component, we decrease ciphertext length. CPA security follows from the DDH assumption in $\mathbb{G}$ via a standard hybrid argument.

Groth-Sahai Proofs. Groth-Sahai (GS) proofs [GS08] are efficient non-interactive witness-indistinguishable[4] (WI) proofs for several types of equations in bilinear groups. We only require *linear pairing-product equations* over variables $W_1, \ldots, W_n \in \mathbb{H}$, which are of the form

$$\prod_{i=1}^n e(A_i, \underline{W_i}) = t, \tag{7}$$

defined by $(A_i)_{i=1}^n \in \mathbb{G}^n$, and $t \in \mathbb{T}$. (As a convention, we always underline the variables.) GS proofs allow a prover to prove that there exists an assignment to the variables that satisfies a given set of equations. Groth-Sahai proofs are perfectly sound (meaning there do not exist proofs for an unsatisfiable set of equations). The instantiation of GS proofs we use is WI under the SXDH assumption. The cost of a proof is 2 elements from $\mathbb{H}$ per variable and 2 elements from $\mathbb{G}$ per equation.

---

[4] Witness-indistinguishability for a proof system for a language L means the following: no PPT adversary that given crs chooses y, w_0, w_1 with $R(y, w_0) = R(y, w_1) = 1$ can distinguish $\pi_0 \leftarrow \mathsf{P}(crs, y, w_0)$ from $\pi_1 \leftarrow \mathsf{P}(crs, y, w_1)$.

5.2   Instantiation

Using ElGamal encryption, we encode pairs $M = (x, m)$ (that is, statement/message pairs which we encrypt in our offline-WE instantiation) as a vector of group elements from $\mathbb{G}^\ell$. We thus assume that there exists an efficiently decodable encoding Cd of pairs (x, m) into $\mathbb{G}^\ell$ [FJT13].

We now construct an SSS-NIZK proof system which allows us to prove that 2 ElGamal ciphertexts under different keys encrypt the same message M. We assume that the ciphertexts are always different from $(1, \ldots, 1)$, which for honestly generated ciphertext is the case as $c_{l+1} \neq 1$ in (6).

A CRS for this system consists of a CRS for GS proofs together with a commitment C to $\mathbf{1}$. An SSS-NIZK proof for the statement y: "$\boldsymbol{c}^{(1)}$ and $\boldsymbol{c}^{(2)}$ encrypt the same message" is a GS proof for the statement

$$\boldsymbol{c}^{(1)} \text{ and } \boldsymbol{c}^{(2)} \text{ encrypt the same message OR } C \text{ commits to } (\boldsymbol{c}^{(1)}, \boldsymbol{c}^{(2)}). \quad (8)$$

Statistical soundness follows from perfect soundness of GS proofs: since C is not a commitment to $(\boldsymbol{c}^{(1)}, \boldsymbol{c}^{(2)}) \neq \mathbf{1}$, the first clause in (8) must hold. Zero-knowledge holds since given a statement $y = (\boldsymbol{c}^{(1)}, \boldsymbol{c}^{(2)})$ the simulator can set the value C in the CRS to a commitment to y; a proof for y can then be simulated by using use the second clause in (8). Since this is (in an information-theoretic sense) the only statement that can be simulated, statistical simulation-soundness (SSS) holds as well. We now present the details.

Language. A statement for our language L_{enc} defined in Eq. (4) is of the form $(\boldsymbol{X}^{(1)}, \boldsymbol{X}^{(2)}, \boldsymbol{c}^{(1)}, \boldsymbol{c}^{(2)})$, where $\boldsymbol{X}^{(1)}, \boldsymbol{X}^{(2)} \in \mathbb{G}^\ell$ are ElGamal encryption keys and $\boldsymbol{c}^{(1)}, \boldsymbol{c}^{(2)} \in \mathbb{G}^{\ell+1}$ are ElGamal encryptions of the same message. Since the public keys are hard-coded in the description of $D_{sk_j, crs}(c, w)$ (defined in (5)), we need not include them in the statement. We therefore construct a proof system for the language

$$L_{pk_1, pk_2} := \left\{ (c_1, c_2) \;\middle|\; \begin{array}{l} \exists\, (M, r_1, r_2) \in \mathbb{G}^\ell \times (\mathbb{Z}_p^*)^r : c_1 = \mathsf{PK.Enc}(pk_1, M; r_1) \\ \qquad\qquad\qquad\qquad \wedge\, c_2 = \mathsf{PK.Enc}(pk_2, M; r_2) \end{array} \right\},$$

where M is an encoding of (x, m).

Commitment. We define a non-interactive commitment scheme that lets us commit to a message $(\boldsymbol{c}^{(1)}, \boldsymbol{c}^{(2)}) \in \mathbb{G}^{2\ell+2}$ as follows:

- The commitment key is $ck = (K_1^{(1)}, \ldots, K_{\ell+1}^{(1)}, K_1^{(2)}, \ldots, K_{\ell+1}^{(2)}) \leftarrow \mathbb{G}^{2\ell+2}$.
- A commitment $\mathsf{Com}(ck, (\boldsymbol{c}^{(1)}, \boldsymbol{c}^{(2)}))$ to a message $(\boldsymbol{c}^{(1)}, \boldsymbol{c}^{(2)}) \in \mathbb{G}^{2\ell+2}$ is computed by picking $r_c \leftarrow \mathbb{Z}_p$ and setting

$$\boldsymbol{C} = \left((C_j^{(i)} := c_j^{(i)} \cdot (K_j^{(i)})^{r_c})_{j=1 \ldots \ell+1}^{i=1,2}, C' := g^{r_c} \right).$$

A commitment can be opened by publishing the "opening" $W = h^{r_c}$, which allows verifying that $\boldsymbol{C}$ is a commitment to $(\boldsymbol{c}^{(1)}, \boldsymbol{c}^{(2)})$ by checking

$$e(C_j^{(i)} \cdot (c_j^{(i)})^{-1}, h) = e(K_j^{(i)}, W) \quad \text{for } i = 1, 2 \,,\, j = 1 \ldots, \ell+1 \text{ and}$$

$$e(C', h) = e(g, W).$$

This yields a perfectly binding commitment scheme for messages from $\mathbb{G}^{2\ell+2}$, and, as the commitment is an ElGamal encryption, it is computationally hiding under the DDH assumption in $\mathbb{G}$.

Using Com we now define our SSS proof system for showing that two ciphertexts as in (6) encrypt the same message $\boldsymbol{M}$.

CRS Generation. A CRS is generated by computing a CRS for GS proofs $crs_{\mathrm{GS}} \leftarrow \mathsf{GS.G}(\Lambda)$, picking a commitment key $ck \leftarrow \mathbb{G}^{2\ell+2}$ computing $\boldsymbol{C} \leftarrow \mathsf{Com}(ck,(1,\dots,1))$ and outputting $crs := (crs_{\mathrm{GS}}, ck, \boldsymbol{C})$.

Proof. We show how to prove, under CRS $(crs_{\mathrm{GS}}, (\boldsymbol{K}^{(1)}, \boldsymbol{K}^{(2)}), \boldsymbol{C})$, a statement $(\boldsymbol{c}^{(1)}, \boldsymbol{c}^{(2)}) \in L_{\boldsymbol{X}^{(1)}, \boldsymbol{X}^{(2)}}$, using as witness (r_1, r_2) such that $\boldsymbol{c}^{(i)} = ((M_j \cdot (X_j^{(i)})^{r_i})_{j=1}^{\ell}, g^{r_i})$ for some $\boldsymbol{M} \in \mathbb{G}^{\ell}$. Consider the following set of linear pairing-product equations in variables $H_c, H_e, W_1, W_2, W_c \in \mathbb{H}$:

$$e(g, \underline{H_c})\,e(g, \underline{H_e}) = e(g, h) \tag{9}$$

$$e(C_j^{(i)} \cdot (c_j^{(i)})^{-1}, \underline{H_c}) = e(K_j^{(i)}, \underline{W_c}) \quad \text{for } i = 1, 2 \,,\, j = 1 \dots, \ell+1 \tag{10}$$

$$e(C', \underline{H_c}) = e(g, \underline{W_c}) \tag{11}$$

$$e(c_j^{(1)} \cdot (c_j^{(2)})^{-1}, \underline{H_e}) = e(X_j^{(1)}, \underline{W_1})\,e((X_j^{(2)})^{-1}, \underline{W_2}) \quad \text{for } j = 1, \dots, \ell \tag{12}$$

$$e(c_{\ell+1}^{(i)}, \underline{H_e}) = e(g, \underline{W_i}) \text{ for } i = 1, 2 \tag{13}$$

A proof of our SSS-NIZK proof system is a (witness-indistinguishable) GS proof of satisfiability of the above equation system and is computed by using witness (r_1, r_2) and setting the variables to

$$H_c := 1, \qquad H_e := h, \qquad W_c := 1, \qquad W_1 := h^{r_1}, \qquad W_2 := h^{r_2}. \tag{14}$$

Verification. A proof π for statement $(\boldsymbol{c}^{(1)}, \boldsymbol{c}^{(2)})$ under CRS $(crs_{\mathrm{GS}}, ck, \boldsymbol{C})$ is verified by verifying the GS proof π under crs_{GS} of satisfiability of equations (9)–(13) defined by the values in $\boldsymbol{c}^{(1)}, \boldsymbol{c}^{(2)}, ck = (\boldsymbol{K}^{(1)}, \boldsymbol{K}^{(2)})$ and $\boldsymbol{C} = ((C_j^{(i)})_{j=1\dots\ell+1}^{i=1,2}, C' := g^{r_c})$.

Completeness of our SSS NIZK proof system follows from completeness of GS proofs together with the fact that the values in (14) satisfy (9)–(13).

Soundness. Below we show that a proof of satisfiability of Eqs. (9)–(13) proves that

> – **either** $\boldsymbol{c}^{(1)}$ and $\boldsymbol{c}^{(2)}$ are encryptions of the same message
> – **or** $\boldsymbol{C}$ contained in the CRS is a commitment to $(\boldsymbol{c}^{(1)}, \boldsymbol{c}^{(2)})$. $\qquad$ (15)

Since GS proofs are perfectly sound and an honestly generated CRS contains a commitment to $(1, \dots, 1)$, which is a valid statement, a valid proof shows that the "either" clause above is satisfied, thus $(\boldsymbol{c}^{(1)}, \boldsymbol{c}^{(2)}) \in L_{pk_1, pk_2}$. We now show (15).

– Equation (9) proves that either $H_c \neq 1$ or $H_e \neq 1$; since $e(g, 1)\,e(g, 1) \neq e(g, h)$.

- If $H_c \neq 1$ then (10)–(11) prove that $(C_1^{(1)}, \ldots, C_{\ell+1}^{(1)}, C_1^{(2)}, \ldots, C_{\ell+1}^{(2)}, C')$ commits to $(c_1^{(1)}, \ldots, c_{\ell+1}^{(1)}, c_1^{(2)} \ldots, c_{\ell+1}^{(2)})$:

  Let $\eta, \omega \in \mathbb{Z}_p$, $\eta \neq 0$ (since $H_c \neq 1$), be such that $H_c = h^\eta$ and $W_c = h^\omega$. From (11) we have $C' = g^{\omega/\eta}$, whereas the equations in (10) yield $C_j^{(i)} \cdot (c_j^{(i)})^{-1} = (K_j^{(i)})^{\omega/\eta}$, thus $C_j^{(i)} = c_j^{(i)} \cdot (K_j^{(i)})^{\omega/\eta}$, which together means that $(C_1^{(1)}, \ldots, C_{\ell+1}^{(2)}, C')$ is a commitment to $(c_1^{(1)}, \ldots, c_{\ell+1}^{(2)})$ with randomness $r_c = \omega/\eta$.

- If $H_e \neq 1$ then with $\eta \neq 0, \omega_1$ and ω_2 such that $H_e = h^\eta$ and $W_i = h^{\omega_i}$ the equations in (13) yield that $c_{\ell+1}^{(i)} = g^{\omega_i/\eta}$, for $i = 1, 2$. Set $r_i := \omega_i/\eta$ and let $m_j^{(i)}$ be (the unique values) such that $c_j^{(i)} = g^{m_j^{(i)}} \cdot (X_j^{(i)})^{r_i}$. Then the equations in (12) yield $c_j^{(1)} \cdot (c_j^{(2)})^{-1} = (X_j^{(1)})^{r_1} \cdot (X_j^{(2)})^{-r_2}$, thus $g^{m_j^{(1)}} = g^{m_j^{(2)}}$ for all $j = 1, \ldots, \ell$, meaning $\boldsymbol{c}^{(1)}$ and $\boldsymbol{c}^{(2)}$ encrypt the same message.

Simulation. Given a statement $(\boldsymbol{c}^{(1)}, \boldsymbol{c}^{(2)})$, the simulator sets up the CRS by choosing $r_c \leftarrow \mathbb{Z}_p$ and setting $C := \mathsf{Com}(ck, (\boldsymbol{c}^{(1)}, \boldsymbol{c}^{(2)}); r_c)$. It simulates a proof for statement $(\boldsymbol{c}^{(1)}, \boldsymbol{c}^{(2)}) \in L_{pk_1, pk_2}$ by computing a GS proof for Eqs. (9)–(13) by instantiating the variables as

$$H_c := h, \qquad H_e := 1, \qquad W_c := h^{r_c}, \qquad W_1 := 1, \qquad W_2 := 1.$$

Since the commitment in the CRS is hiding under DDH in $\mathbb{G}$, and since GS proofs are witness-indistinguishable under SXDH, this simulation is also indistinguishable under SXDH (which implies DDH in $\mathbb{G}$). Statistical simulation-soundness holds, since once the CRS is set up, $(\boldsymbol{c}^{(1)}, \boldsymbol{c}^{(2)})$ is the only statement for which a proof using the 2nd clause in (15) can be computed. Any other proof must use the first clause, meaning the statement must be in the language.

5.3 Cost of an Encryption

In standard implementations of bilinear groups for 128-bit security, $\mathbb{G}$ elements are of size 256 bits and $\mathbb{H}$ elements are of size 512 bits. Let ℓ be such that pairs (x, m) are of size $< 128 \cdot \ell$ bits, that is, they can be mapped to $\mathbb{G}^\ell$.

An encryption in our WE scheme then consists of two ElGamal ciphertexts (each in $\mathbb{G}^{\ell+1}$) and a GS proof with 5 variables in $\mathbb{H}$ (requiring 10 elements from $\mathbb{H}$) and $3\ell + 6$ linear equations (requiring $6\ell + 12$ elements from $\mathbb{G}$). Computing an ElGamal encryption requires $\ell + 1$ exponentiations and ℓ group operations in $\mathbb{G}$. The 2 elements from $\mathbb{H}$ required for each variable require 2 exponentiations and one group operation in $\mathbb{H}$. The 2 elements from $\mathbb{G}$ required for each equation are computed using together 4 exponentiations and 2 group operations in $\mathbb{G}$.

With the above instantiation the output of Enc is in $\mathbb{G}^{8\ell+14} \times \mathbb{H}^{10}$. If two group elements suffice to encode pairs (x, m) then one encryption has $\approx 1.6\,\mathrm{kB}$. For every 128-bit increase of the message length, the encryption only grows by 8 elements from $\mathbb{G}$, that is $0.25\,\mathrm{kB}$.

References

[ABG+13] Ananth, P., Boneh, D., Garg, S., Sahai, A., Zhandry, M.: Differing-inputs obfuscation and applications. IACR Cryptology ePrint Archive, 2013:689 (2013)

[AFP15] Abusalah, H., Fuchsbauer, G., Pietrzak, K.: Offline Witness Encryption. Cryptology ePrint Archive, Report 2015/838 (2015). http://eprint.iacr.org/

[AHKM14] Apon, D., Huang, Y., Katz, J., Malozemoff, A.J.: Implementing cryptographic program obfuscation. Cryptology ePrint Archive, Report 2014/779 (2014). http://eprint.iacr.org/

[BCP14] Boyle, E., Chung, K.-M., Pass, R.: On extractability obfuscation. In: Lindell, Y. (ed.) TCC 2014. LNCS, vol. 8349, pp. 52–73. Springer, Heidelberg (2014)

[BGI+01] Barak, B., Goldreich, O., Impagliazzo, R., Rudich, S., Sahai, A., Vadhan, S.P., Yang, K.: On the (im)possibility of obfuscating programs. In: Kilian, J. (ed.) CRYPTO 2001. LNCS, vol. 2139, pp. 1–18. Springer, Heidelberg (2001)

[BGI+12] Barak, B., Goldreich, O., Impagliazzo, R., Rudich, S., Sahai, A., Vadhan, S., Yang, K.: On the (im)possibility of obfuscating programs. J. ACM 59(2), 1–48 (2012)

[BH15] Bellare, M., Hoang, V.T.: Adaptive witness encryption and asymmetric password-based cryptography. In: Katz, J. (ed.) PKC 2015. LNCS, vol. 9020, pp. 308–331. Springer, Heidelberg (2015)

[EGM96] Even, S., Goldreich, O., Micali, S.: On-line/off-line digital signatures. J. Cryptol. 9(1), 35–67 (1996)

[ElG84] El Gamal, T.: A public key cryptosystem and a signature scheme based on discrete logarithms. In: Blakely, G.R., Chaum, D. (eds.) CRYPTO 1984. LNCS, vol. 196, pp. 10–18. Springer, Heidelberg (1985)

[FJT13] Fouque, P.-A., Joux, A., Tibouchi, M.: Injective encodings to elliptic curves. In: Boyd, C., Simpson, L. (eds.) ACISP. LNCS, vol. 7959, pp. 203–218. Springer, Heidelberg (2013)

[GGH13a] Garg, S., Gentry, C., Halevi, S.: Candidate multilinear maps from ideal lattices. In: Johansson, T., Nguyen, P.Q. (eds.) EUROCRYPT 2013. LNCS, vol. 7881, pp. 1–17. Springer, Heidelberg (2013)

[GGH+13b] Garg, S., Gentry, C., Halevi, S., Raykova, M., Sahai, A., Waters, B.: Candidate indistinguishability obfuscation and functional encryption for all circuits. In: 54th FOCS, pp. 40–49. IEEE Computer Society Press, October 2013

[GGHW14] Garg, S., Gentry, C., Halevi, S., Wichs, D.: On the implausibility of differing-inputs obfuscation and extractable witness encryption with auxiliary input. In: Garay, J.A., Gennaro, R. (eds.) CRYPTO 2014, Part I. LNCS, vol. 8616, pp. 518–535. Springer, Heidelberg (2014)

[GGSW13] Garg, S., Gentry, C., Sahai, A., Waters, B.: Witness encryption and its applications. In: Boneh, D., Roughgarden, T., Feigenbaum, J. (eds.) 45th ACM STOC, pp. 467–476. ACM Press, June 2013

[GLW14] Gentry, C., Lewko, A., Waters, B.: Witness encryption from instance independent assumptions. In: Garay, J.A., Gennaro, R. (eds.) CRYPTO 2014, Part I. LNCS, vol. 8616, pp. 426–443. Springer, Heidelberg (2014)

[GPS08] Galbraith, S.D., Paterson, K.G., Smart, N.P.: Pairings for cryptographers. Discrete Appl. Math. **156**(16), 3113–3121 (2008)

[GS08] Groth, J., Sahai, A.: Efficient non-interactive proof systems for bilinear groups. In: Smart, N.P. (ed.) EUROCRYPT 2008. LNCS, vol. 4965, pp. 415–432. Springer, Heidelberg (2008)

[NY90] Naor, M., Yung, M.: Public-key cryptosystems provably secure against chosen ciphertext attacks. In: 22nd ACM STOC, pp. 427–437. ACM Press, May 1990

[Sah99] Sahai, A.: Non-malleable non-interactive zero knowledge and adaptive chosen-ciphertext security. In: 40th FOCS, pp. 543–553. IEEE Computer Society Press, October 1999

[SW05] Sahai, A., Waters, B.: Fuzzy identity-based encryption. In: Cramer, R. (ed.) EUROCRYPT 2005. LNCS, vol. 3494, pp. 457–473. Springer, Heidelberg (2005)

[Zha14] Zhandry, M.: How to avoid obfuscation using witness PRFs. Cryptology ePrint Archive, Report 2014/301 (2014). http://eprint.iacr.org/2014/301

Deterministic Public-Key Encryption Under Continual Leakage

Venkata Koppula[1], Omkant Pandey[2(✉)], Yannis Rouselakis[3],
and Brent Waters[1]

[1] University of Texas at Austin, Austin, USA
{kvenkata,bwaters}@cs.utexas.edu
[2] Drexel University, Philadelphia, USA
omkant@drexel.edu
[3] Microsoft, Redmond, USA
johnysrouss@gmail.com

Abstract. Deterministic public-key encryption, introduced by Bellare, Boldyreva, and O'Neill (CRYPTO 2007), is an important technique for searchable encryption; it allows quick, logarithmic-time, search over encrypted data items. The technique is most effective in scenarios where frequent search queries are performed over a huge database of unpredictable data items. We initiate the study of deterministic public-key encryption (D-PKE) in the presence of *leakage*. We formulate appropriate security notions for leakage-resilient D-PKE, and present constructions that achieve them in the standard model. We work in the *continual* leakage model, where the secret-key is updated at regular intervals and an attacker can learn arbitrary but bounded leakage on the secret key during each time interval. We, however, do not consider leakage during the updates. Our main construction is based on the (standard) linear assumption in bilinear groups, tolerating up to $0.5 - o(1)$ fraction of arbitrary leakage. The leakage rate can be improved to $1 - o(1)$ by relying on the SXDH assumption.

At a technical level, we propose and construct a "continual leakage resilient" version of the *all-but-one* lossy trapdoor functions, introduced by Peikert and Waters (STOC 2008). Our formulation and construction of leakage-resilient lossy-TDFs is of independent general interest for leakage-resilient cryptography.

Keywords: Deterministic public key encryption · Leakage resilient cryptography · Lossy trapdoor functions

1 Introduction

The notion of *semantic security* for public key encryption schemes was introduced in the seminal work of Goldwasser and Micali [24]. While this strong notion of security is desirable in many applications, it requires that the encryption algorithm must be a random process. This creates a significant performance bottleneck if, for example, one wants to perform fast search over many encrypted

© Springer International Publishing Switzerland 2016
M. Manulis et al. (Eds.): ACNS 2016, LNCS 9696, pp. 304–323, 2016.
DOI: 10.1007/978-3-319-39555-5_17

data items. To address this issue, Bellare, Boldyreva, and O'Neill [5] initiated the study of deterministic public-key encryption (D-PKE) schemes. In D-PKE schemes, the encryption algorithm is required to be a deterministic function of the message. Consequently, D-PKE cannot satisfy any meaningful notion of security for low-entropy plaintext distributions. Bellare et al. demonstrated that a strong notion of security can in fact be realized for relatively high-entropy plaintext distributions. Several follow up works then further investigated security notions for deterministic encryption and presented standard model constructions [6, 9, 14, 22, 35, 37, 45].

Deterministic encryption is a promising technique for building "searchable encryption" [41, 42]. It is most effective in scenarios where frequent search queries are performed over a huge database of *unpredictable*, data items (e.g., credit card numbers). This is in fact the ideal setting for deterministic encryption: on one hand, the "hard-to-guess" nature of credit-card numbers ensures that they are well protected even if encryption is deterministic; on the other hand, logarithmic search-time ensures good response-time even if the database is potentially huge and search queries are rather frequent.

We initiate a study of deterministic PKE in the presence of leakage attack where an adversary can learn partial but important information about the secret key of the system (e.g., by means of insider attacks, or side channel attacks [4, 30, 38, 44]). Existing deterministic PKE schemes are not resilient to leakage and assume that the adversary only has black-box access to the decryption box.

We present a thorough study of leakage-resilient D-PKE. We adapt existing security notions for deterministic PKE to the *continual leakage* model [13, 16] and present constructions that achieve them.

Let us note that although several leakage-resilient schemes for *randomized* PKE are known [1, 2, 13, 16, 17, 19, 26, 36], they have no direct implication to determinisitc PKE. This is because the security of randomized PKE crucially relies on the *randomness* of encryption even in the leakage setting and such randomness is simply not present in deterministic PKE. In general—*even without leakage*—there is no direct way of obtaining deterministic PKE schemes from the randomized ones in the standard model; the techniques for constructing deterministic PKE are usually quite different.

The *continual memory leakage* (CML) model was introduced in [13, 16]. In the context of public-key encryption, we envision a system with a *fixed* public-key pk, along with a (variable) secret key sk which is "refreshed" or "updated" at regular time intervals. In each time interval, the adversary can issue a leakage query of its choice, in the form of a polynomial-time computable function $\mathcal{L}$, and learn $\mathcal{L}(sk)$. The adversary can repeat this process for polynomially many time intervals, issuing queries of the form $\mathcal{L}_i$, and learning $\mathcal{L}(sk_i)$ in the i-th interval. To prevent trivially leaking the whole key, the model asserts that the size of all leakage answers in the i-th intervals is bounded by $\rho.|sk_i|$ for every i, where $\rho \in [0, 1)$ is the leakage parameter of the system and sk_i is the secret-key in the i-th interval. It is also required that every sk_i should correctly decrypt the ciphertexts under pk, and be roughly of the same size as the initial key of the system. The higher the ρ for a scheme, the higher the amount of leakage it can tolerate.[1]

The CML model is indeed a very powerful model since it allows the attacker to potentially learn unbounded leakage on the system's secret memory. In addition to constructions of randomized PKE mentioned above, leakage-resilient schemes for several tasks in a variety of leakage models are now known, e.g., digital signatures [12,31,33], identity-based encryption [13,15,32], interactive proofs [3,23,39], secure computation [11,20,25], and so on. We remark that the study of leakage-resilient cryptography was initiated in [19,29,34] as an attempt to provide an *algorithmic* defense against side-channel attacks [4,30,38,44]. Renauld et al. [46] highlight several difficulties in formalizing an appropriate model of leakage for real-world side-channel attacks, and argue that often an algorithmic defense is not possible since the key might have been completely compromised. In such settings, we cannot do anything except for developing alternative methods such as those at the hardware level. However, when the adversary *is* limited to side-channel attacks that do not fully compromise the system, the continual leakage model is essentially as good a model as possible.

Our Results. Our goal is to obtain standard model constructions of deterministic PKE which can deliver meaningful security under the CML attack. The security notions for deterministic PKE have evolved over time. Bellare et al. [5] proposed the notions of PRIV1-IND and PRIV-IND security; the former is the most basic notion of security, while the latter was shown in [6,9] to be one of the strongest notions. In the special setting when plaintext distributions have sufficient *block-wise min-entropy*, these two notions are actually equivalent. Bellare et al. [5] argued that in the general setting, the plaintext distributions cannot depend on the public-key of the system. However, under special constraints over plaintext distributions, this restriction may not be necessary [14,45].

In this work, we stick to the original setting of [5], and reformulate PRIV1-IND and PRIV-IND security in the presence of CML attacks. We then construct a deterministic PKE scheme satisfying the PRIV1-IND security under the CML attack. Our scheme is based on the (standard) *linear* (a.k.a. "matrix DDH") assumption [10,36] in bilinear groups, and it can tolerate a leakage-rate up to $\rho = 0.5 - o(1)$. A simpler variant of this scheme has better system parameters, and can tolerate an almost optimal leakage rate of $\rho = 1 - o(1)$; however, it is based on the (stronger) SXDH assumption.

To construct our deterministic PKE, we formulate and construct a "continual leakage resilient" version of lossy trapdoor functions, abbreviated as CLR-LTDF. Lossy trapdoor functions were introduced by Peikert and Waters [40], and have found a vast number of applications in cryptography. We actually work with the more general notion of lossy TDFs, namely all-but-one (ABO) functions, since the simpler definition (consisting of only two families) cannot tolerate even 1 bit of leakage. We believe that our formulation of CLR-LTDF is of independent general interest especially with regard to constructing other leakage-resilient schemes.

---

[1] We note that in our model no leakage is allowed during *update* phase. However, the most general model allows leakage during the update phase as well.

We remark that unlike the standard setting where lossy TDFs almost immediately imply D-PKE [9], CLR-LTDFs do not immediately imply a leakage-resilient D-PKE. The leakage setting is more challenging and the proof that such a reduction is possible, is not straight forward.

1.1 An Overview of Our Approach

Bellare et al. [5] show that, in the random-oracle model [8], a semantically secure (randomized) PKE also implies a PRIV-IND secure deterministic PKE; the reduction simply replaces the randomness of encryption by $H(m)$ where H is a random-oracle and m is the message to be encrypted. By using a LR (randomized) PKE in this reduction, we immediately get a LR D-PKE. However, in the standard model, no such general reduction is known. In general, due to the deterministic nature of encryption, D-PKE generally require their own set of techniques.

A prominent technique for constructing deterministic PKE (in the standard model) is based on *lossy trapdoor functions* [40]; it was given by Boldyreva et al. [9]. Recall that, lossy TDFs define two function families $\{F_{\mathrm{inj}}\}$ and $\{F_{\mathrm{lossy}}\}$. Functions in the first family are always *injective* and can be efficiently inverted using a trapdoor. Functions in the other family are always *lossy*: meaning that the range-size of every function in $\{F_{\mathrm{lossy}}\}$ is much smaller than its domain-size. Therefore, functions in the second family necessarily loose a lot of information about their input. In addition, these two families are computationally indistinguishable: it is hard to decide whether a (properly sampled) function belongs to the injective family or the lossy family. Boldyreva et al. [9] observe that if the lossy mode also acts as a *universal* hash function then the functions from the injective family (of a lossy TDF) act as a PRIV1-IND secure deterministic-PKE. Furthermore, following [18], they show that even if the lossy mode is not universal, it still leads to a secure scheme *provided* that the message is first permuted using a pairwise independent permutation. They prove this by extending the crooked LHL of [18] to work with lossy functions and average conditional min-entropy.

A natural idea is to suitably adapt this approach to the leakage setting. Unfortunately, lossy TDFs cannot be leakage-resilient as defined: just one bit of leakage on the trapdoor suffices to tell injective functions from the lossy ones. To make this approach work, we first need to re-formulate the notion of lossy TDFs in the leakage setting and then suitably modify the approach of [9] to obtain a deterministic PKE.

Leakage-Resilient Lossy TDFs. Since lossy TDFs cannot be leakage-resilient as defined, we work with *all-but-one* (ABO) functions also introduced in [40]. ABO functions define only one family $\{F\}$ where each $f \in F$ takes two inputs. The first input is called a *branch* b taken from a branch space $\mathcal{B}$. As the name suggests, there exists a unique branch $b^* \in \mathcal{B}$ such that the single input function $F(b, \cdot)$ is lossy when $b = b^*$ and injective otherwise. We consider a notion similar to ABO functions. Specifically, we consider a family of functions $\{F\}$ which take two inputs where the first input is a branch b. We require that at least one branch b defines a lossy function $F(b, \cdot)$, and the fraction of all lossy branches is negligible. All other branches define an injective function.

Intuitively, leakage resilience for our functions, should mean that given $(f, \mathcal{L}_f(t), b)$, where is t is the trapdoor, it is hard to decide whether b is lossy or injective; here $\mathcal{L}_f$ is the leakage function which can depend on f (but not b, since otherwise we will have the same problem as before). We note that it is of independent interest to consider such functions under various models for leakage $\mathcal{L}_f$. However, motivated by our application of deterministic PKE, we will consider the most demanding CML model. Since the CML model requires that the trapdoor should refreshed or updated after each time interval, our functions will have an *update* algorithm in addition to usual ones for ABO.

The attack model for our functions will then work as follows. Once the description of f is fixed, the adversary will be able to ask (bounded) leakage during each time-interval; the trapdoor for the function f will be *updated* after each time interval. Once the leakage is complete, the adversary will enter a challenge phase in which it will be given either a lossy branch b^* or an injective branch $b \neq b^*$; the adversary wins if it successfully guesses the type of the branch. The adversary is not allowed any queries once the challenge branch is given. The formal description appears in later sections.

As mentioned earlier, we call such functions *continual leakage-resilient lossy-trapdoor functions* or CLR-LTDF. We construct CLR-LTDF under the linear assumption tolerating a leakage fraction of $\rho = 0.5 - o(1)$. A simpler variant of this construction based on SXDH assumption can tolerate almost optimal leakage of $\rho = 1 - o(1)$.

Achieving Leakage-Resilient D-PKE from CLR-LTDF. Although our formulation of CLR-LTDF seems natural, it remains to be seen if it can prove useful in constructing D-PKE. Let us see if we can use an approach along the lines of Boldyreva et al. [9].

Suppose that we are given a family of CLR-TDFs. The functions in the family require a branch for evaluation. We need to find a *deterministic* method to sample the branch. If a branch is chosen and provided with public-parameters, we will not have any leakage-resilience. The adversary can simply check if the branch is lossy or injective via leakage queries. A better idea, following [9], would be to let the branch $b = h(m)$ and then encrypt $\pi(m)$ where m is the message to be encrypted, h is a universal hash function, and π a pairwise independent permutation; both (h, π) are sampled at the time of setup. If m has sufficient entropy the branch looks random due to (standard) LHL; further if m has enough entropy *conditioned* on $(h, h(m))$, we might hope to use the analysis from [9] (which relies on "generalized crooked LHL") to argue security.[2]

Unfortunately, the analysis from [9] does not quite work since it crucially relies on the fact that the family is a lossy TDF *without branches*. (If ABO

---

[2] Note that here it is important that distribution of m does not depend on h, π. This is indeed the case since (h, π) are part of the public-key and m is not allowed to depend on public-key in our setting.

functions are used, then a single branch must be chosen as part of the public-parameters, and used for all evaluations for their analysis to work.) In contrast, in our proposed scheme, the branch changes for almost every sampled message. This results in two main difficulties. Consider the reduction in which the proof will try to reduce the security of our proposed construction to that of the CLR-LTDF. That is, the reduction attempts to correctly guess whether a challenge branch b' is injective or lossy with the help of an adversary A who breaks our proposed scheme. The reduction will somehow need to use b' to create a correctly generated challenge ciphertext c. For example, in the simplest type of reduction, we may try to ensure that c is an encryption under the branch b' for some message, say m. Then, the reduction must ensure that: (1) $h(m) = b'$, and (2) m comes from one distribution if b' is injective and from the other distribution if it is lossy.

It turns out rather non-trivial to show that we can design such a reduction and the proposed construction indeed works. However, making this construction work requires us to consider a slightly strengthened version of CLR-LTDFs where the challenge branches can be sampled using an arbitrary, possibly adversarial, algorithm as long as the sampling results in independent and correctly distributed branches. The security is then required to hold even in the presence of some auxiliary information about the challenge branch.

1.2   How to Construct CLR-LTDF

We now present an overview of our construction of CLR-LTDFs. Our starting point is the ABO construction of [40] which works as follows. It samples a $n \times n$ matrix $\mathbf{A}$ whose entries are, roughly speaking, (ElGamal) encryptions of 0. The function description is then set to $g^{\mathbf{M}}$ where $\mathbf{M} = \mathbf{A} + b^*\mathbf{I}$, $\mathbf{I}$ denotes the identity matrix, and b^* is lossy branch. The function evaluation on $(b, \mathbf{x})$ is $g^{(\mathbf{M}-b\mathbf{I})\mathbf{x}}$, which is easily inverted if $\mathbf{x} \in \{0, 1\}^n$, given $\mathbf{A}, b, b^*$. To ensure lossiness when $b = b^*$, the randomness of the ElGamal encryptions are "correlated" in a special manner.

A natural idea is to replace the ElGamal encryption with an appropriate continual LR PKE scheme. The hope is that leakage-resilience of ABO can now be reduced to leakage-resilience of the PKE in use. The central difficulty such a reduction faces is as follows. The reduction needs to provide the adversary, say A, the description of a function f from the family in the beginning, and a challenge branch b' in the end. Clearly, whether b' is injective or lossy, should somehow depend on whether the challenge ciphertext c obtained from the PKE-challenger encrypts 0 or 1.[3] Since c is not known ahead of time, the reduction must be able to find a b' when c becomes known, yet this b' should make the function injective or lossy depending on what c encrypts.

We do not know if such a black-box reduction is possible in general. However, it might be possible to make this approach work by relying on specific

---

[3] For the PW construction, we will need to use n such ciphertexts, one for each diagonal entry; this can be handled using a hybrid argument.

constructions of LR PKE. Our construction uses a similar approach and uses BKKV encryption instead of ElGamal. A key property of this encryption scheme is that it supports (almost) additive homomorphic encryptions. This allows us to use the branches as a one-time pad to mask the diagonal entries. However, we still cannot obtain an injective or lossy branch from a challenge ciphertext of BKKV in a black-box manner. Instead, we directly work with "matrix DDH" challenger, and use the ideas from BKKV, to directly prove that our construction is leakage-resilient. More specifically, our reduction directly works with the matrix DDH challenger, but relies on the structure of BKKV encryption and the fact that *random subspaces are leakage resilient* (Theorem 2.1, [13]) to answer the leakage queries of the adversary. The reduction only knows a key from a random subspace of the entire key space, and therefore can fail to decrypt some special ciphertexts. These special cipertexts will correspond to the DDH challenges, and used to define the challenge branch b'. A description of BKKV encryption scheme is given in the preliminaries.

Related Work on Lossy TDFs. There has been a significant follow up work on extending lossy TDFs such as all-but-N functions defined by Hemnway et al. [27], all-but-many functions defined by Hofheinz [28], and identity-based lossy TDFs defined by Bellare et al. [7]. Likewise, in addition to the constructions in these works, several other works have presented constructions of (standard) lossy TDFs based on a variety of assumptions [21,47]. Qin et al. [43] propose an alternate type of leakage-resilient lossy-TDF in which a master-key mk is selected first; injective/lossy functions f are chosen later, and mk generates trapdoors for injective f. Leakage is allowed only on mk, and no leakage is allowed after f is fixed. It is not clear how to use this version for our application of deterministic-PKE.

2   Preliminaries

Due to space constraints, we defer some of the preliminaries to the full version of this paper.

New Notation. We will use two types of matrices: matrices of scalars, denoted by uppercase letters $A = [a_{ij}]$ and matrices of *vectors*, denoted by bold uppercase letters $\mathbf{A} = [\mathbf{a}_{ij}]$. When we want to be explicit about the dimension of a matrix $\mathbf{A}$, we will write $\mathbf{A}_{m \times n}$; define $A_{m \times n}$ similarly. Let $\mathbf{A}_{m \times n} = [\mathbf{a}_{ij}]$ be a matrix of vectors, and $\mathbf{x} = (x_1, \ldots, x_n)^{\mathsf{T}}$ be a column vector (with scalar coordinates), then we define:

$$\mathbf{A}\mathbf{x} = \mathbf{Y}_{m \times 1} = (\mathbf{y}_1, \ldots, \mathbf{y}_m)^{\mathsf{T}} \quad \text{where} \quad \mathbf{y}_i = \sum_{j \in [n]} x_j \mathbf{a}_{ij}$$

for every $i \in [m]$. That is, each $\mathbf{y}_i$ is a linear combination of the vectors in the i-th row of matrix $\mathbf{A}$, where the scalars of the linear combination are the coordinates of vector $\mathbf{x}$.

Let $\mathbb{G}$ be a group of prime order p, and g be its generator. For $\mathbf{x} = (x_1, \ldots, x_n) \in \mathbb{Z}_p^n$, we define $g^{\mathbf{x}} := (g^{x_1}, \ldots, g^{x_n})$; similarly, we define matrices $g^A := [g^{a_{ij}}]$ and $g^{\mathbf{A}} := [g^{\mathbf{a}_{ij}}]$ where A is a matrix of scalars $a_{ij} \in \mathbb{Z}_p$, and $\mathbf{A}$ is a matrix of vectors $\mathbf{a}_{ij} \in \mathbb{Z}_p^\ell$ (for some $\ell \in \mathbb{N}$) for all values of i and j.

Finally, when dealing with vectors $\mathbf{x} = (x_1, \ldots, x_n)$ and $\mathbf{y} = (y_1, \ldots, y_n)$ both in $\mathbb{Z}_p^n$, we denote by $+$, $-$, and $\cdot$ the *component-wise* addition, subtraction, and multiplication modulo p. In particular, $\mathbf{x} \cdot \mathbf{y} = (x_1 y_1, \ldots, x_n y_n)$ with product taken modulo p. However, when we deal with vectors $\mathbf{u} = (u_1, \ldots, u_n)$ and $\mathbf{v} = (v_1, \ldots, v_n)$ both in $\mathbb{G}^n$ for some group $\mathbb{G}$, we use $\cdot$ to denote the group operation of $\mathbb{G}$ and define $\mathbf{u} \cdot \mathbf{v} = (u_1 \cdot v_1, \ldots, u_n \cdot v_n)$ as the component-wise group operation.

Bilinear Groups and the Matrix DDH Assumption. We work with multiplicative groups $\mathbb{G}, \mathbb{G}_T$ of prime order p, equipped with a non-degenerate bilinear map $e : \mathbb{G} \times \mathbb{G} \to \mathbb{G}_T$ satisfying the following property: for every $(a, b) \in \mathbb{Z}_p^2$ and generator $g \in \mathbb{G}$, $e(g^a, g^b) = e(g, g)^{ab}$. We require that the group operation and the map e are efficiently computable. We will assume an efficient generation algorithm $\mathcal{G}$, which on input a security parameter λ, outputs the description of groups $\mathbb{G}, \mathbb{G}_T$ of order p, the map e, and a generator g where p is a prime number of length $O(\lambda)$.

The "matrix DDH" assumption [10,36], also known as the 3-linear assumption,[4] states that it is hard to tell whether a randomly chosen matrix $A \in \mathbb{Z}_p^{n \times 3}$ has rank 2 or 3 when given only g^A where $g \in \mathbb{G}$ is the generator of a prime-oder bilinear group $\mathbb{G}$. Formally, for every polynomial $n := n(\lambda)$, we have that distributions

$$\mathcal{D}_2(\lambda, n) \equiv \left\{ (\mathsf{aux}, g^A) : A \xleftarrow{\$} \mathsf{Rank}_2^{n \times 3}(\mathbb{Z}_p) \right\}_{\lambda, n},$$

$$\mathcal{D}_3(\lambda, n) \equiv \left\{ (\mathsf{aux}, g^A) : A \xleftarrow{\$} \mathsf{Rank}_3^{n \times 3}(\mathbb{Z}_p) \right\}_{\lambda, n}$$

are computationally indistinguishable, where $\mathsf{aux} := (p, \mathbb{G}, \mathbb{G}_T, g, e) \leftarrow \mathcal{G}(\lambda)$ and $\lambda \in \mathbb{N}$. It follows from this assumption [36] that for all polynomially bounded $n, \ell \geq 3, r \geq 2, t \geq 0$, a random rank-$r$ matrix is computationally indistinguishable from a random rank-$(r + t)$ matrix when given in the exponent.

Random Subspaces are Leakage-Resilient [13]. Brakerski et al. [13] prove the following theorem which serves as as important tool in building their continual leakage resilient PKE scheme. The theorem roughly states that random subspaces of $\mathbb{Z}_p^n$ are "leakage resilient" provided that the leakage is "small" and independent of the subspace. More formally, let $X \subseteq \mathbb{Z}_p^n$ be a random subspace, $\mathbf{x}_1, \mathbf{x}_2$ two random vectors in X and $\mathbf{u}_1, \mathbf{u}_2$ two random vectors from the entire space. Let $\mathcal{L} : \mathbb{Z}_p^n \to W$ be a leakage function independent of X. The theorem states that if leakage is bounded (i.e. $|W|$ is small), then $\mathcal{L}(\mathbf{x})$ is *statistically close* to $\mathcal{L}(\mathbf{u})$ *even* given the subspace X.

---

[4] We use the therms "matrix DDH assumption" and "linear assumption" interchangeably throughout the paper.

Theorem 1 ([13]). *Let $n, \ell \in \mathbb{N}$, $n \geq \ell \geq 4$ and p be a prime. Let $X \xleftarrow{\$} \mathbb{Z}_p^{n \times \ell}$, $T \xleftarrow{\$} \mathsf{Rank}_2^{\ell \times 2}(\mathbb{Z}_p)$ and let $Y \xleftarrow{\$} \mathbb{Z}_p^{n \times 2}$. Let $\mathcal{L} : \mathbb{Z}_p^{n \times 2} \to W$ be some function independent of X such that $|W| \leq p^{\ell-3} \cdot \epsilon^2$ for a constant $\epsilon \in (0,1)$. Then, $\Delta((X, \mathcal{L}(X \cdot T), (X, \mathcal{L}(Y))) \leq \epsilon$.*

BKKV Encryption Scheme. Our result uses the BKKV encryption which works as follows. The key generation algorithm chooses two uniformly random ℓ-dimensional vectors v_1 and v_2 with elements from $\mathbb{Z}_p$, and another vector t uniformly at random from the orthogonal subspace of v_1 and v_2. The public key is set to be (g^{v_1}, g^{v_2}) and the secret key is g^t, where g is a generator of a bilinear pairing group $\mathbb{G}$ and exponentiation happens component-wise: $g^t = (g^{t_1}, g^{t_2}, \ldots, g^{t_\ell})^\mathsf{T} \in \mathbb{G}^\ell$. To encrypt the bit 0, the encryption algorithm outputs a linear combination of v_1 and v_2 in the exponent: $g^{c_1 v_1 + c_2 v_2}$. The encryption of 1 is a completely random vector in the exponent. Notice that encryptions of 0 have exponents orthogonal to the secret key, while exponents of encryptions of 1 are not orthogonal to the secret key with overwhelming probability. During decryption, the respective components from the secret key and the ciphertext are paired via the bilinear pairing and the results are multiplied. As a result, if the vectors in the exponent are orthogonal, the result is the identity element. Otherwise, it is a random group element.

An important property of this encryption scheme is that it is almost *additively homomorphic*. It is easily shown that multiplying component-wise an encryption of $b_1 \in \{0, 1\}$ with an encryption of $b_2 \in \{0, 1\}$ provides an encryption of $b_1 + b_2$, except when $b_1 = b_2 = 1$ where you get an encryption of 1.

3   Lossy TDF under Continual Leakage

3.1   Our Model

As noted earlier, we will define a "branch" based version of lossy trapdoor functions. To evaluate the function, an evaluator must specify a branch in addition to the input to the function. Some branches will be "lossy" whereas most other will be injective. The set of branches will be denoted $\mathcal{B}_\lambda$ for security parameter λ.

This primitive is closer to the all-but-one (ABO) primitive of Peikert and Waters [40]; the only difference is that in our formulation more than one branch might be lossy. In fact, there may exist branches which are neither injective nor "sufficiently lossy." Nevertheless, fraction of such branches will be negligible, and a random branch will be injective with overwhelming probability.

The leakage-resilience is formulated by requiring that it is hard to distinguish lossy branches from injective *even* under a continual leakage attack on the trapdoor. We will use a parameter $\rho \in [0, 1)$ to capture the leakage as the *fraction* of the length the secret-key. That is, in any given time period, the adversary can learn any PPT leakage function of the trapdoor t with output length at most $\rho|t|$. We now present the formal definition.

Lossy Trapdoor Functions Resilient to Continual Memory Leakage. Let $\lambda \in \mathbb{N}$ be the security parameter, and $n := n(\lambda)$ and $k := k(\lambda)$ be polynomials in λ. Parameter n denotes the length of the input to the function(s) and k is the *lossiness* parameter. For convenience, we define the *residual* information parameter $r := r(\lambda) = n(\lambda) - k(\lambda)$. Let $\rho := \{0,1\}^{\mathrm{poly}(\lambda)} \to [0,1)$ be a *leakage tolerance* parameter, representing the length of the leakage function as a fraction of the length the trapdoor. Finally, let $\{\mathcal{B}_\lambda\}_\lambda \in \mathbb{N}$ be the ensemble of branch-spaces, where $\mathcal{B}_\lambda = \{0,1\}^{\mathrm{poly}(\lambda)}$.[5]

A collection of (n,k,ρ)-*continual leakage resilient lossy trapdoor functions* (CLR-LTDF) with the domain $\{0,1\}^n$ and branch collection $\mathcal{B} = \{\mathcal{B}_\lambda\}$ is given by a tuple of four (possibly probabilistic) polynomial-time (in λ) algorithms (Setup, Eval, Inv, Update) with the following specifications:

Setup$(1^\lambda, b^*)$ takes as input 1^λ and a branch $b^* \in \mathcal{B}_\lambda$, and outputs (pp, t) where
  pp is a function index and t is its trapdoor.
Eval(pp, b, x) is a deterministic algorithm which, given pp, a branch $b \in \mathcal{B}_\lambda$, and
  an input $x \in \{0,1\}^n$, outputs a value y.
Update(pp, t) is a randomized algorithm which, given pp, and a trapdoor t for pp,
  outputs a new trapdoor t' such that $|t'| = |t|$. We call t' to be the *refreshed*
  or *updated* trapdoor.
Inv(pp, t^*, y) is a deterministic algorithm which given pp, a trapdoor t^*, and
  a value y, outputs either $x \in \{0,1\}^n$ or $\bot$. Usually, either $t^* = t$ or t^* is
  obtained by repeated (at most polynomial) application of Update$(\mathsf{pp}, \cdot)$.

We require that the following correctness and lossiness requirements hold.

1. *Injective, and invertible, on almost all branches:* except for a negligible fraction of $b \in \mathcal{B}_\lambda \setminus \{b^*\}$, algorithm Eval$(\mathsf{pp}, b, \cdot)$ computes a (deterministic) injective function, which can be inverted using either the trapdoor t or *any of its polynomially-many refreshings*. That is, for every polynomial $q := q(\lambda)$, every sufficiently large λ, every $x \in \{0,1\}^n$, and every $b^* \in \mathcal{B}_\lambda$,

$$\Pr\left[\mathsf{Inv}\left(\mathsf{pp}, t_q, \mathsf{Eval}(\mathsf{pp}, b, x)\right) \neq x \,\middle|\, \mathcal{E}\right] \leq \mu(\lambda),$$

where $\mathcal{E}$ is the event that $(\mathsf{pp}, t) \leftarrow \mathsf{Setup}(1^\lambda, b^*), b \leftarrow \mathcal{B}_\lambda, t_q$ is obtained by repeatedly applying the function Update$(\mathsf{pp}, \cdot)$ to its own output (with fresh randomness) q times, starting from the initial input t and μ is a negligible function.[6]

---

[5] We can also consider more structured sets instead of $\{0,1\}^{\mathrm{poly}(\lambda)}$. For example, a very intuitive and convenient choice is $\mathcal{B}_\lambda = \mathbb{Z}_p^m$; i.e., the branches vectors in $\mathbb{Z}_p^m$ for some $m = \mathrm{poly}(n)$ and p is a prime of length λ. However, too much structure in $\mathcal{B}_\lambda$ should be avoided to ensure non-triviality and usefulness of the primitive.

[6] We note that this formulation does ensure that Eval$(\mathsf{pp}, b, \cdot)$ is indeed an injective function for all but a negligible fraction of (pp, b) since inversion must almost always succeed for *every* given x.

2. *Lossy at the given branch b^*:* for every $b^* \in \mathcal{B}_\lambda$, except with negligible probability over the randomness of Setup, we have: $|\mathsf{Eval}(\mathsf{pp}, b^*, \cdot)| \leq 2^{n-k}$, where $(\mathsf{pp}, t) \leftarrow \mathsf{Setup}(1^\lambda, b^*)$.

Finally, we require the following *hardness* properties.

1. *Indistinguishability of lossy branch under continual memory leakage:* We require that for every PPT algorithm A, it holds that

$$\left\{\mathbf{Game}_A^\rho(1^\lambda, 0)\right\}_{\lambda \in \mathbb{N}} \equiv_c \left\{\mathbf{Game}_A^\rho(1^\lambda, 1)\right\}_{\lambda \in \mathbb{N}} \tag{1}$$

where the variable $\mathbf{Game}_A^\rho(1^\lambda, d)$ is defined for $d \in \{0,1\}$ as follows:

$\mathbf{Game}_A^\rho(1^\lambda, d)$: The game proceeds between a challenger and adversary A in following stages:

(a) INIT: The challenger chooses two branches (b, b^*) uniformly from the set $\mathcal{B}_\lambda$ and samples $(\mathsf{pp}, t) \leftarrow \mathsf{Setup}(1^\lambda, b^*)$. It sends pp to A.

(b) LEAKAGE QUERIES: A sends polynomially many leakage queries (in the form polynomial-sized circuits) $\mathcal{L}_1, \ldots, \mathcal{L}_s$ where $\mathcal{L}_i$ has output length at most $\rho|t|$, and $i \in [s]$ for some $s = \mathrm{poly}(\lambda)$. The queries are chosen *adaptively* and answered as follows. At the start of this phase, the challenger sets $i = 1$ and $t_1 = t$. Upon receiving a leakage function $\mathcal{L}_i$ for $i \in [s]$, the challenger computes $\sigma_i = \mathcal{L}_i(t_i)$, $t_{i+1} \leftarrow \mathsf{Update}(\mathsf{pp}, t_i)$, and increases the counter i to $i+1$. It then returns σ_i to A and waits for the next leakage function.

(c) CHALLENGE: Finally, if $d = 0$ the challenger sends b, and if $d = 1$ it sends b^* to the adversary.

The output of the game is whatever A outputs: w.l.o.g. the output is a *single* bit.

2. *Hard to sample a non-injective branch even given the inversion trapdoor:* roughly speaking, we require that no PPT algorithm A, given (pp, t) sampled by $\mathsf{Setup}(1^\lambda, b^*)$ for a *random* b^*, can compute a branch b such that the function $\mathsf{Eval}(\mathsf{pp}, b, \cdot)$ is *not* injective except with negligible probability. Formally, for every PPT algorithm A and every sufficiently large $\lambda \in \mathbb{N}$,

$$\Pr\left[b \in \mathcal{B}_\lambda \wedge |\mathsf{Eval}(\mathsf{pp}, b, \{0,1\}^n)| \neq 2^n \Big| \mathcal{E}\right] \leq \mu(\lambda),$$

where $\mathcal{E}$ denotes the event $b^* \leftarrow \mathcal{B}_\lambda$, $(\mathsf{pp}, t) \leftarrow \mathsf{Setup}(1^\lambda, b^*)$, $b \leftarrow A(\mathsf{pp}, t)$ and μ is a negligible function.

It is straightforward to extend this definition to allow leakage during setup and update phases.

Allowing General Sampling Algorithms. Our current formulation works with two uniform and independent branches (b, b^*) without worrying about *how* they are sampled. We consider a slightly more general definition where the algorithm for sampling the branches, say *Samp*, outputs an *encoded* branch (instead of the actual branch); a public decoding function is then used to compute the actual branch from the encoding. Two independent executions of $Samp$ are used to sample branch encodings, which are then decoded. We require that the distribution of the decoded branches be statistically close to uniform over $\mathcal{B}_\lambda \times \mathcal{B}_\lambda$. In addition, during the CHALLENGE phase, the challenger sends the *encoding* of the challenge branch.

Formally, in the general definition, an (n, k, ρ)-CLR-LTDF is defined as above, except that we modify $\mathbf{Game}_A^\rho(1^\lambda, d)$ as follows.[7] For a non-uniform polynomial time algorithm $Samp$ (with advice z) and a collection of decoding functions $\mathcal{H}$, we change the INIT phase as follows. The challenger samples a random decoding function $h \leftarrow \mathcal{H}$. It then samples two encodings $e \leftarrow Samp(1^\lambda, z)$ and $e^* \leftarrow Samp(1^\lambda, z)$ to define the branches $b = h(e)$ and $b^* = h(e^*)$. Branch b^* is used as the lossy branch (as before). We require that for a randomly chosen h, $(h(e), h(e^*))$ is statistically close to the uniform distribution over the pair of branches, and call $(Samp, \mathcal{H})$ to be *good* if they satisfy this requirement. Both h and pp are sent during INIT phase. During the CHALLENGE phase, if $d = 0$, encoding e is sent, otherwise e^* is sent. We require that (1) holds for all good $(Samp, \mathcal{H})$.

3.2 Our Construction

We now present our construction. As described in Sect. 1.2, our construction of CLR-LTDF is inspired by the ABO functions of [40] which samples a $n \times n$ matrix $\mathbf{A}$ whose entries are (ElGamal) encryptions of 0 with correlated randomness. The function description is then set to $g^{\mathbf{M}}$ where $\mathbf{M} = \mathbf{A} + b^*\mathbf{I}$, $\mathbf{I}$ denotes the identity matrix, and b^* is lossy branch. The function evaluation on $(b, \mathbf{x})$ is $g^{(\mathbf{M}-b\mathbf{I})\mathbf{x}}$.

Our construction uses a similar approach and uses BKKV encryption instead of ElGamal. The branches in our construction will be a collection of n vectors, denoted by a matrix $\mathbf{B}_{n \times 1} = (\mathbf{b}_1, \ldots, \mathbf{b}_n)^\mathsf{T}$ where every $\mathbf{b}_i \in \mathbb{Z}_p^\ell$. Each $\mathbf{b}_i$ can be interpreted as a BKKV encryption of 1, and it can also be used as a one-time pad for the diagonal elements of $\mathbf{A}$. Matrix $\mathbf{M}$ will now be matrix $\mathbf{A}$ whose diagonal entries are "masked", i.e., set to $\mathbf{a}_{ii} + \mathbf{b}_i$ for $i \in [n]$.

The Construction. We will be working with prime-order bilinear groups. It will be convenient to assume the existence of a universal setup algorithm $\mathcal{G}(\lambda)$ which sets up some universal parameters such as the bilinear groups, bilinear map, a generator, and the set of branches $\mathcal{B}_\lambda$. That is, $\mathcal{G}(1^\lambda)$ is a randomized algorithm which outputs global parameters params $= (p, \mathbb{G}, \mathbb{G}_T, g, e)$ where p is a random prime of length λ, $\mathbb{G}$ and $\mathbb{G}_T$ groups of order p, and g is a generators of $\mathbb{G}$. Let n, k, ρ be functions of λ, as defined earlier.

We define the set of branches to be $\mathcal{B}_\lambda = \{\mathbb{Z}_p^\ell\}^n$. That is, a branch $\mathbf{B} \in \mathcal{B}_\lambda$ is a collection of vectors (denoted as a matrix as per our notation) as: $\mathbf{B}_{n \times 1} = (\mathbf{b}_1, \ldots, \mathbf{b}_n)^\mathsf{T}$ where $\mathbf{b}_i \in \mathbb{Z}_p^\ell$ for $i \in [n]$. We will assume that all algorithms

---

[7] We abuse the notation and continue to denote this modified game by $\mathbf{Game}_A^\rho$.

described below has access to the global parameters params.[8] The four algorithms of our CLR-LTDF $\Pi_{\mathsf{clr-ltdf}} := (\mathsf{Setup}, \mathsf{Eval}, \mathsf{Inv}, \mathsf{Update})$ are as follows.[9]

$\mathsf{Setup}(1^\lambda, \mathbf{B}^*)$. Sample two uniformly random vectors $\mathbf{v}_1$ and $\mathbf{v}_2$ in $\mathbb{Z}_p^\ell$, and two uniformly random $n \times n$ matrices of rank one, namely $R = [r_{ij}]$ and $S = [s_{ij}]$ from $\mathsf{Rank}_1^{n \times n}(\mathbb{Z}_p)$. Let $\mathbf{M} = [\mathbf{m}_{ij}]$ be a $n \times n$ matrix so that $\mathbf{m}_{ij} = r_{ij}\mathbf{v}_1 + s_{ij}\mathbf{v}_2$ for every valid i, j. The cell-entries of $\mathbf{M}$ are therefore vectors in $\mathsf{span}(\mathbf{v}_1, \mathbf{v}_2)$.

Let $\mathbf{B}^* = (\mathbf{b}_1^*, \ldots, \mathbf{b}_n^*)^\mathsf{T} \in (\mathbb{Z}_p^\ell)^n$. Compute the matrix $\mathbf{A} := \mathbf{M} \boxplus \mathbf{B}^* := [\mathbf{a}_{ij}]$ as follows:

$$\mathbf{a}_{ij} = \begin{cases} \mathbf{m}_{ij} + \mathbf{b}_i^* & i = j \\ \mathbf{m}_{ij} & i \neq j \end{cases}$$

Note that the operation $\boxplus$ affects only the diagonal entries of $\mathbf{M}$. The public-parameter is defined to be $\mathsf{pp} = g^\mathbf{A}$. To compute the trapdoor, choose a matrix $T \xleftarrow{\$} \mathsf{kernel}^2(\mathbf{v}_1, \mathbf{v}_2)$; that is, T has two rows each of which is a vector in $\mathsf{kernel}(\mathbf{v}_1, \mathbf{v}_2)$. The trapdoor is set to $g^T \in \mathbb{G}^{2 \times \ell}$. Output (pp, g^T).

$\mathsf{Eval}(\mathsf{pp}, \mathbf{B}, \mathbf{x})$. Let $\mathbf{x} \in \{0,1\}^n$ be a bit vector. The algorithm outputs $g^\mathbf{Y}$ such that:

$$g^\mathbf{Y} := (g^{\mathbf{y}_1}, \ldots, g^{\mathbf{y}_n})^\mathsf{T} = g^{\mathbf{A}'\mathbf{x}} \quad \text{where} \quad \mathbf{A}' = \mathbf{A} \boxplus (-\mathbf{B}).$$

Note that $g^{\mathbf{A}'}$ is easily computed given $(g^\mathbf{A}, \mathbf{B})$; likewise, $g^\mathbf{Y}$ is easily computed given $(g^{\mathbf{A}'}, \mathbf{x})$.[10]

$\mathsf{Update}(\mathsf{pp}, g^T)$. Choose a full rank matrix $V \in \mathbb{Z}_p^{2 \times 2}$ and output $T' = g^{VT}$. The update operation essentially samples two random vectors in the row-span of T.

$\mathsf{Inv}(\mathsf{pp}, g^T, g^\mathbf{Y})$. Let $g^\mathbf{Y} = (g^{\mathbf{y}_1}, \ldots, g^{\mathbf{y}_n})^\mathsf{T}$ and let the two rows of g^T be $g^{\mathbf{t}_1}$ and $g^{\mathbf{t}_2}$. Output a bit vector $\mathbf{z} = (z_1, \ldots, z_n)$ where, for every $i \in [n]$, bit $z_i = 0$ if $\mathbf{y}_i$ is orthogonal to both $\mathbf{t}_1$ and $\mathbf{t}_2$; otherwise $z_i = 1$. Recall that if $g^\mathbf{y} = (g^{y_1}, \ldots, g^{y_\ell}) \in \mathbb{G}^\ell$ and $g^\mathbf{t} = (g^{t_1}, \ldots, g^{t_\ell}) \in \mathbb{G}^\ell$ for $\mathbf{y} \in \{\mathbf{y}_1, \ldots, \mathbf{y}_n\}$ and $\mathbf{t} \in \{\mathbf{t}_1, \mathbf{t}_2\}$, then $\mathbf{y}$ is orthogonal $\mathbf{t}$ if and only if $\prod_i e(g^{y_i}, g^{t_i}) = 1$.

This completes the description of our function. The main theorem of this section is stated below. As noted earlier, the proof makes use of the fact that branches act as a one-time pad to successfully program that a future BKKV challenge can be appropriately mapped to either an injective or a lossy branch while still allowing the reduction to answer leakage queries. To be precise,

---

[8] We note that assuming such a $\mathcal{G}$ is only for convenience and without loss of generality. Indeed, we can assume $\mathcal{G}$ to be a part of the Setup algorithm. Since the length of the generated prime p is independent of p and only depends on λ, we can set $\mathcal{B}_\lambda = \left(\left(\{0,1\}^{\lfloor \lg p \rfloor}\right)^\ell\right)^n$ which is independent of p and always a subset of $(\mathbb{Z}_p^\ell)^n$.

[9] We remind the reader that uppercase letters, such as A, R, S, denote matrices of scalars (e.g., elements of $\mathbb{Z}_p$), whereas bold uppercase letters, such as $\mathbf{A}$, denote matrices of *vectors* (e.g. elements of $\mathbb{Z}_p^\ell$ or $\mathbb{G}^\ell$). Bold lowercase letter such as $\mathbf{x}$ represent vectors with only scalar entries.

[10] Recall that i-th row of $\mathbf{A}'\mathbf{x}$ contains a vector in the span of the vectors in the i-th row of $\mathbf{A}'$. See Sect. 2.

the reduction works directly with a "matrix DDH" challenger instead of BKKV challenges. This is because the proof requires several steps that are specific to lossy trapdoor functions; it is unclear whether a "semi automatic" reduction to BKKV exists.

Theorem 2. *Under the validity of the matrix DDH assumption, the tuple* (Setup, Eval, Update, Inv) *specifies a* (n, k, ρ)-*CLR-LTDF over the domain* $\{0,1\}^n$ *for every polynomial* n *where* $k = n - 2\lg p$ *and* $\rho = \frac{1}{2} - \frac{3+\gamma}{\ell}$ *for every* $\ell \geq 7, \gamma > 0$

Proof. Let us first verify the correctness and lossiness of our construction. For any given branch $\mathbf{B}$ and input $\mathbf{x}$, consider the matrix $\mathbf{Y} = (\mathbf{y}_1, \ldots, \mathbf{y}_n)^\mathsf{T} = \mathbf{A}'\mathbf{x} = (\mathbf{M} \boxplus (\mathbf{B}^* - \mathbf{B}))\mathbf{x}$. Letting $\mathbf{B} = (\mathbf{b}_1, \ldots, \mathbf{b}_n)$, and expanding, we see that:

$$\mathbf{y}_i = x_i(\mathbf{b}_i^* - \mathbf{b}_i) + \mathbf{Mx}[i] \tag{2}$$

where $i \in [n]$ and $\mathbf{Mx}[i]$ denotes the i-th row of $\mathbf{Mx}$ (which is a vector in span$(\mathbf{v}_1, \mathbf{v}_2)$). By construction, if $x_i = 0$ then $\mathbf{y}_i$ is orthogonal to both (trapdoor) vectors $\{\mathbf{t}_1, \mathbf{t}_2\}$, and if $x_i = 1$ it is not *except* when $(\mathbf{b}_i^* - \mathbf{b}_i)$ is also orthogonal to $\{\mathbf{t}_1, \mathbf{t}_2\}$. But the later happens with exactly $1/p^2$ probability (since there are two vectors) for a random $\mathbf{B}$. It follows that Inv works correctly (for all refreshings of the trapdoor) and the function is injective on almost all $\mathbf{B}$.

To see that the function is lossy when $\mathbf{B} = \mathbf{B}^*$, observe that in this case $\mathbf{Y} = \mathbf{Mx}$. Recall that $\mathbf{M}$ was constructed using matrices R and S of rank 1. In particular, $\mathbf{Mx}[i] = (R\mathbf{x}[i]) \cdot \mathbf{v}_1 + (S\mathbf{x}[i]) \cdot \mathbf{v}_2$. The range of both $R\mathbf{x}$ and $S\mathbf{x}$ is of size at most p, and therefore the size of the range of $\mathbf{Mx}$ is at most p^2. The function is lossy with $k = n - 2\lg p$.

The following lemmata prove the security properties of the construction; the proofs are given in the appendix.

Lemma 1. *For every PPT adversary* A^*, $\{\mathbf{Game}_{A^*}^\rho(1^\lambda, 0)\}_{\lambda \in \mathbb{N}}$ $\equiv_c$ $\{\mathbf{Game}_{A^*}^\rho(1^\lambda, 1)\}_{\lambda \in \mathbb{N}}$ *provided that* $\rho < \frac{1}{2} - \frac{3}{\ell}$ *for every* $\ell \geq 7$.

Lemma 2. *It is hard to sample a non-injective branch against our scheme.*

An interesting property of our functions is that they are actually universal on the lossy branches. I.e., they have a low collision probability. We prove this extra feature in the full version of our paper.

Remark. Our proof is not sensitive to *how* the branches are sampled in the game, so long as they are uniform and independent over the branch space. Therefore, it actually proves the general version of the definition where the branch encodings are sampled using an arbitrary non-uniform PPT sampler *Samp*, and then decoded efficiently using a random function from $\mathcal{H}$.

4   Leakage Resilient Deterministic PKE

In this section, we define leakage-resilient D-PKE and its security, and show that our CLR-LTDF yield such a scheme when branch b is set to $h(m)$ provided certain conditions on h and the entropy of m are met.

4.1   Modeling Deterministic PKE Under Continual Leakage

A deterministic public-key encryption scheme is a triple of polynomial-time algorithms $\Pi = (\mathsf{KG}, \mathsf{Enc}, \mathsf{Dec}, \mathsf{Update})$. The key-generation algorithm KG is a randomized algorithm which on input the security parameter 1^λ outputs a pair (pk, sk) of a public key pk and a secret key sk. The encryption algorithm Enc is *deterministic*, takes as input 1^λ, a public key pk, and a plaintext $m \in \{0,1\}^{n(\lambda)}$, and outputs a ciphertext $c \in \{0,1\}^{t(\lambda)}$. The (possibly deterministic) decryption algorithm Dec takes as input 1^λ, a secret key sk, and a ciphertext $c \in \{0,1\}^{t(\lambda)}$, and outputs either a plaintext $m \in \{0,1\}^{n(\lambda)}$ or the special symbol $\bot$.

Algorithm $\mathsf{Update}(pk, sk')$ is a randomized update algorithm which, given pk, and a secret-key sk' for pk, outputs a new secret-key sk'' such that $|sk''| = |sk'|$; input sk' is either sk or one of the outputs of Update. We call sk' to be the *refreshed* or *updated* secret-key. We require that the outputs of Dec is identical on sk or sk' (which is output of Update). For succinctness, we will always assume 1^λ as an implicit input to all algorithms and refrain from explicitly specifying it.

We now define our security notion, namely CLR-PRIV1-IND security. It is essentially a direct extension of the standard PRIV1-IND definition in the leakage-free setting. PRIV1-IND is the "single challenge" version of the PRIV-IND definition which requires that, roughly speaking, the encryptions of two sequences of messages be computationally indistinguishable provided that each message has sufficient min-entropy and the sequences have same "equality pattern." Formally, these requirements are captured by defining a α-*source q-message adversary*, which is also relevant to our definition.[11]

The α-Source q-Message Adversary. Let $A = (A_1, A_2)$ be a probabilistic polynomial-time algorithm, and let $\alpha = \alpha(\lambda)$ and $q = q(\lambda)$ be functions of the security parameter $\lambda \in \mathbb{N}$. For any $\lambda \in \mathbb{N}$ denote by $(\mathcal{M}_\lambda^{(0)}, \mathcal{M}_\lambda^{(1)}, \mathcal{STATE}_\lambda)$ the distribution corresponding to the output of $A_1(1^\lambda)$. Then, A is a α-*source q-message adversary* if the following properties hold:

1. $\mathcal{M}_\lambda^{(b)} = \left(\mathcal{M}_{1,\lambda}^{(b)}, \ldots, \mathcal{M}_{q,\lambda}^{(b)} \right)$ is a distribution over sequences of q plaintexts for each $b \in \{0, 1\}$.

---

[11] We will only focus on the single challenge setting; it is straightforward to extend our definition to deal with sequence of messages and get the corresponding notion CLR-PRIV-IND. However, our construction only satisfies the single message definition, and we do not know if our scheme can be shown to satisfy security for multiple messages.

2. For any $\lambda \in \mathbb{N}$, $i, j \in [q]$, and for every triplet $\left(\left(m_1^{(0)}, \ldots, m_q^{(0)}\right),\right.$ $\left.\left(m_1^{(1)}, \ldots, m_q^{(1)}\right), \mathsf{state}\right)$ that is produced by $A_1(1^\lambda)$ it holds that $m_i^{(0)} = m_j^{(0)}$ if and only if $m_i^{(1)} = m_j^{(1)}$.

3. For any $\lambda \in \mathbb{N}$, $b \in \{0,1\}$, $i \in [q]$, and $\mathsf{state} \in \{0,1\}^*$ it holds that $\mathcal{M}_{i,\lambda}^{(b)}|_{\mathcal{STATE}_\lambda = \mathsf{state}}$ is a $\alpha(\lambda)$-source.

We are now ready to define the continual-leakage-resilient version of PRIV1-IND security, namely CLR-PRIV1-IND. The definition is same as PRIV1-IND security except that the adversary is allowed to ask leakage queries *before* receiving the challenge encryption.

CLR-PRIV1-IND Security. A deterministic public-key encryption scheme $\Pi = (\mathsf{KG}, \mathsf{Enc}, \mathsf{Dec}, \mathsf{Update})$ is *CLR-PRIV1-IND-secure for $\alpha(\lambda)$-source 1-message adversaries* with leakage-parameter ρ if for any probabilistic polynomial-time $\alpha(\lambda)$-source 1-message adversary $A = (A_1, A_2)$ there exists a negligible function $\nu(\lambda)$ such that

$$\mathbf{Adv}_{\Pi,A,\lambda}^{\mathsf{CLR-PRIV1-IND}} \stackrel{\text{def}}{=} \left| \begin{array}{l} \Pr\left[\mathsf{Expt}_{\Pi,A,\lambda}^{\mathsf{CLR-PRIV1-IND}}(0) = 1\right] \\ - \Pr\left[\mathsf{Expt}_{\Pi,A,\lambda}^{\mathsf{CLR-PRIV1-IND}}(1) = 1\right] \end{array} \right| \leq \nu(\lambda)$$

for all sufficiently large $\lambda \in \mathbb{N}$, where $\mathsf{Expt}_{\Pi,A,\lambda}^{\mathsf{CLR-PRIV1-IND}}(b)$ is defined as follows:

1. INIT: sample $(pk, sk) \leftarrow \mathsf{KG}(1^\lambda)$, and send pk to A_2.
2. LEAKAGE QUERIES: set $i = 1$ and $sk_1 = sk$; interact with A_2, answering every leakage query $\mathcal{L}_i$ whose output length is at most $\rho \cdot |sk|$, as follows. Send $\sigma_i = \mathcal{L}_i(sk_i)$ to A_2, and set $sk_{i+1} \leftarrow \mathsf{Update}(pk, sk_i)$ and $i = i + 1$.
3. CHALLENGE: sample $(m_0, m_1, \mathsf{state}) \leftarrow A_1(1^\lambda)$ and set $c \leftarrow \mathsf{Enc}_{pk}(m_b)$; send (c, state) to A_2. Output of A_2 is the output of the experiment.

Remark. It is not necessary to sample $(m_0, m_1, \mathsf{state}) \leftarrow A_1(1^\lambda)$ in the CHALLENGE phase. Instead, they can be sampled during the INIT phase so long as they are kept completely outside the view of the adversary; CHALLENGE phase then only computes c and sends (c, state) to A_2. From here on, we shall work with this modified version. Also, the advantage can also be mentioned in terms of probability p of correctly guessing which distribution the encrypted message comes from; it is easy to see that the advantage above comes out to be $|2p - 1|$.

4.2   Our Deterministic Public-Key Encryption Scheme

The Construction. Let $\Pi_{\mathrm{clr-ltdf}} := (\mathsf{Setup}, \mathsf{Eval}, \mathsf{Inv}, \mathsf{Update})$ be a (n, k, ρ)-CLR-LTDF which satisfies the universal hash property with respect to lossy branches. Let $s = s(\lambda)$ be a polynomial describing the length of branches $b \in \mathcal{B}_\lambda$.[12] Let $\mathcal{H} = \{h : \{0,1\}^n \to \{0,1\}^s\}$ be a family of universal hash functions,

---

[12] W.l.o.g. we can assume s to be quite small if necessary. If the length requires a large string to describe the branch, we can use pseudorandom generators of sufficient stretch.

and perm be a family of pairwise independent permutations which are easy to invert.[13] The message space of the scheme is $\{0,1\}^n$.

The key-generation algorithm KG samples $h \leftarrow \mathcal{H}$, $\pi \leftarrow$ perm, $b^* \leftarrow \mathcal{B}_\lambda$, $(\text{pp}, t) \leftarrow \text{Setup}(1^\lambda, b^*)$. It outputs $pk = (h, \pi, \text{pp})$ and $sk = t$. The encryption algorithm Enc takes as input pp and a message $x \in \{0,1\}^n$. It outputs $y = \text{Eval}(\text{pp}, b, \pi(x))$ where $b = h(x)$ is used as the branch. The decryption algorithm Dec takes as input y, sk, and $pk = (h, \pi, \text{pp})$. It outputs $x = \pi^{-1}(\text{Inv}(\text{pp}, sk, y))$ if x is valid and $\bot$ otherwise. The update algorithm of the scheme is the same as Update.

We denote this scheme by $\Pi_{\text{clr-de}} := (\text{KG}, \text{Enc}, \text{Dec}, \text{Update})$. It is easy to verify the correctness of this scheme.

Theorem 3. *Scheme $\Pi_{\text{clr-de}}$ is a CLR-PRIV1-IND secure scheme for $\alpha(\lambda)$- source 1-message adversary with leakage parameter ρ provided that $\Pi_{\text{clr-ltdf}}$ is a (n, k, ρ)-CLR-LTDF and: $\alpha(\lambda) \geq n(\lambda) - k(\lambda) + s(\lambda) + 2\lg(1/\epsilon)$, where ϵ is an arbitrary negligible function in λ.*

Due to space constraints, the proof of this theorem is given in the full version of our paper.

References

1. Akavia, A., Goldwasser, S., Vaikuntanathan, V.: Simultaneous hardcore bits and cryptography against memory attacks. In: Reingold, O. (ed.) TCC 2009. LNCS, vol. 5444, pp. 474–495. Springer, Heidelberg (2009)
2. Alwen, J., Dodis, Y., Naor, M., Segev, G., Walfish, S., Wichs, D.: Public-key encryption in the bounded-retrieval model. In: Gilbert, H. (ed.) EUROCRYPT 2010. LNCS, vol. 6110, pp. 113–134. Springer, Heidelberg (2010)
3. Ananth, P., Goyal, V., Pandey, O.: Interactive proofs under continual memory leakage. In: Garay, J.A., Gennaro, R. (eds.) CRYPTO 2014, Part II. LNCS, vol. 8617, pp. 164–182. Springer, Heidelberg (2014)
4. Anderson, R.J., Kuhn, M.G.: Low cost attacks on tamper resistant devices. In: Christianson, B., Crispo, B., Lomas, M., Roe, M. (eds.) Security Protocols. LNCS, pp. 125–136. Springer, Heidelberg (1997)
5. Bellare, M., Boldyreva, A., O'Neill, A.: Deterministic and efficiently searchable encryption. In: Menezes, A. (ed.) CRYPTO 2007. LNCS, vol. 4622, pp. 535–552. Springer, Heidelberg (2007)
6. Bellare, M., Fischlin, M., O'Neill, A., Ristenpart, T.: Deterministic encryption: definitional equivalences and constructions without random oracles. In: Wagner, D. (ed.) CRYPTO 2008. LNCS, vol. 5157, pp. 360–378. Springer, Heidelberg (2008)
7. Bellare, M., Kiltz, E., Peikert, C., Waters, B.: Identity-based (lossy) trapdoor functions and applications. In: Pointcheval, D., Johansson, T. (eds.) EUROCRYPT 2012. LNCS, vol. 7237, pp. 228–245. Springer, Heidelberg (2012)
8. Bellare, M., Rogaway, P.: Random oracles are practical: a paradigm for designing efficient protocols. In: Proceedings of the 1st Annual ACM Conference on Computer and Communications Security. pp. 62–73 (1993)

---

[13] Such permutations are known.

9. Boldyreva, A., Fehr, S., O'Neill, A.: On notions of security for deterministic encryption, and efficient constructions without random oracles. In: Wagner, D. (ed.) CRYPTO 2008. LNCS, vol. 5157, pp. 335–359. Springer, Heidelberg (2008)
10. Boneh, D., Boyen, X., Shacham, H.: Short group signatures. In: Franklin, M. (ed.) CRYPTO 2004. LNCS, vol. 3152, pp. 41–55. Springer, Heidelberg (2004)
11. Boyle, E., Goldwasser, S., Jain, A., Kalai, Y.T.: Multiparty computation secure against continual memory leakage. In: STOC. pp. 1235–1254 (2012)
12. Boyle, E., Segev, G., Wichs, D.: Fully leakage-resilient signatures. In: Paterson, K.G. (ed.) EUROCRYPT 2011. LNCS, vol. 6632, pp. 89–108. Springer, Heidelberg (2011)
13. Brakerski, Z., Kalai, Y.T., Katz, J., Vaikuntanathan, V.: Overcoming the hole in the bucket: public-key cryptography resilient to continual memory leakage. In: FOCS. pp. 501–510 (2010)
14. Brakerski, Z., Segev, G.: Better security for deterministic public-key encryption: the auxiliary-input setting. In: Rogaway, P. (ed.) CRYPTO 2011. LNCS, vol. 6841, pp. 543–560. Springer, Heidelberg (2011)
15. Chow, S.S.M., Dodis, Y., Rouselakis, Y., Waters, B.: Practical leakage-resilient identity-based encryption from simple assumptions. In: ACM Conference on Computer and Communications Security. pp. 152–161 (2010)
16. Dodis, Y., Haralambiev, K., López-Alt, A., Wichs, D.: Cryptography against continuous memory attacks. In: FOCS. pp. 511–520 (2010)
17. Dodis, Y., Kalai, Y.T., Lovett, S.: On cryptography with auxiliary input. In: STOC. pp. 621–630 (2009)
18. Dodis, Y., Smith, A.: Correcting errors without leaking partial information. In: STOC 2005. pp. 654–663 (2005)
19. Dziembowski, S., Pietrzak, K.: Leakage-resilient cryptography. In: FOCS. pp. 293–302 (2008)
20. Faust, S., Rabin, T., Reyzin, L., Tromer, E., Vaikuntanathan, V.: Protecting circuits from leakage: the computationally-bounded and noisy cases. In: Gilbert, H. (ed.) EUROCRYPT 2010. LNCS, vol. 6110, pp. 135–156. Springer, Heidelberg (2010)
21. Freeman, D.M., Goldreich, O., Kiltz, E., Rosen, A., Segev, G.: More constructions of lossy and correlation-secure trapdoor functions. In: Proceedings of the 13th International Conference on Practice and Theory in Public Key Cryptography. pp. 279–295 (2010)
22. Fuller, B., O'Neill, A., Reyzin, L.: A unified approach to deterministic encryption: new constructions and a connection to computational entropy. In: Cramer, R. (ed.) Theory of Cryptography. Lecture Notes in Computer Science, vol. 7194, pp. 582–599. Springer, Heidelberg (2012). Cryptology ePrint Archive, Report 2012/005
23. Garg, S., Jain, A., Sahai, A.: Leakage-resilient zero knowledge. In: Rogaway, P. (ed.) CRYPTO 2011. LNCS, vol. 6841, pp. 297–315. Springer, Heidelberg (2011)
24. Goldwasser, S., Micali, S.: Probabilistic encryption. J. Comput. Syst. Sci. **28**(2), 270–299 (1984)
25. Goldwasser, S., Rothblum, G.N.: How to compute in the presence of leakage. In: FOCS. pp. 31–40 (2012)
26. Hazay, C., López-Alt, A., Wee, H., Wichs, D.: Leakage-resilient cryptography from minimal assumptions. In: Johansson, T., Nguyen, P.Q. (eds.) EUROCRYPT 2013. LNCS, vol. 7881, pp. 160–176. Springer, Heidelberg (2013)

27. Hemenway, B., Libert, B., Ostrovsky, R., Vergnaud, D.: Lossy encryption: constructions from general assumptions and efficient selective opening chosen ciphertext security. In: Lee, D.H., Wang, X. (eds.) ASIACRYPT 2011. LNCS, vol. 7073, pp. 70–88. Springer, Heidelberg (2011)

28. Hofheinz, D.: All-but-many lossy trapdoor functions. In: Pointcheval, D., Johansson, T. (eds.) EUROCRYPT 2012. LNCS, vol. 7237, pp. 209–227. Springer, Heidelberg (2012)

29. Ishai, Y., Sahai, A., Wagner, D.: Private circuits: securing hardware against probing attacks. In: Boneh, D. (ed.) CRYPTO 2003. LNCS, vol. 2729, pp. 463–481. Springer, Heidelberg (2003)

30. Kocher, P.C.: Timing attacks on implementations of Diffie-Hellman, RSA, DSS, and other systems. In: Koblitz, N. (ed.) CRYPTO 1996. LNCS, vol. 1109, pp. 104–113. Springer, Heidelberg (1996)

31. Lewko, A.B., Lewko, M., Waters, B.: How to leak on key updates. In: STOC (2011)

32. Lewko, A., Rouselakis, Y., Waters, B.: Achieving leakage resilience through dual system encryption. In: Ishai, Y. (ed.) TCC 2011. LNCS, vol. 6597, pp. 70–88. Springer, Heidelberg (2011)

33. Lewko, A.B., Waters, B.: On the insecurity of parallel repetition for leakage resilience. In: FOCS. pp. 521–530 (2010)

34. Micali, S., Reyzin, L.: Physically observable cryptography. In: Naor, M. (ed.) TCC 2004. LNCS, vol. 2951, pp. 278–296. Springer, Heidelberg (2004)

35. Mironov, I., Pandey, O., Reingold, O., Segev, G.: Incremental deterministic publickey encryption. In: Pointcheval, D., Johansson, T. (eds.) EUROCRYPT 2012. LNCS, vol. 7237, pp. 628–644. Springer, Heidelberg (2012)

36. Naor, M., Segev, G.: Public-key cryptosystems resilient to key leakage. In: Halevi, S. (ed.) CRYPTO 2009. LNCS, vol. 5677, pp. 18–35. Springer, Heidelberg (2009)

37. O'Neill, A.: Deterministic public-key encryption revisited. Eprint Report 2010/533 (2010)

38. Osvik, D.A., Shamir, A., Tromer, E.: Cache attacks and countermeasures: the case of AES. In: Pointcheval, D. (ed.) CT-RSA 2006. LNCS, vol. 3860, pp. 1–20. Springer, Heidelberg (2006)

39. Pandey, O.: Achieving constant round leakage-resilient zero-knowledge. In: Lindell, Y. (ed.) TCC 2014. LNCS, vol. 8349, pp. 146–166. Springer, Heidelberg (2014)

40. Peikert, C., Waters, B.: Lossy trapdoor functions and their applications. In: STOC. pp. 187–196 (2008)

41. Popa, R.A., Redfield, C.M.S., Zeldovich, N., Balakrishnan, H.: Cryptdb: protecting confidentiality with encrypted query processing. In: SOSP. pp. 85–100 (2011)

42. Popa, R.A., Redfield, C.M.S., Zeldovich, N., Balakrishnan, H.: Cryptdb: processing queries on an encrypted database. Commun. ACM 55(9), 103–111 (2012)

43. Qin, B., Liu, S., Chen, K., Charlemagne, M.: Leakage-resilient lossy trapdoor functions and public-key encryption. In: AsiaPKC (2013)

44. Quisquater, Jean-Jacques, Samyde, David: Electromagnetic analysis (EMA): measures and counter-measures for smart cards. In: Attali, S., Jensen, T. (eds.) E-smart 2001. LNCS, vol. 2140, pp. 200–210. Springer, Heidelberg (2001)

45. Raghunathan, A., Segev, G., Vadhan, S.: Deterministic public-key encryption for adaptively chosen plaintext distributions. In: Johansson, T., Nguyen, P.Q. (eds.) EUROCRYPT 2013. LNCS, vol. 7881, pp. 93–110. Springer, Heidelberg (2013)

46. Renauld, M., Standaert, F.-X., Veyrat-Charvillon, N., Kamel, D., Flandre, D.: A formal study of power variability issues and side-channel attacks for nanoscale devices. In: Paterson, K.G. (ed.) EUROCRYPT 2011. LNCS, vol. 6632, pp. 109–128. Springer, Heidelberg (2011)

47. Wee, H.: Dual projective hashing and its applications — lossy trapdoor functions and more. In: Pointcheval, D., Johansson, T. (eds.) EUROCRYPT 2012. LNCS, vol. 7237, pp. 246–262. Springer, Heidelberg (2012)

Computing on Encrypted Data

Better Preprocessing for Secure Multiparty Computation

Carsten Baum[1]([✉]), Ivan Damgård[1], Tomas Toft[2], and Rasmus Zakarias[1]

[1] Department of Computer Science, Aarhus University, Aarhus, Denmark
cbaum@cs.au.dk
[2] Danske Bank, Copenhagen, Denmark

Abstract. We present techniques and protocols for the preprocessing of secure multiparty computation (MPC), focusing on the so-called SPDZ MPC scheme [14] and its derivatives [1,11,13]. These MPC schemes consist of a so-called preprocessing or offline phase where correlated randomness is generated that is independent of the inputs and the evaluated function, and an online phase where such correlated randomness is consumed to securely and efficiently evaluate circuits. In the recent years, it has been shown that such protocols (such as [5,17,18]) turn out to be very efficient in practice.

While much research has been conducted towards optimizing the online phase of the MPC protocols, there seems to have been less focus on the offline phase of such protocols (except for [11]). With this work, we want to close this gap and give a toolbox of techniques that aim at optimizing the preprocessing. We support both instantiations over small fields and large rings using somewhat homomorphic encryption and the Paillier cryptosystem [19], respectively. In the case of small fields, we show how the preprocessing overhead can basically be made independent of the field characteristic. In the case of large rings, we present a protocol based on the Paillier cryptosystem which has a lower message complexity than previous protocols and employs more efficient zero-knowledge proofs that, to the best of our knowledge, were not presented in previous work.

Keywords: Efficient multiparty computation · Preprocessing · Paillier encryption

1 Introduction

During the recent years, secure two- and multiparty computation ([16,21]) has evolved from a merely academic research topic into a practical technique for secure function evaluation (see e.g. [6]). Multiparty computation (MPC) aims

The authors acknowledge support from the Danish National Research Foundation and The National Science Foundation of China (under the grant 61061130540) for the Sino-Danish Center for the Theory of Interactive Computation, within which part of this work was performed; and also from the CFEM research center (supported by the Danish Strategic Research Council) within which part of this work was performed.

© Springer International Publishing Switzerland 2016
M. Manulis et al. (Eds.): ACNS 2016, LNCS 9696, pp. 327–345, 2016.
DOI: 10.1007/978-3-319-39555-5_18

at solving the following problem: How can a set of parties $\mathcal{P}_1, ..., \mathcal{P}_n$, where each party $\mathcal{P}_i$ has a secret input value x_i, compute a function $y = f(x_1, ..., x_n)$ on their values while not revealing any other information than the output y? Such function could e.g. compute a statistic on the inputs (to securely compute a mean or median) or resemble an online auction or election. Ideally, all these parties would give their secret to a trusted third party (which is incorruptible), that evaluates the function f and reveals the result y to each participant. Such a solution in particular guarantees two properties:

Privacy: Even if malicious parties collude, as long as they cannot corrupt the trusted third party they cannot gain any information except y and what they can derive from it using their inputs.

Correctness: After each party sent their input, there is no way how malicious parties can interfere with the computation of the trusted third party in such a way as to force it to output a specific result y' to the parties that are honest.

A secure multiparty computation protocol replaces such a trusted third party by an interactive protocol among the n parties, while still guaranteeing the above properties. In recent years, it has been shown that even if $n - 1$ of the n parties can be corrupted, the efficiency of secure computation can be dramatically improved by splitting the protocol into different phases: During a *preprocessing* or *offline* phase, *raw material* or so-called correlated randomness is generated. This computation is both independent of f and the inputs x_i and can therefore be carried out any time before the actual function evaluation takes place. This way, a lot of the *heavy* computation that relies e.g. on public-key primitives (which we need to handle dishonest majority) will be done beforehand and need not be performed in the later *online* phase, where one can rely on *cheap* information-theoretic primitives.

This approach led to very efficient MPC protocols such as [11,13,14,17,18] to just name a few. In this work, we will primarily focus on variants of the so-called SPDZ protocol [11,14] and their preprocessing phases. They are secure against up to $n-1$ static corruptions, which will also be our adversarial model. For the preprocessing, they rely on very efficient lattice-based homomorphic cryptosystems that allow to perform both additions and multiplications on the encrypted ciphertexts and can pack a large vector of plaintexts into one ciphertext. Unfortunately, the current implementations of the preprocessing has several (non-obvious) drawbacks in terms of efficiency which we try to address in this work:

- The complexity of the preprocessing phase depends upon the size of the field over which the function f will be evaluated: It is much less efficient for small fields. The main reason behind it is that SHE schemes have no efficient reliable distributed decryption algorithm, so since the output from the preprocessing depends in part on decryption results, it must be checked for correctness. This is done by sacrificing some part of the computed data to check the remainder, but this approach only yields security inversely proportional to the field size.

Hence, especially for small fields, one has to repeat that procedure multiple times which introduces noticeable overhead.

- If the goal in the end is to do secure computation over the integers, one needs to use large fields or rings to avoid overflow. Unfortunately, the parameter sizes of SHE schemes grow very quickly if one increases the size of the underlying field, rendering them very slow in practice. This makes it interesting to investigate a preprocessing scheme using Paillier encryption, which comes with a very large ring as plaintext space.

1.1 Contributions and Technical Overview

In this work, we address the aforementioned problems and show the following results:

(1) We present a novel way of checking the correctness of shared multiplication triples for SHE schemes. In particular, we need to sacrifice only a constant fraction of the data to do the checking, where existing methods need to sacrifice a fraction $\Theta(1 - 1/\kappa)$ for error probability $2^{-\kappa}$.

(2) We show how the linearly homomorphic encryption scheme of Paillier and Damgård-Jurik [10,19] can be used more efficiently to produce multiplication triples by representing the data as polynomials and thereby reducing the amount of complex zero-knowledge proofs. Moreover, we also present zero-knowledge proofs for, e.g., plaintext knowledge that only require players to work modulo N even if the ciphertexts are defined modulo N^2. Though the technique may already be known, this did not appear in previous published work.

In the full version of this work [2] we also show a technique that improves the efficiency of the zero-knowledge proofs as used in [11,14]. Moreover, we present an optimized distributed decryption routine as it is required for our Paillier-based preprocessing. We will explain our contributions and techniques in more detail now.

Verifying Multiplicative Relations. Our goal is (somewhat simplified) to produce encrypted vectors x, y, z such that $x \odot y = z$, where $\odot$ denotes the coordinate-wise product, or Schur product. The SPDZ protocol for creating such data uses distributed decryption during which errors may be introduced. To counter this, we encode the plaintexts in such a way that we can check the result later: We will let x, y be codewords of a linear code. Those vectors can be put into SIMD ciphertexts of the SPDZ preprocessing scheme. Note that multiplying x and y coordinate-wise yields a codeword in a related code (namely its so-called Schur transform). Now we do a protocol to obtain an encryption of z, which, however, uses unreliable decryption[1] underway. The next step is then to check

---

[1] With unreliable decryption, we mean that the result is only correct if no party acts maliciously during the decryption procedure.

if z is indeed codeword as expected, This can be done almost only by linear operations - which are basically *free* in the SPDZ MPC scheme, because they can all be done as local operations and do not involve sending messages.

Checking whether the result is a codeword is not sufficient, but if z is in the code and not equal to the codeword $x \odot y$, then an adversary would have to have cheated in a large number of positions (the minimum distance of the code). Thus, given the resulting vector z is a codeword, one checks a small number of random positions of the vector to see if it contains the product of corresponding positions in x and y. During each check we have a constant probability of catching the adversary, and this quickly amplifies to our desired security levels.

Note that the only assumption that we have to make on the underlying field is that appropriate codes with good distance can be defined.

Paillier-Based Preprocessing for SPDZ. Paillier's encryption scheme is linearly homomorphic, so does not allow to perform multiplications of the plaintexts of two or more ciphertexts directly. On the other hand, it has a reliable decryption routine which is what we will make use of. Computing products of encryptions using linearly homomorphic encryption schemes is a well-known technique and works as follows: Assume $\mathcal{P}_1$ published some encryption $[\![a_1]\!], [\![b_1]\!]$, $\mathcal{P}_2$ published $[\![a_2]\!], [\![b_2]\!]$ and they want to compute values c_1, c_2 where $\mathcal{P}_1$ holds c_1 and $\mathcal{P}_2$ c_2 such that $(a_1 + a_2) \cdot (b_1 + b_2) = c_1 + c_2$.

In a protocol, $\mathcal{P}_2$ would send an encryption $[\![c'_2]\!] := b'_2 \cdot [\![a_1 + a_2]\!] + [\![-x_2]\!]$ to $\mathcal{P}_1$ and prove (among other things) that this b'_2 is the same as the plaintext inside $[\![b_2]\!]$ (where $[\![x_2]\!]$ is an auxiliary value). $\mathcal{P}_1$ similarly sends $[\![c'_1]\!] := b'_1 \cdot [\![a_1 + a_2]\!] + [\![-x_1]\!]$ to $\mathcal{P}_2$ and proves a related statement. Afterwards, both use the distributed decryption to safely decrypt the value $c'_1 + c'_2$, which does not reveal any information about the product if x_1, x_2 were appropriately chosen. $\mathcal{P}_1$ now sets $c_1 = c'_1 + c'_2 + x_1$ as her share, while $\mathcal{P}_2$ chooses $c_2 = x_2$. These shares do individually not reveal any information about the product.

Our approach is, instead of sampling all a_i, b_i independently, to let the factors be evaluations of a polynomial (that is implicitly defined), and then multiply these factors *unreliably*: Instead of giving a zero-knowledge proof that $b'_2 = b_2$, we only need to prove that $\mathcal{P}_2$ knows b'_2, x_2 such that the above equation is satisfied, which reduces the complexity of the proof. This means that the result is only correct if all parties honestly follow the multiplication protocol.

The products computed using unreliable multiplication now all lie on a polynomial as well, and using Lagrange interpolation one can evaluate the polynomial in arbitrary points. This can be used to efficiently (and almost locally) check if all products are correct.

We want to remark that this approach is asymptotically as efficient as existing techniques, but relies on zero-knowledge proofs with lower message complexity. It is an interesting open question how these approaches compare in practice.

1.2 Related Work

In an independent work, Frederiksen et al. showed how to preprocess data for the SPDZ MPC scheme using oblivious transfer ([15]). Their approach can make use of efficient OT-extension, but does only allow fields of characteristic 2. While this has some practical applications, it does not generalize (efficiently) to arbitrary fields. On the contrary, our techniques are particularly efficient for other use-cases when binary fields cannot be used to compute the desired function efficiently. Therefore, both results complement each other.

Our technique for checking multiplicative relations is related to the work in [4] for secret shared values in honest majority protocols and in [9] for committed values in 2-party protocols. To the best of our knowledge, this type of technique has not been used before for dishonest majority MPC.

Paillier Encryption: The Paillier encryption scheme has been used in MPC preprocessing before such as in [5]. Moreover it was also employed in various MPC schemes such as [6,8,12] to just name a few. The particular instance of the scheme that we use is from [10].

2 Preliminaries

Throughout this work, we assume that a secure point-to-point channels between the parties exist and that a broadcast channel is available. We make commitments abstractly available using the functionality $\mathcal{F}_{\text{COMMIT}}$ and assume the existence of a random oracle, which will be used in the coin-flipping protocol $\mathcal{P}_{\text{PROVIDERANDOM}}$ [2]. Both $\mathcal{F}_{\text{COMMIT}}, \mathcal{P}_{\text{PROVIDERANDOM}}$ can be found in the full version [2]. We use $\odot$ for point-wise multiplication of vector entries, $(g, h) = d$ to denote that d is the greatest common divisor of g, h and let $[r]$ be defined as the set $[r] := \{1, ..., r\}$. We will denote vectors in bold lower-case letters such as e.g. $\boldsymbol{b}$ whereas matrices are bold upper-case letters such as $\boldsymbol{M}$. $[\![m]\!]$ denotes an encryption of a message m where the randomness is left implicit.

2.1 The SPDZ Multiparty Computation Protocol

We start out with a short primer on the [14] MPC protocol which we will mostly refer to as SPDZ. This we use not just as motivation for our results, but also to make the reader familiar with the notation.

SPDZ evaluates an arithmetic circuit C over a field $\mathbb{Z}_p$ on a gate-level, where there are addition and multiplication gates. Each value $c \in \mathbb{Z}_p$ of the computation (which is assigned to a wire in the process of the evaluation) is MACed using a uniformly random MAC secret MAC key α as $\alpha \cdot c$ and both of these values are then sum-shared among all parties. This MAC key α is fixed for all such shared values, and α is additionally sum-shared among the parties, where party $\mathcal{P}_i$ holds share α_i such that $\alpha = \sum_{i=1}^{n} \alpha_i$.

---

[2] In practice, this can be implemented in several ways, e.g. using a pseudorandom function and the commitment scheme $\mathcal{F}_{\text{COMMIT}}$.

To make the above more formal, we define the $\langle \cdot \rangle$-representation of a shared value as follows:

Definition 1. *Let $r, s, e \in \mathbb{Z}_p$, then the $\langle r \rangle$-representation of r is defined as*

$$\langle r \rangle := ((r_1, ..., r_n), (\gamma(r)_1, ..., \gamma(r)_n))$$

where $r = \sum_{i=1}^{n} r_i$ and $\alpha \cdot r = \sum_{i=1}^{n} \gamma(r)_i$. Each player $\mathcal{P}_i$ will hold his shares $r_i, \gamma(r)_i$ of such a representation. We define

$$\langle r \rangle + \langle s \rangle := ((r_1 + s_1, ..., r_n + s_n), (\gamma(r)_1 + \gamma(s)_1, ..., \gamma(r)_n + \gamma(s)_n))$$

$$e \cdot \langle r \rangle := ((e \cdot r_1, ..., e \cdot r_n), (e \cdot \gamma(r)_1, ..., e \cdot \gamma(r)_n))$$

$$e + \langle r \rangle := ((r_1 + e, r_2, ..., r_n), (\gamma(r)_1 + e \cdot \alpha_1, ..., \gamma(r)_n + e \cdot \alpha_n))$$

This representation is closed under linear operations:

Proposition 1. *Let $r, s, e \in \mathbb{Z}_p$. We say that $\langle r \rangle \hat{=} \langle s \rangle$ if both $\langle r \rangle, \langle s \rangle$ reconstruct to the same value. Then it holds that*

$$\langle r \rangle + \langle s \rangle \hat{=} \langle r + s \rangle \quad and \quad e \cdot \langle r \rangle \hat{=} \langle e \cdot r \rangle \quad and \quad e + \langle r \rangle \hat{=} \langle e + r \rangle$$

In order to multiply two representations, we rely on a technique due to Beaver [3]: Let $\langle r \rangle, \langle s \rangle$ be two values where we want to calculate a representation $\langle t \rangle$ such that $t = r \cdot s$. Assume the availability of a triple[3] $(\langle a \rangle, \langle b \rangle, \langle c \rangle)$ such that a, b are uniformly random and $c = a \cdot b$. To obtain $\langle t \rangle$, one can use the procedure as depicted in Fig. 1. Correctness and privacy of this procedure were established before, e.g. in [14]. This already allows to compute on shared values, and inputting information into such a computation can also easily be achieved using standard techniques[4]. Checking that a value was indeed reconstructed correctly will be done using $\mathcal{P}_{\text{CHECKMAC}}$ which allows to check the MAC of the opened value without revealing the key α.

Procedure $\mathcal{P}_{\text{MULT}}$

Multiply($\langle r \rangle, \langle s \rangle, \langle a \rangle, \langle b \rangle, \langle c \rangle$):
  (1) The players calculate $\langle \gamma \rangle = \langle r \rangle - \langle a \rangle, \langle \delta \rangle = \langle s \rangle - \langle b \rangle$.
  (2) The players publicly reconstruct γ, δ.
  (3) Each player locally calculates $\langle t \rangle = \langle c \rangle + \delta \langle a \rangle + \gamma \langle b \rangle + \gamma \delta$.
  (4) Return $\langle t \rangle$ as the representation of the product.

Fig. 1. Procedure $\mathcal{P}_{\text{MULT}}$ to generate the product of two $\langle \cdot \rangle$-shared values.

---

[3] We will also refer to those triples as *multiplication triples* throughout this paper.
[4] Open a random value $\langle r \rangle$ to a party that wants to input x. That party then broadcasts $x - r$ and the parties jointly compute $(x - r) + \langle r \rangle = \langle x \rangle$.

This checking procedure will fail to detect an incorrect reconstruction with probability at most $2/p$ over fields of characteristic p, and similarly with probability $2/q$ over rings $\mathbb{Z}_N$ where q is the smallest prime factor of N. This in essence is captured by the following Lemma which we will also need in other cases (Fig. 2):

Lemma 1. *Assume that* $\mathcal{P}_{\text{CHECKMAC}}$ *is executed over the field* $\mathbb{Z}_p$. *The protocol* $\mathcal{P}_{\text{CHECKMAC}}$ *is correct and sound: It returns 1 if all the values* v_i *and their corresponding MACs* $\gamma(v_i)$ *are correctly computed and rejects except with probability* $2/p$ *in the case where at least one value or MAC is not correctly computed.*

Procedure $\mathcal{P}_{\text{CHECKMAC}}$

CheckOutput($v_1, ..., v_t, m$):
(1) The parties compute $r \leftarrow \mathcal{P}_{\text{PROVIDERANDOM}}.\text{ProvideRandom}(m, t)$.
(2) Each $\mathcal{P}_i$ computes $v = \sum_{i=1}^{t} r[i] \cdot v_i$ and $\gamma_i = \sum_{j=1}^{t} r[j] \cdot \gamma(v_j)$.
(3) Each $\mathcal{P}_i$ computes $\sigma_i = \gamma_i - \alpha_i \cdot v$ and commits to σ_i using $\mathcal{F}_{\text{COMMIT}}$ as c_i'.
(4) Each c_i' is opened towards all players using $\mathcal{F}_{\text{COMMIT}}$.
(5) If $\sigma = \sum_{i=1}^{n} \sigma_i$ is 0 then return 1, otherwise return 0.

Fig. 2. Procedure $\mathcal{P}_{\text{CHECKMAC}}$ to check validity of MACs.

Proof. See e.g. [11].

For some of our settings we will choose p to be rather small (i.e. of constant size in the security parameter). In this case, one can extend the $\langle \cdot \rangle$−representation as in Definition 1 by having a larger number of MACs and then check all of these MACs in parallel.

2.2 (Reed-Solomon) Codes

Let $q, k, m \in \mathbb{N}^+, m > k$ and q be a prime power. Consider the two vector spaces $\mathbb{F}_q^k, \mathbb{F}_q^m$ and a monomorphism $C : \mathbb{F}_q^k \to \mathbb{F}_q^m$ together as a *code*, i.e. $c = C(x)$ as an encoding of x in $\mathbb{F}_q^m$. We assume that it is efficiently decidable whether $c' \in C$ (error checking), where $c' \in C \Leftrightarrow \exists x' \in \mathbb{F}_q^k : C(x') = c'$ and the minimum distance d of two codewords $x, y \in C$ should be large (meaning that the difference of any two distinct codewords should be nonzero in as many positions as possible). Such a code is called an $[m, k, d]$ code.

If, for every message $x \in \mathbb{F}_q^k$ the message x reappears directly in $C(x)$ then the code is called *systematic*. Without loss of generality, one can assume that the first m positions of a codeword are equal to the encoded message in that case. The mapping of C can be represented as multiplication with a matrix G (called the *generator matrix*), and one can write the encoding procedure as $C : x \mapsto Gx$ where $G \in \mathbb{F}_q^{m \times k}$. Similarly, we assume the existence of a *check matrix* $H \in \mathbb{F}_q^{(m-k) \times m}$ where $Hx = 0 \Leftrightarrow x \in C$.

For a $[m, k, d]$ code C, define the *Schur transform* (as in [13]) as $C^* = span(\{\boldsymbol{x} \odot \boldsymbol{y} \mid \boldsymbol{x}, \boldsymbol{y} \in C\})$. C^* is itself a code where the message length k' cannot be smaller than k. On the contrary, C^* has a smaller minimum distance $d' \leq d$. The actual values k', d' depend on the properties of the code C.

A code with small loss $d - d'$ with respect to the Schur transform (as we shall see later) is the so-called *Reed-Solomon* code ([20]), where the encoding C works as follows: Fix pairwise distinct and nonzero $z_1, ..., z_m \in \mathbb{F}_q$ and define the matrices $\boldsymbol{A_1} = V(z_1, ..., z_k)^{-1}$ and $\boldsymbol{A_2} = V(z_1, ..., z_m)$ where $V(\cdot)$ is the Vandermonde matrix. We then define the encoding as

$$C : \mathbb{F}_q^k \to \mathbb{F}_q^m$$
$$x \mapsto \boldsymbol{A_2 A_1 x}$$

This encoding can be made efficient since the matrices are decomposable for certain values $z_1, ..., z_k$ using the *Fast Fourier Transform* (FFT). The decoding works essentially the same way, where one computes $\boldsymbol{y}^\top \boldsymbol{A_2}^{-1} \boldsymbol{A_1}^{-1}$.

The intuition behind the encoding procedure is as follows: The k values uniquely define a polynomial f of degree at most $k - 1$, whose coefficients can be computed using $\boldsymbol{A_1}$ (as an inverse FFT). One evaluates the polynomial in the remaining $m - k$ positions using $\boldsymbol{A_2}$. The minimum distance d is exactly $m - k + 1$, since two polynomials of degree at most $k - 1$ are equal if they agree in at least k positions. Now, by letting $\boldsymbol{A_2}$ be another FFT matrix, the pointwise multiplication of codewords from C yields a codeword in C^* which is a polynomial of degree at most $2(k - 1)$ and the code C^* therefore has minimum distance $d' = m - 2k + 1$.

2.3   The Paillier Cryptosystem

We use the Paillier encryption scheme as defined in [10,19] (with some practical restrictions). Let $N = p \cdot q$ be the product of two odd, τ-bit safe-primes with $(N, \phi(N)) = 1$ (we choose τ such that the scheme has λ bit security). Paillier encryption of a message $x \in \mathbb{Z}/N\mathbb{Z}$ with randomness $r \in \mathbb{Z}/N\mathbb{Z}^*$ is defined as:

$$\mathsf{Enc}_{pk}(x, r) := r^N \cdot (N + 1)^x \bmod N^2$$

Knowing the factorization of N allows decryption of ciphertext $c \in \mathbb{Z}/N^2\mathbb{Z}^*$, e.g., by determining the randomness used,

$$r = c^{N^{-1} \bmod \phi(N)} \bmod N.$$

The decryption then proceeds as

$$x = ((c \cdot r^{-N} \bmod N^2) - 1)/N \bmod N$$

The KG algorithm samples an RSA modulus $N = p \cdot q$, and we let the public key be $pk = (N)$ and the secret key be $sk = (p, q, f = N^{-1} \bmod \varphi(N))$. The encryption scheme is additively homomorphic and IND-CPA secure given the Composite Residuosity problem $CR[N]$ is hard.

Functionality $\mathcal{F}_{\mathrm{KGD}}$

Generate key:

(1) On input (generate_key, τ, κ) by all parties, randomly sample two different primes $p, q \in \mathbb{P}$ of bit length approximately τ. Let $N = p \cdot q$ and compute $f = N^{-1} \bmod \varphi(N)$.

(2) Sample key shares $f_1, ..., f_n \in \mathbb{Z}/2^{\kappa} N\mathbb{Z}$.

(3) Output (N, f_i) to party $\mathcal{P}_i$, and save $(N, f, f_1, ..., f_n)$ locally.

Distributed decryption:

(1) When receiving (decrypt, f_i, c) from each party $\mathcal{P}_i$, check whether some $(N, f, f_1, ..., f_n)$ was stored. If not, return $\perp$.

(2) Send $(x, r) \leftarrow \mathsf{Dec}_{sk}(c)$ to the adversary. Upon receiving $x' \in \{(x, r), \perp\}$ from the adversary, send (result, x') to all players.

Fig. 3. Functionality $\mathcal{F}_{\mathrm{KGD}}$ that provides shared keys and decrypts ciphertexts.

During the decryption of a ciphertext as described above one does completely recover the randomness used during encryption. This gives rise to a reliable distributed decryption algorithm, which we describe in the full version of this work[5] Both key generation and distributed decryption are described in the functionality Fig. 3.

Observe that the distributed decryption does also output the randomness used in the ciphertext. This can be harmful in some applications, but is sufficient for our application.

3   More Efficient Preprocessing from SHE

In this section, we present an improved preprocessing protocol for SPDZ over large fields. Towards achieving this, we overhaul the triple generation in a way that allows more efficient checks of correctness. This check uses the original SPDZ preprocessing as a black box[6] (see Fig. 4). Our approach introduces some computational overhead, but we show how this overhead can be reduced. In the full version of this work ([2]), we additionally present a technique to improve the zero-knowledge proofs of plaintext knowledge used in [11].

Offline Phase Protocol. Let C be some $[m, k, d]$ Reed-Solomon code as described in the previous section. Moreover, let C^* be its $[m, k', d']$ Schur transform. We assume the existence of a functionality that samples *faulty correlated*

---

[5] One can also find such an algorithm in [10], but our solution allows for a much simpler decryption routine. In particular, no zero-knowledge proofs are involved in the decryption process.

[6] We therefore abstain from introducing the concept of SHE in this work and refer the reader to [2,14] for more details on the subject.

Functionality $\mathcal{F}_{\text{TripleGen}}$

This functionality generates a shared MAC key α and (potentially faulty) $\langle \cdot \rangle$-representations.

Initialize: On input (init, p, C) from all players, the functionality stores the prime p and a description of the code C. $\mathcal{A}$ chooses the set of parties $\mathcal{I} \subset \{1, \ldots, n\}$ he corrupts.

   (1) For all $i \in \mathcal{I}$, $\mathcal{A}$ inputs $\alpha_i \in \mathbb{Z}_p$, while for all $i \notin \mathcal{I}$, the functionality chooses $\alpha_i \leftarrow \mathbb{Z}_p$ at random.

   (2) Set they key $\alpha = \sum_{i=1}^{n} \alpha_i$ and send α_i to $\mathcal{P}_i, i \notin \mathcal{I}$.

Triples: On input (triples) from all parties, the functionality does the following to generate triples:

   (1) For $i \notin \mathcal{I}$, the functionality samples $\boldsymbol{a}_i, \boldsymbol{b}_i \in C$ at random.

   (2) For $i \in \mathcal{I}$, $\mathcal{A}$ inputs $\boldsymbol{a}_i, \boldsymbol{b}_i, \boldsymbol{c}_i, \boldsymbol{\delta}, \boldsymbol{\Delta}_{\gamma,a}, \boldsymbol{\Delta}_{\gamma,b}, \boldsymbol{\Delta}_{\gamma,c} \in \mathbb{Z}_p^m$. If $\boldsymbol{a}_i, \boldsymbol{b}_i \notin C$ then stop.

   (3) Define $\boldsymbol{a} = \sum_{j=1}^{n} \boldsymbol{a}_j, \boldsymbol{b} = \sum_{j=1}^{n} \boldsymbol{b}_j$.

   (4) Let $j \notin \mathcal{I}$ be the smallest index of an honest player. For all $i \notin \mathcal{I}, i \neq j$ choose $\boldsymbol{c}_i \in \mathbb{Z}_p^m$ uniformly at random. For $\mathcal{P}_j$ let $\boldsymbol{c}_j = \boldsymbol{a} \odot \boldsymbol{b} + \boldsymbol{\delta} - \sum_{i \in [n], i \neq j} \boldsymbol{c}_i$. Send $\boldsymbol{a}_i, \boldsymbol{b}_i, \boldsymbol{c}_i$ to each honest $\mathcal{P}_i$.

   (5) Run the macros
$$\langle \boldsymbol{a} \rangle \leftarrow \text{Angle}(\boldsymbol{a}_1, \ldots, \boldsymbol{a}_n, \alpha, \boldsymbol{\Delta}_{\gamma,a}, m, p),$$
$$\langle \boldsymbol{b} \rangle \leftarrow \text{Angle}(\boldsymbol{b}_1, \ldots, \boldsymbol{b}_n, \alpha, \boldsymbol{\Delta}_{\gamma,b}, m, p),$$
$$\langle \boldsymbol{c} \rangle \leftarrow \text{Angle}(\boldsymbol{c}_1, \ldots, \boldsymbol{c}_n, \alpha, \boldsymbol{\Delta}_{\gamma,c}, m, p).$$

   (6) Return $(\langle \boldsymbol{a} \rangle, \langle \boldsymbol{b} \rangle, \langle \boldsymbol{c} \rangle)$.

$\text{Angle}(\boldsymbol{r}_1, \ldots, \boldsymbol{r}_n, \alpha, \boldsymbol{\Delta}_\gamma, m, p)$: This macro will be run to create $\langle \cdot \rangle$-representations.

   (1) Define $\boldsymbol{r} = \sum_{i=1}^{n} \boldsymbol{r}_i$

   (2) For $i \in \mathcal{I}$, $\mathcal{A}$ inputs $\boldsymbol{\gamma}_i \in \mathbb{Z}_p^m$, and for $i \notin \mathcal{I}$, the functionality chooses $\boldsymbol{\gamma}_i \leftarrow \mathbb{Z}_p^m$ at random except for $\boldsymbol{\gamma}_j$, with j being the smallest index not in $\mathcal{I}$.

   (3) Set $\boldsymbol{\gamma} = \alpha \cdot \boldsymbol{r} + \boldsymbol{\Delta}_\gamma$ and $\boldsymbol{\gamma}_j = \boldsymbol{\gamma} - \sum_{j \neq i=1}^{n} \boldsymbol{\gamma}_i$. For every honest party $\mathcal{P}_i$, send $\boldsymbol{\gamma}_i$.

   (4) Define $\langle \boldsymbol{r} \rangle = (\boldsymbol{r}_1, \ldots, \boldsymbol{r}_n, \boldsymbol{\gamma}_1, \ldots, \boldsymbol{\gamma}_n)$. Return $\langle \boldsymbol{r} \rangle$.

Fig. 4. Functionality $\mathcal{F}_{\text{TripleGen}}$ that generates potentially faulty triples.

randomness and which is depicted in Fig. 4. It generates random codewords as the shares of factors $\boldsymbol{a}, \boldsymbol{b}$ of multiplication triples and also enforces that malicious parties choose such codewords as their shares. The functionality then computes a product and shares it among all parties, subject to the constraint that $\mathcal{A}$ can arbitrarily modify the sum and the shares of malicious parties. Figure 4 can be implemented using a SHE scheme as was shown in [14]. As a twist, the zero-knowledge proofs must be slightly extended to show that the vectors inside the ciphertexts contain codewords from C. Based on this available functionality, we show that one can implement $\mathcal{F}_{\text{FullTripleGen}}$ as depicted in Fig. 5 using our protocol $\Pi_{\text{TripleCheck}}$. $\mathcal{F}_{\text{FullTripleGen}}$ is similar to $\mathcal{F}_{\text{TripleGen}}$ but additionally ensures that all multiplication triples are correct.

Functionality $\mathcal{F}_{\text{FullTripleGen}}$

Let $\mathcal{I}$ be the set of parties that are controlled by $\mathcal{A}$, $u \in \mathbb{N}^+$. This functionality generates a shared MAC key α and $\langle \cdot \rangle$-representations. It uses the macro Angle as depicted in $\mathcal{F}_{\text{TripleGen}}$.

Initialize: On input (init, p, u) from all players, the functionality stores the prime p and the vector dimension u. $\mathcal{A}$ chooses the set of parties $\mathcal{I} \subset [n]$ he corrupts.
  (1) For all $i \in \mathcal{I}$, $\mathcal{A}$ inputs $\alpha_i \in \mathbb{Z}_p$, while for all $i \notin \mathcal{I}$, the functionality chooses $\alpha_i \leftarrow \mathbb{Z}_p$ at random.
  (2) Set they key $\alpha = \sum_{i=1}^n \alpha_i$ and send α_i to $\mathcal{P}_i, i \notin \mathcal{I}$.

Triples: On input (triples) the functionality does the following
  (1) Let $\mathcal{A}$ input $a_i, b_i, c_i, \Delta_{\gamma,a}, \Delta_{\gamma,b}, \Delta_{\gamma,c} \in \mathbb{Z}_p^u$ for each $i \in \mathcal{I}$.
  (2) Choose $a_i, b_i \in \mathbb{Z}_p^u$ for each honest $\mathcal{P}_i$ uniformly at random. Set $a = \sum_i a_i, b = \sum_i b_i$ and define $c = a \odot b$.
  (3) Let j be the smallest number in $[n] \backslash \mathcal{I}$. Choose uniformly random $c_i \in R^u$ for each $\mathcal{P}_i$ with $i \in [n] \backslash \mathcal{I}, i \neq j$ and set $c_j = c - \sum_{i \in [n], i \neq j} c_i$.
  (4) Run the macros
      $\langle a \rangle \leftarrow \text{Angle}(a_1, \ldots, a_n, \alpha, \Delta_{\gamma,a}, u, p)$,
      $\langle b \rangle \leftarrow \text{Angle}(b_1, \ldots, b_n, \alpha, \Delta_{\gamma,b}, u, p)$,
      $\langle c \rangle \leftarrow \text{Angle}(c_1, \ldots, c_n, \alpha, \Delta_{\gamma,c}, u, p)$.
  (5) Return $(\langle a \rangle, \langle b \rangle, \langle c \rangle)$.

Fig. 5. Functionality $\mathcal{F}_{\text{FullTripleGen}}$ that generates correct triples.

The main idea of this protocol follows the outline as presented in the introduction:

(1) Check that the output vector c is a codeword of C^*. If so, then the error vector δ is also a codeword, meaning that either it is $\mathbf{0}$ or *it has weight at least d'*.
(2) Open a fraction of the triples to check whether they are indeed correct. If so, then δ must be the all-zero vector with high probability.

Due to the lack of space, the proof of security of $\Pi_{\text{TripleCheck}}$ is postponed to the full version of this work [2], where the security is proven in the UC framework [7].

Fast and Amortized Checks. In the protocol presented in Fig. 7, we check each potential code vector separately. Let $H \in \mathbb{Z}_p^{l \times m}$ be the check matrix of the Schur transform of the code. Multiplication with a check matrix H can be done in $O(m^2)$ steps - but assuming that this must be carried out for a number of e.g. m vectors this leads to $O(m^3)$ operations, if done trivially. Let us put all the l input vectors $a_1, ..., a_l$ into a matrix $A = [a_1 || a_2 || ... || a_l]$. If all vectors are drawn from the code, then $HA = \mathbf{0}$.

Now consider another generator matrix $G \in \mathbb{Z}_p^{m' \times l}$ for a Reed-Solomon code of message dimension l, where we denote the redundancy as $d \in O(m)$ again (we can easily assume that $m' \in O(m)$). Multiplication of each of the matrices H, A with G can be done in time $m'^2 \cdot \log(m')$ using the FFT, and one can precompute GH before the actual computation takes place. $GHAG^\top$ is a zero matrix if A

Procedure $\mathcal{P}_{\text{MatrixMultCheck}}$

CheckMultiplication(H, A):
   (1) Compute the matrices GH and $AG^\top$.
   (2) For $j \in [m']$ select a pair $(x_j, y_j) \in \{1, ..., m'\}^2$.
   (3) For $j \in [m']$, compute z_j as the inner product of the x_jth row of GH and the y_jth column of $AG^\top$.
   (4) If all z_i are 0 return *accept*, otherwise *reject*.

Fig. 6. Procedure $\mathcal{P}_{\text{MatrixMultCheck}}$ to check whether a matrix product is zero.

Protocol $\Pi_{\text{TripleCheck}}$

Let H be the check matrix of C^* and $t \in \mathbb{N}^+, t < k - 1$ be the upper bound on the number of opened triples. We assume that both C, C^* are in systematic form, and are over the field $\mathbb{Z}_p$.

Initialize:
   (1) All parties send (init, p, C) to $\mathcal{F}_{\text{TripleGen}}$ to receive their shares α_i of α.

Triples:
   (1) All parties send (triples) to $\mathcal{F}_{\text{TripleGen}}$ and obtain $(\langle a \rangle, \langle b \rangle, \langle c \rangle)$.
   (2) Let c_i be $\mathcal{P}_i$s share of $\langle c \rangle$. Each party locally computes $\sigma_i = Hc_i$ and commits to σ_i using $\mathcal{F}_{\text{Commit}}$.
   (3) Each party $\mathcal{P}_i$ opens its commitments to σ_i towards all parties. Check if $0 = \sum_i \sigma_i$. If not, abort.
   (4) Let $A = [m]$. For $j \in [t]$ all parties do the following
      (4.1) Sample the uniformly random value $r \leftarrow \text{ProvideRandom}(m, 1)$. Set $A \leftarrow A \backslash \{r\}$.
      (4.2) Each party $\mathcal{P}_i$ commits to its shares $a_i[r], b_i[r], c_i[r]$ using $\mathcal{F}_{\text{Commit}}$.
      (4.3) Each party opens its commitments towards all other parties.
      (4.4) Each party checks that $(\sum_i a_i[r]) \cdot (\sum_i b_i[r]) = \sum_i c_i[r]$. If not, then they abort.
   (5) Let $U = [m] \backslash A$, where $U = \{u_1, ..., u_l\}$. Compute $d \leftarrow \mathcal{P}_{\text{CheckMac}}.\text{CheckOutput}(\sigma, a[u_1], b[u_1], c[u_1], ..., a[u_l], b[u_l], c[u_l])$. If $d \neq 0$ the parties return $\bot$.
   (6) Let $O \subset A$ be the smallest $k - t - 1$ indices of A. The parties output $(\langle a[O] \rangle, \langle b[O] \rangle, \langle c[O] \rangle)$.

Fig. 7. Protocol $\Pi_{\text{TripleCheck}}$ that checks the correctness of triples.

only consists of codewords. On the other hand, consider $\boldsymbol{GHA}$: If one row is not a codeword, then it will be encoded to a vector with weight at least d due to the distance of the code. Multiplying with $\boldsymbol{G}^{\top}$ will then yield a matrix where at least d^2 entries are nonzero. Since both $m', d \in O(m)$, the fraction $\frac{d^2}{m'^2}$ is constant. One can compute both $\boldsymbol{GH}$ and $\boldsymbol{AG}^{\top}$ in time $m'^2 \cdot \log(m^{prime})$ using the FFT, and then choose rows/columns from both product matrices for which one then computes the scale product. In case that at least one $\boldsymbol{a}_i$ is not a codeword, it will be nonzero with constant probability. Repeating this experiment $\Omega(m')$ times yields 0 in all cases only with probability negligible in m' (Fig. 6). We refer to [13] for more details on this technique.

4   Preprocessing from Paillier Encryption

In this section we present a novel approach to produce multiplication triples using Paillier's cryptosystem. In comparison to previous work which uses heavy zero-knowledge machinery to prove that multiplications are done correctly, we choose a somewhat different approach that is related to the preprocessing protocol from the previous section. Moreover, we present two zero-knwoledge proofs which are used in the protocol. In comparison to previous work, they will require to send less bits per proof instance.

Protocol Π_{ZKPoPK}

$\mathcal{P}$ proves the relation R_{ZKPoPK}.

(1) $\mathcal{P}$ chooses $s \leftarrow \mathbb{Z}/N\mathbb{Z}^*$ and sends $t = s^N \mod N$ to $\mathcal{V}$.
(2) $\mathcal{V}$ chooses $e \leftarrow \mathbb{Z}/N\mathbb{Z}$ and sends it to $\mathcal{P}$.
(3) $\mathcal{P}$ sends $k = s \cdot r^e \mod N$ to $\mathcal{V}$.
(4) $\mathcal{V}$ accepts if $k^N = c^e \cdot t \mod N$ and otherwise rejects.

Fig. 8. Protocol Π_{ZKPoPK} to prove knowledge of plaintexts of Paillier encryptions.

4.1   Proving Statements About Paillier Ciphertexts

First, consider a regular proof of plaintext knowledge. For Paillier encryption, one would prove the following relation:

$$R_{\text{ZKPoPK}} = \{(a, w) \mid a = (c, pk) \land w = (x, r) \land x \in \mathbb{Z}/N\mathbb{Z} \land$$
$$r \in \mathbb{Z}/N\mathbb{Z}^* \land c = \text{Enc}_{pk}(x, r)\}$$

Throughout the protocol, the parties must compute products with ciphertexts, where we want to establish that a party *knows* which value it multiplied in. This can be captured as follows:

$$R_{\text{PoM}} = \{(a, w) \mid a = (z, \hat{z}, pk) \land w = (b, c, r) \land b, c \in \mathbb{Z}/N\mathbb{Z} \land$$
$$r \in \mathbb{Z}/N\mathbb{Z}^* \land \hat{z} = z^b \cdot \mathsf{Enc}_{pk}(c, r) \bmod N^2\}$$

Protocol Π_{PoM}

$\mathcal{P}$ proves the relation R_{PoM}.

(1) $\mathcal{P}$ generates $t, u \in \mathbb{Z}/N\mathbb{Z}, v \in \mathbb{Z}/N\mathbb{Z}^*$. He then sends $f = z^t \cdot \mathsf{Enc}_{pk}(u, v) \bmod N^2$ to $\mathcal{V}$.

(2) $\mathcal{V}$ chooses a uniformly random $e \in \mathbb{Z}/N\mathbb{Z}$ and sends it to $\mathcal{P}$.

(3) $\mathcal{P}$ computes $g = t + e \cdot b \bmod N, h = u + e \cdot c \bmod N, i = v \cdot r^e \bmod N$ and and sends (g, h, i) to $\mathcal{V}$.

(4) $\mathcal{V}$ accepts if $z^g \cdot \mathsf{Enc}_{pk}(h, i) = \hat{z}^e \cdot f \bmod N^2$, and rejects otherwise.

Fig. 9. Protocol Π_{PoM} to prove linear relation on ciphertexts.

In the following, we present honest-verifier perfect zero-knowledge proofs for both $R_{\text{ZKPoPK}}, R_{\text{PoM}}$ between a prover $\mathcal{P}$ and verifier $\mathcal{V}$. In order to use them in the preprocessing protocol, one can either make them non-interactive using the Fiat-Shamir transformation in the Random Oracle Model, or use the secure coin-flip protocol $\mathcal{P}_{\text{ProvideRandom}}$ to sample the challenge e. Since during a protocol instance, many proofs are executed in parallel, one can use the same challenge for all instances and so the complexity of doing the coin-flip is not a significant cost.

For practical implementations, one can choose the random value e from a smaller interval like e.g. $[0, 2^\kappa]$ where κ is the statistical security parameter. This also yields negligible cheating probability[7]. The proof that $\Pi_{\text{ZKPoPK}}, \Pi_{\text{PoM}}$ are in fact honest-verifier zero-knowledge proofs for the relations $R_{\text{ZKPoPK}}, R_{\text{PoM}}$ can be found in the full version of this work.

4.2   Computing and Checking Triples

Our protocol $\Pi_{\text{PaillierTripleGen}}$, on a high level, runs in the following phases:

(1) In a first step, every party encrypts uniformly random values.

(2) Take $k + 2$ values which define a polynomial A of degree $k + 1$ uniquely (when considered as evaluations in the points $1, ..., k + 2$). Interpolate this polynomial A in the next $k + 2$ points locally, encrypt these points and prove that the encrypted values are indeed points that lie on A. Then the same is done for a polynomial B.

---

[7] For the soundness of the proof, we rely on the fact that $(e - e', N) = 1$ which indeed is always true if $e, e' \ll \sqrt{N}$ and N is a safe RSA modulus.

Protocol $\Pi_{\text{PAILLIERTRIPLEGEN}}$ (Part 1)

A protocol to perform preprocessing for the SPDZ protocol using Paillier encryption.

Initialize: On input $(\text{init}, \mathbb{Z}/N\mathbb{Z}, k)$ the parties do the following:
  (1) Each party $\mathcal{P}_i$ picks $\alpha_i \in \mathbb{Z}/N\mathbb{Z}$ uniformly at random, broadcasts a fresh encryption $[\![\alpha_i]\!]$ and proves knowledge of plaintext of $[\![\alpha_i]\!]$ using Π_{ZKPoPK}.
  (2) The parties compute $[\![\alpha]\!] \leftarrow \prod_{i=1}^{n}[\![\alpha_i]\!]$.
  (3) Each $\mathcal{P}_i$ stores $[\![\alpha]\!]$ as the encrypted MAC key and its share α_i of the MAC key.

Triples: On input (triples) the parties do the following:
  (1) For $j \in [k + 2]$ each $\mathcal{P}_i$ picks $A_i(j), B_i(j) \in \mathbb{Z}/N\mathbb{Z}$ uniformly at random, computes $[\![A_i(j)]\!], [\![B_i(j)]\!]$ and broadcasts $([\![A_i(j)]\!], [\![B_i(j)]\!])_{j \in [k+2]}$ together with proofs of Π_{ZKPoPK}.
  (2) For $j \in [k + 2]$ every party $\mathcal{P}_i$ defines the polynomials $A_i(\cdot), B_i(\cdot)$ using $A_i(j), B_i(j)$ as evaluations. Each party computes and broadcasts $([\![A_i(l)]\!], [\![B_i(l)]\!])_{l=k+3,\dots,2k+2}$ together with proofs of plaintext knowledge using Π_{ZKPoPK}.
  (3) The parties locally compute

$$[\![A(l)]\!] = \prod_{i=1}^{n}[\![A_i(l)]\!] \text{ and } [\![B(l)]\!] = \prod_{i=1}^{n}[\![B_i(l)]\!]$$

  (4) The parties sample $\beta \leftarrow \mathcal{P}_{\text{PROVIDERANDOM}}$. ProvideRandom$(N-2k-3, 1)+2k+3$ so that $\beta \in \mathbb{Z}/N\mathbb{Z} \setminus \{0, \dots, 2k + 2\}$.
  (5) Define $A^{\top}(\beta)$ to be the value $A(\beta)$ computed using Lagrange interpolation and the values $A(1), \dots, A(k + 2)$ and similarly $A^{\perp}(\beta)$ to be $A(\beta)$ computed using $A(1), \dots, A(2k + 2)$. Every $\mathcal{P}_i$ locally computes

$$[\![A^{\dagger}(\beta)]\!] = [\![A^{\top}(\beta)]\!]/[\![A^{\perp}(\beta)]\!] \text{ and } [\![B^{\dagger}(\beta)]\!] = [\![B^{\top}(\beta)]\!]/[\![B^{\perp}(\beta)]\!]$$

  (6) The parties decrypt $[\![A^{\dagger}(\beta)]\!], [\![B^{\dagger}(\beta)]\!]$ and check whether $A^{\dagger}(\beta) = B^{\dagger}(\beta) = 0 \bmod N$. Otherwise they abort.

Fig. 10. Protocol $\Pi_{\text{PAILLIERTRIPLEGEN}}$ to generate correct random triples out of random single values, Part 1.

(3) An unreliable point-wise multiplication of A, B is performed. The resulting polynomial C is interpolated in a random point β, and it is checked whether the multiplicative relation holds. This is enough to check correctness of all triples due to the size of N.
(4) Share the points of C among all parties as random shares.
(5) For all of the shares of A, B, C that were generated in the protocol, products with the MAC key α are computed. Correctness of the multiplication with α is checked and if the check is passed, the MACs are reshared among the parties in the same way as the points of C.

Protocol $\Pi_{\text{PAILLIERTRIPLEGEN}}$ (Part 2)

Triples:

(7) For $j \in [2k+2]$ each $\mathcal{P}_i$ chooses $r_{i,j} \leftarrow \mathbb{Z}/N\mathbb{Z}^*$, computes encryptions

$$[\![\hat{c}_{i,j}]\!] \leftarrow [\![A(j)]\!]^{B_i(j)} \text{Enc}_{pk}(0, r_{i,j})$$

broadcasts the $[\![\hat{c}_{i,j}]\!]$ and proves the relation using Π_{PoM}.

(8) For $j \in [2k+2]$ each $\mathcal{P}_i$ picks $\tilde{c}_{i,j} \in \mathbb{Z}/N\mathbb{Z}$ uniformly at random, computes $[\![\tilde{c}_{i,j}]\!]$ and broadcasts $([\![\tilde{c}_{i,j}]\!])_{j \in \{0,\ldots,2k+3\}}$ together with proofs of Π_{ZKPoPK}.

(9) For $j \in [2k+2]$ the parties locally compute

$$[\![\hat{c}_j]\!] = \prod_{i=1}^{n} [\![\hat{c}_{i,j}]\!] / \prod_{i=1}^{n} [\![\tilde{c}_{i,j}]\!]$$

and publicly decrypt $\hat{c}_j$.

(10) For $j \in [2k+2]$ each party $\mathcal{P}_i$ sets

$$[\![C_1(j)]\!] = [\![\tilde{c}_{1,j}]\!] \cdot [\![\hat{c}_j]\!] \qquad \text{and} \qquad [\![C_i(j)]\!] = [\![\tilde{c}_{t,j}]\!]$$

for $t \in [n], t \neq 1$ and $[\![C(j)]\!] = \prod_{i=1}^{n} [\![C_i(j)]\!]$ and its share of $C(j)$ as

$$C_i(j) = \begin{cases} \tilde{c}_{1,j} + \hat{c}_j & \text{if } i = 1 \\ \tilde{c}_{i,j} & \text{else} \end{cases}$$

(11) The parties sample $\beta \leftarrow \mathcal{P}_{\text{PROVIDERANDOM}}.\text{ProvideRandom}(N - k - 1, 1) + k + 1$ so that $\beta \leftarrow \mathbb{Z}/N\mathbb{Z} \setminus \{0, \ldots, k\}$.

(12) The parties compute $[\![A(\beta)]\!], [\![B(\beta)]\!], [\![C(\beta)]\!]$ locally using Lagrange interpolation and then decrypt these values.

(13) If $A(\beta) \cdot B(\beta) \neq C(\beta) \mod N$ then abort.

(14) Each $\mathcal{P}_i$ picks $s_i \in \mathbb{Z}/N\mathbb{Z}$ uniformly at random, computes $[\![s_i]\!]$ and broadcasts $[\![s_i]\!]$ together with a proof of Π_{ZKPoPK}. Let $s = \sum_i s_i$.

(15) We define the following abbreviation:

$$t_{i,j} \leftarrow \begin{cases} s_i \text{ for } j = 0 \\ A_i(j) \text{ for } j = 1, \ldots, k \\ B_i(j) \text{ for } j = k+1, \ldots, 2k \\ C_i(j) \text{ for } j = 2k+1, \ldots, 3k \end{cases} \quad \text{and} \quad t_j \leftarrow \begin{cases} s \text{ for } j = 0 \\ A(j) \text{ for } j = 1, \ldots, k \\ B(j) \text{ for } j = k+1, \ldots, 2k \\ C(j) \text{ for } j = 2k+1, \ldots, 3k \end{cases}$$

Fig. 11. Protocol $\Pi_{\text{PAILLIERTRIPLEGEN}}$ to generate correct random triples out of random single values, Part 2.

The protocol $\Pi_{\text{PAILLIERTRIPLEGEN}}$ can be found in Figs. 10, 11 and 12. The proof of security in the UC framework [7] as well as a short introduction into the UC framework can be found in the full version of this work.

Protocol $\Pi_{\text{PaillierTripleGen}}$ (Part 3)

Triples:

(16) For $j = 0, \dots, 3k$ each $\mathcal{P}_i$ picks $r_{i,j} \in \mathbb{Z}/N\mathbb{Z}^*$ uniformly at random and computes

$$[\![t_{i,j} \cdot \alpha]\!] \leftarrow [\![\alpha]\!]^{t_{i,j}} \cdot \mathsf{Enc}_{pk}(0, r_{i,j})$$

then broadcasts $([\![t_{i,j} \cdot \alpha]\!])$ and proves the relation using Π_{PoM}.

(17) For $j = 0, \dots, 3k$, $\mathcal{P}_1, \dots, \mathcal{P}_n$ compute

$$[\![t_j \cdot \alpha]\!] \leftarrow \prod_{i=1}^{n} [\![t_{i,j} \cdot \alpha]\!]$$

(18) The parties sample $\beta \leftarrow \mathcal{P}_{\text{ProvideRandom}} \cdot \text{ProvideRandom}(N, 1)$.

(19) All parties compute

$$[\![v]\!] \leftarrow \prod_{j=0}^{3k} [\![t_j]\!]^{\beta^j} \text{ and } [\![v']\!] \leftarrow \prod_{j=0}^{3k} [\![t_j \cdot \alpha]\!]^{\beta^j}$$

(20) The parties jointly decrypt $[\![v]\!]$ to v and check that the decryption was correct.

(21) The parties jointly decrypt

$$[\![M]\!] \leftarrow [\![\alpha]\!]^v / [\![v']\!]$$

and verify that $M = 0$, otherwise they abort. All parties verify correctness of decryption.

(22) For $j \in [3k]$ each $\mathcal{P}_i$ picks $m_{i,j} \in \mathbb{Z}/N\mathbb{Z}$ uniformly at random, computes $[\![m_{i,j}]\!]$ and broadcasts $([\![m_{i,j}]\!])_{j \in [3k]}$ together with proofs of Π_{ZKPoPK}.

(23) For each $j \in [3k]$, the parties compute

$$[\![O_j]\!] \leftarrow [\![t_j \cdot \alpha]\!] / \prod_{i=1}^{n} [\![m_{i,j}]\!]$$

and publicly decrypt $[\![O_j]\!]$. All parties verify correctness of decryption.

(24) For each $j \in [3k]$, each $\mathcal{P}_i$ determines its share $\gamma(t_j)_i$, of the MAC $\gamma(t_j)$ of t_j as

$$\gamma(t_j)_i \leftarrow \begin{cases} O_j + m_{i,j} & \text{for } i = 1 \\ m_{i,j} & \text{for } 1 < i \leq n \end{cases}$$

(25) Each party $\mathcal{P}_i$ uses $t_{i,j}, \gamma(t_j)_i$ as its shares of $\langle t_j \rangle$.

Fig. 12. Protocol $\Pi_{\text{PaillierTripleGen}}$ to generate correct random triples out of random single values, Part 3.

References

1. Baum, C., Damgård, I., Orlandi, C.: Publicly auditable secure multi-party computation. In: Abdalla, M., De Prisco, R. (eds.) SCN 2014. LNCS, vol. 8642, pp. 175–196. Springer, Heidelberg (2014)
2. Baum, C., Damgård, I., Toft, T., Zakarias, R.: Better preprocessing for secure multiparty computation (2016). https://eprint.iacr.org/2016/048

3. Beaver, D.: Efficient multiparty protocols using circuit randomization. In: Feigenbaum, J. (ed.) CRYPTO 1991. LNCS, vol. 576, pp. 420–432. Springer, Heidelberg (1992)
4. Ben-Sasson, E., Fehr, S., Ostrovsky, R.: Near-linear unconditionally-secure multiparty computation with a dishonest minority. In: Safavi-Naini, R., Canetti, R. (eds.) CRYPTO 2012. LNCS, vol. 7417, pp. 663–680. Springer, Heidelberg (2012)
5. Bendlin, R., Damgård, I., Orlandi, C., Zakarias, S.: Semi-homomorphic encryption and multiparty computation. In: Paterson, K.G. (ed.) EUROCRYPT 2011. LNCS, vol. 6632, pp. 169–188. Springer, Heidelberg (2011)
6. Bogetoft, P., et al.: Secure multiparty computation goes live. In: Dingledine, R., Golle, P. (eds.) FC 2009. LNCS, vol. 5628, pp. 325–343. Springer, Heidelberg (2009)
7. Canetti, R.: Universally composable security: a new paradigm for cryptographic protocols. In: Proceedings of 42nd IEEE Symposium on Foundations of Computer Science, 2001, pp. 136–145. IEEE (2001)
8. Cramer, R., Damgård, I.B., Nielsen, J.B.: Multiparty computation from threshold homomorphic encryption. In: Pfitzmann, B. (ed.) EUROCRYPT 2001. LNCS, vol. 2045, pp. 280–300. Springer, Heidelberg (2001)
9. Cramer, R., Damgård, I., Pastro, V.: On the amortized complexity of zero knowledge protocols for multiplicative relations. In: Smith, A. (ed.) ICITS 2012. LNCS, vol. 7412, pp. 62–79. Springer, Heidelberg (2012)
10. Damgård, I., Jurik, M.: A generalisation, a simplification and some applications of Paillier's probabilistic public-key system. PKC 2001. LNCS, vol. 1992, pp. 119–136. Springer, Heidelberg (2001)
11. Damgård, I., Keller, M., Larraia, E., Pastro, V., Scholl, P., Smart, N.P.: Practical covertly secure MPC for dishonest majority – or: breaking the SPDZ limits. In: Crampton, J., Jajodia, S., Mayes, K. (eds.) ESORICS 2013. LNCS, vol. 8134, pp. 1–18. Springer, Heidelberg (2013)
12. Damgård, I.B., Nielsen, J.B.: Universally composable efficient multiparty computation from threshold homomorphic encryption. In: Boneh, D. (ed.) CRYPTO 2003. LNCS, vol. 2729, pp. 247–264. Springer, Heidelberg (2003)
13. Damgård, I., Zakarias, S.: Constant-overhead secure computation of boolean circuits using preprocessing. In: Sahai, A. (ed.) TCC 2013. LNCS, vol. 7785, pp. 621–641. Springer, Heidelberg (2013)
14. Damgård, I., Pastro, V., Smart, N., Zakarias, S.: Multiparty computation from somewhat homomorphic encryption. In: Safavi-Naini, R., Canetti, R. (eds.) CRYPTO 2012. LNCS, vol. 7417, pp. 643–662. Springer, Heidelberg (2012)
15. Frederiksen, T.K., Keller, M., Orsini, E., Scholl, P.: A unified approach to MPC with preprocessing using OT. In: Iwata, T., Cheon, J.H. (eds.) ASIACRYPT 2015. LNCS, vol. 9452, pp. 711–735. Springer, Heidelberg (2015). doi:10.1007/978-3-662-48797-6_29
16. Goldreich, O., Micali, S., Wigderson, A.: How to play any mental game. In: Proceedings of the Nineteenth Annual ACM Symposium on Theory of Computing, pp. 218–229. ACM (1987)
17. Lindell, Y., Pinkas, B., Smart, N.P., Yanai, A.: Efficient constant round multiparty computation combining BMR and SPDZ. In: Gennaro, R., Robshaw, M. (eds.) CRYPTO 2015. LNCS, vol. 9216, pp. 319–338. Springer, Heidelberg (2015)
18. Nielsen, J.B., Nordholt, P.S., Orlandi, C., Burra, S.S.: A new approach to practical active-secure two-party computation. In: Safavi-Naini, R., Canetti, R. (eds.) CRYPTO 2012. LNCS, vol. 7417, pp. 681–700. Springer, Heidelberg (2012)

19. Paillier, P.: Public-key cryptosystems based on composite degree residuosity classes. In: Stern, J. (ed.) EUROCRYPT 1999. LNCS, vol. 1592, pp. 223–238. Springer, Heidelberg (1999)
20. Reed, I.S., Solomon, G.: Polynomial codes over certain finite fields. J. Soc. Ind. Appl. Math. **8**(2), 300–304 (1960)
21. Yao, A.C.-C.: How to generate and exchange secrets. In: 27th Annual Symposium on Foundations of Computer Science, 1986, pp. 162–167. IEEE (1986)

Trinocchio: Privacy-Preserving Outsourcing by Distributed Verifiable Computation

Berry Schoenmakers[1], Meilof Veeningen[2(✉)], and Niels de Vreede[1]

[1] Department of Mathematics and Computer Science, TU Eindhoven,
Eindhoven, The Netherlands
[2] Philips Research, Eindhoven, The Netherlands
meilof.veeningen@philips.com

Abstract. Verifiable computation allows a client to outsource computations to a worker with a cryptographic proof of correctness of the result that can be verified faster than performing the computation. Recently, the highly efficient Pinocchio system was introduced as a major leap towards practical verifiable computation. Unfortunately, Pinocchio and other efficient verifiable computation systems require the client to disclose the inputs to the worker, which is undesirable for sensitive inputs. To solve this problem, we propose Trinocchio: a system that distributes Pinocchio to three (or more) workers, that each individually do not learn which inputs they are computing on. We fully exploit the almost linear structure of Pinochhio proofs, letting each worker essentially perform the work for a single Pinocchio proof; verification by the client remains the same. Moreover, we extend Trinocchio to enable joint computation with multiple mutually distrusting inputters and outputters and still very fast verification. We show the feasibility of our approach by analysing the performance of an implementation in a case study.

1 Introduction

Recent cryptographic advances are starting to make verifiable computation more and more practical. The goal of verifiable computation is to allow a client to outsource a computation to a worker and cryptographically verify the result with less effort than performing the computation itself. Based on recent ground-breaking ideas [Gro10,GGPR13], Pinocchio [PHGR13] was the first implemented system to achieve this for some realistic computations. Recent works have improved the state-of-the-art in verifiable computation, e.g., by considering better ways to specify computations [BSCG+13], or adding access control [AJCC15].

However, one feature not yet available in practical verifiable computation is privacy, meaning that the worker should not learn the inputs that it is computing on. This feature would enable a client to save time by outsourcing computations, even if the inputs of those computations are so sensitive that it does not want to disclose them to the worker. Also, it would allow verifiable computation to be used in settings where multiple clients do not trust the worker or each other, but still want to perform a joint computation over their respective inputs and be sure of the correctness of the result.

© Springer International Publishing Switzerland 2016

M. Manulis et al. (Eds.): ACNS 2016, LNCS 9696, pp. 346–366, 2016.
DOI: 10.1007/978-3-319-39555-5_19

While privacy was already defined in the first paper to formalize verifiable computation [GGP10], it has not been shown so far how it is efficiently achieved, with existing constructions relying on efficient cryptographic primitives. By outsourcing a computation to multiple workers, it *is* possible to guarantee privacy (if not all workers are corrupted) and correctness, but existing constructions from the multiparty literature lose the most appealing feature of verifiable computation: namely, that computations can be verified very quickly, even in time independent from the computation size. This leads to the central question of this paper: can we perform verifiable computation with the *correctness* and *performance* guarantees of [PHGR13], but while also getting *privacy* against corrupted workers?

1.1 Our Contributions

In this paper, we introduce Trinocchio to show that indeed, it is possible to outsource a computation in a privacy-preserving way to multiple workers, while retaining the fast verification offered by verifiable computation. Trinocchio uses state-of-the-art [PHGR13]-style proofs, but distributes the computation of these proofs to, e.g., three workers such that no single worker learns anything about the inputs. The client essentially gets a normal Pinocchio proof, so we keep Pinocchio's correctness guarantees and fast verification. The critical observation is that the almost linear structure of Pinocchio proofs (supporting verification based on bilinear maps) allows us to distribute the computation of Pinocchio proofs such that individual workers perform essentially the same work as a normal Pinocchio prover in the non-distributed setting. Specifically, our contributions are:

– We show how to distribute the production of Pinocchio proofs in a privacy-preserving way to multiple workers, thereby achieving privacy-preserving verifiable computation in the setting with one client.
– We extend our system to settings with multiple distrusting input and result parties.
– We provide a precise security model capturing the security guarantees of our protocols: privacy, correctness, but also input independence.
– We demonstrate the practical feasibility of our approach by implementing a case study: we demonstrate Trinocchio's low overhead by repeating the multivariate polynomial evaluation case study of [PHGR13]'s.

While our Trinocchio protocol ensures correct function evaluation, it only fully protects privacy against semi-honest workers. This is a realistic attacker model; in particular, it means that side channel attacks on individual workers are ineffective because each individual worker's communication and computation are completely independent from the sensitive inputs. However, even if an adversary should be able to obtain sensitive information, they are unable to manipulate the result thanks to the use of verifiable computation. In this way, our protocol *hedges* against the risk of more powerful adversaries.

1.2 Related Work

Privacy-preserving outsourcing to single workers has been considered in the literature, but constructions in this setting rely on inefficient cryptographic primitives like fully homomorphic encryption [GGP10, CKKC13, FGP14], functional encryption [GKP+13], and multi-input attribute-based encryption [GKL+15]. (This is not surprising: indeed, even without guaranteeing correctness, letting a single worker perform a computation on inputs it does not know would intuitively seem to require some form of fully homomorphic encryption.) Some of these works also consider a multi-client setting [CKKC13, GKL+15].

A large body of works considers multiparty computation for privacy-preserving outsourcing (see, e.g., [KMR12, PTK13, CLT14, JNO14]). These works do not consider verifiability and achieve correctness at best in the case that *all-but-one* workers are corrupt (due to inherent limitations of the underlying protocols). We stress that this is rather unsatisfactory for the outsourcing scenario, where one naturally wishes to cover the case that *all* workers are corrupt—dispensing of the need to trust any particular worker.

Concerning outsourcing to multiple workers, [ACG+14] presents a verifiable computation protocol combining privacy and correctness; but unfortunately, they guarantee neither privacy nor correctness if all workers are corrupted and may collude; and it places a much higher burden on the workers than, e.g., [PHGR13]. Alternatively, recent works [BDO14, dHSV16, SV15], like us, guarantee correctness independent of worker corruption, but privacy only under some conditions. Our work offers a substantial performance improvement over these works by fully exploiting a set-up that needs to be trusted both for guaranteeing privacy and for guaranteeing correctness.

We should mention that the notion of verifiability exists in various forms and the field has a richer background than presented here, however, we focus entirely on the notion of verifiable computation first formalized by [GGP10], because it is tailored to the outsourcing scenario.

1.3 Outline

We first briefly define the security model for privacy-preserving outsourced computation in Sect. 3. In Sect. 4, we show how Trinocchio distributes the proof computation of Pinocchio in the single-client scenario, and prove security of the construction. We generalise Trinocchio to the setting with multiple, mutually distrusting inputters and outputters in Sect. 5. Finally, we demonstrate the feasibility of Trinocchio in Sect. 6 by analysing its performance in a case study, computing a multivariate polynomial evaluation. We finish with a discussion and conclusions in Sect. 7.

For convenience, we also provide a brief overview of the Pinocchio protocol [PHGR13] for verifiable computation based on quadratic arithmetic programs in Sect. 2.

2   Verifiable Computation from QAPs

In this section, we discuss the protocol for verifiable computation based on quadratic arithmetic programs from [GGPR13,PHGR13].

2.1   Modelling Computations as Quadratic Arithmetic Programs

A quadratic arithmetic program, or QAP, is a way of encoding arithmetic circuits, and some more general computations, over a field $\mathbb{F}$ of prime order q. It is given by a collection of polynomials over $\mathbb{F}$.

Definition 1 [PHGR13]. *A quadratic arithmetic program Q over a field $\mathbb{F}$ is a tuple $Q = (\{v_i\}_{i=0}^k, \{w_i\}_{i=0}^k, \{y_i\}_{i=0}^k, t)$, with $v_i, w_i, y_i, t \in \mathbb{F}[x]$ polynomials of degree $\deg v_i, \deg w_i, \deg y_i < \deg t = d$. The polynomial t is called the* target *polynomial. The* size *of the QAP is k; the* degree *is the degree d of t.*

In the remainder, for ease of notation, we adopt the convention that $x_0 = 1$.

Definition 2. *Let $Q = (\{v_i\}, \{w_i\}, \{y_i\}, t)$ be a QAP. A tuple $(x_1, \ldots, x_k)$ is a* solution *of Q if t divides $(\sum_{i=0}^k x_i v_i) \cdot (\sum_{i=0}^k x_i w_i) - (\sum_{i=0}^k x_i y_i) \in \mathbb{F}[x]$.*

In case t splits, i.e., $t = (x - \alpha_1) \cdot \ldots \cdot (x - \alpha_n)$, a QAP can be seen as a collection of rank-1 quadratic equations for $(x_1, \ldots, x_k)$; that is, equations $v \cdot w - y$ with $v, w, y \in \mathbb{F}[x_1, \ldots, x_k]$ of degree at most one. Namely, $(x_1, \ldots, x_k)$ is a solution of Q if t divides $(\sum_i x_i v_i) \cdot (\sum_i x_i w_i) - (\sum_i x_i y_i)$, which means exactly that, for every α_j, $(\sum_i x_i v_i(\alpha_j)) \cdot (\sum_i x_i w_i(\alpha_j)) - (\sum_i x_i y_i(\alpha_j)) = 0$: that is, each α_j gives a rank-1 quadratic equation in variables $(x_1, \ldots, x_k)$. Conversely, a collection of d such equations (recall $x_0 \equiv 1$)

$$(v_0^j \cdot x_0 + \ldots + v_k^j \cdot x_k) \cdot (w_0^j \cdot x_0 + \ldots + w_k^j \cdot x_k) - (y_0^j \cdot x_0 + \ldots + y_k^j \cdot x_k)$$

can be turned into a QAP by selecting d distinct elements $\alpha_1, \ldots, \alpha_d$ in $\mathbb{F}$, setting target polynomial $t = (x - \alpha_1) \cdot \ldots \cdot (x - \alpha_d)$, and defining v_0 to be the unique polynomial of degree smaller than d for which $v_0(\alpha_j) = v_0^j$, etcetera.

A QAP is said to compute a function $(x_{l+1}, \ldots, x_{l+m}) = f(x_1, \ldots, x_l)$ if the remaining x_i give a solution exactly if the function is correctly evaluated.

Definition 3 [PHGR13]. *Let $Q = (\{v_i\}, \{w_i\}, \{y_i\}, t)$ be a QAP, and let $f : \mathbb{F}^l \to \mathbb{F}^m$ be a function. We say that Q computes f if $(x_{l+1}, \ldots, x_{l+m}) = f(x_1, \ldots, x_l) \Leftrightarrow \exists (x_{l+m+1}, \ldots, x_k)$ such that $(x_1, \ldots, x_k)$ is a solution of Q.*

For any function f given by an arithmetic circuit, we can easily construct a QAP that computes the function f. Indeed, we can describe an arithmetic circuit as a series of rank-1 quadratic equations by letting each multiplication gate become one equation. Apart from circuits containing just addition and multiplication gates, we can also express circuits with some other kinds of gates directly as QAPs. For instance, [PHGR13] defines a "split gate" that converts a number a into its k-bit decomposition $a_1, \ldots, a_k$ with equations $a = a_1 + 2 \cdot a_2 + \ldots + 2^{k-1} \cdot a_k$, $a_1 \cdot (1 - a_1) = 0$, $\ldots$, $a_k \cdot (1 - a_k) = 0$.

2.2 Proving Correctness of Computations

If QAP $Q = (\{v_i\}, \{w_i\}, \{y_i\}, t)$ computes a function f, then a prover can prove that $(x_{l+1}, \ldots, x_{l+m}) = f(x_1, \ldots, x_l)$ by proving knowledge of values $(x_{l+m+1}, \ldots, x_k)$ such that $(x_1, \ldots, x_k)$ is a solution of Q, i.e., t divides $(\sum_i x_i v_i) \cdot (\sum_i x_i w_i) - (\sum_i x_i y_i)$. [PHGR13] gives a construction of a proof system which does exactly this. The proof system assumes discrete logarithm groups $\mathbb{G}_1, \mathbb{G}_2, \mathbb{G}_3$ with a pairing $e : \mathbb{G}_1 \times \mathbb{G}_2 \to \mathbb{G}_3$ for which the $(4d+4)$-PDH, d-PKE and $(8d+8)$-SDH assumptions [PHGR13] hold, with d the degree of the QAP. Moreover, the proof is in the common reference string (CRS) model: the CRS consists of an *evaluation key* used to produce the proof, and a *verification key* used to verify it. Both are public, i.e., provers can know the verification key and vice versa.

To prove that t divides $p = (\sum_i x_i v_i) \cdot (\sum_i x_i w_i) - (\sum_i x_i y_i)$, the prover computes quotient polynomial $h = p/t$ and basically provides evaluations "in the exponent" of h, $(\sum_i x_i v_i)$, $(\sum_i x_i w_i)$, and $(\sum_i x_i y_i)$ in an unknown point s that can be verified using the pairing. More precisely, given generators g_1 of $\mathbb{G}_1$ and g_2 of $\mathbb{G}_2$ (written additively) and polynomial $f \in \mathbb{F}[x]$, let us write $\langle f \rangle_1$ for $g_1 \cdot f(s)$ and $\langle f \rangle_2$ for $g_2 \cdot f(s)$. The evaluation key in the CRS, generated using random $s, \alpha_v, \alpha_w, \alpha_y, \beta, r_v, r_w, r_y = r_v \cdot r_w \in \mathbb{F}$, is:

$$\langle r_v v_i \rangle_1, \langle r_v \alpha_v v_i \rangle_1, \langle r_w w_i \rangle_2, \langle r_w \alpha_w w_i \rangle_1, \langle r_y y_i \rangle_1, \langle r_y \alpha_y y_i \rangle_1,$$
$$\langle r_v \beta v_i + r_w \beta w_i + r_y \beta y_i \rangle_1, \langle s^j \rangle_1.$$

where i ranges over $l + m + 1, l + m + 2, \ldots, k$ and j runs from 0 to the degree of t. The proof contains the following elements:

$$
\begin{aligned}
\langle V_{\mathrm{mid}} \rangle_1 &= \sum_i \langle r_v v_i \rangle_1 \cdot x_i, & \langle \alpha_v V_{\mathrm{mid}} \rangle_1 &= \sum_i \langle r_v \alpha_v v_i \rangle_1 \cdot x_i, \\
\langle W_{\mathrm{mid}} \rangle_2 &= \sum_i \langle r_w w_i \rangle_2 \cdot x_i, & \langle \alpha_w W_{\mathrm{mid}} \rangle_1 &= \sum_i \langle r_w \alpha_w w_i \rangle_1 \cdot x_i, \\
\langle Y_{\mathrm{mid}} \rangle_1 &= \sum_i \langle r_y y_i \rangle_1 \cdot x_i, & \langle \alpha_y Y_{\mathrm{mid}} \rangle_1 &= \sum_i \langle r_y \alpha_y y_i \rangle_1 \cdot x_i, \\
\langle Z \rangle_1 &= \sum_i \langle r_v \beta v_i + r_w \beta w_i + r_y \beta y_i \rangle_1 \cdot x_i, & \langle H \rangle_1 &= \sum_j \langle s^j \rangle_1 \cdot h_j,
\end{aligned}
\tag{1}
$$

where i ranges over $l + m + 1, l + m + 2, \ldots, k$, and h_j are the coefficients of polynomial $h = p/t$.

To verify that t divides $(\sum_i x_i v_i) \cdot (\sum_i x_i w_i) - (\sum_i x_i y_i)$ and hence $(x_{l+1}, \ldots, x_{l+m}) = f(x_1, \ldots, x_l)$, a verifier uses the following verification key from the CRS:

$$\langle \alpha_v \rangle_2, \langle \alpha_w \rangle_2, \langle \alpha_y \rangle_2, \langle \beta \rangle_1, \langle \beta \rangle_2, \langle r_v v_i \rangle_1, \langle r_w w_i \rangle_2, \langle r_y y_i \rangle_1, \langle r_y t \rangle_2,$$

where i ranges over $1, 2, \ldots, l + m$[1]. Given the verification key, a proof, and values $x_1, \ldots, x_{l+m}$, the verifier proceeds as follows. First, it checks that

---

[1] In [PHGR13], several terms of the verification key includes a value γ; however, a careful look at [PHGR13]'s proof reveals that γ is actually not needed. We remove it because it simplifies notation, especially for our multi-client protocols.

$$e(\langle V_{\mathrm{mid}}\rangle_1, \langle \alpha_v\rangle_2) = e(\langle \alpha_v V_{\mathrm{mid}}\rangle_1, \langle 1\rangle_2);$$
$$e(\langle \alpha_w\rangle_1, \langle W_{\mathrm{mid}}\rangle_2) = e(\langle \alpha_w W_{\mathrm{mid}}\rangle_1, \langle 1\rangle_2); \qquad (2)$$
$$e(\langle Y_{\mathrm{mid}}\rangle_1, \langle \alpha_y\rangle_2) = e(\langle \alpha_y Y_{\mathrm{mid}}\rangle_1, \langle 1\rangle_2):$$

intuitively, under the d-PKE assumption, these checks guarantee that the prover must have constructed $\langle V_{\mathrm{mid}}\rangle_1$, $\langle W_{\mathrm{mid}}\rangle_2$, and $\langle Y_{\mathrm{mid}}\rangle_1$ using the elements from the evaluation key. It then checks that

$$e(\langle V_{\mathrm{mid}}\rangle_1 + \langle Y_{\mathrm{mid}}\rangle_1, \langle \beta\rangle_2) \cdot e(\langle \beta\rangle_1, \langle W_{\mathrm{mid}}\rangle_2) = e(\langle Z\rangle_1, \langle 1\rangle_2): \qquad (3)$$

under the PDH assumption, this guarantees that the same coefficients x_i were used in $\langle V_{\mathrm{mid}}\rangle_1$, $\langle W_{\mathrm{mid}}\rangle_2$, and $\langle Y_{\mathrm{mid}}\rangle_1$. Finally, the verifier computes evaluations $\langle V\rangle_1$ of $\sum_{i=0}^{k} x_i v_i$ as $\langle V_{\mathrm{mid}}\rangle_1 + \sum_{i=1}^{l+m}\langle r_v v_i\rangle_1 \cdot x_i$; $\langle W\rangle_2$ of $\sum_{i=0}^{k} x_i w_i$ as $\langle W_{\mathrm{mid}}\rangle_2 + \sum_{i=1}^{l+m}\langle r_w w_i\rangle_2 \cdot x_i$; and $\langle Y\rangle_1$ of $\sum_{i=0}^{k} x_i y_i$ as $\langle Y_{\mathrm{mid}}\rangle_1 + \sum_{i=1}^{l+m}\langle r_y y_i\rangle_1 \cdot x_i$, and verifies that

$$e(\langle V\rangle_1, \langle W\rangle_2) \cdot e(\langle Y\rangle_1, \langle 1\rangle_2)^{-1} = e(\langle H\rangle_1, \langle r_y t\rangle_2): \qquad (4)$$

under the $(8d + 8)$-SDH assumption, this guarantees that, for the polynomial h encoded by $\langle H\rangle_1$, $t \cdot h = (\sum_i x_i v_i) \cdot (\sum_i x_i w_i) - (\sum_i x_i y_i)$ holds.[2]

Theorem 1 ([GGPR13], **Informal**). *Given QAP $Q = (\{v_i\}, \{w_i\}, \{y_i\}, t)$ and values $x_1, \ldots, x_{l+m}$, the above is a non-interactive argument of knowledge of $(x_{l+m+1}, \ldots, x_k)$ such that $(x_1, \ldots, x_k)$ is a solution of Q.*

2.3   Making the Proof Zero-Knowledge

The above proof can be turned into a zero-knowledge proof, that reveals nothing about the values of $(x_{l+m+1}, \ldots, x_k)$ other than that t divides $(\sum_i x_i v_i) \cdot (\sum_i x_i w_i) - (\sum_i x_i y_i)$ for some h, by performing randomisation. Namely, instead of proving that $t \cdot h = (\sum_i x_i v_i) \cdot (\sum_i x_i w_i) - (\sum_i x_i y_i)$, we prove that $t \cdot \tilde{h} = (\sum_i x_i v_i + \delta_v \cdot t) \cdot (\sum_i x_i w_i + \delta_w \cdot t) - (\sum_i x_i y_i + \delta_y \cdot t)$ with $\delta_v, \delta_w, \delta_y$ random from $\mathbb{F}$. Precisely, the evaluation key needs to contain additional elements:

$$\langle r_v t\rangle_1, \langle r_v \alpha_v t\rangle_1, \langle r_w t\rangle_2, \langle r_w \alpha_w t\rangle_1, \langle r_y t\rangle_1, \langle r_y \alpha_y t\rangle_1, \langle r_v \beta t\rangle_1, \langle r_w \beta t\rangle_1, \langle r_y \beta t\rangle_1, \langle t\rangle_1.$$

Compared to the original proof, we let

$$\langle V'_{\mathrm{mid}}\rangle_1 = \langle V_{\mathrm{mid}}\rangle_1 + \langle r_v t\rangle_1 \cdot \delta_v, \quad \langle \alpha_v V'_{\mathrm{mid}}\rangle_1 = \langle \alpha_v V'_{\mathrm{mid}}\rangle_1 + \langle r_v \alpha_v t\rangle_1 \cdot \delta_v,$$
$$\langle W'_{\mathrm{mid}}\rangle_2 = \langle W_{\mathrm{mid}}\rangle_2 + \langle r_w t\rangle_2 \cdot \delta_w, \quad \langle \alpha_w W'_{\mathrm{mid}}\rangle_1 = \langle \alpha_w W_{\mathrm{mid}}\rangle_1 + \langle r_w \alpha_w t\rangle_1 \cdot \delta_w,$$
$$\langle Y'_{\mathrm{mid}}\rangle_1 = \langle Y_{\mathrm{mid}}\rangle_1 + \langle r_y t\rangle_1 \cdot \delta_y, \quad \langle \alpha_y Y'_{\mathrm{mid}}\rangle_1 = \langle \alpha_y Y_{\mathrm{mid}}\rangle_1 + \langle r_y \alpha_y t\rangle_1 \cdot \delta_y,$$
$$\langle Z'\rangle_1 = \langle Z\rangle_1 + \langle r_v \beta t\rangle_1 \cdot \delta_v + \langle r_w \beta t\rangle_1 \cdot \delta_w + \langle r_y \beta t\rangle_1 \cdot \delta_y, \langle H'\rangle_1 = \sum_j \langle s^j\rangle_1 \cdot \tilde{h}_j,$$

with $\tilde{h}_j$ the coefficients of $h + \delta_v w_0 + \sum_i \delta_v x_i \cdot w_i + \delta_w v_0 + \sum_i \delta_w x_i \cdot v_i + \delta_v \delta_w \cdot t - \delta_y$. Verification remains exactly the same.

---

[2] We remark that, as shown in [PHGR13], a verifier who has generated the evaluation and verification keys, can use the randomness from the generation process to save several of the above pairing checks. We do not consider this optimisation here.

Secure function evaluation:

- Honest parties send inputs x_i to trusted party
- Adversary sends inputs x_i of corrupted parties to trusted party (active adversary may modify them)
- Trusted party computes function $(y_1, \ldots, y_m) = f(x_1, \ldots, x_m)$ (where $y_1 = \ldots = \perp$ if any $x_i = \perp$)
- Trusted party provides outputs y_i for corrupted parties to adversary
- Trusted party provides outputs y_i to honest parties
- Honest parties output received value; corrupted parties output $\perp$; adversary chooses own output

Correct function evaluation:

- Honest parties send inputs x_i to trusted party
- Adversary sends inputs x_i of corrupted parties to trusted party (active adversary may modify them)
- Trusted party computes function $(y_1, \ldots, y_m) = f(x_1, \ldots, x_m)$ (where $y_1 = \ldots = \perp$ if any $x_i = \perp$)
- Trusted party provides all inputs x_i to adversary
- Adversary gives subset of honest parties to trusted party (passive adversary gives all honest parties)
- Trusted party sends outputs y_i to given honest parties, $\perp$ to others
- Honest parties output received value; corrupted parties output $\perp$; adversary chooses own output

Fig. 1. Ideal-world executions of secure (left) and correct (right) function evaluation. The highlighted text indicates where the two differ (Color figure online).

Theorem 2 ([GGPR13], **Informal**). *Given QAP $Q = (\{v_i\}, \{w_i\}, \{y_i\}, t)$ and values $x_1, \ldots, x_{l+m}$, the above is a non-interactive zero-knowledge argument of knowledge of $(x_{l+m+1}, \ldots, x_k)$ such that $(x_1, \ldots, x_k)$ is a solution of Q.*

3   Security Model for Privacy-Preserving Outsourcing

In this section, we define security for privacy-preserving outsourcing. Because we have interactive protocols between multiple parties (as opposed to a cryptographic scheme, like verifiable computation above), we define security using the ideal/real-paradigm [Can00a]. In our setting, the parties are several *result parties* that wish to obtain the result of a computation on inputs held by several *input parties*, who are willing to enable the computation, but not to divulge their private input values to anybody else. Therefore, they outsource the computation to several *workers*. (Input and result parties may overlap.) The simplest case is the "single-client scenario" in which one party is the single input/result party.

We consider protocols operating in three phases: an *input phase* involving the input parties and workers; a *computation phase* involving only the workers; and a *result phase* involving the workers and result parties. The work of the input parties and output parties should depend only on the number of other parties and the size of their own in/outputs.

To define security, we will re-use the existing definition framework for secure function evaluation [Can00a]. These definitions not specific to the outsourcing setting; but the outsourcing setting will become apparent when we claim that a protocol, e.g., implements secure function evaluation *if at most X workers are corrupted*. Secure function evaluation is the problem to evaluate $(y_1, \ldots, y_m) = f(x_1, \ldots, x_m)$ with m parties such that the ith party inputs x_i and obtains y_i, and no party learns anything else. (In outsourcing, result parties have non-empty output, input parties have non-empty inputs, and workers have empty in- and outputs.) A protocol π *securely evaluates function f* if the outputs of the parties and adversary $\mathcal{A}$ in a real-world execution of the protocol can be emulated by the outputs of the parties and an adversary $\mathcal{S}_\mathcal{A}$ in an idealised execution, where f is computed by a trusted party that acts as shown in Fig. 1. Security is guaranteed because the trusted party correctly computes the function. Privacy is guaranteed because the adversary in the idealised execution does not learn anything it should not. Secure evaluation also implies *input independence*, meaning that an input party cannot let its input depend on that of another, e.g., by copying the input of another party; this is guaranteed because the adversary needs to provide the inputs of corrupted parties without seeing the honest inputs. Typically, protocols achieve secure function evaluation for a given, restricted class of adversaries, e.g., adversaries that are passive and only corrupt a certain number of workers. Protocols can require set-up assumptions; these are captured by giving protocol participants access to a set of functions $g_1, \ldots, g_k$ that are always evaluated correctly. In this case, we say that the protocol securely evaluates the function *in the $(g_1, \ldots, g_k)$-hybrid model*. For details, see [Can00a].

We only achieve secure function evaluation if not too many workers are corrupted; we still need to formalise that in all other cases, we still guarantee that the function was evaluated correctly. This weaker security guarantee, which we call *correct function evaluation*, captures security and input independence, as above, but not privacy. It is formalised by modifying the ideal-world execution as shown in Fig. 1. Namely, after evaluating f, the trusted party provides all inputs to the adversary (modelling that the computation may leak the inputs), who, based on these inputs, can decide which honest parties are allowed to see their outputs. Hence, we guarantee that, *if* an honest party gets a result, then it gets the correct result of the computation on independently chosen inputs, but not that the inputs remain hidden, or that it gets a result at all. Note that, in this definition, the adversary has complete control over which result parties see an output and which ones do not.

4   Distributing the Prover Computation

In this section, we present the single-client version of our Trinocchio protocol for privacy-preserving outsourcing. In Trinocchio, a client distributes computation of a function $x_2 = f(x_1)$ to n workers (we consider here single-valued input and output, but the generalisation is straightforward). Trinocchio guarantees correct function evaluation (regardless of corruptions) and secure function evaluation (if at most θ workers are passively corrupted, where $n = 2\theta + 1$). Trinocchio in effect distributes the proof computation of Pinocchio; the number of workers to obtain privacy against one semi-honest worker is three, hence its name.

4.1   Multiparty Computation Using Shamir Secret Sharing

To distribute the Pinocchio computation, Trinocchio employs multiparty computation techniques based on Shamir secret sharing [BGW88]. Recall that in (θ, n) Shamir secret sharing, a party shares a secret s among n parties so that $\theta + 1$ parties are needed to reconstruct s. It does this by taking a random degree-$\leq \theta$ polynomial $p(x) = \alpha_\theta x^\theta + \ldots + \alpha x + s$ with s as constant term and giving $p(i)$ to party i. Since $p(x)$ is of degree at most θ, $p(0)$ is completely independent from any θ shares but can be easily computed from any $\theta + 1$ shares by Lagrange interpolation. We denote such a sharing as $[\![s]\!]$. Note that Shamir-sharing can also be done "in the exponent", e.g., $[\![\langle a \rangle_1]\!]$ denotes a Shamir sharing of $\langle a \rangle_1 \in \mathbb{G}_1$ from which $\langle a \rangle_1$ can be computed using Lagrange interpolation in $\mathbb{G}_1$.

Shamir secret sharing is linear, i.e., $[\![a + b]\!] = [\![a]\!] + [\![b]\!]$ and $[\![\alpha a]\!] = \alpha [\![a]\!]$ can be computed locally. When computing the product of $[\![a]\!]$ and $[\![b]\!]$, each party i can locally multiply its points $p_a(i)$ and $p_b(i)$ on the random polynomials p_a and p_b. Because the product polynomial has degree at most 2θ, this is a $(2\theta, n)$ sharing, which we write as $[a \cdot b]$ (note that reconstructing the secret requires $n = 2\theta + 1$ parties). Moreover, the distribution of the shares of $[a \cdot b]$ is not independent from the values of a and b, so when revealed, these shares reveal information about a and b. Hence, in multiparty computation, $[a \cdot b]$ is typically converted back into a random (θ, n) sharing $[\![a \cdot b]\!]$ using an interactive protocol due to [GRR98]. Interactive protocols for many other tasks such as comparing two shared value also exist (see, e.g., [dH12]).

4.2   The Trinocchio Protocol

We now present the Trinocchio protocol. Trinocchio assumes that Pinocchio's KeyGen has been correctly performed: formally, Trinocchio works in the KeyGen-hybrid model. Furthermore, Trinocchio assumes pairwise private, synchronous communication channels. To obtain $x_2 = f(x_1)$, a client proceeds in four steps:

- The client obtains the verification key, and the workers obtain the evaluation key, using hybrid calls to KeyGen.
- The client secret shares $[\![x_1]\!]$ of its input to the workers.
- The workers use multiparty computation to compute secret-shares $[\![x_2]\!]$ of the output and $[\![\langle V_{\mathrm{mid}} \rangle_1]\!]$, $[\![\langle \alpha_v V_{\mathrm{mid}} \rangle_1]\!]$, $[\![\langle W_{\mathrm{mid}} \rangle_2]\!]$, $[\![\langle \alpha_w W_{\mathrm{mid}} \rangle_1]\!]$, $[\![\langle Y_{\mathrm{mid}} \rangle_1]\!]$, $[\![\langle \alpha_y Y_{\mathrm{mid}} \rangle_1]\!]$, $[\![\langle Z \rangle_1]\!]$, $[\![\langle H \rangle_1]\!]$ of the Pinocchio proof, as we explain next; and sends these shares to the client.
- The client recombines the shares into $\langle V_{\mathrm{mid}} \rangle_1$, $\langle \alpha_v V_{\mathrm{mid}} \rangle_1$, $\langle W_{\mathrm{mid}} \rangle_2$, $\langle \alpha_w W_{\mathrm{mid}} \rangle_1$, $\langle Y_{\mathrm{mid}} \rangle_1$, $\langle \alpha_y Y_{\mathrm{mid}} \rangle_1$, $\langle Z \rangle_1$, $\langle H \rangle_1$ by Lagrange interpolation, and accepts x_2 as computation result if Pinocchio's Verify returns success.

Algorithm 1 shows in detail how the secret-shares of the function output and Pinocchio proof are computed. The first step is to compute function output $x_2 = f(x_1)$ and values $(x_3, \ldots, x_k)$ such that $(x_1, \ldots, x_k)$ is a solution of the QAP (line 4). This is done using normal multiparty computation protocols based on secret sharing. If function f is represented by an arithmetic circuit, then it is evaluated

---

Algorithm 1. Trinocchio's Compute protocol

1: $\triangleright \mathcal{S} = \{\alpha_1, \ldots, \alpha_d\}$ denotes the list of roots of the target polynomial of the QAP
2: $\triangleright \mathcal{T} = \{\beta_1, \ldots, \beta_d\}$ denotes a list of distinct points different from $\mathcal{S}$
3: **function** Compute($\mathsf{EK}_f = \{\langle r_v v_i \rangle_1\}_i, \ldots, \{\langle s^j \rangle_1\}_j; [\![x_1]\!]$)
4:      $([\![x_2]\!], \ldots, [\![x_k]\!]) \leftarrow f([\![x_1]\!])$
5:      $[\![v]\!] \leftarrow \{\sum_i v_i(\alpha_j) \cdot [\![x_i]\!]\}_j$; $[\![V]\!] \leftarrow \mathsf{FFT}_{\mathcal{S}}^{-1}([\![v]\!])$; $[\![v']\!] \leftarrow \mathsf{FFT}_{\mathcal{T}}([\![V]\!])$
6:      $[\![w]\!] \leftarrow \{\sum_i w_i(\alpha_j) \cdot [\![x_i]\!]\}_j$; $[\![W]\!] \leftarrow \mathsf{FFT}_{\mathcal{S}}^{-1}([\![w]\!])$; $[\![w']\!] \leftarrow \mathsf{FFT}_{\mathcal{T}}([\![W]\!])$
7:      $[\![y]\!] \leftarrow \{\sum_i y_i(\alpha_j) \cdot [\![x_i]\!]\}_j$; $[\![Y]\!] \leftarrow \mathsf{FFT}_{\mathcal{S}}^{-1}([\![y]\!])$; $[\![y']\!] \leftarrow \mathsf{FFT}_{\mathcal{T}}([\![Y]\!])$
8:      $[\![h']\!] \leftarrow \{([\![v_j']\!] \cdot [\![w_j']\!] - [\![y_j']\!])/t(\beta_j)\}_j$; $[\![H]\!] \leftarrow \mathsf{FFT}_{\mathcal{T}}^{-1}([\![h']\!])$
9:      $[\![\langle V_{\mathrm{mid}}\rangle_1]\!] \leftarrow \sum_i \langle r_v v_i \rangle_1 \cdot [\![x_i]\!]$
10:     $[\![\langle \alpha_v V_{\mathrm{mid}}\rangle_1]\!] \leftarrow \sum_i \langle r_v \alpha_v v_i \rangle_1 \cdot [\![x_i]\!]$
11:     $[\![\langle W_{\mathrm{mid}}\rangle_2]\!] \leftarrow \sum_i \langle r_w w_i \rangle_2 \cdot [\![x_i]\!]$
12:     $[\![\langle \alpha_w W_{\mathrm{mid}}\rangle_1]\!] \sum_i \langle r_w \alpha_w w_i \rangle_1 \cdot [\![x_i]\!]$
13:     $[\![\langle Y_{\mathrm{mid}}\rangle_1]\!] \leftarrow \sum_i \langle r_y y_i \rangle_1 \cdot [\![x_i]\!]$
14:     $[\![\langle \alpha_y Y_{\mathrm{mid}}\rangle_1]\!] \leftarrow \sum_i \langle r_y \alpha_y y_i \rangle_1 \cdot [\![x_i]\!]$
15:     $[\![\langle Z\rangle_1]\!] \leftarrow \sum_i \langle r_v \beta v_i + r_w \beta w_i + r_y \beta y_i \rangle_1 \cdot [\![x_i]\!]$
16:     $[\![\langle H\rangle_1]\!] = \sum_j \langle s^j \rangle_1 \cdot [\![H_j]\!]$
17:     **return** $([\![x_2]\!]; [\![\langle V_{\mathrm{mid}}\rangle_1]\!], [\![\langle \alpha_v V_{\mathrm{mid}}\rangle_1]\!], [\![\langle W_{\mathrm{mid}}\rangle_2]\!], [\![\langle \alpha_w W_{\mathrm{mid}}\rangle_1]\!],$
18:            $[\![\langle Y_{\mathrm{mid}}\rangle_1]\!], [\![\langle \alpha_y Y_{\mathrm{mid}}\rangle_1]\!], [\![\langle Z\rangle_1]\!], [\![\langle H\rangle_1]\!])$

---

using local addition and scalar multiplication, and the multiplication protocol from [GRR98]. If f is represented by a circuit using more complicated gates, then specific protocols may be used: e.g., the split gate discussed in Sect. 2.1 can be evaluated using multiparty bit decomposition protocols [DFK+06,ST06]. Any protocol can be used as long as it guarantees privacy, i.e., the view of any θ workers is statistically independent from the values represented by the shares.

The next task is to compute, in secret-shared form, the coefficients of the polynomial $h = ((\sum_i x_i v_i) \cdot (\sum_i x_i w_i) - (\sum_i x_i y_i))/t \in \mathbb{F}[x]$ that we need for proof element $\langle H\rangle_1$. In theory, this computation could be performed by first computing shares of the coefficients of $(\sum_i x_i v_i) \cdot (\sum_i x_i w_i) - (\sum_i x_i y_i)$, and then dividing by t, which can be done locally using traditional polynomial long division. However, this scales quadratically in the degree of the QAP and hence leads to unacceptable performance. Hence, we take the approach based on fast Fourier transforms (FFTs) from [BSCG+13], and adapt it to the distributed setting. Given a list $\mathcal{S} = \{\omega_1, \ldots, \omega_d\}$ of distinct points in $\mathbb{F}$, we denote by $P = \mathsf{FFT}_{\mathcal{S}}(p)$ the transformation from coefficients p of a polynomial p of degree at most $d - 1$ to evaluations $p(\omega_1), \ldots, p(\omega_d)$ in the points in $\mathcal{S}$. We denote by $p = \mathsf{FFT}_{\mathcal{S}}^{-1}(P)$ the inverse transformation, i.e., from evaluations to coefficients. Deferring specifics to later, we mention now that the FFT is a linear transformation that, for some $\mathcal{S}$, can be performed locally on secret shares in $\mathcal{O}(d \cdot \log d)$.

With FFTs available, we can compute the coefficients of h by evaluating h in d distinct points and applying FFT^{-1}. Note that we can efficiently compute evaluations v of $v = (\sum_i x_i v_i)$, w of $w = (\sum_i x_i w_i)$, and y of $y = (\sum_i x_i y_i)$ in the zeros $\{\omega_1, \ldots, \omega_d\}$ of the target polynomial. Namely, the values $v_k(\omega_i)$, $w_k(\omega_i)$, $y_k(\omega_i)$ are simply the coefficients of the quadratic equations represented by the QAP, most of which are zero, so these sums have much fewer than k

elements (if this were not the case, then evaluating v, w, and y would take an unacceptable $O(d \cdot k)$). Unfortunately, we cannot use these evaluations directly to obtain evaluations of h, because this requires division by the target polynomial, which is zero in exactly these points ω_i. Hence, after determining v, w, and y, we first use the inverse FFT to determine the coefficients V, W, and Y of v, w, and y, and then again the FFT to compute the evaluations v', w', and y' of v, w, and y in another set of points $T = \{\Omega_1, \ldots, \Omega_k\}$ (lines 5–7). Now, we can compute evaluations h' of h in T using $h(\Omega_i) = (v(\Omega_i) \cdot w(\Omega_i) - y(\Omega_i))/t(\Omega_i)$. This requires a multiplication of (θ, n)-secret shares of $v(\Omega_i)$ and $w(\Omega_i)$, hence the result is a $(2\theta, n)$-sharing. Finally, the inverse FFT gives us a $(2\theta, n)$-sharing of the coefficients H of h (line 8).

Given secret shares of the values of x_i and coefficients of h, it is straightforward to compute secret shares of the Pinocchio proof. Indeed, $\langle V_{\text{mid}} \rangle_1, \ldots, \langle H \rangle_1$ are all computed as linear combinations of elements in the evaluation key, so shares of these proof elements can be computed locally (lines 9–16), and finally returned by the respective workers (lines 17–18).

Note that, compared to Pinocchio, our client needs to carry out slightly more work. Namely, our client needs to produce secret shares of the inputs and recombine secret shares of the outputs; and it needs to recombine the Pinocchio proof. However, according to the micro-benchmarks from [PHGR13], this overhead is small. For each input and output, Verify includes three exponentiations, whereas Combine involves four additions and two multiplications; when using [PHGR13]'s techniques, this adds at most a 3 % overhead. Recombining the Pinocchio proof involves 15 exponentiations at around half the cost of a single pairing. Alternatively, it is possible to let one of the workers perform the Pinocchio recombining step by using the distributed zero-knowledge variant of Pinocchio (Sect. 2.3) and the techniques from Sect. 5. In this case, the only overhead for the client is the secret-sharing of the inputs and zero-knowledge randomness, and recombining the outputs.

Parameters for Efficient FFTs. To obtain efficient FFTs, we use the approach of [BSCG+13]. There, it is noted that the operation $P = \text{FFT}_S(p)$ and its inverse can be efficiently implemented if $S = \{\omega, \omega^2, \ldots, \omega^d = 1\}$ is a set of powers of a primitive dth root of unity, where d is a power of two. (We can always demand that QAPs have degree $d = 2^k$ for some k by adding dummy equations.) Moreover, [BSCG+13] presents a pair of groups $\mathbb{G}_1, \mathbb{G}_2$ of order q such that $\mathbb{F}_q$ has a primitive 2^{30}th root of unity (and hence also primitive 2^kth roots of unity for any $k < 30$) as well as an efficiently computable pairing $e : \mathbb{G}_1 \times \mathbb{G}_2 \to \mathbb{G}_3$. Finally, [BSCG+13] remarks that for $T = \{\eta\omega, \eta\omega^2, \ldots, \eta\omega^d = \eta\}$, operations FFT_T^{-1} and FFT_T^{-1} can easily be reduced to FFT_S and FFT_S^{-1}, respectively. In our implementation, we use exactly these suggested parameters.

4.3   Security of Trinocchio

Theorem 3. *Let f be a function. Let $n = 2\theta + 1$ be the number of workers used. Let d be the degree of the QAP computing f used in the Trinocchio protocol. Assuming the d-PKE, $(4d + 4)$-PDH, and $(8d + 8)$-SDH assumptions:*

- *Trinocchio correctly evaluates f in the KeyGen-hybrid model.*
- *Whenever at most θ workers are passively corrupted, Trinocchio securely evaluates f in the KeyGen-hybrid model.*

The proof of this theorem is easily derived as a special case of the proof for the multi-client Trinocchio protocol later. Here, we present a short sketch.

Proof (Sketch). To prove correct function evaluation, we need to show that for every real-world adversary $\mathcal{A}$ interacting with Trinocchio, there is an ideal-world simulator $\mathcal{S}_\mathcal{A}$ that interacts with the trusted party for correct function evaluation such that the two executions give indistinguishable results. The only interesting case is when the client is honest and some of the workers are not. In this case, the simulator receives the input of the honest party, and needs to choose whether to provide the output. To this end, the simulator simply simulates a run of the actual protocol with $\mathcal{A}$, until it has finally obtained function output x_2 and the accompanying Trinocchio proof. If the proof verifies, it tells the trusted party to provide the output to the client; otherwise, it tells the trusted party not to. Finally, the simulator outputs whatever $\mathcal{A}$ outputs. Because Trinocchio is secure, except with negligible probability a verifying proof implies that the real-world output of the client (as given by the adversary) matches the ideal-world output of the client (as computed by the trusted party); and by construction, the outputs of $\mathcal{A}$ and $\mathcal{S}_\mathcal{A}$ are distributed identically. This proves correct function evaluation.

For secure function evaluation, again the only interesting case is if the client is honest and some of the workers are passively corrupted. In this case, because corruption is only passive, correctness of the multiparty protocol used to compute f and correctness of the Pinocchio proof system used to compute the proof together imply that real-world executions (like ideal-world executions) result in the correct function result and a verifying proof. Hence, we only need to worry about how $\mathcal{S}_\mathcal{A}$ can simulate the view of $\mathcal{A}$ on the Trinocchio protocol without knowing the client's input. However, note that the workers only use a multiparty computation to compute f (which we assume can be simulated without knowing the inputs), after which they no longer receive any messages. Hence simulating the multiparty computation for f and receiving any messages that $\mathcal{A}$ sends is sufficient to simulate $\mathcal{A}$. This proves secure function evaluation.   □

Privacy Against Active Attacks. We remark that actually, Trinocchio in some cases provides privacy against corrupted workers as well. Namely, suppose that the protocol used to compute f does not leak any information to corrupted workers in the event of an active attack (even though in this case it may not guarantee correctness). For instance, this is the case for the protocol from [GRR98]: the attacker can manipulate the shares that it sends, which makes the computation

---

Algorithm 2. ProofBlock

1: **function** ProofBlock(BK; $\boldsymbol{x}$; $\delta_v, \delta_w, \delta_y$)
2:    $\langle V \rangle_1 \leftarrow \langle r_v t \rangle_1 \delta_v + \sum_i \langle r_v v_i \rangle_1 x_i$; $\langle V' \rangle_1 \leftarrow \langle r_v \alpha_v t \rangle_1 \delta_v + \sum_i \langle r_v \alpha_v v_i \rangle_1 x_i$
3:    $\langle W \rangle_2 \leftarrow \langle r_w t \rangle_2 \delta_w + \sum_i \langle r_w w_i \rangle_2 x_i$; $\langle W' \rangle_1 \leftarrow \langle r_w \alpha_w t \rangle_1 \delta_w + \sum_i \langle r_w \alpha_w w_i \rangle_1 x_i$
4:    $\langle Y \rangle_1 \leftarrow \langle r_y t \rangle_1 \delta_y + \sum_i \langle r_y y_i \rangle_1 x_i$; $\langle Y' \rangle_1 \leftarrow \langle r_y \alpha_y t \rangle_1 \delta_y + \sum_i \langle r_y \alpha_y y_i \rangle_1 x_i$
5:    $\langle Z \rangle_1 \leftarrow \langle r_v \beta t \rangle_1 \delta_v + \langle r_w \beta t \rangle_1 \delta_w + \langle r_y \beta t \rangle_1 \delta_y + \sum_i \langle r_v \beta v_i + r_w \beta w_i + r_y \beta y_i \rangle_1 x_j$
6:    **return** $(\langle V \rangle_1, \langle V' \rangle_1, \langle W \rangle_2, \langle W' \rangle_1, \langle Y \rangle_1, \langle Y' \rangle_1, \langle Z \rangle_1)$

---

return incorrect results; but since the attacker always learns only θ many shares of any value, it does not learn any information. Because the attacker learns no additional information from producing the Pinocchio proof, the overall protocol still leaks no information to the adversary. (And security of Pinocchio ensures the client notices the attacker's manipulation.)

This crucially relies on the workers not learning whether the client accepts the proof: if the workers would learn whether the client obtained a validating proof, then, by manipulating proof construction, they could learn whether a modified version of the tuple $(x_1, \ldots, x_k)$ is a solution of the QAP used, so corrupted workers could learn one chosen bit of information about the inputs (cf. [MF06]).

5   Handling Mutually Distrusting In- and Outputters

We now consider the scenario where there are multiple (possibly overlapping) input and result parties. There are some significant changes between this scenario and the single-client scenario. In particular, we need to extend Pinocchio to allow verification not based on the actual input/output values (indeed, no party sees all of them) but on some kind of representation that does not reveal them. Moreover, we need to use the zero-knowledge variant of Pinocchio (Sect. 2.3), and we need to make sure that input parties choose their inputs independently from each other.

5.1   Multi-client Proofs and Keys

Our multi-client Trinocchio proofs are a generalisation of the zero-knowledge variant of Pinocchio (Sect. 2.3) with modified evaluation and verification keys. Recall that in Pinocchio, the proof terms $\langle V_{\mathrm{mid}} \rangle_1$, $\langle \alpha_v V_{\mathrm{mid}} \rangle_1$, $\langle W_{\mathrm{mid}} \rangle_2$, $\langle \alpha_w W_{\mathrm{mid}} \rangle_1$, $\langle Y_{\mathrm{mid}} \rangle_1$, $\langle \alpha_y Y_{\mathrm{mid}} \rangle_1$, and $\langle Z \rangle_1$ encode circuit values $x_{l+m+1}, \ldots, x_k$; in the zero-knowledge variant, these terms are randomised so that they do not reveal any information about $x_{l+m+1}, \ldots, x_k$. In the multi-client case, additionally, the inputs of all input parties and the outputs of all result parties need to be encoded such that no other party learns any information about them. Therefore, we extend the proof with *blocks* of the above seven terms for each input and result party, which are constructed in the same way as the seven proof terms above. Although some result parties could share a block of output values, for simplicity we assign each result party its own block in the protocol.

Algorithm 3. CheckBlock

1: **function** CheckBlock(BV; $\langle V \rangle_1, \langle V' \rangle_1, \langle W \rangle_2, \langle W' \rangle_1, \langle Y \rangle_1, \langle Y' \rangle_1, \langle Z \rangle_1$)
2:     **if** $e(\langle V \rangle_1, \langle \alpha_v \rangle_2) = e(\langle V' \rangle_1, \langle 1 \rangle_2)$
3:         $\wedge e(\langle \alpha_w \rangle_1, \langle W \rangle_2) = e(\langle W' \rangle_1, \langle 1 \rangle_2)$
4:         $\wedge e(\langle Y \rangle_1, \langle \alpha_y \rangle_2) = e(\langle Y' \rangle_1, \langle 1 \rangle_2)$
5:         $\wedge e(\langle Z \rangle_1, \langle 1 \rangle_2) = e(\langle V \rangle_1 + \langle Y \rangle_1, \langle \beta \rangle_2)e(\langle \beta \rangle_1, \langle W \rangle_2)$ **then**
6:         **return** $\top$
7:     **else**
8:         **return** $\bot$

To produce a block containing values x, a party first samples three random field values δ_v, δ_w, and δ_y and then executes ProofBlock, cf. Algorithm 2. The BK argument to this algorithm is the *block key*; the subset of the evaluation key terms specific to a single proof block. Because each input party should only provide its own input values and should not affect the values contributed by other parties, each proof block must be restricted to a subset of the wires. This is achieved by modifying Pinocchio's key generation such that, instead of a sampling a single value β, one such value, β_j, is sampled for each proof block j and the terms $\langle r_v \beta_j v_i + r_w \beta_j w_i + r_y \beta_j y_i \rangle_1$ are only included for wires indices i belonging to block j. That is, the jth block key is

$$BK_j = \{ \langle r_v v_i \rangle_1, \langle r_v \alpha_v v_i \rangle_1, \langle r_w w_i \rangle_2, \langle r_w \alpha_w w_i \rangle_1, \langle r_y y_i \rangle_1, \langle r_y \alpha_y y_i \rangle_1,$$
$$\langle r_v \beta_j v_i + r_w \beta_j w_i + r_y \beta_j y_i \rangle_1, \langle r_v \beta_j t \rangle_1, \langle r_w \beta_j t \rangle_1, \langle r_y \beta_j t \rangle_1 \},$$

with i ranging over the indices of wires in the block. Note that ProofBlock only performs linear operations on its x, δ_v, δ_w and δ_y inputs. Therefore this algorithm does not have to be modified to compute on secret shares.

A Trinocchio proof in the multi-client setting now consists of one block $Q_i = (\langle V_i \rangle_1, \ldots, \langle Z_i \rangle_1)$ for each input and result party, one block $Q_{\text{mid}} = (\langle V_{\text{mid}} \rangle_1, \ldots, \langle Z_{\text{mid}} \rangle_1)$ of internal wire values, and Pinocchio's $\langle H \rangle_1$ element. Verification of such a proof consists of checking correctness of each block, and checking correctness of $\langle H \rangle_1$. The validity of a proof block can be verified using CheckBlock, cf. Algorithm 3. Compared to the Pinocchio verification key, our verification key contains "block verification keys" BV_i (i.e., elements $\langle \beta_j \rangle_1$ and $\langle \beta_j \rangle_2$) for each block instead of just $\langle \beta \rangle_1$ and $\langle \beta \rangle_2$. Apart from the relations inspected by CheckBlock, one other relation is needed to verify a Pinocchio proof: the divisibility check of Eq. (4) (Sect. 2.2). In the protocol, the algorithm that verifies this relation will be called CheckDiv. We denote the modified setup of the evaluation and verification keys by hybrid call MKeyGen.

5.2 Protocol Overview

We will proceed with a protocol overview. Pseudocode and a more detailed description of the protocol are given in the full version. The multi-client variant of our Trinicchio protocol makes use of private channels, just as the single-client variant, to privately communicate in- and output values, and to let the workers carry out the computation. We need some additional communication to ensure input independence and fix the input parties' values. For this we use a bulletin board. To achieve input independence, we first have the input parties commit to a representation of their input and then reveal these, which requires the use of a commitment scheme.

Apart from key set-up there are three phases to the multi-client Trinocchio protocol.

– In the *input phase*, the input parties provide representations of their input on the bulletin board. These representations are later used as part of the proof to verify the computation results. They also serve to ensure that each input party provides its value independent of the other input values. The input parties then secret share their input values to the workers. The workers verify that the secret shared input values are consistent with their representations on the bulletin board, to prevent malicious input parties from providing a different value.

– The *computation phase* is very similar to the single-client variant of Trinocchio. In this phase the workers perform multi-party computation to carry out the actual computation and obtain secret shares of intermediate and result wire values. They then use these secret shared wire values to construct shares of the proof elements. These are then posted on the bulletin board, instead of being communicated directly to the result parties to ensure that all result parties receive a consistent result. In order to prevent these proof elements from revealing any information about the wire values, the zero-knowledge variant of the proof is used (Sect. 2.3).

– In the *result phase* the workers privately send the shares of the result values to the result parties. The result parties recombine the proof shares from the bulletin board and check whether the proof verifies. The result parties further check whether the recombined shares of the result are consistent with the information on the bulletin board. The result parties only accept the result received from the workers if both checks are satisfied.

5.3   Security of the Trinocchio Protocol

Analogously to the single-client case, we obtain the following result:

Theorem 4. *Let f be a function. Let $n = 2\theta + 1$ be the number of workers used. Let d be the degree of the QAP computing f used in the multi-client Trinocchio protocol. Assuming the d-PKE, $(4d + 4)$-PDH, and $(8d + 8)$-SDH assumptions:*

– *Trinocchio correctly evaluates f in the* (ComGen, MKeyGen)*-hybrid model.*
– *Whenever at most θ workers are passively corrupted, Trinocchio securely evaluates f in the* (ComGen, MKeyGen)*-hybrid model.*

We stress that "at most θ workers are passively corrupted" includes both the case when the adversary is passively corrupted, and corrupts at most θ workers (as well as arbitrarily many input and result parties); and the case when the adversary is actively corrupted, and corrupts no workers (but arbitrarily many input and result parties)

We give a proof of this theorem in the full version of the paper [SVdV15]. To prove secure function evaluation, we obtain privacy by simulating the multiparty computation of the proof with respect to the adversary without using honest inputs. To prove correct function evaluation, we run the protocol together with the adversary: if this gives a fake Pinocchio proof, then one of the underlying problems can be broken.

In the single-client case, we remarked that Trinocchio actually provides security against up to θ *actively* corrupted workers. Namely, although θ actively corrupted workers may manipulate the computation of the function and proof, they do not learn any information from this because they do not see the resulting proof that the client gets. In our multi-client protocol, it is less natural to assume that the workers cannot see the resulting proof; and in fact, in our protocol, corrupted workers *do* see the full proof as it is posted on the bulletin board. It should be possible to obtain some privacy guarantees against actively malicious workers (who do not collude with any result parties) by letting the result parties provide proof contributions directly to the result parties instead of posting them on the bulletin board. We leave an analysis for future work.

6   Performance

In this section, we show that our approach indeed adds privacy to verifiable computation with little overhead. We demonstrate this in a case study: we take the "MultiVar Poly" application from [PHGR13], and show that using Trinocchio, this computation can be outsourced in a private and correct way at essentially the same cost as letting three workers each perform the Pinocchio computation. In the full version of the paper we present a second case study in which we show that, using Trinocchio, the performance of "verification by validation" due to [dHSV16] can be considerably improved: in particular, we improve the client's performance by several orders of magnitude.

In our experiments, one client outsources the computation to three workers. In particular, we use multiparty computation based on $(1,3)$ Shamir secret sharing. As discussed in Sects. 4.3 and 5.3, this guarantees privacy against one passively corrupted worker (or, in the single-client case against θ actively corrupted workers when the multiparty computation protocol does not leak any information). We did not implement the multiple client scenario; this would add small overhead for the workers, with verification effort growing linearly in he number of input and result parties but remaining small and independent from the computation size. To simulate a realistic outsourcing scenario, we distribute computations between three Amazon EC2 "m3.medium" instances[3] around the world: one in Oregon, United States; one in Ireland; and one in Tokyo, Japan.

---

[3] Running Intel Xeon E5-2670 v2 Ivy Bridge with 4 GB SSD and 3.75 GiB RAM.

Multiparty computation requires secure and private channels: these are implemented using SSL.

6.1 Case Study: Multivariate Polynomial Evaluation

In [PHGR13], Pinocchio performance numbers are presented showing that, for some applications, Pinocchio verification is faster than native execution. One of these applications, "MultiVar Poly", is the evaluation of a constant multivariate polynomial on five inputs of degree 8 ("medium") or 10 ("large"). In this case study, we use Trinocchio to add privacy to this outsourcing scenario.

We have made an implementation[4] of Trinocchio's Compute algorithm (Algorithm 1) that is split into two parts. The first part performs the evaluation of the function f (line 4), given as an arithmetic circuit, using the secret sharing implementation of VIFF (We use the arithmetic circuit produced by the Pinocchio compiler, hence f is exactly the same as in [PHGR13].) Note that, because f is an arithmetic circuit, this step does not leak any information against actively corrupted workers. Hence, in the single-client outsourcing scenario of Sect. 4, we achieve privacy against one actively corrupted worker. The second part is a completely new implementation of the remainder of Trinocchio using [Mit13]'s implementation of the discrete logarithm groups and pairings from [BSCG+13].

Table 1 shows the performance numbers of running this application in the cloud with Trinocchio. Significantly, evaluating the function f using passively secure multiparty computation (i.e., line 4 of Compute) is more than twenty times cheaper than computing the Pinocchio proof (i.e., lines 5–16 of Comp). Moreover, we see that computing the Pinocchio proof in the distributed setting takes around the same time (per party) as in the non-distributed setting. Indeed, this is what we expect because the computation that takes place is exactly the same as in the non-distributed setting, except that it happens to take place on shares rather than the actual values itself. Hence, according to these numbers, the cost of privacy is essentially that the computation is outsourced to three different workers, that each have to perform the same work as one worker in the non-private setting. Finally, as expected, verification time completely vanishes compared to computation time.

Our performance numbers should be interpreted as estimates. Our Pinocchio performance is around 8–9 times worse than in [PHGR13]; but on the other hand, we could not use their proprietary elliptic curve and pairing implementations; and we did not spend much time optimising performance. Note that, as expected, our Pinocchio and Trinocchio implementations have approximately the same running time. If Trinocchio would be based on Pinocchio's code base, we would expect the same. Moreover, apart from combining the proofs from different workers, the verification routines of Pinocchio and Trinocchio are exactly the same, so achieving faster verification than native computation as in [PHGR13] should be possible with Trinocchio as well. We also note that VIFF is not known

---

[4] Implementation available at http://meilof.home.fmf.nl/.

Table 1. Performance of multivariate polynomial evaluation with Trinocchio: number of multiplications in f; time for single-worker proof; time per party for computing f and proof, and total; and verification time (all times in seconds)

	# mult	Pinoc.	Dist f	Dist π	Trinoc.	Verif.
MultiVar poly, medium	203428	2102	96	2092	2187	0.04
MultiVar poly, large	571046	6458	275	6427	6702	0.05

for its speed, so replacing VIFF with a different multiparty computation framework should considerably speed up the computation of f.

7   Discussion and Conclusion

In this paper, we have presented Trinocchio, a system that adds privacy to the Pinocchio verifiable computation scheme essentially at the cost of replicating the Pinocchio proof production algorithm at three (or more) servers. Trinocchio has the same correctness and security guarantees as Pinocchio; distributing the computation between $2\theta + 1$ workers gives privacy if at most θ of them are corrupted. We have shown in a case study that the overhead is indeed small.

As far as we are aware, our work is the first to deliver efficient verifiable computation (i.e., with cryptographic guarantees of correctness and practical verification times independent of the computation size) with privacy guarantees. Although privacy is only guaranteed if not too many of the workers are corrupt, the use of verifiable computation ensures that the outcome of the protocol cannot be manipulated by the workers. This allows us to hedge against an adversary being more powerful than anticipated in a real world scenario.

As discussed, existing verifiable computation constructions in the single-worker setting [GGP10, GKP+13, FGP14] use very expensive cryptography, while multiple-worker efforts to provide privacy [ACG+14] do not guarantee correctness if all workers are corrupted. In contrast, existing works from the area of multiparty computation [BDO14, SV15, dHSV16] deliver privacy and correctness guarantees, but have much less efficient verification.

A major limitation of Pinocchio-based approaches is that they assume trusted set-up of the (function-dependent) evaluation and verification keys. In the single-client setting, the client could perform this set-up itself, but in the multiple-client setting, it is less clear who should do this. In particular, whoever has generated the evaluation and verification keys can use the values used during key generation as a trapdoor to generate proofs of false statements. Even though key generation can likely be distributed using the same techniques we use to distribute proof production, it remains the case that all generating parties together know this trapdoor. Unfortunately, this seems inherent to the Pinocchio approach.

Our work is a first step towards privacy-preserving verifiable computation, and we see many promising directions for future work. Recent work in verifiable computation has extended the Pinocchio approach by making it easier to specify computations [BSCG+13], and by adding access control functionality [AJCC15]. In future work, it would be interesting to see how these kind of techniques can be used in the Trinocchio setting. Also, recent work has focused on applying verifiable computation on large amounts of data held by the server (and possibly signed by a third party) [CTV15]; assessing the impact of distributing the computation (in particular when aggregating information from databases from several parties) in this scenario is also an important future direction. It would also be interesting to base Trinocchio on the (much faster) Pinocchio codebase [PHGR13] and more efficient multiparty computation implementations, and see what kind of performance improvements can be achieved. Another interesting direction is to investigate the possibility of practical universally composable [Can00b, CCL15] distributed verifiable computation; or to use the universal composability framework to obtain a more generic framework for combining multiparty computation with verifiable computation (even with only standalone guarantees).

Acknowledgements. This work was supported in part through the FP7 programme under grant 609611 (PRACTICE) and through the H2020 programme under grant 643964 (SUPERCLOUD).

References

[ACG+14] Ananth, P., Chandran, N., Goyal, V., Kanukurthi, B., Ostrovsky, R.: Achieving privacy in verifiable computation with multiple servers – without FHE and without pre-processing. In: Krawczyk, H. (ed.) PKC 2014. LNCS, vol. 8383, pp. 149–166. Springer, Heidelberg (2014)

[AJCC15] Alderman, J., Janson, C., Cid, C., Crampton, J.: Access control in publicly verifiable outsourced computation. In: Proceedings of ASIACCS (2015)

[BDO14] Baum, C., Damgård, I., Orlandi, C.: Publicly auditable secure multi-party computation. In: Abdalla, M., De Prisco, R. (eds.) SCN 2014. LNCS, vol. 8642, pp. 175–196. Springer, Heidelberg (2014)

[BGW88] Ben-Or, M., Goldwasser, S., Wigderson, A.: Completeness theorems for non-cryptographic fault-tolerant distributed computation. In: Proceedings of STOC (1988)

[BSCG+13] Ben-Sasson, E., Chiesa, A., Genkin, D., Tromer, E., Virza, M.: SNARKs for C: verifying program executions succinctly and in zero knowledge. In: Canetti, R., Garay, J.A. (eds.) CRYPTO 2013, Part II. LNCS, vol. 8043, pp. 90–108. Springer, Heidelberg (2013)

[Can00a] Canetti, R.: Security and composition of multi-party cryptographic protocols. J. Cryptology **13**(1), 143–202 (2000)

[Can00b] Canetti, R.: Universally composable security: a new paradigm for cryptographic protocols. Cryptology ePrint Archive, Report 2000/067 (2000)

[CCL15] Canetti, R., Cohen, A., Lindell, Y.: A simpler variant of universally composable security for standard multiparty computation. In: Gennaro, R., Robshaw, M. (eds.) CRYPTO 2015. LNCS, vol. 9216, pp. 3–22. Springer, Heidelberg (2015)

[CKKC13] Choi, S.G., Katz, J., Kumaresan, R., Cid, C.: Multi-client non-interactive verifiable computation. In: Sahai, A. (ed.) TCC 2013. LNCS, vol. 7785, pp. 499–518. Springer, Heidelberg (2013)

[CLT14] Carter, H., Lever, C., Traynor, P.: Whitewash: outsourcing garbled circuit generation for mobile devices. In: Proceedings of ACSAC (2014)

[CTV15] Chiesa, A., Tromer, E., Virza, M.: Cluster computing in zero knowledge. In: Oswald, E., Fischlin, M. (eds.) EUROCRYPT 2015. LNCS, vol. 9057, pp. 371–403. Springer, Heidelberg (2015)

[DFK+06] Damgård, I.B., Fitzi, M., Kiltz, E., Nielsen, J.B., Toft, T.: Unconditionally secure constant-rounds multi-party computation for equality, comparison, bits and exponentiation. In: Halevi, S., Rabin, T. (eds.) TCC 2006. LNCS, vol. 3876, pp. 285–304. Springer, Heidelberg (2006)

[dH12] de Hoogh, S.: Design of large scale applications of secure multiparty computation: secure linear programming. Ph.D. thesis, Eindhoven University of Technology (2012)

[dHSV16] de Hoogh, S., Schoenmakers, B., Veeningen, M.: Guaranteeing correctness in privacy-friendly outsourcing by certificate validation. In: Proceedings of AFRICACRYPT (2016)

[FGP14] Fiore, D., Gennaro, R., Pastro, V.: Efficiently verifiable computation on encrypted data. In: Proceedings of CCS (2014)

[GGP10] Gennaro, R., Gentry, C., Parno, B.: Non-interactive verifiable computing: outsourcing computation to untrusted workers. In: Rabin, T. (ed.) CRYPTO 2010. LNCS, vol. 6223, pp. 465–482. Springer, Heidelberg (2010)

[GGPR13] Gennaro, R., Gentry, C., Parno, B., Raykova, M.: Quadratic span programs and succinct NIZKs without PCPs. In: Johansson, T., Nguyen, P.Q. (eds.) EUROCRYPT 2013. LNCS, vol. 7881, pp. 626–645. Springer, Heidelberg (2013)

[GKL+15] Gordon, S.D., Katz, J., Liu, F.-H., Shi, E., Zhou, H.-S.: Multi-client verifiable computation with stronger security guarantees. In: Dodis, Y., Nielsen, J.B. (eds.) TCC 2015, Part II. LNCS, vol. 9015, pp. 144–168. Springer, Heidelberg (2015)

[GKP+13] Goldwasser, S., Kalai, Y.T., Popa, R.A., Vaikuntanathan, V., Zeldovich, N.: Reusable garbled circuits and succinct functional encryption. In: Proceedings of STOC (2013)

[Gro10] Groth, J.: Short pairing-based non-interactive zero-knowledge arguments. In: Abe, M. (ed.) ASIACRYPT 2010. LNCS, vol. 6477, pp. 321–340. Springer, Heidelberg (2010)

[GRR98] Gennaro, R., Rabin, M.O., Rabin, T.: Simplified VSS and fact-track multiparty computations with applications to threshold cryptography. In: Proceedings of PODC (1998)

[JNO14] Jakobsen, T.P., Nielsen, J.B., Orlandi, C.: A framework for outsourcing of secure computation. In: Proceedings of CCSW (2014)

[KMR12] Kamara, S., Mohassel, P., Riva, B.: Salus: a system for server-aided secure function evaluation. In: Proceedings of CCS (2012)

[MF06] Mohassel, P., Franklin, M.K.: Efficiency tradeoffs for malicious two-party computation. In: Yung, M., Dodis, Y., Kiayias, A., Malkin, T. (eds.) PKC 2006. LNCS, vol. 3958, pp. 458–473. Springer, Heidelberg (2006)

[Mit13] Mitsunari, S.: A fast implementation of the optimal ate pairing over BN curve on Intel Haswell processor. Cryptology ePrint Archive, Report 2013/362 (2013)

[PHGR13] Parno, B., Howell, J., Gentry, C., Raykova, M.: Pinocchio: nearly practical verifiable computation. In: Proceedings of S&P (2013)

[PTK13] Peter, A., Tews, E., Katzenbeisser, S.: Efficiently outsourcing multiparty computation under multiple keys. IEEE Trans. Inf. Forensics Secur. 8(12), 2046–2058 (2013)

[ST06] Schoenmakers, B., Tuyls, P.: Efficient binary conversion for Paillier encrypted values. In: Vaudenay, S. (ed.) EUROCRYPT 2006. LNCS, vol. 4004, pp. 522–537. Springer, Heidelberg (2006)

[SV15] Schoenmakers, B., Veeningen, M.: Universally verifiable multiparty computation from threshold homomorphic cryptosystems. In: Liu, S., et al. (eds.) ACNS 2015. LNCS, vol. 9092, pp. 3–22. Springer, Heidelberg (2015). doi:10.1007/978-3-319-28166-7_1

[SVdV15] Schoenmakers, B., Veeningen, M., de Vreede, N.: Trinocchio: privacy-friendly outsourcing by distributed verifiable computation. Cryptology ePrint Archive, Report 2015/480 (2015)

Verifiable Multi-party Computation with Perfectly Private Audit Trail

Édouard Cuvelier[✉] and Olivier Pereira

ICTEAM/ELEN – Crypto Group, Univeristé Catholique de Louvain,
1348 Louvain-la-Neuve, Belgium
edouard.cuvelier@uclouvain.be

Abstract. We propose an efficient protocol for the evaluation of functions getting their inputs from multiple parties in a way that guarantees the result correctness. In our setting, a worker is trusted with the confidentiality of the inputs and, given this assumption, our protocol guarantees perfect privacy to the clients.

Our protocol offers an interesting middle ground between traditional verifiable computation protocols, that usually do not come with privacy guarantees and focus on one or a small number of clients, and secure multi-party computation protocol that distribute the privacy trust between a number of parties, at the cost of much more expensive protocols (especially for NP functions and functions that do not admit an efficient static circuit representation) and a demanding infrastructure of independently managed servers interacting in multiple rounds. By contrast, our protocol is single-pass: the clients submit their inputs asynchronously, and everyone can collect the result at any later time.

We present three unrelated applications of our technique: solving a system of linear equations, an auction scheme and the search of the shortest path in a shared graph. These examples illustrate the ease of use and the advantage in terms of complexity of our approach. We made a prototype implementation that illustrates the practicality of our solution.

1   Introduction

We investigate the well-known problem of a set of clients holding private inputs and looking for an efficient solution for the evaluation of a function of these inputs.

In most practical cases, e.g., auctions, health information management systems, benchmarking services, or cloud services in general, this problem is handled by delegating all the confidential inputs to a trusted third party, or worker, who is in charge of computing and distributing the output of the computation to the clients. The trust encompasses two different aspects: the correctness of the computation, and the confidentiality of the inputs.

Several important lines of work addressed these two forms of trust in different settings. Secure Multi-Party Computation (SMC) addresses the confidentiality issue by distributing the computation between several workers (who can also be the clients) and often also addresses the correctness aspect through

© Springer International Publishing Switzerland 2016
M. Manulis et al. (Eds.): ACNS 2016, LNCS 9696, pp. 367–385, 2016.
DOI: 10.1007/978-3-319-39555-5_20

zero-knowledge proofs. Despite tremendous improvements in terms of efficiency that happened during the last few years, e.g., through the "SPDZ" protocol of Damgård et al. [1] and its publicly verifiable improvement proposed by Baum et al. [2], there remain important practical obstacles to the broad deployment of these techniques. First, a large computational and communication overhead seems inevitable due to the need to perform the whole computation process step by step in a distributed fashion. This concern becomes even stronger when the function that needs to be evaluated does not admit a simple static circuit representation, as it is the case when efficient solutions require non-uniform data-dependent branching (see examples from Aly et al. for instance [3]). Besides, from an organizational point of view, it is often difficult to obtain that the various workers independently deploy and manage servers on a common high-speed network. For example, the sugar beet auction in Denmark [4] was performed between three parties representing farmers, buyers and the SMC project promoters, who were trusted by all the clients. This is also the case in some cryptographic voting systems such as Helios [5] where, despite the simplicity of the function that is evaluated (a sum), the tallying is performed by a small set of trustees sharing the private key of a distributed encryption scheme.

As a second line of work, Verifiable Computation (VC) addresses this infrastructure problem by investigating solutions based on a single worker, who could be a cloud service provider. For instance, the "Pinocchio" protocol proposed by Parno et al. [6], and its refinement "Gepetto" [7] are highly efficient solutions that offer public verifiability in a single client-worker setting. However the protocol does not aim at providing privacy of the inputs. Even more efficient than "Pinocchio", Backes et al. [8] developed a three-party protocol where a worker is requested to prove computations to a client over authenticated data received from a single trusted source. The construction of Parno has also been used by Zhang et al. [9] in "Alitheia", a single-client verifiable computation system for graph problems such as the shortest path studied in this paper.

The addition of confidentiality constraints in VC, that is, considering a single worker that is not trusted for confidentiality, has been formalized by Gennaro et al. [10] in the single client setting, then extended by Choi et al. [11] who achieve non-interactive multi-client verifiable computation by relying on garbled circuits, oblivious transfer and fully homomorphic encryption. In the follow-up works of Goldwasser et al. [12] and Gordon et al. [13], the solution uses functional encryption and indistinguishability obfuscation. These works have a largely theoretical flavor, and do not provide any concrete efficiency analysis.

Our Contributions. Our setting aims at practical solutions and focuses on an interesting middle-ground between the two forms of VC described above. Our unique worker performs verifiable computation, and the proof of correctness of its outputs preserves the privacy of the inputs (in an information theoretic way). Still, our worker is trusted to preserve the privacy of the inputs.

Trusting the worker for confidentiality has serious practical benefits: the worker is able to compute efficiently on cleartext data, and the function evaluation therefore does not come with any overhead. The proof of correctness is based on cryptographic primitives but, in many practical applications, is considerably cheaper than the computation itself: these applications include most problems in NP, and even simple standard problems like sorting. Besides, it makes it possible to perform the computation using highly sophisticated algorithms, circumventing issues related to functions that do not have a static circuit representation, and allowing the worker to use its own proprietary and confidential solution.

The level of interaction in our protocol is minimal: the clients submit their inputs to the worker as a single message, and the result and a single publicly verifiable proof is made available at the end of the computation. This makes our solution practical even for applications based on a web interface, which clients could use to submit their input, and later retrieve the outcome of the computation.

We define the security properties of our scheme through ideal functionalities for secure function evaluation. Our protocol guarantees the correctness of the output, even if the worker is corrupted. Furthermore, our protocol guarantees information theoretic privacy if the worker is honest.

We illustrate our technique via three test applications: solving a system of linear equations, electronic auctions and finding the shortest path in a graph. Finally, we give some insight on the performances obtained for these applications by a prototype implementation realized in Python.

Related Works. Besides the works described above, and very close to our technique, Rabin et al. [14,15] present a secrecy-preserving proof of correctness scheme for the evaluation of any function with straight line computation through an agreed public circuit. Indeed, similar to what is done in this paper, they propose to perform the proof of correctness on the commitments on the inputs of the function. A parallel circuit is evaluated by a worker on the commitments and every operation is validated by a zero-knowledge proof of knowledge. While the schemes proposed there rely on symmetric cryptography and a split-value representation to perform cut-and-choose proofs, we show in this work better timing results as well as more compact proofs using homomorphic cryptography based on elliptic curves.

2   Verifiable Multi-party Function Evaluation

The Ideal Protocol. In this section, we specify our protocol in terms of an ideal functionality, following the notations and definitions of Canetti [16]. We will then require our protocol to offer the same security features as that functionality.

In this regard, let us consider a set of clients $\mathcal{C} = \{C_1, \ldots, C_n\}$. Each C_i has a private input $x_i \in I$, the input space. We define our *ideal functionality* $\mathcal{F}^f$ as a process that privately receives inputs from the clients and then evaluates the function $f : I^n \to O$ on these inputs (O is the output space), and outputs that result to all parties. So, correctness is always guaranteed by this functionality.

We consider two corruption models for our protocol, which lead to two flavors of our functionality. In the case of a honest-but-curious (also often called "passive") adversary $\mathcal{A}_p$, that is, an adversary who learns the internal state of the corrupted parties but lets them follow the protocol, the functionality $\mathcal{F}^f_{\mathcal{A}_p}$ also guarantees that the clients do not learn anything about each other's inputs (apart from what might be derived from the output of the function). In the case of an active adversary $\mathcal{A}_a$, correctness remains guaranteed, but the client's inputs are leaked to the adversary, and confidentiality is therefore not guaranteed anymore.

The ideal functionalities $\mathcal{F}^f_{\mathcal{A}_p}$ and $\mathcal{F}^f_{\mathcal{A}_a}$

---

1. Upon receiving (Send, C_i, x_i) from a client C_i or adversary $\mathcal{S}$, if $x_i \in I$, store x_i, otherwise abort. Then, in the case of
   - a *honest-but-curious adversary*, send C_i to adversary $\mathcal{S}$ and halt.
   - an *active adversary*, send (C_i, x_i) to adversary $\mathcal{S}$ and halt.
2. Upon receiving Compute from $\mathcal{S}$, evaluate $y := f(x_1, \ldots, x_n)$. Send y to every client C_i and $\mathcal{S}$, then halt.

The Real Protocol. We now turn to the design of our real-world protocol, that realizes the ideal functionalities.

We require our protocol to produce a perfectly private audit trail (PPAT) of its computation, that is, the privacy guarantees offered by our protocol will be perfect in the sense of information theory. For simplicity, we focus on the case of static corruption: corruption of parties happen before the beginning of the protocol, and not dynamically as the protocol executes.

We build the protocol Π^f_{PPAT} which realizes these functionalities in the real world in the presence of honest-but-curious and active adversaries. In this protocol, most of the work of the functionality is performed by an entity called the Worker $\mathcal{W}$. However, contrary to the ideal functionality, the worker can be corrupted by the adversary and, in the case of an active adversary, might be willing to evaluate a function different of f.

Designing a protocol that implements our functionality in the presence of an honest-but-curious adversary is fairly immediate: clients hand their inputs to the worker through a secure channel (which can be realized by means of a CPA-secure encryption scheme), then the worker simply outputs the result.

The case of an active adversary is more demanding: in order to make sure that an invalid output of the worker will not be accepted by the clients, our protocol requires the worker to provide a proof of the correctness of the output. And, in order to ensure that every client receives the same result at the end of the protocol, this proof will be posted on a Public Bulletin Board **PB**, which maintains publicly available every input sent to him by any parties.

The most immediate way of building the proof would be to use zero-knowledge proofs computed from the encrypted inputs of the clients. This has two downsides, however. In terms of efficiency, secure encryption is length increasing, which will typically lead to more expensive proofs, since they need to apply to larger statements. In terms of security, the ciphertexts that will be needed to verify the proofs are only computationally hiding, meaning that the inputs of the client will eventually become available through data that are published as part of the protocol.

An alternative approach, which we adopt, is to work on perfectly hiding commitments: they do not need to be length increasing, potentially leading to more efficient proofs, and they do not cause any weakening of privacy. Perfectly hiding commitments can only be computationally binding, but this is a much lower concern, since the workers only have a relatively short period of time for producing their proofs, making any future computational breakthrough innocuous.

So, our protocol will rely on a commitment scheme, that is, a triple of algorithms $\Pi_C := (\text{Gen}_C, \text{Com}, \text{Verify})$. Algorithm Com, on input x and public key cpk generated by Gen_C, produces d, o where d is the commitment and o is the opening value used afterwards to open the commitment through the Verify algorithm. The perfectly hiding property of the commitment scheme means that for any commitment d, we can find, for any value x in the input space, an opening o such that $\text{Verify}(d, o, x)$ accepts. In other words, it implies that no single piece of information from x could be extracted from d. We also require the commitments to be computationally binding: it must be hard to produce a commitment d, two messages $x \neq x'$ and two opening values o, o' on which d can be opened.

As a first step in our protocol, the clients send a commitment $d_i \leftarrow \text{Com}(x_i)$ on their private inputs x_i to **PB**. Along with the commitment d_i, each client must produce a proof denoted $\pi_{\text{ver}}(d_i)$ that ensures non-malleability [17], under the form of a Σ-proof of knowledge (see [18]). Non-malleability will be used to enforce the independence of the inputs posted by the clients [18], preventing one client from choosing his input as a function of someone else's input, which could have devastating effects in some contexts (e.g., auctions). In some cases, the proof $\pi_{\text{ver}}(d_i)$ can also be designed to be more than just a proof of knowledge: for instance, a Σ-proof of membership can be used to ensure the validity of x_i.

In parallel with the posting of these commitments and proofs, all clients submit an opening of their commitment to the worker W, using a private channel. From these inputs, W posts the evaluation of f on **PB**. And, in order to capture an actively corrupted W, we require that W also publishes a proof denoted π_{cor} of the correctness of the evaluation y of f on the inputs. The key point is that the verification of π_{cor} relies on the commitments $d_1, \ldots, d_n$ posted by the clients on **PB**. In the general case, this verification involves the computation of a commitment d_y that must be a commitment on y computed from $d_1, \ldots, d_n$. With this requirement, an active adversary who would be willing to cheat during the function evaluation process would need to be able to break the binding property of the commitment scheme or the soundness of the proof π_{cor}.

Protocol Π_{PPAT}^f and Formal Security. The proofs we are referring to here are built from the notion of sigma (or Σ)-protocols [19]. In the following, we define relations R in a formal NP-language such as $R \subset \mathcal{L}_{\text{NP}} \times W(s)$ where s is called the statement and $w \in W(s)$ a witness of s.

We rely on the Fiat-Shamir/Blum transformation [20,21] to turn Σ-protocols into non-interactive zero-knowledge proofs of knowledges (NIZKPK). This heuristic relies on the existence of an efficient hash function which is used to create the challenge of the Σ-protocol. Careful attention must be paid on the choice of the values thrown into the hash function [18].

Definition 1 (Non-interactive Zero-Knowledge Proof of Knowledge). *A Non-Interactive Zero-Knowledge Proof of Knowledge π for a relation R on an NP-language $\mathcal{L}_{NP}$ is a couple of efficient algorithms* (Prove, Check) *such that:*

Prove(s, w): *on inputs $(s, w) \in R$, outputs a transcript* t.
Check(s, t): *on inputs a statement s and a transcript t, outputs 0 or 1.*

where Prove *is probabilistic and* Check *is deterministic. The next properties hold:*

Completeness: $\forall (s, w) \in R, \forall t \leftarrow$ Prove(s, w), *we have that* Check$(s, t) = 1$ *with overwhelming probability.*
Soundness: *there exists a polynomial time extractor E such that, when E receives on inputs two valid transcripts t, t' with respect to the same s, E returns a correct witness w.*
Perfect Zero-Knowledge: *there exists a probabilistic polynomial time simulator $\mathcal{M}$ that produces simulated transcripts that are perfectly indistinguishable from real transcripts produced through the* Prove *algorithm.*

The parties involved in the protocol Π_{PPAT}^f will publish on **PB** transcripts of NIZKPK to prove some relations. We describe in Sect. 3 the relations we aim to prove and how to build specific proofs for our applications.

The relations for the NIZKPK π_{cor} and $\pi_{ver}(d_i)$ mentioned in Π_{PPAT}^f are defined as follows: $R^{cor} := \{((y, d_1, \ldots, d_n), (x_1, o_1, \ldots, x_n, o_n)) | y = f(x_1, \ldots, x_n) \bigwedge_i$ Verify$(d_i, o_i, x_i) = 1\}$ and $R^{ver} := \{(d, (x, o)) | $Verify$(d, o, x) = 1 \land x \in I\}$

where the algorithm Verify(d, o, x) of the commitment scheme returns 1 only if d is a commitment on x with opening o.

These proofs are published on **PB** and π_{cor} will be checked by each C_i at the end of the protocol to convince itself of the correctness of the function's computation. We are now ready to define protocol Π_{PPAT}^f which realizes functionalities $\mathcal{F}_{\mathcal{A}_p}^f$ and $\mathcal{F}_{\mathcal{A}_a}^f$ in the presence of $\mathcal{A}_p$ and $\mathcal{A}_a$ respectively.

We show in Sect. 3.3 how to build protocol Π_{PPAT}^f for any function f and how $\mathcal{W}$ can prepare the proof π_{cor}. Note that, in step 2, it is crucial for $\mathcal{W}$ to verify that the commitments on **PB** are consistent with the private inputs. Indeed, if a cheating client published a commitment that is not consistent with his private input, then $\mathcal{W}$ will not be able to provide a correct proof π_{cor} on the result since this proof is bound to the commitments. In the full version of this paper, we point out two modifications of the protocol that achieve slightly different functionalities. The first one keeps the outcome y secret so that the function evaluation can be used as a subroutine of a larger function without revealing intermediary results. The second one aims at encountering active adversaries that dynamically chooses the inputs of the corrupted clients as a function of the inputs of honest clients.

Protocol Π_{PPAT}^f

Input: Each C_i has his private input $x_i \in I$ for $i = 1, \ldots, n$.
Output: Each C_i receives $y := f(x_1, \ldots, x_n)$.

1. Each C_i computes a perfectly hiding commitment on x_i : $d_i, o_i \leftarrow \mathsf{Com}(x_i)$ as well as a proof $\pi_{\mathsf{ver}}(d_i)$ on some property that x_i must meet. C_i publishes d_i and $\pi_{\mathsf{ver}}(d_i)$ on **PB**. Then, C_i sends x_i, o_i to $\mathcal{W}$ through the *secure channel*.
2. $\mathcal{W}$ runs $\mathsf{Check}_{\mathsf{ver}}$ of $\pi_{\mathsf{ver}}(d_i)$ on each d_i and aborts if one of the check is false. $\mathcal{W}$ runs the Verify algorithm on each triple (d_i, o_i, x_i) and aborts if one verification fails. Otherwise, on inputs $x_1, \ldots, x_n, o_1, \ldots, o_n$, $\mathcal{W}$ computes $y := f(x_1, \ldots, x_n)$ and a proof of correctness π_{cor} of the result. Then, $\mathcal{W}$ publishes y and π_{cor} on **PB**.
3. Each C_i runs $\mathsf{Check}_{\mathsf{ver}}$ of $\pi_{\mathsf{ver}}(d_j)$ on each d_j (for $j = 1, \ldots, n$ and $j \neq i$) and $\mathsf{Check}_{\mathsf{cor}}$ of π_{cor} on $(y, d_1, \ldots, d_n)$. If each verification accepts, then C_i accepts output y, otherwise C_i aborts.

One can see that the security of the protocol in the presence of a passive adversary $\mathcal{A}_p$ rests on the fact that every piece of information present on **PB** is either perfectly hiding or zero-knowledge. However, in the presence of an active adversary $\mathcal{A}_a$ the privacy of the scheme is not guaranteed: a corrupted worker could disclose all the client inputs. Nevertheless, in this scenario, we assert that the verifiability property still stands. In other words, $\mathcal{A}_a$ could leak the private inputs but is not able to tamper with the correctness of the function evaluation.

Our first result shows that protocol Π_{PPAT}^f, executed with an ideal bulletin board, realizes the functionality $\mathcal{F}_{\mathcal{A}_p}^f$ in the presence of passive adversary $\mathcal{A}_p$, and has a perfectly private audit trail.

Theorem 1. *Let $\Pi_\mathsf{C} := (\mathsf{Gen}_\mathsf{C}, \mathsf{Com}, \mathsf{Verify})$ be a perfectly hiding commitment scheme and π_{cor} and π_{ver} be perfect zero-knowledge proofs. Then, for any set of corrupted clients, there is a simulator such that, for any environment, the views resulting from the following two situations are* **identical**:

- *interacting with the bulletin board, the clients and the worker playing the Π_{PPAT}^f protocol.*
- *interacting with the ideal functionality $\mathcal{F}_{\mathcal{A}_p}^f$ and the simulator.*

The view of the environment includes its accesses to the bulletin board (controlled by the simulator in the second case), submitting the input x_i to the clients (or to $\mathcal{F}_{\mathcal{A}_p}^f$), and obtaining the outcome y in return.

Proof. Informal. We proceed by a set of game hops to show that the view of the environment and the adversary is indistinguishable between the real execution of the protocol and the ideal execution simulating the functionality $\mathcal{F}_{\mathcal{A}_p}^f$. The key points are that

1. the commitments published on **PB** reveal no information whatsoever about the committed values.
2. the proofs of knowledge on **PB** are perfect zero-knowledge and cannot be used by an adversary to extract information.
3. the proof π_{cor} present on **PB** computationally ensures the result soundness.
4. the three first points combined form a perfectly private audit trail of the function evaluation that is computationally sound.

The complete proof can be found in the full version of this paper.

Our second result shows that Protocol Π_{PPAT}^f, executed with an ideal bulletin board, realizes the functionality $\mathcal{F}_{\mathcal{A}_a}^f$ in the presence of an active adversary $\mathcal{A}_a$ who controls the worker.

Theorem 2. *Let $\Pi_C := (\mathsf{Gen}_C, \mathsf{Com}, \mathsf{Verify})$ be a binding commitment scheme and π_{cor} and π_{ver} be computationally sound proofs. Then, for a corrupted worker and any set of corrupted clients, there is a simulator such that, for any environment, the views resulting from the two situations below are* **indistinguishable***:*

- *interacting with the bulletin board, the clients and the corrupted worker playing the Π_{PPAT}^f protocol.*
- *interacting with the ideal functionality $\mathcal{F}_{\mathcal{A}_a}^f$ and the simulator.*

The view of the environment includes its accesses to the bulletin board (controlled by the simulator in the second case), submitting the input x_i to the clients (or to $\mathcal{F}_{\mathcal{A}_a}^f$), and obtaining the outcome y in return, and every communication that the corrupted worker would make.

Proof. Informal. The demonstration follows the same pattern of Theorem 1 with the major difference that the privacy of the inputs is no longer guaranteed due to the adversary ability to corrupt the worker. However, the soundness of the proof π_{cor} remains ensuring the correctness of the result. We show that it is still essential that **PB** displays the computationally binding commitments of the clients. This condition enforces an adversary to produce a proof of knowledge on these commitments. As a result the audit trail present on **PB** is not perfectly hiding anymore but is still computationally sound.

The complete proof can be found in the full version of this paper.

3   Building Blocks for Perfectly Private Audit Trail

The interactions between the clients and the worker involve the exchange of private inputs and the publication on a Public Bulletin Board **PB** of some trail that will be used to perform further audit of the process. Depending on the properties one wants to achieve in different scenarios, we propose to use a primitive introduced by Cuvelier et al. in [22] called *commitment consistent encryption*. The primitive is a combination of an encryption scheme and a commitment scheme. It allows one to send its private inputs through a ciphertext while publicly committing on the same inputs for further public verification.

3.1 Commitment Consistent Encryption Scheme

A Commitment Consistent Encryption (CCE) scheme is a traditional public key encryption scheme that offers an extra feature: from any CCE ciphertext, it is possible to derive a commitment on the encrypted message, and the private key can also be used to obtain an opening of that commitment.

Definition 2 (CC Encryption). *A commitment consistent encryption scheme Π is a tuple of efficient algorithms* (Gen, Enc, Dec, DerivCom, Open, Verify) *defined as follows:*

- Gen(1^λ): *Given a security parameter λ, output a triple* (pp, pk, sk), *respectively the public parameters, the public key and the secret key.*
- Enc$_{pk}(m)$: *Output a ciphertext c which is an encryption using the public key* pk *of a message m chosen in the plaintext space* **M** *defined by* pp.
- Dec$_{sk}(c)$: *From a ciphertext c, output a message m using the secret key* sk.
- DerivCom$_{pk}(c)$: *Output a commitment d from a ciphertext c using* pk.
- Open$_{sk}(c)$: *Output an auxiliary value o using the secret key* sk. *This auxiliary value can be considered as part of an opening for a commitment.*
- Verify$_{pk}(d, o, m)$: *From a message m, a commitment d with respect to key* pk *and an auxiliary value o, output a bit. This algorithm checks the validity of the opening (m, o) with respect to d and* pk.

It is implicit that pp *is given to each algorithm apart from* Gen.

Correctness: *for any* (pp, pk, sk) $\leftarrow$ Gen(1^λ), *any message $m \in$ **M** and any ciphertext $c \leftarrow$ Enc$_{pk}(m)$, it holds with overwhelming probability in λ that* Dec$_{sk}(c) = m$ *and that* Verify$_{pk}($DerivCom$_{pk}(c),$ Open$_{sk}(c),$ Dec$_{sk}(c)) = 1$.

The security properties that we can expect from the encryption part of the CCE scheme are the traditional ones. We refer to the work [22] for a more complete description of CCE scheme. This paper also presents a CCE scheme that is built from a Pedersen commitment and a Paillier encryption as well as two other optimal constructions of CCE based on elliptic curves.

In some settings such as e-voting, an homomorphic encryption scheme that allows threshold decryption is mandatory while in other settings, the encryption scheme could be superfluous when using a physically secure channel between the clients and the workers. In this last case, one may be just fine with a commitment scheme alone. However, in most cases, we are in an intermediate situation where the inputs are sent to the worker through a not-so-secure network where encryption is not a luxury. For this reason a CCE scheme comes in handy.

We note that, when encryption is used instead of a secure channel, we must make sure that the adversary cannot submit inputs that he actually ignores by copying CCE ciphertexts. This can be prevented by using the non-malleability offered by sigma proofs to prevent any re-randomization of commitments, and by declaring duplicate commitments invalid (see [22] for details).

For readability, in the rest of the paper, we do not differentiate the commitments obtained through the DerivCom algorithm from other commitments produced in the proofs below, and, without loss of generality, we assume that the Com algorithm stands either for the contraction of DerivCom(Enc) when a CCE scheme is used either for some commitment scheme when a secure channel is set up for the inputs transmission. In both cases, we assume a homomorphic perfectly hiding and computationally binding commitment scheme.

3.2   Non Interactive Zero-Knowledge Proof of Knowledge

The second tool that we need is non-interactive zero-knowledge proof of knowledge (NIZKPK). Below we explicit the different relations for the proofs that we use in our construction.

The first NIZKPK is the classical or-proof of knowledge [23] denoted $\pi_{or}(d)$. Another kind of well-known NIZKPK is the proof of equality of discrete logarithms between two commitments [24] that we refer to as $\pi_{DL}(d_1, d_2)$. The proof of the opening of the commitment is denoted $\pi_{ope}(d)$. We also rely on proofs for multiplications $\pi_{mul}(d_1, d_2, d_3)$, on range proofs $\pi_{ran}(d, I)$ and on comparison proofs[1] $\pi_<(d_1, d_2, d_3)$ which are essentially range proofs. We give the relations for these proofs respectively:

$$R^{or} := \{(d, (x, o)) | \mathsf{Verify}(d, o, x) = 1 \wedge (x = 0 \vee x = 1)\}$$
$$R^{DL} := \{((d_1, d_2), (x, o_1, o_2)) | \mathsf{Verify}(d_1, o_1, x) = 1 \wedge \mathsf{Verify}(d_2, o_2, x) = 1\}$$
$$R^{ope} := \{(d, (x, o)) | \mathsf{Verify}(d, o, x) = 1\}$$
$$R^{mul} := \{((d_1, d_2, d_3), (x_1, o_1, x_2, o_2, x_3, o_3)) | x_3 = x_1 x_2 \wedge_i \mathsf{Verify}(d_i, o_i, x_i) = 1\}$$
$$R^{ran} := \{(d, (x, o)) | \mathsf{Verify}(d, o, x) = 1 \wedge x \in I\}$$
$$R^< := \{((d_1, d_2, d_3), (x_1, o_1, x_2, o_2, x_3, o_3)) | x_3 = x_1 < x_2 \wedge_i \mathsf{Verify}(d_i, o_i, x_i) = 1\}$$

The details of the Σ-protocols for relations R^{mul}, R^{ran} and $R^<$ are given in the full version of this paper. Note that the soundness of the proof π_{mul} relies on the binding property of the commitment scheme since d_3 could theoretically open to any value. A direct way to obtain a range proof that $x \in [0, 2^{k+1}[$ is by composing k proofs $\pi_{or}(b_i)$ where b_i is the binary decomposition of x.

3.3   Generic Construction of Π_{PPAT}^f

Commitment consistent encryption and NIZKPK are the building blocks of protocol Π_{PPAT}^f.

The protocol is fairly simple: each client computes a $c_i \leftarrow \mathsf{Enc}(x_i)$ of his private input. From c_i, C_i derives a perfectly hiding commitment $d_i \leftarrow \mathsf{DerivCom}(c_i)$ and, computes a $\pi_{ver}(d_i)$, for example $\pi_{or}(d_i)$, $\pi_{ran}(d_i, I)$ or by

---

[1] Since committed values belong to $\mathbb{Z}_q$, this comparison operator makes sense only on a small interval of $\mathbb{Z}_q$ where one can define a natural order. Typically an interval centred in $0 \in \mathbb{Z}_q$.

default, $\pi_{\text{ope}}(d_i)$. Then, C_i publishes d_i and $\pi_{\text{ver}}(d_i)$ on **PB**, and sends c_i to W. After having decrypted every c_i to get the clients' private inputs, W computes $y := f(x_1, \ldots, x_n)$. From the commitments published on **PB**, W computes $d_y := f(d_1, \ldots, d_n)$ as well as the NIZKPK-s for each operator of f (except for $+$ and $-$ which are natural operators in the commitment space): the set of the NIZKPK and all the intermediary commitments created for the needs of the proofs are executed in parallel to form π_{cor}. W publishes y and π_{cor} on **PB**. Finally, each C_i verifies the correctness of π_{cor} in regards to y and the reconstruction of d_y.

As we will see in the next section, this is not the most efficient way to achieve the perfectly private audit trail since there are lots of cases where the verification of the output of the function can be done without recomputing the entire function in the commitment space.

4   Applications

Until now, we have seen how to generate a perfectly private audit trail of computation from the blueprint of any function. As we will see through several examples, there is a more direct way to provide the π_{cor} that guarantees the correctness of the output. The main idea is that, once given the result of the function it is much simpler to verify that it is correct. For example, once you are told that 8128 is the square root of $66,064,384$, it costs you only one squaring to agree while finding the square root by hand calculus is trickier.

In the following applications, we show how to use this trick to reduce the complexity of the proof for the client compared with the original complexity of the algorithm computing the result as it must be done in classical SMC. We selected unrelated problems to illustrate the ease of application of our technique and we point out in the full version of this paper other examples that may turn into good candidates.

4.1   System of Linear Equations

The first application is solving a system of linear equations. It is involved as a subroutine in many algorithms as, among others, in the Lagrange polynomial interpolation or in linear programming techniques. In linear programming, the goal is to optimize a solution under a set of linear constraints. This kind of scenario fits very well in a multi-party setting. We illustrate it by an example in which a set of companies in a production line agree to cooperate in order to optimize the production of some goods but do not wish to divulge their internal work flow to each other. The gain for the companies is lower costs and the ability to reallocate resources. Nowadays, all the solutions impair the privacy in one way or another, thus preventing such benefits.

Consider the following system of linear equations L:

$$L \equiv \begin{cases} \alpha_{1,1}z_1 + \cdots + \alpha_{1,n}z_n = b_1 \\ \cdots \qquad\qquad\qquad \cdots \\ \alpha_{m,1}z_1 + \cdots + \alpha_{m,n}z_n = b_m \end{cases} \Leftrightarrow AZ = B$$

where $A \in \mathbf{M}^{m \times n}$, $B \in \mathbf{M}^{m \times 1}$, $\mathbf{M}$ is the coefficient space, and Z is the matrix of variables of dimension $(n \times 1)$. The unique solution, if it exists, is $Z_s = A^{-1}B$. When the matrix is not invertible, one might produce Z_{nts} a non trivial solution of the homogeneous system $AZ = 0$.

In a multi-party setting, the constraints are given by the clients. Here we consider K clients where $K = mn$. The clients are indexed by $i = (1,1), \ldots, (m,n)$ as are the coefficients α_i of the matrix A. The simplest scenario is that α_i is the private input of client C_i while the independent coefficients b_j for $j = 1, \ldots, m$, are known to everyone.

Each C_i computes $c_i \leftarrow \mathsf{Enc}(\alpha_i)$ and derives from it a commitment on α_i: $d_i \leftarrow \mathsf{DerivCom}(c_i)$. The d_i-s are published on $\mathbf{PB}$ as well as a proof $\pi_{\mathsf{ope}}(d_i)$ computed by C_i. The encryptions c_i are passed on to $\mathcal{W}$. We can combine each d_i on $\mathbf{PB}$ to form the matrix D which can be seen as a commitment on A. After having decrypted each c_i to get α_i, $\mathcal{W}$ computes the inverse matrix A^{-1} with his favourite method and thus the solution $Z_s = A^{-1}B$. The worker then publishes Z_s on $\mathbf{PB}$ along with π_{cor}. This proof consists of a list of m openings $o_1, \ldots, o_m$ where o_j is the opening of $b'_j = d_{j,1}z_1 + \cdots + d_{j,n}z_n$. Indeed, to verify the result, each client computes $B' := DZ_s$ and checks that the opening of each entry of this $(m, 1)$-matrix is valid and that B' opens on the values of B. In the case of a non trivial solution Z_{nts} occurring when A is not invertible, the worker opens $B' := DZ_{nts}$ which must be a series of commitments on zero.

One might also want to include B in the private inputs of the clients. In this case, the π_{cor} is a bit different. Instead of giving the openings o_j, $\mathcal{W}$ provides a $\pi_{\mathsf{DL}}(b'_j, b_j)$ that b'_j commits on the same value as b_j for $j = 1, \ldots, m$.

π_{cor} **is Zero-Knowledge:**

- *Completeness*: It is clear that, given $o_1, \ldots, o_m$, any client can verify that Z_s is indeed the solution of the linear system.
- *Soundness*: This relies on the computationally binding property of the commitment scheme.
- *Perfect ZK*: As the commitment scheme is perfectly hiding, the openings of the commitments must be uniformly distributed in the space of openings.

Complexity. For the client, the complexity cost is exactly linear in the number of clients. In fact, the complexity bottleneck of the protocol is how to find Z. Either by inverting A, by the Gauss-Jordan elimination or more efficiently by the LU decomposition method, computing Z_s requires about $O(n^3)$ operations (or $O(n^{2.373}$ with the best current algorithm). It is also noteworthy that these algorithms often require branching when for example, searching the pivot in a row. However, when performed in SMC, these operations may become costly.

4.2   Auctions

Another type of problem that benefits from our approach is electronic auctions. We consider a setting of simple auctions where n clients submit one bid each. The result of the auction consists of a list of the sorted bids. More precisely, each C_i computes $c_i \leftarrow \mathsf{Enc}(x_i)$ where the bid $x_i \in I = [0, L[$. From

c_i, C_i derives $d_i \leftarrow \mathsf{DerivCom}(c_i)$ and computes $\pi_{\mathsf{ran}}(d_i, I)$. While c_i is sent to W, each C_i publishes d_i and $\pi_{\mathsf{ran}}(d_i, I)$ on **PB**. W computes the sorted list $(x'_1, \ldots, x'_n)$ from $(x_1, \ldots, x_n)$ with his favourite algorithm. From the sorted list, W rearranges the d_i to produce a sorted list of commitments $d'_1, \ldots, d'_n$. Then, W computes $n - 1$ commitments $e_1, \ldots, e_{n-1}$ where $e_i := d_i \geq d_{i+1}$ which requires $n - 1$ proofs $\pi_{\mathsf{ran}}(d_i - d_{i+1},]-L, L[)$ denoted π_i. Thus, $\pi_{\mathsf{cor}} := ((e_1, o_1, \pi_1) \wedge \cdots \wedge (e_{n-1}, o_{n-1}, \pi_{n-1}))$ where o_i is an opening of r_i which must imply that r_i commits on 1. W publishes π_{cor} on **PB** along with $d'_1, \ldots, d'_n$. Then, each client verifies π_{cor} to validate the result of the auction.

Note that, while there is a strong guarantee for the client that the winner(s) of the auction are legitimate winner(s), the winning bid and every other bids remain perfectly private. However, if required, W could also have revealed the winning bids by publishing the openings of the commitments. It is possible to transform this protocol into a sorting protocol that does not reveal which client's bid arrives in which position. This can be done by, first, randomizing the commitments on **PB** and, then, providing a proof of shuffle that the sorted list of commitments comes from the randomized list. The work of Terelius and Wilkström [25] proposes such an efficient technique that adapts our commitment consistent approach. In this way, one could use the protocol as a subroutine of an algorithm that needs sorting.

π_{cor} is **ZK**: This is clear since π_{cor} is formed by a series of NIZKPK.

Complexity. As in the case of the linear system, the complexity for the client is linear in the number of clients. For the worker though, the highest complexity comes from the sorting algorithm (for example $O(n \log(n))$ in the case of Quicksort). However, as it is done on clear values, the cost is marginal compared with the linear number of range proofs to compute.

4.3   Shortest Path

In this third example, we aim at showing that realizing more complex protocols can be done without much difficulty. In the case of the shortest path, we consider a directed graph with m vertices and n weighted edges. The goal is to find the shortest path from a source node to a target node which is the path that minimizes the sum of the weights. We denote by $v_1, \ldots, v_m$ the vertices, while $e_k^{i,j}$ is the edge from v_i to v_j, numbered k in the edges list. Similarly, we denote $w_k^{i,j}$ the positive weight of edge $e_k^{i,j}$.

This problem has been studied in **SMC** since it offers a potential solution to privacy-preserving GPS guidance in which the guided person does not want to reveal its location to the service provider. In a multi-party setting involving more than two players, one can imagine the following scenario. A set of concurrent delivering companies possessing connections with spare room available for goods might be appealed to work together to offer a joined transport solution to a client without disclosing private information.

The Bellman-Ford algorithm solves the shortest path problem in $O(mn)$ operations. This algorithm maintains two lists: a predecessors list **pred** and a distances list **dist**. While the algorithm executes, $pred_i$ designates the predecessor vertex of v_i while $dist_i$ stores the distance of v_i which is the weight of the current shortest path from the source to v_i.

In a multi-party setting we assume that each client C_i has w_i as private input. It is possible to turn Bellman-Ford algorithm in its secure version using classical SMC or using our technique. As previously, the derived commitment $d_i \leftarrow \mathsf{DerivCom}(c_i)$ are published on **PB**, while $\mathcal{W}$ gathers the $c_i \leftarrow \mathsf{Enc}(w_i)$ of the clients private inputs. Then $\mathcal{W}$ decrypts and computes the shortest path. The algorithm requires a supremum value denoted $\top$ which is the maximum weight a path might have plus one. We define $\top$ as $n.L - n + 1$, where L is the bound on the weights of the edges: $w_i < L$. As a result, we also require C_i to publish with d_i, a $\pi_{\mathsf{ran}}(d_i, L)$ on **PB**. This proof must later be verified by the other clients and $\mathcal{W}$.

Let us now focus on the computation of π_{cor} by $\mathcal{W}$. This is done by computing Algorithm 1 on the commitments and by providing an NIZKPK when necessary.

Algorithm 1. Secure shortest path based on Bellman-Ford's algorithm

---

Input: A graph $G = (V, E)$ where V is the list of vertices $v_1, \ldots, v_m$ and E the list of edges $e_1, \ldots, e_n$ associated to a list of committed weights $d_1, \ldots, d_n$. One of the vertex is labelled *source*.

Output: The predecessors list **pred** and/or the total distances list **dist**.

1 **for** $i \leftarrow 1$ **to** m **do**
2      $pred_i \leftarrow \mathsf{Com}(i)$
3   **if** $v_i = source$ **then** $dist_i \leftarrow \mathsf{Com}(0)$;
4   **else** $dist_i \leftarrow \mathsf{Com}(\top)$;
5 **end**
6 **for** $k \leftarrow 1$ **to** m **do**
7   **for** $l \leftarrow 1$ **to** n **do**
8         $e_l^{i,j} = e_l$; $z \leftarrow dist_i - dist_j + d_l$; $x \leftarrow z < \mathsf{Com}(0)$;
9         $dist_j \leftarrow dist_j + x \cdot z$; $pred_j \leftarrow pred_j + x \cdot (\mathsf{Com}(i) - pred_j)$;
10   **end**
11 **end**

The predecessor of a vertex is represented by a commitment to the number of the vertex (lines 2 and 8) as well as the commitments on 0 and $\top$ on lines 3, and 7. These commitments can be computed once and then reused when needed. Their openings should also be given in π_{cor}. The comparison on line 7 requires a π_{ran} and the two multiplications on lines 8 require each a π_{mul}. All these proofs are aggregated in π_{cor}.

π_{cor} is **ZK**: This is clear by the generic construction of π_{cor} (see Sect. 3.3).

Complexity. The verification algorithm has exactly the same complexity as the algorithm itself since it is a secure version of it. As a result the complexity of the verification of the proof is $O(mn)$ for the client. Of course, depending on the context, various shortest path algorithms exists some of which are more efficient than Bellman-Ford. However, we ignore if a verification proof simpler in terms of complexity than the best computation algorithm exists. Nevertheless, this example shows that it is always possible to obtain a complexity equal to the complexity of the algorithm.

5   Prototype Implementation

A generic implementation of the protocol has been realized in Python. The main objective was to create a simple framework to emulate the clients-worker interaction and measure the load of work of each party in different scenarios. Our entire code is available at https://github.com/mpfeppat/mpfeppat. We also provide the code of the applications tested in this paper to facilitate the reproduction of our results. In the full version of this paper, we point out precautions that must be taken prior to using an implementation of our technique. We indicate which part of the code on the client's and on the worker's side must be audited and how.

The implementation aims to be light and reasonably efficient by using optimized algorithms and techniques. Our implementation is a prototype. However it is already a good indicator of performance. Nevertheless, one might expect a nice efficiency gain when using optimized code in C for example. This should be worth for specifically designed applications. In this regard, we do not claim that we have the best known time results for our applications.

The CCE scheme of [22] is implemented through Elliptic Curves (EC). We denote $\mathbb{F}_p$ the prime field where p is a λ-bit prime. The Pedersen-like commitment part and the ElGamal-like encryption part of the CCE scheme are performed respectively in $G_1 := E(\mathbb{F}_p)$ and $G_2 \subset E'(\mathbb{F}_{p^2})$, two prime order q groups where $E(\mathbb{F}_p), E'(\mathbb{F}_{p^2})$ are elliptic curves. Complete details are provided in the full version of this paper and the complexity analysis of our three test applications is given in the full version of this paper.

In Table 1, we list the cost of different tools we use in our algorithms. For each NIZKPK, we split the cost between the computation and the verification. The proofs are computed in parallel whenever possible which imply that the computational cost of π_{cor} is not always the sum of the cost of each intermediate proof but rather a fraction of this sum.

Several tests were performed on a standard laptop: Intel® Core i5-3320M CPU @ 2.60 GHz ×4 with 7.7 GB of RAM. For these tests, the security parameter λ is 256-bit long. Even though this is the current security requirement for EC based cryptosystems, we argue that we do not need such a high security parameter for our protocol. Indeed, a polynomial time adversary that would be able to break the correctness of the scheme needs to run an attack against the binding property of the commitment scheme (in our case, break the DDH problem). However, at the time scale of the protocol execution, this attack has to be performed in a short amount of time. For this reason, we suspect that a smaller security parameter would still allow a high level of security and decrease the computational burden of the participants.

The time results including all the computations are presented in Table 2. The results show clearly the linearity in the number of clients in the first two

Table 1. Complexity and size cost for primitives and NIZKPK.

Legend		Computation	Verification	Size
A: EC Point addition	Enc	$8Sm_p + 3A$	\	$5U + 3$
in G_1	Com	$2Sm_p + 1A$	$2Sm_p + 1A$	$U + 1$
Sm_p, Sm: EC scalar	π_{ope}	$2Sm_p + 1A$	$Sm + 2Sm_p + 2A$	$3U$
multiplication in G_1	π_{or}	$4Sm_p + 2A$	$2Sm + 3Sm_p + 3A$	$4U$
with an without	π_{DL}	$4Sm_p + 2A$	$2Sm + 4Sm_p + 4A$	$4U$
precomputation	π_{mul}	$6Sm_p + 3A$	$4Sm + 5Sm_p + 6A$	$6U$
U: λ-bit long integer	$\pi_{ran}(2^{k+1})$	$6kSm_p + 3kA$	$(3k-1)Sm + 3kSm_p$ $+(4k-1)A$	$5kU + k$

Table 2. Timings (in seconds) and proof size for the three applications – the proof sizes are computed for a security parameter λ of 256-bit long.

	Number of clients $|\mathcal{C}|$	Parameters	Worker	Client	Proof size
Linear system solving	16	Square system of size $\sqrt{|\mathcal{C}|} \times \sqrt{|\mathcal{C}|}$	$1.86e10^{-1}$	$4.14e10^{-2}$	384 B
	256		3.03	$5.62e10^{-1}$	1.54 KB
	4096		52.34	8.8	6.14 KB
Auctions	10		$3.94e10^{-1}$	$3.87e10^{-1}$	22.79 KB
	100		4	4.17	250.5 KB
	1000		40.08	42.04	2.53 MB
Shortest path	4	Number of vertices = number of edges = $|\mathcal{C}|$	$2.57e10^{-1}$	$4.81e10^{-1}$	54.81 KB
	16		2.57	6.85	864.7 KB
	64		35.03	105.7	13.79 MB

applications while the complexity of the shortest path follows the quadratic complexity of the algorithm. The main limitations of efficiency might come from our use of Python and the generic Gmpy package for basic modular operations of addition and multiplication as these do not provide algebraic computations optimized for finite fields of a given characteristic. As a point of comparison, the auctions protocol of Rabin et al. [14] based on symmetric cryptography and cut-and-choose proofs achieve a 100 bids auctions with a security parameter of size 40. The worker needs 4.11 min to prepare the proof and the clients, less than one minute to verify it while the proof in itself weight for 1.45 GB.

6   Conclusion

Current progress and real world applications in the field of secure multi-party computations and multi-party verifiable computation are positive indicators for this branch of cryptography. Faster and reliable but also user-friendly solutions are provided to meet the needs of an emerging sector of activity.

This work aims at proposing a simple and efficient solution to evaluate multiparty function in a clients-worker setting where the clients want a strong guarantee over the correctness of the result. Our solution is based on perfectly hiding commitments posted on a public bulletin board for which a worker will be bound to and will provide a computationally sound proof of correctness. We combine this commitment with an encryption in a primitive called *commitment consistent encryption* to provide a generic and easy-to-set up protocol that is secure against passive adversary for the privacy and secure against active adversary for the correctness of the function evaluation. As a result, our protocol provides a *perfectly private audit trail*.

Moreover, we show that this setting allows the clients to gain in complexity for the verification of the proof when this verification is cheaper than the algorithm used to compute the result. As a side effect, the worker is able to use his own algorithm to compute the result of the function without disclosing the intellectual property of his algorithm. This is of particular interest when the worker is a company specialized in algorithmic optimization. We illustrate the ease of use of our technique by three – rather simple but already used in real world – applications. We also provide timing results measured on our prototype implementation that indicate efficiency even though we point out that improvements could be achieved with clever optimizations.

Acknowledgements. This work has been funded by the Brussels Region INNOVIRIS project SeCloud. Part of this work was done while Édouard Cuvelier was funded by a FRIA grant of the F.R.S.-FNRS. The authors are grateful to the anonymous reviewers for their constructive feedback. They also like to thank Sylvie Baudine for her help in improving the paper.

References

1. Damgård, I., Keller, M., Larraia, E., Pastro, V., Scholl, P., Smart, N.P.: Practical covertly secure MPC for dishonest majority – or: breaking the SPDZ limits. In: Crampton, J., Jajodia, S., Mayes, K. (eds.) ESORICS 2013. LNCS, vol. 8134, pp. 1–18. Springer, Heidelberg (2013)
2. Baum, C., Damgård, I., Orlandi, C.: Publicly auditable secure multi-party computation. IACR Cryptology ePrint Archive 2014/75 (2014)
3. Aly, A., Cuvelier, E., Mawet, S., Pereira, O., Van Vyve, M.: Securely solving simple combinatorial graph problems. In: Sadeghi, A.-R. (ed.) FC 2013. LNCS, vol. 7859, pp. 239–257. Springer, Heidelberg (2013)
4. Bogetoft, P., et al.: Secure multiparty computation goes live. In: Dingledine, R., Golle, P. (eds.) FC 2009. LNCS, vol. 5628, pp. 325–343. Springer, Heidelberg (2009)
5. Adida, B., De Marneffe, O., Pereira, O., Quisquater, J.J.: Electing a university president using open-audit voting: analysis of real-world use of Helios. EVT/WOTE **9**, 10–10 (2009)

6. Parno, B., Howell, J., Gentry, C., Raykova, M.: Pinocchio: nearly practical verifiable computation. In: IEEE Symposium on Security and Privacy (SP), pp. 238–252. IEEE (2013)

7. Costello, C., Fournet, C., Howell, J., Kohlweiss, M., Kreuter, B., Naehrig, M., Parno, B., Zahur, S.: Geppetto: versatile verifiable computation. In: Proceedings of the IEEE Symposium on Security and Privacy. IEEE, May 2015

8. Backes, M., Barbosa, M., Fiore, D., Reischuk, R.M.: Adsnark: nearly practical and privacy-preserving proofs on authenticated data. Cryptology ePrint Archive, Report 2014/617 (2014). http://eprint.iacr.org/

9. Zhang, Y., Papamanthou, C., Katz, J.: Alitheia: towards practical verifiable graph processing. In: Proceedings of the 2014 ACM SIGSAC Conference on Computer and Communications Security, pp. 856–867. ACM (2014)

10. Gennaro, R., Gentry, C., Parno, B.: Non-interactive verifiable computing: outsourcing computation to untrusted workers. In: Rabin, T. (ed.) CRYPTO 2010. LNCS, vol. 6223, pp. 465–482. Springer, Heidelberg (2010)

11. Choi, S.G., Katz, J., Kumaresan, R., Cid, C.: Multi-client non-interactive verifiable computation. In: Sahai, A. (ed.) TCC 2013. LNCS, vol. 7785, pp. 499–518. Springer, Heidelberg (2013)

12. Goldwasser, S., et al.: Multi-input functional encryption. In: Nguyen, P.Q., Oswald, E. (eds.) EUROCRYPT 2014. LNCS, vol. 8441, pp. 578–602. Springer, Heidelberg (2014)

13. Gordon, S.D., Katz, J., Liu, F.-H., Shi, E., Zhou, H.-S.: Multi-client verifiable computation with stronger security guarantees. In: Dodis, Y., Nielsen, J.B. (eds.) TCC 2015, Part II. LNCS, vol. 9015, pp. 144–168. Springer, Heidelberg (2015)

14. Rabin, M.O., Servedio, R.A., Thorpe, C.: Highly efficient secrecy-preserving proofs of correctness of computation, US Patent App. 12/105, 508, 18 April 2008

15. Parkes, D.C., Rabin, M.O., Shieber, S.M., Thorpe, C.: Practical secrecy-preserving, verifiably correct and trustworthy auctions. Electron. Commer. Res. Appl. **7**(3), 294–312 (2008)

16. Canetti, R.: Universally composable security: a new paradigm for cryptographic protocols. In: IEEE 54th Annual Symposium on Foundations of Computer Science, pp. 136–136. IEEE Computer Society (2001)

17. Dolev, D., Dwork, C., Naor, M.: Non-malleable cryptography. In: SIAM Journal on Computing, pp. 542–552 (1998)

18. Bernhard, D., Pereira, O., Warinschi, B.: How not to prove yourself: Pitfalls of the Fiat-Shamir heuristic and applications to Helios. In: Wang, X., Sako, K. (eds.) ASIACRYPT 2012. LNCS, vol. 7658, pp. 626–643. Springer, Heidelberg (2012)

19. Damgård, I.: On Σ-protocols (2004). http://www.daimi.au.dk/ivan/Sigma.ps

20. Fiat, A., Shamir, A.: How to prove yourself: practical solutions to identification and signature problems. In: Odlyzko, A.M. (ed.) CRYPTO 1986. LNCS, vol. 263, pp. 186–194. Springer, Heidelberg (1987)

21. Bellare, M., Rogaway, P.: Random oracles are practical: a paradigm for designing efficient protocols. In: Proceedings of the 1st ACM Conference on Computer and communications security, pp. 62–73. ACM (1993)

22. Cuvelier, É., Pereira, O., Peters, T.: Election verifiability or ballot privacy: do we need to choose? In: Crampton, J., Jajodia, S., Mayes, K. (eds.) ESORICS 2013. LNCS, vol. 8134, pp. 481–498. Springer, Heidelberg (2013)

23. Cramer, R., Damgård, I.B., Schoenmakers, B.: Proof of partial knowledge and simplified design of witness hiding protocols. In: Desmedt, Y.G. (ed.) CRYPTO 1994. LNCS, vol. 839, pp. 174–187. Springer, Heidelberg (1994)

24. Chaum, D., Pedersen, T.P.: Wallet databases with observers. In: Brickell, E.F. (ed.) CRYPTO 1992. LNCS, vol. 740, pp. 89–105. Springer, Heidelberg (1993)
25. Terelius, B., Wikström, D.: Proofs of restricted shuffles. In: Bernstein, D.J., Lange, T. (eds.) AFRICACRYPT 2010. LNCS, vol. 6055, pp. 100–113. Springer, Heidelberg (2010)

Practical Fault-Tolerant Data Aggregation

Krzysztof Grining$^{(\boxtimes)}$, Marek Klonowski, and Piotr Syga

Faculty of Fundamental Problems of Technology,
Wrocław University of Technology, Wrocław, Poland
{krzysztof.grining,marek.klonowski,piotr.syga}@pwr.edu.pl

Abstract. During Financial Cryptography 2012 Chan et al. presented a novel privacy-protection fault-tolerant data aggregation protocol. Comparing to previous work, their scheme guaranteed provable privacy of individuals and could work even if some number of users refused to participate.

In our paper we demonstrate that despite its merits, their method provides unacceptably low accuracy of aggregated data for a wide range of assumed parameters and cannot be used in majority of real-life systems. To show this we use both analytic and experimental methods.

Additionally, we present a precise data aggregation protocol that provides provable level of security even when facing massive failures of nodes. Moreover, the protocol requires significantly less computation (limited exploiting of heavy cryptography) than most of currently known fault tolerant aggregation protocols and offers better security guarantees that make it suitable for systems of limited resources (including sensor networks). To obtain our result we relax however the model and allow some limited communication between the nodes.

Keywords: Data aggregation · Differential privacy · Fault tolerance

1 Introduction

Aggregation of data is a fundamental problem that has been approached from different perspectives. Recently there were many papers published, that presented methods of data aggregation that preserve privacy of individual users. More precisely, the goal of the protocol is to reveal some general aggregated statistics (like an average value) while keeping value of each individual secret, even if the aggregator is untrusted (e.g., tries to learn input of individual users). The general notion is to design a protocol that allows the aggregator to learn a perturbed sum, but no intermediate results.

P. Syga—The study is cofounded by the European Union from resources of the European Social Fund. Project PO KL "Information technologies: Research and their interdisciplinary applications", Agreement UDA-POKL.04.01.01-00-051/10-00. Contribution of the M. Klonowski is supported by Polish National Science Center - DEC 2013/09/B/ST6/02258.

© Springer International Publishing Switzerland 2016
M. Manulis et al. (Eds.): ACNS 2016, LNCS 9696, pp. 386–404, 2016.
DOI: 10.1007/978-3-319-39555-5_21

In [1] Shi et al. have introduced a new approach to aggregation of information in distributed systems based on combining cryptographic techniques and typical "methods of differential privacy", that was originally used for protecting privacy of individuals in statistical data bases after some data was revealed. The privacy preservation is usually realized by adding some carefully prepared noise to the aggregated values. Similar approach has been independently proposed in [2].

Those papers put a new light on the problem of privacy preserving data aggregation – the authors constructed a protocol that can be very useful, however its applicability is limited to some narrow class of scenarios due to few shortcomings. One of them is the fact that **all** of the members of a group of users have to cooperate to compute the aggregated data. Thus, this approach is not appropriate for a dynamic, real-life systems (e.g. mobile sensor networks), even though it seems to be a perfect solution for fixed, small system of devices, where a series of data is generated periodically for a long time and the number of failures is always small (e.g. collecting measurements of electricity consumption in a neighborhood).

Another important protocol, called Binary Protocol, has been introduced in [3], wherein authors presented the first privacy preserving aggregation protocol that is, to some extent, fault tolerant. In our paper we focus on showing some shortcomings of the solution from [3] (by pointing out the extent to which it is fault tolerant) as well as present our approach to privacy preserving and fault tolerant data aggregation.

1.1   Our Contribution and Organization of the Paper

In Subsect. 2 we briefly describe the model assumed in our paper and provide some notation used throughout it as well as introduce some definitions we use further on. In Sect. 3 we recall the Binary Protocol by Chan et al. presented in [3], followed by discussion of its disadvantages in Sect. 4. In Sect. 5 we present and analyze our protocol addressing some of the Binary Protocol's issues. Section 6 is devoted to recalling some of the previous work related to the problem addressed in the paper. Finally, in Sect. 7 we conclude and indicate some possible future work. The contribution of our paper is twofold.

- We show that the fault tolerant protocol from [3] (called Binary Protocol) offers very low level of accuracy of aggregated data even for small number of faults for any reasonable size of the network. This holds despite very good asymptotic guarantees.
- On the positive side we construct a modified protocol that offers much better accuracy and significantly lower computational requirements. We assume however a weaker security model where users may trust a few others and we allow some limited, local communication between users. This assumption is justified in various scenarios, specifically when users have some **local** knowledge about few other participants. This is a natural assumption in electricity meters, where privacy concerns is that the adversary can deduce i.e. the sleep/work habits or the number of inhabitants in the household. Your neighbors knows

your habits anyway. Similarly, in cloud services or social network, where you naturally have some friends or users to whom you give your data on your own free will. More precisely, **all** my neighbors/friends can break my privacy cooperating easier than any outer party.

2   Definitions and Tools

Below we present some definitions and facts that will be used throughout this paper. We will denote the set of real numbers by $\mathbb{R}$, integers by $\mathbb{Z}$ and natural numbers by $\mathbb{N}$.

Definition 1 *(Symmetric Geometric Distribution). Let $\alpha > 1$. We denote by $Geom(\alpha)$ the symmetric geometric distribution that takes integer values such that the probability mass function at $k \in \mathbb{Z}$ is $\frac{\alpha-1}{\alpha+1} \cdot \alpha^{-|k|}$.*

Fact 1 *(From [3]). Let $\epsilon > 0$. Let u, v be integers such that $|u - v| \leq \Delta$ for fixed $\Delta \in \mathbb{N}^+$. Let r be a random variable having distribution $Geom(\exp(\frac{\epsilon}{\Delta}))$. Then for any integer k*

$$Pr[v + r = k] \leq \exp(\epsilon) \Pr[u + r = k].$$

Definition 2 *(Diluted Geometric Distribution). Let $\alpha > 1$ and $0 < \beta \leq 1$. A random variable has β-diluted Geometric distribution $Geom^\beta(\alpha)$ if with probability β it is sampled from $Geom(\alpha)$, and with probability $1 - \beta$ is set to 0.*

In the same manner as in [3], we use *computational differential privacy* as a measure of privacy protection. This notion has been introduced (in a similar form) in [4] and is in fact a computational counterpart of differential privacy from [5].

Definition 3 *(Computational Differential Privacy Against Compromise (from [3])). Suppose the users are compromised by some underlying randomized process $\mathcal{C}$, and we use C to denote the information obtained by the adversary from the compromised users. Let $\varepsilon, \delta > 0$. A (randomized) protocol Π preserves computational (ε, δ)-differential privacy (against the compromising process $\mathcal{C}$) if there exists a negligible function $\eta : \mathbb{N} \to \mathbb{R}^+$ such that for all $\lambda \in \mathbb{N}$, for all $i \in \{1, 2, \ldots, n\}$, for all vectors $x, y \in \{0, 1\}^n$ that differ only at position i, for all probabilistic polynomial-time Turing machines $\mathcal{A}$, for any output $b \in \{0, 1\}$,*

$$\Pr_{\mathcal{C}_i} [\mathcal{A} (\Pi (\lambda, x), C) = b] \leq e^\varepsilon \Pr_{\mathcal{C}_i} [\mathcal{A} (\Pi (\lambda, x), C) = b] + \delta + \eta (\lambda) \ ,$$

where the probability is taken over the randomness of $\mathcal{A}$, Π and $\mathcal{C}_i$, which denotes the underlying compromising process conditioning on the event that user i is uncompromised.

In a similar manner to regular differential privacy, we say that protocol Π preserves computational ε-differential privacy if it preserves computational $(\varepsilon, 0)$-differential privacy. The intuition behind this definition is as follows. Every party has some bit b. From observing some processing of data, it is not feasible for any computationally bounded adversary to learn too much about b. This should hold with probability at least $1 - \delta$.

3 Protocol by Chan et al. – Description

In the paper [3] authors propose a fault tolerant, privacy preserving data aggregation protocol which they named Binary Protocol. The purpose of the protocol is to allow some untrusted Aggregator **AGG**, to learn the sum of values x_i, $1 \leq i \leq n$, where x_i is kept by the i-th user. We will denote i-th user by $\mathbf{N}_i$. The idea is based on earlier work [1], in particular the Block Aggregation protocol. In this setting, we do not have a trusted party who can collect the data and perform some specific actions to preserve privacy (i.e. add noise of appropriate magnitude). The users themselves have to be responsible for securing their privacy by adding noise from some specific distribution, encrypting the noisy value and sending it to the Aggregator. This problem requires combination of both cryptographic and privacy preserving techniques. See that we have essentially two adversaries here. First is an external one, against whom we have to use cryptography to protect the communication between users and the Aggregator. This external adversary should not be able to decipher anything, including noisy sum of all data. On the other hand, the Aggregator himself is an adversary as well. This adversary, however, should be able to decrypt only the noisy sum (not the single user noisy values) and should not be able to compromise the privacy of any single user. The general notion behind Block Aggregation is to generate a random secret key sk_i for each of n users as well as an additional sk_0 given to the Aggregator, such that $\sum_{i=0}^{n} sk_i = 0$. Before sending the encrypted data, i-th user adds noise r_i coming from Diluted Geometric Distribution (Definition 2 in Sect. 2). We will denote the noisy data of i-th user by $\tilde{x}_i = x_i + r_i$. Namely, each user transmits $\mathrm{Enc}_{sk_i}(\tilde{x}_i)$ so that upon receiving all shares and having sk_0, the secret keys cancel out and the Aggregator is left with the desired noisy sum. One may easily note that as long as each user transmits its value, **AGG** may use sk_0 to decipher the sum. The symmetric geometric distribution $Geom(\alpha)$ can be viewed as a discrete version of Laplace distribution, which is widely used in differential privacy papers. Having discrete values is essential for the cryptography part of the protocol. The dilution parameter β is the probability that a specific user will add noise from $Geom(\alpha)$. This is done because, intuitively, we want at least one user to add a geometric noise, but we do not want too many of these noises to keep the necessary noise sufficiently small. The problem that occurred with so-called Block Aggregation is that whenever a single user fails to deliver their share (and what is really important – their sk_i), the blindings do not cancel out, hence making it impossible for the Aggregator to decipher the desired value.

Binary Protocol presented in [3] addresses the incompleteness of the data by arranging the users in a virtual binary tree. One may visualize each user as a leaf of a binary tree, with all the tree-nodes up to the root being virtual. The Aggregator is identified with an additional tree-node, which is located "above" the root and is connected only to the tree-root. In order to simulate the tree structure, the users and **AGG** are equipped with appropriate secret keys and generate random noises for each of the tree-layer, where layer is equivalent to the depth the tree-node is at, i.e., the first layer consists of root, second layer consists of two direct children of the root, and so on. Finally, at the $\lceil \log n \rceil + 1^{st}$ layer consists of the leaves. Finally, each user performs Block Aggregation protocol for each of the layers, i.e., they generate their block $\mathrm{Enc}_{sk_i}(\tilde{x}_i)$ for the $\lceil \log n \rceil + 1^{st}$ layer and their shares for larger blocks of higher layers. In each of the layers, the noise r_i is taken from a different distribution, namely β parameter for diluted geometric distribution is derived as follows: $\beta = \min\left(\frac{1}{|B|} \ln \frac{1}{\delta_0}, 1\right)$, where $|B|$ is the number of tree-nodes in the layer and $\delta_0 > 0$ is a privacy parameter. One may note that, the more tree-nodes in the layer, the blinding becomes sparser. If all users present their shares the problem is reduced to the original Block Aggregation. Namely, the Aggregator may decrypt the root-layer block, obtaining the sum of all the $\tilde{x}_i$ with the blinding canceled out. However, if at least one user $\mathbf{N}_i$ fails, all the blocks containing $\mathbf{N}_i$ will suffer the same issues as Block Aggregation with a missing user. Namely, large, uncanceled random disturbance. In order to provide the aggregation of the working users, the authors allow the Aggregator to find such a covering of the tree from the blocks of different layers that all the working users are covered, none of the failed users is included and that **AGG** is able to recover the result.

Binary Protocol provides security under computational differential privacy model and results in $\mathrm{O}\left(n \log n\right)$ communications exchanged in the network and guarantees $\tilde{\mathrm{O}}\left((\log n)^{\frac{3}{2}}\right)$ error. This notion hides significant constants. Nevertheless in a practical setting, those results are less satisfying than one would expect. The issues concerning the privacy and the resulting error are raised in Sect. 4.

4   Analysis of Chan et al.'s Protocol – The Magnitude of Error

In this section we will show that the error magnitude in Binary Protocol is significant for moderate number of participants. Note that in [3] the authors assumed that each user has data $x_i \in \{0, 1\}$, which means that the range of the sum of aggregated data is $[0, n]$. Thus, error of magnitude γn shall be regarded large already for moderate constant γ. They have also shown that the magnitude of error is $o(n)$ asymptotically. However, in practical applications we are also interested in performance of this protocol for moderate values of n, i.e. $n \leqslant 2^{14}$. We will show that for a reasonable range of values of the number of users n and number of failures κ the error is large (γn for some constant γ) with significant probability. Obviously, as the n increases, the Binary Protocol becomes better because of the asymptotic guarantees. However, our aim here is to show, that if the number of participants is at most moderate (i.e. 2^{12}) or the number of failures is significant (i.e. $\kappa = \log_2(n)$, $\kappa = \lfloor \frac{n}{2^6} \rfloor$) then the accuracy of Binary Protocol is too low to be used. Furthermore, if the number of users is quite small (i.e. 2^{10} or less), then even for $\kappa = 5$ the errors generated are unacceptably high.

We aim to show a precise magnitude of error in the Binary Protocol. To achieve this, we will use some subtler method than these presented by the authors of [3]. To support our analytic analysis we show results of simulations. Note that in [3] the authors described only simulations without failures, even though their protocol is specifically designed to handle failed users.

4.1 Analytical Approach

The size of error depends on the number of failed users and the way they are distributed amongst all participants. Let us fix n as the number of participants. Like the authors of [3], we assume for simplicity that n is a power of 2. Our reasoning can be however generalized for every n. We also assume that κ users have failed. We assume that these failed users are uniformly distributed amongst all participants, which seems to be reasonable in most scenarios. The error generated during the Binary Protocol is the sum of all noises in the aggregated blocks. Throughout this section we will use following notation, $\delta_0 = \frac{\delta}{\lfloor \log_2(n) \rfloor + 1}$, where δ is a privacy parameter. Also we have $\beta_i = \min\left(\frac{1}{|B_i|} \ln \frac{1}{\delta_0}, 1\right)$, where B_i is size of the node on ith level of the tree. Because we assumed that n is a power of 2, so the binary tree is full, then B_i is essentially the number of leaves being descendants of any node on ith level of the tree. In our analysis, first we show an exact formula for the expected value of the number of noises added by individual nodes. The exact formula is given in the following theorem.

Theorem 1. *Let Y be a random variable which denotes the number of noises added during the Binary Protocol. Let $\kappa > 0$ and fix n as the number of participants. Then, the expected value of random variable Y is given by the following formula:*

$$EY = n - \kappa + n \cdot \sum_{i=1}^{\log_2(n)-1} \left(\frac{\binom{n-\frac{n}{2^i}}{\kappa}}{\binom{n}{\kappa}} \cdot (\beta_i - \beta_{i+1}) \right),$$

where $\beta_i = \min\left(\frac{1}{|B_i|} \ln \frac{1}{\delta_0}, 1\right)$.

Proof of this theorem can be found in full version of our paper [6]. It is based on combinatorial and probabilistic techniques. Now we show a lower bound for this value for limited range of n. We present it in the following

Lemma 1. *Let $2^4 \leqslant n \leqslant 2^{21}$ and $\delta = 0.05$, then EY has a following lower bound:*

$$EY \geqslant n - \kappa - n \cdot \left(e^{-\frac{8\kappa}{n}} + \frac{\ln\left(\frac{\log_2(n)+1}{\delta}\right)}{8} \cdot \left(e^{-\frac{16\kappa}{n}} - e^{-\frac{8\kappa}{n}} \right) \right).$$

Note that if $n < 2^4$ then we have $\beta_i = 0$, which means that every remaining user has to add noise (even if there are no failures, i.e. $\kappa = 0$). There is no need to give a lower bound in that case, because then the number of noisy inputs is exactly $n - \kappa$. Note also that even though we fixed a specific δ that is used broadly in previous papers (including [3]), similar reasoning can be made for different values of δ.

We can use this bound to obtain a following

Corollary 1. *Fix $\delta = 0.05$. For $n \leqslant 2^{10}$ and $\kappa = \log_2(n)$, we have $EY \geqslant 0.1n$. Similarly, if $\kappa = \lfloor \frac{n}{2^6} \rfloor$, then for $2^6 \leqslant n \leqslant 2^{12}$ we have $EY \geqslant 0.16n$.*

This comes immediately from Lemma 1 and an observation that $\frac{EY}{n}$ is a decreasing function of n. After plugging the greatest value of n that is allowed by assumptions we obtain these bounds.

Having an exact formula and also a lower bound for the expected number of noises generated, we can calculate the error. Let us assume that we have m noises generated. Recall that each of them comes from symmetric geometric distribution $Geom(\alpha)$ with $\alpha > 1$, which is comprehensively described both in [1] and [3]. We denote the sum of all noises as Z. One can easily see that $EZ = 0$ due to symmetry of distribution. However the expected additional error i.e., $E|Z|$ might be, and we will show that it often is, quite large.

Theorem 2. *Consider Binary Protocol with fixed α and let m denote the number of noises generated. Then let Z be a random variable which denotes the value of generated noises. We have*

$$E|Z| = \int\limits_{0}^{\infty} \frac{4 \cdot a \cdot m \cdot \sin t \cdot (\alpha - 1)^{2m}}{t \cdot \pi \cdot (\alpha^2 - 2\alpha \cos t + 1)^{m+1}} dt.$$

The proof of this theorem is in Appendix of the full version of our paper [6]. It is based on techniques comprehensively described in [7]. We also show a lower bound for $E|Z|$ in a following

Lemma 2. *For fixed n and ϵ, which is a privacy parameter, and provided that $m = \gamma n$, for $\gamma \in [0, 1]$ we have*

$$E|Z| \geqslant c_{n,\epsilon} \cdot \sqrt{\gamma} \cdot \frac{\log_2(n) \cdot \sqrt{n}}{\epsilon \sqrt{\pi}} - 0.1,$$

where $c_{n,\epsilon}$ is a constant, which is at least 1.4 for moderate values of n and ϵ.

Having all useful theorems and lemmas we can obtain a following

Corollary 2. *Consider Binary Protocol for $\delta = 0.05$, $\epsilon = 0.5$, $n \leqslant 2^{10}$ and $\kappa = \log_2(n)$. Let $|Z|$ be the absolute value of all noises aggregated during this protocol. We have $E|Z| \geqslant 0.15 \cdot n$.*
Moreover, if we take $\kappa = \frac{n}{2^6}$ and $2^6 \leqslant n \leqslant 2^{12}$ we have $E|Z| \geqslant 0.12 \cdot n$.

This is an immediate result from Lemma 2, we can see that $\frac{E|Z|}{n}$ is a decreasing function of n, so it is enough to plug $n = 2^{10}$ into lower bound for $E|Z|$ for the first part of the corollary and $n = 2^{12}$ for the second part of the corollary.

This clearly shows that even if we consider the lower bound for the number of noises and their magnitude, the Binary Protocol is far from perfect for many realistic scenarios, i.e. when the number of participants is moderate. Even worse conclusions will be drawn in Subsect. 4.2, where we use the exact formulas given in Theorems 1 and 2 to numerically analyze the errors generated in this protocol.

4.2 Experimental Approach

In Subsect. 4.1 we gave both exact formulas and lower bounds for the number of noises generated and their sum. Note that the lower bounds are not very tight for many n. In this subsection we will show that the errors generated are, in fact, even larger. We will use the exact formulas to precisely calculate the errors numerically. First let us consider the case where $n \leqslant 2^{10}$, $\kappa = \lfloor \log_2(n) \rfloor$, and privacy parameters are $\epsilon = 0.5$, $\delta = 0.05$. See Fig. 1. It clearly shows that the error magnitude in Binary Protocol is, in fact, significantly greater than the lower bound given in Corollary 2. Now let $2^6 \leqslant n \leqslant 2^{12}$, $\kappa = \frac{n}{2^6}$ and privacy parameters stays the same. See Fig. 2. Again we can see that the error magnitude is unacceptably high, greater than $0.2n$. Note that the noise is independent from the data, so such error could be very problematic, especially if the sum of the real data is small (e.g. $o(n)$). In such case the noise could be greater than the data itself. We can also check how great the errors will be for constant value of $\kappa = 5$. See Fig. 3.

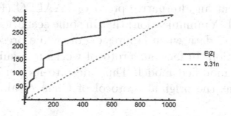

Fig. 1. Error magnitude in Binary Protocol with $\epsilon = 0.5$, $\delta = 0.05$ and $\kappa = \lfloor \log_2(n) \rfloor$.

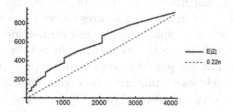

Fig. 2. Error magnitude in Binary Protocol with $\epsilon = 0.5$, $\delta = 0.05$ and $\kappa = \lfloor \frac{n}{2^6} \rfloor$.

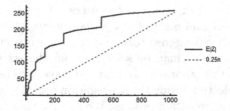

Fig. 3. Error magnitude in Binary Protocol with $\epsilon = 0.5$, $\delta = 0.05$ and $\kappa = 5$.

4.3   Some Other Shortcomings

Note that in [3], but also in numerous other papers concerning data aggregation with untrusted aggregator, we have a constant privacy parameter δ (i.e. $\delta = 0.05$). This significantly decreases the amount of noises generated, but is fundamentally incorrect in terms of classic differential privacy standards. Such approach allows choosing δ fraction of the database and revealing their data to everyone. In fact, the magnitude of δ should be $o(\frac{1}{n})$, where n is the number of users. This is necessary to ensure that the probability of leakage is negligible. More information about this can be found in [8]. Furthermore, we assumed that no participants collude with the aggregator. We used the same regime as in [1] with γ being a lower bound for fraction of non-colluding participants, the magnitude of added noises would be even greater.

5   Precise Aggregation Algorithm with Local Communication

In this part we present an alternative protocol PAALEC (Precise Aggregation Algorithm with Local Communication) that in some scenarios offers much better accuracy of aggregated data when failures occur, while preserving high level of users' privacy protection. In fact our protocol works in a substantially different way and for slightly modified model. Thus, despite its performance and accuracy that outperforms the original protocol of Chan et al., they are not fully comparable.

First of all, we assume that users may communicate (also in order to bypass the lower bound pointed out in [9]). Let us stress that the communication is limited to a small circle of "neighbors". The idea behind the presented construction is to take advantage of some natural structures emerging in distributed systems (e.g. social networks) wherein, apart from logical connections between each user and a server/aggregator there are also some direct links between individual users. Clearly, such model is not adequate for some real-life problems discussed in [3], for example in sensor fields with unidirectional communication. Thus there are applications where the original protocol from [3] is the only one possible.

5.1   Modified Model

We assume that the network consists of n users - $V = \{v_1, v_2, \ldots, v_n\}$ as well as the aggregator **AGG** and a set of $k < n$ *local aggregators* **Agg**$_1, \ldots,$ **Agg**$_k$. Please note that the local aggregators may be separate entities but without any significant changes they may be selected from the set of regular users V. The only issue with this approach is that we have to ensure that the local aggregator is either selected during the aggregation round or it cannot fail during **a single** execution of aggregation process. We assume that each user is assigned to **exactly one** local aggregator. We denote the set of nodes assigned to the local aggregator **Agg**$_i$ by V_i. An example of the network's topology is depicted in Fig. 4.

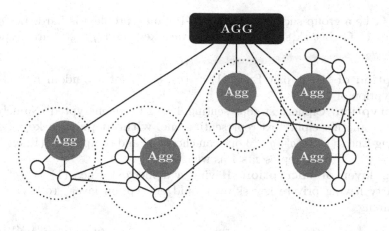

Fig. 4. Example of a clusterized network with global aggregator (**AGG**) and local aggregators (**Agg**) marked.

We can derive a graph $G = (V, E)$ from the network structure, where V are all the nodes and the set of edges is created based on the ability to establish communication (e.g., transmission range in a sensor network, friendship relation in a social network). Namely, the edge $\{v, v'\} \in E$ if and only if v and v' are *neighbors* and can communicate via a private channel. In our protocol we assume that each node can perform some basic cryptographic operations and has access to a source of randomness. By $N(v)$ we denote a set of such vertices v' of G that the edge $\{v, v'\} \in E$. Security of the protocol described in Sect. 5.3 depends on the structure of graph G, and how many parties the adversary can corrupt. Discussion on security of the protocol can be found in Sect. 5.4.

Adversary. The adversary may corrupt a subsets of users, local aggregators and the aggregator. It can read all messages the controlled parties sent or received. The aim of the adversary is to learn about individual contributions of uncorrupted users.

5.2 Building Blocks

Similarly to previous papers, for obtaining high level of data privacy we combine cryptographic techniques with data perturbation methods typical for research concentrated on differential privacy of databases.

The first technique we use in our protocol is a homomorphic encryption scheme based on original ElGamal construction enriched by some extra techniques introduced in [10]. More precisely, encrypted messages can be "aggregated" and re-encrypted. Moreover one can "add" an extra encryption layer to a given ciphertext, in such way that the message can be decrypted only using both respective keys. Clearly this operation preserves the homomorphic property.

Let $\mathbf{G}$ be a group such that the Diffie-Hellman problem is hard. Let g be a generator of $\mathbf{G}$. Let $\mathrm{sk}, \mathrm{sk}'$ be a some private keys and $g^{\mathrm{sk}}, g^{\mathrm{sk}'}$ are respective public keys.

Encryption of '1'. A pair $\mathrm{Enc}_{\mathrm{sk}}(1) = (g^r, g^{r \cdot \mathrm{sk}})$ for a random $r \in \mathbf{G}$ is an encryption of 1.

Re-encryption. Ciphertext representing 1 can be re-encrypted. Namely, one can get another ciphertext representing one, **without private key**. Namely having $\mathrm{Enc}_{\mathrm{sk}}(1) = (g^r, g^{r \cdot \mathrm{sk}})$ one can choose r' and compute $\mathrm{Re}(\mathrm{Enc}_{\mathrm{sk}}(1)) = (g^{r \cdot r'}, g^{r \cdot r' \cdot \mathrm{sk}})$ that represents 1 as well.

Adding layer of encryption. Having a ciphertext $\mathrm{Enc}_{\mathrm{sk}}(1) = (g^r, g^{r \cdot \mathrm{sk}})$ a party having private key sk' can "add encryption layer" to a ciphertext obtaining

$$\mathrm{Enc}_{\mathrm{sk}+\mathrm{sk}'}(1) = ((g^r)^{r'}, (g^{r \cdot \mathrm{sk}})^{r'} \cdot (g^r)^{r' \mathrm{sk}'}) = (g^{r \cdot r'}, g^{r \cdot r' \cdot (\mathrm{sk}+\mathrm{sk}')}).$$

Filling the ciphertext. Having $\mathrm{Enc}_{\mathrm{sk}}(1) = (g^r, g^{r \cdot \mathrm{sk}})$ one can compute $\mathrm{Enc}_{\mathrm{sk}+\mathrm{sk}'}(C) = (g^r, g^{r \cdot \mathrm{sk}} \cdot C)$.

Partial decryption. Having $\mathrm{Enc}_{\mathrm{sk}}(C) = (g^{r \cdot r'}, g^{r \cdot r' \cdot (\mathrm{sk}+\mathrm{sk}')}C)$ and a private key sk' one can "remove one layer of encryption" and obtain

$$\mathrm{Enc}_{\mathrm{sk}}(C) = \left(g^{r \cdot r'}, \frac{g^{r \cdot r' \cdot (\mathrm{sk}+\mathrm{sk}')}C}{(g^{r \cdot r'})^{\mathrm{sk}'}} \right) = (g^{r \cdot r'}, g^{r \cdot r' \cdot \mathrm{sk}}C).$$

For the sake of clarity we skip some technical details (i.e., choice of the group size, generators etc.) as well as full security discussion of this encryption scheme. Note that these are quite standard techniques used in many papers including [10,11].

Similarly to previous papers (including [1,3]) we utilize the following method: if we know that each user $v \in V$ has a value from an interval of moderate size $\xi_v \in [0, \Delta]$ then the sum of values of all ξ_v's cannot exceed $n\Delta$. Thus one can find a discreet logarithm for $g^{\sum_{v \in V} \xi_v}$ even if finding a discreet logarithm of g^r is not feasible if r is a random element of $\mathbf{G}$. Using Pollard's Rho method this can be completed in average time $O(\sqrt{n\Delta})$.

5.3   Protocol Description

During the protocol, we assume that the aggregator **AGG** has a private key sk, moreover each of the local aggregators **Agg**$_i$ has its own private key sk$_i$. We also assume that there is a public parameter g, that is a generator of some finite group $\mathbf{G}$, in which Diffie-Hellman problem is hard. By $\mathrm{Enc}_{\mathrm{sk}}(c)$ we denote the encryption structure introduced in Sect. 5.2. Let us assume that each user v has a private value ξ_v from the range $[0, \Delta]$. The final aim is to provide **AGG** the sum $\sum_{v \in V} \xi_v$ perturbed in such way that the privacy (expressed in terms of differential privacy) of all $v \in V$ is preserved. Clearly, the privacy of users can be endangered both by reveling the output as well as by collecting information about the aggregation process.

Setup

- **AGG** broadcasts to the local aggregators $\text{Enc}_{\text{sk}}(1)$.
- Each of the local aggregators $\textbf{Agg}_i$ constructs $\text{Enc}_{\text{sk}+\text{sk}_i}(1)$ and publishes it for all users from V_i.

The setup phase is performed only once during network's lifetime. Moreover if needed, each $\textbf{Agg}_i$ may provide a non-interactive proof that the operations were performed correctly and honestly [12,13].

Aggregation

Algorithm for node v

- For each node $v' \in N(v)$ generate a random value $x^v_{v'} \in \mathbf{G}$.
- Using a private channel send each value $x^v_{v'}$ to the appropriate neighbor v'.
- Having received all $x^{v'}_v$ from each of the neighbors, select random r_v from $Geom^\beta(\alpha)$ and calculate

$$c_v = \sum_{v' \in N(v)} x^{v'}_v - \sum_{v' \in N(v)} x^v_{v'} + r_v + \xi_v.$$

- Compute $\text{Re}(\text{Enc}_{\text{sk}+\text{sk}_i}(g^{c_v}))$ and send it to $\textbf{Agg}_i$.

An example of node's communication is shown in Fig. 5.

Algorithm for local aggregator $\textbf{Agg}_i$

- Having received $\text{Enc}_{\text{sk}+\text{sk}_i}(g^{c_v})$ from all nodes from V_i, compute

$$\text{Enc}_{\text{sk}}(g^{c_v}) = \left(g^{r_i}, \frac{g^{r_i(\text{sk}+\text{sk}_i)+c_v}}{g^{r_i \cdot \text{sk}_i}} \right).$$

This operations result in obtaining shares

$$\text{Enc}_{\text{sk}}(g^{c_{v_1}}) = (g^{r_{v_1}}, g^{r_{v_1} \cdot \text{sk}+c_{v_1}}), \ldots, \text{Enc}_{\text{sk}}(g^{c_{v_l}}) = (g^{r_{v_l}}, g^{r_{v_l} \cdot \text{sk}+c_{v_l}})$$

of all $l = |V_i|$ users from $|V_i|$.
- Compute

$$\text{Enc}_{\text{sk}}\left(g^{c_{v_1}+\cdots+c_{v_l}} \right) = \left(\prod_{i=1}^{l} g^{r_i}, \prod_{i=1}^{l} g^{r_i \text{sk}+c_{v_i}} \right) = \left(g^{\sum_{i=1}^{l} r_i}, g^{(\sum_{i=1}^{l} r_i)\text{sk}+\sum_{i=1}^{l} c_{v_i}} \right).$$

- Send the value $\text{Enc}_{\text{sk}}\left(g^{c_{v_1}+\cdots+c_{v_l}} \right)$ to the aggregator **AGG**.

Final aggregation

- Having received the aggregated values from each V_i, for each of those values **AGG** calculate $y_i = g^{\sum_{v \in V_i} c_v}$, using its private key sk for each $i = 1, \ldots, k$. Then compute

$$y = \prod_{i}^{k} y_i = \prod_{i} g^{\sum_{v \in V_i} c_{v_i}} = g^{\sum_{v \in V} c_{v_i}}.$$

- Then **AGG** compute discrete logarithm of y as a final (perturbed) value being a sum of all $\sum_{v \in V} \xi_v$.

Note that the protocol depends on two security parameters β and α. They strongly depend on the topology of the underlying graph. We discuss this issue in the next subsection.

5.4 Comparison and Analysis

In this section we outline the analysis of the presented aggregation protocol with respect to correctness, level of privacy provided and error of the result obtained by the aggregator. The analysis is slightly more complicated since the parameters of the protocol strongly depend on the underlying network. We argue however that they offer very good properties for wide classes of networks.

Correctness. First, let us look at the result obtained by the aggregator **AGG** in the last step of the protocol. This is a discrete logarithm of $g^{\sum_{v \in V} c_{v_i}}$. Let us observe that

$$
\sum_{v \in V} c_v = \sum_{v \in V} \left(\sum_{v' \in N(v)} x_v^{v'} - \sum_{v' \in N(v)} x_{v'}^v + r_v + \xi_v \right)
$$
$$
= \sum_{v \in V} \sum_{v' \in N(v)} x_v^{v'} - \sum_{v \in V} \sum_{v' \in N(v)} x_{v'}^v + \sum_{v \in V} \xi_v + \sum_{v \in V} r_v = \sum_{v \in V} \xi_v + \sum_{v \in V} r_v.
$$

The value $\sum_{v \in V} \xi_v$ is the exact sum of values kept by nodes and sum of all the noises $\sum_{v \in V} r_v$. This leads to two conclusions. First, the result is correct.

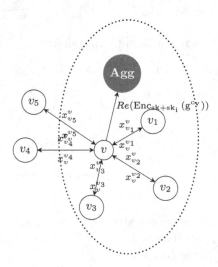

Fig. 5. An example of communication in a single aggregation round from a perspective of node v. The dotted line marks the set of nodes assigned to a single local aggregator **Agg**. Note that neighbors may have different local aggregators.

Second, retrieving the data using Pollard's Rho method (or even brute force method) is feasible since the absolute value of the first sum has to be smaller than $n\Delta$. One can easily see that the sum of added noises is of the magnitude $O(n)$ with high probability (as a sum of independent geometric distributions).

Privacy protection. We assume that the encryption scheme $\text{Enc}_{sk}()$ is *semantically secure*. In particular after re-encryption operation one cannot retrieve any non-trivial information about the plaintext without the private key sk possibly except some negligible probability $\eta(\lambda)$ with respect to the key-length λ or some other security parameters. In particular, in our protocol, the local aggregator $\textbf{AGG}_i$ cannot learn the contributions sent to $\textbf{AGG}_j$ for $i \neq j$ without access to keys sk_j and sk.

For the simplicity of analysis of the privacy protection let us consider the simplest case when $k = 1$, i.e. there is only one aggregator. In such case we may assume $\textbf{AGG}_1 = \textbf{AGG}$. Let $V^H \subset V$ be the set of uncompromised users. Note that all neighboring users exchange a purely random values $x_v^{v'}$'s that finally cancel-out, however as long as they remain unknown to the adversary, they perfectly obfuscate the results sent to the aggregator (exactly in the same manner as the one-time pad cipher). This can be easily adopted to our protocol to get the following fact.

Fact 2. *Let us assume that the adversary can control* $\textbf{AGG}$ *and a subset of users* $V \backslash V^H$. *Let* S *be a connected component of the subgraph of* $\mathcal{G} = (V, E)$ *induced by the subset* V^H. *Then, the adversary can learn nothing but* $\sum_{v \in S}(\xi_v + r_v)$ *about the values* ξ_v's *from the execution of PAALEC for any* $v \in V^H$.

Theorem 3. *Let us assume that PAALEC with parameter* $\alpha = \exp(\frac{\epsilon}{\Delta})$ *is executed in the network represented by a graph* $\mathcal{G} = (V, E)$ *and* $\mathcal{G}'$ *is a subgraph of* $\mathcal{G}$ *induced by the set of uncompromised users* V^H. *Moreover we assume that each user* v *contributes a value* $\xi_v \in [0, \Delta]$.

If in each connected component S *of* $\mathcal{G}'$ *there is a user* s, *such that its added noise* r *is taken from* $Geom(\exp(\frac{\epsilon}{\Delta}))$, *then PAALEC preserves computational* $(\varepsilon, 0)$-*differential privacy.*

Proof. Let $\Xi = \sum_{s \in S} \xi_s$ and let Ξ' be the same sum with changed a single value ξ_s. By the assumption about the range of the aggregated values we get $|\Xi' - \Xi| \leq \Delta$. Let r be a random variable taken from the symmetric geometric distribution $Geom(\exp(\frac{\epsilon}{\Delta}))$. From Fact 1 we know that $Pr[\Xi + r = k]$ may differ from $Pr[\Xi' + r = k]$ by at most a multiplicative factor $\exp(\epsilon)$. However, from Fact 2 we know that the adversary may learn nothing more than the sum of all values from the component S. To complete the proof it is enough to recall that we assumed that probability of gaining some other knowledge if weak parameters of the cipher are chosen is at most negligible function $\eta(\lambda)$.

From this theorem follows next corollary.

Corollary 3. *If PAALEC is executed on a graph such that a subgraph induced by the set of uncompromised users* V^H *is connected and with probability at least*

$1 - \delta$ *at least one uncompromised users adds its value* r *from* $Geom(\exp(\frac{\epsilon}{\Delta}))$ *then PAALEC computationally preserves* (ε, δ)*-differential privacy.*

Translating into real terms Theorem 3 with Corollary 3 say if the connections between honest users are dense enough and we can somehow guarantee that at least one honest node adds the noise, the system is secure. The core of the problem is judge if a real-world networks are dense enough and what parameters of adding noise are sufficient. This problem is discussed in the next paragraph.

Accuracy. The level of accuracy and security in this protocol strongly depends on the graph topology and chosen security parameters. We will consider a random graph, where each of possible edge is independently added with probability p. Moreover the adversary controls up to $n - m$ randomly chosen users.

Theorem 4. *Let us consider a random network with* n *nodes. Each of possible* $\binom{n}{2}$ *connections (edges) is independently added to the network with probability* $p \geq \frac{8 \log n}{n}$. *Let* S *be a subgraph induced by a subset of at least* $m \geq n/2$ *randomly chosen nodes. Then* S *is connected with probability at least* $1 - 1/n$.

Note that the presented model boils down to the classic Erdős-Rényi model [14]. For the sake of completeness and to get explicit constants we present the proof in the appendix of the full version of our paper [6].

From Theorem 4 we learn that a "typical" network of n nodes with random connections such that the average number of neighbors is $8 \log n = \Theta(\log n)$ is dense enough even if the adversary is able to compromise as much as $n/2$ nodes.

If we have guaranteed at least $n/2$ honest (uncompromised and working) nodes one may note that the probability that none of them adds the noise is at least $(1-\beta)^{n/2}$. To have $(1-\beta)^{n/2} \leq \delta$ one needs to have β such that $\log(1-\beta) \leq \frac{2 \log \delta}{n}$. Since $\log(1+x) \leq x$ for $x > -1$ it is enough to use $\beta \geq \frac{2\log(1/\delta)}{n}$. Clearly the expected error cannot exceed $2\sqrt{\log(1/\delta)}$ for $\beta = \frac{2\log(1/\delta)}{n}$. Using standard methods one can also show that the expected error is concentrated.

Remarks and Extensions. We proved that the proposed protocol guarantees a very good accuracy even facing a massive failures and compromising of nodes. Half of nodes may failed or cooperate with the adversary (In fact this result can be generalized to any constant fraction of users). The analysis and the model can be relaxed/extended in many directions. One can instantly observe that the analysis can be extended for smaller δ for the price of moderate increasing of the expected noise. Note that the value of δ set to a celebrated magic constant 0.05 seems to be definitely too big for practice. Indeed, this implies that one out of each 20 may loos its privacy.

We believe that this approach can be useful for other graphs-including those representing social networks. Note that if a graph guarantees a specific level of privacy then more dense graph (with some added edges) offers at least the same level of privacy. Thus it is enough if each users adds something like $\Theta(\log n)$ "randomly" chosen neighbors to protect the privacy in any network.

Note that our protocol is not immune against an adversarial nodes that sends incoherent random data. To the best of our knowledge all protocols of this type (including [1,3]) are prone to so called *contaminating* attacks. To mitigate this problem as in other cases one may apply orthogonal methods presented in [15].

6   Previous and Related Work

Data aggregation in distributed networks has been thoroughly studied due to practical importance of such protocols. Measuring the target environment, aggregating data and rising alarm are arguably three most important functionalities of distributed sensing networks, and with the increased number of personal mobile devices, the aggregation becomes of greatest interest among the three. Exemplary protocols that do not address security nor privacy may be found in [16,17], with the latter being often presented as a model aggregation algorithm.

There are several settings considering data aggregation. They differ in both, the abilities and constraints of the nodes performing the aggregation, as well as the issues that the algorithm addresses. Some of the adversities that may be addressed include data confidentiality (i.e., protecting the data from disclosure), privacy of the nodes (inability to learn exact values of each node), node failure and spontaneous node joining the network as well as data poisoning (i.e., injecting malicious data by the adversary that allows them to significantly influence the outcome of the algorithm or learning more information about the execution that they would not gain when following the protocol honestly).

Our paper follows the model considered in [3], where the nodes have constrained abilities and their energy pool is limited. Authors present a privacy preserving aggregation protocol that assumes malicious aggregator, moreover they claim tolerance for failures and joins, hence addressing majority of the issues. Similar problems that focus on narrower range of properties have been also studied in [1,2]. In [18,19] authors present some aggregation protocols that preserve privacy, however they do not consider dynamic changes inside of the network. The latter also considers data poisoning attacks, however the authors do not provide rigid proofs. A different approach was presented in [20,21], where the authors present a framework for some aggregation functions and consider the confidentiality of the result, however leaving nodes' privacy out of scope of their papers. On the other hand, there is bulk of research that focuses on fault tolerance that leaves privacy and security issues either out of scope or just mentioned, not keeping it as a priority. Examples of such work may be found in [22–24]. In [9] the authors present an asymptotic lower bound on the error of the aggregation that preserves privacy, showing that in order to reduce the errors, one has to resign from perfect privacy and focus rather on computational variant of the privacy preservation.

An example of work on secure data aggregation in stronger models may be found in [25,26], where the authors consider data aggregation in a smart grid. Another fruitful branch of the research on data aggregation considers data aggregation in vehicular ad hoc networks (VANET). The research in this field is motivated by the increasing number of "smart-cars" with internal computational unit. One of the first works addressing this issue was [27–29]. A practical scenario for data aggregation in VANET has been presented in [30]. The security issue in VANET data-aggregation has been mentioned in [31,32]. A survey of the known protocols has been performed in [33]. One may note that retrieving encrypted or blinded data by one entity, that requires cooperation of others is similar to cryptographic secret-sharing. Some of the most important work on secret sharing may be found in [34,35], however in our paper we draw from the Universal Re-encryption method presented in [10].

7 Conclusions

In our paper we provided a precise analysis of accuracy of the data aggregation protocol presented in [3]. We have shown that in many cases its accuracy may not be sufficient even if the number of faults is moderate. We constructed another fault tolerant, privacy preserving aggregation protocol that offers much better precision. In order to obtain this, we allowed a moderate communication between the nodes. This assumption deviates from the classic model.

We believe that our approach and security model is justified in many real-life scenarios, however much research is left to be done in the field. First of all, our protocol as well as all other similar protocols we are aware of, is not immune against so called data poisoning attack. Another problem is finding solution for statistics other than sum. Authors of aggregating schemes usually limit the scope of their work to sum, product and average of the values of all nodes in the network. In many cases we need however other statistics, e.g. minimum or the median. We suppose that finding more general statistics with guaranteed privacy of individuals is possible using methods explored in e-voting protocols. They however are very demanding in terms of required resources. From the theoretical point of view the important question is about the possible trade-offs between privacy protection, volume of communication and possible accuracy of the results of aggregation.

References

1. Shi, E., Chow, R., Hubert Chan, T-H., Song, D., Rieffel, E.: Privacy-preserving aggregation of time-series data. In: NDSS (2011)
2. Rastogi, V., Nath, S.: Differentially private aggregation of distributed time-series with transformation and encryption. In: Proceedings of the 2010 ACM SIGMOD International Conference on Management of Data, SIGMOD 2010, pp. 735–746. ACM, New York (2010)
3. Chan, T.-H.H., Shi, E., Song, D.: Privacy-preserving stream aggregation with fault tolerance. In: Keromytis, A.D. (ed.) FC 2012. LNCS, vol. 7397, pp. 200–214. Springer, Heidelberg (2012)
4. Mironov, I., Pandey, O., Reingold, O., Vadhan, S.: Computational differential privacy. In: Halevi, S. (ed.) CRYPTO 2009. LNCS, vol. 5677, pp. 126–142. Springer, Heidelberg (2009)

5. Dwork, C., McSherry, F., Nissim, K., Smith, A.: Calibrating noise to sensitivity in private data analysis. In: Halevi, S., Rabin, T. (eds.) TCC 2006. LNCS, vol. 3876, pp. 265–284. Springer, Heidelberg (2006)
6. Grining, K., Klonowski, M., Syga, P.: Practical fault-tolerant data aggregation. CoRR abs/1602.04138 (2016). http://arxiv.org/abs/1602.04138
7. Pinelis, I.: Characteristic function of the positive part of a random variable and related results, with applications. Stat. Probab. Lett. 106, 281–286 (2015)
8. Dwork, C., Roth, A.: The algorithmic foundations of differential privacy. Found. Trends Theor. Comput. Sci. 9(3–4), 211–407 (2014)
9. Chan, T.H.H., Shi, E., Song, D.: Optimal lower bound for differentially private multi-party aggregation. IACR Cryptology ePrint Archive 2012 373 informal publication (2012)
10. Golle, P., Jakobsson, M., Juels, A., Syverson, P.F.: Universal re-encryption for mixnets. In: Okamoto, T. (ed.) CT-RSA 2004. LNCS, vol. 2964, pp. 163–178. Springer, Heidelberg (2004)
11. Gomułkiewicz, M., Klonowski, M., Kutyłowski, M.: Onions based on universal re-encryption – anonymous communication immune against repetitive attack. In: Lim, C.H., Yung, M. (eds.) WISA 2004. LNCS, vol. 3325, pp. 400–410. Springer, Heidelberg (2005)
12. Goldreich, O., Oren, Y.: Definitions and properties of zero-knowledge proof systems. J. Cryptology 7(1), 1–32 (1994)
13. Blum, M., Feldman, P., Micali, S.: Non-interactive zero-knowledge and its applications. In: Proceedings of the Twentieth Annual ACM Symposium on Theory of Computing, STOC 1988, pp. 103–112. ACM, New York (1988)
14. Janson, S., Luczak, T., Rucinski, A.: Random Graphs. Wiley Series in Discrete Mathematics and Optimization. Wiley, New York (2011)
15. Chan, H., Perrig, A., Przydatek, B., Song, D.: Sia: Secure information aggregation in sensor networks. J. Comput. Secur. 15(1), 69–102 (2007)
16. Heinzelman, W.R., Kulik, J., Balakrishnan, H.: Adaptive protocols for information dissemination in wireless sensor networks. In: Proceedings of the 5th Annual ACM/IEEE International Conference on Mobile Computing and Networking, MobiCom 1999, pp. 174–185. ACM, New York (1999)
17. Madden, S., Franklin, M.J., Hellerstein, J.M., Hong, W.: Tag: A tiny aggregation service for ad-hoc sensor networks. SIGOPS Oper. Syst. Rev. 36(SI), 131–146 (2002)
18. PDA: privacy-preserving data aggregation in wireless sensor networks. In: INFOCOM 2007. 26th IEEE International Conference on Computer Communications. IEEE (2007)
19. He, W., Liu, X., Nguyen, H., Nahrstedt, K.: A cluster-based protocol to enforce integrity and preserve privacy in data aggregation. In: ICDCS Workshops, pp. 14–19. IEEE Computer Society (2009)
20. Roy, S., Conti, M., Setia, S., Jajodia, S.: Secure data aggregation in wireless sensor networks: Filtering out the attacker's impact. Trans. Info. For. Sec. 9(4), 681–694 (2014)
21. Papadopoulos, S., Kiayias, A., Papadias, D.: Exact in-network aggregation with integrity and confidentiality. IEEE Trans. Knowl. Data Eng. 24(10), 1760–1773 (2012)
22. Feng, Y., Tang, S., Dai, G.: Fault tolerant data aggregation scheduling with local information in wireless sensor networks. Tsinghua Sci. Technol. 16(5), 451–463 (2011)

23. Jhumka, A., Bradbury, M., Saginbekov, S.: Efficient fault-tolerant collision-free data aggregation scheduling for wireless sensor networks. J. Parallel Distrib. Comput. **74**(1), 1789–1801 (2014)

24. Larrea, M., Martin, C., Astrain, J.: Hierarchical and fault-tolerant data aggregation in wireless sensor networks. In: 2nd International Symposium on Wireless Pervasive Computing, ISWPC 2007 (2007)

25. Jawurek, M., Kerschbaum, F.: Fault-tolerant privacy-preserving statistics. In: Fischer-Hübner, S., Wright, M. (eds.) PETS 2012. LNCS, vol. 7384, pp. 221–238. Springer, Heidelberg (2012)

26. Rottondi, C., Verticale, G., KrauÃ§, C.: Distributed privacy-preserving aggregation of metering data in smart grids. IEEE J. Sel. Areas Commun. (JSAC) - JSAC Smart Grid Commun. Ser. **31**(7), 1342–1354 (2013)

27. Hermann.: SOTIS - a self-organizing traffic information system. In: Proceedings of the IEEE Vehicular Technology Conference Spring, pp. 2442–2246 (2003)

28. Nadeem, T., Dashtinezhad, S., Liao, C., Iftode, L.: Trafficview: Traffic data dissemination using car-to-car communication. SIGMOBILE Mob. Comput. Commun. Rev. **8**(3), 6–19 (2004)

29. Wischhof, L., Ebner, A., Rohling, H.: Information dissemination in Self-Organizing intervehicle networks. IEEE Trans. Intell. Transp. Syst. **6**(1), 90–101 (2005)

30. Caliskan, M., Graupner, D., Mauve, M.: Decentralized discovery of free parking places. In: Proceedings of the 3rd International Workshop on Vehicular Ad Hoc Networks, VANET 2006, pp. 30–39. ACM, New York (2006)

31. Antolino Rivas, D., Barceló-Ordinas, J.M., Guerrero Zapata, M., Morillo-Pozo, J.D.: Security on VANETs: Privacy, misbehaving nodes, false information and secure data aggregation. J. Netw. Comput. Appl. **34**(6), 1942–1955 (2011)

32. Han, Q., Du, S., Ren, D., Zhu, H.: SAS: A secure data aggregation scheme in vehicular sensing networks. In: Proceedings of IEEE International Conference on Communications, ICC 2010, Cape Town, South Africa, pp. 23–27. IEEE ,1–5 May 2010

33. Mohanty, S., Jena, D.: Secure data aggregation in vehicular-adhoc networks: A survey. Procedia Technol. **6**, 922–929 (2012). 2nd International Conference on Communication, Computing and Security [ICCCS-2012]

34. Benaloh, J.C.: Secret sharing homomorphisms: keeping shares of a secret secret. In: Odlyzko, A.M. (ed.) CRYPTO 1986. LNCS, vol. 263, pp. 251–260. Springer, Heidelberg (1987)

35. Beimel, A.: Secret-sharing schemes: a survey. In: Chee, Y.M., Guo, Z., Ling, S., Shao, F., Tang, Y., Wang, H., Xing, C. (eds.) IWCC 2011. LNCS, vol. 6639, pp. 11–46. Springer, Heidelberg (2011)

Accelerating Homomorphic Computations on Rational Numbers

Angela Jäschke[✉] and Frederik Armknecht

University of Mannheim, Mannheim, Germany
{jaeschke,armknecht}@uni-mannheim.de

Abstract. Fully Homomorphic Encryption (FHE) schemes are conceptually very powerful tools for outsourcing computations on confidential data. However, experience shows that FHE-based solutions are not sufficiently efficient for practical applications yet. Hence, there is a huge interest in improving the performance of applying FHE to concrete use cases. What has been mainly overlooked so far is that not only the FHE schemes themselves contribute to the slowdown, but also the choice of data encoding. While FHE schemes usually allow for homomorphic executions of algebraic operations over finite fields (often $\mathbb{Z}_2$), many applications call for different algebraic structures like signed rational numbers. Thus, before an FHE scheme can be used at all, the data needs to be mapped into the structure supported by the FHE scheme.

We show that the choice of the encoding can already incur a significant slowdown of the overall process, which is independent of the efficiency of the employed FHE scheme. We compare different methods for representing signed rational numbers and investigate their impact on the effort needed for processing encrypted values. In addition to forming a new encoding technique which is superior under some circumstances, we also present further techniques to speed up computations on encrypted data under certain conditions, each of independent interest. We confirm our results by experiments.

Keywords: Confidential machine learning · Fully homomorphic encryption · Encoding · Implementation

1 Introduction

Fully Homomorphic Encryption (FHE) is a very promising field of research because it allows arbitrary computations on encrypted data. This means that data can be outsourced securely without sacrificing functionality, as any operation one would like to perform on the data can also be performed on the encrypted data by a third party without divulging information. With a powerful enough encryption scheme, this third party may even apply its own proprietary algorithm, like a machine learning algorithm, to the encrypted data such that the result divulges nothing about the algorithm that was applied - this is the setting we will assume. While multiparty computation also offers this kind of

© Springer International Publishing Switzerland 2016
M. Manulis et al. (Eds.): ACNS 2016, LNCS 9696, pp. 405–423, 2016.
DOI: 10.1007/978-3-319-39555-5_22

confidential computation, it requires frequent interaction between the involved parties, which seems unfortunate for the goal of outsourcing computation. For this reason, we instead focus on FHE, which allows a non-interactive solution. Unfortunately, FHE-based solutions today are still very slow and thus not very practical. Since a ciphertext can become undecryptable if too many consecutive multiplications are computed, multiplicative depth is often key in FHE computations. In so-called leveled FHE schemes, one can adjust the encryption scheme to support a predetermined multiplicative depth, where the scheme becomes slower the larger the depth is. Thus, minimizing depth is one of our goals in this paper. Another approach for handling the problems that come with consecutive multiplications, which we opted for because of very large depths in our use cases, is called bootstrapping. Here, the ciphertext is "cleaned up" after multiplication, but this operation takes very long and constitutes the bottleneck when used. Hence, minimizing the total number of multiplications is another of our goals.

Because of these efficiency problems, there is currently much research on improving the efficiency of the schemes themselves on the one hand, and on designing algorithms that are particularly suited to FHE, i.e., through minimal multiplicative depth, on the other hand. While this is certainly a valuable contribution for some use cases, we feel that in general the algorithms one wants to perform on the data are predetermined and not up for discussion. At first glance, this might seem to imply that there is little potential for improvement apart from improving the schemes themselves, but we show that this is indeed not the case.

Generally, suppose one has an FHE scheme $\mathcal{E} = (\mathsf{Gen}, \mathsf{Enc}, \mathsf{Dec})$ with plaintext space $\mathcal{M}$ and ciphertext space $\mathcal{C}$, and there is a function $g : \mathcal{M}^z \to \mathcal{M}$ for some $z \in \mathbb{N}$. Then a Fully Homomorphic Encryption scheme promises that there exists a corresponding function $g^* : \mathcal{C}^z \to \mathcal{C}$ with

$$\mathsf{Dec}(\mathsf{sk}, g^*(\mathsf{Enc}(\mathsf{pk}, m_1), \ldots, \mathsf{Enc}(\mathsf{pk}, m_z))) = g(m_1, \ldots, m_z).$$

However, plaintext spaces for encryption schemes are usually some finite field $GF(p^d)$ for some prime p and power d, so if we want to work with elements from a different structure S (like the rational numbers), we must first map them[1] to the plaintext space using an encoding $\pi : S \to \mathcal{M}^k$ and then perform a function on the plaintext values that emulates the function on S. For a better understanding, suppose we have an encryption scheme like above. Then, if we want to evaluate a function $f : S^n \to S$ on encrypted data, we must first turn f into a function $g : (\mathcal{M}^k)^n \to \mathcal{M}^k$ on the plaintext space (where $\mathcal{M}^k$ emulates S) and then execute the function $g^* : (\mathcal{C}^k)^n \to \mathcal{C}^k$ that corresponds to g. This is illustrated in Fig. 1.

As it turns out, there is often no unique function g for a given function f, but instead several different ones which depend on the chosen encoding function π. This also means that the most we can aim for in terms of efficiency in evaluating a function f on encrypted data is not f itself, but rather its emulation g on

---

[1] For example, if $S = \{x \in \mathbb{Z} | 0 \leq x \leq 7\}$ (i.e., numbers representable by 3 bits) but the plaintext space of the encryption scheme is only $\mathcal{M} = \{0, 1\}$, we could map $\pi : S \to \mathcal{M}^3$.

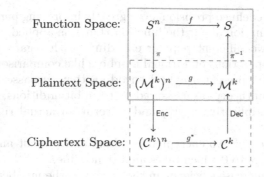

Fig. 1. Steps in homomorphic evaluation

the plaintext space. As it turns out, the increase here is not negligible: While the Perceptron, which we evaluate in Sect. 6.3 on encrypted data, runs almost instantaneously (roughly 0.004 s) for ten rounds when computing on unencrypted rational numbers, the evaluation of the same algorithm emulated on the plaintext space (i.e., still unencrypted) takes over 120 s for the same parameters even with our most efficient encoding in the plaintext space. This shows that though largely ignored until now, the overhead that comes from switching from the function f to g can be substantial and must equally be addressed to make FHE applications as efficient as possible. Thus, while previous work on making computations with FHE more efficient has focused primarily on the area inside the dashed red rectangle in Fig. 1, we investigate how to improve efficiency through the right choice of π and subsequently g, represented by the solid green rectangle. Motivated by the idea of outsourcing actual data and running existing algorithms on it, we face the challenges of encoding rational numbers (as opposed to elements of finite fields or unsigned integers) and of incorporating basic operations like addition, multiplication and comparison, which are needed for many popular algorithms.

1.1 Our Contribution

We address the above challenges and try to minimize total number of multiplications (and the multiplicative depth) of g through appropriate choices in π. We also examine some further optimizations which increase efficiency under certain assumptions and are of independent interest. As a concrete application, we apply our results to two use cases from machine learning, the Perceptron and the Linear Means Classifier, and see that the right choice of π can make a significant difference in terms of multiplicative depth, total number of multiplications, and in terms of runtime, for which we encrypted the data with the HElib library. To this end:

– We present a new method for working with encrypted rational numbers by solving the problem that the number of digits of precision doubles with each multiplication. We show how to remove the extra digits and bring the number back down to a predefined precision level, greatly improving performance without leaking information about the function that was applied.

- We investigate two different popular encodings with regard to efficiency in emulating basic operations on rational numbers like comparison, addition and multiplication, and present a hybrid encoding that surpasses the two traditional ones both in theory (as measured by total bit additions, multiplications and required multiplicative depth) and in terms of actual runtime for large sizes.
- We the comparison of two encrypted numbers and present an easier way for comparing numbers to 0 which takes almost no time.
- We show how to increase efficiency in the case that the numbers are bounded, like in real-world applications where values lie in some known range.
- We confirm our results by implementing the Perceptron, a fundamental algorithm in machine learning, and running it using the different encodings, as well as a polynomial like that used for Linear Means Classification.

As a quick preview, consider Fig. 2, which shows theoretical bounds on the number of bitwise additions and multiplications as well as extrapolated runtime needed to apply a Linear Means Classifier with each of the three encodings for different numbers of features. We can see that our new hybrid encoding mechanism is superior in all three aspects, making it an attractive choice.

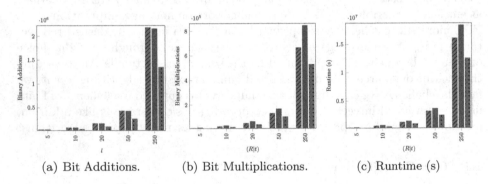

(a) Bit Additions.　　　(b) Bit Multiplications.　　　(c) Runtime (s)

Fig. 2. Bounds for the number of bitwise additions and multiplications as well as runtime for evaluating Linear Means Classifier with l features of length 30 for different l using Two's Complement • (lines), Sign-Magnitude • (solid) and Hybrid Encoding • (dotted) (Color figure online)

1.2 Outline

We start by giving an overview of related work in Sect. 2. In Sect. 3, we give some background on Fully Homomorphic Encryption and the challenges faced when working with rational numbers, as well as on the two encodings we use. In Sect. 4, we show how to emulate the addition, multiplication and comparison of encoded numbers using just binary additions and multiplications and analyze complexity. Section 5 presents different ways of accelerating computations on encrypted data, and Sect. 6 gives some motivation and necessary background on machine learning before using two algorithms from this field to demonstrate the effects of our improvements. Lastly, Sect. 7 gives our conclusion and an insight into future work.

2   Related Work

While encryption schemes that allow one type of operation on ciphertexts are well understood and have a comprehensive security characterization [4], Fully Homomorphic Encryption, which allows both unlimited additions and multiplications, was only first solved in [19]. Since then, numerous other schemes have been developed, for example [9,10,13,14,16,21,26]. An overview can be found in [3]. There have been several works concerning actual implementation of FHE, like [20] (homomorphically evaluating the AES circuit), [7] (predictive analysis on encrypted medical data), or [22] (machine learning on encrypted data), and there are two publicly available libraries [1,18]. [24] discusses whether FHE will ever be practical and gives a number of possible applications, including encrypted machine learning. Most recently, two publications regarding encoding rational numbers for FHE have appeared, illustrating what an important topic this is: [12] examines encoding rational numbers through continued fractions (restricted to positive rationals and evaluating linear multivariate polynomials), whereas [15] focuses on most efficiently embedding the computation into a single large plaintext space. Another work that explores similar ideas as [15] and also offers an implementation is [17].

While the idea of being able to privately evaluate machine learning algorithms is certainly intriguing, the overwhelming majority of work in this area considers multiparty computation, which requires interaction between the client and the server during computation and is thus a different model. Examples include [8,25,28], and works like [23,27] concern themselves with efficiency measures and circuit optimizations specific to multiparty computation. Another line of research regarding confidential machine learning, e.g. [7] and again [8], focuses on a scenario where the model being computed and/or evaluated is publicly known - a scenario we explicitly exclude. Other work like [11] restricts itself to unsigned integers, making all involved circuits much less complex. Work like [5] considers recommender systems, but in a scenario which becomes insecure if too many fresh encryptions are available. Closest to our work is [22], which restricts itself to machine learning algorithms like the Linear Means Classifier and Fishers Linear Discriminant Classifier, which can be expressed as polynomials of low degree, and focuses on the classification, not the derivation of the model. Their encoding of input data is also restricted to functions with few multiplications.

We stress that until now, all approaches dealing with rational numbers either restrict computations to positive integers, or the multiplicative depth of the computation must be know beforehand. Our approach is the first to actually tackle the problem of computing on rational numbers with no further assumptions, and offers other improvements if some assumptions can be made.

3   Background

3.1   FHE and Efficiency Metrics

Fully Homomorphic Encryption (FHE) describes a class of encryption schemes that allow arbitrary operations on encrypted data. This would, in theory, enable outsourcing of encrypted data to an untrusted cloud service provider, who could still perform any operations the user wishes. This means that we can protect privacy (as opposed to uploading the data in unencrypted form) while maintaining functionality (as opposed to uploading data encrypted under conventional schemes). Unfortunately, FHE today it is still rather slow, although huge advancements have been made in the last six years.

Because of this, one of our measures for efficiency is the number of bit additions and multiplications performed, as this would translate directly into the number of homomorphic additions and multiplications performed if the data were encrypted. Note that in schemes today, homomorphic multiplication tends to be computationally more expensive than addition.

In our analysis of computational effort, we also include the multiplicative depth: Many publications today use *Leveled Fully Homomorphic Encryption*, which is related to Fully Homomorphic Encryption in that arbitrary functions f can be performed on the encrypted data, but the multiplicative depth of f must be known beforehand, and efficiency of the encryption scheme decreases as this number increases. Multiplicative depth measures how many consecutive multiplications are performed. For example, the polynomial $x_1 \cdot x_2 + x_1 \cdot x_3 + x_2 \cdot x_3$ has 3 multiplications in total, but a multiplicative depth of only 1. These leveled schemes can be more efficient than pure FHE schemes for small depths, but if more than the allowed number of consecutive multiplications are performed, decryption may return the wrong result. To this end, we include multiplicative depth in our analysis and aim to minimize it as one of our goals. We would, however, like to point out that if one uses bootstrapping, as we did in our implementations, depth becomes less of an issue and the total number of multiplications is the main factor determining runtime.

3.2   From Unsigned Integers to Rationals of Arbitrary Precision

In previous work (e.g. [6], see also Sect. 2), rational numbers have often been approximated by multiplying with a power of 10 and rounding, but note that when multiplying two rational numbers with k bits of precision, we obtain a number with $2k$ bits of precision (whereas addition does not change the precision). If we are working on unencrypted numbers, we might just round to obtain k bits of precision again, or we could truncate (truncation after k bits yields the same accuracy as rounding to $k-1$ bits). However, things become more difficult if we will be operating on encrypted data, as rounding is generally not possible here and thus these extra bits of precision accumulate. To see this, suppose a precision of k digits is required. One would usually multiply the rational number with 10^k and round (or truncate) to the nearest integer, which is then encoded and encrypted. Dividing the decrypted decoded number by 10^k again yields the rounded rational. However, the problem of doubling precision with multiplication is prevalent here. Consider what would happen if we were to multiply two such numbers: Suppose we have two rational numbers a and b that we would like to encode as integers a' and b' with k digits of precision, so we get $a' = a \cdot 10^k$ and $b' = b \cdot 10^k$ (rounded to the nearest integer). Multiplying a' and b', we get $c'' = a' \cdot b' = a \cdot 10^k \cdot b \cdot 10^k = (a \cdot b) \cdot 10^{2k}$. Thus, having reversed the encoding, the obtained value c'' must be divided by 10^{2k}. This is a problem because we cannot remove the extra bits by dividing by 10^k, so the party performing the algorithm must now divulge what power of 10 to divide the obtained result by. This leaks information about the multiplicative depth of the function used and thus constitues a privacy breach for the computing party. Additionally, there is also the problem during computation that the sizes of the encoded numbers will increase substantially.

To solve this problem, we propose the following approach: Instead of scaling by a power of 10, we multiply by a power of 2 and truncate to obtain an integer that we will encode in binary fashion, so that we can later encrypt each bit separately. This eliminates the above problem: Multiplying two numbers a' and b' with k bits of precision still yields $c'' = (a \cdot b) \cdot 2^{2k}$, but since we are encoding bit by bit, dividing by 2^k and truncating corresponds to merely deleting the last k (encrypted) bits of the product. Thus, the party performing the computations can bring the product c'' back down to the required precision after every step by discarding the last k bits and thus obtaining $c' = a \cdot b \cdot 2^k$, meaning that the party which holds the data must always divide the decoded result by 2^k no matter what operations were applied. This has the benefit of not only hiding the data from the computing party, but also hiding the function from the party with the data.

3.3 Two's Complement

Having determined that we will be encoding bit for bit to support arbitrary precision without information leakage, we must now decide on how exactly we want to represent a rational number (which has been scaled to be a signed integer). For unsigned integers, binary representation is well known: Given an integer $a \geq 0$, we write it as $a = \sum_{i=0}^{n} a_i \cdot 2^i$ where $n = \lfloor \log_2(|a|) \rfloor$ and $a_i \in \{0, 1\}$ to obtain a $n + 1$-bit string $a_n a_{n-1} \ldots a_1 a_0$.

To incorporate negative numbers, the most popular encoding is called *Two's Complement*: Here, we write an integer a as $a = a_{n+1} \cdot (-2^{n+1}) + \sum_{i=0}^{n} a_i \cdot 2^i$ where $n = \lfloor \log_2(a) \rfloor$ and $a_i \in \{0, 1\}$. This means that the most significant bit (MSB) encodes the negative value -2^{n+1} and is thus 1 exactly when $a < 0$. As an example, consider the bitstring 1011, which encodes $1 \cdot (-2^3) + 0 \cdot 2^2 + 1 \cdot 2 + 1 \cdot 1 = -8 + 2 + 1 = -5$.

The most notable aspect for Two's Complement is that for multiplication to work, the inputs must first be encoded as numbers of the length that the output will have, i.e., when multiplying numbers of lengths n and m, both inputs lengths need to be increased to $n + m$ before multiplication. This procedure, called *sign extension*, is done by replacing the first bit with the appropriate number of copies if itself. In the above example, if we needed to extend the 4-bit string 1011 to length 8, it would result in 11111011, which still encodes -5.

3.4   Sign-Magnitude

While Two's Complement may be the most popular encoding of signed integers, it is not the only one: *Sign-Magnitude* encoding formalizes the most intuitive idea of having an extra bit that determines the sign. Conventionally, this is the most significant bit, which is 1 when a number is negative and 0 when a number is positive. Thus, for example, the number $5 = 0101$ and $-5 = 1101$. This notation suffers from the fact that there are two encodings of 0 ($0 = 00\ldots00$ and $-0 = 10\ldots00$) and is seldom used, but we will later see how this slightly unconventional encoding can help us.

We would like to point out that addition in this encoding is much more involved than in Two's Complement: Here, we need to add the absolute values and keep the sign bit if both inputs have equal signs, and otherwise compare the two inputs, subtract the smaller from the larger absolute value, and keep the sign of the input with the larger absolute value. Obviously, expressing this operation as a polynomial is considerably more involved than the straightforward addition used in Two's Complement. However, in multiplication, Sign-Magnitude encoding does not need sign extension, and addition of the rows in multiplication can use the straightforward addition instead of the above one, so this problem does not carry over to multiplication.

4   Basic Operations and Their Performance

Having introduced two different ways of encoding, this section will now examine both the theoretical complexity and actual performance of elementary operations. All computations were done on a virtual machine with 5 GB of RAM running Ubuntu 14.04 LTS (running on a Lenovo Yoga 2 Pro with a Intel i7-4500U processor with 1.8 GHz and 8 GB of RAM with Windows 8.1). We give the number of binary additions and multiplications as well as multiplicative depth required for these elementary operations. Due to space limitations, we omit how these values were determined, but we used straightforward methods to turn the functions into polynomials over $\{0, 1\}$ and derived the number of bit additions and multiplications as well as the multiplicative depth. We note that we also implemented all our functions with a subroutine that counts these values to ensure that the formulas are correct. Runtimes were obtained for values encrypted with the HElib library [1].

4.1 Note on Comparisons

As already mentioned, Sign-Magnitude uses a comparison in its addition function, making the comparison function an important building block. We note, however, that when comparing a number with 0, there is an easier way (see Sect. 5.2). For the general case (and used in Sign-Magnitude's addition procedure), the effort of comparing two arbitrary numbers is:

Two's Complement:
- $3n$ binary additions
- $n + 1$ binary multiplications
- a multiplicative depth of n

Sign-Magnitude:
- $10n - 3$ binary additions
- $6n - 2$ binary multiplications
- a multiplicative depth of $2n - 1$

We can see that Two's Complement is more efficient for comparing encrypted numbers.

4.2 Addition

We will now compare addition of two n-bit numbers for Two's Complement and Sign-Magnitude encoding. The computational effort is:

Two's Complement:
- $5n - 2$ binary additions
- n binary multiplications
- a multiplicative depth of n

Sign-Magnitude:
- $73n - 17$ binary additions
- $28n + 4$ binary multiplications
- a multiplicative depth of $2n + 2$

As we can see, Two's Complement again does better in theory. In practice (i.e., counted by our program), we get as values the number of operations and runtime as shown in Fig. 3. These diagrams show that Two's Complement is indeed superior to Sign-Magnitude where addition is concerned.

4.3 Multiplication

In this section, we will examine the multiplication of an n-bit number with an m-bit number. Heuristically, we expect Sign-Magnitude to do better here: Instead of the costly "normal" Sign-Magnitude addition operation which uses a comparison circuit, we can use regular textbook binary addition to add up the rows encountered in multiplication, so the fact that addition of two n-bit Sign-Magnitude numbers is much more expensive than that of two n-bit Two's Complement numbers does not weigh in here. On the other hand, because of the sign extension necessary in Two's Complement multiplication, not only are the rows longer ($n + m$ as compared to n), but there are also more of them ($n + m$ as opposed to m), so we must do more additions of longer bitstrings. We examine the effort required:

Two's Complement:

- $\frac{5(m^2+n^2)-19(m+n)}{2} + 5mn + 10$ binary additions
- $\frac{(m+n-3)(m+n)}{2} + mn + 1$ binary multiplications
- a multiplicative depth of $\lceil \log_2(m+n) \rceil \cdot (m+n-1) - 2^{\lceil \log_2(m+n) \rceil} + 2$

Sign-Magnitude: Due to changing intermediate lengths during row additions (which depend on both n and m instead of just $n+m$ as in Two's Complement), an exact formula would be very involved and hardly informative. Thus, we present a formula for an upper bound which already shows that SM is superior to TC for multiplication. To this end, we now have two data sets for Sign-Magnitude in the diagrams 3b, d and f in Fig. 3 regarding the number of operations: One shows the exact numbers as counted by an instruction in our program (and verified manually), and one shows the bounds as given by the following formulas:

- $(2^{\lceil \log_2(m-1) \rceil} - 1) \cdot (5n - 7) + (2^{\lceil \log_2(m-1) \rceil - 1} - 1) \cdot 5 \cdot \lceil \log_2(m-1) \rceil$
  binary additions at most
- $(n-1) \cdot (m-1) + (2^{\lceil \log_2(m-1) \rceil} - 1) \cdot (n-1) + (2^{\lceil \log_2(m-1) \rceil - 1} - 1) \cdot \lceil \log_2(m-1) \rceil$
  binary multiplications at most
- A multiplicative depth of at most
  $\frac{1}{2} \lceil \log_2(m-1) \rceil \cdot (\lceil \log_2(m-1) \rceil + 2n - 5) + 2^{\lceil \log_2(m-1) \rceil}$

Concrete values and runtimes can be seen in Fig. 3 and as we can see, Two's Complement performs much worse, as expected. *Thus, Two's Complement encoding is superior for addition and comparison, but inferior for multiplication.*

5   Accelerating Computations

In this section, we will discuss several optimizations to make computations on encrypted data more efficient.

5.1   Hybrid Encoding

Since we have seen in the previous sections that Two's Complement encoding always performs better than Sign-Magnitude except for multiplication (where it is much worse), we propose the following approach, called Hybrid Encoding: We work with Two's Complement encoding, but when we want to multiply, we convert the numbers to their representations in Sign-Magnitude, perform the multiplication there, and convert the result back. As we will see, this is indeed more efficient than regular Two's Complement multiplication. To do this, we must first determine how to convert numbers from their representation in Two's Complement to their Sign-Magnitude form and vice versa, so suppose we have a number a under one encoding α (either Two's Complement or Sign-Magnitude), denoted a_α, and wish to transform it into its representation under the other encoding β, denoted a_β. For numbers with MSB 0, both encodings are actually the same ($a_\alpha = a_\beta$), so in this case we do nothing. If the number has a MSB of

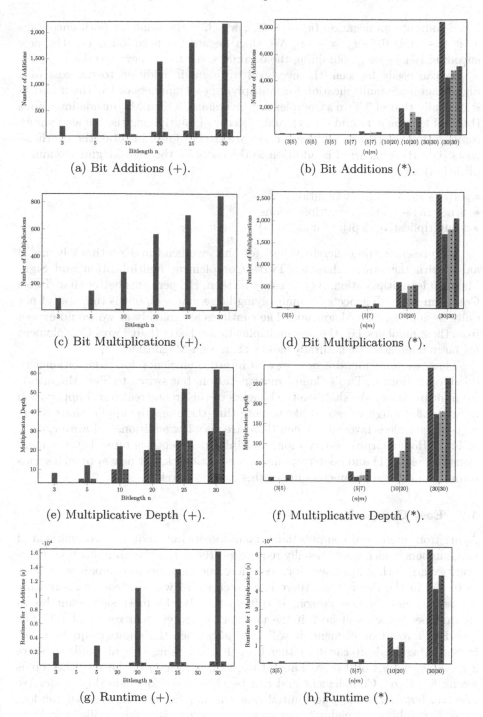

(a) Bit Additions (+).

(b) Bit Additions (*).

(c) Bit Multiplications (+).

(d) Bit Multiplications (*).

(e) Multiplicative Depth (+).

(f) Multiplicative Depth (*).

(g) Runtime (+).

(h) Runtime (*).

Fig. 3. Comparison of addition (+) and multiplication (*) for Two's Complement ● (lines), exact values for Sign-Magnitude (counted by program) ● (solid), upper bound for Sign-Magnitude for multiplication ● (dotted) and our new Hybrid Encoding (● (dotted). Runtimes for data encrypted with HElib (Color figure online).

1, we compute its negation $(a_\alpha \mapsto -a_\alpha)$, which is the same for both encodings as it has MSB 0 $(-a_\alpha = -a_\beta)$. We then negate the negation under the new encoding $(-a_\beta \mapsto a_\beta)$, obtaining the original value in the new encoding.

As can easily be seen, the overhead we incur in addition to the cost of a Sign-Magnitude multiplication for multiplying two numbers of lengths n and m is basically that of 3 Two's Complement inversions, 3 Sign-Magnitude inversions (both of lengths n, m and $n + m$), and the cost of multiplying the boolean values representing whether the different cases are true or false. In total, the overhead costs (i.e., those incurred in addition to the costs for the Sign-Magnitude multiplication) are:

- $14(n + m) - 7$ binary additions
- $6(n + m) - 3$ binary multiplications
- a multiplicative depth of $\max\{n, m\} + 1 + n + m$

We present some concrete values for this overhead and runtimes in Fig. 3 along with the same values for Two's Complement multiplication and Sign-Magnitude multiplication. As can easily be seen, HE performs better than Two's Complement in all aspects for multiplying large numbers, but is (naturally) not quite as good as Sign-Magnitude. The runtimes are roughly as we would expect from these numbers, i.e., the new multiplication is faster than Two's Complement for large numbers, but naturally slower than Sign-Magnitude.

Thus, we have found a new way to improve efficiency for large bitlengths: do all operations in Two's Complement notation, but switch to Sign-Magnitude for multiplication. We shall see the benefits of this in our real-world application in Sect. 6.3, though we would like to note that there may be applications where Sign-Magnitude is favorable (when there are very few additions). However, since in Fully Homomorphic Encryption, multiplicative depth is often key (as mentioned in Sect. 3.1) and bootstrapping is the bottleneck, our new approach seems favorable for large parameters under this aspect as well.

5.2   Easy Comparison

Apart from numerical computations, many algorithms require a comparison of two numbers, which would usually require a rather expensive computation. However, we argue that in some use cases where one only has to compare a number to 0, like in the Perceptron, there is a much easier way. Instead of computing a costly circuit for comparison, it suffices to take the most significant bit of the number, which will be 0 if the number is greater than zero and 1 if it is less. For Two's Complement, it will be 0 also when the number equals 0, but in Sign-Magnitude it can be either 0 or 1 when using this method, as there are two encodings of 0 here. Thus, if the sum is exactly 0, the resulting bit is wrong for Two's Complement and can be either case for Sign-Magnitude. We observe, however, that when initializing the weights $w_1, \ldots, w_l$ with random rational numbers, a weighted sum $w_1 x_1 + \cdots + w_l x_l$ is highly unlikely to be 0. Thus, in this case there should be no change whether the condition for an operation is $w_1 x_1 + \cdots + w_l x_l > 0$ or $w_1 x_1 + \cdots + w_l x_l \geq 0$ and the easy comparison should return the correct result with overwhelming probability. If the weights are initialized with 0 (as could be chosen in the Perceptron) or integers in the more general case, a more involved formula should be used.

5.3 Improved Multiplication

As the reader may have noticed, the sign extension in Two's Complement introduces costly redundancy, which can be avoided by carefully copying values to appropriate locations instead of computing them from scratch every time. Of course, as Sign-Magnitude multiplication works without sign extension, this improvement only applies to Two's Complement. However, the following further improvements hold for both encodings:

Having computed the matrix whose rows we want to sum up, we can apply a $\log(n+m)$-depth circuit for adding the $n+m$ rows. It is noteworthy that we can save computation power by modifying the addition operation: As can easily be seen, we are always adding rows of different lengths. While the naive approach of padding the right-hand side of the shorter number with 0's and applying normal addition would also work, we can save some effort by copying the excess bits of the longer number and then performing addition on the remaining shorter equal-length parts. Generally, when using this second approach, we only perform an addition of the length of the shorter input, which is an important factor in depth optimization.

In the simpler case where one value is known, i.e., multiplication by a constant, we do not need to do as much work: For simplicity, assume that the input b is known. We again first need to do sign extension for Two's Complement, but in the next step instead of having to compute $n \cdot m$ terms $a_i \cdot b_j$ as before, we can just copy the string a for every bit that is 1 in b, shifting to the left with each bit. This way, we save $n \cdot m$ multiplications from the generation of the matrix and reduce the depth by one. Also, note that we now don't need to add as many rows, as we only write down those that correspond to the non-zero bits in b. Thus, we only need to do $\mathrm{hm}(b)$ row additions, where $\mathrm{hm}(b)$ is the hamming weight of b. Of course, the complexity and multiplicative depth now depend on the value of b and are the same as for regular multiplication in the worst case. However, on average we will only have to do half as many row additions.

5.4 Managing Length

By default, each addition and each multiplication increase the bitlength: Addition increases it by 1, whereas multiplication results in a bitlength that is the sum of the two input lengths. When performing several multiplications consecutively, this can easily lead to enormous bitlengths. However, in a scenario where the size of the values can be estimated, there is a way around this. One such scenario is machine learning, where the person working on the data is the person who has the algorithm for building the model and it is a reasonable assumption that some factors of the model are known, e.g. from experience. For example, in the data set we worked with [2], the value w_0 always took some value near

10000 no matter what subset of test subjects we chose. In such cases, the service provider who is doing the computations can put a bound on the lengths (i.e., he is certain that the weights will not be larger in absolute value than 2^q for some q). When this is the case, we can reduce the bitlength of the encrypted values to this size $q + 1$ by discarding the excess bits: In Two's Complement, we can delete the most significant bits (which will all be 0 for a positive and 1 for a negative number) until we reach the desired length, whereas for Sign-Magnitude we discard the bits following the MSB (which will all be 0). More specifically, we actually integrated this into our multiplication routine, such that we not only save space, but also effort, as we only compute until we reach the bound in each step. This can be viewed as the inversion of the sign extension operation introduced in Sect. 3.3 and makes the entire algorithm significantly faster, as we have elimninated linear growth in the bitlength.

6   Applications

In this section, we demonstrate the performance increase on two concrete use cases.

6.1   Background and Motivation

Fully Homomorphic Encryption allows the computation of arbitrary functions on encrypted data while keeping the data hidden from the computing party. While FHE does not in principle offer to keep the function private (e.g., if the data and the function belong to the same party, who wishes to have the computation done by a different party with more computing power), it can hide the function that was applied in the following case: If the data belongs to one party and the function belongs to the computing party, then FHE schemes that are "circuit private" guarantee that a ciphertext divulges nothing about the function that was applied to it. Since circuit privacy is often a goal for FHE schemes, it makes sense to extend this requirement to the encoding choices to achieve privacy for the end result. This then means that the data owner learns nothing about the applied function except for what he can derive from the result, and the function owner learns nothing about the data. In this spirit, machine learning has often been cited as an application of Fully Homomorphic Encryption (see Sect. 2). Machine learning describes a field of research focused on extracting information from data, e.g. in the form of models. In this paper we consider the following scenario: Suppose Alice has a machine learning algorithm which takes data as input and returns a predictive model, and Bob has some data and would like either to obtain a model based on his data, or apply said model to further data (though he does not obtain the model in that case, e.g. allowing the service provider to bill him for each classification of his data). However, Alice does not want to reveal her algorithm for building the model to Bob, and Bob wishes to keep his data secret. With Fully Homomorphic Encryption, Bob could encrypt his (training) data and send it to Alice, who then performs her algorithm on the encrypted data. The output is an encryption of the model, which Alice can apply to new encrypted data instances from Bob and Bob only receives the result of applying the model to his data (first case), or the whole model is sent to Bob (second case), in which case only Bob can decrypt the model. Thus, with an adequately secure Fully Homomorphic Encryption scheme, Alice has learned nothing about Bob's data and Bob has learned nothing about Alice's algorithm except what he can deduce from the result of the evaluation.

In the following, we consider two use cases, one for each of the above scenarios. For the first case, we take up a use case already presented in [22]: the Linear Means Classifier, where we assume that the model has already been built. Alice receives Bob's encrypted data, which she classifies by evaluating a polynomial of degree 2. This use case showcases our new Hybrid Encoding, which performs significantly better in this general case where the results are not bounded.

For the second case, we examine the Perceptron and show how to improve efficiency in evaluating it (i.e., obtaining the model), showcasing our results regarding choice of encoding and tweaks in multiplication. The Perceptron is an important fundamental algorithm in machine learning upon which many others are built, so being able to efficiently homomorphically evaluate it is mandatory before we can move on to more advanced machine learning algorithms.

The given runtimes are estimates for data encrypted with HElib [1], as runtimes are still very large: We measured the time for operations like addition and multiplication for different parameters and extrapolated the time it would take to compute the entire function. For example, given the function $f(x_1, x_2, x_3, x_4) = x_1 \cdot x_2 + x_3 \cdot x_4$ on inputs of length n, we would calculate the runtime as that of 2 multiplications of n-bit numbers plus one addition of numbers of lengths $2n$ (in the unbounded case). We confirmed our computations by actually running the Perceptron for lengths $n = 3$ and $n = 5$ for all three encodings to make sure that our computations reflect reality. However, we point out that these runtimes depend greatly on the characteristics of HElib: If one used a different encryption scheme that takes longer or shorter to perform bootstrapping, the results would vary greatly. However, our theoretical results are independent of the scheme that was used.

6.2 Linear Means Classifier

In this section, we examine the Linear Means Classifier to showcase the first use case, where the Service Provider retains the encrypted model and the user may send further encrypted data which is then classified by the encrypted model and only the encrypted result is returned to the user.

The Linear Means Classifier: Like [22], we consider the case where there are two classes, which are determined by the sign of the score function, which is a polynomial of degree 2. More concretely, the model consists of a vector $w = (w_1, \ldots, w_l)$ and a constant c, and the data to be classified is a l-dimensional real-valued vector $x = (x_1, \ldots, x_l)$. The score function is then computed as $\langle w, x \rangle + c = w_1 x_1 + w_2 x_2 + \cdots + w_l x_l + c$, and the sign of the result determines which class the data instance belongs to. As can easily be seen, this is closely related to the classification function of the Perceptron from the next section, where the focus is on determining w and c instead of computing the score function for given (encrypted and thus unknown) values for w and c as we do here.

Performance: Using the Linear Means Classifier, we examine the effects of using different encodings in the unbounded case (i.e., when the product of two n-bit numbers has length $2n$). To this end, we compute both the effort required in terms of bit operations and depth and the runtime of evaluating the score function for inputs of bitlength 30 for different numbers l of features. As explained above, we computed these runtimes from their components (i.e., the runtime for multiplying two 30-bit numbers without bounds, and the runtime for adding two 60-bit numbers) as the numbers are quite large. The results can be found in Fig. 2 in Sect. 1.1. As we can see, Two's Complement is better than Sign-Magnitude, and using our new Hybrid Encoding significantly improves all aspects except depth, which is about halfway between the other two encodings. This did not matter in our case as we bootstrapped after every multiplication.

6.3 Homomorphically Evaluating the Perceptron

In this section, we examine the first use case where the Perceptron is evaluated to return an encrypted model.

The Perceptron: The Perceptron is an algorithm based on neural networks and basically works by computing a weighted sum of the input traits (usually rational numbers) for each subject and then classifying into one of two classes depending on whether this weighted sum is above a certain threshold or not. In the training phase, the weights are adjusted if the computed classification does not match the known classification of the training instance. After training, the model can be used to classify future inputs with no known classification. The model consists of the weights, and the threshold can either be predetermined or flexible (and thus part of the model being computed). We will work with the latter approach, which enables us to compare the inner product to 0.

Performance: We will now examine how the optimizations from Sect. 5 affect the Perceptron, as shown in Fig. 4. We can see that bounding the values makes a huge difference, especially since these values are only for the first round and would grow exponentially in further rounds. Sign-Magnitude is consistently the worst choice, and in the unbounded case, Hybrid Encoding is fastest (as already evident from Sect. 6.2). In the bounded case, however, Two's Complement is fastest, and this makes sense: The fact that we have integrated the bounding into our multiplication procedure and stop computing in each line as soon as the bound is reached negates the sign extension that incurs the slowdown for multiplication in Two's Complement encoding. This means that we expect bounded Two's Complement multiplication to be almost as fast as Sign-Magnitude multiplication, which was confirmed by our experiments. Due to this, there is no efficiency gain through our new encoding in the bounded case, but the graph still

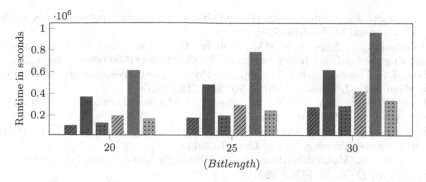

Fig. 4. Extrapolated runtimes for one subject for one round of the encrypted Perceptron for Two's Complement (● (lines) for bounded, ● (lines) for unbounded values), Sign-Magnitude (● (solid) for bounded, ● (solid) for unbounded values) and using our new Hybrid Encoding (● (dotted) for bounded, ● (dotted) for unbounded values) (Color figure online).

illustrates the importance of choosing the right encoding, as Sign-Magnitude is significantly slower here due to its costly addition.

7   Conclusion and Future Work

In conclusion, we have presented a way of working with encrypted rational numbers, to our knowledge being the first to not restrict ourselves to unsigned integers. We have presented a new hybrid encoding technique that vastly improves efficiency for FHE on rational numbers both in theory and for real-world applications like the Linear Means Classifier, and other optimizations that improve efficiency for more complicated functions like the Perceptron. Since our results are independent of the scheme used, they hold with maximum generality and can thus be beneficial for anyone looking to evaluate a function homomorphically. For future research, we believe that this hybrid approach may be transferable to plaintext spaces other than $\{0, 1\}$, although the elementary operations will be considerably more involved. Further, we imagine that it could be beneficial to take a step back from established encodings and come up with a new one from scratch, which could be specially tailored to FHE computations.

References

1. HeLib Library: https://github.com/shaih/HELib
2. Pima Dataset: https://archive.ics.uci.edu/ml/datasets/Pima+Indians+Diabetes
3. Armknecht, F., Boyd, C., Carr, C., Gjøsteen, K., Jäschke, A., Reuter, C.A., Strand, M.: A guide to fully homomorphic encryption. IACR Cryptology ePrint Archive (2015/1192)
4. Armknecht, F., Katzenbeisser, S., Peter, A.: Group homomorphic encryption: characterizations, impossibility results, and applications. DCC **67**(2), 209–232 (2013)

5. Armknecht, F., Strufe, T.: An efficient distributed privacy-preserving recommendation system. In: Med-Hoc-Net (2011)
6. Aslett, L.J.M., Esperança, P.M., Holmes, C.C.: Encrypted statistical machine learning: new privacy preserving methods. CoRR abs/1508.06845 (2015)
7. Bos, J.W., Lauter, K.E., Naehrig, M.: Private predictive analysis on encrypted medical data. J. Biomed. Inform. **50**, 234–243 (2014)
8. Bost, R., Popa, R.A., Tu, S., Goldwasser, S.: Machine learning classification over encrypted data. In: NDSS (2015)
9. Brakerski, Z., Gentry, C., Vaikuntanathan, V.: Fully homomorphic encryption without bootstrapping. ECCC **18**, 111 (2011)
10. Brakerski, Z., Vaikuntanathan, V.: Efficient fully homomorphic encryption from (standard) LWE. In: FOCS (2011)
11. Cheon, J.H., Kim, M., Lauter, K.: Homomorphic computation of edit distance. In: Brenner, M., Christin, N., Johnson, B., Rohloff, K. (eds.) FC 2015 Workshops. LNCS, vol. 8976, pp. 194–212. Springer, Heidelberg (2015)
12. Chung, H., Kim, M.: Encoding rational numbers for fhe-based applications. IACR Cryptology ePrint Archive (2016/344)
13. Coron, J.-S., Lepoint, T., Tibouchi, M.: Scale-invariant fully homomorphic encryption over the integers. In: Krawczyk, H. (ed.) PKC 2014. LNCS, vol. 8383, pp. 311–328. Springer, Heidelberg (2014)
14. Coron, J.-S., Naccache, D., Tibouchi, M.: Public key compression and modulus switching for fully homomorphic encryption over the integers. In: Pointcheval, D., Johansson, T. (eds.) EUROCRYPT 2012. LNCS, vol. 7237, pp. 446–464. Springer, Heidelberg (2012)
15. Costache, A., Smart, N.P., Vivek, S., Waller, A.: Fixed point arithmetic in SHE scheme. IACR Cryptology ePrint Archive (2016/250)
16. van Dijk, M., Gentry, C., Halevi, S., Vaikuntanathan, V.: Fully homomorphic encryption over the integers. In: Gilbert, H. (ed.) EUROCRYPT 2010. LNCS, vol. 6110, pp. 24–43. Springer, Heidelberg (2010)
17. Dowlin, N., Gilad-Bachrach, R., Laine, K., Lauter, K., Naehrig, M., Wernsing, J.: Manual for using homomorphic encryption for bioinformatics. Technical report MSR-TR-2015-87, Microsoft Research (2015)
18. Ducas, L., Micciancio, D.: FHEW: bootstrapping homomorphic encryption in less than a second. In: Oswald, E., Fischlin, M. (eds.) EUROCRYPT 2015. LNCS, vol. 9056, pp. 617–640. Springer, Heidelberg (2015)
19. Gentry, C.: A fully homomorphic encryption scheme. Ph.D. thesis, Stanford University (2009)
20. Gentry, C., Halevi, S., Smart, N.P.: Homomorphic evaluation of the AES circuit. In: Canetti, R., Safavi-Naini, R. (eds.) CRYPTO 2012. LNCS, vol. 7417, pp. 850–867. Springer, Heidelberg (2012)
21. Gentry, C., Sahai, A., Waters, B.: Homomorphic encryption from learning with errors: conceptually-simpler, asymptotically-faster, attribute-based. In: Canetti, R., Garay, J.A. (eds.) CRYPTO 2013, Part I. LNCS, vol. 8042, pp. 75–92. Springer, Heidelberg (2013)
22. Graepel, T., Lauter, K., Naehrig, M.: ML confidential: machine learning on encrypted data. In: Kwon, T., Lee, M.-K., Kwon, D. (eds.) ICISC 2012. LNCS, vol. 7839, pp. 1–21. Springer, Heidelberg (2013)
23. Henecka, W., Kögl, S., Sadeghi, A., Schneider, T., Wehrenberg, I.: TASTY: tool for automating secure two-party computations. In: CCS (2010)
24. Naehrig, M., Lauter, K.E., Vaikuntanathan, V.: Can homomorphic encryption be practical? In: CCSW (2011)

25. Sadeghi, A.-R., Schneider, T.: Generalized universal circuits for secure evaluation of private functions with application to data classification. In: Lee, P.J., Cheon, J.H. (eds.) ICISC 2008. LNCS, vol. 5461, pp. 336–353. Springer, Heidelberg (2009)
26. Smart, N.P., Vercauteren, F.: Fully homomorphic encryption with relatively small key and ciphertext sizes. In: Nguyen, P.Q., Pointcheval, D. (eds.) PKC 2010. LNCS, vol. 6056, pp. 420–443. Springer, Heidelberg (2010)
27. Songhori, E.M., Hussain, S.U., Sadeghi, A., Schneider, T., Koushanfar, F.: Tinygarble: highly compressed and scalable sequential garbled circuits. In: SP (2015)
28. Wu, D.J., Feng, T., Naehrig, M., Lauter, K.E.: Privately evaluating decision trees and random forests. IACR Cryptology ePrint Archive (2015/386)

Non-Interactive Proofs and PRFs

New Techniques for Non-interactive Shuffle and Range Arguments

Alonso González[1(✉)] and Carla Ráfols[2]

[1] DCC, Universidad de Chile, Santiago, Chile
alonso.gon@gmail.com
[2] DTIC, Universitat Pompeu Fabra, Barcelona, Spain

Abstract. We construct the most efficient non-interactive *Argument of Correctness of a Shuffle* and *Range Argument* under falsifiable assumptions in asymmetric bilinear groups. Our constructions use as a common building block a novel quasi-adaptive argument for proving that n commitments open to messages in a public set S, with proof-size independent of n.

1 Introduction

Zero-knowledge proofs are proofs which yield nothing beyond the validity of a certain statement. Although one can prove every NP statement in zero-knowledge (going through a proof of circuit satisfiability, for instance), the literature has extensively explored more efficient alternatives for concrete statements which appear often in practice. Among them, some of the most important are: proofs of membership in linear spaces [13,14,16,17], range proofs [3,4,20], membership in a set [2,20], or correctness of a shuffle [5,7,10,18].

These problems have been studied following a variety of approaches and techniques. For instance, they have been studied both in the interactive [1,3,9] and the non-interactive setting [4,7,10,18,20], and in the latter setting, both under falsifiable (but not always standard) [10,20] and non-falsifiable assumptions [4,7,18] (like knowledge of exponent type of assumptions).

Generally speaking, non-interactive zero-knowledge proofs under falsifiable assumptions remain more inefficient than other approaches for the same problem (one notable exception being the recent QA-NIZK arguments of membership in linear spaces of [14,16,17]). However, this is the most desirable alternative from a cryptographic point of view. Indeed, interaction is not so convenient in practice and further, there is the additional problem of non-transferability (a proof might not convince a third party who cannot check if the challenges were computed correctly). On the other hand, non-falsifiable assumptions are very strong assumptions whose use is, at the very least, controversial. Although it might still be interesting to use these assumptions in practice, from a theoretical

A. González—Funded by CONICYT, CONICYT-PCHA/Doctorado Nacional/2013-21130937.

© Springer International Publishing Switzerland 2016
M. Manulis et al. (Eds.): ACNS 2016, LNCS 9696, pp. 427–444, 2016.
DOI: 10.1007/978-3-319-39555-5_23

viewpoint it is definitely worth to explore how to improve efficiency based only on standard assumptions.

This paper focuses on obtaining efficiency improvements for non-interactive arguments based on falsifiable assumptions for two of the interesting examples discussed above, namely, range proofs and proofs of correctness of a shuffle.

An argument of Correctness of a Shuffle is an essential tool in the construction of *Mix-nets* [5]. A Mix-net consists of a series of *mixers*, each of which receives as input a set of n ciphertexts and outputs a *shuffle* of the input ciphertexts. That is, a *rerandomization* of the set of ciphertexts obtained after applying a *random permutation* to the input set of ciphertexts. To enforce the honest behavior of mixers they are required to produce a zero-knowledge argument that the shuffle was correctly computed.

A Range argument is a tool often required in e-voting and e-cash scenarios, with the purpose of showing that the opening y of some commitment c is an integer in some interval $[A, B]$. For simplicity, the range considered is usually $[0, 2^n - 1]$ since a proof in any interval can be reduced to a proof in this interval.

To derive efficiency improvements for these two languages we develop specific techniques that we can apply to both problems. Our resulting proofs are more efficient in terms of proof size and are based on more standard assumptions, but they have a rather large common reference string. They build on the recent arguments for membership in linear spaces of [14,16,17] and the argument for proving that some commitment to a vector of integers in $\mathbb{Z}_q^n$ opens to $\{0,1\}^n$ due to [8].

1.1   Our Techniques

All our results are in a bilinear group $gk := (q, \mathbb{G}_1, \mathbb{G}_2, \mathbb{G}_T, e, \mathcal{P}_1, \mathcal{P}_2)$, where $\mathbb{G}_1, \mathbb{G}_2$ and $\mathbb{G}_T$ are groups of prime order q, $\mathcal{P}_\gamma$ generates $\mathbb{G}_\gamma$ for $\gamma \in \{1, 2\}$ and $e : \mathbb{G}_1 \times \mathbb{G}_2 \to \mathbb{G}_T$ is an efficiently computable, non-degenerate bilinear map. Given a generator $\mathcal{P}_\gamma$ of $\mathbb{G}_\gamma$, for any $x \in \mathbb{Z}_q$ we define $[x]_\gamma := x\mathcal{P}_\gamma$. We simply write $[x]_1 [y]_2$ to denote $e([x]_1, [y]_2)$.

Note that in bilinear groups we could use Groth-Sahai proofs to prove any the statements we consider (quadratic equations allow to prove every statement in NP, [11]). However, a naive use of GS proofs results in a large proof size ($\Theta(n^2)$ for shuffles, $\Theta(n)$ for range proofs) and in fact, as we discuss below, they have always been combined with other strategies to obtain improved asymptotic efficiency.

A Common Building Block. Our starting point is the observation that range and shuffle proofs can be constructed by using as a common building block a "zero-knowledge aggregated set membership argument". This is achieved by slightly modifying some previous strategies used for shuffle and range proofs.

More specifically, given some publicly known set S, such an argument proves that n commitments $c_1, \ldots, c_n$ open to values $x_1, \ldots, x_n \in S$. The set S is of polynomial size and is either $[0, d-1] \subset \mathbb{Z}_q$ or a subset of $\mathbb{G}_\gamma, \gamma \in \{1, 2\}$. In other words, an aggregated set membership argument proves that each $c_1, \ldots, c_n$ is in the language

$$\mathcal{L}_{ck,S} := \{c : \exists x \in S, \mathbf{w} \in \mathbb{Z}_q^r \text{ s.t. } c = \mathsf{Com}_{ck}(x; \mathbf{w})\}, \text{ where } ck \leftarrow \mathcal{K}, \qquad (1)$$

and $c = \mathsf{Com}_{ck}(x; \mathbf{w})$ is a Groth-Sahai commitment to x with randomness $\mathbf{w}$. The proof is Quasi-Adaptive [13], in the sense that the common reference string depends on ck and S, which are assumed to be sampled from some distribution $\mathcal{D}$ and further, the marginal distribution of ck is assumed to be witness samplable, which essentially means it can be sampled along with its discrete logarithms. The argument is said to be *aggregated* because the size of the proof is independent of n ($\Theta(\log d)$ when $S = [0, d-1]$ and $\Theta(|S|)$ when $S \subset \mathbb{G}_\gamma$). However, in the soundness proof we will loose a factor of n in the reduction.

Before discussing how to construct such an argument, we show how to use it as a building block for range and shuffle proofs.

Range Argument: Let $n, d \in \mathbb{N}$, $m := \log d$, and $\ell := n/m$. A commitment c opens to an integer x in the range $[0, 2^n - 1]$ if $\exists x_1, \ldots, x_\ell \in [0, d-1]$ and $x = \sum_{i \in [\ell]} x_i d^{i-1}$. Indeed, since $x_i \in [0, d-1]$, $x = \sum_{i \in [\ell]} x_i d^{i-1} \in [0, d^\ell - 1]$ and $[0, d^\ell - 1] = [0, (d^{1/\log d})^n - 1] = [0, 2^n - 1]$. The statement $\exists x_1, \ldots, x_\ell \in [0, d-1]$ can be proven by showing that $(c_1, \ldots, c_\ell) \in \mathcal{L}_{ck,[0,d-1]}^\ell$, where $c_i = \mathsf{Com}_{ck}(x_i)$, with an aggregated set membership proof, and the statement $x = \sum_{i \in [\ell]} d^{i-1} x_i$ can be proven using standard techniques.

While this way of constructing range arguments has been widely used in the literature, with the addition of our techniques we get a smaller proof size. Indeed, the total cost of the range proof is $\Theta(\ell) + \Theta(m)$ (ℓ is due to the size of the commitments $c_1, \ldots, c_\ell$ and m to the size of an aggregated proof of membership in $\mathcal{L}_{ck,[0,d-1]}^\ell$). Setting $d = n^k$ for arbitrary k leads to a proof size of $\Theta(\frac{n}{k \log n})$. Compared to previous approaches, the novelty of ours is that the cost of proving that $x_1, \ldots, x_\ell \in [0, d-1]$ is significantly reduced.

Shuffle Argument: The proof is partially inspired by the non-interactive shuffle of [10]. The statement we want to prove in a correctness of a shuffle argument is: "Given two vectors of ciphertexts which open, respectively, to vectors of plaintexts $[\mathbf{m}_1]_2, [\mathbf{m}_2]_2$, prove that $[\mathbf{m}_2]$ is a permutation of $[\mathbf{m}_1]$". Roughly, our strategy is the following: (1) publish some vector of group elements $[\mathbf{s}]_1 = ([s_1]_1, \ldots, [s_n]_1)^\top$ (which we identify with the set S of its components) in the common reference string, where $\mathbf{s}$ is sampled from some distribution $\mathcal{D}_{n,1}$; (2) the prover commits to $[\mathbf{x}]_1 = ([x_1]_1, \ldots, [x_n]_1)^\top$, a permutation of the set S and proves that the commitments to $[\mathbf{x}]_1$ are in $\mathcal{L}_{ck,S}^n$; (3) the prover proves that $\sum_{i \in [n]} [x_i]_1 = \sum_{i \in [n]} [s_i]_1$; (4) finally, the prover outputs a proof that:[1]

$$[\mathbf{s}^\top]_1 [\mathbf{m}_1]_2 = [\mathbf{x}^\top]_1 [\mathbf{m}_2]_2. \qquad (2)$$

---

[1] This is a slightly oversimplified explanation. Actually, a prover (a mixer) does not know the randomness nor the decryptions of the ciphertexts but only the randomness of the re-encryptions, so it cannot prove exactly this statement.

The underlying computational assumption is that it is infeasible to find a non-trivial combination of elements of S which adds to 0, that is, given $[\mathbf{s}]_1$ it is infeasible to find $[\mathbf{k}]_2 \neq [\mathbf{0}]_2$ such that $\mathbf{s}^\top \mathbf{k} = \mathbf{0}$ (this is the $\mathcal{D}_{n,1}$-KerMDH Assumption of [19], which is a generalization of the Double Pairing Assumption, which is weaker than DDH).

Soundness goes as follows. First, by the soundness of the aggregated set membership proof, $[\mathbf{x}]_1 \in S^n$ and from the fact that $\sum_{i \in [n]} x_i = \sum_{i \in [n]} s_i$, it holds that if $\mathbf{x}$ is not a permutation of $\mathbf{s}$, then one can extract in the soundness game (assuming the extractor knows ck) a non-trivial linear combination of elements of S which adds to 0, which contradicts the security assumption. Finally, if $\mathbf{x}$ is a permutation of $\mathbf{s}$, then Eq. (2) implies that the shuffle is correct, or, again, one can extract from $[\mathbf{m}_1]_2, [\mathbf{m}_2]_2$ the coefficients of some non-trivial combination of elements of S which is equal to 0 (breaking the $\mathcal{D}_{n,1}$-KerMDH Assumption).

This soundness argument is an augmentation and translation into asymmetric groups of the argument of Groth and Lu [10]. Essentially, the argument there also consists of two parts: one devoted to proving that some GS commitments open to a permutation of some set in the CRS (in [10] this is done via the (non-standard) pairing permutation assumption), while the second part (Step 4) is proven very similarly (in particular, its soundness also follows from some Kernel Assumption secure in symmetric bilinear groups).

We note that it is crucial for our soundness argument that it is possible to decrypt the ciphertexts (otherwise we cannot extract solutions to the Kernel problems). This is possible in our case because public key for encryption is assumed to be witness-samplable and the argument is quasi-adaptive. This explains why we do not refer to the notion of culpable soundness, as in [7,10].

Set Membership Proofs. Before we move to aggregated set membership proofs, we give a characterization of $\mathcal{L}_{ck,S}$, defined as in Eq. (1), which is key to obtain our results. We observe that membership in S can be written as:

- If $S \subset \mathbb{G}_\gamma$, and we identify S with $[\mathbf{s}]_\gamma = ([s_1]_\gamma, \ldots, [s_m]_\gamma)^\top$ then, $c \in \mathcal{L}_{ck,S}$ if and only if $\exists \mathbf{b} \in \mathbb{Z}_q^m$ such that

$$1)\mathbf{b} \in \{0,1\}^m, \quad 2)c = \mathsf{Com}_{ck}(x; w), \quad 3)x = \mathbf{s}^\top \mathbf{b}, \quad 4) \sum_{i \in [m]} b_i = 1.$$

- If $S = [0, d-1]$ and $m := \log d$, then: $c \in \mathcal{L}_{ck,S}$ if and only if $\exists \mathbf{b} \in \mathbb{Z}_q^m$ such that:

$$1)\mathbf{b} \in \{0,1\}^m, 2)c = \mathsf{Com}_{ck}(x; w), \quad 3)x = (1, 2, \ldots, 2^{m-1})\mathbf{b}.$$

That is, both languages can be written in a similar way, except that when $S \subset \mathbb{G}_\gamma$ there is an additional linear constraint that $\mathbf{b}$ must satisfy (condition 4)).

To avoid distinguishing all the time between both types of subsets, we note that both languages can be seen as special case of the language $\mathcal{L}_{[\mathbf{M}]_1,[\mathbf{N}]_1,\Lambda,\alpha} \subseteq \mathbb{G}_1^{\ell_1}$, defined as: $[\mathbf{x}]_1 \in \mathcal{L}_{[\mathbf{M}]_1,[\mathbf{N}]_1,\Lambda,\alpha}$ if and only if $\exists \mathbf{b} \in \mathbb{Z}_q^m, \mathbf{w} \in \mathbb{Z}_q^{\ell_2}$ such that

$$1)\mathbf{b} \in \{0,1\}^m \wedge 2) \begin{pmatrix} \mathbf{c} \\ \alpha \end{pmatrix} = \begin{pmatrix} \mathbf{M} & \mathbf{N} \\ \Lambda & 0_{\ell_3 \times \ell_2} \end{pmatrix} \begin{pmatrix} \mathbf{b} \\ \mathbf{w} \end{pmatrix}.$$

The basic idea is that a GS commitment is a linear combination of the commitment keys whose coefficients are the randomness and the committed values, i.e. a commitment to a scalar $x \in \mathbb{Z}_q$ is defined as $\mathsf{Com}_{ck}(x; w) = x[\mathbf{u}_1]_1 + w[\mathbf{u}_2]_1$, for $ck = (\mathbf{u}_1, \mathbf{u}_2)$, so essentially membership in this space amounts to some "linear conditions" plus proving that $\mathbf{b}$ is binary. For instance in the case where $S = [0, d-1]$, it should hold that: $\mathbf{c} = (\mathbf{M}\ \mathbf{N})\left(\begin{smallmatrix}\mathbf{b}\\w\end{smallmatrix}\right)$ where $\mathbf{M} = \mathbf{u}_1\left(2^0\ 2^1\ \ldots\ 2^{m-1}\right)$ and $\mathbf{N} = \mathbf{u}_2$. (In this case, because there is no condition 4), $\boldsymbol{\Lambda}$ and $\boldsymbol{\alpha}$ are zero and are ignored).

Proof Strategy. The most efficient strategy we are aware of for proving this type of statements follows a commit-and-prove approach. Namely, to prove that such a vector $\mathbf{b}$ exists, one computes GS commitments $[\mathbf{d}_i]_1$, $i \in [m]$, to all coordinates of $\mathbf{b}$ and then it proves two independent statements, namely that:

- $\exists \mathbf{b} \in \mathbb{Z}_q^m, \mathbf{r} \in \mathbb{Z}_q^m$ such that 1')$\mathbf{b} \in \{0,1\}^m$ and 3')$\forall i \in [m], \mathbf{d}_i = \left(\mathbf{u}_1\ \mathbf{u}_2\right)\left(\begin{smallmatrix}b_i\\r_i\end{smallmatrix}\right)$,
- $\exists \widetilde{\mathbf{b}} \in \mathbb{Z}_q^m, \widetilde{\mathbf{r}} \in \mathbb{Z}_q^m, \mathbf{w} \in \mathbb{Z}_q^{\ell_2}$ such that 2')$\left(\begin{smallmatrix}\mathbf{c}\\\boldsymbol{\alpha}\end{smallmatrix}\right) = \left(\begin{smallmatrix}\mathbf{M}&\mathbf{N}\\\boldsymbol{\Lambda}&\mathbf{0}_{\ell_3 \times \ell_2}\end{smallmatrix}\right)\left(\begin{smallmatrix}\widetilde{\mathbf{b}}\\\mathbf{w}\end{smallmatrix}\right)$ and 3')$\forall i \in [m], \mathbf{d}_i = \left(\mathbf{u}_1\ \mathbf{u}_2\right)\left(\begin{smallmatrix}\widetilde{b}_i\\r_i\end{smallmatrix}\right)$.

For the first, one can use the QA-NIZK argument for bit-strings of [8], and for the second, the QA-NIZK argument for linear spaces of [14,16] (for the latter, note that conditions 2') and 3') can be written down as a single system of equations with a large matrix $\widetilde{\mathbf{M}}$. Satisfiability of 2') and 3') is equivalent to $(\mathbf{c}^\top, \boldsymbol{\alpha}^\top, \mathbf{d}_1^\top, \ldots, \mathbf{d}_m^\top)^\top$ being in the span of this matrix $\widetilde{\mathbf{M}}$).

Since both proofs are constant-size, the resulting proof size is dominated by the cost of the commitments to b_i, which is $\Theta(m)$. For soundness, the important point here is that we never prove that $\mathbf{b} = \widetilde{\mathbf{b}}$, but, since GS commitments are perfectly binding (or, said otherwise, because $(\mathbf{u}_1\ \mathbf{u}_2)$ has full rank), equality holds. This immediately proves the statement.

Aggregated Set Membership Proofs. An aggregated set membership proof amounts to proving membership in $\mathcal{L}_{[\mathbf{M}]_1, [\mathbf{N}]_1, \boldsymbol{\Lambda}, \boldsymbol{\alpha}}^n$. By definition, $([\mathbf{c}_1]_1, \ldots, [\mathbf{c}_n]_1) \in \mathcal{L}_{[\mathbf{M}]_1, [\mathbf{N}]_1, \boldsymbol{\Lambda}, \boldsymbol{\alpha}}^n$ if and only if $\forall j \in [n], \exists \mathbf{b}_j \in \mathbb{Z}_q^m, \mathbf{w}_j \in \mathbb{Z}_q^{\ell_2}$ such that

$$1)\mathbf{b}_j \in \{0,1\}^m \wedge 2)\left(\begin{smallmatrix}\mathbf{c}_j\\\boldsymbol{\alpha}\end{smallmatrix}\right) = \left(\begin{smallmatrix}\mathbf{M}&\mathbf{N}\\\boldsymbol{\Lambda}&\mathbf{0}_{\ell_3 \times \ell_2}\end{smallmatrix}\right)\left(\begin{smallmatrix}\mathbf{b}_j\\\mathbf{w}_j\end{smallmatrix}\right).$$

Recall that we want a proof size independent of n. This rules out the naive approach of computing GS commitments to all the coordinates of $\mathbf{b}_j$, for all $j \in [n]$, as the cost is $\Theta(nm)$. Therefore, to improve on the asymptotic size of the proof, we are forced to use shrinking commitments to $b_{i,j}$. We stress that it is far from clear how to do this, as it might break down the soundness argument completely (e.g. in the single proof, we used in a fundamental way the uniqueness of the commitment openings). In fact, overcoming this problem is one of the main technical contributions of this paper.

Our idea is to use as a shrinking commitment a two-dimensional generalization of Multi-Pedersen commitments, which was used implicitly by González et al. [8]. Given some matrix $\mathbf{G} \in \mathbb{Z}_q^{2 \times (n+1)}$ sampled from some distribution $\mathcal{D}_{2,n+1}$, MP.Com$(\mathbf{y} \in \mathbb{Z}_q^n; r \in \mathbb{Z}_q) := [\mathbf{G}]_1 \left(\begin{smallmatrix} \mathbf{b} \\ r \end{smallmatrix} \right)$. The special thing about these commitments is that one can set a "hidden" linearly independent column of $\mathbf{G}$, and thus commitments are perfectly binding at some coordinate $j^* \in [n]$ which is computationally hidden to the adversary.

Define the matrix $\mathbf{B} = (\mathbf{b}_1 || \ldots || \mathbf{b}_n) \in \{0,1\}^{m \times n}$ and let $\mathbf{b}_i^*$ be the ith row of $\mathbf{B}$. To prove $([\mathbf{c}_1]_1, \ldots, [\mathbf{c}_n]_1) \in \mathcal{L}_{[\mathbf{M}]_1,[\mathbf{N}]_1,\Lambda,\alpha}^n$, we first compute MP commitments $[\mathbf{d}_i]_1$, $i \in [m]$, to $\mathbf{b}_i^*$. As before, the proof actually consists of two independent statements:

- $\exists \mathbf{r} \in \mathbb{Z}_q^m, \mathbf{B} \in \mathbb{Z}_q^{m \times n}$ such that $1''$)$\mathbf{B} \in \{0,1\}^{m \times n}$ and $3''$)$\forall i \in [m], \mathbf{d}_i = \mathbf{G} \left(\begin{smallmatrix} \mathbf{b}_i^* \\ r_i \end{smallmatrix} \right)$,

- $\exists \widetilde{\mathbf{r}} \in \mathbb{Z}_q^m, \mathbf{w}_1, \ldots, \mathbf{w}_n \in \mathbb{Z}_q^{\ell_2}, \widetilde{\mathbf{B}} \in \mathbb{Z}_q^{m \times n}$, (whose rows are denoted as $\widetilde{\mathbf{b}}_i^*$, $i \in [m]$, and the columns $\widetilde{\mathbf{b}}_j$, $j \in [n]$), such that $2''$)$\forall i \in [n], \left(\begin{smallmatrix} \mathbf{c}_j \\ \alpha \end{smallmatrix} \right) = \left(\begin{smallmatrix} \mathbf{M} & \mathbf{N} \\ \Lambda & \mathbf{0}_{\ell_3 \times \ell_2} \end{smallmatrix} \right) \left(\begin{smallmatrix} \mathbf{b}_j \\ \mathbf{w}_j \end{smallmatrix} \right)$ and $3''$)$\forall i \in [m], \mathbf{d}_i = \mathbf{G} \left(\begin{smallmatrix} \widetilde{\mathbf{b}}_i^* \\ \widetilde{r}_i \end{smallmatrix} \right)$.

Again, for the first we use a slight modification[2] of [8] and for the second, (after rewriting the equations) a QA-NIZK argument for linear spaces. With this approach, the proof remains of size $\Theta(m)$, the size of the commitments, while the rest of the proof is constant.

The interesting part is the soundness argument. The previous reasoning for the non-aggregated case (when $n = 1$) fails here because now there is no guarantee that $\mathbf{B} = \widetilde{\mathbf{B}}$ (as the openings of $[\mathbf{d}_i]_1$ are not unique). However, as we said, the distribution of the MP commitment key can be chosen so that it is binding at some coordinate j^*. This implies that for all i, the j^*th coordinate of $\mathbf{b}_i^*$ and $\widetilde{\mathbf{b}}_i^*$ is equal, i.e. the j^*th column of $\mathbf{B}$ and $\widetilde{\mathbf{B}}$ must be equal.

Thus, we have that for the coordinate j^*, the proof is sound (because $\mathbf{b}_j^*$ is uniquely determined, which was the uniqueness of openings which was necessary to prove soundness for $n = 1$). That is, the adversary cannot break soundness for any tuple $([\mathbf{c}_1]_1, \ldots, [\mathbf{c}_n]_1)$ such that $[\mathbf{c}_j^*]_1 \notin \mathcal{L}_{[\mathbf{M}]_1,[\mathbf{N}]_1,\Lambda,\alpha}$. But since j^* is computationally hidden from the adversary, we can reduce soundness to one coordinate soundness with a loss in the reduction of $1/n$.

1.2   Related Work

Zero Knowledge Set Membership Arguments. Camenisch et al. constructed $\Theta(1)$ interactive Zero-Knowledge set membership arguments using Boneh-Boyen Signatures, and they prove them secure under the q-SDH assumption [3]. Bayer and Groth constructed $\Theta(\log |S|)$ interactive Zero-Knowledge arguments for polynomial evaluation, which can be used to construct set membership arguments, relying only on the discrete logarithm assumption [2].

---

[2] For details on the modification and why we cannot use the argument directly, see Sects. 4 and 4.1.

However, none of the previous constructions have addressed the problem of aggregating many proofs, and a direct use of them will end up with a proof of size $\Omega(n)$.

NIZK Shuffle and Range Arguments. The most efficient NIZK Shuffle argument under falsifiable assumptions is the one from Groth and Lu [10], which works for BBS ciphertexts. The proof size is linear in the number of ciphertexts, specifically $15n + 120$ group elements in Type I groups. The security of their construction relies on two assumptions: the *Paring Product Assumption* and the *Permutation Pairing Assumption*. The first assumption is a $\mathcal{D}_{n,2}$-KerMDH Assumption, when $\mathbf{M} \leftarrow \mathcal{D}_{n,2}$ is of the form $\mathbf{M}^\top := \begin{pmatrix} x_1, \ldots, x_n \\ x_1^2, \ldots, x_n^2 \end{pmatrix}$ for $x_i \leftarrow \mathbb{Z}_q$, $i \in [n]$. The second assumption is proven generically secure in [10] but it seems to be unrelated with any other assumption.

Using non-falsifiable assumptions (i.e. Knowledge of Exponent type of assumptions), Lipmaa and Zhang [18] constructed a shuffle argument with communication $6n|\mathbb{G}_1| + 11|\mathbb{G}_2|$, and recently Fauzi and Lipmaa [7] constructed a shuffle argument with communication $(5n + 2)|\mathbb{G}_1| + 2n|\mathbb{G}_2|$.

Rial, Kohlweiss, and Preneel constructed a range argument in $[0, 2^n - 1]$ with communication $\Theta(\frac{n}{\log n - \log \log n})$ and prove it secure under the q-HSDH assumption [20]. One might get rid of the q-HSDH assumption replacing the *P-signature* with any *Structure Preserving Signature*, but, since the proof requires $\frac{n}{\log n - \log \log n}$ Groth-Sahai proofs of satisfiability of the signature's verification equation and the signature's size is at least 7 group elements [15], the resulting protocol is far less efficient. Using non-falsifiable assumptions, Chaabouni, Lipmaa, and Zhang constructed a range argument with constant communication [4].

A detailed comparison of our Shuffle and Range arguments with the most efficient constructions under falsifiable assumptions is depicted in Table 1.

Table 1. Comparison of our Shuffle, Π_{shuffle}, and Range, $\Pi_{\text{range-proof}}$, arguments with the literature. To increase readability, for $\Pi_{\text{range-proof}}$ we include only the leading part of the sizes, that is, we write $f(n)$ and we mean $f(n) + o(f(n))$. Notation (x, y) means x elements of $\mathbb{G}_1$ and y elements of $\mathbb{G}_2$. "PP" stands for the Permutation Pairing assumption. The prover's computation is measured by the number of exponentiations (i.e. $z[x]_i$) and the verifier's computation is measured by the number of pairings.

	Shuffle Argument		Range Argument	
	[10]	Π_{shuffle}	[20]	$\Pi_{\text{range-proof}}$
CRS size	$2n + 8$	$(n^2 + 24n + 36, 23n + 37)$	$\Theta(\frac{n}{\log n - \log \log n})$	$(6n^2, 6n^2)$
Proof size	$15n + 120$	$(4n + 17, 14)$	$\Theta(\frac{n}{\log n - \log \log n})$	$(\frac{2n}{k \log n}, 10)$
P's comp.	$51n + 246$	$11n + 17$	$\Theta(\frac{n}{\log n - \log \log n})$	$2n$
V's comp.	$75n + 282$	$13n + 55$	$\Theta(\frac{n}{\log n - \log \log n})$	$\frac{4n}{k \log n}$
Assumption	PP	SXDH+SSDP	q-HSDH	SXDH+SSDP

2   Preliminaries

Let Gen_a be some probabilistic polynomial time algorithm which on input 1^λ, where λ is the security parameter, returns the *group key* which is the description of an asymmetric bilinear group $gk := (q, \mathbb{G}_1, \mathbb{G}_2, \mathbb{G}_T, e, \mathcal{P}_1, \mathcal{P}_2)$, where $\mathbb{G}_1, \mathbb{G}_2$ and $\mathbb{G}_T$ are groups of prime order q, the elements $\mathcal{P}_1, \mathcal{P}_2$ are generators of $\mathbb{G}_1, \mathbb{G}_2$ respectively, and $e : \mathbb{G}_1 \times \mathbb{G}_2 \to \mathbb{G}_T$ is an efficiently computable, non-degenerate bilinear map.

Elements in $\mathbb{G}_s$, are denoted implicitly as $[a]_s := a\mathcal{P}_s$, where $s \in \{1, 2, T\}$ and $\mathcal{P}_T := e(\mathcal{P}_1, \mathcal{P}_2)$. The pairing operation will be written as a product $\cdot$, that is $[a]_1 \cdot [b]_2 = [a]_1[b]_2 = e([a]_1, [b]_2) = [ab]_T$. Vectors and matrices are denoted in boldface. Given a matrix $\mathbf{T} = (t_{i,j})$, $[\mathbf{T}]_s$ is the natural embedding of $\mathbf{T}$ in $\mathbb{G}_s$, that is, the matrix whose (i,j)th entry is $t_{i,j}\mathcal{P}_s$. We denote by $|\mathbb{G}_s|$ the bit-size of the elements of $\mathbb{G}_s$.

$\mathbf{I}_{n \times n}$ refers to the identity matrix in $\mathbb{Z}_q^{n \times n}$, $\mathbf{0}_{m \times n}$ and $\mathbf{1}_{m \times n}$ the all-zero and all-one matrices in $\mathbb{Z}_q^{m \times n}$, respectively, and $\mathbf{e}_i^n$ the ith element of the canonical basis of $\mathbb{Z}_q^n$ (simply $\mathbf{I}$, $\mathbf{0}$, $\mathbf{1}$, and $\mathbf{e}_i$, respectively, if m and n are clear from the context). Given some matrices $\mathbf{A} \in \mathbb{Z}_q^{m \times t}, \mathbf{A}_1 \in \mathbb{Z}_q^{m_1 \times t}, \ldots, \mathbf{A}_n \in \mathbb{Z}_q^{m_n \times n}$, we define the operations $\mathbf{A}_1 \oplus \ldots \oplus \mathbf{A}_n := \begin{pmatrix} \mathbf{A}_1 \\ \vdots \\ \mathbf{A}_n \end{pmatrix}$ and $\mathbf{A}^n := \begin{pmatrix} \mathbf{A} & & 0 \\ & \ddots & \\ 0 & & \mathbf{A} \end{pmatrix}$.

2.1   Decisional Assumptions

Definition 1. *Let $\ell, k \in \mathbb{N}$. We call $\mathcal{D}_{\ell,k}$ a matrix distribution if it outputs (in poly time, with overwhelming probability) matrices in $\mathbb{Z}_q^{\ell \times k}$. We define $\mathcal{D}_k := \mathcal{D}_{k+1,k}$.*

For the following decisional assumption to hold, it is a necessary condition that $\ell > k$. However, in other contexts, we might need $\mathcal{D}_{\ell,k}$ distributions where $\ell \geq k$.

Definition 2 (Matrix Diffie-Hellman Assumption in $\mathbb{G}_\gamma$, $\gamma \in \{1, 2\}$ [6]). *Let $\mathcal{D}_{\ell,k}$ be a matrix distribution and $gk \leftarrow \mathsf{Gen}_a(1^\lambda)$. We say that the $\mathcal{D}_{\ell,k}$-Matrix Diffie-Hellman ($\mathcal{D}_{\ell,k}$-MDDH$_{\mathbb{G}_\gamma}$) Assumption holds relative to Gen_a if for all PPT adversaries D,*

$$\mathbf{Adv}_{\mathcal{D}_{\ell,k}, \mathsf{Gen}_a}(\mathsf{D}) := |\Pr[\mathsf{D}(gk, [\mathbf{A}]_\gamma, [\mathbf{Aw}]_\gamma) = 1] - \Pr[\mathsf{D}(gk, [\mathbf{A}]_\gamma, [\mathbf{z}]_\gamma) = 1]|$$

is negligible in k, where the probability is taken over $gk \leftarrow \mathsf{Gen}_a(1^\lambda)$, $\mathbf{A} \leftarrow \mathcal{D}_{\ell,k}, \mathbf{w} \leftarrow \mathbb{Z}_q^k, [\mathbf{z}]_\gamma \leftarrow \mathbb{G}_\gamma^\ell$ and the coin tosses of adversary D.

In this paper we will refer to the following matrix distributions:

$$\mathcal{L}_k : \mathbf{A} = \begin{pmatrix} a_1 & 0 & \ldots & 0 \\ 0 & a_2 & \ldots & 0 \\ \vdots & \vdots & \ddots & \vdots \\ 0 & 0 & \ldots & a_k \\ 1 & 1 & \ldots & 1 \end{pmatrix}, \quad \mathcal{U}_{\ell,k} : \mathbf{A} = \begin{pmatrix} a_{1,1} & \ldots & a_{1,k} \\ \vdots & \ddots & \vdots \\ a_{\ell,1} & \ldots & a_{\ell,k} \end{pmatrix},$$

where $a_i, a_{i,j} \leftarrow \mathbb{Z}_q$. The $\mathcal{L}_k$-MDDH Assumption is the k-linear family of Decisional Assumptions and corresponds to the Decisional Diffie-Hellman (DDH) Assumption in $\mathbb{G}_\gamma$ when $k = 1$. The SXDH Assumption states that DDH holds in $\mathbb{G}_\gamma$ for all $\gamma \in \{1, 2\}$. The $\mathcal{U}_{\ell,k}$ Assumption is the *Uniform* Assumption and is the weakest of all assumptions of size $\ell \times k$.

Further, given any matrix distribution $\mathcal{D}_k$, $m \in \mathbb{N}$ and any $i \in [m]$, we will repeatedly make reference to the distribution $\mathcal{D}_k^{m,i}$, which is defined as follows:

$$\mathcal{D}_k^{m,0} : \mathbf{A} = (\, \mathbf{B}\mathbf{w}_1 \, \dots \, \mathbf{B}\mathbf{w}_m \, \mathbf{B} \,) \qquad \mathcal{D}_k^{m,i} : \mathbf{A} = (\, \mathbf{B}\mathbf{w}_1 \, \dots \, \mathbf{B}\mathbf{w}_{i-1} \, \mathbf{z} \, \mathbf{B}\mathbf{w}_{i+1} \, \dots \, \mathbf{B}\mathbf{w}_m \, \mathbf{B} \,)$$

where $\mathbf{B} \leftarrow \mathcal{D}_k$, $\mathbf{w}_i \leftarrow \mathbb{Z}_q^k$ and $\mathbf{z} \leftarrow \mathbb{Z}_q^{k+1}$. The following are two trivial properties of the $\mathcal{D}_k^{m,i}$ distribution.

Lemma 1. *Under the $\mathcal{D}_k$-MDDH Assumption in $\mathbb{G}_\gamma$, for any $0 < i \leq n$, the distribution of $[\mathbf{A}]_\gamma$ when $\mathbf{A} \leftarrow \mathcal{D}_k^{m,0}$ and when $\mathbf{A} \leftarrow \mathcal{D}_k^{m,i}$ are computationally indistinguishable. Further, if $\ell > k$, for any $i > 0$, if $\mathbf{A} \leftarrow \mathcal{D}_k^{m,i}$, then with overwhelming probability its ith column is linearly independent of the rest.*

2.2 Computational Assumptions

Additionally, we will be using the following family computational assumptions:

Definition 3 (Kernel Diffie-Hellman Assumption in $\mathbb{G}_\gamma$ [19]). *Let $gk \leftarrow \mathsf{Gen}_a(1^\lambda)$. The Kernel Diffie-Hellman Assumption in $\mathbb{G}_\gamma$ ($\mathcal{D}_{\ell,k}$-KerMDH$_{\mathbb{G}_\gamma}$) says that every PPT Algorithm has negligible advantage in the following game: given $[\mathbf{A}]_\gamma$, where $\mathbf{A} \leftarrow \mathcal{D}_{\ell,k}$, find $[\mathbf{x}]_{3-\gamma} \in \mathbb{G}_{3-\gamma}^\ell$, $\mathbf{x} \neq \mathbf{0}$, such that $[\mathbf{x}]_{3-\gamma}^\top [\mathbf{A}]_\gamma = [\mathbf{0}]_T$.*

The Simultaneous Pairing Assumption in $\mathbb{G}_\gamma$ (SP$_{\mathbb{G}_\gamma}$) is the $\mathcal{U}_1$-KerMDH$_{\mathbb{G}_\gamma}$ Assumption. The Kernel Diffie-Hellman assumption is a generalization and abstraction of this assumption to other matrix distributions. The $\mathcal{D}_{\ell,k}$-KerMDH$_{\mathbb{G}_\gamma}$ Assumption is weaker than the $\mathcal{D}_{\ell,k}$-MDDH$_{\mathbb{G}_\gamma}$ Assumption, since a solution to the former allows to decide membership in $\mathbf{Im}([\mathbf{A}]_\gamma)$.

In asymmetric bilinear groups, there is a natural variant of this assumption which was introduced in [8].

Definition 4 (Split Kernel Diffie-Hellman Assumption). *Let $gk \leftarrow \mathsf{Gen}_a(1^\lambda)$. The Split Kernel Diffie-Hellman Assumption in $\mathbb{G}_1, \mathbb{G}_2$ ($\mathcal{D}_{\ell,k}$-SKerMDH) says that every PPT Algorithm has negligible advantage in the following game: given $([\mathbf{A}]_1, [\mathbf{A}]_2)$, $\mathbf{A} \leftarrow \mathcal{D}_{\ell,k}$, find a pair of vectors $([\mathbf{r}]_1, [\mathbf{s}]_2) \in \mathbb{G}_1^\ell \times \mathbb{G}_2^\ell$, $\mathbf{r} \neq \mathbf{s}$, such that $[\mathbf{r}]_1^\top [\mathbf{A}]_2 = [\mathbf{s}]_2^\top [\mathbf{A}]_1$.*

While the Kernel Diffie-Hellman Assumption says one cannot find a non-zero vector in one of the groups which is in the co-kernel of $\mathbf{A}$, the split assumption says one cannot find a pair of vectors in $\mathbb{G}_1^\ell \times \mathbb{G}_2^\ell$ such that the difference of the vector of their discrete logarithms is in the co-kernel of $\mathbf{A}$. As a particular case we consider the *Split Simultaneous Double Pairing Assumption in $\mathbb{G}_1, \mathbb{G}_2$* (SSDP) which is the $\mathcal{RL}_2$-SKerMDH Assumption, where $\mathcal{RL}_2$ is the distribution which results of sampling a matrix from $\mathcal{L}_2$ and replacing the last row by random elements.

2.3   Groth-Sahai NIZK Proofs

The GS proof system allows to prove satisfiability of a set of quadratic equations in a bilinear group. The admissible equation types must be in the following form:

$$\sum_{j=1}^{m_y} f(\alpha_j, \mathsf{y}_j) + \sum_{i=1}^{m_x} f(\mathsf{x}_i, \beta_i) + \sum_{i=1}^{m_x} \sum_{j=1}^{m_y} f(\mathsf{x}_i, \gamma_{i,j}\mathsf{y}_j) = t, \tag{3}$$

where $\boldsymbol{\alpha} \in A_1^{m_y}$, $\boldsymbol{\beta} \in A_2^{m_x}$, $\boldsymbol{\Gamma} = (\gamma_{i,j}) \in \mathbb{Z}_q^{m_x \times m_y}$, $t \in A_T$, and $A_1, A_2, A_T \in \{\mathbb{Z}_q, \mathbb{G}_1, \mathbb{G}_2, \mathbb{G}_T\}$ are equipped with some bilinear map $f : A_1 \times A_2 \to A_T$.

We give more details about GS proofs in the full version. Next, we introduce the GS commitment scheme.

Definition 5. *The Groth-Sahai commitment scheme in the SXDH instantiation in the group $\mathbb{G}_\gamma$, $\gamma \in \{1, 2\}$, is specified by the following three algorithms* $(\mathsf{GS.K}, \mathsf{GS.Com}, \mathsf{GS.Vrfy})$ *such that:*

- *$\mathsf{GS.K}$ is a randomized algorithm, which on input the group key gk and the (optional and if not given assumed to be* true*) flag* binding*, outputs a commitment key $ck := [\mathbf{U}]_\gamma = [(\mathbf{u}_1 \| \mathbf{u}_2)]_\gamma \in \mathbb{G}_\gamma^{2 \times 2}$. It samples $\mathbf{u}_2 \leftarrow \mathcal{L}_1$ and $\mu \leftarrow \mathbb{Z}_q$, and, if* binding $=$ true*, $[\mathbf{U}]_\gamma$ is the perfectly binding key and $\mathbf{u}_1 := \mu \mathbf{u}_2$ and else it is the perfectly hiding key and $\mathbf{u}_1 := \mu \mathbf{u}_2 - \mathbf{e}_2$.*
- *$\mathsf{GS.Com}$ is a randomized algorithm which, on input a commitment key $ck = [\mathbf{U}]_\gamma$, and a message m in the message space $\mathcal{M}_{ck} = \mathbb{Z}_q \cup \mathbb{G}_\gamma$, it proceeds as follows. If $\mathsf{m} = m \in \mathbb{Z}_q$, it samples $r \leftarrow \mathbb{Z}_q$ and outputs a commitment $[\mathbf{c}]_\gamma := m[\mathbf{e}_2 + \mathbf{u}_1]_\gamma + r[\mathbf{u}_2]_\gamma$ in the commitment space $\mathcal{C}_{ck} = \mathbb{G}_\gamma^2$ and an opening $Op = r$. If $\mathsf{m} = [m]_\gamma \in \mathbb{G}_\gamma$, it samples $\mathbf{r} \leftarrow \mathbb{Z}_q^2$ and outputs a commitment $[\mathbf{c}]_\gamma := [m]_\gamma \mathbf{e}_2 + [\mathbf{U}]_\gamma \mathbf{r}$ in the commitment space $\mathcal{C}_{ck} = \mathbb{G}_\gamma^2$ and an opening $Op = \mathbf{r}$.*
- *$\mathsf{GS.Vrfy}$ is a deterministic algorithm which, on input the commitment key $ck = [\mathbf{U}]_\gamma$, a commitment $[\mathbf{c}]_\gamma$, a message $m \in \mathcal{M}_{ck}$ and an opening Op, outputs 1 if $[\mathbf{c}]_\gamma = \mathsf{GS.Com}_{ck}(m; Op)$ and 0 otherwise.*

Theorem 1 ([12]). *If $ck \leftarrow \mathsf{K}(gk)$ (resp. $ck \leftarrow \mathsf{K}(gk, \mathsf{false})$) the Groth-Sahai commitment scheme is perfectly binding (resp. computationally binding) and computationally hiding (resp. perfectly hiding).*

2.4   Quasi-Adaptive NIZK Arguments

A Quasi-Adaptive NIZK proof system [13] enables to prove membership in a language defined by a relation $\mathcal{R}_\rho$, which in turn is completely determined by some parameter ρ sampled from a distribution $\mathcal{D}_{gk}$. We say that $\mathcal{D}_{gk}$ is *witness samplable* if there exists an efficient algorithm that samples (ρ, ω) from a distribution $\mathcal{D}_{gk}^{\mathsf{par}}$ such that ρ is distributed according to $\mathcal{D}_{gk}$, and membership of ρ in the *parameter language* $\mathcal{L}_{\mathsf{par}}$ can be efficiently verified with ω. While the Common Reference String can be set based on ρ, the zero-knowledge simulator is required to be a single probabilistic polynomial time algorithm that works for the whole collection of relations $\mathcal{R}_{gk}$.

The details of the QA-NIZK definition can be found in the full version.

QA-NIZK Argument for Linear Subspaces. In this section we describe the languages for which there exist constant-size QA-NIZK arguments of membership which will be used as building blocks in our constructions. These languages are (1) linear subspaces of $\mathbb{G}_s^m$, $s \in \{1, 2\}$ [14,16,17], (ii) linear subspaces of $\mathbb{G}_1^m \times \mathbb{G}_2^n$ [8], (iii) equal commitment opening [8], and (iv) *sum in subspace* [8]. More specifically, the languages are defined as follows for $\gamma, \nu \in \{1, 2\}$,

$$\mathcal{L}_{[\mathbf{M}]_\gamma} := \{[\mathbf{x}]_\gamma \in \mathbb{G}_\gamma^n : \exists \mathbf{w} \in \mathbb{Z}_q^t, \ \mathbf{x} = \mathbf{M}\mathbf{w}\}, \tag{i}$$

$$\mathcal{L}_{[\mathbf{M}]_1,[\mathbf{N}]_2} := \{([\mathbf{x}]_1, [\mathbf{y}]_2) \in \mathbb{G}_1^m \times \mathbb{G}_2^n : \exists \mathbf{w} \in \mathbb{Z}_q^t, \ \mathbf{x} = \mathbf{M}\mathbf{w}, \ \mathbf{y} = \mathbf{N}\mathbf{w}\}, \tag{ii}$$

$$\mathcal{L}_{ck,ck',\mathsf{com}} := \left\{ ([\mathbf{c}]_\gamma, [\mathbf{d}]_\nu) : \exists (\mathbf{w}, \mathbf{r}, \mathbf{s}) \in \mathbb{Z}_q^n \times \mathbb{Z}_q^{t_1} \times \mathbb{Z}_q^{t_2}, \begin{array}{l} [\mathbf{c}]_\gamma = \mathsf{Com}_{ck}(\mathbf{w}; \mathbf{r}), \\ [\mathbf{d}]_\nu = \mathsf{Com}_{ck'}(\mathbf{w}; \mathbf{s}) \end{array} \right\}, \tag{iii}$$

$$\mathcal{L}_{[\mathbf{M}]_1,[\mathbf{N}]_2,\mathsf{sum}} := \{([\mathbf{x}]_1, [\mathbf{y}]_2) : \exists \mathbf{w}, \mathbf{x} + \mathbf{y} = (\mathbf{M} + \mathbf{N})\mathbf{w}\}. \tag{iv}$$

In the above definitions, $\mathbf{M} \in \mathbb{Z}_q^{m \times t_1}$, $\mathbf{N} \in \mathbb{Z}_q^{n \times t_2}$ and ck (resp. ck') defines some commitments to vectors of $\mathbb{Z}_q^n$ where the randomness space is $\mathbb{Z}_q^{t_1}$ (resp. $\mathbb{Z}_q^{t_2}$). In (iv), $t_1 = t_2$. The commitment scheme Com is assumed to be of the form $\mathsf{Com}_{ck}(\mathbf{w}; \mathbf{r}) = [\mathbf{A}]_\gamma \mathbf{w} + [\mathbf{B}]_\gamma \mathbf{r}$, for some matrices $[\mathbf{A}]_\gamma, [\mathbf{B}]_\gamma$ defined in ck.

We denote indistinctly by Π_{lin} the proof systems for (i) and (ii), by Π_{com} the proof system for (iii), and by Π_{sum} the proof system for (iv).

To compute the proof sizes of our constructions, we will use the most efficient instantiations for each of these languages, which are described in Table 2. We note that the argument of [8] for $\mathcal{L}_{ck,ck',\mathsf{com}}$ is for the case $\gamma = 1, \nu = 2$. It is not hard to see that when $\nu = \gamma$, membership in $\mathcal{L}_{ck,ck',\mathsf{com}}$ (for commitments of the form we specified) amounts to prove membership in some linear space in $\mathbb{G}_\gamma$, which explains the second row of the table.

Table 2. QA-NIZK arguments for linear subspaces used in this work. When the proof size is given by (a, b) it means a elements of $\mathbb{G}_1$ and b elements of $\mathbb{G}_2$, otherwise $|\mathbb{G}_\gamma|$ means one element of $\mathbb{G}_\gamma$.

Proof system	Language	Proof Size	Assumption
[14,16]	$\mathcal{L}_{[\mathbf{M}]_s}$	$|\mathbb{G}_\gamma|$	$\mathsf{SP}_{\mathbb{G}_{3-\gamma}}$
	$\mathcal{L}_{ck,ck',,}, \gamma = \nu$	$|\mathbb{G}_\gamma|$	$\mathsf{SP}_{\mathbb{G}_{3-\gamma}}$
[8]	$\mathcal{L}_{[\mathbf{M}]_1,[\mathbf{N}]_2}$	$(2,2)$	SSDP
	$\mathcal{L}_{ck,ck',,}, \gamma \neq \nu$	$(2,2)$	SSDP
	$\mathcal{L}_{[\mathbf{M}]_1,[\mathbf{N}]_2,\mathsf{sum}}$	$(2,2)$	SSDP

3 Extended Multi-Pedersen Commitments

In this Section we introduce a new commitment scheme which is a generalization of Multi-Pedersen commitments and which was implicitly used in [8].

Given a vector $\mathbf{m} \in \mathbb{Z}_q^m$, the Multi-Pedersen commitment in $\mathbb{G}_\gamma$ is a single group element $[c]_\gamma := \sum_{i \in [m]} m_i [g_i]_\gamma + r[g_{m+1}]_\gamma \in \mathbb{G}_\gamma$, where $[g_i]_\gamma \in \mathbb{G}_\gamma$, $i \in [m+1]$, and $r \leftarrow \mathbb{Z}_q$.[3] The $(k+1)$-dimensional Multi-Pedersen commitment differs only in that the keys and the resulting commitments are in $\mathbb{G}_\gamma^{k+1}$, for $k \geq 1$.

While the original MP commitments are perfectly hiding, the interest of the new commitments is that, if the keys come from the distribution $\mathcal{D}_k^{m,i}$ defined in Sect. 2.1, they are perfectly binding at coordinate i. Intuitively, the new commitment is defined in a larger space so that not all the information about the witness is destroyed (in an information-theoretic sense).

Definition 6. *The $(k+1)$-dimensional Multi-Pedersen commitment scheme in the group $\mathbb{G}_\gamma$ is specified by the following three algorithms* $\mathsf{MP} = (\mathsf{MP.K}, \mathsf{MP.Com}, \mathsf{MP.Vrfy})$:

– *$\mathsf{MP.K}$ is a randomized algorithm, which on input the group key gk, a natural number $m \in \mathbb{N}$, and the description of some matrix distribution $\mathcal{D}_{k+1,m+k}$, outputs a commitment key $ck := [\mathbf{G}]_\gamma$, where $\mathbf{G} \leftarrow \mathcal{D}_{k+1,m+k}$.*
– *$\mathsf{MP.Com}$ is a randomized algorithm which, on input a commitment key $ck = [\mathbf{G}]_\gamma$, and a message $\mathbf{m}$ in the message space $\mathcal{M}_{ck} = \mathbb{Z}_q^m$, samples $\mathbf{r} \leftarrow \mathbb{Z}_q^k$ and outputs a commitment $[\mathbf{c}]_\gamma := [\mathbf{G}]_\gamma \left(\begin{smallmatrix} \mathbf{m} \\ \mathbf{r} \end{smallmatrix} \right)$ in the commitment space $\mathcal{C}_{ck} = \mathbb{G}_\gamma^{k+1}$ and an opening $Op = \mathbf{r}$.*
– *$\mathsf{MP.Vrfy}$ is a deterministic algorithm which, on input the commitment key $ck = [\mathbf{G}]_\gamma$, a commitment $[\mathbf{c}]_\gamma$, a message $\mathbf{m} \in \mathbb{Z}_q^m$ and an opening $Op = \mathbf{r} \in \mathbb{Z}_q^k$, outputs 1 if $[\mathbf{c}]_\gamma = [\mathbf{G}]_\gamma \left(\begin{smallmatrix} \mathbf{m} \\ \mathbf{r} \end{smallmatrix} \right)$ and 0 otherwise.*

Theorem 2. *The MP scheme is computationally binding if the discrete logarithm assumption holds in $\mathbb{G}_\gamma$. Further, if $\mathcal{D}_{k+1,m+k} = \mathcal{D}_k^{m,i}$, it holds that:*

– *If $i = 0$, then MP is perfectly hiding,*
– *If $i \in [m]$, then MP is statistically binding at coordinate i, which means that for each $[\mathbf{c}]_\gamma \in \mathbb{G}_\gamma^{k+1}$, there exists a unique $\tilde{m}_i \in \mathbb{Z}_q$ such that for all $\mathbf{m} \in \mathbb{Z}_q^m, \mathbf{r} \in \mathbb{Z}_q^k$ such that $[\mathbf{c}]_\gamma = [\mathbf{G}]_\gamma \left(\begin{smallmatrix} \mathbf{m} \\ \mathbf{r} \end{smallmatrix} \right)$, $m_i = \tilde{m}_i$. Further, the scheme is perfectly hiding at the rest of coordinates.*

The proof is not hard to derive from the definition of the $\mathcal{D}_k^{m,i}$ distribution, and can be found in the full version.

4 QA-NIZK for Bit-Strings, Revisited

We construct a QA-NIZK argument of membership in the language

$$\mathcal{L}_{ck,\mathsf{bits}} := \{[\mathbf{c}]_1 \in \mathbb{G}_1^{k+1} : \exists \mathbf{b} \in \{0,1\}^m, \mathbf{r} \in \mathbb{Z}_q^k \text{ s.t. } [\mathbf{c}]_1 = \mathsf{MP.Com}_{ck}(\mathbf{b}; \mathbf{r})\},$$

---

[3] Written in the usual multiplicative notation $c = \prod_{i \in [m]} g_i^{m_i} \cdot g_{m+1}^r$.

where $ck := [\mathbf{G}]_1$ and $\mathbf{G}$ is a matrix sampled from some distribution $\mathcal{D}_k^{m,i}$. For simplicity, in the exposition we restrict ourselves to the case $\mathcal{D}_k = \mathcal{L}_1$ so $\mathbf{G}$ is sampled from $\mathcal{L}_1^{m,i}$, for some $0 \le i \le m$.

It is important to note that, as an extended MP commitment is at best only binding at one coordinate, a priori showing that it opens to $\mathbf{b} \in \{0,1\}^m$ is not very meaningful, as it does open to other values as well. However, when combined with external protocols that univocally define $\mathbf{b}$, it becomes a key building block to obtain the rest of the results of the paper.

The argument is implicit in [8], where the authors construct a QA-NIZK argument for proving that a perfectly binding commitment opens to a bit-string. More technically, to prove that a perfectly binding commitment $[\mathbf{c}']_1$ opens to a bit-string $\mathbf{b}$, the argument in [8] takes the following steps: (1) construct two MP commitments $[\mathbf{c}]_1$; $[\mathbf{d}]_2$ to $\mathbf{b}$ (2) prove that $[\mathbf{c}]_1$ and $[\mathbf{c}']_1$ open to the same string; (3) prove that the two MP commitments $[\mathbf{c}]_1$ and $[\mathbf{d}]_2$ open to the same string; (4) prove that $\mathbf{c}(\mathbf{d} - \sum_{j \in [m]} \mathbf{h}_j)^\top \in \mathbf{Span}(\{\mathbf{g}_i \mathbf{h}_j^\top : i, j \in [m+1]\}) \setminus \{\mathbf{g}_i \mathbf{h}_i^\top : i \in [m]\})$, where $ck := [(\mathbf{g}_1, \ldots, \mathbf{g}_{m+1})]_1$ and $ck' := [(\mathbf{h}_1, \ldots, \mathbf{h}_{m+1})]_2$. The last step guarantees that $b_i(b_i - 1) = 0$ for all $i \in [m]$. Indeed, $\mathbf{c}(\mathbf{d} - \sum_{j \in [m]} \mathbf{h}_j)^\top$ can be written as a linear combination of the vectors $\{\mathbf{g}_i \mathbf{h}_j^\top\}$ where the coefficient of $\mathbf{g}_i \mathbf{h}_i^\top$ is $b_i(b_i - 1)$. Intuitively, an adversary will be able to prove that $\mathbf{c}(\mathbf{d} - \sum_{j \in [m]} \mathbf{h}_j)^\top$ is in the span of the vectors $\{\mathbf{g}_i \mathbf{h}_j^\top\}$ without those pairs where $i = j$ only if $b_i(b_i - 1) = 0$ for all $i \in [m]$.

The argument we need for our results eliminates the perfectly binding commitment, which of course also means that step 2 disappears. Additionally, in the original scheme of [8], the distribution of $ck = [\mathbf{G}]_1$ is $\mathcal{L}_1^{m,0}$, while in our argument of membership in $\mathcal{L}_{ck,\text{bits}}$, $\mathbf{G}$ can follow any distribution $\mathcal{L}_1^{m,i}$ for some $0 \le i \le m$. However, it is not hard to adapt the original proof to these distributions (in fact, in the soundness proof of [8], there is a game where the distribution of $\mathbf{G}$ is changed to $\mathcal{L}_1^{m,i}$, for some $i \leftarrow [m]$). The proof that $\mathcal{L}_{ck,\text{bits}}$ admits a constant-size QA-NIZK argument essentially reuses parts of the proof of [8]. In summary, in the full version of this work we prove the following result, which heavily draws on the work of [8].

Theorem 3. *There exists a QA-NIZK argument Π_{bits} for membership in $\mathcal{L}_{ck,\text{bits}}$ with proof size $8|\mathbb{G}_1| + 10|\mathbb{G}_2|$ with perfect completeness, perfect-zero knowledge and computational soundness.*

4.1   Constant-Size Argument for $\mathcal{L}_{ck,\text{bits}}^n$

We give a QA-NIZK argument of membership in the language $\mathcal{L}_{ck,\text{bits}}^n = \mathcal{L}_{ck,\text{bits}} \times \ldots \times \mathcal{L}_{ck,\text{bits}}$ with a proof size which is independent of n (but with a loss factor in the proof of soundness of n). The result will be crucial to get improved proof sizes for more complex statements. More specifically, we prove:

Theorem 4. *There exists a QA-NIZK argument $\Pi_{\text{bits},n}$ for membership in $\mathcal{L}_{ck,\text{bits}}^n$ with proof size $10|\mathbb{G}_1| + 10|\mathbb{G}_2|$ with perfect completeness, perfect-zero knowledge and computational soundness.*

The description of the protocol and the full proof of Theorem 4 are in the full version.

5   Aggregated NIZK Set Membership Arguments

In this section we construct a QA-NIZK argument that many commitments open to elements in a set $[0, d-1] \subset \mathbb{Z}_q$ or $S \subset \mathbb{G}_\gamma$. We first express both languages in a unified way.

Definition 7. *Denote by* $\mathcal{L}_{[\mathbf{M}]_1,[\mathbf{N}]_1,\Lambda,\alpha} \subseteq \mathbb{G}_1^{\ell_1}$ *the language parameterized by* $[\mathbf{M}]_1 \in \mathbb{G}_1^{\ell_1 \times m}, [\mathbf{N}]_1 \in \mathbb{G}_1^{\ell_1 \times \ell_2}, \Lambda \in \mathbb{Z}_q^{\ell_3 \times m}$, *and* $\alpha \in \mathbb{Z}_q^{\ell_3}$ *such that*

$$[\mathbf{c}]_1 \in \mathcal{L}_{[\mathbf{M}]_1,[\mathbf{N}]_1,\Lambda,\alpha} \iff \exists \mathbf{b} \in \{0,1\}^m, \mathbf{w} \in \mathbb{Z}_q^{\ell_2} \; s.t. \; \begin{pmatrix} \mathbf{c} \\ \alpha \end{pmatrix} = \begin{pmatrix} \mathbf{M} & \mathbf{N} \\ \Lambda & \mathbf{0}_{\ell_3 \times \ell_2} \end{pmatrix} \begin{pmatrix} \mathbf{b} \\ \mathbf{w} \end{pmatrix}. \quad (4)$$

Additionally, we require $(\mathbf{N}, [\mathbf{N}]_1)$ *to be efficiently samplable and that membership in* $\mathcal{L}_{[\mathbf{M}]_1,[\mathbf{N}]_1,\Lambda,\alpha}$ *is efficiently testable with the trapdoor* $\mathbf{N}$*, that is, that there exists an efficient algorithm* F *such that* $\mathsf{F}([\mathbf{M}]_1, \mathbf{N}, [\mathbf{c}]_1) = 1 \iff [\mathbf{c}]_1 \in \mathcal{L}_{\mathbf{M},\mathbf{N},\Lambda,\alpha}$*. The witness of* $[\mathbf{c}]_1 \in \mathcal{L}_{[\mathbf{M}]_1,[\mathbf{N}]_1,\Lambda,\alpha}$ *is* $(\mathbf{b}, \mathbf{w})$*, and the bit-witness is* $\mathbf{b}$*. The size of the bit-witness is* m*.*

Example 1. The language of GS commitments to group elements in the set $S := \{[s_1]_1, \ldots, [s_m]_1\} \subset \mathbb{G}_1$, $\mathcal{L}_{ck,S}$, where $ck := ([\mathbf{u}_1]_1 || [\mathbf{u}_2]_1)$, is equal to $\mathcal{L}_{[\mathbf{M}]_1,[\mathbf{N}]_1,\Lambda,\alpha}$, where $\mathbf{M} := \begin{pmatrix} 0 & \cdots & 0 \\ s_1 & \cdots & s_m \end{pmatrix}$, $\mathbf{N} := (\mathbf{u}_1 || \mathbf{u}_2)$, $\alpha = 1$, and $\Lambda = (1, \ldots, 1)$. The bit-witness size is $|S|$ and membership $\mathcal{L}_{ck,S}$ is efficiently testable given $\mathbf{u}_1, \mathbf{u}_2 \in \mathbb{Z}_q^2$ (assuming $|S| = \mathsf{poly}(\lambda)$).

Example 2. The language of GS commitments to integers in the range $[0, d-1]$, $\mathcal{L}_{ck,[0,d-1]}$, where $ck := ([\mathbf{u}_1]_1 || [\mathbf{u}_2]_1)$, is equal to $\mathcal{L}_{[\mathbf{M}]_1,[\mathbf{N}]_1,\Lambda,\alpha}$, where $\mathbf{M} := (\mathbf{e}_2 + \mathbf{u}_1)(2^0, 2^1, \ldots, 2^{\log d - 1}) \in \mathbb{Z}_q^{2 \times \log d}$, $\mathbf{N} := \mathbf{u}_2 \in \mathbb{Z}_q^2$, and $\ell_3 := 0$. The bit-witness size is $\log d$ and membership in $\mathcal{L}_{ck,[0,d-1]}$ is easily testable given $\mathbf{u}_2 \in \mathbb{Z}_q^2$ (assuming $d = \mathsf{poly}(\lambda)$).

The general idea of how to prove membership in $\mathcal{L}_{[\mathbf{M}]_1,[\mathbf{N}]_1,\Lambda,\alpha}$ was explained in Sect. 1.1. As we discussed there the total size of the proof is $2m|\mathbb{G}_1| + \Theta(1)$.

5.1   QA-NIZK Argument of Membership in $\mathcal{L}^n_{\mathbf{M},\mathbf{N},\Lambda,\alpha}$

The main result of this Section is a proof, of roughly the same size as in the last Section ($2m|\mathbb{G}_1| + \Theta(1)$), that $([\mathbf{c}_1]_1, \ldots, [\mathbf{c}_n]_1)$ is in $\mathcal{L}^n_{[\mathbf{M}]_1,[\mathbf{N}]_1,\Lambda,\alpha}$.

For all $j \in [n]$, let $(\mathbf{b}_j, \mathbf{w}_j) \in \{0,1\}^m \times \mathbb{Z}_q^{\ell_2}$ be the witness of $\mathbf{c}_j \in \mathcal{L}_{[\mathbf{M}]_1,[\mathbf{N}]_1,\Lambda,\alpha}$. Let $\mathbf{B} = (\mathbf{b}_1 || \ldots || \mathbf{b}_n)$ and let $\mathbf{b}_i^*$, $i \in [m]$ the ith row of $\mathbf{B}$. To get a proof of size independent of n we commit to $\mathbf{B}$ "compressing the rows", that is, the proof includes MP commitments $[\mathbf{d}_i]_1$, $i \in [n]$ to $\mathbf{b}_i^*$.[4] Further, as announced in Sect. 1.1, the proof consists of two independent statements:

---

[4] To get a constant-size proof, it would be tempting to compress the commitments to all of $\mathbf{B}$, but we do not know how to prove soundness in this case.

- $\exists \mathbf{r} \in \mathbb{Z}_q^m, \mathbf{B} \in \mathbb{Z}_q^{m \times n}$ such that 1")$\mathbf{B} \in \{0,1\}^{m \times n}$ and 3")$\forall i \in [m] : \mathbf{d}_i = \mathbf{G}\left(\begin{smallmatrix} \mathbf{b}_i^* \\ r_i \end{smallmatrix}\right)$,
- $\exists \widetilde{\mathbf{r}} \in \mathbb{Z}_q^m, \mathbf{w}_1, \ldots, \mathbf{w}_n \in \mathbb{Z}_q^{\ell_2}, \widetilde{\mathbf{B}} \in \mathbb{Z}_q^{m \times n}$ such that 2")$\forall j \in [n], \left(\begin{smallmatrix} \mathbf{c}_j \\ \alpha \end{smallmatrix}\right) = \left(\begin{smallmatrix} \mathbf{M} & \mathbf{N} \\ \Lambda & \mathbf{0} \end{smallmatrix}\right)\left(\begin{smallmatrix} \widetilde{\mathbf{b}}_j \\ \mathbf{w}_j \end{smallmatrix}\right)$ and 3")$\forall i \in [m], \mathbf{d}_i = \mathbf{G}\left(\begin{smallmatrix} \widetilde{\mathbf{b}}_i^* \\ \widetilde{r}_i \end{smallmatrix}\right)$.

For the first statement we use the constant-size argument for $\mathcal{L}_{ck,\mathrm{bits}}^m$ of Sect. 4. For the second statement, we write conditions 2"), 3") as a single system of equations and use Π_{lin} to prove that it can be satisfied.

The soundness argument follows from the arguments exposed in Sect. 1.1. The full description of the argument together with the proof of the following theorem are in the full version.

Theorem 5. *There exists a QA-NIZK argument Π_{set} for membership in the language $\mathcal{L}_{[\mathbf{M}]_1,[\mathbf{N}]_1,\Lambda,\alpha}^n$ with proof size $(2m+11)|\mathbb{G}_1| + 10|\mathbb{G}_2|$, perfect completeness, perfect-zero knowledge and computational soundness.*

6   Proof of Correctness of a Shuffle

In a NIZK Shuffle argument one wants to prove that two lists of ciphertexts open to the same values when the second list is permuted under some hidden permutation. We represent each list of ciphertexts as a matrix in $\mathbb{G}_2^{2 \times n}$ where each column is an El-Gamal ciphertext under public key $pk := [\mathbf{v}]_2 \in \mathbb{G}_2^2$ and we write $\mathsf{Enc}_{pk}([\mathbf{m}^\top]_2; \mathbf{r}^\top) := (\mathsf{Enc}_{pk}([m_1]_2; r_1)||\cdots||\mathsf{Enc}_{pk}([m_n]_2; r_n))$, where $[\mathbf{m}]_2 \in \mathbb{G}_2^n$, $\mathbf{r} \in \mathbb{Z}_q^n$, and $\mathsf{Enc}_{pk}([m]_2; r) := [m]_2\mathbf{e}_2 + r[\mathbf{v}]_2$. Similarly, through this section we will sometimes write $\mathsf{GS.Com}_{ck}([\mathbf{x}^\top]_\gamma; \mathbf{R}) :=$ $(\mathsf{GS.Com}_{ck}([x_1]_\gamma; \mathbf{r}_1)||\cdots||\mathsf{GS.Com}_{ck} ([x_n]_\gamma; \mathbf{r}_n))$, where $\mathbf{R} = (\mathbf{r}_1||\cdots||\mathbf{r}_n) \in \mathbb{Z}_q^{2 \times n}$.

The language of correct shuffles under public key $[\mathbf{v}]_2 \in \mathbb{G}_2^2$ can can be defined as

$$\mathcal{L}_{[\mathbf{v}]_2, n, \mathsf{shuffle}} := \{([\mathbf{C}]_2, [\mathbf{D}]_2) \in \mathbb{G}_2^{2 \times n} \times \mathbb{G}_2^{2 \times n} :$$

$$\exists \mathbf{P} \in \mathcal{S}_n, \delta \in \mathbb{Z}_q^n \text{ s.t. } [\mathbf{C}]_2\mathbf{P} - [\mathbf{D}]_2 = \mathsf{Enc}_{pk}([\mathbf{0}_{1 \times n}]_2; \delta^\top)\},$$

where $\mathcal{S}_n$ is the set of permutation matrices of size $n \times n$.

6.1   Our Construction

Our proof system builds on a proof that a set of GS commitments open to elements in the set $S = \{[s_1]_1, \ldots, [s_n]_1\}$, where $\mathbf{s} := (s_1, \ldots, s_n)^\top \leftarrow \mathcal{D}_{n,1}$ and the $\mathcal{D}_{n,1}$-KerMDH Assumption holds in $\mathbb{G}_1$. Given $[\mathbf{F}]_1 \in \mathbb{G}_1^{2 \times n}$, where the ith column is $[\mathbf{f}_i]_1 \leftarrow \mathsf{GS.Com}([x_i]_1)$, let $\mathbf{x} := (x_1, \ldots, x_n)^\top = \mathbf{Ps}$, for some permutation matrix $\mathbf{P}$. Given a commitment to $[y]_1 := [\mathbf{s}^\top]_1\delta$, we prove that $([\mathbf{C}]_2, [\mathbf{D}]_2) \in \mathcal{L}_{[\mathbf{v}]_2, n, \mathsf{shuffle}}$ as follows: (a) show that $[\mathbf{F}]_1 \in \mathcal{L}_{ck,S}^n$, where $ck \leftarrow \mathsf{GS.K}(gk)$; (b) give a GS proof for the satisfiability of $\sum_{i \in [n]}[s_i]_1 - \sum_{j \in [n]}[x_j]_1 = [0]_1$; (c) give a GS proof for the satisfiability of $[\mathbf{x}^\top]_1[\mathbf{C}^\top]_2 - [\mathbf{s}^\top]_1[\mathbf{D}^\top]_2 = [y]_1[\mathbf{v}^\top]_2$.

Soundness Intuition. Conditions (a) and (b) imply that $\mathbf{x}$ is a permutation of $\mathbf{s}$ or equivalently, $\mathbf{x} = \mathbf{Ps}$ and $\mathbf{P}$ is a permutation matrix. Note that $\mathbf{P}$ is a permutation matrix iff $\mathbf{P}$ is a binary matrix and for each row and column there is at most one 1. Let's see in more detail why $\mathbf{x}$ is a permutation of $\mathbf{s}$. Condition (a) implies that each x_i is an element from $\{s_1, \ldots, s_n\}$, which can be written as $\mathbf{x} = \mathbf{Ps}$, $\mathbf{P} \in \{0,1\}^{n \times n}$, where each row of $\mathbf{P}$ has at most one 1. But, given that there might be repeated elements, there might be also more than one 1 in some column of $\mathbf{P}$. For example, if $S = \{s_1, s_2, s_3\}$, it may be that $\mathbf{x} = \begin{pmatrix} s_2 \\ s_3 \\ s_1 \end{pmatrix} = \begin{pmatrix} 0 & 1 & 0 \\ 0 & 0 & 1 \\ 1 & 0 & 0 \end{pmatrix} \begin{pmatrix} s_1 \\ s_2 \\ s_3 \end{pmatrix}$ but also $\mathbf{x} = \begin{pmatrix} s_2 \\ s_3 \\ s_3 \end{pmatrix} = \begin{pmatrix} 0 & 1 & 0 \\ 0 & 0 & 1 \\ 0 & 0 & 1 \end{pmatrix} \begin{pmatrix} s_1 \\ s_2 \\ s_3 \end{pmatrix}$. Condition (b) implies that there are no repeated x_is unless one can break the $\mathcal{D}_{n,1}$-KerMDH assumption. Indeed, there are repeated x_is iff $(1, \ldots, 1)\mathbf{P}$ (the row vector of "frequencies" of $\mathbf{x}$, which in the first example is $(1, 1, 1)$ and in the second $(0, 1, 2)$) is not equal to $(1, \ldots, 1)$. Given that (b) is equivalent to $((1, \ldots, 1) - (1, \ldots, 1)\mathbf{P})[\mathbf{s}]_1 = [0]_1$, then $((1, \ldots, 1) - (1, \ldots, 1)\mathbf{P})^\top$ is a solution to the $\mathcal{D}_{n,1}$-KerMDH problem. We conclude that $\mathbf{P}$ is a permutation matrix and thus $\mathbf{x}$ is a permutation of $\mathbf{s}$.

The remainder of the proof follows essentially the proof from [10]. Suppose that $[\mathbf{C}]_2 = \mathsf{Enc}_{[\mathbf{v}]_2}([\mathbf{m}^\top]_2)$ and $[\mathbf{C}]_2 = \mathsf{Enc}_{[\mathbf{v}]_2}([\mathbf{n}^\top]_2)$. Let $\mathbf{k} = (-v_2/v_1, 1)^\top$ the "decryption key" (i.e. $\mathbf{v}^\top \mathbf{k} = 0$ and $(0, 1)\mathbf{k} = 1$)[5]. We multiply by $\mathbf{k}$ on the right the equation from condition (c) to "decrypt" $[\mathbf{C}]_2$ and $[\mathbf{D}]_2$. We get that $[\mathbf{s}^\top]_1 \mathbf{P}^\top [\mathbf{m}]_2 - [\mathbf{s}^\top]_1 [\mathbf{n}]_2 = [0]_T$, which implies that $\mathbf{P}^\top [\mathbf{m}]_2 = [\mathbf{n}]_2$ unless $\mathbf{P}^\top [\mathbf{m}]_2 - [\mathbf{n}]_2$ is a solution to the $\mathcal{D}_{n,1}$-KerMDH. Finally this implies that $[\mathbf{C}]_2 \mathbf{P} - [\mathbf{D}]_2$ is an encryption of $[\mathbf{0}_{n \times 1}]_2$ and thus $([\mathbf{C}]_2, [\mathbf{D}]_2) \in \mathcal{L}_{[\mathbf{v}]_2, n, \mathsf{shuffle}}$.

A detailed description and the proof of security of our construction can be found in the full version.

7 Range Argument in the Interval $[0, 2^n - 1]$

We want to prove that a GS commitment $[\mathbf{c}]_1$ opens to some integer y in the range $[0, 2^n - 1]$. That is, construct a NIZK proof system for the language

$$\mathcal{L}_{ck, [0, 2^n - 1]} := \{[\mathbf{c}]_1 \in \mathbb{G}_1^2 : \exists y, r \in \mathbb{Z}_q \text{ s.t. } [\mathbf{c}]_1 = \mathsf{GS.Com}_{ck}(y; r) \wedge y \in [0, 2^n - 1]\},$$

where $ck := ([\mathbf{u}_1]_1, [\mathbf{u}_2]_1) \leftarrow \mathsf{GS.K}(1^\lambda)$. Our proof is as follows: (a) commit to $y_1, \ldots y_\ell$, (b) show that $y_i \in [0, d-1]$, for each $i \in [\ell]$, (c) show that $y = \sum_{i \in [\ell]} y_i d^{i-1}$. Given that it must hold that $\ell = n / \log d$, the total size of the proof is $\mathsf{S}_{[0, d-1]}(\ell) + \Theta(\ell)$, where $\mathsf{S}_{[0, d-1]}(\ell)$ is the size of ℓ Range Proofs in the interval $[0, d-1]$.

7.1 Our Construction

Note that (b) is equivalent to show that $(\mathsf{GS.Com}_{ck}(y_1) || \cdots || \mathsf{GS.Com}_{ck}(y_\ell)) \in \mathcal{L}_{ck, [0, d-1]}^\ell$. Thus, using the proof system from Sect. 5 we are able to aggregate ℓ

---

[5] The availability of the decryption key $\mathbf{k}$ in the soundness reduction is possible since the reduction samples by itself the language parameter $\mathbf{v}$. Correspondingly Groth and Lu [10] proved *Culpable Soundness* (also called co-soundness), which essentially requires the soundness adversary to produce the decryption key.

Range Proofs in the interval $[0, d-1]$ into a single proof of size $\Theta(\log d)$. Choosing $d = n^k$ we get that $\mathsf{S}_{[0,d-1]}(\ell) = \Theta(k \log n)$ and $\ell = n/\log n^k = \frac{n}{k \log n}$, and thus the size of our Range Proof is $\Theta(\frac{n}{k \log n})$ for an arbitrarily chosen $k \in \mathbb{N}$. One would be tempted to choose $d = 2^{\sqrt{n}}$ to obtain a proof of size $\Theta(\sqrt{n})$. However, the proof system from Sect. 5 requires membership in $\mathcal{L}_{ck,[0,d-1]}$ to be efficiently testable, which seems to be infeasible as when $d = 2^{\sqrt{n}}$.

A detailed description and the security proofs of our proof system can be found in the full version.

References

1. Bayer, S., Groth, J.: Efficient zero-knowledge argument for correctness of a shuffle. In: Pointcheval, D., Johansson, T. (eds.) EUROCRYPT 2012. LNCS, vol. 7237, pp. 263–280. Springer, Heidelberg (2012)
2. Bayer, S., Groth, J.: Zero-Knowledge argument for polynomial evaluation with application to blacklists. In: Johansson, T., Nguyen, P.Q. (eds.) EUROCRYPT 2013. LNCS, vol. 7881, pp. 646–663. Springer, Heidelberg (2013)
3. Camenisch, J.L., Chaabouni, R., Shelat, A.: Efficient protocols for set membership and range proofs. In: Pieprzyk, J. (ed.) ASIACRYPT 2008. LNCS, vol. 5350, pp. 234–252. Springer, Heidelberg (2008)
4. Chaabouni, R., Lipmaa, H., Zhang, B.: A non-interactive range proof with constant communication. In: Keromytis, A.D. (ed.) FC 2012. LNCS, vol. 7397, pp. 179–199. Springer, Heidelberg (2012)
5. Chaum, D.: Untraceable electronic mail, return addresses, and digital pseudonyms. Commun. ACM **24**, 84–88 (1981)
6. Escala, A., Herold, G., Kiltz, E., Ràfols, C., Villar, J.: An algebraic framework for diffie-hellman assumptions. In: Canetti, R., Garay, J.A. (eds.) CRYPTO 2013, Part II. LNCS, vol. 8043, pp. 129–147. Springer, Heidelberg (2013)
7. Fauzi, P., Lipmaa, H.: Efficient culpably sound nizk shuffle argument without random oracles. Cryptology ePrint Archive, Report 2015/1112 (2015). http://eprint.iacr.org/
8. González, A., Hevia, A., Ràfols, C.: QA-NIZK arguments in asymmetric groups: new tools and new constructions. In: Iwata, T., Cheon, J.H. (eds.) ASIACRYPT 2015, Part I. LNCS, vol. 9452, pp. 605–629. Springer, Heidelberg (2015). doi: 10.1007/978-3-662-48797-6_25
9. Groth, J.: Efficient zero-knowledge arguments from two-tiered homomorphic commitments. In: Lee, D.H., Wang, X. (eds.) ASIACRYPT 2011. LNCS, vol. 7073, pp. 431–448. Springer, Heidelberg (2011)
10. Groth, J., Lu, S.: A non-interactive shuffle with pairing based verifiability. In: Kurosawa, K. (ed.) ASIACRYPT 2007. LNCS, vol. 4833, pp. 51–67. Springer, Heidelberg (2007)
11. Groth, J., Ostrovsky, R., Sahai, A.: Perfect non-interactive zero knowledge for NP. In: Vaudenay, S. (ed.) EUROCRYPT 2006. LNCS, vol. 4004, pp. 339–358. Springer, Heidelberg (2006)
12. Groth, J., Sahai, A.: Efficient noninteractive proof systems for bilinear groups. SIAM J. Comput. **41**(5), 1193–1232 (2012)
13. Jutla, C.S., Roy, A.: Shorter quasi-adaptive NIZK proofs for linear subspaces. In: Sako, K., Sarkar, P. (eds.) ASIACRYPT 2013, Part I. LNCS, vol. 8269, pp. 1–20. Springer, Heidelberg (2013)

14. Jutla, C.S., Roy, A.: Switching lemma for bilinear tests and constant-size NIZK proofs for linear subspaces. In: Garay, J.A., Gennaro, R. (eds.) CRYPTO 2014, Part II. LNCS, vol. 8617, pp. 295–312. Springer, Heidelberg (2014)
15. Kiltz, E., Pan, J., Wee, H.: Structure-Preserving signatures from standard assumptions, revisited. In: Gennaro, R., Robshaw, M. (eds.) CRYPTO 2015, Part II. LNCS, vol. 9216, pp. 275–295. Springer, Heidelberg (2015)
16. Kiltz, E., Wee, H.: Quasi-Adaptive NIZK for linear subspaces revisited. In: Oswald, E., Fischlin, M. (eds.) EUROCRYPT 2015, Part II. LNCS, vol. 9057, pp. 101–128. Springer, Heidelberg (2015)
17. Libert, B., Peters, T., Joye, M., Yung, M.: Non-malleability from malleability: simulation-sound quasi-adaptive NIZK proofs and CCA2-Secure encryption from homomorphic signatures. In: Nguyen, P.Q., Oswald, E. (eds.) EUROCRYPT 2014. LNCS, vol. 8441, pp. 514–532. Springer, Heidelberg (2014)
18. Lipmaa, H., Zhang, B.: A more efficient computationally sound non-interactive zero-knowledge shuffle argument. In: Visconti, I., De Prisco, R. (eds.) SCN 2012. LNCS, vol. 7485, pp. 477–502. Springer, Heidelberg (2012)
19. Morillo, P., Ràfols, C., Villar, J.L.: Matrix computational assumptions in multi-linear groups. Cryptology ePrint Archive, Report 2015/353 (2015). http://eprint.iacr.org/2015/353
20. Rial, A., Kohlweiss, M., Preneel, B.: Universally composable adaptive priced oblivious transfer. In: Shacham, H., Waters, B. (eds.) Pairing 2009. LNCS, vol. 5671, pp. 231–247. Springer, Heidelberg (2009)

Constrained PRFs for Unbounded Inputs with Short Keys

Hamza Abusalah[1(✉)] and Georg Fuchsbauer[2]

[1] Institute of Science and Technology Austria, Klosterneuburg, Austria
habusalah@ist.ac.at
[2] Inria, ENS, CNRS and PSL Research University, Paris, France
georg.fuchsbauer@ens.fr

Abstract. A constrained pseudorandom function (CPRF) $F \colon \mathcal{K} \times \mathcal{X} \to \mathcal{Y}$ for a family $\mathcal{T}$ of subsets of $\mathcal{X}$ is a function where for any key $k \in \mathcal{K}$ and set $S \in \mathcal{T}$ one can efficiently compute a short constrained key k_S, which allows to evaluate $F(k, \cdot)$ on all inputs $x \in S$, while the outputs on all inputs $x \notin S$ look random even given k_S.

Abusalah et al. recently constructed the first constrained PRF for inputs of arbitrary length whose sets S are decided by Turing machines. They use their CPRF to build broadcast encryption and the first ID-based non-interactive key exchange for an unbounded number of users. Their constrained keys are obfuscated circuits and are therefore large.

In this work we drastically reduce the key size and define a constrained key for a Turing machine M as a short signature on M. For this, we introduce a new signature primitive with constrained signing keys that let one only sign certain messages, while forging a signature on others is hard even when knowing the coins for key generation.

Keywords: Constrained PRFs · Unbounded inputs

1 Introduction

Constrained PRFs. A pseudorandom function (PRF) [15] is a keyed function $F \colon \mathcal{K} \times \mathcal{X} \to \mathcal{Y}$ for which no efficient adversary, given access to an oracle $\mathcal{O}(\cdot)$, can decide whether $\mathcal{O}(\cdot)$ is $F(k, \cdot)$ with a random key $k \in \mathcal{K}$, or whether $\mathcal{O}(\cdot)$ is a uniformly random function $\mathcal{X} \to \mathcal{Y}$. A PRF F is called *constrained* [7,10,17] for a predicate family $\mathcal{P}$ if additionally there exists a PPT constraining algorithm $k_p \leftarrow F.\mathsf{Constr}(k, p)$ that, on input a key k and a predicate $p \colon \mathcal{X} \to \{0, 1\}$ specifying a subset $S_p = \{x \in \mathcal{X} \mid p(x) = 1\}$ of potentially exponential size, derives a constrained key k_p. The latter allows computing $F(k, x)$ on all $x \in S_p$, while even given keys for $p_1, \ldots, p_\ell$, values $F(k, x)$ for $x \notin \bigcup_i S_{p_i}$ still look random. Note that if all sets S_p are polynomial-size, a simple solution would be

---

H. Abusalah—Research supported by the European Research Council, ERC starting grant (259668-PSPC) and ERC consolidator grant (682815 - TOCNeT).

© Springer International Publishing Switzerland 2016
M. Manulis et al. (Eds.): ACNS 2016, LNCS 9696, pp. 445–463, 2016.
DOI: 10.1007/978-3-319-39555-5_24

to set $k_p := \{F(k,x) \mid x \in S_p\}$, which would achieve the desired security. The challenge is to have short keys for potentially big sets.

The simplest type of constrained PRFs (CPRF) are puncturable PRFs [18], where for any input $x \in \{0,1\}^*$ one can derive a key k_{x^*} that allows evaluation everywhere except on x^*, whose image is pseudorandom even given k_{x^*}. The most general CPRF is one that is constrained w.r.t. a Turing-machine (TM) predicate family $\mathcal{M}$, where $M \in \mathcal{M}$ defines a subset of inputs of arbitrary length $S_M = \{x \in \{0,1\}^* \mid M(x) = 1\}$. In a TM-constrained PRF a constrained key k_M can be derived for any set S_M defined by a TM M.

Abusalah et al. (AFP) [2] construct a (selectively secure) TM-constrained PRF and show how to use it to construct broadcast encryption (BE) [8,11] where there is no a priori bound on the number of possible recipients and the first identity-based non-interactive key-exchange scheme [7,12,19] with no a priori bound on the number of parties that agree on a key.

The main shortcoming of their construction is that a constrained key k_M for a TM M is an obfuscated circuit and is therefore not short but typically huge. This translates to large user keys in the BE and ID-NIKE schemes built from their CPRF. In this paper we overcome this and reduce the key size drastically by defining a constrained key k_M for M as simply a signature on M.

TM-Constrained PRFs with Short Keys. The AFP TM-constrained PRF in [2] is built from puncturable PRFs, succinct non-interactive arguments of knowledge (SNARKs), which let one prove knowledge of an NP witness via a short proof, collision-resistant hashing and public-coin differing-input obfuscation ($di\mathcal{O}$) [16]. The latter lets one *obfuscate* programs, so that one can only distinguish obfuscations of two equal-size programs if one knows an input on which those programs' outputs are different. Moreover, if for two programs it is hard to find such a differing input, *even when knowing the coins used to construct the programs*, then their obfuscations are indistinguishable.

Relying on essentially the same assumptions, we enhance the AFP construction and obtain short constrained keys. Let us look at their CPRF F first, which is defined as $F(k,x) := PF(k, H(x))$, where PF is a puncturable PRF, and H is a hash function (this way they map unbounded inputs to constant-size inputs for a puncturable PRF). A constrained key for a TM M is a $di\mathcal{O}$ obfuscation of the circuit P_M that on input (h, π) outputs $PF(k, h)$ iff π is a valid SNARK proving the following statement: $(*)$ $\exists x : h = H(x) \wedge M(x) = 1$. So P_M only outputs the PRF value if the evaluator knows such an input x.

We also define our TM-CPRF as $F(k,x) := PF(k, H(x))$. However at setup, we publish as a public parameter once and for all a $di\mathcal{O}$-obfuscated circuit P that on input (h, π, M, σ) outputs $PF(k, h)$ iff π is a valid SNARK for $(*)$ and additionally σ is a valid signature on M. A constrained key k_M for a TM M is a signature on M and a party holding $k_M := \sigma$ can generate a SNARK π, as in the AFP construction, and additionally use M, σ to run P to evaluate F.

The intuition behind the construction is simple: in order to evaluate F on x, one needs a signature on a machine M with $M(x) = 1$. Unforgeability of such signatures should guarantee that without a key for such an M the PRF value of x should be pseudorandom. However, actually proving this turns out quite tricky.

In the selective security game for CPRFs, the adversary first announces an input x^* and can then query keys for sets that do not contain x^*, that is, sets decided by TMs M with $M(x^*) = 0$. The adversary then needs to distinguish the PRF image of x^* from random. To argue that $F(k, x^*)$ is pseudorandom, we replace the circuit P by P^* for which F looks random on x^*, because it uses a key that is punctured at $H(x^*)$. Intuitively, since P is obfuscated, an adversary should not notice the difference. However, to formally prove this we need to construct a sampler that constructs P and P^* and argue that it is hard to find a differing input (h, π, M, σ) even when given the coins to construct the circuits.

One such differing input would be one containing a signature $\hat{\sigma}$ on a machine $\hat{M}$ with $\hat{M}(x^*) = 1$. Since $\hat{\sigma}$ is a key for a set containing x^*, P outputs the PRF value, while P^* does not, as its key is punctured. As the adversary only obtains signatures for M's with $M(x^*) = 0$, $\hat{\sigma}$ intuitively is a forgery. But the sampler that computes P and P^* also computed the signature verification key. So how can it be hard to construct a differing input containing $\hat{\sigma}$ for someone knowing the coins that also define the secret key?

We overcome this seeming contradiction by introducing a new primitive called *functional signatures with obliviously samplable keys* (FSwOSK). To produce the circuits P, P^*, the sampler needs to answer the adversary's key queries, that is, compute signatures on M's with $M(x^*) = 0$. FSwOSK lets the sampler create a pair of verification and signing keys, of which the latter only allows to sign such machines M; and security for FSwOSK guarantees that *even when knowing the coins used to set up the keys*, it is hard to create a signature on a message $\hat{M}$ with $\hat{M}(x^*) = 1$.

2 Preliminaries

2.1 Constrained and Puncturable PRFs

Definition 1 (Constrained Functions). *A family of keyed functions* $\mathcal{F}_\lambda = \{F: \mathcal{K} \times \mathcal{X} \to \mathcal{Y}\}$ *over a key space* $\mathcal{K}$, *a domain* $\mathcal{X}$ *and a range* $\mathcal{Y}$ *is efficiently computable if there exist a probabilistic polynomial-time (PPT) sampler* F.Smp *and a deterministic PT evaluator* F.Eval *as follows:*

- $k \leftarrow$ F.Smp(1^λ): *On input a security parameter* λ, F.Smp *outputs a key* $k \in \mathcal{K}$.
- $y :=$ F.Eval(k, x): *On input a key* $k \in \mathcal{K}$ *and* $x \in \mathcal{X}$, F.Eval *outputs* $y = F(k, x)$.

The family $\mathcal{F}_\lambda$ *is constrained w.r.t. a family* $\mathcal{S}_\lambda$ *of subsets of* $\mathcal{X}$, *with constrained key space* $\mathcal{K}_\mathcal{S}$ *such that* $\mathcal{K}_\mathcal{S} \cap \mathcal{K} = \emptyset$, *if* F.Eval *accepts inputs from* $(\mathcal{K} \cup \mathcal{K}_\mathcal{S}) \times \mathcal{X}$ *and there exists the following PPT algorithm:*

$k_S \leftarrow$ F.Constr(k, S): *On input a key* $k \in \mathcal{K}$ *and a (short) description of a set* $S \in \mathcal{S}_\lambda$, F.Constr *outputs a constrained key* $k_S \in \mathcal{K}_\mathcal{S}$ *such that*

$$\text{F.Eval}(k_S, x) = \begin{cases} F(k, x) & \text{if } x \in S \\ \bot & \text{otherwise.} \end{cases}$$

$\mathbf{Exp}_{\mathcal{F},\mathcal{A}}^{\mathcal{O},b}(\lambda):$

$k \leftarrow \mathsf{F.Smp}(1^\lambda); C, E := \emptyset$

$(x^*, st) \leftarrow \mathcal{A}_1^{\mathcal{O}_1}(1^\lambda)$

If $x^* \in E$, then abort

If $b = 1$ then $y := \mathsf{F.Eval}(k, x^*)$;

else $y \leftarrow \mathcal{Y}$

$C := C \cup \{x^*\}$

Return $b' \leftarrow \mathcal{A}_2^{\mathcal{O}_2}(st, y)$

Oracle $\mathrm{CONSTR}(S):$

If $S \notin \mathcal{S}_\lambda \vee S \cap C \neq \emptyset$

  Return $\bot$

$E := E \cup S$

$k_S \leftarrow \mathsf{F.Constr}(k, S)$

Return k_S

Oracle $\mathrm{EVAL}(x):$

If $x \notin \mathcal{X} \vee x \in C$

  Return $\bot$

$E := E \cup \{x\}$

$y = \mathsf{F.Eval}(k, x)$

Return y

Fig. 1. The security game for constrained PRFs

Definition 2 (Security of Constrained PRFs). *A family of constrained functions* $\mathcal{F}_\lambda = \{F: \mathcal{K} \times \mathcal{X} \to \mathcal{Y}\}$ *is selectively pseudorandom, if for every PPT adversary* $\mathcal{A} = (\mathcal{A}_1, \mathcal{A}_2)$ *in* $\mathbf{Exp}_{\mathcal{F},\mathcal{A}}^{\mathcal{O},b}$, *defined in Fig. 1, with* $\mathcal{O}_1 = \emptyset$ *and* $\mathcal{O}_2 = \{\mathrm{CONSTR}(\cdot), \mathrm{EVAL}(\cdot)\}$, *it holds that*

$$\mathsf{Adv}_{\mathcal{F},\mathcal{A}}^{\mathcal{O}}(\lambda) := \left| \Pr\left[\mathbf{Exp}_{\mathcal{F},\mathcal{A}}^{\mathcal{O},0}(\lambda) = 1\right] - \Pr\left[\mathbf{Exp}_{\mathcal{F},\mathcal{A}}^{\mathcal{O},1}(\lambda) = 1\right] \right| = \mathsf{negl}(\lambda). \qquad (1)$$

Furthermore, $\mathcal{F}_\lambda$ *is adaptively pseudorandom if the same holds for* $\mathcal{O}_1 = \mathcal{O}_2 = \{\mathrm{CONSTR}(\cdot), \mathrm{EVAL}(\cdot)\}$.

Remark 1. We require $\mathbf{Exp}_{\mathcal{F},\mathcal{A}}^{\mathcal{O},b}$ of Fig. 1 to be efficient. Thus when sets are described by Turing machines then every machine M queried to CONSTR must terminate on x^* within a polynomial number of steps T (as the oracle must check whether $S \cap \{x^*\} \neq \emptyset$, that is, $M(x^*) = 1$).

Puncturable PRFs [18]. These are simple constrained PRFs whose domain is $\{0,1\}^n$ for some n and whose constrained keys are for sets $\{\{0,1\}^n \setminus \{x_1, \ldots, x_m\} \mid x_1, \ldots, x_m \in \{0,1\}^n, m = \mathsf{poly}(\lambda)\}$, i.e., a punctured key can evaluate the PRF on all except polynomially many inputs. We only require selective pseudorandomness. A formal definition is given in the full version [1].

Selectively secure puncturable PRFs are easily obtained from selectively secure prefix-constrained PRFs, which were constructed from the GGM PRF [15] in [7,10,17]. In this work we only require selectively secure puncturable PRFs.

2.2 Public-Coin Differing-Input Obfuscation

Public-coin differing-input (di) obfuscation guarantees that if for pairs of *publicly* sampled programs it is hard to find an input on which they differ then their obfuscations are computationally indistinguishable. We follow [16] by first defining public-coin di samplers that output programs whose obfuscations are indistinguishable.

Definition 3 (Public-Coin DI Sampler [16]). *A non-uniform PPT sampler Samp is a public-coin differing-input sampler for a family of polynomial-size* *circuits* C_λ *if the output of* Samp *is in* $C_\lambda \times C_\lambda$ *and for every non-uniform PPT extractor* $\mathcal{E}$ *it holds that*

$$\Pr\left[\begin{matrix} r \leftarrow \{0,1\}^{poly(\lambda)} \\ (C_0, C_1) := Samp(1^\lambda, r); \ x \leftarrow \mathcal{E}(1^\lambda, r) \end{matrix} : \ C_0(x) \neq C_1(x)\right] = negl(\lambda). \quad (2)$$

Definition 4 (Public-Coin diO [16]). *A uniform PPT algorithm* diO *is a public-coin differing-input obfuscator for a family of poly-size circuits* C_λ *if:*

- *For all* $\lambda \in \mathbb{N}$, $C \in C_\lambda$ *and* x: $\Pr[\tilde{C} \leftarrow diO(1^\lambda, C) : C(x) = \tilde{C}(x)] = 1.$
- *For every public-coin di sampler* Samp *for a family of poly-size circuits* C_λ, *every non-uniform PPT distinguisher* $\mathcal{D}$ *and every* $\lambda \in \mathbb{N}$:

$$\big| \Pr\left[r \leftarrow \{0,1\}^{poly(\lambda)}; (C_0, C_1) := Samp(1^\lambda, r); \tilde{C} \leftarrow diO(1^\lambda, C_0) : 1 \leftarrow \mathcal{D}(r, \tilde{C})\right] -$$
$$\Pr\left[r \leftarrow \{0,1\}^{poly(\lambda)}; (C_0, C_1) := Samp(1^\lambda, r); \tilde{C} \leftarrow diO(1^\lambda, C_1) : 1 \leftarrow \mathcal{D}(r, \tilde{C})\right]\big|$$
$$= negl(\lambda). \quad (3)$$

Ishai et al. [16] conjecture that Garg et al.'s [13] $i\mathcal{O}$ construction satisfies their notion of public-coin $di\mathcal{O}$.

2.3 Non-interactive Proof Systems

An efficient non-interactive proof system in the *common-random-string* (CRS) model for a language $L \in \mathsf{NP}$ consists of PPT prover P and verifier V sharing a uniformly random string crs. On input a statement and a witness, P outputs a proof; V, on input a statement and a proof outputs 0 or 1. We require proof systems to be complete (honestly generated proofs verify) and sound (no adversary can produce a a valid proof of a false statement).

A non-interactive proof system is *zero-knowledge* if proofs of true statements reveal nothing beyond their validity. This is formalized by requiring the existence of a PPT simulator $\mathsf{S} = (\mathsf{S}_1, \mathsf{S}_2)$ that on input a true statement produces a CRS and a proof that are computationally indistinguishable from real ones.

Definition 5 (NIZK). *A tuple of PPT algorithms* NIZK $= (\mathsf{G}, \mathsf{P}, \mathsf{V}, \mathsf{S})$ *is a statistically sound non-interactive zero-knowledge (NIZK) proof system in the common-random-string model for* $L \in \mathsf{NP}$ *with witness relation* R *if we have:*

1. *Perfect completeness: For every* (η, w) *such that* $R(\eta, w) = 1$, *it holds that*

$$\Pr\left[\mathrm{crs} \leftarrow \{0,1\}^{poly(\lambda)} ; \ \pi \leftarrow \mathsf{P}(\mathrm{crs}, \eta, w) : \mathsf{V}(\mathrm{crs}, \eta, \pi) = 1\right] = 1.$$

2. *Statistical soundness:*

$$\Pr\left[\mathrm{crs} \leftarrow \{0,1\}^{poly(\lambda)} : \exists (\eta, \pi) \ s.t. \ \eta \notin L \wedge \mathsf{V}(\mathrm{crs}, \eta, \pi) = 1\right] = negl(\lambda). \quad (4)$$

3. *Computational zero-knowledge: For every* (η, w) *such that* $R(\eta, w) = 1$, *and non-uniform PPT adversary* $\mathcal{A}$, *it holds that*

$$\big| \Pr\left[\mathrm{crs} \leftarrow \{0,1\}^{poly(\lambda)}; \ \pi \leftarrow \mathsf{P}(\mathrm{crs}, \eta, w) : \mathcal{A}(\mathrm{crs}, \eta, \pi) = 1\right] -$$
$$\Pr\left[(\mathrm{crs}, \tau) \leftarrow \mathsf{S}_1(1^\lambda, \eta); \ \pi \leftarrow \mathsf{S}_2(\mathrm{crs}, \tau, \eta) : \mathcal{A}(\mathrm{crs}, \eta, \pi) = 1\right]\big| = negl(\lambda). \quad (5)$$

A succinct non-interactive argument of knowledge (SNARK) is a computationally sound NI proof-of-knowledge system with universally succinct proofs. A proof for a statement η is *succinct* if its length and verification time are bounded by a fixed polynomial in the statement length $|\eta|$. We define SNARK systems in the common-random-string model following Bitansky et al. [5,6,16].

Definition 6 (The Universal Relation $\mathcal{R}_\mathcal{U}$ [3]). *The universal relation $\mathcal{R}_\mathcal{U}$ is the set of instance-witness pairs of the form $((M, m, t), w)$ where M is a TM accepting an input-witness pair (m, w) within t steps. In particular $|w| \leq t$.*

Definition 7 (SNARK). *A pair of PPT algorithms (P, V), where V is deterministic, is a succinct non-interactive argument of knowledge (SNARK) in the common-random-string model for a language $\mathcal{L}$ with witness relation $\mathcal{R} \subseteq \mathcal{R}_\mathcal{U}$ if there exist polynomials p, ℓ, q independent of $\mathcal{R}$ such that the following hold:*

1. *Completeness: For every $(\eta = (M, m, t), w) \in \mathcal{R}$, it holds that*

$$\Pr\left[\mathrm{crs} \leftarrow \{0,1\}^{\mathsf{poly}(\lambda)}; \ \pi \leftarrow \mathsf{P}(\mathrm{crs}, \eta, w) : \mathsf{V}(\mathrm{crs}, \eta, \pi) = 1\right] = 1.$$

   Moreover, P runs in time $q(\lambda, |\eta|, t)$.

2. *(Adaptive) Soundness: For every PPT adversary $\mathcal{A}$:*

$$\Pr\left[\mathrm{crs} \leftarrow \{0,1\}^{\mathsf{poly}(\lambda)}; \ (\eta, \pi) \leftarrow \mathcal{A}(\mathrm{crs}) : \eta \notin \mathcal{L} \wedge \mathsf{V}(\mathrm{crs}, \eta, \pi) = 1\right] = \mathsf{negl}(\lambda).$$

3. *(Adaptive) Argument of knowledge: For every PPT adversary $\mathcal{A}$ there exists a PPT extractor $\mathcal{E}_\mathcal{A}$ such that*

$$\Pr\left[\begin{array}{l} \mathrm{crs} \leftarrow \{0,1\}^{\mathsf{poly}(\lambda)}; \ r \leftarrow \{0,1\}^{\mathsf{poly}(\lambda)} \\ (\eta, \pi) := \mathcal{A}(\mathrm{crs}; r); \ w \leftarrow \mathcal{E}_\mathcal{A}(1^\lambda, \mathrm{crs}, r) \end{array} : \begin{array}{l} (\eta, w) \notin \mathcal{R} \wedge \\ \mathsf{V}(\mathrm{crs}, \eta, \pi) = 1 \end{array}\right] = \mathsf{negl}(\lambda).$$

4. *Succinctness: For all $(\mathrm{crs}, \eta, w) \in \{0,1\}^{\mathsf{poly}(\lambda)} \times \mathcal{R}$, the length of an honestly generated proof $\pi \leftarrow \mathsf{P}(\mathrm{crs}, \eta, w)$ is bounded by $\ell(\lambda, \log t)$ and the running time of $\mathsf{V}(\mathrm{crs}, \eta, \pi)$ is bounded by $p(\lambda + |\eta|) = p(\lambda + |M| + |m| + \log t)$.*

Bitansky et al. [5] construct SNARKs for $\mathcal{R}_c \subset \mathcal{R}_\mathcal{U}$ where $t = |m|^c$ and c is a constant, based on knowledge-of-exponent assumptions [6] and extractable collision-resistant hash functions (ECRHF) [5]. These are both non-falsifiable assumptions, but Gentry and Wichs [14] prove that SNARKs cannot be built from falsifiable assumptions via black-box reductions. Relying on exponentially hard one-way functions and ECRHF, [5] construct SNARKs for $\mathcal{R}_\mathcal{U}$.

2.4 Commitment Schemes

A commitment scheme CS for a message space $\mathcal{M} \not\ni \perp$ consists of the following PPT algorithms: On input 1^λ, Setup outputs a commitment key ck; on input ck and a message $m \in \mathcal{M}$, Com outputs a commitment c and an opening d; on input ck, c and d, Open opens c to a message m or $\perp$. Besides correctness (commitments open to the committed message), we require *computational hiding* (no PPT adversary can distinguish commitments to messages of his choice) and *statistical binding* (no unbounded adversary can find some c and two openings d, d', which open c to two different messages, except with negligible probability over the choice of ck). A formal definition is given in the full version [1].

2.5 Collision-Resistant Hash Functions

A family of hash functions is *collision-resistant* (CR) if for a uniformly sampled function H it is hard to find two values that map to the same image under H. It is *public-coin* CR if this is hard even when given the coins used to sample H. A formal definition is given in the full version [1].

2.6 Functional Signatures

Functional signatures were introduced by Boyle et al. [10]. They generalize the concept of digital signatures by letting the holder of a secret key sk derive keys sk_f for functions f.[1] Such a key sk_f enables signing (only) messages in the range of f: running $\mathsf{Sign}(f, sk_f, w)$ produces a signature on $f(w)$.

Definition 8 (Functional Signatures [10]). *A functional signature scheme for a message space $\mathcal{M} \not\ni \bot$ and a function family $\mathcal{F}_\lambda = \{f \colon \mathcal{D}_f \to \mathcal{R}_f\}_\lambda$ with $\mathcal{R}_f \subseteq \mathcal{M}$ is a tuple of PPT algorithms $\mathsf{FS} = (\mathsf{Setup}, \mathsf{KeyGen}, \mathsf{Sign}, \mathsf{Verify})$ where:*

- $(msk, mvk) \leftarrow \mathsf{Setup}(1^\lambda)$: *On input a security parameter 1^λ, Setup outputs a master signing and verification key.*
- $sk_f \leftarrow \mathsf{KeyGen}(msk, f)$: *On input msk and a function $f \in \mathcal{F}_\lambda$, KeyGen outputs a signing key sk_f.*
- $(f(w), \sigma) \leftarrow \mathsf{Sign}(f, sk_f, w)$: *On input $f \in \mathcal{F}_\lambda$, a signing key sk_f for f, and $w \in \mathcal{D}_f$, Sign outputs a signature on $f(w) \in \mathcal{M}$.*
- $b = \mathsf{Verify}(mvk, m, \sigma)$: *On input a master verification key mvk, a message $m \in \mathcal{M}$, and signature σ, Verify outputs $b \in \{0, 1\}$.*

A functional signature is *correct* if correctly generated signatures verify, and is secure if it satisfies *unforgeability, function privacy,* and *succinctness.*

Unforgeability states that even given oracles that generate signatures and functional signing keys, it must be hard to produce a valid signature on a message that was not submitted to the signing oracle and that cannot be signed using a key obtained from the key oracle. *Function privacy* states that signatures neither reveal the function associated to the secret key nor the used preimage w. *Succinctness* requires that the size of a signature is independent of $|w|$ and $|f|$. A formal security definition is given in the full version [1].

Boyle et al. [10] construct functional signatures based on zero-knowledge SNARKs.

3 Functional Signatures with Obliviously Samplable Keys

We introduce and construct a new primitive we call *functional signatures with obliviously samplable keys* (FSwOSK), which will be central to achieving short

---

[1] In [10], f is given as a circuit, but in their construction of functional encryption, Boyle et al. [9] allow f to be a Turing machine. In this work we adopt the latter definition.

$\mathbf{Exp}_{S,\mathcal{A}}^{ind\text{-}b}(\lambda)$	$\mathbf{Exp}_{S,\mathcal{A}}^{obl\text{-}uf}(\lambda)$
$(st, m) \leftarrow \mathcal{A}_1(1^\lambda)$	$(st, m) \leftarrow \mathcal{A}_1(1^\lambda)$
If $b = 0$	$r \leftarrow \{0,1\}^{\mathsf{poly}(\lambda)};\ (\mathsf{vk}, \sigma) \leftarrow \mathsf{OSmp}(1^\lambda, m; r)$
$\quad (\mathsf{vk}, \mathsf{sk}) \leftarrow \mathsf{KeyGen}(1^\lambda);\ \sigma \leftarrow \mathsf{Sign}(\mathsf{sk}, m)$	$(m^*, \sigma^*) \leftarrow \mathcal{A}_2(st, r)$
Else $(\mathsf{vk}, \sigma) \leftarrow \mathsf{OSmp}(1^\lambda, m)$	Return 1 iff $m^* \neq m$
Return $b' \leftarrow \mathcal{A}_2(st, \mathsf{vk}, \sigma)$	$\qquad\qquad \wedge \mathsf{Verify}(\mathsf{vk}, m^*, \sigma^*) = 1$

Fig. 2. The oblivious-indist. game   **Fig. 3.** The oblivious-unforgeability game

keys for CPRF with unbounded inputs. We first extend a (standard) signature scheme by an extra functionality that given a message m allows one to sample a verification key together with a signature on m in an oblivious way. This means that, while the key and the signature look like regularly generated ones, it is hard to forge a signature on a different message under this key, even when given the coins used to sample the key/signature pair. We call this primitive *signatures with obliviously samplable signatures* (SwOSS) and construct it from one-way functions and NIZK by adapting a signature scheme due to Bellare and Goldwasser [4]. We then combine this scheme with SNARKs in order to construct our FSwOSK following the construction of a (standard) functional signature scheme of Boyle et al. [10].

3.1   Signature Schemes with Obliviously Samplable Signatures

Definition 9 (SwOSS). *Let* $S = (\mathsf{KeyGen}, \mathsf{Sign}, \mathsf{Verify})$ *be a (standard) signature scheme that is existentially unforgeable under chosen-message attacks (EUF-CMA) with message space* $\mathcal{M} \not\ni \perp$. *We say* S *has obliviously samplable signatures if there exists a PPT algorithm* OSmp *such that:*

- $(\mathsf{vk}, \sigma) \leftarrow \mathsf{OSmp}(1^\lambda, m)$: *On input security parameter* 1^λ *and a message* $m \in \mathcal{M}$, OSmp *outputs a verification key* vk *and a signature* σ *on* m.

SwOSS S *is secure if it satisfies (with experiments defined in Figs. 2 and 3):*

1. *Indistinguishability: For every PPT algorithm* $\mathcal{A} = (\mathcal{A}_1, \mathcal{A}_2)$ *in* $\mathbf{Exp}_{S,\mathcal{A}}^{ind\text{-}b}(\lambda)$

$$\left| \Pr\left[\mathbf{Exp}_{S,\mathcal{A}}^{ind\text{-}0}(\lambda) = 1 \right] - \Pr\left[\mathbf{Exp}_{S,\mathcal{A}}^{ind\text{-}1}(\lambda) = 1 \right] \right| = negl(\lambda). \qquad (6)$$

2. *Oblivious unforgeability: For every PPT* $\mathcal{A} = (\mathcal{A}_1, \mathcal{A}_2)$ *in* $\mathbf{Exp}_{S,\mathcal{A}}^{obl\text{-}uf}(\lambda)$

$$\Pr\left[\mathbf{Exp}_{S,\mathcal{A}}^{obl\text{-}uf}(\lambda) = 1 \right] = negl(\lambda). \qquad (7)$$

Construction 1 (SwOSS). *Let* $\mathcal{F}_\lambda = \{F : \mathcal{K} \times \{0,1\}^n \to \mathcal{Y}\}$ *be a family of PRFs,* $\mathsf{CS} = (\mathsf{Setup}, \mathsf{Com}, \mathsf{Open})$ *a perfectly binding commitment scheme for message space* $\mathcal{M}$, *and* $\mathsf{NIZK} = (\mathsf{G}, \mathsf{P}, \mathsf{V}, \mathsf{S}$ *a statistically sound NIZK scheme for*

$$L_\eta := \left\{ (ck, c_0, c_1, y, m) \,\middle|\, \begin{array}{c} \exists\, (k, r) : \big(c_0 = \mathsf{CS.Com}_1(ck, k; r) \wedge y = F(k, m) \big) \\ \vee\ c_1 = \mathsf{CS.Com}_1(ck, m; r) \end{array} \right\} \qquad (8)$$

(where Com_1 *denotes the first output of* Com*). Let* $\top \in \mathcal{M}$ *be such that* $\top \notin \mathcal{K}$ *and* $\top \notin \{0,1\}^n$. *Our signatures-with-obliviously-samplable-signatures scheme* $\mathsf{OS} = (\mathsf{KeyGen}, \mathsf{Sign}, \mathsf{Verify}, \mathsf{OSmp})$ *is defined as follows:*

$\underline{(\mathsf{sk}, \mathsf{vk}) \leftarrow \mathsf{KeyGen}(1^\lambda)}$: *On input a security parameter* 1^λ, *compute*

- $k \leftarrow \mathsf{F.Smp}(1^\lambda)$; $crs \leftarrow \{0,1\}^{poly(\lambda)}$; $ck \leftarrow \mathsf{CS.Setup}(1^\lambda)$;
- $(c_0, d_0) := \mathsf{CS.Com}(ck, k)$; $(c_1, d_1) := \mathsf{CS.Com}(ck, \top)$;

return $\mathsf{sk} := (k, r_0), \mathsf{vk} := (crs, ck, c_0, c_1)$

$\underline{\sigma \leftarrow \mathsf{Sign}(\mathsf{sk}, m)}$: *On input* $\mathsf{sk} = (k, r_0)$ *and* $m \in \mathcal{M}$ *compute*

- $y := F(k, m)$;
- $\pi \leftarrow \mathsf{NIZK.P}(crs, \eta := (ck, c_0, c_1, y, m), (k, r_0))$, *where* $\eta \in L_\eta$ *from* (8);

return $\sigma := (y, \pi)$.

$\underline{b := \mathsf{Verify}(\mathsf{vk}, m, \sigma)}$: *On input* $\mathsf{vk} = (crs, ck, c_0, c_1)$, *m and* $\sigma = (y, \pi)$,

return $b := \mathsf{NIZK.V}(crs, \eta = (ck, c_0, c_1, y, m), \pi)$.

$\underline{(\mathsf{vk}, \sigma) \leftarrow \mathsf{OSmp}(1^\lambda, m)}$: *On input* 1^λ *and* $m \in \mathcal{M}$, *compute*

- $r := r_0 \| r_1 \| r_y \| r_{\mathsf{Setup}} \| crs \| r_\mathsf{P} \leftarrow \{0,1\}^{poly(\lambda)}$,
- $y \leftarrow_{r_y} \mathcal{Y}$ // r_y *is used to sample* y *from* $\mathcal{Y}$,
- $ck := \mathsf{CS.Setup}(1^\lambda; r_{\mathsf{Setup}})$,
- $(c_0, d_0) := \mathsf{CS.Com}(ck, \top; r_0)$; $(c_1, d_1) := \mathsf{CS.Com}(ck, m; r_1)$,
- $\pi := \mathsf{NIZK.P}(crs, \eta := (ck, c_0, c_1, y, m), w := (m, r_1); r_\mathsf{P})$;

return $\mathsf{vk} := (crs, ck, c_0, c_1)$ *and* $\sigma := (y, \pi)$.

Theorem 1. *Scheme* OS *in Construction 1 is an EUF-CMA-secure signature scheme with obliviously samplable signatures.*

Proof. We need to show that $(\mathsf{KeyGen}, \mathsf{Sign}, \mathsf{Verify})$ is (standard) EUF-CMA-secure and prove indistinguishability (6) and oblivious unforgeability (7). The proof of EUF-CMA is analogous to that of Bellare and Goldwasser's [4] (noting that the second clause in (8) is always false) and is therefore omitted.

Indistinguishability: Let $\mathcal{A} = (\mathcal{A}_1, \mathcal{A}_2)$ be a PPT adversary that non-negligibly distinguishes honestly generated $(\mathbf{Exp}_{\mathsf{OS},\mathcal{A}}^{\mathsf{ind}\text{-}0}(\lambda))$ and obliviously sampled verification key-signature pairs $(\mathbf{Exp}_{\mathsf{OS},\mathcal{A}}^{\mathsf{ind}\text{-}1}(\lambda))$. Our proof will be by game hopping and we define a series of games $\mathbf{Exp}^{(0)} := \mathbf{Exp}_{\mathsf{OS},\mathcal{A}}^{\mathsf{ind}\text{-}0}(\lambda)$, $\mathbf{Exp}^{(1)}, \ldots, \mathbf{Exp}^{(5)} := \mathbf{Exp}_{\mathsf{OS},\mathcal{A}}^{\mathsf{ind}\text{-}1}(\lambda)$ and show that for $c = 0, \ldots, 4$, $\mathbf{Exp}^{(c)}$ and $\mathbf{Exp}^{(c+1)}$ are computationally indistinguishable. In $\mathbf{Exp}^{(0)}$ the adversary obtains vk output by KeyGen and σ output by Sign as defined in Construction 1.

$\mathbf{Exp}_{\mathsf{FS},\mathcal{A}}^{\mathsf{ind}\text{-}b}(\lambda)$

$(st, f) \leftarrow \mathcal{A}_1(1^\lambda)$
If $b = 0$
  $(msk, mvk) \leftarrow \mathsf{KeyGen}(1^\lambda)$
  $sk_f \leftarrow \mathsf{KeyGen}(msk, f)$
Else $(mvk, sk_f) \leftarrow \mathsf{OSmp}(1^\lambda, f)$
Return $b' \leftarrow \mathcal{A}_2(st, mvk, sk_f)$

$\mathbf{Exp}_{\mathsf{FS},\mathcal{A}}^{\mathsf{obl}\text{-}\mathsf{uf}}(\lambda)$

$(st, f) \leftarrow \mathcal{A}_1(1^\lambda)$
$r \leftarrow \{0, 1\}^{\mathsf{poly}(\lambda)}$
$(mvk, sk_f) \leftarrow \mathsf{OSmp}(1^\lambda, f; r)$
$(m^*, \sigma^*) \leftarrow \mathcal{A}_2(st, r)$
Return 1 iff $m^* \notin \mathcal{R}_f$
    $\wedge\ \mathsf{Verify}(mvk, m^*, \sigma^*) = 1$

Fig. 4. The oblivious-indist. game   **Fig. 5.** The oblivious-unforgeability game

$\mathbf{Exp}^{(1)}$ differs from $\mathbf{Exp}^{(0)}$ in that the CRS for the NIZK and the proof π are simulated. By zero knowledge of NIZK the game is indistinguishable from $\mathbf{Exp}^{(0)}$.
$\mathbf{Exp}^{(2)}$ differs from $\mathbf{Exp}^{(1)}$ in that c_0 commits to $\top$ rather than a PRF key k. By computational hiding of CS, this is indistinguishable for PPT adversaries (note that r_0 is not used elsewhere in the game).
$\mathbf{Exp}^{(3)}$ differs from $\mathbf{Exp}^{(2)}$ in that c_1 commits to m rather than $\top$. Again, by hiding of CS (and since r_1 is not used anywhere), this is indistinguishable.
$\mathbf{Exp}^{(4)}$ differs from $\mathbf{Exp}^{(3)}$ in that $y \leftarrow \mathcal{Y}$ is random rather than $y := \mathsf{F}(k, m)$. Pseudorandomness of F guarantees this change is indistinguishable to PPT adversaries (note that k is not used anywhere else in the game).
$\mathbf{Exp}^{(5)}$ differs from $\mathbf{Exp}^{(4)}$ in that the CRS crs for the NIZK is chosen at random (rather than simulated) and π is computed by NIZK.P. Again, this is indistinguishable by zero knowledge of NIZK.

Oblivious unforgeability. This follows from soundness of NIZK and the binding property of CS. OSmp sets c_0 to a commitment of $\top$ and c_1 to a commitment of m. If $\mathcal{A}$ manages to output a signature (y^*, π^*) that is valid on message $m^* \neq m$, i.e., NIZK.V$(crs, (ck, c_0, c_1, y^*, m^*), \pi^*) = 1$, then by soundness of NIZK, $(ck, c_0, c_1, y^*, m^*) \in L_\eta$ (8), meaning that either c_0 is a commitment to a valid PRF key or c_1 is a commitment to m^*. Either case would contradict the binding property of the commitment scheme.

This proves Theorem 1. A formal proof is given in the full version [1].

3.2 Functional Signature Schemes with Obliviously Samplable Keys

Definition 10. (FSwOSK). *Let* $\mathsf{FS} = (\mathsf{Setup}, \mathsf{KeyGen}, \mathsf{Sign}, \mathsf{Verify})$ *be a functional signature scheme (Definition 8). FS has obliviously samplable keys if there exists a PPT algorithm:*

$(mvk, sk_f) \leftarrow \mathsf{OSmp}(1^\lambda, f)$*: On input* 1^λ *and a function* $f \in \mathcal{F}_\lambda$*, OSmp outputs a master verification key mvk and a functional signing key sk_f for f.*

FSwOSK FS is secure if it is a secure functional signature scheme that additionally satisfies the following:

1. *Indistinguishability: For every PPT* $\mathcal{A} = (\mathcal{A}_1, \mathcal{A}_2)$ *in* $\mathbf{Exp}_{FS,\mathcal{A}}^{ind-b}(\lambda)$ *(Fig. 4):*

$$| \Pr\left[\mathbf{Exp}_{FS,\mathcal{A}}^{ind-0}(\lambda) = 1\right] - \Pr\left[\mathbf{Exp}_{FS,\mathcal{A}}^{ind-1}(\lambda) = 1\right]| - negl(\lambda).$$

2. *Oblivious unforgeability: For every PPT* $\mathcal{A} = (\mathcal{A}_1, \mathcal{A}_2)$ *in* $\mathbf{Exp}_{FS,\mathcal{A}}^{obl-uf}(\lambda)$ *(Fig. 5):*

$$\Pr\left[\mathbf{Exp}_{FS,\mathcal{A}}^{obl-uf}(\lambda) = 1\right] = negl(\lambda).$$

We next show that if in the construction of functional signatures of Boyle et al. [10] we replace the signature scheme by a SwOSS (Definition 9) then we obtain a FSwOSK. As a first step Boyle et al. [10, Theorem 3.3] construct FS' = (Setup', KeyGen', Sign', Verify'), which does not satisfy function privacy nor succinctness, but which is unforgeable if the underlying signature scheme is EUF-CMA. Relying on adaptive zero-knowledge SNARKs for NP, they then transform FS' into a secure FS scheme [10, Theorem 3.4].

We first enhance their scheme FS' by an oblivious sampler OSmp' so it also satisfies indistinguishability and oblivious unforgeability, as defined in Definition 10.

Construction 2. *Let* OS = (KeyGen, Sign, Verify, OSmp) *be a secure SwOSS and* SS *an EUF-CMA-secure signature scheme. For a message space* $\mathcal{M} \not\ni \perp$ *and a function family* $\mathcal{F}_\lambda = \{f : \mathcal{D}_f \to \mathcal{R}_f \subseteq \mathcal{M}\}_\lambda$, *we construct* FS' *as follows:*

$(msk, mvk) \leftarrow$ FS'.Setup(1^λ) : $Return(msk, mvk) \leftarrow$ OS.KeyGen(1^λ).

$sk_f \leftarrow$ FS'.KeyGen(msk, f) : *On input* msk *and* $f \in \mathcal{F}_\lambda$, *compute* $(sk, vk) \leftarrow$
   SS.KeyGen(1^λ), $\sigma_{f\|vk} \leftarrow$ OS.Sign$(msk, f\|vk)$; *return* $sk_f := (f\|vk, \sigma_{f\|vk}, sk)$.

$(f(w), \sigma) \leftarrow$ FS'.Sign(f, sk_f, w) : *On input* $f \in \mathcal{F}_\lambda$, *key* $sk_f = (f\|vk, \sigma_{f\|vk}, sk)$ *for*
   f *and* $w \in \mathcal{D}_f$, *compute* $\sigma_w \leftarrow$ SS.Sign(sk, w); *return* $\sigma := (f\|vk, \sigma_{f\|vk}, w, \sigma_w)$.

$b =$ FS'.Verify(mvk, m, σ) : *Given* mvk, $m \in \{0,1\}^*$, $\sigma = (f\|vk, \sigma_{f\|vk}, w, \sigma_w)$;
   return OS.Verify$(mvk, f\|vk, \sigma_{f\|vk}) = 1 =$ SS.Verify$(vk, w, \sigma_w) \wedge m = f(w)$.

$(mvk, sk_f) \leftarrow$ FS'.OSmp$(1^\lambda, f)$: *Given* 1^λ *and* $f \in \mathcal{F}_\lambda$, *pick* $r_G, r_O \leftarrow \{0,1\}^{poly(\lambda)}$,
   set $(sk, vk) :=$ SS.KeyGen$(1^\lambda; r_G)$, $(mvk, \sigma_{f\|vk}) :=$ OS.OSmp$(1^\lambda, f\|vk; r_O)$;
   return mvk *and* $sk_f := (f\|vk, \sigma_{f\|vk}, sk)$.

Theorem 2. FS' *of Construction 2 is a FSwOSK that satisfies correctness, unforgeability, indistinguishability and oblivious unforgeability (but neither function privacy nor succinctness).*

Theorem 2 is formally proved in the full version [1] and we give some proof intuition here. Theorem 3.3 in [10] proves that (FS'.Setup, FS'.KeyGen, FS'.Sign, FS'.Verify) is a functional signature scheme that is correct and unforgeable. What remains then is to show that FS.OSmp' satisfies both indistinguishability (Item 1. in Definition 10) and oblivious unforgeability (Item 2.).

Note that a FSwOSK master verification key is a SwOSS verification key, and a FswOSK functional signing key is a SwOSS signature; thus an obliviously samplable pair for FSwOSK translates to a pair for SwOSS; indistinguishability for FSwOSK reduces thus to indistinguishability for SwOSS. Similarly, oblivious unforgeability for FSwOSK reduces to oblivious unforgeability of SwOSS (note that in this game the adversary cannot ask for functional signatures, so EUF-CMA of the regular signature scheme is not needed).

Next we show that the transformation of [10] applies to our scheme FS', and therefore the transformed FS is a FSwOSK satisfying Definition 10.

Theorem 3. *Assuming an adaptive zero-knowledge SNARK system for NP, FS' from Construction 2 can be transformed into a secure FSwOSK scheme FS.*

Proof (Proof sketch). The construction and proof of the theorem are exactly the same as those of Theorem 3.4 of [10], and therefore we only give an intuitive argument and refer the reader to [10] for more details.

First observe that in FS' a signature $\sigma := (f\|vk, \sigma_{f\|vk}, w, \sigma_w)$ on $f(w)$ contains both f and w in the clear and is therefore neither function-private nor succinct. In the new scheme FS a signature on m is instead a zero-knowledge SNARK proof π of knowledge of the following: f, vk, a signature $\sigma_{f\|vk}$ on $f\|vk$ that verifies under mvk, an element w such that $f(w) = m$, and a signature σ on w, valid under vk. Now function privacy reduces to zero knowledge and succinctness of signatures reduces to succinctness of the underlying SNARK.

4   Constrained PRFs for Unbounded Inputs

In this section we construct a family of constrained PRFs for unbounded inputs such that a constrained key is simply a (functional) signature on the constraining TM M. As a warm-up, we review the construction of [2] where a constrained key is a $di\mathcal{O}$ obfuscation of a circuit that depends on the size of the constraining TM M. In particular, the circuit verifies a SNARK for the following relation.

Definition 11 (R_{legit}). *We define the relation $R_{legit} \subset \mathcal{R}_\mathcal{U}$ (with $\mathcal{R}_\mathcal{U}$ from Definition 6) to be the set of instance-witness pairs $(((H,M),h,t),x)$ such that M and H are descriptions of a TM and a hash function, $M(x) = 1$ and $H(x) = h$ within t steps. We let L_{legit} be the language corresponding to R_{legit}. For notational convenience, abusing notation, we write $((H,M,h),x) \in R_{legit}$ to mean $(((H,M),h,t),x) \in R_{legit}$ while implicitly setting $t = 2^\lambda$.*

Remark 2. Let $t = 2^\lambda$ in the definition of R_{legit}; then by succinctness of SNARKs (Definition 7), the length of a SNARK proof is bounded by $\ell(\lambda)$ and its verification time is bounded by $p(\lambda + |M| + |H| + |h|)$, where p, ℓ are a priori fixed polynomials that do not depend on R_{legit}.

Construction 3 [2]. *Let $\mathcal{PF}_\lambda = \{PF\colon \mathcal{K} \times \{0,1\}^n \to \mathcal{Y}\}$ be a selectively secure puncturable PRF, $\mathcal{H}_\lambda = \{H\colon \{0,1\}^* \to \{0,1\}^n\}_\lambda$ a family of public-coin CR hash functions, diO a public-coin $di\mathcal{O}$ obfuscator for a family of polynomial-size circuits $\mathcal{P}_\lambda$, and SNARK a SNARK system for R_{legit} (Definition 11). A family of selectively secure PRFs $\mathcal{F}_\lambda = \{F\colon \mathcal{K} \times \{0,1\}^* \to \mathcal{Y}\}$ constrained w.r.t. to any polynomial-size family of TMs $\mathcal{M}_\lambda$ is defined as follows:*

$\underline{K \leftarrow \mathsf{F.Smp}(1^\lambda)}$: *Sample* $k \leftarrow \mathsf{PF.Smp}(1^\lambda)$, $H \leftarrow \mathsf{H.Smp}(1^\lambda)$, crs $\leftarrow \{0,1\}^{poly(\lambda)}$;
return $K := (k, H, \text{crs})$.
$\underline{k_M \leftarrow \mathsf{F.Constr}(K, M)}$: *On input* $K = (k, H, \text{crs})$ *and* $M \in \mathcal{M}_\lambda$, *define*

$$P_{M,H,\text{crs},k}(h, \pi) := \begin{cases} \mathsf{PF.Eval}(k, h) & \textit{if } \mathsf{SNARK.V}(\text{crs}, (H, M, h), \pi) = 1 \\ \bot & \textit{otherwise} \end{cases} \qquad (9)$$

compute $\widetilde{P} \leftarrow \mathsf{diO}(1^\lambda, P_{M,H,\text{crs},k})$ *and output* $k_M := (M, \widetilde{P}, H, \text{crs})$.
$\underline{y := \mathsf{F.Eval}(\kappa, x)}$: *On input* $\kappa \in \mathcal{K} \cup \mathcal{K}_\mathcal{M}$ *and* $x \in \{0,1\}^*$, *do the following:*

- *If* $\kappa \in \mathcal{K}$, $\kappa = (k, H, \text{crs})$: *return* $\mathsf{PF.Eval}(k, H(x))$.
- *If* $\kappa = (M, \widetilde{P}, H, \text{crs}) \in \mathcal{K}_\mathcal{M}$: *if* $M(x) = 1$, *let* $h := H(x)$ *(thus* $(H, M, h) \in L_{legit}$), $\pi \leftarrow \mathsf{SNARK.P}(\text{crs}, (H, M, h), x)$ *and return* $y := \widetilde{P}(h, \pi)$.

The drawback of Construction 3 is that a constrained key for a TM M is a *diO*-obfuscated circuit and is therefore large. In our construction below we use FSwOSK to define a constrained key k_M simply as a functional signature on M. As in Construction 3, our constrained PRF F is defined as $\mathsf{F}(k, x) = \mathsf{PF}(k, H(x))$, where PF is a puncturable PRF and H is a collision-resistant hash function. To enable evaluating F given a constrained key k_M, in the setup we output as a public parameter a *diO*-obfuscation of a circuit P (defined in (10) below) that on input (M, h, π, σ) outputs $\mathsf{PF}(k, h)$ which is equal to $\mathsf{F}(k, x)$ if π is a valid SNARK proving knowledge of some x such that $M(x) = 1$ and $h = H(x)$, and moreover σ is a valid functional signature on M; and outputs $\bot$ otherwise.

Construction 4 (TM CPRF with short keys). *Let* $\mathcal{PF}_\lambda = \{\mathsf{PF}\colon \mathcal{K} \times \{0,1\}^n \to \mathcal{Y}\}$ *be a selectively secure puncturable PRF* , $\mathcal{H}_\lambda = \{H\colon \{0,1\}^* \to \{0,1\}^n\}_\lambda$ *a family of public-coin collision-resistant hash functions,* $\mathsf{FS} = (\mathsf{Setup}, \mathsf{KeyGen}, \mathsf{Sign}, \mathsf{Verify}, \mathsf{OSmp})$ *a FSwOSK scheme, diO a public-coin differing-input obfuscator for a family of poly-size circuits* $\mathcal{P}_\lambda$, *and SNARK a SNARK system in the common-random-string model for* R_{legit} *(cf. Definition 11).*
We construct a family of PRFs $\mathcal{F}_\lambda = \{\mathsf{F}\colon \mathcal{K} \times \{0,1\}^* \to \mathcal{Y}\}$ *constrained w.r.t. to a polynomial-size family of Turing machines* $\mathcal{M}_\lambda$ *as follows:*

$\underline{K \leftarrow \mathsf{F.Smp}(1^\lambda)}$:

- $H \leftarrow \mathsf{H.Smp}(1^\lambda)$.
- crs $\leftarrow \{0,1\}^{poly(\lambda)}$.
- $(\text{msk}, \text{mvk}) \leftarrow \mathsf{FS.Setup}(1^\lambda)$.
- $sk_{f_I} \leftarrow \mathsf{FS.KeyGen}(\text{msk}, f_I)$ *where* $f_I(M) := M$.
- $k \leftarrow \mathsf{PF.Smp}(1^\lambda)$.
- $\widetilde{P} \leftarrow \mathsf{diO}(1^\lambda, P)$ *where* $P = P_{H,\text{crs},\text{mvk},k} \in \mathcal{P}_\lambda$ *is defined as:*

$$P(M, h, \pi, \sigma) := \begin{cases} \mathsf{PF.Eval}(k, h) & \textit{if } \mathsf{SNARK.V}(\text{crs}, (H, M, h), \pi) = 1 \\ & \quad \wedge \mathsf{FS.Verify}(\text{mvk}, M, \sigma) = 1 \\ \bot & \textit{otherwise} \end{cases} \qquad (10)$$

- *Set* $pp = (H, crs, mvk, \widetilde{P})$ *and return* $K := (k, sk_{f_I}, pp)$.

$k_M \leftarrow \mathsf{F.Constr}(K, M)$: *On input* $K = (k, sk_{f_I}, pp)$ *and* $M \in \mathcal{M}_\lambda$, *compute* $(M, \sigma) \leftarrow \mathsf{FS.Sign}(I, sk_{f_I}, M)$ *and return* $k_M := (M, \sigma, pp)$.

$y := \mathsf{F.Eval}(\kappa, x)$: *On input* $\kappa \in \mathcal{K} \cup \mathcal{K}_\mathcal{M}$ *and* $x \in \{0,1\}^*$:

- *If* $\kappa \in \mathcal{K}$, $\kappa = (k, sk_{f_I}, pp = (H, crs, mvk, \widetilde{P}))$: *set* $y := \mathsf{PF.Eval}(k, H(x))$.
- *If* $\kappa \in \mathcal{K}_\mathcal{M}$, $\kappa = (M, \sigma, (H, crs, mvk, \widetilde{P}))$: *if* $M(x) = 1$, *set* $h := H(x)$ *(thus* $(H, M, h) \in L_{legit}$), *compute* $\pi \leftarrow \mathsf{SNARK.P}(crs, (H, M, h), x)$, *and return* $y := \widetilde{P}(M, h, \pi, \sigma)$.

Remark 3. The public parameters pp are computed once and for all. As the model for CPRFs defines no public parameters, we formally include them in k_M. Note that $\mathcal{P}_\lambda$ is a circuit family with input length $|M| + n + |\pi| + |\sigma|$ where $|\pi|$ is upper bounded by $\ell(\lambda)$ even for an exponentially long x (cf. Remark 2).

Let us now argue why we need functional signatures with obliviously samplable keys in order to prove our construction secure.

If we could replace the PRF key k by a punctured one $k^* := k_{H(x^*)}$ then $\mathsf{F}(k, x^*)$ would look random, as required for selective security of F. The obfuscated circuit P would thus use k^* instead of k. But obfuscations of P_k and P_{k^*} are only indistinguishable if it is hard to find an input on which they differ. And, since we use public-coin diO, this should be even hard when given all coins used to produce P_k and P_{k^*}.

In the security experiment the adversary can query keys for machines M with $M(x^*) = 0$ and when fed to P_k and P_{k^*}, both output the same. However, if the adversary manages to forge a signature on some $\hat{M}$ with $\hat{M}(x^*) = 1$ then P_k outputs $\mathsf{F}(k, x^*)$, but P_{k^*}, using a punctured key, outputs $\bot$.

The tricky part is to break some unforgeability notion when this happens. The differing-input sampler that computes P_k and P_{k^*} must simulate the experiment for $\mathcal{A}$ and thus create signatures to answer key queries. This is why we need functional signatures, as then the sampler can use a signing key sk_{f^*}, which only allows signing of machines with $M(x^*) = 0$, to answer key queries. FS unforgeability guarantees that even given such a key it is hard to compute a signature on some $\hat{M}$ with $\hat{M}(x^*) = 1$.

The next problem is that finding a differing input (and thus a forgery on $\hat{M}$) should be hard *even when given all coins*, so in particular the coins to create the signature verification key mvk contained in P_k and P_{k^*}; thus it would be easy to "forge a signature". This is why we need FSwOSK, as they allow to sample a verification key together with sk_{f^*} and even given the coins, forgeries should be hard.

Theorem 4. $\mathcal{F}_\lambda$ *of Construction 4 is a selectively secure family of constrained PRFs with input space* $\{0,1\}^*$ *for which constrained keys can be derived for any set that can be decided by a polynomial-size Turing machine.*

$\mathbf{Exp}^{b,(c)}_{\mathcal{F},\mathcal{A}}(\lambda)$ // $c \in \{0,1,2,3,4\}$

$(x^*, st) \leftarrow \mathcal{A}_1(1^\lambda)$

$H \leftarrow \mathsf{H.Smp}(1^\lambda);\ crs \leftarrow \{0,1\}^{\mathsf{poly}(\lambda)}$

If $c \leq 1$

    $(msk, mvk) \leftarrow \mathsf{FS.Setup}(1^\lambda)$

    Define f_I and f_{x^*} as in (11) and pad

        them to the same length.

    $sk_{f_I} \leftarrow \mathsf{FS.KeyGen}(msk, f_I)$

    $sk_{f_{x^*}} \leftarrow \mathsf{FS.KeyGen}(msk, f_{x^*})$

Else

    $(mvk, sk_{f_{x^*}}) \leftarrow \mathsf{FS.OSmp}(1^\lambda, f_{x^*})$

$k \leftarrow \mathsf{PF.Smp}(1^\lambda)$

$k_{h^*} \leftarrow \mathsf{PF.Constr}(k, \{0,1\}^n \setminus \{H(x^*)\})$

If $c \leq 2$ then

    $P := P_{H,crs,mvk,k}$ as defined in (10)

Else

    $P := P_{H,crs,mvk,k_{h^*}}$ as defined in (10)

$\widetilde{P} \leftarrow \mathsf{diO}(1^\lambda, P)$

$pp := (H, crs, mvk, \widetilde{P})$

If $b = 1$, $y^* := \mathsf{PF.Eval}(k, H(x^*))$, else $y^* \leftarrow \mathcal{Y}$

$b' \leftarrow \mathcal{A}_2^{\mathrm{Constr}(\cdot),\mathrm{Eval}(\cdot)}(st, y^*)$; return b'

Oracle $\mathrm{Constr}(M)$

If $M \notin \mathcal{M}_\lambda \vee M(x^*) = 1$

    Return $\perp$

If $c = 0$

    $(M, \sigma) \leftarrow \mathsf{FS.Sign}(f_I, sk_{f_I}, M)$

Else

    $(M, \sigma) \leftarrow \mathsf{FS.Sign}(f_{x^*}, sk_{f_{x^*}}, M)$

Return $k_M := (M, \sigma, pp)$

Oracle $\mathrm{Eval}(x)$

If $x = x^*$

    Return $\perp$

If $c \leq 3$

    $y := \mathsf{PF.Eval}(k, H(x))$

Else

    If $H(x) = H(x^*)$, abort

    Else $y := \mathsf{PF.Eval}(k_{h^*}, H(x))$

Return y

Fig. 6. Hybrids used in the proof of Theorem 4

Proof. Let $\mathcal{A}$ be a PPT adversary for the game $\mathbf{Exp}^{(\emptyset,\{\mathrm{Constr},\mathrm{Eval}\}),b}_{\mathcal{F},\mathcal{A}}(\lambda)$, as defined in Fig. 6, which we abbreviate as $\mathbf{Exp}^b$. We need to show that $\mathbf{Exp}^0$ and $\mathbf{Exp}^1$ are indistinguishable. Our proof will be by game hopping and we define a series of hybrid games $\mathbf{Exp}^{b,(0)} := \mathbf{Exp}^b$, $\mathbf{Exp}^{b,(1)}, \mathbf{Exp}^{b,(2)}$, $\mathbf{Exp}^{b,(3)}$, $\mathbf{Exp}^{b,(4)}$ and show that for $b = 0, 1$ and $c = 0, 1, 2, 3$ the games $\mathbf{Exp}^{b,(c)}$ and $\mathbf{Exp}^{b,(c+1)}$ are indistinguishable. Finally we show that $\mathbf{Exp}^{0,(4)}$ and $\mathbf{Exp}^{1,(4)}$ are also indistinguishable, which concludes the proof. All games are defined in Fig. 6, using the following definitions:

$$f_I : M \mapsto M, \qquad\qquad f_{x^*} : M \mapsto \begin{cases} M & \text{if } M(x^*) = 0 \\ \perp & \text{otherwise} \end{cases} \qquad (11)$$

$\mathbf{Exp}^{b,(0)}$ is the original game $\mathbf{Exp}^{b,(\emptyset,\{\mathrm{Constr},\mathrm{Eval}\})}_{\mathcal{F},\mathcal{A}}(\lambda)$ for Construction 4. (Note that we padded f_I but, by succinctness, functional signatures (returned by Constr) are independent of the length of f.)

$\mathbf{Exp}^{b,(1)}$ differs from $\mathbf{Exp}^{b,(0)}$ by replacing the signing key sk_{f_I} with $sk_{f_{x^*}}$, which only allows to sign machines M with $M(x^*) = 0$.

$\mathbf{Exp}^{b,(2)}$ differs from $\mathbf{Exp}^{b,(1)}$ by replacing the verification/signing key pair $(mvk, sk_{f_{x^*}})$ with an obliviously sampled one.

$\mathbf{Exp}^{b,(3)}$ differs from $\mathbf{Exp}^{b,(2)}$ by replacing the full key of the puncturable PRF PF with one that is punctured at $H(x^*)$ in the definition of P.

$\mathbf{Exp}^{b,(4)}$ differs from $\mathbf{Exp}^{b,(3)}$ by answering EVAL queries using the punctured key k_{h^*} and aborting whenever the adversary queries EVAL on a value that collides with x^* under H.

Intuitively, $\mathbf{Exp}^{b,(0)}(\lambda)$ and $\mathbf{Exp}^{b,(1)}(\lambda)$ are computationally indistinguishable as the only difference between them is the use of the signing key sk_{f_I} and $sk_{f_{x^*}}$, respectively, in answering constraining queries. The CONSTR oracle only computes signatures on TMs M with $M(x^*) = 0$. Therefore, f_{x^*} coincides with f_I on all such legitimate queries. By function privacy of FS, signatures generated with f_{x^*} and f_I are computationally indistinguishable.

Proposition 1. $\mathbf{Exp}^{b,(0)}$ *and* $\mathbf{Exp}^{b,(1)}$ *are computationally indistinguishable for* $b = 0, 1$ *if* FS *is a functional signature scheme satisfying function privacy and succinctness.*

The only difference between $\mathbf{Exp}^{b,(1)}$ and $\mathbf{Exp}^{b,(2)}$ is in how mvk and $sk_{f_{x^*}}$ are computed. In $\mathbf{Exp}^{b,(1)}$ the keys mvk (used to define P) and $sk_{f_{x^*}}$ (used to answer CONSTR queries) are generated by FS.Setup and FS.KeyGen, resp., whereas in $\mathbf{Exp}^{b,(2)}$ they are obliviously sampled together. Indistinguishability of honestly generated and obliviously sampled pairs (Definition 10) of verification/signing key pairs guarantees that this change is indistinguishable to PPT adversaries.

Proposition 2. $\mathbf{Exp}^{b,(1)}$ *and* $\mathbf{Exp}^{b,(2)}$ *are computationally indistinguishable for* $b = 0, 1$ *if* FS *is a FS scheme with obliviously samplable keys.*

It is in the next step that we use the full power of our new primitive FSwOSK. The only difference between $\mathbf{Exp}^{b,(2)}$ and $\mathbf{Exp}^{b,(3)}$ is in the definition of the circuit P that is obfuscated. In $\mathbf{Exp}^{b,(2)}$ the circuit $P =: P^{(2)}$ is defined as in (10), with $k \leftarrow \mathsf{PF.Smp}(1^\lambda)$. In $\mathbf{Exp}^{b,(3)}$, the key k in circuit $P =: P^{(3)}$ is replaced by a punctured key $k_{h^*} \leftarrow \mathsf{PF.Constr}(k, \{0,1\}^n \setminus \{H(x^*)\})$.

The two games differ thus in whether $\tilde{P}$ is an obfuscation of $P^{(2)}$ or $P^{(3)}$. By public-coin diO, these are indistinguishable, if for a sampler Samp that outputs $P^{(2)}$ and $P^{(3)}$, no extractor, even when given the coins used by Samp, can find a differing input $(\hat{M}, \hat{h}, \hat{\pi}, \hat{\sigma})$.

Suppose there exists an extractor $\mathcal{E}$ outputs such a tuple. By correctness of PF, $P^{(2)}$ and $P^{(3)}$ only differ on inputs $(\hat{M}, \hat{h}, \hat{\pi}, \hat{\sigma})$, where

$$\hat{h} = H(x^*), \tag{12}$$

as that is where the punctured key behaves differently. Moreover, the signature $\hat{\sigma}$ must be valid on $\hat{M}$, as otherwise both circuits output $\perp$. Intuitively, unforgeability of functional signatures should guarantee that

$$\hat{M}(x^*) = 0, \tag{13}$$

as the adversary only obtains a signature from its CONSTR oracle when it submits machines satisfying (13), so a valid $\hat{\sigma}$ on $\hat{M}$ with $\hat{M}(x^*) = 1$ would be a forgery.

To construct $P^{(2)}$ and $P^{(3)}$, Samp must simulate the experiment for $\mathcal{A}$, during which it needs to answer $\mathcal{A}$'s CONSTR queries and thus create signatures. This shows the need for a functional signature scheme: we need to enable Samp to create signatures on M's with $M(x^*) = 0$ (by giving it $sk_{f_{x^*}}$) while still arguing that it is hard to find a signature on $\hat{M}$ with $\hat{M}(x^*) = 1$.

Finally, if we used standard functional signatures then we would need to embed a master verification key (under which the forgery will be) into Samp, but this would require diO *with auxiliary inputs*. We avoid this using FSwOSK, which let Samp create mvk (together with sk_{f^*}) itself, and which ensure that for $\mathcal{E}$, even given Samp's coins, it is hard to find a forgery $\hat{\sigma}$. It follows that (13) must hold with overwhelming probability.

Finally the proof $\hat{\pi}$ must be valid for $(H, \hat{M}, \hat{h})$, as otherwise both circuits output $\perp$. By SNARK extractability, we can therefore extract a witness $\hat{x}$ for $(H, \hat{M}, \hat{h}) \in L_{legit}$, that is, (i) $\hat{M}(\hat{x}) = 1$ and (ii) $H(\hat{x}) = \hat{h}$. Now (i) and (13) imply $\hat{x} \neq x^*$ and (ii) and (12) imply $H(\hat{x}) = H(x^*)$. Together, this means $(\hat{x}, x^*)$ is a collision for H.

Overall, we showed that an extractor can only find a differing input for $P^{(2)}$ and $P^{(3)}$ with negligible probability. By security of diO (Definition 4), we thus have that obfuscations of $P^{(2)}$ and $P^{(3)}$ are indistinguishable.

Proposition 3. $\mathbf{Exp}^{b,(2)}$ *and* **$\mathbf{Exp}^{b,(3)}$** *are computationally indistinguishable for $b = 0, 1$, if* diO *is a public-coin differing-input obfuscator, FS a FSwOSK satisfying oblivious unforgeability and $\mathcal{H}$ is public-coin collision-resistant.*

For the game hop from games $\mathbf{Exp}^{b,(3)}$ to $\mathbf{Exp}^{b,(4)}$, indistinguishability follows directly from collision resistance of $\mathcal{H}$, as the only difference is that $\mathbf{Exp}^{b,(4)}$ aborts when $\mathcal{A}$ finds a collision.

Proposition 4. $\mathbf{Exp}^{b,(3)}$ *and* **$\mathbf{Exp}^{b,(4)}$** *are computationally indistinguishable for $b = 0, 1$, if $\mathcal{H}$ is CR.*

We have now reached a game, $\mathbf{Exp}^{b,(4)}$, in which the key k is only used to create a punctured key k_{h^*}. The experiment can thus be simulated by an adversary $\mathcal{B}$ against selective security of $\mathcal{PF}$, who first asks for a key for the set $\{0,1\}^n \setminus \{H(x^*)\}$ and then uses $\mathcal{A}$ to distinguish $y^* = \mathsf{PF.Eval}(k, H(x^*))$ from random.

Proposition 5. $\mathbf{Exp}^{0,(4)}$ *and* **$\mathbf{Exp}^{1,(4)}$** *are indistinguishable if $\mathcal{PF}$ is a selectively secure family of puncturable PRFs.*

Theorem 4 now follows from Propositions 1–5, which are proven in the full version [1].

References

1. Abusalah, H., Fuchsbauer, G.: Constrained PRFs for unbounded inputs with short keys. Cryptology ePrint Archive, Report 2016/279 (2016)
2. Abusalah, H., Fuchsbauer, G., Pietrzak, K.: Constrained PRFs for unbounded inputs. In: Sako, K. (ed.) Topics in Cryptology - CT-RSA 2016. LNCS, vol. 9610, pp. 413–428. Springer, Heidelberg (2016). http://eprint.iacr.org/2014/840
3. Barak, B., Goldreich, O.: Universal arguments and their applications. SIAM J. Comput. **38**(5), 1661–1694 (2008)
4. Bellare, M., Goldwasser, S.: New paradigms for digital signatures and message authentication based on non-interactive zero knowledge proofs. In: Brassard, G. (ed.) CRYPTO 1989. LNCS, vol. 435, pp. 194–211. Springer, Heidelberg (1990)
5. Bitansky, N., Canetti, R., Chiesa, A., Goldwasser, S., Lin, H., Rubinstein, A., Tromer, E.: The hunting of the SNARK. IACR Cryptology ePrint Archive, 2014:580 (2014)
6. Bitansky, N., Canetti, R., Chiesa, A., Tromer, E.: Recursive composition and bootstrapping for SNARKS and proof-carrying data. In: Boneh, D., Roughgarden, T., Feigenbaum, J. (eds.) 45th ACM STOC, pp. 111–120. ACM Press, New York (2013)
7. Boneh, D., Waters, B.: Constrained pseudorandom functions and their applications. In: Sako, K., Sarkar, P. (eds.) ASIACRYPT 2013, Part II. LNCS, vol. 8270, pp. 280–300. Springer, Heidelberg (2013)
8. Boneh, D., Waters, B., Zhandry, M.: Low overhead broadcast encryption from multilinear maps. In: Garay, J.A., Gennaro, R. (eds.) CRYPTO 2014, Part I. LNCS, vol. 8616, pp. 206–223. Springer, Heidelberg (2014)
9. Boyle, E., Chung, K.-M., Pass, R.: On Extractability obfuscation. In: Lindell, Y. (ed.) TCC 2014. LNCS, vol. 8349, pp. 52–73. Springer, Heidelberg (2014)
10. Boyle, E., Goldwasser, S., Ivan, I.: Functional signatures and pseudorandom functions. In: Krawczyk, H. (ed.) PKC 2014. LNCS, vol. 8383, pp. 501–519. Springer, Heidelberg (2014)
11. Fiat, A., Naor, M.: Broadcast encryption. In: Stinson, D.R. (ed.) CRYPTO 1993. LNCS, vol. 773, pp. 480–491. Springer, Heidelberg (1994)
12. Freire, E.S.V., Hofheinz, D., Paterson, K.G., Striecks, C.: Programmable hash functions in the multilinear setting. In: Canetti, R., Garay, J.A. (eds.) CRYPTO 2013, Part I. LNCS, vol. 8042, pp. 513–530. Springer, Heidelberg (2013)
13. Garg, S., Gentry, C., Halevi, S., Raykova, M., Sahai, A., Waters, B.: Candidate indistinguishability obfuscation and functional encryption for all circuits. In: 54th FOCS, pp. 40–49. IEEE Computer Society Press (2013)
14. Gentry, C., Wichs, D.: Separating succinct non-interactive arguments from all falsifiable assumptions. In: Fortnow, L., Vadhan, S.P. (eds.) 43rd ACM STOC, pp. 99–108. ACM Press, June 2011
15. Goldreich, O., Goldwasser, S., Micali, S.: How to construct random functions. J. ACM **33**(4), 792–807 (1986)
16. Ishai, Y., Pandey, O., Sahai, A.: Public-Coin differing-inputs obfuscation and its applications. In: Dodis, Y., Nielsen, J.B. (eds.) TCC 2015, Part II. LNCS, vol. 9015, pp. 668–697. Springer, Heidelberg (2015)
17. Kiayias, A., Papadopoulos, S., Triandopoulos, N., Zacharias, T.: Delegatable pseudorandom functions and applications. In: Sadeghi, A.-R., Gligor, V.D., Yung, M. (eds.) ACM CCS 13, pp. 669–684. ACM (2013)

18. Sahai, A., Waters, B., How to use indistinguishability obfuscation: deniable encryption, and more. In: Shmoys, D.B. (ed.) 46th ACM STOC, pp. 475–484. ACM Press, May/June 2014
19. Sakai, R., Ohgishi, K., Kasahara, M.: Cryptosystems based on pairing. In: SCIS 2000, Okinawa, Japan, January 2000

Symmetric Ciphers

Wide Trail Design Strategy
for Binary MixColumns
Enhancing Lower Bound of Number of Active S-boxes

Yosuke Todo[(⊠)] and Kazumaro Aoki

NTT Secure Platform Laboratories, Tokyo, Japan
todo.yosuke@lab.ntt.co.jp

Abstract. AES is one of the most common block ciphers and many AES-like primitives have been proposed. Recently, many lightweight symmetric-key cryptographic primitives have also been proposed. Some such primitives require the diffusion using element-wise XORs, which are called *binary matrices* in this paper, rather than that using MDS matrices because the element-wise XOR is efficiently implemented in a lightweight environment. However, since the branch number of binary matrices is generally lower than that of MDS matrices, such primitives require more rounds to guarantee security against several cryptanalyses. In this paper, we focus on binary matrices and discuss useful cryptographic properties of binary matrices. Specifically, we focus on AES-like primitives with *binary MixColumns*, whose output is computed using a binary matrix. One of the benefit of AES-like primitives is that four rounds guarantee $\mathcal{B}^2$ differentially and linearly active S-boxes, where $\mathcal{B}$ denotes the branch number of the matrix. We argue that there is a binary MixColumns in which the lower bound of the number of active S-boxes is more than $\mathcal{B}^2$ in the 4-round characteristic. For some binary matrices, the lower bound is improved from $\mathcal{B}^2$ to $\mathcal{B}(\mathcal{B}+2)$.

Keywords: Differential attack · Linear attack · Active S-box · AES-like primitive · MDS · Binary MixColumns

1 Introduction

Many symmetric key cryptographic primitives, e.g., block ciphers, compression functions of hash functions, and core functions of authenticated encryptions, have been proposed. Specifically, AES [1] is one of the most common block ciphers. The state is represented as a 4×4 matrix whose elements take 8-bit values. After AES was standardized by NIST, many AES-like primitives have been proposed [2,5, 10,17,19–21]. Their state is represented as an $n \times m$ matrix, and its elements take not only 8-bit values. We call such primitives (n, m)-AES-like primitives. PHOTON [19] can be considered as $(5,5)$, $(6,6)$, ..., $(8,8)$-AES-like primitives, and PRIMATEs [2], FIDES [5], Grøstl [17], LED [20], and Prøst [21] adopt various (n, m)-AES-like primitives other than $(4, 4)$-AES-like primitives, for example.

© Springer International Publishing Switzerland 2016
M. Manulis et al. (Eds.): ACNS 2016, LNCS 9696, pp. 467–484, 2016.
DOI: 10.1007/978-3-319-39555-5_25

Table 1. Lower bounds of 4-round (n, m)-AES-like primitives when $n \leq m$.

Dimension n	Type	Best branch number	Classical bound	Enhanced bound
4	MDS	5	25	-
	Binary	4	16	16 (max)
5	MDS	6	36	-
	Binary	4	16	17 (max)
6	MDS	7	49	-
	Binary	4	16	24 (max)
7	MDS	8	64	-
	Binary	4	16	24^{a}
8	MDS	9	81	-
	Binary	5	25	32 (max)

^{a} Enhancement is maximized for AES-like primitive with an $(7, 7)$ matrix state.

Recently, many lightweight primitives have been proposed, and they are expected to perform well in area-constrained and low-power environments as well as high-end environments. MixColumns in the original AES adopts a 4×4 Maximum Distance Separable code (MDS) matrix and its elements only take '1', '2', and '3', which is one of the best choices with respect to the cost of multiplication in a Galois field and branch number [30]. However, if the area is very constrained, even the multiplication of an MDS matrix becomes disadvantage for lightweight implementation. There are two methods for reducing the cost of multiplication for both lightweight and high-end environments. One involves a recursive approach [2,19,20] and the other involves a binary matrix similar to Camellia P-function [3,5,31]. In the recursive approach, an MDS matrix is generated by an iterating lightweight matrix, and it is superior to classical MDS matrices for area-constrained lightweight implementation. However, the execution time tends to be slow, which means that it also requires high power consumption because of the recursive operation [15]. On the other hand, the use of a binary matrix is also superior to classical MDS matrices for both constrained and non-constrained environments because it can be implemented only by element-wise XORs[1]. Unfortunately, the branch number of a binary matrix is lower than that of an MDS matrix. For instance, when $\mathcal{B}$ denotes the differential and linear branch number of the matrix, AES-like primitives guarantee at least $\mathcal{B}^2$ active S-boxes in 4-round differential and linear characteristics [10]. Therefore, AES-like primitives with a binary matrix have fewer active S-boxes than those with an MDS matrix, and it requires more rounds to guarantee security against several cryptanalyses.

---

[1] When a matrix is an $n \times n$ matrix whose elements take ℓ-bit value, both an MDS and a "binary" matrices are also represented by binary matrices on $(\mathbb{F}_2)^{\ell n \times \ell n}$. Then, the Hamming weight of MDS matrix is always greater than ℓn^2, but that of "binary" matrix is smaller than ℓn^2.

Our Contribution. In this paper, we focus on binary matrices and discuss useful cryptographic properties of binary matrices. We specifically focus on AES-like primitives with *binary MixColumns*, whose output is computed using a binary matrix.

If the number of active S-boxes per specific number of rounds increases, we can efficiently guarantee that the block cipher with fewer rounds has immunity against several cryptanalyses. In previous design criteria, we only care about the branch number of binary matrices because the classical proof only guarantees $\mathcal{B}^2$ active S-boxes in the 4-round characteristic. However, we argue that the classical lower bound is not tight for some binary matrices. Namely, there are binary matrices such that the lower bound is more than $\mathcal{B}^2$.

In this paper, we exhaustively search $n \times n$ binary matrices with $n \in \{4, 5, \ldots, 8\}$ and show some instances whose lower bound is more than $\mathcal{B}^2$. We first discuss cryptographic properties of binary matrices. Then, we propose an algorithm to evaluate a more accurate lower bound by using these properties. Our algorithm efficiently evaluates the lower bound for a given binary matrix, and some matrices enhance the lower bound from $\mathcal{B}^2$ to $\mathcal{B}(\mathcal{B} + 2)$. Specifically, our algorithm finds some binary matrices whose lower bounds become 16, 17, 24, 24, and 32 for $n = 4, 5, 6, 7$, and 8, respectively. We summarize the enhanced lower bounds in Table 1. Since the highest branch number of binary matrices is 4 for $n \in \{4, 5, \ldots, 7\}$, the classical proof only guarantees 16 active S-boxes. Moreover, since the highest branch number is 5 for $n = 8$, the classical proof only guarantees 25 active S-boxes. Therefore, we can enhance the lower bounds for $n \in \{5, 6, 7, 8\}$. We also evaluate the limit of the enhancement. We guarantee that the enhancement in Table 1 is maximized for all (n, n)-AES-like primitives with $n \in \{4, 5, \ldots, 8\}$. Moreover, for all (n, m)-AES-like primitives with $n < m$, we also guarantee that the enhancement is maximized for $n \in \{4, 5, 6, 8\}$.

2   Preliminaries

2.1   Definitions

Notations. Let $x = (x_1, x_2, \ldots, x_n)$ be an n-dimensional vector over $\mathbb{F}_{2^\ell}$. Let $x[j] = (x_1[j], x_2[j], \ldots, x_n[j])$ be an n-dimensional vector over $\mathbb{F}_2$, where $x_i[j]$ denotes the jth bit in x_i. Let $\tilde{x} \in (\mathbb{F}_2)^n$ be the truncation of $x \in (\mathbb{F}_{2^\ell})^n$ such that the ith element of $\tilde{x}$, i.e., $\tilde{x}_i$ takes 0 if $x_i = 0$ and takes 1 if $x_i \neq 0$. The Hamming weight of $x_i \in \mathbb{F}_{2^\ell}$ is calculated as $hw(x_i) = \sum_{j=1}^{\ell} x_i[j]$, where the addition is calculated over $\mathbb{Z}$. Moreover, the Hamming weight of $x \in (\mathbb{F}_{2^\ell})^n$ is calculated based on the truncated vector, i.e., it is calculated as $hw(x) = \sum_{i=1}^{n} \tilde{x}_i$. For any $a \in \mathbb{F}_2^n$ and $b \in \mathbb{F}_2^n$, let $a \succeq b$ if $a \vee b = a$, where $\vee$ denotes a bit-wise OR. Note that an element in $\mathbb{F}_{2^\ell}$ is represented as an ℓ-bit vector in $\mathbb{F}_2^\ell$, and it is naturally converted using an appropriate basis.

Active S-boxes. When we evaluate security against differential and linear cryptanalyses, we often evaluate the number of active S-boxes. An S-box that has a non-zero input difference is called a *differentially active S-box*, and an S-box that has a non-zero output linear mask is called a *linearly active S-box*. We can show the "provable security" against the differential and linear cryptanalyses by guaranteeing the lower bound of the number of active S-boxes.

The Substitution Permutation Network (SPN) cipher based on the wide trail design strategy [12] consists of a confusion layer and diffusion layer, where parallel applications of S-boxes and matrix multiplications are used in the confusion layer and diffusion layer, respectively. When ℓ-bit S-boxes are applied in the confusion layer, the diffusion matrix M is represented as $(\mathbb{F}_{2^\ell})^{n \times n}$ matrix. Let $x \in (\mathbb{F}_{2^\ell})^n$ be the input of the diffusion represented by an M. Then, the output is calculated as $y^T = Mx^T$. To evaluate the security of the diffusion matrix, we often focus on the branch number.

Definition 1 (Branch Number [30]). *Let M be an $n \times n$ matrix over $\mathbb{F}_{2^\ell}$. Then, a differential branch number of M is defined as $\mathcal{B}_d = \min\{hw(x) + hw(Mx^T) \mid x \in (\mathbb{F}_{2^\ell})^n \setminus \{0\}\}$. Similarly, a linear branch number of M is defined as $\mathcal{B}_l = \min\{hw(yM) + hw(y) \mid y \in (\mathbb{F}_{2^\ell})^n \setminus \{0\}\}$.*

Note that $\mathcal{B}_d$ and $\mathcal{B}_\ell$ is always less than or equal to $n + 1$. In the following sections, we only consider differential cryptanalysis unless otherwise noted. For linear cryptanalysis, similar discussion can be made because of the duality of these cryptanalyses [27].

We call that two $n \times n$ matrices M and M' are permutation-homomorphic [24] to each other if there is a row permutation ρ and a column permutation γ satisfying $\rho(\gamma(M)) = \gamma(\rho(M)) = M'$.

Lemma 1 [24]. *Let M and M' be matrices that are permutation-homomorphic to each other. Then M and M' have the same differential and linear branch number.*

In cryptographic applications, an MDS matrix has good properties and is defined in the context of coding theory. Its definition is equivalent as the following theorem for our context.

Theorem 1 [30]. *Let M be an $n \times n$ MDS matrix, the differential and linear branch number is $n + 1$.*

It is very useful to use the MDS matrix in the diffusion layer since the branch number takes the maximum possible value. However, it is inefficient for light-weight implementation because the multiplication by the MDS matrix requires the multiplication in a Galois field. On the other hand, if all elements of the matrix consist of binary elements, we can efficiently implement the multiplication because it only requires ℓ-bitwise XORs. Unfortunately, such a binary matrix does not generate an MDS matrix except for the trivial MDS matrix, i.e., $n = 1$. Nevertheless, there are concrete ciphers that adopt binary matrices. For example, Camellia uses an 8×8 binary matrix [3], and the designers showed that the maximum branch number of 8×8 binary matrices is 5 from computation using a PC. Kwon et al. summarized the maximum branch number of binary matrix with $n = 4, 5, 6, 7$, and 8 as $4, 4, 4, 4$, and 5, respectively, and they call such matrices *Maximum Distance Binary Linear (MDBL) matrices* [25].

2.2   AES-Like Primitives

The state of AES is represented as a 4×4 matrix whose elements take 8-bit values, i.e., the block length is 128 bits. Many cryptographic primitives use similar state expressions, and we call them AES-like primitives [2,5,10,17,19–21].

We only focus on the property of AES-like primitives independent of a choice of S-boxes. For convenience, let ℓ be the bit length of the input and output of an S-box. We introduce (n, m)-AES-like primitives, where the numbers of rows and columns are scaled like [8].

Definition 2 ((n, m)-AES-Like Primitives). *The AES-like primitives are parameterized by n and m, where the state is represented as an $n \times m$ matrix and $m \geq n$. The round function consists of four component functions: SubBytes, ShiftRows, MixColumns, and AddRoundKey. Each function is defined as follows:*

- *SubBytes (SB) substitutes each ℓ-bit value in the matrix into another ℓ-bit value by an S-box.*
- *ShiftRows (SR) rotates each ℓ-bit value located at row i by i positions to the left.*
- *MixColumns (MC) diffuses n ℓ-bit values within each column by a linear function.*
- *AddRoundKey (AK) XORs the round key with the state.*

Then, the round function of an AES-like primitive is defined as

$$Y \leftarrow (MC \circ SR \circ SB)(X) \oplus RK,$$

where X, Y, and RK denote the input, output, and round key, respectively. When a cryptographic permutation is designed, a constant is XORed to the matrix state instead of a round key.

We also focus on the following MixColumns.

Definition 3 (Binary MixColumns). *When the AES-like primitive uses a binary matrix in the MixColumns, we call such MixColumns binary Mix-Columns.*

Figure 1 shows 4-round AES-like primitives, which are equivalently transformed with regard to counting the number of active S-boxes. When analyzing 4-round AES-like primitives, we divide the primitive into three layers; front, middle, and back, as shown in Fig. 1. We often focus on the so-called *super-S-box* [13,18], which is defined as follows:

Definition 4 (Super-S-box). *Let a super-S-box consist of two S-box layers and one MixColumns. First, n S-boxes are applied. Then, a diffusion matrix M is applied. Finally, n S-boxes are applied again.*

If the branch number of M is $\mathcal{B}$, an active super-S-box has at least $\mathcal{B}$ active S-boxes. Moreover, both the front and the back layers of the AES-like primitives have m super-S-boxes, respectively.

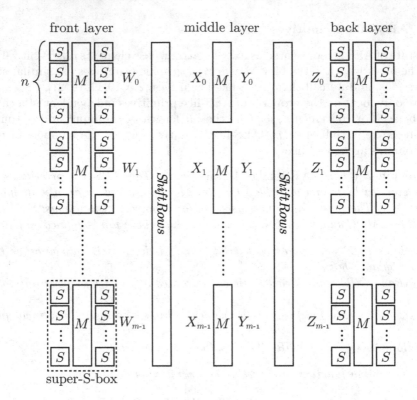

Fig. 1. Proof for 4-round AES-like primitives

Number of Active S-boxes. A good property of AES-like primitives is that the number of active S-boxes in the 4-round characteristic independent of a choice of S-boxes and AddRoundKey can be guaranteed[2]. First, all (n, m)-AES-like primitives have the following characteristic.

Lemma 2. *Let M be an $n \times n$ matrix over $\mathbb{F}_{2^\ell}$. Let $\mathcal{B}$ be the branch number of M. When M is adopted in MixColumns of AES-like primitives, there is always a 4-round characteristic whose number of active S-boxes is lower than or equal to $(n + 1)\mathcal{B}$ active S-boxes.*

Proof. Let us focus on the middle layer in Fig. 1. Since the branch number of M is $\mathcal{B}$, there is always a 4-round characteristic satisfying $hw(X_0) + hw(Y_0) = \mathcal{B}$. Then, $hw(X_0) + hw(Y_0)$ super-S-boxes are active, and each super-S-box has at most $n + 1$ active S-boxes. Therefore, there is always a 4-round characteristic whose number of active S-boxes has at most

$$(n + 1)hw(X_0) + (n + 1)hw(Y_0) = (n + 1)(hw(X_0) + hw(Y_0)) = (n + 1)\mathcal{B}.$$

□

---

[2] Any part of this paper does not consider the trivial characteristic that has no active S-box.

Next, let us consider the lower bound of the number of active S-boxes.

Lemma 3 [11]. *Let M be an $n \times n$ matrix over $\mathbb{F}_{2^\ell}$. Let $\mathcal{B}$ be the branch number of M. When M is applied to the MixColumns in AES-like primitives, there are at least $\mathcal{B}^2$ active S-boxes in the 4-round characteristic.*

Lemmas 2 and 3 derive the following theorem.

Theorem 2. *Assuming that M is an MDS matrix with branch number $\mathcal{B}$, there are at least $\mathcal{B}^2$ active S-boxes in the 4-round characteristic, and it is tight.*

Theorem 2 shows that there is no MDS matrix in which the minimum number of active S-boxes is more than $\mathcal{B}^2$ in the 4-round characteristic. However, if binary MixColumns is used, there is a possibility that the minimum number of active S-boxes is more than $\mathcal{B}^2$ because $\mathcal{B}^2 < (n+1)\mathcal{B}$. For instance, if a 5×5 binary matrix is used, $\mathcal{B}^2 = 16$ and $(n+1)\mathcal{B} = 24$, and there is a possibility that the minimum number of active S-boxes can be improved to 24.

3 Properties of Binary Matrices

We now discuss useful properties of binary matrices. Let $x \in (\mathbb{F}_{2^\ell})^n \setminus \{0\}$ be the input difference. Specifically, we focus on the propagation $x \xrightarrow{M} Mx^T$. Assume that the branch number of M is $\mathcal{B}$, i.e., $hw(\tilde{x}) + hw(\widetilde{Mx^T})$ is at least $\mathcal{B}$. Then, an enhanced propagation is defined as follows.

Definition 5 (Enhanced Propagation). *For a binary matrix $M \in (\mathbb{F}_{2^\ell})^{n \times n}$ with branch number $\mathcal{B}$, $x \in (\mathbb{F}_{2^\ell})^n \setminus \{0\}$ denotes the input difference of the diffusion by M. We say that the propagation $x \xrightarrow{M} Mx^T$ is an enhanced propagation, when $hw(\tilde{x}) + hw(\widetilde{Mx^T}) > \mathcal{B}$.*

When we consider all possible propagations from x, the minimum of $hw(\tilde{x}) + hw(\widetilde{Mx^T})$ is $\mathcal{B}$ because of the branch number. However, some propagations have $hw(\tilde{x}) + hw(\widetilde{Mx^T}) > \mathcal{B}$. Moreover, we define the following two propagations.

Definition 6 (Direct and Indirect Propagations). *For a binary matrix $M \in (\mathbb{F}_{2^\ell})^{n \times n}$, $x \in (\mathbb{F}_{2^\ell})^n \setminus \{0\}$ denotes the input difference of the diffusion by M. We say that the propagation $x \xrightarrow{M} Mx^T$ is a direct (resp. indirect) propagation, when $\widetilde{Mx^T} = M\tilde{x}^T$ (resp. $\widetilde{Mx^T} \neq M\tilde{x}^T$).*

In the direct propagation, $\widetilde{Mx^T}$ can be directly calculated from $\tilde{x}$ as $M\tilde{x}^T$. In the indirect propagation, we cannot calculate $\widetilde{Mx^T}$ from only $\tilde{x}$ and have to calculate it from the difference x.

3.1   Indirect Branch Number

We now want to evaluate the propagation $x \xrightarrow{M} Mx^T$, and let us consider the condition in which the propagation becomes an enhanced propagation. We first define a variant of the branch number as follows.

Definition 7 (Indirect Branch Number). *Let M be an $n \times n$ binary matrix over $\mathbb{F}_{2^\ell}$. Let $x \in (\mathbb{F}_{2^\ell})^n \setminus \{0\}$ be the input difference of the diffusion by M. For all indirect propagations, i.e., all $x \xrightarrow{M} Mx^T$ satisfying $\widetilde{Mx^T} \neq M\tilde{x}^T$, the indirect branch number denotes the minimum of $hw(\tilde{x}) + hw(\widetilde{Mx^T})$.*

We can obtain a useful lemma about the indirect branch number.

Lemma 4. *Let M be an $n \times n$ binary matrix over $\mathbb{F}_{2^\ell}$. Let $\mathcal{B}$ be the branch number of M, and assume $\mathcal{B} > 2$. Then, the indirect branch number is at least $\mathcal{B} + 2$.*

Proof. Let y be the output vector, i.e., $y^T = Mx^T$. When the propagation $x \xrightarrow{M} y$ is indirect propagation, i.e., $\tilde{y}^T \neq M\tilde{x}^T$, there are always two non-zero $x[i]$ and $x[j]$ satisfying $x[i] \neq x[j]$, and $hw(\tilde{x}) \geq hw(x[i] \vee x[j])$. Similarly, let $y[i]^T = Mx[i]^T$ and $y[j]^T = Mx[j]^T$, and $hw(\tilde{y}) \geq hw(y[i] \vee y[j])$. Without loss of generality, assume $hw(x[j]) + hw(y[j]) \geq hw(x[i]) + hw(y[i])$.

First, assuming that $hw(x[j]) + hw(y[j]) \geq \mathcal{B} + 2$, the sum of the Hamming weight of $\tilde{x}$ and that of $\tilde{y}$ is at least $\mathcal{B} + 2$.

Second, assume that $hw(x[j]) + hw(y[j]) = \mathcal{B} + 1$. When $x[j] \not\succeq x[i]$, $hw(x[i] \vee x[j]) \geq hw(x[j]) + 1$. Moreover, when $y[j] \not\succeq y[i]$, $hw(y[i] \vee y[j]) \geq hw(y[j]) + 1$. Therefore, when $x[j] \not\succeq x[i]$ or $y[j] \not\succeq y[i]$, the sum of the Hamming weight of $\tilde{x}$ and that of $\tilde{y}$ is at least $\mathcal{B} + 2$ because

$$hw(x[i] \vee x[j]) + hw(y[i] \vee y[j]) \geq hw(x[j]) + hw(y[j]) + 1 = \mathcal{B} + 2.$$

Finally, when $x[j] \succeq x[i]$ and $y[j] \succeq y[i]$,

$$hw(x[i] \oplus x[j]) + hw(y[i] \oplus y[j]) = hw(x[j]) - hw(x[i]) + hw(y[j]) - hw(y[i])$$
$$\leq \mathcal{B} + 1 - \mathcal{B} = 1,$$

where $(y[i] \oplus y[j])^T = M(x[i] \oplus x[j])^T$. Therefore, this is contradictory because the branch number is greater than 2.

Third, assuming that $hw(x[j]) + hw(y[j]) = \mathcal{B}$, $hw(x[i]) + hw(y[i]) = \mathcal{B}$. Without loss of generality, assume $hw(x[j]) \geq hw(x[i])$. When $hw(x[i]) = hw(x[j])$, $hw(x[i] \vee x[j]) \geq hw(x[j]) + 1$ because $x[i] \neq x[j]$. Moreover, $hw(y[i] \vee y[j]) \geq hw(y[j]) + 1$ because $y[i] \neq y[j]$. Therefore, the sum of the Hamming weight of $\tilde{x}$ and that of $\tilde{y}$ is at least $\mathcal{B} + 2$ because

$$hw(x[i] \vee x[j]) + hw(y[i] \vee y[j]) \geq hw(x[j]) + 1 + hw(y[j]) + 1 = \mathcal{B} + 2.$$

When $hw(x[i]) + 1 = hw(x[j])$, then $hw(y[i]) = hw(y[j]) + 1$. If $x[j] \not\succeq x[i]$, $hw(x[i] \vee x[j]) \geq hw(x[j]) + 1 = hw(x[i]) + 2$. Moreover, if $y[i] \not\succeq y[j]$, $hw(y[i] \vee$

$y[j]) \geq hw(y[i]) + 1 = hw(y[j]) + 2$. Therefore, when $x[j] \not\succeq x[i]$ or $y[i] \not\succeq y[j]$, the sum of the Hamming weight of $\tilde{x}$ and that of $\tilde{y}$ is at least $\mathcal{B} + 2$. Finally, when $x[j] \succeq x[i]$ and $y[i] \succeq y[j]$,

$$hw(x[i] \oplus x[j]) + hw(y[i] \oplus y[j]) = hw(x[j]) - hw(x[i]) + hw(y[i]) - hw(y[j])$$
$$= 1 + 1 = 2.$$

Therefore, this is contradictory because the branch number is greater than 2. When $hw(x[i]) + 2 \leq hw(x[j])$, then the sum of the Hamming weight of $\tilde{x}$ and that of $\tilde{y}$ is at least $\mathcal{B} + 2$ because

$$hw(x[i] \vee x[j]) + hw(y[i] \vee y[j]) \geq hw(x[i]) + 2 + hw(y[i]) = \mathcal{B} + 2.$$

$\square$

Lemma 4 shows that the indirect propagation is always an enhanced propagation when $\mathcal{B} > 2$.

3.2   Propagation on Restricted Input and Output Differences

When we consider the propagation $x \xrightarrow{M} Mx^T$, $hw(\tilde{x}) + hw(\widetilde{Mx^T})$ is generally lower-bounded by branch number. However, if Hamming weight of input difference or that of output difference is restricted, it is not always lower-bounded by the branch number, i.e., it may have higher lower bounds.

Lemma 5. *Let M be an $n \times n$ binary matrix over $\mathbb{F}_{2^\ell}$. Let $\mathcal{B}$ be the branch number. Let $x \in (\mathbb{F}_{2^\ell})^n \setminus \{0\}$ be the input difference of the diffusion by M. Then, assuming that $hw(\tilde{x}) \leq 2$,*

$$hw(\tilde{x}) + hw(\widetilde{Mx^T}) \geq hw(\tilde{x}) + hw(M\tilde{x}^T).$$

Similarly, assuming that $hw(\widetilde{Mx^T}) \leq 2$,

$$hw(\tilde{x}) + hw(\widetilde{Mx^T}) \geq hw(M^{-1}(\widetilde{Mx})^T) + hw(\widetilde{Mx^T}).$$

Proof. We prove the first part of the lemma. Both left- and right-hand sides of the inequality include the term $hw(\tilde{x})$; thus, it is sufficient to prove $hw(\widetilde{Mx^T}) \geq hw(M\tilde{x}^T)$. Both $\widetilde{Mx^T}$ and $M\tilde{x}^T$ can be regarded as a truncated difference, so we focus on these truncated differences. For the right-hand side, $M\tilde{x}^T$, only $\mathbb{F}_2$-operations are performed. For the left-hand side, $\widetilde{Mx^T}$, we need to consider the following steps; 1. convert the truncated difference to (full) difference, 2. multiply matrix M, and 3. reconvert the difference to truncated difference. Therefore, we need to consider the following "special" operation for truncated differences 0 and 1: $0 \oplus 0 = 0$, $0 \oplus 1 = 1$, $1 \oplus 0 = 1$, and $1 \oplus 1 = 0$ or 1. Recall that we are evaluating Hamming weight. Thus, when $1 \oplus 1 = 1$, the left-hand side is greater than the right-hand side; otherwise they are equal. The second part of the lemma can be obtained to substitute x and M with Mx^T and M^{-1}, respectively. $\square$

Assuming that the Hamming weight of the input difference or that of the output difference is at most 2, Lemma 5 shows that $hw(\tilde{x}) + hw(\widetilde{Mx^T})$ can be lower-bounded by the corresponding direct propagation. Therefore, we can effectively guarantee the lower bound of $hw(\tilde{x}) + hw(\widetilde{Mx^T})$. Specifically, let us consider the time complexity to guarantee the lower bound. Then, the time complexity is $O(n)$ when the Hamming weight is at most 1, and it is $O(n(n-1))$ when the Hamming weight is at most 2.

4   Number of Active S-boxes in AES-Like Primitives with Binary MixColumns

From Lemma 2, there is always a 4-round characteristic whose number of active S-boxes is lower than or equal to $(n+1)\mathcal{B}$, and the use of MDS matrices is the best choice because $\mathcal{B}^2 = \mathcal{B}(n+1)$. However, if a binary MixColumns is used, there is a gap between $\mathcal{B}^2$ and $\mathcal{B}(n+1)$ since $\mathcal{B} < n+1$. In this section, we guarantee more accurate lower bound of the number of active S-boxes in the 4-round characteristic. Note that our proof is independent of the choice of S-boxes.

4.1   Intuition of Idea

First, we revisit the proof that there are at least $\mathcal{B}^2$ differentially and linearly active S-boxes in the 4-round characteristic of the AES-like primitives. We focus on the propagation in the middle layer, and we assume that the ith MixColumns is active. Then $hw(\tilde{x}) + hw(\widetilde{Mx^T})$ is at least $\mathcal{B}$, and there are at least $\mathcal{B}$ active super-S-boxes in the 4-round characteristic because of the property of SR. Since every active super-S-box has $\mathcal{B}$ active S-boxes, there are at least $\mathcal{B}^2$ active S-boxes in the 4-round characteristic.

Now, we consider an AES-like primitive whose MixColumns uses a binary matrix with branch number $\mathcal{B}$.

First, we consider the case in which there is an indirect propagation in the middle layer. Since the indirect branch number is $\mathcal{B}+2$ from Lemma 4, there are at least $\mathcal{B}+2$ active super-S-boxes in the 4-round characteristic. This also implies that there are at least $\mathcal{B}(\mathcal{B}+2)$ active S-boxes in the 4-round characteristic.

Next, we consider the case in which there is an only direct propagation in the middle layer. We focus on the number of active MixColumns in the middle layer, and i active MixColumns denote the case in which i MixColumns are active in the middle layer. Then, the minimum number of active S-boxes is proven using different methods depending on the number of active MixColumns. In more detail, let us consider the following cases, where the notation in Fig. 1 is used, and Fig. 2 shows the outline. First, we assume i active MixColumns with $i \le 2$. Then, at most two elements in W_i and Z_i are active for any i because of the construction of SR. Therefore, we effectively guarantee the minimum number of active S-boxes in every super-S-box using Lemma 5. Next, we assume i active

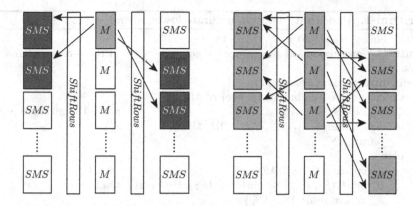

Fig. 2. Proof Strategy. When the number of active MixColumns is at most two (see the left figure), we use a binary matrix M such that super-S-boxes in the front and back layers always have enhanced propagation. When the number of active MixColumns is at least three (see the right figure), we use an M such that the characteristics always have many active super-S-boxes.

MixColumns with $i \geq 3$. We choose binary matrices such that the number of active super-S-boxes is beyond $\mathcal{B}$ for all characteristics.

Section 4.2 shows an algorithm to efficiently evaluate a more accurate lower bound of a given binary matrix.

4.2 Algorithm to Obtain Accurate Lower Bound

We guarantee the lower bound for a given binary matrix $M \in \mathbb{F}_{2^t}^{n \times n}$, and Algorithm 1, the validity of which is shown later in this section, shows the procedure to evaluate a more accurate lower bound. Here, AS_i and ASS_i are defined as follows.

Definition 8 (AS_i : Accurate lower bound of number of active S-boxes under i active MixColumns on direct propagation). *We only consider the 4-round characteristic whose propagation does not have the indirect propagation. For any characteristic with i active MixColumns in the middle layer, AS_i denotes the accurate lower bound of the number of active S-boxes in the 4-round characteristic.*

Definition 9 (ASS_i : Accurate lower bound of number of active super-S-boxes under i active MixColumns on direct propagation). *We only consider the 4-round characteristic whose propagation does not have the indirect propagation in the middle layer. For any characteristic with i active MixColumns in the middle layer, ASS_i denotes the accurate lower bound of the number of active super-S-boxes in the 4-round characteristic.*

Both AS_i and ASS_i only focus on characteristics whose middle layer has direct propagations. Moreover, AS_i only focuses on the characteristic whose super-S-boxes have direct propagations, but the bound $\mathcal{B} \times ASS_i$ takes into account

---

Algorithm 1. Algorithm to obtain accurate lower bound

Input: A binary matrix $M \in \mathbb{F}_{2^\ell}^{n \times n}$.

Output: The lower bound of the number of active S-boxes in the 4-round characteristic.

```
1: procedure AccurateBound(M)
2:      Calculate B as the branch number of M.
3:      Calculate AS₁ and ASS₂.                          ▷ See Definitions 8 and 9.
4:      if  AS₁ ≤ min{B × ASS₂, B(B + 2)}  then
5:          return AS₁
6:      else
7:          Calculate AS₂ and ASS₃.
8:          if  min{AS₁, AS₂} ≤ min{B × ASS₃, B(B + 2)}  then
9:              return min{AS₁, AS₂}
10:         else
11:             return min{B × ASS₃, B(B + 2)}
12:         end if
13:     end if
14: end procedure
```

---

characteristics whose super-S-boxes have indirect propagations. Therefore, $\mathcal{B} \times ASS_i \leq AS_i$. Moreover, ASS_i monotonically increases as a value of i.

For any binary matrix M with branch number $\mathcal{B}$, the number of active S-boxes in the 4-round characteristic is lower-bounded by

$$\min\{\mathcal{B} \times ASS_1, \mathcal{B}(\mathcal{B} + 2)\}. \tag{1}$$

Here, $\mathcal{B} \times ASS_1$ and $\mathcal{B}(\mathcal{B} + 2)$ denote the lower bound in which the middle layer has an only direct propagation and indirect propagation, respectively. Note that since $ASS_1 = \mathcal{B}$, the number of active S-boxes is lower-bounded by $\mathcal{B} \times ASS_1 = \mathcal{B}^2$.

We first calculate AS_1 to obtain a more accurate lower bound. Since AS_1 only focuses on the characteristic whose propagations do not have indirect propagations and there is at most one active MixColumns, it can be computed by counting the number of Hamming weights of the column vector of M and M^{-1} by considering the computation of the multiplication by M and M^{-1}.

$$AS_1 = \min_{\tilde{x} \in \mathbb{F}_2^n \setminus \{0\}} \left\{ \sum_{i=1}^{n} (hw((M^{-1})_i)\tilde{x}_i + hw(M_i)(M\tilde{x}^T)_i) \right\},$$

Note that M_i and $(M^{-1})_i$ denote the ith column vector in M and M^{-1}, respectively, and AS_1 does not depend on the position of the active MixColumns in the middle layer. Therefore, we can obtain AS_1 with $O(2^n)$ time complexity. Since Lemma 5 enables us only to consider the case of direct propagations, we can replace $\mathcal{B} \times ASS_1$ with $\min\{AS_1, \mathcal{B} \times ASS_2\}$ in (1). Then, the number of active S-boxes is lower-bounded by

$$\min\{AS_1, \mathcal{B} \times ASS_2, \mathcal{B}(\mathcal{B} + 2)\}. \tag{2}$$

Note that there is always a characteristic whose number of active S-boxes is AS_1. Therefore, AS_1 is a tight lower bound if $AS_1 \leq \min\{\mathcal{B} \times ASS_2, \mathcal{B}(\mathcal{B}+2)\}$. Otherwise, $\min\{\mathcal{B} \times ASS_2, \mathcal{B}(\mathcal{B}+2)\}$ is a new lower bound, but we do not guarantee whether or not it is tight.

When $AS_1 > \mathcal{B} \times ASS_2$, there is a possibility that the lower bound can be further improved. Lemma 5 shows that we can replace $\mathcal{B} \times ASS_2$ with $\min\{AS_2, \mathcal{B} \times ASS_3\}$ in (2). Then, the number of active S-boxes is lower-bounded by

$$\min\{AS_1, AS_2, \mathcal{B} \times ASS_3, \mathcal{B}(\mathcal{B}+2)\}. \tag{3}$$

Since both AS_2 and ASS_2 depend on truncated differentials of two active Mix-Columns and the difference between positions of two active MixColumns, we can obtain them with $O((n-1) \times 2^{2n})$ time complexity. Similarly, since ASS_3 depends on truncated differentials of three active MixColumns and the difference among positions of three active MixColumns, we can obtain it with $O((n-1)(n-2) \times 2^{3n})$ time complexity. Note that there are always characteristics whose number of active S-boxes is AS_2. Therefore, $\min\{AS_1, AS_2\}$ is a tight lower bound if $\min\{AS_1, AS_2\} \leq \min\{\mathcal{B} \times ASS_3, \mathcal{B}(\mathcal{B}+2)\}$. Otherwise, $\min\{\mathcal{B} \times ASS_3, \mathcal{B}(\mathcal{B}+2)\}$ is a new lower bound, but we cannot guarantee whether or not it is tight. Note that tightness is not efficiently guaranteed because we cannot use Lemma 5 for three active MixColumns.

For linear cryptanalysis, we also execute the same procedure for the binary matrix M^T because of the duality between differential and linear cryptanalyses (see Appendix A).

5   Best Binary Matrices

We now want to evaluate all $n \times n$ binary matrices and efficiently obtain binary matrices whose number of active S-boxes is maximized in the 4-round characteristic.

5.1   Efficient Search

The number of $n \times n$ binary matrices is 2^{n^2}, and e.g., since 2^{64} for $n = 8$, it is infeasible to exhaustively evaluate all matrices. However, in the application to Mix-Columns, we usually prefer to use binary matrices with the highest branch number. Therefore, we exhaustively search binary matrices with the highest branch number from $n = 4$ to $n = 8$ by using a similar technique to that by Guo et al. [16].

Fact 1. *For binary matrices with* $n = 4, 5, 6, 7,$ *and* 8, *the numbers of binary matrices with the highest differential and linear branch number are* $4! \approx 2^{4.6}$, $22 \times 5! \approx 2^{11.4}$, $49032 \times 6! \approx 2^{25.1}$, $279631988 \times 7! \approx 2^{40.4}$, *and* $18527040 \times 8! \approx 2^{39.4}$, *respectively.*

Moreover, we only consider invertible binary matrices.

Algorithm 1 requires much time complexity. Note that there is always a characteristic whose number of active S-boxes is equal to AS_1. Then, the lower bound of the number of active S-boxes is always upper-bounded by at most AS_1. Therefore, we first exhaustively search all binary matrices with the highest branch number and only evaluate AS_1. Table 2 shows AS_1, where columns in DC and those in LC have AS_1 of M and that of M^T, respectively. Columns in DC corresponds to the case for differential characteristics and columns in LC corresponds to the case for linear characteristics. Moreover, Table 2 does not include the case in which AS_1 for DC is greater than that for LC. When the number of columns is greater than or equal to the number of rows, we can calculate AS_1 independent of the number of columns. Therefore, from Table 2, we obtain the following fact.

Table 2. AS_1 of all $MDBL$ matrices with $n = 4, 5, \ldots, 8$.

n	DC	LC	# of matrices	n	DC	LC	# of matrices	n	DC	LC	# of matrices
4	16	16	24	7	17	19	49796596080	7	22	24	9671760
5	16	16	2160	7	17	20	10055893680	7	22	25	50400
5	17	17	480	7	17	21	640024560	7	23	24	6325200
6	16	16	5650560	7	17	22	27649440	7	23	25	161280
6	16	17	4364640	7	17	23	70560	7	24	24	4969440
6	16	18	1011600	7	18	18	200729783520	7	24	25	30240
6	16	19	15840	7	18	19	105763669200	7	25	25	40320
6	16	20	2160	7	18	20	29003380560	8	25	25	126252403200
6	17	17	9405360	7	18	21	2736417600	8	25	26	99931668480
6	17	18	2821680	7	18	22	160644960	8	25	27	9902471040
6	17	19	90720	7	18	23	1547280	8	25	28	214462080
6	18	18	2586240	7	18	24	594720	8	25	29	1290240
6	18	19	244800	7	19	19	88863979680	8	26	26	191120630400
6	18	20	27360	7	19	20	36434255760	8	26	27	58113216000
6	19	19	275040	7	19	21	5529872880	8	26	28	3361276800
6	19	20	54720	7	19	22	483537600	8	26	29	38868480
6	20	20	103680	7	19	23	9051840	8	27	27	53379285120
6	21	21	11520	7	19	24	1149120	8	27	28	9583176960
6	22	22	2880	7	20	20	24798715200	8	27	29	503193600
6	24	24	720	7	20	21	6400180080	8	27	30	1612800
7	16	16	22453467120	7	20	22	923988240	8	28	28	7646042880
7	16	17	43355400480	7	20	23	33405120	8	28	29	1739808000
7	16	18	34791593760	7	20	24	3417120	8	28	30	16450560
7	16	19	9488802960	7	21	21	3160795680	8	29	29	1305642240
7	16	20	1606162320	7	21	22	795795840	8	29	30	37900800
7	16	21	70817040	7	21	23	60490080	8	30	30	109992960
7	16	22	2716560	7	21	24	4929120	8	30	31	33546240
7	16	24	90720	7	21	25	10080	8	31	31	229985280
7	17	17	126753399360	7	22	22	445440240	8	31	32	1290240
7	17	18	132789625920	7	22	23	64506960	8	32	32	5806080

DC: # of differentially active S-boxes, LC: # of linearly active S-boxes

Fact 2. *For all 4-round (n,m)-AES-like primitives, AS_1 is upper-bounded by 16, 17, 24, 25, and 32 for $n = 4, 5, 6, 7$, and 8, respectively.*

Therefore, there are not exist binary matrices such that the lower bound is 17, 18, 25, 26, and 33 for $n = 4, 5, 6, 7$, and 8, respectively.

Finally, we exhaustively search all $n \times n$ binary matrices. First, we evaluate AS_1, and if AS_1 is not maximum possible, we prune the matrix. Then, we evaluate the accurate lower bound by using Algorithm 1. If we can find a binary matrix whose lower bound is the same as AS_1, it is one of the best binary matrices. On the other hand, if we cannot find such a matrix, we also evaluate binary matrices whose AS_1 is not maximum possible by using Algorithm 1.

5.2   Examples

Table 3 shows each example of binary matrices with an enhanced lower bound.

When $n = 4$, there is no binary matrix such that the lower bound of the number of active S-boxes is enhanced. On the other hand, for $n > 4$, we find such matrices. Specifically, when $n = 5, 6$, and 8, the enhancement is maximized because of Fact 2. When $n = 7$, we cannot obtain binary matrices such that the number of active S-boxes is lower-bounded by 25. However, for $m = n$, we also exhaustively evaluate the lower bound of AS_2 and AS_3 because there is always a characteristic whose number of active S-boxes is AS_2 or AS_3. As a result, since there is no binary matrix such that the number of active S-boxes is lower-bounded by 25, the enhancement is maximized. For $(7, m)$-AES-like primitives with $7 < m$, it may be possible that the number of active S-boxes is lower-bounded by 25. However, since Lemma 4 only guarantees $4 \times 6 = 24$ active S-boxes, we have to consider the indirect propagation in the middle layer if we guarantee that the number of active S-boxes is lower-bounded by 25.

5.3   Future Work

Essentially, binary matrices with enhanced lower bound tends to have high Hamming weight. For the lightweight implementation, it is important to consider binary matrices that we can compute the multiplication with low XOR count. We have to consider good trade-off.

Our algorithm deeply utilizes the structure of an AES-like primitive and its properties, and this accelerates the algorithm to compute the bounds and derives good matrices. On the other hand, our algorithm is customized for 4-round AES-like primitives, and the mixed-integer linear programming approach [28] seems useful for more round primitives.

We focused on the number of active S-boxes, which implies "provable security" [22] against differential and linear cryptanalyses. Towards the ultimate security against differential and linear cryptanalysis, there is a long way to evaluate our construction. Differential [26], linear hull [29], and plateau characteristics [14] are the topic of this area. Moreover, a "good" cipher should have a similar security level for each cryptanalysis. Therefore, the next problem we

Table 3. Examples of binary matrices with enhanced lower bound.

Binary matrix	4×4	5×5	6×6	7×7	8×8
Example	$\begin{bmatrix} 0\,1\,1\,1 \\ 1\,0\,1\,1 \\ 1\,1\,0\,1 \\ 1\,1\,1\,0 \end{bmatrix}$	$\begin{bmatrix} 1\,1\,1\,0\,0 \\ 1\,0\,1\,1\,0 \\ 1\,1\,0\,1\,1 \\ 1\,0\,1\,0\,1 \\ 0\,1\,1\,1\,1 \end{bmatrix}$	$\begin{bmatrix} 1\,1\,1\,1\,1\,0 \\ 1\,1\,1\,1\,0\,1 \\ 1\,1\,0\,1\,1\,1 \\ 0\,1\,1\,1\,1\,1 \\ 1\,1\,1\,0\,1\,1 \\ 1\,0\,1\,1\,1\,1 \end{bmatrix}$	$\begin{bmatrix} 1\,1\,1\,1\,0\,0\,0 \\ 1\,1\,0\,1\,0\,1\,0 \\ 1\,0\,1\,0\,1\,1\,1 \\ 1\,1\,0\,1\,1\,0\,0 \\ 0\,0\,1\,1\,1\,1\,1 \\ 0\,1\,1\,0\,1\,1\,1 \\ 1\,1\,0\,1\,0\,0\,1 \end{bmatrix}$	$\begin{bmatrix} 1\,1\,1\,1\,1\,0\,0\,0 \\ 1\,1\,1\,0\,0\,1\,1\,0 \\ 1\,0\,1\,1\,1\,1\,1\,0 \\ 1\,1\,1\,1\,0\,0\,1\,1 \\ 0\,1\,0\,1\,1\,0\,1\,1 \\ 1\,1\,0\,1\,1\,1\,0\,1 \\ 1\,0\,0\,0\,1\,1\,1\,1 \\ 0\,1\,1\,0\,1\,1\,1\,1 \end{bmatrix}$
Lower bound	16	17	24	24	32

need to analyze is to confirm security against other cryptanalyses, e.g., impossible differential [4], integral [23], and zero-correlation cryptanalyses [6].

6   Conclusion

We investigated the number of active S-boxes in differential and linear characteristics for 4-round AES-like primitive with binary MixColumns. The number is lower-bounded by $\mathcal{B}^2$ when the branch number of the binary MixColumns is $\mathcal{B}$. However, we showed that the lower bound is not always tight for AES-like primitives with binary MixColumns. To analyze the bound, we first introduced *enhanced propagation* and *(in)direct propagations*, and showed useful properties of binary matrix. Then, we showed how to evaluate an accurate lower bound for a given binary matrix. As a result, we showed that some binary matrices enhance the lower bound from $\mathcal{B}^2$ to $\mathcal{B}(\mathcal{B}+2)$. Specifically, for (n, m)-AES-like primitives with $n = 5, 6, 7$, and 8, we find binary matrices whose lower bound is 17, 24, 24, and 32, respectively. Moreover, we also evaluated the limit of the enhancement, and the enhancement is maximized for all (n, n)-AES-like primitives with $n \in \{4, 5, \ldots, 8\}$. Moreover, for all (n, m)-AES-like primitives with $n < m$, we also guarantee that the enhancement is maximized for $n \in \{4, 5, 6, 8\}$.

A   Duality Between Differences and Linear Masks

The duality between differential and linear cryptanalyses was pointed out, and several meanings of duality are known [7,27]. When constructing a differential characteristic, we should know the differential propagation rule for XOR and branch operation. That is, $\Delta z = \Delta x \oplus \Delta y$, where $z \leftarrow x \oplus y$, and $\Delta x = \Delta y = \Delta z$, where $x \leftarrow z$ and $y \leftarrow z$. For linear cryptanalysis, we have $\Gamma x = \Gamma y = \Gamma z$, where $z \leftarrow x \oplus y$, and $\Gamma x \oplus \Gamma y = \Gamma z$, where $x \leftarrow z$ and $y \leftarrow z$ [9,27]. We generalize this propagation rule to any linear transformation.

Let $M \in \mathbb{F}_2^{n \times n}$ be a binary matrix, and let $x \in \mathbb{F}_2^n$ be the input of the diffusion represented by an M. Then, let $y \in \mathbb{F}_2^n$ be the output of the diffusion represented by M as $y^T = Mx^T$. For the differential propagation, $(\Delta y)^T = M(\Delta x)^T$ trivially holds. For the linear mask propagation, we want to know the linear mask Γx and $\Gamma y \in \mathbb{F}_2^n$ such that $\Gamma y \bullet y = \Gamma x \bullet x$ with probability 1. Using the matrix multiplication, the equation can be written as $\Gamma y y^T = \Gamma x x^T$. That is, $\Gamma y (Mx^T) = (\Gamma y M)x^T = \Gamma x x^T$. Thus, $\Gamma y M = \Gamma x \Leftrightarrow M^T (\Gamma y)^T = (\Gamma x)^T$ should hold and is the propagation rule for the linear mask.

References

1. Specification for the Advanced Encryption Standard (AES): U.S. Department of Commerce/National Institute of Standards and Technology, Federal Information Processing Standards Publication 197 (2001)
2. Andreeva, E., Bilgin, B.B., Bogdanov, A., Luykx, A., Mendel, F., Mennink, B., Mouha, N., Wang, Q., Yasuda, K.: PRIMATEs. CAESAR Proposal (2014). http://primates.ae/
3. Aoki, K., Ichikawa, T., Kanda, M., Matsui, M., Moriai, S., Nakajima, J., Tokita, T.: *Camellia*: a 128-bit block cipher suitable for multiple platforms - design and analysis. In: Stinson, D.R., Tavares, S. (eds.) SAC 2000. LNCS, vol. 2012, pp. 39–56. Springer, Heidelberg (2001)
4. Biham, E., Biryukov, A., Shamir, A.: Cryptanalysis of Skipjack reduced to 31 rounds using impossible differentials. In: Stern, J. (ed.) EUROCRYPT 1999. LNCS, vol. 1592, pp. 12–23. Springer, Heidelberg (1999)
5. Bilgin, B., Bogdanov, A., Knežević, M., Mendel, F., Wang, Q.: FIDES: lightweight authenticated cipher with side-channel resistance for constrained hardware. In: Bertoni, G., Coron, J.-S. (eds.) CHES 2013. LNCS, vol. 8086, pp. 142–158. Springer, Heidelberg (2013)
6. Bogdanov, A., Rijmen, V.: Zero-correlation linear cryptanalysis of block ciphers. IACR Cryptology ePrint Archive 2011, 123 (2011). http://eprint.iacr.org/2011/123
7. Chabaud, F., Vaudenay, S.: Links between differential and linear cryptanalysis. In: De Santis, A. (ed.) EUROCRYPT 1994. LNCS, vol. 950, pp. 356–365. Springer, Heidelberg (1995)
8. Cid, C., Murphy, S., Robshaw, M.: Small scale variants of the AES. In: Gilbert, H., Handschuh, H. (eds.) FSE 2005. LNCS, vol. 3557, pp. 145–162. Springer, Heidelberg (2005)
9. Daemen, J., Govaerts, R., Vandewalle, J.: Correlation matrices. In: Preneel, B. (ed.) FSE 1994. LNCS, vol. 1008, pp. 275–285. Springer, Heidelberg (1995)
10. Daemen, J., Knudsen, L.R., Rijmen, V.: The block cipher SQUARE. In: Biham, E. (ed.) FSE 1997. LNCS, vol. 1267, pp. 149–165. Springer, Heidelberg (1997)
11. Daemen, J., Rijmen, V.: AES Proposal: Rijndael (1998)
12. Daemen, J., Rijmen, V.: The Design of Rijndael: AES - The Advanced Encryption Standard. Information Security and Cryptography. Springer, Heidelberg (2002). doi:10.1007/978-3-662-04722-4
13. Daemen, J., Rijmen, V.: Understanding two-round differentials in AES. In: De Prisco, R., Yung, M. (eds.) SCN 2006. LNCS, vol. 4116, pp. 78–94. Springer, Heidelberg (2006)
14. Daemen, J., Rijmen, V.: Plateau characteristics. IET Inf. Secur. **1**(1), 11–17 (2007)
15. Dinu, D., Corre, Y.L., Khovratovich, D., Perrin, L., Großschädl, J., Biryukov, A.: Triathlon of lightweight block ciphers for the internet of things. In: Lightweight Cryptography Workshop 2015 (2015)

16. Gao, Y., Guo, G.: Unified approach to construct 8×8 binary matrices with branch number 5. In: CDEE, pp. 413–416. IEEE (2010)
17. Gauravaram, P., Knudsen, L.R., Matusiewicz, K., Mendel, F., Rechberger, C., Schläffer, M., Thomsen, S.S.: Grøstl. a SHA-3 candidate (2011). http://groestl.info/specification.html
18. Gilbert, H., Peyrin, T.: Super-sbox cryptanalysis: improved attacks for AES-like permutations. In: Hong, S., Iwata, T. (eds.) FSE 2010. LNCS, vol. 6147, pp. 365–383. Springer, Heidelberg (2010)
19. Guo, J., Peyrin, T., Poschmann, A.: The PHOTON family of lightweight hash-functions. In: Rogaway, P. (ed.) CRYPTO 2011. LNCS, vol. 6841, pp. 222–239. Springer, Heidelberg (2011)
20. Guo, J., Peyrin, T., Poschmann, A., Robshaw, M.: The LED block cipher. In: Preneel, B., Takagi, T. (eds.) CHES 2011. LNCS, vol. 6917, pp. 326–341. Springer, Heidelberg (2011)
21. Kavun, E.B., Lauridsen, M.M., Leander, G., Rechberger, C., Schwabe, P., Yalçın, T.: Prøst. CAESAR Proposal (2014). http://proest.compute.dtu.dk
22. Knudsen, L.R.: Practically secure Feistel ciphers. In: Anderson, R. (ed.) FSE 1993. LNCS, vol. 809, pp. 211–221. Springer, Heidelberg (1994)
23. Knudsen, L.R., Wagner, D.: Integral cryptanalysis. In: Daemen, J., Rijmen, V. (eds.) FSE 2002. LNCS, vol. 2365, pp. 112–127. Springer, Heidelberg (2002)
24. Koo, B.-W., Jang, H.S., Song, J.H.: Constructing and cryptanalysis of a 16×16 binary matrix as a diffusion layer. In: Chae, K.-J., Yung, M. (eds.) WISA 2003. LNCS, vol. 2908, pp. 489–503. Springer, Heidelberg (2004)
25. Kwon, D., Sung, S.H., Song, J.H., Park, S.: Design of block ciphers and coding theory. Trends Math. **8**(1), 13–20 (2005)
26. Lai, X., Massey, J.L.: Markov ciphers and differential cryptanalysis. In: Davies, D.W. (ed.) EUROCRYPT 1991. LNCS, vol. 547, pp. 17–38. Springer, Heidelberg (1991)
27. Matsui, M.: On correlation between the order of S-boxes and the strength of DES. In: De Santis, A. (ed.) EUROCRYPT 1994. LNCS, vol. 950, pp. 366–375. Springer, Heidelberg (1995)
28. Mouha, N., Wang, Q., Gu, D., Preneel, B.: Differential and linear cryptanalysis using mixed-integer linear programming. In: Wu, C.-K., Yung, M., Lin, D. (eds.) Inscrypt 2011. LNCS, vol. 7537, pp. 57–76. Springer, Heidelberg (2012)
29. Nyberg, K.: Linear approximation of block ciphers. In: De Santis, A. (ed.) EUROCRYPT 1994. LNCS, vol. 950, pp. 439–444. Springer, Heidelberg (1995)
30. Rijmen, V., Daemen, J., Preneel, B., Bosselaers, A., De Win, E.: The cipher SHARK. In: Gollmann, D. (ed.) FSE 1996. LNCS, vol. 1039, pp. 99–111. Springer, Heidelberg (1996)
31. Sasaki, Y., Todo, Y., Aoki, K., Naito, Y., Sugawara, T., Murakami, Y., Matsui, M., Hirose, S.: Minalpher. CAESAR Proposal (2014). http://info.isl.ntt.co.jp/crypt/minalpher/index.html

Automatic Search of Linear Trails in ARX with Applications to SPECK and Chaskey

Yunwen Liu[1,2], Qingju Wang[1,3(✉)], and Vincent Rijmen[1]

[1] ESAT/COSIC, KU Leuven and iMinds, Leuven, Belgium
qingju.wang@esat.kuleuven.be
[2] Department of Science, National University of Defence Technology,
Changsha, China
[3] Department of Computer Science and Engineering, Shanghai Jiao Tong University,
Shanghai, China

Abstract. In this paper, we study linear cryptanalysis of the ARX structure by means of automatic search. To evaluate the security of ARX designs against linear cryptanalysis, it is crucial to find (round-reduced) linear trails with maximum correlation. We model the problem of finding optimal linear trails by the boolean satisfiability problem (SAT), translate the propagation of masks through ARX operations into bitwise expressions and constraints, and then solve the problem using a SAT solver. We apply the method to find optimal linear trails for round-reduced versions of the block cipher SPECK and the MAC algorithm Chaskey. For SPECK with block size 32/48/64/96/128, we can find optimal linear trails for 22/11/13/9/9 rounds respectively, which largely improves previous results, especially on larger versions. A 3-round optimal linear trail of Chaskey is presented for the first time as far as we know. In addition, our method can be used to enumerate the trails in a linear hull, and we present two linear hulls with the distributions of trails for round-reduced SPECK32. Our work provides designers with more accurate evaluation against linear cryptanalysis on ARX designs, especially for primitives with large block sizes and many rounds.

Keywords: Linear cryptanalysis · ARX structure · Boolean satisfiability problem

1 Introduction

Many symmetric key primitives are proposed with the ARX design strategy which only uses three operations: Additions ($\boxplus$), Rotations ($\lll$) and XORs ($\oplus$). These operations are very simple and efficient in software implementation, but interactively provide non-linearity. The ARX structure can be found in a large number of symmetric key designs, including hash functions BLAKE [2] and Skein [9], which are two of the five SHA-3 finalists, stream ciphers such as Salsa20 [5] and ChaCha [4], block ciphers such as TEA [27], XTEA [18], HIGHT [12] and SPECK [3], and MAC algorithm Chaskey [16]. Even though the ARX

© Springer International Publishing Switzerland 2016
M. Manulis et al. (Eds.): ACNS 2016, LNCS 9696, pp. 485–499, 2016.
DOI: 10.1007/978-3-319-39555-5_26

structure receives a considerable amount of attention due to its elegance and efficiency, it remains a difficult problem to evaluate its security margin against known attacking techniques.

Differential cryptanalysis [6] and linear cryptanalysis [15] are two main techniques used in the analysis of symmetric primitives, including ARX designs. Differential characteristics (resp. linear trails) with optimal probability (resp. correlation) can lead to efficient attacks with complexity better than the brute force searching. Hence the resistance against differential cryptanalysis and linear cryptanalysis is a crucial feature to consider for both designers and attackers. Among the methods and algorithms proposed in finding good differential characteristics and linear trails, automatic searching is a popular and efficient way. Several automatic toolkits dedicated to the searching of differential characteristics in ARX are proposed in the literature [7,14]. Comparing to the significant efforts which have been dedicated to the automatic search of differential characteristics, the searching tool of linear trails in ARX designs fell behind. The first paper on this topic as far as we know is presented by Yao *et al.* [28], where an algorithm based on branch and bound is used to find optimal (round-reduced) linear trails in SPECK32, and short linear trails of larger versions of SPECK.

Our motivation is to model the problem of searching optimal linear trails in an ARX structure as a boolean satisfiability problem [24]. The boolean satisfiability problem is widely used to determine whether the boolean variables in a given set of boolean conditions have valid assignments such that the conditions evaluate to TRUE. Specifically, in order to construct linear trails with nonzero correlation, the idea is to explore the bit-level conditions on the bits of the masks when passing through every operation of an ARX structure, render them into boolean satisfiability language, and call solvers to obtain valid linear trails with certain correlations. Our work can be applied to general ARX designs and has good performance in finding linear trails with best correlation for round-reduced primitives. Therefore it could provide a rigorous security evaluation for some ARX primitives against linear cryptanalysis.

Table 1. The number of covered rounds in finding optimal linear trails for SPECK family and Chaskey

Cipher	#covered rounds [28]	#covered rounds this paper	#total rounds
SPECK32	22	22	22
SPECK48	7	11	22/23
SPECK64	5	13	26/27
SPECK96	4	9	28/29
SPECK128	4	9	32/33/34
Chaskey	-	3	8

In this paper, our method is applied to the linear cryptanalysis of round-reduced SPECK family and Chaskey. Table 1 gives an overview of the number of rounds for which optimal linear trails are found in SPECK and Chaskey. Note that there is no previous research on finding optimal linear trails in round-reduced Chaskey.

This paper is organised as follows. In Sect. 2, we recall linear cryptanalysis and the boolean satisfiability problem. We study the propagation of bits in masks through operations of the ARX structure and transform them using boolean satisfiability language such that they can be solved automatically in Sect. 3. In Sect. 4, we apply the method to block cipher SPECK and MAC algorithm Chaskey, and find linear hulls for round-reduced SPECK32. Finally, we conclude in Sect. 5.

2   Preliminaries

We denote an n-bit boolean vector by $x = (x_{n-1}, \cdots, x_1, x_0)$, where x_0 is the least significant bit. For two n-bit boolean vectors x and y, the inner product is $x \cdot y = \bigoplus_{i=0}^{n-1} x_i y_i$. The partial order $\preccurlyeq$ is defined by $x \preccurlyeq y \Leftrightarrow x_i \leq y_i, \forall i \in \{0, \cdots, n-1\}$. The characteristic function $1_{x \preccurlyeq y}$ is defined as

$$1_{x \preccurlyeq y} = \begin{cases} 1, & \text{if } x \preccurlyeq y, \\ 0, & \text{otherwise.} \end{cases}$$

Logical operations OR, AND, NOT, XOR are referred to as $\vee, \wedge, \neg, \oplus$, respectively. All linear masks are hexadecimal, and we omit the 0x symbol.

2.1   Linear Cryptanalysis

Linear cryptanalysis investigates linear relations among the parities of plaintext, ciphertext and the secret key. Let $f : \mathbb{F}_{2^n} \to \mathbb{F}_{2^m}$ be a vectorial boolean function. Assume that masks for input x and output $f(x)$ are Γ_{in} and Γ_{out}. The *correlation* of the linear approximation is defined as

$$C(\Gamma_{in}, \Gamma_{out}) = 2 \cdot \Pr(\Gamma_{in} \cdot x \oplus \Gamma_{out} \cdot f(x) = 0) - 1.$$

Equivalently, the correlation can also be written as a Walsh transformation,

$$C(\Gamma_{in}, \Gamma_{out}) = 2^{-n} \sum_{x \in \mathrm{GF}(2^n)} (-1)^{\Gamma_{in} \cdot x \oplus \Gamma_{out} \cdot f(x)}.$$

Let $g = f_{r-1} \circ \cdots \circ f_1 \circ f_0$ be an iterated permutation which is the composition of r round functions f_i. Linear approximations (γ_i, γ_{i+1}) of a single round f_i can be concatenated into a *linear trail* $(\gamma_0, \gamma_1, \cdots, \gamma_r)$ of g.

Lemma 1 ([8]). *Let $(\gamma_0, \gamma_1, \cdots, \gamma_r)$ be a linear trail of an iterated permutation. Then the correlation of the linear trail can be calculated as*

$$C(\gamma_0, \gamma_r) = \prod_{i=0}^{r-1} C(\gamma_i, \gamma_{i+1})$$

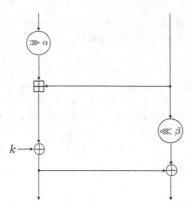

Fig. 1. Round function of SPECK

We call a linear trail over a (round-reduced) cipher with maximum correlation amplitude an *optimal linear trail*.

A linear approximation $(\Gamma_{in}, \Gamma_{out})$ of a block cipher is called a linear hull [19], which contains all linear trails with input mask Γ_{in} and Γ_{out}. The *potential* (averaged linear probability over the key space $\mathcal{K}$) of a linear hull is defined as

$$ALP(\Gamma_{in}, \Gamma_{out}) = \frac{1}{|\mathcal{K}|} \sum_{k \in \mathcal{K}} C(\Gamma_{in}, \Gamma_{out})^2,$$

and gives the expected value of the data complexity of a linear attack.

2.2 Description of SPECK and Chaskey

The lightweight block cipher SPECK family was designed by the NSA in 2013. The block sizes are defined as $2n$ with $n \in \{16, 24, 32, 48, 64\}$, and key size as mn with $m \in \{2, 3, 4\}$ depending on n. The instances corresponding to a block size $2n$ and key size mn are denoted by SPECK$2n/mn$. Since we do not explore the key schedule in this paper, the instances of SPECK will simply be referred to as SPECK$2n$. The round function of SPECK with inputs x and y, a round key k is defined as:

$$F_k(x, y) = (f_k(x, y), f_k(x, y) \oplus (y \lll \beta))$$

where $f_k(\cdot, \cdot)$ is defined as $f_k(x, y) = ((x \ggg \alpha) \boxplus y) \oplus k$, the rotation offset (α, β) is $(7, 2)$ for SPECK32, and $(8, 3)$ for the larger instances. One round of SPECK is depicted in Fig. 1. For more details, we refer to the design [3].

Chaskey is a permutation-based MAC algorithm presented by Mouha *et al.* in 2014. The underlying permutation is an Even-Mansour block cipher with the ARX structure. The block size is 128-bits, which is separated into four 32-bit words. The design of Chaskey is inspired by Siphash [1], and has a structure similar to the block cipher Threefish [9]. The total number of rounds is 8, and

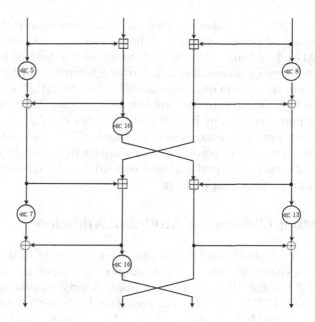

Fig. 2. Round function of Chaskey

there are four modular addition operations and some rotation operations in each round. The round function of the Chaskey permutation is showed in Fig. 2.

2.3 Boolean Satisfiability Problem

The boolean satisfiability problem is often called SAT. It considers whether there is a valid assignment to boolean variables satisfying a given set of boolean clauses. A Boolean clause consists of boolean variables (called literals), operators AND, OR, NOT, and parentheses. For example, the clause x AND (NOT y) is satisfiable since $x =$ TRUE, $y =$ FALSE is a valid assignment.

The SAT problem is NP-complete. However for most practical situations, the solutions can be found in reasonable time. There are a large number of heuristic SAT solvers, and all of them accept DIMACS CNF (Conjunctive Normal Form) files as the standard input format. In CNF format, all clauses are literals with logical operation OR and NOT, while the clauses are concatenated by AND. The output is either *satisfiable* or *unsatisfiable*, when satisfiable, the solver can also return a valid assignment to all literals. More specifically, SAT solvers will start searching with an initial assignment, then calculate the number of conflicting clauses, based on which the search tree of the SAT solver decides the next step of searching to eliminate possible conflicts until a valid or no solution is found. It is believed that, for cryptographic problems, the time for *unsatisfiable* decision is much longer than that of *satisfiable*, because the search is roughly brute-force before returning the decision of *unsatisfiable* [23].

In some applications, we also consider arithmetic operations, for instance, the arithmetic sum of boolean variables, which leads to the satisfiability modulo theory (SMT) problem. SMT has certain similarity with the 0-1 integer programming problem or mixed integer linear programming (MILP), while the underlying ideas to solve them differ significantly. For the MILP problem, linear programming solvers first regard the problem as a general linear programming problem in real numbers, then by Branch and Cut, they carefully rule out illegal branches and then limit the solution to 0-1 integers. SMT solvers try to translate the problem to SAT, then solve it within a binary field. Due to the different methodologies of solvers, the performances depend heavily on the background and structure of the underlying problem.

3   Translating Clauses for Modular Addition

The behaviours of masks through linear operations are easy to describe, since the correlation is either zero or ± 1. For example, with input masks Γ_a, Γ_b and output mask Γ_c, the condition for being a linear approximation of XOR with nonzero correlation is $\Gamma_a = \Gamma_b = \Gamma_c$. The condition for being a nontrivial linear approximation of three-fork branching is $\Gamma_a \oplus \Gamma_b \oplus \Gamma_c = 0$, and the conditions for rotational circular shift is the equality on each corresponding bit of masks.

However for the nonlinear operation modular addition, it is necessary to have a better understanding on the nature of addition modulo 2^n.

3.1   Propagation of Masks Through Modular Addition

The milestone works on linear correlation of modular addition are by Wallén et al. [20,26]. They propose a recursive method to calculate the correlation of a linear approximation in addition modulo 2^n efficiently by an automaton. The only drawback of the recursive automaton is that it is very difficult to translate the expression into bit-level linear relations in masks, i.e. every bit is dependent on all previous bits, which leads to a huge number of complex constraints. Therefore, even though there are several papers discussing the heuristic search methods of differentials, no previous result is on finding linear trails in ARX ciphers with SAT theory.

In order to avoid the recursive expression, an explicit result on calculating the correlation of linear approximations in modular addition is proven by Schulte-Geers [21]. Despite the recursive property of the carry, modular addition is CCZ-equivalent to a vectorial quadratic boolean function. A more natural formula to calculate the correlation in addition modulo 2^n is given in Proposition 1.

Proposition 1 ([21]). *Let z be an n-bit vector satisfying $z \oplus (z \gg 1) \oplus ((u \oplus v \oplus w) \gg 1) = 0$, $z_{n-1} = 0$, where u is the output mask, v, w are the input masks in a linear approximation of addition modulo 2^n. Then the correlation of the linear approximation is given by*

$$cor(u, v, w) = 1_{u \oplus v \preccurlyeq z} 1_{u \oplus w \preccurlyeq z} (-1)^{(u \oplus w) \cdot (u \oplus v)} 2^{-|z|}.$$

Comparing to a recursive algorithm, the Hamming weight of z determines the amplitude of the correlation directly, while each bit of z can be explicitly calculated from input and output masks. Next, we will mainly focus on the absolute value of the correlation.

From Proposition 1, to obtain a valid linear approximation, the input masks v, w and output mask u through addition modulo 2^n need to follow the constraints below.

$$\begin{aligned}
z_{n-1} &= 0, \\
z_{n-2} &= u_{n-1} \oplus v_{n-1} \oplus w_{n-1}, \\
z_j &= z_{j+1} \oplus u_{j+1} \oplus v_{j+1} \oplus w_{j+1}, \\
z_i &\geq u_i \oplus v_i, \\
z_i &\geq u_i \oplus w_i,
\end{aligned} \tag{1}$$

where $0 \leq i \leq n - 1$, $0 \leq j \leq n - 3$.

3.2   From Linear Relations Towards SATisfiability

When considering problems in cryptanalysis, XOR is one of the most common operations. If we translate XOR clauses into CNF, a sentence $a \oplus b$ becomes two clauses $(\neg a \vee \neg b) \wedge (a \vee b)$. In general, the XOR of n boolean variables will give 2^{n-1} clauses in CNF format. Even if the expressions are logically equivalent, the underlying structure of the XOR equation system is missing in terms of the CNF format. A system of XOR equations is in fact a linear equation system on GF(2), therefore, it can be solved by Gaussian elimination in time $O(n^3)$, where n is the number of variables. In many circumstances, Gaussian elimination is much more efficient than translating XOR into operations $\vee$ and $\wedge$. One SAT solver called Cryptominisat4 [23] is specially designed to be compatible with XOR operations and solve the XOR equation system by Gaussian elimination.

The remaining constraints in Eq. (1) are inequalities. Consider the inequality in boolean variables, $z \geq a \oplus b$. It is equivalent to *if $a \oplus b$, then z*, which is logically consistent with $(\neg a \vee b \vee z) \wedge (a \vee \neg b \vee z)$.

Recall that in order to find good linear trails with large correlation values, we need to minimize the Hamming weight of z. By the piling-up lemma, the sum of z in every round $\sum_{i,r} z_i^r$ is the objective function to be minimized. Addition over integers is an unnatural operation in SAT language, which is not easy to describe with only OR and AND. In SAT/SMT theory, Constraints like objective function $\sum_i x_i \leq k$, where $k \geq 1$, are called cardinality constraints, which belongs to an even larger class called Pseudo Boolean constraints (PB-constraints). There are two directions to handle the cardinality constraints: one is to develop new PB-solvers dedicated to cardinality constraints, the other one is to convert cardinality constraints into CNF format, which is what we adopt in this paper.

One plain method is enumerating all the possible combinations of no more than k out of n variables being true, i.e. the conjunction of $\binom{n}{k+1}$ clauses $\bigwedge_{i_1,\dots,i_{k+1}} (\neg x_{i_1} \vee \cdots \vee \neg x_{i_{k+1}})$. However it is not applicable when n, k are large. Throughout the literature, a large number of methods to encode the cardinality

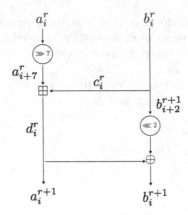

Fig. 3. Notation of masks in round function of SPECK32

constraints are presented. The basic idea is to add new variables to reduce the number of constraints. Since it is a tradeoff between the number of new variables needed and the number of clauses, while the sizes of variables and clauses both have a significant influence on the efficiency of solving, it is critical to find a good encoding method. In this paper, we use sequential encoding method [22], as shown in Eq. (2). For $\sum_i x_i \leq k$, new dummy variables $\{u_{i,j}\}_{1\leq i\leq n-1, 1\leq j\leq k}$ are introduced to return contradiction when the cardinality is larger than k.

$$\begin{cases} (\neg x_1 \vee u_{1,1}) \wedge (\neg u_{1,j}), \\ (\neg x_i \vee u_{i,1}) \wedge (\neg u_{i-1,1} \vee u_{i,1}) \wedge (\neg x_i \vee \neg u_{i-1,j-1} \vee u_{i,j}) \\ \qquad \wedge (\neg u_{i-1,j} \vee u_{i,j}) \wedge (\neg x_i \vee \neg u_{i-1,k}), \\ \neg x_n \vee \neg u_{n-1,k}, \end{cases} \quad (2)$$

where $1 < j \leq k, 1 < i < n$. The sequential encoding of cardinality constraints is one of the best methods, with relatively small amount of additional variables and a great reduction of clauses.

When $k = 0$, all variables are zero, which can be translated to n clauses as $\neg x_i, 1 \leq i \leq n$.

4   Applications

4.1   Application to the SPECK Family

For simplicity, we take SPECK32 as an illustration. Figure 3 shows the notation of the masks in round r. From Eq. (1), we can derive the constraints on linear approximation of SPECK32 in round r as

$$z_{15}^r = 0,$$
$$z_{14}^r = a_6^r \oplus c_{15}^r \oplus d_{15}^r,$$
$$z_j^r = z_{j+1}^r \oplus a_{j+8}^r \oplus c_{j+1}^r \oplus d_{j+1}^r,$$
$$z_i^r \geq a_{i+7}^r \oplus d_i^r, \tag{3}$$
$$z_i^r \geq c_i^r \oplus d_i^r,$$
$$d_i^r = a_i^{r+1} \oplus b_i^{r+1},$$
$$c_i^r = b_i^r \oplus b_{i+2}^{r+1},$$

where $0 \leq i \leq 15$, $0 \leq j \leq 13$, and $\sum_{r,i} z_i^r$ is to be minimized.

Since usually the time for *unsatisfiable* decision is much longer than that for *satisfiable*, we follow Algorithm 1 below to find linear trails with optimal correlation, which ensures that the most time-consuming part *unsatisfiable* only appears once during the search.

Algorithm 1. Find optimal linear trail

Input: An optimal linear trail L with correlation $2^{-\ell}$ of an r round-reduced cipher
Output: The correlation of the optimal linear trail in $r + 1$ round-reduced cipher

1: Append a 1-round trail at the end of L to extend it into a $r + 1$ round valid linear
    trail L' with correlation $2^{-\ell'}$
2: **while** the problem is *satisfiable* with $\sum_{r,i} z_i^r \leq \ell'$ **do**
3:    $\ell' \leftarrow \ell' - 1$
    return $2^{-(\ell'+1)}$

Table 2 gives an overview of the correlation of optimal linear trails in round-reduced SPECK ciphers.[1] We confirm all the correlations of optimal linear trails in [28]. Moreover, our method covers significantly more rounds in larger versions of SPECK: 11/13/9/9 rounds comparing to 7/5/4/4 rounds in previous paper [28] for SPECK48/64/96/128.

We also show examples of linear trails with best correlation for round-reduced SPECKs in Table 3. Sometimes without further constraints, input and output masks may have very high Hamming weight. By setting cardinality constraints on the Hamming weights of the masks, we can obtain trails with input and output masks of the lowest Hamming weight under a given correlation and number of rounds, an example is the linear trail of 11-round SPECK32 in Table 3.

4.2 Application to Chaskey

The designers of Chaskey did not give a security evaluation against linear cryptanalysis in their paper. Using our method, we are able to find the correlation

---

[1] Our experiments for searching optimal linear trails are performed on a PC with 8 Intel® Core™ i7 clocked at 3.40 GHz. In order to speed up the searching for linear hulls by utilising the parallel mode in Cryptominisat4, we run the program on a cruncher with 40 Intel® Xeon™ E5-2687W v3 clocked at 3.1 GHz.

Table 2. Correlation of best linear trail in SPECK family.

R	SPECK32	R	SPECK32	R	SPECK48	SPECK64	SPECK96	SPECK128
1	1	12	2^{-20}	1	1	1	1	1
2	1	13	2^{-22}	2	1	1	1	1
3	2^{-1}	14	2^{-24}	3	2^{-1}	2^{-1}	2^{-1}	2^{-1}
4	2^{-3}	15	2^{-26}	4	2^{-3}	2^{-3}	2^{-3}	2^{-3}
5	2^{-5}	16	2^{-28}	5	2^{-6}	2^{-6}	2^{-6}	2^{-6}
6	2^{-7}	17	2^{-30}	6	2^{-8}	2^{-9}	2^{-9}	2^{-9}
7	2^{-9}	18	2^{-34}	7	2^{-12}	2^{-13}	2^{-13}	2^{-13}
8	2^{-12}	19	2^{-36}	8	2^{-15}	2^{-17}	2^{-18}	2^{-18}
9	2^{-14}	20	2^{-38}	9	2^{-19}	2^{-19}	2^{-22}	2^{-22}
10	2^{-17}	21	2^{-40}	10	2^{-22}	2^{-21}		
11	2^{-19}	22	2^{-42}	11	2^{-25}	2^{-24}		
				12		2^{-27}		
				13		2^{-30}		

of the best linear trail for the round-reduced Chaskey permutation, as shown in Table 4. Table 5 is an example trail for 3-round Chaskey. Notations a, b, c, d are the masks on each 32-bit branch.

4.3   Enumerating Linear Trails in a Linear Hull

For most SAT solvers, if the problem is *satisfiable*, they can print all the solutions. However, due to the additional variables introduced by encoding methods in generating the CNF files, the solvers may output duplicated solutions which represent the same trail, as also observed by Kölbl *et al.* in [13]. To avoid inaccuracy, we generate the solutions one by one:

Step 1: Generate the CNF file for the problem, ask the solver to give one solution $\bar{s}$ if it exists.

Step 2: Append a new clause to the current CNF file in order to rule out $\bar{s}$.

Step 3: Ask solver to give a solution, repeat step 2 until the solver returns *unsatisfiable*.

In Table 6, we give the best linear hulls found and their corresponding distribution of trails for 9-round, 10-round SPECK32, where ALP is the estimated averaged linear probability. The experimental average ALP with 128 random keys for the above linear hulls are $2^{-28.9}$ and $2^{-31.1}$ respectively.

4.4   Comparison of Solvers

In some previous papers on automatic searching of differential and linear trails, e.g. [17,25], the searching idea is modelled as a MILP problem and solved

Table 3. Linear trail with best correlation in reduced-round SPECK.

R	SPECK32		SPECK48		SPECK64	
1	4000	00b0	800121	158021	00101800	00001812
2	0000	00c0	018100	200101	00001000	00000010
3	0300	0300	000100	000001	00000018	00000000
4	0c1e	0818	000001	000000	d8000000	c0000000
5	f000	d010	098000	080000	04100006	04800006
6	4683	4743	406100	406800	0026d030	0420c030
7	00a0	0629	00024b	00420a	01070101	21073781
8	78a0	18a1	001040	5e1042	01b00100	00318601
9	0090	6021	9082c0	f082d0	01800001	0181b000
10	6080	4081	000018	80d09b	01000000	00018000
11	0080	0001	de84dc	c684dc	00010000	00000000
12	0001	0000			00000d00	00000c00
13					00006065	00006068

R	SPECK96		SPECK128	
1	000001800120	140000018021	000000001800120	1400000000018021
2	000000018100	200000000101	000000000018100	2000000000000101
3	000000000100	000000000001	000000000000100	0000000000000001
4	000000000001	000000000000	000000000000001	0000000000000000
5	098000000000	080000000000	0d00000000000000	0c00000000000000
6	404000000000	404800000000	6040000000000000	604c000000000000
7	000000000002	004000000002	0000000000000003	0060000000000003
8	180000000010	1a0000000010	1800000000000018	1b00000000000018
9	009000000080	108000000080	00900000000000c0	18800000000000c0
10	440458000404	840480000404	000000004045e06	c404800000000606
11				

Table 4. Correlation of optimal linear trails in round-reduced Chaskey.

R	1	2	3	4
Best cor.	2^{-1}	2^{-2}	2^{-9}	-

Table 5. A linear trail with optimal correlation in 3-round Chaskey.

R	a	b	c	d
1	00000020	00000000	0001800d	08018189
2	00000000	00000000	00010000	00010000
3	00800000	00000000	00000081	00000000
4	0260c080	18208006	01010260	18208000

Table 6. The Distribution of linear trails in best found 9-/10-round SPECK32 linear hull.

Cor.	9-round[a] #trails	Cor.	10-round[b] #trails
2^{-14}	0	2^{-17}	1
2^{-15}	1	2^{-18}	1
2^{-16}	0	2^{-19}	6
2^{-17}	3	2^{-20}	16
2^{-18}	2	2^{-21}	81
2^{-19}	21	2^{-22}	344
2^{-20}	69	2^{-23}	1298
2^{-21}	346	2^{-24}	4873
2^{-22}	1196	2^{-25}	17781
2^{-23}	4461	2^{-26}	$\geq$60480
2^{-24}	15241	2^{-27}	$\geq$23951
2^{-25}	48397	2^{-28}	$\geq$11272
2^{-26}		2^{-29}	$\geq$3789
2^{-27}		2^{-30}	$\geq$5883
2^{-28}		2^{-31}	$\geq$48951
ALP	$2^{-29.1}$	ALP	$\geq 2^{-32.1}$

[a] input masks: 0010, 1400, output masks: 0b00, 0800
[b] input masks: 0000, 0306, output masks: 0b00, 0800

by CPLEX. To compare the performance of CPLEX and Cryptominisat4, we encode the same constraints with MILP language and CNF without optimisation. Despite the connection between the MILP and the SAT problem with an objective function, our method has an advantage over CPLEX. For instance, to find an optimal linear trail in 6-round SPECK32, it takes over 4000 s on CPLEX, comparing to about 2 s on Cryptominisat4.[2]

Another commonly used solver is STP [11], which is a SMT solver and also a CNF generator. It can encode constraints into CNF file inside the solver based on SMTLIB2 language, and then call a SAT solver to solve the problem. Unlike Cryptominisat4, STP does not support XOR clauses and Gaussian elimination, therefore all clauses involving XOR are translated into standard CNF format. Thus, with exactly the same constraints derived in Sect. 3.1, we generate different

---

[2] Recently, the MILP-based method was applied to the search of differential characteristics and linear trails of SPECK [10]. The formulae describing the linear approximations differ from those of this paper, and dedicated technics are used to improve their search. In addition, the authors concatenate two or three shorter linear trails to attack more rounds, while this paper focuses on finding optimal trails in reduced-round primitives.

Table 7. Comparison between the runtime of CNF files generated by Sect. 3 and STP on the searching problems of SPECK128.

Round	Section 3		STP	
	time1	time2	time1	time2
4	0.05s	0.09s	2s	2s
5	0.8s	1s	4s	7s
6	8s	10s	18s	19s
7	4m44s	1m56s	6m2s	4m20s
8	2s	643m55s	55m4s	114m26s
9	53m51s	16523m	10m27s	12184m

CNF files encoded by STP and our method, and compare their performances on the searching problem of SPECK by considering the number of variables and clauses in corresponding CNF file, as well as the run time for getting optimal linear trails and *unsatisfiable* decision. Both CNF files run on Cryptominisat4.

In most cases, the CNF file encoded by our method has a smaller number of variables and clauses than the STP-generated ones, and the difference can be two times for problems in SPECK with larger block sizes. Although the size of the problem and the speed of solving are not strictly proportional, in general, less variables and clauses are preferable. Table 7 shows the comparison between the runtime of CNF files generated by the method in Sect. 3 and STP solver, where time1 is the time to find an optimal linear trail, and time2 is the time to return *unsatisfiable*. In general, the performance of both methods is comparable. However it is interesting to notice that, it takes 2 s to find one optimal trail for 8-round SPECK128 by our method while STP uses around one hour. It shows that the performance of CNF files depends heavily on the encoding method and the underlying problem, therefore our method may provide an alternative way to solve problems which are not solvable using other solvers.

5   Conclusion

In this paper, we focus on how to find linear trails with optimal correlations in the ARX structures. We model the question as a boolean satisfiability problem, translate the propagation of masks through ARX operations into bitwise expressions and CNF constraints, and then solve the problem by SAT solvers. We apply the automatic search method to the block cipher SPECK and MAC proposal Chaskey, and obtain the correlation of optimal linear trails for 22/11/13/9/9-round reduced SPECK32/48/64/96/128 and 3-round Chaskey, where the analysis of optimal linear trails on Chaskey is presented for the first time so far. In addition, our method is applied to enumerate linear trails in two linear hulls of 9-round and 10-round SPECK32.

Our work provides a searching tool with improved performance towards analysing the security of ARX designs against linear cryptanalysis, which is meaningful to both designers and attackers.

Acknowledgements. We would like to thank the anonymous reviewers for their valuable comments and suggestions. This work was supported in part by the Research Council KU Leuven: GOA TENSE (GOA/11/007) and the Research Fund KU Leuven OT/13/071. Yunwen Liu is partially supported by the China Scholarship Council. Qingju Wang is in part sponsored by National Natural Science Foundation of China (61472250, U1536103) and Major State Basic Research Development Program (973 Plan) of China (2013CB338004).

References

1. Aumasson, J.-P., Bernstein, D.J.: SipHash: a fast short-input PRF. In: Galbraith, S., Nandi, M. (eds.) INDOCRYPT 2012. LNCS, vol. 7668, pp. 489–508. Springer, Heidelberg (2012)
2. Aumasson, J.-P., Henzen, L., Meier, W., Phan, R.C.W.: SHA-3 proposal BLAKE. Submission to NIST (2008)
3. Beaulieu, R., Shors, D., Smith, J., Treatman-Clark, S., Weeks, B., Wingers, L.: The SIMON and SPECK lightweight block ciphers. In: Proceedings of the 52nd Annual Design Automation Conference, DAC 2015, pp. 175:1–175:6. ACM (2015)
4. Bernstein, D.J.: ChaCha, a variant of Salsa20. http://cr.yp.to/chacha.html
5. Bernstein, D.J.: The Salsa20 family of stream ciphers. In: Robshaw, M., Billet, O. (eds.) New Stream Cipher Designs. LNCS, vol. 4986, pp. 84–97. Springer, Heidelberg (2008)
6. Biham, E., Shamir, A.: Differential cryptanalysis of DES-like cryptosystems. J. Cryptol. **4**(1), 3–72 (1991)
7. Biryukov, A., Velichkov, V.: Automatic search for differential trails in ARX ciphers. In: Benaloh, J. (ed.) CT-RSA 2014. LNCS, vol. 8366, pp. 227–250. Springer, Heidelberg (2014)
8. Daemen, J., Govaerts, R., Vandewalle, J.: Correlation matrices. In: Preneel, B. (ed.) FSE 1994. LNCS, vol. 1008, pp. 275–285. Springer, Heidelberg (1995)
9. Ferguson, N., Lucks, S., Schneier, B., Whiting, D., Bellare, M., Kohno, T., Callas, J., Walker, J.: The Skein hash function family. Submission to NIST (round 3) (2010)
10. Fu, K., Wang, M., Guo, Y., Sun, S., Hu, L.: MILP-based automatic search algorithms for differential and linear trails for SPECK. In: Fast Software Encryption, FSE 2016. Springer (2016, to appear)
11. Ganesh, V.: STP constraint solver: Simple theorem prover SMT solver. http://stp.github.io
12. Hong, D., Sung, J., Hong, S.H., Lim, J.-I., Lee, S.-J., Koo, B.-S., Lee, C.-H., Chang, D., Lee, J., Jeong, K., Kim, H., Kim, J.-S., Chee, S.: HIGHT: a new block cipher suitable for low-resource device. In: Goubin, L., Matsui, M. (eds.) CHES 2006. LNCS, vol. 4249, pp. 46–59. Springer, Heidelberg (2006)
13. Kölbl, S., Leander, G., Tiessen, T.: Observations on the SIMON block cipher family. In: Gennaro, R., Robshaw, M. (eds.) CRYPTO 2015. LNCS, vol. 9215, pp. 161–185. Springer, Heidelberg (2015)

14. Leurent, G.: Construction of differential characteristics in ARX designs application to Skein. In: Canetti, R., Garay, J.A. (eds.) CRYPTO 2013, Part I. LNCS, vol. 8042, pp. 241–258. Springer, Heidelberg (2013)

15. Matsui, M.: Linear cryptanalysis method for DES cipher. In: Helleseth, T. (ed.) EUROCRYPT 1993. LNCS, vol. 765, pp. 386–397. Springer, Heidelberg (1994)

16. Mouha, N., Mennink, B., Van Herrewege, A., Watanabe, D., Preneel, B., Verbauwhede, I.: Chaskey: an efficient MAC algorithm for 32-bit microcontrollers. In: Joux, A., Youssef, A. (eds.) SAC 2014. LNCS, vol. 8781, pp. 306–323. Springer, Heidelberg (2014)

17. Mouha, N., Wang, Q., Gu, D., Preneel, B.: Differential and linear cryptanalysis using mixed-integer linear programming. In: Wu, C.-K., Yung, M., Lin, D. (eds.) Inscrypt 2011. LNCS, vol. 7537, pp. 57–76. Springer, Heidelberg (2012)

18. Needham, R.M., Wheeler, D.J.: TEA extensions. Technical report (1997)

19. Nyberg, K.: Linear approximation of block ciphers. In: De Santis, A. (ed.) EUROCRYPT 1994. LNCS, vol. 950, pp. 439–444. Springer, Heidelberg (1995)

20. Nyberg, K., Wallén, J.: Improved linear distinguishers for SNOW 2.0. In: Robshaw, M. (ed.) FSE 2006. LNCS, vol. 4047, pp. 144–162. Springer, Heidelberg (2006)

21. Schulte-Geers, E.: On CCZ-equivalence of addition mod 2^n. Des. Codes Crypt. **66**(1–3), 111–127 (2013)

22. Sinz, C.: Towards an optimal CNF encoding of Boolean cardinality constraints. In: van Beek, P. (ed.) CP 2005. LNCS, vol. 3709, pp. 827–831. Springer, Heidelberg (2005)

23. Soos, M.: A blog about SAT solving and cryptography. http://www.msoos.org

24. Soos, M., Nohl, K., Castelluccia, C.: Extending SAT solvers to cryptographic problems. In: Kullmann, O. (ed.) SAT 2009. LNCS, vol. 5584, pp. 244–257. Springer, Heidelberg (2009)

25. Sun, S., Hu, L., Wang, P., Qiao, K., Ma, X., Song, L.: Automatic security evaluation and (related-key) differential characteristic search: application to SIMON, PRESENT, LBlock, DES(L) and other bit-oriented block ciphers. In: Sarkar, P., Iwata, T. (eds.) ASIACRYPT 2014. LNCS, vol. 8873, pp. 158–178. Springer, Heidelberg (2014)

26. Wallén, J.: Linear approximations of addition modulo 2^n. In: Johansson, T. (ed.) FSE 2003. LNCS, vol. 2887, pp. 261–273. Springer, Heidelberg (2003)

27. Wheeler, D.J., Needham, R.M.: TEA, a tiny encryption algorithm. In: Preneel, B. (ed.) FSE 1994. LNCS, vol. 1008, pp. 363–366. Springer, Heidelberg (1995)

28. Yao, Y., Zhang, B., Wu, W.: Automatic search for linear trails of the SPECK family. In: López, J., Mitchell, C.J. (eds.) ISC 2015. LNCS, vol. 9290, pp. 158–176. Springer, Heidelberg (2015)

Square Attack on 7-Round Kiasu-BC

Christoph Dobraunig[(✉)], Maria Eichlseder, and Florian Mendel

Graz University of Technology, Graz, Austria
christoph.dobraunig@iaik.tugraz.at

Abstract. Kiasu-BC is a tweakable block cipher presented within the TWEAKEY framework at AsiaCrypt 2014. Kiasu-BC is almost identical to AES-128, the only difference to AES-128 is the tweak addition, where the 64-bit tweak is xored to the first two rows of every round-key. The security analysis of the designers focuses primarily on related-key related-tweak differential characteristics and meet-in-the-middle attacks. For other attacks, they conclude that the security level of Kiasu-BC is similar to AES-128. In this work, we provide the first third-party analysis of Kiasu-BC. We show that we can mount Square attacks on up to 7-round Kiasu-BC with a complexity of about $2^{48.5}$ encryptions, which improves upon the best published 7-round attacks for AES-128. Furthermore, we show that such attacks are applicable to the round-reduced ΘCB3-like mode of the CAESAR candidate Kiasu. To be specific, we show a key-recovery attack on 7-round Kiasu$\neq$ with a complexity of about 2^{82} encryptions.

Keywords: Cryptanalysis · TWEAKEY · Kiasu · Square attack

1 Introduction

In contrast to standard block ciphers, tweakable block ciphers provide an additional input called tweak. This tweak is usually public and is used to select one specific instance of the block cipher. The concept of tweakable block ciphers was first formalized by Liskov et al. [15,16]. Since then, tweakable block ciphers have proven to be a valuable building block of cryptographic schemes for various applications, like encryption, authentication, or authenticated encryption. For example, several of the authenticated encryption schemes in the ongoing CAESAR competition [19] are based on tweakable block ciphers [8,12,13].

Recently, Jean et al. presented the TWEAKEY framework [10] for designing tweakable block ciphers. The extended version of their paper [11] specifies three instances: Deoxys-BC, Joltik-BC, and Kiasu-BC. Kiasu-BC is a tweakable variant of AES-128, accepting a 64-bit tweak T in addition to the 128-bit key and 128-bit data block. The specification of Kiasu-BC is essentially identical to AES-128, except that T is xored to the first two rows of every round key. Hence, Kiasu-BC exactly matches AES-128 if $T = 0$. This has several advantages. First of all, it allows easy reuse or updates of existing implementations of AES-128. Moreover, the trust of the industry and academia in AES-128 has been steadily

© Springer International Publishing Switzerland 2016
M. Manulis et al. (Eds.): ACNS 2016, LNCS 9696, pp. 500–517, 2016.
DOI: 10.1007/978-3-319-39555-5_27

growing over the past years and it might be easier in practice to promote the use of AES-128 with slight modifications instead of proposing new tweakable block ciphers. Another advantage of the similarity of Kiasu-BC and AES-128 is that AES-128 has been very thoroughly analyzed due to its prominence and widespread adoption. Since Kiasu-BC corresponds to AES-128 if $T = 0$, existing and also new analysis results for AES-128 directly carry over to Kiasu-BC. However, it is not trivial to determine the effects of the tweak on the security of the design. Therefore, we provide—to the best of our knowledge—the first third-party analysis of Kiasu-BC.

The existing cryptanalysis of Kiasu-BC by its designers [9,11] focuses mainly on meet-in-the-middle attacks and related-key related-tweak differential attacks. The designers argue that the existing meet-in-the-middle attacks for AES-128 also apply to Kiasu-BC. Regarding related-key related-tweak differential characteristics, the designers were able to show that the minimum number of active S-boxes for 7 rounds of Kiasu-BC is 22 and thus, an upper bound for the probability is 2^{-132}. Since this bound is not tight, the designers conclude that Kiasu-BC suffers at most one round security loss compared to AES [9] in the framework of related-key related-tweak differential attacks. For the remaining types of attacks, the designers claim: *"As we keep the original round function and key schedule of AES, we believe that the security level of KIASU-BC against the remaining types of attacks stays the same"* [9]. In Table 1, we have listed some of these remaining attacks. The best-performing attacks that cover 7 rounds of AES-128 fall into the category of impossible differential and meet-in-the-middle attacks. Our goal is to find stronger attacks than these.

All our attacks are based on the Square attack [1]. In the attack, a so-called Λ-set of 256 different plaintexts is observed during the encryption. In the case of AES, it is possible to construct 3-round distinguishers based on the Square property [2,3]. This leads to efficient 6-round key-recovery attacks on AES-128 by prepending 1 round and appending 2 rounds to the 3-round distinguisher [6]. To extend these attacks, we use the additional freedom introduced by the tweak of Kiasu-BC to create a Square-based distinguisher covering 4 rounds. This leads to 7-round attacks on Kiasu-BC (shown in Table 2), which are significantly better

Table 1. Excerpt of best attacks on AES-128.

Rounds	Type	Data (CP)	Time	Ref
6	Partial sum	$2^{34.6}$	2^{44}	[6]
7	Partial sum	$2^{128-\varepsilon}$	2^{120}	[6]
7	Collisions	2^{32}	$2^{128-\varepsilon}$	[7]
7	Impossible differential	$2^{112.2}$	$2^{117.2}$ MA	[17]
7	Meet-in-the-middle	2^{80}	2^{123}	[4]
7	Impossible differential	$2^{106.2}$	$2^{110.2}$	[18]
7	Meet-in-the-middle	2^{97}	2^{99}	[5]

MA – memory accesses

Table 2. Dedicated attacks on round-reduced Kiasu-BC and Kiasu≠.

Target	Rounds	Type	Data (CP)	Time	Ref
Kiasu-BC	7/10	Square	2^{40}	2^{82}	4.1
	7/10	Square	$2^{43.6}$	$2^{48.5}$	4.2
Kiasu≠	7/10	Square	$2^{28} \times 2^{16}$	2^{82}	5.2

than the best published attacks on 7 rounds of AES-128 (see Table 1 for an overview of attacks on AES-128). Furthermore, we show that variants of our Square attack are also applicable to round-reduced variants of an authenticated encryption mode of the CAESAR candidate Kiasu [9]. To be more specific, we target a round-reduced variant of Kiasu≠, which uses 7-round Kiasu-BC in a ΘCB3-like [14] mode of operation. The attacks on round-reduced Kiasu≠ are performed in a nonce-respecting scenario, and also comply with the very low data complexity limits imposed by Kiasu≠.

The remainder of the paper is organized as follows. First, we describe the design of Kiasu-BC in Sect. 2. Afterwards, we construct a 4-round distinguisher based on the Square attack (Sect. 3), followed by two key-recovery attacks on 7-round Kiasu-BC in Sect. 4. Next, we demonstrate the applicability of variants of the key-recovery attacks on the mode of operation Kiasu≠ in Sect. 5. Finally, we conclude in Sect. 6.

2   Description of Kiasu-BC

The tweakable block cipher Kiasu-BC was introduced as building block of the Kiasu authenticated cipher family [9], a candidate in the CAESAR competition [19]. Kiasu-BC is an instantiation of the TWEAKEY framework [10], a general construction framework for tweakable block ciphers. For each 128-bit key and public 64-bit tweak, Kiasu-BC defines a 128-bit permutation.

Kiasu-BC is essentially identical to AES, except that the 64-bit tweak value is xored to the state in each round after the round-key addition. Thus, like for AES, the 128-bit Kiasu-BC state S is represented as a 4×4 matrix of bytes, labeled $x_0, \ldots, x_{15}$:

$$S = \begin{array}{|c|c|c|c|}
\hline
x_0 & x_4 & x_8 & x_{12} \\
\hline
x_1 & x_5 & x_9 & x_{13} \\
\hline
x_2 & x_6 & x_{10} & x_{14} \\
\hline
x_3 & x_7 & x_{11} & x_{15} \\
\hline
\end{array}.$$

In each of Kiasu-BC's 10 rounds, the round operations SubBytes, ShiftRows, MixColumns and AddRoundTweakey are applied to the state in turn. Except for AddRoundTweakey, they are identical to the AES round operations:

- SubBytes: Applies the 8-bit AES S-box $\mathcal{S}$ to each of the 16 state bytes.
- ShiftRows: Rotates row i of the state, $0 \leq i \leq 3$, by i bytes to the left.
- MixColumns: Multiplies each byte column of the state by the MDS-matrix M over $\mathbb{K} = \mathbb{F}_2[\alpha]/(\alpha^8 + \alpha^4 + \alpha^3 + \alpha + 1)$,

$$
M = \begin{pmatrix} \alpha & \alpha+1 & 1 & 1 \\ 1 & \alpha & \alpha+1 & 1 \\ 1 & 1 & \alpha & \alpha+1 \\ \alpha+1 & 1 & 1 & \alpha \end{pmatrix} = \begin{pmatrix} 02 & 03 & 01 & 01 \\ 01 & 02 & 03 & 01 \\ 01 & 01 & 02 & 03 \\ 03 & 01 & 01 & 02 \end{pmatrix}
$$

- AddRoundTweakey: In round i, xors the 128-bit round key RK_i and the tweak T to the state, where

$$
\mathsf{RK}_i = \begin{array}{|c|c|c|c|} \hline \mathsf{RK}_{i0} & \mathsf{RK}_{i4} & \mathsf{RK}_{i8} & \mathsf{RK}_{i12} \\ \hline \mathsf{RK}_{i1} & \mathsf{RK}_{i5} & \mathsf{RK}_{i9} & \mathsf{RK}_{i13} \\ \hline \mathsf{RK}_{i2} & \mathsf{RK}_{i6} & \mathsf{RK}_{i10} & \mathsf{RK}_{i14} \\ \hline \mathsf{RK}_{i3} & \mathsf{RK}_{i7} & \mathsf{RK}_{i11} & \mathsf{RK}_{i15} \\ \hline \end{array}, \quad T = \begin{array}{|c|c|c|c|} \hline T_0 & T_2 & T_4 & T_6 \\ \hline T_1 & T_3 & T_5 & T_7 \\ \hline & & & \\ \hline & & & \\ \hline \end{array}.
$$

We omit the details of the AES key schedule that derives the round subkeys RK_i from the key K, since they are not relevant for our attack. Note that there is no tweak schedule, i.e., the same tweak T is xored in each round. So for the all-zero tweak $T = 0$, Kiasu-BC is equivalent to AES-128.

To refer to intermediate states of Kiasu-BC, we denote by S_i the state after i rounds: $S_0 = P \oplus T \oplus \mathsf{RK}_0$, S_1, ..., $S_{10} = C$. In addition, the state after SubBytes of round i is denoted S_i^{SB}, after ShiftRows S_i^{SR}, after MixColumns S_i^{MC}, and after AddRoundTweakey $S_i^{\mathsf{AK}} = S_i$. So the states of full-round Kiasu-BC are

$$
P \xrightarrow{\mathsf{AK}} S_0 \xrightarrow{\mathsf{SB}} S_1^{\mathsf{SB}} \xrightarrow{\mathsf{SR}} S_1^{\mathsf{SR}} \xrightarrow{\mathsf{MC}} S_1^{\mathsf{MC}} \xrightarrow{\mathsf{AK}} S_1
$$

$$
\vdots
$$

$$
S_9 \xrightarrow{\mathsf{SB}} S_{10}^{\mathsf{SB}} \xrightarrow{\mathsf{SR}} S_{10}^{\mathsf{SR}} \xrightarrow{\mathsf{AK}} S_{10} = C \ .
$$

3   Distinguisher for 4 Rounds of Kiasu-BC

The distinguisher presented in this section is based on the Square attack. This attack, originally demonstrated for the block cipher Square [1], is also applicable to AES [2,3]. As in the Square attack on AES, we will observe a Λ-set of 256 different plaintexts through the encryption. By making use of the tweak input of Kiasu-BC, we show that a distinguisher for 4 rounds can be created. This is one round more than the distinguisher used in the Square attack on AES. Before giving the distinguisher, we recall the effect of the round functions of AES on Λ-sets.

3.1   Preliminaries

For the Square attack, we will make statements about the 256 values for single byte positions x_i of a Λ-set. We index the individual byte value of byte position i in Λ-set element k as $x_i[k]$, where the index k is in the range from 0 to 255. We call a byte of a Λ-set active (A) if it takes all possible 256 values; constant (C) if all 256 values are equal; balanced (B) if the sum of all 256 values is 0; or unknown (?) if we cannot make any statements about the 256 values for this byte position.

SubBytes. SubBytes affects each byte of the state individually. Therefore, we can put our focus on the effects of the S-box on our four different byte states: active, constant, balanced, and unknown. The AES S-box is a permutation. Hence, if the input of the S-box iterates over all 256 possible values, then so will the output. Thus, an active byte remains active after SubBytes. Since the AES S-box is deterministic, a certain value at the input of the S-box will always map to the same value at the output. This means a constant byte remains constant after SubBytes. However, a balanced byte becomes unknown, because the S-box is non-linear. An unknown byte remains, of course, unknown.

ShiftRows. The ShiftRows operation works on byte-level. To be more concrete, it simply reorders the bytes of the state. Hence, our statements about the bytes remain the same, just the position differs after ShiftRows.

MixColumns. MixColumns is a linear transformation that mixes the single bytes of one column. Clearly, an all-constant input set will be mapped to an all-constant output set. Furthermore, if at least one of the input byte positions of the set is unknown, the entire output will be unknown.

Since MixColumns is based on an MDS matrix, it has a branch number of 5. This implies that if two input columns differ only in one byte, the output will differ in all 4 bytes. In particular, if the 4 input byte positions of a set are all constant except for one active byte, then all output bytes will be active. (Assume that one byte is not active, but takes one particular value twice. The corresponding pair of inputs will have a difference in only 1 input byte and at most 3 output bytes, violating the branch number property.) The same reasoning also clearly applies for the inverse operation of MixColumns.

AddRoundTweakey. Here, the specific round key as well as the tweak are xored to the state. Our attacks are performed in the single-key setting, so each key byte is constant. This means that an active byte of the state remains active, a constant byte constant, a balanced byte balanced (since the constant key is added an even number of times and cancels out), and an unknown byte remains unknown.

The situation changes if we take a look at the tweak addition. For the distinguisher, we want to use Λ-sets where one byte of the tweak is active, so we have to consider the following situations. The xor of an active byte with an active byte definitely results in a balanced byte. If the tweak byte as well as the state byte are active and $T_i[k] \oplus x_i[k] = c$ for each k, the byte gets constant. The xor of an active byte with a balanced byte results in a balanced byte.

3.2 The 4-Round Distinguisher

The distinguisher used in the Square attack against AES [2,3] spans over 3 rounds. It starts with a Λ-set that is active in one byte of the plaintext and constant in the rest of the state. The distinguisher ends after the key addition of the third round with an all-balanced state. By introducing an active tweak byte, we are able to extend the distinguisher by one round. However, the condition we get after round 4 is slightly more difficult to exploit (see Fig. 1).

As shown in Fig. 1, we start with a Λ-set of 256 plaintexts P, where one byte is active and the others remain constant. Additionally, we require that byte T_0 of the tweak is active as well. Since always the same tweak is xored to every round key, every resulting round key xored with the tweak can be described as a Λ-set that is active at byte 0 and constant in the rest of the bytes. The tweak and plaintext values have to be chosen in a way that the xor of the tweak and the plaintext is constant. For instance, $T_0[k]$ can always be chosen to be equal to the

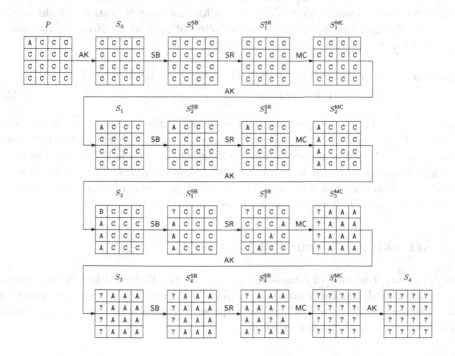

Fig. 1. Distinguisher for 4 rounds of Kiasu-BC.

first byte of the plaintext $x_0[k]$ for all 256 values of k. In this way, it is ensured that state S_0 is constant at every byte position. The state remains constant until S_1, where byte x_0 becomes active again due to the addition of the tweak.

The second round of our distinguisher for Kiasu-BC corresponds to the first round of the distinguisher used in the AES Square attack, except for the addition of the active tweak byte at the end. Since SubBytes and ShiftRows affect neither active nor constant bytes, we get to state S_2^{SR}, where still only the byte at position 0 remains active. The rest of the state is still constant. The next MixColumns operation leads to an active column in state S_2^{MC}. In contrast to the first tweak addition, the tweak addition at the end of round 2 leads to a balanced byte at position 0. We get a balanced byte here, because we cannot make any assumption on the concrete ordering of the 256 values of x_0 of state S_2^{MC}.

In the third round, we have one balanced byte before SubBytes. This byte becomes unknown after the S-box application. The ShiftRows operation shifts the active bytes away from the first column. So we have at state S_3^{SR} one unknown, and three constant bytes in the first column and one active, and 3 constant bytes in every other column. This leads to one completely unknown first column, and three completely active columns in state S_3^{MC}. The next tweak addition does not change anything.

For the fourth round, we only go with active or unknown bytes through the S-box layer, thus SubBytes does not influence our knowledge about the Λ-set at this point. ShiftRows shifts one unknown byte to every column, so we get a completely unknown state S_4^{MC} if we only limit our view to single byte positions. Hence, we have to take a closer look at the MixColumns operation. To do so, we represent the bytes of S_4^{SR} as x_i and the bytes of S_4^{MC} as y_i. Now, let us take a look at what happens if we xor y_1 with y_2:

$$\begin{aligned} y_1 \oplus y_2 &= 01 \cdot x_0 \oplus 02 \cdot x_1 \oplus 03 \cdot x_2 \oplus 01 \cdot x_3 \oplus 01 \cdot x_0 \oplus 01 \cdot x_1 \oplus 02 \cdot x_2 \oplus 03 \cdot x_3 \\ &= 03 \cdot x_1 \oplus 01 \cdot x_2 \oplus 02 \cdot x_3 \end{aligned} \tag{1}$$

As shown in (1), x_0 cancels and thus does not influence $y_1 \oplus y_2$. In the first column of S_4^{SR}, x_0 is the only byte which is unknown. The rest of the bytes are active. Since (1) only contains active coefficients, $y_1 \oplus y_2$ is balanced. The next key and tweak addition is an addition with constant bytes. This addition with constant values does not influence the balanced property and therefore, also the xor of byte 1 and 2 of state S_4 is balanced.

4   Attacking 7 Rounds of Kiasu-BC

For attacking 7 rounds of Kiasu-BC, we extend the distinguisher by one round in the backward and two rounds in the forward direction. At first we present a basic version of the attack. Then, we improve the attack by using partial sums in a similar way as Ferguson et al. [6].

4.1   Basic Square Attack

The key-recovery attack is based on a set of plaintexts with differences only on one of the diagonals of the state, combined with a set of tweaks with differences only in the top left byte T_0. Figure 2 shows the trail we use to attack 7 rounds of Kiasu-BC, where rounds 2 to 5 correspond to the distinguisher explained in Sect. 3. To perform this attack, we first collect the encryption of all 2^{32} plaintexts P where the diagonal bytes $(x_0, x_5, x_{10}, x_{15})$ loop through all possible values, whereas the remaining 12 bytes are fixed to some constant. Each of these plaintexts is encrypted under all 2^8 possible tweaks where all bytes except T_0 are fixed to some constant, and T_0 loops through all values. Thus, in total, we require the ciphertext for $2^8 \cdot 2^{32} = 2^{40}$ plaintext-tweak combinations.

Building Λ-sets. Next, we want to group this data into suitable Λ-sets, so that the previously introduced distinguisher can be applied to state S_1. This has to be done separately for each possible key guess of the 32 key bits $\mathsf{RK}_{0,0}$, $\mathsf{RK}_{0,5}$, $\mathsf{RK}_{0,10}$, and $\mathsf{RK}_{0,15}$, which determine the values of the first column of state S_1^{MC}.

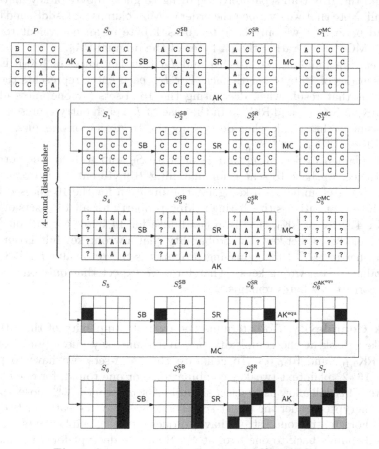

Fig. 2. Square attack for 7 rounds of Kiasu-BC.

What we want to achieve is that this first column has only 1 active byte in x_0, and that this activity is canceled by AddRoundTweakey. Thus, we can fix the 3 constant bytes x_1, x_2, x_3 in S_1^{MC} to some arbitrary value, and set $x_0 = T_0$ for each of the 2^8 tweaks. If we decrypt these 2^8 set elements by 1 round, MixColumns will produce 4 active S-boxes in S_5^{SR}, which will be shifted to active S-boxes in x_0, x_5, x_{10}, x_{15} in state S_0. Depending on the different tweak bytes T_0 and the current key guess for the partial first-round key RK_0, we get a Λ-set of 2^8 plaintexts. We can repeat this procedure for a few different constant values in S_1^{MC} in order to build 16 Λ-sets for each of the 2^{32} key guesses of RK_0. For the correct key guess, all 16 Λ-sets will follow the 4-round distinguisher from Sect. 3.

Applying the Distinguisher. We now want to partially decrypt all ciphertexts of each Λ-set back to state S_5, in order to verify the distinguishing property. Remember that we are interested in computing the xor sum $y_1 \oplus y_2$ of each Λ-set, marked in black (y_1) and gray (y_2) in Fig. 2. To do so, we have to calculate all intermediate values marked in black and gray in Fig. 2. We can do this for the black and the gray trail separately, requiring to guess 5 byte of key material for each trail. Note that we swapped the order of MixColumns and AddRoundTweakey in round 6, so that we only have to guess 1 byte of an equivalent round-key $RK_6^{equ} = MC^{-1}(RK)$, rather than 4 bytes of the original RK_6.

We end up building two lists L_1 and L_2 (per key guess of RK_0). Each list has 2^{40} entries of 16-byte length each. For L_1, each entry represents the 16 xor sums of y_1 that result when decrypting the 16 Λ-sets for one guess of $RK_{7,3}$, $RK_{7,6}$, $RK_{7,9}$, $RK_{7,12}$, and $RK_{6,13}^{equ}$. In the case of L_2, each entry represents the 16 xor sums of y_2 that result when decrypting the 16 Λ-sets for one guess of $RK_{7,2}$, $RK_{7,5}$, $RK_{7,8}$, $RK_{7,15}$, and $RK_{6,10}^{equ}$.

As explained in Sect. 3, y_1 and y_2 of state S_5 sum to 0 for the correct key guess. Hence, we have to search for matching 16-byte entries between lists L_1 and L_2. A match indicates a key guess combination for the 10 guessed bytes of RK_6^{equ}, RK_7 that satisfies the distinguishing property for all 16 Λ-sets of one key guess for 4 bytes of RK_0; that is, a candidate for 14 bytes (or 112 bits) of key material for the correct key. The probability that a wrong key fulfills our 16-byte distinguisher is 2^{-128} (distinguishing property is the zero value for 128 bits, all other values reveal wrong keys). Therefore, we expect that only one candidate for the correct key bytes remains.

Attack Complexity. To determine the overall complexity of this attack, we first take a look at the complexity per first-round key guess (guess of $RK_{0,0}$, $RK_{0,5}$, $RK_{0,10}$, and $RK_{0,15}$). To generate the 16 Λ-sets, we have to partially decrypt $16 \cdot 2^8$ plaintext-tweakey combinations for one round, for one column of the state. This will allow us to select suitable Λ-sets from the 2^{40} chosen-plaintext queries encrypted under the target key. Then, we have to create our two lists L_1 and L_2. For creating one list, we have to decrypt $2^4 \cdot 2^8$ ciphertexts for 2^{40} key guesses 2 rounds back to one byte at S_5. Since we decrypt for 2 rounds to one byte, we only have to look at one column of the state. Hence, we estimate the costs for such a partial decryption with half a Kiasu-BC round. So, creating one list has approximately the complexity of $2^4 \cdot 2^8 \cdot 2^{40} = 2^{52}$ half-round decryptions, which corresponds to less than 2^{49} 7-round Kiasu-BC decryptions. For creating both lists, we require about 2^{50} 7-round Kiasu-BC decryptions. This complexity dominates both the complexity of 2^{12} one-round encryptions for creating the 16 Λ-sets and the complexity for finding a match between the two lists, which is approximately $40 \cdot 2^{40}$ comparison operations for sorting one list and $40 \cdot 2^{40}$ memory look-ups for finding a match.

Since we have to build the two lists for each of the 2^{32} first-round key guesses, we end up having a total attack complexity of 2^{82} 7-round Kiasu-BC encryptions. For carrying out this attack, we have to query $2^8 \cdot 2^{32} = 2^{40}$ chosen plaintexts. In addition to the plaintext-ciphertext pairs, we have to store our two lists L_1 and L_2. One entry of the lists corresponds to the memory complexity of storing one plaintext. Thus, we have an additional memory requirement of roughly 2^{41} Kiasu-BC states.

4.2 Improvements Using Partial Sums

Ferguson et al. [6] showed that the complexity of the Square attack on AES can be significantly improved by using the partial sum technique. Their first observation is that for AES, the effort of guessing the 32 bits of RK_0 can be traded for summing over larger sets (of all 2^{32} plaintexts, rather than only 2^8 Λ-set messages), thus reducing the complexity by a factor of 2^8. Then, as a second improvement, the increased number of operations necessary for evaluating the distinguisher can be rearranged into partial sums to significantly cut down the computational complexity. In this section, we will show that a similar reasoning applies to Kiasu-BC, and that the techniques of Ferguson et al. [6] can be adapted to improve the complexity of the attack on 7-round Kiasu-BC significantly.

Summing All Messages. In the basic attack, we had to guess 4 bytes of the first round key RK_0 in order to select a suitable Λ-set of 2^8 plaintext-tweak combinations and apply the distinguisher. For such a Λ-set, which is characterized by a single active byte x_0 in state S_1^{MC} and a constant difference between this byte and tweak byte T_0 (e.g., $x_0 = T_0$), we know that in S_5, the values $y_1 \oplus y_2$ sum to 0. Clearly, the same distinguishing property also applies if we sum not just over one, but over several Λ-sets.

Now consider again our set of $2^8 \cdot 2^{32}$ plaintext-tweak combinations. This set can actually be grouped into $2^8 \cdot 2^{24}$ Λ-sets as follows. For every value of T_0, the state bytes x_0, x_1, x_2, x_3 in state S_1^{MC} take all 2^{32} values. Therefore, for each of the 2^{24} fixed constant values of x_1, x_2, x_3 and each fixed value $x_0 \oplus T_0$ in state S_1^{MC}, we can find exactly 2^8 plaintext-tweak combinations that map to this state, where x_1, x_2, x_3 and $x_0 \oplus T_0$ are constant. Each of these 2^8 plaintext-tweak combinations fulfills our conditions for a Λ-set. Thus, if we sum over all plaintext-tweak combinations, we actually sum over many Λ-sets, so the distinguishing property for $y_1 \oplus y_2$ will apply – and we do not have to guess the round key RK_0

in order to evaluate it. In other words, we can trade guessing the 32 key bits of RK_0 for summing over 2^{40} instead of 2^8 messages. Unfortunately, in contrast to the original attack on AES [6], this first improvement described so far does not, by itself, decrease the attack complexity, since we have to sum over all values of T_0. However, as we will show next, this modified distinguisher can be evaluated in an optimized way by reorganizing the order of summation.

Adapting the Distinguisher. To evaluate the distinguisher, we now need to decrypt our 2^{40} ciphertexts back to y_1 and y_2. To identify valid key candidates, we calculate the sum in y_1 for each key guess of $RK_{7,3}$, $RK_{7,6}$, $RK_{7,9}$, $RK_{7,12}$, and $RK_{6,13}$, storing the result in L_1 (indexed by the key guess); and we do the same for y_2 in L_2, based on all guesses of $RK_{7,2}$, $RK_{7,5}$, $RK_{7,8}$, $RK_{7,15}$, and $RK_{6,10}$. Since we guess in total 10 bytes of key material, a 1-byte distinguisher is not enough to filter all wrong key guesses. Hence, we repeat the whole procedure for a total of 12 collections (of 2^{40} ciphertexts each), so that L_1 and L_2 are in the end populated with 12-byte entries (and indexed by 5-byte key guesses). We expect only one 12-byte match between L_1 and L_2, providing us with the correct 10 bytes of key material.

We now want to optimize the costs for calculating the entries of L_1 and L_2, which dominate the overall runtime by making use of the partial-sum technique described by Ferguson et al. [6]. They show that the cost for computing the 2^{40} sums (for each key guess) of one byte located 2 AES rounds before the end (similar to our case, y_1 or y_2 of State S_5), using 2^{32} ciphertexts, can be reduced to approximately 2^{50} S-box applications. Assuming that one encryption under a new key is equivalent to 2^8 S-box applications, the overall cost is only about 2^{42} encryptions. In contrast to the original attack, we actually want to sum over 2^{40} values, and additionally have to consider the tweak input. However, it turns out that the original partial-sum technique can be adapted to allow this with no significant computational overhead.

First, observe that in each AddRoundTweakey step, the different values of T_0 only influence the first byte x_0 of the state; and in the AddRoundTweakey^{equ} step that we apply in round 6, T_0 modifies the equivalent round key of the first column (state bytes x_0, x_1, x_2, x_3). As illustrated in Fig. 2, neither L_1 nor L_2 depend on these state bytes, so we do not need to know T_0 in order to partially decrypt. Second, note that for building L_1 (or L_2), we are only interested in 32 bits of each of the 2^{40} encrypted messages (per collection). Thus, instead of decrypting each message with each key guess, we can count how often each possible 32-bit value occurs among the encrypted messages, and then only decrypt based on each 32-bit value once. Furthermore, since the effects of two occurrences of the same 32-bit value will simply cancel out in the final xor-sum, it is sufficient to count occurrences modulo 2. We can store the counters in a 2^{32}-bit vector $\delta^{\text{cccc}} = (\delta_0^{\text{cccc}}, \ldots, \delta_{2^{32}-1}^{\text{cccc}})$, indexed by the possible values $x = x_0 \| x_1 \| x_2 \| x_3$.

Equipped with these two observations, we can now directly apply Ferguson et al.'s partial-sum technique, which we summarize below.

Ferguson et al.'s Partial Sums [6]. Consider the byte y_1 we need to evaluate for one entry of L_1, i.e., the sum over the 2^{40} messages of one collection. If we denote the 4 relevant (black) ciphertext bytes of message i in state S_7 by $c_{i,0}, \ldots, c_{i,3}$ and the 5 guessed round-key bytes (after xoring the known tweak) by $k_0, \ldots, k_4$, and summarize the inverse SubBytes in round 7 and the constant multiplications by MixColumns in round 6 in the bytewise functions $S_0, \ldots, S_3$, then the value we want to compute is

$$\sigma = \bigoplus_{i=0}^{2^{40}-1} S^{-1}[S_0[c_{i,0} \oplus k_0] \oplus S_1[c_{i,1} \oplus k_1] \oplus S_2[c_{i,2} \oplus k_2] \oplus S_3[c_{i,3} \oplus k_3] \oplus k_4]$$

$$= \bigoplus_{x=0}^{2^{32}-1} \delta_x^{cccc} \cdot S^{-1}[S_0[x_0 \oplus k_0] \oplus S_1[x_1 \oplus k_1] \oplus S_2[x_2 \oplus k_2] \oplus S_3[x_3 \oplus k_3] \oplus k_4].$$

To optimize this computation, we first count for every key guess of k_0 and k_1 the modulo-2 frequency of the values $(S_0[c_{i,0} \oplus k_0] \oplus S_1[c_{i,1} \oplus k_1], c_{i,2}, c_{i,3})$ and store it in the 2^{24}-bit vector δ^{scc}. This vector can easily be computed from δ^{cccc} as

$$\delta_{x_0,x_1,x_2}^{scc} = \bigoplus_{s=0}^{2^8-1} \delta_{s,S_1^{-1}[x_0 \oplus S_0[s \oplus k_0]] \oplus k_1, x_1, x_2}^{cccc}. \tag{2}$$

Similarly, after guessing k_2 and subsequently k_3, we can compute the frequency δ^{sc} of $(S_0[c_{i,0} \oplus k_0] \oplus S_1[c_{i,1} \oplus k_1] \oplus S_2[c_{i,2} \oplus k_2], c_{i,3})$ (2^{16} entries) and then δ^s of $(S_0[c_{i,0} \oplus k_0] \oplus S_1[c_{i,1} \oplus k_1] \oplus S_2[c_{i,2} \oplus k_2] \oplus S_3[c_{i,3} \oplus k_3])$ (2^8 entries) via

$$\delta_{x_0,x_1}^{sc} = \bigoplus_{s=0}^{2^8-1} \delta_{s,S_2^{-1}[x_0 \oplus s] \oplus k_2, x_1}^{scc}, \tag{3}$$

$$\delta_{x_0}^{s} = \bigoplus_{s=0}^{2^8-1} \delta_{s,S_3^{-1}[x_0 \oplus s] \oplus k_3}^{sc}. \tag{4}$$

Finally, we guess k_4 and compute the desired result byte via

$$\sigma = \bigoplus_{s=0}^{2^8-1} \delta_s^s \cdot S^{-1}[s \oplus k_4]. \tag{5}$$

The same procedure can be applied to compute the entries of L_2, and needs to be repeated for each of the 12 collections. Afterwards, L_1 and L_2 can be sorted and matched as before to identify the correct partial key for 10 bytes of key material. The remaining 6 bytes of key information can be recovered with a brute-force approach.

Overall Complexity. The data complexity for the improved attack is $12 \cdot 2^{40} \approx 2^{43.6}$ chosen plaintext-tweak combinations. Per list and collection, we have the following complexity. The original 2^{32}-bit vector δ^{cccc} can be constructed with negligible overhead to each chosen-plaintext query. The 2^{24}-bit vector δ^{scc} is computed for 2^{16} key guesses, and requires $2 \cdot 2^8 \cdot 2^{24} = 2^{33}$ S-box lookups, so the computations of (2) contribute 2^{49} S-box lookups per list and collection. Similarly, computations (3), (4) and (5) contribute 2^{48} S-box lookups each. Overall, computing lists L_1 and L_2 require $2 \cdot 12 \cdot (2^{49} + 3 \cdot 2^{48}) \approx 2^{54.9}$ S-box lookups, or roughly $2^{46.9}$ 7-round encryptions.

Sorting the 2^{40} entries of L_1 and L_2 can be implemented, for example, with less than $40 \cdot 2^{40} \approx 2^{45.3}$ comparisons (worst-case) and $2 \cdot 2^{40.1}$ Kiasu-BC states of memory per list via MergeSort, or a total of $2^{46.3}$ comparisons and $2^{41.7}$ memory for both lists. Finding all matches between the sorted lists takes a negligible $2 \cdot 2^{40}$ comparisons (worst-case).

We expect to find only one match, and guessing the remaining 6 bytes of key information takes, in the worst case, 2^{48} encryptions (assuming that the known 10 bytes of key information can be combined efficiently). In total, the worst-case attack complexity is about $2^{48.5}$ 7-round Kiasu-BC encryptions, and requires about $2^{41.7}$ Kiasu-BC states of memory, and $2^{43.6}$ chosen-plaintext-tweak queries.

5   Application to Authenticated Cipher Kiasu$\neq$

In this section, we show that variants of the previously presented Square attacks are applicable when Kiasu-BC is used in a ΘCB3-like [14] mode of operation. To be specific, we demonstrate the feasibility of a variant of the attack presented in the previous section on Kiasu$\neq$. Kiasu$\neq$ is one of two proposed modes of the CAESAR candidate Kiasu [9], which only claims security when used in a nonce-respecting way. Thus, the attacks presented in this section follow this restriction and never require the nonce to be equal for queries on the encryption oracle. Before describing the attack, we give a short description of Kiasu$\neq$.

5.1   Description of Kiasu$\neq$

Figure 3 shows the plaintext processing part of the authenticated encryption scheme Kiasu$\neq$. Here, each plaintext block P_i is encrypted with the help of Kiasu-BC using always a different value for its tweak. The tweak value is constructed by concatenating a 3-bit 0, the 32-bit nonce N and a 29-bit value representing the index i of the plaintext block P_i that is encrypted. To generate the tag T, the sum of the plaintext blocks is encrypted and xored with Auth, which is derived from processing the authenticated data.

5.2   A Key-Recovery Attack on Round-Reduced Kiasu$\neq$

Our attack targets the encryption of the plaintexts blocks. For the attack to be carried out, we need an encryption oracle that encrypts plaintexts chosen by the attacker. We use the block counter to iterate over the tweak byte T_7 to construct our Λ-sets. Since the least significant byte of the block counter is xored to byte

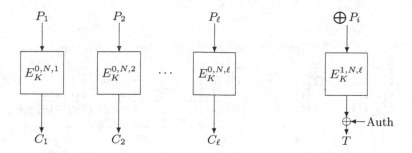

Fig. 3. Plaintext processing for the nonce-respecting mode Kiasu$\neq$ for a multiple of the block length.

13 of the state, we have to use a slightly different distinguisher, which is shown in Fig. 4. Similar to the attacks presented in Sect. 4, we prepend one round to the distinguisher and append two rounds. Then, we can apply a slight modification of the Square attack described in Sect. 4.1.

The attack of Sect. 4.1 can be partitioned in two phases. The first one is the generation of 16 Λ-sets under a specific guess of 32-bits of RK_0, the second part is the evaluation of the Λ-sets to see if the distinguishing property holds for partial guesses of RK_6 and RK_7. While this evaluation of the Λ-sets works equivalent as in Sect. 4.1 for the attack on Kiasu$\neq$, we have to change the way we built our Λ-sets. For building the Λ-sets, the attack of Sect. 4.1 uses the same 2^8 tweak values for every Λ-set. This is no longer an option, since the attacks on round-reduced Kiasu$\neq$ are performed in a nonce-respecting setting. Therefore, we have to build each Λ-set using different tweak values and respecting the data limits of Kiasu$\neq$, which limit the number of encrypted blocks per message to 2^{29}, and the total number of encrypted messages to 2^{32}. Next, we will describe how to select suitable plaintexts to obtain Λ-sets under these constraints.

Observe that for a single multi-block plaintext message, the tweaks used for encrypting the individual plaintext blocks will be constant in the first 35 bits, where 32 bits represent the nonce value. Dependent on the attack model, the nonce may be known before we make an encryption query (e.g., it is implemented as a counter, to avoid collisions of the very short nonces), or the oracle picks a random nonce. Note that one byte of the nonce at tweak position T_1 influences our key guess at $\mathsf{RK}_{0,1}$ in the upcoming attack. Hence, for sake of simplicity, we assume that the nonce value is known before we make each encryption query (we discuss the case of unpredictable nonces at the end of this section). The remaining bits of the tweak represent a 29-bit block counter and are always known in advance. In our attack we want to use the least significant 8 counter bits in T_7 for the active tweak byte. Since the counter starts with a value of 1, we actually can only start building Λ-sets from block 256 on. So the first Λ-set includes blocks $256, \ldots, 511$, i.e., $T_6 = 1$ and T_7 is active. Now, we need to define suitable plaintext blocks to query, so that the ciphertext blocks of one 511-block message will allow us to evaluate the distinguisher.

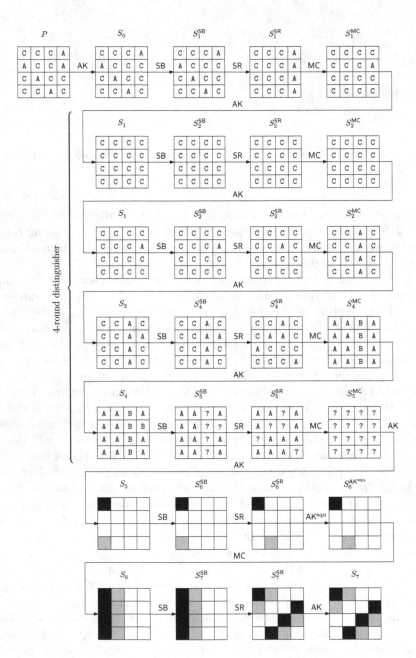

Fig. 4. Attack for 7 rounds of Kiasu≠.

Let p_i denote the individual state bytes of the plaintext, x_i the bytes of S_1^{MC}, and z_i the bytes of the state right after adding the tweak (but before adding the round key). We start by choosing some arbitrary constant value for the bytes $z_{12}, z_{13}, z_{14}, z_{15}$. Then, we apply the inverse tweak-addition to obtain $x_{12}, \ldots, x_{15}$, which will add a constant value of $T_6 = 1$ to z_{12}, and an active $T_7 = 0, \ldots, 255$ to z_{13}. The inverse first round will map this column to some set of states with 4 active bytes in S_0. For one key guess of $RK_{0,1}$, $RK_{0,6}$, $RK_{0,11}$, and $RK_{0,12}$, we obtain a set of 256 values for $(p_1, p_6, p_{11}, p_{12})$. The only other active byte, p_{13}, needs to be chosen so that the difference $p_{13} \oplus T_7$ is fixed, e.g., by setting $p_{13} = T_7$. The rest of the state can be chosen as some arbitrary constant. The resulting plaintext blocks have to be encrypted by the encryption oracle at block positions P_{256} to P_{511} and form a Λ-set for the right guess of $RK_{0,1}$, $RK_{0,6}$, $RK_{0,11}$, and $RK_{0,12}$.

The second part of the attack is evaluating the constructed Λ-sets. Since we changed the position of the active tweak byte from T_0 to T_7 compared to the original attack of Sect. 4.1, we also need to adapt the distinguishing property and evaluate, for instance, $y_0 \oplus y_3$ in state S_5, instead of $y_1 \oplus y_2$. The indices of the guessed round keys and ciphertext bytes need to be adapted accordingly, but otherwise, the attack procedure remains the same. This modification also has no influence on the attack runtime, so the computational complexity is still a total of 2^{82} encryptions to recover 12 bytes of key information.

Accomodating the Data Complexity Limit. Note that with the above strategy, we would need to encrypt $16 \cdot 2^{32}$ messages to obtain 16 Λ-sets per 32-bit guess of RK_0. Thus, we would exceed the maximum number of messages that can be encrypted per key. However, it is possible and necessary to build more than one Λ-set per message following block 511, so that we do not exceed the maximum number of possible messages in our attack. Assume we construct 2^8 Λ-sets per message. This means the first Λ-set covers blocks $256, \ldots, 511$, so $T_6 = 1$ and T_7 is active, the second Λ-set covers blocks $512, \ldots, 767$, so $T_6 = 2$ and T_7 is active, and so on, until we have 2^8 Λ-sets. Thus, every message we query has a length of $2^{16} + 255$ blocks. This means we need 2^{28} chosen messages sent to the encryption oracle, corresponding to $2^{44} + 2^{36}$ chosen plaintext blocks for the attack.

Adaptation for Unpredictable Nonces. For simplicity, we assumed that the nonce value for each encryption query is predictable, since we needed the value of the nonce byte at tweak position T_1 in order to derive the plaintext values p_1 for each key guess of $RK_{0,1}$. However, the attack can also be adapted for cases where the nonce is not known as follows. The attacker assumes $T_1 = 0$ and simply queries one message per guess of RK_0. The actual values of T_1 will be random, so for each value of $RK_{0,6}, RK_{0,11}, RK_{0,12}$, the attacker effectively queried sets for 2^8 random values of $RK_{0,1}$. Due to possible collisions, these queries will, on average, cover a fraction of about $1 - \frac{1}{e} \approx 63.2\,\%$ of all 2^8 possible values of $RK_{0,1}$. The attack is only successful if the correct value of $RK_{0,1}$ is among the covered fraction, so the success probability of the overall attack will be about 63.2 %. This can be improved by asking several queries per key guess, e.g., 4 queries for a success probability of about $1 - \frac{1}{e^4} \approx 98.2\,\%$, at the cost of an increase in data complexity by a factor of 2^2 (but no increase in computational complexity).

An alternative, deterministic approach is to query 2^8 Λ-sets per guess of $RK_{0,1}$, one for each possible value of T_1. All 2^8 Λ-sets need to be queried in one message, to get a constant nonce value and thus definitely cover the correct guess of T_1. Each message now contains $2^{24} + 255$ blocks, and we query a total of $2^{52} + 2^{36}$ blocks. Again, the computational complexity remains at 2^{82} encryptions.

6   Conclusion

In this work, we presented the first third-party analysis of Kiasu-BC. We showed that the additional tweak input can be exploited to create a distinguisher based on the Square property spanning 4 rounds. This is one more round compared to the distinguisher used in Square attacks on AES-128. Hence, we were able to perform key-recovery attacks on 7-round Kiasu-BC with a computational complexity of only about $2^{48.5}$ encryptions, which is faster than the best 7-round attacks for AES-128. However, we cannot attack more rounds compared to AES-128 and hence our analysis does not contradict the claim of the designers that Kiasu-BC has a sufficient security margin.

Variants of the Square attacks on Kiasu-BC are also applicable if Kiasu-BC is used in one of its recommended modes of operation. We demonstrated this with a nonce-respecting key-recovery attack on Kiasu$\neq$, a ΘCB3-like mode of the CAESAR candidate Kiasu. The computational complexity of this attack is approximately 2^{82} encryptions for 7-round Kiasu-BC, and the attack also respects the low data query limits.

Acknowledgements

 The research leading to these results has received funding from the European Union's Horizon 2020 research and innovation programme under grant agreement No 644052 (HECTOR).

Furthermore, this work has been supported in part by the Austrian Science Fund (project P26494-N15) and by the Austrian Research Promotion Agency (FFG) under grant number 845589 (SCALAS).

References

1. Daemen, J., Knudsen, L.R., Rijmen, V.: The block cipher SQUARE. In: Biham, E. (ed.) FSE 1997. LNCS, vol. 1267, pp. 149–165. Springer, Heidelberg (1997)
2. Daemen, J., Rijmen, V.: AES proposal: Rijndael. National Institute of Standards and Technology (1998)
3. Daemen, J., Rijmen, V.: The Design of Rijndael: AES - The Advanced Encryption Standard. Information Security and Cryptography. Springer, Heidelberg (2002)

4. Demirci, H., Taşkın, I., Çoban, M., Baysal, A.: Improved Meet-in-the-Middle Attacks on AES. In: Roy, B., Sendrier, N. (eds.) INDOCRYPT 2009. LNCS, vol. 5922, pp. 144–156. Springer, Heidelberg (2009)
5. Derbez, P., Fouque, P.-A., Jean, J.: Improved key recovery attacks on reduced-round AES in the single-key setting. In: Johansson, T., Nguyen, P.Q. (eds.) EUROCRYPT 2013. LNCS, vol. 7881, pp. 371–387. Springer, Heidelberg (2013)
6. Ferguson, N., Kelsey, J., Lucks, S., Schneier, B., Stay, M., Wagner, D., Whiting, D.L.: Improved cryptanalysis of Rijndael. In: Schneier, B. (ed.) FSE 2000. LNCS, vol. 1978, pp. 213–230. Springer, Heidelberg (2001)
7. Gilbert, H., Minier, M.: A collision attack on 7 rounds of Rijndael. In: AES Candidate Conference, pp. 230–241 (2000)
8. Grosso, V., Leurent, G., Standaert, F., Varici, K., Journault, A., Durvaux, F., Gaspar, L., Kerckhof, S.: SCREAM. Submission to the CAESAR competition (2015). http://competitions.cr.yp.to/round2/screamv3.pdf
9. Jean, J., Nikolic, I., Peyrin, T.: KIASU. Submission to the CAESAR competition (2014). http://competitions.cr.yp.to/round1/kiasuv1.pdf
10. Jean, J., Nikolic, I., Peyrin, T.: Tweaks and keys for block ciphers: the TWEAKEY framework. In: Sarkar, P., Iwata, T. (eds.) ASIACRYPT 2014, Part II. LNCS, vol. 8874, pp. 274–288. Springer, Heidelberg (2014)
11. Jean, J., Nikolic, I., Peyrin, T.: Tweaks and keys for block ciphers: the TWEAKEY framework. IACR Cryptology ePrint Archive 2014, 831 (2014). http://eprint.iacr.org/2014/831
12. Jean, J., Nikolic, I., Peyrin, T.: Deoxys. Submission to the CAESAR competition (2015). http://competitions.cr.yp.to/round2/deoxysv13.pdf
13. Jean, J., Nikolic, I., Peyrin, T.: Joltik. Submission to the CAESAR competition (2015). http://competitions.cr.yp.to/round2/joltikv13.pdf
14. Krovetz, T., Rogaway, P.: The software performance of authenticated-encryption modes. In: Joux, A. (ed.) FSE 2011. LNCS, vol. 6733, pp. 306–327. Springer, Heidelberg (2011)
15. Liskov, M., Rivest, R.L., Wagner, D.: Tweakable block ciphers. In: Yung, M. (ed.) CRYPTO 2002. LNCS, vol. 2442, pp. 31–46. Springer, Heidelberg (2002)
16. Liskov, M., Rivest, R.L., Wagner, D.: Tweakable block ciphers. J. Cryptology 24(3), 588–613 (2011)
17. Lu, J., Dunkelman, O., Keller, N., Kim, J.-S.: New impossible differential attacks on AES. In: Chowdhury, D.R., Rijmen, V., Das, A. (eds.) INDOCRYPT 2008. LNCS, vol. 5365, pp. 279–293. Springer, Heidelberg (2008)
18. Mala, H., Dakhilalian, M., Rijmen, V., Modarres-Hashemi, M.: Improved impossible differential cryptanalysis of 7-round AES-128. In: Gong, G., Gupta, K.C. (eds.) INDOCRYPT 2010. LNCS, vol. 6498, pp. 282–291. Springer, Heidelberg (2010)
19. The CAESAR committee: CAESAR: Competition for authenticated encryption: Security, applicability, and robustness (2014). http://competitions.cr.yp.to/caesar.html

On the Design Rationale of SIMON Block Cipher: Integral Attacks and Impossible Differential Attacks against SIMON Variants

Kota Kondo[1], Yu Sasaki[2], and Tetsu Iwata[1(✉)]

[1] Nagoya University, Nagoya, Japan
k_kondo@echo.nuee.nagoya-u.ac.jp, iwata@cse.nagoya-u.ac.jp
[2] NTT Secure Platform Laboratories, Tokyo, Japan
sasaki.yu@lab.ntt.co.jp

Abstract. SIMON is a lightweight block cipher designed by NSA in 2013. NSA presented the specification and the implementation efficiency, but they did not provide detailed security analysis nor the design rationale. The original SIMON has rotation constants of $(1, 8, 2)$, and Kölbl et al. regarded the constants as a parameter (a, b, c), and analyzed the security of SIMON block cipher variants against differential and linear attacks for all the choices of (a, b, c). This paper complements the result of Kölbl et al. by considering integral and impossible differential attacks. First, we search the number of rounds of integral distinguishers by using a supercomputer. Our search algorithm follows the previous approach by Wang et al., however, we introduce a new choice of the set of plaintexts satisfying the integral property. We show that the new choice indeed extends the number of rounds for several parameters. We also search the number of rounds of impossible differential characteristics based on the miss-in-the-middle approach. Finally, we make a comparison of all parameters from our results and the observations by Kölbl et al. Interesting observations are obtained, for instance we find that the optimal parameters with respect to the resistance against differential attacks are not stronger than the original parameter with respect to integral and impossible differential attacks. We also obtain a parameter that is better than the original parameter with respect to security against these four attacks.

Keywords: SIMON · Lightweight block cipher · Integral attack · Impossible differential attack · Design rationale · Rotation constant

1 Introduction

Lightweight cryptography has been discussed actively to provide secure communication for various communication devices with constraint resources, such as RFID tags and sensor network. In fact, quite a few lightweight ciphers, hash functions, message authentication codes (MACs) etc. have been designed recently.

© Springer International Publishing Switzerland 2016
M. Manulis et al. (Eds.): ACNS 2016, LNCS 9696, pp. 518–536, 2016.
DOI: 10.1007/978-3-319-39555-5_28

Among a large variety of lightweight block ciphers, SIMON and SPECK [6], which were designed by NSA in 2013, achieve overwhelming performance and thus attract a lot of attention. Meanwhile, the designers of SIMON and SPECK do not provide any security discussion and design rationale. Thus it is necessary to carry out security analysis and to study design rationale so that the community can have more confidence on those designs.

Yang *et al.* investigated a performance aspect of SIMON, and proposed another block cipher SIMECK which optimizes the performance of SIMON by slightly modifying its round function and key schedule [27]. As a drawback, security of SIMECK is known to be weaker than SIMON, thus evaluating security of SIMECK is also important.

In general, security of block ciphers is evaluated by deriving lowerbounds and upperbounds of the cipher's security against particular cryptanalysis. Here, lowerbounds are derived by applying cryptanalysis. Regarding SIMON, a large number of attacks have been applied since its proposal including differential cryptanalysis [2,8,17,22,23,25], linear cryptanalysis [1,4,5,10,11,20,22], algebraic analysis [3,19], integral attack [24,26], impossible differential attack [9,12,26], zero-correlation attack [26], known-key attack [13] and so on.

Design rationale of block cipher is often provided by the designers. If it is not the case, there still exists an approach for the third party to study the design rationale. For example, an evaluator parameterizes some part of the target cipher, e.g. rotation constants, and evaluates the security for all parameter choices. If the original parameter shows the highest security, it can be said that the original parameters have been chosen in good rationale. For example, Pramstaller *et al.* evaluated the design rationale of SHA-1 by evaluating all the rotation constants [18]. Regarding SIMON, Kölbl *et al.* regarded three rotation constants $(1, 8, 2)$ of SIMON as a parameter (a, b, c), and evaluated security of SIMON variants denoted by SIMON$_{a,b,c}$ against differential and linear cryptanalysis for all choices of (a, b, c) [16]. As a result, it turned out that the original rotation constants in SIMON are not one of the strongest. Kölbl *et al.* concluded that considering only differential and linear cryptanalysis is not sufficient to explain the design rationale, and further security evaluation with other cryptanalysis approach were left open.

Our Contributions. In this paper, we study design rationale of SIMON32; a member of the SIMON family whose block size is 32 bits. We extend the analysis by Kölbl *et al.* [16] to integral attack and impossible differential attack. Namely, we apply those attacks to SIMON$_{a,b,c}$ for all the choices of rotation constants (a, b, c).

Regarding integral attacks on SIMON, Wang *et al.* experimentally evaluated the number of rounds covered by integral distinguishers [26]. In more details, Wang *et al.* choose 2^{31} plaintexts and encrypt them with several keys to check if the sum of the corresponding internal states after some rounds is always zero in some bits. In this paper, we use the same approach to evaluate all the choices of rotation constants. Here, the difficulty is expensive computational cost of this experiment. To overcome this problem, we introduce equivalence classes for rotation constants and sets of 2^{31} plaintexts, which make the experiment feasible for a supercomputer. Moreover, we point out that the method of choosing 2^{31} plaintexts by Wang *et al.* [26] does not cover all the cases, thus may miss an optimal attack. In this paper, we enlarge the search space so that wider classes of 2^{31} plaintext sets are examined. The obtained results contain many interesting features. Several parameters can be distinguished even after 32 rounds, which is the default number of rounds for SIMON32. We show that original rotation constants in SIMON have reasonably good resistance against the integral attack, while several other choices have stronger resistance.

Regarding impossible differential attacks, we derive the number of rounds for impossible differential characteristics with the miss-in-the-middle approach. Many round constant choices lead to impossible differential characteristics of length between 9 rounds to 17 rounds, while the original SIMON parameter allows 11-round distinguishers.

At the last part of this paper, we compare strength of rotation constants by considering integral attacks and impossible differential attacks from our paper and differential cryptanalysis and linear cryptanalysis by Kölbl *et al.* [16]. We classify strength of each parameter with respect to the number of rounds covered by distinguishers. This identifies several interesting properties, for example, any rotation constant having better resistance against integral and impossible differential attacks than original SIMON is not as strong as original SIMON with respect to differential and linear cryptanalysis. It turns out that original rotation constants in SIMON are fairly well by taking into account four kinds of cryptanalysis, yet we find that rotation constant $(5, 12, 3)$ is better than original SIMON, and thus interesting to investigate more details in future.

Paper Outline. The rest of this paper is organized as follows. We describe notations used in this paper, specification of SIMON and basic concepts of integral and impossible differential attacks in Sect. 2. Integral attacks on $SIMON_{a,b,c}$ are shown in Sect. 3. Impossible differential attacks on $SIMON_{a,b,c}$ are shown in Sect. 4. We then compare strength of parameters to study the design rationale of SIMON in Sect. 5. Finally, we conclude this paper in Sect. 6.

2   Preliminaries

2.1   Notation

The set $\{0, 1, \ldots, n - 1\}$ is written as Z_n, and the set $\{n' \mid 1 \leq n' \leq n, \gcd(n', n) = 1\}$ is written as Z_n^*. The d-bit circular rotation of a bit string x to the left is written as $S^d(x)$.

2.2   Specification of SIMON

SIMON is a lightweight block cipher suitable for hardware implementation that was designed by NSA in 2013 [6]. The SIMON block cipher with a $2n$-bit block is

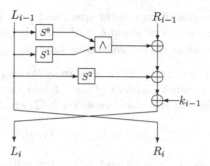

Fig. 1. The $(i-1)$-st round function of SIMON

denoted SIMON$2n$, where $n \in \{16, 24, 32, 48, 64\}$. SIMON$2n$ with an m-word key (mn bits) is denoted SIMON$2n/mn$. In this paper, we are only concerned with the case $n = 16$ and $m = 4$.

The round function of SIMON is composed of three operations: AND ($\wedge$), rotation (S) and XOR ($\oplus$). Let v denote the n-bit input word of the round function F, where F is defined as

$$F(v) = (S^1(v) \wedge S^8(v)) \oplus S^2(v).$$

Let (L_{i-1}, R_{i-1}) denote the $2n$-bit input state of the $(i-1)$-st round, which is encrypted into (L_i, R_i) as:

$$L_i = F(L_{i-1}) \oplus R_{i-1} \oplus k_{i-1},$$
$$R_i = L_{i-1},$$

where k_{i-1} is the subkey of the $(i-1)$-st round. The plaintext is (L_0, R_0), and if the number of rounds is r, then (L_r, R_r) is the ciphertext. We note that the index of the round starts with 0 and the last round is the $(r-1)$-st round. Figure 1 shows the round function of SIMON. The key schedule is irrelevant in our analysis and we omit the details, which can be found in [6].

2.3 SIMON Block Cipher Variants

In [16], Kölbl *et al.* introduced SIMON block cipher variants by regarding the three rotation constants $(1, 8, 2)$ of SIMON as a parameter (a, b, c). Then they proved a structural equivalence among the round functions with different parameters. Furthermore, they showed the detailed security analysis of SIMON block cipher variants against differential attacks for a large set of parameters.

The round function of SIMON block cipher variants is defined as:

$$F_{a,b,c}(v) = (S^a(v) \wedge S^b(v)) \oplus S^c(v),$$

where $a, b, c \in Z_n$. We exclude the case $a = b$ since the encryption algorithm becomes a linear transformation. We also assume that $a < b$ from the symmetry of AND operation. The size of parameter space is $\binom{16}{2} \times 16 = 1920$, where $\binom{16}{2}$ is the number of combinations of a and b, and 16 is the number of choices of c.

The structural equivalence is formalized as follows.

Proposition 1 ([16]). *Let T be a permutation of the bits of an n-bit word that corresponds to an affine transformation of the bit-indices. Thus there are $s \in Z_n$ and $t \in Z_n$ such that bit i is translated to $s \cdot i + t$. Then*

$$T(F_{a,b,c}(v)) = F_{sa,sb,sc}(T(v)).$$

The equivalence relation of Proposition 1 is written with $\Leftrightarrow$, and the set of all distinct equivalence classes is written as $\mathcal{SV}$. In Sects. 3.3 and 4.1, we will point out that if the round functions are equivalent, attack characteristics we consider are also equivalent. Therefore we can reduce the size of parameter space that we must search by computers. The size of parameter space after the reduction is 509 $(= |\mathcal{SV}|)$.

As the results of the analyses by Kölbl *et al.*, the following 20 parameters are optimal with respect to 10 rounds differential characteristics.

$$\begin{array}{ccccc}
(0,1,2) & (0,1,3) & (1,2,3) & (3,4,5) & (0,5,10) \\
(0,5,15) & (4,5,3) & (0,7,14) & (6,7,5) & (1,8,3) \\
(3,8,14) & (7,8,5) & (5,10,15) & (6,11,1) & (1,12,7) \\
(5,12,3) & (7,12,1) & (0,13,10) & (0,13,7) & (8,13,2)
\end{array}$$

Among these parameters, $(0,1,2)$ and $(5,12,3)$ are also optimal with respect to linear characteristics for 10 rounds. SIMECK, a variant of SIMON block cipher proposed by Yang *et al.* [27], has the equivalent structure as SIMON and its parameter corresponds to $(a,b,c) = (0,5,1)$. As a result, Kölbl *et al.* found that SIMON and SIMECK are not optimal with respect to differential characteristics.

2.4   Basic Consepts of Integral and Impossible Differential Attacks

The integral attack [15] is a chosen-plaintext attack against block ciphers. It is composed of *integral distinguishers* and the *key recovery* step. Suppose that a set of plaintexts is encrypted. An integral distinguisher refers to an event where certain bits of the XOR of all ciphertexts is always 0. Integral distinguishers are often constructed by evaluating the propagation characteristic of the integral property, which is the property for a multiset of the internal state. The integral property is classified as follows:

- All ($\mathcal{A}$): Every value appears the same number of times in the multiset.
- Balance ($\mathcal{B}$): The XOR of all texts in the multiset is 0.
- Const ($\mathcal{C}$): The value is fixed to a constant for all texts in the multiset.
- Unknown (*): The multiset is indistinguishable from one of random values.

In this paper, we focus on the search of integral distinguishers for all the SIMON block cipher variants.

Table 1. Computation environment

Computation node	Fujitsu PRIMEHPC FX100
processor	- Fujitsu SPARC64 XIfx (2.2 GHz) 32 cores
- the memory capacity	- 32 GiB
The total number of nodes (cores)	2880 nodes (92160 cores)
The total computing performance	3.2 PFlop/s
The total memory capacity	90 TiB
Programming language	C
MPI library	Fujitsu MPI

The impossible differential attack [7] is a chosen-plaintext attack against block ciphers. An adversary attempts to recover the right key by using impossible differential characteristics, which are the differential characteristics where an input difference can never result in an output difference. In this paper, we focus on the search of impossible differential characteristics for all the SIMON block cipher variants.

3   Integral Attacks

In general, the propagation of integral properties cannot be evaluated efficiently in SIMON because of its computational structure in which the round function is computed without S-box. Wang *et al.* [26] addressed the issue by experimentally searching the number of rounds of integral distinguishers of SIMON32. The algorithm they used is shown in Sect. 3.1. However, it is computationally difficult to apply it to all parameters (Sect. 3.2). Therefore we introduce equivalence classes for rotation constants and sets of 2^{31} plaintexts (Sect. 3.3). The search result is shown in Sect. 3.4.

In Table 1, we show the computing environment we used to carry out the experiments in this section.

3.1   Integral Distinguisher Searching Algorithm

We use the following algorithm by Wang *et al.* [26] to search the number of rounds of integral distinguishers of a SIMON block cipher variant.

1. Generate 2^t plaintexts ($t \geq 16$) by setting all (16) bits of the right half and $(t - 16)$ bits of the left half of the input in round 1 to be property $\mathcal{A}$ (each bit is called active), while keeping the remaining bits as constant.
2. (a) Choose the private key randomly. Encrypt 2^t plaintexts by r rounds and check whether certain bits of the output are balanced (i.e., for each of these bits, the XOR sum of the bit over 2^t output states is 0). If yes, keep this as an integral candidate.

(b) Repeat (a) for K times and verify if the integral candidate always holds. If not, discard it. Here, K is the number of random keys.

3. If there is an integral candidate for all the structures with the same pattern (i.e., with the same t active bits), regard this as an r-round integral distinguisher of SIMON32.

Straightforward implementation of the above algorithm executes Step 3 after iterating Steps 2 (a) and (b) for K times. However, we see that Steps 2 (b) and 3 can be merged into a single step by fixing the constant bit of round 1 to an arbitrary value and randomly choosing the private key, and our implementation takes this approach. We note that $K = 2^{13}$ was used in [26], and it is argued that if the 2^{31} plaintexts yield the same balanced bits for all the K random keys, then with a high probability, we obtain an integral distinguisher. From the results, we observe that for large t (i.e., if the number of active bits is large), the number of rounds of integral distinguishers becomes large.

This is also the case for SIMON block cipher variants. Therefore we use this algorithm in which t is fixed to 31 because we are interested in maximizing the number of rounds of integral distinguishers.

In [14], the same experimental search was performed for SIMON48/96 with $K = 96$, where the rationale here is that it is sufficient if K is at least the key length of the block cipher. In this paper, we follow the approach in [14] and use $K = 64$. An example of an integral distinguisher against SIMON$_{5,12,3}$ that we obtain by applying this algorithm with $r = 15$ is shown in Fig. 2. In Step 1, we prepare plaintexts that have the integral property of $(\mathcal{C}, \mathcal{A}, \ldots, \mathcal{A})$ as the input of round 1, and this means that the number of rounds can be extended by one round compared to the case where we use $(\mathcal{C}, \mathcal{A}, \ldots, \mathcal{A})$ as the integral property of round 0.

3.2   Necessity for Reducing the Search Space

We first estimate the time complexity for the search of all parameters by using the algorithm in Sect. 3.1. We first observe that even if the round functions $F_{a,b,c}$ are equivalent, this may not guarantee that we have the equivalence between the corresponding integral distinguishers, and we thus need to consider 1920 parameters. From Sect. 3.1, there are 16 choices for the sets of chosen plaintexts. Then the time complexity of the algorithm is 64×2^{31} r-round SIMON$_{a,b,c}$ encryptions, implying that the time complexity for the search of all parameters and plaintext sets is estimated as $1920 \times 16 \times 64 \times 2^{31} \simeq 2^{51.91}$ r-round SIMON$_{a,b,c}$ encryptions.

We implement the algorithm in Sect. 3.1 on a computer system shown in Table 1, and we estimate the number of necessary cores to search over all parameter choices, assuming that one core carries out the algorithm in Sect. 3.1. Then one node has 32 cores under our environment. Now we observe that we need to consider 1920 parameters and 16 choices for the sets of chosen plaintexts. Thus naive implementation requires $1920 \times 16 = 30{,}720$ cores, and this corresponds to 960 nodes.

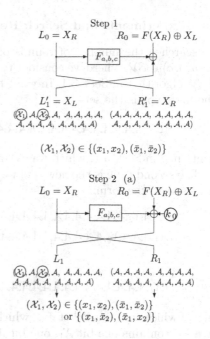

Fig. 3. Applying the algorithm in Sect. 3.1 to the new set with 2^{31} plaintexts

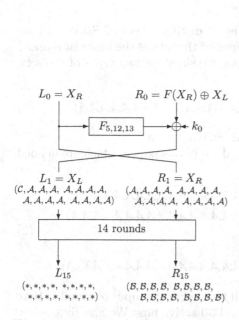

Fig. 2. 15-round integral distinguisher of $\text{SIMON}_{5,12,3}$

3.3 Finding Equivalent Parameters

We present the following property regarding the equivalence.

Property 1. Let T be a permutation of the bits of an n-bit word that corresponds to an affine transformation of the bit-indices. Thus there are $s \in Z_n$ and $t \in Z_n$ such that bit i is translated to $s \cdot i + t$. Let

$$(\mathcal{L}_0, \mathcal{R}_0) \rightarrow (\mathcal{L}_r, \mathcal{R}_r)$$

be an r-round integral distinguisher against $\text{SIMON}_{a,b,c}$. Then

$$(T(\mathcal{L}_0), T(\mathcal{R}_0)) \rightarrow (T(\mathcal{L}_r), T(\mathcal{R}_r))$$

is an r-round integral distinguisher against $\text{SIMON}_{sa,sb,sc}$.

The proof is not obvious but elementary and omitted. From Property 1, the number of parameters to consider is reduced to 509. By letting $s = 1$ in Property 1, we observe that we only have to consider an integral distinguisher with the input of round 1 of the form

$$(\mathcal{C}AAAAAAAAAAAAAAA, AAAAAAAAAAAAAAAA).$$

This means that we only have to consider one set of plaintexts, and hence the time complexity is estimated $509 \times 1 \times 64 \times 2^{31} \simeq 2^{45.99}$ r-round $\text{SIMON}_{a,b,c}$ encryptions. Then the number of necessary cores in the implementation is 509, which amounts to 16 nodes.

3.4 Experiments and Search Results

We searched the number of rounds of integral distinguishers of $\text{SIMON}_{a,b,c}$ for all $(a, b, c) \in \mathcal{SV}$, where we consider two types of the sets of the input of round 1 in the algorithm in Sect. 3.1. In what follows, we show the two types of the sets. The first type is the set

$$(\mathcal{C}\mathcal{A}\mathcal{A}\mathcal{A}\mathcal{A}\mathcal{A}\mathcal{A}\mathcal{A}\mathcal{A}\mathcal{A}\mathcal{A}\mathcal{A}\mathcal{A}\mathcal{A}\mathcal{A}, \mathcal{A}\mathcal{A}\mathcal{A}\mathcal{A}\mathcal{A}\mathcal{A}\mathcal{A}\mathcal{A}\mathcal{A}\mathcal{A}\mathcal{A}\mathcal{A}\mathcal{A}\mathcal{A}\mathcal{A}\mathcal{A}), \tag{1}$$

mentioned in Sect. 3.1, which was searched by Wang *et al.*

The second type is the new sets we introduce in this paper, which are defined as 15 sets of the form:

$$(\mathcal{X}_1\mathcal{A}\mathcal{X}_2\mathcal{A}\mathcal{A}\mathcal{A}\mathcal{A}\mathcal{A}\mathcal{A}\mathcal{A}\mathcal{A}\mathcal{A}\mathcal{A}\mathcal{A}\mathcal{A}\mathcal{A}, \mathcal{A}\mathcal{A}\mathcal{A}\mathcal{A}\mathcal{A}\mathcal{A}\mathcal{A}\mathcal{A}\mathcal{A}\mathcal{A}\mathcal{A}\mathcal{A}\mathcal{A}\mathcal{A}\mathcal{A}\mathcal{A})$$

$$(\mathcal{X}_1\mathcal{A}\mathcal{A}\mathcal{A}\mathcal{X}_2\mathcal{A}\mathcal{A}\mathcal{A}\mathcal{A}\mathcal{A}\mathcal{A}\mathcal{A}\mathcal{A}\mathcal{A}\mathcal{A}, \mathcal{A}\mathcal{A}\mathcal{A}\mathcal{A}\mathcal{A}\mathcal{A}\mathcal{A}\mathcal{A}\mathcal{A}\mathcal{A}\mathcal{A}\mathcal{A}\mathcal{A}\mathcal{A}\mathcal{A}\mathcal{A})$$

$$\vdots \tag{2}$$

$$(\mathcal{X}_1\mathcal{A}\mathcal{A}\mathcal{A}\mathcal{A}\mathcal{A}\mathcal{A}\mathcal{A}\mathcal{A}\mathcal{A}\mathcal{A}\mathcal{A}\mathcal{A}\mathcal{A}\mathcal{A}\mathcal{A}, \mathcal{A}\mathcal{A}\mathcal{A}\mathcal{A}\mathcal{A}\mathcal{A}\mathcal{A}\mathcal{A}\mathcal{A}\mathcal{A}\mathcal{A}\mathcal{A}\mathcal{A}\mathcal{A}\mathcal{X}_2\mathcal{A})$$

each of which contains 2^{31} states, which will be used as the input of round 1. Here each set contains one bit $\mathcal{X}_1$, one bit $\mathcal{X}_2$, and 30 active bits. We first fix the two bits indicated with $\mathcal{X}_1$ and $\mathcal{X}_2$ to any value $(x_1, x_2) \in \{(0,0), (0,1), (1,0), (1,1)\}$, and this yields 2^{30} states from the 30 active bits. We then consider another set of 2^{30} states by fixing the two bits to $(\bar{x}_1, \bar{x}_2)$, and the actual set of 2^{31} states consists of the whole above mentioned states. Here, we let $\bar{x} = x \oplus 1$ for a bit x. In Fig. 3, we show how the algorithm in Sect. 3.1 is applied to (2). In Step 1, we obtain 2^{31} plaintexts by decrypting the set of the input of round 1 satisfying property (2) without the subkey (or equivalently, by assuming that the subkey is zero). In Step 2 (a), we encrypt the obtained plaintexts in Step 1. Here, if the corresponding bits of subkey in round 0 have value $(0,0)$ or $(1,1)$, the corresponding bits of the input of round 1 have values of the form (x_1, x_2) and $(\bar{x}_1, \bar{x}_2)$. If the corresponding bits of subkey in round 0 have value $(0,1)$ or $(1,0)$, they have the value of the form $(x_1, \bar{x}_2)$ and $(\bar{x}_1, x_2)$. However, we observe that both cases still have the property indicated in (2).

Since we consider two types, namely the 16 sets in total with 2^{31} chosen plaintexts, the time complexity is estimated as $509 \times 16 \times 64 \times 2^{31} \simeq 2^{49.99}$ r-round $\text{SIMON}_{a,b,c}$ encryptions from Sect. 3.3.

We show the number of rounds of integral distinguishers and the number of corresponding parameters as the result of the experiment in Table 2 and Fig. 4. Note that small number of rounds implies the stronger resistance against integral attack.

In our implementation of this experiments, we set r to $r_{\max}$ which is a sufficiently large number in the algorithm in Sect. 3.1. In Step 2 (a) we check if certain bits are balanced for $r_{\max}$ rounds, and save all the intermediate states so that we obtain the number of rounds of integral distinguishers. With respect to the running time, when the number of cores is 509, $r_{\max} = 26$, and with (1), it

Table 2. Search result of integral distinguishers

The number of rounds	14	15	16	18	19	20	22	33	≥ 53	∞	Sum
The number of parameters	97	112	62	4	15	18	16	6	15	164	509

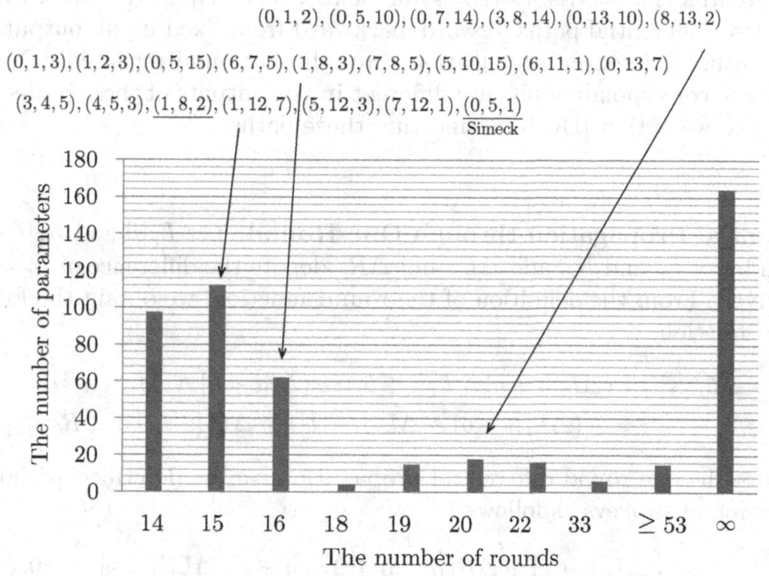
(0, 1, 2), (0, 5, 10), (0, 7, 14), (3, 8, 14), (0, 13, 10), (8, 13, 2)
(0, 1, 3), (1, 2, 3), (0, 5, 15), (6, 7, 5), (1, 8, 3), (7, 8, 5), (5, 10, 15), (6, 11, 1), (0, 13, 7)
(3, 4, 5), (4, 5, 3), (1, 8, 2), (1, 12, 7), (5, 12, 3), (7, 12, 1), (0, 5, 1)
Simeck
The number of parameters
180
160
140
120
100
80
60
40
20
0
14
15
16
18
19
20
22
33
≥ 53
∞
The number of rounds

Fig. 4. Search result of integral distinguishers and comparison with parameter in [16]. The listed parameters are 20 parameters from [16] and the parameters for SIMON and SIMECK, and the 20 parameters are optimal with respect to 10 rounds differential characteristics.

took 18 h 8 m 31 s. When the number of cores is 345 and $r_{\max} = 36$, each of (2) took about a day, and for instance the first case of (2) took 25 h 5 m 52 s.

We also note that "≥ 53" means that the maximum value of $r_{\max}$ was set to 53, as we stopped the program due to the time constraint. Thus parameters in this class have integral distinguishers with the number of rounds that is larger than 53, but the precise value is unknown at this moment. Moreover, we observe that when a, b, and c are all odd or all even, then the cipher has integral distinguisher of infinite number of rounds.

A detailed result shows an interesting fact. Most of the results are obtained by using (1). However, it turns out that there are cases where (2) outperforms (1). In more detail, for parameters $(1, 6, 4)$, $(1, 14, 12)$, $(2, 3, 12)$ and $(2, 7, 4)$, we obtain larger number of rounds with (2) than (1), and this was obtained when both $\mathcal{X}_1$ and $\mathcal{X}_2$ belong to the left half of the input of round 1.

In Sect. 5, we use the result to make a comparison of the strength of SIMON block cipher variants.

4 Impossible Differential Attacks

4.1 Impossible Differential Characteristic (IDC) of $\text{SIMON}_{a,b,c}$

In this paper, we use the *miss-in-the-middle approach* [26] to search impossible differential characteristics (IDCs) of SIMON block cipher variants. First, we extend two differential paths forward/backward from fixed input/output difference by using differential propagation through one round repeatedly. Next, we check if the corresponding bits are different in the outputs of these paths. If this is the case, we obtain IDC by connecting these paths.

Differential Propagation through One Round. Let $L_r[i]$ and $R_r[i]$ denote the i-th bit of L_r and R_r, and ΔL_r and ΔR_r denote the difference of L_r and R_r, respectively. From the definition of the round function, we obtain the following bitwise equation.

$$\Delta L_{r+1}[i] = (\Delta L_r[i+a] \wedge L_r[i+b]) \oplus (L_r[i+a] \wedge \Delta L_r[i+b])$$
$$\oplus (\Delta L_r[i+a] \wedge \Delta L_r[i+b]) \oplus \Delta L_r[i+c] \oplus \Delta R_r[i] \qquad (3)$$

Therefore the one round differential propagation can be described without any information of subkeys as follows:

$$\Delta L_{r+1}[i] = \begin{cases} \Delta L_r[i+c] \oplus \Delta R_r[i] & \text{if } (\Delta L_r[i+a], \Delta L_r[i+b]) = (0,0) \\ ? \text{ (Unknown)} & \text{otherwise} \end{cases} \qquad (4)$$

$$\Delta R_{r+1}[i] = \Delta L_r[i]$$

We extend the differential path by using (4) along the encryption direction. We call it a forward differential path.

As to the decryption direction, we use the following equation.

$$\Delta L_{r-1}[i] = \Delta R_r[i]$$

$$\Delta R_{r-1}[i] = \begin{cases} \Delta R_r[i+c] \oplus \Delta L_r[i] & \text{if } (\Delta R_r[i+a], \Delta R_r[i+b]) = (0,0) \\ ? \text{ (Unknown)} & \text{otherwise} \end{cases} \qquad (5)$$

We call paths extended by using (5) backward differential paths.

Furthermore, it is obvious that if the round functions have equivalent parameters, there is a corresponding equivalent differential path, and hence we also have the IDC.

IDC Search Algorithm. We use the following algorithm to search the number of rounds of IDCs of a SIMON block cipher variant. We denote a $2n$-bit input difference to the input/output differential paths by $\Delta \text{input}_0 / \Delta \text{output}_0$. Then, $2n$-bit difference after r rounds of input/output differential paths are denoted by $\Delta \text{input}_r / \Delta \text{output}_r$. In the following algorithm, we obtain the number of rounds of IDCs by updating a temporal variable $r_{\max}$, which is initialized to 0.

R	Left	Right
0	0000, 0000, 0000,0000	1000, 0000, 0000, 0000
1	1000, 0000, 0000, 0000	0000, 0000, 0000, 0000
2	0000, ?000, 000?, 0100	1000, 0000, 0000, 0000
3	1?00, 00?0, ?010, 000?	0000, ?000, 000?, 0100
4	0?0?, ??01, 00??, ?0?0	1?00, 00?0, ?010, 000?
5	???0, 1???, ??1?, ?0??	0?0?, ??01, 00??, ?0?0
6	????, ????, ????, ????	???0, 1???, ??1?, ?0??
5	00?0, ???0, 100?, ??0?	????, **01**??, ???1, ??0?
4	?1?0, 000?, 0?01, 0000	00?0, ???0, 100?, ??0?
3	0000, 0?00, 0000, ?010	?1?0, 000?, 0?01, 0000
2	0100, 0000, 0000, 0000	0000, 0?00, 0000, ?010
1	0000, 0000, 0000, 0000	0100, 0000, 0000, 0000
0	0100, 0000, 0000, 0000	0000, 0000, 0000, 0000

Fig. 5. 11-round IDC of $\text{SIMON}_{5,12,3}$ (R is the number of extended rounds)

1. Extend a forward differential path for given Δinput_0 by using (4) until all the bits of the state become unknown. Let r_{in} be the number obtained by subtracting 1 from the number of extended rounds. The subtraction is to consider a path whose bits are not all unknown.
2. Extend a backward differential path for given Δoutput_0 by using (5) until all the bits of the state become unknown. Let r_{out} be the number obtained by subtracting 1 from the number of extended rounds. Let $r_{\text{tmp}} \leftarrow r_{\text{in}} + r_{\text{out}}$.
3. Check if there are different values between the corresponding bits in $\Delta\text{input}_{r'_{\text{in}}}$ and $\Delta\text{output}_{r'_{\text{out}}}$ for all $(r'_{\text{in}}, r'_{\text{out}})$ satisfying $r'_{\text{in}} + r'_{\text{out}} = r_{\text{tmp}}$. If not, update r_{tmp} to $r_{\text{tmp}} - 1$ and iterate this step.
4. If $r_{\text{tmp}} > r_{\text{max}}$, update r_{max} to r_{tmp}.
5. Apply Steps 1 to 4 to all $(\Delta\text{input}_0, \Delta\text{output}_0) = (S^l(0\ldots01), S^m(0\ldots01))$ satisfying $l, m \in Z_{2n}$.

We then obtain the number of rounds of IDC as r_{max}. We note the reason why it is sufficient to consider the differences of the form $(\Delta\text{input}_0, \Delta\text{output}_0) = (S^l(0\ldots01), S^m(0\ldots01))$ only. Notice that if we have more bits with 1 or unknown in a certain state, then we have more bits with unknown in the next state. Thus the number of extended rounds of each differential path is reduced. Therefore it is sufficient that we search paths starting with input and output differences of low Hamming weight. An example of IDC that we obtain by applying this algorithm is shown in Fig. 5. Notice that bold bits are always different, which indicates that the differential propagation is impossible.

4.2 Experiments and Search Results

We searched the number of rounds of IDCs of $\text{SIMON}_{a,b,c}$ for all $(a, b, c) \in \mathcal{SV}$. We show the maximum number of rounds of IDCs and the number of corresponding parameters in Table 3 and Fig. 6. Smaller number of rounds that corresponds to

Table 3. IDC search result

The number of rounds	9	10	11	12	13	17	∞	Sum
The number of parameters	42	85	111	28	48	31	164	509

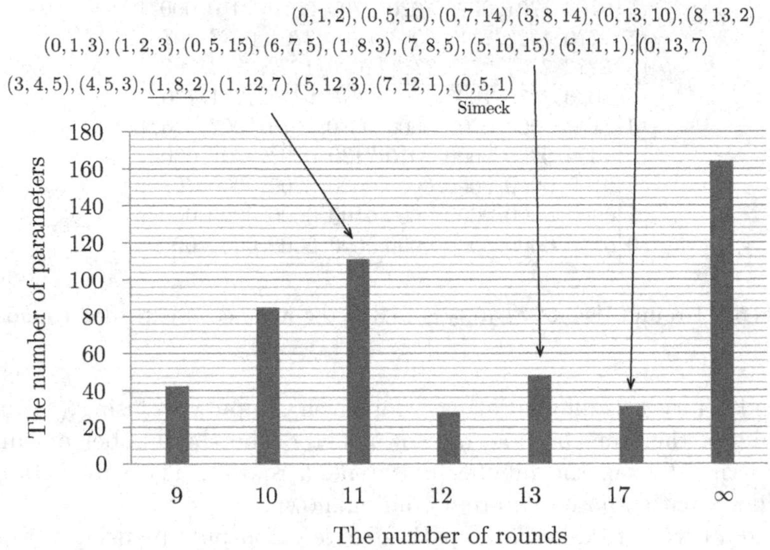
(0, 1, 2), (0, 5, 10), (0, 7, 14), (3, 8, 14), (0, 13, 10), (8, 13, 2)
(0, 1, 3), (1, 2, 3), (0, 5, 15), (6, 7, 5), (1, 8, 3), (7, 8, 5), (5, 10, 15), (6, 11, 1), (0, 13, 7)
(3, 4, 5), (4, 5, 3), (1, 8, 2), (1, 12, 7), (5, 12, 3), (7, 12, 1), (0, 5, 1)
Simeck
180
160
140
120
100
80
60
40
20
0
The number of parameters
9
10
11
12
13
17
∞
The number of rounds

Fig. 6. IDC search result

the parameters in the left part of Fig. 6 implies the stronger resistance against impossible differential attack. We note that the same observation as the integral distinguisher holds here, that is, when a, b, and c are all odd or all even, then the cipher has IDC of infinite number of rounds.

In this experiment, we use a computer of which CPU is Core i5-4210M, capacity of mounted memory (RAM) is 8 GB and OS is Windows 7.

In Sect. 5, we use the result to make a comparison of the strength of Simon block cipher variants.

5 Discussions

From the results presented in Fig. 4, Table 2, Fig. 6, and Table 3, in Table 4, we list all 345 parameters that have integral distinguishers and IDCs of finite number rounds and write in boldface the parameters that are optimal with respect to differential attacks. We classify the parameters into Groups A, B, . . . , T according to the number of rounds of integral distinguishers and IDCs, and they are summarized in Fig. 7.

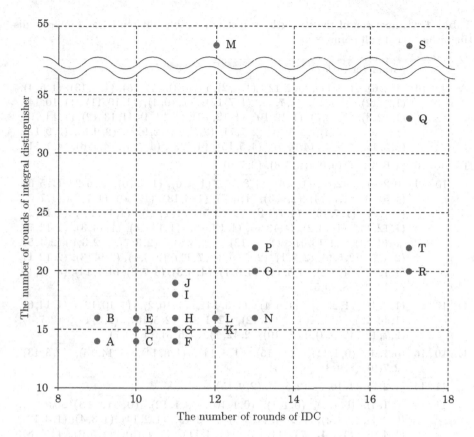

Fig. 7. Comparison of the strength against impossible differential and integral distinguisher among all parameters

We describe some observations and the notable parameters as follows:

- Note that there are many parameters in the lower left of Fig. 7.
- We observe that Group G that contains SIMON and SIMECK is not placed in the bottom left part of the figure, implying that the resistance against integral and impossible differential attacks was not given the highest priority when defining the rotation constants of these block ciphers.
- The number of parameters equivalent to original SIMON and SIMECK in resistance against these attacks is larger than any other parameters of which distinguishers have finite round.
- The default number of rounds of SIMON32 is 32, and we see that all SIMON block cipher variants in Groups M, S, and Q are distinguishable with the integral distinguishers even if they have the default number of rounds. They are also less resistant against impossible differential attacks.
- Parameters in Groups N and R have the highest resistance against differential attacks but low resistance against integral and impossible differential attacks.

Table 4. Comparison of the strength against impossible differential and integral distinguisher among all parameters

	*	&	parameter (a, b, c)
A	9	14	$(1,2,6)$, $(1,2,11)$, $(1,2,12)$, $(1,4,2)$, $(1,4,3)$, $(1,4,5)$, $(1,4,13)$, $(1,5,4)$, $(1,5,12)$, $(1,6,2)$, $(1,7,4)$, $(1,7,12)$, $(1,10,4)$, $(1,10,11)$, $(1,10,14)$, $(1,12,3)$, $(1,12,5)$, $(1,12,10)$, $(1,12,13)$, $(1,13,4)$, $(1,13,12)$, $(1,14,10)$, $(2,3,6)$, $(2,5,4)$, $(2,5,6)$, $(2,5,7)$, $(2,7,6)$, $(2,9,3)$, $(2,9,6)$, $(2,9,12)$, $(4,5,1)$, $(4,5,9)$, $(4,5,10)$, $(4,5,15)$, $(4,7,3)$, $(4,7,5)$, $(4,7,6)$, $(4,7,11)$
B	9	16	$(1,6,8)$, $(1,14,0)$, $(2,3,8)$, $(2,7,0)$
C	10	14	$(0,2,5)$, $(1,2,5)$, $(1,3,6)$, $(1,3,14)$, $(1,4,6)$, $(1,4,10)$, $(1,5,2)$, $(1,5,6)$, $(1,5,10)$, $(1,5,14)$, $(1,6,3)$, $(1,6,7)$, $(1,6,13)$, $(1,7,0)$, $(1,7,2)$, $(1,7,6)$, $(1,7,8)$, $(1,7,10)$, $(1,7,14)$, $(1,10,5)$, $(1,11,2)$, $(1,11,10)$, $(1,12,2)$, $(1,12,14)$, $(1,13,2)$, $(1,13,6)$, $(1,13,10)$, $(1,13,14)$, $(1,14,3)$, $(1,14,7)$, $(1,14,13)$, $(1,15,4)$, $(1,15,12)$, $(2,3,5)$, $(2,3,7)$, $(2,3,9)$,$(2,4,5)$, $(2,4,7)$, $(2,5,9)$, $(2,7,1)$, $(2,7,5)$, $(2,7,11)$, $(2,8,1)$, $(2,9,13)$, $(2,12,1)$, $(2,12,3)$, $(4,5,2)$, $(4,5,14)$, $(4,6,1)$, $(4,6,3)$, $(4,7,2)$, $(4,7,14)$, $(4,10,1)$, $(4,10,3)$, $(8,10,5)$
D	10	15	$(1,2,4)$, $(1,2,10)$, $(1,6,4)$, $(1,6,14)$, $(1,10,2)$, $(1,10,12)$, $(1,14,6)$, $(1,14,12)$, $(2,3,10)$, $(2,3,12)$, $(2,4,3)$, $(2,5,10)$, $(2,5,12)$, $(2,7,4)$, $(2,7,10)$, $(2,9,4)$, $(2,9,10)$, $(2,12,7)$, $(4,6,5)$, $(4,10,7)$
E	10	16	$(0,1,6)$, $(0,1,11)$, $(1,6,15)$, $(1,8,11)$, $(1,8,14)$, $(1,14,15)$, $(2,3,13)$, $(2,7,9)$, $(8,9,3)$, $(8,9,14)$
F	11	14	$(1,2,7)$, $(1,10,7)$, $(2,5,3)$, $(2,9,15)$
G	11	15	$(0,1,4)$, $(0,1,5)$, $(0,1,7)$, $(0,1,10)$, $(0,1,12)$, **(0, 1, 13)**(SIMECK), $(0,4,1)$, $(0,4,3)$, $(1,2,8)$, $(1,2,9)$, $(1,2,13)$, $(1,2,14)$, $(1,3,4)$, $(1,3,12)$, $(1,4,0)$, **(1, 4, 7)**, $(1,4,8)$, $(1,4,11)$, $(1,4,15)$, $(1,5,0)$, $(1,5,8)$, $(1,6,5)$, $(1,6,9)$, $(1,6,10)$, $\underline{(1,8,2)}$, $(1,8,4)$, $(1,8,5)$, $(1,8,7)$, $(1,8,12)$, $(1,8,13)$, $(1,10,0)$, $\underline{(1,10,6)}$, $\underline{(1,10,9)}$, $(1,10,13)$, $(1,11,4)$, $(1,11,12)$, $(1,12,0)$, **(1, 12, 7)**, $(1,12,8)$, $(1,12,11)$, $(1,12,15)$, $(1,13,0)$, $(1,13,8)$, $(1,14,2)$, $(1,14,5)$, $(1,14,9)$, $(2,3,11)$, $(2,3,14)$, $(2,3,15)$, $(2,5,0)$, $(2,5,1)$, $(2,5,13)$, $(2,5,14)$, $(2,7,3)$, $(2,7,14)$, $(2,7,15)$, $(2,9,1)$, $(2,9,5)$, $(2,9,8)$, $(2,9,14)$, $(2,14,1)$, $(2,14,3)$, $(2,14,5)$, $(2,14,7)$, $(4,5,0)$, $(4,5,3)$, $(4,5,7)$, $(4,5,8)$, $(4,5,11)$, $(4,7,0)$, $(4,7,1)$, $(4,7,8)$, $(4,7,9)$, $(4,7,13)$, $(4,8,1)$, $(4,8,3)$, $(8,9,2)$, $(8,9,4)$, $(8,9,5)$, $(8,9,12)$, $(8,9,13)$, $(8,9,15)$, $(8,12,1)$, $(8,12,3)$
H	11	16	$(1,6,12)$, $(1,14,4)$, $(2,3,4)$, $(2,7,12)$
I	11	18	$(1,4,9)$, $(1,12,9)$, $(4,5,13)$, $(4,7,15)$
J	11	19	$(0,1,8)$, $(0,1,9)$, $(0,2,1)$, $(1,4,12)$, $(1,8,0)$, $(1,8,9)$, $(1,12,4)$, $(1,15,0)$, $(1,15,8)$, $(2,8,5)$, $(4,5,12)$, $(4,7,12)$, $(8,9,0)$, $(8,9,1)$, $(8,10,1)$
K	12	15	$(2,4,1)$, $(2,6,1)$, $(2,6,3)$, $(2,6,5)$, $(2,6,7)$, $(2,12,5)$, $(4,6,7)$, $(4,10,5)$
L	12	16	$(1,3,0)$, $(1,3,8)$, $(1,4,14)$, $(1,6,0)$, $(1,11,0)$, $(1,11,8)$, $(1,12,6)$, $(1,14,8)$, $(2,3,0)$, $(2,7,8)$, $(4,5,6)$, $(4,7,10)$
M	12	53	$(1,9,2)$, $(1,9,6)$, $(1,9,10)$, $(1,9,14)$, $(2,10,1)$, $(2,10,3)$, $(2,10,5)$, $(2,10,7)$

(Continued)

Table 4. *(Continued)*

	*	&	parameter (a, b, c)
N	13	16	**(0, 1, 3)**, **(0, 1, 14)**, $(0,2,3)$, $(0,2,7)$, **(1, 2, 3)**, $(1,2,15)$, $(1,3,2)$, $(1,3,10)$, $(1,6,11)$, **(1, 8, 3)**, $(1,8,6)$, **(1, 10, 3)**, $(1,10,15)$, $(1,11,6)$, $(1,11,14)$, $(1,14,11)$, $(1,15,2)$, $(1,15,6)$, $(1,15,10)$, $(1,15,14)$, $(2,3,1)$, $(2,5,11)$, $(2,5,15)$, $(2,7,13)$, $(2,8,3)$, $(2,8,7)$, $(2,9,7)$, $(2,9,11)$, $(8,9,6)$, $(8,9,11)$, $(8,10,3)$, $(8,10,7)$
O	13	20	$(1,6,1)$, $(1,6,6)$, $(1,14,1)$, $(1,14,14)$, $(2,3,2)$, $(2,3,3)$, $(2,7,2)$, $(2,7,7)$
P	13	22	$(1,4,1)$, $(1,4,4)$, $(1,12,1)$, $(1,12,12)$, $(4,5,4)$, $(4,5,5)$, $(4,7,4)$, $(4,7,7)$
Q	17	33	$(0,1,0)$, $(0,1,1)$, $(1,8,1)$, $(1,8,8)$, $(8,9,8)$, $(8,9,9)$
R	17	20	**(0, 1, 2)**, $(0,1,15)$, $(1,2,0)$, **(1, 8, 10)**, $(1,8,15)$, $(1,10,8)$, $(2,5,8)$, $(2,9,0)$, $(8,9,7)$, $(8,9,10)$
S	17	53	$(0,8,1)$, $(1,9,0)$, $(1,9,4)$, $(1,9,8)$, $(1,9,12)$, $(4,12,1)$, $(4,12,3)$
T	17	22	$(1,2,1)$, $(1,2,2)$, $(1,10,1)$, $(1,10,10)$, $(2,5,2)$, $(2,5,5)$, $(2,9,2)$, $(2,9,9)$

*: The number of rounds of impossible differential characteristic
&: The number of rounds of integral distinguisher

Interestingly, we find that two parameters $(1, 4, 7)$ and $(5, 12, 3) \Leftrightarrow (1, 12, 7)$ (both in Group G) are better than original SIMON from the following reasons.

- $(1, 4, 7)$ and $(5, 12, 3)$ belong to the 20 parameters with optimal security against differential attack, while SIMON or SIMECK are not optimal.
- $(1, 4, 7)$ and $(5, 12, 3)$ have the same level of security against integral and impossible differential attacks as the original SIMON.

Additionally, $(5, 12, 3)$ is optimal with respect to linear attacks, and hence this can be an alternative parameter to the original one. However, it should be noted that we only focus on the security aspect against the four attacks only, and the implementation characteristic is not considered here.

Links Between Impossible Differential and Integral Attacks. In 2015, Sun *et al.* [21] showed that impossible differential characteristics lead to integral distinguishers for any Feistel cipher adopting an *SP*-round function. Actually, for all parameters from Fig. 7, we observe that integral distinguishers cover more rounds than impossible differential characteristics, which agrees with the observation by Sun *et al.* Thus we are interested in if we can view our results with the context of the link.

Sun *et al.* assumes that the domain and range sizes of the *S*-layer is a word size, n. To fit the round function of SIMON$_{a,b,c}$ into this framework, we have to regard the entire round function as S and then P is an identity transformation. Otherwise, concatenation of bit-wise AND is the only possible candidate as S, leading to $2n$-bit to n-bit S-layer which does not match the framework. By regarding the entire round function as S, we can only examine a set of 2^n plaintexts, in which $n = 16$ for SIMON32. At this level, the link in [21] can be applied to SIMON. However, we carried out our experiments, considering the details of $F_{a,b,c}$. At this level, any links between integral distinguishers and impossible differential characteristics has not been discovered.

6   Conclusions

In this paper, we searched the number of rounds of integral distinguishers and impossible differential characteristic for all parameters $(a, b, c) \in \mathcal{SV}$. As a result, we clarified that original rotation constants $(1, 8, 2)$ are not chosen to optimize resistance against integral and impossible differential attacks. Furthermore, from our experiments and investigations by Kölbl *et al.*, we found that $(a, b, c) = (5, 12, 3)$ is a possible alternative parameter to the original parameter.

Acknowledgments. The authors thank the anonymous ACNS 2016 reviewers for helpful comments. The work was partially carried out during ASK 2015 (Asian-workshop on Symmetric Key Cryptography) and Dagstuhl seminar 16021. The work by Tetsu Iwata was supported in part by JSPS KAKENHI, Grant-in-Aid for Scientific Research (B), Grant Number 26280045. The experiment in Sect. 3 was conducted using a supercomputer system at Information Technology Center of Nagoya University.

References

1. Abdelraheem, M.A., Alizadeh, J., AlKhzaimi, H.A., Aref, M.R., Bagheri, N., Gauravaram, P.: Improved linear cryptanalysis of reduced-round SIMON-32 and SIMON-48. In: Biryukov, A., Goyal, V. (eds.) Progress in Cryptology – INDOCRYPT 2015. LNCS, vol. 9462, pp. 153–179. Springer, Heidelberg (2015)
2. Abed, F., List, E., Lucks, S., Wenzel, J.: Differential cryptanalysis of round-reduced simon and speck. In: Cid, C., Rechberger, C. (eds.) FSE 2014. LNCS, vol. 8540, pp. 525–545. Springer, Heidelberg (2015)
3. Ahmadian, Z., Rasoolzadeh, S., Salmasizadeh, M., Aref, M.R.: Automated Dynamic Cube Attack on Block Ciphers: Cryptanalysis of SIMON and KATAN. Cryptology ePrint Archive, Report 2015/040 (2015). http://eprint.iacr.org/
4. Alizadeh, J., Alkhzaimi, H.A., Aref, M.R., Bagheri, N., Gauravaram, P., Kumar, A., Lauridsen, M.M., Sanadhya, S.K.: Cryptanalysis of SIMON variants with connections. In: Sadeghi, A.-R., Saxena, N. (eds.) RFIDSec 2014. LNCS, vol. 8651, pp. 90–107. Springer, Heidelberg (2014)
5. Ashur, T.: Improved Linear Trails for the Block Cipher Simon. Cryptology ePrint Archive, Report 2015/285 (2015). http://eprint.iacr.org/
6. Beaulieu, R., Shors, D., Smith, J., Treatman-Clark, S., Weeks, B., Wingers, L.: The SIMON and SPECK Families of Lightweight Block Ciphers. Cryptology ePrint Archive, Report 2013/404 (2013). http://eprint.iacr.org/
7. Biham, E., Biryukov, A., Shamir, A.: Cryptanalysis of skipjack reduced to 31 rounds using impossible differentials. J. Crypt. **18**(4), 291–311 (2005)
8. Biryukov, A., Roy, A., Velichkov, V.: Differential analysis of block ciphers SIMON and SPECK. In: Cid, C., Rechberger, C. (eds.) FSE 2014. LNCS, vol. 8540, pp. 546–570. Springer, Heidelberg (2015)

9. Boura, C., Naya-Plasencia, M., Suder, V.: Scrutinizing and improving impossible differential attacks: applications to CLEFIA, Camellia, LBlock and Simon. In: Sarkar, P., Iwata, T. (eds.) ASIACRYPT 2014. LNCS, vol. 8873, pp. 179–199. Springer, Heidelberg (2014)
10. Chen, H., Wang, X.: Improved Linear Hull Attack on Round-Reduced Simon with Dynamic Key-guessing Techniques. Cryptology ePrint Archive, Report 2015/666 (2015). http://eprint.iacr.org/
11. Chen, H., Wang, X.: Improved Linear Hull Attack on Round-Reduced Simon with Dynamic Key-guessing Techniques. In: Pre-Proceedings of FSE 2016 (2016). https://fse.rub.de/index.html
12. Chen, Z., Wang, N., Wang, X.: Impossible Differential Cryptanalysis of Reduced Round SIMON. Cryptology ePrint Archive, Report 2015/286 (2015). http://eprint.iacr.org/
13. Hao, Y., Meier, W.: Truncated Differential Based Known-Key Attacks on Round-Reduced Simon. Cryptology ePrint Archive, Report 2016/020 (2016). http://eprint.iacr.org/
14. Iizuka, H., Todo, Y., Morii, M.: Integral Attack against SIMON48. In: SCIS 2015 2E1-3 (2015) (in Japanese)
15. Knudsen, L.R., Wagner, D.: Integral cryptanalysis. In: Daemen, J., Rijmen, V. (eds.) FSE 2002. LNCS, vol. 2365, pp. 112–127. Springer, Heidelberg (2002)
16. Kölbl, S., Leander, G., Tiessen, T.: Observations on the SIMON block cipher family. In: Gennaro, R., Robshaw, M. (eds.) Advances in Cryptology – CRYPTO 2015. LNCS, vol. 9215, pp. 161–185. Springer, Heidelberg (2015)
17. Mourouzis, T., Song, G., Courtois, N., Christofii, M.: Advanced Differential Cryptanalysis of Reduced-Round SIMON64/128 Using Large-Round Statistical Distinguishers. Cryptology ePrint Archive, Report 2015/481 (2015). http://eprint.iacr.org/
18. Pramstaller, N., Rechberger, C., Rijmen, V.: Impact of rotations in SHA-1 and related hash functions. In: Preneel, B., Tavares, S.E. (eds.) SAC 2005. LNCS, vol. 3897, pp. 261–275. Springer, Heidelberg (2006)
19. Raddum, H.: Algebraic analysis of the simon block cipher family. In: Lauter, K., Rodríguez-Henríquez, F. (eds.) LatinCrypt 2015. LNCS, vol. 9230, pp. 157–169. Springer, Heidelberg (2015)
20. Shi, D., Hu, L., Sun, S., Song, L., Qiao, K., Ma, X.: Improved Linear (hull) Cryptanalysis of Round-reduced Versions of SIMON. Cryptology ePrint Archive, Report 2014/973 (2014). http://eprint.iacr.org/
21. Sun, B., Liu, Z., Rijmen, V., Li, R., Cheng, L., Wang, Q., AlKhzaimi, H., Li, C.: Links among impossible differential, integral and zero correlation linear cryptanalysis. In: Gennaro, R., Robshaw, M. (eds.) Advances in Cryptology – CRYPTO 2015. LNCS, vol. 9215, pp. 95–115. Springer, Heidelberg (2015)
22. Sun, S., Hu, L., Wang, M., Wang, P., Qiao, K., Ma, X., Shi, D., Song, L., Fu, K.: Constructing Mixed-integer Programming Models whose Feasible Region is Exactly the Set of All Valid Differential Characteristics of SIMON. Cryptology ePrint Archive, Report 2015/122 (2015). http://eprint.iacr.org/
23. Sun, S., Hu, L., Wang, P., Qiao, K., Ma, X., Song, L.: Automatic security evaluation and (related-key) differential characteristic search: application to SIMON, PRESENT, LBlock, DES(L) and other bit-oriented block ciphers. In: Sarkar, P., Iwata, T. (eds.) Advances in Cryptology – ASIACRYPT 2014. LNCS, vol. 8873, pp. 158–178. Springer, Heidelberg (2014)
24. Todo, Y., Morii, M.: Bit-Based Division Property and Application to Simon Family. In: Pre-Proceedings of FSE 2016 (2016). https://fse.rub.de/index.html

25. Wang, N., Wang, X., Jia, K., Zhao, J.: Differential Attacks on Reduced SIMON Versions with Dynamic Key-guessing Techniques. Cryptology ePrint Archive, Report 2014/448 (2014). http://eprint.iacr.org/
26. Wang, Q., Liu, Z., Varici, K., Sasaki, Y., Rijmen, V., Todo, Y.: Cryptanalysis of reduced-round SIMON32 and SIMON48. In: Meier, W., Mukhopadhyay, D. (eds.) Progress in Cryptology – INDOCRYPT 2014. LNCS, vol. 8885, pp. 143–160. Springer, Heidelberg (2014)
27. Yang, G., Zhu, B., Suder, V., Aagaard, M.D., Gong, G.: The simeck family of lightweight block ciphers. In: Güneysu, T., Handschuh, H. (eds.) CHES 2015. LNCS, vol. 9293, pp. 307–329. Springer, Heidelberg (2015)

Correlation Power Analysis of Lightweight Block Ciphers: From Theory to Practice

Alex Biryukov, Daniel Dinu$^{(\boxtimes)}$, and Johann Großschädl

SnT, University of Luxembourg, 6, rue Richard Coudenhove-Kalergi,
1359 Luxembourg, Luxembourg
{alex.biryukov,dumitru-daniel.dinu,johann.groszschaedl}@uni.lu

Abstract. Side-Channel Analysis (SCA) represents a serious threat to the security of millions of smart devices that form part of the so-called Internet of Things (IoT). Choosing the "right" cryptographic primitive for the IoT is a highly challenging task due to the resource constraints of IoT devices and the variety of primitives. An important criterion to assess the suitability of a lightweight cipher with respect to SCA is the amount of leakage available to an adversary. In this paper, we analyze the efficiency of different selection functions that are commonly used in Correlation Power Analysis (CPA) attacks on symmetric primitives. To this end, we attacked implementations of the lightweight block ciphers AES, Fantomas, LBlock, Piccolo, PRINCE, RC5, Simon, and Speck on an 8-bit AVR processor. By exploring the relation between the nonlinearity of the studied selection functions and the measured leakages, we discovered some imperfections when using nonlinearity to quantify the resilience against CPA. Then, we applied these findings in an evaluation of the "intrinsic" CPA-resistance of unprotected implementations of the eight mentioned ciphers. We show that certain implementation aspects can influence the leakage level and try to explain why. Our results shed new light on the resilience of basic operations executed by these ciphers against CPA and help to bridge the gap between theory and practice.

Keywords: CPA · Selection function · Leakage · Nonlinearity

1 Introduction

Side-Channel Analysis (SCA) [21] belongs to the genre of physical attacks and exploits some auxiliary information (e.g. the power consumption leaking from a device that executes a cryptographic algorithm) to recover the secret key. The history of SCA stretches back 20 years when Kocher described the first timing attacks [24] and thereafter introduced the basics of Differential Power Analysis (DPA) [23]. Since then, non-invasive attacks exploiting the power consumption or electromagnetic emanations of a target device have been steadily improved by using better leakage models and advanced analysis techniques to recover the secret key. Notable milestones in the evolution of power analysis attacks in the

© Springer International Publishing Switzerland 2016
M. Manulis et al. (Eds.): ACNS 2016, LNCS 9696, pp. 537–557, 2016.
DOI: 10.1007/978-3-319-39555-5_29

past 15 years include Correlation Power Analysis (CPA) [7], Template Attacks (TA) [10], and Mutual Information Analysis (MIA) [16].

The study of "lightweight" symmetric primitives has been a hot topic in the cryptographic community in the past few years, driven primarily by the rapid growth of the Internet of Things (IoT) [14] and the demand for security at low cost in terms of execution time, power consumption, RAM requirements, and code size. A significant portion of the smart devices that will soon populate the IoT in large quantities are equipped with an 8-bit microcontroller and feature only a few kB of RAM (e.g. wireless sensor nodes). Such resource constraints pose a massive challenge for the implementation of measures to minimize side-channel leakage, which makes IoT devices an easy target for attacks [22]. It is widely believed in the cryptographic community that side-channel attacks are primarily an implementation problem rather than a design problem, i.e. there is little that can be done from a designer's perspective to eliminate or reduce the leakage of sensitive information. However, some recent research results start to challenge this view, and so does the present work.

Previous research at the intersection between lightweight cryptography and SCA focussed (almost) exclusively on the AES, i.e. there exist only few papers that deal with attacks or countermeasures for other ciphers. In particular, the study of the SCA-resistance of software implementations of lightweight ciphers did not keep pace with the high number of new proposals. In [1], the resilience of the AES and three lightweight block ciphers that share some characteristics (namely KLEIN, LED, and PRESENT) is investigated against profiled single-trace attacks. Unprotected hardware implementations of Simon and LED were analyzed with respect to DPA in [34]. An evaluation of both an unmasked and a masked implementation of Simon for FPGAs was reported in [5]. In [33], the vulnerability of PRINCE and RECTANGLE against DPA is studied. A second line of research focussed on the design of new ligthweight primitives that can be efficiently protected against DPA via masking; representative examples include PICARO [30], Zorro [15], and the LS-designs Robin and Fantomas [17].

The above-mentioned studies on DPA attacks against (lightweight) ciphers other than the AES were mainly "isolated" efforts in the sense that they were carried out on different execution platforms with different measurement setups and different analysis frameworks. A comparative (and consistent) study of the DPA-vulnerability of lightweight block ciphers based on power traces acquired with the same target device is, to our knowledge, still missing. However, such a study would allow one to answer the question of whether different ciphers are equally difficult to attack or not (and if not, why not). Furthermore, we could not find a detailed analysis of the power leakage of basic operations (e.g. arithmetic and logical computations, table look-ups) executed in the round function of common lightweight ciphers. Thus, in this paper, we first try to answer the following questions: (1) How do the theoretical metrics used to assess leakage relate to real-world attack results? (2) Which operation leaks more? Then, we apply the answers of these questions to illustrate how eight lightweight ciphers (namely AES, Fantomas, LBlock [37], Piccolo [35], PRINCE [6], RC5 [32], as well as Simon and Speck [2]) behave with respect to CPA. These eight ciphers were selected from the portfolio of lightweight symmetric algorithms evaluated in [13] using the FELICS framework [11]. The two main selection criteria were high performance and to have a variety of different design strategies.

All results and findings we describe in this paper are based on CPA attacks performed with power consumption traces that were captured on an evaluation board equipped with an 8-bit AVR microcontroller. Our choice for this specific platform is motivated by the widespread use of the 8-bit AVR architecture in resource-limited environments and its particular relevance in the context of the IoT (e.g. wireless sensor nodes). A better understanding of the actual leakage of different operations on 8-bit AVR microcontrollers could influence the design of new lightweight ciphers for the IoT and the implementation of more effective and less costly SCA countermeasures. For example, it is a known fact that the AES leaks significantly due to its highly nonlinear S-box [8], but modern lightweight ciphers generally use smaller S-boxes with lower nonlinearity compared to the AES, and thus one might expect that they leak less. However, an actual confirmation of this assumption with measured traces is still lacking.

We remark that the evaluation of candidates for the NIST SHA-3 standard considered besides security and performance on various hardware and software platforms also SCA resistance as a selection criterion (see e.g. [4,39] for some concrete results). Currently, a number of standardization bodies, including the NIST, are either considering or have already started the process to standardize lightweight symmetric primitives for the IoT. In this context, it makes sense to compare different aspects of potential candidates, including the SCA resistance of (unprotected) software implementations, before deploying them on millions or even billions of devices. Furthermore, we hope that our work will contribute to a better understanding of how to design lightweight block ciphers that have a better *intrinsic* resistance against side-channel attacks.

Research Contributions. Firstly, we quantify the leakage generated by the execution of different instructions on an AVR processor, aiming to identify the instructions that leak most. Then, we compare the power consumption leakage of basic operations widely used by lightweight ciphers. For each operation, we analyze the relation between our experimental results, the nonlinearity of the operation, and the size (in bits) of the attacked intermediate value.

Secondly, we provide a fair comparison of the resilience of eight lightweight block ciphers against CPA attacks. Knowing which instructions and operations leak more, and knowing all implementation details of the eight ciphers helps to identify the weakest point of each cipher, which can be attacked with maximal efficiency. Our experimental results show that, in some cases, the actual leakage is lower than expected due to certain implementation-related aspects.

The practical approach we follow has the benefit that it gives more realistic results compared with simulated power traces, where the noise is modeled in a deterministic way, which favors the attacker. Thus, our work sheds new light on the resilience of different operations against CPA attacks, and we illustrate this for a set of eight lightweight block ciphers. To the best of our knowledge, there has been no similar effort published in the literature.

2   Preliminaries

Unless specified otherwise, we will use the notation defined in this section. We use the following operators for the corresponding (bitwise) logical operations: "$\cdot$" for AND, "$+$" for OR, "$\oplus$" for XOR. The operators "$\boxplus$" and "$\boxminus$" denote a modular addition and a modular subtraction, respectively. The two functions $\mathsf{MSB}(x)$ and $\mathsf{LSB}(x)$ are used to extract the most and the least significant byte from a stream of bits x, respectively. We represent the S-box layer of a block cipher α by S_α, which may involve the application of one or more S-boxes in parallel, depending on the input size and the specifications of the cipher. The symbol $L_{i,Fantomas}^{-1}$ stands for the result of the inverse linear layer of Fantomas computed with L-box i, where $i \in \{0,1\}$. Finally, $\mathsf{HW}(x)$ denotes the Hamming weight of x, whereas $\mathsf{HD}(x,y) = \mathsf{HW}(x \oplus y)$ is the Hamming distance between x and y.

Definition 1 (Iterated Block Cipher). *An iterated block cipher, sometimes called a product cipher, is a block cipher obtained by iterating r times a round function $R : \{0,1\}^n \to \{0,1\}^n$, each time with its own key $K_i \in \mathcal{K}$, where $\mathcal{K}$ is called round key space. The cipher block size is n bits, the number of rounds is equal to r, $X^{(0)}$ is the plaintext, and $X^{(r)}$ is the ciphertext. It works as follows:*

$$X^{(i)} = R_{K_i}(X^{(i-1)}) \, for \, 1 \leq i \leq r$$

Definition 2 (Selection Function). *In the context of side-channel attacks, a selection function gives the intermediate result, also referred to as sensitive value $\phi_k = \varphi(x,k)$, which is used by the attacker to recover the secret key. It depends on a known part x of the input $X^{(i-1)}$ of the round function R_{K_i} and on an unknown part k of the round key K_i.*

The attacker computes the intermediate values ϕ_k for a fixed (either known or chosen) input x and for all possible subkeys k. The bit-size $|k|$ of the subkey k determines the memory complexity m of the side-channel attack. Then, she uses the sensitive values $\phi_1, \phi_2, \ldots, \phi_{2^{|k|}}$ and the side-channel leakage to guess the subkey k^* used during the actual computations on the target device. The higher the number of inputs x for which the attacker manages to measure the leakage, the higher the chances to recover the subkey k^*. Usually, the selection functions are chosen to be easy to compute, typically at the first round of the encryption or decryption operation.

Definition 3 (Correlation Power Analysis (CPA)). *Given a set of power traces and the corresponding sets of intermediate values $\phi_1, \phi_2, \ldots \phi_{2^{|k|}}$, Correlation Power Analysis (CPA) aims at recovering the secret subkey k^* using a correlation factor between the measured power samples and the power model of the computed sensitive values.*

The concept of CPA was studied as an improvement of DPA and formalized in [7]. A power model is used to describe the hypothetical power consumption of the target device as a function of the intermediate value ϕ_k considering the device's power consumption characteristics. The Hamming weight (HW) model is more common for software implementations, whereas the Hamming distance (HD) model is generally used for hardware devices.

2.1 Theoretical Metrics for the SCA Resistance of S-Boxes

In the definitions introduced in this subsection, we denote by "+" the addition of integers in $\mathbb{Z}$ and by "$\oplus$" the addition mod 2. We will also use "+" for the addition of two vectors in $\mathbb{F}_2^n$ since there is no ambiguity. For a pair of vectors $a = (a_1, a_2, \ldots, a_m)$ and $b = (b_1, b_2, \ldots, b_m)$ from $\mathbb{F}_2^m$, the scalar product $a \cdot b$ is defined as $a \cdot b = \oplus_{i=1}^m a_i \cdot b_i$.

One way to achieve nonlinearity in symmetric cryptographic primitives is to use S-boxes. Formally, an S-box is an (n, m) function $F : \mathbb{F}_2^n \mapsto \mathbb{F}_2^m$ that maps n input bits to m output bits. If $m = 1$, then F is nothing else than a Boolean function. For any given (n, m) function F, we denote by $(F_1, F_2, \ldots, F_m)$ the coordinate functions of F, such that $F(x) = (F_1(x), F_2(x), \ldots, F_m(x))$, where $F_i : \mathbb{F}_2^n \mapsto \mathbb{F}_2$ for $1 \le i \le m$. The *derivative* of F with respect to a vector a in $\mathbb{F}_2^n$ is the function $D_a F : \mathbb{F}_2^n \mapsto \mathbb{F}_2^m$ such that $D_a F(x) = F(x) + F(x + a)$. The *Walsh transform* of F is the function $W_F(u, v) = \sum_{x \in \mathbb{F}_2^n} (-1)^{v \cdot F(x) + u \cdot x}$, while the *cross-correlation transform* of Boolean functions F_i and F_j with respect to a vector $a \in \mathbb{F}_2^n$ is defined as $C_{F_i, F_j}(a) = \sum_{x \in \mathbb{F}_2^n} (-1)^{F_i(x) + F_j(x + a)}$.

Definition 4 (Nonlinearity). *The nonlinearity of an (n, m) function F is defined as:*

$$\mathsf{NL}(F) = 2^{n-1} - \frac{1}{2} \max_{\substack{u \in \mathbb{F}_2^n \\ v \in F_2^{m*}}} |W_F(u, v)| \tag{1}$$

Nonlinearity characterizes the resistance of F against linear cryptanalysis [27]. The higher the nonlinearity of a function, the more resistant the function is to linear cryptanalysis. It is widely accepted that the higher the nonlinearity of a function F, the more information it leaks through side channels.

Definition 5 (Transparency Order). *The Transparency Order of an (n, m) function F, where n and m are two positive integers, is:*

$$\mathsf{TO}(F) = \max_{\beta \in \mathbb{F}_2^m} \left(\left| m - 2\mathsf{HW}(\beta) \right| - \frac{1}{2^{2n} - 2^n} \sum_{a \in \mathbb{F}_2^{n*}} \left| \sum_{\substack{v \in \mathbb{F}_2^m \\ \mathsf{H}(v) = 1}} (-1)^{v \cdot \beta} W_{D_a F}(0, v) \right| \right)$$

The *Transparency Order* was introduced in [31] to "quantify" the resistance of an S-box against DPA attacks using the Hamming weight power model. In general, the smaller the transparency order of F, the higher is its resistance to DPA attacks. $\mathsf{TO}(F)$ satisfies the following relation: $0 \le \mathsf{TO}(F) \le m$.

Definition 6 (Improved Transparency Order). *The Improved Transparency Order of a balanced (n, m) function F is defined as:*

$$\mathsf{ITO}(F) = \max_{\beta \in \mathbb{F}_2^m} \left(m - \frac{1}{2^{2n} - 2^n} \sum_{a \in \mathbb{F}_2^{n*}} \sum_{j=1}^m \left| \sum_{i=1}^m (-1)^{\beta_i + \beta_j} C_{F_i, F_j}(a) \right| \right)$$

The *Improved Transparency Order* addresses the limitations identified in the initial definition of TO [9].

Definition 7 (DPA Signal-to-Noise Ratio). *The DPA Signal-to-Noise Ratio of function F is defined as:*

$$\mathsf{SNR}(F) = m 2^{2n} \left(\sum_{a \in \mathbb{F}_2^n} \left(\sum_{i=0}^{m-1} \left(\sum_{x \in \mathbb{F}_2^n} (-1)^{F_i(x) + x \cdot a} \right) \right)^4 \right)^{-\frac{1}{2}}$$

The *DPA Signal-to-Noise Ratio* was proposed in [18] as a way to model the information leakage of CMOS circuits using the tools of traditional cryptanalysis. The SNR increases when the resistance of an S-box to linear and differential cryptanalysis increases. A novel definition of the SNR based on the maximum likelihood estimator was introduced in [19].

3   Evaluation Framework

Measurement Setup. All experiments reported in this paper were performed on an evaluation board equipped with an 8-bit ATmega2561 processor clocked at 16 MHz. A regulated power supply provides the 5 V supply voltage required for the operation of the board. The evaluation board and the computer used to control the measurements are connected through optical fiber. We placed the board in a Faraday cage to reduce the environmental noise. The measurements of the power traces were performed with a LeCroy waveRunner 104MXi digital sampling oscilloscope using a differential probe.

We mounted the CPA attacks against the ANSI C implementations of the selected ciphers available in the FELICS framework [11]. The only modification of the original C source codes we made was the insertion of a trigger signal to indicate the beginning and the end of the side-channel relevant portion of the power traces. To have a common ground for comparison, we assumed that the attacker needs to recover the 32 bits of the round key $K_1 = $ 0x01234567 for all eight block ciphers. Note that, in all of our experiments, we acquired the same number of traces, namely q for the encryption of q known plaintexts.

Metrics. To ensure a fair and uniform side-channel evaluation of the selected ciphers, we used the evaluation methodology for key-recovery attacks proposed in [36]. In that paper, two different types of evaluation metrics are defined: an information-theoretic metric quantifying the amount of information that leaks from a given implementation, and an actual security metric, which quantifies how well the leaked information can be used by the attacker.

Since we conducted a practical evaluation based on leakages acquired from a target board using the described setup instead of attacks based on simulated power traces, the actual security metrics (i.e. success rate and guessing entropy) are sound for our study. We do not use the information-theoretic metric from [36] (i.e. conditional entropy) because it involves profiling the target device in order to approximate the probability distribution of the leakage, which reduces the applicability of the attack to a certain class of devices. Moreover, both the template creation and the approximation of the probability distribution for all leakage samples are computationally intensive.

We recall that side-channel attacks are generally performed using a divide-and-conquer approach. The adversary attacks a subkey class κ with $|\kappa| \ll |\mathcal{K}|$ using the selection function $\varphi(x, k)$ and q measurements. As result she gets a guess vector $g = [g_1, g_2, \ldots, g_{2^{|k|}}]$ for the subkey k with the possible candidates sorted in descending order, the most-likely subkey candidate being g_1, and the least-likely subkey candidate being $g_{2^{|k|}}$. The following two metrics quantify the amount of effort required to recover the correct subkey k^* from the guess vector. Consequently, they serve as an indicator of how efficient an attack is in the case of q measurement queries.

Definition 8 (Success Rate). *The success rate of order o, $o \leq 2^{|k|}$, of a side-channel key recovery attack is defined as:*

$$\mathsf{SR}_o(k^*, g) = \begin{cases} 1, & \text{if } k^* \in [g_1, g_2, \ldots, g_o] \\ 0, & \text{otherwise} \end{cases}$$

Definition 9 (Guessing Entropy). *The guessing entropy of a side-channel key recovery attack is:*

$$\mathsf{GE}(k^*, g) = log_2 i, \text{ such that } k^* = g_i \text{ for } g_i \in [g_1, g_2, \ldots, g_{2^{|k|}}]$$

Given an implementation $\mathcal{C}$ to be evaluated using N experiments with the maximum number of measurement queries q, the memory complexity m, and the time complexity t, Algorithm 1 shows in detail how the mean success rate of order o, i.e. $\overline{\mathsf{SR}_o^i}$, and the mean guessing entropy, i.e. $\overline{\mathsf{GE}^i}$, can be computed for i power consumption traces. The results are accompanied by the respective standard errors $\mathsf{SE}_{\overline{\mathsf{SR}_o^i}}$ and $\mathsf{SE}_{\overline{\mathsf{GE}^i}}$. Unless otherwise specified, the results in this paper are based on $N = 100$ experiments, each with $q = 2000$ queries. Both the time complexity t and memory complexity m were determined by guesses of at most 8-bit subkeys of the round key K_1, where k^* is the actual key used by the implementation $\mathcal{C}$.

4   Quantifying the Leakage

Using the measurement environment described before, we quantify the leakage of different instructions to find out which instruction gives the "best" target in

---

Algorithm 1. CPA Evaluation Algorithm

Data: $\mathcal{C}, k^*, q, m, t, N$
Result: $\overline{SR_o^i}, \overline{GE^i}, SE_{\overline{SR_o^i}}, SE_{\overline{GE^i}}$
for j *in* $[1, N]$ **do**
    AcquirePowerTraces$(\mathcal{C}, k^*, q)$;
    for i *in* q **do**
        $g = \text{CPA}(\mathcal{C}, i, m, t)$;
        compute and store $SR_o^{j,i}(k^*, g), GE^{j,i}(k^*, g)$;
    end
end
for i *in* $[5, q]$ **do**
    compute $\overline{SR_o^i} = \frac{1}{N}\sum_{j=1}^{N} SR_o^{j,i}(k^*, g), \overline{GE^i} = \frac{1}{N}\sum_{j=1}^{N} GE^{j,i}(k^*, g)$;
    compute $SE_{\overline{SR_o^i}}, SE_{\overline{GE^i}}$;
end

---

the power traces when performing a CPA attack. For this purpose, we define the *correlation coefficient difference* $\delta = c_{k^*} - c_{k^\circ}$ as the difference between the correlation coefficient of the correct key k^*, i.e. c_{k^*}, and the correlation coefficient of the most likely key guess k°, i.e. c_{k°, with $k^\circ \neq k^*$.

For the measurements we used a simple Assembly code fragment that contains the targeted Assembly instruction guarded by several **nop** instructions to reduce the noise from other operations such as the communication between the board and the computer or the peaks of the trigger signal. The measurements were done with values of the correct key k^* such that $\mathsf{HW}(k^*)$ runs through all possible values once. For a fixed value of the input plaintext x and key k^*, we averaged eight power measurements of the analyzed instruction to get a single power trace. The plaintext took all possible values from 0x00 up to 0xFF; thus the number of traces q is 256. We performed $N = 10$ experiments for each value of k^*.

4.1 Understanding the Device's Leakage

Understanding the device's leakage requires to understand how different Assembly instructions executed by the processor can impact the power consumption of the device. For this purpose, we evaluated two instructions that operate on registers (namely **and** and **add**) as well as three instructions that require access to memory (namely **lpm**, **ld**, and **st**). The **and** instruction performs a bitwise AND of two 8-bit words, while the **add** instruction executes a modular addition of two 8-bit words. Loading an 8-bit word from the Flash memory of the device into a register can be achieved through the **lpm** instruction, whereas loading an 8-bit quantity from RAM into a register requires a **ld** instruction. Finally, the **st** instruction writes the content of an 8-bit register to memory. We used the AES S-box with the index value given by the plaintext XORed with the key to perform the memory accesses.

Table 1. Correlation coefficient difference $\delta = c_{k^*} - c_{k^\circ}$ between the correlation of the correct key (i.e. c_{k^*}) and the correlation of the most likely key (i.e. c_{k°) where $k^\circ \neq k^*$ for different Hamming weights of the correct key k^* ($\bar{\delta}$ and $\mathsf{SE}_{\bar{\delta}}$ are the mean and the standard error for a 95 % confidence interval, respectively).

Instr.	Correct key									$\bar{\delta}$	$\mathsf{SE}_{\bar{\delta}}$
	0x00	0x01	0x03	0x07	0x0F	0x1F	0x3F	0x7F	0xFF		
and	−0.798	−0.643	−0.577	−0.518	−0.465	−0.392	−0.329	−0.178	−0.016	−0.435	0.183
add	0.190	−0.218	−0.160	−0.079	−0.053	0.001	0.049	0.041	0.001	−0.025	0.093
lpm	0.376	0.312	0.271	0.219	0.174	0.169	0.164	0.156	0.143	0.220	0.062
ld	0.244	0.200	0.178	0.225	0.215	0.226	0.215	0.195	0.222	0.213	0.015
st	0.596	0.581	0.578	0.577	0.566	0.594	0.603	0.585	0.592	0.586	0.008

Our results given in Table 1 show that the memory-access instructions leak a lot more information about the secret key than the register instructions. The writing of a register to memory leaks most, followed by the loading of a word from memory. At the other end of the spectrum is the and instruction, which is leaking approximately 20 times less than the add instruction (see Table 1 and Fig. 1). We also observed that increasing the number of power traces does not significantly change the values of δ.

Although these experiments may remind the reader about template attacks (where the attacker creates in the profiling phase leakage templates for various instructions), we stress that we did not perform actual template attacks, but we used a technique inspired by classical template attacks to quantify the leakage of different Assembly instructions. Our results indicate that an attacker should target the store of a sensitive value to increase the success rate of the attack.

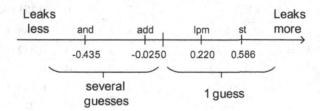

Fig. 1. Correlation coefficient difference spectrum

4.2 Comparison of Different Selection Functions

We now extend the previous experiments to different selection functions, whereby we target the writing of the selection function's result to memory using the st instruction, which, as we saw, has the highest leakage. Table 2 summarizes the nonlinearity NL and the mean correlation coefficient difference $\bar{\delta}$ for a total of 16 different selection functions, which are divided into four groups. Detailed values for different correct keys can be found in Table 5.

The first group of selection functions comprises the three logical operations AND, OR, and XOR, which all have a negative value for the mean correlation coefficient difference $\bar{\delta}$. This means that using one of these logical operations as a selection function for a CPA attack is not a very good option. As our results show, only the AND and OR, but not XOR, are sometimes able to recover the correct key k^*, whereby AND is slightly more efficient than OR.

One can notice the contrast between the huge nonlinearity of the AND and OR selection functions on the one side, and all other selection functions listed in Table 2 on the other side. It is also interesting to note that these high values of nonlinearity are accompanied by (relatively) poor values for the correlation coefficient difference. In the case of the bitwise logical operations, it seems the high nonlinearity values do not provide the useful leakage one normally would expect. This contrasts with the conventional wisdom saying that the higher the nonlinearity of a selection function, the more information it leaks in SCA.

Table 2. Leakages of different selection functions (n and m are the input and output size of the selection function in bits, NL is the nonlinearity of the selection function, $\bar{\delta}$ is the mean correlation coefficient difference, and $\mathsf{SE}_{\bar{\delta}}$ is the standard error for a 95 % confidence interval).

Selection function	n	m	NL	$\bar{\delta}$	$\mathsf{SE}_{\bar{\delta}}$
$\varphi_1(x,k) = x \cdot k$	16	8	16384	−0.005	0.074
$\varphi_2(x,k) = x + k$	16	8	16384	−0.018	0.060
$\varphi_3(x,k) = x \oplus k$	16	8	0	−0.153	0.168
$\varphi_4(x,k) = x \boxplus k$	16	8	0	0.127	0.011
$\varphi_5(x,k,c) = x \boxplus k \boxplus c$	17	8	0	0.121	0.010
$\varphi_6(x \oplus k) = S_{AES}(x \oplus k)$	8	8	112	0.586	0.008
$\varphi_7(x \oplus k) = S_{LBlock}(x \oplus k)$	4	4	4	0.342	0.008
$\varphi_8(x \oplus k) = S_{LBlock}(x \oplus k)$	8	8	64	0.235	0.006
$\varphi_9(x \oplus k) = S_{Piccolo}(x \oplus k)$	4	4	4	0.339	0.019
$\varphi_{10}(x \oplus k) = S_{Piccolo}(x \oplus k)$	8	8	64	0.259	0.006
$\varphi_{11}(x \oplus k) = S_{PRINCE}(x \oplus k)$	4	4	4	0.269	0.010
$\varphi_{12}(x \oplus k) = S_{PRINCE}(x \oplus k)$	8	8	64	0.138	0.004
$\varphi_{13}(x \oplus k) = \mathsf{LSB}(L^{-1}_{1,Fantomas}(x \oplus k))$	8	8	0	0.087	0.015
$\varphi_{14}(x \oplus k) = \mathsf{MSB}(L^{-1}_{1,Fantomas}(x \oplus k))$	8	8	0	0.041	0.014
$\varphi_{15}(x \oplus k) = \mathsf{LSB}(L^{-1}_{2,Fantomas}(x \oplus k))$	8	8	0	0.136	0.007
$\varphi_{16}(x \oplus k) = \mathsf{MSB}(L^{-1}_{2,Fantomas}(x \oplus k))$	8	8	0	0.083	0.018

The modular addition is similar to the XOR operation; the main difference is the carry propagation in the case of modular addition. Although the nonlinearity of the two modular addition selection functions in Table 2 is zero, there are components of these functions that reach high nonlinearity because of the carry propagation. For clarity, it should be mentioned that all the components of the XOR selection function have a nonlinearity equal to zero, and that the nonlinearity of an (n, m) function is determined by the component having the lowest nonlinearity. By nonlinearity of a component of an (n, m) function F, we mean the nonlinearity of F computed for a fixed vector $v \in \mathbb{F}_2^{m*}$ as shown in Eq. (1); see Table 6 for details. This exhibits another imperfection of the nonlinearity metric when used to compare various selection functions regarding side-channel leakage. We note that considering the carry bit c from a previous operation when using selection function φ_5 (adc instruction) does not improve the correlation coefficient difference compared with φ_4 (add instruction). The modular addition selection function successfully recovered the secret key in all our test cases and should thus be preferred over logical operations.

A further group of selection functions is composed of the substitution layers of different lightweight block ciphers. These selection functions clearly leak the most with respect to CPA. In fact, the selection function using the S-box of the AES has the highest leakage among all studied selection functions. For ciphers using 4-bit S-boxes, we considered two different selection functions: one with an 8-bit input and one with a 4-bit input. The 8-bit selection functions based on the substitution layer of LBlock, Piccolo and PRINCE leak two times less than the selection function using the AES S-box. Surprisingly, although our target device has an 8-bit architecture, the 4-bit selection functions φ_7, φ_9, φ_{11} leak more than the 8-bit selection functions of the same substitution layers.

The selection functions based on the L-boxes of Fantomas are analyzed in a fourth group since they are linear operations, which are generally expected to leak less than nonlinear operations. To our surprise, this group (which consists of the last four selection functions listed in Table 2) leaks more than the logical operations and is on a similar level with the modular addition. Thus, they can be considered as selection functions when performing CPA attacks.

We remark that in [25], the basic algebraic group operations XOR, addition modulo 2^n, and modular multiplication are studied in the context of multi-bit CPA attacks using simulated power traces. Then, selection functions based on the addition modulo 2^{16} and multiplication modulo $2^{16} + 1$ are applied to an implementation of IDEA running on an 8-bit AVR processor. In the case of the modular addition, the characteristics of the correlation coefficients for practical attacks do not correspond to the simulated ones due to signal superposing.

Through these experiments, we revealed some interesting aspects about the leakage of the studied selection functions with respect to CPA. In contradiction to intuitions based on nonlinearity, we made the following observations: (1) the bitwise logical AND and OR operations leak much less than expected and do not always reveal the secret key; (2) for block ciphers that use 4-bit S-boxes, a 4-bit selection function is more efficient than an 8-bit selection function; (3) the linear lookup tables (i.e. L-boxes) used by Fantomas leak more than expected and can be considered as selection functions for CPA attacks.

The lessons we learned from these experiments helped us a lot to select the appropriate leakage functions to attack the eight lightweight block ciphers we briefly describe in the following section.

5   Analyzed Ciphers

We chose the eight lightweight ciphers included in our evaluation according to the following criteria. Firstly, we selected the ciphers from those that achieved good software performance in the Triathlon competition [13]. Besides selecting the ciphers for our CPA study from the ones evaluated in [13], we also used the provided C source codes. This approach has the advantage that all ciphers are implemented according to a common set of guidelines and by the same team of developers, and therefore all implementations had undergone a similar level of optimization. Secondly, we chose our ciphers from the two major structural classes, namely Feistel Networks (FN) and Substitution-Permutation Networks (SPN) with the goal of having many different design approaches with unique features or properties. For example, PRINCE introduced the α-reflection property, which means that a message encrypted under a certain key can only be decrypted with a related key. RC5 introduced data-dependent rotations, while Fantomas is the first instance of the so-called LS-designs.

The main characteristics of the studied ciphers are given in Table 3. In the following, we provide a brief description of each cipher (we refer the reader to the original papers for more details). Half of the eight ciphers use substitution boxes; Table 4 summarizes the most important properties of each S-box.

Table 3. Main characteristics of the analyzed lightweight ciphers.

Cipher	Block size (bits)	Key size (bits)	Rounds	Structure	Target platform	Attacked operation
AES	128	128	10	SPN	SW, HW	S-box lookup
Fantomas	128	128	12	SPN	SW	L-box lookup
LBlock	64	80	32	Feistel	HW, SW	S-box lookup
Piccolo	64	80	25	Feistel	HW	S-box lookup
PRINCE	64	128	12	SPN	HW	S-box lookup
RC5	64	128	20	Feistel	SW	modular addition
Simon	64	96	42	Feistel	HW, SW	bitwise AND
Speck	64	96	26	Feistel	SW, HW	modular subtraction

AES: Based on the Rijndael block cipher [12], the AES [29] is to date the most important symmetric algorithm. It uses a block size of 128 bits and three different key sizes: 128, 192, and 256 bits. In each round (except for the final round) the `SubBytes`, `ShiftRows`, `MixColumns`, and `AddRoundKey` transformations are applied to a 4 × 4 byte state matrix. The final round does not include the `MixColumns` transformation. The key schedule expands the master key into the round keys using the `SubWord` and `RotWord` transformations.

Table 4. Properties of the S-boxes of four analyzed ciphers. The values of TO, ITO, and SNR have a similar behavior as the value of NL for different S-boxes, but they have a different granularity. Thus, the study of NL with respect to CPA holds also for TO, ITO, and SNR, which are variations of NL.

Cipher	S-box	NL	TO	ITO	SNR
AES	S	112	7.860	6.916	9.600
LBlock	s_0	4	3.667	2.567	2.946
	s_1	4	3.667	2.567	2.807
	s_2	4	3.667	2.567	2.807
	s_3	4	3.667	2.567	2.946
	s_4	4	3.667	2.567	2.946
	s_5	4	3.667	2.567	2.807
	s_6	4	3.667	2.567	2.946
	s_7	4	3.667	2.567	2.946
Piccolo	S	4	3.667	2.567	3.108
PRINCE	S	4	3.400	2.333	2.129

Selection function: The 8-bit selection function we used in our experiments targets the result of the S-box lookup in the first round of encryption.

Fantomas: Fantomas [17] is the non-involutive instance of a newly-crafted class of lightweight block ciphers, called LS-designs, that is specialized towards efficient Boolean masking. LS-designs facilitate the masking countermeasure to protect against DPA attacks by combining a linear diffusion layer in the form of a lookup table (L-box) with a bitsliced confusion layer. The 8-bit bitsliced S-box is an unbalanced Feistel network built from a 3-bit and a 5-bit S-box as in MISTY [28]. On the other hand, the 16-bit L-box has a branch number of 8 as explained in [17, Sect. 2.2] and was built from a systematic generator of the Reed-Muller code $RM(2,5)$. Fantomas does not have a key schedule. The family of LS-designs was very recently extended to XLS-designs [20], which aim to improve the security margins while retaining the implementation efficiency.

Selection function: Because there are four possible 8-bit inputs for the same MSB or LSB of the output of the mentioned 16-bit L-boxes, we had to attack both the MSB and LSB to recover the key. The selection function targets the inverse linear layer at the first round of decryption.

LBlock: LBlock [37] is based on a Feistel structure with a 64-bit block and an 80-bit key. At each round, the left branch goes through the round function F, while the right branch is rotated by 8 to the left. The two Feistel branches are swapped after each round, except for the last one. F consists of a substitution layer applied to the permutation of the left branch XORed with the round key. The confusion function includes eight 4-bit S-boxes used in parallel, while the diffusion function is defined as a permutation of eight 4-bit words.

This 4-bit permutation can be implemented efficiently in both hardware and software environments. The key schedule of LBlock is designed in the form of a stream cipher and uses a left-rotation by 29 bits, two 4-bit S-boxes, and an XOR.

Selection function: The 4-bit selection function is given by the result of the substitution layer at the first round of encryption.

Piccolo: Piccolo [35] is a 64-bit block cipher supporting 80-bit and 128-bit keys and is suitable for restricted environments thanks to its high efficiency in hardware. It has a generalized Feistel structure with four 16-bit branches and a permutation-based key schedule. Due to its involution property, Piccolo can support decryption with little extra cost. The round function is very light and consists of two S-box layers, separated by a diffusion matrix. Piccolo also uses an 8-bit word-based permutation between rounds to improve diffusion.

Selection function: The 4-bit selection function targets the result of the first substitution layer of the first round function of encryption.

PRINCE: PRINCE [6] is a 64-bit block cipher with 128-bit keys based on the so-called FX construction. It is optimized for latency when implemented in hardware and allows the encryption of data within one clock cycle. PRINCE is suitable for pervasive applications with real-time security needs. The overhead for decryption on top of encryption is negligible due to the α-reflection property: decryption for one key corresponds to encryption with a related key. The key schedule expands the 128-bit key k to 192 bits, out of which the first two 64-bit subkeys k_0, k_0' are used as whitening keys, while the third subkey k_1 is used as a round key for the 12-round cipher called $PRINCE_{core}$. Each round of $PRINCE_{core}$ comprises an S-box layer, a linear layer, an addition of a round constant, and a key addition.

Selection function: The 4-bit selection function we used targets the substitution layer applied to the initial state XORed with the whitening key k_0 and round key k_1 at the first round of $PRINCE_{core}$. Thus, the attacker recovers the key $k^* = k_0 \oplus k_1$.

RC5: The RC5 [32] encryption algorithm is a Feistel-based cipher suitable for hardware and software implementation. A distinguishing feature of RC5 is the use of data-dependent rotations as a source of cryptographic strength. The rotation distance depends on the input data and is not predetermined. RC5 is parameterized and supports many implementation options; RC5-$w/r/b$ denotes a variant that operates on $2w$-bit blocks, has a key size of b bits, and performs r rounds. The encryption operation uses only three simple operations: addition modulo 2^w, bitwise XOR, and rotation to the left. However, the key expansion is quite complex and has a certain amount of "one-wayness." In our evaluation we used the same instance of RC5 as in [13], namely RC5-32/20/16, which is RC5 with 32-bit words, 20 rounds, and a 16-byte key.

Selection function: The selection function for RC5 targets the modular addition of the round key before the first encryption round. To avoid correlations with the reading the round key from memory instead of modular additions, we wrote the selection function in Assembly language to measure just the leakage generated by the targeted operation.

Simon: Simon [2,3] is a family of lightweight block ciphers tuned for good performance in hardware, without sacrificing the performance in software too much. Simon $2n/mn$ denotes a Simon instance with a $2n$-bit block size and an mn-bit key, where n can be 16, 24, 32, 48, or 64. Designed to be very small in hardware and easy to serialize at many levels, it uses an extremely simple and low-complexity round function, which employs bitwise AND, bitwise XOR, and circular shifts applied to n-bit data words. The nonlinearity is provided by the bitwise AND. Simon's key schedule uses a sequence of 1-bit round constants to eliminate slide properties and circular shift symmetries.

Selection function: To increase leakage, we attacked the composition of the XOR and AND operations at the end of the first round of decryption because at that time the intermediate value is written to memory.

Speck: Speck [2,3] is a family of software-optimized block ciphers that is also efficient in hardware. An instance with a $2n$-bit block and a mn-bit key is referred to as Speck $2n/mn$, where n can be 16, 24, 32, 48, or 64. The round function comprises bitwise XOR, addition modulo 2^n, and rotations applied to n-bit data. Speck gets its nonlinearity solely from the modular additions. The key schedule uses the encryption round function to generate the round keys.

Selection function: The used selection function gives the result of the modular subtraction of the two Feistel branches in the first decryption round. The attacker can take advantage of the memory-write operation of the result of the selection function rotated by 8 bits to the left.

6 Experimental Results

We distinguish between two main classes of lightweight ciphers with respect to their implementations' resistance against CPA. The first class contains ciphers that are implemented using lookup tables, while the second class comprises the ARX-based designs, whose operations generally leak less than table lookups.

First class: The first class can be further divided into three different categories of ciphers. The *first category* contains the AES, whose 8-bit S-box leaks much more than any other considered selection function. Our attacks required only 59 power traces to recover the four key-bytes with 100 % success rate. The *second category* consists of the three lightweight ciphers LBlock, Piccolo, and PRINCE, each using one or more 4-bit S-boxes for the substitution layer. All members of this category leak enough information to make the recovery of the key with a small number of traces possible. On average, a little bit more than 100 traces were enough to get the subkeys of these ciphers with 100 % success rate. However, two subkeys of LBlock and two subkeys of Piccolo required a lot more traces since the sensitive results of the selection functions are not written to memory after the targeted operation and hence the attacker correlates the reading of the S-box content (i.e. ld instruction) instead of the writing of the S-box output (i.e. st instruction). The *third category* is represented by ciphers that use linear lookup tables, e.g. Fantomas. Our attack against the implementation of Fantomas is a multi-target attack [26] because a normal attack failed to recover two bits of each attacked subkey. The multi-target attack enabled us to reveal the four key-bytes using 165 traces with 100 % success rate.

Second class: The second class covers the ARX designs RC5, Simon, and Speck, for which we were not able to recover the full secret key due to reduced leakage. If we consider, for example, the attacks to obtain the fourth key byte $k^* = 0\mathrm{x}67$ using $q = 2000$ traces, our experiments for RC5 and Simon gave a mean guessing entropy $\overline{GE}$ of 1.58 and 3.05, respectively. However, in the case of Speck, we managed to reveal k^* using 1345 traces with 100 % success rate.

The Assembly code generated from the C implementations of these ciphers executes four consecutive st instructions, which entails signal superposing. We tried to "cancel" this effect by reducing the frequency of the processor, but we had no success. Although the insertion of nop instructions between the stores improved the results, we decided to not use these modified implementations in our experiments because they give the attacker an unreasonable advantage and affect therefore the fair comparison with the ciphers from the first class.

Given the small size of the state of the ARX designs and the rather simple operations they carry out, we investigated the possibility of keeping the whole state in registers during the entire encryption process. The 64-bit block version of both Simon and Speck can be implemented in Assembly without having to execute a single st instruction between the start and the end of the encryption operation. This approach significantly reduces the amount of leakage available to the attacker. But this leakage reduction optimization can not be applied to 128-bit block implementations of RC5, Simon, and Speck due to the restricted register space available on an 8-bit microcontroller. For RC5, we also tried the butterfly attack proposed in [38] on the modular addition, but the results were worse than when using the classical CPA attack.

We performed the described attacks also with a "low-cost" setup consisting of an Arduino Uno board and an Analog Discovery oscilloscope with a built-in differential probe. The Arduino board gets its supply voltage through an USB connection, which is also used for the communication with the computer that controls the trace acquisition process. We did not employ any noise reduction techniques. The experiments with the low-cost setup produced similar results for the ciphers in the first class, except for Fantomas, but required more traces due to the increased noise levels. For example, the AES key could be recovered with 80 % success rate using 36 power traces with the first setup, but 58 traces were necessary with the second (i.e. low-cost) setup. Similarly, to retrieve the PRINCE key with the same success rate, the first setup needed 65 traces, while the second setup required 85 traces. For the ciphers from the second class, the low-cost setup yielded much worse results. When using 5000 traces, the mean guessing entropy for the attack against RC5 increased from 3.68 (low noise) to

22.29 (high noise). Similarly, for Simon we got $\overline{GE} = 9.97$ in the noise-reduced setting and $\overline{GE} = 16.44$ with the cheap equipment.

All our experiments were conducted on unprotected implementations of the ciphers. However, many security-critical applications require countermeasures against SCA attacks, e.g. masking. In this context, it is known that linear and Boolean operations, such as those performed by Fantomas, RC5, Simon, and Speck, can be masked with relatively low overheads in terms of execution time and code size. On the other hand, masking a nonlinear S-box like that of AES generally entails a significant performance and code-size penalty. Somewhere in the middle between these two extremes are LBlock, Piccolo, and PRINCE.

7 Conclusions

Following a practical approach, we investigated the leakage of various selection functions widely used in existing lightweight ciphers for an 8-bit processor. We analyzed how these results relate to the intuition about side-channel leakages based on the nonlinearity of the selection function. Thereby, we identified three imperfections of leakage evaluation based on nonlinearity, namely for AND and OR bitwise operations, for 4-bit S-boxes, and for linear lookup tables.

Using the knowledge gained from the evaluation of selection functions, we attacked unprotected software implementations of eight well-known lightweight ciphers, namely AES, Fantomas, LBlock, Piccolo, PRINCE, RC5, Simon, and Speck. We grouped the results of our experiments into two classes according to the observed resistance against CPA attacks. The unprotected implementation of AES was broken with the smallest number of power traces, followed by the implementations of lightweight ciphers using 4-bit S-boxes, and thereafter the implementation of Fantomas, whose L-boxes required slightly more traces than the 4-bit S-boxes. On the other hand, the ARX-based designs RC5, Simon, and Speck leaked less as we could not recover the full key for any of them. We also demonstrated that different implementation options can increase the resilience of lightweight block ciphers against power analysis attacks.

The software implementations of the three ARX designs we considered are characterized by a certain level of "intrinsic" resilience against CPA. They can also be efficiently masked with relatively small impact on execution time and code size. These features make ARX constructions excellent candidates for the implementation of lightweight block ciphers for the IoT.

Acknowledgements. We thank Yann Le Corre and André Stemper for their help with the measurement setup. The work of Daniel Dinu is supported by the CORE project ACRYPT (ID C12-15-4009992) funded by the Fonds National de la Recherche (FNR) Luxembourg.

A   Additional Tables

Table 5. Detailed leakages for different selection functions φ_i as defined in Table 2.

Selection function	Correct key								
	0x00	0x01	0x03	0x07	0x0F	0x1F	0x3F	0x7F	0xFF
φ_1	−0.225	0.098	0.086	0.057	−0.031	−0.052	−0.001	0.011	0.007
φ_2	0.006	−0.005	−0.002	−0.073	−0.002	0.026	0.015	0.072	−0.202
φ_3	−0.145	−0.160	−0.173	−0.190	−0.167	−0.152	−0.142	−0.125	−0.124
φ_4	0.129	0.134	0.134	0.127	0.150	0.125	0.117	0.096	0.131
φ_5	0.121	0.120	0.147	0.125	0.113	0.109	0.111	0.141	0.110
φ_6	0.597	0.582	0.578	0.577	0.566	0.595	0.603	0.586	0.593
φ_7	0.341	0.343	0.338	0.354	0.337	−	−	−	−
φ_8	0.234	0.223	0.228	0.249	0.230	0.245	0.244	0.233	0.234
φ_9	0.319	0.331	0.361	0.350	0.338	−	−	−	−
φ_{10}	0.252	0.245	0.264	0.256	0.263	0.268	0.264	0.255	0.268
φ_{11}	0.265	0.257	0.273	0.273	0.278	−	−	−	−
φ_{12}	0.139	0.135	0.146	0.143	0.136	0.142	0.129	0.145	0.131
φ_{13}	0.094	0.089	0.079	0.061	0.061	0.080	0.105	0.099	0.120
φ_{14}	0.036	0.027	0.026	0.028	0.018	0.047	0.060	0.062	0.069
φ_{15}	0.144	0.121	0.137	0.127	0.129	0.145	0.134	0.151	0.143
φ_{16}	0.078	0.073	0.072	0.037	0.074	0.093	0.120	0.100	0.100

Table 6. Nonlinearity (NL) of the components of the modular addition (selection functions φ_4 and φ_5 from Table 2). By nonlinearity of a component of an (n, m) function F, we mean the nonlinearity of F computed for a fixed vector $v \in \mathbb{F}_2^{m*}$ as in Eq. (1). "Number" denotes how many components have the given nonlinearity NL, "Proportion (%)" is the proportion of the given nonlinearity NL with respect to the nonlinearity of all components of F.

(a) $\varphi_4 : \mathbb{F}_2^{16} \mapsto \mathbb{F}_2^8, \varphi_4(x, k) = x \boxplus k$

NL	Number	Proportion (%)
0	1	0.39
16384	26	10.20
24576	100	39.22
28672	112	43.92
30720	16	6.27

(b) $\varphi_5 : \mathbb{F}_2^{17} \mapsto \mathbb{F}_2^8, \varphi_5(x, k, c) = x \boxplus k \boxplus c$

NL	Number	Proportion (%)
0	1	0.39
32768	26	10.20
49152	100	39.22
57344	112	43.92
61440	16	6.27

References

1. Banciu, V., Oswald, E., Whitnall, C.: Exploring the resilience of some lightweight ciphers against profiled single trace attacks. In: Mangard, S., Poschmann, A.Y. (eds.) COSADE 2015. LNCS, vol. 9064, pp. 51–63. Springer, Heidelberg (2015)
2. Beaulieu, R., Shors, D., Smith, J., Treatman-Clark, S., Weeks, B., Wingers, L.: The SIMON and SPECK Families of Lightweight Block Ciphers. IACR Cryptology ePrint Archive (2013)
3. Beaulieu, R., Shors, D., Smith, J., Treatman-Clark, S., Weeks, B., Wingers, L.: SIMON and SPECK: Block Ciphers for the Internet of Things. In: NIST Lightweight Cryptography Workshop (2015)
4. Benoît, O., Peyrin, T.: Side-channel analysis of six SHA-3 candidates. In: Mangard, S., Standaert, F.-X. (eds.) CHES 2010. LNCS, vol. 6225, pp. 140–157. Springer, Heidelberg (2010)
5. Bhasin, S., Graba, T., Danger, J.-L., Najm, Z.: A Look into SIMON from a side-channel perspective. In: IEEE International Symposium on Hardware-Oriented Security and Trust (HOST), pp. 56–59. IEEE (2014)
6. Borghoff, J., Canteaut, A., Güneysu, T., Kavun, E.B., Knezevic, M., Knudsen, L.R., Leander, G., Nikov, V., Paar, C., Rechberger, C., Rombouts, P., Thomsen, S.S., Yalçın, T.: PRINCE – A low-latency block cipher for pervasive computing applications. In: Wang, X., Sako, K. (eds.) ASIACRYPT 2012. LNCS, vol. 7658, pp. 208–225. Springer, Heidelberg (2012)
7. Brier, E., Clavier, C., Olivier, F.: Correlation power analysis with a leakage model. In: Joye, M., Quisquater, J.-J. (eds.) CHES 2004. LNCS, vol. 3156, pp. 16–29. Springer, Heidelberg (2004)
8. Carlet, C.: On highly nonlinear S-boxes and their inability to thwart DPA attacks. In: Maitra, S., Veni Madhavan, C.E., Venkatesan, R. (eds.) INDOCRYPT 2005. LNCS, vol. 3797, pp. 49–62. Springer, Heidelberg (2005)
9. Chakraborty, K., Maitra, S., Sarkar, S., Mazumdar, B., Mukhopadhyay, D., Prouff, E.: Redefining the Transparency Order. Cryptology ePrint Archive, Report 2014/367 (2014)
10. Chari, S., Rao, J.R., Rohatgi, P.: Template attacks. In: Kaliski Jr., B.S., Koç, Ç.K., Paar, C. (eds.) CHES 2002. LNCS, vol. 2523, pp. 13–28. Springer, Heidelberg (2003)
11. CryptoLUX Team.FELICS – Fair Evaluation of Lightweight Cryptographic Systems (2015). https://www.cryptolux.org/index.php/FELICS
12. Daemen, J., Rijmen, V.: The Design of Rijndael: AES-The Advanced Encryption Standard. Springer Science & Business Media (2013)
13. Dinu, D., Le Corre, Y., Khovratovich, D., Perrin, L., Großschädl, J., Biryukov, A.: Triathlon of Lightweight Block Ciphers for the Internet of Things. Cryptology ePrint Archive, Report 2015/209 (2015). http://eprint.iacr.org/
14. Evans, D.: The Internet of Things: How the Next Evolution of the Internet is Changing Everything.Cisco IBSG white paper (2011). http://www.cisco.com/web/about/ac79/docs/innov/IoT_IBSG_0411FINAL.pdf
15. Gérard, B., Grosso, V., Naya-Plasencia, M., Standaert, F.-X.: Block ciphers that are easier to mask: how far can we go? In: Bertoni, G., Coron, J.-S. (eds.) CHES 2013. LNCS, vol. 8086, pp. 383–399. Springer, Heidelberg (2013)
16. Gierlichs, B., Batina, L., Tuyls, P., Preneel, B.: Mutual information analysis. In: Oswald, E., Rohatgi, P. (eds.) CHES 2008. LNCS, vol. 5154, pp. 426–442. Springer, Heidelberg (2008)

17. Grosso, V., Leurent, G., Standaert, F.-X., Varıcı, K.: LS-designs: Bitslice encryption for efficient masked software implementations. In: Cid, C., Rechberger, C. (eds.) FSE 2014. LNCS, vol. 8540, pp. 18–37. Springer, Heidelberg (2015)

18. Guilley, S., Hoogvorst, P., Pacalet, R.: Differential power analysis model and some results. In: Quisquater, J.-J., et al. (eds.) CARDIS 2004. IFIP, vol. 153, pp. 127–142. Springer, Heidelberg (2004)

19. Guilley, S., Hoogvorst, P., Pacalet, R., Schmidt, J.: Improving side-channel attacks by exploiting substitution boxes properties. In: International Workshop on Boolean Functions: Cryptographyand Applications, pp. 1–25 (2007)

20. Journault, A., Standaert, F.-X., Varici, K.: Improving the Security and Efficiency of Block Ciphers based on LS-Designs. Designs, Codes and Cryptography (2016)

21. Joye, M., Olivier, F.: Side-channel analysis. In: Encyclopedia of Cryptography and Security, pp. 1198–1204 (2011)

22. Kasper, T., Oswald, D., Paar, C.: Sweet dreams and nightmares: security in the internet of things. In: Naccache, D., Sauveron, D. (eds.) WISTP 2014. LNCS, vol. 8501, pp. 1–9. Springer, Heidelberg (2014)

23. Kocher, P.C., Jaffe, J., Jun, B.: Differential power analysis. In: Wiener, M. (ed.) CRYPTO 1999. LNCS, vol. 1666, pp. 388–397. Springer, Heidelberg (1999)

24. Kocher, P.C.: Timing attacks on implementations of Diffie-Hellman, RSA, DSS, and other systems. In: Koblitz, N. (ed.) CRYPTO 1996. LNCS, vol. 1109, pp. 104–113. Springer, Heidelberg (1996)

25. Lemke, K., Schramm, K., Paar, C.: DPA on n-bit sized boolean and arithmetic operations and its application to IDEA, RC6, and the HMAC-construction. In: Joye, M., Quisquater, J.-J. (eds.) CHES 2004. LNCS, vol. 3156, pp. 205–219. Springer, Heidelberg (2004)

26. Mather, L., Oswald, E., Whitnall, C.: Multi-target DPA attacks: pushing DPA beyond the limits of a desktop computer. In: Sarkar, P., Iwata, T. (eds.) ASIACRYPT 2014. LNCS, vol. 8873, pp. 243–261. Springer, Heidelberg (2014)

27. Matsui, M.: Linear cryptanalysis method for DES cipher. In: Helleseth, T. (ed.) EUROCRYPT 1993. LNCS, vol. 765, pp. 386–397. Springer, Heidelberg (1994)

28. Matsui, M.: New block encryption algorithm MISTY. In: Biham, E. (ed.) FSE 1997. LNCS, vol. 1267, pp. 54–68. Springer, Heidelberg (1997)

29. NIST. Advanced Encryption Standard (AES). Federal Information Processing Standards Publication (FIPS) 197, 2001

30. Piret, G., Roche, T., Carlet, C.: PICARO – A block cipher allowing efficient higher-order side-channel resistance. In: Bao, F., Samarati, P., Zhou, J. (eds.) ACNS 2012. LNCS, vol. 7341, pp. 311–328. Springer, Heidelberg (2012)

31. Prouff, E.: DPA attacks and S-boxes. In: Gilbert, H., Handschuh, H. (eds.) FSE 2005. LNCS, vol. 3557, pp. 424–441. Springer, Heidelberg (2005)

32. Rivest, R.L.: The RC5 encryption algorithm. In: Preneel, B. (ed.) FSE 1994. LNCS, vol. 1008. Springer, Heidelberg (1995)

33. Selvam, R., Shanmugam, D., Annadurai, S.: Vulnerability analysis of PRINCE and RECTANGLE using CPA. In: ACM Workshop on Cyber-Physical System Security, pp. 81–87 (2015)

34. Shanmugam, D., Selvam, R., Annadurai, S.: Differential power analysis attack on SIMON and LED block ciphers. In: Chakraborty, R.S., Matyas, V., Schaumont, P. (eds.) SPACE 2014. LNCS, vol. 8804, pp. 110–125. Springer, Heidelberg (2014)

35. Shibutani, K., Isobe, T., Hiwatari, H., Mitsuda, A., Akishita, T., Shirai, T.: *Piccolo*: An ultra-lightweight blockcipher. In: Preneel, B., Takagi, T. (eds.) CHES 2011. LNCS, vol. 6917, pp. 342–357. Springer, Heidelberg (2011)

36. Standaert, F.-X., Malkin, T.G., Yung, M.: A unified framework for the analysis of side-channel key recovery attacks. In: Joux, A. (ed.) EUROCRYPT 2009. LNCS, vol. 5479, pp. 443–461. Springer, Heidelberg (2009)
37. Wu, W., Zhang, L.: LBlock: A lightweight block cipher. In: Lopez, J., Tsudik, G. (eds.) ACNS 2011. LNCS, vol. 6715, pp. 327–344. Springer, Heidelberg (2011)
38. Zohner, M., Kasper, M., Stöttinger, M.: Butterfly-attack on Skein's modular addition. In: Schindler, W., Huss, S.A. (eds.) COSADE 2012. LNCS, vol. 7275, pp. 215–230. Springer, Heidelberg (2012)
39. Zohner, M., Kasper, M., Stöttinger, M., Huss, S.: Side channel analysis of the SHA-3 finalists. In: Design, Automation & Test in Europe Conference & Exhibition (DATE), pp. 1012–1017. IEEE (2012)

Cryptography in Software

Assisted Identification of Mode of Operation in Binary Code with Dynamic Data Flow Slicing

Pierre Lestringant[1,2]([✉]), Frédéric Guihéry[1], and Pierre-Alain Fouque[2,3]

[1] AMOSSYS, R&D Security Lab, Rennes, France
pierre.lestringant@amossys.fr
[2] Université de Rennes 1, Rennes, France
[3] Institut Universitaire de France, Paris, France

Abstract. Verification of software security properties, when conducted at the binary code level, is a difficult and cumbersome task. This paper is focused on the reverse engineering task that needs to be performed prior to any thorough analysis. A previous line of work has been dedicated to the identification of cryptographic primitives. Relying on the techniques that have been proposed, we devise a semi-automated solution to identify modes of operation. Our solution produces a concise representation of the data transfers occurring within a cryptographic scheme. Inspired by program slicing techniques, we extract from a dynamic data flow a slice defined as the smallest subgraph that is distance preserving for the set of cryptographic parameters. We apply our solution to several modes of operation including CBC, CTR, HMAC and OCB. For each of them, we successfully obtain a complete and readable representation. Moreover, we show with an example that our solution can be applied on non standard schemes to quickly discover security flaw.

Keywords: Binary analysis · Reverse engineering · Cryptography

1 Introduction

1.1 Problem Statement

Modes of operation are critical from a security perspective, since they have to guarantee the confidentiality, the integrity and the authenticity of sensitive data. However, they are subtle to securely devise and implement and they are subject to many security vulnerabilities. For instance, Katz and Schneier described an attack on OpenPGP which was applicable to many other e-mail encryption protocols [14]. Using a *chosen-ciphertext attack* on the Cipher Feedback (CFB) mode of operation, they were able to decrypt any message without recovering the secret key. It is also well-known that the padding used in modes of operation is highly sensitive. Bad paddings have led to devastating attacks on many IETF standards [30] by Vaudenay. A practical attack has been successfully implemented using timing information [8]. Later, Paterson described many such attacks by carefully studying the interplay between modes of operation and various security protocols against TLS [25], against IPsec [11] and against SSH [1].

© Springer International Publishing Switzerland 2016
M. Manulis et al. (Eds.): ACNS 2016, LNCS 9696, pp. 561–579, 2016.
DOI: 10.1007/978-3-319-39555-5_30

Therefore, to ensure that the security properties provided by modes of operation are truly effective, security experts have to analyze their design and their implementations. When the source code is not available, this analysis needs to be conducted at the binary level. For instance, in black box security audits, security experts are limited to publicly available information about the target. The objective of such audits is to simulate real-world scenarios. Unfortunately, even with a good understanding of the machine language, binary code analysis is still a difficult and time consuming task mostly due to the lack of high level structure. It would be highly beneficial for security analysts if some parts of the analysis could be automated. In particular, before digging into the details of padding verification or before looking for possible side channels, analysts have to identify the mode of operation and to locate its main components. In this paper we propose a solution to facilitate this first step.

1.2   Related Work

To the best of our knowledge the only previous work to address the problem of finding modes of operation in binary code, is CipherXRay [17]. CipherXRay is based on the avalanche effect of cryptographic functions. It identifies memory buffers that are highly dependent on one another. Specific dependencies patterns are proposed to distinguish some modes of operation. The problem of identifying modes of operation can be related to wider research fields such as generic algorithm identification and more generally binary analysis. Algorithm identification has been studied in the past few years for various reasons ranging from intellectual property protection to malware analysis and to vulnerability discovery. Identification techniques can be classified according to which code abstraction(s) they use to represent and compare binary code. The main abstractions are: bytes value [13], instruction mnemonics [27], Control Flow Graph (CFG) [6], program dependence graphs [23] and observations of runtime behavior [3]. One of the most recent result in that domain is Rendezvous [15] that relies on several abstractions: data constant, instruction mnemonics and CFG subgraphs.

In the case of modes of operation, it seems interesting to devise a specific solution. In fact, symmetric cryptographic algorithms share common characteristics. For instance, their implementations try to avoid conditional statements as much as possible due to performance and security considerations (typically to resist timing attacks). By taking them into account, a dedicated identification method will have a better efficiency and produce more relevant results. A previous line of work, dealing with primitive identification, provides a good starting point. The main primitive identification techniques are presented along with their advantages and drawbacks in Sect. 3.

1.3   Solution Overview

We choose to rely on the Data Flow Graph (DFG) to identify modes of operation. Modes of operation specify how cryptographic primitives are applied on data to achieve security properties. Thus, the data dependencies between the cryptographic primitives and, more generally, their organization in the data flow, are essential to identify modes of operation. We present our data flow model and how it can be obtained from a program execution in Sect. 2.

A classical approach would be to search for distinctive data flow patterns using automated pattern matching techniques [9]. However, this approach lacks flexibility and robustness. It is ineffective against modes of operation that have been modified or that have never been encountered before. Besides, these techniques often produce fully processed results that may be hard to seize by human analysts if they want to continue the analysis manually. Instead of using signatures to identify modes of operation, we chose to produce a synthetic representation of the data transfers occurring between the cryptographic primitives. The interpretation of the synthetic representation is left to the human analyst. This solution seems ideal to bridge the gap between automated processing and manual analysis. Furthermore, human interpretation is much more flexible than any automated pattern matching techniques. This synthetic representation, called a slice, must contain enough information to accurately identify modes of operation and, at the same time, must be easily readable by a human analyst. A slice is defined in Sect. 4 as the smallest subgraph of the DFG that is distance preserving for the set of cryptographic parameters. A practical heuristic to extract a slice from a DFG is described in Sect. 4. Experimental results are presented in Sect. 5. Finally, three use cases are detailed in Sect. 6: the first one is about OCB an authenticated encryption mode, the second one deals with an uncommon use of a cryptographic primitive as part of an IV-replacement attack and the third one is about and instant messaging application that uses a custom encryption scheme. In summary, this paper makes the following contributions:

- We propose to facilitate the analysis of modes of operation by computing a representation that summarizes the data dependencies between the cryptographic primitives.
- We give a formal definition for this representation and we propose a practical algorithm to compute it. We discuss why this definition is a good tradeoff between completeness and readability.
- We present experimental results obtained for several modes of operation including CBC, CTR, HMAC and OCB on well-known cryptographic libraries.

2   Data Flow

In this section we describe our data flow model and explain how it can be computed. As mentioned in the introduction, symmetric cryptographic algorithms try to avoid conditional statements as much as possible. Apart from the number of iterations over the message blocks, we do not expect the control flow to change significantly from one execution to one another. To take advantage of this observation we assume that the code to be analyzed is a sequence of instructions that is executed from the first to the last. This hypothesis, greatly simplify the data flow computation. Straight line code can be easily obtained in practice by recording a particular execution.

2.1   Data Flow Model

The data flow is represented by a directed graph. A vertex corresponds to an operation, and an edge to a data dependency between two operations. An operation depends on its operand(s). An input variable or a constant has no dependency. A memory access does not depend on its address but only on the value it reads or writes. Let us consider the following x86 assembly code snippet:

mov eax, [**ebp** + 8]
mov ebx, [**ebp** + 16]

Taking load-address dependencies into account results in *eax* and *ebx* being connected through *ebp*. But as far as we know, *eax* and *ebx* may be perfectly independent (despite the fact that they are stored side by side). In the end, there is a risk that everything becomes interconnected through the stack pointer (at least when arguments are passed on the stack). Thus, we discard this type of dependency. In our model, a memory read depends only on the last value that was written at its address (if there is any, otherwise it is considered as an input value). This is essential to track values as they are written and read from memory. However, to build these dependencies, one has to find which memory accesses are performed at the same address. This issue is discussed in Sect. 2.2. In our data flow model we do not consider implicit dependencies. An example of implicit dependency is illustrated in the following code line:

for (y = 0; y < x; y++);

The final value of y is equal to the value of x, yet there is no direct assignment from x to y. This is an implicit dependency. As explained in the introduction there should be almost no conditional statements on cryptographic data. Thus, for simplicity we ignore implicit dependencies. Finally, it goes without saying that if the result of an operation is constant it will not depend on its operands. A typical example in x86 code is:

xor eax, **eax**

2.2   Concrete Memory Addresses

To obtain correct load-value dependencies we must be able to compare the address of memory accesses. It can be done either statically or dynamically.

Static Approach. Given two addresses, the goal is to over-approximate their difference. That is to say, to find a set that contains all the possible values that their difference could take. If this set is equal to the zero singleton, the two addresses are equal. If it does not contain the zero value, they are different. Otherwise, it is impossible to conclude. Thus, it is important to find the smallest over-approximation possible. One of the most advanced techniques for over-approximating memory addresses in binary code is Value Set Analysis (VSA) [2]. In our case, due to the straight line hypothesis, this technique can be greatly simplified.

One important design principle was to limit the analysis to a code window. In fact, we already know, where modes of operation are located in the program (code regions surrounding the cryptographic primitives call sites). Besides, applying analysis (such as VSA) to the whole program will dramatically increase the complexity of our solution without providing any guarantee on the information we will retrieve from it. However, lack of context information greatly reduces the efficiency of static address over-approximations. In fact, modes of operation manipulate several data buffers (at least plaintext, ciphertext, key and nonce), the address of which is usually defined outside of the analysis window. Hence, whatever method is used, no good over-approximation can be computed for these addresses. Since these buffers are accessed for mixed reads and writes, aliasing issues arise. For instance, because we cannot decide if the address of the ciphertext buffer is different from the address of the key, any write access to the ciphertext buffer might also overwrite the key.

Dynamic Approach. In order to be context sensitive without needing to analyze the whole program, we use concrete memory addresses. The resulting DFG reflects the particular execution, where the concrete memory addresses were recorded, and not necessarily the generic behavior of the program. However, the generality loss is not a big concern since we do not expect many addresses to be dependent on input values. A typical example of an address that depends on an input value is a substitution box. But implementations of modes of operation should be free of any substitution box access. Any complex transformation occurring inside the code of the mode can be seen as a distinct cryptographic primitive and be dealt with separately.

3   Identification of the Primitives and the Parameters

As a preliminary condition, the parameters and the code of the cryptographic primitives need to be identified and located inside the DFG. With this last requirement, concerning the code of the primitive, our goal is to be able to dissociate the data flow of the primitive from the external data flow of the mode of operation. Since we are only interested in the data connections happening at the mode level, we must be able to exclude the internal data flow of the primitive from our analysis.

3.1   Existing Techniques

Cryptographic primitive identification has already been studied and practical solutions have been proposed. A first solution, described in [12] and [7], is based on the unique relationship that exists between the input and the output values of a cryptographic algorithm. If the data manipulated by a program fits that relationship, then we have not only identified the algorithm but also its parameters. However this solution suffers from a high combinatorial complexity. In fact, no good solution has been proposed to aggregate registers and memory accesses together in order to obtain parameters than can be test against standard implementations. CipherXRay (already mentioned in the introduction) is a second solution. It takes advantage of the avalanche effect of cryptographic functions. According to this effect, each byte of the input is expected to influence all the bytes of the output. CipherXRay searches for couples of memory buffers (continuous memory location accessed within a code fragment) that are subject to the avalanche effect. A third solution, presented in [16], is relying on DFG to build signatures for cryptographic algorithms. The DFG is first normalized using code rewrite mechanisms and then compared to the signatures of a database using a subgraph isomorphism algorithm. Signatures are a distinctive subgraphs. Parameter of cryptographic primitives are automatically identified as part of the signature boundary.

3.2   Selected Technique: DFG Signatures

We choose to rely on DFG signatures to retrieve cryptographic code and cryptographic parameters. The DFG model used in our method for mode identification is similar to the one that is used for primitive identification. Thus, it will only have to be created once for both methods. Moreover, this method has proven to be fast (execution time does not exceed a couple of seconds), efficient for non obfuscated programs and it does not require heavy instrumentation. And most of all, since it is based on DFG isomorphism, it tells very precisely which vertices and edges are part of the primitive and which ones are part of the mode.

4   Slicing

As explained in the introduction, to make it possible for a human analyst to interpret the data flow easily, it needs to be simplified. To this end, we propose to extract parts of the data flow that are connected to the cryptographic parameters. Described as such, this step can be seen as a program slicing process. As in program slicing, our goal is to extract parts of the program that are affected by or have an effect on points of interest (which are, in our case, the cryptographic parameters). But unlike the usual definitions of program slicing [29], we do not impose the slice to maintain semantics of the original program with respect to the points of interest. In fact, we favor readability over semantic equivalence. Thus, not every part of the data flow that is connected with the cryptographic parameters, is transcribed in the extracted graph. Because of the proximity to the program slicing domain, we borrow the terminology and call the extracted graph a slice. This section is structured as follow: first we give a formal definition of a slice; then we justify why this definition is a good compromise between completeness and readability; finally we describe a practical algorithm to compute an approximated slice.

4.1   Problem Formalization

Given a DFG $D = (V_D, E_D)$ and a set of cryptographic parameters $P \subset V_D$, a slice $S = (V_S, E_S)$ is the smallest subgraph of D such that $P \subset V_S$ and:

$\forall (u, v) \in P^2, dst_D(u, v) = dst_S(u, v)$ (where dst_D and dst_S denotes respectively the distance in D and S). We define the distance between two vertices as the number of edges on the shortest *undirected* path.

4.2 Completeness-Readability Tradeoff

Completeness. A slice is said to be *complete* if it contains enough information to identify the mode of operation. The completeness is due to the distance preserving property. If two parameters are connected in the DFG, then they will also be connected in the slice. A first naive approach would be to consider a less generic definition where the slice is made only of predefined connections (instead of generic undirected paths) between subsets of cryptographic parameters. For instance, based on the CBC mode, it could be tempting to only extract the smallest directed path from an output parameter to an input parameter (chaining between two executions of the block cipher) and the lowest common ancestor between two input parameters (same key for two executions of the block cipher). However, there is a risk for this list of predefined connections to be incomplete and to become more and more complex as new types of connections are added. For instance, let us consider the simple construct to make a block cipher *tweakable*: $E_k(M \oplus h(T)) \oplus h(T)$ described in [22]. Part of the DFG for this construct is given in Fig. 1. None of the connections previously mentioned for the CBC mode can describe the path between the input and the output of the block cipher in that case. To obtain complete slices without a priori knowledge of the types of connections that may be encountered, we consider undirected paths between every pair of parameters.

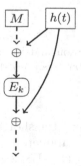

Fig. 1. DFG of a possible construct to obtained a tweakable block cipher from a block cipher. The connection between the input and the output is neither a directed path nor a lowest common ancestor

So far we have justified why the proposed definition is necessary to obtain complete slices with a large variety of modes of operation. Unfortunately, due to the minimality property, this definition does not guarantee the slice to always be complete. For instance, if one is interested in a particular path between two parameters, only the smallest is guaranteed to be reported. In the next section, this issue is illustrated by an example. In practice, as showed in Sects. 5 and 6, this definition has given good results.

Readability. A slice is said to be *readable*, if it does not contain significantly more information than what is strictly required to identify the mode of operation. The readability is ensured by the minimality property. It guarantees that the slice is free of irrelevant elements, that is to say, vertices or edges that are not connected to any cryptographic parameters.

However, the minimality property may also cause some perfectly relevant elements to be discarded. In fact, if they are not located on the shortest path between a pair of cryptographic parameters, they will not be included in the slice. This scenario is illustrated by an example in Fig. 2. On the left there is a possible data flow of a CTR mode and on the right its corresponding slice. The counter is implemented using two variables, as it could be the case for a 128-bit counter on 64-bit architecture. For a large majority of executions, including the one used to build the data flow of the example, only the least significant part is being incremented. Of the two existing paths between the input of the block cipher, only the shortest is included in the slice. Thus, the information about the addition, which is useful to identify the CTR mode, is lost.

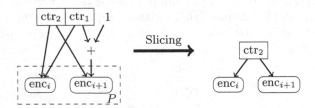

Fig. 2. DFG of a CTR implementation and its corresponding slice. The counter is implemented using two variables: ctr_1 (resp. ctr_2) is the least significant part (resp. most significant part).

Including any paths and not only the shortest one, is not a possible solution to this problem. In fact for some parameters, there are a lot of paths that are strictly equivalent. For instance, the AES128 round key buffer is made of 44 32-bit words. Thus, there would be 44 paths for each pair of encryptions sharing the same round key buffer. To avoid redundant elements (representing the same information several times) we stick with the original slice definition.

4.3   Practical Greedy Algorithm

Finding a minimum distance preserving subgraph is a difficult task. A basic idea is to search for a shortest path for every pair of P^2 and to take their union. Since the path length is measured as the number of edges, a Breadth First Search

(BFS) algorithm can be used to compute the shortest path between two vertices. For a sparse graph with a number of edges linear to the number of vertices (as it is the case in our DFG model) the complexity of the BFS algorithm is linear to the number of vertices. Thus, the overall complexity of this simplistic algorithm is $\mathcal{O}(|V_G|.|P|^2)$. However, the resulting subgraph is not necessarily the smallest. If there are several smallest paths for a pair of vertices, the size of the union may depend on which one is chosen. It is illustrated by an example in Fig. 3. We want to find a slice for the data flow on the left assuming a set of parameters $P = \{enc_i, enc_j, enc_k\}$. By using the algorithm we just described, we may obtain the slice given on the top right which is equal to the union of (enc_i, key_2, enc_j), (enc_i, key_1, enc_k) and (enc_j, key_2, enc_k). However, the slice given on the bottom right is smaller. This problem is common in practice. In fact, a cryptographic parameter is almost always defined by a set of vertices. For instance on a 32-bit architecture, a 128-bit plaintext is usually split into four 32-bit fragments. One shortest path for each of these fragments is to be expected. Back to the example of Fig. 3, key_1 and key_2 could be two fragments of a same key parameter.

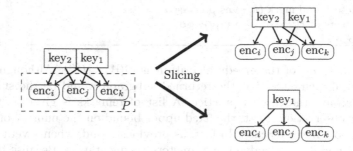

Fig. 3. A data flow with two possible distance preserving subgraphs

In the field of graph spanner, Coppersmith and Elkin [10] describe an approximate algorithm to compute pair-wise preservers. Given a graph $G = (V, E)$ and a set P^2 of pairs of vertices in P, a pair-wise preserver of G with respect to P is a subgraph $G' = (V, E')$ that is distance preserving for the elements of P. Their algorithm produces pair-wise preserver the size of which is bounded by $\mathcal{O}(|V| + \sqrt{|V|}|P^2|)$. The idea behind their algorithm is to modify slightly the weight of the edges to enforce the uniqueness of the shortest paths. If this upper bound is relevant from the graph spanner perspective, in our case it does not provide any guarantee at all. The DFG is already sparse. Thus, all its subgraphs are under that bound. Apart from this work, we have not been able to find any work or study addressing directly our problem.

An exact solution can be computed using the following algorithm. First, search for the set of shortest paths for every pair of parameters. Then, pick one path from each set, such that their union is minimum. This algorithms suffers from a high complexity. The number of shortest paths can be exponential to the number of vertices. Evaluating every possible selection of paths to find the smallest union has also an exponential complexity.

To reduce its complexity and make it tractable in practice, we make the following modifications. First, we limit to a fixed amount the number of paths returned by the BFS shortest path computation. Second, we used a greedy algorithm to find the set of paths with the smallest union. Iteratively, for each pair of P^2, we insert its shortest path that shares the largest number of edges with the current selection. A pseudo-code for this new algorithm, called the greedy algorithm, is given in Algorithm 1.

Algorithm 1. Greedy Algorithm

for all pairs (u, v) of P^2 **do**
    $path_{u,v} = minPath(u, v)$
end for
Initialize $S = (V_S, E_S)$ as an empty graph
repeat
    pick an unprocessed pair (u, v) such that $|path_{u,v}|$ is minimal
    pick a path $p \in path_{u,v}$ such that $|V_S \cup p|$ is minimal
    add p to S and mark (u, v) as processed
until all pairs of P^2 have been processed
return S

The complexity of the greedy algorithm is $\mathcal{O}(|V_G|.|P^2|)$. Although there is no theoretical guarantee that the returned subgraph would be the smallest, it is almost always the case in practice. A list of remarks is given as follow to justify this observation. First, the fixed upper bound on the number of shortest paths is almost never reached. In fact, as previously said, when several shortest paths are found it is often due to parameters fragmentation. Because fragments are rarely mix together outside of the cryptographic primitives, the number of shortest paths is almost always linear to the number of fragments. Second, not every pair of parameters has several shortest paths. Thus, the greedy selection mechanism starts with a non empty set of edges. As a consequence, the first path has not been chosen randomly and more generally we think it helps to stabilize the result. Finally, some sets of shortest paths are disjoints. For instance, for a usual mode of operation, the plaintext path will not intersect the key path. It mitigates the effect of the selection algorithm on the solution.

5   Experimental Evaluation

From an implementation perspective, we divided our solution into two parts. The first one, collects an execution trace of a program, using the PIN [24] framework. This execution trace contains the sequence of executed instructions along with the concrete memory addresses. The computation of the DFG and the extraction of the slice are performed off-line, in the second part. Results are printed in the DOT graph description language.

This section describes the experiments we conducted to evaluate our method. The data set is made of cryptographic implementations of some well-known cryptographic libraries.

5.1 Methodology

To save some space, we do not detail every slice that was obtained. Instead, to assess their usability by a human analyst, we provide measure of their completeness and their readability. These two notions are defined with respect to what should be an optimal data flow pattern in order to identify the mode of operation. The slice is called S, S_{opt} is the optimal pattern and Mcs is a function that returns, for a pair of graphs, its maximum common subgraph. The completeness Cp and the readability Rd are defined as follows:

$$\mathrm{Cp}(S) = \frac{|\mathrm{Mcs}(S, S_{opt})|}{|S_{opt}|} \qquad \mathrm{Rd}(S) = \frac{|\mathrm{Mcs}(S, S_{opt})|}{|S|}$$

Here, the size of a graph (denoted by $|.|$) is equal to its number of edges. If the slice is equal to the optimal pattern then both the completeness and the readability are equal to 1. During our experiments, the completeness and the readability were computed manually.

We performed experiments for three modes of operation: CBC (encryption and decryption), CTR and HMAC. We give in Fig. 4 what we consider to be an optimal pattern for each of these modes. In that representation, the * label may refer not only to any vertices but also to any path that does not intersect the rest of the graph. Some edges have a label to specify to which parameter of the cryptographic primitives they are connected. These patterns contain only the minimal number of executions of the cryptographic primitives to be recognizable. If the analysis window contains more, they will need to be extended. A short explanation for each of these patterns is given as follows.

CBC. For both encryption and decryption, the pattern contains two executions of the block cipher. In both cases, they have the same key parameter. For encryption, the input of the second execution of the block cipher, depends on the output of the first. For decryption, the input of the first execution an the output of the second have a common descendant.

CTR. The pattern contains two executions of the encryption primitive. They have the same key parameter and their input, both depends on the counter initial value.

HMAC. The pattern contains four executions of the compression function (two for each execution of the hash function). The first message block for the inner and outer hash function, are both dependent on the key. The second message block of the outer hash function depends on the output of the inner hash function. The others edges are due to the Merkle-Damgård hash construction. The dashed edge marks the place where the pattern would have to be extended if a larger code window were to be analyzed.

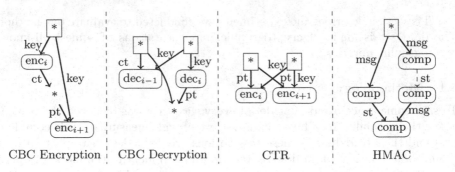

Fig. 4. Optimal data flow pattern for CBC, CTR and HMAC modes of operation

5.2 Results

We evaluated our method against the following cryptographic libraries: Crypto++ [18], LibTomCrypt [21], Nettle [19] and OpenSSL [20]. To be as close as possible to the reality, we did not recompiled these libraries, but took them as they were distributed in their respective Debian package. The CBC and CTR modes were tested with the AES and XTEA block cipher (when available) and the HMAC was tested with the MD5 hash function. For each scenario, we wrote a very simple program that calls the right library function on a small amount of data. We expected the same kind of results on larger programs. In fact, the analysis is limited to a small code window. For cryptographic libraries, this code window is not going to change depending on the amount of code surrounding it. Efficient heuristics that may be used to extract relevant code windows, are presented in Sect. 6.

Table 1. Measures of the completeness Cp and the readability Rd

	CBC	CTR	HMAC
Crypto++ 5.6.1	Cp = 1, Rd = 1	Cp = 1, Rd = 1	Cp = 1, Rd = 1
LibTomCrypt 1.17	Cp = 1, Rd = 1	Cp = 1, Rd = 1	Cp = 1, Rd = 1
Nettle 2.7.1	Cp = 1, Rd = 1	Cp = 1, Rd = 1	Cp = 1, Rd = 0.71
OpenSSL 1.0.1f	Cp = 1, Rd = 1	Cp = 1, Rd = 1	Cp = 1, Rd = 0.83

The completeness and the readability measures are given in Table 1. The completeness is always equal to one. It means that the slicing process has not missed any important connection specified by the optimal pattern. The majority of the readability values are also equal to one, meaning that the corresponding slices do not contain superfluous connections. However, smaller readability values were obtained for some HMAC implementations (Nettle and OpenSSL). These slices contain a common ancestor between the last block of the two executions of the hash function. After a thorough investigation, it appears that this common ancestor is the size of a message block. In fact, by the specification $k \oplus$ opad and $k \oplus$ ipad have the same size than a message block. Thus, the size of the messages $k \oplus$ opad$||H(k \oplus$ ipad$||m)$ and $k \oplus$ ipad$||m$ both depend on the size of a message block. Since the message padding includes the length of the message, it is perfectly legitimate for the last block to depend on the size of a block. Nevertheless we count it as a superfluous connection since it can be misleading for inexperienced analysts.

To conclude, our method have given promising results. In particular, every elements necessary to identify the mode of operation were obtained and the percentage of superfluous elements was never overwhelming.

6   Detailed Uses Cases

In this section we detail three application scenarios. First, we apply our solution on an OCB implementation to demonstrate that it can scale to more complex modes of operation. Second, we show that our solution can be used to quickly identify a malicious CBC implementation containing a backdoor. Finally, we confront our solution with an instant messaging application, to illustrate how it can be used on larger programs.

6.1   Authenticated Encryption: OCB

There are three versions of OCB. This example is based on the implementation of LibTomCrypt which corresponds to the first version, described in [26]. The slice given in Fig. 5, was obtained after encrypting a 34-byte message with AES OCB.

To justify why this slice correctly reflects the algorithm and to underline some of its imprecisions we divide the graph into four parts. The first part, colored in blue at the top, computes the first offset which is defined by the following expression: $E_k(N \oplus E_k(0^n))$, where N denotes the nonce, E_k the encryption under the key k and 0^n n bits set to 0. The two AES executions and the XOR operation in between are visible in the graph. The second part, colored in orange at the bottom left, encrypts the two first message blocks by evaluating the expression: $E_k(M[i] \oplus Z[i]) \oplus Z[i]$, where $M[i]$ is the ith message block and $Z[i]$ the ith offset (random mask). Here again the slice perfectly transcribes the algorithm specification. The two message blocks correspond to the two LOAD vertices at the center of the graph. The offset $Z[i]$ is XORed two times, before and after the encryption. The OR and PART1_8 operators are due to size changes from 32-bit to 8-bit variables and conversely. The third part, colored in violet on the right, corresponds to the last block encryption defined by: $E_k(len(M) \oplus L(-1) \oplus Z[m]) \oplus M[m]$. The last message block $M[m]$ does not appear in the graph. $M[m]$ is read only once for the whole scheme. Thus, it does not belong to any path between cryptographic parameters and it was not reported in the slice. The last part, colored in green at the bottom right, computes the authentication tag defined

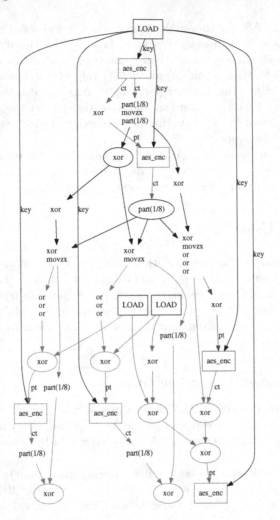

Fig. 5. Experimental slice obtained for the AES OCB implementation of the TomCrypt library executed on a three block message

by: $E_k(M[1] \oplus \ldots \oplus M[m-1] \oplus (C[m]||0^*) \oplus Y[m] \oplus Z[m])$, where $C[m]||0^*$ is the last encrypted block padded with zeros and $Y[m] = E_k(len(M) \oplus L(-1) \oplus Z[m])$. As previously said, the message used for this slice is 34-bytes long. Thus, the size of $C[m]$ is 2 bytes. These two bytes are obviously not on any shortest path, since they involved an additional XOR operation compared to $Y[m]$. With this remark in mind, the slice appears to contain the right dependencies: the two message blocks, $Y[m]$ and $Z[m]$ are XORed together and the result is encrypted. For brevity, we will not dig into how the different offsets are generated. As far as we have conducted our analysis, no inconsistency between the slice and the specifications has been found.

To conclude, our slicing model was able to capture most of the interesting connections even though some are missing (the XOR with $C[m]||0^*$ for instance). Obviously the complexity of this mode reduces the advantage of a graph representation for a human analyst. However, as demonstrated in the last paragraph, it is still possible to understand it with the help of the specifications.

6.2 IV-Replacement Attack

Algorithm Substitution Attack (ASA) consists in replacing the original encryption algorithm by a malicious one containing backdoor capabilities. There has been a renewed attention in the last past years for ASA, as shown by recent publications in that domain [4,5]. Closed source implementations of symmetric cryptography are attractive targets for ASA. Thus, while evaluating binary software, security experts could be interested in detecting ASA. This example shows that our method can automatically discloses an IV-replacement attack.

An IV-substitution attack is a simple ASA that was first described in [5]. It can be used against any encryption scheme that surfaces its IV, such as CBC or CTR. Two keys are used: the legitimate encryption key k defined by the user and a second key k' known only by the attacker. The IV is replaced by k encrypted under k'. Anyone with the knowledge of k' can decrypt the IV, recover k and finally decrypt the data.

For this experiment, we have implemented a very simple AES CBC encryption subject to an IV-replacement attack. The encryption key k is also encrypted using AES. It is a simplistic example, since in reality one will probably use public key cryptographic to correctly conceal the encryption key k. To start the analysis, we located the AES key schedule and the AES encryption, using primitive identification methods. The slice that was returned by our method is given in Fig. 6a. It is easy to recognize three CBC patterns in the middle: encryption executions are chained by XOR operations. Notice that encryptions depend on both the result of the key schedule and the key (LOAD labels in the graph). It is perfectly correct since the first four round keys are equal to the key. The key schedule is executed two times: one for each k and k'. The IV generation happens on the top left corner: we noticed that the first AES encryption takes as a plaintext parameter a value read form the memory that is later used as input by a key schedule execution. This is the encryption key k. The IV-substitution pattern is thus clearly visible.

6.3 Instant Messaging Application

For simplicity reasons, every results provided so far were obtained on wrapper applications that just call few functions from cryptographic libraries. In this section, we apply our solution on a much larger program: the Telegram client for Linux. Telegram is an instant messaging service that uses a custom encryption scheme called MtProto [28]. Brief specifications of this protocol can be found on editor's website. Client applications are available for several operating systems and they are all open source. Thus, it will be easy to check the validity of our results.

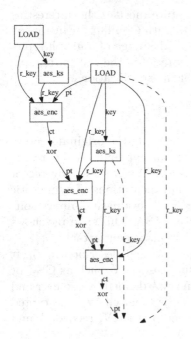

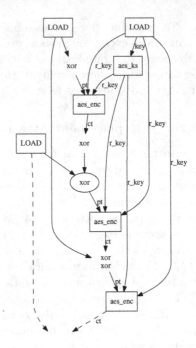

(a) AES CBC encryption subject to an IV-replacement attack.

(b) AES IGE used by Telegram to encrypt messages.

Fig. 6. Experimental slices

To extract interesting code fragments for our analysis, we use three simple heuristics. First, we looked for large basic blocks (more 40 instructions). Symmetric cryptography algorithms have very few conditional statements resulting in large basic blocks. Second, we filtered the basic blocks that had a low ratio of logical bitwise instructions. Finally, we kept only functions that did not call any sub function and, of course, contained at least one of the previously selected basic blocks. These three heuristics returned, for an execution trace of nearly a billion dynamic instructions and more than 130000 basic blocks, only a dozen of functions. Among them, we found AES (encryption and decryption), SHA1 and MD5. The others are checksum or compression functions.

The slice we obtained for the encryption part of protocol is given in Fig. 6b. It covers the encryption of the first two blocks of a message. The IGE mode of operation is perfectly recognizable. The two blocks of message (corresponding to the LOAD vertexes on the left), are XORed with their previous ciphertext block, encrypted and XORed with their previous plaintext block.

7   Conclusion

In this paper we have presented an automated solution to produce synthetic representations of the principal data transfers occurring in modes of operation. A formal definition ensures that this representation, called a slice, is both, sufficiently complete to reliably identify the mode of operation and, easily readable to benefit from the flexibility of human interpretation. We have described how slices can be computed. First we generate a dynamic DFG from an execution trace containing the executed instructions and the concrete memory addresses. Then, we locate in the DFG, the code and the parameters of the cryptographic primitives, using a signature-based identification technique. Finally, we apply a greedy algorithm to find the smallest representation possible.

We have demonstrated with experimental results on CBC, CTR and HMAC that, in practice, the slices produced by our method are complete and readable. In the last section, we have described in details three application scenarios to illustrate the capability of our solution. For the three scenarios, a complex mode of operation, a modified one with a security flaw and a real world program, our method performed well. Security analysts can take advantage of the results provided our solution, to quickly identify modes of operation and to get a good understanding of their internal structure. As such it should be highly profitable for black box audits and any other activities that require to reverse engineer the binary code of mode of operation.

References

1. Albrecht, M.R., Paterson, K.G., Watson, G.J.: Plaintext recovery attacks against SSH. In: 30th IEEE Symposium on Security and Privacy (S&P 2009), pp. 16–26 (2009)
2. Balakrishnan, G., Reps, T.: Analyzing memory accesses in x86 executables. In: Duesterwald, E. (ed.) CC 2004. LNCS, vol. 2985, pp. 5–23. Springer, Heidelberg (2004)
3. Bayer, U., Comparetti, P.M., Hlauschek, C., Krügel, C., Kirda, E.: Scalable, behavior-based malware clustering. In: Proceedings of the Network and Distributed System Security Symposium, NDSS 2009 (2009)
4. Bellare, M., Jaeger, J., Kane, D.: Mass-surveillance without the state: strongly undetectable algorithm-substitution attacks. In: Proceedings of the 22nd ACM SIGSAC Conference on Computer and Communications Security, pp. 1431–1440 (2015)
5. Bellare, M., Paterson, K.G., Rogaway, P.: Security of symmetric encryption against mass surveillance. IACR Cryptology ePrint Archive 2014, 438 (2014)
6. Bonfante, G., Kaczmarek, M., Marion, J.: Morphological detection of malware. In: 3rd International Conference on Malicious and Unwanted Software, MALWARE 2008, pp. 1–8 (2008)
7. Calvet, J., Fernandez, J.M., Marion, J.: Aligot: cryptographic function identification in obfuscated binary programs. In: The ACM Conference on Computer and Communications Security, CCS 2012, pp. 169–182 (2012)

8. Canvel, B., Hiltgen, A.P., Vaudenay, S., Vuagnoux, M.: Password interception in a SSL/TLS channel. In: Boneh, D. (ed.) CRYPTO 2003. LNCS, vol. 2729, pp. 583–599. Springer, Heidelberg (2003)

9. Conte, D., Foggia, P., Sansone, C., Vento, M.: Thirty years of graph matching in pattern recognition. IJPRAI 18(3), 265–298 (2004)

10. Coppersmith, D., Elkin, M.: Sparse sourcewise and pairwise distance preservers. SIAM J. Discrete Math. 20(2), 463–501 (2006)

11. Degabriele, J.P., Paterson, K.G.: On the (in)security of IPsec in MAC-then-encrypt configurations. In: Proceedings of the 17th ACM Conference on Computer and Communications Security, CCS 2010, pp. 493–504 (2010)

12. Gröbert, F., Willems, C., Holz, T.: Automated identification of cryptographic primitives in binary programs. In: Sommer, R., Balzarotti, D., Maier, G. (eds.) RAID 2011. LNCS, vol. 6961, pp. 41–60. Springer, Heidelberg (2011)

13. Hemel, A., Kalleberg, K.T., Vermaas, R., Dolstra, E.: Finding software license violations through binary code clone detection. In: Proceedings of the 8th International Working Conference on Mining Software Repositories, MSR 2011, pp. 63–72 (2011)

14. Katz, J., Schneier, B.: A chosen ciphertext attack against several e-mail encryption protocols. In: 9th USENIX Security Symposium (2000)

15. Khoo, W.M., Mycroft, A., Anderson, R.: Rendezvous: a search engine for binary code. In: Proceedings of the 10th Working Conference on Mining Software Repositories, MSR 2013, pp. 329–338 (2013)

16. Lestringant, P., Guihéry, F., Fouque, P.: Automated identification of cryptographic primitives in binary code with data flow graph isomorphism. In: Proceedings of the 10th ACM Symposium on Information, Computer and Communications Security, ASIA CCS 2015, pp. 203–214 (2015)

17. Li, X., Wang, X., Chang, W.: Cipherxray: exposing cryptographic operations and transient secrets from monitored binary execution. IEEE Trans. Dependable Sec. Comput. 11(2), 101–114 (2014)

18. Crypto++. http://www.cryptopp.com/

19. Nettle. http://www.lysator.liu.se/~nisse/nettle/

20. Openssl. https://www.openssl.org/

21. Libtomcrypt. http://libtom.org/

22. Liskov, M., Rivest, R.L., Wagner, D.: Tweakable block ciphers. In: Yung, M. (ed.) CRYPTO 2002. LNCS, vol. 2442, pp. 31–46. Springer, Heidelberg (2002)

23. Liu, C., Chen, C., Han, J., Yu, P.S.: GPLAG: detection of software plagiarism by program dependence graph analysis. In: Proceedings of the Twelfth ACM SIGKDD International Conference on Knowledge Discovery and Data Mining, pp. 872–881 (2006)

24. Luk, C., Cohn, R.S., Muth, R., Patil, H., Klauser, A., Lowney, P.G., Wallace, S., Reddi, V.J., Hazelwood, K.M.: Pin: building customized program analysis tools with dynamic instrumentation. In: Proceedings of the ACM SIGPLAN 2005 Conference on Programming Language Design and Implementation, pp. 190–200 (2005)

25. Paterson, K.G., AlFardan, N.J.: Plaintext-recovery attacks against datagram TLS. In: 19th Annual Network and Distributed System Security Symposium, NDSS 2012 (2012)

26. Rogaway, P., Bellare, M., Black, J., Krovetz, T.: OCB: a block-cipher mode of operation for efficient authenticated encryption. In: Proceedings of the 8th ACM Conference on Computer and Communications Security, CCS 2001, pp. 196–205 (2001)

27. Sæbjørnsen, A., Willcock, J., Panas, T., Quinlan, D.J., Su, Z.: Detecting code clones in binary executables. In: Proceedings of the Eighteenth International Symposium on Software Testing and Analysis, ISSTA 2009, pp. 117–128 (2009)
28. Telegram. https://telegram.org/
29. Tip, F.: A survey of program slicing techniques. J. Prog. Lang. 3(3) (1995). http://compscinet.dcs.kcl.ac.uk/JP/jp030301.abs.html
30. Vaudenay, S.: Security flaws induced by CBC padding - applications to SSL, IPSEC, WTLS. In: Knudsen, L.R. (ed.) EUROCRYPT 2002. LNCS, vol. 2332, pp. 534–545. Springer, Heidelberg (2002)

Parallel Implementation of BDD Enumeration for LWE

Elena Kirshanova$^{(\boxtimes)}$, Alexander May, and Friedrich Wiemer

Horst Görtz Institute for IT-Security, Faculty of Mathematics,
Ruhr University Bochum, Bochum, Germany
{elena.kirshanova,alex.may,friedrich.wiemer}@rub.de

Abstract. One of the most attractive problems for post-quantum secure cryptographic schemes is the LWE problem. Beside combinatorial and algebraic attacks, LWE can be solved by a lattice-based Bounded Distance Decoding (BDD) approach. We provide the first parallel implementation of an enumeration-based BDD algorithm that employs the Lindner-Peikert and Linear Length pruning strategies. We ran our algorithm on a large variety of LWE parameters, from which we derive the following interesting results. First, our parallel enumeration achieves almost perfect speed-up, which allows us to provide for the first time practical cryptanalytic results on standard LWE parameters of meaningful size. Second, we conclude that lattice-based attacks perform better than recent advanced BKW-type algorithms even for small noise, while requiring way less samples. Third, we experimentally show weaknesses for a binary matrix LWE proposal of Galbraith.

Keywords: Lwe security · Bounded distance decoding · Lattices

1 Introduction

Estimating the hardness of the *Learning with Errors Problem* (LWE) is of great importance in cryptography since its introduction by Regev [1]. Nowadays, the standard way to check concrete hardness of an LWE instance is by comparison with tables in LWE cryptanalysis papers (see [2–4] for lattice-based attacks, [5–7] for combinatorial attacks of BKW-type, [8] for an algebraic attack). Also, [9] provides a publicly available LWE-estimator that collects all known attacks and predicts their running-times on given LWE parameters. Due to the large memory- and sample-complexity of combinatorial algorithms, the lattice-based approach seems more practical. This belief was questioned by a recent result on BKW of Kirchner and Fouque [7], where an LWE instance of dimension 128 was solved in 13 hours. Currently, this is the record for combinatorial attacks on LWE. So it is reasonable to ask whether a similar result can be achieved by lattice-based attacks.

In this paper we present results on a parallel implementation of lattice-based attacks on LWE. We view the LWE problem as a BDD instance on a q-ary lattice.

© Springer International Publishing Switzerland 2016
M. Manulis et al. (Eds.): ACNS 2016, LNCS 9696, pp. 580–591, 2016.
DOI: 10.1007/978-3-319-39555-5_31

From here there are two approaches to go for: one can solve a BDD instance either via Kannan's embedding [10], or via reducing a lattice basis first and then solving a CVP problem on a reduced basis (reduce-then decode). While Kannan's embedding performs well for small dimensions [11], its complexity grows with the dimension since the algorithm calls an SVP solver as a subroutine.

We take the reduce-then-decode approach because the decoding part contains a tree-traversal algorithm that can be almost perfectly parallelized.

Our main contribution is a parallelization of BDD enumeration [3,4]. From our experiments we conclude that:

1. BDD enumeration can be almost perfectly parallelized, i.e. with n processors the achieved speed-up is roughly n.
2. For standard LWE-settings (e.g. uniform secret) instances with dimension of order $n = 100$ can be broken in several hours (see Sect. 5)
3. Lattice-based techniques are more efficient than current combinatorial algorithms even for binary secret.
4. Small error rates in BDD (binary or ternary error-vectors) allow for a much more efficient decoding.
5. A concrete instance of a space-efficient LWE variant of Galbraith [12] is weaker than previously thought (see Sect. 4)

To the best of our knowledge, our implementation provides the first results for lattice-based enumeration attacks on *concrete* LWE instances. Our attack is carried out in combination with the BKZ algorithm implemented in the NTL library [13]. Further improvements of lattice reduction (like in [14]) would in combination with our parallel BDD implementation certainly speed-up the attacks even further. Our code will be made available online.[1]

The remainder of this paper is organized as follows. Section 2 covers notations and background. In Sect. 3 we describe Babai's enumeration algorithm and its generalization. Our main algorithm, the parallelized BDD enumeration, is described in Sect. 3. Section 4 discusses variants of LWE and differences to the standard BDD attack. Our implementation results are presented in Sect. 5.

2 Background

We use bold lower-case letters for vectors $\mathbf{b}$ and we let $\|\mathbf{b}\|$ denote their Euclidean norm. For vectors $(\mathbf{b}_1, \ldots, \mathbf{b}_k)$, we construct a basis matrix $\mathbf{B}$ consisting of rows $\mathbf{b}_i$. For linearly independent $(\mathbf{b}_1, \ldots, \mathbf{b}_k) \in \mathbb{R}^m$, the *fundamental domain* $\mathcal{P}_{1/2}(\mathbf{B})$ is $\left\{ \sum_{i=1}^k c_i \mathbf{b}_i \colon c_i \in [-\frac{1}{2}, \frac{1}{2}) \right\}$. The *Gram-Schmidt orthogonalization* $\widetilde{\mathbf{B}} = (\widetilde{\mathbf{b}}_1, \ldots, \widetilde{\mathbf{b}}_k)$ is obtained iteratively by setting $\widetilde{\mathbf{b}}_1 = \mathbf{b}_1$ and $\widetilde{\mathbf{b}}_i$ as the orthogonal projection of $\mathbf{b}_i$ on $(\mathbf{b}_1, \ldots, \mathbf{b}_{i-1})^{\perp}$ for $i = 2, \ldots, k$. This orthogonalization process can be described via matrix-decomposition $\mathbf{B} = \mu \widetilde{\mathbf{B}}$, where μ is a lower-triangular matrix with $\mu_{i,j} = \langle \mathbf{b}_i, \widetilde{\mathbf{b}}_j \rangle / \|\widetilde{\mathbf{b}}_j\|^2$ for $i \geq j$.

---

[1] https://github.com/pfasante/cvp-enum.

We deal with a q-ary lattice with basis $\mathbf{B}$:

$$\Lambda_q(\mathbf{B}) = \Big\{ \mathbf{y} \in \mathbb{Z}^m : \mathbf{y} = \sum_{i=1}^{k} z_i \cdot \mathbf{b}_i \mod q : z_i \in \mathbb{Z} \Big\}.$$

Vectors from this lattice are in $\mathrm{Im}(\mathbf{B})$. The kernel of matrix $\mathbf{B}$ forms another lattice $\Lambda_q^{\perp}(\mathbf{B}) = \{ \mathbf{x} \in \mathbb{Z}^k : \mathbf{x}\mathbf{B} = 0 \mod q \}$. For a lattice $\Lambda(\mathbf{B})$, the first successive minimum $\lambda_1(\Lambda(\mathbf{B}))$ is the length of its shortest vector.

In this paper we describe an algorithm to solve the so-called *Bounded Distance Decoding Problem* (BDD) and the most cryptographically relevant instance of it, the *Learning with Errors Problem* (LWE). BDD asks to find a lattice point $\mathbf{v}$ closest to a given point $\mathbf{t} \in \mathbb{R}^m$ under the promise that $\|\mathbf{v} - \mathbf{t}\| = \|\mathbf{e}\| \le R$, where R is usually much smaller than the lattice's packing radius. In the LWE case, we know in addition that the error-vector $\mathbf{e}$ is distributed as a *discrete Gaussian* i.e. its probability distribution, denoted D_s, is proportional to $\exp(-\pi\|\mathbf{e}\|^2/s^2)$. In LWE it suffices to consider the integer lattice $\mathbb{Z}$ as a support for the error distribution, so we used the Ziggurat Algorithm implemented in [15] for the sampling. A discrete Gaussian sampler over *any* lattice can be found in [16].

Apart from the scaled standard deviation s, the LWE problem is parametrized by a dimension $n \ge 1$, an integer modulus $q = \mathrm{poly}(n)$ and the number of LWE samples m. For secret $\mathbf{s} \in \mathbb{Z}_q^n$, an LWE sample is obtained by choosing a vector $\mathbf{a} \in \mathbb{Z}_q^n$ uniformly at random, an error $e \leftarrow D_s$, and outputting m pairs $(\mathbf{a}, t = \langle \mathbf{a}, \mathbf{s} \rangle + e \mod q) \in \mathbb{Z}_q^n \times \mathbb{Z}_q$. Typically a cryptosystem reveals $m = \Theta(n)$ samples (commonly as a public key) and for lattice-based attack we consider $m \le 2n$.

We write the obtained m pairs as $(\mathbf{A}, \mathbf{t} = \mathbf{s}\mathbf{A} + \mathbf{e} \mod q) \in \mathbb{Z}^{n \times m} \times \mathbb{Z}^m$ for $\mathbf{t} = (t_1, \ldots, t_m)$, $\mathbf{e} = (e_1, \ldots, e_m)$ and the columns of matrix $\mathbf{A}$ are composed of the $\mathbf{a}_i$. From this it is easy to see that (the search version of) the LWE problem is an average-case hard Bounded Distance Decoding problem for the q-ary lattice $\Lambda(\mathbf{A}) = \{ \mathbf{z} \in \mathbb{Z}^m : \exists \mathbf{s} \in \mathbb{Z}_q^n \text{ s.t. } \mathbf{z} = \mathbf{s}\mathbf{A} \mod q \}$, i.e. $\mathbf{t}$ is close to a linear combination of rows of $\mathbf{A}$. Assuming $\mathbf{A}$ is full-rank (which is the case w.h.p.), its determinant is $\det(\Lambda(\mathbf{A})) = q^{m-n}$ and the rows of the matrix below form its basis over $\mathbb{Z}^m$

$$\mathbf{B} = \begin{pmatrix} \mathbf{A}' & \mathbf{I}_{m-n} \\ q\mathbf{I}_{m-n} & \mathbf{0} \end{pmatrix} \in \mathbb{Z}^{m \times m}, \tag{1}$$

where $\mathbf{A} = (\mathbf{A}'|\mathbf{I}_{m-n})$ and $\mathbf{A}' \in \mathbb{Z}^{n \times n}$ is a row-reduced echelon form of $\mathbf{A}$.

Reduce-then-decode is our approach to solve LWE in practice. For the reduction step, we β-BKZ reduce the basis defined in Eq. (1). The reduction's running time is determined by m and the running time of an SVP-solver on a lattice of dimension β. Our decoding step is described in the subsequent section.

3   Enumeration Tree

Let us describe our implementation of the tree-traversal algorithm for the BDD enumeration. Recall that a BDD instance is given by a (BKZ-reduced) basis

$\mathbf{B} \in \mathbb{Z}^{m \times m}$ and a target $\mathbf{t} \in \mathbb{Z}^m$ that is close to a lattice point $\mathbf{v} = \sum_{k=1}^{m} v_k \mathbf{b}_k$. Our goal is to find the coordinates v_k. Knowing that $\mathbf{t} - \mathbf{v} = \mathbf{e}$ is short, we enumerate over all coefficient vectors $(v_m, \ldots, v_1)$ that result in a vector close to $\mathbf{t}$. A way to find the coordinates v_k via iterative projections is the Nearest Plane Algorithm of Babai [17]. In the k-th iteration ($k = m, \ldots, 1$), the target $\mathbf{t}$ is projected onto $\mathrm{Span}(\mathbf{b}_1, \ldots, \mathbf{b}_{k-1})^{\perp}$ choosing the closest translate of the sub-lattice $\Lambda(\mathbf{b}_1, \ldots, \mathbf{b}_{k-1})$ (line 4, Algorithm 1) and the projected vector becomes a new target (line 5). The procedure results in a closest vector $\mathbf{v}$, s.t. $\|\mathbf{e}\| \leq 1/2 \sqrt{\sum_{k=1}^{m} \|\widetilde{\mathbf{b}}_k\|^2}$. An iterative version of the Nearest Plane Algorithm is presented in Algorithm 1.

Algorithm 1. Babai's NearestPlane $(\mathbf{B}, \mathbf{t})$

Input: $\mathbf{B} = (\mathbf{b}_1, \ldots, \mathbf{b}_m) \in \mathbb{Z}^{m \times m}, \mathbf{t} \in \mathbb{Z}^m$
Output: $\mathbf{v} \in \mathcal{L}(\mathbf{B})$ close to $\mathbf{t}$ and $e = \|\mathbf{e}\| = \|\mathbf{t} - \mathbf{e}\|$
1: $\mathbf{t}^{(m)} \leftarrow \mathbf{t}, e^{(m)} \leftarrow 0, k \leftarrow m$.
2: Let $\widetilde{\mathbf{B}} \leftarrow \mathrm{GSO}(\mathbf{B})$
3: **while** $k > 0$ **do**
4:     $c^{(k)} \leftarrow \langle \mathbf{t}^{(k)}, \frac{\widetilde{\mathbf{b}}_k}{\|\widetilde{\mathbf{b}}_k\|^2} \rangle$ $\triangleright$ Compute the closest hyperplane $U^{(k)}$
5:     $\mathbf{t}^{(k-1)} \leftarrow \mathbf{t}^{(k)} - \lceil c^{(k)} \rfloor \mathbf{b}_k$ $\triangleright$ Project onto $U^{(k)} = c^{(k)} \widetilde{\mathbf{b}}_k + \mathrm{Span}(\mathbf{b}_1, \ldots, \mathbf{b}_{k-1})$
6:     $e^{(k-1)} \leftarrow e^{(k)} + (c^{(k)} - \lceil c^{(k)} \rfloor)^2 \|\widetilde{\mathbf{b}}_k\|^2$ $\triangleright$ Compute the squared error-length
7:     $k \leftarrow k - 1$
8: **return** $(\mathbf{t} - \mathbf{t}^{(0)}, e^0)$

While the above Nearest Plane procedure is very efficient even for large m, the output $\mathbf{t}^{(0)}$ is the correct one only if $\mathbf{e} \in \mathcal{P}_{1/2}(\mathbf{B})$. As a given basis $\mathbf{B}$ may be 'far away' from being orthogonal, the choice of the closest hyperplane (line 4, Algorithm 1) may not lead to the actual closest vector. On each iteration, the additive factor to the squared error-length can be as large as $\frac{1}{2}\|\widetilde{\mathbf{b}}\|^2$.

To mitigate the non-orthogonality of the input basis, Lindner and Peikert [3] proposed to project on *several* close hyperplanes, i.e. in Step 5 of Algorithm 1, $c_i^{(k)}$, $1 \leq i \leq d_k$ are chosen, resulting in d_k new targets $t_i^{(k-1)}$. To guarantee a constant success probability, d_k must be chosen such that $d_k \cdot \|\widetilde{\mathbf{b}}_k\| > 2e_k$, i.e. the error-vector $\mathbf{e}$ must be contained in the stretched fundamental parallelepiped $\mathcal{P}_{1/2}(\mathbf{B} \cdot \mathrm{diag}(d_1, \ldots d_m))$. For the LWE-case the sequence $(d_i)_{i=1,\ldots,m}$ can be computed given $(\|\widetilde{\mathbf{b}}_i\|)_{i=1,\ldots,m}$ and the parameter s.

Our algorithm is implemented as a depth-first tree traversal where each level-k node ($k = m, \ldots, 1$), represents a partial assignment $(c^{(m)}, \ldots, c^{(k)})$ of the target $\mathbf{t}^{(k)} = \mathbf{t} - \sum_{i=k}^{m} c^{(i)} \mathbf{b}_i$. A children-set for this node is generated by projecting $\mathbf{t}^{(k)}$ onto d_{k-1} closest hyperplanes $U_i^{(k-1)} = c_i^{(k-1)} \widetilde{\mathbf{b}}_{k-1} + \mathrm{Span}(\mathbf{b}_1, \ldots, \mathbf{b}_{m-k})$, $i = 1, \ldots, d_{k-1}$. Each leaf is a candidate-solution $v = \sum_{i=1}^{m} c^{(i)} \mathbf{b}_i$, whose corresponding error is checked against the currently shortest. Figure 1a. represents the case $m = 3$, $d_1 = 3$, $d_2 = 2$, $d_1 = 1$.

Note that the length of an error-vector is not explicitly bounded by the Lindner-Peikert enumeration tree. Instead, one imposes a restriction on its

LWE Decoding

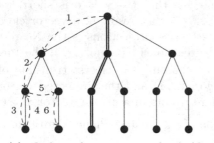
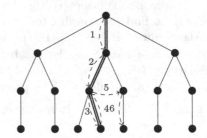

(a) Order of tree-traversal of Algorithm 2. The left-most children are visited first.

(b) Order of tree-traversal of the implemented best-first search.

Fig. 1. Orders of tree-traversal

individual coordinates e_i. In Liu and Nguyen's Length Pruning Algorithm [4], the number of children for a node is determined only by the length of the error accumulated so far and hence, as opposed to the Lindner-Peikert strategy, might differ for two nodes on the same level. For Gaussian error, one would expect that on level k the value $e^{(k-1)}$ (line 6, Algorithm 1) satisfies $e^{(k-1)} < R_k \approx s^2(m-k+1)$ resulting in $e^{(0)} = \|\mathbf{e}\| = s^2 m$. This strategy is called *Linear Pruning* and is used in our experiments. We do not consider the so-called *Extreme Pruning* strategy where the bounds satisfy $R_k \ll s^2(m-k+1)$ (i.e. the success probability is very low, but boosted via re-randomizing the basis and repeating). While Extreme Pruning proved to be more efficient in the SVP setting [18], in the BDD case re-randomizing an instance causes re-running the expensive BKZ reduction (as the re-randomization distorts the reducedness).

Both enumeration strategies, Lindner-Peikert and Length Pruning, can be generalized by considering a family of bounding functions $B^{(k)} : \mathbb{Q} \to \mathbb{Q}$, $1 \leq k \leq m$ that take a squared error-length as input and output the remaining allowed length depending on the chosen strategy. From the value $B^{(k)}(e^{(k)})$, one can compute the number of children for a node on level k (line 6, Algorithm 2). The Lindner-Peikert bounding function ignores the error-length setting $B^{(k)} = (d_k \|\widetilde{\mathbf{b}}_k\|)^2$ by having d_k children for *all* k-level nodes. For the Length Pruning of [4], we set $B^{(k)} = R_k - e^{(k)}$. Our BDD Enumeration in Algorithm 2 describes the depth-first tree-traversal under this generalization.

Algorithm 2 constructs an enumeration tree with a k-level node storing a target-vector $\mathbf{t}^{(k-1)}$, a coefficient vector $c^{(k)}$ of a candidate-solution $\sum_{k=1}^{m} c^{(k)}\mathbf{b}_k$ and an accumulated error-length $e^{(k-1)}$ (lines 10–12). A path from a root ($k = m$) to a leaf ($k = 1$) gives one candidate-solution $\mathbf{v} = \sum_{k=1}^{m} c^{(k)}\mathbf{b}_k$ with error-length $e^{(0)} = \mathbf{t} - \mathbf{v}$. The path with the minimal error-value is the output of the algorithm.

Notice that different paths have different success probabilities: the path corresponding to Babai's solution $\sum_{k=1}^{m} c^{(k)}\mathbf{b}_k$ is the most promising one. So instead

---

Algorithm 2. BDD Enumeration $(\mathbf{B}, \mathbf{t}, B^{(k)})$

Input: $\mathbf{B} = (\mathbf{b}_1, \ldots, \mathbf{b}_m) \in \mathbb{Z}^{m \times m}, \mathbf{t} \in \mathbb{Z}^m$, a family of bounding functions $B^{(k)} : \mathbb{Q} \rightarrow \mathbb{Q}$
Output: $\mathbf{v} \in \mathcal{L}(\mathbf{B})$ close to $\mathbf{t}$ and $e = \|\mathbf{e}\| = \|\mathbf{t} - \mathbf{e}\|$

1:    $\mathbf{t}^{(m)} \leftarrow \mathbf{t}, e^{(m)} \leftarrow 0, k \leftarrow m$.
2:    Let $\widetilde{\mathbf{B}} \leftarrow \text{GSO}(\mathbf{B})$
3:    $(\mathbf{t}^{(0)}, \text{minLen}) \leftarrow \text{NearestPlane}(\mathbf{B}, \mathbf{t})$
4: **while** (true) **do**
5:     **if** $(k > 0)$ **then**
6:       $Int \leftarrow \sqrt{B^{(k)}(e^{(k)})}/\|\widetilde{\mathbf{b}}_k\|$ $\triangleright$ Number of children
7:       $c^* \leftarrow \langle \mathbf{t}^{(k)}, \widetilde{\mathbf{b}}_k \rangle / \|\widetilde{\mathbf{b}}_k\|^2$
8:       $c_{\min} \leftarrow \lceil c^* - \frac{1}{2} Int \rceil$ $\triangleright$ Left-most child
9:       $c_{\max} \leftarrow \lfloor c^* + \frac{1}{2} Int \rfloor$ $\triangleright$ Right-most child
10:      $c^{(k)} \leftarrow c_{\min}$
11:      $\mathbf{t}^{(k-1)} \leftarrow \mathbf{t}^{(k)} - c^{(k)} \mathbf{b}_k$ $\triangleright$ Project onto $U^{(k)} = c^{(k)} \widetilde{\mathbf{b}}_k + \text{Span}(\mathbf{b}_1, \ldots, \mathbf{b}_{k-1})$
12:      $e^{(k-1)} \leftarrow e^{(k)} + (c^{(k)} - c^*)^2 \|\widetilde{\mathbf{b}}_k\|^2$ $\triangleright$ Compute the squared error-length
13:      $k \leftarrow k - 1$ $\triangleright$ Go down the tree
14:     **else** $\triangleright$ On a leaf
15:      **if** $(e^{(k)} < \text{minLen})$ **then**
16:       $\mathbf{v} \leftarrow \sum_{i=1}^{k} c^{(i)} \mathbf{b}_i$ $\triangleright$ Current best solution
17:       $\text{minLen} = e^{(k)}$
18:      **repeat** $\triangleright$ Traverse up
19:       **if** $(k = 0$ AND $c^{(k)} > c_{\max})$ **then** $\triangleright$ On the root, no right siblings
20:        **return** $(\mathbf{v}, \text{minLen})$
21:       $k \leftarrow k + 1$
22:      **until** $(c^{(k)} \geq c_{\max})$
23:      $c^{(k)} \leftarrow c^{(k)} + 1$ $\triangleright$ Traverse to the right sibling
24:      $\mathbf{t}^{(k-1)} \leftarrow \mathbf{t}^{(k)} - \lceil c^{(k)} \rfloor \mathbf{b}_k$
25:      $e^{(k-1)} \leftarrow e^{(k)} + (c^{(k)} - \lceil c^{(k)} \rfloor)^2 \|\widetilde{\mathbf{b}}_k\|^2$
26: **return** $(\mathbf{t}^{(0)}, e^{(0)})$

---

of choosing the left-most child and traversing its sub-tree, the implemented tree-traversal algorithm chooses Babai's path first, i.e. a 'middle' child of a node, and then examines all nearby paths. This strategy of ordering the paths by decreasing success probability is called *Length best first search* (see Fig. 1b).

3.1 Parallel Implementation

In Algorithm 2, sub-tree traversals for two different nodes on the same level are independent, so we can parallelize the BDD Enumeration. Let #NThreads be the number of threads (processors) available. Our goal is to determine the upper-most level k having at least as many nodes #N(k) as #NThreads. Then we can traverse the #N(k) sub-trees in parallel by calling Algorithm 2 on each thread.

We start traversing the enumeration tree in a *breadth-first* manner using a queue. In a breadth-first traversal, once all the nodes of level k are visited, the queue contains all their children (i.e. all the nodes of level $k + 1$), thus their number $\#N(k+1)$ can be computed. Once a level k with $\#N(k) \geq c \cdot \#NThreads$ for some small constant $c \geq 1$ is found, we stop the breadth-first traversal and start Algorithm 2 for each of the $\#N(k)$ sub-trees in an own thread. The benefit of having $c > 1$ is that whenever one of the threads finishes quickly, it can be assigned to traverse another sub-tree. This strategy compensates for imbalanced sizes of sub-trees.

This breadth-first traversal is described in Algorithm 3. At the root we have $\#N(m) = 1$. The associated data to each node are the target $\mathbf{t}^{(m-1)}$, the error-length $e^{(m-1)}$ and the partial solution $\mathbf{s}^{(m-1)}$. We store them in queues Q_t, Q_e, Q_s. Traversing the tree down is realized via dequeuing the first element from a queue (line 9) and enqueuing its children into the queue. When Algorithm 3 terminates, we spawn a thread that receives as input a target $\mathbf{t}^{(k)}$ from Q_t, an accumulated so far error-length $e^{(k)} \in Q_e$, a partial solution $\mathbf{s}^{(k-1)} \in Q_s$, GSO-lengths $(\|\widetilde{\mathbf{b}}_{k-1}\|, \ldots, \|\widetilde{\mathbf{b}}_1\|)$ and bounding functions $B^{(i)}$, $1 \leq i \leq k-1$. Since the number of possible threads is usually a small constant, there is no blow-up in memory usage in the breadth-first traversal.

Note that for a family of bounding functions $B^{(k)}$ that allows to compute the number of children per node without actually traversing the tree, e.g. the Lindner-Peikert bounding strategy, it is easy to find the level where we start parallelization. In case of Lindner-Peikert, $\#N(k) = \prod_{i=m}^{m-k} d_i$ and hence, we simply compute the largest level k where $\#N(k) \geq c \cdot \#NThreads$.

Algorithm 3. Traverse Breadth-First $(\mathbf{B}, \mathbf{t}, B^{(k)})$

Input: $\mathbf{B} = (\mathbf{b}_1, \ldots, \mathbf{b}_m) \in \mathbb{Z}^{m \times m}, \mathbf{t} \in \mathbb{Z}^m$, a family of bounding functions $B^{(k)}$, $\#NThreads \in \mathbb{Z}, c \in \mathbb{Z}$
Output: An array $(\mathbf{t}^{(k)})_i$ of size $\#N(k)$, where $\#N(k) \geq c \cdot \#NThreads$, an array of associated error-length $(e^{(k)})_i$, an array of associated partial solutions $(\mathbf{s}^{(k)})_i$, $1 \leq i \leq \#N(k)$.

```
 1:  Initialize queues Q_t, Q_e, Q_s
 2:  Q_t.Enqueue(t), Q_e.Enqueue(0), Q_s.Enqueue(0)
 3:  Let B̃ ← GSO(B)
 4:  #N(m) ← 1
 5:  k ← m - 1
 6:  while (#N(k + 1) < c · #NThreads) do
 7:      #N(k) ← 0
 8:      for j = 1 ... #N(k + 1) do
 9:          t ← Q_t.Dequeue(), e ← Q_e.Dequeue(), s ← Q_s.Dequeue()
10:          #N(k) ← #N(k) + ⌈√(B^(m)(e))/‖b̃_m‖⌉
11:          c* ← ⟨t, b̃_m⟩/‖b̃_m‖²
12:          for i = 0 ... ⌈√(B^(m)(e))/‖b̃_m‖⌉ - 1 do
13:              Q_t.Enqueue(t - ⌈c* ± i⌋b_k)
14:              Q_e.Enqueue(e + (c* - ⌈c* ± i⌋)²‖b̃_k‖²)
15:              Q_s.Enqueue(s + ⌈c* ± i⌋b_k)
16:      k ← k - 1
17:  return (Q_t, Q_e, Q_s)
```

4   Variants of LWE

Binary Secret LWE. Recent results on the BKW algorithm for LWE [6,7] show that BKW's running time can be significantly sped up for small LWE secret vectors **s**. For a binary secret, the complexity drops from fully exponential to $2^{\mathcal{O}(n/\log\log n)}$, and Kirchner and Fouque [7] report on a successful secret-recovery for $n = 128$ within 13 hours using 2^{28} LWE samples.

Lattice-based techniques in turn can also profit from the fact that the secret is small (smaller than the error). As described by Bai and Galbraith [2], one transforms a BDD instance $(\Lambda(\mathbf{A}), \mathbf{b} = \mathbf{sA} + \mathbf{e})$ with error **e** into a BDD instance

$$\left(\Lambda_q^{\perp}\begin{pmatrix}\mathbf{I}_m \\ \mathbf{A}\end{pmatrix}, (\mathbf{b}, \mathbf{0}^n)\right) \tag{2}$$

with error $(\mathbf{e}, \mathbf{s})$. The instance is correctly defined since

$$((\mathbf{e}, \mathbf{s}) - (\mathbf{b}, \mathbf{0}^n))\begin{pmatrix}\mathbf{I}_m \\ \mathbf{A}\end{pmatrix} = 0 \mod q.$$

The lattice $\Lambda_q^{\perp}\begin{pmatrix}\mathbf{I}_m \\ \mathbf{A}\end{pmatrix} \in \mathbb{Z}^{n+m}$ is generated by the rows of $\mathbf{A}^{\perp}$, where

$$\mathbf{A}^{\perp} = \begin{pmatrix}-\mathbf{A}|\mathbf{I}_n \\ q\mathbf{I}_{n+m}\end{pmatrix}.$$

We run the BDD Enumeration of Algorithm 2 on instances defined by Eq. (2) (see Sect. 5, Table 1).

Binary Matrix. To implement an LWE-based encryption on lightweight devices, Galbraith [12] proposed not to store the whole random matrix $\mathbf{A} \in \mathbb{Z}_q^{n \times m}$, but to generate the entries of a *binary* $\mathbf{A} \in \mathbb{Z}_2^{n \times m}$ via some PRNG. Galbraith's ciphertexts are of the form $(C_1, C_2) = (\mathbf{Au}, \langle \mathbf{u}, \mathbf{b}\rangle + m\lceil q/2\rceil \mod q)$ for a message $m \in \{0, 1\}$, some random $\mathbf{u} \in \{0, 1\}^m$ and a modulus $q \in \mathbb{Z}$. The task is to recover **u** given $(\mathbf{A}, \mathbf{Au})$.

Let us describe a simple lattice-attack on the instance $(\mathbf{A}, \mathbf{Au})$. Notice that $C_1 = \mathbf{Au}$ holds over $\mathbb{Z}$ and, hence, over $\mathbb{Z}_q$ for large enough modulus q since we expect to have $\mathbf{Au} \approx m/4$. First, we find any solution **w** for $\mathbf{Aw} = C_1 \mod q$. Note that

$$(\mathbf{w} - \mathbf{u}) \in \ker(\mathbf{A}).$$

So we have a BDD instance $(\Lambda_q^{\perp}(\mathbf{A}), \mathbf{w})$, with **u** as the error-vector of length $m/2$ and a lattice with $\det(\Lambda_q^{\perp}(\mathbf{A})) = q^n$. Since we can freely choose q to be as large as we want, we can guarantee that $\lambda_1(\Lambda_q^{\perp}(\mathbf{A})) \gg m/2$. Such an instance can be solved by first running β-BKZ for some small constant β and then Babai's CVP algorithm.

As a challenge, Galbraith proposes a parameter-set $(n = 256, m = 400)$ and estimates that computing **u** from $\mathbf{Au}$ should take around one day. We solve this instance using NTL's BKZ implementation with $\beta = 4$ and $q = 500009$ in 4.5 hours (see Table 1).

5   Implementation Results

We implemented our BDD enumeration step with Lindner-Peikert's Nearest Planes and Liu-Nguyen's Linear Length Pruning. All programs are written in C++ and we used C++11 STL for implementing the threading. Our tests were performed on the Ruhr-University's "Crypto Crunching Cluster" (C3) which consists of one master node to schedule jobs and four computing nodes. Each computing node has four AMD Bulldozer Opteron 6276 CPUs, and thus 64 cores, running at 2.3 GHz and 256 GByte of RAM. The results of our experiments are presented in Table 1.

Our experiments are run on

1. standard LWE parameters (top part of Table 1),
2. LWE with binary- and ternary-error (middle part),
3. binary secret LWE,
4. the space-efficient proposal of Galbraith (bottom).

Let us describe the results of our experiments in more details.

1. For the standard LWE case and Gaussian error, the dimensions we success- fully attacked in several hours are within the interval $n \in [70, 100]$. We achieve an almost perfect speed-up – the gained factor in the running times is roughly equal to the number of processors (#NThreads). This shows that our distribution of processors balances the workload. The largest success- fully decoded parameters are $(n = 100, s = 4)$. For comparison, the instance $(n = 192, s = 9)$ achieves 2^{87}-security level as estimated in [3].
2. Not surprisingly, once the error is changed from Gaussian to binary or ternary, the decoding attack performs better, but balancing the BKZ-reduction and BDD steps becomes more subtle, since a smaller error is more favourable for the decoding. Hence, such an instance can be attacked with a less reduced basis than a similar LWE instance with Gaussian noise. To balance the reduc- tion and enumeration steps, we first choose a smaller block-size β for the reduction and, second, choose fewer than $2n$ samples. Our choice for m addi- tionally lowers the running time of BKZ-reduction, while it still guarantees suc- cessful decoding. The maximal dimension achieved in this regime is $n = 130$. Binary and ternary errors are especially interesting for cryptanalysis of NTRU [21] and for special variants of LWE considered by Micciancio and Peikert [19] and Buchmann et al. [20].
3. For binary secret we are able to attack dimensions $n \in [100, 140]$. In contrast to the BKW attack of Kirchner and Fouque [7], we choose as few samples as possible to aid the reduction step (while keeping a unique solution). More concretely, for $n = 130$, we used only $m = 150$ samples, as opposed to $m = 2^{28}$ samples required in the BKW attack. Our attack takes only 7.6h, which is faster than the reported 13h in [7]. Moreover, we are able to attack dimension $n = 140$ for which we benefit again from parallelization.
4. For the space-efficient binary-matrix case of [12], we choose $q = 50009$ and solve the instance $(n = 256, m = 400)$ in 4.5h with $\beta = 4$ and Babai's CVP algorithm.

Table 1. Running-times of the BDD-decoding attack on LWE.The superscript B indicates that Babai's Nearest Plane Algorithm already solved the instance. Uniform binary and ternary error distributions are denoted by $s = \{0,1\}$ and $s = \{-1,0,1\}$.

LWE-parameters						BKZ-reduction	Lindner-Peikert		Length Pruning	
n	q	s	m	β	T		#NThreads	T	#NThreads	T
70	4093	6	140	15	41min		—	—	1	14h
70	4093	6	140	15	41min		10	9.6h	10	1.5h
70	4093	6	140	20	65min		—	—	1	44min
70	4093	6	140	20	65min		—	—	10	5min
80	4093	5	150	25	4.3h		1	55h	1	13h
80	4093	5	150	25	4.3h		10	45h	10	1.5h
80	4093	5	150	25	4.3h		20	12h	20	50min
90	4093	4	170	22	11.3h		—	—	1	35.5h
90	4093	4	170	22	11.3h		20	49.5h	10	3.6h
100	4093	4	200	20	6.9h		24	3.0h	24	2.7h
Binary error [19, 20]										
100	4093	$\{0,1\}$	140	4	1h		—	—	1	2.5min
110	4093	$\{0,1\}$	160	5	1.4h		1	5.7h	1	3.1h
120	4093	$\{0,1\}$	170	10	1.6h		—	—	1	27min
130	4093	$\{0,1\}$	190	18	4.5h		—	—	1	13.5h
130	4093	$\{0,1\}$	190	18	4.5h		—	—	10	1.7h
130	4093	$\{0,1\}$	200	10	3.1h		—	—	1	1h
130	4093	$\{0,1\}$	260	20	30.3h		16	1.8min	16	75s
Ternary error [21]										
100	4093	$\{-1,0,1\}$	140	10	50min		1	5.6h	1	9min
100	4093	$\{-1,0,1\}$	200	7	2.2h		1	17s	1	17s
110	4093	$\{-1,0,1\}$	180	7	1.5h		1	10min	1	10min
120	4093	$\{-1,0,1\}$	240	7	4.5h		20	13h	20	14min
128	4093	$\{-1,0,1\}$	256	20	28.8h		30	92s	30	43s
Binary secret										
120	16411	7	150	10	2.3h		—	—	1	2h
130	16411	5	150	15	6.6h		—	—	1	1h
140	16411	5	170	15	12h		—	—	1	16.3h
140	16411	5	170	15	12h		—	—	10	1.7h
Binary matrix SIS [12]										
256	500009	–	400	4	4.5h		1	2min[B]	—	—
280	500009	–	440	4	6.5h		1	3min[B]	—	—

All our experiments confirm that Linear Length Pruning works much more efficient than Lindner-Peikert Decoding for most of the considered variants of LWE. Another observation is that lowering the number of samples significantly speeds up the reduction in practice and slows down the decoding step. Since the latter can be parallelized, a proper choice of the number of samples leads to a better trade-off between the reduction and enumeration.

Acknowledgments. We thank Gottfried Herold and the anonymous reviews for their helpful feedback and valuable suggestions. Elena Kirshanova and Friedrich Wiemer were supported by UbiCrypt, the research training group 1817/1 funded by the DFG.

References

1. Regev, O.: On lattices, learning with errors, random linear codes, cryptography. In: STOC 2005, pp. 84–93. ACM (2005)
2. Bai, S., Galbraith, S.D.: Lattice decoding attacks on binary LWE. In: Susilo, W., Mu, Y. (eds.) ACISP 2014. LNCS, vol. 8544, pp. 322–337. Springer, Heidelberg (2014). https://eprint.iacr.org/2013/839
3. Lindner, R., Peikert, C.: Better key sizes (and attacks) for lwe-based encryption. In: Kiayias, A. (ed.) CT-RSA 2011. LNCS, vol. 6558, pp. 319–339. Springer, Heidelberg (2011). https://eprint.iacr.org/2010/613
4. Liu, M., Nguyen, P.Q.: Solving BDD by enumeration: an update. In: Dawson, E. (ed.) CT-RSA 2013. LNCS, vol. 7779, pp. 293–309. Springer, Heidelberg (2013)
5. Albrecht, M.R., Cid, C., Faugère, J., Fitzpatrick, R., Perret, L.: On the complexity of the BKW algorithm on LWE. Des. Codes Crypt. **74**(2), 325–354 (2015)
6. Guo, Q., Johansson, T., Stankovski, P.: Coded-BKW: solving LWE using lattice codes. In: Gennaro, R., Robshaw, M. (eds.) CRYPTO 2015. LNCS, vol. 9215, pp. 23–42. Springer, Heidelberg (2015). doi:10.1007/978-3-662-47989-6_2
7. Kirchner, P., Fouque, P.-A.: An improved BKW algorithm for LWE with applications to cryptography and lattices. In: Gennaro, R., Robshaw, M. (eds.) CRYPTO 2015. LNCS, vol. 9215. Springer, Heidelberg (2015). doi:10.1007/978-3-662-47989-6_3. https://eprint.iacr.org/2015/552
8. Arora, S., Ge, R.: New algorithms for learning in presence of errors. In: Aceto, L., Henzinger, M., Sgall, J. (eds.) ICALP 2011, Part I. LNCS, vol. 6755, pp. 403–415. Springer, Heidelberg (2011)
9. Albrecht, M.R., Player, R., Scott, S.: On the concrete hardness of learning with errors. J. Math. Cryptology **9**(3), 169–203 (2015). https://eprint.iacr.org/2015/046
10. Kannan, R.: Minkowski's convex body theorem, integer programming. In: Mathematics of Operations Research 12.3 , pp. 415–440. ISSN: 0364765X, 15265471 (1987)
11. Luzzi, L., Stehlé, D., Ling, C.: Decoding by embedding: correct decoding radius and DMT optimality. IEEE Trans. Inf. Theory **59**(5), 2960–2973 (2013)
12. Galbraith, S. D.: Space-efficient variants of cryptosystems based on learning with errors. https://www.math.auckland.ac.nz/~sgal018/compact-LWE.pdf
13. Shoup, V.: Number theory library 9.6.2 (NTL) for C++. http://www.shoup.net/ntl/
14. Chen, Y., Nguyen, P.Q.: BKZ 2.0: better lattice security estimates. In: Lee, D.H., Wang, X. (eds.) ASIACRYPT 2011. LNCS, vol. 7073, pp. 1–20. Springer, Heidelberg (2011). https://www.iacr.org/archive/asiacrypt2011/70730001/70730001.pdf
15. Buchmann, J., Cabarcas, D., Göpfert, F., Hülsing, A., Weiden, P.: Discrete ziggurat: a time-memory trade-off for sampling from a gaussian distribution over the integers. In: Lange, T., Lauter, K., Lisoněk, P. (eds.) SAC 2013. LNCS, vol. 8282, pp. 402–417. Springer, Heidelberg (2014). https://eprint.iacr.org/2013/510

16. Gentry, C., Peikert, C., Vaikuntanathan, V.: Trapdoors for hard lattices, new cryptographic constructions. In: Dwork, C. (ed.) STOC 2008, pp. 197–206. ACM (2008)
17. Babai, L.: On Lovász lattice reduction, the nearest lattice point problem. In: Mehlhorn, K. (ed.) STACS 1985. LNCS, vol. 182, pp. 13–20. Springer, Heidelberg (1985)
18. Gama, N., Nguyen, P.Q., Regev, O.: Lattice enumeration using extreme pruning. In: Gilbert, H. (ed.) EUROCRYPT 2010. LNCS, vol. 6110, pp. 257–278. Springer, Heidelberg (2010). https://www.iacr.org/archive/eurocrypt2010/66320257/66320257.pdf
19. Micciancio, D., Peikert, C.: Hardness of SIS and LWE with small parameters. In: Canetti, R., Garay, J.A. (eds.) CRYPTO 2013, Part I. LNCS, vol. 8042, pp. 21–39. Springer, Heidelberg (2013). https://eprint.iacr.org/2013/069
20. Buchmann, J., Göpfert, F., Player, R., Wunderer, T.: On the hardness of LWE with binary error: revisiting the hybrid lattice-reduction and meet-in-the-middle attack. In: Pointcheval, D., Nitaj, A., Rachidi, T. (eds.) AFRICACRYPT 2016. LNCS, vol. 9646, pp. 24–43. Springer, Heidelberg (2016). doi:10.1007/978-3-319-31517-1_2. https://eprint.iacr.org/2016/089
21. Hoffstein, J., Pipher, J., Silverman, J.H.: NTRU: a ring-based public key cryptosystem. In: Buhler, J.P. (ed.) ANTS 1998. LNCS, vol. 1423, pp. 267–288. Springer, Heidelberg (1998)

Memory Carving in Embedded Devices: Separate the Wheat from the Chaff

Thomas Gougeon[1]([⊠]), Morgan Barbier[1], Patrick Lacharme[1], Gildas Avoine[2,3], and Christophe Rosenberger[1]

[1] Normandie Univ, ENSICAEN, UNICAEN, CNRS, GREYC, 14000 Caen, France
thomas.gougeon@ensicaen.fr
[2] INSA Rennes, IRISA UMR 6074, Rennes, France
[3] Institut Universitaire de France, Paris, France

Abstract. This paper investigates memory carving techniques for embedded devices. Given that cryptographic material in memory dumps makes carving techniques inefficient, we introduce a methodology to distinguish meaningful information from cryptographic material in small-sized memory dumps. The proposed methodology uses an adaptive boosting technique with statistical tests. Experimented on EMV cards, the methodology recognized 92% of meaningful information and 98 % of cryptographic material.

Keywords: Forensics · Memory carving · Randomness · Embedded devices · Smartcards · Privacy

1 Introduction

Embedded devices usually gather and store personal data about the behaviours of their holders. They are typically low-cost devices including (but not limited to) credit cards, mass transportation passes, electronic passports, keyless entry and start systems, and ski passes. They usually gather and store a lot of personal data, for example an electronic passport contains the identity and the picture of its holder [2], a mass transportation pass may store the last trips of its holder [4], a ski pass may also contain the location of the ski lifts the skier used [21], an EMV card records the last payments done by the customer [8], a car ignition key in recent vehicle contains plenty of information about the car and the behaviour of the driver, including the monthly fuel consumption, the external temperature during the last trip, and the average engine speed. In most cases, the personal data contained in these devices are accessible without requiring any authentication, and can be obtained using, for example, the ISO/IEC 7816 interface or by sniffing a genuine communication between the device and a reader.

Interpreting the meaning of the captured raw data is hard when the system specifications are not available. However, such a task is important today when investigations must be carried out. It can be to find digital evidence for example

© Springer International Publishing Switzerland 2016
M. Manulis et al. (Eds.): ACNS 2016, LNCS 9696, pp. 592–608, 2016.
DOI: 10.1007/978-3-319-39555-5_32

in connection with criminal investigations – when information related to a suspect is stored in a device – or to verify that a system complies with the national privacy regulations.

A large body of literature exists in the field of memory forensics. Many off-the-shelf tools exist, too. The analyses typically focus on hard drives [18] and volatile memories [3]. Analyses of hard drives are typically based on file carving, i.e. a technique that consists in searching for files in the considered data. The main difficulty is the file fragmentation in the system. File carving is consequently performed using machine learning techniques, the entropy of the blocks, or the file headers and footers. The technique targets specific file formats, e.g., PDF, ZIP [5], or file systems such as NTFS [26]. Analyses of volatile memories consist in searching for special strings or signatures, interpreting internal kernel structures, or enumerating and correlating all page frames, in order to retrieve running and terminated processes, open ports, sockets, hidden data, etc.

The analysis of the non-volatile memory of an embedded device differs from classical memory forensics techniques for several reasons. (i) First of all, the memory typically consists of a few kilobits only. (ii) The data available in these devices are poorly structured: in most cases, there are no file headers, sentinels, or field separators. (iii) Home-made encoding systems are commonly used in practice to save memory or to naively hide information. (iv) Performing a bit-by-bit copy of the memory is rarely possible because the only way to access the memory is to use the application program interface (API) or to eavesdrop a genuine communication. This means that the captured data is not necessarily a perfect copy of the memory.

A naive technique to interpret data retrieved from embedded devices (called a dump) consists in applying several encoding functions to the dumps until retrieving the correct one for each information stored. Due to the nature of the dumps, there is unfortunately no oracle that can efficiently determine whether the decoding of the information is correct. As a consequence, the technique outputs many false positives that renders it unusable in practice. Most existing contributions on the memory carving problem for embedded devices consider ad-hoc, hand-made analyses, e.g., for retrieving keys hidden in an EEPROM [6].

There exist few techniques designed for an automatic analysis of embedded devices. A seminal work, though, is due to Ton Van Deursen et al. [25], who investigated the memory carving problem for sets of memory dumps, and applied it to public transportation cards. It is worth noting that they obtained the memory dumps using the API of the cards, meaning that there is no guarantee that the dumps are indeed bit-by-bit copy of the memory. The authors aimed to singulate the memory data fields using the concept of commonalities and dissimilarities applied to a dump set. A commonality occurs for a given bit position if the value of the bit is the same for all the dumps of a given set, whereas a dissimilarity occurs otherwise. Using these commonalities and dissimilarities, as well as contextual information (as data printed on the coupon), the technique deduces the data fields. Once the data fields are singulated, a manual investigation is needed to retrieve the encoding function. The authors applied their technique to the

E-Go System (the public transportation card in Luxembourg) and retrieved a dozen of fields, e.g., the date and time of the last validation. Their work does not provide an automatic interpretation of the data and it requires contextual information to complete the analysis. Another work related to ours is due to Jean-Louis Lanet et al. [14], who investigated the reverse engineering of EEP-ROM in Java Cards. They aim to retrieve the location of the source code and data related to the language(package, class, instance ...). The index of coincidence [10] is used to locate the source code. This approach is not very efficient, though. Still worse, in our case, real-life dumps are generally generated using several (unknown) encoding functions. This makes the calculation of the index of coincidence meaningless. To retrieve the data related to the language [14] uses a pattern matching technique applied to the headers (or metadata), which differ for each type of data. Unfortunately, there is neither header nor metadata in our dumps.

Given the difficulty to retrieve personal data from the memory dump of an embedded device, this work focuses on a narrower problem that consists in distinguishing meaningful information (encoded with ASCII, BCD, etc.) from cryptographic material (ciphered data, hash value, secret key, etc.). The ratio-nale behind this restriction is that cryptographic materials generate many false positives and no personal information can be obtained from these values, assum-ing the algorithms used to create the materials are cryptographically secure. As a consequence, we introduce a technique that *separates the wheat from the chaff*, namely a preliminary step in the forensics process that distinguishes meaningful information from cryptographic materials, considered as random data. Unfortu-nately, the size of the considered dumps does not allow to naively use classical tools (e.g., NIST's statistical tests [19]) that usually require several kilobytes of data to make the statistical tests relevant. Moreover, the tests cannot be directly applied to the data because the considered dumps contain data fields, which must be analysed separately. For the same reason, techniques for locat-ing cryptographic keys hidden in gigabytes of sparse data, proposed by [20] and based on the entropy computation, are not possible on such dumps.

This paper introduces a statistical and automatic recognition technique that distinguishes meaningful information from cryptographic material, obtained from non-volatile memory dumps of embedded devices. The technique, based on a machine learning method, called boosting [9], requires information neither on the dump structure, nor on the application context, for the classification between these two sets of data. The technique is then improved by comparing dumps of different devices belonging to the same application. Our technique reaches quite a high success rate: we applied it to EMV-based dumps and Calypso-based dumps, obtaining a 99 % success rate.

2   Dump Examples

To illustrate the problem considered in this paper, Sect. 2 provides details on two dumps extracted from EMV and Calypso cards. The cards contain elemen-tary files that have been retrieved using the cards' APIs. The files are made of

records. Files can be *linear fixed* (linear data structure of fixed length), *linear variable* (linear data structure of variable length), or *cyclic* (oldest data are erased to store newest data). The information is contained in (non-necessarily contiguous) **fields**, e.g., holder's name, holder's zip code, a cryptographic key, etc. A pedestrian approach has been used to analyse the dumps, given that there does not exist automatic tools that can achieve this task.

2.1 EMV Dump

Figure 1 is a (partial) anonymised dump of a credit card compliant with the EMV specifications [8]. Each numbered line represents a record. The underlined sequences are fields that contain the holder name, the issuer's public key modulus, the amount, and the date of the last transactions.

```
 1.  9F3602004D
 2.  9F13020046
 3.  9F170103
 4.  9F4F109F02069F27019F1A025F2A029A039C01
 5.  70615F201A4A4F484E2F534D4954482E4D5220202020202020202020202020205F300202018C1B9F02069F03069
      F1A0295055F2A029A039C019F37049F45029F4C088D1A8A029F02069F03069F1A0295055F2A029A039C019F37
      049F4C08
 6.  9F49039F3704701A5F25030911015F24031003315A0849750000075922345F340100
 7.  70369F0702FF008E0E00000000000000000020301031F009F0D059800B420009F0E0500504800009F0F05B820B
      4F8005F280202509F4A0182
 8.  70329F080200028F01069F32010392243459245 1B87DA8C05BA7F1DE5DC802BF59D394D6CC034A046F46995E0
      245E437AED7B899
 9.  00000000135040025009781 0032600
10.  00000000177040025009781 0032600
11.  00000000209040025009781 0032500
12.  00000000770740025009781 0032400
```

Fig. 1. Extract of an anonymised credit card dump.

Holder Name. The underlined sequence of the 5th record represents the name of the holder of the credit card (*MR John Smith*) encoded using ASCII and padded with the repeated pattern 0x20.

Issuer's Public Key Modulus. The underlined sequence of the 8th record represents the issuer public key modulus used by the authentication protocol.

Transactions. Records 9 to 12 represent the last four transactions (cash withdrawal) made by the card. The first underlined sequence represents the transaction amount (13.50 euros for the 9th record) and the second one is the date of the transaction (2010/03/26 for the 9th record).

The EMV card contains a cyclic file that stores information on the transactions. For any new transaction, the information in the cyclic file is rotated such that the record about the oldest transaction is discarded to save room for the newest transaction.

2.2   Calypso Dump

Figure 2 is a (partial) anonymised dump of a transportation card compliant with the Calypso specifications [4]. The record names (ICC, Holder1, Holder2, etc.) are available in the specifications, but the content of the records is not defined by Calypso. The content is indeed let to the discretion of the public transportation operator. The provided example illustrates that a single card may contain several encoding rules, and the information in the card is not necessarily byte-aligned.

```
ICC      00 00 00 00 00 00 00 04 00 71 B3 00 00 00 00 00 01 B8 B2 4A 02 50 00 33 01 1A 13 43 00

Holder1  04 00 98 E5 94 C8 02 0D 60 C9 65 C7 D5 90 00 00 00 00 00 00 00 19 75 08 10 92 82 D2 CF
Holder2  F3 6A 68 88 00 00 00 00 00 00 00 00 00 00 00 00 00 00 00 00 00 00 00 00 00 00 00 00 00

EnvHol1  08 38 2B 00 08 BD 59 2A 46 60 C4 81 98 E5 94 C8 02 0D 60 C9 65 C6 41 F4 00 00 00 00 00
EnvHol2  00 00 00 00 00 00 00 00 00 00 00 00 00 00 00 00 00 00 00 00 00 00 00 00 00 00 00 00 00

EvLog1   09 0E E5 92 04 20 60 86 60 00 00 00 00 1C D6 DD 56 40 00 01 C0 00 00 51 08 66 E0 00 00
EvLog2   09 0E E5 7A 04 20 60 86 60 00 00 00 00 1C D6 DD 56 40 00 01 80 00 00 11 08 66 E0 00 00
EvLog3   09 0E E5 5A 04 20 60 86 60 00 00 00 00 1C D6 DD 56 40 00 01 40 00 00 91 08 66 E0 00 00

ConList  11 2B 40 01 80 00 00 00 00 00 00 00 00 00 00 00 00 00 00 00 00 00 00 00 00 00 00 00 00
```

Fig. 2. Anonymised transportation car dump.

On the Holder1 line, the first underlined sequence represents the BCD-encoded birth date of the holder: 1975/08/10. The second underlined sequence that continues on the Holder2 line represents the name of the holder, namely "James Smith". To decode this information the binary representation of the sequence must be split into 5-bit pieces (omitting the first bit of the sequence), which are then decoded with the rule (decimal representation): A=1, B=2, C=3, etc. This information is not byte-aligned.

EvLog1, EvLog2, and EvLog3 are the last three trips performed by the card, stored in a cyclic file. For example, the first underlined sequences in the EvLog lines correspond to the validation time, which is "11:53 am" for EvlLog1. This information is retrieved using the binary representation of 0x592 (omitting the last bit), and converting it to an integer that represents the number of minutes since the beginning of the day. The second underlined sequence in each log represents the validation date of the card during the trip: 2008/12/09, for EvlLog1. This information is retrieved by using the binary representation of 0x5108 (omitting the two first bits) and by converting it to an integer that represents the number of days since 1997/01/01. Other information on this line are the transportation means (metro, bus, tramway), the bus line number, the number of travellers who shared the card for that trip, the station, etc. Additional information can be found in the dump, e.g., the serial number of the card, the manufacturer, the date of manufacture, etc.

3   Statistical Analysis

Retrieving the meaningful information from a dump using a statistical analysis is a difficult problem. In particular, the meaningful information is drowned in a mass of information that include pseudo-random values generated by crypto-graphic means. This paper consequently focuses on a preliminary step in the forensics process that distinguishes meaningful information from cryptographic materials. To start with, we explain below the difficulty to use statistical tests to perform this task in our framework.

3.1   Statistical Tests for (Pseudo-) Random Generators

There exist many statistical tests for random and pseudo-random number gen-erators. The NIST statistical test suite [19] includes the most important ones, while keeping small the redundancy between them. We consequently decided to consider this suite for our experiments.

A statistical test aims to verify a given *null hypothesis*, which is *data are random* in our experiments. A p-value represents the strength of the evidence against the null hypothesis. This p-value is computed from the reference distri-bution of the tested statistical property. NIST uses an asymptotic distribution.

The hypothesis is rejected if the p-value is lower than the level of significance of the test (for example 0.01 or 0.001). Thus, a threshold of 0.01 means that one sequence among 100 sequences is expected to be rejected. A p-value greater than this threshold (respectively lower) indicates that the sequence is considered to be random (respectively non-random) with a 99 % confidence.

The NIST proposes two methods to decide whether or not a generator is suitable for a cryptographic use. A set of sequences is produced by the generator, and its quality is evaluated by means of statistical tests. The result is determined from the rate of sequences that successfully pass each test (p-value greater than the level of significance), or from the uniformity of the p-values.

Even if tests like the *monobit test*, the *longest runs test*, or the *approximate entropy test* could be theoretically applied to short sequences (100 bits), the recommended length is 20, 000-bit long according to the NIST, because asymp-totic approximations are used to determine the limiting distribution. Additional information on these statistical tests can be found in [19].

Moreover, some tests like the *linear complexity test* or the *random excursions test* require at least 10^6 bits to be applied. For short sequences, the NIST sug-gests that asymptotic distribution would be inappropriate and would need to be replaced by exact distributions that, according to them, would commonly be difficult to compute. Thus, [1,7,23] introduce new tests with their exact distri-bution, and [24] suggests a new method to take the decision of randomness for short sequences. Unfortunately, although these approaches can deal with short sequence, they require a significantly large set of such sequences.

3.2 Statistical Tests in Our Context

Dumps obtained from embedded devices typically contain information fields whose lengths are between 1 bit and 1, 024 bits (the size of an entire dump is typically 100-bit to 40, 000-bit long).

Each sequence tested can be seen as an output of a different generator (name, date, ciphered or hashed data, etc.), then for a dump, only one sequence per generator can be tested. Section 3.1 and the above-mentioned arguments justify that most of statistical tests are not suited to short sequences, and the technique used by the NIST to decide whether or not a sequence is random is therefore not applicable. Moreover, there is no technique that use a combination of statistical tests to take the decision of randomness. In our context, the decision of the classification of each bit into meaningful information or cryptographic material is only done by directly comparing a p-value to a threshold, but this threshold need to be determined.

4   Distinguish Cryptographic Materials from Meaningful Information

A first step to distinguish meaningful information from cryptographic materials in a memory dump of an embedded device consists in establishing a methodology to apply the statistical tests. Applying the tests to the entire dump is inefficient. Instead, tests should be applied to each field of the considered dumps. Unfortunately, neither the location nor the size of the fields of the dump are known. The methodology consequently consists in classifying the data (*meaningful* or *cryptographic*) bit by bit, instead of field by field.

A second step consists in performing a learning phase where the methodology is applied to dumps for which the classification of bits is known. This ground truth allows us to determine the decision threshold: the statistical tests provide a score to each bit of the considered dump, and the score is compared to the threshold to decide whether a bit is classified *meaningful* or *cryptographic*.

Then, a boosting algorithm [12] is used, namely a machine learning approach that identifies the most appropriate statistical tests to be applied and how to combine their results.

The identified tests can then be applied to dumps whose ground truth is unknown.

Finally, comparing the classification obtained by this combination of statistical tests on different dumps of the same application, we propose a technique that improves the classification for each dump of the application.

4.1 Applying Statistical Tests to Dumps

Given dumps cannot be split into fields, the classification of the data has to be done bit by bit. However statistical tests are not applicable to single bits. As a consequence, bits need to be grouped into sequences. A methodology that separates a dump into several overlapping sequences is thus proposed.

Let D be a n-bit dump (bits indexed from 1 to n), a *sequence length* ℓ, and a *shift* s, with $0 < s \leq \ell \leq n$. The *shift* represents the distance between two start bits of two consecutive tested sequences. The $i+1$-th tested sequence of D is from the bit index $(i \times s + 1)$ to $i \times s + \ell$ with $0 \leq i \leq \lfloor \frac{n-\ell}{s} \rfloor$. In the case where s does not divide $n - \ell$, the bits from $\lceil \frac{n-\ell}{s} \rceil \times s + l - s + 1$ to n are never tested, and so a last sequence from index $n - \ell + 1$ to n is tested. For each tested sequence, the *statistical test* returns a p-value. Due to the use of a *shift* s potentially shorter than the *sequence length* ℓ, each bit of D is tested in at most $\lceil \frac{\ell}{s} \rceil$ different sequences. All bits of D are therefore related to a variable number of p-values. However, the classification method used in Sect. 4.2 works with the same number of scores per bit. A *score function* that takes p-values as input and outputs a single score is therefore applied to the p-values of each bit. The function can be for example the mean of the p-values.

As a consequence, the previous parameters, namely *sequence length*, *shift*, and *score function* play an important role in the quality on the classifier. Furthermore, some statistical tests require an *internal parameter*. For example, the *serial test* looking at the proportion of each possible block of m bits in the tested sequence, takes m as additional input. It leads to a set of N features, $\mathbf{F} = \{F_j, 1 \leq j \leq N\}$ where each feature is defined by a 5-tuple (*statistical test*, *sequence length*, *shift*, *score function*, *internal parameter*). Applying a feature F_j to D outputs a score set $S_j = \{s_i^j, 1 \leq i \leq n\}$ – as presented in Fig. 3 – where s_i^j is the score assigned by F_j to the i-th bit of D. Applying all the features F_j of $\mathbf{F}$ so generates a set $\mathbf{S} = \{s_i^j, 1 \leq j \leq N, 1 \leq i \leq n\}$ as presented in Fig. 4.

4.2 Bits Classification Using Statistical Tests

In order to decide whether a bit in a dump should be classified as *cryptographic* or *meaningful*, scores returned by each feature need to be compared to a threshold. This process that determines the class of each bit using the scores and a pre-definite threshold is a classifier. Given a n-bit dump D and its score set S_j obtained by applying a feature F_j, and the predetermined threshold t, the classifier C_j computes the prediction $P_j = \{p_i^j \in \{cryptographic, meaningful\}, 1 \leq i \leq n\}$ for D where the prediction of the class of the i-th bit of D is done as following:

$$p_i^j = \begin{cases} cryptographic, & \text{if } s_i^j > t \\ meaningful, & \text{otherwise} \end{cases}$$

Using scores returned by each F_j together with the ground truth of D, represented by $G = \{g_i \in \{cryptographic, meaningful\}, 1 \leq i \leq n\}$, a learning process determines the best threshold to use. We use the learning process described in [22] whose complexity is $\mathcal{O}(n)$ in our case. The best threshold is the one that leads to the classification which is the most similar to the ground truth. Namely, the classification that maximises the recognition rate R_j, where R_j is computed as following:

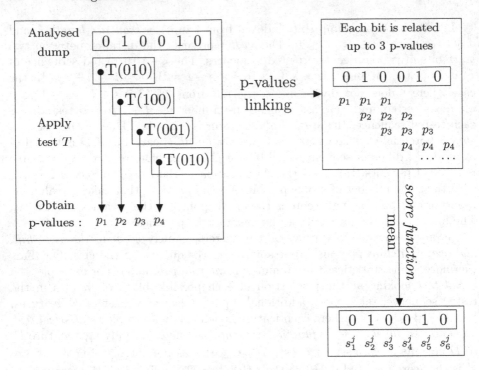

Fig. 3. Applying a feature $F_j = (T, 3, 1, \text{mean}, .)$ on a 6-bit dump D. The process assigns the score set $S_j = \{s_i^j, \ 1 \le i \le 6\}$ to D.

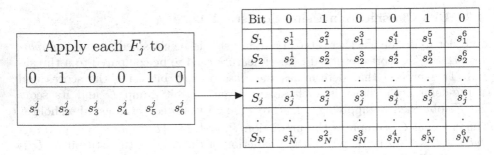

Fig. 4. Set $\mathbf{S} = \{s_i^j, \ 1 \le j \le N\}$ of scores obtained after applying all features F_j of the set $\mathbf{F}$ to a short dump D of 6 bits length.

$$R_j = \frac{\sum_i^n r_i^j}{n} \quad \text{with} \quad r_i^j = \begin{cases} 1, & \text{if } G_i = p_i^j \\ 0, & \text{otherwise} \end{cases}$$

Applying the learning process to all F_j leads to a set of classifier $\mathbf{C} = \{C_j, \ 1 \le j \le N\}$, where each C_j is related to the feature F_j.

4.3 Boosting of Statistical Tests

In order to determine the best features F_j to use, we propose to use the boosting technique that is a machine learning technique to combine several classifiers of the set $\mathbf{C}$ into a final classifier $\widehat{C}$.

More precisely, we propose here to use the AdaBoost algorithm [9] which is the most popular boosting method. Given a dump, AdaBoost first selects the best classifier of $\mathbf{C}$ and adds it to the final classifier $\widehat{C}$. The best classifier of the set $\mathbf{C}$ is the one that leads to the best recognition rate respecting the ground truth of the dump. Then looking at the obtained classification, misclassified bits by $\widehat{C}$ receive a more important weight. The boosting then selects the new best classifier taking into account the bit weights (thus this second classifier focuses on misclassified bits) and adds it to $\widehat{C}$. The weights of the bits misclassified by $\widehat{C}$ are updated. Repeating those actions until all the bits are correctly classified, or a certain preset number of classifiers in $\widehat{C}$ is reached. AdaBoost does not return the optimal classifier $\widehat{C}$ because it behaves as a greedy algorithm but it is efficient whereas the naive optimal algorithm is computationally infeasible. AdaBoost's complexity is $\mathcal{O}(|\mathbf{C}|L)$, where L is the complexity of the learning algorithm.

The final classifier provided by the boosting is then used to distinguish *cryptographic material* from *meaningful information* in dumps where the ground truth is unknown.

4.4 Merging Classifications in a Set of Dumps

Dumps belonging to the same application share similarities on their data. However, the prediction $\widehat{P}$ obtained by the final classifier is done independently for each dump. Therefore a merging technique is proposed to combine their classification in order to improve the recognition rate.

A set of dumps of the same application can be obtained by dumping memory of different cards belonging to several holders. It can also be acquired by dumping the same card at different time of the card lifetime, e.g. before and after a cash withdrawal for bank cards.

One may expect that dumps belonging to a given application to be identically structured, i.e. containing the same fields, in the same locations. For example, in some Calypso dumps, the name, the birth date, and the postal code of the holder or details of his last trips are always located at the same place in the dump, with the same encoding. The data of these fields vary for each dump but the class (meaningful information or cryptographic material) is the same. The merging process is also applied to cyclic records, because they contain the same fields in the same locations. Therefore a classification of the bits of the application is computed rather than a classification for each dump.

Given a set $\mathbf{D} = \{D_k, 1 \leq k \leq d\}$ of d dumps of length n bits belonging to the same application the merging process creates a prediction $P_{merging}$ that replaces all the prediction of the final classifier. The prediction $P_{merging}$ is computed as follows:

$$P_{merging} = \{Majority(\widehat{P}_i^1, \widehat{P}_i^2, \ldots \widehat{P}_i^d),\ 1 \le i \le n\}$$

where $\widehat{P}_i^k$ represents the prediction of the final classifier for the i-th bit of the dump D_k, and *Majority* represents the application of a majority vote to the classes. The $P_{merging}$ obtained has a better recognition rate than the prediction obtained independently for each dump of **D**.

5 Experiments

We present the data and the values of the features used by our boosting experiment. The final classifier obtained by AdaBoost is applied to real EMV dumps. The merging process finally allows us to reach a recognition rate greater than 99 % on these EMV dumps.

5.1 Generating Data for the Learning Phase

When fitting the classifiers, AdaBoost requires a sufficient amount of data belonging to each class (i.e. *meaningful information* and *cryptographic material*) from different embedded objects, to be representative of all the existing embedded devices.

We have extracted the data of about 300 devices (using CardPeek [16] or RFIDIOT [15]) from various applications: access control, transportation, banking, health insurance and loyalty cards, train tickets, e-passports, ski passes, etc. Unfortunately, only a small part of these data can be used for the learning phase, because the ground truth of a large part of these data is unknown. In order to solve this problem, we set up a large synthetic dump containing data similar to real dumps, inspired by our 300 dumps. This synthetic dump is modeled by several sequences of variable lengths, containing cryptographic materials (hashed or ciphered data, cryptographic keys, etc.) or meaningful information (dates, names, etc.).

A generated synthetic dump is 100,000-bit long. It contains approximately 65 % of meaningful information, where sequences are between 80 and 300-bit long. Cryptographic materials are generated from various cryptographic algorithms as RSA, AES, SHA-1, etc. They are truncated to obtain the expected length. Meaningful information includes dates with different encoding, e.g., ASCII, BCD, and various formats like YYYY-MM-DD, YY/MM/DD, etc. There are also names, textual information, and zip codes with various encoding techniques.

5.2 Considered Features

Given each feature is described by 5 parameters (*Statistical test, Sequence length, Shift, Score function, Internal parameter*) and each parameter can be assigned with various values, the set **F** contains approximately 10,000 features.

Statistical Test: It is the statistical test that is applied to the dump sequences. All these tests are the NIST tests except those that require 10^6 bits or a specific pattern to test. These NIST tests represent 8 tests: *monobit, runs, block frequency, serial, discrete Fourier transform, approximate entropy, cumulative sum,* and *longest runs.* These 8 tests provided in the NIST suite are completed by the *autocorrelation* [13] and tests suited to short sequences: *TBT* [1] and *saturation point* [23]. There is so 11 tests in total.

Sequence Length: We have decided to lower bound the sequences to 32 bits because tests on too short sequences are not relevant. Sequence lengths used in our experiments are thus chosen in the set $\{32, 48, 76, 100, 128, 192, 256\}$.

Shift: 10 different shifts are used, represented by a percentage of the sequence length: $10\%, 20\% \dots 100\%$.

Score Function: It represents the method that computes the score from the set of p-values of each bit. The functions mean, min, max, and the geometric mean are used here.

Internal Parameter: When the test requires an internal parameter, several values are considered for this parameter. For example, for the serial test the parameter is the block length. When it is applied to a sequence of 256 bits, the possible size of the blocks are from 2 to 6 bits.

5.3   Learning with AdaBoost

The boosting algorithm must be set with a parameter that is the number of classifiers of the final classifier. This parameter must be well suited to the context to avoid overfitting the final classifier. This phenomenon occurs when the final classifier is too adapted to the data used for fitting, which leads to a poor recognition rate on other data. We have experimented with a number of classifiers from 1 to 50.

Two synthetic dumps are generated, one represents the learning set and the second the validation one. The boosting creates a final classifier $\widehat{C}$ from the learning dump and then this classifier is applied to the validation one. Then, varying the number of classifiers in $\widehat{C}$ on the learning dump, each obtained $\widehat{C}$ is applied to the validation one. The $\widehat{C}$ which leads to the best recognition rate on the validation dump is saved.

The final classifier obtained after learning with AdaBoost is composed of five tests with their parameters, described as following:

- Approximate Entropy on sequences of 192 bits by blocks of 2 bits and a *shift* of 19 bits, the *score function* is *max.*
- Longest runs on sequences of 256 bits by blocks of 8 bits and a *shift* of 25 bits, the *score function* is *min.*

- TBT on sequences of 256 bits by blocks of 4 bits and a *shift* of 76 bits, the *score function* is *mean*.
- Serial test on sequences of 256 bits by blocks of 3 bits and a *shift* of 76 bits, the *score function* is *mean*.
- Cumulative sum on sequences of 256 bits with a *shift* of 230 bits, the *score function* is *max*.

The recognition rate of these tests is 91.7 % on the learning dump and 90.7 % on the validation one.

The boosting algorithm selects the most pertinent statistical tests in relation to our context of short sequences belonging to memory dumps. Note that, slightly varying the learning data, the boosting algorithm returns other strong classifiers (with different statistical tests and parameters) providing similar recognition rate. Namely, generating three dumps D_1, D_2, and D_3, then applying the boosting to the scores obtained by the features on D_1 and D_2 creates two final classifier C_{F_1} and C_{F_2}. These two classifiers can consist in different statistical tests but when they are applied to the dump D_3 they provide similar recognition rate. Using more statistical tests in the final classifier improves the recognition rate on the learning dump, we obtain 98.1 % with 50 statistical tests, but the recognition rate on the validation one is 90.0 %, it is a case of overfitting. Using only one statistical test in the final classifier leads to a recognition rate of 89.9 % on the learning dump and a recognition rate of 87.7 % on the validation one. One can notice that these statistical tests use more than 200 bits to take their decision, but they are able to detect the class of sequences that are shorter than 200 bits, because all bits are tested several times due to the shift between tested sequences.

Experiments have been done with our own python program using the AdaBoost-SAMME.R algorithm [11] from Scikit-learn [17]. Calculating the p-values array on a large dump of 100, 000 bits for our set of 10, 000 features took several hours. Calculations have been made on a 64-core processor (4 AMD Opteron 6282SE 2.6 GHz) with 512 GB of RAM available. Running the AdaBoost algorithm, on a single core, takes between a few minutes (when $|\widehat{C}| = 1$) and two hours (when $|\widehat{C}| = 50$).

5.4   Recognition on Real Dumps

In this subsection, the classifier trained on synthetic data is used to classify meaningful information and cryptographic materials on real dumps of memory. This set is applied to more than 30 EMV dumps [8], 2 VITALE dumps (the French health insurance card) and 7 Calypso dumps. In these cards, the meaning of an important part of the data is publicly known (EMV, VITALE) or a previous work of the authors allows to determine it, so, the ground truth (i.e. theoretical classification of the data) is easily accomplished. It represents more than 600, 000 bits of data with 140, 000 cryptographic bits and 500, 000 bits of meaningful information. As result, we obtained a recognition rate of 92.1% for cryptographic bits and 98.6% for bits of meaningful information. When the final classifier is applied to Calypso cards, we get 100 % of recognition. Note that there are only bits of *meaningful information* in our Calypso dumps. Applying the final classifier to these dumps, is almost instantaneous, for large dumps (40,000 bits), it takes less than 2 s.

Some further analysis can improve the results, for example if a single cryptographic bit (resp. meaningful bit) is surrounded by a significant amount of meaningful bits (resp. cryptographic bits), then this bit is likely misclassified. Errors are often localised on the frontier between two fields, one containing cryptographic material and another one containing meaningful information.

Table 1. Detection of cryptographic bits and meaningful bits in EMV, VITALE, and Calypso dumps

Dump type	Cryptographic bits	Recognition rate	Meaningful bits	Recognition rate
EMV	131,384	92.3 %	379,352	98.0 %
VITALE	9,168	90.0 %	126,160	99.9 %
Calypso	0	–	9,681	100.0 %

5.5 Merging Process on EMV Cards

Table 1 shows that our method applied to a single dump already provides good results. We now still improve the results by analysing in parallel several dumps obtained from the same application. We call this improvement the *merging process*.

In the following experiments, 10 fields representing in total 3,560 bits are selected, split as 3,312 cryptographic bits and 248 bits of meaningful information. These fields are information about the holder, the card or cryptographic materials. Since they are repeated numerous time in each dump (cyclic records) and our database is composed of 34 EMV dumps, the merging process takes the decision of the classification of the fields using 21,120 bits of meaningful information and 124,512 cryptographic bits. Applying the merging process to all these fields, we obtain a 100 % recognition rate. Merging 3 to 5 dumps is usually enough to reach a 100 % recognition rate.

Table 2 provides the results of the merging process for each selected field from EMV cards, where the class is M for meaningful information and C for cryptographic material. The classic rate column is the mean of recognition rates of the analysis applied to each dump separately. The merging rate column represents the recognition rate when applying the merging process.

Note that the memory structure of the dumps of a given application is not always the same in practice: some records are possibly missing, or are not of the same length, the number of repetitions of cyclic records can vary or the data stored in a field is not always of the same length and the value of the

Table 2. Recognition rate of the merging process on several fields of EMV cards.

Field name	Class	Length (bits)	Classic rate	Merging rate
Issuer PK Certificate	C	1,024	93.1 %	100.0 %
Signed Static App. Data	C	960	93.8 %	100.0 %
ICC PK Certificate	C	1,024	93.1 %	100.0 %
ICC PK Remainder	C	144	83.2 %	100.0 %
Issuer PK Remainder	C	160	86.2 %	100.0 %
App. Label	M	16	99.0 %	100.0 %
App. Preferred Name	M	16	97.3 %	100.0 %
App. Effective Date	M	24	97.6 %	100.0 %
App. Expiration Date	M	24	99.5 %	100.0 %

non-used bits of the allocated space for the field is uncertain. For example, Mifare cards own always the same structure in their memory which is separated into several sectors of fixed length. Whereas EMV cards are made of files that contain records, and depending on the bank, these files and records can differ. They do not store necessarily the same number of transactions, do not contain all possible records of the EMV specification, the field of the name is padded with 0x20 when the name is shorter than the allocated space, etc. Consequently, a pre-processing phase is needed to identify the records in each dump of the application. In our dumps, all records are separated due to the data recovery technique. This pre-process aims to match the records between the dumps. This operation does not require the knowledge of the card specification, because it is performed by analysing the structure of the data of the dump and the data into the record. It includes the size and the location of the records in the dump, combined with the presence of runs of 0 or 1 separating fields in the record.

6   Conclusion and Perspectives

This paper investigates memory carving techniques for embedded devices. Given that cryptographic material in memory dumps makes carving techniques ineffi-cient, we introduce a methodology to distinguish meaningful information from cryptographic material in memory dumps. We propose a technique to apply sta-tistical tests to memory dump from embedded devices. Our approach uses an adaptive boosting algorithm based on results of statistical tests for randomness. We obtained a recognition rate of about 95 % on real dumps from EMV, Vitale and Calypso cards. We also suggested to analyse several dumps in parallel, which increases the recognition rate up to 100.0 % on EMV cards. Merging the classifi-cation of several dumps of the same application reaching a rate of 100.0 % with only 3 merged dumps for considered fields.

References

1. Alcover, P.M., Guillamón, A., del Ruiz, M.C.: A new randomness test for bit sequences. Informatica **24**(3), 339–356 (2013)
2. Avoine, G., Kalach, K., Quisquater, J.-J.: ePassport: securing international contacts with contactless chips. In: Tsudik, G. (ed.) FC 2008. LNCS, vol. 5143, pp. 141–155. Springer, Heidelberg (2008)
3. Burdach, M.: Physical memory forensics (2006). https://www.blackhat.com/presentations/bh-usa-06/BH-US-06-Burdach.pdf
4. Calypso CNA: Calypso. http://www.calypsostandard.net/
5. Cohen, M.I.: Advanced carving techniques. Digital Invest. **4**(3), 119–128 (2007)
6. Coisel, I., Sanchez, I., Shaw, D.: Physical attacks against the lack of perfect forward secrecy in dect encrypted communications and possible countermeasures. In: International Wireless Communications and Mobile Computing Conference (IWCMC). pp. 594–599 (2015)
7. Doğanaksoy, A., Çalık, C., Sulak, F., Turan, M.S.: New randomness tests using random walk. In: National Cryptology Symposium II (2006)
8. EMVCo: EMV integrated circuit card specifications for payment systems, June 2008
9. Freund, Y., Schapire, R., Abe, N.: A short introduction to boosting. J. Jpn. Soc. Artif. Intell. **14**(5), 771–780 (1999)
10. Friedman, W.F.: The Index of Coincidence and its Applications in Cryptanalysis. Aegean Park Press, California (1987)
11. Hastie, T., Rosset, S., Zhu, J., Zou, H.: Multi-class adaboost. Stat. Interface **2**(3), 349–360 (2009)
12. Kajdanowicz, T., Kazienko, P.: Boosting-based sequential output prediction. New Gener. Comput. **29**(3), 293–307 (2011)
13. Knuth, D.E.: The Art of Computer Programming: Seminumerical Algorithms, vol. 2. Addison-Wesley, Reading (1997)
14. Lanet, J.L., Bouffard, G., Lamrani, R., Chakra, R., Mestiri, A., Monsif, M., Fandi, A.: Memory forensics of a java card dump. Smart Card Research and Advanced Applications. LNCS, vol. 8968, pp. 3–17. Springer, Heidelberg (2014)
15. Laurie, A.: Rfidiot. http://rfidiot.org/
16. Pannetrat, A.: Cardpeek. http://pannetrat.com/Cardpeek/
17. Pedregosa, F., Varoquaux, G., Gramfort, A., Michel, V., Thirion, B., Grisel, O., Blondel, M., Prettenhofer, P., Weiss, R., Dubourg, V., et al.: Scikit-learn: machine learning in python. J. Mach. Learn. Res. **12**, 2825–2830 (2011)
18. Poisel, R., Tjoa, S.: A comprehensive literature review of file carving. In: 2013 Eighth International Conference on Availability, Reliability and Security (ARES), pp. 475–484. IEEE (2013)
19. Rukhin, A., Soto, J., Nechvatal, J., Smid, M., Barker, E., Leigh, S., Levenson, M., Vangel, M., Banks, D., Heckert, A., Dray, J., Vo, S.: A statistical test suite for random and pseudorandom number generators for cryptographic applications. Technical report, DTIC Document April 2010
20. Shamir, A., van Someren, N.: Playing hide and seek with stored keys. In: Franklin, M.K. (ed.) FC 1999. LNCS, vol. 1648, pp. 118–124. Springer, Heidelberg (1999)
21. SKIDATA AG: Skidata. http://www.skidata.com/en.html
22. Su, J., Zhang, H.: A fast decision tree learning algorithm. AAAI **6**, 500–505 (2006)
23. Sulak, F.: A new statistical randomness test: saturation point test. Int. J. Inf. Secur. Sci. **2**(3), 81–85 (2013)

608 T. Gougeon et al.

24. Sulak, F., Doğanaksoy, A., Ege, B., Koçak, O.: Evaluation of randomness test results for short sequences. In: Carlet, C., Pott, A. (eds.) SETA 2010. LNCS, vol. 6338, pp. 309–319. Springer, Heidelberg (2010)
25. Van Deursen, T., Mauw, S., Radomirovic, S.: mCarve: carving attributed dump sets. In: USENIX Security Symposium. pp. 107–121 (2011)
26. Yoo, B., Park, J., Lim, S., Bang, J., Lee, S.: A study on multimedia file carving method. Multimedia Tools Appl. **61**(1), 243–261 (2012)

Security for Human Use

CAPTCHaStar! A Novel CAPTCHA
Based on Interactive Shape Discovery

Mauro Conti, Claudio Guarisco, and Riccardo Spolaor(✉)

University of Padua, Padua, Italy
{conti,rspolaor}@math.unipd.it, cguarisc@gmail.com

Abstract. Over the last years, most websites on which users can register (e.g., email providers and social networks) adopted CAPTCHAs (Completely Automated Public Turing test to tell Computers and Humans Apart) as a countermeasure against automated attacks. The battle of wits between designers and attackers of captchas led to current ones being annoying and hard to solve for users, while still being vulnerable to automated attacks.

In this paper, we propose CAPTCHaStar, a new image-based captcha that relies on user interaction. This novel captcha leverages the innate human ability to recognize shapes in a confused environment. We assess the effectiveness of our proposal for the two key aspects of captchas, i.e., usability, and resiliency to automated attacks. In particular, we evaluated the usability, carrying out a thorough user study, and we tested the resiliency of our proposal against several types of automated attacks: traditional ones; designed ad-hoc for our proposal; and based on machine learning. Compared to the state of the art, our proposal is more user friendly (e.g., only some 35 % of the users prefer current solutions, such as text-based captchas) and more resilient to automated attacks.

Keywords: Usable security · Image-based captcha · Access control

1 Introduction

Many public services on the Internet are subject to automated attacks, i.e., an automated program can exploit a vulnerable on-line service, pretending to be a legitimate user. As an example, an attacker may create multiple accounts on an e-mail provider and use them to send spam messages. In the last years, an increasing number of websites adopted countermeasures against these malicious attacks. The most common method consists in allowing access to a service only to users able to solve a CAPTCHA (Completely Automated Public Turing Test to Tell Computers and Humans Apart). The main purpose of a captcha is to distinguish a human user from a software robot (from now on also referred as "bot") that runs automated tasks. In order to do that, researchers leverage the existing gap between human abilities and the current state of the art of software, including also Artificial Intelligence techniques [25]. A captcha is a program that generates a test, which has the property to be easily solvable by humans, but

© Springer International Publishing Switzerland 2016
M. Manulis et al. (Eds.): ACNS 2016, LNCS 9696, pp. 611–628, 2016.
DOI: 10.1007/978-3-319-39555-5_33

hardly solvable by a bot [39] (if not employing a significant amount of resources and time). As an example, a bot cannot easily understand the meaning of a sentence (or a picture), while humans can carry out this task with negligible effort.

The design of a good captcha is not a trivial task. Indeed, both usability to legitimate users and resiliency against automated attacks must be simultaneously satisfied. Attackers of captcha usually improve automated attacks over time. For this reason, designers use to improve their captchas in order to reduce the success rate of novel attacks. Unfortunately, these improvements usually cause a dramatic decrease in usability [10]. Researchers put a significant effort in understanding the trade-off between usability and resiliency to attacks [8]. Also, in order to measure the effective usability of a captcha, Yan et al. [41] presented a set of metrics that we also consider in this paper: *success rate, completion time* and *ease of understanding.*

The contribution of this paper is as follow:

- We present CAPTCHaStar[1], a novel captcha based on shape recognition and user interaction. CAPTCHaStar prompts the user with some "stars" inside a square. The position of these stars changes according to the position of the cursor. The user must move the cursor, until the stars aggregate in a recognizable shape. Our captcha leverages the innate human ability to recognize a shape in a confused environment. Indeed, a machine cannot easily emulate this ability [20]. This makes CAPTCHaStar easy solvable by humans while remaining difficult for bots.
- We assess the usability of our proposal via a user study, considering an extensive set of parameters. The results show that CAPTCHaStar users achieve a success rate higher than 90 %
- We assess the security of our proposal. In particular, we first studied the resiliency of our CAPTCHaStar against traditional attacks (such as exhaustion and leak of the database). Then, we present some possible ad-hoc attack strategies and discuss their effectiveness against our proposal. Finally, we also assessed the resiliency of CAPTCHaStar against attacks based on machine learning. In all these studies, our solution showed promising results, comparable or even better than state of the art solutions.
- We compare the features of CAPTCHaStar with other existing captchas. In particular, we compare our proposal against some of the most famous image-based designs in the literature. For each of these designs, we discuss the protection that it offers against various attack strategies. The results of our comparison underline that our design improves the state of the art.

Our work suggests that CAPTCHaStar is promising for a practical wide adoption (particularly for mobile devices, where the use of keyboard is more difficult and error-prone [33]), as well as motivate further research along the same direction.

---

[1] A demo is available at http://captchastar.math.unipd.it/demo.php.

Organization. The rest of this paper is organized as follows. In Sect. 2, we report an overview of the current state of the art. In Sect. 3, we describe in details CAPTCHaStar, our novel captcha. In Sect. 4, we evaluate its usability features, while in Sect. 5, we assess its resiliency to automated attacks. In Sect. 6, we compare CAPTCHaStar with other image-based captchas in the literature, and we discuss limitations and possible future work. Finally, in Sect. 7, we draw some conclusions summarizing the contributions of our research.

2   Related Work

In this section, we discuss the main techniques in the literature to design captchas, along with their pros and cons. This section is not intended to be a comprehensive review of the whole literature. Interested readers can refer to the work in [36] for an extensive survey of the state of the art. Henceforth, we refer to a single instance of a captcha test prompted to a user with the term *challenge*. In the following sections, we divide captchas in two main categories, according to the skill required to solve them: *text-based* (Sect. 2.1), when they require text recognition, and *image-based* (Sect. 2.2), when they challenge the user to recognize images. For each category, we briefly describe their usability, traditional attack strategies, and possible countermeasures. Recently, Google proposed noCaptcha, a system that uses an "advanced risk analysis back-end that considers the engagement of the user" and prompts the user with either a text-based or an image-based challenge [3]. Unfortunately, there is not yet much technical information available (as well as research papers) to understand how exactly it works, nor to run a proper comparison. As far as we know, the actual captcha prompted to the user seems independent from the actual "risk assessment", i.e., even CAPTCHaStar might be used!

2.1   Text-Based Captchas

A text-based captcha presents an obfuscated word in the form of an image, and asks the user to read and rewrite it, usually in a text box. Baird et al. [6] proposed the first text-based captcha in 2002. Several researchers focused on improving the resiliency against automated attacks [7,16,21]. Currently, text-based captchas are the most widely used [11].

Usability features. The first implementations of text-based captchas had a very short completion time and high success rate for legitimate users. Unfortunately, the introduction of countermeasures to new automated attacks have dramatically lowered these usability features, highlighting the need for new designs [17]. The instructions to solve text-based captchas are really easy to understand. Users need to type the answer using a keyboard, except for particular designs (e.g., iCaptcha [38]). Unfortunately, inputting the answer with a keyboard undermine the usability of a captcha on smartphone or tablet. Indeed, in such devices, a single-handed touch-based interaction style is dominant [32].

Attacks and countermeasures. The most common way to automatically solve text-based captchas is to use an OCR (Optical Character Recognition) software. In the past few years, captchas designers and attackers took part in a battle of wits. This battle led to an improvement of OCR software, hence making OCR a very effective threat [12] to text-based captchas. Another effective approach to solve captcha is the so-called *relay attack*: some companies sells real-time human labor to solve captchas [28]. This approach has a really high success rate and it costs only one U.S. dollar per thousand captchas [10].

Looking at the literature, the attack strategies against text-based captchas can be classified as follows:

(A01) Forward the challenge to paid humans that solve it (i.e., relay attack).
(A02) In case the answer is a word of sense, use OCR technology combined with a dictionary.
(A03) Use OCR software on a single character separately.
(A04) Segment the word, in order to obtain a single image for every character.
(A05) Remove smaller lines added as an obstacle to the segmentation process.
(A06) Fill hollow spaces inside each character, to improve OCR effectiveness.
(A07) Repair characters outline by fixing broken lines. This method leverages on analyzing the distance between pixels.

Attackers may combine two or more of these attack strategies in order to achieve a higher success rate.

captcha designers reacted to these attacks proposing several improvements to mitigate their effectiveness. Some examples follow (between parenthesis we indicate the attack for which the mitigation strategy could be effective):

- Add more layers of interaction between user and captcha (could be effective for threat A01 above).
- Add more distortion to the letters, e.g., warping, scaling, rotating (against A02 and A06).
- Use of English-like or totally random words (against A03).
- Add more pollution to the image, e.g., ticker lines over the letters (against A04 and A05).
- Increment noise, e.g., degrading the quality of resulting image (against A07).

Unfortunately, some of these mitigation strategies have been shown to be ineffective [9,14].

2.2   Image-Based Captchas

Image-based captchas usually ask the user to recognize an image or to interact with on-screen objects to find a solution. Unlike text-based captchas, every image-based design is substantially different from each other. For this reason, a user who faces a captcha design for the first time needs a little more effort to understand how it works. Studies suggest that image-based captchas are more appreciated by users [18]. Indeed, image-based captchas usually have a high success rate and they are less challenging than text-based ones [29]. In the following, we report some examples of image-based captcha that we could group in three sub-categories: static, motion, and interactive.

One of the representative static image-based captchas was Asirra [15], which was discontinued in fall 2014. Asirra asks the user to distinguish between cats and dogs, on twelve different photos randomly taken from an external website. Another static image-based captcha is Collage [34]: it requests to click on a specific picture, among six pictures randomly taken. Deep captcha [29] prompts the user with six 3D models of real world objects and it asks to sort them by their size.

Some designers focus on captcha that requires video recognition rather than static image recognition. For example, Motion captcha [35] shows the user a randomly chosen video from a database, then it asks the user to identify the action performed by the person in the video. Similarly, YouTube Videos captcha [23] leverages on real video in YouTube service, and it asks the user to write three tags related to the content of the video.

Interactive captchas mitigate the relay attack threat. For example, Noise captcha [31] presents a transparent noisy image overlapped to a noisy background. The user needs to drag this image until he can recognize a well formed text. Cursor captcha [37] changes the appearance of mouse cursor into another random object. The user needs to overlap the cursor on the identical object placed in a random generated image. Jigsaw captcha [18] reprises the classical jigsaw puzzle. Indeed, the user needs to correctly rearrange the pieces of a jigsaw. Finally, PlayThru [1] asks the user to solve a randomly generated mini-game. These mini-games require to drag objects on their correct spots.

Usability features. Since image-based captchas are different from each other, the usability may change depending on the considered design. Usually, image-based captchas do not require to type on a keyboard. For this reason, smartphone and tablet users prefer image-based captchas over text-based ones [33]. The instructions for each different captcha design are usually short and intuitive. Finally, on the server-side, resources required and setup time should be as small as possible. However, some image-based captchas need many external libraries and may require a large amount of computational power (for example, the design proposed in [42] requires more than two minutes to generate a single challenge).

Attacks and countermeasures. The attacks designed to automatically solve image-based captchas are usually very specific, i.e., the attacker has to exploit weak points of each specific captcha design. The main attack strategies used against image-based captchas are the following (to avoid confusion and have a unique numbering for attack strategies—also considering the ones for text-based captchas—we continue from A08):

(A08) Some captchas (especially the ones based on games) hide the solution on client-side. Henceforth, an attacker might run what we call *indirect attack*: get the solution from the client-side (e.g., via reverse engineering of the client application).

(A09) Some captchas rely on a pool of pre-computed challenges, stored in a database. A malicious attacker can perform the *exhaustion of the database* using real humans (e.g., via Amazon Mechanical Turk).

(A10) Similarly, an attacker can make queries to a *leaked database* to identify the solution of a challenge.

(A11) An attacker can use *machine learning* techniques (e.g., Support Vector Machine) to recognize the objects that compose a challenge and solve it.

(A12) In case of a limited number of possible answers, an attacker could simply rely on a *random chance* obtaining a decent success rate.

(A13) captchas solvable with a single interaction are prone to *pure relay attacks*. Indeed, attackers can simply send a screenshot of the challenge to an external paid human.

(A14) Given a heavily interactive captcha, a bot can synchronously relay the data stream from the server over to a human solver, and then relay back the input of the user to the server. This strategy is defined as *stream relay attack* [27].

Several improvements are possible to mitigate the previous weaknesses. Some examples follow:

- Use code obfuscation or encryption (against A08).
- Use Web crawlers to have a self-growing database (against A09).
- Process objects stored in the database before presenting them in the challenge. This makes it unfeasible to match the original object with the one presented in the challenge (against A09 and A10).
- Enlarge the search space to increase the computational cost to find a solution (against A11) or increase the number of possible answers (against A12).
- Analyze the behavioral features, identifying suspicious pattern of movement [26] (against A13 and A14).

3   Our Proposal: CAPTCHaStar

In this section, we present CAPTCHaStar, a novel image-based captcha. The aim of our proposal is to provide a high level of usability, while improving security. In the following, we first provide an overview of the system (Sect. 3.1), then we discuss the implementation of the prototype (Sect. 3.2).

3.1   CAPTCHaStar Overview

Our captcha prompts the user with several small white squares, randomly placed inside a squared black space. From now on, we refer to a single white square as a *star*, and to the squared black space as the *drawable space*. The position of each star changes according to the current coordinates of the cursor, inside the drawable space. Given a challenge, we define as *state* a snapshot of the stars location on the drawable space, relative to a specific cursor position. The challenge asks the user (who wants to be recognized as a human) to change the position of the stars, by moving her cursor, until she is able to recognize a shape (which is not predictable). In particular, CAPTCHaStar creates such a shape starting from a picture randomly chosen among a huge set of pictures. Figure 1a illustrates an example of a picture with ideal features: two colors and a limited number of small details.

Our system decomposes the selected picture in several stars using a sampling algorithm (described later in Sect. 3.2). For each star, the system sets its movement pattern, in a way such that the stars can aggregate together, forming the shape of the sampled picture. This happens only when the cursor is on a secret position. We refer to that position as the *solution* of the challenge. In general, a single CAPTCHaStar challenge can include more than one shape, each of them having its own solution (i.e., secret position of the cursor), at which becomes visible.

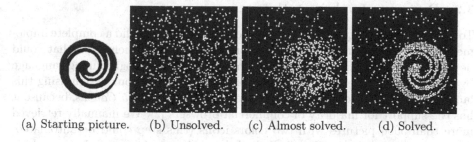

(a) Starting picture.   (b) Unsolved.   (c) Almost solved.   (d) Solved.

Fig. 1. A process of solving a CAPTCHaStar challenge: an example.

When the position of the cursor is far from the solution, the stars appear randomly scattered on the black space. Figure 1b shows an example, obtained from the stars that compose the picture in Fig. 1a. The user has to move the cursor inside the drawable space until she recognizes a meaningful shape. As the distance between the cursor and the solution decreases significantly, the stars aggregate together in a more and more detailed shape (see Fig. 1c). The user needs to adjust the position of the cursor, until she is confident that the resulting shape is detailed enough (see Fig. 1d). Finally, the user confirms the current cursor position as her final answer. The system compares the solution with the final answer (allowing a small margin of error), eventually assessing whether the interaction was made by human.

To make the solution of the captcha more difficult for a bot, in addition to the stars forming the original shape (*original stars*), we add also *noisy stars*: i.e., stars that will be in random position when the shape is complete. The number of the noisy stars can be tuned according to a specific parameter.

The system stores on server-side the solution of the challenge, and performs the check only when the user confirms her answer, that is considered as final and irrevocable. For the sake of usability, CAPTCHaStar considers as a valid answer also a pair of coordinates that is close enough to the actual solution (more details in Sect. 3.2).

The generation phase of a challenge involves some parameters to tune usability and security:

- *Noise* (ψ): the percentage of noisy stars added to the scheme, with respect to the number of original stars.
- *Sensitivity* (δ): the relationship between the amount of displacement of the cursor (in pixel) and the movement of each star (more details in Sect. 3.2).
- *NSol*: the number of possible solutions (i.e., secret positions) of the challenge. Each solution corresponds to a different shape.
- *PicSize*: the maximum value between width and height on the sampled picture, expressed in number of pixels.
- *Rotation*: Boolean value that indicates whether the picture is rotated by a random degree.

3.2   Prototype Implementation

To assess the feasibility and effectiveness of our solution, we did a complete implementation. In particular, we aimed at providing an implementation that could be widely deployed. Since *PHP* is the most supported programming language by web servers [4], we implemented the server-side part of our design using this language. We implemented the client-side part using *HTML5 Canvas*, because it has the support for majority of commercial browsers [2]. We manually retrieved more than 5000 pictures with two colors icons (this step could be automated, e.g., with web crawlers). We collected all these pictures in a pool. For a real life deployment of that system, we recommend using a pool as large as possible. In the following, we first describe how a challenge is generated on the server-side, then we describe how it is presented to the user on the client-side.

Generation of a Challenge. Each challenge is composed by original stars (generated from the base shape) and noisy stars (generated randomly). The steps to generate a challenge are as follows: (i) Picture selection and pre-process; (ii) Picture decomposition; (iii) Trajectory computation. Our system repeats these steps for a number of times equal to the value of the parameter *NSol*.

Picture selection and pre-process. Our system randomly chooses one of the pictures from the pool, and resizes it according to the value of the parameter *PicSize*. If the *Rotation* parameter is enabled, CAPTCHaStar rotates the picture by a random degree. At this point, our system converts the picture in black and white (i.e., binarization).

Picture decomposition. The sampling algorithm first divides the picture in 5x5 pixel tiles, then it counts the number of black pixels inside each tile. A tile will result in an original star when it matches one of the following conditions:(i) if the tile is filled with black pixels (i.e., having $5 \times 5 = 25$ black pixels), our system generates an original star and places it at the center of the tile; (ii) if the tile has a number of black pixels between 9 and 24, our system generates an original star and places it in a position that is shifted from the center of the tile, toward the position where there are the majority of black pixels. Our system places the final shape composed by stars inside the *drawable space*, in a random position (such that all the original stars lie inside).

Trajectory computation. We define the solution *sol* of the challenge as the pair of coordinates (sol_x, sol_y). Our system generates sol_x and sol_y at random, within the range of $[5, 295]$. We adopted such range for the sake of usability.In particular, this guarantees that the solution will not appear on the edges of the drawable area (which is 300x300 pixel). For each original star i, our system also defines (P_x^i, P_y^i) as the coordinates of the position that the star i takes when the cursor is in coordinates (sol_x, sol_y). For each star i, our system randomly generates four coefficients $(m_{x,x}^i, m_{x,y}^i, m_{y,x}^i, m_{y,y}^i)$, that relates the coordinates of the star with the coordinates of the cursor: m_{ab}^i associates the coordinate of the star i in axis a, with the coordinate of the cursor in axis b. The values of these coefficients are picked in the range $[-\frac{\delta}{10}, \frac{\delta}{10}]$ (we remind that δ is the *sensitivity* value).

Our system computes a pair of constants, (C_x^i, C_y^i), for each original star i as follows:

$$C_x^i = P_x^i - sol_y \cdot m_{x,y}^i - sol_x \cdot m_{x,x}^i \quad \text{and} \quad C_y^i = P_y^i - sol_y \cdot m_{y,y}^i - sol_x \cdot m_{y,x}^i.$$

CAPTCHaStar generates the noisy stars in a similar way, but their coordinates (P_x, P_y) having random values. The number of noisy stars is equal to the percentage ψ of the number of original stars. Henceforth, we define as *trajectories parameters* of star i, the following set of parameters: $m_{x,x}^i, m_{x,y}^i, C_x^i, m_{y,x}^i, m_{y,y}^i, C_y^i$. The only information that the client needs from the server in order to calculate the position of the stars, whenever the user moves her cursor, is the trajectories parameters. We underline that noisy and original stars are mixed together, i.e., they are indistinguishable from client side.

Presentation of a Challenge. Whenever the user moves the cursor, our system uses the cursor coordinates $cur = (cur_x, cur_y)$ to compute the new coordinates of each star i, as follows:

$$x^i = m_{x,y}^i \cdot cur_y + m_{x,x}^i \cdot cur_x + C_x^i \quad \text{and} \quad y^i = m_{y,x}^i \cdot cur_x + m_{y,y}^i \cdot cur_y + C_y^i.$$

When the user confirms her answer (e.g., with a mouse click), the client passes *cur* to a simple server-side script, via HTTP GET parameter. For the sake of usability, on mobile devices the submission of the answer is performed by tapping on a button, which is external to the drawable space.

Our server-side script calculates Δ as the euclidean distance between *sol* and *cur*. We define *usability tolerance* as a threshold, in terms of euclidean distance from *sol*. When the value Δ is below the *usability tolerance*, the system considers the test as passed (failed otherwise). From our experiments, we found that a reasonable value for *usability tolerance* is five. We highlight that the position of each star varies linearly with the movement of the cursor. For this reason, humans can easily build a mental map [30] of the stars' behavior, hence moving the cursor toward the position that is closer to a real shape.

4   User Study

In order to evaluate our proposal, we ran a user study according to the usability metrics proposed in [41], and an exhaustive set of parameter combinations. In particular, we compare our solution with text-based captchas taken directly from reCaptcha 2015 [5]. In the following, we describe in detail how we ran the user study and discuss the obtained results.

4.1   Survey Design and Implementation

We designed a web-based survey page, in order to collect data from a large number of participants. We built a survey composed of eight different tests: six CAPTCHaStar challenges (named from T1 to T6) and two text-based ones (T7 and T8). Tests from T1 to T6 are randomly generated (i.e., starting from a random image) using the value of parameters reported in Table 1. Tests T4 and T5 have more than one solutions, i.e., two and three, respectively. Test T4 requires the user to find both of its solutions, while for T5, it is enough to find only one of the three existing solutions.

Table 1. Values of ψ, δ, *NSol* and *Rotation* for the survey.

Test	T1	T2	T3	T4	T5	T6
ψ	0 %	70 %	70 %	10 %	0 %	250 %
δ	5	7	7	7	10	5
NSol	1	1	1	2	3	1
Rotation	Off	Off	On	Off	Off	Off

The last two tests are random text-based captchas from reCaptcha, with one and two words (i.e., T7 and T8, respectively). In order to minimize the learning effect [24], we prompt the user with the eight tests selected in a random order. At the beginning of the survey, we prompt users with a description of our proposal and a simple demo. Then, we ask the participants to fill out a form with their demographic information: age, gender, nationality, level of education, years passed using Internet, and frequency of Internet use. We gather this data in order to understand whether factors like the experience of the user affects the performances in solving CAPTCHaStar challenges. In the same page, we also ask the participants to read and accept an informed consent statement, where we declare how we intend to use the collected data and that we do not intend to disclose private information to third parties. For each test in the survey, we ask the user to rate the perceived difficulty of that test on a scale from 1 (easy) to 5 (hard). We design this survey in a way that each session should last less than 10 min.

4.2   Participants

All the participants took the survey unsupervised using their own devices, in order to recreate the natural conditions of use of CAPTCHaStar. We recruited the participants with an invitation (including a public link to the survey) that we broadcast on mailing lists and on social networks (i.e., Facebook, Google+, Twitter, and LinkedIn), in order to collect usage data for a large number of participants. We did not give any reward for the participation. 281 users took part in our survey, 81 % male and 19 % female). The average age of the participants was 25.5. The education level was distributed as follows: 32 % high school diploma, 29 % bachelor degree, 26 % master degree, 9 % PhD, and 4 % none of the previous ones. The totality of the participants used Internet daily, 49 % from 5 to 10 years, 33 % for more than 10 to 15 years, 28 % for more than 15 years.

4.3   Results and Discussion

Among all the participants, only 35 % of them preferred traditional captchas rather than CAPTCHaStar. Table 2 reports the success rate and the average solving time for each of the eight challenges described above.

Table 2. Survey results for CAPTCHaStar and text-based (Text) captchas.

Test		CAPTCHaStar						Text	
		T1	T2	T3	T4	T5	T6	T7	T8
Success Rate (%)		77.0	87.1	91.0	46.4	82.7	75.5	59.4	50.4
Perceived difficulty		1.9	2.4	2.5	3.4	2.9	3.2	2.4	2.7
Success	Avg time (s)	15.0	18.8	23.1	59.5	32.8	31.1	11.6	15.1
	Std	10.0	10.2	16.6	39.1	25.6	24.5	6.2	6.4
Fail	Avg time (s)	17.4	22.1	31.6	49.3	39.0	40.4	13.1	21.9
	Std	11.7	14.5	20.5	35.3	28.1	29.1	8.4	17.3

In most cases, when considering failed tests, the average completion time is higher than successfully passed ones. In general, the standard deviation of these completion times is quite high (more than 25 for most of the tests): a possible reason for this could be users having different abilities in solving CAPTCHaStar challenges. We highlight that 5 out of 6 CAPTCHaStar tests (i.e., T1 to T6, but T4) have a success rate higher than T7 and T8 (i.e., text-based with two words), and only for T4 the success rate is lower than the one of T7 (i.e., text-based with one word). We believe that users found T4 more difficult to be solved because it requires to discover two images (i.e., original stars for two images, plus the *noisy stars*). In particular, T3 shows a success rate that is some 90 %, which is higher than the 84 % for text-based captchas reported in [10]. We underline that in our text-based captchas T7 and T8 (where we used current reCaptcha used

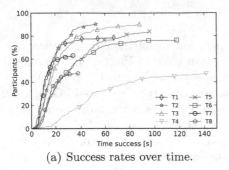
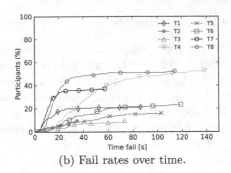

(a) Success rates over time.   (b) Fail rates over time.

Fig. 2. Success and fail rate over time.

by Google), we observed a success rate of 62.7 % (for the simpler test with only one word). In Figs. 2a and 2b, we report in the domain of time the percentages of the participants that solved and failed a challenge, respectively.

We highlight that text-based challenges (T7 and T8) rapidly approach to their maximum within some 20 sec, while CAPTCHaStar challenges reach a higher success rate in just a few more seconds. Indeed, the average time to solve T2 is some 18 sec, which is some 7 sec higher than the best time for text-based captchas (i.e., 11 sec for T7). We believe that this is an acceptable value.

5   Resiliency to Automated Attacks

An important feature of a good captcha is the resiliency to automated attacks. In the following, we investigate the resiliency of our proposal against several attacks, such as: traditional attacks (Sect. 5.1); automated attacks using ad-hoc heuristics (Sect. 5.2) and attacks based on machine learning (Sect. 5.3).

5.1   Traditional Attacks

In this section, we discuss how CAPTCHaStar withstands traditional attack strategies for captchas (we listed those strategies in Sect. 2.2).

- *Indirect Attack* (A08): An indirect attack is not feasible, since all the information about the solution are not available on the client-side. CAPTCHaStar generates the challenge randomly on the server-side, and passes to the client only the description of the behavior of each star with respect to the current cursor position. We remind that the coordinates (sol_x, sol_y), corresponding to the solution of the challenge, are never revealed to the client. Our system checks the correctness of the final answer on the server-side, only after the user confirms it.
- *Exhaustion of Database* (A09): Our system generates a challenge starting from a .png picture, randomly chosen among more than five thousand candidates. Moreover, this database can be automatically enriched with the help of a web crawler, but we consider this as a future work.

- *Leak of Database* (A10): An attacker who tries to match a challenge with its original picture faces a more complex problem than actually solving the challenge. Indeed, the attacker has to solve the challenge in order to input the complete shape to a matching algorithm. Moreover, we highlight that during the generation phase the system alters the original picture, as described in Sect. 3.1.
- *Machine Learning* (A11): In order to understand the feasibility of this attack, we actually trained a classifier to beat our captcha. Results suggest that this approach could be a serious threat, but it needs an unpractical amount of time and resources to be performed. We provide more detailed study about this specific attack in Sect. 5.3.
- *Random Choice* (A12): For the sake of usability, CAPTCHaStar also accepts as a correct answer the neighborhood of the solution (according to the value of *usability tolerance* parameter). Nevertheless, the probability of success of a random guess is some 0.09% with *usability tolerance* equal to five.
- *Pure Relay Attack* (A13): The solution discovery requires constant interaction with the captcha. For this reason, a single screenshot sent to a third party is surely not enough to put a relay attack into practice.
- *Stream Relay Attack* (A14): As we introduced in Sect. 2.2, a stream relay attack needs to synchronously stream the current state to a human third party. CAPTCHaStar needs a constant and immediate feedback system on each cursor movement. Streaming a large number of frames over a (usually) slow connection between the bot and the solvers machine may reduce solving accuracy and increase the response time. Unfortunately, this attack strategy remains the most effective against captchas (including our proposal).

5.2   Automated Attacks Using Ad-hoc Heuristics

In this section, we describe the design of a CAPTCHaStar automatic solver, in order to test the reliability of our design. While retrieving all the possible states of a challenge is a trivial task (an attacker can simply take a snapshot for each cursor position), identifying the specific state corresponding to the solution is not simple. Indeed, the core task of an automatic solver is to recognize the presence of a shape in a given state. In the following, we report some ad-hoc heuristics we came up with to perform this task (of course, we cannot exclude better solutions that could be proposed in the future). We created a program that given a state, it aims to quantify the dispersion of the stars. We consider as a candidate solution the state that minimizes the score given by the applied heuristic. For each heuristic, we evaluate the automatic solver in terms of success rate and average time for at least 250 challenges. For this evaluation, we use the same value of parameters as in test T3 in the usability survey in Sect. 4 (we chose these parameters since test T3 was the test with the highest success rate). In this evaluation, we used a PC with a 2.3 GHz Intel Pentium B970 and 4 GB memory.

Minimize the distribution (MinDistribution). The main idea under this heuristic consists of dividing the drawable space for a state k into T^k tiles, and evaluating the stars dispersion on each tile: $MinDistr(k) = \sum_{t \in T^k} |2 \cdot \sum_{i=1}^{25} \sum_{j=1}^{25} t_{ij} - 25^2|$.

Minimize the sum of distances (MinSumDist). This heuristic aims to detect when stars are clustered together, even in different groups according to their euclidean distance: $MinSumDist(k) = \sum_{s \in S^k} \min_{r \in S^k} d(s, r)$.

Minimize the sum of all distances (AllSumDist). We modify the previously discussed heuristic in order to consider all distances. The heuristic is defined as: $AllSumDist(k) = \sum_{s \in S^k} \sum_{r \in S^k} d(s, r)$.

From Table 3, we observe that even if the variation of execution time is very high (from 65 sec of MinDistribution, to 1500 of AllSumDist ones), the success rate is always smaller than 2 %. In order to reduce the search space, and thus the execution time, we could consider just a sub-set of coordinates by sampling the original set of possible cursor positions. However, we underline that these attacks will remain useless, since their performance is less than 2 % of success. We expect that such sampling would further reduce this success rate.

Table 3. Execution time and Success ($\psi = 70\,\%$; $\delta = 7$).

Strategy	MinDistribution	MinSumDist	AllSumDist
Time (s)	65	765	1500
Success rate	0.07 %	0.50 %	1.92 %

5.3   Attacks Based on Machine Learning

In order to assess the resiliency of CAPTCHaStar against machine learning-based attacks, we designed a tool that tries to find the solution of a challenge. The procedure to recognize a shape is similar to the one reported in [19]. For the sake of attack feasibility (in terms of both occupied memory and execution time), from a search space composed of all possible states, we sub-sample it to a subset K, according to the value of *usability tolerance* (i.e., from 290^2 possible states to 60^2, in our specific implementation). This, in order to ensure that we have at least one solution among the states in K. Similarly to attacks based on ad-hoc heuristic (showed in Sect. 5.2), classifiers return a score for each state in K. We observed experimentally that the distribution of scores often presents multiple local maximums and large plateaus. Since a challenge allows only one answer (final and irrevocable), an attacker must find the state with the globally maximum score. In this evaluation, we ran the attacks on a test set of 200 challenges (with $\psi = 70\,\%$ and $\delta = 7$) on a high end PC with a 3.16 GHz Intel Xeon X5460 and 32 GB of RAM. Readers interested in additional implementation details (not reported here due to space limitation) can refer to our technical report [13].

The attack with the best success rate uses a SVM classifier and it achieves a success rate of 78.1 %. The time required to build the features vectors for the states in K remains stable at around 340 sec. This means that an attack on a single challenge will have around 78 % of success rate, but it will require 421 sec in total to be performed. We recall that a human user can solve a challenge with a success rate of more than 90 % in an average time of 27 sec (56 seconds in the worst case). Therefore, the problem for a bot of automatically recognizing a solution state of a challenge of CAPTCHaStar is hard to treat in a limited amount of time and resources. We underline that, as recently reported in [9], machine learning based attacks achieve some 50 % success rate in only two seconds against Baidu and eBay CAPTCHAs. Since our attack takes 0.1 seconds to evaluate a single state, within two seconds it is able to evaluate only 20 states, which corresponds to a success rate of 0.39 %. To reach a success rate of 50 %, our attack must evaluate at least 2560 states, and to perform this evaluation it takes 256 seconds (i.e., more than four minutes).

6   Discussion

In this section, we first compare our solution with other image-based captchas, then we discuss limitations of CAPTCHaStar and possible future work.

6.1   Comparison with Other Image-Based Captchas

Comparing our solution with the state-of-the-art of image-based captchas (presented in Sect. 2.2), our proposal turns out to be more resilient against attacks. In particular, Table 4 reports the comparison considering the common weaknesses of image-based captchas, reviously discussed in Sect. 2.2. In the table we indicate whether the design is protected against the following attacks: *indirect attack*, *exhaustion of DB*, *leak of DB*, and *pure relay attack*. In addition, for *stream relay attack* and *machine learning* based attacks, we report the cost to perform such attack, in terms of computational time and resources.

We notice that most of the designs in the literature limit their focus to a specific threat, but they offer less protection against others. On the other hand, our proposal is designed to resist all of them, while maintaining a high usability level.

6.2   Limitations and Future Work

Unfortunately, we (as well as other captcha proposers) are not able to prove that our captcha is secure against all the possible attacks. We believe the best a researcher can do in such cases is to consider both current traditional attacks (see our Sect. 5.1) and ad-hoc ones (see our Sects. 5.2 and 5.3). As an example, Asirra [15] has been later proven to be breakable [19,42]. The same goes for other captchas, such as ReCaptcha (both versions of 2011 and 2013) and the ones employed by CNN, Wikipedia, Yahoo, Microsoft [40] and PlayThru [1].

As a future work, we plan to further increase the resiliency of CAPTCHaStar by analyzing the pattern of mouse movements during the resolution of a challenge. We believe this analysis will be meaningful in order to better discriminate human users and automatic programs. Finally, we plan to investigate the

Table 4. Protection against the threats in Sect. 2.2.

captcha design	Indirect attack	Database exhaustion	Database leak	Pure relay	Stream relay	Machine learning	Random chance
Asirra [15]	✓	✓	✗	✗	low	low	0.02 %
Collage [34]	✓	✗	✗	✗	low	high	16.60 %
Deep [29]	✓	✓	✓	✗	low	high	0.20 %
Motion [35]	✓	✗	✗	✓	low	high	25.00 %
Video [23]	✓	✓	✗	✗	low	high	0.30 %
Noise [31]	✓	✓	✓	✓	mid	mid	< 0.01 %
Cursor [37]	✓	✓	✓	✓	low	low	< 0.01 %
Jigsaw [18]	✓	✗	✗	✗	low	mid	6.66 %
PlayThru [1]	✗	✗	✗	✓	high	high	< 0.01 %
CAPTCHaStar	✓	✓	✓	✓	**high**	**high**	**0.09 %**

possibility of leveraging additional gaps between human abilities and automatic programs. For example, we intend to involve in a challenge the semantic meaning of the final shape. This means to rely on the innate human ability to relate objects with their semantic, which is hardly imitable by a machine [42].

7   Conclusions

In this paper, we proposed CAPTCHaStar, a novel image-based captcha that leverages the innate human ability to recognize shapes in a confused environment [22]. Our study demonstrates that our proposal meets both security and usability requirements for a good captcha design. We described in detail our prototype implementation and the selection of parameters involved in challenge generation. Data collected from our user study confirmed the usability of our proposal. Indeed, users were able to obtain a success rate higher than 90 %, which is better than the success rates of captchas currently used in websites [10] such as mail.ru and Microsoft. Finally, the majority of the users who participated in our survey preferred CAPTCHaStar over classical text-based captchas. These results motivate further research in this direction.

In this paper, we also assessed the resiliency of CAPTCHaStar against traditional and automated ad-hoc attacks. Indeed, these attacks were shown to be ineffective (for a proper setting of our parameters). We also performed an attack leveraging a machine learning classifier, which we optimized by reducing as much as possible the research space.Despite this optimization of the attack and its execution on a high end PC, the resulting average execution time is still unacceptable, i.e., more than six minutes to find the solution for a single challenge (with a success probability of 78 %). We recall that users are able to complete CAPTCHaStar challenges in an average time of 23.1 seconds (with a success probability of some 91 %).

References

1. AreYouAHuman - game based CAPTCHAs (2013). http://areyouahuman.com
2. Canvas (basic support) (2014). http://caniuse.com/#feat=canvas
3. Introducing "NoCAPTCHA reCAPTCHA", December 2014. http://google onlinesecurity.blogspot.co.uk/2014/12/are-you-robot-introducing-no-captcha.html
4. Usage of server-side programming languages for websites (2014). http://w3techs.com/technologies/overview/programming_language/all/
5. recaptcha plugins, December 2015. https://developers.google.com/recaptcha
6. Baird, H.S., Coates, A.L., Fateman, R.J.: Pessimalprint: a reverse turing test. IJDAR **5**, 2–3 (2003)
7. Baird, H.S., Riopka, T.P.: ScatterType: a reading CAPTCHA resistant to segmentation attack. In: Proceedings of EI. SPIE (2005)
8. N. Ben-Asher, J. Meyer, S. Moller, and R. Englert.: An experimental system for studying the tradeoff between usability and security. In: Proceedings of IEEE ARES (2009)
9. Bursztein, E., Aigrain, J., Moscicki, A., Mitchell, J.C.: The end is nigh: generic solving of text-based captchas. In: Proceedings of USENIX WOOT (2014)
10. Bursztein, E., Bethard, S., Fabry, C., Mitchell, J.C., Jurafsky, D.: How good are humans at solving CAPTCHAs? a large scale evaluation. In: Proceedings of IEEE SP (2010)
11. Bursztein, E., Martin, M., Mitchell, J.: Text-based CAPTCHA strengths and weaknesses. In: Proceedings of ACM CCS (2011)
12. Chellapilla, K., Larson, K., Simard, P.Y., Czerwinski, M.: Computers beat humans at single character recognition in reading based human interaction proofs (HIPs). In: Proceedings of CEAS (2005)
13. Conti, M., Guarisco, C., Spolaor, R.: Captchastar! a novel CAPTCHA based on interactive shape discovery (2015). eprint arXiv:1503.00561
14. El Ahmad, A.S., Yan, J., Marshall, L.: The robustness of a new captcha. In: Proceedings of ACM EuroSys (2010)
15. Elson, J., Douceur, J.R., Howell, J., Saul, J.: Asirra: a captcha that exploits interest-aligned manual image categorization. In: Proceedings of ACM CCS (2007)
16. Ferzli, R., Bazzi, R., Karam, L.J.: A captcha based on the human visual systems masking characteristics. In: Proceedings of IEEE ICME (2006)
17. Fidas, C.A., Voyiatzis, A.G., Avouris, N.M.: On the necessity of user-friendly CAPTCHA. In: Proceedings of ACM SIGCHI CHI (2011)
18. Gao, H., Yao, D., Liu, H., Liu, X., Wang, L.: A novel image based CAPTCHA using jigsaw puzzle. In: Proceedings of IEEE CSE (2010)
19. Golle, P.: Machine learning attacks against the asirra CAPTCHA. In: Proceedings of ACM CCS (2008)
20. Hinton, G.E.: To recognize shapes, first learn to generate images. Prog. Brain Res. **165**, 535–547 (2007)
21. Ince, I.F., Yengin, I., Salman, Y.B., Cho, H.-G., Yang, T.-C.: Designing captcha algorithm: splitting and rotating the images against ocrs. In: Proceedings of IEEE ICCIT (2008)
22. Kanizsa, G., Kanizsa, G.: Organization in vision: Essays on Gestalt perception. Praeger, New York (1979)
23. Kluever K.A. Zanibbi, R.: Balancing usability and security in a video CAPTCHA. In: Proceedings of ACM SOUPS (2009)

24. Kosara, R., Healey, C.G., Interrante, V., Laidlaw, D.H., Ware, C.: User studies: why, how, and when? IEEE Comput. Graphics Appl. **23**, 20–25 (2003)
25. Lopresti, D.P.: Leveraging the CAPTCHA problem. In: Baird, H.S., Lopresti, D.P. (eds.) HIP 2005. LNCS, vol. 3517, pp. 97–110. Springer, Heidelberg (2005)
26. Mohamed, M., Gao, S., Saxena, N., Zhang, C.: Dynamic cognitive game captcha usability and detection of streaming-based farming. In: Proceedings of the NDSS USEC (2014)
27. Mohamed, M., Sachdeva, N., Georgescu, M., Gao, S., Saxena, N., Zhang, C., Kumaraguru, P., van Oorschot, P.C., Chen, W.-B.: A three-way investigation of a game-captcha: automated attacks, relay attacks and usability. In: Proceedings of ACM AsiaCCS (2014)
28. Motoyama, M., Levchenko, K., Kanich, C., McCoy, D., Voelker, G.M., Savage, S.: Re: Captchas understanding captcha solving services in an economic context. In: Proceedings of USENIX Security (2010)
29. Nejati, H., Cheung, N.-M., Sosa, R., Koh, D.C.: DeepCAPTCHA: an image CAPTCHA based on depth perception. In: Proceedings of ACM MSC (2014)
30. Norman, D.A.: The design of everyday things: Revised and expanded edition. Basic books, New York (2013)
31. Okada, M., Matsuyama, S.: New captcha for smartphones and tablet pc. In: Proceedings of IEEE CCNC (2012)
32. Poslad, S.: Ubiquitous computing: smart devices, environments and interactions. John Wiley & Sons, New York (2011)
33. Reynaga, G., Chiasson, S.: The usability of CAPTCHAs on smartphones. In: Proceedings of SECRYPT (2013)
34. Shirali-Shahreza, M., Shirali-Shahreza, S.: Advanced collage captcha. In: Proceedings of IEEE ITNG (2008)
35. Shirali-Shahreza, M. Shirali-Shahreza, S.: Motion captcha. In: Proceedings of IEEE HSI (2008)
36. Shirali-Shahreza, M.H., Shirali-Shahreza, S.: Distinguishing Human Users from Bots. IGI Global, Hershey (2014)
37. Thomas, V., Kaur, K.: Cursor CAPTCHA implementing CAPTCHA using mouse cursor. In: Proceedings of IEEE WOCN (2013)
38. Truong, H.D., Turner, C.F., Zou, C.C.: iCAPTCHA: the next generation of CAPTCHA designed to defend against 3rd party human attacks. In: Proceedings of IEEE ICC (2011)
39. Ahn, L., Blum, M., Langford, J.: Telling humans and computers apart automatically. Commun. ACM **47**, 56–60 (2004)
40. Yan, J., El Ahmad, A.S.: A low-cost attack on a microsoft CAPTCHA. In: Proceedings of ACM CCS (2008)
41. Yan, J., El Ahmad, A.S.: Usability of CAPTCHAs or usability issues in CAPTCHA design. In: Proceedings of ACM SOUPS (2008)
42. Zhu, B.B., Yan, J., Li, Q., Yang, C., Liu, J., Xu, N., Yi, M., Cai, K.: Attacks and design of image recognition CAPTCHAs. In: Proceedings of ACM CCS (2010)

TMGuard: A Touch Movement-Based Security Mechanism for Screen Unlock Patterns on Smartphones

Weizhi Meng[1](✉), Wenjuan Li[2], Duncan S. Wong[3], and Jianying Zhou[1]

[1] Infocomm Security Department, Institute for Infocomm Research,
Singapore, Singapore
{mengw,jyzhou}@i2r.a-star.edu.sg
[2] Department of Computer Science, City University of Hong Kong,
Hong Kong, China
wenjuan.li@my.cityu.edu.hk
[3] Applied Science and Technology Research Institute (ASTRI), Hong Kong, China
duncanwong@astri.org

Abstract. Secure user authentication is a big challenge for smartphone security. To overcome the drawbacks of knowledge-based method, various graphical passwords have been proposed to enhance user authentication on smartphones. Android unlock patterns are one of the Android OS features aiming to authenticate users based on graphical patterns. However, recent studies have shown that attackers can easily compromise this unlock mechanism (i.e., by means of smudge attacks). We advocate that some additional mechanisms should be added to improve the security of unlock patterns. In this paper, we first show that users would perform a touch movement differently when interacting with the touchscreen and that users would perform somewhat stably for the same pattern after several trials. We then develop a touch movement-based security mechanism, called *TMGuard*, to enhance the authentication security of Android unlock patterns by verifying users' touch movement during pattern input. In the evaluation, our user study with 75 participants demonstrate that *TMGuard* can positively improve the security of Android unlock patterns without compromising its usability.

Keywords: Mobile security · User authentication · Android unlock patterns · Usability · Touch gestures · Behavioral biometric

1 Introduction

Smartphones like Android phones and iPhones have become extremely popular in our daily lives and routines, where the Android phones and iPhones captured nearly 82.8% and 13.9% global smartphone market share each in Q2 2015 [11]. With the increasing capability of current phones, users are likely to store their personal information such as passwords and credit card numbers on

© Springer International Publishing Switzerland 2016
M. Manulis et al. (Eds.): ACNS 2016, LNCS 9696, pp. 629–647, 2016.
DOI: 10.1007/978-3-319-39555-5_34

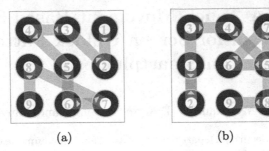

(a)   (b)

Fig. 1. Cases of 9-dot Android unlock pattern generated by Berkeley Churchill.

their phones [12], and use the phones for sensitive tasks such as mobile banking [21]. However, according to a survey of mobile phone users in 2012 [24], among the most common issues, 67 % of respondents had dealt with lost or stolen mobile devices. In this case, user authentication on smartphones has become very crucial to protect the stored private and sensitive data.

At present, the most commonly used method for user authentication is based on text or PIN codes, in which users are required to input correct characters for authentication. However, several studies indicated that this kind of authentication had drawbacks regarding both usability and security [6]. For instance, users have difficulty in remembering complex and random passwords which is known as long-term memory (LTM) limitations [26]. Therefore, users are likely to choose a simple password to reduce the burden of memory. According to a report from SplashData, the worst password used in 2013 is "123456" [22].

To mitigate the drawbacks of the knowledge-based passwords, graphical passwords (*GPs*) have been developed as an alternative aiming to enhance the process of user authentication. Several psychological studies like [18] have indicated that the human brain was better at remembering and recognizing images than text. Current smartphones using the Android operating systems adopt a type of screen unlock mechanism that requires users to input correct patterns to unlock the phones within a 3 × 3 touch-enabled grid. Users can start touching on any one of the dots, swipe the fingers to touch more dots and construct a pattern. For example, Fig. 1 shows two patterns generated by an unlock pattern generator from Berkeley Churchill [3]. The number from 1 to 9 indicates the sequence of dots during the touch movement.

Motivations. Due to the popularity of the Android unlock patterns, many adversarial techniques have been explored in the literature aiming to compromise this mechanism. For instance, since users can only choose a minimum of 4 and a maximum of 9 dots to generate such a pattern, the total number of possible patterns is 389,112 [2], where it is still feasible for a brute-force attack. What is worse, by means of several other types of attacks, the password space of the unlock patterns can be greatly reduced. The details of potential attacks can be referred to Sect. 2.2. Therefore, it is very crucial for Android unlock patterns to improve its authentication security in practical usage.

Contributions. To enhance the authentication security of Android unlock patterns, it is reasonable that some additional mechanisms should be added to securing these patterns. Motivated by work [8, 15, 28, 30], we believe that behavioral biometric is one of the potential solutions. Our main goal is to complement the existing solutions in enhancing authentication security on smartphones. The contributions of our work can be summarized as below:

- In this work, we begin by conducting a study with 50 participants to investigate how users would perform in creating unlock patterns. It is found that different users would input unlock patterns differently regarding touch movement, in which the average speed of touch movement may be varied. On the other hand, it is found that users are able to perform a more stable movement for inputting the same pattern after several trials.
- We then develop a security mechanism based on touch movement, called *TMGuard*, to authenticate users in terms of both their input patterns and extracted information from touch movement. Distinguished from other work, we develop two approaches of *dot-dot pattern computation* and *proportional matching* in order to better model and compare users' touch movements.
- In the evaluation, we conduct a user study with a total of 75 participants and it is found that *TMGuard* can enhance the authentication security of unlock patterns with good usability in practice.

The remaining parts of this paper are organized as follows. In Sect. 2, we introduce the background of Android unlock patterns and present some potential attacks. Section 3 presents our first study to investigate how users would perform touch movement when inputting unlock patterns. Section 4 describes the proposed security mechanism of *TMGuard* in detail, and presents another user study to evaluate its performance. Finally, we conclude the paper in Sect. 5.

2   Background and Related Work

2.1   Android Unlock Patterns

Android unlock patterns are one of the graphical password schemes that requires users to swipe their finger to construct a pattern and unlock the device. Specifically, it is a modified version of Pass-Go [20] in order to adapt for the small touchscreens on typical smartphones. It allows users to create a pattern by means of 4 dots at least and 9 dots at most, within a 3×3 grid on the touchscreen, and to use it to unlock a mobile device. To create a valid unlock pattern, three major rules are applied as follows [19, 23]: (1) One cannot use a dot more than once, since it is virtually removed after selection. In Fig. 1(b), it is shown that *dot 1* can be only selected once when touching back from *dot 2* to *dot 3*. (2) At least 4 dots must be chosen and only straight lines are allowed. (3) It is not possible to create a line using three dots, without selecting the middle one, unless the latter has been previously visited.

Based on these rules described above, it is not easy to compute the number of total patterns directly, but one can enumerate all possible patterns: there are 389,112 (2^{19}) possible patterns [2]. These possible patterns would be sufficient if users can select the patterns uniformly, however, the situation is much worse in practice (i.e., it offers less security than a three digit PIN [23]).

After users input one unlock pattern, this mechanism will convert the pattern to byte array, transform it to the SHA-1 hash function and save it in the phone (e.g., the stored file name is *gesture.key*). Due to the popularity of this mechanism, it has been available not only in Android OS, but also in iOS. For example, *Cydia Tweak* [25] currently allows users to add an Android-inspired pattern unlock system to a jailbroken iPhone handset.

2.2   Potential Attacks

Since an Android unlock pattern is composed of several dots, this mechanism suffers from the issue of 'hot-dot'. In [1], a pilot study has shown that users have some preferences on the *start points* and *end points* when drawing the pattern. For instance, they reported that about 52.08 % of the participants preferred to start their patterns from the top left node. In addition, Aviv et al. [2] indicated that unlock patterns can be retrieved by launching smudge attacks. The basic idea is that users may leave an oily residue or smudges when swiping their fingers on the device. In the experiments, they concluded that intentionally cleaning with cloth or putting the phone to pocket was not enough to prevent pattern retrieval. Therefore, an attacker can easily capture a photo of the touchscreen and perform necessary contrast and brightness adjustments to the captured photo to retrieve the pattern.

In addition, Android unlock patterns have an inherent limitation, in which only 9 touch dots can be used during the pattern creation. In such case, the total number of possible patterns is 389,112, which makes brute force attacks still feasible if a weak pattern is chosen by users. For instance, Pereira Botelho [19] conducted a preliminary study to explore the performance of 4-dot unlock patterns against brute force attacks. The experimental results indicated that the maximin time needed to crack a 4-dot pattern is less than 4 min.

As there are only 9 touch dots for creating an Android unlock pattern, we consider that additional mechanisms could be added to enhance the authentication security of unlock patterns. One of the possible solutions is to use *behavioral biometrics*, which use measurements from human actions [4]. As discussed in previous research such as [8,15,17,28,30], users may perform differently when using their phones, so that it is feasible to authenticate users based on their gestures. In this work, we thus aim to improve the authentication security of Android unlock patterns by combining it with users' touch behavior.

3   Study on Touch Movement for Unlock Patterns

As shown in Fig. 1, Android unlock patterns consist of 9 nodes in a 3 × 3 grid. In practice, to construct a valid pattern, users should use one touch movement

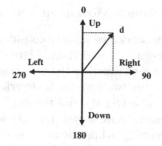

Fig. 2. (a) The interface of CyanogenMod Android OS; (b) The screen of Android unlock patterns; (c) An instance of raw data collection.

Fig. 3. Directions for a touch movement.

to draw a pattern by selecting dots in a certain sequence. A *basic* question here is how users would input patterns when performing touch movements on their phones. We have two intuitive hypotheses:

Hypothesis 1. Distinct users may perform the touch movement differently when inputting the patterns.

Hypothesis 2. Through some input trials, one user's touch behavior may become more stable.

To verify these hypothesis, we conduct a user study with 50 participants. In this section, we introduce how to collect raw data, select and define features for a touch movement, and analyze the collected results.

3.1 Data Collection

Although the unlock patterns will be hashed and stored in a pre-defined file like *gesture.key*, we do not use it directly in this work. Instead, to record and collect the input data, we used a modified Google/HTC Nexus One Android phone with a capacitive touchscreen (resolution 480×800 px). Specifically, we updated the phone with a modified Android OS version 2.2 based on *CyanogenMod*.[1] The modification consists of changes to the application framework layer to record raw data from the touchscreen, such as the timing of touch inputs, the coordinates of x and y, and the type of the input (e.g., single-touch or touch movement).

To facilitate the real observation, we installed a *log application* allowing us to more easily extract the recorded data from the phone. A Beta version of our customized-Android OS can be downloaded at Sourceforge website.[2] The major advantage of using our data collection is that we can collect all raw data during a user's input including users' behavioral data and input patterns, and then compute the related features, while using *gesture.key* can only extract those patterns. The interface of the *CyanogenMod* Android OS can be seen in Fig. 2(a), the interface of Android unlock patterns can be referred to Fig. 2(b), and an instance of raw data collection is given in Fig. 2(c).

---

[1] http://www.cyanogenmod.com/.

[2] https://sourceforge.net/projects/touchdynamicsauthentication/files/Android_OS/.

3.2   Touch Movement Features

In this work, we mainly consider 4 standard directions for a touch movement: up, down, left and right. Figure 3 defines each direction and thus we can use a degree d to describe the direction of a touch movement.

We use two features to describe a specific touch movement: the speed of touch movement (STM) and the angle of touch movement (ATM). Suppose a touch movement selects two dots $D1$ and $D2$ with coordinates (x1, y1) and (x2, y2) respectively, while the event system time is $S1$ and $S2$. As shown below, Eq. (1) describes how to calculate STM and Eq. (2) describes how to calculate ATM (e.g., with an angle d).

$$STM = \frac{\sqrt{(x2 - x1)^2 + (y2 - y1)^2}}{S2 - S1} \tag{1}$$

$$ATM\ (d) = \arctan\frac{y2 - y1}{x2 - x1}, \theta \in [0, 360°] \tag{2}$$

3.3   Study Design and Result Analysis

In the study, we have recruited 50 participants who are volunteers and interested in this topic. Among them, 60 % are males and the remainder are females. All participants are regular mobile phone users and aged between 15 and 60. Among them, 76 % currently use Android OS while the others use iOS. But all of them have used or experienced Android unlock patterns before. As incentives, $20 gift vouchers were given to each participant. The detailed information of participants is shown in Table 1.

More specifically, we introduced our objectives to all participants before they joined the study, showed what kind of data would be collected and acknowledged that all data collected in the study was used in an anonymized way. Overall, there are two phases in the user study:

- *Phase1*. Each participant has to create a total of 3 different patterns, while for each pattern they should re-enter it three times (recorded) after two practice (not recorded) in one day. This makes us collect 150 patterns and 450 trials in total.
- *Phase2*. We provide each participant with an Android phone equipped with our modified Android OS. Each participant should choose one of their created patterns in *Phase1* as the phone's unlock pattern, and freely use the phone for another 2 days. After that, all participants were asked to return and input their patterns in our lab for three times.

The objective of *Phase1* is to explore whether users can perform touch movement differently when inputting the patterns, while the objective of *Phase2* is to investigate whether users can input the pattern stably after a number of trials.

We show the average speed of touch movement ($ASTM$) for different users in Fig. 4. In particular, Fig. 4(a) shows the $ASTM$ for user ID from 1 to 25 while

Table 1. Participants' information in the first user study.

Age range	Male	Female
< 25	7	5
25–35	13	9
35–45	6	3
> 45	4	3

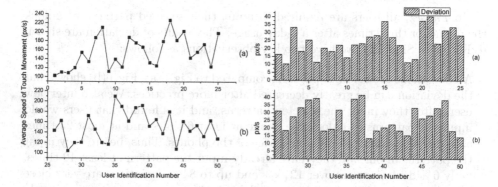

Fig. 4. Average speed of touch movement (users from 1 to 50).

Fig. 5. Deviation for average speed of touch movement (users from 1 to 50).

Fig. 4(b) shows the *ASTM* for user ID from 26 to 50. The calculation of average movement speed is based on the collected 9 trials for each user. The average speed is ranged from nearly 100 px/s to 230 px/s. The figure shows that users would perform differently when swiping their fingers on the touchscreen. For example, it is seen that User 8, 18, 25 and 35 could perform a high movement speed over 200 px/s, while User 1, 3, 28 and 44 might perform a very slow speed less than 100 px/s. Others may perform a speed between these two.

In addition, as shown in Fig. 5, we compute the deviations for each user based on their 9 trials. It is noticeable that several users like User 2, 6, 10, 18, 19, 38 and 50 could perform more stably than other users (i.e., the deviation is less than 15 px/s), but some users like User 15, 20, 21, 30, 31, 36, 37 and 48 would perform not stably (i.e., the deviation is more than 35 px/s). The results reveal that users would not perform consistently when inputting different patterns, which is in line with our common sense. However, our interests are focus on whether users would perform consistently to draw a same pattern, or whether the deviations are below an appropriate threshold. To explore these questions, we further compute the deviations for all users when drawing the same pattern (3 trials for the same pattern) in Fig. 6(a). We have two key observations based on the comparison between Fig. 6(a) and Fig. 5:

– The deviation for the same pattern is much lower than that for inputting all patterns (by comparing Fig. 6(a) with Fig. 5). This is reasonable as users may perform different movement speeds according to distinct patterns. For example, for a complex pattern, users may slow down the speed while for ' some 'easy' patterns, users may perform a touch movement fast.

– Nearly 75 % deviations are below 25 px/s while only 3.3 % deviations are over 30 px/s. This observation shows that users could perform more consistently to some degree, when inputting the same pattern as compared to inputting different patterns. It also shows that the speed of touch movement can be used to distinguish different users when inputting unlock patterns.

In *Phase2*, all users are required to input their selected patterns to unlock the phone for three times after a 2-day usage. The results of deviation are shown in Fig. 6(b). Similarly, we have two key observations as follows:

– All deviations are below 17 px/s. As compared to Fig. 6(a), Fig. 6(b) shows that the deviation can be greatly decreased after more practices. We also interview users after they input the selected patterns, and it is found that users would input the patterns to unlock the phone at least 6 times and at most 25 times each day, depending on different usage of the phones. Thus, before they input the patterns in our lab, they have already input the pattern at least 12 times.

– Only 6 % deviations are over 12 px/s and up to 84 % deviations are very close to, or even below 10 px/s. As compared to Fig. 6(a), this observation positively indicates that users would perform a touch movement much more stably after a period of time. Based on this observation, we believe that it is feasible and promising to enhance the authentication security of Android unlock patterns by combining it with behavioral biometrics.

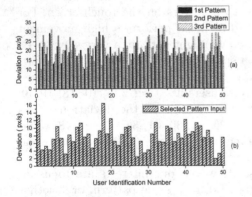

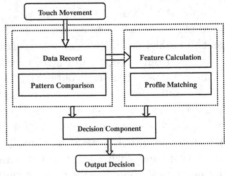

Fig. 6. Deviation for average speed of touch movement (users from 1 to 50): (a) Deviation in *Phase1* and (b) Deviation in *Phase2*.

Fig. 7. The high-level architecture of TM-Guard.

3.4   Discussions

The results illustrated above demonstrate the feasibility of applying behavioral biometrics to improving the security of Android unlock patterns. From the study, we verify our two hypothesis: users would perform a touch movement differently when inputting the patterns and they would perform more stably after inputting a pattern several times. These users' behavioral habits benefit the application of touch gestures in user authentication on smartphones.

However, we should still pay attention to an issue. It is noted that the average touch speed of some users may be similar. For example, based on Fig. 4, we find that User 1 can perform an *ASTM* of 102.5 px/s while User 28 can perform an *ASTM* of 104.2 px/s. Therefore, it is still too vague for a mechanism to use *ASTM* only to distinguish different users without considering their deviations. Otherwise, this problem can cause many usability problems (e.g., a high false rejection rate). To mitigate this issue, motivated by [9,15,16], we believe that some parameters/features like the *angle of touch movement* can be combined to better distinguish users.

What is more, we further develop and introduce two methods called *dot-dot pattern computation* and *proportional matching* in our proposed security mechanism (see next section) to maintain a balance between security and usability. The *dot-dot pattern computation* aims to describe a user's touch movement more accurately by separating a pattern into several segments while the *proportional matching* attempts to provide better usability through allowing reasonable touch deviations.

4   TMGuard: A Security Mechanism for Android Unlock Patterns

As illustrated above, it is identified that distinct users would perform the touch movement differently when drawing a pattern, while they would perform more stably for the same pattern after several trials. Based on the observations, it is feasible to apply behavioral biometrics to enhancing the security of Android unlock patterns. In this section, we therefore develop a security mechanism based on touch movement, called *TMGuard*, attempting to improve the authentication security of drawing unlock patterns. This mechanism can be utilized to complement the existing security solutions.

4.1   Mechanism Design

We present the high-level architecture of *TMGuard* in Fig. 7, which consists of five major components: *Data Record, Feature Calculation, Pattern Comparison, Profile Matching* and *Decision Component*.

- *Data Record.* This component is mainly used to record users' input when they interact with the touch screen and to collect relevant data for speed and angle calculation (e.g., timing and coordinates).

- *Feature Calculation.* This component is responsible for calculating the speed and angle of a touch movement based on the collected data.
- *Pattern Comparison.* This component is used to compare the unlock pattern input with the stored pattern and to report the result like acceptance or decline to the *Decision Component*.
- *Profile Matching.* This component is responsible for establishing the normal profile of users' input (e.g., touch movement) and matching the current input behavior with the normal profile. The result will be forwarded to the *Decision Component*.
- *Decision Component.* This component is responsible for collecting the results and making the final decision whether the current user is legitimate. Users can only be authenticated by both inputting the correct pattern and passing the examination of *Profile Matching*.

4.2   Profile Matching

As discussed earlier, it is not good enough to use only one *ASTM* to distinguish different users due to false rates. To address this issue, we add the *angle of touch movement* (*ATM*) in the profile construction. Moreover, in order to establish a more reliable normal profile, we develop another method called *dot-dot pattern computation*. This method aims to construct an accurate normal profile by separating a pattern into several segments. That is, it records pairs of (*STM, ATM*) for any two sequential touched dots in a pattern.

Dot-Dot Pattern Computation. Taking the pattern in Fig. 1 as an example, our mechanism records the speed and angle when the finger swipes from *dot 1* to *dot 2*. When the finger swipes from *dot 2* to *dot 3*, *TMGuard* then calculates the speed and angle for this movement in-between. Similarly, all pairs of (*STM, ATM*) will be recorded during the construction of a pattern. In this case, when the pattern is finished, *TMGuard* would log a collection of pairs regarding average touch speed and touch angle between any two sequential touched dots in a pattern. For a 9-dot pattern, there will be 8 pairs (or segments) to construct a normal profile.

In real usage, *TMGuard* will record three trials from users in inputting their patterns, and use the average value to establish the normal profile aiming to improve the reliability. In this case, the construction of a normal profile can be represented by means of Eq. (3).

$$Profile = \{\bigcup^{j}(ASTM,\ AATM)_i^{i+1}\}\ \ (4 \leq j \leq 9; i = 1, ..., j) \tag{3}$$

In the equation, j means the number of selected dots in an Android unlock pattern, i means dot number (or dot sequence number). *ASTM* means the average speed of touch movement between *dot i* and *dot i + 1*, while *AATM* means the average angle of touch movement between *dot i* and *dot i+1*. Thus for a j-dot pattern, the number of collected pairs is $j - 1$. There are two major objectives of using the *dot-dot pattern computation* in *TMGuard*:

- We identify that it is not reliable to authenticate users by means of only one *ASTM* for the whole pattern. In this case, the use of *dot-dot pattern computation* can provide more segments of *STM* during the authentication, so that users' touch behavior can be examined more precisely. In other words, *dot-dot pattern computation* attempts to describe a touch movement more accurately by recording the data between any two dots. This can improve the authentication security of Android unlock patterns.
- The same in our previous user study, it is found that the overall *ASTM* can be significantly affected by an abnormal (or unexpected) touch movement between two dots. Therefore, separating these dots and computing their *ASTM* respectively may eliminate these negative effects to some extent and improve the usability of *TMGuard*.

To authenticate a user, the component of *profile matching* will record his/her current inputs, calculate the pairs of $(ASTM, AATM)$ between any two touched dots, and compare these pairs with the stored normal profile.

Tradeoffs Between Security and Usability. Traditionally, users should perform a similar touch movement to unlock the pattern with the same pairs of $(ASTM, ATM)$ in a right sequence. However, we notice that users are often hard to exactly perform the same behavior. For example, the speed and angle of a touch movement between two dots may be a bit different. This is actually a big challenge for behavioral biometric authentication. It is also a big difference between *pattern comparison* and *profile matching*. If we do not improve the traditional profile matching, it can definitely increase false rejection rate and decrease usability. Thus, tradeoffs should be made between security and usability. Below we develop a novel scheme for profile matching.

Proportional Matching Scheme. For many existing behavioral biometric schemes like [9,15,28], machine learning techniques have been widely used in profile matching. But a major limitation is that it is hard to train an appropriate classifier in real scenario [13]. To avoid this issue, in this work, we develop a statistic-based scheme in *TMGuard*, called *proportional matching*, aiming to improve its usability, and make a balance between security and usability.

This method specifically utilizes a *confidence threshold* during the authentication. That is, users are only allowed to perform a touch movement within a defined deviation. For instance, if we set the *confidence threshold* to 0.98, thus, it is allowed a deviation less than 0.02 $(= 1 - 0.98)$ as compared to the stored normal profile. For a numerical example, if we have a pair of $(110.5, 23°)$, with a *confidence threshold* of 0.98, users then can be authenticated if the touch movement speed and the angle fall into an interval of $[108.3, 112.7]$ and $[22.54°, 23.46°]$ respectively. The effectiveness of this scheme is based on our observation that users would perform more stably when they have several input trials.

We have two major objectives of developing such a scheme in *TMGuard*:

- Users' inconsistent behaviors are a big challenge (open problem) for any behavioral biometric authentication scheme, which can significantly reduce the effectiveness of behavioral authentication. *TMGuard* attempts to provide another protection for Android unlock patterns, so that we do not expect to compromise the usability; otherwise, users may lose interests in using the application. The *proportional matching scheme* is thus used with the purpose of improving the usability of *TMGuard*.

- During the previous user study, it is found that users may perform more stably after inputting the selected patterns several times. This makes us believe that loosing the profile matching appropriately would not compromise the authentication security. On the other hand, according to specific scenarios, it is very easy to adjust the *confidence threshold* of the *proportional matching scheme*, making *TMGuard* more flexible in practical applications.

4.3 User Study for TMGuard

To investigate the performance of *TMGuard*, we conduct another user study with a total of 75 participants. All participants are regular mobile phone users and 40 % of them were joined our previous study in drawing unlock patterns. There are 45 males and 30 females and aged in the range from 18 to 60. Among them, 66.67 % are students while the others are company employees, senior citizens and businessmen. As incentives, $20 gift vouchers were given to each participant. The detailed information is shown in Table 2.

Table 2. Participants' information in the second user study.

Information	Male	Female	Occupation	Male	Female
Age < 25	10	7	Students	26	24
Age 25–35	20	15	Company employees	3	2
Age 35–45	9	5	Business people	8	4
Age > 45	6	3	Senior citizens	5	3

During the lab study, all participants were provided with our modified Android phones to avoid any implementation differences. There are two major phases in the study.

- *Phase1: in-lab study.* Users require to create a 4-dot and 9-dot pattern respectively and re-draw the pattern for three times. *TMGuard* will collect these trials, calculate the data and build the corresponding normal profile. The *confidence threshold* is set to 0.9. Then after 5 practice trials, users input the same pattern for another three real trials for authentication.
- *Phase2: out-of-lab study.* Users can freely create a pattern as their phone lock (note that they should also re-draw the pattern for three times to build normal profiles) in the lab and freely use the phone for another 2 days out of lab. When users input patterns, records will be stored. Finally, they should input the same pattern for three times in our lab.

The objective of *phase1* is to explore the initial performance of *TMGuard* and investigate how to decide an appropriate *confidence threshold*, while the latter aims to study the performance of *TMGuard* in a real scenario.

Result Analysis for Phase1. In this phase, each user can perform the authentication three times for both 4-dot and 9-dot pattern respectively, so that we can obtain 225 trials for each pattern. We show the results of authentication attempts differentiated by gender in Table 3. The table shows that male participants can achieve a successful login with a rate of 98.5 % for a 4-dot pattern, while they can reach a successful rate of 97.8 % for a 9-dot pattern. The slight decrease is due to that more pairs should be authenticated for a 9-dot pattern (e.g., 8 pairs of dot-dot patterns) as compared to a 4-dot pattern (e.g., 3 pairs of dot-dot patterns). The results are reasonable as more pairs of dot-dot patterns will increase the uncertainty during a touch movement (i.e., increasing the deviation of inputting patterns). Regarding female participants, it is noticed that they perform very similarly for 9-dot pattern, but achieve better performance for 4-dot pattern than males.

After the user study, we interviewed all users and found that 78.7 % of the participants are satisfied with the login experience, and encouragingly 80 % of them consider that *TMGuard* can improve the security of Android unlock patterns. In addition, 73.3 % of them acknowledge that they would like to try this mechanism in regular use. As this is a scientific and security related study, we notice that users' answers may be affected by the environment. Even so, the feedback can still positively support the performance of *TMGuard*.

In contrast, Table 4 shows the authentication results if we do not use *dot-dot pattern computation*. It is noticeable that the successful authentication rate decreases significantly for both male and female participants. Taking 9-dot patterns as an example, the successful rate is decreased from 97.8 % to 91.1 % for males and from 97.8 % to 88.9 % for females respectively. To study the effect of *proportional matching scheme*, we further present the authentication results with different *confidence thresholds* for the 9-dot patterns in Fig. 8(a). The figure

Table 3. Authentication results of users' trials with *TMGuard* including *confidence threshold* and *dot-dot pattern computation*.

Successful rate	4-dot pattern	9-dot pattern
Males	133/135 (98.5 %)	132/135 (97.8 %)
Females	90/90 (100 %)	88/90 (97.8 %)

Table 4. Authentication results of users' trials without *dot-dot pattern computation*.

Successful rate	4-dot pattern	9-dot pattern
Males	127/135 (94.1 %)	123/135 (91.1 %)
Females	83/90 (92.2 %)	80/90 (88.9 %)

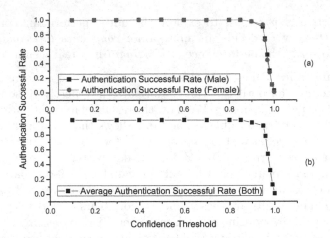

Fig. 8. Authentication results of users' trials with different *confidence thresholds*.

shows that the *confidence threshold* can make a crucial impact on user authentication. We have three major observations:

- On the whole, the authentication rate will be decreased through increasing the *confidence threshold*. When the *confidence threshold* reaches 1, which means conducting the user authentication without *proportional matching scheme* where users should exactly input their patterns, it is found that the authentication rate will be significantly reduced below 1%. This observation demonstrates the importance of *proportional matching scheme* on improving the usability of *TMGuard*.
- In Fig. 8(b), we compute the average authentication successful rate for both 4-dot and 9-dot patterns. It is found that 0.9 is a turning point, where before this point, the authentication rate can be quickly increased to 1, while after this point, the authentication rate would have a quick drop. At this point, Table 3 presents that the successful authentication rate is about 98%. Thus, we consider that it is an appropriate threshold in *TMGuard*.
- In addition, we find that there is no significant statistical difference between male and female participants. The collected data shows that gender information would not greatly affect the performance of *TMGuard*.

Result Analysis for Phase2. In this phase, we expect to simulate a real scenario on how users may use their phones. We have two collected datasets. (1) After an informal interview, we find that all users have input their selected patterns to unlock their phones 10 times at least and 33 times at most during the 2 days, and a total of 1856 trials were collected after analyzing the record. (2) In addition, since all users should input their patterns three times in our lab, we can further record 225 real trials in the lab. The *confidence threshold* is also set to 0.9. It means that there allows a 20 px/s deviation for a high speed at 200 px/s and a 10 px/s deviation for a low speed at 100 px/s.

For the first dataset, we present the successful authentication rate in Fig. 9. The figure shows that the successful authentication rate keeps increasing and becomes much stable after 4 trials. In addition, we show the DET curve regarding the false rejection rate (FRR) and false acceptance rate (FAR) with different *confidence thresholds* in Fig. 10, based on the recorded 1856 trials. The FAR and FAR are computed by authenticating all users trials against their templates under different thresholds. It is seen that when the *confidence threshold* is 0.9, a better FAR of 2.12 % and FRR of 2.23 % could be achieved.

Table 5. Authentication results of users' trials with *TMGuard* in *Phase2*.

Gender	Trials and successful rate
Males	135/135 (100 %)
Females	90/90 (100 %)

Similarly, for the second dataset collected in our lab, we compute the results of authentication attempts in Table 5, which shows a perfect authentication rate that all users can successfully input the patterns and unlock their phones. After interviewing with the participants, we found that many participants would pay attention to their touch behavior when inputting the patterns. They indicated that this may bring a little burden for them, but it is not a hard job for them to keep their behavior within the threshold. That is, users can adapt to a new mechanism when they pay attention to it and practice with several trials. This is the major reason for the perfect authentication results. It is worth noting that increasing user awareness is one of the important factors to improve the authentication security [5].

Based on the results in our study, we believe that setting the *confidence threshold* to 0.9 is appropriate without compromising the usability of inputting unlock patterns. These results also showed that the use of *dot-dot pattern computation* and *proportional matching* can encouragingly improve the usability of *TMGuard* in real applications.

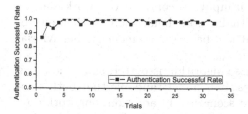

Fig. 9. Authentication results of users' performance with 1856 trials in *Phase2*.

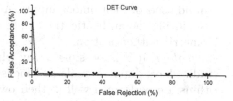

Fig. 10. DET curve shows how FRR and FAR vary when different confidence thresholds are used.

Discussions. In the literature, De Luca et al. [8] proposed an implicit approach to improve unlock patterns by extracting touchscreen data including pressure, size, X-coordinate, Y-coordinate and timings. They then conducted two studies and gave a conclusion: it is possible to distinguish users and improve the security of password patterns and screen unlocks by integrating behavioral biometrics. In their studies, the top user could reach an accuracy of 96 %, while the overall accuracy is 77 % for all users. Their work is the most referred and similar one to our work in the following aspects:

- Both research studies advocate that the security of unlock patterns should be improved by integrating an additional layer.
- Both research studies attempt to combine behavioral biometrics with Android unlock patterns.
- Both studies employ a non-machine-learning approach in the process of profile matching, where our work uses statistic-based method while De Luca et al. [8] use dynamic time warping (DTW).[3]

Although the main idea of these research studies are similar, it is not applicable to directly compare the results of these two articles. For example, the authentication accuracy in our work is above 97 % in average, but the results in [8] are much lower (i.e., 77 %). However, we should notice that the evaluation processes and research focuses are different. Those differences can be summarized as below:

- *Goals.* The main goal of [8] is to investigate the feasibility of applying behavioral biometrics to unlock patterns, while thanks to their conclusion, the goal of our work is to design a better mechanism to enhance the security of Android unlock patterns.
- *Schemes.* According to different goals, in [8], they did not propose a specific scheme to process the collected data while only apply dynamic time warping to the data. In contrast, our work first conducts a study to learn user behaviors during inputting Android unlock patterns and then designs a concrete mechanism based on touch movement.
- *Evaluation.* Obviously, the evaluation steps are different in these two studies. Moreover, behind the evaluation, the two articles have different views on user awareness. In [8], they would like to reduce users awareness in which users can perform not the same for a pattern input. In contrast, our work aims to remind users of their unlock inputs. Actually, user should increase their awareness during the authentication, since it is a basic requirement for behaviorial biometric authentication.
- *Algorithms.* It is impossible to say whose algorithm is better, since these two studies have different goals and focuses. It is understandable that both algorithms are performed well in their own scenarios. In addition, our work dose not aim to replace the existing algorithms, but provide alternatives for enhancing the security of unlock patterns.

---

[3] Dynamic time warping (DTW) is an algorithm for measuring similarity between two temporal sequences which may vary in time or speed.

Overall, [8] is a feasibility study that provides useful insights for combining behavioral biometrics with Android unlock patterns, and its results are positive and encouraging. Thanks to this, our work designs a more specific scheme in data processing and uses a statistic-based approach in profile matching. In practice, these two studies are complementary to each other. For example, our work does not include pressure and size, which can be considered in our future studies.

5 Conclusion and Future Work

In this paper, we develop a security mechanism, called *TMGuard*, attempting to enhance the authentication security of Android unlock patterns by combining it with behavioral biometrics. We totally conduct two studies in this work. In the first study, we find that users would perform touch movement differently when interacting with the touchscreen and that users would perform touch movement more stably for the same pattern after several trials. In the second user study, the experimental results and users' feedback demonstrate that *TMGuard* can promisingly improve the authentication security of Android unlock patterns without compromising its usability. Future work includes adding more features to our mechanism (i.e., from accelerometer and sensors [7,10]) and simulating advanced attacks. Our efforts aim to complement the existing solutions and to stimulate more research in this area.

Acknowledgments. We would like to thank all participants for their hard work and collaboration in the user studies such as data collection, and thank all anonymous reviewers for their helpful comments.

References

1. Andriotis, P., Tryfonas, T., Oikonomou, G., Yildiz, C.: A pilot study on the security of pattern screen-lock methods, soft side channel attacks. In: Proceedings of WiSec, pp. 1–6. ACM (2013)
2. Aviv, A.J., Gibson, K., Mossop, E., Blaze, M., Smith, J.M.: Smudge attacks on smartphone touch screens. In: Proceedings of the 4th USENIX Conference on Offensive Technologies, pp. 1–7. USENIX Association (2010)
3. Churchill , B.:Unlock Pattern Generator (2013). https://www.berkeleychurchill.com/software/android-pwgen/pwgen.php
4. Bergadano, F., Gunetti, D., Picardi, C.: User authentication through keystroke dynamics. ACM Trans. Inf. Syst. Secur. 5(4), 367–397 (2002)
5. Bisson, D.: The state of security-Authentication and awareness: the anti-cybercrime duo, 30 October 2014. http://www.tripwire.com/state-of-security/security-awareness/authentication-and-awareness-the-anti-cybercrime-duo/
6. Brown, A.S., Bracken, E., Zoccoli, S., Douglas, K.: Generating and remembering passwords. Appl. Cogn. Psychol. **18**, 641–651 (2004)
7. Conti, M., Zachia-Zlatea, I., Crispo, B.: Mind how you answer me! (transparently authenticating the user of a smartphone when answering or placing a call). In: Proceedings of the 6th ASIACCS, pp. 249–259 (2011)

8. De Luca, A., Hang, A., Brudy, F., Lindner, C., Hussmann, H.: Touch me once and i know it's you!: implicit authentication based on touch screen patterns. In: Proceedings of CHI, pp. 987–996. ACM (2012)
9. Frank, M., Biedert, R., Ma, E., Martinovic, I., Song, D.: Touchalytics: on the applicability of touchscreen input as a behavioral biometric for continuous authentication. IEEE Trans. Inf. Forensics Secur. 8(1), 136–148 (2013)
10. Giuffrida, C., Majdanik, K., Conti, M., Bos, H.: I sensed it was you: authenticating mobile users with sensor-enhanced keystroke dynamics. In: Dietrich, S. (ed.) DIMVA 2014. LNCS, vol. 8550, pp. 92–111. Springer, Heidelberg (2014)
11. IDC. Smartphone OS Market Share, Q2 2015, December 2015. http://www.idc.com/prodserv/smartphone-os-market-share.jsp
12. Karlson, A.K., Brush, A.B., Schechter, S. Can i borrow your phone?: understanding concerns when sharing mobile phones. In: Proceedings of the 27th CHI, pp. 1647–1650. ACM (2009)
13. Kotthoff, L., Gent, I.P., Miguel, I.: An evaluation of machine learning in algorithm selection for search problems. AI Commun. 25(3), 257–270 (2012)
14. Li, L., Zhao, X., Xue, G.: Unobservable re-authentication for smartphones. In: Proceedings of the 20th Annual Network and Distributed System Security Symposium (NDSS), pp. 1–16 (2013)
15. Meng, Y., Wong, D.S., Schlegel, R., Kwok, L.: Touch gestures based biometric authentication scheme for touchscreen mobile phones. In: Kutyłowski, M., Yung, M. (eds.) INSCRYPT 2012. LNCS, vol. 7763, pp. 331–350. Springer, Heidelberg (2013)
16. Meng, W., Wong, D.S., Kwok, L.F.: The effect of adaptive mechanism on behavioural biometric based mobile phone authentication. Inf. Manag. Comput. Secur. 22(2), 155–166 (2014)
17. Meng, W., Wong, D.S., Furnell, S., Zhou, J.: Surveying the development of biometric user authentication on mobile phones. IEEE Commun. Surv. Tutorials 17(3), 1268–1293 (2015)
18. Nelson, D.L., Reed, V.S., Walling, J.R.: Pictorial superiority effect. J. Exp. Psychol.: Hum. Learn. Mem. 2(5), 523–528 (1976)
19. Pereira Botelho, B.A., Nakamura, E.T., Uto, N.: Security analysis of touch inputted passwords. In: Lopez, J., Huang, X., Sandhu, R. (eds.) NSS 2013. LNCS, vol. 7873, pp. 714–720. Springer, Heidelberg (2013)
20. Tao, H., Adams, C.: Pass-go: a proposal to improve the usability of graphical passwords. Int. J. Netw. Secur. 7(2), 273–292 (2008)
21. Van Thanh, D.: Security issues in mobile eCommerce. In: Proceedings of the 11th International Workshop on Database and Expert Systems Applications (DEXA), pp. 412–425 (2000)
22. SplashData Inc, Password unseated by "123456" on SplashData's annual Worst Passwords list (2013). http://splashdata.com/press/worstpasswords2013.htm
23. Uellenbeck, S., Dürmuth, M., Wolf, C., Holz, T.: Quantifying the security of graphical passwords: the case of Android unlock patterns. In: Proceedings of the 2013 ACM Conference on Computer and Communications Security (CCS), pp. 161–172 (2013)
24. Webroot. SURVEY: Mobile Threats are Real and Costly (2012). http://www.webroot.com/shared/pdf/byod-mobile-security-study.pdf
25. J. White. Cydia Tweak: How To Add An Android-Inspired Pattern Unlock Screen To The iPhone, 26 June 2013. http://appadvice.com/appnn/2013/06/cydia-tweak-how-to-add-an-android-inspired-pattern-unlock-screen-to-the-iphone

26. Yan, J., Blackwell, A., Anderson, R., Grant, A.: Password memorability and security: empirical results. IEEE Secur. Priv. **2**(5), 25–31 (2004)
27. Yan, Q., Han, J., Li, Y., Zhou, J., Deng, R.: Designing leakage-resilient passwordentry on touchscreen mobile devices. In: Proceedings of the 8th Asia CCS, pp. 37–48 (2013)
28. Zahid, S., Shahzad, M., Khayam, S.A., Farooq, M.: Identification, keystroke-based user on smart phones. In: Proceedings of RAID, pp. 224–243 (2009)
29. Zhang, Y., Xia, P., Luo, J., Ling, Z., Liu, B., Fu, X.: Fingerprint attack against touch-enabled devices. In: Proceedings of the 2nd ACM Workshop on Security and Privacy in Smartphones and Mobile Devices, pp. 57–68 (2012)
30. Zhao, X., Feng, T., Shi, W., Kakadiaris, I.A.: Mobile user authentication using statistical touch dynamics images. IEEE Trans. Inf. Forensics Secur. **9**(11), 1780–1789 (2014)

Gesture-Based Continuous Authentication for Wearable Devices: The Smart Glasses Use Case

Jagmohan Chauhan[1,2](✉), Hassan Jameel Asghar[2], Anirban Mahanti[2], and Mohamed Ali Kaafar[2]

[1] UNSW, Sydney, Australia
[2] Data61, CSIRO, Sydney, Australia
{jagmohan.chauhan,hassan.asghar,anirban.mahanti,
dali.kaafar}@data61.csiro.au

Abstract. We study the feasibility of touch gesture behavioural biometrics for implicit authentication of users on smart glasses by proposing a continuous authentication system on Google Glass using two classifiers: SVM with RBF kernel, and a new classifier based on Chebyshev's concentration inequality. Based on data collected from 30 users, we show that such authentication is feasible both in terms of classification accuracy and computational load on Glass. We achieve a classification accuracy of up to 99 % with only 75 training samples using behavioural biometric data from four different types of touch gestures. To show that our system can be generalized, we test its performance on touch data from smartphones and found the accuracy to be similar to Glass. Finally, our experiments on the permanence of gestures show that the negative impact of changing user behaviour with time on classification accuracy can be best alleviated by periodically replacing older training samples with new randomly chosen samples.

1 Introduction

Since many wearable devices store highly sensitive user information such as health data, a secure and usable authentication mechanism to restrict access to unauthorized users is paramount. A straightforward solution is *entry-point* authentication relying on personal identification numbers (PINs), passwords or graphical patterns [18]. However, frequent use of entry-point authentication potentially disrupts user activities [2,4]. Moreover, in comparison to smartphones, unlocking patterns on wearable devices such as Google Glass are more vulnerable to *shoulder-surfing* [14,19] since the Glass touchpad is easily observable from a distance.

An alternative is to use an implicit and continuous authentication system, which runs in the background without disrupting the user, and authenticates

---

The full version of this paper is available at http://arxiv.org/abs/1412.2855.

© Springer International Publishing Switzerland 2016
M. Manulis et al. (Eds.): ACNS 2016, LNCS 9696, pp. 648–665, 2016.
DOI: 10.1007/978-3-319-39555-5_35

the user whenever he/she performs a designated action, which in our case is using the touchpad. The system only triggers entry-point authentication if an intrusion is detected. Provided the method is reliable, this approach reduces the number of times a legitimate user needs to undergo entry-point authentication. Many continuous authentication schemes have previously been proposed in the literature for smartphones [7,9,10,19], however, they may not provide similar accuracy or may be computationally heavy on wearables such as Glass. A smaller touchpad of Glass compared to a smartphone is likely to show less variation in gestures across different users, thereby impacting accuracy. Also, running computationally expensive applications can deplete the battery faster on Glass [11].

These factors motivate a feasibility study of continuous authentication on wearables. Towards this goal, in this paper, we assess the feasibility of continuous authentication on Glass. Our key contributions are as follows. First, to the best of our knowledge, we are the first to study the feasibility of touch gesture based continuous authentication on smart glasses in terms of classification accuracy and computational cost by using Google Glass as a use case. Although Glass itself may or may not be continued as a product, our work is still relevant since our scheme can be extended to other smart glasses with touchpads namely RECON, SiME, GlassUP, ORA-S and Icis, as well as other touchpad devices, e.g., smartphones. Second, we model a touch gesture as one or more *forces* applied on the touchpad by the user's finger over the duration of the gesture. A resulting novel feature is the *downward force feature* which is a product of pressure and size values extracted from the device's touch event.

Third, to authenticate the user, besides using support vector machine (SVM) with Gaussian radial basis function (RBF) classifier (widely used for continuous authentication on smartphones), we introduce a new classifier based on *Chebyshev's concentration inequality*. Previous research on touch gesture based continuous authentication on smartphones has shown that during testing (authentication), instead of using features from a single sample of a gesture, using features from a *block* of samples of the gesture shows improved classification accuracy [7,10,15]. We note that this observation implicitly uses the assumption that the average value of a feature over a block is more likely to be concentrated around the mean. The justification of this comes from concentration inequalities, which give probabilistic bounds on the deviation of the average of identically distributed random variables from their true mean. This led us to propose the Chebyshev classifier. Lastly, by extending our experiments to smartphone touch data, we find that the size of the touchpad has an effect on classification accuracy; smaller touchpads, as in smart glasses, exhibit less variation across users.

2   Related Work

Entry Point Authentication: Zheng et al. [20] collected the tapping behaviour of 80 different users when entering PINs on smartphones and extracted four features (acceleration, pressure, size, and time) from the collected data, achieving a 3.65 % equal error rate. Shahzad et al. [16] created a system named GEAT. However, unlike the scheme proposed by Zheng et al., GEAT differentiates the user on the basis of their sliding behaviour and uses unique features such as finger velocity, device acceleration, and slide time, achieves a 0.5 % equal error rate. Similarly, Luca et al. [6] exploit user sliding behaviour while unlocking smartphone patterns, achieving an accuracy of around 50 %. In comparison to the these works, our study focuses on continuous authentication.

Continuous Authentication: Numerous schemes [3,7,10,19] have been proposed for continuous authentication on smartphones. Hui et al. [19] collected data from 31 volunteers for different touch operations such as keystroke, slide, pinch and handwriting to test their continuous authentication scheme and showed that the slide gesture is the best in classifying users, while handwriting performs the worst. Similarly, Frank et al. [7] proposed a scheme using a set of 30 touch-based features and tested it on 41 users. Their classifier achieved a median equal error rate of 0 % within the same usage session and 2–3 % across different sessions. The reason why these two schemes achieve exceptionally high authentication accuracy might be due to the fact that users were static and were given specific tasks to be performed. In comparison, we did not enforce any such restriction on the users. Li et al. tested a continuous authentication scheme based on sliding and tap gestures [10] and extracted features such as the position and area of first touch, duration and average curvature of slide. SilentSense [3] used finger movements and user motion patterns and achieved 99 % accuracy. In contrast to our study, the temporal effect of user behaviour on accuracy is not studied in the last two schemes. A more recent work from Mondal and Bours [12] uses a trust-based approach for continuous authentication, where instead of waiting for a fixed number of gestures from the user before making a decision, the system updates its trust value, about the current user being the target user, with every gesture and locks the user when the trust value falls below a pre-defined threshold. This approach can be applied to any continuous authentication mechanism including ours.

A somewhat related topic is the recently introduced sensor-enhanced keystroke dynamics [8], which augments traditional timing-based keystroke dynamics with motion sensors available on smart devices. Not only does this approach increase the accuracy of traditional keystroke dynamics and gesture-based authentication [8], it has also been shown to be more resistant to statistical attacks using general population statistics [17].

Overall our work is different from previous works in three major ways: (1) we assess the feasibility of touch gestured based continuous authentication on smart glasses. Smart glasses, such as Google Glass, present unique challenges such as smaller form factor and lesser computational power compared to smartphones, (2) we propose a new classifier based on concentration inequalities, and (3) we propose new force-based features.

3   Background

The Google Glass: Google Glasses (cf. Fig. 1a) contain an optical display mounted on the lens, which contains a small screen (cf. Fig. 1b). The user can navigate using voice commands or by interacting with the touchpad located on the side through taps or swipes (forward, backward or downward). Swipes can be done through one, two or three fingers. Note that not all apps (cards) and their menu items can be interacted using voice and require a touch gesture.

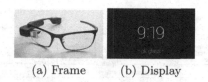

(a) Frame   (b) Display

Fig. 1. The Google glass (images courtesy of Wikipedia and Google).

Definitions: For the rest of this paper, a *gesture* is defined as a tap or a swipe with one finger on the touchpad. For each gesture, the set of data recorded by the Glass touchpad, e.g., the point of contact, is called a *sample*. A sample contains a time-ordered sequence of one or more *readings*, which correspond to data recorded at different discrete time intervals during the duration of a gesture. Each reading contains data corresponding to one or more variables called *features*. The authentication mechanism takes as input a set of gestures and either (implicitly) accepts or rejects the user depending on whether or not the set matches the gestures of the target user. True positive rate (TPR) is defined as the fraction of times the target user is correctly accepted. False positive rate (FPR) is defined as the fraction of times the attacker is (wrongly) accepted as the target user. Equal error rate (EER) is defined as the rate at which both acceptance and rejection *errors* are equal, i.e., when $1 - \text{TPR} = \text{FPR}$. EER is widely used as a measure of classification accuracy. A related measure is the average error rate (AER), which is defined as $\frac{1}{2}(1 - \text{TPR} + \text{FPR})$ and is useful when EER is unknown. Receiver operating characteristic (ROC) curve shows the trend of TPR against FPR. Variability in these rates is introduced by changing different parameter values of the authentication system.

4   Continuous Authentication for Google Glass

4.1   Architecture

The proposed system architecture, as shown in Fig. 2, has a training and a testing phase. The system listens for gesture events that are triggered whenever the user performs gestures on the touchpad. Once an event is triggered, elementary features such as the start and end point of gestures are extracted. From the start and end points, the gesture type (tap, forward, backward or downward swipe) is identified, after which higher-level features, e.g., force exerted on the touchpad, are derived. Some of the features in our system are derived as a function of time and require further processing for consistent inter-comparison. After going through this post-processor, our system feeds the resulting features to the classifier. During training, the classifier generates different classification models for different gesture combinations. During the testing phase, real-time gesture data from the current user is processed to obtain the feature sets as above, which are then fed to the classifier for prediction.

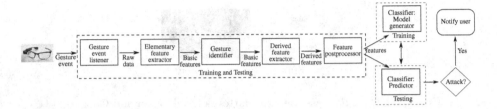

Fig. 2. System architecture.

4.2 Data Collection

We collected data for four gestures: tap, forward swipe, backward swipe, and downward swipe from the Glass touchpad (v 18.1, Android) using a background process, which reads the raw touch data values at runtime. Glass is equipped with the Synaptics T1320 touchpad. More technical details, such as the structure of touch packets, are given in the full paper. We selected 30 volunteers consisting of 8 females and 22 males within the 18–45 age bracket and asked them to use Google Glass for a few hours. All were colleagues and students with a computer science background. They were free to explore Glass as they liked and use any application installed on the device. Each user was trained how to operate Glass prior to data collection. Table 1 shows the quantity of gesture data collected from the users. Forward swipe is the most frequently used gesture, followed by the tap; downward swipe being the least frequent gesture. Backward swipes can be used in place of forward swipes to navigate in the opposite direction, explaining their relatively less usage. Moreover, downward swipes are mostly used for quitting an app or cancelling an action and hence their frequency is the lowest.

Table 1. Total number of samples, average and minimum sample size per user, and average gap (in seconds) for gestures obtained in our user study.

Gesture	Total	Ave. sample size	Min. sample size	Average gap
Tap (T)	4932	164.4	60	13
Forward swipe (F)	7874	262.46	67	8
Backward swipe (B)	3257	108.56	37	17
Downward swipe (D)	1525	50.83	11	32

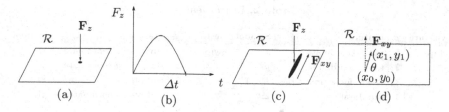

Fig. 3. Force based gesture models: (a) the tap force, (b) the magnitude of the force curve $F_z(t)$ over the interval Δt, (c) the two forces active during a swipe, and (d) the source of the force $\mathbf{F}_{xy}$ estimated through the angle θ.

4.3 Gesture Model and Feature Extraction

We model the touchpad as a rectangle $\mathcal{R}$ on a two dimensional xy-plane, where the origin is the bottom-left corner. We distinguish between two types of gestures, tap (T) and swipe. Swipe is further divided into forward (F), backward (B) and downward (D). We model each gesture as one or more forces (exerted by user's finger) acting over the course of a gesture. Our main assumption is that the *magnitude and source of these forces over the time duration* of the gesture are characteristics of a user.

Modelling the Tap Gesture: The tap is characterised by the downward force applied by the finger on the touchpad. This force, denoted $\mathbf{F}_z$, acts downwards on $\mathcal{R}$, i.e., along the z-axis. The source is the point on $\mathcal{R}$ where the user taps. This is shown in Fig. 3a. The magnitude of $\mathbf{F}_z$ is calculated using pressure P and area (size) A readings from the touch event as $F_z = PA$. Note that our hypothesis is that it is the correlation between the pressure and area values that is expected to be consistent across samples, instead of treating the two separately, as is done in [6] for instance. As the tap is performed over a time interval, say Δt, we denote the magnitude of $\mathbf{F}_z$ over time as $F_z(t)$, which is a *time series*. Figure 3b visualises the possible shape of F_z over the duration of tap. $F_z(t)$ can be calculated over discrete points t in the interval Δt through corresponding pressure and area values. We also use tap duration (Δt) as a feature.

Modelling the Swipe Gesture: We model a swipe as two forces acting on $\mathcal{R}$ simultaneously. The first is $\mathbf{F}_z$, the force acting downwards on $\mathcal{R}$, as in the case of tap. The second, denoted $\mathbf{F}_{xy}$, is a force acting along the direction of swipe (xy-plane). These two forces are visualized in Fig. 3c. To estimate the source of $\mathbf{F}_z$, we use the start point (x_0, y_0) and the end point (x_1, y_1) of the swipe. The source of the force $\mathbf{F}_{xy}$ is estimated as the angle θ between the straight line joining these two points and the y-axis as shown in Fig. 3d. To estimate the duration of the forces, in addition to the swipe duration Δt, we also include the swipe length l. The magnitude of $\mathbf{F}_z$ is again estimated as the time series $F_z(t)$ of individual pressure and area (PA) values. The magnitude of $\mathbf{F}_{xy}$ is also modelled as a time series $F_{xy}(t)$ with the difference that individual values are the magnitude of *velocity* at discrete time intervals. This is done since in classical mechanics, force

Table 2. List of features.

Gesture	#	Feature	Symbol	Gesture	#	Feature	Symbol
Tap	1	tap x-coordinate	x	Swipe	1	start pt. x-coordinate	x_0
	2	tap y-coordinate	y		2	start pt. y-coordinate	y_0
	3	down. force time series	$F_z(t)$		3	end pt. x-coordinate	x_1
	4	tap duration	Δt		4	end pt. y-coordinate	y_1
					5	angle	θ
					6	down force time series	$F_z(t)$
					7	planar force time series	$F_{xy}(t)$
					8	swipe duration	Δt
					9	swipe length	l

is considered proportional to acceleration which can be determined by change in velocity. Table 2 summarizes the list of features.

Post-processing the Time Series: The time series for the magnitude of force ($F_z(t)$ and $F_{xy}(t)$) can be misaligned due to the non-uniform sampling rate of the device and difference in duration of the gesture. To get a consistent comparison of time series from different readings, we do the following: (a) we align the first sample of the two time series at time $t = 0$; (b) we resample each time series at intervals of $t_{int} = 0.01$ s (slightly lower than the system average of ≈ 0.012 s) similar to the approach is used in [16]; (c) we use a cut-off point $t_{off} = 0.3$, after which all values are discarded. Most time series span an interval Δt, which is less than t_{off}. For such cases, all values at time $\Delta t < t < t_{off}$ are mapped to 0.

4.4 Chebyshev Classifier

Many researchers have indicated that a *block* of samples used for testing shows an improved performance over using individual samples [7,10,15], where the average reading of the feature over the block is used as a single instance for input to the classifier. We note that if a sample block is to be used, a classifier based on *concentration inequalities* can be employed. A concentration inequality bounds the probability that a random variable deviates from its expected value. The deviation from the expected value decreases (probabilistically) with an increase in the block size of identically distributed random variables. We thus propose a one class classifier based on the concentration inequality called Chebyshev's inequality. The use of this inequality is not unprecedented in anomaly or outlier detection in a somewhat different manner [1]. A further advantage of Chebyshev's inequality is that it does not make any assumptions on the probability distribution of data (which may be unimodal or multimodal).

Let X be a random variable representing a unitary feature, i.e., any feature other than a time-series based feature. Let $\mathbf{x} = (x_1, \ldots, x_n)$ denote n samples of this unitary feature. The corresponding random variables are denoted $X_1, \ldots, X_n$. We assume that these random variables are independent and identically distributed (i.i.d.), since they correspond to different samples (of the same gesture type). Let $E[X] = \mu_X$ and $Var[X] = \sigma_X^2$ denote the expected value (mean) and variance of X, respectively. Then for any $\tau > 0$, $\Pr\left[|X - \mathrm{E}[X]| \geq \tau\right] \leq \frac{\mathrm{Var}[X]}{\tau^2} \Rightarrow$ $\Pr\left[|X - \mu_X| \geq \tau\right] \leq \frac{\sigma_X^2}{\tau^2}$ is known as Chebyshev's inequality [13, Sect. 8, p. 431]. Consider the random variable $\overline{S}_n = \frac{1}{n}\sum_{i=1}^{n} X_i$. Since the X_i's are i.i.d., we have $\mathrm{E}[\overline{S}_n] = \frac{1}{n}\sum_{i=1}^{n} \mathrm{E}[X_i] = \frac{n}{n}\mu_X = \mu_X$, and $\mathrm{Var}[\overline{S}_n] = \mathrm{Var}\left[\frac{1}{n}\sum_{i=1}^{n} X_i\right] = \frac{1}{n^2}\mathrm{Var}\left[\sum_{i=1}^{n} X_i\right] = \frac{1}{n^2}\sum_{i=1}^{n} \mathrm{Var}[X_i] = \frac{n}{n^2}\sigma_X^2 = \frac{\sigma_X^2}{n}$. Using Chebyshev's inequality on $\overline{S}_n$ and the above two results, we get

$$\Pr\left[|\overline{S}_n - \mathrm{E}[\overline{S}_n]| \geq \tau\right] \leq \frac{\mathrm{Var}[\overline{S}_n]}{\tau^2} \Rightarrow \Pr\left[\left|\frac{1}{n}\sum_{i=1}^{n} X_i - \mu_X\right| \geq \tau\right] \leq \frac{\sigma_X^2}{n\tau^2} \quad (1)$$

for any $\tau > 0$. A qualitative explanation of this inequality is that as n increases, the average of a sample is more likely to be concentrated around the mean. Now, let $\rho = \frac{\sigma_X^2}{n\tau^2}$. Rearranging we get $\tau = \frac{\sigma_X}{\sqrt{n\rho}}$. By specifying a value of ρ in this equation, i.e., a bound on probability, we can obtain a corresponding threshold τ. This then gives us a straightforward classification method for features: Given a sample $x_1', x_2', \ldots, x_n'$, purported to be generated from the same distribution as X, we calculate the sample mean and see if this lies within the threshold τ determined by ρ. If yes, then the sample is classified as belonging to the target user; otherwise it is rejected. Similarly, for a time-series based feature we can use this classifier with slight modification as detailed in the full version of the paper. Thus given an n-element sample $\mathbf{x} = (x_1, x_2, \ldots, x_n)$ and the parameter ρ, we have the *Chebyshev feature classifier* $f(\mathbf{x}, \rho)$ which outputs 1 if the sample belongs to the target user and 0 otherwise. To make an overall decision given samples from a set of m features $\chi = \{\mathbf{x}_1, \ldots, \mathbf{x}_m\}$, we have the following classifier, which we call the *Chebyshev classifier*:

$$g(\chi, \rho, \epsilon) = \begin{cases} 1, & \text{if } \sum_{i=1}^{m} f(\mathbf{x}_i, \rho) > \epsilon m \\ 0, & \text{otherwise} \end{cases} \quad (2)$$

We call ϵ the *decision threshold* and ϵm the *decision boundary*. Through our experiments we found $\epsilon = \frac{2}{3}$ to give the best EER.

4.5 SVM Classifier

Our second classifier is the binary class SVM with Gaussian radial basis function (RBF) kernel. We used its implementation available through the LIBSVM library [5]. To construct the feature space for SVM, we represented the time series based features as $\frac{t_{\text{off}}}{t_{\text{int}}} = 30$ dimensional vectors. The whole feature space of the SVM is then a vector of all unitary features and time series based features represented in the aforementioned way. Constructed in this way, the SVM classifier is given training data. To obtain the best classification results, we performed a grid search with 10-fold cross validation on the training data to find the optimal values for its parameters, i.e., C and γ [5]. Notice that the training phase needs data both from the legitimate (target) user and other users (represented as the second class). As this type of data represents unbalanced data (more data from the second class), we used a weighted scheme SVM. After a user model has been created by the SVM, the authentication phase or testing phase can be carried out. Let χ be a set of samples of features to be tested against the user model, where we assume the sample size of each feature to be $n \geq 1$. For each feature $\mathbf{x} \in \chi$ with n samples denoted by $\mathbf{x} = (x_1, \ldots, x_n)$, the average value $\frac{1}{n}\sum_{i=1}^{n} x_i$ is used in the final feature vector.

5   Evaluation and Results

5.1   Experimental Setup

To evaluate the performance of Chebyshev classifier, we consider three sets of users denoted by U_1, U_2, and U_3, containing 10, 20 and 30 users, respectively. For all user sets, our experimental setup is as follows. To obtain the True Positive Rate (TPR), we randomly select a target user, and use a random set of 50 samples from this user as the training set. The test set used for authentication, consists of the remaining samples. Given a fixed value of n, a random sample of length n is obtained from the test set. The random test sample is then fed to the classifier, which was trained using the training data. The decision from the classifier is then logged. This process was repeated 500 times each with a new random target user. Note that due to randomness, the training set for the same user is different over different trials. Finally, the number of times, out of the 500 tests, the target user was accepted was used to compute TPR.

The False Positive Rate (FPR) is calculated in the same manner as TPR except that the classifier was given a test sample of size n from all the samples of a random attacker selected from U_1 (respectively from U_2, and U_3), excluding the target user. FPR was calculated as the rate at which the attacker was accepted. The size of the training set for tap and forward swipe was 50, whereas backward swipe and downward swipe had training set sizes of 25 and 10, respectively, since for these gestures we had lower number of available samples (see Table 1).

For the SVM classifier we divided the pool of 30 users into three disjoint sets. The first set, labelled U_1, consists of 10 target users for whom we had *at least* 75 samples for all gesture types and is fixed. The remaining 20 users are modelled as attackers and are assigned to two sets labelled U_2 (10 attackers) and U_3 (20 attackers). For each user in U_1, the training data consists of a random sample of a fixed size from the user's data. This constitutes positive samples for the target user required for binary class SVM training. The negative samples for the target user came from the data of the remaining 9 target users in U_1. That is, the data from the remaining 9 users was used in the training phase to model the *mock* attacker. The data of the users from U_2 and U_3 is used to compute FPR.

5.2   Chebyshev Classifier Results

First, we empirically determined the decision threshold ϵ in Eq. 2. For this, we used the user set U_1, and chose tap and forward swipes as gestures. Since tap and forward swipes have a total of $m = 13$ features (cf. Table 2), ϵm ranges from 6 (majority decision) to 12 (unanimous decision). We construct a ROC curve for each of these cases. As n increases we observe that majority decision does not produce the best result. Figure 4a shows the ROC curves when $n = 15$. The different values of FPR and TPR are obtained by varying the probability parameter ρ in the Chebyshev classifier from 1.00 to 0.1 with steps of 0.05. The dashed line in the figure is the line with $TPR = 1 - FPR$, which meets the ROC curve at the EER value.

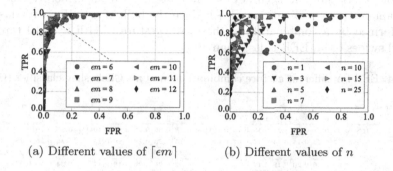

(a) Different values of $\lceil \epsilon m \rceil$ (b) Different values of n

Fig. 4. ROC curves - Chebyshev classifier.

We can see no significant improvement beyond $m = 9$. Since $\epsilon m = 9$ implies $\epsilon \approx 0.69$, we use the nearest approximation $\epsilon = \frac{2}{3}$ and the decision boundary $\lceil \epsilon m \rceil$ for the Chebyshev classifier in Eq. 2. This corresponds to the two-third majority rule. Table 3 shows the decision boundaries for various combination of gestures used in our evaluation which are obtained by choosing $\epsilon = \frac{2}{3}$.

Table 3. The decision boundaries corresponding to the decision threshold $\epsilon = \frac{2}{3}$ for different combination of gestures from the Chebyshev classifier.

Combination	$\lceil \epsilon m \rceil$	m	Combination	$\lceil \epsilon m \rceil$	m
T	3	4	T + F + B	15	22
F/B/D	6	9	T + F + B + D	21	31
T + F	9	13			

Next, we studied the impact of n on the EER. Figure 4b shows the EER for the combination T + F against different values of n with the user set U_1 (notice that there are n taps and n forward-swipes in each test sample). The ROC curves show improvement as n increases, starting with an EER of about 30 % for $n = 1$ and an EER of around 3 % for $n = 25$. The trend of improving EER with increasing n is shown by all gesture combinations and all user sets, U_1, U_2 and U_3, as shown in Table 4. Note that for a gesture combination containing multiple gestures, e.g., T + F, authentication can trigger as soon as it collects a *minimum* of n samples for each gesture. From Table 4, we observe that the tap gesture as a standalone gesture performs worse in terms of EER as compared to the swipes. The EER of the forward and backward swipes are comparable, with forward swipes narrowly edging out. The downward swipe performs worse than the other two swipe types, which is potentially due to fewer data points available for training. The EER deteriorates by 3 to 4 percent when using the data sets U_2 (20 users) and U_3 (30 users) as compared to data set U_1 (10 users). However, we do not see a noticeable deterioration in EER when comparing data sets U_2 and U_3, which suggests that adding more number of users to the system does not deteriorate the accuracy of the system by a huge factor. Our most important gesture combination is T + F since the bulk of activities on Glass can be performed by a combination of these two gestures. With $n = 10$ taps and forward swipes each, EER is less than 10 %.

Table 4. EER for different gesture combinations and n - Chebyshev classifier (Glass).

Combination	Set	n							Set	n					Set	n				
		1	3	5	7	10	15	25		1	3	5	7	10		1	3	5	7	10
T	U_1	0.35	0.27	0.23	0.21	0.18	0.16	0.13	U_2	0.38	0.32	0.25	0.23	0.19	U_3	0.37	0.29	0.25	0.22	0.20
F		0.32	0.23	0.15	0.14	0.12	0.07	0.07		0.35	0.23	0.18	0.16	0.13		0.33	0.25	0.18	0.18	0.14
B		0.32	0.22	0.17	0.14	0.12	-	-		0.34	0.26	0.21	0.18	0.16		0.36	0.28	0.24	0.22	0.19
D		0.33	0.26	0.20	0.19	0.17	-	-		0.32	0.26	0.20	0.18	0.17		0.34	0.23	0.20	0.20	0.14
T + F		0.29	0.18	0.14	0.09	0.09	0.05	0.03		0.33	0.21	0.16	0.13	0.12		0.32	0.20	0.18	0.14	0.10
T + F + B		0.27	0.16	0.09	0.08	0.04	-	-		0.30	0.17	0.13	0.11	0.07		0.30	0.22	0.15	0.10	0.07
T + F + B + D		0.25	0.13	0.09	0.07	0.03	-	-		0.27	0.13	0.11	0.07	0.06		0.26	0.16	0.09	0.07	0.06

Finally we also looked at the relationship of EER with ρ, and found that for a given n and gesture combination a fixed value of ρ can be used which appears independent of the size of the user set. Details are in the full version of the paper.

5.3 SVM Classification Results

The accuracy of the SVM classifier as measured by the average error rate (AER) is shown in Table 5. The classification accuracy is varied against two parameters: training size $|T|$ and testing size n for each gesture combination listed in the table. The training set size was varied from 25 to 75 at intervals of 25. Note that AER for all gesture combinations decreases with increasing training size, since it gives the classification algorithm more information for accurate prediction. However, this may also lead to *overfitting*, which is indeed the case with downward swipe with training set of size 75. The AER of the SVM classifier also improves with increasing number of test samples, i.e., n. The tap gesture performs the worst amongst all the individual gestures and forward swipe outperforms all other gestures, which is consistent with the observation from the Chebyshev classifier. As observed with Chebyshev classifier earlier, the AER does not significantly deteriorate with more number of users in the system (U_3 against U_2).

5.4 Distinguishing Features

To determine if individual features have distinguishing capabilities, we use the Chebyshev feature classifier f on user set U_2 to obtain true positive (TP) and

Table 5. AER for different gesture combinations and n - SVM classifier (Glass).

Combination	Training Size	Set	n					Set	n				
			1	3	5	7	10		1	3	5	7	10
T	25	U_2	0.40	0.32	0.30	031	0.26	U_3	0.37	0.34	0.32	0.29	0.30
	50		0.30	0.32	0.28	0.29	0.30		0.36	0.31	0.30	0.26	0.27
	75		0.30	0.29	0.27	0.28	0.27		0.32	0.31	0.30	0.28	0.27
F	25		0.32	0.25	0.20	0.20	0.19		0.31	0.26	0.21	0.19	0.18
	50		0.27	0.21	0.21	0.22	0.20		0.26	0.21	0.19	0.18	0.18
	75		0.28	0.21	0.18	0.19	0.15		0.23	0.22	0.19	0.18	0.16
B	25		0.33	0.32	0.31	0.31	0.30		0.33	0.35	0.29	0.31	0.29
	50		0.28	0.27	0.26	0.27	0.23		0.32	0.29	0.26	0.23	0.21
	75		0.29	0.27	0.27	0.25	0.21		0.31	0.28	0.25	0.24	0.21
D	25		0.33	0.27	0.23	0.20	0.16		0.34	0.26	0.20	0.19	0.16
	50		0.30	0.21	0.18	0.16	0.17		0.30	0.22	0.17	0.16	0.14
	75		0.30	0.28	0.27	0.30	0.32		0.31	0.28	0.29	0.29	0.29
T + F	25		0.35	0.24	0.20	0.18	0.17		0.32	0.23	0.19	0.19	0.18
	50		0.30	0.21	0.18	0.16	0.17		0.29	0.21	0.17	0.17	0.15
	75		0.26	0.17	0.12	0.11	0.11		0.30	0.13	0.12	0.11	0.10
T + F + B	25		0.28	0.20	0.16	0.14	0.14		0.29	0.21	0.18	0.16	0.15
	50		0.29	0.14	0.11	0.10	0.07		0.27	0.14	0.10	0.08	0.06
	75		0.23	0.12	0.10	0.10	0.09		0.20	0.14	0.10	0.09	0.08
T + F + B + D	25		0.25	0.18	0.16	0.13	0.12		0.28	0.17	0.16	0.15	0.15
	50		0.21	0.09	0.06	0.04	0.03		0.22	0.12	0.09	0.08	0.07
	75		0.15	0.08	0.04	0.03	0.01		0.16	0.09	0.06	0.05	0.03

false positive (FP) frequencies for the features of all four gestures as shown in
Fig. 5. The x-axis shows 31 features (4 for tap plus 9 each for forward, backward
and downward swipes). The TP frequencies are above 400 (out of 500) for all
gesture types except the downward swipe (last nine features in the figure), which
is most likely due to its small training set size, i.e., 10. Nevertheless, observe that
the FP frequencies are lower than the corresponding TP frequencies for all features. We therefore included all features for classification as each can effectively
distinguish between users. For more details of the setup and exact frequencies,
see the full version of the paper.

5.5 Comparison of the Two Classifiers

To compare the two classifiers in terms of classification accuracy, we use EER
readings from the Chebyshev classifier based on the set of 20 users, i.e., the set
U_2 shown in Table 4, and we use the AER readings from SVM based on training
set of size 50 from Table 5.[1] We first consider $n = 10$ for the purpose of our

---

[1] Note that when $1 - \text{TPR} = \text{FPR}$ (as is the case with EER), AER and EER are the
same and hence comparable.

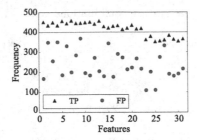

Fig. 5. TP & FP frequencies obtained via Chebyshev feature classifier for all features.

comparison. By looking at Tables 4 and 5 we can see that compared to the SVM classifier, Chebyshev's error rate is lower for taps, forward swipes and backward swipes. For all other combinations the two classifiers have similar error rates. For other values of n, we observe that the SVM classifier performs slightly better when $n = 1$, but the Chebyshev classifier's performance rapidly improves with increasing n, outperforming SVM in the three aforementioned gesture types. For combination of gestures, the performance of the two is very similar. These findings suggest that in terms of accuracy both classifiers are effective on Glass and hence can be used on similar wearables.

To compare the computational overhead of the two classifiers, we evaluated the time taken by model generation and prediction. Both these components are illustrated in Fig. 2. We first implemented both components of the two classifiers on a desktop computer. The SVM classifier was implemented in Java (via LIBSVM), whereas we used Python to implement the Chebyshev classifier. The results of the model generation and prediction time are shown in Table 6.

Table 6. Model generation and prediction time (ms) for gestures on a PC.

	Tap	Swipe		Tap	Swipe
Chebyshev Model	11	20	Chebyshev Predictor	0.04	0.095
SVM Model	38,000	49,000	SVM Predictor	9	9.4

Not surprisingly, for both the classifiers model generation takes longer than prediction. For both model generation and prediction, the Chebyshev classifier is many orders of magnitude faster than SVM. This suggests that using SVM for training on Glass can be computationally expensive in terms of power and heat generation. However, three important points need to be considered here. First, high model generation time is not inherent to SVM. In fact, it is due to the use of the RBF kernel; a linear SVM is likely to yield much lower model generation time. Secondly, we do not consider the high model generation time as a drawback of the SVM classifier, as (a) model generation is done infrequently, and (b) model generation can be outsourced to the Cloud (depending on connectivity). Lastly, a smaller grid search, i.e., restricting the ranges of the parameters C and γ, may result in faster model generation time, at the possible expense of accuracy. Alternatively, although the optimum range of these SVM parameters depend on user data, it may be possible to experimentally determine whether the optimum values lie within narrow ranges for touch based gestures. Nevertheless, our focus was more on accuracy than speed.

We, therefore, chose to implement only the predictor component of SVM on Glass to check the actual performance. The classification models were generated offline on a desktop computer and loaded on to the Glass. On the other hand, for Chebyshev classifier we implemented both the model generator and predictor on Glass. The results from our experiment are shown in Table 7. As can be seen, Chebyshev is faster than SVM in terms of prediction time and needs little time for model generation on Glass. Having said that, the prediction time for SVM is also small enough to be practical. In terms of space requirements, both classifiers require storing gesture data which is in the order of a few kilobytes. For the model, Chebyshev classifier needs to store the means, variances and co-variances for all features, whereas the SVM classifier needs to store the support vectors. The model space complexity also increases with gesture combinations. Typically, the model size ranges from 15 KB for a simple tap to 400 KB for all gestures. In any case, Glass has 8 GB of storage capacity, and the total space required by the classifiers is only in the order of a few megabytes. The main advantage of using the Chebyshev classifier, in our opinion, is its ease of implementation (as it requires standard functions and therefore does not require external libraries).

Table 7. Model generation and prediction time (ms) for different gestures on Glass.

	T	F	T + F	T + F + B	T + F + B + D
Chebyshev Model	150	325	499	838	1,172
Chebyshev Predictor	0.80	0.32	1.13	1.89	2.74
SVM Predictor	24	40	70	90	110

5.6   Generalization: Results on Smartphone Data

To test the generalizability of our proposed system on smartphones, we used publicly available smartphone gesture data which was collected by the authors of [19].[2] The data consists of 120 taps, and 20 forward, backward and downward-swipes each for 31 users. We chose 30 of the 31 users for our study. We further fixed training size of 50 for taps and 10 for all swipe gestures. The rest of the data was used as the testing set. The other details of the experimental setup remain the same as in Sect. 5.1. The results of applying Chebyshev and SVM on the smartphone data are shown in Tables 8 and 9, respectively.

The trends observed in the results for both the classifiers on the smartphone data remain similar to Glass data. We observe that the accuracy of the system

---

[2] The data is available from http://xuhui.me/.

Table 8. EER for different gesture combinations and n - Chebyshev classifier (phone).

Combination	Set	n					Set	n					Set	n				
		1	3	5	7	10		1	3	5	7	10		1	3	5	7	10
T	U_1	0.43	0.30	0.24	0.23	0.15	U_2	0.39	0.27	0.21	0.18	0.15	U_3	0.36	0.26	0.22	0.17	0.16
F		0.17	0.05	0.06	0.03	0.03		0.16	0.07	0.07	0.06	0.04		0.16	0.10	0.07	0.07	0.04
B		0.20	0.13	0.12	0.11	0.09		0.16	0.12	0.10	0.11	0.10		0.22	0.15	0.11	0.10	0.11
D		0.20	0.11	0.08	0.06	0.06		0.21	0.13	0.09	0.08	0.07		0.18	0.10	0.09	0.08	0.07
T + F		0.16	0.09	0.06	0.04	0.03		0.16	0.08	0.05	0.05	0.04		0.16	0.08	0.06	0.04	0.05
T + F + B		0.15	0.05	0.02	0.03	0.03		0.12	0.04	0.02	0.02	0.02		0.12	0.05	0.04	0.03	0.02
T + F + B + D		0.09	0.03	0.01	0.02	0.01		0.08	0.03	0.02	0.01	0.01		0.09	0.03	0.02	0.01	0.02

Table 9. AER for different gesture combinations and n - SVM classifier (phone).

Combination	Set	n					Set	n				
		1	3	5	7	10		1	3	5	7	10
T	U_2	0.43	0.41	0.38	036	0.35	U_3	0.44	0.40	0.38	0.38	0.36
F		0.12	0.06	0.05	0.04	0.04		0.10	0.05	0.04	0.04	0.04
B		0.21	0.14	0.12	0.11	0.11		0.19	0.16	0.15	0.11	0.10
D		0.14	0.08	0.07	0.05	0.03		0.12	0.08	0.06	0.05	0.05
T + F		0.28	0.19	0.10	0.05	0.03		0.27	0.19	0.08	0.05	0.03
T + F + B		0.19	0.10	0.06	0.04	0.03		0.20	0.10	0.05	0.04	0.03
T + F + B + D		0.15	0.10	0.04	0.03	0.02		0.20	0.10	0.04	0.04	0.02

increases with increasing testing size, i.e., n. The system is able to achieve accuracy of 98 %-99 % with $n \geq 7$ with all 4 gestures combined. We also observed two marked differences in the accuracy of the classifier between the smartphone data and Glass data. First, the accuracy of the system on all the swipe gestures on the smartphone is better than Glass. However, this might be due to the fact that the total number of swipe gestures were smaller, i.e., 20, in the smartphone data. Secondly, the accuracy of the system is less impacted with increasing number of users on smartphone than Glass. A plausible reason for these two differences might be due to the difference in touchpad size of the two devices. Bigger touchpad size allows for more variation in the gesture patterns. It is interesting to investigate whether other gesture-based authentication mechanisms proposed for smartphones exhibit a similar trend on smart glasses.

5.7 Effect of Behavioural Evolution on Classification Accuracy

As the gesture behaviour of users may change over time, we studied its evolution through an extended study on three users asking them to use Glass for five days over two weeks. The five days were spaced as: day 1, 2, 3, 7 and 14. We used a fixed training size of 20. To test the permanence of a user's gesture model, We experimented with the following three scenarios related to how the training model was generated. (a) *Same Day*: This scenario serves as the benchmark.

The testing data is matched against training data collected from the same day. (b) *First Day*: In this scenario, each user model is generated using data from day one. The model is then tested against data collected on subsequent days. For instance, day seven against day one. (c) *Adaptive*: In this scenario, the user model is updated every day, by iteratively replacing a fixed number of samples in the training data of previous days with random samples from the data of the same day. For example, to create the training data for day 3, we randomly replaced 8 samples from the training data of day one with 4 samples from day two and 4 samples from day three.

For the Chebyshev classifier, for each simulation run we use one random user as the target user and the remaining two as the attack users. In case of the SVM classifier, each of the three user is taken as a target user. The training data for the target user consists of a random sample of a fixed size from the target user's data. This constitutes positive samples for the target user required for SVM training. The negative samples for the target user come from the data of the remaining two target users. The attackers' data come from a fixed set of three users who did not participate in the evolution study and whose data was collected for earlier experiments. The results are shown in Fig. 6 for both the classifiers. As expected, the same day scenario achieves the highest accuracy amongst all the scenarios for a given day. We can also observe that the accuracy of the first day scenario is the worst, suggesting that the touch biometrics are not quite stable over time and hence an adaptive approach should be considered to maintain accuracy over time. Using adaptive approach in our experiments clearly shows performance improvements over the first day scenario, especially for the Chebyshev classifier. Note that replacing older samples with newer ones means that the classifiers need to be re-trained. For the Chebyshev classifier, this is not an issue since re-training takes around 1 s at worst (cf. Table 7). For SVM, training takes longer, but this is not a substantial hurdle due to the reasons discussed in Sect. 5.5.

6 Some Limitations and Discussion

We did not consider the effect of user posture, e.g., walking versus sitting, on touch gestures. Although this difference may not be as profound as in the case of smartphones, since the Glass is mounted on the user's head and is relatively stable, it needs to be experimentally determined. Since the focus of our research has been touch gesture based continuous authentication, we have overlooked voice characteristics (as mentioned before, the user can also perform certain operations in Glass through voice commands) or readings from other sensors such as accelerometer and gyroscope. Our continuous authentication system can be augmented by including distinguishing features from voice or other sensors. Also, as is the case for any behaviour biometric system, it is important to test our system on the larger population to validate its accuracy, a feat we were unable to perform due to limited resources.

Since the Chebyshev classifier is based on a concentration inequality, it will be interesting to employ other concentration inequalities such as Hoeffding or

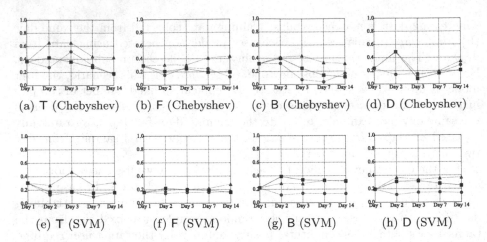

Fig. 6. The evolution of EER - Chebyshev classifier and AER - SVM classifier. Legend: ● *same day* training data; ■ *adaptive* training data; ▲ *first day* training data.

Bernstein's inequalities to compare the results. As a classifier's performance is also dependent on the features being used, it will be interesting to expand on the feature model introduced in this paper. For instance, one may model the swipe feature as an interaction between the two forces (downward and planar), instead of taking the two forces separately. A resulting feature could be a three dimensional magnitude of force over time.

7   Conclusion

Due to smaller touchpad size and relatively meagre resources of current smart glasses hardware (CPU, battery) compared to modern smartphones, it is not straightforward to assume that gesture based implicit authentication systems proposed for smartphones would yield high classification accuracy and low computational load on smart glasses, such as Google Glass. The results of our study indicate that gesture based continuous authentication is indeed both computationally and accuracy-wise feasible on Glass. Among other contributions of our work is the proposal of a new classifier based on Chebyshev's concentration inequality, which can be added to other classifiers used in the field of implicit authentication. Our secondary contributions include modelling touch gestures in a new way from which we extract new features such as downward (as measured by pressure and area readings) and planar (as measured by velocity readings) force as a function of time, and the finding that classification accuracy is dependent on the size of the touchpad.

References

1. Amidan, B.G., Ferryman, T.A., Cooley, S.K.: Data outlier detection using the chebyshev theorem. In: IEEE Aerospace Conference, pp. 3814–3819 (2005)

2. Ben-Asher, N., Kirschnick, N., Sieger, H., Meyer, J., Ben-Oved, A., Möller, S.: On the need for different security methods on mobile phones. In: MobileHCI 2011, pp. 465–473. ACM (2011)
3. Bo, C., Zhang, L., Li, X.Y., Huang, Q., Wang, Y.: SilentSense: silent user identification via touch and movement behavioral biometrics. In: MobiCom 2013, pp. 187–190 (2013)
4. Burgbacher, U., Hinrichs, K.: An implicit author verification system for text messages based on gesture typing biometrics. In: CHI 2014, pp. 2951–2954. ACM (2014)
5. Chang, C.C., Lin, C.J.: LIBSVM: a library for support vector machines. ACM Trans. Intell. Syst. Technol. **2**(3), 27:1–27:27 (2011)
6. De Luca, A., Hang, A., Brudy, F., Lindner, C., Hussmann, H.: Touch me once and i know it's you!: implicit authentication based on touch screen patterns. In: CHI 2012, pp. 987–996. ACM (2012)
7. Frank, M., Biedert, R., Ma, E., Martinovic, I., Song, D.: Touchalytics: on the applicability of touchscreen input as a behavioral biometric for continuous authentication. IEEE Trans. Inf. forensics Secur. **8**(1), 136–148 (2013)
8. Giuffrida, C., Majdanik, K., Conti, M., Bos, H.: I sensed it was you: authenticating mobile users with sensor-enhanced keystroke dynamics. In: Dietrich, S. (ed.) DIMVA 2014. LNCS, vol. 8550, pp. 92–111. Springer, Heidelberg (2014)
9. Jakobsson, M., Shi, E., Golle, P., Chow, R.: Implicit authentication for mobile devices. In: HotSec 2009, p. 9. USENIX (2009)
10. Li, L., Zhao, X., Xue, G.: Unobservable re-authentication for smartphones. In: NDSS 2013. Internet Society (2013)
11. LiKamWa, R., Wang, Z., Carroll, A., Lin, F.X., Zhong, L.: Draining our glass: an energy and heat characterization of google glass. In: APSys 2014, pp. 10:1–10:7. ACM (2014)
12. Mondal, S., Bours, P.: Swipe gesture based continuous authentication for mobile devices. In: ICB 2015, pp. 458–465. IEEE (2015)
13. Ross, S.M.: A First Course in Probability, 4th edn. Prentice Hall, Upper Saddle River (2002)
14. Schaub, F., Deyhle, R., Weber, M.: Password entry usability and shoulder surfing susceptibility on different smartphone platforms. In: MUM 2012, pp. 13:1–13:10. ACM (2012)
15. Serwadda, A., Phoha, V.V., Wang, Z.: Which verifiers work?: a benchmark evaluation of touch-based authentication algorithms. In: BTAS 2013, pp. 1–8. IEEE (2013)
16. Shahzad, M., Liu, A.X., Samuel, A.: Secure unlocking of mobile touch screen devices by simple gestures: you can see it but you can not do it. In: MobiCom 2013, pp. 39–50. ACM (2013)
17. Stanciu, V.D., Spolaor, R., Conti, M., Giuffrida, C.: On the effectiveness of sensor-enhanced keystroke dynamics against statistical attacks. In: CODASPY 2016, pp. 105–112. ACM (2016)
18. Uellenbeck, S., Dürmuth, M., Wolf, C., Holz, T.: Quantifying the security of graphical passwords: the case of android unlock patterns. In: CCS 2013, pp. 161–172. ACM (2013)
19. Xu, H., Zhou, Y., Lyu, M.R.: Towards continuous and passive authentication via touch biometrics: an experimental study on smartphones. In: SOUPS 2014, pp. 187–198. ACM (2014)
20. Zheng, N., Bai, K., Huang, H., Wang, H.: You are how you touch: User verification on smartphones via tapping behaviors. In: ICNP 2014, pp. 221–232. ACM (2014)

Author Index

Printed in the United States
By Bookmasters

Printed in the United States
By Bookmasters